# MODERN SCIEN EVIDENCE

## EVIDENCE

## Forensics

---

## 2008 Student Edition

By

**DAVID L. FAIGMAN**
*University of California*
*Hastings College of the Law*

**MICHAEL J. SAKS**
*Arizona State Univerisity*
*College of Law*

**JOSEPH SANDERS**
*University of Houston*
*Law Center*

**EDWARD K. CHENG**
*Brooklyn Law School*

*For Customer Assistance Call 1-800-328-4880*

**ISBN:** 978–0–314–18415–3

# Dedication

---

*For Lisa*
(DLF)

*For Roselle*
(MJS)

*For Mary*
(JS)

*For Jenny*
(EKC)

# Preface

For the rational study of the law the blackletter man may be the man of the present, but the man of the future is the man of statistics and the master of economics.

— Oliver Wendell Holmes[1]

The intellectual life of the whole of western society is increasingly being split into two polar groups.... Literary intellectuals at one pole—at the other scientists.... Between the two a gulf of mutual incomprehension.

— C.P. Snow[2]

Judges and lawyers, in general, are not known for expertise in science and mathematics. Nor is science a subject given significant attention in American law schools. The reasons are manifold. Despite Justice Holmes' prescient and often-quoted statement, the legal profession has perceived little need for lawyers to have a grounding in the scientific method. Indeed, law students, as a group, seem peculiarly averse to math and science. The American educational system is partly at fault, for students routinely divide, or are divided, into two separate cultures early in their training. Students who display a talent in math and science typically pursue careers in medicine, engineering, biology, chemistry, computer science, and similar subjects. Students with less inclination toward quantitative analysis very often go to law school. It is perhaps not surprising that the student who excels in the humanities soon learns that the best job opportunities for a graduate in Nineteenth Century Russian Literature can be found through law school. Whatever its origins, the legal profession today is a particularly salient example of a literary culture that remains largely ignorant of scientific culture.

Increasingly, however, there are signs that a "third culture" is emerging in the law.[3] This third culture would be one that integrates a sophisticated understanding of science into legal decisionmaking. Perhaps the most visible sign of this emerging integration is the United States Supreme Court's decision in *Daubert v. Merrell*

---

[1] Oliver Wendell Holmes, Jr., *The Path of the Law*, 10 HARV. L. REV. 457, 469 (1897).

[2] C.P. Snow, *The Two Cultures and the Scientific Revolution* 3 (Rede Lecture 1959).

[3] Cf. JOHN BROCKMAN, THE THIRD CULTURE (1995) (chronicling the emergence of a "third culture" in society generally, through the increasing numbers of scientists writing for a general audience); STEVEN GOLDBERG, CULTURE CLASH: LAW AND SCIENCE IN AMERICA (1994) (exploring the many contexts in which law and science overlap in practice).

*Dow Pharmaceuticals, Inc.*[4] The Court, for the first time in its history, considered the standard for evaluating the admissibility of scientific expert testimony. Briefly, the *Daubert* Court held that under the Federal Rules of Evidence, trial court judges must act as "gatekeepers," and evaluate the validity of the basis for proffered scientific expertise before permitting the expert to testify. In two subsequent cases—*General Electric Co. v. Joiner*[5] and *Kumho Tire Ltd. v. Carmichael*[6]—the Court further explicated the obligations that this gatekeeping role demands. These obligations were codified in the Federal Rules of Evidence in 2000. Moreover, states have increasingly followed the Supreme Court's lead, with many adopting *Daubert* outright, and still others incorporating the insights of *Daubert's* validity standard into their preexisting tests for admission of expert testimony.

Application of the *Daubert* standard requires an understanding of scientific research. Whether the Court intended to change the way the law responds to scientific evidence, or had more modest expectations, is impossible to know. Without doubt, however, the many judges, lawyers and scholars who have written on the decision have discovered a revolution of sorts. This revolution is one of perspective, and it affects profoundly not only the judges who guard the gate, but also the lawyers who seek to enter through it.

Until *Daubert*, courts had applied a variety of tests, with most courts being deferential to the scientists in their respective fields of expertise. This role was most closely associated with the general acceptance test articulated in *Frye v. United States*.[7] *Frye* instructed judges to admit scientific evidence only after it had achieved general acceptance in its field. The *Daubert* Court, in contrast, found that the Federal Rules of Evidence require judges themselves to determine the scientific validity of the basis for expert opinion. The shift in perspective is subtle yet profound. Whereas *Frye* required judges to survey the pertinent field to assess the validity of the proffered scientific evidence, *Daubert* calls upon judges to assess the merits of the scientific research supporting an expert's opinion. Implicitly, as well, the *Daubert* standard contemplates that lawyers will have sufficient expertise to explain the science to judges when they make admissibility arguments. The *Daubert* perspective immediately raised the spectre, as Chief Justice Rehnquist decried it, of judges assuming the role of "amateur scientists."[8] The gatekeeping role, he feared, was one most judges were ill-suited to fill.

*Daubert* has not come to mean that judges must be trained as scientists to carry out admissibility decisions. No one expects judges to join physicists soon in the

---

[4] 509 U.S. 579, 113 S.Ct. 2786, 125 L.Ed.2d 469 (1993).

[5] 522 U.S. 136, 118 S.Ct. 512, 139 L.Ed.2d 508 (1997).

[6] 526 U.S. 137, 119 S.Ct. 1167, 143 L.Ed.2d 238 (1999).

[7] 293 F. 1013 (D.C. Cir. 1923).

[8] 113 S.Ct. at 2800 (Rehnquist, C.J., concurring in part and dissenting in part).

search for grand unified theories.[9] But there is considerable space between being a trained scientist and being ignorant of science. Although *Daubert* does not expect judges and lawyers to be scientists, it does expect them to be sophisticated consumers of science. This book was formulated with that goal in mind. It is intended to introduce students to the rigors and details underlying scientific expert testimony, to offer an entry point to a host of scientific fields that are highly relevant to the law. It is not intended to provide simple "answers" or final "conclusions." Instead, it is designed and organized to acquaint aspiring lawyers with scientific fields that will be crucial to their practices.

This volume is part of a special student edition of a much larger work intended for a professional audience, our five volume treatise, MODERN SCIENTIFIC EVIDENCE: THE LAW AND SCIENCE OF EXPERT TESTIMONY (2008). There are two volumes in the student edition. The first volume, *Standards, Statistics and Research Issues,* concentrates on the background issues in both law and science that lie behind the sundry contexts in which experts are employed. The second volume, *Forensic Science Issues*, concentrates on an array of important forensic subjects. We hope that the two volumes will be of service either standing alone or as companions to regular texts in a variety of classes. If *Daubert* stands for the proposition that judges and lawyers must henceforth understand science well enough to integrate it successfully into the law, then the educational process that will allow this to occur must begin in law school.

The chapters follow one of two formats. Several chapters provide general overviews of the subject. Most chapters, however, are divided into two sections, one dedicated to the legal relevance of the particular field and the second concerned with the state of the art of the research in that field. The first section is authored by the editors and the second is authored by one or more eminent scientists. The sections on the state of the science are all written largely following a similar organizational scheme. We asked the contributors to discuss the scientific questions or hypotheses posited by the researchers, the methods brought to bear to study these hypotheses, the areas of scientific agreement, the areas of scientific disagreement, and the likely future directions for scientific research in the area. Some scientific topics lend themselves to this scheme better than others. Nonetheless, our guiding objective was to make the science accessible to the non-scientifically trained generalist.

*Daubert*, perhaps, represents nothing more, nor *less*, than that the legal culture must assimilate the scientific culture. As compared to the sciences, the law obviously has different objectives, values, and time tables in which to work. The law should not, nor could it, adopt the scientific perspective wholly and without qualifications. Science is merely a tool that the law can and must use to achieve its own

---

[9] See generally STEVEN WEINBERG, DREAMS OF A FINAL THEORY: THE SEARCH FOR THE FUNDAMENTAL LAWS OF NATURE (1992).

objectives. Science cannot dictate what is fair and just. We can confidently conclude, however, that science has become, and will forever more be, a tool upon which the law must sometimes rely to do justice.

DAVID L. FAIGMAN
MICHAEL J. SAKS
JOSEPH SANDERS
EDWARD K. CHENG

February, 2008

# Acknowledgments

At the conclusion of *The Adventures of Huckleberry Finn*, Huck states, ". . . and so there ain't nothing more to write about, and I am rotten glad of it, because if I'd a knowed what a trouble it was to make a book I wouldn't a tackled it and ain't agoing to no more."[1] We, perhaps, suffer Huck's lament more than he, for he never knew the pain of periodic supplements, as are planned for these volumes. However, we have had the immeasurable assistance of a score of colleagues and students who have made our task less trouble. We wish to thank all of the people who contributed so much to both the first and second editions.

At the University of California, Hastings College of the Law, we wish to thank our colleagues Mary Kay Kane, William Schwarzer, Roger Park, and Eileen Scallen for their support, encouragement and comments on various parts of this book. In addition, much is owed the student research assistants who spent innumerable hours on the project, including Tamara Costa, Kathryn Davis, Jamie Tenero, Paula Quintiliani, Amy Wright, Ali Graham, Cliff Hong, Lucia Sciaraffa, Faith Wolinsky and Sara Zalkin. Finally, we owe a considerable debt to Ted Jang and, especially, Barbara Topchov for secretarial support.

At Arizona State University, College of Law, we thank Gail Geer, Sonja Quinones and Rosalind Pearlman for secretarial support and Vivian Chang and James Pack for research assistance.

At the University of Iowa, College of Law, we thank research assistants "Max" Wilkinson, Alec Hillbo, and Patricia Fowler.

At the University of Houston Law Center, we wish to thank the students in the Spring 1996 Scientific Evidence seminar who did much in assisting on the toxic tort sections of the first edition: Angela Beavers, Chris Blanton, Armi Easterby, Nellie Fisher, Stephanie Hall, Jim Hildebrandt, Lynn Huston, Preston Hutson, Dino Ioannides, Candice Kaiser, Bill Long, Helen O'Conor, Ruth Piller, Larry Pinsky, John Powell, Jane Starnes, Donna Woodruff, and Kirk Worley. On the second edition, we extend our grateful appreciation to the research assistance of William Campbell, Mary Chapman, Alison Chein, Cynthia DeLaughter, Linda Garza, Linda Glover, Jamie Liner, Laura Moore, Jason Pinkall, Scott Provinse, Amanda Snowden and Angela Williams. Special thanks goes to Bethany Fitch who helped to cite check and proof read the manuscript.

At Brooklyn Law School, we thank Nancy Fayed and Sylvia Simson for research assistance.

Outside of our respective home institutions, we have had the generous assistance of many colleagues and institutions. At the Federal Judicial Center, we wish to thank Joe Cecil for his support and encouragement of this project. We are also indebted to Bert Black, for both his assistance in identifying authors and his generous sharing of ideas on a variety of topics.

---

[1] Mark Twain, Adventures of Huckleberry Finn 363 (Random House 1996).

# Summary of Contents

# Table of Contents

# CHAPTER 2.   DNA TYPING

## I.  LEGAL ISSUES

# CHAPTER 3.  FINGERPRINT IDENTIFICATION

## I.  LEGAL ISSUES

## II.  SCIENTIFIC STATUS

# CHAPTER 4.   HANDWRITING IDENTIFICATION

## I.   LEGAL ISSUES

## II.   SCIENTIFIC STATUS

# CHAPTER 5.  FIREARMS AND TOOLMARK IDENTIFICATION

## I.  LEGAL ISSUES

## II.  SCIENTIFIC ISSUES

# CHAPTER 6.  IDENTIFICATION FROM BITEMARKS

## I.  LEGAL ISSUES

## II.  SCIENTIFIC ISSUES

# CHAPTER 7.  TALKER IDENTIFICATION

## I.  LEGAL ISSUES

## II.  SCIENTIFIC STATUS

# CHAPTER 8.  POLYGRAPH TESTS

## I.  LEGAL ISSUES

## II.  SCIENTIFIC STATUS

### A.  THE CASE FOR POLYGRAPH TESTS

## B.    THE CASE AGAINST POLYGRAPH TESTS

# CHAPTER 9.  FIRES, ARSONS AND EXPLOSIONS

## I.  LEGAL ISSUES

## II.  SCIENTIFIC STATUS

# Chapter 1

# The General Assumptions and Rationale of Forensic Identification

*by*

*John I. Thornton\* & Joseph L. Peterson\*\**

## I. INTRODUCTION

## II. COMPARISON

## III. IDENTIFICATION AND INDIVIDUALIZATION

## IV. EVALUATION OF SOURCE

## V. SCIENCE AND THE SCIENTIFIC METHOD

\*John Thornton, D.Crim., is an Emeritus Professor of Forensic Science at the University of California at Berkeley. He worked in an operational crime laboratory for 15 years and taught at Berkeley for 24 years. He also has taught forensic science in Colombia, Israel, Mexico, India, and the People's Republic of China. He is a past president of the California Association of Criminalists and past chairman of the Criminalistics Section of the American Academy of Forensic Sciences.

\*\*Joseph L. Peterson, D.Crim., is Director, School of Criminal Justice and Criminalistics, California State University, Los Angeles. His research has tracked the evolution of the forensic sciences over the past thirty years, focusing on the quality of results emanating from crime laboratories, ethical dilemmas facing scientists, and the impact of science on legal decision making. Previously, he served as Executive Director of the Forensic Sciences Foundation and directed the criminal justice research center at John Jay College of Criminal Justice in New York.

## I.  INTRODUCTION

### § 1:1  Generally

The identification of items of physical evidence is a routine practice in any forensic laboratory. These identifications are not, however, made in a vacuum of the intellect. They are made in a conglomerate and frequently disheveled atmosphere of science, inference, knowledge, supposition, assumption, rationalization, and bias. In an ideal world, all forensic endeavors would be true palaces of clarity, constructed and imbued only with the purest scientific spirit and unsullied by less noble considerations. Alas, it is not to be. In short, forensic science is subject to the same real-world considerations as any other applied science. Being caught permanently in the cross fire of the adversary system has not made matters any better.

Most forensic examinations are conducted in government-funded laboratories, usually located within law enforcement agencies, and typically for the purpose of building a case for the prosecution. Police agencies investigate most crime scenes and recover the evidence that is submitted to the laboratory for analysis and interpretation. Laboratory resources are limited, however, and priorities dictate which evidence is examined and in what order. A recent census of the nation's 351 publicly funded crime laboratories found they received more than 2.7 million new cases in 2002, but had over 500,000 backlogged requests at year end.[1] The laboratory procedures followed in examining evidence and the content of laboratory reports are determined by local practice and professional guidelines. Quite apart from these organizational factors, the properly trained forensic scientist attempts to remain independent from various pressures that may influence the scientist to bias results. The courts set standards for assessing the reliability and admissibility of scientific evidence. The evidence that is presented before the court may also be reviewed by defense counsel, whose ability to interpret and possibly re-examine that evidence is severely limited by resources available to hire independent experts. Forensic examiners who deliver court testimony may engage opposing experts in their effort to explain to the court the significance of their examinations.

If forensic science is to maintain a high quality ethic in the conduct of its affairs, the processes by means of which forensic identifications are effected must be understood and controlled. This applies to those processes that are noble as well as those that are less so. The assumptions and rationale of forensic identifications are of critical importance in bringing coherence to this important subject.

Forensic science is, in many ways, an untidy, scruffy sort of discipline. In an anthropomorphic sense, it has dirty fingernails and hair growing out of its ears. Those using forensic science have had trouble in deciding what they want from it, and those practicing it have had trouble deciding what they will allow themselves to become. In any discussion of forensic science, it is inevitable that when focusing on one aspect, another aspect will, amoeba-like, bulge out somewhere else. Forensic science is not a subject that lends itself well to orderly analysis, and anyone who attempts to confine in a close space the general assumptions and the rationales of the forensic sciences is certain to be a very busy shepherd.

This situation arises because physical evidence is without scope or dimension. Physical evidence runs the gamut from the commonplace to the virtually unique, and the forensic scientist is expected to deal with it all. At one time or another, virtually anything can represent a form of physical evidence, from badger hairs to billiard balls, from bloodstains to bullets. This diversity in the form of physical evidence makes forensic science a necessarily messy, disheveled sort of thing. The forensic scientist has no control over what constitutes physical evidence—it is thrust upon him by the vagaries of life itself.[2]

Forensic science has historically been troubled by a serious deficiency in that a

------

**[Section 1:1]**

[1]Joseph L. Peterson and Matthew J. Hickman, Census of Publicly Funded Forensic Crime Laboratories, 2002 (U.S. Department of Justice, Bureau of Justice Statistics, Washington, DC, 2005).

[2]The authors are forensic scientists, but only

one sort of a forensic scientist—they are criminalists. The reader of this work will understand that there are many other types of forensic scientists— forensic accountants, forensic linguists, forensic engineers, and experts in everything from pornography to potholes. The present writers do not presume to understand or even appreciate all of the issues that pertain to every facet of what we

heterogeneous assemblage of technical procedures, a pastiche of sorts, however effective or virtuous they may be in their own right, has frequently been substituted for basic theory and principles. There are, nevertheless, certain features of forensic science that are common to all forensic examinations—common denominators that cut across the various disciplines that comprise the totality of the forensic sciences.

## § 1:2    What makes something "forensic?"

An analysis of the term forensic science will help us understand what is meant by the term. "Forensic" comes to us from the Latin *forensus*, meaning "of the forum." In Ancient Rome, the forum was where governmental debates were held, but it was also where trials were held. It was the courthouse. So forensic science has come to mean the application of the natural and physical sciences to the resolution of conflicts within a legal context. "Science" also comes to us in a roundabout fashion from the Latin *scire*, meaning "to know." The classical definition of science is that it is an orderly body of knowledge with principles that are clearly enunciated. This definition will suffice for many of our purposes, but will collapse when it is applied to some specific physical evidence types. Again, this will be discussed in more detail below.

What then, of the forensic *scientist*? The single feature that distinguishes forensic scientists from any other scientist is the expectation that they will appear in court and testify to their findings and offer an opinion as to the significance of those findings. The forensic scientist will, or should, testify not only to what things *are*, but to what things *mean*. Forensic science is science exercised on behalf of the law in the just resolution of conflict. It is therefore expected to be the handmaiden of the law, but at the same time this expectation may very well be the marina from which is launched the tension that exists between the two disciplines.

## § 1:3    What is expected of the forensic sciences?

The clients of the forensic sciences—the police, the attorneys, and the courts—have somewhat conflicting expectations of what science is likely to provide. By and large, forensic science is selfishly viewed in strictly utilitarian terms, i.e., how is this going to help me? Although the police may aggressively pursue their investigations, they will, with a minimum of ritual whining, generally accept what a forensic laboratory is able to provide. The courts are interested in forensic science only from the standpoint of how science may be used by the trier of fact to resolve technical issues.

But there is a fundamental conflict here. The classical goal of science is the production of *truth*, while the goal of law is the achievement of *justice*.

Few forensic scientists harbor serious misgivings about the expectation of good science on the part of their clients, be they the police, the prosecution, or the defense bar; indeed, most forensic scientists are rather cynical on this point. The clients want good science and the truth if it will help their case. If good science and the truth will not help their case, they will willingly settle for poor science and something less than the absolute truth.

Most forensic scientists accept the reality that while truthful evidence derived from scientific testing is useful for establishing justice, justice may nevertheless be negotiated. In these negotiations, and in the just resolution of conflict under the law, truthful evidence may be subordinated to issues of fairness, and truthful evidence may be manipulated by forces beyond the ability of the forensic scientist to control or perhaps even to appreciate fully.

---

broadly call "forensic science." The comments here center around physical evidence in connection with criminal matters, because that is what the authors understand best.

## § 1:4 Subordination of "scientific truth" to "legal truth"

Forensic scientists recognize that they are but the hired help, and that forensic science is but the handmaiden of the legal system. The validity of facts testified to in a court of law by non-expert witnesses is perpetually subject to challenge. When facts are introduced into a court of law by a scientist, however, they are likewise subject to the same challenge. Scientific "truths" are established when the validity of a proposition is proven to the satisfaction of a prudent and rational mind. Legal "truths" are not established by the exercise of the scientific method, but by the processes of the adversary system.

The role of physical evidence in the administration of justice may reasonably be described as follows: Science offers a window through which the law may view the technological advances of our age. Science spreads out a smorgasbord of (hopefully) valid facts and, having proudly displayed its wares, stands back. The law now picks out those morsels that appear most attractive to it, applying selection criteria that may or may not have anything to do with science. These selection criteria may appear sensible, even obligatory to the law, but may appear illogical or even whimsical to science.

## § 1:5 Scientific evidence effects on criminal justice

Research completed in the 1980s in the United States and England investigated the value of forensic evidence to police investigators and to the courts. In four American cities, Peterson et al.[1] found (controlling for other factors) that clearance rates for robberies and burglaries were about three times higher for cases where physical evidence was scientifically examined than in cases for which it was not. A British study found forensic laboratories generated helpful information in about three-quarters of cases where suspects had been identified, but in only 40% of cases without suspects.[2] The introduction of DNA testing and the development of large population data bases have increased those figures dramatically, with DNA now making major contributions to the solution of thousands of personal and property crimes.[3] In a separate study at the court level, Peterson et al.[4] found that conviction rates did not vary appreciably if forensic evidence was or was not gathered and examined, but found it increased the likelihood that convicted felons are sentenced to longer periods of incarceration.

Having discussed the part that forensic science plays in the broader drama of the administration of justice, we may now proceed to address how this role is played out.

## II. COMPARISON

## § 1:6 Generally

Physical evidence at the scene of a crime may serve to associate that scene with a particular individual. Such evidence frequently is termed *associative evidence*. A fingerprint of the suspect at the crime scene is the archetypal example. If the suspect's fingerprints are found at the crime scene, he is unquestionably (or as

**[Section 1:5]**

[1]Joseph Peterson et al., Forensic Evidence and the Police: The Effects of Scientific Evidence on Criminal Investigations (Washington, D.C.: National Institute of Justice, 1984).

[2]M. Ramsay, The Effectiveness of the Forensic Science Service (Home Office Research Study No.92, London: Her Majesty's Stationery Office,

1987).

[3]The Forensic Science Service, Annual Report and Accounts, 2004–05 (2006) at 18. Available at http://www.forensic.gov.uk/forensic_t/inside/about/docs/04_05.pdf.

[4]Peterson et al., The Uses and Effects of Forensic Science in the Adjudication of Felony Cases, 32 J. Forensic Sci. 1730 (1987).

nearly unquestionable as things get) associated with the scene in some way. The suspect may have had legitimate access to the scene, or the suspect may have been at the scene at some previous time, but the issue of the fundamental presence of the suspect at the scene is essentially unassailable. Associative evidence works both ways—something belonging to the suspect may be found at the scene, or something from the scene may later be found on or in the possession of the suspect after the suspect has left the scene. An example of the latter is a bloodstain of a victim on the clothing of the suspect. The forensic scientist undertakes to compare evidence found at the crime scene to evidence known to belong to a suspect.

### § 1:7   Class and individual characteristics

In the comparison of physical evidence, it is often helpful to make use of the concepts of *class characteristics* and *individual characteristics*. Class characteristics are general characteristics that separate a group of objects from a universe of diverse objects. In a comparison process, class characteristics serve the very useful purpose of screening a large number of items by eliminating from consideration those items that do not share the characteristics common to all of the members of that group. Class characteristics do not, and cannot, establish uniqueness. Individual characteristics, on the other hand, are those exceptional characteristics that may establish the uniqueness of an object. It should be recognized that an individual characteristic, taken in isolation, might not in itself be unique. The uniqueness of an object may be established by an ensemble of individual characteristics. A scratch on the surface of a bullet, for example, is not a unique event; it is the arrangement of the scratches on the bullet that mark it as unique.

An example of a class characteristic is "red." The characteristic "red" separates red items from those of all other colors. Class characteristics may be chained together to further refine the screening or elimination process.[1] "Red Buick" will instantly exclude from consideration any other vehicle, but will not distinguish among a sub-population of red Buicks. There is a fundamental mathematical foundation to this type of elimination, which resides in the "either/or" logic of Boolean algebra. Any vehicle that is not a red Buick may be eliminated because it is "either" of another manufacturer "or" it is of some other color.

An example of an individual characteristic would be the VIN number of the vehicle. The license plate number might be an individual characteristic, but the remote possibility exists that there would be some duplication of license plate numbers among different states and possibly between different countries. Examples of a few other class and individual characteristics for a number of evidence categories are given in Table 1.

### Table 1. Class and Individual Characteristics

| Class Characteristic | Individual Characteristic |
| --- | --- |
| Fingerprint pattern (e.g., loop, whorl, arch). | Ridge ending, bifurcation, dot. |
| Number of lands and grooves of a firearm. | Striations on the surface of a fired bullet. |
| Thickness of a shard of glass. | Irregular fracture margin. |
| Width of a prying tool (e.g., screwdriver). | Striations within the toolmark. |
| Tread pattern of an automobile tire. | Cuts and tears acquired through use. |

---

[Section 1:7]

[1]It should be apparent that the "class" in "class characteristic" and the "class" in "classification" are derived from the same root.

The trick is to recognize class and individual characteristics for what they are, and not to confuse the two. Frequently this is easily accomplished. In other instances, however, this is not easily realized, and may call upon and challenge the experience of the examiner. An example of this is to be found in the area of handwriting examination. An examiner may note an unusual letter formation, which in the experience of that examiner seems to be unique. The natural tendency would be to categorize the letter form as an individual characteristic, as an idiosyncratic expression of the writing of a particular person to the exclusion of all other people, but it may be that every schoolchild in a Bulgarian town was taught to execute that particular letter formation. The characteristic may be obscure, but it is still a class characteristic, not an individual characteristic, and should be given only the weight that a class characteristic deserves and not the additional weight that ordinarily would be given to an individual characteristic.

Individual characteristics may arise out of different considerations. They may result from natural phenomena which are poorly understood or not understood at all, such as the origin of fingerprints, or earprints, or lip prints. They may arise from manufacturing processes, which are understood but which are unintentional in their expression, such as marks associated with the machining of tools. Or they may reflect the career and history of an item after the manufacturing process—the use and the abuse of the item. Examples of the latter would be uneven wear and tear on the patterned sole of a shoe, or a screwdriver that has suffered some damage by having been used as a prying tool.

In the process of the comparison of an evidence item and an exemplar item, the analyst typically will check to see that the class characteristics agree before proceeding to the individual characteristics. It would be senseless, for example, to spend hours examining the striations on two bullets if one was a .22 caliber bullet and the other was a .38 caliber bullet. It is not obligatory in every case, however, to ensure that the class characteristics between the two items agree. For example, in the comparison of fingerprints, the class characteristic of pattern might not be apparent in a fragmentary fingerprint. The individual characteristics, i.e., the detailed pattern of the fingerprint ridges, may nevertheless be compared and an identification effected. If the patterns were apparent, however, one would not proceed to a comparison of the fingerprint ridges if one print was a loop and the other was a whorl.

## § 1:8 Features

Forensic scientists are concerned, even obsessed, with features. A feature is a quality, property, or trait that is used to characterize an object or a source. Some features are dichotomous, that is, they are either present or absent. Other features are quantifiable, and may take on values which are continuous, quasi-discrete, or discrete. Of whatever sort, it must be recognized that some features are rather ephemeral in how they are perceived and recognized by the eye and the mind. These include some of the features upon which we rely the most in forensic practice—visual, two-dimensional images of the features in shoeprint impressions, fingerprint minutiae, handwriting characteristics, and firearms striae. These features may be evaluated and tested, but the manner in which these patterns are recognized by the human mind is not well understood.

Forensic scientists are (hopefully) adept at recognizing features by means of which items are identified, e.g., pine pollen under the microscope, 00 Buckshot, a

Greek "$\epsilon$" in handwriting. It is reasonable to ask what are the limits that apply to the ability to identify things by sight. (Further analysis may of course follow). The answer is that we don't really know, but almost certainly the number of things that can be identified by the inspection of visible features alone would number in the thousands. One possibly appropriate analogy is Chinese characters. The ability to recognize two or three thousand characters will allow a person to read a Chinese newspaper. Scholars may, on the other hand, recognize upwards of ten thousand.

## § 1:9   Feature independence

The soundness of a hypothesis increases when the prediction it makes is supported by several lines of evidence that have no relationship to one another. This is the condition of independence. If, on the other hand, one feature of the evidence is correlated with another feature, then the observation of one can predict, to a greater or lesser extent, the second feature. This is the condition of dependence.

If features are dependent, the forensic scientist is not justified in multiplying the frequencies of their individual occurrences to calculate the discriminating power of the features for the purpose of determining identity of source. For forensic identifications, the most valuable features are those that are demonstrably independent. Studies testing the independence of features exist for only a few evidence categories (e.g., blood types, glass density and refractive index, and gunshot residue). Where no studies exist, which is true for the preponderance of physical evidence types, prudence argues for caution in the interpretation of the evidence.

## III.  IDENTIFICATION AND INDIVIDUALIZATION

### § 1:10   Generally

Forensic science is classically described as being concerned with the analysis, identification, and interpretation of physical evidence. We find that in the English language, there are two somewhat different connotations associated with the term *identification*. In one sense, identification refers to the process of placing an item in a category. One may say, "I identified the specimen as an *Ursus horribilis*." That will establish that the animal is a grizzly bear. We now know that the animal is not a polar bear, or a panda, or a Himalayan Sun bear. But at this point, the bear could be any one of a number of grizzly bears. In the same sense of the word, one may identify a specimen of *Cannabis sativa*, or one may identify an automobile as a red Buick.

But rarely is the forensic scientist satisfied with this level of identity. In most situations, it is desirable to extend the level of discrimination beyond merely placing the item in a category. It is not sufficient to identify a firearm as a Smith & Wesson, if the issue is whether that *particular* firearm, to the exclusion of all other Smith & Wesson firearms, was responsible for having fired the fatal bullet. It is not sufficient to identify a vehicle as a red Buick if the issue is whether that particular red Buick is the one that ran down a hit-and-run victim.

To extend the discrimination to the level desired, i.e., uniqueness, the concept of *individualization* is required. Individualization is the process of placing an object in a unit category which consists of a single unit. Individualization implies uniqueness; identification, strictly speaking, does not require it. As discussed below, though individualization is clearly the goal toward which forensic science strives, it can be achieved only in a probabilistic sense, of reducing uncertainty to the smallest possible amount.

But in everyday usage, the term identification often is used when the concept of individualization is intended. One may hear testimony of the sort, "I identified the latent fingerprint as having been made from the right ring finger of the defendant."

The intent of the witness here is to declare clearly that the latent fingerprint was that of the defendant, to the total exclusion of all other fingers of all of the other people in the world. The use of the term "identified" here is not the most precise usage of the word; the term "individualized" would be more felicitous. But the use of term "individualization" and various other forms of the word would only confuse matters. If, in response to the question, "Did you have occasion to identify the suspect's fingerprint on the knife?" the witness were to answer, "No, I individualized it," communication would be thwarted and the listener confused.

This is a constraint imposed by our language, and there is probably no feasible remedy. Forensic scientists are accustomed to the use of the term identification when what actually is meant is individualization, and few forensic scientists will go to the bother of correcting another person who uses the terms casually.[1] It should be appreciated, however, that the process of identification means one thing to the forensic scientist, and another thing to the botanist or the zoologist.

## § 1:11  Identification processes v. comparison processes

In the "identification" mode, the forensic scientist examines an item of evidence for the presence or absence of specific characteristics that have been previously abstracted from authenticated items. Identifications of this sort are legion, and are conducted in forensic laboratories so frequently and in connection with so many different evidence categories that the forensic scientist is often unaware of the specific steps that are taken in the process. It is not necessary that those authenticated items be in hand, but it is necessary that the forensic scientist have access to the abstracted information. For example, an obscure 19th Century Hungarian revolver may be identified as an obscure 19th Century Hungarian revolver, even though the forensic scientist has never actually seen one before and is unlikely ever to see one again. This is possible because the revolver has been described adequately in the literature and the literature is accessible to the scientist. Their validity rests on the application of established tests which have been previously determined to be accurate by exhaustive testing of known standard materials.

In the "comparison" mode, the forensic scientist compares a questioned evidence item with another item. This second item is a "known item." The known item may be a standard reference item which is maintained by the laboratory for this purpose (e.g., an authenticated sample of cocaine), or it may be an exemplar sample which itself is a portion of the evidence in a case (e.g., a sample of broken glass or paint from a crime scene). This item must be in hand. Both questioned and known items are compared, characteristic by characteristic, until the examiner is satisfied that the items are sufficiently alike to conclude that they are related to one another in some manner, or, alternatively, until the examiner is satisfied of a lack of commonality.

In the comparison mode, the characteristics that are taken into account may or may not have been previously established. Whether they have been previously established and evaluated is determined primarily by: (1) the experience of the examiner; and (2) how often that type of evidence is encountered. The forensic scientist must first determine what the characteristics are to be compared, then determine the weight to be ascribed to them, and then decide upon the number of matching characteristics that must be noted before a conclusion can be reached. This is more easily said than achieved, and may require de novo research in order to come to grips with the significance of observed characteristics. For example, a fo-

---

**[Section 1:10]**

[1]In the ensuing discussion, "identification" will be used in the more-or-less common use of the word, despite the fact that uniqueness is implied.

rensic scientist compares a shoe impression from a crime scene with the shoes of a suspect. Slight irregularities in the tread design are noted, but the examiner is uncertain whether those features are truly individual characteristics unique to this shoe, or a mold release mark common to thousands of shoes produced by this manufacturer. Problems of this type are common in the forensic sciences, and are anything but trivial.

In a strict sense, the identification mode is actually a form of the comparison mode. The identification mode does in fact involve a comparison, but a comparison of an evidence item with a hypothetical ideal instead of a tangible example.

### § 1:12  Explicable differences

Differences exist between all objects, even those that are exceedingly similar in their outward appearance. The document examiner does not expect replicate signatures from one person to be totally superimposable; the firearms examiner does not expect replicate test firings from a particular firearm to agree in every striae on the surfaces of the two bullets. It follows, then, that total agreement between evidence and exemplar is not to be expected; some differences will be seen even if the objects are from the same source or the product of the same process. It is experience that guides the forensic scientist in distinguishing between a truly significant difference and a difference that is likely to have occurred as an expression of natural variation.

But forensic scientists universally hold that in a comparison process, differences between evidence and exemplar should be explicable. There should be some rational basis to explain away the differences that are observed, or else the value of the match is significantly diminished.

A danger exists that, once the examiner has become satisfied that a match does exist between the evidence and the exemplar, any differences will be dismissed as trivial and insignificant. A different, and more forgiving, set of criteria may be employed to rationalize away the differences than that originally employed in establishing the match. This is a situation where the training and experience of the examiner is at a premium, and the examiner must be attentive to the natural tendency to defend one's opinion against any and all challenges.

## IV.  EVALUATION OF SOURCE

### § 1:13  Generally

The forensic scientist often is called upon to compare evidence items to determine whether they did, or could have, come from the same source. Consider, for example, a case where a hair is found in an automobile suspected of having been used as the getaway car in a bank robbery. The hair is recovered by a police investigator, and the forensic laboratory is requested to compare the hair with exemplar hair of a suspect. The issue of identity here is not a question of "What is it?" but rather it is a question of "Where did it come from?"[1] Here it is *identity of source* that occupies our attention, not *identity of the object*.

The concept of identity of source presents some other complications, arising from the fact that there is not just one singular relationship between an object and its source.[2] An object may be related to its source because of *production* considerations, or because of *segment* considerations, or because of *alteration*, or because of

---

[Section 1:13]

[1]The question has been phrased here in a commonly encountered but inelegant fashion. A more precise formulation of the appropriate question would be "Given the undeniable fact that this is a hair, from whom did the hair originate?"

[2]The entire landscape of how criteria are established for association and exclusion, as well

considerations of *spatial location*; often the relationships operate alone, but situations commonly arise in which the relationships are interwoven, with no single relationship dominating the tapestry.

Production considerations are straightforward. The source produces the object, and the composition of the raw material utilized in the production are then expressed in the object. An example would be a sample of glass in which the principal components of silica, soda, and lime also contained, inadvertently, traces of the elements Manganese, Iron, and Copper. Finding these elements in an evidence sample of glass at the same concentration as the putative source would establish a relationship between the evidence and the source. (Whether the same concentration of these elements establishes *uniqueness* to the evidence is another matter.)

A segment relationship exists when a source is somehow dismantled and parts of the whole are somehow scattered. If a fragment of glass located at the scene of a hit-and-run accident is found to match an irregular edge of a broken headlight of the vehicle belonging to the suspect, a relationship between the evidence and the source is thereby established. In this instance, the composition of the glass as dictated by production considerations is not relevant.

An alteration relationship exists when a source is an agent or a process that alters or modifies an object. For example, in the commission of a burglary, a surface is acted upon by a prying tool. In this process, the surface is marked in a unique fashion by the tool. Subsequent comparison of the marks at the scene with test marks from the suspected tool may establish that a particular tool, to the total exclusion of all other tools in the world, was responsible for the evidence marks. In this sense, the tool may be viewed as having altered the otherwise pristine surface; the tabula rasa of the surface has now been altered so as to register a unique signature of the responsible tool.

The fourth type of relationship between a putative source and an object is the relationship of spatial location. A "source" may be a point in space as well as a tangible physical object. Just as a river has a source, an object of evidence may have its origin at a particular spatial location. For example—was the shooter in front of the murder victim, or behind? Does the broken glass on the roadway indicate the specific point of impact to a hit-and-run victim?

### § 1:14  "Same as that" vs. "born of that"

A useful tool in the conceptualization of physical evidence is the "same as that" versus "born of that" dialectic which comes to us from the Sanskrit. The Sanskrit word *tatsam* means "same as that." The word *tadbhav* means "born of that." Ancient Indian philosophers found the two concepts to be useful, and indeed the concepts appear to have a good deal of utility in how physical evidence can be regarded.

In the comparison of two items of physical evidence, the evidence may be of the "same as that" type, or of the "born of that" type. An obvious example of the "born of that" type is a fired bullet. The bullet may be identified as having been fired through a particular gun barrel, to the total exclusion of all other gun barrels in the world. In a literal as well as figurative sense, the bullet has been "born" of the gun barrel. But when cocaine is identified, the analyst is comparing a set of observations derived from the evidence against a set of observations derived from known cocaine. The chemical reactivity of the unknown is the same as that of known cocaine, as is the mass and infrared spectrum. So the unknown is the "same as that," i.e., the known

---

as how physical evidence is conceptualized by the forensic scientist, has been developed elegantly by Cwicklik, An Evaluation of the Significance of Transfers of Debris: Criteria for Association and Exclusion, 44 J. Forensic Sci. 1136 (1999).

cocaine, and the identification is thereby effected. Physical evidence can almost always be ascribed to one or the other of these appellations, and the effort in doing so is frequently rewarded in terms of the clarity with which the evidence may be regarded.

### § 1:15  Uniqueness

Forensic scientists have struggled with the concept of uniqueness, but then so have others—philosophers, logicians, Boolean algebra mathematicians, and rare coin dealers. Each of these groups has made an uneasy peace with the concept.

It is generally held that no two snowflakes are exactly the same.[1] Based on the same type of not very rigorous observation, it is held that no two fingerprints have ever been found to have the same ridge positioning.[2] In the same fashion, no two firearms have ever been found that have exactly the same configuration, and no two panes of glass have ever been observed to fracture into shards of identical shape and size.[3] Observations such as these have gradually become tenets of the beliefs of the forensic scientist of the uniqueness of all objects. In some quarters, these tenets have been scooped up and extended into a single, all-encompassing, generalized principle of uniqueness, which states that "Nature never repeats itself."[4]

This principle is probably true, although it would not seem susceptible of rigorous proof. But the general principle cannot be substituted for a systematic and thorough investigation of a physical evidence category. For convenience in discussion, one may posit that no two snowflakes are alike, but it does not immediately follow that no two shoe soles are alike, since snowflakes are made in clouds and shoes are not. If it is absolutely true that no two shoe soles are alike, the basis for this uniqueness must rest on other grounds, and those grounds must be identified and enunciated.

## V.  SCIENCE AND THE SCIENTIFIC METHOD

### § 1:16  Generally

The scientific method and how it is invoked and applied has occupied the thoughts

---

**[Section 1:15]**

[1]This is, of course, not known with certitude to be true. Indeed, snowflakes that are indistinguishably alike have been reported. N.C. Knight, No Two Alike? 69 Bull. Am. Meteorological Soc'y 496 (1988) (finding "apparent contradiction of the long-accepted truism that no two snow crystals are alike.") For a less-than-serious discussion of the uniqueness of snowflakes within a forensic context, see Thornton, The Snowflake Paradigm, 31 J. Forensic Sci. 399 (1986).

[2]See §§ 3:1 et seq. for important qualifications to this statement. Some number of matching points on different fingers occurs and errors occur where examiners think prints from different fingers came from the same finger.

[3]In practice, uniqueness is more an assumption than an observation. Most areas of forensic practice provide no occasion for testing the assumption, because examiners do not compare evidence in any one case to evidence in every other case. The one exception is fingerprints, where an evidence print is systematically compared to a huge database of other prints. Examiners of firearms and broken glass have no comparable system and therefore no comparable opportunity for detecting coincidental matches. Where systematic studies are undertaken to look for identical snowflakes, or indistinguishable forensic evidence, such as handwritten signatures, the findings unsettle the assumptions. See Harris, How Much Do People Write Alike? A Study of Signatures, 48 J. Crim. L & Criminology 647 (1958). DNA typing has taken a radically different approach, sidestepping this difficult problem by making no heroic assumptions and instead calculating probabilities of coincidental matches.

[4]This is an ancient dogma, and has seen many expressions. Leibniz said: "it is necessary, indeed, that each monad [object] be different from each other. For there are never in nature two beings which are exactly alike and in which is it not possible to find an internal difference." Gottfried W. von Leibniz, Monadology, Section ix, 4th lettre a' Clarke, sect. 4/6 (1951). And, in particular reference to physical evidence, Kirk and Grunbaum have stated: ". . . all items of the universe are in some respect different from other similar items, so that ultimately it may be possible to individualize any object of interest. . . ." Kirk & Grunbaum, Individuality of Blood and Its Forensic Significance, in Legal Medicine Annual 288 (Cyril Wecht ed., 1968).

of many of the world's greatest intellects, and the present authors do not presume to attempt to join their company.[1] But an understanding of the basic tenets of the scientific method is essential to the understanding of how a forensic scientist approaches or *ought* to approach problems.

## § 1:17  Science

There is a difference between *science* and the *scientific method*, a difference that even scientists may not fully appreciate. The latter is generally the means to the former, but the two concepts are at best loosely related. The classical definition of a science is "an orderly body of knowledge with principles that are clearly enunciated." While this definition will suffice for most purposes, it is generally conceded that a few other qualifiers may be necessary. For example, additional requirements commonly added specify that the subject be susceptible of testing, and that it be reality-oriented. When these two additional provisos are added, religion, for example, fails to qualify, regardless of how clearly its principles have been enunciated or how orderly those principles may appear.

## § 1:18  Scientific method

The scientific method, on the other hand, is not a body of knowledge; it is a way of looking at things. The scientific method has been embraced by the modern world because of its incredible power and utility—it is useful for answering many questions concerning the real world. Prior to the modern era, the explanation of many natural phenomena was based on the exercise of the imagination. Thunder was Thor tossing lightning bolts through the heavens. Demented people were possessed by evil spirits.

Gradually, progressive thinkers began to look for intrinsic evidence of the truth of various propositions, and this skepticism eventually spawned the development of the scientific method. The foundation of the scientific method, the most fundamental aspect, is the formulation and testing of hypotheses.[1] Since the laws of nature do not change from day to day, certain phenomena should therefore be repeatable, with a predictable outcome. This is a fundamental premise of the scientific method, but its practical application to forensic problems is not as straightforward as might be imagined.

Little of what goes on in forensic science resembles the classical description of how science develops theories, tests hypotheses, and revises its ideas and understandings. That is partly because the scientific method is a description of pure, or basic, science (knowledge building), while forensic science is an *applied* science. Ideally, forensic scientists would apply the best knowledge borrowed from basic research that *has* employed the scientific method. Additional reasons are discussed below.

---

**[Section 1:16]**

[1]Reference works on the history of science, and the philosophy of science, are legion. A good primer is to be found in Karl Popper, Conjectures and Refutations: The Growth of Scientific Knowledge (5th ed. 1989). A painless introduction to the scientific method is to be found in Robert Pirsig, Zen and the Art of Motorcycle Maintenance 107–111 (1974).

**[Section 1:18]**

[1]Hypothesis is one of a number of related words of Greek origin that are curiously but consistently pronounced in English in such a manner as to obscure their meaning. *Thesis* denotes an idea or a proposition, and in logic is construed to mean a proposition that may be advanced without proof. *Hypo-* is the Greek root for "less than." The word would be more easily understood if we pronounced it as *hypo-thesis*, which we don't. In the same fashion, we say *an-tith-esis* instead of the more meaningful *anti-thesis*, and *synth-esis* instead of the more descriptive *syn-thesis*. (*Anti-*, "against," and *syn-*, "with.")

## § 1:19  Induction and deduction

Many forensic identifications involve deductive processes, *a la* Sherlock Holmes, through the application of relevant generalizations to a particular set of circumstances. Induction is a type of inference that proceeds from a set of specific observations to a generalization, called a premise. This premise is a working assumption, but it may not always be valid. A deduction, on the other hand, proceeds from a generalization to a specific case, and that is generally what happens in forensic practice. Providing that the premise is valid, the deduction will be valid. But knowing whether the premise is valid is the name of the game here; it is not difficult to be fooled into thinking that one's premises are valid when they are not.

Forensic scientists have, for the most part, treated induction and deduction rather casually. They have failed to recognize that induction, not deduction, is the counterpart of hypothesis testing and theory revision. They have tended to equate a hypothesis with a deduction, which it is not. As a consequence, too often a hypothesis is declared as a deductive conclusion, when in fact it is a statement awaiting verification through testing.

## § 1:20  Failure of the forensic sciences to consistently appreciate the implications of the scientific method

The validity of the scientific method is unassailable; no rational person takes issue with its utility in problem solving. But that does not mean that "science" as it is practiced in the real world is infallible. The scientific method is the means by which much of what we believe has come to be discovered. What we do with that discovered knowledge is another matter. The scientific method has given us the collective knowledge essential to various scientific disciplines—chemistry, physics, geology, botany, biology, etc. It has set the stage for the exercise of science. It sits there, as a way of learning something that would otherwise be unknown, waiting for someone—anyone—to invoke its power.

But those individuals engaged in "scientific" work rarely study the scientific method. To be sure, those engaged in research are expected to pick up the scientific method somewhere along the way; for the most part scientists don't study the implementation of the scientific method. Philosophers of science think about the scientific method. Basic research scientists use it to generate new knowledge. Applied scientists typically study the knowledge that the scientific method has managed to accumulate. For example, the chemist studies the hydrogen bond, and the biologist studies the double helix of DNA, but rarely does either receive instruction concerning the scientific method *per se*. It is not only possible, but indeed is generally the case, that a person with a bachelor's degree in chemistry, geology, biology, or other scientific discipline, has not had a single college lecture on precisely how the scientific method works.

This ultimately works against the best interests of the forensic scientist, who ordinarily does not learn much about how undiscovered information is brought to light. If one wishes to know something about the hydrogen bond or the double helix of DNA, one can after all consult books on those subjects. But if one wishes to understand a unique event in which physical evidence plays a role, one must improvise, using the scientific method as the engine to generate that knowledge.

The failure of scientists in general, and of forensic scientists in particular, to understand how knowledge is acquired and applied, leads to abuse. The problem lies in the fact that the forensic sciences are frequently concerned with unique or highly unusual events. Most other scientific disciplines are concerned with the usual and the typical, and with the manner in which things generally happen. The forensic sciences, on the other hand, are concerned with the unusual and the atypical, and with the ways that things generally do not happen. This requires a change of emphasis, away from the commonplace and toward the unknown. This in return requires a return to the scientific method to answer questions concerning the physical evidence.

Consider an instance in which the relevant physical evidence consists of a broken jar of peanut butter. Looking in the index of a textbook on forensic science under "p" for peanut butter will be to no avail. There are undoubtedly experts on peanut butter, but they are probably few and far between, or expensive, or uninterested in forensic problems, or all of the above. The forensic scientist has no alternative but to learn something about peanut butter. The forensic scientist is unlikely ever to have another peanut butter case in his career, but the necessity of becoming an expert on peanut butter has been thrust upon the examiner. Formal education will provide only a direction; it is the scientific method that will provide the truth. If the scientist understands the scientific method poorly, or does not have the wit or patience to apply it properly, errors of judgment can easily occur. This point seems to have eluded the legal profession entirely—the circumstances surrounding many cases are so unusual, or so specific to a particular case, that a research regimen will be required. It may not be particularly sophisticated research. But it is research nevertheless, and the scientific method, whether full-blown or truncated, must be invoked in how this research is executed.

Also, there is a critical distinction between an observation and its interpretation. An observation is a determination or measurement made under a controlled set of conditions. Interpretation, on the other hand, is the intellectual endeavor that assigns a meaning to the observation in the light of scientific knowledge. These two elements may be summarized as "What things are," and "What things mean." It is an evasion of the responsibility of the forensic scientist to state what something "is" without accompanying that opinion, whenever possible, with a statement as to what it "means." This is not a usurpation of the province of the court. To give a court an opinion without attempting to provide the ability to place that opinion in a sensible perspective would be a disservice to the legal system. The court could be convinced of the technical soundness of the opinion, but would be forced to guess as to how that opinion should be factored into the totality of the case. From the standpoint of the court, or a jury, this would be equivalent to listening to an obscure Japanese *noh* drama without the benefit of the plot.

## § 1:21 Substitution of intuition or experience for defensible scientific fact

Virtually everyone agrees that an expert's bare opinion, unsupported by factual evidence, should be inadmissible in a court of law. And yet, precisely that sort of testimony is allowed every day in courts throughout the country by judges who believe that every statement uttered by a person with a scientific degree or employed by an agency called "scientific" is therefore a scientific opinion. Courts permit expert testimony from those with specialized knowledge. But how is a court to gauge such knowledge? The answer generally lies in the education and experience of the prospective witness.[1] A convenient means is to look for a measure of scientific education, and a university degree in a scientific discipline will ordinarily meet that test.

With an educational requirement satisfied, a court will then look at experience. But experience is very difficult to evaluate. The more experience the better, but

------

**[Section 1:21]**

[1]One of the many myths that is promulgated by the legal system is that *voir dire* and cross-examination, together with judicial discretion, will cull out the scientifically lame and halt. Certainly that does occur. More often, however, the court will not know whether the expert witness received superior grades in relevant courses at a flagship university, or had a "C" average on a football scholarship at some institution that no one in the courtroom has ever heard of. How often is a curriculum vitae checked in the course of a trial? How often is a perjury charge leveled at expert witnesses who puff up their credentials?

rarely is there any effort exerted to distinguish between 10 years of experience and one month of experience repeated 120 times, or one month of experience spread out over 10 years.[2] Furthermore, some experts exploit situations where intuition or mere suspicions can be voiced under the guise of experience. When an expert testifies to an opinion, and bases that opinion on "years of experience," the practical result is that the witness is immunized against effective cross-examination. When the witness testifies that "I have never seen another similar instance in my 26 years of experience . . .," no real scrutiny of the opinion is possible. No practical means exists for the questioner to delve into the extent and quality of that experience. Many witnesses have learned to invoke experience as a means of circumventing the responsibility of supporting an opinion with hard facts. For the witness, it eases cross-examination. But it also removes the scientific basis for the opinion.

Consider the following exchange on cross-examination:

| Question | Answer | Translation |
| --- | --- | --- |
| Is this situation unusual? | I have never seen a similar instance. | You don't know what I have seen and what I haven't, so I can say this and get away with it. |
| What is the basis of your opinion? | My 26 years of experience in the field. | It's really a surmise on my part. I believe it to be true, but I can't really tell you why I think that. It's really more of an impression that I have than anything else but I can't say that it's a surmise or a vague impression, could I? |
| Can you tell us how many cases of this type you have examined? | Many hundreds. | I don't know, and I certainly don't know how many of them would support my current position, and I might not be able to tell even if I went back and pulled the files. |
| Can you supply us with a list of all those cases? | Oh, no, I don't think so. They go back many years. | No way. You don't have any way of smoking those cases out of me, and even if I was ordered to do so, I could come up with plenty of reasons not to comply. |
| Can you supply us with the raw data on all those cases? | I don't think so. Some of them were when I was in my previous job. And some might be on microfilm. And it would take weeks or months to locate all of them. | Not a chance. |

---

[2] A knowledgeable, well-prepared attorney could probably smoke out this point, although whether he or she would win points with a jury is debatable. The fact that forensic scientists get away with this unjustified reliance on experience as often as they do may be a sad reflection on just how few knowledgeable, well-prepared attorneys there are.

| Question | Answer | Translation |
|---|---|---|
| Were those cases subjected to independent scrutiny for technical correctness? | All of them were reviewed by my supervisors. I don't have any reason to believe that their review wasn't adequate. | No. And also, now you're going to have to argue with those nameless, faceless supervisors that I have alluded to but haven't identified. |

Testimony of this sort distances the witness from science and the scientific method. And if the science is removed from the witness, then that witness has no legitimate role to play in the courtroom, and no business being there. Saks argues that expert evidence should be admitted in court *only* if it is accompanied by information that speaks to the accuracy of the expert's opinion, preventing the factfinder from grossly overvaluing the evidence.[3] *If there is no science, there can be no forensic science.*

Experience is neither a liability nor an enemy of the truth; it is a valuable commodity, but it should not be used as a mask to deflect legitimate scientific scrutiny, the sort of scrutiny that customarily is leveled at scientific evidence of all sorts. To do so is professionally bankrupt and devoid of scientific legitimacy, and courts would do well to disallow testimony of this sort. Experience ought to be used to enable the expert to remember the when and the how, why, who, and what. Experience should not make the expert less responsible, but rather more responsible for justifying an opinion with defensible scientific facts.

## § 1:22   Legal skepticism concerning case-oriented research

While many cases will of necessity require a mini-research project to adequately deal with the physical evidence, forensic scientists are frequently frustrated at the lack of respect accorded by courts to their efforts. Courts often have been skeptical of research that is directed toward a particular case. Courts frequently disallow testimony by an expert concerning some experiment specifically conducted to answer an issue raised in a particular case because the experiment did not faithfully duplicate *all* of the conditions of the incident in question, e.g., the temperature or humidity isn't known, or the origin of the test materials may not be identical in all respects to the original evidence. The same court may, however, allow another expert to testify to some vague generalizations based on experience with *none* of the conditions specified or even enunciated. This is lamentable. If legitimate research is accepted in connection with, for example, dinosaurs, or the archeology of Egypt, it is unreasonable to summarily condemn well-crafted research that may not be able to duplicate every fanciful parameter of the investigation. Courts should recognize that the questions posed by case-oriented research are often helpful to the trier of fact, and that the research conducted to answer those questions may be as elegant as any other type of research.

There has been a sharp exchange between legal scholars and forensic scientists in the literature over the past decade regarding law enforcement sponsored research addressing the reliability of fingerprint, handwriting, and hair examination.[1] Before the late 1970s, there was virtually no research that assessed the accuracy of crime laboratory results, and as a practice experts generally portrayed their results as error free. Then, in 1978, the crime laboratory proficiency testing research was

---

[3]Saks, The Legal and Scientific Evaluation of Forensic Science (Especially Fingerprint Expert Testimony), 33 Seton Hall Law Review 1167 (2003).

[Section 1:22]

[1]D. Michael Risinger and Michael J. Saks, A House with No Foundation, Issues in Science and

published that demonstrated laboratories did make errors (this is discussed in detail in Section IX).[2] Since this publication, legal critics and laboratory examiners have tangled over how the tests should be carried out, the level of difficulty of the tests, and how the results should be interpreted. The partisanship of the field became evident. While proficiency testing is a necessary laboratory quality control practice to evaluate the accuracy of examinations, the results of such testing may also be used by case adversaries to challenge evidence reports and diminish the standing and testimony of scientists when they go to court. At the ends of the spectrum, forensic examiners have fought for the "good name" of their profession and defended their practices, and critics have attacked what they see as an "illusion of infallibility" that some forensic examiners attempt to convey in courts of law. All researchers, law based and government laboratory based, need to exercise the utmost care to ensure their research is free from distortion and bias.

## VI. STANDARDS OF OPERATION, STANDARDS OF PERFORMANCE

### § 1:23  Generally

The forensic sciences require adherence to standards of operation and of performance.[1] These standards must be clearly enunciated and must be, at least in their basic form, the consensus of opinion of workers in that particular subject area. Stated differently, forensic scientists are not entitled to indulge whims in the conduct of their work. They must adhere to performance norms which have been previously laid down. A forensic scientist who adopts an extreme position that runs counter to the flow of prevailing opinion on a subject, or who enters an area in which operational norms have not been established, has a burden even greater than usual to justify that position in the light of good scientific practice.

A problem arises when the forensic scientist is confronted with a unique problem, a problem not previously encountered and unlikely ever to occur again in the career of that scientist. This situation arises more commonly than might be thought. The forensic scientist is asked to characterize or examine some peculiar substance—a sample of peanut butter, or a physical match between two minute broken pieces of pine needle, or to extract from tissue or bodily fluids some new drug. The analyst cannot go to a textbook on forensic science for a direct answer. Instead, the analyst must look beyond the horizons of the forensic science discipline and acquire the knowledge necessary to deal with the problem at hand.

But while there may not be established procedures in the forensic laboratory for each one of the myriad of materials that could possibly represent physical evidence in a particular case, there are nevertheless standards of scientific endeavor which are applicable to every situation:

(1)   personal bias must be subdued;

(2)   the problem must be tacked down emphatically;

(3)   a hypothesis must be posed;

---

Technology (August 2003); Letters from Readers, Forum, Issues in Science and Technology (January 2004).

[2]Joseph L. Peterson et al., Crime Laboratory Proficiency Testing Research Program, (U.S. Government Printing Office, Washington, DC, 1978).

**[Section 1:23]**

[1]The notion of standards is certainly not new. In a surprisingly scientific view of things for 450 B.C., Mo Tzu said that:

For any doctrine, some standard must be established. To expound a doctrine without a standard is like determining the directions of sunrise and sunset on a revolving potter's wheel. In this way the distinction of right and wrong and benefit and harm cannot be clearly known. Therefore for any doctrine there must be the three standards:

(1) There must be a basis or foundation,

(2) There must be an examination,

(3) There must be practical application and interpretation.

Wing-Tsit Chan (ed.), A Sourcebook in Chinese Philosophy 222 (1963).

(4) experiments must be conducted to test the hypothesis;

(5) if necessary to clarify an issue, subordinate hypotheses must be developed and tested; and

(6) conclusions must rest on evidence from the experiments.

In addition, the analyst must possess at least a threshold conversancy with the subject. A chemist attempting to identify a plant fragment would be lost; likewise would be a botanist attempting to identify a mineral.

Given the many types of physical evidence that may be collected and submitted to a crime laboratory for analysis and interpretation, forensic examiners argued for decades it was ill advised, if not impossible, to adopt standardized methods of analysis. Examiners feared being confronted at trial by an opponent with a "book of standards" that had not been strictly followed in a given case. After all, criminal acts may be committed in any type of setting, and coupled with varieties of tangible evidence produced, scientific approaches might need to be modified from case to case. But, the introduction of DNA typing in the 1980s, and the need to prepare for challenges to this new technology in court, led the field to embrace guidelines for quality assurance issued by the FBIs Technical Working Group on DNA Analysis Methods (TWGDAM) in 1991.[2] This opened the way for standards efforts in many other forensic specialties. Several other scientific working groups devoted to the formation of educational standards, quality assurance guidelines, and analytical protocols have now been formed in a wide range of evidence testing areas.[3] By 2004, there were nine such active working groups. The American Society for Testing and Materials is another organization that has been active in this area for decades and seeks to develop and publish consensus standards and, through its E-30 committee, works on the development of standards in many forensic areas, including criminalistics, questioned documents, forensic engineering, fire debris analysis, drug testing analysis, and collection and preservation of physical evidence.[4]

## § 1:24  Reliability, validity, precision, and accuracy[1]

The methods utilized by the forensic scientist must be shown by appropriate scientific research to be reliable, valid, precise, and accurate. In general usage by the lay public, these terms have somewhat vague and overlapping meaning, but to the scientist their meanings are clear.

*Reliability* refers to the extent to which a measuring instrument produces the same result when it is used repeatedly to measure the same object or event. If a bathroom scale reports different weight when the same person stands on it repeatedly, then it lacks even reliability. Thus, a parade of forensic scientists who make the same subjective judgment, or a series of machines that give the same readings in response to the same evidence sample, can only be said to be reliable.

*Validity* refers to the degree to which a measuring instrument measures what it purports to measure. A reliable watch set to California time will not be valid in Massachusetts or Guam. Even a bathroom scale that is highly reliable will not be valid if it is used to measure intelligence. Similarly, forensic scientists or machines that are in agreement may be highly reliable (in agreement with each other) without

[2]Technical Working Group on DNA Analysis Methods (TWGDAM) Guidelines for Quality Assurance Program for DNA Analysis, 18 Crime Laboratory Digest 44 (1991).

[3]Dwight Adams and Kevin Lothridge, Scientific Working Groups, 2 Forensic Science Communications (July 2000).

[4]ASTM International, 100 Barr Harbor Drive, PO Box C700, West Conshohocken, PA, 19428-2959, USA.

**[Section 1:24]**

[1]John Keenan Taylor, Quality Assurance of Chemical Measurements (1987); G. Kateman & F.W. Pijpers, Quality Control in Analytical Chemistry (1981).

being valid (without reaching the correct answer). They can all be wrong.

*Accuracy* implies conformity to a standard. If one accepts the bull's-eye of a dartboard as the standard, and if all of the darts hit the bull's-eye, then accuracy has been achieved. If, on the other hand, all of the darts hit the board in a one inch cluster at 7 o'clock but 4 inches from the bull's-eye, then the accuracy is poor.

*Precision* refers to the refinement of a measure. How precise a measure needs to be depends on the task at hand. The nearest whole pounds will suffice to weigh players on a football team; it is too gross a measure for weighing samples of drugs.

## § 1:25    Expression of certainty of opinions

Forensic scientists have an obligation to express their opinions in a manner which is as clear as possible. A disservice is rendered to the legal system if the court, jury, or client attorney is forced to guess as to the certainty to which the expert's conclusions are intended.

In most instances, the forensic scientist will be unable to express an opinion in terms of mathematical probabilities. There are few exceptions. Because allele frequencies are known for many populations, a DNA analyst may be able to state something along the lines of "the alleles in this bloodstain may be expected to occur randomly once in 1.2 billion Caucasians, in 0.8 billion Blacks, and in 1.4 billion Hispanics." The ability to express an opinion in a quantifiable fashion is limited to just a few physical evidence categories. But in most physical evidence categories, there simply are no defensible probability models that may be applied, and conclusions must be framed verbally rather than mathematically. Moreover, the difference is not merely one of expression, but of the basis of the opinion. While for DNA analysis there are data on which to base objective probability calculations, for most forensic sciences examiners have to intuit their own subjective probability estimates. This is often a frustration to the user of the opinion—court or jury—who would prefer a more finite expression of certainty (and uncertainty).

Any opinion rendered by a forensic scientist must have in it an associated or embedded statement as to the conviction of the scientist as to the reliance that may be placed on the opinion. In practice, this is difficult to achieve. An opinion may be emphatic, e.g., "A comparison of the questioned text with the exemplar writing reveals sufficient agreement to establish the suspect as having written the questioned text." Or it may justifiably be far less than emphatic, e.g., "A comparison of the questioned text with the exemplar writing reveals some minimal agreement with respect to handwriting characteristics; the amount of agreement is insufficient to establish the suspect as having written the questioned text." The user of the opinion—court, jury, or bar—is understandably interested in knowing where on the continuum of relative certainty the forensic scientist would have his or her opinion pegged. But problems exist with nomenclature, and problems exist in communicating the certainty with which the scientist has embraced the opinion. In one study,[1] researchers asked test subjects to ascribe a mathematical probability, 0 to 1, to the phrase "quite likely." The mean response was 0.79. The mean response for the phrase "quite unlikely," was, however 0.11. The two values should add up to unity. This asymmetry in how common verbal phrases are associated with probability is common in our language. Slow, reluctant efforts are being made within the forensic sciences, however, to standardize to a greater extent the language in which opinions are couched.[2]

The emergence of DNA as the new "gold standard" of scientific evidence has been

---

**[Section 1:25]**

[1]S. Lichtenstein & J. Newman, Empirical Scaling of Common Verbal Phrases Associated with Numerical Probabilities, 9 Psychonomic Sci. 563 (1967).

[2]D. A. Rudram, Interpretation of Scientific

pronounced by legal practitioners and forensic scientists alike. DNA typing was heavily scrutinized in the 1980s and 1990s by forensic examiners and jurists, and has emerged as a scientifically robust and legally accepted form of individualizing evidence. Its role in reversing erroneous convictions, which sometimes had resulted from been less than adequate forensic science evidence, also did much to propel it into judicial and public acceptance. While the sensitivity and specificity of DNA typing is unparalleled, what it has also done is bring attention to the *weaknesses* of some of the other forensic disciplines. DNA examiners could evaluate the strength of matches and nonmatches of biological materials on empirical scientific grounds. Authors such as Saks and Koehler have called on the forensic field to apply the standards and academic rigor of DNA typing to other specialties like firearms, bite marks, and fingerprints, and to experimentally "test the core assumptions" of these fields.[3] They have challenged the field to build the necessary empirical foundations that would enable forensic examiners to express probabilistic assessments of "matching" evidence. Rudin and Inman have replied that while DNA typing has raised the bar for all scientific evidence presented in today's judicial system, the construction of data bases for other pattern evidence categories is an extremely complex task, and the quantitative probability models of DNA typing may not be appropriate for non-biological, pattern evidence.[4] What is clear is that thoughtful legal scholars and research minded forensic scientists should collaborate on developing a long range research agenda (that private and public funding agencies will embrace) to answer some of these challenging scientific evidentiary problems.

## § 1:26    The mismeasure of evidence

Everyone connected with the justice system expects forensic science to be infallible. It is not. The law would prefer hard facts, inviolate and certain. But science, however pure it may be in the abstract, must be practiced in the real world by fallible human beings using imperfect tools. The standard expectation that pertains to any forensic endeavor is that the work is exemplary. The analyst is expected to deliver quality work, and anything else will be criticized or even rejected. But to consistently deliver quality work over a long period of time will require an enormous dedication of resources—time, effort, care, and money. Consistently high quality work can be provided, but the cost will be high. Quality work on a shoestring is an oxymoron. If adequate resources are not provided and an error in analysis or interpretation occurs, typically the blame is placed on the analyst rather than the withholder of resources.

Techniques exist by means of which error may be measured and managed, but error is never entirely absent. Any forensic scientist who believes that he or she will complete a satisfying and rewarding professional career without making a serious mistake will eventually be taught otherwise, and will suffer treble recompense for their arrogance. The trick is to try to keep the error out of the courtroom. Most mistakes in the laboratory are the result of inexperience, inadequate training of the analyst, the analyst being in a hurry, or the analyst simply wanting to please and be helpful. Some errors are inherent in the nature of evidence and limitations of analytical methods.

It is possible to *minimize* the possibility of error, however. The means typically employed to accomplish this are an ensemble of techniques—the technical review of the work of the forensic scientist, proficiency testing, accreditation of laboratories, and certification of analysts.

---

Evidence, 36 Sci. & Just. 133 (1996).

[3]Saks and Koehler, The Coming Paradigm Shift in Forensic Identification Science, 309 Science 892 (2005).

[4]Norah Rudin and Keith Inman, The Shifty Paradigm, The CAC News, Part I (4th Quarter 2005) and Part II (1st Quarter 2006).

## § 1:27   Proficiency testing as a means of ensuring quality in technical procedures

Proficiency testing is a means by which the preceding qualities can be measured. Evidence created by one laboratory (the "manufacturer") may be submitted to forensic scientists for their testing and their results can be compared with the known values from the manufacturer. To use this procedure effectively, the analyst is not informed of the "true" answer until after the test has been completed. In this manner, errors, or potential sources of error, may be identified.

Error is a concept that causes a good deal of consternation in the minds of forensic scientists. Modern science embraces error forthrightly—error is measured and is managed. Forensic science in general, however, has tended to deal with error by burying its head in the sand; clearly it will not be permitted to continue to do so in the future.

Koppl has presented an interesting critique of forensic laboratories, attributing the problem of error to their institutional structure and the lack of sufficient incentives to produce high quality work.[1] As an alternative, he proposes a new system of "competitive self-regulation." He argues the forensic sciences have been largely structured to eliminate the competitiveness present in the scientific world at large. The forensic enterprise has had nearly a monopoly on tests introduced into court and this sometimes leads to complacency and unconscious bias. While others have argued for the independence of forensic laboratories from law enforcement, either under the courts or another governmental agency, Koppl calls for "competitive self regulation" wherein redundancy of examinations among different laboratories would supply the examiner with the motive to find the truth and apply appropriate scientific standards.

Proficiency testing, the most appropriate means for the identification of sources of error, was unpopular with forensic science practitioners in general because of a widespread belief that a missed proficiency testing sample will be used to discredit them in court. This belief is not entirely without justification. The potential exists that in court, counsel for the opposing side will in a self-serving fashion misconstrue, pervert and abuse a missed proficiency test. Certainly in a court of law, where testimony is given in response to posed questions, and where the witness ordinarily is unable to exercise any significant control over the issues under discussion, the ability of an expert witness to defend against this type of supposed self-righteous indignation is severely hampered.

Consequently, many forensic scientists viewed proficiency testing with considerable anxiety because they feared that a single, isolated substandard proficiency test will compromise their entire career.[2] Under the adversary system of justice it is the legitimate function of opposing counsel to attempt to discredit the testimony of the expert witness, whether the witness is correct or not, and whether or not the attorney personally believes that the witness is correct. It is the function of the expert, on the other hand, to be technically correct just as often as is humanly possible, and in recognition of this fact most forensic scientists consent, somewhat reluctantly and with trepidation, to a program of proficiency testing. Increasingly, however, forensic scientists have come to recognize that the solution to the issue of

---

[Section 1:27]

[1]Koppl, How to Improve Forensic Science, 20 European J. L. and Econ. 255 (2005).

[2]Forensic scientists are often quite touchy on this issue. Forensic scientists, when questioned about proficiency tests they have taken, would like to be able to ask their cross-examiner, "Have you ever lost a case? It doesn't matter if it was years ago, it doesn't matter if the case was hopeless to begin with, it doesn't matter that you were tired, or simply didn't have time to prepare adequately, or were hampered by a lack of investigative resources. The question to you is: Have you ever lost a case? Because if you have, then how could you possibly expect this jury to accept anything you say?"

proficiency testing lies not in avoidance, but in acceptance. Proficiency testing is simply the cost of doing business in the forensic science profession; it cannot be avoided.[3]

A point that has eluded the legal system, however, is that proficiency testing samples may be made so easy that everyone would get them correct, or they could be made so difficult that no one would get them correct. To ferret out error, proficiency tests should be of varying degrees of difficulty, arranged so as to represent a reasonable challenge to the analyst. Additionally, some proficiency tests should be *extremely* challenging, designed to severely tax the skills, knowledge, and ingenuity of the analyst. In the casual parlance of the forensic science community, these are referred to as "stinker" tests. It is to be expected that no analyst will achieve perfect results on these particularly challenging tests, and a less-than-perfect performance on those tests should garner no blame on the part of the analyst. The analyst, however, has reason to suspect that in court his nose will be rubbed in the muffed test, and that he will be unfairly stigmatized.

## § 1:28  Signal detection theory and proficiency testing

Signal detection theory (SDT) is a means for reviewing decision-making in forensic examinations and is designed to disentangle the two components of accuracy in ambiguous decision situations: (1) the examiner's diagnostic/discrimination abilities; and (2) the decision threshold of the examiner. Two examiners with identical technical skills will arrive at different answers if they employ different threshold criteria in terms of what constitutes an identity or a match.[1] Discrimination ability is actually determined by two components—the examiner's technical skills and the quality of the evidence itself. Technical ability is dependent upon the examiner's training, the laboratory's resources (instrumentation, equipment, etc.), and the types of tests being performed. Decision threshold will similarly be influenced by two factors: prior probability (or expectancies) of a positive conclusion, and utilities associated with a particular outcome (what might be termed motivation). What is the frequency that a comparison yields a positive (match) or negative (nonmatch) conclusion? What are the real world consequences of an examiner's conclusion that items do or do not share a common origin? The forensic scientist's conclusions can have profound consequences for parties involved.

Lower decision thresholds will yield more "hits" but will also produce more false positives. Higher decision thresholds will produce more correct rejections, but more false negatives. We know, too, with forensic evidence that certain types of evidence, such as fingerprints, bear features more reliably measured and interpreted than evidence such as handwriting that is less distinctive and has more variability from the same source. (A person's signature will vary slightly every time they write it.) Examiners may employ criteria that are not published, agreed upon, or for that matter clearly articulated. It would be extremely helpful to the field of forensic science to know if variations in decisional accuracy are the result of differences in examiners' backgrounds and training, or merely the employment of different decision thresholds. Do decision thresholds vary among forensic specialties, or might the thresholds vary for the same examiner depending upon the case or the types of other evidence present? Peterson et al.[2] have found that examiners in different laboratories prepare exclusionary reports at very different rates, compared with the

---

[3]Today, proficiency testing is widely accepted in the field. In fact, the recent BJS census of Crime Laboratories found 97% of labs engaged in this practice. Joseph L. Peterson and Matthew J. Hickman, Census of Publicly Funded Crime Laboratories (2005).

[Section 1:28]

[1]Phillips et al., The Application of Signal Detection Theory to Decision-Making in Forensic Science, 46 J. Forensic Sci. 294 (2001).

[2]Joseph L. Peterson et al., Forensic Evidence

fraction of time they may conclude their findings are merely inconclusive. There are many factors that influence examiners' projected estimates of likely matches—from the presence of suspects in cases to the use of computerized data bases that may have already assigned a priority value to an item of evidence in terms of its degree of fit with the unknown sample.

What SDT can do is assist in sorting out the "raw diagnostic skill" of examiners from "decision thresholds." The capabilities of examiners with different backgrounds, training and experience may be determined. The factors that cause decision thresholds to rise or fall could be studied. No systematic study yet exists to determine if the organizational home of a forensic examiner (e.g., government examiner or defense expert) influences the decision thresholds employed. A major change that would be needed to enable proficiency testing data to be of greater utility in something like SDT would be to have examiners give their conclusions a "confidence rating" (perhaps on a scale of certainty from 1 to 10) which could help set the decision thresholds used by different examiners. We would also need to introduce changes to enable the data from the same individuals or laboratories to be linked over successive examinations. It would also be helpful to have an expert rating/assessment of the level of difficulty of the test being administered. There are many reasons why SDT should be employed by the forensic field to aid in research on forensic science decision making.

## VII.   ISSUES OF PROFESSIONAL PRACTICE

### § 1:29   Documentation of findings

Forensic science cannot be viewed solely in terms of its products; it is also judged by the legitimacy of the processes by which evidence is examined and interpreted. Any opinion rendered by a forensic scientist in a written report or in court testimony must have a basis in fact and theory. Without such a basis, any conclusions reached are bereft of validity and should be treated with derision.

The forensic scientist must always bear the burden of responsibility of justifying an opinion, and the work that has led to that opinion. If this work is not properly documented, it deserves to be rejected. It is not within the prerogatives of the forensic scientist to waive this requirement, and no one has the right to release the forensic scientist from this burden. Notetaking and other forms of documentation are as important to the forensic scientist as a proper grounding in chemistry, biology or other discipline. In general, documentation to support conclusions must be such that in the absence of the original examiner, another competent examiner could evaluate what was done and interpret the data. The standard here, which should be met, is whether an entry in laboratory notes would be intelligible to another analyst without additional explanation.

### § 1:30   Statistical basis for evidence evaluation

Behind every opinion rendered by a forensic scientist there is a statistical basis. We may not know what that basis is, and we may have no feasible means of developing an understanding of that basis, but it is futile to deny that one exists.

In the forensic sciences, there is an incredible amount of difficulty attached to the development of a statistical basis for evidence evaluation.[1] It is not because the forensic science community lacks the wit to develop these statistics or is too lazy to

---

and The Police (National Institute of Justice,     Statistics in Forensic Science (1991).
1984).

[Section 1:30]

[1]C.G.G. Aitken & D.A. Stoney, The Use of

commence the process. It is because the types of examination that are often conducted in forensic laboratories do not lend themselves to analysis by conventional statistics.[2] There are exceptions, however, as in blood group typing, DNA typing, and some aspects of gunshot residue models.

The lack of such data has consequences that help us to better appreciate what forensic individualization science aims to do and what it is able to achieve. The most common and coherent theory of forensic identification is that where there is a high degree of variation among attributes (of toolmark striations, writing, friction ridges on skin, and so on), then where a "match" is observed the probability that the match is coincidental rather than reflecting a shared source will be very small. Forensic sciences that have such data can actually calculate the probability of a coincidental match, and report that probability to the judge and jury. Forensic individualization sciences that lack actual data, which is most of them, have no choice but to either intuitively estimate those underlying probabilities and calculate the coincidental match probability from those subjective probabilities, or simply to assume the conclusion of a minuscule probability of a coincidental match (and in fact they do the latter). Moreover, since the basis of all forensic identification is probability theory, examiners can never really assert a conclusion of an "identification to the exclusion of all others in the world," but at best can only assert a very small (objective or subjective) probability of a coincidental match. Those forensic scientists who claim to have identified something "to the exclusion of all others in the world" are offering more of a hope or an overstatement than an opinion that rests on a scientifically meaningful basis. Most, or at least many, forensic scientists understand this well enough that they can explain it to a judge or jury if someone were to ask them to do so. It is ironic that those areas of forensic science that have real underlying data offer more modest statements of individualization, while those limited to subjective or impressionistic data make the strongest statements, sometimes of absolute certainty. Finally, the probabilistic basis of forensic identification means that debates over whether there really literally are "no two alike" in some area of forensic science are not relevant to the real issue in an identification: what the probability is of a coincidental match.

## § 1:31 Personal bias in observation and interpretation

Personal bias and the influence of expectations caused by knowing "too much" about a case have an unknown impact on the judgments of forensic scientists. Well trained and well managed forensic scientists try to reduce it to a very low level, but no prudent scientist would claim that it was forever absent.[1] Bias that would cause the forensic scientist to embrace a position concerning the guilt or innocence of an accused is clearly improper. That sort of bias is easily recognized for its evil *en se*, however. More insidious is the sort of bias in which an analyst will engage to protect findings once they have been developed, or where the results of a test are expected to the extent that the expected results are observed even when they are absent or only marginally present. For example, an analyst might present data in a graphical form in which small effects appear major by stretching the axis. It is pos-

---

[2]The late Paul Kirk put it thusly:

[Forensic science] is concerned with the unlikely and the unusual. Other sciences are concerned primarily with the likely and the usual. The derivation of equations, formulas, and generalizations summarizing the normal behavior of any system in the universe is a major goal of the established sciences . . . . Mathematical analysis is even more necessary for interpreting the significance of each fact that is elicited relative to the evidence. However, we do not yet know how to make such an analysis, despite technical success in determining the actual facts of a crime through study of physical evidence.

Paul L. Kirk, Criminalistics, 40 Science 367 (1963).

**[Section 1:31]**

[1]See Risinger, Saks, Rosenthal & Thompson, The *Daubert/Kumho* Implications of Observer Effects in Forensic Science: Hidden Problems of Expectation and Suggestion, 90 Cal. L. Rev. 1 (2002).

sible that the analyst might not even be consciously aware of the implications of these types of delinquencies. The potential exists here for diverse sorts of rationalization, with the consequent application of a more forgiving set of criteria when faced with unexpected results.

This type of bias is nurtured by the analyst working in an atmosphere where external sources of feedback are not in place. The remedy is to have the work of the analyst reviewed by peers or supervisors, where subtle and insidious mechanisms of bias may be unveiled and brought to light. Earlier, we referenced the proposal by Koppl who extends the call for external review of examiners' findings to routine checks of forensic examinations by outside, competing forensic laboratories.

The 2004 Madrid terrorist bombing case and the FBIs misidentification of a crime scene latent print with a candidate fingerprint from an automated fingerprint identification system led to an international team's review of the procedures followed in the case, and a report by the FBIs Quality Assurance and Training Unit. The report spoke of the influence of the automated system's initial designation of the incorrect print as a candidate on the original examiner, the pressures inherent in such a high profile case, and the mindset formed by those latent print examiners who subsequently confirmed the initial erroneous match. This appears to be a classic case of confirmation bias (or context effect) in which the expectations of those approaching the examination of the prints affected their perceptions of the evidence.[2]

Dror et al.'s recent article empirically verifies, albeit in a small study, the threats posed by extraneous biasing information on forensic comparisons. Five fingerprint examiners, in different areas of the world, were each presented with a different pair of fingerprints that they had found to match five years before. These identifications were independently verified by other examiners. In the experiment, they were presented with the same set of fingerprints, but were told they were the ones the FBI had mistakenly matched in the Madrid bombing. (These examiners were unfamiliar with the actual prints in this case.) This time, four of the five examiners reported the prints did <u>not</u> match, contradicting the conclusions they had reached previously.[3]

To diminish personal bias, forensic scientists can make use of many of the same sorts of checks that are utilized in many other scientific disciplines, viz., blind proficiency testing, replicate testing within the laboratory or in another laboratory, confirmation of observations by other analysts, and marking of samples in a manner so that the outcome of a particular test cannot be anticipated.[4] Several states (New York, Oklahoma, and Texas) have formed oversight commissions to review and accredit crime laboratories in their jurisdictions. A provision in the Illinois Advisory Committee Act (Public Act 093-0784) which went into effect January 1, 2005, acknowledges one of the purposes of the Act is to ensure laboratory examiners are not "inadvertently influenced" by extraneous information.

## § 1:32   Physical evidence is not the property of one side or the other

Good science requires that physical evidence not be considered as chattel; it is not the exclusive property of one side or the other in a contested matter, but must be held in trust for both sides. The side that gets to it first must recognize a responsibility to conserve and to preserve the evidence for an independent examination by the other side. Whether or not a jurisdiction accepts this as a legal procedural rule, it is

---

[2]Robert B. Stacey, Report on the Erroneous Fingerprint Individualization in the Madrid Training Bombing Case, Forensic Science Communications, Volume 7, Number 1, January 2005.

[3]Dror at al., Contextual Information Renders Experts Vulnerable to Making Erroneous Identifications, 156 Forensic Sci. Int'l 74 (2006).

[4]See generally Saks et al., Context Effects in Forensic Science: A Review and Application of the Science of Science to Crime Laboratory Practice in the Untied States, 43 Science & Justice 77 (2003).

an ethical principle of forensic science and a maxim of science in general.

## VIII.  SUBJECTIVE TESTS VS. OBJECTIVE TESTS

### § 1:33  Generally

Many of the examinations conducted in a forensic science laboratory are rather subjective. A subjective test[1] calls upon the experience of the examiner for the proper interpretation of the test results. This is a troublesome area for the forensic scientist, or at least it *should* be. Clearly it is a troublesome area for the courts and for attorneys.

"Subjectivity" typically occurs in two stages of forensic science individualization. First, the examiner makes a complex judgment as to whether there is a match. Second, the examiner must estimate the improbability of occurrence of such a match in order to evaluate the likelihood that the questioned and the known share a common source or match as a matter of coincidence. The first of these steps could and perhaps some day will be done by optical scanners and computers. For now it is done by the exercise of human perception and cognitive processing to compare patterns, and that makes it "subjective." These cognitive tasks actually are something that humans generally are extremely good at. The second stage is more troublesome and should be the heart of the problem for forensic science and for law. This second stage is interpretation of the meaning of a match. That problem is that in order to estimate the probability, or improbability of something, one needs data about the population from which it came—more precisely, data about each of the elements on which comparison has been made—and the appropriate statistical calculus must be applied. For every area of forensic identification science (except DNA typing), because there exist no relative frequency data ("objective probabilities"), examiners have no choice but to intuit, to rely on "experience," in other words, to guesstimate what those values are and therefore to reach judgments of the probability of a coincidental match based on what literally are known as "subjective probabilities." This second stage involves human judgmental tasks that humans are generally quite poor at.[2]

Of course, the classical definition of subjective raises at least the possibility of caprice, of personal bias, of conditioning by the personal characteristics of the mind of the analyst, and of other motivation, which might range from the merely inexplicit to the wholly sinister. But this is an unfortunate consequence of the English language, rather than a fundamental defect of reason. The opposite of subjective is *objective*,[3] which carries the connotation of detachment and impartiality. But the cliché "a lack of objectivity" does not reflect back on the antonym "subjectivity," but implicitly suggests personal bias.

There is a tendency to view subjective tests with some measure of skepticism or even distrust. But not all forensic tests are equivalent in the amount of subjectivity that is involved. Two issues are involved. The first issue is how much subjectivity exists, and the second issue is whether a higher level of subjectivity is correlated with a higher level of unreliability.

Cognitive scientists have developed methods for studying subjective phenomena

---

**[Section 1:33]**

[1]Webster's New Collegiate Dictionary gives, as the second definition of the word subjective, the following: "**2.** Exhibiting or affected by personal bias, emotional background, etc.; as a *subjective* judgment." (Italics in original).

[2]See the considerable body of research on decision heuristics.

[3]Webster's New Collegiate Dictionary gives, as the second definition of the word objective, the following: "**2.** Exhibiting or characterized by emphasis upon or the tendency to view events, phenomena, ideas, etc., as external and apart from self-consciousness; not subjective; hence, detached; impersonal unprejudiced; as, an *objective* discussion; *objective* criteria." (Italics in original).

and have produced massive amounts of research for well over a century.[4] Relevant to the problem of subjective judgment in many areas of forensic work, that research has studied the conditions under which such judgments are more stable and consistent within and across observers as well as the factors that produce distortions in the perception of complex stimuli, methods of eliciting judgments that maximize sensitivity and consistency, and ways of translating subjective experience into objective criteria.[5]

Ironically, given the importance of subjective judgments in the forensic sciences, there has not been much research into the implications of subjective testing, nor much borrowing from cognitive science research (as there has been in other fields involving subjective pattern recognition, such as radiology and sonar). The factors that could be expected to influence subjectivity—the nature of the task, the nature of the evidence, training, experience, alienation, fatigue, the potential for rationalization when confronted with apparent error, indifference on the part of laboratory administrators, an inclination to please one's superiors—have not been addressed within the forensic science profession. Reliability and validity of subjective judgments can be measured. But in forensic science, little work has been done on the problem. As we begin a new millennium, this remains one of the major challenges to the forensic sciences.

It is possible to construct an array of physical evidence types, and indicate roughly how much subjectivity is to be expected, as in Figure 1.[6] At the lower end might be a jigsaw-like "physical match" of two items, where the fit of irregular margins indicates convincingly that the two items were at one time joined. Here the interpretation rests squarely on the items themselves—the objects—hence the examination would rank low in terms of subjectivity. At the other extreme, the comparison of an evidence bullet and a test fired bullet would rank high in terms of subjectivity; here the interpretation has much to do with the training, the experience, and the notions of the examiner.

**Figure 1**

**Relative Subjectivity in Various Forensic Science Specialties**

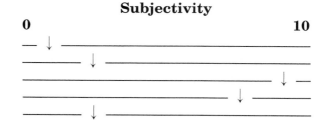

Subjectivity

| | 0 | 10 |

Jigsaw-type Physical Match
Drug and Narcotic Analysis
Handwriting Identification
Firearm and Toolmark Identification
Fingerprint Identification

---

[4]For some older examples, see G.T. Fechner, Elements of Psychophysics (originally published 1860; H.E. Alder trans., 1966); L.L. Thurstone, Attitudes Can be Measured, 33 Am. J. Sociology 529 (1928); H. Gulliksen, Measurement of Subjective Values, 21 Psychometrika 229 (1956).

[5]See D.M. Green & J.A. Swets, Signal Detection Theory And Psychophysics (1966); Lawrence Barsalou, Cognitive Psychology: An Introduction For Cognitive Scientists (1992); Michael Suelzer, Analyses of Human Quantitative Judgment: Models of Sequential Magnitude Estimation (1991); Daniel Algom, Psychophysical Approaches to Cognition (1992); and work appearing in such journals as: Perception and Psychophysics, Cognitive Psychology, Cognitive Science, and Pattern Recognition. See also Phillips et al., The Application of Signal Detection Theory to Decision-Making in Forensic Science, 46 J. Forensic Sci. 294 (2001).

[6]The designations given here are merely approximations; some disagreement within the forensic science community would be expected. This is particularly true if it is someone's personal ox that is being gored.

## Subjectivity

|                                | 0                                                          | 10 |
| ------------------------------ | ---------------------------------------------------------- | -- |

Hair

Fibers

Paint

Glass

Soil

Blood Spatter Interpretation

Serology

Voiceprint

Bitemarks

Fire/Arson

## IX. VULNERABILITY OF PHYSICAL EVIDENCE CATEGORIES IN LIGHT OF *DAUBERT* CRITERIA

### § 1:34  *Daubert* criteria

In *Daubert v. Merrell Dow Pharmaceuticals, Inc.*,[1] the U.S. Supreme Court interpreted the criteria for the admissibility of scientific evidence under the Federal Rules; the implications of this decision have been extensively discussed elsewhere in this work. It is of some interest, however, to see how various evidence categories size up when viewed in the light of these criteria.

The *Daubert* court says that the scientific wheat may be winnowed from the scientific chaff by careful attention to four criteria:

(1)  whether a theory or technique can be (and has been) tested;

(2)  whether the theory or technique has been subjected to peer review and publication (as a means of helping to expose weaknesses in methodology and analysis, as *Daubert*'s discussion of these criteria goes on to explain);

(3)  the known or potential rate of error, and the existence and maintenance of standards controlling the technique's operation; and

(4)  finally, "general acceptance" can yet have a bearing on the inquiry.

Criterion (4) would tend to "grandfather" in many types of forensic examinations. For example, firearms identification is so firmly entrenched that it is unlikely that courts will look askance at it, despite the fact it would be sorely tried to comply with criteria (1) and (3). Criterion (2), if it is understood as most courts have understood it, namely, as being satisfied merely by the fact of publication in peer reviewed journals, is unlikely to pose a problem for most evidence categories. It is in connection with criteria (1) and (3) that *Daubert* poses a threat to many evidence categories. The "known or potential rate of error" alluded to in criterion (3) simply has not been established for the majority of forensic examinations, nor are there good mechanisms in place for attempting to do so. Criterion (1) speaks to whether a method can be (or has been) tested for its validity and for its applicability. Many forensic examinations have been evaluated, but by flawed testing methods. The issue is not whether a particular approach has been tested, but whether the sort of testing that has taken place could pass muster in a court of science. If not, then that approach may not have a legitimate claim to the indulgence of a court of law.

---

**[Section 1:34]**

[1]*Daubert v. Merrell Dow Pharmaceuticals, Inc.*, 509 U.S. 579, 113 S. Ct. 2786, 125 L. Ed. 2d 469, 27 U.S.P.Q.2d 1200, Prod. Liab. Rep. (CCH) P 13494, 37 Fed. R. Evid. Serv. 1, 23 Envtl. L. Rep. 20979 (1993).

In view of the fact that no one has previously attempted to do so, it may be of some benefit to view a number of types of forensic science evidence, assessing them in terms of subjectivity and in terms of *Daubert* criteria (1) and (3). Although this is attempted here for just a few evidence types, this kind of assessment could be accomplished for virtually every category of physical evidence.

### § 1:35　Forensic identification subspecialties—Blood and other physiological fluids[1]

*Subjectivity*: Moderately low.

*Reliability in the minds of forensic scientists*: High. The reliability may be determined with considerable confidence by means of proficiency testing.

*Vulnerability to attack in the light of* Daubert *criteria (1) and (3)*: Moderately low.

Early in the 20th Century it was recognized that the blood of humans displayed a host of genetic markers, some of which could be demonstrated in dried bloodstains. Principal among these markers was the ABO blood group system, and for many years this was the only blood group system for which reliable typing methods for a dried stain were available.

Then, in the middle 1960s, a number of serum isoenzyme and serum protein groups were successfully typed in dried stains; this marked an epoch in the history of forensic serology. To ABO typing was added Phosphoglucomutase (PGM), Esterase D (EsD), Erythrocyte Acid Phosphatase (EAP), Glyoxalase (Glo), Adenylate Kinase (AK), Haptoglobin, Group Specific Component (Gc), and others. While ABO typing was capable of discriminating between individuals at a level of 15 to 48%, the isoenzyme and serum protein groups could typically discriminate between individuals at a level of a few percent down to as refined a level as 0.001%.

All of this was essentially rendered obsolete in the early 1980s, with the introduction of DNA (Deoxyribonucleic acid) typing. DNA typing has eclipsed conventional blood typing, and is widely viewed as being one of the two most important advances in forensic science in the 20th Century.[2] DNA typing is capable of exceedingly high discrimination, and in favorable circumstances it can be shown that only one person in several billion could have been the source of the evidence bloodstain.

DNA profiling was performed initially using restriction fragment length polymorphism (RFLP) analysis that produced the "bar code" pattern familiar to many. This process, while highly discriminating, was time consuming and required a substantial amount of sample in relatively good condition to produce results. Polymerase chain reaction (PCR) based tests became the next generation of profiling that amplified (made copies of) the DNA and proved to be faster and more sensitive than RFLP techniques, and had greater success with older, degraded samples. While laboratories using such techniques have to be more concerned about contamination issues in the handling and analysis of biological evidence, PCR technology created many opportunities to reopen old cases and search for the pres-

---

**[Section 1:35]**

[1]John I. Thornton, DNA Profiling, 67 Chemical & Engineering News (Nov. 20, 1989); Lawrence Kobilinsky, Deoxyribonucleic Acid Structure and Function—A Review, in Forensic Science Handbook, Vol. III, 287 (Richard Saferstein ed., 1993); John S. Waye & Ronald M. Fourney, Forensic DNA Typing of Highly Polymorphic VNTR Loci, in Forensic Science Handbook, Vol. III, 358 (Richard Saferstein ed., 1993); George F. Sensabaugh & Edward T. Blake, DNA Analysis in Biological Evidence: Applications of the Polymerase Chain Reaction, in Forensic Science Handbook, Vol. III 416 (Richard Saferstein ed., 1993). Robert C. Shaler, Modern Forensic Biology, in Forensic Science Handbook, Vol. 1, 2nd ed.; Richard Saferstein, ed., 2002; and Richard Saferstein, Criminalistics: Introduction to Forensic Science, 8th ed., Chapter 13, DNA: The Indispensable Forensic Science Tool, 2004. Also see §§ 2:1 et seq. in this work.

[2]The other would be the automated, computerized single fingerprint identification system.

ence of DNA. During the 1990s the FBI developed its Combined DNA Identification System (CODIS) to which all fifty states contribute convicted offenders' DNA profiles. As of May 2006, CODIS contained over 3.3 million profiles, of which about 3.2 million are of convicted offenders and 140,000 are forensic (crime scene evidence) profiles. The FBI estimates that the CODIS files have assisted in more than 35,000 investigations, and many more hits have been made and investigations aided at the local level.

Short tandem repeat (STR) analysis is the latest and most widely used DNA analysis procedure today. These short, repeating sequences lend themselves very well to forensic casework; they are less susceptible to degradation than other techniques, can be amplified using PCR, and are plentiful in the human genome. The sensitivity of STR testing is about 100 fold greater than what was possible using the RFLP system. Thirteen (13) STRs have now been standardized and are used in CODIS, with each having its own probability of identity. Because STRs are independent, one takes the product of the various frequencies with which they occur in a population. The combination of all STRs used in CODIS yields frequencies of occurrence of about 1 in 575 trillion Caucasians and 1 in 900 trillion African Americans.[3] Mitochondrial DNA is another type of DNA, located outside the nucleus and inherited from the mother. It is much more plentiful, but less discriminating than nuclear DNA, is most time consuming and costly, and is primarily used in cases involving hair, bone, and other samples of degraded human remains.

DNA typing has been subjected to the most rigorous scrutiny by the courts, presumably because its discriminating power is so great and so much is at stake when a suspect is associated to a crime scene only through DNA typing. Or perhaps because (at least some) modern courts or lawyers are more literate about science than they were in the past.

The reliability of DNA testing may be determined by proficiency testing,[4] through which *Daubert* criteria (1) and (3) may be satisfied. Testing of this sort will determine whether the methods used are adequate and whether the techniques used by a particular analyst were proper. There is little if any opportunity for the rationalization of incorrectly reported results when proficiency testing samples are processed according to the methods typically employed in the laboratory. Some

---

[3]Richard Saferstein, Criminalistics: Introduction to Forensic Science, 8th ed., Chapter 13, DNA: The Indispensable Forensic Science Tool, 2004.

[4]Proficiency testing is discussed in greater detail elsewhere in this chapter in connection with specific types of physical evidence, but to clarify the issue of proficiency testing, it is a quality assurance practice in which an analyst is aware it is a test and examines that sample in accordance with the procedures that he or she normally employs. The analyst is not aware of the correct or expected results until after the test has been concluded. In some instances there may be a "blind test" where the analyst is not aware that the sample is a proficiency test. This is not always feasible in forensic practice, however, where the analyst normally has the prerogative to inquire as to the integrity of the evidence, discuss the manner of collection, and explore other extrinsic issues that might relate to the interpretation of the evidence. In the forensic sciences, much of the proficiency testing that is done is accomplished through Collaborative Testing Services (CTS), a private company established in 1971 that is engaged in a wide variety of interlaboratory testing in both the industrial and forensic sectors. As stated in their literature, "all of the tests are designed to assist organizations in achieving and maintaining quality control objectives." Hundreds of forensic laboratories in the United States and throughout the world participate in one or more CTS testing programs. CTS first became engaged in crime laboratory proficiency testing in the mid-1970s when the Forensic Science Foundation (FSF) first received grants from the U.S. Justice Department to develop such a program. CTS became a subcontractor, manufacturing specimens and analyzing test results. This resulted in the publication J. L. Peterson, E. L. Fabricant, K.S. Field & J.I. Thornton, Crime Laboratory Proficiency Testing Program (United States Department of Justice, 1978) that, in turn, stimulated a number of important quality assurance initiatives in the forensic laboratory field. It was also in 1978, with the conclusion of Federal grant support for this testing, that CTS joined with FSF and the American Society of Crime Laboratory Directors (ASCLD) to continue the program on a fee per test specimen basis.

indication of the error rate for the typing of bloodstains is known for both DNA typing and conventional serological methods.

Physiological fluids other than blood include semen, urine, perspiration, milk, feces, and tears. With the exception of semen, there was rarely any attempt to do anything more than to identify the nature of the material. DNA profiling has opened vast new possibilities in the examination of other biological evidence including perspiration, mucus, saliva and urine. The detection level and sensitivity of DNA testing have advanced greatly in the past decade such that only a few cells are needed. This "low copy number" DNA means that not only is the forensic examiner able to work with traditional visible biological stains, but also saliva on envelopes and the rims of drinking cups, mucus in dirty tissues, perspiration on a sweat band, underclothes, and bed linens and pillow cases. In addition, laboratories are deveeloping the ability to find and type DNA from skin or epithelial cells remaining on objects a person has handled or touched, and even to examine the residue (skin cells and amino acids) found in a latent fingerprint.

Semen occurs frequently in cases of sexual assault, and is a valuable form of physical evidence. The identification of a stain as a semen stain may be achieved by a combination of methods, including the demonstration of the enzyme acid phosphatase, the demonstration of the semen-specific protein p30, or the demonstration of intact spermatozoa by means of microscopy. In most instances, semen stains can be subjected to DNA analysis, with a high degree of individuality established. The increased sensitivity of DNA testing affords the sexual assault investigator new opportunities beyond simply typing the semen found within the victim; this includes areas where the offender may have touched or left saliva on the victim, or where the DNA from the victim's vagina may have been transferred to the assailant or his clothing.

As with blood evidence, the reliability of the testing may be determined by means of proficiency testing. Testing of this sort will determine whether the methods used are adequate, and whether the techniques used by a particular analyst were proper. This type of testing ordinarily will satisfy the *Daubert* criteria (1) and (3).[5]

Beginning with blood and physiological fluids, we will briefly summarize the results of Collaborative Testing Services (CTS) proficiency testing of crime laboratories over the past 28 years. Participants grew from 32 laboratories in 1978 to 561 laboratories in 2005—almost an eighteen fold increase. From 1978 to 2005, more than 80 blood and body fluid tests were distributed to laboratories with participation rates (laboratories receiving samples and actually returning results) increasing from 45% in the first set of samples (1978 to 1991) to above 70% in samples from 1992 through 1999. In the tests up through those issued in 1991, laboratories engaged in conventional serological testing, and from 1992 onward, laboratories had the option of testing their DNA proficiency. Participants were commonly issued two or more stains. Typically a stain of known source (from a victim or suspect) and one or more stains of unknown origin found at a crime scene, on a garment, or some other location of importance to the investigation. Laboratory results were compared with values provided by the manufacturer of the proficiency test. The laboratories were asked to determine if the stains could have shared a common origin.[6]

Laboratories improved their typing of biological stains using conventional serologi-

---

[5]While the results of CTS proficiency testing gives an *inkling* of the potential or real error rate that *Daubert* calls for, for several reasons these results cannot be construed as the true error rate. Participation in CTS proficiency testing is voluntary and arguably involves only the better and more progressive forensic laboratories. Additionally, in many laboratories the CTS tests are treated in an entirely different manner than routine physical evidence.

[6]As explained by Peterson & Markham, Crime Laboratory Proficiency Testing Results, 1978–1991, II: Resolving the Questions of Common Origin, 40 J. Forensic Sciences 1009, 1009 (1995), "criterion/unit of measurement . . . is the comparison, whereby one or more questioned (un-

cal techniques during the course of the testing, correctly typing stains about 94% of the time in the period 1978 to 1991, but greater than 98% of the time since then. Using these conventional methods, laboratories correctly ascertained the source of bloodstains about 89% of the time and were incorrect about 6% of the time. In terms of comparing the source of biological and bloodstain *mixtures*, laboratories were only successful about 83% of the time, and were incorrect 11% of the time. In terms of errors, laboratories more frequently stated that stains *could have* had a common source (when they did not) than concluding they *did not*, when in fact they *did*. Mistakes were not as often due to mistyping as they were to the failure of laboratories to employ enough systems to distinguish the samples. Secretor status testing was one area in particular where laboratories performed poorly and which led to improper determinations of common origin. While the introduction of isoenzyme and serum protein systems in the late 1970s led to substantial improvement over straight ABO testing in determinations of source, the introduction of DNA typing in the 1990s provided another quantum level boost in the ability of laboratories to distinguish biological stains.

In the early years of proficiency testing using DNA typing, although determinations of common source were generally correct, they were not perfect. Progressively, though, test results improved. In tests in 1995 to 1996 where laboratories used both conventional serological techniques and DNA typing, a sizeable percentage (from one-fifth to one-half) of laboratories respectively failed to distinguish stains using conventional serology, but using RFLP and PCR, less than 1% of results were inconsistent with manufacturers' specifications. Laboratories did experience some difficulty in simulated sexual assault cases in determining the origin of DNA present in male and female fractions of vaginal swabs. In the mid to late 1990s, typically 98 to 99% of replies were correct, with occasional tests where 2 to 3% of exercises produced inconclusive results. The 1999 test was one of those where less than 1% of replies were in error but around 3% were inconclusive. Clearly, the introduction of DNA typing has enabled laboratories to be much more accurate in differentiating and associating biological stains.

Between the years 2000 to 2005, a total of 32 forensic biology tests were issued to participating laboratories. On average, 339 laboratories subscribed to each test and 306 labs returned results for an overall response rate of 90%. The move from laboratories using conventional serology procedures to DNA typing progressed rapidly in this period. Between the years 2000 to 2001 alone, labs submitting conventional serology grouping results dropped from 93 (for test 00-506) to 55 (for test 01-512); by 2005, the number submitting conventional serology results had dropped to 25. Laboratories using STR typing grew from 307 to 371 between 2000 and 2001 and to 477 by 2005.

Laboratories had the option of supplying: (1) screening test results; (2) serological grouping results; and (3) DNA testing results (see any of the test reports available at www.collaborativetesting.com/forensics/forensics_reports.html). Ordinarily, tests consisted of two "known" stains on white cotton cloth and two unknown stains on different substrates. Screening test results were generally performed well throughout the tests, except for 02-573, an exercise containing canine blood in which of the 270 participants, three reported it to be human blood and 46 reported inconclusive, not determined, or not reported. For the sample containing canine blood, six reported the presence of saliva/amylase in addition to the blood (all samples consisted solely of blood).

Exercise 02-575 illustrates very well the difficulties encountered by some labora-

---

known origin) samples were compared with one or more standard (known) samples." Alternative ways of counting the responses can lead to other reasonable inferences, some indicating higher rates of error. See, e.g., §6:12, at note 1 and accompanying text.

tories with conventional blood grouping systems. One of the two questioned and one of the two known stains were collected from the same individual; this individual was also the biological mother of the donor for the second questioned stain. The other known was from a third unrelated person. Because the three donors shared phenotypes in at least four conventional systems and two of the donors were closely related, a high percentage of the 116 comparisons performed were in error (32 comparisons or 28%), and another 15 (13%) inconclusive.

Test 04-571 consisted of two known stains, one male and one female, and two unknown (questioned) stains, one coming from a different female and one from the same (known) male. Of the 140 conventional serology comparisons performed, 44 (31%) were incorrect. Whereas all participants indicated the male suspect was a possible contributor to the questioned stain on the tablecloth, labs were not able to exclude the female victim or the suspect because they only reported results from a single marker or considered the possibility of a mixture.

The DNA results and their interpretations were in agreement with the manufacturer's specifications 99.4% of the time, out of more than 36,000 comparisons. Inconclusive responses constituted 0.5% of all comparisons and errors only 0.1%. One of the tests having canine blood (02-573) had the highest average percent of inconclusives (about 10%); all inconclusives were for the canine blood sample and led labs not to exclude one of the stains that should have been excluded. For the 8,600 STR results reported for this test, there were only six discrepancies.

Test 05-572 consisted of two known bloodstains and two unknown stains, one of which was human semen. Of the presumptive testing performed, 260/268 (97%) of the results were positive for semen; 241/246 (98%) of the confirmatory tests performed for semen were positive. While all DNA testing on the bloodstains resulted in correct interpretations, there were 23 inconclusive interpretations for the semen stain.

## § 1:36 Forensic identification subspecialties—Glass[1]

*Subjectivity*: Low.

*Reliability in the minds of forensic scientists:* Moderately high to high.

*Vulnerability to attack in the light of* Daubert *criteria (1) and (3):* Moderately high.

In crimes against the person, glass may be broken inadvertently as a result of violent activity. In crimes against property, glass may be purposely broken in order to gain entry. Whether the evidence consists of window glass or beverage bottle glass, automobile headlight glass or a makeup mirror, it may be characterized by physical and optical properties.

The direction of force applied to a broken window can ordinarily be determined with a high degree of certainty, as can the direction of travel of a bullet. The time interval between the breaking of the glass and the collection of the evidence cannot be determined, except in accordance with common sense observations of the extent of accumulation of dust, soil, or other debris.

The greatest number of glass evidence cases, however, involve very small fragments of broken glass that are recovered in the clothing or shoes of a suspect. These fragments are compared on the basis of density, refractive index, fluorescence under short-wavelength ultraviolet illumination, and elemental composition.

---

**[Section 1:36]**

[1]Robert D. Koons et al., Forensic Glass Comparisons, in Forensic Science Handbook, Vol. 1, 2nd edition (Richard Saferstein ed., 2002); David A. Stoney & John I. Thornton, Glass Evidence, in Scientific and Expert Evidence (Edward J. Imwinkelried ed., 1981).

Prevailing opinion is that a match in each of these properties indicates a moderate to high probability that the exemplar and evidence samples have shared a common origin. Fluorescence may in some instances eliminate some glass samples from consideration, but rarely contributes significantly to the issue of commonality of source. Elemental composition is primarily of value in those relatively uncommon instances in which a maverick element, serving as a highly characteristic appellation, occurs in the glass. Density and refractive index are useful because they can be determined on very small quantities of glass, and are susceptible to small changes in the composition of glass. Refractive index may be determined at more than one wavelength of light, resulting in the acquisition of information on the dispersion of the glass. Refractive index and dispersion, together with density, represent the minimum testing that can be justified. Elemental composition alone can never form the basis of an opinion concerning commonality of source.

Most forensic laboratories accept the so-called *Miller Criteria,*[2] which state that for two samples of glass to be consistent with having shared a common origin, they must agree to within ±0.0010 g/cc with respect to density, and in refractive index to within ±0.0002 for the $n_D$ line and ±0.0004 for the $n_C$ and $n_F$ lines. ($n_D$, $n_C$ and $n_F$ are different wavelengths of light).

It is not possible to give a mathematical probability that an evidence sample has shared a common origin with an exemplar sample. No probability model has ever been developed to do so. It is possible, however, to compare the density and refractive index of an evidence sample of glass against a database of these properties to assess whether the sample is a rather prosaic type of glass or is uncommon. This will not deliver a probability, but will enable the analyst to tender an opinion concerning how common those particular values are and to perform a t-test on the hypothesis that the glass samples do not come from the same source.

Blind-trial studies of the incidence of error in forensic laboratories undertaking this type of examination are lacking, but no rational person would claim that the incidence of error is nil. The error rate as countenanced in the *Daubert* criterion (3) is unknown.

Twenty-five different glass comparison exercises were distributed to participating laboratories over the 28 years of CTS testing. Laboratories participating in testing grew from 24 laboratories to 122 in 2005. Laboratories were typically asked to compare two or more glass chips and to determine if they could have shared a common origin. Laboratory performance on these samples ranged widely, depending upon the difficulty of the exercise. From 1978 to 1999, laboratories typically were correct from 90 to 98% of the time, but in about a quarter of the tests laboratories substantially disagreed with the manufacturer's specifications. Three of the problematic exercises involved samples that were produced by the same manufacturer, using the same process, but at different times and/or locations. Such samples had very similar compositions and physical measurements but were, in fact, of different sources. Some of these samples only differed in refractive index measurements to the fourth or fifth decimal place, which exceeded the technical capacity of some laboratories. These tests illustrate well the dilemma of forensic laboratories when examining items such as glass that have been mass produced using stringent quality controls that yield products that will be widely distributed, but which have almost identical properties. Laboratories also experienced difficulty when the test samples gathered from the "crime scene" had actually originated from <u>two</u> different sources, one of the same origin as glass found on a suspect's shoe and one different. Almost a quarter of laboratories failed to complete measurements on all samples. As a result, half of these laboratories reported the sample could have a common source

---

[2]Named for Elmer Miller, the FBI analyst who devoted virtually his entire professional career to the forensic study of glass.

and half said they didn't; the completely correct response would have noted both types of glass.

Up through 2000, laboratories improved their measurements; e.g., their refractive index measures were much "tighter" in later tests than in earlier ones. Such dramatic improvements in refractive index measurements were not always matched by comparable improvements in other methods (color, UV fluorescence, elemental analysis). As in other exercises, the success of laboratories in interpreting this type of physical material was influenced substantially by the difficulty of the test, as in cases where the manufacturer of the proficiency tests issued samples of very similar, but not identical, origin, or when they mixed pieces of different types of glass in the same sample which made for a much more challenging proficiency test. The fact, though, that the proficiency advisory committee decided to issue such challenging samples can be interpreted to mean that glass evidence in actual forensic cases will occasionally involve such complexities.

In the final six tests over the years 2000 to 2005, about 96% of the comparisons were correct, 2% incorrect, and 2% inconclusive. Of laboratory values in disagreement, by a two to one margin, laboratories more often incorrectly stated glass fragments were of a common origin when they were not, than those reporting they were not of a common origin when they actually were. Approximately 50% of these improper comparisons came in exercise 02-548 where participants were presented with three glass fragments, two of which were of the same standard reference material, soda-lime float glass, and the third was tempered window glass obtained from a local glass supply store. Eight participants reported all three shared a common origin, and two reported all three items were of different origin. There were no clear-cut explanations for those reporting all were of common origin, but the two indicating all were of different origin appeared to rely on elemental composition data.

About one-fifth of all the inconclusive determinations occurred in test 05-548, and is a good illustration of the challenge of forensic glass comparisons. The three fragments originated from glass bathroom shelving, two from the same bathroom shelf and the third from another piece of shelving. The density of the fragments of the same shelf was reported as 1.5178, and was 1.5174 for the other fragment—a difference that should have been distinguishable. Precise reasons are unclear, but some laboratories' equipment was inoperable for the exams and others may have relied too greatly on elemental analysis.

## § 1:37  Forensic identification subspecialties—Hair evidence[1]

*Subjectivity:* Very high.

*Reliability in the minds of forensic scientists:* Low.

*Vulnerability to attack in the light of* Daubert *criteria (1) and (3):* High.

In an exclusionary mode, hair is a rather good form of evidence. If the evidence hair is blond, straight, and 12 inches long, it may be emphatically eliminated as having originated from a person whose exemplar hair is black, curly, and two inches long. In an inclusionary mode, however, hair is a miserable form of evidence. The most that can be said about a hair is that it is consistent with having originated from a particular person, but that it would also be consistent with the hair of numerous other people. Stronger opinions are occasionally expressed, but they would not be supportable. An exception would be where the hair was forcibly removed from the skin. In this instance, it may be possible to extend the amount of

---

[Section 1:37]

[1]Richard Bisbing, The Forensic Identification and Association of Human Hair, in 1 Forensic Science Handbook vol, 1, 2nd edition (Richard Saferstein ed., 2002).

information given up by the hair by recovering and amplifying the DNA from the root.

Hair is examined under the optical microscope, in much the same manner that it was examined at the beginning of the century. With the exception of DNA typing, there have been no significant advances in how hair evidence is examined. Not even the scanning electron microscope, with its much greater resolving power, has significantly advanced hair comparison.

Human hair can be rather easily distinguished from animal hair, however, and animal hair of different genera can generally be distinguished reliably by a suitably trained and experienced examiner.

A probability model has been advanced for the interpretation of hair evidence.[2] This model, however, has received a cool reception from the forensic science community. While some aspects of this model are demonstrably valid, criticism of the model has been persuasive.

The validity of hair evidence is susceptible of objective testing, although this has not been accomplished on a scale and in such a manner as to satisfy *Daubert*. The error rate of hair examination is unknown.[3]

In the early sets of proficiency exercises issued by CTS in the 1980s, laboratories, on average,[4] disagreed with the manufacturer in about 8% of their comparisons, and were inconclusive in another 18%. The incorrect determinations were distributed equally between situations where laboratories reported hairs could have shared a common origin when they didn't, and vice versa. Because of difficulties of selecting completely homogeneous samples, and the possibility of "overlapping characteristics" between the victim and suspect samples, the proficiency advisory committee cautioned that in many situations an inconclusive response may be the most appropriate reply. As a result of these difficulties in preparing a fair, yet challenging, proficiency test, CTS discontinued issuing these types of samples in 1989.

## § 1:38  Forensic identification subspecialties—Fiber evidence[1]

*Subjectivity:* High.

*Reliability in the minds of forensic scientists:* Intermediate.

*Vulnerability to attack in the light of* Daubert *criteria (1) and (3):* Moderately high.

Fibers may be encountered at the scenes of crimes, where they may be transferred from one item to another. Typically this is in the case of violent contact between two individuals, where fibers from a garment of one individual are transferred to the garment of the other individual. Depending on the type of fiber, this transfer may be in one direction, or may be in both directions. Forensic scientists have almost universally accepted the *Locard Exchange Principle*. This doctrine was enunciated early in the 20th Century by Edmund Locard, the director of the world's first crime laboratory, in Lyon, France. Locard's Exchange Principle states that with contact

---

[2]Gaudette, An Attempt at Determining Probabilities in Human Scalp Hair Comparison, 19 J. Forensic Sci. 599 (1974); Gaudette, Probabilities and Human Pubic Hair Comparisons, 21 J. Forensic Sci. 514 (1976); Gaudette, Some Further Thoughts on Probabilities and Human Hair Comparisons, 23 J. Forensic Sci. 758 (1978).

[3]In the wake of *Daubert*, at least one court has found hair identification evidence to be so defective as to require vacating a conviction based on hair identification. *Williamson v. Reynolds*, 904 F. Supp. 1529 (E.D. Okla. 1995), aff'd, 110 F.3d 1508 (10th Cir. 1997) and (abrogated on other grounds by, Nguyen v. Reynolds, 131 F.3d 1340 (10th Cir. 1997)) and (rejected on other grounds by, Castro v. Ward, 138 F.3d 810 (10th Cir. 1998)).

[4]§ 1:35, note 6.

[Section 1:38]

[1]James Robertson (ed.), Forensic Examination of Fibers (1992); Barry D. Gaudette, The Forensic Aspects of Textile Fiber Examination, in 2 Forensic Science Handbook (Richard Saferstein ed., 1988).

between two items, there will be an exchange of microscopic material. This certainly includes fibers, but extends to other microscopic materials such as hair, pollen, paint, and soil.

Fibers may be of animal or vegetable origin, or may be synthetic. Examples of animal fibers are wool, mohair, and angora. Examples of vegetable fibers are cotton and linen. The principal synthetic fibers are nylon, polyester, acrylic, and rayon. Animal fibers are hairs utilized in the fabrication of cloth. A wool fiber, for instance, is termed a wool fiber even though fundamentally it is a sheep hair. The identification of animal fiber as to species is by means of the microscope. Other than the morphology of the hair, there are no techniques available at the present time to distinguish one type of animal fiber from another. Further characterization of the animal fiber may be achieved, in the case of fibers that have been dyed, by an assessment of the hue and the degree of saturation (i.e., intensity of the color) of the fiber; this may be accomplished in a strict comparison mode or by means of microspectrophotometry.[2]

Vegetable fibers are identified by their microscopic appearance, and by various staining reactions. No instrumental techniques exist for their identification, nor is the scanning electron microscope of any particular advantage. The identification of vegetable fibers is considered by the forensic science community to be straightforward, although the more obscure vegetable fibers, e.g., sisal, jute, Manila hemp, rarely are encountered and therefore are not likely to be recognized immediately by the analyst. White cotton fibers are so ubiquitous in our environment, however, they are virtually without significance as evidence; typically they are ignored unless there are circumstances that impart to them some special significance.

Synthetic fibers are abundant and represent the single most important type of fiber evidence. The means for the identification and comparison of these synthetic fibers are more diverse. Microscopic examination is essential for morphology and for the assessment of hue. But since these fibers are polymers, they may be approached by instrumental means as well. Fourier Transform Infrared Microspectrophotometry is ideally suited for this purpose, and is non-destructive. Pyrolysis-gas chromatography is perhaps even *more* discriminating, but this test is of a destructive character.

Many synthetic fibers have a characteristic cross-sectional appearance, which may enable the analyst to associate a fiber with a particular manufacturer. This type of examination is only as good as the library of known fibers that is available for reference, however. The major manufacturers of synthetic fibers maintain such libraries—certainly of their own fibers, and, for the purpose of guarding against patent infringement, the fibers of some of their competitors. A comprehensive library of the cross-sectional appearance of synthetic fibers is, however, something that is not ordinarily available to the typical forensic laboratory.

The validity of fiber identification techniques is susceptible of objective testing, although this has not been accomplished on a scale and in such a manner as to satisfy *Daubert*. The error rate of fiber examination is unknown. The validity of the interpretation of the significance of a match in fiber evidence has not been subjected to systematic testing of the sort countenanced by *Daubert*.

Laboratories subscribing to the 22 CTS proficiency exercises generally were asked to identify the types of fibers presented and to answer a question about the origin of two or more fibers.[3] Laboratories were presented with both natural and synthetic fibers used in cordage, clothing, the home and in automobiles. Laboratories employed

---

[2]This is an unusually expressive word. *Micro-*, "small." *spectro-*, "appearance." *photo-*, "light." *metry-*, pertaining to "a means of measurement." So microspectrophotometry is "a means of measuring the appearance of light in a small specimen."

[3]§ 1:35, note 6.

a range of microscopical, chemical and analytical techniques in their examinations. With respect to identification methods, most laboratories performed them quite well, but on occasion misidentified both natural and synthetic fibers. Laboratories sometimes were unable to perform the particular test that would have distinguished fibers, while in other cases they failed to make appropriate observations and interpretations of their data. Of great concern were those few laboratories unable to distinguish between generic classes of fibers, as between polyester and nylon. In some situations, even though laboratories failed to correctly identify the particular fiber category, they were nonetheless able to note differences between one or more fibers and to correctly answer the common origin question.

On the initial eight tests that asked laboratories to determine if two or more fibers originated from the same source, correct comparisons hovered around 85%, while for the next eight challenges, correct comparisons exceeded 90% and, in three tests, exceeded 95%. Similarly, prior to 1990 the rates of incorrect inclusions and exclusions were 10% and higher, while in the 1990s laboratories made fewer outright mistakes and more often failed to distinguish fibers by submitting inconclusive results. In the 1980s, laboratories made more errors and reported fibers could have shared a common origin when they didn't, but in the latter period incorrect inclusions and exclusions were balanced. Two notable exams occurred where a substantial percentage of laboratories were unable to distinguish between two types of nylon fibers (nylon 6 and nylon 6.6) and could not distinguish a dog hair from a mixture of mohair and alpaca hairs. The nylon fibers could have been differentiated by melting point tests that laboratories, not arriving at the correct conclusion, failed to perform. For the animal hairs/fibers exercise, many of the laboratories giving an inconclusive result simply because they did not have the expertise to distinguish such samples (which rarely are presented to crime laboratories as evidence). It appears laboratories were generally able to distinguish fibers that were clearly different, but had difficulty with samples where the fibers were similar but had slight differences in delustering agent, color or construction.

For the exercises in the years 2000 to 2005, laboratories were in agreement with the manufacturer's values in 99% of comparisons made. Participants were asked if two sets of questioned fibers could have shared a common origin with the known fabric or yarn. The 17 comparisons not in agreement with the manufacturer's values were those where respondents stated fibers did *not* originate from a common source when in fact they did. The test accounting for most of the incorrect results was 03-539, where 11 of the 382 reported comparisons incorrectly stated that the individual questioned fiber could not have originated from the section of fabric provided. These laboratories failed to recognize that the fabric in question was composed of two types of polyester fibers, including the fiber type in the sample of questioned origin.

### § 1:39 Forensic identification subspecialties—Paint evidence

*Subjectivity:* Low.

*Reliability in the minds of forensic scientists:* Moderately high.

*Vulnerability to attack in light of* Daubert *criteria (1) and (3):* Moderately high.

Paint is a common form of physical evidence that presents itself in many different crime contexts in the forensic laboratory. Paints of various compositions are used to coat, color and protect surfaces of many products, including automobiles and the interior and exterior of homes and businesses. In the course of hit and run accidents, burglaries, and other crimes involving forcible entry, paint chips and smears are transferred between surfaces of vehicles (and victims), from one object or tool to another, and to the clothing or body of victims and suspects. Forensic examiners will compare questioned and known paint samples to determine their possible origin. Hit and run accidents are unique in that scientists, upon examining a paint chip, may be able to give investigators valuable leads in searching for a particular color, make, and model of vehicle. Forensic paint examination is a very challenging area, owing both to the tremendous variety of materials used in formulating paints and to the quality control efforts of companies to standardize procedures and to manufacture paints of uniformly high quality.

Paint is a mixture of pigments, binders, additives, and solvents for the purpose of coloring and coating surfaces. Pigments, composed of inorganic and organic compounds, give paint its color and opacity, while the polymeric binder gives paint its ability to cover and adhere to a given surface. The pigments, binder, and various other additives are then dissolved in a solvent, which upon application evaporates, leaving behind a hard polymer film. The succession of coatings applied to the steel bodies of automobiles (primers, basecoats, and clearcoats) exhibit a range of chemical and physical properties. Microscopy may be used to examine the color, surface texture, and layering of paints, as well as to determine if fractured paint chips may be physically fitted together. Microchemical tests may be useful in observing how questioned and known paint chips and layers react to various chemical reagents. Layering and physical fits are rare, and chemical tests primarily qualitative, so examiners are typically left to identify the organic and inorganic materials in the paint using instrumentation.

There are several instruments that can be employed during the forensic analysis of paint. Pyrolysis gas chromatography (PGC) is used singly or in tandem with mass spectrometry (PGC-MS) to characterize the organic components of paint. Infrared spectroscopy (IR), specifically Fourier transform infrared spectroscopy (FTIR), can be used to determine the pigments, additives, and binders used during the production of the paint. Scanning electron microscopy in tandem with an energy dispersive X-ray spectrometer (SEM/EDS) is particularly useful in determining the layer structure of the paint sample, as well as its elemental content. The interpretation of these tests of both house and automotive paints is challenging and highly dependent upon the existence and maintenance of appropriate paint data bases. Reference collections are extremely important for training and casework applications. Automobile paint data bases have evolved, beginning with ASTMs in the 1970s, the FBI's collection housed in Quantico, VA, and the RCMP's Paint Data Query (PDQ) system of today.[1] The RCMP's is an improvement in that it stores color, layer structure and spectral information from several worldwide data bases, and makes the information available to forensic laboratories which contribute paint samples to the database.[2]

Typically in the paint proficiency test scenarios, laboratories were issued either two or three paint samples and asked if either (or both) crime scene samples could have originated from the same source as the sample of known paint. The number of laboratories participating in testing grew from about 70 laboratories to more than 200. A range of automotive, household, and marine paints were used. In about the first half of the tests, most samples were actually of different origin even though they were similar in appearance and composition; in the later group of tests, most samples were of common origin. Laboratories had more difficulty with the earlier tests than the later ones. In fact, almost one-fifth of the early tests resulted in incorrect replies—laboratories concluded the samples could have been of common origin when they were not. In the latter group of nine tests in the 1990s only about 2 to 4% of replies were in error, where laboratories reported samples were not of a common source when they actually were. The tests in the 1990s typically consisted of a

---

**[Section 1:39]**

[1]Buckle, et al., PDQ—Paint Data Queries: The History and Technology Behind the Development of the Royal Canadian Mounted Police Laboratory, 30 Canadian Society of Forensic Sci. J. 199 (1997).

[2]Max Houck and Jay Siegel, Fundamentals of Forensic Science, Academic Press (2006), at 431.

known and two "crime scene" samples of unknown origin, and most mistakes occurred where a few laboratories concluded that the samples of the same origin were of different sources. Typically 2 to 6% of replies were inconclusive occurring both in situations where samples were of common origin and those when they were not.

In 12 tests after 2000, comparisons that disagreed with manufacturers' specimens average around 3.5% and inconclusives about 1.5%. Approximately 80% of the incorrect comparisons stated samples could have shared a common origin when they did not, and these were concentrated in tests 01-546 and 04-546, both involving latex paints—one exterior and the other interior. In test 01-546, about 20% of comparisons of black acrylic house paint were found to be of common origin when they were not. Here, instrumental methods such as SEM/EDX, XRS/XRF, XRD or pyrolysis GC were useful in discriminating between samples, but the SEM alone or with organic methods was not as successful.

There were common themes that ran throughout the testing. As a rule, laboratories fared better examining automotive paints than house paints. It became clear that simple stereomicroscopy, color comparisons, and solubility/chemical tests alone were inadequate to differentiate samples with small quantitative differences. Pyrolysis Gas Chromatography and FTIR were two instrumental methods associated with correct results, particularly in distinguishing clearcoat layers of the automotive paints. SEM/EDX, XRS/XRF or XRD were highly effective in other tests. It was also noted on several occasions that laboratories appeared to employ different decision criteria "in the significance attributed to small differences between paint samples."

## § 1:40  Forensic identification subspecialties—Fingerprint evidence[1]

*Subjectivity*: Moderately low.

*Reliability in the minds of forensic scientists:* High.

*Vulnerability to attack in the light of* Daubert *criteria (1) and (3):* Low.

Fingerprints are held up as the ultimate yardstick of uniqueness. When spectroscopists and organic chemists wish to label an area of the infrared spectrum that is capable of uniquely identifying a chemical, they refer to the "fingerprint area" of the spectrum. When molecular biologists refer to the form of DNA typing that demonstrates the seemingly unique character of DNA, they have chosen to call it "DNA fingerprinting."

The palmar surfaces of the hands and fingers, and the dorsal surfaces of the feet and toes, possess ridges. These ridges have a detailed geometry which is considered to be unique to each person. This assumption of uniqueness is based on: (1) empirical evidence; and (2) probability models. The empirical evidence for the uniqueness of fingerprints generally takes the form of: "No two people have ever been found to have the same fingerprints." This statement is certainly true, but it does call out for a qualifier which is seldom appended. It should be recognized that while fingerprints are assumed to be unique, to the exclusion of everyone else in the world, no one is actually intercomparing the fingerprints of everyone in the world. A more precise statement would be: "To the extent that the effort has been made to intercompare fingerprints, no two people have ever been found to have the same fingerprints." Actually, the effort has been considerable, though by no means exhaustive, and no two fingers have ever been found in which the ridges match.

Since the early days of fingerprint identification, fingerprint analysts have ago-

---

**[Section 1:40]**

[1]Robert D. Olsen, Scott's Fingerprint Mechanics (1978). See also §§ 3:1 et seq.

nized over the issue of how many fingerprint characteristics are needed to establish an unequivocal identification. The bottom line is that we still do not know. In the United States, some number between eight and twelve matching characteristics has been widely advanced as the criterion for identification.[2] There is no magic number, but there is a loose convention. While twelve matching characteristics has been adopted as representing a rigorous identification, what twelve matching characteristics really means is simply that the fingerprint examiner can stop counting and write the report.

But if 12 matching characteristics represent a rigorous identification, what about 11? The answer is, yes, that would still constitute an identification. What about one? The answer is no. What about 10? What about nine? Fingerprints at crime scenes vary in clarity and in the expanse of the fingerprint area expressed. As the number of matching characteristics falls, the righteousness of the identification is diminished. Dogma, as currently expressed, is that eight matching characteristics, if they are clear and unambiguous, are adequate for an identification.[3] Six matching characteristics, however, would be sufficient justification for police investigators to channel virtually all of their investigative effort toward that one person.

It should be understood how fingerprint analysts have arrived at this position. If 12 matching characteristics are required, no one will come forward with an instance of apparent misidentification. If the number is dropped to 11, the same situation applies. Ten characteristics, the same result. But this is a slow march toward disaster. At some point, a misidentification would certainly ensue. Every fingerprint examiner has seen fingerprints from two different people that have shown three or four matching characteristics in a local area (although accompanied by many dissimilarities as well). At the number eight, fingerprint examiners have exhausted all of their enthusiasm for having the number lowered.

Although eight or more characteristics might be required for an identification, a fingerprint at a crime scene that matched that of a suspect in six, or five, or perhaps even four characteristics would still represent valuable investigative information. A five-point fingerprint would not satisfy anyone in terms of an absolute identification, but it would certainly justify investigative effort being channeled into the investigation of that one suspect.

So eight matching characteristics, if they are clear and unambiguous, will serve for purposes of identification. A problem, however, is that if the evidence print can be gleaned for no more than eight characteristics, it is likely that the print suffers from some lack of clarity. Evidence fingerprints that possess only eight characteristics, but with those eight characteristics being brilliant and unequivocal, are not commonly encountered. So at the same time that the criterion for identification is being relaxed, the ambiguity of each characteristic is being augmented.

Most fingerprint technicians embrace the "One Dissimilarity Doctrine," which says that a single unexplained dissimilarity precludes an identification. This doctrine was first enunciated in the early days of fingerprint comparison as a means to allay any skepticism about the validity of this form of identification. It was enunciated as a *legal* doctrine, however, not a *scientific* one. There is no scientific basis for the doctrine. The doctrine has the ring of "fairness" to it, but there is no scientific support, one way or the other, for assuming the validity of the doctrine. In practice, the doctrine is abused or violated constantly. Whenever a fingerprint analyst encounters a fingerprint with a dozen or so matching characteristics and one dissimilarity, he will invariably rationalize the dissimilarity somehow, even if the

---

[2]There is no worldwide consensus. Elsewhere, the number varies, and may be as high as 16.

[3]Some bold and venturous examiners might place the number at six; other examiners would view this as teetering on the brink of recklessness.

rationalization is contrived.

Misidentifications based on fingerprint evidence are quite rare, but they do occur, invariably the result of human error. In most instances the sin has been one of misfeasance, with an indistinct evidence fingerprint being misidentified by an examiner who is inexperienced, or in a hurry, or simply anxious to help a police investigator. In a very few instances the sin has been one of malfeasance. It has happened that fingerprint examiners have lost their ethical compass and have reported a fingerprint identification when there was none, and cases are not unknown where a police officer has unscrupulously substituted other fingerprints for evidence fingerprints ostensibly recovered from a crime scene.

Latent fingerprint examiners generally performed very well on the 17 CTS latent fingerprint proficiency tests from 1978 to 1999.[4] Rates of correct identifications are among the highest of any evidence category, usually in the 98% to 99% range. Normally, examiners would receive one or more latent finger or palm prints from a "crime scene" and would be asked if one or more prints could be associated with a set of known prints either from a suspect or the elimination prints of a victim. Actual misidentifications are very rare, amounting to fewer than 0.5% of comparisons. There are three areas of notable exception: (1) situations where the examiner linked the latent to the correct ten fingerprint card, but then designated the wrong finger. These mistakes are usually attributed to carelessness. (2) in another test, laboratories failed to intercompare several latents *with each other*. That is, latents from several different scenes could not be associated with a known set of prints, but were all left by the same individual. In one test, examiners reported only 8% of the intercomparison identifications that were present. (3) the highest rate of incorrect values was in an exercise where the latent prints included those that were taken from twin brothers and 22% of participants made "erroneous identifications." More than 40% of respondents in this exercise failed to identify one or more of the questioned prints. As noted above, the proficiency advisory committee believed many identifications were missed (that is examiners failed to make an identification that was present) due to "procedural restrictions regarding the number of points observed before an identification is established."

From 2000 to 2005, examiners were typically given photographs of from 10 to 12 latent prints and 4 sets of photographs of known finger and palm prints from four individuals; ordinarily, nine to 11 latent (questioned) prints matched one of the known fingerprints and one to three latents did not correspond to any of the fingerprints provided. Examiners matched the latent prints to the correct fingerprint on the card about 98.5% of the time in more than 31,000 comparisons reported. On average, 89% (ranging from 78% to 97%) of the participants correctly identified all (ten or more) identifiable latent prints and did not identify any of the latents that lacked corresponding prints. Over this last six-year period, on average, about 1% of the responses incorrectly eliminated latent prints whose corresponding inked print was provided. Only about 0.4% of all responses incorrectly associated a latent print with the wrong known fingerprint provided. There were an uncharacteristically high number of false exclusions on exercise 01-516 that reflected (in part) examiners concerns over the quality, resolution and lack of detail in the digital photographs, paper and printer technology used in the exercise. There were also a high number of false exclusions in test 02-516 that could be attributed to examiner complaints of the quality and detail of the photographs provided, lab policies that would have required them to request additional (original inked) known prints in actual casework, and carelessness (labs reporting latents corresponding to item numbers that did not exist).

---

[4]§ 1:35, note 6.

### § 1:41 Forensic identification subspecialties—Soil and mineral evidence[1]

*Subjectivity*: Intermediate to moderately high.

*Reliability in the minds of forensic scientists*: Moderately low.

*Vulnerability to attack in the light of* Daubert *criteria (1) and (3):* Moderately high.

Soil is the superficial, weathered covering of the earth. It occurs with moderate frequency as physical evidence, but tends to be underestimated and underutilized by criminal investigators. Soil and minerals are characterized by density, by elemental composition, and by the identification of the parent minerals by means of the polarized light microscope. Even if there is a very high degree of accord in these properties, the most that can be said about soil and mineral evidence is that it is consistent with having shared a common origin with a particular exemplar sample.

The skills required for these types of examinations are rarely seen in those individuals whose training has been in chemistry or the biological sciences. People with specialized training in mineralogy and petrology, those branches of geology concerned with the identification of minerals, rarely enter the province of forensic science. As a consequence, few forensic scientists have the requisite inventory of skills necessary to accomplish examinations of this sort.

The validity of soil and mineral analysis is susceptible of objective testing, although this has not been accomplished on a scale and in such a manner as to satisfy *Daubert*. The error rate for these types of examinations is unknown.

### § 1:42 Forensic identification subspecialties—Handwriting[1]

*Subjectivity:* Very high.

*Reliability in the minds of forensic scientists:* Variable depending upon the nature and extent of the writing, but generally considered to be no better than Intermediate in terms of reliability.

*Vulnerability to attack in the light of Daubert criteria (1) and (3):* High.[2]

Arguments that the identification of handwriting is a science are weak, to the point of being indefensible. Certainly handwriting identification has its scientific elements. It is reality oriented, it involves specialized knowledge, observations are made under controlled conditions, and in some instances hypotheses can be formulated and then tested.

But at that point handwriting identification parts company with other, established scientific disciplines. The classical, and probably outdated, definition of a science is that it is an orderly body of knowledge with principles that can be clearly enunciated.[3] The principles by means of which the handwriting of a particular person can be distinguished from the handwriting of another have not been clearly enunciated. Handwriting identification is more of an art, or a technical skill, than a

---

**[Section 1:41]**

[1]John I. Thornton, Forensic Soil Characterization in Progress in Forensic Science (Andreas Machly & Ray Williams, eds., 1986); Raymond C. Murray and Louis P. Solebollo, Forensic Examination of Soil, in 1 Forensic Science Handbook vol. 1, 2nd ed. (Richard Saferstein, ed., 2002).

**[Section 1:42]**

[1]Richard L. Brunelle, Questioned Document Examination, in 1 Forensic Science Handbook, vol. 1, 2nd ed. (Richard Saferstein ed., 2002). See also §§ 4:1 et seq.

[2]A growing number of courts have determined that handwriting identification evidence fails the *Daubert* test and cannot be regard as a science, and have therefore limited or excluded expert testimony by asserted handwriting experts. The case law is reviewed in §§ 4:1 to 4:4.

[3]Even here, however, some "fuzziness" exists. While this definition satisfies most demands placed on it, it isn't entirely satisfactory. By this definition, science could arguably be applied to library science, astrology, secretarial science, stamp collecting, and the law.

science.

It does not follow, however, that because handwriting identification is not a science that it is devoid of validity. Handwriting identification conducted by a skilled practitioner may possess a high degree of validity. The fact that something is more of an art than a science does not automatically render it disreputable; physicians may diagnose influenza, for example, based on very little information and having applied little or no science in the process. The challenge, of course, is to demonstrate with systematic empirical data (e.g., proficiency tests) that one does reach correct results and therefore is a skilled practitioner. There is no other way to distinguish the skilled from the incompetent.

Handwriting is identified by a comparison of slant, the proportionality of letters to one another, the manner in which letters are formed, and individual letter characteristics. As school children, we are all taught to write in a particular manner. We are expected to emulate the so-called "copybook style" of writing, in which every letter is made in a particular fashion, and in which every letter is of the same size, and every upper and lower loop letter extends above or below the line to the same extent.[4] If the handwriting instruction that school children received was successful, everyone's handwriting would appear the same and no one could ever be identified. But people typically depart from the copybook style by adopting idiosyncratic characteristics that, given time and practice, develop into habits. It is this deviation from copybook style that enables the handwriting examiner to identify the writing of a particular person.

The real problem in handwriting identification is that writing is a dynamic activity. A person's handwriting differs from heroin or a shard of glass. Writing involves numerous muscles and bones that may or may not be acting in concert at a given moment, along with a variable amount of concentration or nonchalance on the part of the writer. This places a great premium on the collection of adequate exemplar handwriting, to document the range and variation of the known writing of the individual. This is not a trivial problem. Added to this, some individuals have little skill in writing, with the result that their exemplar handwriting does not display much in the way of ingrained habit. Without a substantial infusion of ingrained habit, the writing of that person cannot be identified.

The validity of handwriting comparison is susceptible of objective testing. This type of testing has in fact been attempted, although it is arguable whether this testing has been accomplished on a scale and in such a manner as to satisfy *Daubert*. Moreover, a fundamental assumption, the theory of uniqueness in handwriting, has been called into doubt.[5] The true error rate of handwriting comparison under various conditions is unknown, but the available data would not inspire a great deal of confidence.[6]

The 16 CTS questioned document and handwriting proficiency tests from 1978 to 1999 included both exercises where examiners compared questioned and known signatures and writings to determine the authorship of written materials, and other cases where laboratories were asked to examine mechanical impressions, inks and photocopying (rubber stamps, printing, etc.).[7] Examiners made few mistakes with the mechanical impression evidence, with fewer than 5% of responses in error; however, a substantial proportion (10% or more) of replies fell into the inconclusive category. Here, there was a tendency for laboratories to give an inconclusive reply,

---

[4]Numerous copybook styles exist in the United States, such as the Palmer, the Zaner-Bloser, the New Laurel, and the D'Nealian. Different copybook styles come in and out of vogue, like hemlines or sunspot activity.

[5]See Harris, How Much do People Write Alike? A Study of Signatures, 48 J. Crim. Law & Criminology 647 (1958).

[6]The empirical research is reviewed in §§ 4:1 et seq.

[7]§ 1:35, note 6.

particularly where the correct response would have been to exclude the materials as having a common source. Another exercise involving different inks was easily deciphered by all laboratories. With respect to handwriting comparisons, examiners performed very well on the more straightforward tests with correct results approaching 100%. However, in other slightly more challenging tests, a very high percentage of replies (25% and more) were inconclusive. Laboratories also incorrectly associated an author with questioned samples as high as 10% of the time. There was also a high percentage of inconclusives, particularly where the examiner should have excluded a known set of writing but didn't (by saying they couldn't be eliminated as a source). Examiners lacked sophistication in more complicated cases involving multiple authors. That is, they correctly noted one suspect had authored a portion of a document, but failed to mention that a second author penned other sections of the same document.

The questioned document exercises over the 2000 to 2005 period covered a range of situations where examiners were challenged to determine the genuineness of documents where there had been manipulation of paragraphs in the original of a photocopied document, a paper fracture/tear association, and alteration of documents with various pens and ink. Examiners were also asked to determine the manufacturing process used to prepare different areas of questioned checks and to determine the authenticity of a document where the date was in dispute. Results ranged from a high of 99% correct responses on the torn paper and pen/ink alteration exercises to around 90% with photocopier and dating exercises. The exercise where examiners were asked to report the various manufacturing processes to create checks (a request that many of the labs commented was very uncommon) was generally done very well with only one exception, determining the process used to generate the check account logo (Test 04-521). Comments from participating laboratories on all the questioned documents tests ran the gamut, from calling the very same exercise "quite trivial and far from challenging" to a "very challenging and realistic test."

The handwriting exercises from this same period (2000 to 2005) entailed the comparison of questioned and known writings; such comparisons were correct about 92% of the time, in disagreement less than 1%, but inconclusive about 7%. Almost all instances of disagreement were for reporting handwriting was of common origin when it was not, and the inconclusives were failing to identify handwriting comparisons that were in fact different. Two tests accounted for about three-quarters of all incorrect comparisons. One (01-524) involved an exercise in which two questioned entries in a log were genuine and another had been "produced by simulation"—where the individual producing a questioned sample was allowed a day to practice the signature in question. Some labs were clearly fooled. In another exercise (02-524), all but one of the 10 labs which incorrectly associated questioned and known samples were from a country where English was not the first language.

### § 1:43    Forensic identification subspecialties—Narcotics and drugs of abuse[1]

*Subjectivity:* Low.

*Reliability in the minds of forensic scientists:* High.

*Vulnerability to attack in the light of* Daubert *criteria (1) and (3):* Low.

Narcotics and drugs of abuse may be considered together as a group, because identical measures are used for their identification. Each chemical species is capable

---

**[Section 1:43]**

[1]Clarke's Isolation and Identification of Drugs (2d ed., A.E. Moffet ed., 1986); Jay A.

Siegel, Forensic Identification of Controlled Substances in 2 Forensic Science Handbook (Richard Saferstein, ed., 1988).

of being characterized because each material has a unique molecular structure. This structure can be probed with a number of analytical methods, the principal ones being ultraviolet and infrared spectrophotometry, mass spectroscopy, gas chromatography, liquid chromatography, nuclear magnetic resonance, functional group reactivity and optical crystallography. Each of these approaches is extensively utilized in chemistry and other disciplines, and each has a demonstrated history of reliability.

The *Daubert* criteria (1) and (3) may be satisfied by means of proficiency testing.

A total of 42 drug proficiency tests were offered by CTS to subscribing forensic laboratories from 1978 to 1999.[2] Usually the tests challenged laboratories to identify one or more drugs in the presence of other mixtures/diluents. In some cases laboratories were also asked to quantitate the sample if a drug was found. The number of laboratories subscribing to testing increased more than six-fold over the twenty-two years of testing, with more than five hundred laboratories enrolled in drug tests in 1999. Response rates increased substantially over this two-decade period, with rates hovering in the 50% to 60% range in the 1980s, increasing to 80% and higher in the late 1990s. Samples were generally of four types: samples containing a single controlled drug; those containing more than one controlled substance; those with one or more controlled drugs mixed with noncontrolled drugs; and those containing only noncontrolled drugs.

Laboratories generally performed very well in these proficiency tests, correctly identifying the controlled substance in the sample about 96% of the time. The rate of successful identifications increased about three percentage points from 1992 to 1999 compared with the tests from 1978 to 1991. In fourteen of the exercises 100% of the laboratory replies correctly identified the drug in question. Where errors were made, it was far more common for laboratories to fail to identify a drug that was present (false negative) than to erroneously report a drug present when it wasn't (false positive). Laboratories did not perform as well with <u>mixtures</u> where, after identifying the primary controlled drug present, laboratories would sometimes fail to identify the remaining controlled and/or noncontrolled drugs present. In fact, when the success rate of identifying these other noncontrolled drugs is incorporated, the overall successful rate of identification drops about ten percentage points. Laboratories were successful in identifying opiates, stimulants, and depressants about 97% of the time, but had less success with hallucinogens where they were correct about 89% of the time. Laboratories were not particularly successful quantitating drugs, with only about half to two-thirds of laboratories even attempting quantitation (many local laboratories do not regularly perform such tests) and, of these, about 10% producing values outside the limits of acceptability.

Twelve controlled substances proficiency tests were distributed to laboratories in the years 2000 to 2005, with an average of about 400 laboratories returning results for each test. For all 12 exercises combined, about 97% of the results were completely correct. There were two tests (01-502 and 05-502) in which the majority of misidentifications took place. Test 01-502 contained 4-methoxyamphetamine that was misidentified by 11 respondents. Exercise 05-502 consisted of two items, one containing Phentermine HCl (a Schedule IV controlled substance in the U.S.), and the other containing corn starch. Ninety-three percent of the 366 participants in this test correctly identified the Phentermine in Item 1 and no controlled substance in Item 2. However, for Item 1, four laboratories incorrectly identified methamphetamine or identified Phentermine plus another controlled substance, and six failed to find a controlled substance. In Item 2, ten laboratories reported finding Phentermine (suggesting contamination or sample switching) and two others reported finding other substances. Most instances where a controlled substance was present but

---

[2]§ 1:35, note 6.

none was detected occurred in sample 05-501 where one item contained Acetaminophen (noncontrolled) and the other Acetaminophen and 2% Oxycodone HCl (a Schedule II controlled substance). Twenty-three (23) of the 543 participants failed to detect the Oxycodone in the second sample.

### § 1:44   Forensic identification subspecialties—Voiceprints[1]

*Subjectivity:* Very high.

*Reliability in the minds of forensic scientists*: Low.

*Vulnerability to attack in the light of* Daubert *criteria (1) and (3):* High.

Voiceprints, the application of the voice spectrograph to questioned recordings of speech, have failed to garner a significant following outside the community of voiceprint specialists. The forensic science community in general has withheld a certain measure of respect from this type of evidence, and courts have struggled also with the problem of attributing to these procedures the proper extent of reliance.

Voiceprint evidence may eventually satisfy *Daubert*, but at the present time it would be quite vulnerable to *Daubert* criteria (1) and (3), and may have some problems with criteria (2) and (4) as well. The testing of the reliability of voiceprints that was initially conducted has been soundly criticized on the basis of weakness of methodology; it remains to be seen if voiceprints can recover from these false starts.

### § 1:45   Forensic identification subspecialties—Bitemarks[1]

*Subjectivity:* Very high.

*Reliability in the minds of forensic scientists:* Variable, but often low.

*Vulnerability to attack in the light of* Daubert *criteria (1) and (3):* Moderately high.

Bitemark evidence falls within the province of the forensic odontologist. Many bitemark cases involve evidence that is straightforward and unambiguous. In these instances, a photograph (or in some instances a cast) of the bitemark may be shown in juxtaposition with a test impression made by the teeth of a suspect, and the extent of agreement is apparent to everyone, jury included. The only question that remains at that point is the likelihood that another bite is an equally good match, something that has not been tested. In other instances, however, the evidence marks are obscure, or fragmentary, or susceptible to some negotiation or interpretation. In these instances, forensic odontologists have been more successful in convincing courts of the legitimacy of their opinions than they have been in convincing other forensic scientists. Other forensic scientists who routinely compare pattern evidence, e.g., shoeprint evidence, often have difficulty in seeing the agreement claimed by bitemark specialists. The bitemark specialists attribute this blindness to the fact that the other pattern specialist is not a dentist, and therefore is unable to properly interpret the patterns caused by teeth. The pattern specialists counter with the charge that this is The Emperor's New Clothes Syndrome, and the discussions quickly deteriorate. Significant areas of disagreement exist which have not yet been resolved within the forensic science community.

Nevertheless, forensic odontologists have been quite active in promulgating criteria for the identification of bitemarks, and have pursued a vigorous program for

---

**[Section 1:44]**

   [1]§§ 7:1 et seq.

**[Section 1:45]**

   [1]Irvin M. Sopher, Forensic Dentistry (1976); Lester L. Luntz and Phyllys Luntz, Handbook for

Dental Identification (1973). See also §§ 6:1 et seq.

the certification of those engaged in this practice.

The *Daubert* criteria (1) and (3) may be satisfied by proficiency testing.

### § 1:46 Forensic identification subspecialties—Arson and fire evidence[1]

*Subjectivity:* Moderately low.

*Reliability in the minds of forensic scientists:* Moderately high.

*Vulnerability to attack in the light of* Daubert *criteria (1) and (3):* Moderately low.

In the minds of many forensic scientists, the analysis and identification of arson accelerants and of other fire-related phenomena are roughly coextensive with the analysis and identification of drugs and narcotics. Both areas are fundamentally aspects of chemical analysis. The instrumental methods of analysis for the two areas are virtually identical, and the comments in § 29:43 hold as well for the characterization of arson accelerants.

Arson evidence consists of more than the identification of hydrocarbon accelerants, however. The character of heat-crazed glass, the temperature at which various items melt, the processes by which fires progress, are all areas, which involve some application of subjective judgment. In these areas of greater subjectivity, training and experience on the part of the analyst will play a large part.

The *Daubert* criteria (1) and (3) may be satisfied by proficiency testing.

Laboratories experienced difficulties with the flammable proficiency tests, with the fraction of acceptable/correct results varying considerably.[2] The number of laboratories participating in these tests rose about threefold over the 22 years of testing from 1978 to 1991. While laboratories generally performed well in identifying accelerants, of concern was the fact that they reported finding flammables present in more than 10% of samples when in fact none was present in tests up through 1990. A low point of performance also was a sample issued in 1992 in which fewer than 25% of laboratories correctly identified turpentine applied on either of two samples of Oak flooring burned with a Bunsen burner. Only 10% of laboratories correctly found the turpentine on both samples. In another sample involving cotton swabs, first soaked with water and then soaked with lighter fluid, an average of 90% of laboratories correctly identified a "light or medium petroleum distillate" on the two samples. In another sample involving several different classes of flammables applied to simulated fire debris, almost 90% identified kerosene, only about 60% correctly identified the class #1 lighter fluid, and only about half were able to identify the components of a mixture of gas and fuel oil. Problematic recovery techniques were blamed where samples contained wide boiling ranges of petroleum distillates. In exercises containing blank samples (containing no distillates) an average of 1 to 2% of laboratories incorrectly reported the presence of an ignitable fluid even though they contained only distilled water. Laboratories had success stating that a volatile was present, or that two distinct samples contained flammables not of the same source, but were unable to correctly identify the classes of petroleum products present. In another case containing three different types of volatiles, a high (about 95%) percentage of laboratories could identify kerosene and mineral spirits, but fewer that 80% identified lamp oil.

In 2001 to 2005, laboratories were typically issued three Fire Debris PAK(tm) bags, two containing "wicks" with different flammable liquids, and a third containing a clean "wick" as a control. None of these samples of flammables was mixed with other fire debris (burned or unburned). Several laboratories took issue with the

---

**[Section 1:46]**

[1]Charles C. Midkiff, Arson and Explosive Investigation, in 1 Forensic Science Handbook 2nd ed. (Richard Saferstein ed., 2002). See also §§ 9:1 et seq. of this work.

[2]§ 1:35, note 6.

packaging of the samples (small airtight cans were preferred) and the small amount (25ml) of the volatile on the wick; several others felt the tests should include more realistic samples such as carpet padding and wood debris spiked with the flammable liquid. On average, laboratories identified the correct class of flammable material about 89% of the time. Some laboratories did not discriminate among similar classes or subclasses of flammables; e.g., see exercise 02-536 where the new ASTM classification systems puts both classes 4 and 5 into a single category. Other laboratories noted it was their policy and practice not to categorize flammable liquids based on class or subclass.

In exercise 03-536, the manufacturer noted that ASTM advises it may not be possible to distinguish "distillates and de-aromatized distillates" without the use of mass spectrometry, a technique used by 92% of the participants. Participants also noted that some procedures manuals require a standard be used to confirm "positive samples." In several instances, the laboratories lacked the standard and therefore did not report their results. The 05-536 exercise was notable in that 7% of the respondents failed to detect the presence of Methyl Ethyl Ketone, a highly volatile, oxygenated solvent; one possible explanation was that more than half these laboratories did not perform headspace analysis. Others that failed to report an ignitable fluid cited the above noted policy reason (to not report a result without an in-house reference sample confirmation).

## § 1:47   Forensic identification subspecialties—Toolmark and firearms evidence[1]

*Subjectivity:* High.

*Reliability in the minds of forensic scientists*: High.

*Vulnerability to attack in the light of* Daubert *criteria (1) and (3):* Moderate.

Toolmark and firearms evidence has always suffered from the fact that the examination of these types of evidence is highly subjective, and cannot fall back upon a body of independently-derived scientific knowledge.

There is a lack of objective standards in the interpretation of toolmark and firearm evidence. Despite three-quarters of a century, no systematic and comprehensive attempt to codify standards for a minimum toolmark or firearms match has been published. This cannot, however, be attributed to professional lassitude. It reflects instead the nature of toolmark and firearms evidence and the uniqueness of each tool or gun barrel. The markings on the surface of a bullet, for example, are unique because the barrel of the weapon is unique. The very notion of uniqueness thwarts attempts to generalize and categorize, processes which are necessary prolegomena to the development of objective standards.

The problem is not that there are no objective criteria to be applied to the interpretation of toolmark and firearms evidence, but that the criteria, which do exist, are so diffuse. The information that the toolmark and firearms examiner uses to establish that a bullet was fired from a particular weapon or that the mark was created by a particular screwdriver is in large part based on experience that does not, and cannot, come out of books. Consequently it is difficult to transfer one examiner's ability to interpret the microscopic images to another person. Each examiner has to build up a background of experience. A standard of proficiency and a level of expertise may indeed be achieved, but it is very difficult to effectively test the examiner. Nevertheless, it is not impossible.

---

[Section 1:47]

[1]J. Howard Mathews, 1 Firearms Identification (1962); 2 Firearms Identification (1962), 3 Firearms Identification (1973); Julian S. Hatcher, Frank J. Jury & Jac Weller, Firearms Investigation, Identification, and Evidence (1977). See also §§ 5:1 et seq. of this work.

Not all aspects of toolmark and firearms evidence are wholly subjective. The weight of a bullet, its diameter, the width of a toolmark, are all examples of objective features. So are the fine striae on the surface of a bullet. Ten different firearms examiners looking through a comparison microscope will see the same configuration of striae. They may be recorded photographically or by means of contour analysis. Ten people drawn from the general public, given a few minutes of instruction on what to look for, also will see the same striae.

Up to this point, the examination is objective. But now, with striae on the evidence bullet and test fired bullet matching under the microscope, the question becomes one of whether the *extent* of matching of striae justifies a conclusion that both projectiles were fired from the same weapon. This step involves a high degree of subjectivity, but the opinion of the examiner is not made in a vacuum. The matching of striae on bullets or in toolmarks is a form of pattern recognition, and like many other examples of pattern recognition it is harder to describe the process than to perform. But the successful matching of striae is actually the *product*, not the *process*.

Restricting the discussion to firearms evidence, the process begins with the examination of a number of consecutively fired bullets from a single weapon, noting the similarities in the striae on the surfaces of the bullets, and noting the dissimilarities as well. Some dissimilarities are to be expected, and the extent of both accord and discord must be determined. The next step is to examine bullets fired from other weapons of the same manufacture and model. Profound dissimilarities are to be expected in this situation, and again the nature and number of these dissimilarities must be determined. Any attack on the validity of firearms evidence would have to address the accord in the former instance and the lack of it in the latter.

This process of examination of known weapons and projectiles may, in the case of a new firearms examiner, be repeated for scores of cycles before the examiner begins to forge a notion of uniqueness. The process is subjective, but criteria for the identification of striated evidence do exist as the projection of a gestalt of past experience. Training of this sort is probably more systematic in its application than any course of instruction that any of us have received on, for example, how to distinguish our own house from others on the street.

The *Daubert* criteria (1) and (3) may be satisfied by proficiency testing.

Firearms constitute a major portion of cases crime laboratories receive in violent crimes. Laboratories participating in tests grew from about 20 laboratories in 1978 to over 200 in 1999, practically a 10-fold increase.[2] Laboratories typically performed their comparisons well, with a fairly low rate of incorrect comparisons (2 to 3%), but with a substantial percentage (10 to 13%) of inconclusive responses. There were two exercises where inconclusive responses exceeded 50% of replies. The majority of scenarios involved tests in which examiners were asked to compare test fired bullets and/or cartridge cases with evidence projectiles found at the scenes of crimes. There were also three cases in which laboratories were asked to estimate the approximate distance between the cloth provided and the muzzle of the firearm used to fire the bullet. Laboratories generally performed well on these exercises, although many reported they would not issue a formal report in such cases if they did not have the actual weapon and ammunition to perform their own tests (which they did not in these cases).

For the 12 firearms proficiency tests from 2000 to 2005, laboratories averaged less than 1% incorrect responses but still maintained a considerable number of inconclusive responses (10%). Tests 00-527, 01-526, 04-526, and 04-527 stood out with higher than average comparisons (approximately 2%) that disagreed with

---

[2]§ 1:35, note 6.

manufacturer's specifications. In addition, 29% of comparisons in 01-526 were inconclusive. There were four items in this latter exercise: three were single expended 9 mm caliber questioned bullets from "crime scenes" and the fourth item consisted of three known 9 mm bullets test-fired from a "suspect weapon." Seven participants incorrectly associated one or both of the questioned bullets with the known bullets that had been fired from the "known" weapon. Laboratory practice and policy often prevented these labs from excluding bullets that should be excluded because they did not have access to the actual firearm.

Most of the inconclusive replies for the firearms tests occurred in situations where bullets/cartridge cases were actually of *different* origin, but laboratories did not report proper results. The high rate of inconclusive replies may be attributed to the fact that laboratories were not issued a firearm to perform their own test fires, the difficulty of the test and clarity of the instructions given laboratories. In most scenarios, however, the manufacturer checked about 10% of specimens before they were issued to laboratories to insure they were suitable for comparison. While acknowledging that an inconclusive reply is sometimes the appropriate response to ambiguous evidence, "it is not when sufficient data for a conclusive answer is available." As with other examination areas, it is clear the field lacks firm criteria/thresholds for distinguishing cases of common origin from inconclusives from those of different origin.

Laboratories were invited to examine a wide variety of toolmarks over the study period; they included marks made by screwdrivers, bolt cutters, drill bits, hammers, chisels, and hand stamps. In some cases the manufacturer supplied the suspect tool to participants, but in many cases laboratories were given only test marks. In such situations, the manufacturer would check all or a percentage of the marks to insure an identification was (or was not) indicated. The number of participating laboratories grew from 17 in 1981 to 205 in 1999, a 10-fold increase. Early in testing around 50% of laboratories returned replies, but in the late 1990s, upwards of 75% returned answer sheets.

Typically, fewer than 5% of replies were incorrect, with many with rates as low as 1%. One test involved the comparison of a suspect handstamp impression in lead with four other hand stamp impressions, and only two of 178 responding laboratories incorrectly reported none of the suspect tools making impressions 1 through 4 had made the mark. Another exercise involving bolt cutters asked if either of two copper wires had been cut with the tool. One had and one hadn't and only three of more than 300 reported comparisons were incorrect. Still, some exercises gave laboratories particular problems as did one involving groove joint pliers where 12% of replies incorrectly excluded the supplied tool as having made the marks on a stem of a doorknob. An additional 37% of replies were inconclusive. All marks had been examined before sample mailing to insure they were of sufficient quality for identification. Another exercise involved a pair of pliers and five cut wires and examiners were asked if the pliers could have cut the wires. Forty percent of replies were inconclusive, where laboratories should have excluded the pliers as having made the marks. Often, examiners were reluctant to offer a firm conclusion because they reported they were unsure if the blade of the tool might have undergone changes between the times the different markings had been made. Another theme that extended throughout many of the tests was the suggestion (by the advisory committee) that examiners review/reevaluate their identification criteria. Because there was an effort to review exercises before they were issued to ensure the marks were "identifiable," it became evident examiners were employing different criteria for concluding two or more marks were made by the same tool.

In the last six years of toolmark exercises (2000 to 2005), laboratories averaged about 1% incorrect comparisons, with the exception of tests 00-528, 01-528, and 03-529 where about 2% of the comparisons were in error, and 02-529 where 8.5% of the comparisons were in error. Three-quarters of the errors in the latter exercise occurred where examiners reported the screwdriver provided to them made markings on brass lock strikes that were actually made by another screwdriver. Almost all of the errors in the 01-528 exercise occurred where laboratories stated that the provided bolt cutters had cut aluminum wires that in fact had been cut by other bolt cutters not supplied to the laboratories. Eighty percent of all of the incorrect results occurred where participants reported the provided tool made marks that it truly never made. Toolmark comparisons join firearms as those disciplines with the highest percentage of inconclusive responses. Overall, about 20% of the comparisons were inconclusive (tests 00-528, 01-528, 03-528, 03-529, and 05-529 averaged more than 30% inconclusives), almost all of which occurred where the tool should have been excluded as making the test mark.

The 03-528 exercise involved questioned marks on two brass padlocks and two known tools—both steel chisels. Participants were asked to examine both padlocks and advise if they had been marked by either of the tools. Only one of the two chisels provided to laboratories made one of the two questioned marks. The second chisel made neither mark, and the other mark was made by a chisel that was not provided. The manufacturer speculated the high percentage (32%) of inconclusive responses in this exercise was due to the fact that both chisels were of the same manufacturer and had the same class characteristics.

# APPENDIX 1A

## Glossary of Terms

*Accuracy.* Conformity to a standard of correctness.

*Alteration relationship.* Exists when a source is an agent or a process that alters or modifies an object.

*Associative evidence.* Physical evidence at the scene of a crime that may serve to connect that scene with a particular individual.

*Class characteristics.* General characteristics that separate a group of objects from a universe of diverse objects.

*Forensic science.* Science exercised on behalf of the law.

*Identification.* Refers to the process of placing an item in a category. In common usage, including among forensic scientists, this term is used even when *individualization.* is what is meant.

*Individual characteristics.* Those exceptional characteristics that may establish the uniqueness of an object.

*Individualization.* The process of placing an object in a category which consists of a single, solitary unit. Individualization implies uniqueness; *identification.* does not require it.

*Precision.* The refinement of a measure to a greater or lesser degree.

*Production considerations.* The source produces the object, and the composition of the raw material utilized in the production are then expressed in the object. Finding these elements in an evidence sample at the same concentration as the putative source would establish a relationship between the evidence and the source.

*Proficiency testing.* A quality assurance practice in which an analyst is given a known sample and processes that sample in accordance with usual procedures. The analyst is not aware of the correct or expected results until after the test has been concluded.

*Reliability.* The extent to which a measuring instrument produces the same result when it is used repeatedly to measure the same object or event.

*Segment relationship.* When a source is somehow dismantled and parts of the whole are somehow scattered. The parts retain a relationship to the whole.

*Spatial location.* A type of relationship between a putative source and an object. A "source" may be a point in space as well as a tangible physical object.

*Validity.* Refers to the degree to which a measuring instrument measures what it purports to measure.

# BIBLIOGRAPHY

## GENERAL

P. Deforest, An Introduction to Criminalistics (1983).

B. Fisher, Techniques of Crime Scene Investigation (2000).

H. Lee, Crime Scene Handbook (2001).

R. Saferstein, Handbook of Forensic Science (Vol. 1 1982, Vol. 2 1988, Vol. 3 1993).

R. Saferstein, An Introduction to Forensic Science (2000).

Michael J. Saks & Jonathan J. Koehler, The Coming Paradigm Shift in Forensic Identification Science, 309 Science 892 (2005)

Encyclopedia of Forensic Science (J. Siegel ed., 2000)

B. Turvey, Criminal Profiling (1999).

## BLOOD AND OTHER PHYSIOLOGICAL FLUIDS

I. Alcamo, DNA Technology (2000).

S. Baxter, Immunological Identification of Human Semen, 13 Med. Sci. & Law 155 (1973).

T. Bevel & R. Gardner, Bloodstain Pattern Analysis (1997).

E. Blake & G. Sensabaugh, Genetic Markers in Human Semen: A Review, 21 J. Forensic Sci. 784 (1976).

E. Blake, J. Mihalovich, R. Higuchi, P. Walsh & H. Erlich, Polymerase Chair Reaction (PCR) Amplification and Human Leukocyte Antigen (HLA)-DQ CD Oligonucleotide Typing on Biological Evidence Samples: Casework Experience, 37 J. Forensic Sci. 700 (1992).

J. Butler, Forensic DNA Typing (2001).

B. Culliford, The Examination and Typing of Blood Stains in the Crime Laboratory (1971).

C. Comey & B. Budowle, Validation Studies on the Analysis of the HLA DQ CD Locus Using the Polymerase Chain Reaction, 36 J. Forensic Sci. 1633 (1991).

M. Farley & J. Harrington, Forensic DNA Technology (1991).

E. Giblett, Genetic Markers in Human Blood (1969).

P. Gill, A. Jeffreys & D. Werrett, Forensic Application of DNA "Fingerprints," 318 Nature 577 (1985).

H. Harris & D. Hopkinson, Handbook of Enzyme Electrophoresis in Human Genetics (1976).

R. Jonakait, Will Blood Tell? Genetic Markers in Criminal Cases, 31 Emory Law J. 833 (1982).

R. Jonakait, Genetic Analysis in Forensic Science, 29 J. Forensic Sci. 948 (1984).

S. Kaye, The Acid Phosphatase Test for Seminal Stains, 41 J. Crim. L. & Criminol. 834 (1951).

S. Kind, The Acid Phosphatase Test, in 3 Methods of Forensic Science (A. Curry ed., 1964).

L. Kobilinsky, Deoxyribonucleic Acid Structure And Function—A Review, in 3 Forensic Science Handbook (R. Saferstein ed., 1993).

H. Lee, Identification and Grouping of Bloodstains, in 1 Forensic Science Handbook (R. Saferstein ed., 1982).

H. Lee & R. Gaensslen, Forensic Serology, in 1 Advances in Forensic Science (1985).

A. Jeffreys, V. Wilson & S. Thein, Hypervariable "Minisatellite" Regions in Human DNA, 314 Nature 67 (1985).

D. Kaye & G. Sensabaugh, Reference Guide on DNA Evidence (1998).

F. Lundquist, Medicolegal Identification of Seminal Stains Using the Acid Phosphatase Test, 50 Arch. Pathol. 395 (1950).

National Research Council, DNA Technology in Forensic Science (1992).

O. Prokop & G. Uhlenbruck, Human Blood and Serum Groups (1969).

R. Reynolds, G. Sensabaugh & E. Blake, Analysis of Genetic Markers in Forensic DNA Samples Using the Polymerase Chain Reaction, 63 Anal. Chem. 2 (1991).

G. Sensabaugh, Isolation and Characterization of a Semen-Specific Protein from Human Seminal Plasma: A Potential New Marker for Semen Identification, 23 J. Forensic Sci. 106 (1978).

G. Sensabaugh, Biochemical Markers of Individuality, in 1 Forensic Science Handbook (R. Saferstein ed., 1982).

G. Sensabaugh & E. Blake, DNA Analysis in Biological Evidence: Applications of the Polymerase Chain Reaction in 3 Forensic Science Handbook (R. Saferstein ed., 1993).

J. Waye & R. Fourney, Forensic DNA Typing of Highly Polymorphic VNTR Loci, in Forensic Science Handbook (R. Saferstein ed., 1993).

J. Wolson & W. Stuver, Simultaneous Electrophoretic Determination of Phosphoglucomutase Subtypes, Adenose Deaminase, Erthrocyte Acid Phosphatase, and Adenylate Kinase Enzyme Phenotypes, 30 J. Forensic Sci. 904 (1985).

B. Wraxall, Forensic Serology, in Scientific and Expert Evidence (2d ed., E. Imwinkelried ed., 1981).

## GLASS

M. Dabbs & E. Pearson, The Variation in Refractive Index and Density Across Two Sheets of Window Glass, 10 J. Forensic Sci. Soc'y 139 (1970).

W. Fong, The Value of Glass as Evidence, 18 J. Forensic Sci. 398 (1973).

M. Houck, Mute Witness: Trace Evidence Analysis (2001).

S. McJunkins & J. Thornton, Glass Fracture Analysis: A Review, 2 Forensic Sci. 1 (1973).

E. Miller, Forensic Glass Comparisons, in 1 Forensic Science Handbook (R. Saferstein ed., 1982).

S. Ojena & P. DeForest, A Study of the Refractive Index Variations Within and Between Sealed Beam Headlights Using a Precise Method, 17 J. Forensic Sci. 409 (1972).

K. Smalldon & C. Brown, The Discriminating Power of Density and Refractive Index for Window Glass, 13 J. Forensic Sci. Soc'y 307 (1973).

D. Stoney & J. Thornton, Glass Evidence, in Scientific and Expert Evidence (2d ed., E. Imwinkelried ed., 1981).

D. Stoney & J. Thornton, The Forensic Significance of the Correlation of Density and Refractive Index, 29 For. Sci. Inter. 147 (1985).

J. Thornton & P. Cashman, Glass Fracture Mechanisms: A Rethinking, 31 J. Forensic Sci. 818 (1986).

J. Thornton, The Use of k Values in the Interpretation of Glass Density and Refractive Index Data, 34 J. Forensic Sci. 1323 (1989).

F. Tooley, the Handbook of Glass Manufacture (1974).

## HAIR EVIDENCE

C. Aitken & J. Robertson, The Value of Microscopic Features in the Examination of Human Hairs: Statistical Analysis of Questionnaire Returns, 31 J. Forensic Sci. 546 (1986).

C. Aitken & J. Robertson, A Contribution to the Discussion of Probabilities and Human Hair Comparisons, 32 J. Forensic Sci. 684 (1987).

H. Anderson, A Simple Scheme for the Individualisation of Human Hair, 17 Microscope 221 (1969).

P. Barnett & R. Ogle, Probabilities and Human Hair Comparison, 27 J. Forensic Sci. 272 (1982).

R. Bisbing, The Forensic Identification and Association of Human Hair, in 1 Forensic Science Handbook (R. Saferstein ed., 1982).

B. Davis, Phases of the Hair Growth Cycle, 194 Nature 694 (1962).

M. Eddy & J. Raring, Technique in Hair, Fur, and Wool Identification, 15 Proc. Penn. Acad. Sci. 164 (1941).

S. Garn., Types and Distribution of the Hair in Man, 53 Ann. N.Y. Acad. Sci. 498 (1951).

B. Gaudette & E. Keeping, An Attempt at Determining Probabilities in Human Scalp Hair Comparison, 19 J. Forensic Sci. 599 (1974).

B. Gaudette, Some Further Thoughts on Probabilities and Human Hair Comparisons, 23 J. Forensic Sci. 758 (1978).

B. Gaudette, A Supplementary Discussion of Probabilities and Human Hair Comparisons, 27 J. Forensic Sci. 279 (1982).

J. Glaister, A Study of Hairs and Wool Belonging to the Mammalian Group of Animals Including a Special Study of Human Hair Considered from the Medico-legal Aspect (1931).

J. Glaister, Contact Traces, 7 J. Forensic Med. 44 (1960).

L. Hausman, Structural Characteristics of the Hair of Mammals, 54 Amer. Naturalist 496 (1920).

L. Hausman, A Comparative Racial Study of the Structural Elements of Human Head Hair, 59 Amer. Naturalist 529 (1924).

L. Hausman, Histological Variability of Human Hair, 18 Amer. J. Phys. Anthrop. 415 (1934).

K. Hoffman, Statistical Evaluation of the Evidential Value of Human Hairs Possibly Coming from Multiple Sources, 36 J. Forensic Sci. 1053 (1991).

M. Houck, Mute Witness: Trace Evidence Analysis (2001).

D. Hrdy, Quantitative Hair Form Variation in Seven Populations, 39 Amer. J. Phys. Anthrop. 7 (1973).

P. Kirk, Human Hair Studies. I. General Considerations of Hair Individualization and Its Forensic Importance, 31 J. Crim. L. & Criminology 486 (1940).

S. Niyogi, A Study of Human Hairs in Forensic Work—A Review, 9 J. Forensic Med. 27 (1962).

S. Niyogi, A Study of Human Hairs in Forensic Work, 2 Proc. Canad. Soc. For. Sci. 105 (1963).

M. Trotter, A Review of the Classifications of Hair, 24 Amer. J. Phys. Anthrop. 105 (1938).

C. von Beroldingen, G. Sensabaugh & H. Erlich, DNA Typing from Single Hairs, 1988 Nature 332 (1988).

R. Wickenheiser & D. Hepworth, Further Evaluation of Probabilities in Human Scalp Hair Comparisons, 35 J. Forensic Sci. 1323 (1990).

## FIBER EVIDENCE

R. Bressee, Evaluation of Textile Fiber Evidence: A Review, 32 J. Forensic Sci. 510 (1987).

R. Cook & C. Wilson, The Significance of Finding Extraneous Fibers in Contact Cases, 32 Forensic Sci. Int'l. 267 (1982).

L. Forlini & W. McCrone, Dispersion Staining of Fibers, 19 Microscope 243 (1971).

R. Fox & H. Schuetzman, The Infrared Identification of Microscopic Samples of Man-Made Fibers, 13 J. Forensic Sci. 397 (1968).

B. Gaudette, The Forensic Aspects of Textile Fiber Examination, in 2 Forensic Science Handbook (R. Saferstein ed., 1988).

M. Grieve, Fibers and Forensic Science—New Ideas, Developments, and Techniques, 6 Forensic Sci. Rev. 59 (1994).

M. Grieve, The Role of Fibers in Forensic Science Examinations, 28 J. Forensic Sci. 877 (1983).

M. Grieve & L. Cabiness, The Recognition and Identification of Modified Acrylic Fibers, 29 For. Sci. Int'l. 129 (1985).

M. Grieve, J. Dunlop & P. Haddock, An Assessment of the Value of Blue, Red, and Black Cotton Fibers as Target Fibers in Forensic Science Investigations, 33 J. Forensic Sci. 1331 (1988).

M. Grieve, J. Dunlop & P. Haddock, Transfer Experiments with Acrylic Fibers, 40 Forensic Sci. Int'l. 267 (1989).

M. Grieve, Fibers and Their Examination in Forensic Science, in 4 Forensic Science Progress (A. Maehly & R. Williams eds., 1990).

M. Houck, Mute Witness: Trace Evidence Analysis (2001).

R. Janiak & K. Damerau, The Application of Pyrolysis and Programmed Temperature Gas Chromatography to the Identification of Textile Fibers, 59 J. Crim. Law, Criminology & Police Sci. 434 (1968).

A. Longhetti & G. Roche, Microscopic Identification of Man-Made Fibers from the Criminalistics Point of View, 3 J. Forensic Sci. 303 (1958).

C. Lowrie & G. Jackson, Recovery of Transferred Fibers, 50 For. Sci. Int'l. 111 (1991).

J. Robertson, C. Kidd & H. Parkinson, The Persistence of Textile Fibers Transferred During Simulated Contacts, 22 J. Forensic Sci. Soc. 353 (1982).

K. Smalldon, The Identification of Acrylic Fibers by Polymer Composition as Determined by Infrared Spectroscopy and Physical Characteristics, 18 J. Forensic Sci. 69 (1973).

M. Tungol, E. Bartick, & A. Montaser, Analysis of Single Polymer Fibers by Fourier Transform Infrared Microscopy: The Results of Case Studies, 36 J. Forensic Sci. 1027 (1991).

## Fingerprint Evidence

J. Almog & A. Gabay, A Modified Super Glue Technique—The Use of Polycyanoacrylate for Fingerprint Development, 31 J. Forensic Sci. 250 (1986).

J. Almog, A. Hirshfeld & J. Klug, Reagents for the Chemical Development of Latent Fingerprints: Synthesis and Properties of Some Ninhydrin Analogues, 27 J. Forensic Sci. 912 (1982).

D. Ashbaugh, Quantitative-Qualitative Finger Ridge Analysis (1999).

F. Cherill, The Fingerprint System at Scotland Yard (1954).

J. Cowger, Friction Ridge Skin (1983).

H. Cummins & C. Midlo, Finger Prints, Palms and Soles (1976).

B. Dalrymple, J. Duff & R. Menzel, Inherent Luminescence of Fingerprints by Laser, 22 J. Forensic Sci. 106 (1977).

F. Galton, Finger Prints (1892).

Home Office Scientific Research and Development Branch, Manual of Fingerprint Development Techniques (1986).

H. Lee And R. Gaensslen, Advances in Fingerprint Technology (1991).

R. Menzel, The Development of Fingerprints, in Scientific and Expert Evidence (2d ed., Edward Imwinkelried ed., 1981)

A. Moenssens, Fingerprints and the Law (1969).

A. Moenssens, Fingerprint Technique (1971).

R. Olsen, Scott's Fingerprint Mechanics (1978).

D. Stoney & J. Thornton, A Critical Analysis of Quantitative Fingerprint Individuality Models, 31 J. Forensic Sci. 1187 (1986).

H. Wilder & B. Wentworth, Personal Identification (1918).

## Soil And Mineral Evidence

W. Graves, A Mineralogical Soil Classification Technique for the Forensic Scientist, 24 J. Forensic Sci. 323 (1979).

C. Hurlbut, Dana's Manual of Mineralogy (18th ed.1971).

W. McCrone & J. Delly, The Particle Atlas (1973).

R. Murray & J. Tedrow, Forensic Geology, Earth Sciences and Criminal Investigation (1975).

R. Murray, Forensic Examination of Soil, in 1 Forensic Science Handbook (R. Saferstein ed., 1982).

J. Thornton & F. Fitzpatrick, Forensic Characterization of Sand, 20 J. Forensic Sci. 460 (1975).

J. Thornton & A. McLaren, Enzymatic Characterization of Soil Evidence, 20 J. Forensic Sci. 674 (1975).

J. Thornton, Forensic Soil Characterization, in 1 Forensic Science Progress (A. Maehly & R. Williams eds., 1986).

## HANDWRITING

R. Brunelle, Questioned Document Examination, in 1 Forensic Science Handbook (R. Saferstein ed., 1982).

Maureen Casey, Questioned Document Examination, in Modern Legal Medicine, Psychiatry, and Forensic Science (W. Curran, A. McGarry & C. Petty eds., 1980).

J. Conway, Evidential Documents (1959).

E. Ellen, the Scientific Examination of Documents (1989).

W. Harrison, Suspect Documents (2nd ed.1966).

W. Harrison, Forgery Detection: A Practical Guide (1964).

O. Hilton, Scientific Examination of Questioned Documents (Revised ed. 1982).

O. Hilton, How Individual are Personal Writing Habits?, 28 J. Forensic Sci. 683 (1983).

O. Hilton, The Evolution of Questioned Document Examination in the Last 50 Years, 33 J. Forensic Sci. 1310 (1988).

J. Kelly, Questioned Document Examination, in Scientific and Expert Evidence (2d ed., Edward Imwinkelried ed., 1981).

J. Levinson, Questioned Documents (2000).

T. McAlexander, J. Beck & R. Dick, The Standardization of Handwriting Opinion Terminology, 36 J. Forensic Sci. 311 (1991).

R. Muehlberger, Identifying Simulations: Practical Considerations, 35 J. Forensic Sci. 368 (1990).

C. Mitchell, Handwriting and Its Value as Evidence, J. Royal Soc. of Arts 81 (1923).

R. Morris, Forensic Handwriting Identification (2000).

A. Osborn, Questioned Documents (2nd ed.1929).

D. Purtell, Modern Handwriting Instructions, Systems, and Techniques, 8 J. Police Sci. & Admin. 66 (1980).

Michael J. Saks & Holly VanderHaar, On the "General Acceptance" of Handwriting Identification Principles, 50 Journal of Forensic Sciences 119 (2005)

E. Smith, Principles of Forensic Handwriting Identification and Testimony (1984).

F. Whiting, Inconclusive Opinions: Refuge of the Questioned Document Examiner, 35 J. Forensic Sci. 938 (1990).

## NARCOTICS AND DRUGS OF ABUSE

F. Bailey & H. Rothblatt, Handling Narcotic and Drug Cases (1972).

D. Bernheim, Defense of Narcotics Cases (1983).

C. Fulton, Modern Microcrystal Tests for Drugs (1969).

T. Gough, the Analysis of Drugs of Abuse (1991).

E. Horwood, Analytical Methods in Forensic Chemistry (1990).

M. Kurzman & D. Fullerton, Drug Identification, in Scientific and Expert Evidence (2d ed., E. Imwinkelried ed., 1981).

T. Mills, W. Price, P. Price & J. Roberson, Instrumental Data for Drug Analysis (1981–1994).

R. Saferstein, Forensic Applications of Mass Spectrometry, in 1 Forensic Science Handbook (R. Saferstein ed., 1982).

J. Siegel, Forensic Identification of Controlled Substances, in 2 Forensic Science Handbook (R. Saferstein ed., 1988).

R. Smith, Forensic Applications of High-Performance Liquid Chromatography, in 1 Forensic Science Handbook (R. Saferstein ed., 1982).

I. Sunshine, Handbook of Analytical Toxicology (1969).

J. Yinon, Forensic Mass Spectrometry (1987).

## VOICEPRINT

R. Bolt, R. Cooper, E. David, P. Denes, J. Pickett & K. Stevens, Speaker Identification by Speech Spectrograms: A Scientist's View of its Reliability for Legal Purposes, 47 J. Acoustical Soc. Amer. 597 (1970).

R. Bolt, F. Cooper, E. David, P. Denes, J. Pickett & K. Stevens, Speaker Identification by Speech Spectrograms: Some Further Observations, 54 J. Acoustical Soc. Amer. 531 (1973).

H. Hollien, the Acoustics of Crime: the New Science of Forensic Phonetics (1990).

L. Kersta, Speaker Recognition and Identification by Voiceprints, 40 Conn. Bar J. 586 (1966).

L. Kersta, Voiceprint Identification, 196 Nature 1253 (1962).

L. Kersta, Voiceprint Identification Infallibility, 34 J. Acoustical Soc. Amer. 1978 (1962).

B. Koenig, Spectrographic Voice Identification: A Forensic Survey, 79 J. Acoustical Soc. Amer. 2088 (1986).

B. Koenig, Spectrographic Voice Identification, 13 FBI Crime Lab Digest 105 (Oct.1986).

National Academy of Sciences, On the Theory and Practice of Voice Identification (1979).

K. Thomas, Voiceprint—Myth or Miracle, in Scientific and Expert Evidence (2d ed., Edward Imwinkelried ed., 1981).

O. Tosi, Voice Identification: Theory and Legal Applications (1979).

O. Tosi, Voice Identification, in Scientific and Expert Evidence (2d ed., E. Imwinkelried ed., 1981).

O. Tosi, H. Oyer, W. Lashbrook, C. Pedrey, J. Nicol & E. Nash, Experiment on Voice Identification, 51 J. Acoustical Soc. Amer. 2030 (1972).

O. Tosi, Fundamental of Voice Identification, in Modern Legal Medicine, Psychiatry, and Forensic Science (W. Curran, A. McGarry & C. Petty eds., 1980).

Voice Identification and Acoustic Analysis Subcommittee (VIAAS), Voice Comparison Standards, 41 J. Forensic Identification 373 (1991).

## BITEMARKS

American Board of Forensic Odontology, Guidelines for Bite Mark Analysis, 112 J. Amer. Dental Assoc. 383 (1986).

J. Beckstead, R. Rawson & W. Giles, A Review of Bite Mark Evidence, 99 J. Amer. Dental Assoc. 69 (1979).

B. Benson, J. Cottone, T. Bomberg, & N. Sperber, Bite Mark Impressions: A Review of Techniques and Materials, 33 J. Forensic Sci. 1238 (1988).

J. Camerson & B. Sims, Forensic Dentistry (1974).

Outline of Forensic Dentistry (J. Cottone & S. Standish eds., 1982).

G. Gustafson, Forensic Odontology (1966).

W. Harvey, Dental Identification and Forensic Odontology (1976).

W. Hyzer & T. Krauss, The Bite Mark Standard Reference Scale ABFO No. 2, 33 J. Forensic Sci. 498 (1988).

L. Levine, Bitemark Evidence, 21 Dental Clinics of N. Am. 145 (1977).

L. Luntz & P. Luntz, Handbook for Dental Identification (1973).

R. Rawson, R. Ommen, G. Kinard, J. Johnson & A. Yfantis, Statistical Evidence for the Individuality of the Human Dentition, 29 J. Forensic Sci. 245 (1984).

R. Rawson, G. Vale, E. Herschaft, N. Sperber & S. Dowell, Analysis of Photographic Distortion in Bite Marks: A Report of the Bite Mark Guidelines Committee, 31 J. Forensic Sci. 1261 (1986).

R. Rawson, G. Vale, N. Sperber, E. Herschaft, & A. Yfantis, Reliability of the Scoring System of the American Board of Forensic Odontology for Human Bite Marks, 31 J. Forensic Sci. 1235 (1986).

I. Sopher, Forensic Dentistry (1976).

N. Sperber, Forensic Odontology, in Scientific and Expert Evidence (2d ed., E. Imwinkelried ed., 1981).

## ARSON AND FIRE EVIDENCE

T. Aldridge & M. Oates, Fractionation of Accelerants and Arson Residues by Solid Phase Extraction, 31 J. Forensic Sci. 666 (1986).

J. Andrasko, The Collection and Detection of Accelerant Vapors Using Porous Polymers and Curie Point Pyrolysis Wires Coated with Active Carbon, 28 J. Forensic Sci. 330 (1983).

B. Beland, Comments on Fire Investigation Procedures, 29 J. Forensic Sci. 191 (1984).

W. Bennett & K. Hess, Investigating Arson (1984).

D. Berry, Fire Litigation Handbook (1984).

D. Berry, Characteristics and Behavior of Fire, 34 Def. Law. J. 243 (1985).

P. Kirk, Fire Investigation (3rd ed., J. DeHaan ed., 1991).

Law Enforcement Assistance Administration (LEAA), Arson and Arson Investigation (1978).

D. Mabley, Arson Investigation and Prosecution (1982).

C. Midkiff, Arson and Explosive Investigation, in 1 Forensic Science Handbook (R. Saferstein ed., 1982).

V. Reeve, J. Jeffrey, D. Weihs, & W. Jennings, Developments in Arson Analysis: A Comparison of Charcoal Adsorption and Direct Headspace Injection Techniques Using Fused Silica Capillary Gas Chromatography, 31 J. Forensic Sci. 479 (1986).

R. Smith, Mass Chromatographic Analysis of Arson Accelerants, 28 J. Forensic Sci. 318 (1983).

S. Swab, Incendiary Fires: A Reference Manual for Fire Investigators (1983).

## TOOLMARK AND FIREARM EVIDENCE

Association of Firearm and Toolmark Examiners (AFTE), Glossary (1980).

A. Biasotti, A Statistical Study Of the Individual Characteristics of Fired Bullets, 4 J. Forensic Sci. 34 (1959).

A. Biasotti, The Principles of Evidence Evaluation as Applied to Firearms and Tool Mark Identification, 9 J. Forensic Sci. 428 (1964).

D. Burd & P. Kirk, Tool Marks: Factors Involved in Their Comparison and Use as Evidence, 32 J. Crim. Law & Criminology 679 (1942).

D. Burd & R. Greene, Tool Mark Comparisons in Criminal Investigations, 39 J. Crim. Law & Criminology 379 (1948).

D. Burd & R. Greene, Tool Mark Examination Techniques, 2 J. Forensic Sci. 297 (1957).

G. Burrard, The Identification of Firearms and Forensic Ballistics (1962).

P. Ceccaldi, The Examination Of Firearms and Ammunition, in 1 Methods of Forensic Science (F. Lundquist ed., 1962).

J. Davis, Tool Marks, Firearms, And The Striagraph (1958).

W. Deinet, Studies Of Models Of Striated Marks Generated by Random Processes, 26 J. Forensic Sci. 35 (1981).

C. Goddard, Scientific Identification of Firearms and Bullets, 17 J. Crim. Law, Criminology & Police Sci. 254 (1926).

E. Flynn, Toolmark Identification, 2 J. Forensic Sci. 95 (1957).

J. Gunther & C. Gunther, The Identification of Firearms (1935).

J. Hatcher, F. Jury & J. Weller, Firearms Investigation, Identification, and Evidence (1957).

M. Josserand & J. Stevenson, Pistols, Revolvers, and Ammunition (1967).

D. Macpherson, Bullet Penetration (1994).

J. Mathews, Firearms Identification (Vols. 1–2, 1962; Vol. 3, 1973).

E. Matunas, American Ammunition and Ballistics (1979).

W. Rowe, Firearms Identification, in 2 Forensic Science Handbook (R. Saferstein ed., 1988).

E. Springer, Toolmark Examination—A Review of Its Development in the Literature, 40 J. Forensic Sci. 964 (1995).

R. Wilhelm, General Considerations of Firearms Identification and Ballistics, in Scientific and Expert Evidence (2d ed., Edward Imwinkelried ed., 1981).

# Chapter 2

# DNA Typing[*]

## I. LEGAL ISSUES

## II. SCIENTIFIC STATUS

---

[*]This chapter is a revised and expanded version of David H. Kaye & George F. Sensabaugh, Jr., Reference Guide on DNA Evidence, in Reference Manual on Scientific Evidence 485 (Federal Judicial Center, 2d ed.2000).

## I.  LEGAL ISSUES

### § 2:1  Introduction

Deoxyribonucleic acid, or DNA, is a molecule that encodes the genetic information in all living organisms. Its chemical structure was elucidated in 1954. More than 30 years later, samples of human DNA began to be used in the criminal justice system, primarily in cases of rape or murder. The evidence has been the subject of extensive scrutiny by lawyers, judges, and the scientific community.[1] It is now admissible in virtually all jurisdictions,[2] but debate lingers over the safeguards that should be

---

**[Section 2:1]**

[1]At the request of various government agencies, the National Research Council empaneled two committees for the National Academy of Sciences that produced book-length reports on forensic DNA technology, with recommendations for enhancing the rigor of laboratory work and improving the presentation of the evidence in court. Committee on DNA Technology in Forensic Science, National Research Council, DNA Technology in Forensic Science (1992) [hereinafter NRC I]; Committee on DNA Forensic Science: An Update, National Research Council, The Evaluation of Forensic DNA Evidence (1996) [hereinafter NRC II].

[2]For reviews of the challenges to admissibility, see Giannelli, The DNA Story: An Alternative View, 88 J. Crim. L. & Crimin. 380 (1997) (concluding that courts were too willing to admit an untested technology); Kaye, DNA Evidence: Probability, Population Genetics, and the Courts, 7 Harv. J. L. & Tech. 101 (1993) (suggesting that the principal objection to the computations of random match probabilities was exaggerated); Thompson, Evaluating the Admissibility of New Genetic Identification Tests: Lessons from the "DNA War", 84 J. Crim. L. & Crimin. 22 (1993) (reviewing the debate on population structure but not discussing studies indicating that the effect is generally minor). Some of the leading opinions are reproduced in D.H. Kaye, Science in Evidence

required in testing samples and in presenting the evidence in court.[3] Moreover, there are many types of DNA analysis, and still more are being developed.[4] New problems of admissibility arise as advancing methods of analysis and novel applications of established methods are introduced.

This chapter identifies the legal issues pertaining to the admissibility of and weight of DNA evidence of identity, and it describes the science and technology of forensic DNA analysis.[5] Sections 2:1 to 2:19 discuss the major objections that have been raised to the admission of DNA evidence. § 2:21 outlines the types of scientific expertise that go into the analysis of DNA samples.

Sections 2:21 to 2:23 give an overview of the scientific principles behind DNA typing. They describe the structure of DNA and how this molecule differs from person to person. These are basic facts of molecular biology. These sections also define the more important scientific terms. They explain at a general level how DNA differences are detected. These are matters of analytical chemistry and laboratory procedure. Finally, these sections indicate how it is shown that these differences permit individuals to be identified. This is accomplished with the methods of probability and statistics.

The next two groups of sections outline basic methods used in DNA testing. Sections 2:24 to 2:26 describe methods that begin by using the polymerase chain reaction (PCR) to make many copies of short segments of DNA. Sections 2:27 to 2:29 examine the theory and technique of the older procedure of measuring restriction fragment length polymorphisms (RFLPs) due to variable number tandem repeats (VNTRs).

Sections 2:30 to 2:33 consider issues of sample quantity and quality common to all methods of DNA profiling. Sections 2:34 to 2:39 deal with laboratory performance. They outline the types of information that a laboratory should produce to establish that it can analyze DNA reliably and that it has adhered to established laboratory protocols.

Sections 2:40 to 2:50 examine issues in the interpretation of laboratory results. To assist the courts in understanding the extent to which the results incriminate the defendant, they enumerate the hypotheses that need to be considered before concluding that the defendant is the source of the crime-scene samples, and they explore the issues that arise in judging the strength of the evidence. They focus on questions of statistics, probability, and population genetics.

Sections 2:51 to 2:58 take up novel applications of DNA technology, such as the forensic analysis of nonhuman DNA. They identify questions that can be useful in judging whether a new method or application has the scientific merit and power claimed by the proponent of the evidence. An appendix provides detail on technical material, and the glossary defines selected terms and acronyms encountered in genetics, molecular biology, and forensic DNA work.[6]

## § 2:2  Objections to DNA evidence

The usual objective of forensic DNA analysis is to detect variations in the genetic

---

(1997).

[3]See D.H. Kaye, DNA, NAS, NRC, DAB, RFLP, PCR, and More: An Introduction to the Symposium on the 1996 NRC Report on Forensic DNA Evidence, 37 Jurimetrics J. 395 (1997); William C. Thompson, Guide to Forensic DNA Evidence, in Expert Evidence: A Practitioner's Guide to Law, Science, and the FJC Manual 185 (Bert Black & Patrick W. Lee eds., 1997).

[4]See National Commission on the Future of DNA Evidence, The Future of Forensic DNA

Testing: Predictions of the Research and Development Working Group (2000); §§ 2:21 to 2:23.

[5]Leading cases are collected in tables in Committee on DNA Forensic Science: An Update, National Research Council, The Evaluation of Forensic DNA Evidence at 205–211(1996).

[6]The glossary defines the words and phrases that are italicized in the text as well as a number of other terms that may be used by experts in these fields.

material that differentiate individuals one from another.[1] Laboratory techniques for isolating and analyzing DNA have long been used in scientific research and medicine. Applications of these techniques to forensic work usually involve comparing a DNA sample obtained from a suspect with a DNA sample obtained from the crime scene. Often, a perpetrator's DNA in hair, blood, saliva, or semen can be found at a crime scene,[2] or a victim's DNA can be found on or around the perpetrator.[3]

In many cases, defendants have objected to the admission of testimony of a match or its implications.[4] Under *Daubert v. Merrell Dow Pharmaceuticals, Inc.*,[5] the district court, in its role as "gatekeeper" for scientific evidence, then must assure that the expert's methods are scientifically valid and reliable. Under *Frye v. United States*,[6] the question is narrowed to whether the methods are general accepted in the relevant scientific community.

Because the basic theory and most of the laboratory techniques of DNA profiling are so widely accepted in the scientific world, disputed issues involve features unique to their forensic applications or matters of laboratory technique.[7] These include the extent to which standard techniques have been shown to work with crime-scene samples exposed to sunlight, heat, bacteria, and chemicals in the

---

**[Section 2:2]**

[1]Biologists accept as a truism the proposition that, except for identical twins, human beings are genetically unique. Consequently, in principle, DNA samples can be used to distinguish all individuals who are not identical twins from all other human beings.

[2]E.g., *U.S. v. Beasley*, 102 F.3d 1440, 46 Fed. R. Evid. Serv. 1 (8th Cir. 1996) (two hairs were found in a mask used in a bank robbery and left in the abandoned get-away car); *U.S. v. Two Bulls*, 918 F.2d 56, 31 Fed. R. Evid. Serv. 855 (8th Cir. 1990) (semen stain on victim's underwear).

[3]E.g., *U.S. v. Cuff*, 37 F. Supp. 2d 279, 51 Fed. R. Evid. Serv. 557 (S.D. N.Y. 1999) (scrapings from defendant's fingernails); *State v. Bible*, 175 Ariz. 549, 858 P.2d 1152 (1993) (blood stains on defendant's shirt); *People v. Castro*, 144 Misc. 2d 956, 545 N.Y.S.2d 985 (Sup 1989) (bloodstains on defendant's watch). For brevity, we refer only to the typical case of a perpetrator's DNA at a crime scene. The scientific and legal issues in both situations are the same.

[4]Exclusion of the testimony can be sought before or during trial, depending on circumstances and the court's rules regarding pretrial motions. Pretrial requests for discovery and the appointment of experts to assist the defense also can require judicial involvement. See, e.g., *Dubose v. State*, 662 So. 2d 1189 (Ala. 1995) (holding that due process was violated by the failure to provide an indigent defendant with funds for an expert); *Cade v. State*, 658 So. 2d 550 (Fla. Dist. Ct. App. 5th Dist. 1995) (abuse of discretion under state statute to deny defense request for appointment of DNA expert even though there was no showing of specific need, but only the general observation that I can't tell the Court what I'm looking for because "it's so complicated"); *State v. Scott*, 33 S.W.3d 746 (Tenn. 2000) (trial court erred in not

appointing an expert for an indigent defendant where the rule requiring a showing of "particularized need" for an expert to assist defense counsel with regard to mitochondrial DNA testing had been shown); Committee on DNA Forensic Science: An Update, National Research Council, The Evaluation of Forensic DNA Evidence at 167–169 (1996); Giannelli, Book Review, The DNA Story: An Alternative View, 88 J. Crim. L. & Criminology 380, 414–417 (1997) (criticizing the reluctance of state courts to appoint defense experts and to grant discovery requests); Giannelli, Criminal Discovery, Scientific Evidence, and DNA, 44 Vand. L. Rev. 791 (1991); Zollinger, Comment, Defense Access to State-Funded DNA Experts: Considerations of Due Process, 85 Calif. L. Rev. 1803 (1997).

[5]*Daubert v. Merrell Dow Pharmaceuticals, Inc.*, 509 U.S. 579, 113 S. Ct. 2786, 125 L. Ed. 2d 469, 27 U.S.P.Q.2d 1200, Prod. Liab. Rep. (CCH) P 13494, 37 Fed. R. Evid. Serv. 1, 23 Envtl. L. Rep. 20979 (1993).

[6]Frye v. U.S., 293 F. 1013, 34 A.L.R. 145 (App. D.C. 1923) (rejected by, State v. Walstad, 119 Wis. 2d 483, 351 N.W.2d 469 (1984)) and (rejected by, State v. Brown, 297 Or. 404, 687 P.2d 751 (1984)) and (rejected by, Nelson v. State, 628 A.2d 69 (Del. 1993)) and (rejected by, State v. Alberico, 116 N.M. 156, 861 P.2d 192 (1993)) and (rejected by, State v. Moore, 268 Mont. 20, 885 P.2d 457 (1994)) and (rejected by, State v. Faught, 127 Idaho 873, 908 P.2d 566 (1995)) and (rejected by, People v. Shreck, 22 P.3d 68, 90 A.L.R.5th 765 (Colo. 2001)).

[7]An overview of the technical issues written for defense attorneys is William C. Thompson et al., Evaluating Forensic DNA Evidence: Essential Elements of a Competent Defense Review, Champion, Apr. 2003, at 16 (pt. 1); May, 2003, at 24 (pt. 2).

environment;[8] the extent to which the specific laboratory has demonstrated its ability to follow protocols that have been validated to work for crime-scene samples;[9]

---

[8]The extent to which a particular implementation of a standard technique is subject to *Frye* or *Daubert* has been a bone of contention in several cases. For example, in *U.S. v. Ewell*, 252 F. Supp. 2d 104 (D.N.J. 2003), aff'd, 189 Fed. Appx. 120 (3d Cir. 2006), cert. denied, 127 S. Ct. 989, 166 L. Ed. 2d 747 (U.S. 2007), the district court rejected defendant's challenge to the admissibility of STR testing. Noting that "[t]here is little doubt that . . . with proper procedures an expert can determine the allelic types of given DNA samples at the thirteen core STR loci" (*U.S. v. Ewell*, 252 F. Supp. 2d 104, 111 (D.N.J. 2003), aff'd, 189 Fed. Appx. 120 (3d Cir. 2006), cert. denied, 127 S. Ct. 989, 166 L. Ed. 2d 747 (U.S. 2007)), the court observed that "[d]efendant's argument here is focused on the Profiler Plus and Cofiler kits. Defendant maintains that there are no validation studies of either kit from which one could determine their reliability." *U.S. v. Ewell*, 252 F. Supp. 2d 104 (D.N.J. 2003), aff'd, 189 Fed. Appx. 120 (3d Cir. 2006), cert. denied, 127 S. Ct. 989, 166 L. Ed. 2d 747 (U.S. 2007) The court reasoned that whether the manufacturer's "kits" of chemicals were the subject of sufficient scientific study fell outside the ambit of *Daubert* because they "merely provide the materials necessary to perform the PCR amplification process, and thus, the kits need not independently meet the *Daubert* standard of admissibility . . . . Accordingly, challenges as to the efficacy and reliability of the materials kits go to the weight of the evidence and not to admissibility." *U.S. v. Ewell*, 252 F. Supp. 2d 104 (D.N.J. 2003), aff'd, 189 Fed. Appx. 120 (3d Cir. 2006), cert. denied, 127 S. Ct. 989, 166 L. Ed. 2d 747 (U.S. 2007). Nevertheless, the court went on to find that the use of the kits was scientifically valid under *Daubert*.

In *State v. Traylor*, 656 N.W.2d 885 (Minn. 2003), defendant argued that the refusal of a company to disclose the sequence of its primers, which it wished to protect as a trade secret (see Mellon, Note, Manufacturing Convictions: Why Defendants Are Entitled to the Data Underlying Forensic DNA Kits, 51 Duke L.J. 1097, 1103 (2001)), meant that its kit was not generally accepted for use in the field of forensic science. The trial court rejected this argument, reasoning that "the particular machine and kits only need to be shown to have been used in accordance with appropriate and accepted standards." *State v. Traylor*, 656 N.W.2d 885, 892 (Minn. 2003). On appeal from the ensuing conviction, the Minnesota Court of Appeals applied a "two-pronged" version of *Frye*, which looks not only to the general acceptance of the method, but also to its application in a specific occasion. It found that PCR-STR typing itself was generally accepted, but that the accepted standards in DNA forensic science required disclosure of the primer sequences used

in polymerase chain reaction. As a result, it held the laboratory findings were inadmissible. The Minnesota Supreme Court reversed, finding that the scientific community did not demand publication of specific sequences. *State v. Traylor*, 656 N.W.2d 885, 897–898 (Minn. 2003); cf. *State v. Whittey*, 149 N.H. 463, 821 A.2d 1086 (2003) (arguments about the validation of a particular primer set are not subject to *Frye*).

Treating the disclosure issue as merely involving the specific application of a generally accepted method, as in *Ewell* and *Traylor*, is dangerous. In jurisdictions that do not require proof that an accepted method is implemented correctly, it means that the design of the device can escape serious scrutiny. Indeed, other courts have concluded that there is no need to demonstrate general acceptance of particular instrumentation that is said to implement accepted theories and principles. *People v. Hill*, 89 Cal. App. 4th 48, 107 Cal. Rptr. 2d 110, 119 (2d Dist. 2001) (PCR-based STR typing is generally accepted, and the particular instrument, "Profiler Plus," used to do it need not be validated because it "does not embrace new scientific techniques"); *State v. Faulkner*, 103 S.W.3d 346, 358–59 (Mo. Ct. App. S.D. 2003) (distinguishing *Traylor* in that Missouri's *Frye* rule has no specific-application prong). This departs from *Frye*, which should be understood to mean that the proponent must demonstrate that the apparatus is at least capable of doing what is claimed for it. In a case like *Traylor*, the requirement of general acceptance should apply to the generic question of whether scientists are willing to rely on data from STR kits without knowing the primer sequences. See D.H. Kaye et al., The Modern Wigmore, A Treatise on Evidence: Expert Evidence § 8.1.3(d) (2004); see also *Ex parte Taylor*, 825 So. 2d 769 (Ala. 2002) (PCR-STR with Perkin-Elmer kits had to be shown to be reliable).

[9]In *U.S. v. Ewell*, 252 F. Supp. 2d 104 (D.N.J. 2003), aff'd, 189 Fed. Appx. 120 (3d Cir. 2006), cert. denied, 127 S. Ct. 989, 166 L. Ed. 2d 747 (U.S. 2007), the district court rejected the argument that because "the Government has not offered evidence as to how often the laboratory actually reaches the wrong result due to human errors, instrument errors and errors due to the failure to follow FBI protocol," *U.S. v. Ewell*, 252 F. Supp. 2d 104, 113 (D.N.J. 2003), aff'd, 189 Fed. Appx. 120 (3d Cir. 2006), cert. denied, 127 S. Ct. 989, 166 L. Ed. 2d 747 (U.S. 2007), STR testing is not scientifically valid. The court reasoned that:

Laboratory error may only form the basis for exclusion of an expert opinion if a reliable methodology was so altered as to skew the methodology itself. The defendant's argument is not based on evidence of actual errors by the laboratory, but instead has simply challenged the Government's failure to quantify the rate of laboratory error. To the con-

possible ambiguities that might interfere with the interpretation of test results; and the validity and possible prejudicial impact of estimates of the probability of a match between the crime-scene samples and innocent suspects. As explained below, some of these objections—particularly those involving probability and statistics—generally have proved more effective than others.

## § 2:3   Objections to DNA evidence—Historical overview

The history of the judicial treatment of DNA evidence can be divided into at least five phases.[1] The first phase was one of rapid and sometimes uncritical acceptance. Initial praise for RFLP testing in homicide, rape, paternity, and other cases was effusive. Indeed, one judge proclaimed "DNA fingerprinting" to be "the single greatest advance in the 'search for truth' . . . since the advent of cross-examination."[2] In this first wave of cases, expert testimony for the prosecution rarely was countered, and courts readily admitted RFLP findings.[3]

In a second wave of cases, however, defendants pointed to problems at two levels—controlling the experimental conditions of the analysis and interpreting the results.[4] Some scientists questioned certain features of the procedures for extracting and analyzing DNA employed in forensic laboratories. It became apparent that determining whether RFLPs in VNTR loci in two samples actually match can be complicated by measurement variability or missing or spurious bands.[5] Despite these concerns,

---

trary, the Government has demonstrated the scientific method has a virtually zero rate of error, and that it employs sufficient procedures and controls to limit laboratory error and thus, maintain the integrity of the method.

Defendant's argument on this score exhibits a fundamental misunderstanding of the principles of *Daubert*. The Court's concern under Rule 702 and *Daubert* is the reliability of the scientific methodology at issue, not the reliability of the laboratory performing the test. Put simply, a laboratory's error rate is a measure of its past proficiency and is of little value in determining whether a test has methodological flaws. What the defendant has sought to do here is challenge the proficiency of the tester rather than the reliability of the test. Such challenges go to the weight of the evidence, not its admissibility.

*U.S. v. Ewell*, 252 F. Supp. 2d 104, 113–114 (D.N.J. 2003), aff'd, 189 Fed. Appx. 120 (3d Cir. 2006), cert. denied, 127 S. Ct. 989, 166 L. Ed. 2d 747 (U.S. 2007) (internal quotation marks, citations, and notes omitted).

**[Section 2:3]**

[1]This history of the judicial reception of DNA evidence is adapted from 1 McCormick on Evidence § 205 (John Strong ed., 5th ed 1999), and Imwinkelried & Kaye, DNA Typing: Emerging or Neglected Issues, 76 Wash. L. Rev. 413 (2001).

[2]*People v. Wesley*, 140 Misc. 2d 306, 533 N.Y.S.2d 643 (County Ct. 1988), aff'd, 183 A.D.2d 75, 589 N.Y.S.2d 197 (3d Dep't 1992), order aff'd, 83 N.Y.S.2d 417, 611 N.Y.S.2d 97, 633 N.E.2d 451 (1994).

[3]*Andrews v. State*, 533 So. 2d 841 (Fla. Dist. Ct. App. 5th Dist. 1988); *People v. Wesley*, 140 Misc. 2d 306, 533 N.Y.S.2d 643 (County Ct. 1988),

aff'd, 183 A.D.2d 75, 589 N.Y.S.2d 197 (3d Dep't 1992), order aff'd, 83 N.Y.S.2d 417, 611 N.Y.S.2d 97, 633 N.E.2d 451 (1994); *Spencer v. Com.*, 238 Va. 275, 384 S.E.2d 775, 84 A.L.R.4th 293 (1989) (early version of DQα test properly admitted where "[t]he record is replete with uncontradicted expert testimony that no 'dissent whatsoever (exists) in the scientific community' "); *State v. Woodall*, 182 W. Va. 15, 385 S.E.2d 253 (1989) (taking judicial notice of general scientific acceptance where there was no expert testimony, but holding that inconclusive results were properly excluded as irrelevant); Admissibility of DNA identification evidence, 84 A.L.R.4th 313.

[4]For a comprehensive survey of possible sources of error and ambiguity in VNTR profiling, see William Thompson & Simon Ford, The Meaning of a Match: Sources of Ambiguity in the Interpretation of DNA Prints, in Forensic DNA Technology 93 (M.A. Farley & J.J. Harrington eds., 1990).

[5]See *U.S. v. Yee*, 134 F.R.D. 161 (N.D. Ohio 1991), aff'd, 12 F.3d 540, 38 Fed. R. Evid. Serv. 688 (6th Cir. 1993); Anderson, DNA Fingerprinting on Trial, 342 Nature 844 (1989); Thompson & Ford, Is DNA Fingerprinting Ready for the Courts?, New Scientist, Mar. 31, 1990, at 38; Gina Kolata, Some Scientists Doubt the Value of "Genetic Fingerprint" Evidence, N.Y. Times, Jan. 29, 1990, at A1 col. 1 (reporting that "[l]eading molecular biologists say a technique promoted by the nation's top law-enforcement agency for identifying suspects in criminal trials through the analysis of genetic material is too unreliable to be used in court"; but the accuracy of this report is seriously questioned in Andre Moenssens, DNA Evidence and Its Critics—How Valid Are the Challenges?, 31 Jurimetrics J. 87 (1990)).

most cases continued to find forensic RFLP analyses to be generally accepted,[6] and a number of states provided for admissibility of DNA tests by legislation.[7] Concerted attacks by defense experts of impeccable credentials, however, produced a few cases rejecting specific proffers on the ground that the testing procedure was not sufficiently rigorous.[8] Moreover, a minority of courts, perhaps concerned that DNA evidence might well be conclusive in the minds of jurors, added a "third prong" to the general acceptance standard.[9] This augmented *Frye* test requires not only proof of the general acceptance of the ability of science to produce the type of results offered in court, but also a showing of the proper application of an approved method on the particular occasion.[10] Whether this inquiry is properly part of the special screening of scientific methodology, however, is debatable.[11]

---

[6]E.g., *U.S. v. Yee*, 134 F.R.D. 161 (N.D. Ohio 1991), aff'd, 12 F.3d 540, 38 Fed. R. Evid. Serv. 688 (6th Cir. 1993); *State v. Pennington*, 327 N.C. 89, 393 S.E.2d 847 (1990) (uncontradicted expert testimony that false positives are impossible); *Glover v. State*, 787 S.W.2d 544 (Tex. App. Dallas 1990), petition for discretionary review granted, (Sept. 12, 1990) and judgment aff'd, 825 S.W.2d 127 (Tex. Crim. App. 1992) (admissible in light of other decisions where "[a]ppellant did not produce any expert testimony").

[7]Md. Code Ann., Cts. & Jud. Proc. § 10-915 ("In any criminal proceeding, the evidence of a DNA profile is admissible to prove or disprove the identity of any person"); Minn. Stat. Ann. § 634.25 ("In a criminal trial or hearing, the results of DNA analysis . . . are admissible in evidence without antecedent expert testimony that DNA analysis provides a trustworthy and reliable method of identifying characteristics in an individual's genetic material upon a showing that the offered testimony meets the standards for admissibility set forth in the Rules of Evidence."); Kenneth E. Melson, Legal and Ethical Considerations, in DNA Fingerprinting: An Introduction 189, 199–200 (Lorne T. Kirby ed., 1990).

[8]*People v. Castro*, 144 Misc. 2d 956, 545 N.Y.S.2d 985, 995 (Sup 1989) (principles of DNA testing generally accepted, but "[i]n a piercing attack upon each molecule of evidence presented, the defense was successful in demonstrating to this court that the testing laboratory failed in its responsibility to perform the accepted scientific techniques and experiments"); *State v. Schwartz*, 447 N.W.2d 422, 428 (Minn. 1989) ("DNA typing has gained general acceptance in the scientific community," but "the laboratory in this case did not comport" with "appropriate standards"); Colin Norman, Maine Case Deals a Blow to DNA Fingerprinting, 246 Science 1556 (1989); Sherman, DNA Tests Unravel?, Nat'l L.J., Dec. 18, 1989, at 1, 24–25.

Some commentators have assumed or argued that some or all of these issues are aspects of admissibility under Rule 702. E.g., Imwinkelried, The Debate in the DNA Cases over the Foundation for the Admission of Scientific Evidence: The Importance of Human Error as a Cause of Forensic Misanalysis, 69 Wash. U. L.Q.

19 (1991); Scheck, DNA and *Daubert*, 15 Cardozo L. Rev. 1959, 1979–1987 (1994); William C. Thompson, Accepting Lower Standards: The National Research Council's Second Report on Forensic DNA Evidence, 37 Jurimetrics J. 405, 417 (1997). This reading of *Daubert* is rejected in *U.S. v. Shea*, 957 F. Supp. 331, 340–341, 46 Fed. R. Evid. Serv. 1375 (D.N.H. 1997), aff'd, 159 F.3d 37, 50 Fed. R. Evid. Serv. 516 (1st Cir. 1998), but the protocols of a specific laboratory and the proficiency of its analysts are factors that affect probative value under Rule 403. See Berger, Laboratory Error Seen Through the Lens of Science and Policy, 30 U.C. Davis L. Rev. 1081 (1997); Imwinkelried, The Case Against Evidentiary Admissibility Standards that Attempt to "Freeze" the State of a Scientific Technique, 67 U. Colo. L. Rev. 887 (1996).

[9]This innovation was introduced in *People v. Castro*, 144 Misc. 2d 956, 545 N.Y.S.2d 985 (Sup 1989). It soon spread. See *U.S. v. Two Bulls*, 918 F.2d 56, 61, 31 Fed. R. Evid. Serv. 855 (8th Cir. 1990) ("it was error for the trial court to determine the admissibility of the DNA evidence without determining whether the testing procedures . . . were conducted properly"), vacated for rehearing en banc, app. dismissed due to death of defendant, 925 F.2d 1127 (8th Cir.1991); *Ex parte Perry*, 586 So. 2d 242 (Ala. 1991). For cases declining to graft a "third prong" onto *Frye*, see, for example, *State v. Bible*, 175 Ariz. 549, 858 P.2d 1152 (1993); *Hopkins v. State*, 579 N.E.2d 1297 (Ind. 1991); *State v. Ferguson*, 20 S.W.3d 485, 495 (Mo. 2000); *State v. Vandebogart*, 136 N.H. 365, 616 A.2d 483 (1992); *State v. Cauthron*, 120 Wash. 2d 879, 846 P.2d 502 (1993).

[10]Later, some courts insisted on such a showing as part of the demonstration of scientific soundness required under *Daubert*. E.g., *U.S. v. Martinez*, 3 F.3d 1191, 37 Fed. R. Evid. Serv. 863 (8th Cir. 1993) (rejected by, Taylor v. State, 1995 OK CR 10, 889 P.2d 319 (Okla. Crim. App. 1995)).

[11]For an analysis concluding that such matters are better handled not as part of the special test for scientific evidence, but as aspects of the balancing of probative value and prejudice, see Berger, Laboratory Error Seen Through the Lens of Science and Policy, 30 U.C. Davis L. Rev. 1081 (1997).

A different attack on DNA profiling that began in cases during this period proved far more successful and led to a third wave of cases in which many courts held that estimates of the probability of a coincidentally matching VNTR profile were inadmissible.[12] These estimates relied on a simplified population-genetics model for the frequencies of VNTR profiles that treats each race as a large, randomly mating population. Some prominent scientists claimed that the applicability of the model had not been adequately verified.[13] A heated debate on this point spilled over from courthouses to scientific journals and convinced the supreme courts of several states that general acceptance was lacking.[14] A 1992 report of the National Academy of Sciences proposed a more "conservative" computational method as a compromise,[15] and this seemed to undermine the claim of scientific acceptance of the less conservative procedure that was in general use.[16]

---

[12]See Committee on DNA Forensic Science: An Update, National Research Council, The Evaluation of Forensic DNA Evidence at 205–211(1996) (exhaustively tabulating cases); Kaye, DNA Evidence: Probability, Population Genetics, and the Courts, 7 Harv. J. L. & Tech. 101 (1993). A source of confusion in some cases was the fallacious assumption that the relevant population in which to estimate a profile frequency is the defendant's racial or ethnic group (rather than all the groups from which the perpetrator of the crime might have come). This fallacious assumption continues to insinuate itself into opinions. See U.S. v. Morrow, 374 F. Supp. 2d 51, 55 (D.D.C. 2005) (in response to defendant's objection to "being included in the 'African-American' population of the United States since he is Jamaican by birth," the government promised to "run the samples found that matched for defendant Palmer using the [sic] a Caribbean population group data base, which includes individuals from Jamaica, Trinidad and the Bahamas"); Darling v. State, 808 So. 2d 145 (Fla. 2002) (assuming that simply because the defendant was from Bahama, a Bahamanian database was more appropriate than the Hispanic database—even though the crime was committed in the United States, not the Bahamas); cf. People v. Prince, 36 Cal. Rptr. 3d 300 (Cal. App. 5th Dist. 2005), review granted and opinion superseded, 42 Cal. Rptr. 3d 1, 132 P.3d 210 (Cal. 2006) and review dismissed, cause remanded, 49 Cal. Rptr. 3d 208, 142 P.3d 1184 (Cal. 2006) (error to introduce ethnic frequencies without proof of the ethnicity of the actual perpetrator), criticized, Kaye, Logical Relevance: Problems with the Reference Population and DNA Mixtures in People v. Pizarro, 3 L., Probability & Risk 211 (2004), disapproved, People v. Wilson, 38 Cal. 4th 1237, 45 Cal. Rptr. 3d 73, 136 P.3d 864 (2006).

[13]See Kaye, DNA Evidence: Probability, Population Genetics, and the Courts, 7 Harv. J. L. & Tech. 101 (1993); Thompson, Evaluating the Admissibility of New Genetic Identification Tests: Lessons from the "DNA War", 84 J. Crim. L. & Crimin. 22 (1993). In the light of the totality of information on the distribution of various genes in populations, the criticism of the simple random-

mating model may have been overblown. See Bernard Devlin & Kathryn Roeder, DNA Profiling: Statistics and Population Genetics, in 1 Modern Scientific Evidence: The Law and Science of Expert Testimony 710 (David Faigman et al. eds., 1997).

In addition to questioning the model for combining allele frequencies, a few experts testified that no meaningful conclusions can be drawn in the absence of random sampling. E.g., People v. Soto, 21 Cal. 4th 512, 88 Cal. Rptr. 2d 34, 981 P.2d 958 (1999); State v. Anderson, 118 N.M. 284, 881 P.2d 29, 39 (1994). The Arizona Supreme Court accepted this argument but later retreated from its implications. See Kaye, Bible Reading: DNA Evidence in Arizona, 28 Ariz. St. L.J. 1035 (1996). The scientific basis for the argument is considered in Kaye, Bible Reading: DNA Evidence in Arizona, 28 Ariz. St. L.J. 1035 (1996) and §§ 2:40 to 2:52.

Another related concern was that the early, nonrandom samples were too small to give good estimates of allele frequencies. This argument generally proved unpersuasive. E.g., U.S. v. Shea, 957 F. Supp. 331, 46 Fed. R. Evid. Serv. 1375 (D.N.H. 1997), aff'd, 159 F.3d 37, 50 Fed. R. Evid. Serv. 516 (1st Cir. 1998); People v. Soto, 35 Cal. Rptr. 2d 846 (App. 4th Dist. 1994), as modified on denial of reh'g, (Dec. 22, 1994) and review granted and opinion superseded, 39 Cal. Rptr. 2d 406, 890 P.2d 1115 (Cal. 1995) and aff'd, 21 Cal. 4th 512, 88 Cal. Rptr. 2d 34, 981 P.2d 958 (1999); State v. Dishon, 297 N.J. Super. 254, 687 A.2d 1074, 1090 (App. Div. 1997); State v. Copeland, 130 Wash. 2d 244, 922 P.2d 1304, 1321 (1996).

[14]See Kaye, DNA Evidence: Probability, Population Genetics, and the Courts, 7 Harv. J. L. & Tech. 101 (1993).

[15]Committee on DNA Technology in Forensic Science, National Research Council, DNA Technology in Forensic Science (1992).

[16]See Kaye, The Forensic Debut of the National Research Council's DNA Report: Population Structure, Ceiling Frequencies and the Need for Numbers, 96 Genetica 99 (1995), published in slightly different form in 34 Jurimetrics J. 369 (1994).

At this juncture the history was poised to enter a fourth phase. In response to the population-genetics criticism and the 1992 National Academy of Sciences report came an outpouring of both critiques of the report and new studies of the distribution of VNTR alleles in many population groups. Relying on the burgeoning literature, a second National Academy panel concluded in 1996 that the usual method of estimating frequencies of VNTR profiles in broad racial groups was sound.[17] In the fourth phase of judicial scrutiny of DNA evidence, the courts almost invariably returned to the earlier view that the statistics associated with VNTR profiling are generally accepted and scientifically valid both in major population groups[18] and in subgroups.[19]

The fifth phase of the judicial evaluation of DNA evidence is well underway. As results obtained with the new PCR-based methods enter the courtroom, it becomes necessary to ask whether each such method rests on a solid scientific foundation or is generally accepted in the scientific community.[20] Sometimes, the answer will be obvious even without an extensive pretrial hearing.[21] The opinions are practically

---

[17]Committee on DNA Forensic Science: An Update, National Research Council, The Evaluation of Forensic DNA Evidence (1996). The 1996 report provides more refined methods for estimating allele frequencies in ethnic subpopulations.

[18]See, e.g., *People v. Soto*, 21 Cal. 4th 512, 88 Cal. Rptr. 2d 34, 981 P.2d 958, 974 (1999) ("Several developments since the filing of *Barney* indicate the controversy over population substructuring and use of the unmodified product rule has dissipated."); *People v. Miller*, 173 Ill. 2d 167, 219 Ill. Dec. 43, 670 N.E.2d 721, 731–732 (1996) (abrogated on other grounds by, In re Commitment of Simons, 213 Ill. 2d 523, 290 Ill. Dec. 610, 821 N.E.2d 1184 (2004)) ("while there has been some controversy over the use of the product rule in calculating the frequency of a DNA match, that controversy appears to be dissipating"); *Armstead v. State*, 342 Md. 38, 673 A.2d 221, 238 (1996) ("the debate over the product rule essentially ended in 1993"); *Com. v. Fowler*, 425 Mass. 819, 685 N.E.2d 746 (1997) (product rule with and without ceilings for VNTRs now meets test of scientific reliability in light of 1996 NRC Report), *departing from Com. v. Lanigan*, 413 Mass. 154, 596 N.E.2d 311 (1992) (dispute over population structure evinces lack of general acceptance).

   Despite these reassuring statements, the "basic product rule" (see §§ 2:40 to 2:52) is an approximation that is not universally appropriate. A more refined method for handling population structure is available. See §§ 2:40 to 2:52.

[19]A few cases approve of applying the frequency data for major population groups to subgroups with the ordinary product rule. *U.S. v. Santiago Santiago*, 156 F. Supp. 2d 145, 57 Fed. R. Evid. Serv. 867 (D.P.R. 2001) (scientifically valid to use Hispanic database for Puerto Rican subgroup). However, this approach is open to question, and courts have approved the use of a number of modifications. First, some courts have approved of using the "ceiling" procedure recommended in the 1992 *Darling v. State*, 808 So. 2d 145 (Fla. 2002) (lack of a Bahamian database was

not fatal to a modified ceiling calculation). Second, random-match probabilities using the $F_{ST}$ adjustment described in the 1996 NRC Report have been held to satisfy *U.S. v. Gaines*, 979 F. Supp. 1429, 48 Fed. R. Evid. Serv. 419 (S.D. Fla. 1997); *U.S. v. Shea*, 957 F. Supp. 331, 343, 46 Fed. R. Evid. Serv. 1375 (D.N.H. 1997), aff'd, 159 F.3d 37, 50 Fed. R. Evid. Serv. 516 (1st Cir. 1998); *Com. v. Gaynor*, 443 Mass. 245, 820 N.E.2d 233, 254 (2005). Finally, to estimate frequencies in the subgroup of interest, experts have used data on other, arguably similar subgroups. *U.S. v. Chischilly*, 30 F.3d 1144, 1158 n.29, 40 Fed. R. Evid. Serv. 289 (9th Cir. 1994) (responding to the concern that the FBI had insufficient data on VNTR allele frequencies among Navajos); cf. *Government of Virgin Islands v. Byers*, 941 F. Supp. 513, 515, 45 Fed. R. Evid. Serv. 1247 (D.V.I. 1996) (crediting FBI testimony that the distribution of VNTR alleles in African-Americans is similar to that in Afro-Caribbeans); *Government of Virgin Islands v. Penn*, 838 F. Supp. 1054, 1071 (D.V.I. 1993) ("any concern that the St. Thomas' black population's bin frequencies are drastically different from those of the United States black population is unwarranted").

[20]E.g., *Harrison v. State*, 644 N.E.2d 1243 (Ind. 1995) (error not to hold *Frye* hearing on PCR-based method). D.H. Kaye et al., The Modern Wigmore, A Treatise on Evidence: Expert Evidence § 8.1.3(d) (2003). But see *State v. Scott*, 33 S.W.3d 746 (Tenn. 2000) (a state statute providing that "the results of DNA analysis . . . are admissible in evidence without antecedent expert testimony that DNA analysis provides a trustworthy and reliable method of identifying characteristics in an individual's genetic material upon a showing that the offered testimony meets the standards of admissibility set forth in the Tennessee Rules of Evidence" made a hearing on the scientific soundness of mitochondrial DNA testing unnecessary).

[21]For example, a procedure may be so similar to accepted protocols that acceptance or validity can be inferred from previous cases. See *U.S. v. Johnson*, 56 F.3d 947, 41 Fed. R. Evid. Serv. 1181

unanimous in holding that the more commonly used PCR-based laboratory procedures satisfy these standards[22] and that the basic "product rule" for estimating

(8th Cir. 1995) (in response to a defense expert's testimony that a police department's variation on the FBI protocol for RFLP-VNTR testing had not been validated, the court held that the variation did not preclude admission where an FBI analyst testified that the difference was of no significance); *People v. Oliver*, 306 Ill. App. 3d 59, 239 Ill. Dec. 196, 713 N.E.2d 727, 734 (1st Dist. 1999) ("the minor variations . . . in the . . . second RFLP test did not render it a new scientific technique for the purposes of *Frye*."). A closer case is *People v. Hill*, 89 Cal. App. 4th 48, 107 Cal. Rptr. 2d 110, 119 (2d Dist. 2001) (PCR-based STR typing is generally accepted, and the particular instrument, "Profiler Plus," used to do it need not be validated because it "does not embrace new scientific techniques"); cf. *State v. Gore*, 143 Wash. 2d 288, 21 P.3d 262 (2001), as amended, (Mar. 29, 2001) and as amended, (Apr. 6, 2001) and (overruled on other grounds by, State v. Hughes, 154 Wash. 2d 118, 110 P.3d 192 (2005)) ("We decline to hold that each time new loci are involved in DNA testing, a *Frye* hearing must be held"). In general, trial courts have considerable "latitude in deciding how to test an expert's reliability, and to decide whether or when special briefing or other proceedings are needed to investigate reliability." *Kumho Tire Co., Ltd. v. Carmichael*, 526 U.S. 137, 119 S. Ct. 1167, 143 L. Ed. 2d 238, 50 U.S.P.Q.2d 1177, Prod. Liab. Rep. (CCH) P 15470, 50 Fed. R. Evid. Serv. 1373, 29 Envtl. L. Rep. 20638 (1999).

[22]*U.S. v. Ewell*, 252 F. Supp. 2d 104 (D.N.J. 2003), aff'd, 189 Fed. Appx. 120 (3d Cir. 2006), cert. denied, 127 S. Ct. 989, 166 L. Ed. 2d 747 (U.S. 2007) (STRs satisfy *Daubert* and are generally accepted); *U.S. v. Trala*, 162 F. Supp. 2d 336, 57 Fed. R. Evid. Serv. 1266 (D. Del. 2001) (same); *Ex parte Taylor*, 825 So. 2d 769 (Ala. 2002) (commercial kit used for PCR amplification and for typing six genetic locations DQ Alpha, LDLR, GYPA, HBGG, D758, and GC had to be shown to satisfy *Daubert*, and the state did so); *Ex parte Taylor*, 825 So. 2d 769 (Ala. 2002) (PCR-STR testing with Perkin-Elmer kits had to be shown to be reliable, and it was); *People v. Henderson*, 107 Cal. App. 4th 769, 132 Cal. Rptr. 2d 255 (4th Dist. 2003) (all aspects of STR testing satisfy *Frye*); *People v. Smith*, 107 Cal. App. 4th 646, 132 Cal. Rptr. 2d 230 (2d Dist. 2003) (STR testing generally accepted); *People v. Hill*, 89 Cal. App. 4th 48, 107 Cal. Rptr. 2d 110 (2d Dist. 2001) (PCR-based STR typing is generally accepted); *People v. Allen*, 72 Cal. App. 4th 1093, 85 Cal. Rptr. 2d 655 (2d Dist. 1999) (STR testing); *People v. Shreck*, 22 P.3d 68, 90 A.L.R.5th 765 (Colo. 2001), as modified, (May 14, 2001) (concluding that D1S80 and STR multiplex typing is generally accepted and valid); *Lemour v. State*, 802 So. 2d 402 (Fla. Dist. Ct. App. 3d Dist. 2001) (STR-testing method generally accepted in scientific community); *People v.*

*Rokita*, 316 Ill. App. 3d 292, 249 Ill. Dec. 363, 736 N.E.2d 205, 211 (5th Dist. 2000); *Overstreet v. State*, 783 N.E.2d 1140, 1151 (Ind. 2003) ("[T]he trial court was within its discretion to admit the STR evidence."); *Com. v. Rosier*, 425 Mass. 807, 685 N.E.2d 739 (1997) (STR testing); *Com. v. Sok*, 425 Mass. 787, 683 N.E.2d 671, 672–673 (1997) (abrogated on other grounds by, Case of Canavan, 432 Mass. 304, 733 N.E.2d 1042 (2000)) (DQ Polymarker, and D1S80 analysis "meet the test of scientific reliability"); *Hughes v. State*, 735 So. 2d 238 (Miss. 1999) (unspecified PCR method deemed reliable); *State v. Faulkner*, 103 S.W.3d 346 (Mo. Ct. App. S.D. 2003) (STR typing with commercial "kits" is generally accepted); *State v. Traylor*, 656 N.W.2d 885, 900 (Minn. 2003) ("PCR-STR DNA testing is generally accepted in the relevant scientific community . . . ."); *State v. Jackson*, 255 Neb. 68, 582 N.W.2d 317 (1998) (STR testing); *State v. Whittey*, 149 N.H. 463, 821 A.2d 1086 (2003) ("[B]ased upon the evidence presented during the *Frye* hearings and the overwhelming acceptance of PCR-based STR DNA testing in other cases, we affirm the trial court's ruling that the methods and techniques used in PCR-based STR DNA testing are generally accepted in the scientific community."); *State v. Harvey*, 151 N.J. 117, 699 A.2d 596 (1997) (DQα and Polymarker tests generally accepted); *State v. Lyons*, 324 Or. 256, 924 P.2d 802 (1996) (DQα admissible under relevancy standard); *State v. Moeller*, 1996 SD 60, 548 N.W.2d 465 (S.D. 1996) (DQα admissible under *Daubert* standard); *State v. Butterfield*, 2001 UT 59, 27 P.3d 1133 (Utah 2001) (STRs satisfy Utah's reliability standard); *State v. Gore*, 143 Wash. 2d 288, 21 P.3d 262 (2001), as amended, (Mar. 29, 2001) and as amended, (Apr. 6, 2001) and (overruled on other grounds by, State v. Hughes, 154 Wash. 2d 118, 110 P.3d 192 (2005)) (DQ-alpha, polymarker, and D1S80 are generally accepted, as is the basic product rule for these loci).

Attacks on the scientific validity or acceptance, in general, of STR analysis of mixed stains also have been rebuffed. E.g., *U.S. v. Trala*, 162 F. Supp. 2d 336, 349, 57 Fed. R. Evid. Serv. 1266 (D. Del. 2001) ("In light of the controls to reduce the effects of inherent flaws such as stutter or allelic drop out [in analyzing mixed stains], the court finds that the defendant's challenges are directed to the weight of the evidence and not its admissibility."); *People v. Henderson*, 107 Cal. App. 4th 769, 132 Cal. Rptr. 2d 255, 270 (4th Dist. 2003) ("capillary electrophoresis has gained general acceptance as a fast and accurate method of forensic DNA testing" for STRs with mixtures"); *People v. Smith*, 107 Cal. App. 4th 646, 132 Cal. Rptr. 2d 230, 249–50 (2d Dist. 2003) ("mixed sample analysis of deoxyribonucleic acid by means of short tandem repeats utilizing Profiler Plus and COfiler in conjunction with the Applied Biosystems Prism 310 Genetic Analyzer is accepted by

the frequencies of genotypes in major populations groups is scientifically sound and generally accepted for the loci investigated in PCR-based tests.[23]

In sum, in little more than a decade, DNA typing has made the transition from a novel set of methods for identification to a relatively mature and well studied forensic technology. However, one should not lump all forms of DNA identification together. New techniques and applications continue to emerge. These range from the use of new genetic systems and new analytical procedures to the typing of DNA from plants and animals. Before admitting such evidence, it will be necessary to inquire into the biological principles and knowledge that would justify inferences from these new technologies or applications.[24] For example, a court's prior approval of RFLP testing by gel electrophoresis or reverse dot blot testing of PCR-amplified fragments containing the HLA DQ$\alpha$ gene does not dictate the conclusion that the court also must accept testing at STR loci or mitochondrial DNA sequencing. The newer technologies are gaining judicial approval,[25] but a court should not confer approval until it is satisfied that the specific technology meets the applicable standard.[26]

the scientific community"); *Wynn v. State*, 791 So. 2d 1258, 1259 (Fla. Dist. Ct. App. 5th Dist. 2001) (because "[t]here was no evidence offered to suggest the unreliability of the analysis of mixed samples, [t]he court's determination that the procedure used met the *Frye* standard even as it related to mixed samples was not error.").

[23]*People v. Baylor*, 97 Cal. App. 4th 504, 118 Cal. Rptr. 2d 518 (4th Dist. 2002), opinion modified on denial of reh'g, (May 6, 2002) (product rule acceptable for different types of tests); *People v. Reeves*, 91 Cal. App. 4th 14, 109 Cal. Rptr. 2d 728 (1st Dist. 2001), as modified on denial of reh'g, (Aug. 28, 2001) (product rule is generally accepted for PCR-based typing as well as for VNTRs); *Butler v. State*, 842 So. 2d 817, 829 (Fla. 2003) ("case law . . . continues to uphold the validity of the product rule"); *State v. Miller*, 666 N.W.2d 703 (Minn. 2003) (product rule is generally accepted for use with STRs as indicated by 1996 NRC report); *State v. Gore*, 143 Wash. 2d 288, 21 P.3d 262 (2001), as amended, (Mar. 29, 2001) and as amended, (Apr. 6, 2001) and (overruled on other grounds by, State v. Hughes, 154 Wash. 2d 118, 110 P.3d 192 (2005)) (basic product rule is generally accepted for use with DQ-alpha, polymarker, and D1S80 loci). But see *Roberts v. State*, 841 So. 2d 558 (Fla. Dist. Ct. App. 4th Dist. 2003) (remanding for *Frye* hearing on statistics for a PCR-based test).

[24]For suggestions to assist in this endeavor, see §§ 2:53 to 2:60.

[25]On STR testing, see supra note 22. On mitochondrial DNA testing, see *U.S. v. Beverly*, 369 F.3d 516, 64 Fed. R. Evid. Serv. 357, 2004 FED App. 0136P (6th Cir. 2004) (admissible even though laboratory not yet accredited); *U.S. v. Coleman*, 202 F. Supp. 2d 962 (E.D. Mo. 2002) (mt-DNA testing satisfies *Daubert*, and a finding of a match can be presented fairly to reveal that the type is not unique); *State v. Pappas*, 256 Conn. 854, 776 A.2d 1091 (2001) (mt-DNA testing is admissible under *Daubert*; and the upper bound of a confidence interval for the frequency of the

mt-DNA type in the Caucasian population provided an admissible statistic that the jury could understand"); *Magaletti v. State*, 847 So. 2d 523 (Fla. Dist. Ct. App. 2d Dist. 2003) (mt-DNA testing and an estimated population frequency (the upper confidence limit) are generally accepted); *Wagner v. State*, 160 Md. App. 531, 864 A.2d 1037 (2005); *People v. Holtzer*, 255 Mich. App. 478, 660 N.W.2d 405 (2003) (mt-DNA testing admissible despite the trial judge's concerns about the adequacy of a particular laboratory's work); *Adams v. State*, 794 So. 2d 1049 (Miss. Ct. App. 2001) (mt-DNA testing is reliable); *People v. Ko*, 304 A.D.2d 451, 757 N.Y.S.2d 561 (1st Dep't 2003), cert. granted, judgment vacated on other grounds, 542 U.S. 901, 124 S. Ct. 2839, 159 L. Ed. 2d 265 (2004) (upholding finding of reliability of mt-DNA testing); *State v. Council*, 335 S.C. 1, 515 S.E.2d 508, 518 (1999) ("[T]he trial judge was well within his discretion in finding the results of the mt-DNA analysis admissible under [*Daubert*-like] factors and Rule 702."). The first appellate case upholding the admission of mt-DNA evidence appears to be *State v. Ware*, 1999 WL 233592 (Tenn. Crim. App. 1999) (unpublished opinion holding that notwithstanding testimony from a defense expert that mt-DNA sequencing had not been adequately validated for forensic use, the FBI's mt-DNA testing was properly admitted under the scientific soundness standard). Mark Curriden, A New Evidence Tool: First Use of Mitochondrial DNA Test in a U.S. Criminal Trial, A.B.A.J., Nov.1996, at 18.

Objections to the probabilities or counts associated with mt-DNA matches can be expected. See Kaestle et al., Database Limitations on the Evidentiary Value of Forensic Mitochondrial DNA Evidence, 43 Am. Crim. L. Rev. 53 (2006); Bandelt & Bravi, Problems in FBI mtDNA Database, 305 Science 1402 (2004). For the FBI's reply to Bandelt and Bravi, see Budowle & Polanskey, FBI mtDNA Database: A Cogent Perspective, 307 Science 845 (2005).

[26]Some courts could be tempted to avoid this fundamental requirement by pretending that as

### § 2:4 Objections to DNA evidence—Ascertaining DNA matches— Subjectivity and ambiguity in ascertaining the profile

Even if a generally accepted or valid method of analyzing individuating features of DNA has been employed properly, the interpretation of the laboratory results could be objectionable. Examiners sometimes disagree as to the profile of a DNA sample. Bona fide disagreements certainly would go to the weight of the evidence and might bear on its admissibility through Federal Rule of Evidence 403. It also can be argued that such disagreements pertain to admissibility under *Daubert*—to the extent that "adequate scientific care" necessitates "an objective and quantitative procedure for identifying the pattern of a sample," and that "[p]atterns must be identified separately and independently in suspect and evidence samples. By and large, however, courts have not been inclined to treat procedures that allow for subjective judgment in ascertaining the profiles as fatal to admissibility.

### § 2:5 Objections to DNA evidence—Ascertaining DNA matches— Measurement variability and VNTRs

VNTRs are characterized by the variation in their lengths. The measurement process that uses gel electrophoresis ends with pictures that reveals these variations in the form of "bands" located at different heights on a photographic film.[1] However, just as it is impossible to measure the height of a person to the last decimal place, the measurement process for VNTRs is not perfectly precise. The same DNA fragment can appear at slightly different heights on successive measurements. To account for this measurement variability, most laboratories use a statistically determined *match window*: They declare that two fragments match if the bands appear to match visually, and if they fall within a specified distance of one another.[2] The FBI's match window has been challenged as being too inclusive. Because the window has reasonable, empirically validated error rates,[3] however, these attacks have not prevailed.[4]

Match windows should not be confused with "bins." A "bin" is simply a range of

---

long as PCR technology is used to amplify the DNA in the original sample, new analytical methods need not be scrutinized. Indeed, court opinions often read as if PCR is itself an analytical method. E.g., *State v. Begley*, 956 S.W.2d 471, 477 (Tenn. 1997) (stating that "the PCR method of DNA analysis [is] an inherently trustworthy and reliable method of identification."). The problem with relying on such ill-phrased dicta is that STR testing uses different loci and a different method of typing the alleles than earlier technologies that begin with PCR amplification. These differences are significant enough to preclude automatically extending the cases on the earlier methods to the newer ones.

Fortunately, most courts recognize that the letters PCR are not a ticket to admission for new methods that happen to start with the PCR step. See, e.g., *U.S. v. Ewell*, 252 F. Supp. 2d 104 (D.N.J. 2003), aff'd, 189 Fed. Appx. 120 (3d Cir. 2006), cert. denied, 127 S. Ct. 989, 166 L. Ed. 2d 747 (U.S. 2007) (analyzing the admissibility of STR identification procedures separately from those of PCR amplification); *Ex parte Taylor*, 825 So. 2d 769 (Ala. 2002) (commercial kit used for PCR amplification and for typing six genetic locations DQ Alpha, LDLR, GYPA, HBGG, D758, and GC had to be shown to satisfy *Daubert*, and the

state did so); *People v. Henderson*, 107 Cal. App. 4th 769, 132 Cal. Rptr. 2d 255, 263 (4th Dist. 2003) (applying *Frye* to capillary electrophoresis in STR testing because "PCR amplification and electrophoresis are two distinct parts of the overall DNA testing process"); cf. *State v. Roman Nose*, 649 N.W.2d 815 (Minn. 2002) (trial court erred in not conducting a hearing on the general acceptance of STR typing).

**[Section 2:5]**

[1]§ 2:28.

[2]§ 2:42.

[3]§ 2:42; Hans Zeisel & David Kaye, Prove It with Figures: Empirical Methods in Law and Litigation 204–206 (1997); Kaye, DNA Evidence: Probability, Population Genetics, and the Courts, 7 Harv. J. L. & Tech. 101 (1994); Kaye, The Relevance of Matching DNA: Is the Window Half Open or Half Shut?, 85 J. Crim. L. & Criminology 676 (1995). *Contra*, Thompson, Evaluating the Admissibility of the New Genetic Tests: Lessons from the "DNA War", 84 J. Crim. L. & Criminology 22 (1993); § 2:42.

[4]See *U.S. v. Yee*, 134 F.R.D. 161 (N.D. Ohio 1991), aff'd, 12 F.3d 540, 38 Fed. R. Evid. Serv. 688 (6th Cir. 1993); *U.S. v. Jakobetz*, 747 F. Supp. 250, 31 Fed. R. Evid. Serv. 1007 (D. Vt. 1990),

sizes of VNTR fragments, and bins are used to determine the proportion of VNTR alleles of various sizes seen in a database of DNA samples. These proportions then are combined to estimate a profile frequency (the profile typically being composed of six to 10 VNTR alleles).[5] For this purpose, the bins used to count allele frequencies should span at least the width of the two adjacent match windows that would lead to a match being declared. Figure 1 shows why.

---

judgment aff'd, 955 F.2d 786, 34 Fed. R. Evid. Serv. 876 (2d Cir. 1992); *U.S. v. Perry*, No. CR 91-395-SC (D.N.M. Sept. 7, 1995).

[5]§ 2:47.

## Figure 1
## The relationship between floating bin width and match window

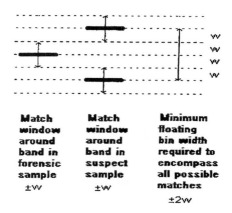

Match
window
around
band in
forensic
sample
±w

Match
window
around
band in
suspect
sample
±w

Minimum
floating
bin width
required to
encompass
all possible
matches
±2w

The failure of the FBI to observe this precept prompted the California Supreme Court to affirm the reversal of a conviction for rape and related offenses in *People v. Venegas*.[6] The court recognized the need for a line between mistakes that are so fundamental as to preclude admissibility and less serious errors,[7] but it deemed the use of too narrow a bin width as a fatal methodological flaw under *Frye*.[8]

## § 2:6    Objections to DNA evidence—Presenting incriminating DNA results

Even if the laboratory determination that defendant's DNA matches that found at a crime scene is accurate, the manner in which this finding is presented could be prejudicial. For example, the presentation of a very small "probability of a random match" in the general population, even if validly computed, has been said to be misleading for a variety of reasons. The next several sections discuss the legal question of which of the various scientifically defensible probabilities[1] should be admissible in court. Assuming that the probabilities are computed according to a method that meets *Daubert*'s demand for scientific validity and reliability and thus satisfies Rule 702, the major issue arises under Rule 403: To what extent will the presentation assist the jury to understand the meaning of a match so that the jury can give the evidence the weight it deserves? This question involves psychology and law, and we summarize the assertions and analyses that have been offered with respect to the various probabilities and statistics that can be used to indicate the probative value of DNA evidence.

## § 2:7    Objections to DNA evidence—Presenting incriminating DNA results—Should match probabilities be excluded?—The inherent prejudice of small frequencies or probabilities

The most common form of expert testimony about matching DNA takes the form of an explanation of how the laboratory ascertained that the defendant's DNA has the profile of the forensic sample plus an estimate of the frequency of the profile in

---

[6]*People v. Venegas*, 18 Cal. 4th 47, 74 Cal. Rptr. 2d 262, 954 P.2d 525 (1998).

[7]The court wrote that:

The *Kelly* test's third prong does not, of course, cover all derelictions in following the prescribed scientific procedures. Shortcomings such as mislabeling, mixing the wrong ingredients, or failing to follow routine precautions against contamination may well be amenable to evaluation by jurors without the assistance of expert testimony. Such readily apparent missteps involve "the degree of professionalism" with which otherwise scientifically accepted methodologies are applied in a given case, and so amount only to "[c]areless testing affect[ing] the weight of the evidence and not its admissibility" . . .

*People v. Venegas*, 18 Cal. 4th 47, 74 Cal. Rptr. 2d 262, 284, 954 P.2d 525 (1998) (citations omitted); cf. *State v. Kinder*, 942 S.W.2d 313 (Mo. 1996) ("argument concerning the manner in which the tests were conducted goes more to the credibility of the witness and the weight of the evidence, which is in the first instance a discretionary call for the trial court and ultimately for the jury").

[8]The FBI laboratory determined that defendant's VNTR profile matched the profiles from vaginal swabs and a semen stain, and that the probability of selecting an unrelated individual at random from the Hispanic population with a profile that also matched the samples was approximately 1/31,000. This figure was obtained using the basic product rule with a match window of ±2.5% and a "fixed bin" width of at least ±3%. *People v. Venegas*, 18 Cal. 4th 47, 74 Cal. Rptr. 2d 262, 954 P.2d 525 (1998). The width of these bins was acceptable, since they more than covered the adjacent match windows. However, the FBI examiner also arrived at an estimate of 1/65,000 using the interim ceiling method for combining the allele frequencies and "floating bins" of ±2.5%.

The trial court admitted testimony that the probability of a random match was 1/65,000. Figure 1 shows the most extreme bands in a samples from suspects that could be declared to match. These bands are positioned at 5% above and 5% below the band from the forensic sample. Because all bands within this range could be declared to match the band from the forensic sample, the appropriate size of a floating bin is twice the match window around an individual band, or ±5%. One of defendant's experts pointed out that the floating bin should have been at least as wide as two match windows placed end-to-end (±5% rather than ±2.5%), but the trial court held that the discrepancy merely went to the weight of the evidence.

[Section 2:6]

[1]§§ 2:44 to 2:48.

the population (or the probability that a randomly selected individual in the population will have matching DNA). Many arguments have been offered against this entrenched practice. First, it has been suggested that jurors do not understand probabilities in general,[1] and infinitesimal match probabilities[2] will so bedazzle jurors that they will not appreciate the other evidence in the case or any innocent explanations for the match.[3] Empirical research has failed to confirm this hypothesis,[4] and remedies short of exclusion are available.[5] Thus, no jurisdiction excludes all match probabilities on this basis.[6]

## § 2:8 Objections to DNA evidence—Presenting incriminating DNA results—Should match probabilities be excluded?—The transposition fallacy and the probability of a random match

A more sophisticated variation on this theme is that the jury will misconstrue the random match probability—by thinking that it gives the probability that the match

---

[Section 2:7]

[1]E.g., R.C. Lewontin, Correspondence, 372 Nature 398 (1994).

[2]Reported population frequencies have been measured in the billionths ($10^{-9}$), trillionths ($10^{-12}$), quadrillionths ($10^{-15}$), quintillionths ($10^{-18}$), and even sextillionths ($10^{-21}$). E.g., *Snowden v. State*, 574 So. 2d 960 (Ala. Crim. App. 1990) ("a 'minimum value' of one in 2.5 billion and a 'maximum' value of one in 27 trillion"); *People v. Johnson*, 139 Cal. App. 4th 1135, 43 Cal. Rptr. 3d 587 (5th Dist. 2006), review denied, (Aug. 16, 2006) ("one in 240 quadrillion"); *U.S. v. Jenkins*, 887 A.2d 1013, 1019 (D.C. 2005) ("1 in 870 quintillion in the Caucasian population, . . . and 1 in 4 sextillion in the Southwestern Hispanic population"); *Gibson v. State*, 915 So. 2d 199 (Fla. Dist. Ct. App. 4th Dist. 2005) ("1 in 101 quintillion"); *State v. Watts*, 172 N.C. App. 58, 616 S.E.2d 290 (2005), writ denied, 361 N.C. 179, 641 S.E.2d 689 (2006) and review denied, 361 N.C. 179, 641 S.E.2d 690 (2006) ("million trillion times"); *State v. Buckner*, 125 Wash. 2d 915, 890 P.2d 460 (1995), on reconsideration, 133 Wash. 2d 63, 941 P.2d 667 (1997) ("one Caucasian in 19.25 billion").

[3]Cf. *Government of Virgin Islands v. Byers*, 941 F. Supp. 513, 527, 45 Fed. R. Evid. Serv. 1247 (D.V.I. 1996) ("Vanishingly small probabilities of a random match may tend to establish guilt in the minds of jurors and are particularly suspect."); *Com. v. Curnin*, 409 Mass. 218, 565 N.E.2d 440, 441 (1991) ("Evidence of this nature [a random-match probability of 1 in 59 million] . . . , having an aura of infallibility, must have a strong impact on a jury."). It also been argued—unsuccessfully—that match probabilities are prejudicial if they are too large. *U.S. v. Morrow*, 374 F. Supp. 2d 51 (D.D.C. 2005). For a mock jury experiment suggesting that jurors do not overvalue the DNA statistics, see Nance & Morris, An Empirical Assessment of Presentation Formats for Trace Evidence with a Relatively Large and Quantifiable Random Match Probability, 42 Jurimetrics J. 1 (2002).

[4]See Committee on DNA Forensic Science: An Update, National Research Council, The Evaluation of Forensic DNA Evidence at 197 (1996); Nance & Morris, Juror Understanding of DNA Evidence: An Empirical Assessment of Presentation Formats for Trace Evidence with a Relatively Small Random Match Probability, 34 J. Leg. Stud. 395 (2005); Schklar & Seidman Diamond, Juror Reactions to DNA Evidence: Errors and Expectancies, 23 Law & Hum. Behav. 159, 181–182 (1999).

[5]Suitable cross-examination, defense experts, and jury instructions might reduce the risk that small estimates of the match probability will produce an unwarranted sense of certainty and lead a jury to disregard other evidence. Committee on DNA Forensic Science: An Update, National Research Council, The Evaluation of Forensic DNA Evidence 197 (1996).

[6]E.g., *U.S. v. Chischilly*, 30 F.3d 1144, 40 Fed. R. Evid. Serv. 289 (9th Cir. 1994) (citing cases); *Martinez v. State*, 549 So. 2d 694, 694–695 (Fla. Dist. Ct. App. 5th Dist. 1989) (rejecting the argument that testimony that "one individual in 234 billion" would have the same banding pattern was "so overwhelming as to deprive the jury of its function"); *Reid v. Page*, 47 F. Supp. 2d 1008 (C.D. Ill. 1999) (no fundamental unfairness in admitting a random match probability of one in 17 million); *State v. Roman Nose*, 667 N.W.2d 386 (Minn. 2003) (basic product rule computations resulting in probabilities on the order of one in 63 trillion not unfairly prejudicial even in the absence of cautionary instructions); *Hughes v. State*, 735 So. 2d 238, 262 (Miss. 1999) (rejecting general claim that frequencies are prejudicial); *State v. Weeks*, 270 Mont. 63, 891 P.2d 477, 489 (1995) (rejecting the argument that "the exaggerated opinion of the accuracy of DNA testing is prejudicial, as juries would give undue weight and deference to the statistical evidence" and "that the probability aspect of the DNA analysis invades the province of the jury to decide the guilt or innocence of the defendant"); *State v. Schweitzer*, 533 N.W.2d 156, 160 (S.D. 1995) (reviewing cases).

is random.[1] Suppose that the random match probability $p$ is some very small number such as one in a billion. The words are almost identical, but the probabilities can be quite different. The random match probability is the probability that (A) the requisite genotype is in the sample from the individual tested *if* (B) the individual tested has been selected at random. In contrast, the probability that the match is random is the probability that (B) the individual tested has been selected at random *given that* (A) the individual has the requisite genotype. In general, for two events A and B, P(A *given* B) does not equal P(B *given* A). The claim that it does is known as the fallacy of the transposed conditional.[2]

To appreciate that the equation is fallacious, consider the probability that a

---

**[Section 2:8]**

[1]Numerous opinions or experts present the random match probability in this manner. See, e.g., *U.S. v. Martinez*, 3 F.3d 1191, 1194, 37 Fed. R. Evid. Serv. 863 (8th Cir. 1993) (rejected by, Taylor v. State, 1995 OK CR 10, 889 P.2d 319 (Okla. Crim. App. 1995)) (referring to "a determination of the probability that someone other than the contributor of the known sample could have contributed the unknown sample"); *Engram v. State*, 341 Ark. 196, 15 S.W.3d 678, 680 (2000) (reporting that "the State's DNA expert testified that the probability that the semen recovered from the victim belonged to a person other than the appellant was one in 600 trillion;" *Mixon v. State*, 330 Ark. 171, 954 S.W.2d 214, 215 (1997) ("DNA testing indicated a 99.99% probability that Mixon raped the victim."); *People v. Padilla*, 2002 WL 31518865 (Cal. App. 2d Dist. 2002), unpublished/noncitable, (Nov. 13, 2002) (unpublished opinion stating that "the odds of appellant not being the rapist were one in 74.9 quadrillion, which is about 12 million times greater than the earth's present population") (note omitted); *Morris v. State*, 811 So. 2d 661, 663 (Fla. 2002) (stating that testimony that "the frequency of this DNA pattern in the African-American database would be 1 in 7.1 million" meant that "the chance that the DNA was not from Morris was between 1 in 710,000 to 1 in 71 million"); *Poole v. State*, 254 Ga. App. 271, 562 S.E.2d 239, 242 (2002) (maintaining that "the odds of someone other than [the defendant] being the donor were one in ten billion"); *State v. Foster*, 259 Kan. 198, 910 P.2d 848 (1996) (a DNA analyst testified that "the probability of another person in the Caucasian population having the same banding pattern was 1 in 100,000"); *State v. Robinson*, 2002 ME 136, 803 A.2d 452, 456 (Me. 2002). (DNA analyst "testified that the probability that the semen came from someone other than [defendant] was one in 392 trillion."); *Com. v. McNickles*, 434 Mass. 839, 753 N.E.2d 131 (2001) (interpreting the population geneticist to have stated that "assuming that [the victim] was a contributor to the mixed sample, . . . it was 37,000 times more likely that the defendant was a contributor to the sample than that another unknown person was the contributor"; the correct rendition of the expert's testimony would be that "assuming the victim was a contributor, it was 37,000 times more likely to find

the DNA types that were detected if the defendant was a contributor than if another person was the contributor"); *State v. Ferguson*, 20 S.W.3d 485, 495–96 (Mo. 2000) (referring to a previous trial at which "the state's DNA expert testified that the chances that the semen stain was from someone other than Ferguson were 1 in 1.7 million or 1 in 11 million, depending on the statistical approach used"); *Faison v. State*, 59 S.W.3d 230, 237 (Tex. App. Tyler 2001), petition for discretionary review refused, (Sept. 19, 2001) and petition for discretionary review refused, (Oct. 5, 2001) (stating that "the odds that Appellant or an identical twin brother had not sexually assaulted G.C. were 380 million to one among African-American males"); *State v. Rogers*, 355 N.C. 420, 562 S.E.2d 859, 865 (2002) (claiming that "DNA testing of the blood found on the shirt revealed that there was only one chance in many millions that the blood did not come from the victim"); *State v. Dean*, 76 S.W.3d 352, 360 (Tenn. Crim. App. 2001) (relying on testimony "that the probability that a person other than the defendant had contributed the sperm recovered from the victim was one in forty-one quadrillion"). For more examples of mischaracterizations of the random match probability, see cases and authorities cited, Committee on DNA Forensic Science: An Update, National Research Council, The Evaluation of Forensic DNA Evidence at 198 n. 92 (1996). cf. § 3:5 (describing a form of the fallacy in parentage cases). These statements may be contrasted with the more accurate comments of an FBI examiner in *State v. Freeman*, 1996 WL 608328, at *7 (Neb. Ct. App. 1996), decision aff'd, 253 Neb. 385, 571 N.W.2d 276 (1997), that "[t]he probability of randomly selecting an unrelated individual from the Caucasian population who would have the same DNA profile as I observed in the K2 sample for Mr. Freeman was approximately one in 15 million."

[2]It is also called the "inverse fallacy," or the "prosecutor's fallacy." David J. Balding, Weight-of-Evidence for Forensic DNA Profiles 146 n.1 (2005). The latter expression is rare in the statistical literature, but it is common in the legal literature on statistical evidence. For an exposition of related errors, see Jonathan J. Koehler, Error and Exaggeration in the Presentation of DNA Evidence at Trial, 34 Jurimetrics J. 21 (1993).

lawyer picked at random from all lawyers in the United States is a judge. This "random judge probability" is practically zero. But the probability that a person randomly selected from the current judiciary is a lawyer is one. The "random judge probability" P(judge *given* lawyer) does not equal the transposed probability P(lawyer *given* judge). Likewise, the random match probability P(genotype *given* unrelated source) does not necessarily equal P(unrelated source *given* genotype).

To avoid this fallacious reasoning by jurors, some defense counsel have urged the exclusion of random match probabilities, and some prosecutors have suggested that it is desirable to avoid testimony or argument about probabilities, and instead to present the statistic as a simple frequency—an indication of how rare the genotype is in the relevant population.[3] The 1996 NRC report noted that "few courts or commentators have recommended the exclusion of evidence merely because of the risk that jurors will transpose a conditional probability,"[4] and it observed that "[t]he available research indicates that jurors may be more likely to be swayed by the 'defendant's fallacy' than by the 'prosecutor's fallacy.' When advocates present both fallacies to mock jurors, the defendant's fallacy dominates."[5] Furthermore, the committee suggested that "if the initial presentation of the probability figure, cross-examination, and opposing testimony all fail to clarify the point, the judge can counter both fallacies by appropriate instructions to the jurors that minimize the possibility of cognitive errors."[6]

No court in the United States has excluded a DNA random match probability (or,

---

[3]George W. Clark, Effective Use of DNA Evidence in Jury Trials, Profiles in DNA, Aug. 1997, at 7, 8 ("References to probabilities should normally be avoided, inasmuch as such descriptions are frequently judicially equated with disfavored 'probabilities of guilt' . . . [T]he purpose of frequency data is simply to provide the factfinder with a guide to the relative rarity of a DNA match . . .").

[4]Committee on DNA Forensic Science: An Update, National Research Council, The Evaluation of Forensic DNA Evidence 198 (1996) (citing McCormick on Evidence § 212 (John Strong ed., 5th ed 1999)).

[5]Committee on DNA Forensic Science: An Update, National Research Council, The Evaluation of Forensic DNA Evidence 198 (1996). cf. Koehler, The Psychology of Numbers in the Courtroom: How To Make DNA-match Statistics Seem Impressive or Insufficient, 74 S. Cal. L. Rev. 1275, 1278 (2001):

> When the statistic is framed in the language of probability (e.g., 0.1%) in a way that highlights a particular suspect's chance of matching by coincidence, it tends to be persuasive. But when the statistic is framed in the language of frequencies (e.g., one in one thousand) in a way that highlights the chance that others will match by coincidence, it is much less persuasive. Similarly, DNA match statistics that target an individual suspect are more persuasive than the equivalent statistic that targets a broader population.

The "defendant's fallacy" consists of dismissing or undervaluing the matches with high likelihood ratios because other matches are to be expected in unrealistically large populations of potential suspects. For example, defense counsel might argue that (a) even with a random match

probability of one in a million, we would expect to find 10 unrelated people with the requisite genotypes in a population of 10 million; (b) the defendant just happens to be one of these ten, which means that the chances are 9 out of 10 that someone unrelated to the defendant is the source; so (c) the DNA evidence does nothing to incriminate the defendant. The problem with this argument is that in a case involving non-DNA evidence against the defendant, it is unrealistic to assume that there are 10 million equally likely suspects.

[6]Committee on DNA Forensic Science: An Update, National Research Council, The Evaluation of Forensic DNA Evidence 198 (1996) (footnote omitted). The committee suggested the following instruction to define the random match probability:

> In evaluating the expert testimony on the DNA evidence, you were presented with a number indicating the probability that another individual drawn at random from the [specify] population would coincidentally have the same DNA profile as the [blood stain, semen stain, etc.]. That number, which assumes that no sample mishandling or laboratory error occurred, indicates how distinctive the DNA profile is. It does not by itself tell you the probability that the defendant is innocent.

Committee on DNA Forensic Science: An Update, National Research Council, The Evaluation of Forensic DNA Evidence at 198 n.93 (1996). But see Kaye, The Admissibility of "Probability Evidence" in Criminal Trials—Part II, 27 Jurimetrics J. 160, 168 (1987) ("Nevertheless, because even without misguided advice from counsel, the temptation to compute the probability of criminal identity [by transposition] seems strong, and because the characterization of the population proportion as a [random match probability] does little to make the evidence more intelligible, it

for that matter, an estimate of the small frequency of a DNA profile in the general population) as unfairly prejudicial just because the jury might misinterpret it as a posterior probability that the defendant is the source of the forensic DNA.[7] One court, however, noted the need to have the concept "properly explained,"[8] and prosecutorial misrepresentations of the random match probabilities for other types of evidence have produced reversals.[9]

### § 2:9 Objections to DNA evidence—Presenting incriminating DNA results—Should match probabilities be excluded?—The relevance of small match probabilities in light of other events that could yield false positives

It has been maintained that match probabilities are logically irrelevant when they are far smaller than the probability of a frame-up, a blunder in labeling samples, cross-contamination, or other events that would yield a false positive.[1] The argument is that the jury should concern itself only with the chance that the forensic sample is reported to match the defendant's profile even though the defendant is not the source. Such a report could happen either because another person who is the source of the forensic sample has the same profile or because fraud or error of a kind that falsely incriminates the defendant occurs in the collection, handling, or analysis of the DNA samples. Match probabilities do not express this chance of a match being reported when the defendant is not the source unless the probability of a false-positive report is essentially zero.

Both theoretical and practical rejoinders to this argument about relevance have been given. At the theoretical level, some scientists question a procedure that would prevent the jury from reasoning in a stepwise, eliminative fashion. In their view, a rational juror might well want to know that the chance that another person selected at random from the suspect population has the incriminating genotype is negligible, for this would enable the juror to eliminate the hypotheses of kinship or coincidence.[2] If the juror concludes that there is little chance that the same genotype would exist in the forensic sample if the DNA originated from anyone but the defendant, then the juror can proceed to consider whether that genotype is present because someone has tried to frame the defendant, or whether it is not really present but was reported

---

might be best to bar the prosecution from having its expert state the probability of a coincidental misidentification, as opposed to providing [a simpler] estimate of the population proportion.").

[7]The efforts of English courts to prescribe methods for experts presenting the statistical implications of DNA matches are reviewed in David J. Balding, Weight-of-Evidence for Forensic DNA Profiles 148–154 (2005) and Mike Redmayne, Expert Evidence and Criminal Justice (2001). Additional discussion can be found in D.H. Kaye et al., The Modern Wigmore, A Treatise on Evidence: Expert Evidence § 12 (2004).

[8]*U.S. v. Shea*, 957 F. Supp. 331, 345, 46 Fed. R. Evid. Serv. 1375 (D.N.H. 1997), aff'd, 159 F.3d 37, 50 Fed. R. Evid. Serv. 516 (1st Cir. 1998).

[9]E.g., *U.S. v. Massey*, 594 F.2d 676, 681 (8th Cir. 1979) (in closing argument about hair evidence, "the prosecutor 'confuse(d) the probability of concurrence of the identifying marks with the probability of mistaken identification' ").

**[Section 2:9]**

[1]E.g., Koehler et al., The Random Match Probability in DNA Evidence: Irrelevant and Prejudicial?, 35 Jurimetrics J. 201 (1995); Richard Lewontin & Daniel Hartl, Population Genetics in Forensic DNA Typing, 254 Science 1745, 1749 (1991) ("probability estimates like 1 in 738,000,000,000,000 . . . are terribly misleading because the rate of laboratory error is not taken into account").

[2]E.g., Committee on DNA Forensic Science: An Update, National Research Council, The Evaluation of Forensic DNA Evidence 85 (1996); Committee on DNA Technology in Forensic Science, National Research Council, DNA Technology in Forensic Science 88 (1992); Russell Higuchi, Human Error in Forensic DNA Typing, 48 Am. J. Hum. Genetics 1215 (1991) (letter). Of course, if the defense were to stipulate that a true DNA match establishes identity, there would be no need for probabilities that would help the jury to reject the rival hypotheses of coincidence or kinship.

to be there because DNA samples were mishandled or misanalyzed.[3] These probabilities, they add, are not amenable to objective modeling and should not be mixed with probabilities that are derived from verifiable models of genetics.[4]

At the practical level, there is disagreement about the adequacy of the estimates that have been proposed to express the probability of a false positive result. The opponents of match probabilities usually argue that an error rate somewhat higher than that observed in a series of proficiency tests should be substituted for the match probability,[5] but the extent to which any such figure applies to the case at bar has been questioned.[6] No reported cases have excluded statistics on proficiency tests administered at a specific laboratory as too far removed from the case at bar to be relevant,[7] but neither has it been held that these statistics must be used in place of random match or kinship probabilities.[8]

### § 2:10  Objections to DNA evidence—Presenting incriminating DNA results—Should match probabilities be excluded?—The prejudice of small match probabilities in light of other events that could yield false positives

It also can be argued that very small match probabilities are relevant but unfairly prejudicial. Such prejudice could occur if the jury was so impressed with this single number that it neglected or underweighted the probability of a match arising due to a false-positive laboratory error.[1] Some commentators believe that this prejudice is so likely and so serious that "jurors ordinarily should receive *only* the laboratory's

---

[3]E.g., Bernard Devlin & Kathryn Roeder, DNA Profiling: Statistics and Population Genetics, in 1 Modern Scientific Evidence: The Law and Science of Expert Testimony § 18-5.3, at 743–744 (David Faigman et al. eds., 1997) ("One way to handle the possibility of a laboratory error, which follows the usual presentation of similar types of evidence, is to present the evidence in two stages: Does the evidence suggest that the samples were obtained from the same individual? If so, is there a harmless reason? Either formal calculations or informal analysis could be used to evaluate the possibility of a laboratory error, both of which should be predicated on the facts of the specific case.").

[4]E.g., N.E. Morton, The Forensic DNA Endgame, 37 Jurimetrics J. 477, 480–481 (1997); cf. Committee on DNA Technology in Forensic Science, National Research Council, DNA Technology in Forensic Science at 88 (1992) ("Coincidental identity and laboratory error are different phenomena, so the two cannot and should not be combined in a single estimate.").

[5]But see William C. Thompson, Accepting Lower Standards: The National Research Council's Second Report on Forensic DNA Evidence, 37 Jurimetrics J. 405, 417 (1997) (suggesting that "DNA evidence" should be excluded as "unacceptable scientifically if the probability of an erroneous match cannot be quantified").

[6]See, e.g., David J. Balding, Errors and Misunderstandings in the Second NRC Report, 37 Jurimetrics J. 469, 475–476, 476 n.21 (1997) ("report[ing] a match probability which adds error rates to profile frequencies . . . would clearly be unacceptable since overall error rates are not

directly relevant: jurors must assess on the basis of the evidence presented to them the chance that an error has occurred in the particular case at hand," but "[e]rror rates observed in blind trials may well be helpful to jurors"); Berger, Laboratory Error Seen Through the Lens of Science and Policy, 30 U.C. Davis L. Rev. 1081 (1997). But cf. William C. Thompson, Accepting Lower Standards: The National Research Council's Second Report on Forensic DNA Evidence, 37 Jurimetrics J. 405, 421 (1997) ("While it makes little sense to present a single number derived from proficiency tests as *the* error rate in every case, it makes less sense to exclude quantitative estimates of the error altogether.").

[7]§ 2:16.

[8]See *Armstead v. State*, 342 Md. 38, 673 A.2d 221 (1996) (rejecting the argument that the introduction of a random match probability deprives the defendant of due process because the error rate on proficiency tests is many orders of magnitude greater than the match probability); *Williams v. State*, 342 Md. 724, 679 A.2d 1106 (1996) (disapproved of on other grounds by, Wengert v. State, 364 Md. 76, 771 A.2d 389 (2001)) (reversing because the trial court restricted cross-examination about the results of proficiency tests involving other DNA analysts at the same laboratory).

**[Section 2:10]**

[1]E.g., Koehler et al., The Random Match Probability in DNA Evidence: Irrelevant and Prejudicial?, 35 Jurimetrics J. 201 (1995); William C. Thompson, Accepting Lower Standards: The National Research Council's Second Report on Forensic DNA Evidence, 37 Jurimetrics J. 405,

false positive rate . . . ."[2] The 1996 NRC report is skeptical of this view, especially when the defendant has had a meaningful opportunity to retest the DNA at a laboratory of his choice, and it suggests that judicial instructions can be crafted to avoid this form of prejudice.[3]

Rather than excluding small match probabilities entirely, a court might require the expert who presents them also to report a probability that the laboratory is mistaken about the profiles.[4] Of course, some experts would deny that they can provide a meaningful statistic for the case at hand, but they could report the results of proficiency tests and leave it to the jury to use this figure as best it can in considering whether a false-positive error has occurred.[5] To assist the jury in making sense of two numbers, however, it has been suggested that an expert take the additional step of reporting how the probability that a matching genotype would be found coincidentally *or* erroneously changes given the random match probability and vari-

---

421–422 (1997). However, it has been claimed that student mock jurors and jurists do better at combining error and random match probabilities when the information is already combined in a "natural frequency" format. Lindsey et al., Communicating Statistical DNA Evidence, 43 Jurimetrics J. 147 (2003).

[2]Lempert, Some Caveats Concerning DNA as Criminal Identification Evidence: With Thanks to the Reverend Bayes, 13 Cardozo L. Rev. 303, 325 (1991) (emphasis added); see also Richard Lempert, After the DNA Wars: Skirmishing with NRC II, 37 Jurimetrics J. 439, 447 (1997); Scheck, DNA and *Daubert*, 15 Cardozo L. Rev. at 1997 (1994).

[3]Committee on DNA Forensic Science: An Update, National Research Council, The Evaluation of Forensic DNA Evidence 199 (1996) (notes omitted):

The argument that jurors will make better use of a single figure for the probability that an innocent suspect would be reported to match has never been tested adequately. The argument for a single figure is weak in light of this lack of research into how jurors react to different ways of presenting statistical information, and its weakness is compounded by the grave difficulty of estimating a false-positive error rate in any given case. But efforts should be made to fill the glaring gap in empirical studies of such matters.

The district court in *U.S. v. Shea*, 957 F. Supp. 331, 334–345, 46 Fed. R. Evid. Serv. 1375 (D.N.H. 1997), aff'd, 159 F.3d 37, 50 Fed. R. Evid. Serv. 516 (1st Cir. 1998), discussed some of the available research and rejected the argument that separate figures for match and error probabilities are prejudicial. For more recent research, see Schklar & Seidman Diamond, Juror Reactions to DNA Evidence: Errors and Expectancies, 23 Law & Hum. Behav. at 179 (1999) (concluding that separate figures are desirable in that "[j]urors . . . may need to know the disaggregated elements that influence the aggregated estimate as well as how they were combined in order to evaluate the DNA test results in the context of their background beliefs and the other evidence introduced at trial").

[4]Koehler, DNA Matches and Statistics: Important Questions, Surprising Answers, 76 Judicature 222, 229 (1993) ("A good argument can be made for requiring DNA laboratories to provide fact finders with conservatively high estimates of their false positive error rates when they provide evidence about genetic matches. By the same token, laboratories should be required to divulge their estimated false negative error rate in cases where exclusions are reported."). This argument has prevailed in a few cases. E.g., *U.S. v. Porter*, 1994 WL 742297 (D.C. Super. Ct. 1994) (mem.). Other courts have rejected it. E.g., *U.S. v. Lowe*, 954 F. Supp. 401, 415, 46 Fed. R. Evid. Serv. 316 (D. Mass. 1996).

[5]See Committee on DNA Technology in Forensic Science, National Research Council, DNA Technology in Forensic Science 94 (1992) ("Laboratory error rates should be measured with appropriate proficiency tests and should play a role in the interpretation of results of forensic DNA typing . . . A laboratory's overall rate of incorrect conclusions due to error should be reported with, but separately from, the probability of coincidental matches in the population. Both should be weighed in evaluating evidence."); Committee on DNA Forensic Science: An Update, National Research Council, The Evaluation of Forensic DNA Evidence at 87 (1996) ("[A] calculation that combines error rates with match probabilities is inappropriate. The risk of error is properly considered case by case, taking into account the record of the laboratory performing the tests, the extent of redundancy, and the overall quality of the results."). The district court in *Government of Virgin Islands v. Byers*, 941 F. Supp. 513, 45 Fed. R. Evid. Serv. 1247 (D.V.I. 1996), declined to require proficiency test results as a precondition for admissibility. See also Berger, Laboratory Error Seen Through the Lens of Science and Policy, 30 U.C. Davis L. Rev. 1081, 1093 (1997) ("the rationale for [requiring the prosecution to introduce a pooled error rate] is weak, and . . . such a shift would be inconsistent with significant evidentiary policies.").

ous values for the probability of a false-positive error.[6] Such arguments have not met with much judicial acceptance.[7]

One commentator has proposed that unless the police can eliminate all named relatives as possible culprits, "the defendant should be allowed to name any close relative whom he thinks might have committed the crime," and the state should use the probability "that at least one named relative has DNA like the defendant's" as the sole indication of the plausibility of the hypothesis of kinship.[8] Whether such numbers should be introduced even when there is no proof that a close relative might have committed the crime is, of course, a matter to be evaluated under Federal or Uniform Rules of Evidence 104(b), 401 and 403. The few courts to address the argument have been unwilling to exclude random match probabilities on the basis of uncorroborated arguments about untested relatives.[9]

### § 2:11   Objections to DNA evidence—Presenting incriminating DNA results—Should match probabilities be excluded?—The effect of a database search

States and the federal government are amassing huge databases consisting of the DNA profiles of suspected or convicted offenders.[1] If the DNA profile from a crime-scene stain matches one of those on file, the person identified by this "cold hit" will become the target of the investigation. In many instances, prosecution will follow.

---

[6]See Thompson, Accepting Lower Standards: The National Research Council's Second Report on Forensic DNA Evidence, 37 Jurimetrics J. 405, 421–422 (1997) (footnote omitted):

> For example, an expert could say that if the probability of a random match is .00000001 and the probability of an erroneous match is .001, then the overall probability of a false match is approximately .001 . . . If the probability of an erroneous match is unclear or controversial (as it undoubtedly will be in many cases), then illustrative combinations could be performed for a range of hypothetical probabilities.

Although the mathematics of combining error rates is not complicated, see Thompson et al., How the Probability of a False Positive Affects the Value of DNA Evidence, 48 J. Forensic Sci. 47 (2003), This procedure could lead to arguments about the relevance of the values for the "probability of an erroneous match." Depending on such factors as the record of the laboratory on proficiency tests, the precautions observed in processing the samples, and the availability of the samples for independent testing, the prosecution could contend that the 0.001 figure in this example has no foundation in the evidence.

[7]See *U.S. v. Morrow*, 374 F. Supp. 2d 51, 68 (D.D.C. 2005); *U.S. v. Trala*, 162 F. Supp. 2d 336, 57 Fed. R. Evid. Serv. 1266 (D. Del. 2001); *People v. Reeves*, 91 Cal. App. 4th 14, 109 Cal. Rptr. 2d 728, 753 (1st Dist. 2001), as modified on denial of reh'g, (Aug. 28, 2001).

[8]Lempert, After the DNA Wars: Skirmishing with NRC II, 37 Jurimetrics J. 439, 461 (1997). For example, if the defendant named two brothers and two uncles as possible suspects, then the probability that at least one shares a four-locus genotype (with alleles that each occur in 5% of the population) would be about $(2 \times .006) + (2 \times$

.0000005), or about 0.012. See §§ 2:40 to 2:52.

[9]See, e.g., *Taylor v. Commonwealth of Virginia*, 1995 WL 80189 (Va. Ct. App. 1995) (unpublished) ("Defendant argues that this evidence did not consider the existence of an identical twin or close relative to defendant, a circumstance which would diminish the probability that he was the perpetrator. While this hypothesis is conceivable, it has no basis in the record and the Commonwealth must only exclude hypotheses of innocence that reasonably flow from the evidence, not from defendant's imagination."). The speculative, "unknown twin" defense also failed in *Faison v. State*, 59 S.W.3d 230 (Tex. App. Tyler 2001), petition for discretionary review refused, (Sept. 19, 2001) and petition for discretionary review refused, (Oct. 5, 2001), defendant proved that he had been an adopted child, and his adoptive mother "testified that she did not know whether his birth mother had twins . . . or if he had a brother." *Faison v. State*, 59 S.W.3d 230, 235 (Tex. App. Tyler 2001), petition for discretionary review refused, (Sept. 19, 2001) and petition for discretionary review refused, (Oct. 5, 2001). In rebuttal, the state showed that "the crimes were carried out in a similar manner and that [defendant's] fingerprints or palmprints were found at each of the three crime scenes." *Faison v. State*, 59 S.W.3d 230, 235 (Tex. App. Tyler 2001), petition for discretionary review refused, (Sept. 19, 2001) and petition for discretionary review refused, (Oct. 5, 2001). Fingerprints differ even among identical twins.

### [Section 2:11]

[1]See, e.g., Kaye, Who Needs Special Needs? On the Constitutionality of Collecting DNA and Other Biometric Data from Arrestees, 34 J.L. Med. & Ethics 188 (2006).

These cases have been called "trawl cases"[2] because "the DNA match itself made the defendant a suspect, and the match was discovered only by searching through a database of previously obtained DNA samples."[3]

These database-trawl cases can be contrasted with traditional "confirmation cases" in which "other evidence has made the defendant a suspect and so warranted testing his DNA."[4] In confirmation cases, it makes sense to present statistics such as the estimated frequency of the matching DNA profile in various populations. Such figures assist the jury in appreciating the probative value of the match, since matches of very unusual profiles are obviously more significant than are matches of very common profiles. With rare crime-scene profiles, the suspect is many times more likely to possess the matching profile when he is the source of the crime-scene sample than when he has been picked for testing "at random" (that is, on the basis of factors that are unrelated to his identifying DNA profile).

As more and more criminal cases are resolved with the aid of database searches, however, courts are beginning to confront a surprisingly subtle question—does the fact that the defendant was selected for prosecution by trawling require some adjustment to the usual random match probability? The legal issues are twofold. First, is a particular quantity—be it the unadjusted random match probability or some adjusted probability—a scientifically valid (or generally accepted) statistic in the case of a database search? If not, it must be excluded under the *Daubert* (or *Frye*) standards. Second, is the statistic irrelevant or unduly misleading? If so, it must be excluded under the rules that require all evidence to be relevant and not unfairly prejudicial? To help answer these questions, we begin by summarizing (and simplifying) the statistical literature on this point. Then, we analyze the first reported case on the admissibility of frequencies in a database-trawl case. We conclude that even though the picture is more complicated when the defendant has been located through a database search, the usual statistics are still useful indicators of the probative value of the match.

Whatever variant of the product rule might be used to find the probability of the genotype in a population, subpopulation, or relative, the number is useful only insofar as it establishes that the same DNA profile in the defendant and the crime scene stain is unlikely to occur if the DNA came from someone other than the defendant. Yet, unlikely events happen all the time. An individual wins the lottery even though it was very unlikely that the particular ticket would be a winner. The chance of a particular supertanker running aground and producing a massive spill on a single trip may be very small, but the Exxon Valdez did just that.

The apparent paradox of supposedly low-probability events being ubiquitous results from what statisticians call a "selection effect," "ascertainment bias," or "data mining." If we pick a lottery ticket at random, the probability $p$ that we have the winning ticket is negligible. But if we search through all the tickets, sooner or later we will find the winning one. And even if we search through some smaller number $N$ of tickets, the probability of picking a winning ticket is no longer $p$, but $Np$.[5]

Likewise, there may be a small probability $p$ that a randomly selected individual who is not the source of the forensic sample has the incriminating genotype. That is

---

[2]E.g., Balding, Errors and Misunderstandings in the Second NRC Report, 37 Jurimetrics J. 469 (1997).

[3]Donnelly & Friedman, DNA Database Searches and the Legal Consumption of Scientific Evidence, 97 Mich. L. Rev. 931, 932 (1999).

[4]Donnelly & Friedman, DNA Database Searches and the Legal Consumption of Scientific Evidence, 97 Mich. L. Rev. 931, 932 (1999).

[5]If there are $T$ tickets and one winning ticket, then the probability that a randomly selected ticket is the winner is $p = 1/T$, and the probability that a set of N randomly selected tickets includes the winner is $N/T = Np$, where $1 \leq N \leq T$.

somewhat like having a winning lottery ticket.[6] If $N$ people are included in the search for a person with the matching DNA, then the probability of a match in this group is not $p$, but some quantity that could be as large as $Np$.[7] This type of reasoning led the second NRC committee to recommend that "[w]hen the suspect is found by a search of DNA databases, the random-match probability should be multiplied by N, the number of persons in the database."[8]

The first NAS committee also felt that "[t]he distinction between finding a match between an evidence sample and a suspect sample and finding a match between an evidence sample and one of many entries in a DNA profile databank is important."[9] Rather than proposing a statistical adjustment to the match probability, however, that committee recommended using only a few loci in the databank search, then confirming the match with additional loci, and presenting only "the statistical frequency associated with the additional loci . . . ."[10]

A number of statisticians reject the committees' view that the random match probability should be inflated, either by a factor of $N$ or by ignoring the loci used in the databank search.[11] They argue that, if anything, the DNA evidence against the defendant is slightly stronger when not only has the defendant been shown to possess the incriminating profile, but also a large number of other individuals have been eliminated as possible sources of the crime scene DNA.[12] They conclude that no adjustment is required to protect the defendant.

---

[6]The analysis of the DNA database search is more complicated than the lottery example suggests. In the simple lottery, there was exactly one winner. The trawl case is closer to a lottery in which we hold a ticket with a winning number, but it might be counterfeit, and we are not sure how many counterfeit copies of the winning ticket were in circulation when we bought our $N$ tickets.

[7]See Committee on DNA Forensic Science: An Update, National Research Council, The Evaluation of Forensic DNA Evidence 163–65 (1996). Assuming that the individual who left the trace evidence sample is not in a database of unrelated people, the probability of at least one match is $1–(1–p)^N$, which is equal to or less than $Np$.

[8]Committee on DNA Forensic Science: An Update, National Research Council, The Evaluation of Forensic DNA Evidence 161 (1996) (Recommendation 5.1). The FBI's DNA Advisory Board appears to endorse using $Np$ rather than $p$ for a database-search case. Initially, the Board explained that

> Two questions arise when a match is derived from a database search: (1) What is the rarity of the DNA profile? and (2) What is the probability of finding such a DNA profile in the database searched? These two questions address different issues. That the different questions produce different answers should be obvious. The former question addresses the random match probability, which is often of particular interest to the fact finder. Here we address the latter question, which is especially important when a profile found in a database search matches the DNA profile of an evidence sample.

DNA Advisory Board, Statistical and Population Genetics Issues Aƒecting the Evaluation of the Frequency of Occurrence of DNA Profiles Calculated From Pertinent Population Database(s), 2 Forensic Sci. Commun., July 2000, available at http://www.fbi.gov/hq/lab/fsc/backiss u/july2000/dnastat.htm. After a discussion of the literature as of 2000, the Board wrote that "we continue to endorse the recommendation of the NRC II Report for the evaluation of DNA evidence from a database search."

[9]It used the same $Np$ formula in a numerical example to show that "[t]he chance of finding a match in the second case is considerably higher, because one . . . fishes through the databank, trying out many hypotheses." Committee on DNA Technology in Forensic Science, National Research Council, DNA Technology in Forensic Science 124 (1992).

[10]Committee on DNA Technology in Forensic Science, National Research Council, DNA Technology in Forensic Science 124 (1992) (Table 1.1). The second NAS Committee did not object to this procedure. It proposed the $Np$ adjustment as an alternative that might be useful when there were very few typable loci in the trace evidence sample.

[11]E.g., Balding, The DNA Database Controversy, 58 Biometrics 241 (2002); Dawid, Comment on Stockmarr's "Likelihood Ratios for Evaluating DNA Evidence When the Suspect Is Found Through a Database Search," 57 Biometrics 976 (2001); Donnelly & Friedman, DNA Database Searches and the Legal Consumption of Scientific Evidence, 97 Mich. L. Rev. 931, 933 n.13 (1999).

[12]David W. Balding, Weight-of-Evidence for Forensic DNA Profiles § 2.3.4 (2005); Donnelly & Friedman, DNA Database Searches and the Legal Consumption of Scientific Evidence, 97 Mich. L. Rev. 931, 933, 945, 948, 955, 957 (1999); Ian W. Evett & Bruce S. Weir, Interpreting DNA Evidence: Statistical Genetics for Forensic Scientists 219–22

At its core, the statistical debate turns on how the problem is framed and what type of statistical reasoning is accepted as appropriate. The NAS committees ask how surprising it would be to find a match in a large database if the database does not contain the true source of the trace evidence. The more surprising the result, the more it appears that the database does contain the source. Because it would be more surprising to find a match in a test of a single innocent suspect than it would be to find a match by testing a large number of innocent suspects, the NAS committees conclude that the single-test match is more convincing evidence than the database search match.[13]

The committees' critics do not deny the mathematical truism that examining more innocent individuals increases the chance of finding a coincidental match, but they maintain that the committees have asked the wrong question. They emphasize that the question of interest to the legal system is not whether the database contains the culprit, but whether the one individual whose DNA matches the trace-evidence DNA is the source of that trace, and they note that as the size of a database approaches that of the entire population, finding one and only one matching individual should be more, not less, convincing evidence against that person.[14] Thus, instead of looking at how surprising it would be to find a match in a large group of innocent suspects, this school of thought asks how much the result of the database search enhances the probability that the individual so identified is the source. They reason that the many exclusions in a database search reduce the number of people who might have left the trace evidence if the suspect did not. This additional information, they conclude, increases the likelihood that the defendant is the source, although the effect is indirect and generally small.[15] Thus, these statisticians endorse the random-match probability, but only as a conservative approximation to the probability of the finding that the specific defendant matches (and no one else in the database does) when someone outside the database is the true source of the crime-scene sample.

On the face of it, there would seem to be a distinct division in the scientific community. One group maintains that it is important to consider the probability of finding *any* match in the database. Another contends that what matters is the probability of finding *exactly one* match—the one that points to the defendant and that excludes everyone else in the database. Both groups agree that some adjustment to the random-match probability or the population frequency is, in principle, required to account for the fact that the match results from a database search.

*United States v. Jenkins*, decided by the highest court in the District of Columbia, is the first published opinion to address this statistical issue.[16] Building on statements such as the one from the second NRC report, the defendant argued "that the

---

(1998).

[13]This is a "frequentist" analysis. It describes how frequently trawls through databases of size $N$ for a profile with a population frequency of $p$ would produce matches *when the databases do not contain the true source of the trace evidence.*

[14]See, e.g., Donnelly & Friedman, DNA Database Searches and the Legal Consumption of Scientific Evidence, 97 Mich. L. Rev. 931, 952–53 (1999).

[15]Donnelly & Friedman, DNA Database Searches and the Legal Consumption of Scientific Evidence, 97 Mich. L. Rev. 931, 945 (1999). When the size of the database approaches the size of the entire population, the effect is large. *Id.* at 948.

[16]*Jenkins* was followed in *People v. Johnson*,

139 Cal. App. 4th 1135, 43 Cal. Rptr. 3d 587 (5th Dist. 2006), review denied, (Aug. 16, 2006). This court also contended that *Frye* did not apply to the method of computing a match probability for a database search because "the use of database searches as a means of identifying potential suspects is not new or novel" and "no authority [applies] *Kelly*'s requirements to a mere investigative technique." *People v. Johnson*, 139 Cal. App. 4th 1135, 43 Cal. Rptr. 3d 587 (5th Dist. 2006), review denied, (Aug. 16, 2006). It is true that the initial match in the database will be confirmed by drawing and analyzing a new sample from the individual involved. This is a red herring, however, because the challenge is not to the use of a convicted-offender DNA database as an investigatory tool. The objection is to the use of the random-match probability to gauge the power of

FBI's method of presenting the rarity statistic alone to express the significance of a DNA match of a crime scene sample with a suspect identified through a database search (a so-called 'cold hit') is not generally accepted in the scientific community and is inadmissible under *Frye*."[17]

The trial court agreed that there is a significant controversy over the need to adjust for a database search. It concluded that the *Np* rule endorsed by the second NRC committee and acknowledged by the first committee as one possible "solution" lacks general acceptance because of the controversy it has engendered in the literature.[18] The trial court also found that the limited-loci approach outlined in the first NRC report lacked general acceptance because it is not used by forensic laboratories.[19] Reasoning that neither *p* nor *Np* are admissible and that some statistic is essential, the court excluded proof of the DNA match itself.[20]

In an interlocutory appeal, the District of Columbia Court of Appeals overruled the trial court. It reasoned that *Frye* was beside the point because the dispute involved the relevancy of each statistic rather the computational method. As the court explained:

> At the heart of this debate is a disagreement over the competing questions to be asked, not the methodologies used to answer those questions. [T]here is no controversy in the relevant scientific community as to the accuracy of the various formulas. In other words, the math that underlies the calculations is not being questioned. Each approach to expressing significance of a cold hit DNA match accurately answers the question it seeks to address. The rarity statistic accurately expresses how rare a genetic profile is in a given society. Database match probability accurately expresses the probability of obtaining a cold hit from a search of a particular database. [Another computation] accurately expresses the probability that the person identified through the cold hit is the actual source of the DNA in light of the fact that a known quantity of potential suspects was eliminated through the database search. These competing schools of thought do not question or challenge the validity of the computations and mathematics relied upon by the others. Instead, the arguments raised by each of the proponents simply state that their formulation is more probative, not more correct. Thus, the debate cited by Mr.

---

the confirmatory match.

[17]*U.S. v. Jenkins*, 887 A.2d 1013, 1017 (D.C. 2005). The government countered with affidavits of selected NAS committee members, collected nearly a decade after the committee issued its report, maintaining that the recommendation was not meant to preclude the use of *p*. One committee member (and an editor of this section) provided an affidavit to the defense declining to divine the collective intent of the committee but describing the literature circa 1996 questioning the committee's recommendation. The chair of the committee, who filed an affidavit for the government, had written in 1998 that

> Our most controversial recommendation concerned making calculations when the suspect was found through a database search. We argued that, on the hypothesis that the contributor of the evidence DNA was not in the database, a Bonferroni correction was in order. The probability of finding at least one match in a homogeneous database of size N is $1-(1-p)^N$ where p is the frequency of the profile in the population. This is approximately Np if N is much less than the reciprocal of p.

James Crow, The 1996 NRC Report: Another Look, Proceedings of the Ninth International Symposium on Human Identification, at 110, 112 (Promega Corp ed., 1998), *available at* http://www.promega.com/geneticidproc/ussymp9proc/conten

t/24.pdf.

[18]*United States v. Jenkins*, No. F320-00 (D.C. Super. Ct., Apr. 5, 2005), rev'd, 887 A.2d 1013, 1017 (D.C. 2005).

[19]*United States v. Jenkins.*, No. F320-00 (D.C. Super. Ct., Apr. 5, 2005), rev'd, 887 A.2d 1013, 1017 (D.C. 2005) For reasons that are not apparent, the government itself urged this position on the trial court. But the fact that laboratories do not use the limited-loci approach is an odd reason to deem it inadmissible. They do not use it because their staff do not think they need to, but no one questions the proposition that ignoring loci (or using the *Np* rule) works to the defendant's advantage. The controversy is over the need for any upward adjustment to *p*, not over whether the limited-loci figure or *Np* is an upper bound on the probability of finding a coincidental match in a full search of a database of *N* profiles. Therefore, at most, the controversy affects the admissibility of *p* but not of the larger probabilities.

[20]But see *U.S. v. Jenkins*, 887 A.2d 1013, 1020 (D.C. 2005) ("The trial court did, however, present the government with the opportunity to present the National Research Council's 1992 formulation because it provided a more conservative result than the rarity statistic.").

Jenkins is one of relevancy, not methodology; and . . . there is no basis under *Porter* for the trial court to exclude the DNA evidence in this case.[21]

This reasoning is almost entirely correct. The only problem is that the final conclusion does not follow from the preceding points. True, the general-acceptance standard is not dispositive here.[22] But this does not mean that the random-match probability should be admitted when the match is the product of a search through a large database. The question the courts must resolve is which statistic or statistics will help the jury appreciate the fact of a DNA match, and the debate among scientists and statisticians bears on this quintessentially legal issue. Rather than evaluate the arguments of the disputants as to which questions are logically relevant, the court simply announced that "[t]he likelihood that the suspect is the actual source of the DNA is best expressed through the rarity of a particular profile. Thus, the rarity statistic is highly probative and will always be relevant."[23]

This view of the relevance of the random match probability is open to question. The first NRC committee thought that, as matter of logic, and hence relevance, it is necessary to make a correction to the random-match probability "for . . . multiple [hypothesis] testing."[24] The second committee also asserted that "the calculation of a match probability . . . should take into account the search process."[25] If "[t]here is an important difference between [a single suspect search] and one in which the suspect is initially identified by searching a database to find a DNA profile matching that left at a crime scene,"[26] then the fact that the method of computing a match probability in each separate situation is not in doubt does not tell us which number or numbers logically apply in a database-search case. Thus, the two NRC reports at least suggest that when the match comes from a database search, the random-match probability and the population frequency are *not* relevant and grossly overstate the significance of the match.

The *Jenkins* court begs this question. It simply assumes that the various statistics—the population frequency, the random-match probability, and the database-match probability—are all relevant.[27] It assumes, in other words, that in a database-search case, the jury would benefit from the answers to three distinct questions, which it suggests are connected to these statistics: (1) "how rare a genetic profile is in a given society"; (2) how probable "a cold hit from a search of a particular database" would be when the culprit is not in the database; and (3) how probable it is "that the person identified through the cold hit is the actual source of the DNA in light of the fact that [the defendant's DNA profile matched while] a known quantity of potential suspects was eliminated through the database search"[28]

To determine whether the implicit assumption is valid, we must begin by identifying some relevant proposition on which the evidence of a DNA match bears. Whether the defendant is the source of the DNA recovered at the crime scene (say, a semen stain on the clothing of a woman who has been raped) is certainly relevant. The jury

---

[21]*U.S. v. Jenkins*, 887 A.2d 1013, 1022–23 (D.C. 2005) (footnote omitted). "*Porter*" refers to *U.S. v. Porter*, 618 A.2d 629 (D.C. 1992) (holding that the basic product rule for computing a random-match probability did not satisfy *Frye* and directing the trial court to consider whether the interim-ceiling method was generally accepted as a conservative alternative).

[22]Accord *People v. Johnson*, 139 Cal. App. 4th 1135, 43 Cal. Rptr. 3d 587 (5th Dist. 2006), review denied, (Aug. 16, 2006).

[23]*U.S. v. Jenkins*, 887 A.2d 1013, 1025 (D.C. 2005).

[24]National Research Council Committee on DNA Technology in Forensic Science, DNA Technology in Forensic Science 124 (1992).

[25]Committee on DNA Forensic Science: An Update, National Research Council, The Evaluation of Forensic DNA Evidence 134–35 (1996).

[26]Committee on DNA Forensic Science: An Update, National Research Council, The Evaluation of Forensic DNA Evidence 134–35 (1996).

[27]The same concern applies to the California court of appeals opinion in *People v. Johnson*, 139 Cal. App. 4th 1135, 43 Cal. Rptr. 3d 587 (5th Dist. 2006), review denied, (Aug. 16, 2006).

[28]*U.S. v. Jenkins*, 887 A.2d 1013, 1023 (D.C. 2005).

may agree with the prosecution's position that the defendant is the source, or it could embrace an alternative hypothesis. One alternative hypothesis is that the match is bad luck—the defendant is unrelated to the source and just happens to share the profile of the true source. Evidence that informs the jury of the plausibility of this alternative hypothesis therefore is also relevant—as an aid to understanding the fact of a DNA match.

When the defendant is selected for testing for reasons that have nothing to do with his identifying DNA profile and no one else is tested, the chance of the match under the hypothesis of coincidence is simply the population frequency. If a tiny percentage, say $p = 0.0001\%$, of the population has the profile, then the probability of a match given this hypothesis is just this tiny number. The hypothesis of coincidence thus seems implausible. If a larger percentage of the population has the same profile, however, such coincidences are more likely to occur, and the hypothesis is harder to dismiss. This is why the population frequency estimate, or, equivalently, the random-match probability, is relevant in a case in which the defendant is the only suspect who has been tested. This small size of this number informs the fact-finder that one innocent explanation—a coincidental match of an individual who is unrelated to the actual criminal—is implausible.

This analysis of relevance uses what statisticians call a classical (or frequentist) hypothesis-testing framework. The same conclusion—that the population frequency is relevant—also follows when the probative value of a match is measured in terms of a likelihood ratio. As explained in the next section, evidence supports one hypothesis as compared to another when it is more likely to be observed if the former is true than if the latter is the explanation. If the defendant is the source of the crime-scene stain, then the two DNA profiles must be identical; hence, the probability of matching profiles given the prosecution's hypothesis is one. Under the alternative hypothesis of unrelatedness, however, the probability that the two samples have the same profile is, again, the population frequency $p = 0.0001\%$. Consequently, the chance of match profiles under the prosecution's hypothesis is $1/p$ = 1,000,000 times greater than it is under the alternative hypothesis, indicating, of course, that the rarity of the profile makes a true match extremely probative with respect to these hypotheses.

But in the trawl case the defendant was not the only individual selected for testing, which necessitates some additional analysis to justify using the confirmation-case likelihood ratio as a measure of probative value. The frequentist argument is that because a trawl match is much less surprising than a single confirmation match, the hypothesis of coincidence is much more plausible than the random-match probability $p$ would suggest. If the appropriate database-match probability is much larger than $p$, then the applicable likelihood ratio is much smaller than $1/p$. According to this argument, $p$ is an unfair indicator of probative value.

*Jenkins* does not dispose of this argument for excluding $p$ in a database-search case. The court correctly rejects the claim that general acceptance is a barrier to admitting $p$, but it does not reach the related argument that $p$ is irrelevant and potentially misleading.[29] And, if $p$ is irrelevant, then presenting it along with $Np$ does not make it relevant. Furthermore, the database-search probability $Np$ may

---

[29]Cf. *People v. Johnson*, 139 Cal. App. 4th 1135, 43 Cal. Rptr. 3d 587, 600(5th Dist. 2006), review denied, (Aug. 16, 2006):

Appellant claims, however, that in a cold hit case, the results derived from the product rule do not accurately represent the probability of finding a matching profile by chance. As we understand his argument and the materials of which we have previously taken judicial notice, this is due to ascertain-

ment bias, i.e., the bias that exists when one searches for something rare in a set database. In other words, the fact that many profiles have been searched increases the probability of finding a match, so that conceptually, the more populated the database, the less impressive the match. Appellant contends that there is broad scientific consensus concerning the need to determine differently the statistical significance of profile matches in a cold hit case versus a confirmation case, but says that

not be any more pertinent than $p$. $Np$ indicates how probative the match is with respect to the hypothesis that the database contains the source of the crime-scene DNA as opposed to the alternative hypothesis that the crime-scene DNA came from someone not represented in the database.[30] In other words, it indicates how often searches of databases that do not include the culprit (or close relatives) will generate cold hits. But the database is not on trial. Only the defendant is. A database match is relevant only to the extent that it affects the probability that the defendant—not the database—is the source. Thus, it appears that asking how probable a search of a particular database is to generate a false cold hit is the wrong question.[31] The jury ought to be thinking about how probable the cold hit on the defendant's profile would be when the specific defendant is, and is not, the source of the crime-scene DNA. The likelihood ratio formed with these probabilities is the appropriate measure of the probative value of the database match.

This likelihood ratio is more complex than the $1/p$ figure that pertains to the simple "confirmation case," for the evidence is richer. It includes not only the fact that the defendant matches but also the fact that everyone else in the database has been excluded. It can be shown that when this additional information is incorporated in the likelihood ratio, the resulting number can be no greater than $1/p$.[32] Consequently, introducing $p$ as the indicator of probative value is not prejudicial. It understates the incriminatory power of the DNA evidence.[33] As many of the cases decided in the interregnum of the "interim ceiling principle" demonstrate, a defendant can hardly complain that a relevant probability that understates the significance of the evidence against him is inadmissible.[34]

---

the means of determining the statistical value of a cold hit "is a matter of continuing and strident debate."

*Johnson* and *Jenkins* are at their most persuasive when they argue that the mere existence of a "continuing and strident debate" in the scientific journals does not foreclose the use of suitable "means of determining the statistical value of a cold hit." The opinions are less convincing when they jump to the conclusion that an expert can present a match in a manner allegedly calculated to exaggerate "statistical significance . . . in a cold hit case."

[30]See Committee on DNA Forensic Science: An Update, National Research Council, The Evaluation of Forensic DNA Evidence 164–65 (1996).

[31]The matter invites confusion because only one person in the database has the matching profile, making appear that if we can reject the alternative hypothesis, we can conclude that the defendant is the source. For a formal treatment of the hypotheses and probabilities, see Committee on DNA Forensic Science: An Update, National Research Council, The Evaluation of Forensic DNA Evidence 164–65 (1996).

[32]A simple proof is available in Ian W. Evett & Bruce S. Weir, Interpreting DNA Evidence 219–22 (1998).

[33]A fortiori, the prosecution should be permitted to introduce $Np$ (without indicating that it is the adjusted form of $p$, and hence intimating that the defendant has previous convictions). Even more than $p$, $Np$ understates the force of the DNA evidence against the defendant. In *Jenkins*, the random match probability was in the quintillionths, and $Np$ was in the hundred trillionths or so. Prosecutors ought to be content with such vanishingly small quantities. See *People v. Johnson*, 139 Cal. App. 4th 1135, 43 Cal. Rptr. 3d 587, 601 n.19 (5th Dist. 2006), review denied, (Aug. 16, 2006).

[34]As explained earlier in this chapter, when the 1992 NRC report proposed the "ceiling" method as a device to compute the random match probability for a "structured" population, bitter criticism from population geneticists followed. Pointing to this debate, many defendants argued that no generally accepted method was available for producing a random match probability. However, there was little or no doubt that the ceiling estimates were almost always far less than actual random match probability. They may have been inelegant and inefficient in their use of the data, but they were generally accepted as a way to *over*estimate of the desired number. Once this was recognized, courts had little difficulty admitting the evidence, for they understood that whether to exclude or admit scientific evidence that is presented so as to resolve uncertainties by bending over backwards to favor the defendant is a question of legal policy rather than scientific knowledge.

### § 2:12    Objections to DNA evidence—Presenting incriminating DNA results—Should likelihood ratios be excluded?

A likelihood ratio expresses how many times more likely it would be for matching profiles to exist if the defendant is the source of crime-scene sample than if other hypotheses about the origin of the sample are true.[1] The most commonly considered alternative hypothesis is that an unrelated person is the source (coincidence), but likelihood ratios can be calculated with respect to the hypothesis that a close relative is the source (kinship). The 1996 NRC Report offers the following analysis of the admissibility of such ratios:

> Although LRs [likelihood ratios] are rarely introduced in criminal cases, we believe that they are appropriate for explaining the significance of data and that existing statistical knowledge is sufficient to permit their computation. None of the LRs that have been devised for VNTRs can be dismissed as clearly unreasonable or based on principles not generally accepted in the statistical community. Therefore, legal doctrine suggests that LRs should be admissible unless they are so unintelligible that they provide no assistance to a jury or so misleading that they are unduly prejudicial. As with frequencies and match probabilities, prejudice might exist because the proposed LRs do not account for laboratory error, and a jury might misconstrue even a modified version that did account for it as a statement of the odds in favor of S [the claim that the defendant is the source of the forensic DNA sample]. [But] the possible misinterpretation of LRs as the odds in favor of identity . . . is a question of jury ability and performance to which existing research supplies no clear answer.[2]

Notwithstanding the lack of adequate empirical research, other commentators believe that the danger of prejudice (in the form of the transposition fallacy) warrants the exclusion of likelihood ratios.[3]

Likelihood ratios have been used primarily in the interpretation of mixed stains.[4] In *State v. Garcia*,[5] analysis of the semen stain on the victim's blouse indicated that sperm from two males were present. According to the court of appeals, a population geneticist "provided the jury with likelihood ratios (broken down by population subgroups such as Caucasians, African-Americans, and the like) for three distinct scenarios involving the sources of the DNA mixture found in the stain: (1) victim, defendant and unknown versus victim and two unknowns; (2) victim, defendant and

---

[Section 2:12]

[1]§ 2:52.

[2]Committee on DNA Forensic Science: An Update, National Research Council, The Evaluation of Forensic DNA Evidence at 200–201 (1996). A footnote adds that:

> Likelihood ratios were used in *State v. Klindt*, 389 N.W.2d 670 (Iowa 1986) (overruled on other grounds by, State v. Reeves, 636 N.W.2d 22 (Iowa 2001)) . . . , and are admitted routinely in parentage litigation, where they are known as the 'paternity index' . . . Some state statutes use them to create a presumption of paternity . . . The practice of providing a paternity index has been carried over into criminal cases in which genetic parentage is used to indicate the identity of the perpetrator of an offense . . .

Committee on DNA Forensic Science: An Update, National Research Council, The Evaluation of Forensic DNA Evidence at 200 n. 97 (1996).

[3]See Koehler, On Conveying the Probative Value of DNA Evidence: Frequencies, Likelihood Ratios, and Error Rates, 67 Colo. L. Rev. 859, 880 (1996); Thompson, DNA Evidence in the O.J. Simpson Trial, 67 Colo. L. Rev. 827, 850 (1996).

*Contra* Koehler et al., The Random Match Probability in DNA Evidence: Irrelevant and Prejudicial?, 35 Jurimetrics J. 201 (1995) (proposing the use of a likelihood ratio that incorporates laboratory error).

[4]When a mixed stain can be separated into "primary" and "secondary" contributions, a laboratory may report an estimated frequency for the primary contributor only and not present likelihood ratios for the various other combinations of alleles. See, e.g., *Com. v. Gaynor*, 443 Mass. 245, 820 N.E.2d 233, 252 (2005) ("Likelihood ratio analysis is appropriate for test results of mixed samples when the primary and secondary contributors cannot be distinguished. . . . It need not be applied when a primary contributor can be identified."). Another approach is to state the probability that a randomly selected person would be excluded as a contributor to a mixed stain. See, e.g., *Coy v. Renico*, 414 F. Supp. 2d 744, 751 (E.D. Mich. 2006); *U.S. v. Morrow*, 374 F. Supp. 2d 51, 54–55 (D.D.C. 2005).

[5]*State v. Garcia*, 197 Ariz. 79, 3 P.3d 999 (Ct. App. Div. 1 1999).

unknown versus defendant and two unknowns; and (3) victim, defendant and one unknown versus three unknowns." To illustrate the nature of the testimony with simplified numbers for the first set of hypotheses, the calculations might show the chance of the specified DNA types being present was 100 times greater if (a) the DNA came from the victim, the defendant, and a randomly selected person than if (b) it came from the victim and two randomly selected persons.

The trial court admitted this testimony following a *Frye* hearing at which the state's expert testified to general acceptance. The defendant was convicted. On appeal, he argued that the state had not proved that the specific formulas used to calculate the likelihood ratios had been generally accepted. The court of appeals affirmed the conviction, reasoning that both the concept of the likelihood ratio and the specific formulas were generally accepted, as indicated by publications in the scientific literature.

Although *Garcia* recognizes that the use of likelihood ratios is generally accepted as scientifically valid, the fact remains that an expert can make a mistake in algebraically representing the pertinent conditional probabilities or in working out the algebra that yields the likelihood ratio for a particular problem. Although this sounds like a concern about the implementation of a generally accepted method (so that *Frye* would not apply even in most *Frye* jurisdictions), it also can be characterized as a trans-case, major premise (which would require general acceptance). After all, the formulas in *Garcia* easily could be employed in other cases involving a mixture of DNA from one female and two males. There should be little difficulty admitting them under *Daubert*, for the derivation of the formulas is a straightforward algebraic exercise that can be verified by any number of experts familiar with probability theory. Affidavits from a few such experts should be enough to demonstrate the requisite reliability. Under *Frye*, it is more difficult to introduce even an obviously valid result that has yet to be scrutinized by the relevant portion of the scientific community. Nevertheless, the outcome should be the same.[6]

The Massachusetts Supreme Judicial Court also upheld the admission of expert testimony as to likelihood ratios for mixed stains. The court described the testimony in *Commonwealth v. McNickles*[7] as follows:

Because it was unclear whether [the victim's] own DNA was . . . in the evidence sample, [the expert] performed his calculations to cover both possibilities. Thus he calculated one likelihood ratio on the assumption that [the victim's] DNA was not part of the sample, comparing the likelihood that the sample was comprised of the defendant's DNA and another unknown person's DNA with the likelihood that the sample was comprised of the DNA of two unknown persons. Assuming that [the victim's] DNA was not part of the sample, it was 220 times more likely that the defendant was a contributor to the sample than that he was not a contributor. Then, [the expert] ran the calculations assuming that [the victim] was a contributor to the mixed sample, comparing the likelihood that the sample was comprised of the defendant's DNA and [her] DNA with the likelihood that the sample was comprised of the DNA of an unknown person and [her] DNA. On that assumption, it was 37,000 times more likely that the defendant was

---

[6]In a petition for review, Garcia suggested that although the use of the likelihood ratio has support in the literature, the particular formulas were not previously published. However, there is no general formula for computing a likelihood ratio. It depends on the specific hypotheses being compared. The likelihood ratio for a mixture with two possible men is different from that for a mixture with three, or four, and so on. The same approach produces the appropriate expression in each situation, and arriving at the correct expression is like solving word problems in high school algebra. Everyone agrees that the problems should be solved with formulas derived according to the rules of algebra, but different word problems require different formulas. The use of algebra is generally accepted, but a student can make a mistake applying those rules.

[7]*Com. v. McNickles*, 434 Mass. 839, 753 N.E.2d 131 (2001).

a contributor to the sample than that another unknown person was the contributor.[8]

The trial judge found that this application of likelihood ratios to mixed samples of DNA to be "a valid and reliable scientific method of assigning statistical significance to DNA test results."[9] The Supreme Judicial Court discerned no abuse of discretion in this ruling.[10]

The Montana Supreme Court followed *McNickles* and *Garcia* in *State v. Ayers.*[11] However, in a superficial discussion of the issue, the court merely reasoned that because likelihood ratios were used in previous (typically unreported) cases, because a different likelihood ratio (known as a paternity index) is used in parentage cases, and because the likelihood ratio has been discussed in the legal literature, it is not a novel concept that would need to be shown to be valid or reliable within the meaning of *Daubert*. This view that *Daubert* or *Frye* applies only to evidence that is new to the courts is flawed.[12] Likewise, in *People v. Coy*,[13] a Michigan appellate court upheld the admission of likelihood ratios and other probabilities for mixed stains without requiring these statistics to satisfy the general-acceptance standard applicable to other scientific evidence in that state. The view that the method of arriving at these statistics is not subject to the type of heightened scrutiny normally required of scientific evidence is a minority position[14] that is difficult to justify.[15]

---

[8]*Com. v. McNickles*, 434 Mass. 839, 753 N.E.2d 131, 138 (2001). The characterization of the likelihood ratio in the passage is flawed. The ratio relates to conditional probabilities for the presence of the alleles given the competing hypotheses—not to the conditional probabilities of the hypotheses given the presence of the alleles. the court's description of the likelihood ratios transposes the conditional probabilities involved in the likelihood ratios. Take the statement that "assuming that [the victim] was a contributor to the mixed sample, . . . it was 37,000 times more likely that the defendant was a contributor to the sample than that another unknown person was the contributor." The correct rendition of the expert's testimony would be that "assuming the victim was a contributor, it was 37,000 times more likely to find the DNA types that were detected if the defendant was a contributor than if another person was the contributor."

[9]*Com. v. McNickles*, 434 Mass. 839, 753 N.E.2d 131, 138 (2001).

[10]The defendant argued that by assuming that the victim's DNA was in the sample, the calculation relied on a fact not established by the evidence. The court convincingly disposed of the latter argument by reasoning that

Precisely because the testing had suggested but not definitively confirmed the presence of [the victim's] DNA in the mixed sample, [the analyst] presented statistics for both possible scenarios. He did not "assume" anything, but rather presented statistical analyses for the full range of possibilities presented by the forensic evidence. Had the Commonwealth presented only a calculation based on the assumption that [the victim's] DNA was part of the sample, the defendant's argument would perhaps carry more weight. However, by presenting the . . . same calculation covering the countervailing assumption, the presentation was complete, and did not rely on any particular assumption or finding as to whether

[the victim's] DNA was or was not part of the sample.

*Com. v. McNickles*, 434 Mass. 839, 753 N.E.2d 131, 139 (2001); see also *Com. v. Gaynor*, 443 Mass. 245, 820 N.E.2d 233 (2005); *State v. Manning*, 885 So. 2d 1044 (La. 2004), cert. denied, 544 U.S. 967, 125 S. Ct. 1745, 161 L. Ed. 2d 612 (2005). Contra *People v. Wilson*, 38 Cal. 4th 1237, 45 Cal. Rptr. 3d 73, 136 P.3d 864 (2006).

[11]*State v. Ayers*, 2003 MT 114, 315 Mont. 395, 68 P.3d 768 (2003). See also *Coy v. Renico*, 414 F. Supp. 2d 744 (E.D. Mich. 2006) (use of likelihood ratio and other statistics for a mixed stain were sufficiently accepted in the scientific community to be consistent with due process); *State v. Belton*, 150 N.H. 741, 846 A.2d 526, 530 (2004) (citing *Garcia* and later cases in dicta indicating that likelihood ratios for mixtures would be appropriate).

[12]See, e.g., D.H. Kaye et al., The Modern Wigmore, A Treatise on Evidence: Expert Evidence § 8.1.3(d) (2004).

[13]*People v. Coy*, 258 Mich. App. 1, 669 N.W.2d 831 (2003).

[14]Opinions that adopt this view include *Smith v. State*, 702 N.E.2d 668, 673–74 (Ind. 1998) (argument that laboratory's techniques rendered its frequency calculations scientifically unreliable was a question of weight, not admissibility), and *State v. Kinder*, 942 S.W.2d 313, 327 (Mo. 1996) (criticism of particular methods used to apply product rule pertain to the weight to be given the DNA evidence at trial); cf. *State v. Whittey*, 149 N.H. 463, 821 A.2d 1086, 1097 (2003) ("Even assuming without deciding that Cellmark did misapply the product rule, we disagree with the defendant that this renders the results of PCR-based STR DNA testing inadmissible under *Frye*. The contention that Cellmark failed to follow generally accepted techniques when analyzing DNA

### § 2:13 Objections to DNA evidence—Presenting incriminating DNA results—Should posterior probabilities be excluded?

Match probabilities state the chance that certain genotypes would be present conditioned on specific hypotheses about the source of the DNA (a specified relative, or an unrelated individual in a population or subpopulation). Likelihood ratios express the relative support that the presence of the genotypes in the defendant gives to these hypotheses compared to the claim that the defendant is the source. Posterior probabilities or odds express the chance that the defendant is the source (conditioned on various assumptions). These probabilities, if they are meaningful and accurate, would be of great value to the jury.

Experts have been heard to testify to posterior probabilities. In *Smith v. Deppish*,[1] for example, the state's "DNA experts informed the jury that . . . there was more than a 99 percent probability that Smith was a contributor of the semen,"[2] but how such numbers are obtained is not apparent. If they are instances of the transposition fallacy, then they are scientifically invalid (and objectionable under Rule 702) and unfairly prejudicial (under Rule 403).

However, a meaningful posterior probability can be computed with Bayes' theorem.[3] Ideally, one would enumerate every person in the suspect population, specify the prior odds that each is the source of the forensic DNA and weight those prior odds by the likelihoods (taking into account the familial relationship of each possible suspect to the defendant) to arrive at the posterior odds that the defendant is the source of the forensic sample. But this hardly seems practical. The 1996 NRC report therefore discusses a somewhat different implementation of Bayes' theorem. Assuming that the hypotheses of kinship and error could be dismissed on the basis of other evidence, the report focuses on "the variable-prior-odds method," by which:

> [A]n expert neither uses his or her own prior odds nor demands that jurors formulate their prior odds for substitution into Bayes's rule. Rather, the expert presents the jury with a table or graph showing how the posterior probability changes as a function of the prior probability.[4]

This procedure, it observes, "has garnered the most support among legal scholars and is used in some civil cases."[5] Nevertheless, "very few courts have considered its merits in criminal cases."[6] In the end, the report concludes:

> How much it would contribute to jury comprehension remains an open question, especially considering the fact that for most DNA evidence, computed values of the likelihood ratio (conditioned on the assumption that the reported match is a true match) would swamp any plausible prior probability and result in a graph or table that would

---

under the product rule is an issue that goes to the weight that evidence should be given in a particular case, not the general admissibility under *Frye*.").

[15]See D.H. Kaye et al., The Modern Wigmore, A Treatise on Evidence: Expert Evidence § 7.3 (2004).

**[Section 2:13]**

[1]*Smith v. Deppish*, 248 Kan. 217, 807 P.2d 144 (1991).

[2]See also *State v. Thomas*, 830 S.W.2d 546, 550 (Mo. Ct. App. E.D. 1992) (a geneticist testified that "the likelihood that the DNA found in Marion's panties came from the defendant was higher than 99.99%"); *Com. v. Crews*, 536 Pa. 508, 640 A.2d 395, 402 (1994) (an FBI examiner who

at a preliminary hearing had estimated a coincidental-match probability for a VNTR match "at three of four loci" reported at trial that the match made identity "more probable than not").

[3]§§ 2:40 to 2:52.

[4]Committee on DNA Forensic Science: An Update, National Research Council, The Evaluation of Forensic DNA Evidence 202 (1996) (footnote omitted).

[5]Committee on DNA Forensic Science: An Update, National Research Council, The Evaluation of Forensic DNA Evidence 202 (1996).

[6]Committee on DNA Forensic Science: An Update, National Research Council, The Evaluation of Forensic DNA Evidence 202 (1996) (footnote omitted).

show a posterior probability approaching 1 except for very tiny prior probabilities.[7]

## § 2:14 Objections to DNA evidence—Presenting incriminating DNA results—Which verbal expressions of probative value should be presented?

Having surveyed various views about the admissibility of the probabilities and statistics indicative of the probative value of DNA evidence, we turn to a related issue that can arise under Rules 702 and 403: Should an expert be permitted to offer a non-numerical judgment about the DNA profiles?

Inasmuch as most forms of expert testimony involve qualitative rather than quantitative testimony, this may seem an odd question. Yet, many courts have held that a DNA match is inadmissible unless the expert attaches a scientifically valid number to the figure.[1] In reaching this result, some courts cite the statement in the 1992 NRC report that "[t]o say that two patterns match, without providing any scientifically valid estimate (or, at least, an upper bound) of the frequency with which such matches might occur by chance, is meaningless."[2]

The 1996 report phrases the scientific question somewhat differently. Like the 1992 report, it states that "[b]efore forensic experts can conclude that DNA testing has the power to help identify the source of an evidence sample, it must be shown that the DNA characteristics vary among people. Therefore, it would not be scientifically justifiable to speak of a match as proof of identity in the absence of underlying data that permit some reasonable estimate of how rare the matching characteristics actually are."[3] However, the 1996 report then explains that "determining whether quantitative estimates should be presented to a jury is a different issue. Once science has established that a methodology has some individualizing power, the legal system must determine whether and how best to import that technology into the

---

[7]Committee on DNA Forensic Science: An Update, National Research Council, The Evaluation of Forensic DNA Evidence 202 (1996). For arguments said to show that the variable-prior-odds proposal is "a bad idea," see William C. Thompson, Accepting Lower Standards: The National Research Council's Second Report on Forensic DNA Evidence, 37 Jurimetrics J. 422–423 (1997).

**[Section 2:14]**

[1]E.g., *Peters v. State*, 18 P.3d 1224 (Alaska Ct. App. 2001) (error to introduce "consistent with" testimony for mixed stains unaccompanied by any further indication of probative value); *Com. v. Daggett*, 416 Mass. 347, 622 N.E.2d 272, 275 (1993) (plurality opinion insisting that "[t]he point is not that this court should require a numerical frequency, but that the scientific community clearly does"); *People v. Coy*, 243 Mich. App. 283, 620 N.W.2d 888 (2000) (plain error to present a DNA match in a mixed stain without a qualitative or quantitative estimate of its significance); *State v. Cauthron*, 120 Wash. 2d 879, 846 P.2d 502 (1993) ("probability statistics" must accompany testimony of a match). *Contra Com. v. Crews*, 536 Pa. 508, 640 A.2d 395, 402 (1994) ("The factual evidence of the physical testing of the DNA samples and the matching alleles, even without statistical conclusions, tended to make appellant's presence more likely than it would

have been without the evidence, and was therefore relevant.").

[2]Committee on DNA Technology in Forensic Science, National Research Council, DNA Technology in Forensic Science 74 (1992). For criticism of this statement, see D.H. Kaye, The Forensic Debut of the NRC's DNA Report: Population Structure, Ceiling Frequencies, and the Need for Numbers, 96 Genetica 99, 104–105 (1995), *reprinted in* Human Identification: The Use of DNA Markers 99, 104–105 (Bruce S. Weir ed., 1995):

> [I]t would not be 'meaningless' to inform the jury that two samples match and that this match makes it more probable, in an amount that is not precisely known, that the DNA in the samples comes from the same person. Nor, when all estimates of the frequency are in the millionths or billionths, would it be meaningless to inform the jury that there is a match that is known to be extremely rare in the general population. Courts may reach differing results on the legal propriety of qualitative as opposed to quantitative assessments, but they only fool themselves when they act as if scientific opinion automatically dictates the correct answer.

[3]Committee on DNA Forensic Science: An Update, National Research Council, The Evaluation of Forensic DNA Evidence 192 (1996). As indicated in earlier sections, these "underlying data" have been collected and analyzed for many genetic systems.

trial process."[4]

Since the loci typically used in forensic DNA identification have been shown to have substantial individualizing power, it is scientifically sound to introduce evidence of matching profiles. Nonetheless, even evidence that meets the scientific soundness standard of *Daubert* is not admissible if its prejudicial effect clearly outweighs its probative value. Unless some reasonable explanation accompanies testimony that two profiles match, it is surely arguable that the jury will have insufficient guidance to give the scientific evidence the weight it deserves.[5]

Instead of presenting frequencies or match probabilities obtained with quantitative methods, however, a scientist would be justified in characterizing every four-locus VNTR profile, for instance, as "rare," "extremely rare," or the like.[6] At least one state supreme court has endorsed this qualitative approach as a substitute to the presentation of more debatable numerical estimates.[7]

The most extreme case of a purely verbal description of the infrequency of a profile arises when that profile can be said to be unique. The 1992 report cautioned that "an expert should—given . . . the relatively small number of loci used and the available population data—avoid assertions in court that a particular genotype is unique in the population."[8] Following this advice in the context of a profile derived from a handful of single-locus VNTR probes, several courts initially held that assertions of uniqueness are inadmissible,[9] while others found such testimony less troublesome.[10]

With the advent of more population data and loci, the 1996 NRC report pointedly

---

[4]Committee on DNA Forensic Science: An Update, National Research Council, The Evaluation of Forensic DNA Evidence 192 (1996).

[5]Committee on DNA Forensic Science: An Update, National Research Council, The Evaluation of Forensic DNA Evidence 193 (1996) ("Certainly, a judge's or juror's untutored impression of how unusual a DNA profile is could be very wrong. This possibility militates in favor of going beyond a simple statement of a match, to give the trier of fact some expert guidance about its probative value."). But see *Padgett v. State*, 668 So. 2d 78 (Ala. Crim. App. 1995), as supplemented on reh'g, (May 5, 1995) (exclusion of population frequency statistics evidence to explain DNA evidence was not abuse of discretion); *Brodine v. State*, 936 P.2d 545, 551–52 (Alaska Ct. App. 1997) (no error occurred in presenting DNA typing evidence unaccompanied by statistical estimates, including tests on mixed samples).

[6]Cf. Committee on DNA Forensic Science: An Update, National Research Council, The Evaluation of Forensic DNA Evidence 195 (1996) ("Although different jurors might interpret the same words differently, the formulas provided . . . produce frequency estimates for profiles of three or more loci that almost always can be conservatively described as 'rare.' ").

[7]*State v. Bloom*, 516 N.W.2d 159, 166–167 (Minn. 1994) ("Since it may be pointless to expect ever to reach a consensus on how to estimate, with any degree of precision, the probability of a random match, and that given the great difficulty in educating the jury as to precisely what that figure means and does not mean, it might make sense to simply try to arrive at a fair way of

explaining the significance of the match in a verbal, qualitative, non-quantitative, nonstatistical way."); see also Kreiling, Review—Comment, DNA Technology in Forensic Science, 33 Jurimetrics J. 449 (1993).

[8]Committee on DNA Technology in Forensic Science, National Research Council, DNA Technology in Forensic Science 92 (1992).

[9]See *State v. Buckner*, 125 Wash. 2d 915, 890 P.2d 460, 462 (1995), on reconsideration, 133 Wash. 2d 63, 941 P.2d 667 (1997) (testimony that the profile "would occur in only one Caucasian in 19.25 billion" and that because "this figure is almost four times the present population of the Earth, the match was unique" was improper).

[10]*State v. Zollo*, 36 Conn. App. 718, 654 A.2d 359, 362 (1995) (testimony that the chance "that the DNA sample came from someone other than the defendant was 'so small that . . . it would not be worth considering' " was not inadmissible as an opinion on an ultimate issue in the case "because his opinion could reasonably have aided the jury in understanding the [complex] DNA testimony"); *People v. Heaton*, 266 Ill. App. 3d 469, 203 Ill. Dec. 710, 640 N.E.2d 630, 633 (5th Dist. 1994) (rejected on other grounds by, Franson v. Micelli, 269 Ill. App. 3d 20, 206 Ill. Dec. 399, 645 N.E.2d 404 (1st Dist. 1994)) (an expert who used the product rule to estimate the frequency at 1/52,600 testified over objection to his opinion that the "defendant was the donor of the semen"); *State v. Pierce*, 1990 WL 97596 (Ohio Ct. App. 5th Dist. Delaware County 1990), judgment aff'd, 64 Ohio St. 3d 490, 1992-Ohio-53, 597 N.E.2d 107 (1992) (affirming admission of testimony that the probability would be one in 40 billion "that the match

observed that "we are approaching the time when many scientists will wish to offer opinions about the source of incriminating DNA."[11] Of course, the uniqueness of any object, from a snowflake to a fingerprint, in a population that cannot be enumerated never can be proved directly. The committee therefore wrote that "[t]here is no 'bright-line' standard in law or science that can pick out exactly how small the probability of the existence of a given profile in more than one member of a population must be before assertions of uniqueness are justified. . . . There might already be cases in which it is defensible for an expert to assert that, assuming that there has been no sample mishandling or laboratory error, the profile's probable uniqueness means that the two DNA samples come from the same person."[12]

The report concludes that "[b]ecause the difference between a vanishingly small probability and an opinion of uniqueness is so slight, courts may choose to allow the latter along with, or instead of the former, when the scientific findings support such testimony."[13] Confronted with an objection to an assertion of uniqueness, a court

---

would be to a random occurrence," and "[t]he DNA is from the same individual"); cf. *State v. Bogan*, 183 Ariz. 506, 905 P.2d 515, 517 (Ct. App. Div. 1 1995), as corrected, (Apr. 13, 1995) (it was proper to allow a molecular biologist to testify, on the basis of a PCR-based analysis that he "was confident the seed pods found in the truck originated from" a palo verde tree near a corpse); *Com. v. Crews*, 536 Pa. 508, 640 A.2d 395, 402 (1994) (testimony of an FBI examiner that he did not know of a single instance "where different individuals that are unrelated have been shown to have matching DNA profiles for three or four probes" was admissible under *Frye* despite an objection to the lack of a frequency estimate, which had been given at a preliminary hearing as 1/400).

In *State v. Hummert*, 188 Ariz. 119, 933 P.2d 1187 (1997), VNTR testing performed by the FBI showed that Hummert could have been the source of a semen stain. But the trial court excluded basic product rule estimates of the three-locus profile frequency, and an FBI examiner testified that such a match is "rare" and meant that "[e]ither you're brothers, identical twins, or that would be a very unique experience." A second expert, a geneticist and epidemiologist from the University of California at Berkeley, went further. She testified that "one can, by carefully choosing particular parts of the DNA that vary a lot between people, uniquely identify every person with just a sample of each person's DNA." *State v. Hummert*, 183 Ariz. 484, 905 P.2d 493, 499 (Ct. App. Div. 1 1994), opinion vacated, 188 Ariz. 119, 933 P.2d 1187 (1997). Oddly, the supreme court perceived no testimony that science had established that three-locus VNTR matches demonstrated uniqueness. The majority opinion downplayed the expert testimony, remarking that "[a]t trial, the judge admitted evidence of the match, the criteria for declaring a match, and opinions that Defendant was not excluded by the DNA tests." *State v. Hummert*, 188 Ariz. 119, 933 P.2d 1187, 1189 (1997). Later, the opinion recognizes that more was involved—but not much more: "the . . . conclusions . . . in this case [came] strictly

from personal knowledge and study." *State v. Hummert*, 188 Ariz. 119, 933 P.2d 1187, 1192 (1997). The court reasoned such "personal knowledge" need not meet "the apparent trappings of science, the *Frye* rule, and scientific recognition" but rather "need only meet the traditional requirements of relevance and avoid substantial prejudice, confusion, or waste of time." *State v. Hummert*, 188 Ariz. 119, 933 P.2d 1187, 1195 (1997). This "personal knowledge" exception is criticized in Kaye, Choice and Boundary Problems in Logerquist, Hummert, and Carmichael, 33 Ariz. St. L.J. 41 (2001).

[11]Committee on DNA Forensic Science: An Update, National Research Council, The Evaluation of Forensic DNA Evidence 194 (1996).

[12]As an illustration, the committee cited *State v. Bloom*, 516 N.W.2d 159, 160 (Minn. 1994), a case in which a respected population geneticist was prepared to testify that "in his opinion the nine-locus match constituted 'overwhelming evidence that, to a reasonable degree of scientific certainty, the DNA from the victim's vaginal swab came from the [defendant], to the exclusion of all others.'" Committee on DNA Forensic Science: An Update, National Research Council, The Evaluation of Forensic DNA Evidence 194–195 n.84 (1996); see also *People v. Hickey*, 178 Ill. 2d 256, 227 Ill. Dec. 428, 687 N.E.2d 910, 917 (1997) (given the results of nine VNTR probes plus PCR-based typing, two experts testified that a semen sample originated from the defendant).

[13]Committee on DNA Forensic Science: An Update, National Research Council, The Evaluation of Forensic DNA Evidence 195 (1996). If an opinion as to uniqueness were simply tacked on to a statistical presentation, it might be challenged as cumulative. Cf. Committee on DNA Forensic Science: An Update, National Research Council, The Evaluation of Forensic DNA Evidence 195 (1996) ("Opinion testimony about uniqueness would simplify the presentation of evidence by dispensing with specific estimates of population frequencies or probabilities. If the basis of an opinion were attacked on statistical grounds, however, or if frequency or probability estimates

may need to verify that a large number of sufficiently polymorphic loci have been tested.[14]

Currently, the FBI uses a slightly convoluted procedure to justify opinions that a specific defendant is "the source of an evidentiary sample,"[15] and more and more court opinions contain unqualified statements of uniqueness or of defendant's being the source of the incriminating sample.[16] Although most opinions contain no discussion of the propriety of such testimony,[17] a few courts have addressed aspects of this issue. In *People v. Baylor*,[18] the California court of appeals rejected a claim that a population geneticist should not have been allowed to testify that "defendant had a

---

were admitted, this advantage would be lost.").

[14]The NRC committee merely suggested that a sufficiently small random match probability compared to the earth's population could justify a conclusion of uniqueness. The committee did not propose any single figure, but asked: "Does a profile frequency of the reciprocal of twice the earth's population suffice? Ten times? One hundred times?" Committee on DNA Forensic Science: An Update, National Research Council, The Evaluation of Forensic DNA Evidence 194 (1996). Another approach would be to consider the probability of recurrence in a close relative. Cf. Thomas R. Belin et al., Summarizing DNA Evidence When Relatives are Possible Suspects, 92 J. Am. Stat. Ass'n 706 (1997); Buckleton & Triggs, Relatedness and DNA: Are We Taking It Seriously Enough?, 152 Forensic Sci. Int'l 115 (2005).

[15]Rather than ask whether a profile probably is unique in the world's population, the examiner focuses on smaller populations that might be the source of the evidentiary DNA. When the surrounding evidence does not point to any particular ethnic group or geographic area, the analyst takes the random match probability and multiplies it by ten (to account for any uncertainty due to population structure). The analyst then asks what the probability of generating a population of unrelated people as large as that of the entire U.S. (260 million people) that contains no duplicate of the evidentiary profile would be. If that "no-duplication" probability is 1% or less, the examiner must report that the suspect "is the source of an evidentiary sample." Bruce Budowle et al., Source Attribution of a Forensic DNA Profile, Forensic Science Communications, July 2000, *available at* http://www.fbi.gov/hq/lab/fsc/ba ckissu/july2000/source.htm. Similarly, the FBI computes the no-duplication probability in each ethnic or racial subgroup that may be of interest. If that probability is 1% or less, the examiner must report that the suspect is the source of the DNA. Bruce Budowle et al., Source Attribution of a Forensic DNA Profile, Forensic Science Communications, July 2000, *available at* http://w ww.fbi.gov/hq/lab/fsc/backissu/july2000/source. htm. Finally, if the examiner thinks that a close relative could be the source, and these individuals cannot be tested, standard genetic formulae are used to find the probability of the same profile in

a close relative. Bruce Budowle et al., Source Attribution of a Forensic DNA Profile, Forensic Science Communications, July 2000, *available at* http://www.fbi.gov/hq/lab/fsc/backissu/july2000/so urce.htm. What probability permits the analyst to testify that the suspect is the source in this situation, however, is not specified. This type of testimony is questioned in Ian W. Evett & Bruce S. Weir, Interpreting DNA Evidence: Statistical Genetics for Forensic Scientists 108–18 (1998).

[16]E.g., *People v. Hill*, 89 Cal. App. 4th 48, 107 Cal. Rptr. 2d 110, 113 (2d Dist. 2001) ("appellant's DNA and the sperm DNA taken from [the victim] had a unique genetic profile occurring in only one of 5.89 trillion African-Americans."); *Glass v. State*, 255 Ga. App. 390, 565 S.E.2d 500 (2002) (vaginal swabs revealed the presence of spermatozoa, and DNA testing identified Glass as their "source"); *State v. Watts*, 172 N.C. App. 58, 616 S.E.2d 290, 293 (2005), writ denied, 361 N.C. 179, 641 S.E.2d 689 (2006) and review denied, 361 N.C. 179, 641 S.E.2d 690 (2006) (FBI analyst "testified that, in his opinion, it was scientifically unlikely that the semen found on the minor's underwear originated from anyone other than Defendant."); *Young v. State*, 388 Md. 99, 879 A.2d 44, 45–46 (2005) ("when a DNA method analyzes genetic markers at sufficient locations to arrive at an infinitesimal random match probability, expert opinion testimony of a match and of the source of the DNA evidence is admissible"; hence, it was permissible to introduce a report providing no statistics but stating that "[t]o a reasonable degree of scientific certainty (in the absence of an identical twin), [defendant] is the source of the DNA obtained from the sperm fraction"); *State v. Yarbrough*, 95 Ohio St. 3d 227, 2002-Ohio-2126, 767 N.E.2d 216 (2002) (analysis of semen on a vaginal swab "showed that appellant was the source of the semen.").

[17]Of course, where the prosecutor interprets the DNA match as establishing that the defendant is the source of incriminating stain, the concern that the jury will overvalue an expert's claim of uniqueness is less significant. See *State v. Roman Nose*, 667 N.W.2d 386 (Minn. 2003).

[18]*People v. Baylor*, 97 Cal. App. 4th 504, 118 Cal. Rptr. 2d 518 (4th Dist. 2002), opinion modified on denial of reh'g, (May 6, 2002).

unique DNA profile that 'probably does not exist in anyone else in the world.' "[19] However, the court's analysis is limited because the defendant's objection went to the method of computing a random-match probability and not to the expert's characterization of it. The Massachusetts Supreme Judicial Court spoke more definitively in *Commonwealth v. Girouard*,[20] where it concluded that there was no error in admitting an expert's opinion that "no one other than [the defendant] is the donor of the DNA obtained from the sperm fraction of the vaginal swabs [of the victim]."[21] The court was satisfied because "trial counsel was free to cross-examine the expert, or adduce rebuttal evidence, to establish that the DNA testing performed could not conclusively establish the donor of the sperm."[22]

### § 2:15  Objections to DNA evidence—Proficiency test records[1]

In a validation study, the researchers empirically verify the ability of the technology to identify features of DNA molecules. In a proficiency study, the focus is on how competently the laboratory's analysts apply a technology that already has been validated.[2] The purpose of proficiency testing is to uncover difficulties that a particular technician or a particular laboratory might be encountering in applying established methods.

Proficiency testing raises a variety of legal issues. As indicated in the previous section, some commentators have suggested that participation in a program of proficiency testing ought to be a prerequisite to the admission of evidence from a forensic laboratory,[3] that proficiency test results should be admissible to show how likely it is that the laboratory erred in the test at bar,[4] and that random match probabilities ought to be inadmissible unless they are combined with proficiency test results to estimate the probability of a false match. If the second suggestion is followed, and the defense is allowed to introduce evidence of proficiency tests to suggest that the laboratory is prone to err, a further question arises: Should the prosecution be permitted to present testimony that the defense has not retested or even requested the opportunity to retest the samples?[5]

### § 2:16  Objections to DNA evidence—Proficiency test records—Is proficiency testing a prerequisite to admission?

The first suggestion, that courts condition admissibility on proficiency testing, is a departure from the usual practice. As indicated in the previous section, the scientific

---

[19]*People v. Baylor*, 97 Cal. App. 4th 504, 118 Cal. Rptr. 2d 518, 522 (4th Dist. 2002), opinion modified on denial of reh'g, (May 6, 2002).

[20]*Com. v. Girouard*, 436 Mass. 657, 766 N.E.2d 873 (2002).

[21]*Com. v. Girouard*, 436 Mass. 657, 766 N.E.2d 873, 882 (2002).

[22]*Com. v. Girouard*, 436 Mass. 657, 766 N.E.2d 873, 882 (2002).

**[Section 2:15]**

[1]The discussion in this section is adapted from Imwinkelried & Kaye, DNA Typing: Emerging or Neglected Issues, 76 Wash. L. Rev. 413 (2001). Proficiency testing of DNA laboratories is described more fully in §§ 2:15 to 2:19.

[2]Proficiency testing in forensic genetic testing is designed to ascertain whether an analyst can correctly determine genetic types in a sample the origin of which is unknown to the analyst but is known to a tester. Proficiency is demonstrated

by making correct genetic typing determinations in repeated trials, and not by opining on whether the sample originated from a particular individual. Proficiency tests also require laboratories to report random match probabilities to determine if proper calculations are being made.

[3]See, e.g., Scheck, DNA and *Daubert*, 15 Cardozo L. Rev. 1979–1987 (1994); Thompson, Accepting Lower Standards: The National Research Council's Second Report on Forensic DNA Evidence, 37 Jurimetrics J. 417 (1997).

[4]See, e.g., Koehler, Error and Exaggeration in the Presentation of DNA Evidence at Trial, 34 Jurimetrics J. 37–38 (1993); Scheck, DNA and *Daubert*, 15 Cardozo L. Rev. 1984 n. 93 (1994).

[5]Cf. Wooley & Harmon, The Forensic DNA Brouhaha: Science or Debate?, 51 Am. J. Hum. Genetics 1164 (1992) (letter urging defense experts who criticize laboratory procedures to do their own tests).

validity and general acceptance standards relate to the capacity of an analytical procedure to generate accurate results when properly applied, and not to whether the individual or institution using a valid or generally accepted method is skilled and careful or is instead careless and prone to error.[1] Of course, the latter issue can be of paramount importance, but usually it is said to be a matter affecting the weight of the evidence rather than its admissibility.[2]

## § 2:17 Objections to DNA evidence—Proficiency test records—When are errors on proficiency tests admissible?

The second suggestion, that testimony about proficiency test results be used to reveal the chance of error in the case at bar, presupposes that such evidence is admissible at trial. In its 1992 report, a committee of the National Academy of Sciences took the position that "laboratory error rates must be continually estimated in blind proficiency testing and must be disclosed to juries."[1] Some courts then held that when the prosecution introduces testimony about the probability of a coincidentally matching profile, the defendant is entitled to introduce testimony about the laboratory's proficiency tests.[2] Indeed, it has been held that the opponent must be allowed to cross-examine one laboratory representative about errors committed by other analysts at the laboratory.[3]

In contrast, in a report published in 1996, a second committee of the National Academy declined to take a position on whether evidence of laboratory error rates, as estimated from proficiency studies, should be admissible at trial.[4] However, the report's discussion of proficiency testing raises questions about the probative value of such evidence. For example, the report notes that "[t]he pooling of proficiency-test results across laboratories" could mislead a jury and "penalize the better laboratories."[5] It adds that even a test of the same laboratory might be outdated, since the laboratory may have taken corrective action.[6] In these circumstances, the testimony could be vulnerable to an objection under Federal Rule of Evidence 403, which requires the exclusion of evidence whose probative value is substantially outweighed by the dangers of prejudice, confusion of the issues, or undue consump-

---

**[Section 2:16]**

[1]*U.S. v. Shea*, 957 F. Supp. 331, 340–341, 46 Fed. R. Evid. Serv. 1375 (D.N.H. 1997), aff'd, 159 F.3d 37, 50 Fed. R. Evid. Serv. 516 (1st Cir. 1998).

[2]See Imwinkelried, The Debate in the DNA Cases over the Foundation for the Admission of Scientific Evidence: The Importance of Human Error as a Cause of Forensic Misanalysis, 69 Wash. U. L.Q. 19 (1991). In extreme cases, where the laboratory departs so grossly from accepted practices that the reliability of its findings are in serious doubt, the court may well exclude the evidence on the ground that its probative value is too slight to warrant its admission.

**[Section 2:17]**

[1]Committee on DNA Technology in Forensic Science, National Research Council, DNA Technology in Forensic Science 89 (1992).

[2]E.g., *U.S. v. Porter*, 1994 WL 742297 (D.C. Super. Ct. 1994).

[3]*Williams v. State*, 342 Md. 724, 679 A.2d 1106 (1996) (disapproved of on other grounds by,

Wengert v. State, 364 Md. 76, 771 A.2d 389 (2001)).

[4]The report stated that the committee had chosen to limit its remarks to the question of "what aspects of the procedures used in connection with forensic DNA testing are scientifically valid . . ." Committee on DNA Forensic Science: An Update, National Research Council, The Evaluation of Forensic DNA Evidence 185 (1996).

[5]Committee on DNA Forensic Science: An Update, National Research Council, The Evaluation of Forensic DNA Evidence 86 (1996).

[6]Committee on DNA Forensic Science: An Update, National Research Council, The Evaluation of Forensic DNA Evidence 86 (1996) (asserting that "[a] laboratory is not likely to make the same error again"); see also Committee on DNA Technology in Forensic Science, National Research Council, DNA Technology in Forensic Science 120 (1992) (recognizing that "errors on proficiency tests do not necessarily reflect permanent probabilities of false-positive or false-negative results").

tion of time.[7]

A further objection is that the testimony represents inadmissible character evidence.[8] If the theory of logical relevance is merely that the laboratory's past commission of errors increases the probability that the laboratory erred on the occasion in question, then the theory amounts to forbidden character reasoning.[9] It is precisely the theory of logical relevance generally banned by Federal Rule of Evidence 404.[10] Moreover, to the extent that proficiency test results constitute evidence of specific acts introduced to show a general tendency to make mistakes, they seem to run afoul of Rule 405, which forbids this form of proof of character.[11]

This issue is rarely recognized as a character evidence problem in the trial court,[12] but a trial judge might find it difficult to justify overruling a properly phrased character-evidence objection when the theory of relevance is nothing more than a general tendency of the laboratory to make mistakes. If there is a consensus that the jury sometimes needs the proficiency test results as an antidote to overwhelmingly small random match probabilities, then the federal and state rules governing character evidence should be altered to give the trial court the discretion to admit the evidence.[13]

Moreover, both the bench and bar should appreciate that in some circumstances,

---

[7]Cf. *U.S. v. Lowe*, 954 F. Supp. 401, 415, 46 Fed. R. Evid. Serv. 316 (D. Mass. 1996) (rejecting the argument that an expert *must* present an error rate from proficiency tests along with the random-match probability).

[8]Imwinkelried, Coming to Grips with Scientific Research in *Daubert*'s "Brave New World": The Courts' Need to Appreciate the Evidentiary Differences between Validity and Proficiency Studies, 61 Brook. L. Rev. 1247, 1273–1278 (1995). A number of jurisdictions have abolished the character evidence prohibition as it applies to a defendant's character in certain types of cases such as rape or child abuse. See Fed. R. Evid. 413 to 415; Cal. Evid. Code §§ 1108 to 1109. In these jurisdictions that allow the prosecution to rely on an accused past misconduct as circumstantial proof of the offense that is charged, the defense conceivably could argue that the differential treatment of the accused's inculpatory misconduct and the exculpatory proficiency test results violates the equal protection guarantee. E.g., *Nettles v. State*, 683 So. 2d 9, 12 (Ala. Crim. App. 1996). However, the constitutional attacks on character-evidence restrictions on defense evidence have failed. Edward J. Imwinkelried & Norman M. Garland, Exculpatory Evidence: The Accused's Constitutional Right to Introduce Favorable Evidence Ch. 14 (2d ed. 1996).

[9]See, e.g., *Moorhead v. Mitsubishi Aircraft Intern., Inc.*, 828 F.2d 278, 23 Fed. R. Evid. Serv. 1193 (5th Cir. 1987) (error to admit pilot's low marks at flight school refresher course); see generally 1 McCormick on Evidence § 186 (John Strong ed., 5th ed. 1999).

[10]Federal Rule 404(a) provides that "[e]vidence of a person's character or a trait of his character is not admissible for the purpose of proving that he acted in conformity therewith on a particular occasion . . ." Section (b) of the rule recognizes certain exceptions to this blanket rule

of exclusion, but none are apposite here. There also is an exception permitting a witness's opponent to impeach the witness by questioning the witness about prior untruthful acts. Fed. R. Evid. 608(b). However, those acts relate to the witness's character trait for untruthfulness, rather the trait of competence or proficiency. The Federal Rules expressly carve out the exception for untruthfulness, but there is no comparable exception for the character trait of competence or proficiency.

[11]Federal Rule 405(a) provides that "In all cases in which evidence of character or a trait of character of a person is admissible, proof may be made by testimony as to reputation or by testimony in the form of an opinion. On cross-examination, inquiry is allowable into relevant specific instances of conduct." Section (b) permits specific act evidence only when character is "in issue"—a term of art that has no application to the tendency of laboratory personnel to make mistakes in performing DNA tests. See 1 McCormick on Evidence § 187 (John Strong ed., 5th ed. 1999).

[12]But see *U.S. v. Shea*, 957 F. Supp. 331, 344, 46 Fed. R. Evid. Serv. 1375 (D.N.H. 1997), aff'd, 159 F.3d 37, 50 Fed. R. Evid. Serv. 516 (1st Cir. 1998) ("The parties assume that error rate information is admissible at trial. This assumption may well be incorrect. Even though a laboratory or industry error rate may be logically relevant, a strong argument can be made that such evidence is barred by Fed. R. Evid. 404 because it is inadmissible propensity evidence."); *Unmack v. Deaconess Medical Center*, 1998 MT 262, 291 Mont. 280, 967 P.2d 783 (1998) (going to the brink of explicitly holding that the character evidence prohibition bars this type of testimony).

[13]Courts also generally have not addressed the impact of the character-evidence ban on expert testimony about the conditions under which eyewitness identifications are likely to be in error. Such testimony is unusual, and exclu-

however, proficiency tests of the laboratory involved in the case should be held admissible without relaxing the ban on character evidence. The ban applies only when the sole theory of logical relevance is that the existence of errors in the past suggests a tendency to err that might affect the result in the case at bar. There might be situations in which the defense can use the test data at trial on an entirely different theory of logical relevance. Assume, for instance, that the experts in a case disagree over whether a peak or a band observed in a DNA test is due to an allele or is an artifact. Evidence that spurious peaks or bands have occurred under similar circumstances in proficiency tests of the laboratory on known samples would lend support to the defense theory that the band in the pending case is an artifact. In this situation, proficiency test data are relevant because they provide information about the operating characteristics of the DNA test at that particular laboratory.[14]

### § 2:18 Objections to DNA evidence—Proficiency test records—Must proficiency tests be used to modify random-match probabilities?

The third suggestion relating to proficiency testing is that random-match probabilities should be inadmissible unless accompanied by or blended with the laboratory's error rate.[1] The 1996 committee observed that combining the two figures "would deprive the trier of fact of the opportunity to separately evaluate the pos-

---

sion almost invariably is upheld on appeal. In the rare cases where appellate courts have held that the failure to admit the evidence was an abuse of discretion, they have not mentioned the rule against character-evidence. See *State v. Chapple*, 135 Ariz. 281, 660 P.2d 1208 (1983); *People v. McDonald*, 37 Cal. 3d 351, 208 Cal. Rptr. 236, 690 P.2d 709, 46 A.L.R.4th 1011 (1984) (overruled on other grounds by, People v. Mendoza, 23 Cal. 4th 896, 98 Cal. Rptr. 2d 431, 4 P.3d 265 (2000)). Of course, much of this type of testimony falls outside the character-evidence rule. Thus, the rule does not ban testimony that "weapons focus" interferes with the accuracy of eyewitness identifications any more than it bans testimony that handling DNA samples from the suspect and the crime scene without taking precautions against cross-contamination can produce false matches. On the other hand, testimony that people err in their identifications a specified fraction of the time resembles testimony about the incidence of medical mistakes in hospitals, the safety record of airlines, and the like. These error statistics the law traditionally excludes.

[14]Of course, even when the proficiency test data would be admissible and the defense has a legitimate need to discover this type of information, there might be means of satisfying the need other than by furnishing proficiency test results. By way of example, a sampling of the laboratory's case work could meet the need. However, in most cases permitting discovery of proficiency test data may be preferable. It will likely be more convenient for the laboratory to reveal the proficiency test data, since that data has already been compiled and giving the defense access to actual case work could compromise the privacy of the persons involved in those cases. When the defense needs to discover information about the operating characteristics of a laboratory's test for a purpose

other than merely establishing the laboratory's general error rate, the data could prove to be admissible at trial; hence, the courts would not be justified in denying discovery of proficiency test results on the ground that such discovery cannot lead to the production of admissible evidence at trial.

**[Section 2:18]**

[1]Combining the random-match probability with the probability of a false-positive laboratory error according the rules governing conditional probabilities would give the jury an estimate of the probability that the laboratory would find a match if the source of the crime-scene DNA were neither the defendant nor a close relative. When random-match probabilities are orders of magnitude smaller than estimates of the chance of a laboratory error of some kind, the possible error rate derived from proficiency testing dominates the combined error risk. As explained in Thompson, Accepting Lower Standards: The National Research Council's Second Report on Forensic DNA Evidence, 37 Jurimetrics J. 421 n. 59 (1997):

The overall probability that a match will be declared if the samples are from different people is approximately (although not precisely) the sum of the probability of an erroneous match and the probability of a random match. Let S designate that two samples have the same source and -S that they do not; let M designate that two samples have matching DNA profiles and -M that they do not; and let D designate that a match is declared by a DNA analyst following testing. The overall probability of a false match, $P(D|-S)$, is not simply the sum of the probability of a random match, $P(M|-S)$, and the probability of an erroneous match, $P(D|-M)$, but rather, $P(D|-S) = P(D|M)P(M|-S) + P(D|-M)P(-M|-S)$. Because $P(D|M)$ and $P(-M|-S)$ will usually be close to one, however, the sum of the probability of a random match and an erroneous match is close to the overall probability of a false

sibility that the profiles match by coincidence as opposed to the possibility that they are reported to match by reason of laboratory or handling error."[2] The committee took the position that "a calculation which combines error rates with match probabilities is inappropriate."[3] The reasoning supporting the committee's position essentially sounds under Federal Rule of Evidence 403.[4] If anything, the Rule 403 objection is more substantial here than when it is urged as a basis for excluding testimony offered to impeach the laboratory's competence. In this situation, the questions about the validity of industry-wide error rates and the staleness of even the laboratory's own tests are equally applicable and call into question the probative worth of the testimony. Moreover, there is a heightened risk that the jury will be confused. Error rates and random match probabilities relate to distinct hypotheses, and a lay juror may find it difficult to understand the significance of a computation which merges the rates and the probability. That mode of computation could place even greater strain on the jurors' ability to comprehend the body of evidence submitted to them.[5] The few courts that have addressed the argument that error rates should be used to the exclusion of random-match probabilities have not been persuaded.[6]

## § 2:19    Objections to DNA evidence—Proficiency test records—Is the opportunity to retest a permissible response to defense arguments about proficiency testing?

While defense counsel or experts originated the first three suggestions, the fourth suggestion related to proficiency testing has been made by prosecutors. The thrust of this suggestion is that when the defense is allowed to introduce evidence of proficiency tests of the laboratory employing the prosecution expert to suggest that the laboratory is prone to err, the prosecution should be permitted to present testimony that the defense has not retested or even requested the opportunity to retest the samples analyzed by the prosecution expert.[1]

The testimony would be logically relevant on several theories. To begin with, if a defense expert testifies that the laboratory result is untrustworthy, it would be relevant to impeach the defense expert's credibility on the ground that a scientist who truly doubted the accuracy of the analysis normally would have retested the samples

---

match.

[2]Committee on DNA Forensic Science: An Update, National Research Council, The Evaluation of Forensic DNA Evidence 85 (1996).

[3]Committee on DNA Forensic Science: An Update, National Research Council, The Evaluation of Forensic DNA Evidence 87 (1996).

[4]See generally Berger, Laboratory Error Seen Through the Lens of Science and Policy, 30 U.C. Davis L. Rev. 1081 (1997).

[5]See Schklar & Seidman Diamond, Juror Reactions to DNA Evidence: Errors and Expectancies, 23 Law & Hum. Behav. 130, 179 (1999) (concluding that separate figures are desirable in that "[j]urors . . . may need to know the disaggregated elements that influence the aggregated estimate as well as how they were combined in order to evaluate the DNA test results in the context of their background beliefs and the other evidence introduced at trial.").

[6]E.g., *Armstead v. State*, 342 Md. 38, 673

A.2d 221 (1996) (rejecting the argument that the introduction of a random match probability deprives the defendant of due process because the error rate on proficiency tests is many orders of magnitude greater than the match probability).

**[Section 2:19]**

[1]When the defense argues that the prosecution failed to perform appropriate DNA tests because it feared they would have exonerated the defendant, the prosecution may be permitted to respond that a similar inference can be drawn from the defendant's failure to test material that is made available to it. See *State v. Roman Nose*, 667 N.W.2d 386 (Minn. 2003) (holding that a prosecutor's questions on the availability of samples for retesting was a fair response to defendant's suggestion that the state did not test enough samples); *Hamel v. State*, 803 S.W.2d 878, 880 (Tex. App. Fort Worth 1991), petition for discretionary review refused, (June 12, 1991) (stating that this prosecutorial response is "clearly legitimate" and does not shift the burden of proof to the defendant).

to resolve the matter.[2] Inasmuch as replication is a crucial and common feature of scientific inquiry, it could be argued that neglecting to retest is prior inconsistent conduct. On this theory, the defense would be entitled to a limiting instruction to the effect that the expert's failure to retest is not offered to show that the test result is correct, but only to demonstrate that the defense expert is not sincere in asserting that it is flawed.[3]

The probative value of a failure to retest in showing an expert's insincerity, however, is open to question. It is not uncommon for scientists to question in print or otherwise the adequacy of another researcher's experiment before undertaking to replicate it. And even if such opinions were unheard of in the course of ordinary science, the expert may have been retained for the limited purpose of giving an opinion on the adequacy of the testing that was done rather than redoing that testing. Nevertheless, the inference of insincerity need not be particularly strong for the "inconsistent" conduct to be a proper, logically relevant subject for cross-examination.[4]

Second, if the defense expert offers an opinion that the laboratory's results may be in error, the expert's failure to request or conduct an independent test would be relevant to suggest that the jury should give less weight to that opinion.[5] The prosecution could argue to the jury that an expert who fails to use a more definitive and readily available procedure for ascertaining whether the initial test results are correct has not been thorough in evaluating those results, and that such experts deserve little credence because the basis for the opinion is not as complete as it could be. Again, the inference may be debatable, but the standard of relevance, particularly on cross-examination, is lenient.

Third, whether or not a defense expert discusses proficiency tests, the prosecution could argue that the defense failure to retest (or to request a retest) amounts to an admission by conduct by the defendant.[6] The courts have applied the admission-by-conduct theory to a litigant's failure to present evidence when "it would be natural" for the litigant to introduce such testimony.[7] The prosecution might urge that it would be natural for a defendant affected by a false match to seek retesting and that it would be natural for a DNA expert who entertained serious doubts about the accuracy of a prior test to retest the samples.[8]

In short, there are reasonable arguments for permitting the prosecution to raise the issue of retesting when a defendant questions the laboratory's ability to type DNA samples correctly. But even if the inquiry is probative of the insincerity or lack of thoroughness of the expert, or an admission by the defendant, there are potential objections to this counterthrust by the prosecution. One objection is that the inquiry is inconsistent with the prosecution's burden of proof.[9] To reinforce the allocation of the burden to the government, some courts generally forbid prosecution comment on

---

[2]This theory does not apply if the defense introduces the proficiency test data by cross-examining the prosecution's experts rather than producing its own expert.

[3]Fed. R. Evid. 105.

[4]The impeaching statement or conduct "need only bend in a different direction." John M. Mcnaught & Harold Flannery, Massachusetts Evidence: A Courtroom Reference 13-5 (1988).

[5]Thus, in *People v. Oliver*, 306 Ill. App. 3d 59, 239 Ill. Dec. 196, 713 N.E.2d 727 (1st Dist. 1999), the state was allowed to show that a defense expert who questioned the results of DNA tests had done no testing of his own. See *People v. Oliver*, 306 Ill. App. 3d 59, 239 Ill. Dec. 196, 713

N.E.2d 727, 736 (1st Dist. 1999) ("it was proper for the prosecution to bring out on cross-examination that the defense criticisms of the prosecution's expert witnesses were not based on any independent testing that it had done.").

[6]2 McCormick on Evidence § 264 (John Strong ed., 5th ed. 1999).

[7]2 McCormick on Evidence § 174 (John Strong ed., 5th ed. 1999).

[8]On this theory, the defense is not entitled to a limiting instruction; an admission by conduct qualifies as substantive evidence.

[9]*People v. Harbold*, 124 Ill. App. 3d 363, 79 Ill. Dec. 830, 464 N.E.2d 734, 741 (1st Dist. 1984).

the defense failure to produce evidence.[10] The argument runs that the defense is entitled to rely on the burden and has no obligation to present any evidence at trial. According to this line of argument, it is improper to convert the defense's failure to present testimony into prosecution evidence.[11] Under this line of authority, the defense could bar prosecution comment about the defense's failure to retest the DNA sample. However, even in such a jurisdiction, if the defense overreached, prosecution comment might be permitted as an invited response.[12] In addition, some jurisdictions reject that line of authority and allow comment on the defense's failure to present exculpatory evidence[13] so long as the trial judge clearly instructs the jury that the prosecution has the ultimate burden of proof.

A further objection is that the admission of the testimony is inconsistent with the defendant's attorney-client privilege. A number of jurisdictions apply the attorney-client privilege when, as part of trial preparation, defense counsel hires an expert to evaluate private information from the defendant, such as the defendant's mental or physical condition.[14] The Advisory Committee Note to draft Federal Rule of Evidence 503 endorsed the application of the attorney-client privilege to experts,[15] and some courts have gone to the length of invoking the theory even when the expert did not evaluate information realistically originating from the defendant.[16] Based on these authorities, the defense might contend that the attorney-client privilege applies to a defense expert's retest of a DNA sample. The gist of the objection would be that if the result of a retest would be privileged, it is wrong-minded to penalize the defense for failing to retest.

As with the other suggestions related to proficiency testing, the case law offers little guidance. In principle, it would seem that once the defense has sharpened the issue of the prosecution expert's use of proper test procedures, the prosecution should be allowed to elicit testimony about the defense's failure to retest at least to probe the basis for the expert's opinion and as circumstantial evidence of defendant's belief that retesting would not yield a different result. The fact that the prosecution

---

[10]*Hayes v. State*, 660 So. 2d 257 (Fla. 1995); *People v. Wills*, 151 Ill. App. 3d 418, 104 Ill. Dec. 278, 502 N.E.2d 775, 777–778 (2d Dist. 1986); *State v. Primus*, 341 S.C. 592, 535 S.E.2d 152 (Ct. App. 2000), aff'd in part, rev'd in part on other grounds, 349 S.C. 576, 564 S.E.2d 103 (2002) (overruled by, State v. Gentry, 363 S.C. 93, 610 S.E.2d 494 (2005)).

[11]A related argument looks to the privilege against self-incrimination. *Griffin v. California*, 380 U.S. 609, 614, 85 S. Ct. 1229, 14 L. Ed. 2d 106 (1965), teaches that the prosecution may not comment on the accused invocation of the privilege. However, a prosecutor's statement that the defense has not introduced rebuttal expert testimony would not amount to impermissible comment. Courts have held that similar statements from the prosecution were improper only when the defendant was the only potential witness who could contradict the prosecution. *Bergmann v. McCaughtry*, 65 F.3d 1372, 1377 (7th Cir. 1995); *U.S. v. Martinez*, 937 F.2d 299, 33 Fed. R. Evid. Serv. 334 (7th Cir. 1991). In a case involving DNA, the prosecutor's comments would relate to potential rebuttal testimony by an expert witness rather than any testimony from the accused.

[12]*Wise v. State*, 132 Md. App. 127, 751 A.2d 24 (2000).

[13]*Van Woudenberg ex rel. Foor v. Gibson*, 211

F.3d 560, 570 (10th Cir. 2000) (abrogated on other grounds by, McGregor v. Gibson, 248 F.3d 946 (10th Cir. 2001)) ("The prosecutor may . . . comment on the defendant's failure to present evidence or call witnesses"); *People v. Guzman*, 80 Cal. App. 4th 1282, 96 Cal. Rptr. 2d 87 (4th Dist. 2000).

[14]*Miller v. District Court In and For City and County of Denver*, 737 P.2d 834, 838 (Colo. 1987); *State v. Pratt*, 284 Md. 516, 398 A.2d 421 (1979); *Van White v. State*, 1999 OK CR 10, 990 P.2d 253 (Okla. Crim. App. 1999); Note, Disclosures by Criminal Defendant to Defense-Retained Psychiatrist Held Within Scope of Attorney-Client Privilege Which Defendant Does Not Waive by Pleading Insanity, 9 U. Balt. L. Rev. 99, 111 (1979).

[15]As enacted, Rule 503 leaves the recognition and development of privileges under federal law to the courts. The original draft would have codified and defined the privileges. Its description of the attorney-client privilege remains useful to courts as they continue to define and refine that privilege.

[16]*State v. Riddle*, 155 Or. App. 526, 964 P.2d 1056 (1998), opinion modified on reconsideration, 156 Or. App. 606, 969 P.2d 1032 (1998) and decision rev'd and remanded on other grounds, 330 Or. 471, 8 P.3d 980 (2000) (accident reconstruction expert).

has the burden of persuasion does not make such inferences impermissible.[17] The constitutional requirement for proof beyond a reasonable doubt regulates the quantum of proof the prosecution must present, but no court has invoked the requirement to preclude the prosecution from introducing an otherwise admissible item of evidence. In appropriate circumstances, the majority of courts permit prosecutors to comment on a defendant's failure to produce evidence such as an available witness who would presumably corroborate the defendant's testimony.[18]

Neither should the attorney-client privilege pose an insurmountable barrier. Certainly, the prosecution cannot comment on a defendant's decision to exercise a constitutional privilege,[19] and comment on a defendant's failure to produce a witness is often forbidden when the defendant stands in a privileged relationship with the witness.[20] Consequently, it might be justifiable to apply the attorney-client privilege to a defense expert's actual analysis of material that has become available because of the defendant's exercise of the right to prepare a defense with the assistance of counsel. Perhaps material that both emanates from the defendant and is still confidential would fall into this category. However, these conditions do not seem to be satisfied in this setting. The DNA sample that the defendant suggests has been misanalyzed might be crime-scene material that was not obtained from the defendant, or it could be a sample that the prosecution lawfully acquired from the defendant. In these situations, the attorney-client privilege should not preclude adverse comment on the defense failure to retest.

## § 2:20    Relevant expertise

DNA identification can involve testimony about laboratory findings, about the statistical interpretation of these findings, and about the underlying principles of molecular biology. Consequently, expertise in several fields might be required to establish the admissibility of the evidence or to explain it adequately to the jury. The expert who is qualified to testify about laboratory techniques might not be qualified to testify about molecular biology, to make estimates of population frequencies, or to establish that an estimation procedure is valid.

Trial judges ordinarily are accorded great discretion in evaluating the qualifications of a proposed expert witness, and the decisions depend on the background of each witness. Courts have noted the lack of familiarity of academic experts—such as statisticians or biologists who have done respected work in other fields—with the scientific literature on forensic DNA typing,[1] and on the extent to which their

---

[17]Thus, in *Fluellen v. Campbell*, 683 F. Supp. 186, 25 Fed. R. Evid. Serv. 777 (M.D. Tenn. 1987), judgment aff'd, 842 F.2d 331 (6th Cir. 1988), defense counsel argued that the state's case was weakened by the fact that it failed to have blood tests performed, and the prosecutor remarked in rebuttal "if he thinks that is such good evidence, why didn't he request that it be done?" *Fluellen v. Campbell*, 683 F. Supp. 186, 189, 25 Fed. R. Evid. Serv. 777 (M.D. Tenn. 1987), judgment aff'd, 842 F.2d 331 (6th Cir. 1988). The federal district court found that "this comment in no way imposed upon the jury a presumption which conflicted 'with the overriding presumption of innocence with which the law endows the accused and which extends to every element of the crime.'" *Fluellen v. Campbell*, 683 F. Supp. 186, 189, 25 Fed. R. Evid. Serv. 777 (M.D. Tenn. 1987), judgment aff'd, 842 F.2d 331 (6th Cir. 1988).

[18]Adverse presumption or inference based on party's failure to produce or examine family member other than spouse--modern cases, 80 A.L.R.4th 337, 344; Adverse presumption or inference based on party's failure to produce or examine friend--modern cases, 79 A.L.R.4th 779, 785–786.

[19]Most, but not all jurisdictions also forbid comment on the invocation of a statutory or common-law privilege. 1 McCormick on Evidence § 74.1 (John Strong ed., 5th ed. 1999).

[20]See, e.g., Adverse presumption or inference based on party's failure to produce or examine spouse--modern cases, 79 A.L.R.4th 694.

**[Section 2:20]**

[1]See, e.g., *State v. Copeland*, 130 Wash. 2d 244, 922 P.2d 1304, 1318 (1996) (noting that defendant's statistical expert, Seymour Geisser,

research or teaching lies in other areas.[2] Although such concerns may give trial judges pause, they rarely result in exclusion of the testimony on the ground that the witness simply is not qualified as an expert.[3]

The other side of this coin is technicians or scientists with ample expertise in laboratory methods, but less familiarity with population genetics. For example, in *State v. Harvey*,[4] Nathaniel Harvey was convicted of a brutal murder and sentenced to death. A "senior molecular biologist," and "a microbiologist and supervisor of forensic casework" at a private laboratory[5] testified that DNA tests showed that blood samples recovered at the crime scene were genetically comparable to defendant's DNA and that the genotype was common to one-in-1,400 African-Americans.[6] On appeal, Harvey did not dispute the qualifications of these witnesses as experts in the field of DNA testing, but argued that such witnesses, not being statisticians, were not competent to explain the databases and the formula used to derive this figure.[7]

The qualifications of a scientist or technician to testify to statistical estimates should turn on the familiarity of the expert with the methods used,[8] the complexity of those methods, and the extent to which comparable use of such methods is commonplace. The more complex the methods and the less obvious it is that they are appropriate to the problem at hand, the more the expert should be knowledgeable in statistics. The construction of DNA databases and the estimation of genotype frequencies in most cases is not unduly complex.[9] In *Harvey*, the Supreme Court of New Jersey simply observed that "defendant's own expert . . . did not take issue with [the] databases or . . . mathematical formula" and invoked the legal principle that "the competency of a witness to testify as an expert is an issue remitted to the sound discretion of the trial court."[10] On this basis, it concluded that the admission of the biologists' testimony about DNA databases and the frequency of genetic markers in the population was not an abuse of discretion.[11]

---

"was also unfamiliar with publications in the area," including studies by "a leading expert in the field" who he thought was "a guy in a lab somewhere").

[2]E.g., *State v. Copeland*, 130 Wash. 2d 244, 922 P.2d 1304, 1318 (1996) (noting that defendant's population genetics expert, Laurence Mueller, "had published little in the field of human genetics, only one non-peer reviewed chapter in a general text, had two papers in the area rejected, was uninformed of the latest articles in the field, had misused a statistical model . . . , had no graduate students working under him, had not received any awards in his field in over ten years, had not received a research grant in about eight years, and made about $100,000 testifying as an expert in 1990–1991").

[3]E.g., *Com. v. Blasioli*, 454 Pa. Super. 207, 685 A.2d 151 (1996), aff'd, 552 Pa. 149, 713 A.2d 1117 (1998) (professor of ecology and evolutionary biology was said to be qualified, but "barely").

[4]*State v. Harvey*, 151 N.J. 117, 699 A.2d 596 (1997).

[5]*State v. Harvey*, 151 N.J. 117, 699 A.2d 596 (1997).

[6]*State v. Harvey*, 151 N.J. 117, 699 A.2d 596 (1997).

[7]*State v. Harvey*, 151 N.J. 117, 699 A.2d 596

(1997).

[8]See, e.g., *People v. Contreras*, 246 Ill. App. 3d 502, 186 Ill. Dec. 204, 615 N.E.2d 1261, 1265 (2d Dist. 1993) (noting that a "forensic geneticist" with a bachelor's degree in medical technology had "taken master's level courses in genetics and statistics").

[9]But see Committee on DNA Forensic Science: An Update, National Research Council, The Evaluation of Forensic DNA Evidence 133–134 (1996) (suggesting formulas of greater complexity when "the suspect and other possible sources of the sample belong to the same [ethnic] subgroup").

[10]*State v. Harvey*, 151 N.J. 117, 699 A.2d 596, 637 (1997).

[11]*State v. Harvey*, 151 N.J. 117, 699 A.2d 596, 637 (1997). Likewise, in *State v. Loftus*, 1997 SD 131, 573 N.W.2d 167 (S.D. 1997), a prosecution expert from a private company testified to "the possibility of a random match." The defendant argued that although the expert was qualified "in DNA matching techniques," he "was not qualified to give statistical probability DNA opinion because he is not a population geneticist." *State v. Loftus*, 1997 SD 131, 573 N.W.2d 167, 173 (S.D. 1997). The South Dakota Supreme Court correctly rejected the proposition that it takes a population geneticist to testify to genotype frequencies. It observed, somewhat cursorily, that "[t]here was

Likewise, in *Butler v. State*,[12] the Florida Supreme Court rejected an argument that a DNA analyst was unqualified to estimate the frequency of a DNA profile just because she did not participate in the creation of the database and was not trained in statistics.[13] The court distinguished its decision in *Murray v. State*.[14] "In *Murray*, the expert who testified had no knowledge about the database on which his population frequency calculations were based, repeatedly evaded questions about the procedures he used in his testing, and misled the court as to the scientific community's acceptance of PCR (Polymerase Chain Reaction) DNA testing at that time."[15] The Supreme Court ultimately found the expert was not qualified, and stated that "a sufficient knowledge of the database grounded in the study of authoritative sources" is necessary to testify to the statistical results.[16]

Applying this standard, the court deemed the expert in *Butler* qualified. The opinion, however, does little to demonstrate her familiarity with the statistical method she employed. It describes the witness as "a forensic scientist specializing in DNA serology."[17] Responding to the clearly fallacious argument that a witness must help compile the database to make use of it, the court explained that "[a]lthough she did not participate in the creation of the database, she was familiar with samples from which the database was created. Moreover, [she] stated the Florida Department of Law Enforcement in Tampa conducted validation studies of its own on the database she used. Although these studies were conducted before she began working there, her training consisted of conducting 'revalidations' of those databases."[18] The opinion states that her "testimony quantitatively helped the jury and the trial court understand the importance of a DNA match"[19] and that it was based on valid scientific principles,[20] but it never describes her training, experience, or knowledge with respect to the formula she must have used to provide this quantitative testimony. As such, *Butler*'s treatment of the witness's qualifications to offer a

---

ample evidence before the trial court that [the witness] possessed expert qualifications in the area of DNA, which would include statistical DNA probability analysis." 573 N.W.2d at 173. "Concerning [the expert's] qualifications to present statistical DNA evidence," the Supreme Court wrote only that the expert "testified that he has published several papers including one focusing on some of the 'statistical methods available for determining whether two DNA samples match.'" *State v. Loftus*, 1997 SD 131, 573 N.W.2d 167, 173 n.7 (S.D. 1997).

[12]*Butler v. State*, 842 So. 2d 817 (Fla. 2003).

[13]Cf. *Darling v. State*, 808 So. 2d 145, 158 (Fla. 2002) ("The fact that he was not, himself, a statistician is not a sound basis to exclude his expert testimony regarding the statistical results.").

[14]*Murray v. State*, 692 So. 2d 157 (Fla. 1997).

[15]*Murray v. State*, 692 So. 2d 157, 164 (Fla. 1997).

[16]*Murray v. State*, 692 So. 2d 157, 164 (Fla. 1997).

[17]*Butler v. State*, 842 So. 2d 817, 821 (Fla. 2003).

[18]*Butler v. State*, 842 So. 2d 817, 828 (Fla. 2003).

[19]*Butler v. State*, 842 So. 2d 817, 829 (Fla.

2003).

[20]The court wrote that the serologist "was qualified to testify as an expert because her testimony was based on proven scientific principles." *Butler v. State*, 842 So. 2d 817, 829 (Fla. 2003). See also *State v. Watts*, 172 N.C. App. 58, 616 S.E.2d 290, 295–96 (2005), writ denied, 361 N.C. 179, 641 S.E.2d 689 (2006) and review denied, 361 N.C. 179, 641 S.E.2d 690 (2006) (disposing of the objection that an FBI special agent was not necessarily qualified to opine on statistics simply because the agent "was properly tendered as an expert in the field of forensic DNA analysis. Indeed, the trial court established that [he] had a bachelor's degree in biochemistry, a master's and Ph.D. in microbiology, had undergone additional forensic DNA training through the North Carolina Bureau of Investigation, the Federal Bureau of Investigation, and the Armed Forces, and had conducted DNA analysis in over 400 cases."). But see *Gibson v. State*, 915 So. 2d 199 (Fla. Dist. Ct. App. 4th Dist. 2005) (although the analyst had taken courses in statistics and had testified that she was following the procedure in the 1996 NRC report, the court of appeals "remanded for a limited evidentiary hearing to determine whether the expert had sufficient knowledge of the authoritative sources to present the statistical evidence").

statistical analysis of the DNA results is disappointing.[21]

Of course, even an expert who is well qualified to testify in a particular field may have unusual views. However, the scientific and legal literature on the objections to DNA evidence is extensive.[22] By studying the scientific publications, or perhaps by appointing a special master or expert adviser to assimilate this material, a court can ascertain where a party's expert falls in the spectrum of scientific opinion. Furthermore, an expert appointed by the court under Federal Rule of Evidence 706 could testify about the scientific literature generally or even about the strengths or weaknesses of the particular arguments advanced by the parties.[23]

## II. SCIENTIFIC STATUS
*by David H. Kaye* & George F. Sensabaugh, Jr**

### § 2:21   Overview of variation in DNA and its detection

Deoxyribonucleic acid is a complex molecule that contains the "genetic code" of organisms as diverse as bacteria and humans.[1] This part describes the structure of DNA and how this molecule differs from person to person. It explains at a general level how DNA differences are detected. Finally, we indicate how it is shown that these differences permit individuals to be identified.

### § 2:22   Overview of variation in DNA and its detection—DNA, chromosomes, sex, and genes

DNA is made of subunits that include four *nucleotide bases*, whose names are abbreviated to A, T, G, and C.[1] The physical structure of DNA is described more fully in Appendix A of this chapter, but for general purposes it suffices to say that a DNA

---

[21]See also *State v. Watts*, 172 N.C. App. 58, 616 S.E.2d 290, 295 to 296 (2005), writ denied, 361 N.C. 179, 641 S.E.2d 689 (2006) and review denied, 361 N.C. 179, 641 S.E.2d 690 (2006) (disposing of the objection that an FBI special agent "was properly tendered as an expert in the field of forensic DNA analysis. Indeed, the trial court established that [he] had a bachelor's degree in biochemistry, a master's and Ph.D. in microbiology, had undergone additional forensic DNA training through the North Carolina Bureau of Investigation, the Federal Bureau of Investigation, and the Armed Forced, and had conducted DNA analysis in over 400 cases."). But see *Gibson v. State*, 915 So. 2d 199 (Fla. Dist. Ct. App. 4th Dist. 2005) (although the analyst had taken courses in statistics and had testified that she was following the procedure in the 1996 NRC report, the court of appeals "remanded for a limited evidentiary hearing to determine whether the expert had sufficient knowledge of the authoritative sources to present the statistical evidence.").

[22]See, e.g., Bruce S. Weir, A Bibliography for the Use of DNA in Human Identification, in Human Identification: The Use of DNA Markers 179–213 (Bruce S. Weir ed., 1995); Committee on DNA Forensic Science: An Update, National Research Council, The Evaluation of Forensic DNA Evidence 226–239 (1996) (list of references).

[23]Some courts have appointed experts to address general questions relating to DNA profiling. E.g., *U.S. v. Bonds*, 12 F.3d 540, 38 Fed. R. Evid. Serv. 688 (6th Cir. 1993); *U.S. v. Porter*, 1994 WL 742297 (D.C. Super. Ct. 1994) (mem.). Whether a court should appoint its own expert instead of an expert for the defense when there are more specific disputes is more controversial.

*David H. Kaye is Regents' Professor, Arizona State University College of Law, and Fellow, Center for the Study of Law, Science, and Technology. He was a member of the National Academy of Sciences' Committee on DNA Forensic Science: An Update and was reporter for the Legal Issues Working Group of the National Commission on the Future of DNA Evidence.

**George F. Sensabaugh, Jr., is Professor, School of Public Health, University of California at Berkeley. He was a member of the National Academy of Sciences' Committee on DNA Technology in Forensic Science and its subsequent Committee on DNA Forensic Science: An Update.

[Section 2:21]

[1]Some viruses use a related nucleic acid, RNA, instead of DNA to encode genetic information.

[Section 2:22]

[1]The full names are adenine, thymine, guanine, and cytosine.

molecule is like a long sequence of these four letters, where the chemical structure that corresponds to each letter is known as a *base pair*.

Most human DNA is tightly packed into structures known as *chromosomes*, which are located in the *nuclei* of most cells.[2] If the bases are like letters, then each chromosome is like a book written in this four-letter alphabet, and the nucleus is like a bookshelf in the interior of the cell. All the cells in one individual contain copies of the same set of books. This library, so to speak, is the individual's *genome*.[3]

In human beings, the process that produces billions of cells with the same genome starts with sex. Every sex cell (a sperm or ovum) contains 23 chromosomes. When a sperm and ovum combine, the resulting fertilized cell contains 23 pairs of chromosomes, or 46 in all. It is as if the father donates half of his collection of 46 books, and the mother donates a corresponding half of her collection. During pregnancy, the fertilized cell divides to form two cells, each of which has an identical copy of the 46 chromosomes. The two then divide to form four, the four form eight, and so on. As gestation proceeds, various cells specialize to form different tissues and organs. In this way, each human being has immensely many copies[4] of the original 23 pairs of chromosomes from the fertilized egg, one member of each pair having come from the mother and one from the father.

All told, the DNA in the 23 chromosomes contains over three billion letters (base pairs) of genetic "text."[5] About 99.9% is identical between any two individuals. This similarity is not really surprising—it accounts for the common features that make humans available and identifiable species. The remaining 0.1% is particular to an individual (identical twins excepted). This variation makes each person genetically unique.

A *gene* is a particular DNA sequence, usually from 1,000 to 10,000 base pairs long, that "codes" for an observable characteristic.[6] For example, a tiny part of the sequence that directs the production of the human group-specific complement protein (GC)[7] is

GCAAAATTGCCTGATGCCACACCCAAGGAACTGGCA[8]

This gene always is located at the same position, or *locus*, on chromosome number 4. As we have seen, most individuals have two copies of each gene at a given locus—one from the father and one from the mother.

A locus where almost all humans have the same DNA sequence is called *monomorphic* ("of one form"). A locus at which the DNA sequence varies among individuals is called *polymorphic* ("of many forms"). The alternative forms are called *alleles*. For example, the GC protein gene sequence has three common alleles that result from *single nucleotide polymorphisms* (SNPs, pronounced "snips")—substitutions in the base that occur at a given point.[9] In terms of the metaphor of DNA as text, the gene

---

[2]A few types of cells, such as red blood cells, do not contain nuclei.

[3]Originally, "genome" referred to the set of base pairs in an egg or sperm, but the term also is used to designate the ordered set in the fertilized cell.

[4]The number of cells in the human body has been estimated at more than $10^{15}$ (a million billion).

[5]If the base pairs were listed as letters in a series of books, one piled on top of the other, the pile would be as high as the Washington monument.

[6]The genetic code consists of "words" that are three nucleotides long and that determine the structure of the proteins that are manufactured in cells. See, e.g., Elaine Johnson Mange & Arthur P. Mange, Basic Human Genetics 107 (2d ed. 1999).

[7]This "GC" stands for "group complement," and not for the bases guanine and cytosine.

[8]The full GC gene is nearly 42,400 base pairs in length. The product of this gene is also known as vitamin D-binding protein. GC is one of the five loci included in the polymarker (PM) typing kit, which is widely used in forensic testing.

[9]The three alleles are designated Gc*1F, Gc*1S, and Gc*2, and the sequences at the variable site are shown in Figure 1.

is like an important paragraph in the book; a SNP is a change in a letter somewhere within that paragraph, and the two versions of the paragraph that result from this slight change are the alleles. An individual who inherits the same allele from both parents is called a *homozygote*.[10] An individual with distinct alleles is termed a *heterozygote*.[11]

Regions of DNA used for forensic analysis usually are not genes, but parts of the chromosome without a known function. The "non-coding" regions of DNA have been found to contain considerable sequence variation, which makes them particularly useful in distinguishing individuals. Although the terms "locus," "allele," "homozygous," and "heterozygous" were developed to describe genes, the nomenclature has been carried over to describe all DNA variation—coding and noncoding alike—for both types are inherited from mother and father in the same fashion.

### § 2:23    Overview of variation in DNA and its detection—Types of polymorphisms and methods of detection

By determining which alleles are present at strategically chosen loci, the forensic scientist ascertains the genetic profile, or *genotype*, of an individual. Genotyping does not require "reading" the full DNA sequence; indeed, direct sequencing is technically demanding and time-consuming.[1] Rather, most genetic typing focuses on identifying only those variations that define the alleles and does not attempt to "read out" each and every base as it appears.[2]

For instance, simple sequence variation, such as that for the GC locus, is conveniently detected using a *sequence-specific oligonucleotide* (SSO) *probe*. With GC typing, probes for the three common alleles (which we shall call $A_1$, $A_2$, and $A_3$) are attached to designated locations on a membrane. When DNA with a given allele (say, $A_1$) comes in contact with the probe for that allele, it sticks. To get a detectable quantity of DNA to stick, many copies of the variable sequence region of the GC gene in the DNA sample have to be made.[3] All this DNA then is added to the membrane. The DNA fragments with the allele $A_1$ in them stick to the spot with the $A_1$ probe. To permit these fragments to be seen, a chemical "label" that catalyses a color change at the spot where the DNA binds to its probe can be attached when the

---

**Figure 1**. The variable sequence region of the vitamin D-binding protein gene. The base substitutions that define the alleles are shown in bold.

Allele *2:

GCAAAATTGCCTGATGCCACACCCAAGGAACTGGCA

Allele *1F:

GCAAAATTGCCTGATGCCACACCCACGGAACTGGCA

Allele *1S:

GCAAAATTGCCTGAGGCCACACCCACGGAACTGGCA

See R.L. Reynolds & G.F. Sensabaugh, Use of the Polymerase Chain Reaction for Typing Gc Variants, in 3 Advances in Forensic Haemogenetics 158 (H.F. Polesky & W.R. Mayr eds. 1990); A. Braun et al., Molecular Analysis of the Gene for Human Vitamin-D-binding Protein (Group-specific Component): Allelic Differences of the Common GC Types, 89 Hum. Genetics 401 (1992). These are examples of *point mutations*.

[10] For example, someone with the Gc*2 allele on both number 4 chromosomes is homozygous at the GC locus. This homozygous GC genotype is designated as 2,2 (or simply 2).

[11] For example, someone with the Gc*2 allele on one chromosome and the Gc*1F allele on the other is heterozygous at the GC locus. This heterozygous genotype is designated as 2,1F.

**[Section 2:23]**

[1] However, automated machinery for direct sequencing has been developed and is used at major research centers engaged in the international endeavor to sequence the human genome and the genomes of other organisms. See R. Waterston & J.E. Sulston, The Human Genome Project: Reaching the Finish Line, 282 Science 53 (1998). Further improvements in methods for efficient sequencing have been made and continue to be made.

[2] For example, genetic typing at the GC locus focuses on the sequence region shown in Figure 1; the remainder of the 42,300 base pairs of the GC gene sequence is the same for almost all individuals and is ignored for genetic typing purposes.

[3] The polymerase chain reaction (PCR) is used to make many copies of the DNA that is to be typed. PCR is roughly analogous to copying and pasting a section of text with a wordprocessor. See Appendix 2A Part 4.

copies are made. A colored spot showing that the $A_1$ allele is present thus should appear on the membrane.[4]

Another category of polymorphism is characterized by the insertion of a *variable number of tandem repeats* (VNTR) at a locus.[5] The core unit of a VNTR is a particular short DNA sequence that is repeated many times end-to-end. This repetition gives rise to alleles with length differences; regions of DNA containing more repeats are larger than those containing fewer repeats. Genetic typing of polymorphic VNTR loci employs *electrophoresis*, a technique that separates DNA fragments based on size.[6]

The first polymorphic VNTRs to be used in genetic and forensic testing had core repeat sequences of 15–35 base pairs. Alleles at VNTR loci of this sort generally are too long to be measured precisely by electrophoretic methods—alleles differing in size by only a few repeat units may not be distinguished. Although this makes for complications in deciding whether two length measurements that are close together result from the same allele, these loci are quite powerful for the genetic differentiation of individuals, for they tend to have many alleles that occur relatively rarely in the population. At a locus with only 20 such alleles (and most loci typically have many more), there are 210 possible genotypes.[7] With five such loci, the number of possible genotypes is $210^5$, which is more than 400 billion. Thus, VNTRs are an extremely discriminating class of DNA markers.

Within a decade or so, the attention of the genetic typing community shifted to repetitive DNA characterized by short core repeats, two to seven base pairs in length. These noncoding DNA sequences are known as *short tandem repeats* (STRs).[8] Because STR alleles are much smaller than VNTR alleles, electrophoretic detection permits the exact number of base pairs in an STR to be determined, allowing alleles to be defined as discrete entities. Figure 2 illustrates the nature of allelic variation at a polymorphic STR locus. The first allele has nine tandem repeats, the second has ten, and the third has eleven.[9]

**Figure 2**.

Three Alleles of an STR with the Core Sequence ATTT:

ATTTATTTATTTATTTATTTATTTATTTATTTATTT
ATTTATTTATTTATTTATTTATTTATTTATTTATTT
ATTTATTTATTTATTTATTTATTTATTTATTTATTTATTT

Although there are fewer alleles per locus for STRs than for VNTRs, there are many STRs, and they can be analyzed simultaneously.[10] As more STR loci are included, STR testing becomes more revealing than VNTR profiling at four or five loci.[11]

Full DNA sequencing is employed at present only for mitochondrial DNA

---

[4]This approach can be miniaturized and automated with hybridization chip technology. See the glossary ("chip") at the end of this chapter.

[5]VNTR polymorphisms also are referred to as *minisatellites*.

[6]We describe one form of electrophoresis often used with VNTR loci §§ 2:27 to 2:29.

[7]There are 20 homozygous genotypes and another (20 × 19)/2 = 190 heterozygous ones.

[8]They also are known as *microsatellites*. A valuable reference work that focuses on the STRs now used in forensic typing is John M. Butler, Forensic DNA Typing: Biology and Technology

Behind STR Markers (2001).

[9]To conserve space, the figure uses alleles that are unrealistically short. A typical STR is in the range of 50-350 base pairs in length.

[10]The procedures for simultaneous detection are known as *multiplex* methods. See the Glossary ("capillary electrophoresis," "chip") at the end of this chapter. *Mass spectroscopy* also can be applied to detect STR fragments.

[11]Usually, there are between 7 and 15 STR alleles per locus. Thirteen loci that have 10 STR alleles each can give rise to $55^{13}$, or 42 billion trillion possible genotypes.

(mtDNA).[12] *Mitochondria* are small structures found inside the cell. In these organelles, certain molecules are broken down to supply energy. Mitochondria have a small genome that bears no relation to the chromosomal genome in the cell nucleus.[13] Mitochondrial DNA has three features that make it useful for forensic DNA testing. First, the typical cell, which has but one nucleus, contains hundreds of identical mitochondria.[14] Hence, for every copy of chromosomal DNA, there are hundreds of copies of mitochondrial DNA. This means that it is possible to detect mtDNA in samples containing too little nuclear DNA for conventional typing.[15] Second, the mtDNA contains a sequence region of about a thousand base pairs that varies greatly among individuals. Finally, mitochondria are inherited mother to child,[16] so that siblings, maternal half-siblings, and others related through maternal lineage possess the same mtDNA sequence.[17] This last feature makes mtDNA particularly useful for associating persons related through their maternal lineage— associating skeletal remains to a family, for example.[18]

Just as genetic variation in mtDNA can be used to track maternal lineages, genetic variations on the *Y chromosome* can be used to trace paternal lineages. Y chromosomes, which contain genes that result in development as a male rather than a female, are found only in males and are inherited father to son. Markers on this chromosome include STRs and SNPs,[19] and they have been used in cases involving semen evidence.[20]

In sum, DNA contains the genetic information of an organism. In humans, most of the DNA is found in the cell nucleus, where it is organized into separate chromosomes. Each chromosome is like a book, and each cell has the same library of books of various sizes and shapes. There are two copies of each book of a particular size and shape, one that came from the father, the other from the mother. Thus, there are two copies of the book entitled "Chromosome One," two copies of "Chromosome Two," and so on. Genes are the most meaningful paragraphs in the books, and there are differences (polymorphisms) in the spelling of certain words in the

---

[12]Mitochondrial sequence variations also can be detected with other procedures. See Reynolds et al., Detection of Sequence Variation in the HVII Region of the Human Mitochondrial Genome in 689 Individuals Using Immobilized Sequence-Specific Oligonucleotide Probes, 45 J. Forensic Sci. 1210 (2000); Stoneking et al., Population Variation of Human mtDNA Control Region Sequences Detected by Enzymatic Amplification and Sequence-specific Oligonucleotide Probes, 48 Am. J. Hum. Genetics 370 (1991).

[13]In contrast to the haploid nuclear genome of over three billion base pairs, the mitochondrial genome is a circular molecule 16,569 base pairs long.

[14]There are between 75 to 1,000 or so mitochondria per cell.

[15]Even so, because the mitochondrial genome is so much shorter than the nuclear genome, it is a tiny fraction of the total mass of DNA in a cell.

[16]Although sperm have mitochondria, these are not passed to the ovum at fertilization. Thus the only mitochondria present in the newly fertilized cell originate from the mother.

[17]Evolutionary studies suggest an average mutation rate for the mtDNA control region of one nucleotide difference every 300 generations, or one difference every 6,000 years. Consequently,

one would not expect to see many examples of nucleotide differences between maternal relatives. On the other hand, differences in the bases at a specific sequence position among the copies of the mtDNA within an individual have been seen. This *heteroplasmy*, which is more common in hair than other tissues, counsels against declaring an exclusion on the basis of a single base pair difference between two samples.

[18]See, e.g., Peter Gill et al., Identification of the Remains of the Romanov Family by DNA Analysis, 6 Nature Genetics 130 (1994).

[19]See, e.g., Hammer et al., The Geographic Distribution of Human Y Chromosome Variation, 145 Genetics 787 (1997). The Y chromosome is used in evolutionary studies along with mtDNA to learn about human migration patterns. Hammer & Zegura, The Role of the Y Chromosome in Human Evolutionary Studies, 5 Evolutionary Anthropology 116 (1996). The various markers are inherited as a single package (known as a *haplotype*).

[20]They also were used in a family study to ascertain whether President Thomas Jefferson fathered a child of his slave, Sally Hemmings. See E.A. Foster et al., Jefferson Fathered Slave's Last Child, 396 Nature 27 (1998); Eliot Marshall, Which Jefferson Was the Father?, 283 Science 153 (1999).

paragraphs of different copies of each book. The different versions of the same paragraph are the alleles. Some alleles result from the substitution of one letter for another. These are SNPs. Others come about from the insertion or deletion of single letters, and still others represent a kind of stuttering repetition of a string of extra letters. These are the VNTRs and STRs. In addition to the 23 pairs of books in the cell nucleus, another page or so of text resides in each of the mitochondria, the power plants of the cell.

The methods of molecular biology permit scientists to determine which alleles are present. Sections 2:24 to 2:26 discuss the procedures that can distinguish among all the known alleles at certain loci. Sections 2:27 to 2:29 deal with the "RFLP" procedures that measure the lengths of DNA fragments at a scale that is not fine enough to resolve all the possible alleles.

### § 2:24 DNA profiling with discrete alleles

Simple sequence variations and STRs occur within relatively short fragments of DNA. These polymorphisms can be analyzed with so-called PCR-based tests. The three steps of PCR-based typing are: (1) DNA extraction; (2) amplification; and (3) detection of genetic type using a method appropriate to the polymorphism. This section discusses the scientific and technological foundations of these three steps and the basis for believing that the DNA characteristics identified in the laboratory can help establish who contributed the potentially incriminating DNA.[1]

### § 2:25 DNA profiling with discrete alleles—DNA extraction and amplification

DNA usually can be found in biological materials such as blood, bone, saliva, hair, semen, and urine.[1] A combination of routine chemical and physical methods permit DNA to be extracted from cell nuclei and isolated from the other chemicals in a sample.[2] Thus, the premise that DNA is present in many biological samples and can be removed for further analysis is firmly established.[3]

Just as the scientific foundations of DNA extraction are clear, the procedures for amplifying DNA sequences within the extracted DNA are well established. The first National Academy of Sciences committee on forensic DNA typing described the amplification step as "simple . . . analogous to the process by which cells replicate their DNA."[4] Details of this process, which can make millions of copies of a single DNA fragment, are given in Appendix A of this chapter.

---

[Section 2:24]

[1]The problem of drawing an inference about the source of the evidence DNA, which is common to all forms of DNA profiling, is taken up in §§ 2:40 to 2:52.

[Section 2:25]

[1]See, e.g., Committee on DNA Technology in Forensic Science, National Research Council, DNA Technology in Forensic Science 28 (1992) (Table 1.1).

[2]See, e.g., Comey et al., DNA Extraction Strategies for Amplified Fragment Length Polymorphism Analysis, 39 J. Forensic Sci. 1254 (1994); Akane et al., Purification of Forensic Specimens for the Polymerase Chain Reaction (PCR) Analysis, 38 J. Forensic Sci. 691 (1993).

[3]See, e.g., Committee on DNA Technology in Forensic Science, National Research Council, DNA Technology in Forensic Science 149 (1992) (recommending judicial notice of the proposition that "DNA polymorphisms can, in principle, provide a reliable method for comparing samples," "although the actual discriminatory power of any particular DNA test will depend on the sites of DNA variation examined"); Committee on DNA Forensic Science: An Update, National Research Council, The Evaluation of Forensic DNA Evidence 9 (1996) ("DNA typing, with its extremely high power to differentiate one human being from another, is based on a large body of scientific principles and techniques that are universally accepted.").

[4]Committee on DNA Technology in Forensic Science, National Research Council, DNA Technology in Forensic Science 40 (1992). The second committee used similar language, reporting that "[t]he PCR process is relatively simple and easily carried out in the laboratory." Committee on DNA

For amplification to work properly and yield copies of only the desired sequence, however, care must be taken to achieve the appropriate biochemical conditions and to avoid excessive contamination of the sample.[5] A laboratory should be able to demonstrate that it can faithfully amplify targeted sequences with the equipment and reagents that it uses[6] and that it has taken suitable precautions to avoid or detect handling or carryover contamination.[7]

## § 2:26    DNA profiling with discrete alleles—DNA analysis

To determine whether the DNA sample associated with a crime could have come from a suspect, the genetic types as determined by analysis of the DNA amplified from the crime-scene sample are compared to the genetic types as determined for the suspect. For example, Figure 3 shows the results of STR typing at four loci in a sexual assault case.[1]

---

Forensic Science: An Update, National Research Council, The Evaluation of Forensic DNA Evidence 70 (1996). But see 1992 Report, at 63 ("Although the basic exponential amplification procedure is well understood, many technical details are not, including why some primer pairs amplify much better than others, why some loci cause systematically unfaithful amplification, and why some assays are much more sensitive to variations in conditions."). For these reasons, PCR-based procedures are validated by experiment.

[5]See Committee on DNA Technology in Forensic Science, National Research Council, DNA Technology in Forensic Science at 63–67 (1992); Committee on DNA Forensic Science: An Update, National Research Council, The Evalua-

tion of Forensic DNA Evidence at 71 (1996).

[6]See Committee on DNA Technology in Forensic Science, National Research Council, DNA Technology in Forensic Science 63–64 (1992).

[7]Carryover occurs when the DNA product of a previous amplification contaminates samples or reaction solutions. See Committee on DNA Technology in Forensic Science, National Research Council, DNA Technology in Forensic Science 66 (1992).

**[Section 2:26]**

[1]The initials CTTA refer to these loci, which are known as CPO, TPO, THO, and Amelogenin.

**Figure 3**
**Results of STR Typing at Four Loci in Sexual Assault Case**

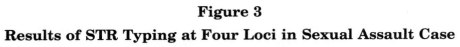
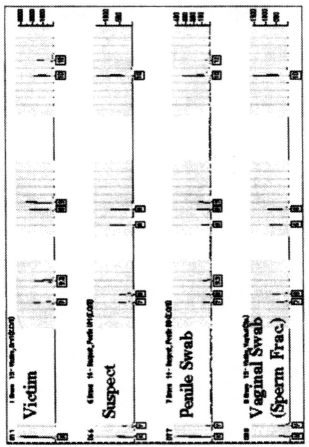

The peaks result from DNA fragments of different sizes.[2] The bottom row shows the profile of sperm DNA isolated from a vaginal swab. These sperm have two alleles at the first locus (indicating that both X and Y chromosomes are present),[3] two alleles at the second locus (consisting of seven and eight repeat units), two at the third locus (a six and an eight), and one (a 10 on each chromosome) at the fourth.[4] The same profile also appears in the DNA taken from the suspect. DNA from a penile swab from the suspect is consistent with a mixture of DNA from the victim and the suspect.

Regardless of the kind of genetic system used for typing—STRs, Amp-FLPs,[5] SNPs, or still other polymorphisms[6]—some general principles and questions can be applied to each system that is offered for courtroom use. As a beginning, the nature of the polymorphism should be well characterized. Is it a simple sequence polymorphism or a fragment length polymorphism? This information should be in the published literature or in archival genome databanks.[7]

Second, the published scientific literature also can be consulted to verify claims that a particular method of analysis can produce accurate profiles under various conditions.[8] Although such "validation studies" have been conducted for all the discrete-allele systems ordinarily used in forensic work, determining the point at which the empirical validation of a particular system is sufficiently convincing to pass scientific muster may well require expert assistance.

Finally, the population genetics of the marker should be characterized. As new marker systems are discovered, researchers typically analyze convenient collections of DNA samples from various human populations[9] and publish studies of the relative frequencies of each allele in these population samples. These database studies give a measure of the extent of genetic variability at the polymorphic locus in the various populations, and thus of the potential probative power of the marker for distinguishing between individuals.

At this point, the existence of PCR-based procedures that can ascertain genotypes accurately cannot be doubted.[10] Of course, the fact that scientists have shown that it is possible to extract DNA, to amplify it, and to analyze it in ways that bear on the

---

[2]The height of (more, precisely, the area under) each peak is related to the amount of DNA in the gel.

[3]The X-Y typing at the first locus is simply used to verify the sex of the source of the DNA. XY is male, and XX is female. That these markers show that the victim is female and the suspect male helps demonstrate that a valid result has been obtained.

[4]Although each sperm cell contains only one set of chromosomes, a collection of many sperm cells from the same individual contains both sets of chromosomes.

[5]"Amp-FLP" is short for "Amplified Fragment Length Polymorphism." The DNA fragment is produced by amplifying a longish sequence with a PCR primer. The longer Amp-FLPs, such as DS180, overlap the shorter VNTRs. In time, PCR methods will be capable of generating longer Amp-FLPs.

[6]See §§ 2:21 to 2:23; Appendix 2 (Table A-1).

[7]Primary data regarding gene sequence variation is increasingly being archived in publically accessible computer databanks, such as GenBank, rather than in the print literature. See

Victor A. McKusick, The Human Genome Project: Plans, Status, and Applications in Biology and Medicine, in Gene Mapping: Using Law and Ethics as Guides 18, 35 (George J. Annas & Sherman Elias eds.1992). This trend is driven by an explosion of new data coupled with the fact that most of the detected variation has no known biological significance and hence is not particularly noteworthy.

[8]Cf. Committee on DNA Technology in Forensic Science, National Research Council, DNA Technology in Forensic Science 72 (1992) ("Empirical validation of a DNA typing procedure must be published in appropriate scientific journals.").

[9]The samples come from diverse sources, such as blood banks, law enforcement personnel, paternity cases, and criminal cases. Reliable inferences probably can be drawn from these samples.

[10]See, e.g., *U.S. v. Shea*, 159 F.3d 37, 50 Fed. R. Evid. Serv. 516 (1st Cir. 1998) (DQA, Polymarker, D1S80); *U.S. v. Lowe*, 145 F.3d 45, 49 Fed. R. Evid. Serv. 687 (1st Cir. 1998) (DQA, Polymarker, D1S80); *U.S. v. Beasley*, 102 F.3d 1440, 1448, 46 Fed. R. Evid. Serv. 1 (8th Cir. 1996) (DQA, Polymarker); *U.S. v. Hicks*, 103 F.3d 837, 46 Fed. R. Evid. Serv. 15 (9th Cir. 1996) (DQA);

issue of identity does not mean that a particular laboratory has adopted a suitable protocol and is proficient in following it. These laboratory-specific issues are considered in §§ 2:34 to 2:39.

## § 2:27  VNTR profiling

VNTR profiling, described in general terms in §§ 2:21 to 2:23, was the first widely used method of forensic DNA testing. Consequently, its underlying principles, its acceptance within the scientific community, and its scientific soundness have been discussed in a great many opinions.[1] Because so much has been written on VNTR profiling, and because the method is being supplanted by more efficient procedures involving discrete allele systems,[2] only the basic steps of the procedure will be outlined here:

1. Like profiling by means of discrete allele systems, VNTR profiling begins with the extraction of DNA from a crime-scene sample. (Because this DNA is not amplified, however, larger quantities of higher quality DNA[3] are required.)

2. The extracted DNA is "digested" by a *restriction enzyme* that recognizes a particular, very short sequence; the enzyme cuts the DNA at these *restriction sites*. When a VNTR falls between two restriction sites, the resulting DNA fragments will vary in size depending on the number of core repeat units in the VNTR region.[4] (These VNTRs are thus referred to as a *restriction fragment length polymorphism*, or RFLP.)

3. The digested DNA fragments are then separated according to size by *gel electrophoresis*. The digest sample is placed in a well at the end of a lane in an agarose gel, which is a gelatin-like material solidified in a slab. Digested DNA from the suspect is placed in another well on the same gel. Typically, control specimens of DNA fragments of known size, and, where appropriate, DNA specimens obtained from a victim, are run on the same gel. Mild electric current applied to the gel slowly separates the fragments in each lane by length, as shorter fragments travel farther in a fixed time than longer, heavier fragments.

4. The resulting array of fragments is transferred for manageability to a sheet of nylon by a process known as Southern blotting.[5]

5. The restriction fragments representing a particular polymorphic locus are "tagged" on the membrane using a sequence-specific probe labeled with a ra-

---

*U.S. v. Gaines*, 979 F. Supp. 1429, 48 Fed. R. Evid. Serv. 419 (S.D. Fla. 1997) (DQA, Polymarker, D1S80); *State v. Hill*, 257 Kan. 774, 895 P.2d 1238 (1995) (DQA); *Com. v. Rosier*, 425 Mass. 807, 685 N.E.2d 739 (1997) (STRs); *State v. Harvey*, 151 N.J. 117, 699 A.2d 596 (1997) (DQA, Polymarker); *State v. Lyons*, 324 Or. 256, 924 P.2d 802 (1996) (DQA); *State v. Moeller*, 1996 SD 60, 548 N.W.2d 465 (S.D. 1996) (DQA); *State v. Begley*, 956 S.W.2d 471 (Tenn. 1997) (DQA); *State v. Russell*, 125 Wash. 2d 24, 882 P.2d 747, 768 (1994) (DQA).

**[Section 2:27]**

[1]See Committee on DNA Forensic Science: An Update, National Research Council, The Evaluation of Forensic DNA Evidence at 205–211 (1996) (listing leading cases and status as of 1995, by jurisdiction). The first reported appellate opinion is *Andrews v. State*, 533 So. 2d 841 (Fla. Dist. Ct. App. 5th Dist. 1988).

[2]§§ 2:24 to 2:26.

[3]"Quality" refers to the extent to which the original, very long strands of DNA are intact. When DNA degrades, it forms shorter fragments. RFLP testing requires fragments that are on the order of at least 20,000–30,000 base pairs long.

[4]§§ 2:21 to 2:60.

[5]This procedure is named after its inventor, Edwin Southern. Either before or during this transfer, the DNA is *denatured* ("unzipped") by alkali treatment, separating each double helix (see infra Appendix, Figure A-1) into two single strands. The weak bonds that connect the two members of a base pair are easily broken by heat or chemical treatment. The bonds that hold a base to the backbone and keep the backbone intact are much stronger. Thus, the double-stranded helix separates neatly into two single strands, with one base at each position.

dioactive or chemical tag.[6]

6. The position of the specifically bound probe tag is made visible, either by autoradiography (for radioactive labels) or by a chemical reaction (for chemical labels). For autoradiography, the washed nylon membrane is placed between two sheets of photographic film. Over time, the radioactive probe material exposes the film where the biological probe has hybridized with the DNA fragments.[7] The result is an *autoradiograph*, or an autorad, a visual pattern of bands representing specific DNA fragments. An autorad that shows two bands in a single lane indicates that the individual who is the source of the DNA is a heterozygote at that locus. If the autorad shows only one band, the person may be homozygous for that allele (that is, each parent contributed the same allele), or the second band may be present but invisible for technical reasons. The band pattern defines the person's genotype at the locus associated with the probe.

Once an appropriately exposed autorad is obtained, the probe is stripped from the membrane, and the process is repeated with a separate probe for each locus tested. Three to five probes are typically used, the number depending in part on the amount of testable DNA recovered from the crime-scene sample. The result is a set of autorads, each of which shows the results of one probe.[8] If the crime-scene and suspect samples yield bands that are closely aligned on each autorad, the VNTR profiles[9] from the two samples are considered to match.[10]

## § 2:28   VNTR profiling—Validity of the underlying scientific theory

The basic theory underlying VNTR profiling is textbook knowledge. The molecular structure of DNA,[1] the presence of highly polymorphic VNTR loci,[2] and the existence of methods to produce VNTR fragments and measure their lengths are not in doubt.[3]

---

[6]This locus-specific probe is a single strand of DNA that binds to its complementary sequence of denatured DNA in the sample. See §§ 2:24 to 2:26. The DNA locus identified by a given probe is found by experimentation, and individual probes often are patented by their developers. Different laboratories may use different probes (i.e., they may test for alleles at different loci). Where different probes (or different restriction enzymes) are used, test results are not comparable.

[7]One film per probe is checked during the process to see whether the process is complete. Because this can weaken the image, the other film is left undisturbed, and it is used in comparing the positions of the bands.

[8]For a photograph of an autorad, see, for example, Committee on DNA Forensic Science: An Update, National Research Council, The Evaluation of Forensic DNA Evidence 9 (1996).

[9]Each autorad reveals a single-locus genotype. The collections of single-locus profiles, one for each single-locus probe, sometimes is called a multi-locus VNTR profile. A "multi-locus probe," however, is a single probe that produces bands on a single autorad by hybridizing with VNTRs from many loci at the same time. It is, in other words, like a cocktail of single-locus probes. Because it is more difficult to interpret autoradiographs from multi-locus probes, these probes have not been used in criminal cases in the United States.

[10]Issues that arise in interpreting autoradiographs and declaring matches are considered §§ 2:40 to 2:52.

**[Section 2:28]**

[1]§§ 2:21 to 2:23.

[2]Studies of the population genetics of VNTR loci are reviewed in Committee on DNA Forensic Science: An Update, National Research Council, The Evaluation of Forensic DNA Evidence 9 (1996). See also §§ 2:40 to 2:52.

[3]See, e.g., Committee on DNA Technology in Forensic Science, National Research Council, DNA Technology in Forensic Science 149 (1992) (recommending judicial notice of the proposition that "DNA polymorphisms can, in principle, provide a reliable method for comparing samples," but cautioning that "the actual discriminatory power of any particular DNA test will depend on the sites of DNA variation examined"); Committee on DNA Forensic Science: An Update, National Research Council, The Evaluation of Forensic DNA Evidence 9 (1996) ("DNA typing, with its extremely high power to differentiate one human being from another, is based on a large body of scientific principles and techniques that are universally accepted."); Committee on DNA Forensic Science: An Update, National Research Council, The Evaluation of Forensic DNA Evidence 36 (1996) ("Methods of DNA profiling are firmly grounded in molecular technology. When profiling

Indeed, some courts have taken judicial notice of these scientific facts.[4] In short, the ability to discriminate between human DNA samples using a relatively small number of VNTR loci is widely accepted.

## § 2:29 VNTR profiling—Validity and reliability of the laboratory techniques

The basic laboratory procedures for VNTR analysis have been used in other settings for many years: "The complete process—DNA digestion, electrophoresis, membrane transfer, and hybridization—was developed by Edwin Southern in 1975 . . . These procedures are routinely used in molecular biology, biochemistry, genetics, and clinical DNA diagnosis . . . ."[1] Thus, "no scientific doubt exists that [these technologies] accurately detect genetic differences."[2]

Before concluding that a particular enzyme-probe combination produces accurate profiles as applied to crime-scene samples at a particular laboratory, however, courts may wish to consider studies concerning the effects of environmental conditions and contaminants on VNTR profiling as well as the laboratory's general experience and proficiency with these probes. And the nature of the sample and other considerations in a particular case can affect the certainty of the profiling. The next two sections outline the type of inquiry that can help assess the accuracy of a profile in a specific case.

## § 2:30 Sample quantity and quality

The primary determinant of whether DNA typing can be done on any particular sample is: (1) the quantity of DNA present in the sample; and (2) the extent to which it is degraded. Generally speaking, if a sufficient quantity of reasonable quality DNA can be extracted from a crime-scene sample, no matter what the nature of the sample, DNA typing can be done without problem. Thus, DNA typing has been performed successfully on old blood stains, semen stains, vaginal swabs, hair, bone, bite marks, cigarette butts, urine, and fecal material. The next several subsections discuss what constitutes sufficient quantity and reasonable quality in the contexts of PCR-based genetic typing and VNTR analysis by Southern blotting. Complica-

---

is done with appropriate care, the results are highly reproducible.").

[4]See, e.g., State v. Fleming, 1997 ME 158, 698 A.2d 503, 507 (Me. 1997) (taking judicial notice that "the overall theory and techniques of DNA profiling [are] scientifically reliable if conducted in accordance with appropriate laboratory standards and controls"); State v. Davis, 814 S.W.2d 593, 602 (Mo. 1991); People v. Castro, 144 Misc. 2d 956, 545 N.Y.S.2d 985, 987 (Sup 1989); cases cited, Committee on DNA Forensic Science: An Update, National Research Council, The Evaluation of Forensic DNA Evidence 172 n. 15 (1996).

**[Section 2:29]**

[1]Committee on DNA Technology in Forensic Science, National Research Council, DNA Technology in Forensic Science 38 (1992).

[2]Office of Technology Assessment, Genetic Witness: Forensic Uses of DNA Tests 59 (1990). The 1992 NRC report therefore recommends that courts take judicial notice that:

[t]he current laboratory procedure for detecting DNA variation (specifically, single-locus probes analyzed on Southern blots without evidence of band shifting) is fundamentally sound, although the validity of any particular implementation of the basic procedure will depend on proper characterization of the reproducibility of the system (e.g., measurement variation) and the inclusion of all necessary scientific controls.

Committee on DNA Technology in Forensic Science, National Research Council, DNA Technology in Forensic Science at 149 (1992). The 1996 report reiterates the conclusion that "[t]he techniques of DNA typing [including RFLP analysis] are fully recognized by the scientific community." Committee on DNA Forensic Science: An Update, National Research Council, The Evaluation of Forensic DNA Evidence 50 (1996). It insists that "[t]he state of the profiling technology and the methods for estimating frequencies and related statistics have progressed to the point where the admissibility of properly collected and analyzed DNA data should not be in doubt." Committee on DNA Forensic Science: An Update, National Research Council, The Evaluation of Forensic DNA Evidence 36 (1996).

tions due to contaminants and inhibitors also are discussed. Finally, the question of whether the sample contains DNA from two or more contributors is considered.

### § 2:31  Sample quantity and quality—Did the sample contain enough DNA?

The amount of DNA in a cell varies from organism to organism. The DNA in the chromosomes of a human cell, for example, is about two thousand times greater than that in a typical bacterium.[1] Within an organism, however, DNA content is constant from cell to cell. Thus, a human hair root cell contains the same amount of DNA as a white cell in blood or a buccal cell in saliva.[2] Amounts of DNA present in some typical kinds of samples are indicated in Table A-2 of Appendix A of this chapter. These vary from a trillionth or so of a gram for a hair shaft to several millionths of a gram for a post-coital vaginal swab. RFLP typing requires a much larger sample of DNA than PCR-based typing. As a practical matter, RFLP analysis requires a minimum of about 50 billionths of a gram of relatively non-degraded DNA,[3] while most PCR test protocols recommend samples on the order of one to five billionths of a gram for optimum yields.[4] Thus, PCR tests can be applied to samples containing 10 to 500-fold less nuclear DNA than that required for RFLP tests.[5] Moreover, mitochondrial DNA analysis works reliably with DNA from even fewer cells. As noted in §§ 2:21 to 2:60, cells contain only one nucleus, but hundreds of mitochondria. Consequently, even though there rarely is sufficient DNA in a hair shaft to allow testing with nuclear DNA markers, the mitochondrial DNA often can be analyzed.[6]

These sample-size requirements help determine the approach to be taken for a DNA typing analysis. Samples which, from experience, are expected to contain at least 50 to 100 billionths of a gram of DNA typically are subjected to a formal DNA extraction followed by characterization of the DNA for quantity and quality. This characterization typically involves gel electrophoresis of a small portion of the extracted DNA. This test, however, does not distinguish human from non-human DNA. Since the success of DNA typing tests depends on the amount of human DNA

---

**[Section 2:31]**

[1] A human egg or sperm cell contains half as much DNA; hence, the haploid human genome is about one thousand larger than the typical bacterial genome.

[2] A human cell contains about six picograms of DNA. (A picogram (pg) is one trillionth (1/1,000,000,000,000) of a gram.) Sperm cells constitute a special case, for they contain half a genetic complement (that which the father passes along to an offspring) and so contain half as much DNA (about 3 pg). The 3 pg of DNA varies from sperm cell to sperm cell because each such cell has a randomly drawn half of the man's chromosomes. The DNA in a semen sample contains many of these cells; being a mixture of the many combinations, it contains all the man's alleles.

[3] RFLP analysis has been performed successfully on smaller amounts of DNA but at a cost of longer autoradiograph exposure times. From the standpoint of the reliability of the typing, what is important is the strength of the banding pattern on the autoradiograph or lumigraph. Threshold amounts of DNA may result in weak bands, and some bands could be missed because they are too weak to be observed.

[4] Although the polymerase chain reaction can amplify DNA from the nucleus of a single cell, chance effects may result in one allele being amplified much more than another. To avoid preferential amplification, a lower limit of about 10 to 15 cells' worth of DNA has been determined to give balanced amplification. PCR tests for nuclear genes are designed to yield no detectable product for samples containing less than about 20 cell equivalents (100–200 pg) of DNA. This result is achieved by limiting the number of amplification cycles.

[5] The great sensitivity of PCR for the detection of DNA, even under these "safe" conditions, is illustrated by the successful genetic typing of DNA extracted from fingerprints. Roland A.H. Van Oorschot & M.K. Jones, DNA Fingerprints from Fingerprints, 387 Nature 767 (1997).

[6] E.g., M.R. Wilson et al., Extraction, PCR Amplification, and Sequencing of Mitochondrial DNA from Human Hair Shafts, 18 Biotechniques 662 (1995). Of course, mitochondrial DNA analysis can be done with other sources of mtDNA.

present, it may be desirable to test for the amount of human DNA in the extract.[7] For samples that typically contain small amounts of DNA, the risk of DNA loss during extraction may dictate the use of a different extraction procedure.[8]

Whether a particular sample contains enough human DNA to allow typing cannot always be predicted in advance. The best strategy is to try; if a result is obtained, and if the controls (small samples of known DNA) have behaved properly, then the sample had enough DNA.

### § 2:32 Sample quantity and quality—Was the sample of sufficient quality?

The primary determinant of DNA quality for forensic analysis is the extent to which the long DNA molecules are intact. Within the cell nucleus, each molecule of DNA extends for millions of base pairs. Outside the cell, DNA spontaneously degrades into smaller fragments at a rate that depends on temperature, exposure to oxygen, and, most importantly, the presence of water.[1] In dry biological samples, protected from air, and not exposed to temperature extremes, DNA degrades very slowly. In fact, the relative stability of DNA has made it possible to extract usable DNA from samples hundreds to thousands of years old.[2]

RFLP analysis requires relatively non-degraded DNA, and testing DNA for degradation is a routine part of the protocol for VNTR analysis. In RFLP testing, a restriction enzyme cuts long sequences of DNA into smaller fragments. If the DNA is randomly fragmented into very short pieces to begin with, electrophoresis and Southern blotting will produce a smear of fragments rather than a set of well-separated bands.[3]

In contrast, PCR-based tests are relatively insensitive to degradation. Testing has proved effective with old and badly degraded material such as the remains of the Tsar Nicholas family (buried in 1918, recovered in 1991)[4] and the Tyrolean Ice Man

---

[7]This test entails measuring the amount of a human-specific DNA probe that binds to the DNA in the extract. This test is particularly important in cases where the sample extract contains a mixture of human and microbial DNA. Vaginal swabs, for example, are expected to contain microbial DNA from the vaginal flora as well as human DNA from the female and sperm donor. Similarly, samples that have been damp for extended periods of time often contain significant microbial contamination; indeed, in some cases, little or no human DNA can be detected even though the extract contains significant amounts of DNA.

[8]Boiling a sample for a few minutes releases DNA, and this DNA is used directly for PCR without first characterizing the DNA. The boiling step usually is conducted in the presence of a resin that absorbs inhibitors of PCR.

[Section 2:32]

[1]Other forms of chemical alteration to DNA are well studied, both for their intrinsic interest and because chemical changes in DNA are a contributing factor in the development of cancers in living cells. Most chemical modification has little effect on RFLP analysis. Some forms of DNA modification, such as that produced by exposure to ultraviolet radiation, inhibit the amplification step in PCR-based tests, while other chemical

modifications appear to have no effect. George F. Sensabaugh & C. von Beroldingen, The Polymerase Chain Reaction: Application to the Analysis of Biological Evidence, in Forensic DNA Technology (M.A. Farley & J.J. Harrington eds., 1991).

[2]This has resulted in a specialized field of inquiry dubbed "ancient DNA." Ancient DNA: Recovery and Analysis of Genetic Material from Paleontological, Archaeological, Museum, Medical, and Forensic Specimens (B. Hermann & S. Hummel eds., 1994); Svante Paaobo, Ancient DNA: Extraction, Characterization, Molecular Cloning, and Enzymatic Amplification, 86 Proc. Nat'l Acad. Sci. USA 1939 (1989).

[3]Practically speaking, RFLP analysis can yield interpretable results if the bulk of the DNA in a sample exceeds 20,000–30,000 base pairs in length. Partial degradation of the DNA can result in the weakening or loss of the signal from large restriction fragments. This effect is usually evident from the appearance of the restriction fragment banding pattern. Another indication of degradation is smearing in the background of the banding pattern. If there is evidence that degradation has affected the banding pattern, the statistical interpretation of a match should account for the possibility that some allelic bands might not have been detected.

[4]Peter Gill et al., Identification of the Remains of the Romanov Family by DNA Analy-

(frozen for some 5,000 years).[5] The extent to which degradation affects a PCR-based test depends on the size of the DNA segment to be amplified. For example, in a sample in which the bulk of the DNA has been degraded to fragments well under 1,000 base pairs in length, it may be possible to amplify a 100 base-pair sequence, but not a 1,000 base-pair target. Consequently, the shorter alleles may be detected in a highly degraded sample, but the larger ones may be missed.[6] As with RFLP analysis, this possibility would have to be considered in the statistical interpretation of the result.

Allelic dropout of this sort does not seem to be a problem for STR loci, presumably because the size differences between alleles at a locus are so small (typically no more than 50 base pairs). If there is a degradation effect on STR typing, it is "locus dropout": in cases involving severe degradation, loci yielding smaller PCR products (less than 180 base pairs) tend to amplify more efficiently than loci yielding larger products (greater than 200 base pairs).[7]

Surprising as it may seem, DNA can be exposed to a great variety of environmental insults without any effect on its capacity to be typed correctly. Exposure studies have shown that contact with a variety of surfaces, both clean and dirty, and with gasoline, motor oil, acids, and alkalis either have no effect on DNA typing or, at worst, render the DNA untypable.[8]

Although contamination with microbes generally does little more than degrade the human DNA,[9] other problems sometimes can occur with both RFLP[10] and PCR-based analyses.[11] Nevertheless, there are procedures that identify or avoid these anomalies.[12] Therefore, the validation of DNA typing systems should include tests for interference with a variety of microbes to see if artifacts occur; if artifacts are

---

sis, 6 Nature Genetics 130 (1994).

[5]O. Handt et al., Molecular Genetic Analyses of the Tyrolean Ice Man, 264 Science 1775 (1994).

[6]For example, typing at a genetic locus such as D1S80, for which the target allelic sequences range in size from 300 to 850 base pairs, may be affected by the non-amplification of the largest alleles ("allelic dropout").

[7]J.P. Whitaker et al., Short Tandem Repeat Typing of Bodies from a Mass Disaster: High Success Rate and Characteristic Amplification Patterns in Highly Degraded Samples, 18 Biotechniques 670 (1995).

[8]Adams et al., Deoxyribonucleic Acid (DNA) Analysis by Restriction Fragment Length Polymorphisms of Blood and Other Body Fluid Stains Subjected to Contamination and Environmental Insults, 36 J. Forensic Sci. 1284 (1991); van Oorschot et al., HUMTHO1 Validation Studies: Effect of Substrate, Environment, and Mixtures, 41 J. Forensic Sci. 142 (1996). Most of the effects of environmental insult readily can be accounted for in terms of basic DNA chemistry. For example, some agents produce degradation or damaging chemical modifications. Other environmental contaminants inhibit restriction enzymes or PCR. (This effect sometimes can be reversed by cleaning the DNA extract to remove the inhibitor.) But environmental insult does not result in the selective loss of an allele at a locus or in the creation of a new allele at that locus.

[9]Webb et al., Microbial DNA Challenge Studies of Variable Number Tandem Repeat

(VNTR) Probes Used for DNA Profiling Analysis, 38 J. Forensic Sci. 1172 (1993).

[10]Autoradiograms sometimes show many bands that line up with the molecular weight sizing ladder bands. (The "ladder" is a set of DNA fragments of known lengths that are placed by themselves in one or more lanes of the gel. The resulting set of bands provides a benchmark for determining the weights of the unknown bands in the samples.) These extra bands can result from contamination of the sample DNA with ladder DNA at the time the samples are loaded onto the electrophoresis gel. Alternatively, the original sample may have been contaminated with a microbe infected with lambda phage, the virus that is used for the preparation of the sizing ladder.

[11]Although PCR primers designed to amplify human gene sequences would not be expected to recognize microbial DNA sequences, much less amplify them, such amplification has been reported with the D1S80 typing system. A. Fernandez-Rodriguez et al., Microbial DNA Challenge Studies of PCR-based Systems in Forensic Genetics, 6 Advances in Forensic Haemogenetics 177 (1995).

[12]Whatever the explanation for the extra sizing bands mentioned, the lambda origin of the bands can be demonstrated by an additional probing with the ladder probe alone or with a human specific probe without the ladder probe. Likewise, the spurious PCR products observed by A. Fernandez-Rodriguez et al., Microbial DNA Challenge Studies of PCR-based Systems in

observed, then control tests should be applied to distinguish between the artifactual and the true results.

### § 2:33 Sample quantity and quality—Does a sample contain DNA from more than one person?

DNA from a single individual can have no more than two alleles at each locus. This follows from the fact that individuals inherit chromosomes in pairs, one from each parent.[1] An individual who inherits the same allele from each parent (a homozygote) can contribute only that one allele to a sample, and an individual who inherits a different allele from each parent (a heterozygote) will contribute those two alleles.[2] Finding three or more alleles at a locus therefore indicates a mixture of DNA from more than one person.[3]

Some kinds of samples, such as post-coital vaginal swabs and blood stains from scenes where several persons are known to have bled, are expected to be mixtures. Sometimes, however, the first indication the sample has multiple contributors comes from the DNA testing. The chance of detecting a mixture by finding extra alleles depends on the proportion of DNA from each contributor as well as the chance that the contributors have different genotypes at one or more loci. As a rule, a minor contributor to a mixture must provide at least 5% of the DNA for the mixture to be recognized.[4] In addition, the various contributors must have some different alleles. The chance that multiple contributors will differ at one or more locus increases with the number of loci tested and the genetic diversity at each locus. Unless many loci are examined, genetic markers with low to moderate diversities do not have much power to detect multiple contributors. Genetic markers that are highly polymorphic are much better at detecting mixtures. Thus, STRs and especially VNTRs are sensitive to mixtures.

Analysis of STRs on the Y-chromosome offers a promising method in rape cases for resolving ambiguities in some mixtures.[5] Men have a Y-chromosome and an X-chromosome, while women have two X-chromosomes. Therefore, if there are, say,

---

Forensic Genetics, 6 Advances in Forensic Haemogenetics 177 (1995), can be differentiated from the true human PCR products, and the same authors have described a modification to the D1S80 typing system that removes all question of the non-human origin of the spurious PCR products. A. Fernandez-Rodriguez et al., D1S80 Typing in Casework: A Simple Strategy to Distinguish Non-specific Microbial PCR Products from Human Alleles, 7 Progress in Forensic Genetics 18 (1997).

**[Section 2:33]**

[1]See §§ 2:21 to 2:23.

[2]Loci on the sex chromosomes constitute a special case. Females have two X chromosomes, one from each parent; as with loci on the other chromosomes, they can be either homozygous or heterozygous at the X-linked loci. Males, on the other hand, have one X and one Y chromosome; hence, they have only one allele at X-linked loci and one allele at Y-linked loci. In cases of trisomy, such as XXY males, multiple copies of loci on the affected chromosome will be present, but this condition is rare and often lethal.

[3]On very rare occasions, an individual exhibits a phenotype with three alleles at a locus. This can be the result of a chromosome anomaly (such as a duplicated gene on one chromosome or a

mutation). A sample from such an individual is usually easily distinguished from a mixed sample. The three-allele variant is seen at only the affected locus, whereas with mixtures, more than two alleles typically are evident at several loci.

[4]With RFLP testing, alleles from a contributor of as little as one percent can be detected at the price of overexposing the pattern from the major contributor. Studies in which DNA from different individuals is combined in differing proportions show that the intensity of the bands reflects the proportions of the mixture. Thus, if bands in a crime-scene sample have different intensities, it may be possible to assign alleles to major and minor contributors. However, if bands are present in roughly equal proportions, this allocation cannot be made, and the statistical interpretation of the observed results must include all possible combinations.

[5]See generally M.F. Hammer et al., Development of the Human Y Chromosome as a Forensic Tool, Final Progress Report, NIJ Research Rev., Sept. 2000; M Prinz et al., Validation and Casework Application of a Y Chromosome Specific STR Multiplex, 120 Forensic Sci. Int'l 177–88 (2001) (reporting on validation experiments for a Y-chromosome-specific STR multiplex system); Tsuji et al., Personal Identification Using

two distinct Y-STRs at the same locus, then one male contributor is responsible for one allele, and the other male is responsible for the second allele.

## § 2:34    Laboratory performance

DNA profiling is valid and reliable, but confidence in a particular result that is establishing that a suspect is (or is not) the source of a sample depends on the quality control and quality assurance procedures in the laboratory and the handling and nature of the samples that are compared.

## § 2:35    Laboratory performance—Quality control and assurance

Quality control refers to measures to help ensure that a DNA-typing result (and its interpretation) meets a specified standard of quality. Quality assurance refers to monitoring, verifying, and documenting laboratory performance.[1] A quality assurance program helps demonstrate that a laboratory is meeting its quality control objectives and thus justifies confidence in the quality of its product.

Professional bodies within forensic science have described procedures for quality assurance. Guidelines have been prepared by two FBI-appointed groups—the Technical Working Group on DNA Analysis Methods (TWGDAM),[2] which has been supplanted by the Scientific Working Group on DNA Analysis Methods (SWGDAM),[3] and the DNA Advisory Board (DAB).[4] The DAB also has encouraged forensic DNA laboratories to seek accreditation,[5] and at least two states require forensic DNA lab-

Y-Chromosomal Short Tandem Repeats From Bodily Fluids Mixed with Semen, 22 Am. J. Forensic Med. Pathology 288 (2001) (reporting that Y-STR haplotype analysis of several mixtures of biological fluids, including semen, proved useful for the identification of the offender in a sex-crime case); Tun et al., Simultaneous Detection of Multiple STR Loci on Sex Chromosomes for Forensic Testing of Sex and Identity, 44 J. Forensic Sci. 772 (1999); cf. Mark A. Jobling & Chris Tyler-Smith, The Human Y Chromosome: An Evolutionary Marker Comes of Age, 4 Nature Reviews Genetics 598 (2003).

**[Section 2:35]**

[1] For general descriptions of quality assurance programs, see Committee on DNA Technology in Forensic Science, National Research Council, DNA Technology in Forensic Science 28 (1992) (Table 1.1) ("Ensuring High Standards of Laboratory Performance"); Committee on DNA Forensic Science: An Update, National Research Council, The Evaluation of Forensic DNA Evidence ch. 4 (1996).

[2] See Technical Working Group on DNA Analysis Methods, Guidelines for a Quality Assurance Program for DNA Analysis, 22 Crime Laboratory Digest 21 (1995); 18 Crime Laboratory Digest 44 (1991).

[3] SWGDAM has promulgated guidelines on STR typing and mitochondrial-DNA testing. Scientific Working Group on DNA Analysis Methods (SWGDAM), Short Tandem Repeat (STR) Interpretation Guidelines, Forensic Sci. Communica-

tions, July 2000; Scientific Working Group on DNA Analysis Methods (SWGDAM), Guidelines for Mitochondrial DNA (mtDNA) Nucleotide Sequence Interpretation, Forensic Sci. Communications, Apr. 2003.

[4] See Federal Bureau of Investigation, Quality Assurance Standards for Forensic DNA Testing Laboratories, July 15, 1998; see also Recommendations of the DNA Commission of the International Society for Forensic Haemogenetics Relating to the Use of PCR-based Polymorphisms, 64 Vox Sang. 124 (1993); 1991 Report Concerning Recommendations of the DNA Commission of the International Society for Forensic Haemogenetics Relating to the Use of DNA Polymorphism, 63 Vox Sang. 70 (1992).

Under the DNA Identification Act of 1994, Pub. L. No. 103-322, 108 Stat. 2065 (codified at 42 U.S.C.A. § 13701 (1994)), to qualify for federal laboratory improvement funds, a forensic DNA laboratory must meet the quality assurance standards recommended by the DAB and issued by the director of the FBI. The DAB membership includes molecular geneticists, population geneticists, an ethicist, and representatives from federal, state, and local forensic DNA laboratories, private sector DNA laboratories, the National Institute of Standards and Technology, and the judiciary. Its recommendations closely follow the 1995 TWGDAM guidelines.

[5] Federal Bureau of Investigation, Quality Assurance Standards for Forensic DNA Testing Laboratories at 1, July 15, 1998 (preface).

oratories to be accredited.[6] The American Association of Crime Laboratory Directors-Laboratory Accreditation Board (ASCLD-LAB) accredits forensic laboratories.[7]

## § 2:36 Laboratory performance—Quality control and assurance—Documentation

The quality assurance guidelines promulgated by TWGDAM, the DAB, and ASCLD-LAB call for laboratories to document laboratory organization and management, personnel qualifications and training, facilities, evidence control procedures, validation of methods and procedures, analytical procedures, equipment calibration and maintenance, standards for case documentation and report writing, procedures for reviewing case files and testimony, proficiency testing, corrective actions, audits, safety program, and review of subcontractors. Of course, maintaining even such extensive documentation and records does not guarantee the correctness of results obtained in any particular case. Errors in analysis or interpretation might occur as a result of a deviation from an established procedure, analyst misjudgment, or an accident. Although case-review procedures within a laboratory should be designed to detect errors before a report is issued, it is always possible that some incorrect result will slip through. Accordingly, determination that a laboratory maintains a strong quality assurance program does not eliminate the need for case-by-case review.

## § 2:37 Laboratory performance—Quality control and assurance—Validation

The validation of procedures is central to quality assurance. "Developmental" validation is undertaken to determine the applicability of a new test to crime-scene samples; it defines conditions that give reliable results and identifies the limitations of the procedure. For example, a new genetic marker being considered for use in forensic analysis will be tested to determine if it can be typed reliably in both fresh samples and in samples typical of those found at crime scenes. The validation would include testing samples originating from different tissues—blood, semen, hair, bone, samples containing degraded DNA, samples contaminated with microbes, samples containing DNA mixtures, and so on. Developmental validation of a new marker also includes the generation of population databases and the testing of allele and genotype distributions for independence. Developmental validation normally results in publication in the scientific literature, but a new procedure can be validated in multiple laboratories well ahead of publication.

"Internal" validation, on the other hand, involves the verification by a laboratory that it can reliably perform an established procedure that already has undergone developmental validation. Before adopting a new procedure, the laboratory should verify its ability to use the system in a proficiency trial.

Both forms of validation build on the accumulated body of knowledge and experience. Thus, some aspects of validation testing need be repeated only to the

---

[6]N.Y. Exec. Law § 995-b; Cal. DNA and Forensic Identification Data Base and Data Bank Act of 1998, Cal. Pen. Code § 297.

[7]See American Society of Crime Laboratory Directors—Laboratory Accreditation Board, ASCLD-LAB Accreditation Manual, Jan. 1997. As of mid-1998, ASCLD-LAB had accredited laboratories in Australia, New Zealand, and Hong Kong as well as laboratories in the United States and Canada. The ASCLD-LAB accreditation program does not allow laboratories to obtain accreditation only for particular services—a laboratory seeking accreditation must qualify for the full range of services it offers. This constraint has slowed some forensic DNA labs from seeking accreditation. As an interim solution, the National Forensic Science Technology Center (NFSTC) has an agreement with ASCLD-LAB to perform certification audits on DNA sections of laboratories for compliance with DAB and ASCLD-LAB standards; this service is available to private sector DNA laboratories as well as government laboratories.

extent required to verify that previously established principles apply. One need not validate the principle of the internal combustion engine every time one brings out a new model of automobile.

## § 2:38   Laboratory performance—Quality control and assurance—Proficiency testing

Proficiency testing in forensic genetic testing is designed to ascertain whether an analyst can correctly determine genetic types in a sample the origin of which is unknown to the analyst but is known to a tester. Proficiency is demonstrated by making correct genetic typing determinations in repeated trials, and not by opining on whether the sample originated from a particular individual. Proficiency tests also require laboratories to report random-match probabilities to determine if proper calculations are being made.

An internal proficiency trial is conducted within a laboratory. One person in the laboratory prepares the sample and administers the test to another person in the laboratory. An external trial is one in which the test sample originates from outside the laboratory—from another laboratory, a commercial vendor, or a regulatory agency. In a declared (or open) proficiency trial the analyst knows the sample is a proficiency sample. In contrast, in a blind (or more properly "full-blind") trial, the sample is submitted so that the analyst does not recognize it as a proficiency sample.[1] It has been argued that full-blind trials provide a better indication of proficiency because the analyst will not give the trial sample any special attention.[2] On the other hand, full-blind proficiency trials for forensic DNA analysis entail considerably more organizational effort and expense than open proficiency trials. Obviously, the "evidence" samples prepared for the trial have to be sufficiently realistic that the laboratory does not suspect the legitimacy of the submission. A police agency and prosecutor's office have to submit the "evidence" and respond to laboratory inquiries with information about the "case." Finally, the genetic profile from a proficiency test must not be entered into regional and national databases.[3]

The DAB recommends that every analyst regularly undergo external, open proficiency testing[4] and that the laboratory take "corrective action whenever proficiency testing discrepancies [or] casework errors are detected."[5] Certification by the American Board of Criminalistics as a specialist in forensic biology DNA analysis requires

---

[Section 2:38]

[1] There is potential confusion over nomenclature with regard to open and blind trials. All proficiency tests are blind in the sense that the analyst does not know the composition of the test sample. In some disciplines, any trial in which the analyst receives "unknowns" from a tester is referred to as a blind trial. With regard to proficiency testing in the forensic area, however, the convention is to distinguish "open" and "blind" trials as described here.

[2] See, e.g., Scheck, DNA and *Daubert*, 15 Cardozo L. Rev. 1980 (1994). Another argument for the full-blind trial is that it tests a broader range of laboratory operations, from submission of the evidence to the laboratory through the analysis and interpretation stages to the reporting out to the submitting agency. However, these aspects of laboratory operations also can be evaluated, at much less cost, by mechanisms such as laboratory audits and random review of case files.

[3] The feasibility of mounting a national, full-blind proficiency trial program was studied as a part of the DNA Identification Act of 1994, Pub. L. No. 103-322, 108 Stat. 2065 (codified at 42 U.S.C.A. § 13701 (1994)). The study concludes that "[i]n the extreme, blind proficiency testing is possible, but fraught with problems (including costs), and it is recommended that a blind proficiency testing program be deferred" while other quality assurance measures are implemented. Peterson et al., The Feasibility of External Blind Proficiency Testing, 48 J. Forensic Sci. 21 (2003).

[4] Standard 13.1 specifies that these tests are to be performed at least as frequently as every 180 days. Federal Bureau of Investigation, Quality Assurance Standards for Forensic DNA Testing Laboratories 16, July 15, 1998. TWGDAM recommended two open proficiency tests per year per analyst. TWGDAM Technical Working Group on DNA Analysis Methods, Guidelines for a Quality Assurance Program for DNA Analysis, 22 Crime Laboratory Digest 21 (1995).

[5] Federal Bureau of Investigation, Quality Assurance Standards for Forensic DNA Testing

one proficiency trial per year. Accredited laboratories must maintain records documenting compliance with required proficiency test standards.[6]

## § 2:39  Laboratory performance—Handling samples

Sample mishandling, mislabeling, or contamination, whether in the field or in the laboratory, is more likely to compromise a DNA analysis than an error in genetic typing. For example, a sample mixup due to mislabeling reference blood samples taken at the hospital could lead to incorrect association of crime-scene samples to a reference individual or to incorrect exclusions. Similarly, packaging two items with wet blood stains into the same bag could result in a transfer of stains between the items, rendering it difficult or impossible to determine whose blood was originally on each item. Contamination in the laboratory may result in artifactual typing results or in the incorrect attribution of a DNA profile to an individual or to an item of evidence. Accordingly, it is appropriate to look at the procedures that have been prescribed and implemented to guard against such error.

Mislabeling or mishandling can occur when biological material is collected in the field, when it is transferred to the laboratory, when it is in the analysis stream in the laboratory,[1] when the analytical results are recorded, or when the recorded results are transcribed into a report. Mislabeling and mishandling can happen with any kind of physical evidence and are of great concern in all fields of forensic science. Because forensic laboratories often have little or no control over the handling of evidence prior to its arrival in the laboratory, checkpoints should be established to detect mislabeling and mishandling along the line of evidence flow.[2] Investigative agencies should have guidelines for evidence collection and labeling so that a chain of custody is maintained. Similarly, there should be guidelines, produced with input from the laboratory, for handling biological evidence in the field. These principles remain the same as in the pre-DNA era.[3]

TWGDAM guidelines and DAB recommendations require documented procedures to ensure sample integrity and to avoid sample mixups, labeling errors, recording errors, and the like. They also mandate case review to identify inadvertent errors before a final report is released. Finally, laboratories must retain, when feasible, portions of the crime-scene samples and extracts to allow reanalysis.[4] However, retention is not always possible. For example, retention of original items is not to be

---

Laboratories 17, July 15, 1998 (standard 14.1).

[6]Proficiency test results from laboratories accredited by ASCLD-LAB are reported also to an ASCLD-LAB Proficiency Review Committee. The committee independently reviews test results and verifies compliance with accreditation requirements. ASCLD-LAB specifies the vendors whose proficiency tests it accepts for accreditation purposes. Since accreditation can be suspended or withdrawn by unacceptable proficiency trial performance, the proficiency test vendors must meet high standards with respect to test-sample preparation and documentation. Yet, in some instances vendors have provided mislabeled or contaminated test samples. See TWGDAM & ASCLD-LAB Proficiency Review Committee, Guidelines for DNA Proficiency Test Manufacturing and Reporting, 21 Crime Laboratory Digest 27–32 (1994).

**[Section 2:39]**

[1]E.g., *U.S. v. Cuff*, 37 F. Supp. 2d 279, 283, 51 Fed. R. Evid. Serv. 557 (S.D. N.Y. 1999).

[2]Committee on DNA Forensic Science: An Update, National Research Council, The Evaluation of Forensic DNA Evidence at 80–82 (1996).

[3]Samples (particularly those containing wet stains) should not be packaged together, and samples should be dried or refrigerated as soon as possible. Storage in the dry state and at low temperatures stabilizes biological material against degradation. George Sensabaugh, Biochemical Markers of Individuality, in Forensic Science Handbook 338, 385 (Richard Saferstein ed., 1982). The only precaution to have gained force in the DNA era is that evidence items should be handled with gloved hands to protect against handling contamination and inadvertent sample-to-sample transfers.

[4]Forensic laboratories have a professional responsibility to preserve retained evidence so as to minimize degradation. See Technical Working Group on DNA Analysis Methods, Guidelines for a Quality Assurance Program for DNA Analysis, 22 Crime Laboratory Digest at 30 (1995) (para. 6.3). Furthermore, failure to preserve potentially exculpatory evidence has been treated as a denial

expected when the items are large or immobile (for example, a wall or sidewalk). In such situations, a swabbing or scraping of the stain from the item would typically be collected and retained. There also are situations where the sample is so small that it will be consumed in the analysis.[5]

Assuming appropriate chain-of-custody and evidence-handling protocols are in place, the critical question is whether there are deviations in the particular case. This may require a review of the total case documentation as well as the laboratory findings.[6]

As the 1996 NRC report emphasizes, an important safeguard against error due to mislabeling and mishandling is the opportunity to retest original evidence items or the material extracted from them.[7] Should mislabeling or mishandling have occurred, reanalysis of the original sample and the intermediate extracts should detect not only the fact of the error but also the point at which it occurred. It is even possible in some cases to detect mislabeling at the point of sample collection if the genetic typing results on a particular sample are inconsistent with an otherwise consistent reconstruction of events.[8]

Contamination describes any situation in which foreign material is mixed with a sample of DNA. Contamination by non-biological materials, such as gasoline or grit, can cause test failures, but they are not a source of genetic typing errors. Similarly, contamination with non-human biological materials, such as bacteria, fungi, or plant materials, is generally not a problem. These contaminants may accelerate DNA degradation, but they do not contribute spurious genetic types.[9]

Consequently, the contamination of greatest concern is that resulting from the addition of human DNA. This sort of contamination can occur three ways:[10]

---

of due process and grounds for suppression. *People v. Nation*, 26 Cal. 3d 169, 161 Cal. Rptr. 299, 604 P.2d 1051 (1980). In *Arizona v. Youngblood*, 488 U.S. 51, 109 S. Ct. 333, 102 L. Ed. 2d 281 (1988), however, the Supreme Court held that a police agency's failure to preserve evidence not known to be exculpatory does not constitute a denial of due process unless "bad faith" can be shown. In *Youngblood*, the police had failed to refrigerate a victim's underwear, precluding the serologic testing of semen then available. DNA testing of the underwear conducted nearly two decades later showed that Youngblood was not the source of the stain. See Barbara Whitaker, DNA Frees Inmate Years After Justices Rejected Plea, N.Y. Times, Aug. 11, 2000.

[5]When small samples are involved, whether it is necessary to consume the entire sample is a matter of scientific judgment.

[6]Such a review is best undertaken by someone familiar with police procedures, forensic DNA analysis, and forensic laboratory operations. Case review by an independent expert should be held to the same scientific standard as the work under review. Any possible flaws in labeling or in evidence handling should be specified in detail, with consideration given to the consequence of the possible error.

[7]Committee on DNA Forensic Science: An Update, National Research Council, The Evaluation of Forensic DNA Evidence 81 (1996).

[8]For example, a mislabeling of husband and

wife samples in a paternity case might result in an apparent maternal exclusion, a very unlikely event. The possibility of mislabeling could be confirmed by testing the samples for gender and ultimately verified by taking new samples from each party under better controlled conditions.

[9]Validation of new genetic markers includes testing on a variety of non-human species. The probes used in VNTR analysis and the PCR-based tests give results with non-human primate DNA samples (apes and some monkeys). This is not surprising given the evolutionary proximity of the primates to humans. As a rule, the validated test systems give no results with DNA from animals other than primates, from plants, or from microbes. An exception is the reaction of some bacterial DNA samples in testing for the marker D1S80. A. Fernandez-Rodriguez et al., Microbial DNA Challenge Studies of PCR-based Systems in Forensic Genetics, 6 Advances in Forensic Haemogenetics 177 (1995). However, this could be an artifact of the particular D1S80 typing system, since other workers have not been able to replicate fully their results, and an alternative D1S80 typing protocol gave no spurious results. S. Ebraham et al., Investigation of the Specificity of the STR and D1S80 Primers on Microbial DNA Samples, Presentation B84, 50th Annual Meeting of the American Academy of Forensic Sciences, San Francisco, Feb. 1998.

[10]Committee on DNA Forensic Science: An Update, National Research Council, The Evaluation of Forensic DNA Evidence 82–84 (1996);

1. The crime-scene samples by their nature may contain a mixture of fluids or tissues from different individuals. Examples include vaginal swabs collected as sexual assault evidence[11] and blood stain evidence from scenes where several individuals shed blood.[12]

2. The crime-scene samples may be inadvertently contaminated in the course of sample handling in the field or in the laboratory. Inadvertent contamination of crime-scene DNA with DNA from a reference sample could lead to a false inclusion.[13]

3. Carry-over contamination in PCR-based typing can occur if the amplification products of one typing reaction are carried over into the reaction mix for a subsequent PCR reaction. If the carry-over products are present in sufficient quantity, they could be preferentially amplified over the target DNA.[14] The primary strategy used in most forensic laboratories to protect against carry-over contamination is to keep PCR products away from sample materials and test reagents by having separate work areas for pre-PCR and post-PCR sample handling, by preparing samples in controlled air-flow biological safety hoods, by using dedicated equipment (such as pipetters) for each of the various stages of sample analysis, by decontaminating work areas after use (usually by wiping down or by irradiating with ultraviolet light), and by having a one-way flow of sample from the pre-PCR to post-PCR work areas.[15] Additional protocols are used to detect any carry-over contamination.[16]

In the end, whether a laboratory has conducted the appropriate tests properly

---

Committee on DNA Technology in Forensic Science, National Research Council, DNA Technology in Forensic Science 65–67 (1992) (Table 1.1); G.F. Sensabaugh & E.T. Blake, DNA Analysis in Biological Evidence: Applications of the Polymerase Chain Reaction, in 3 Forensic Science Handbook 416, 441 (Richard Saferstein ed., 1993); G.F. Sensabaugh & C. vonBeroldingen, The Polymerase Chain Reaction: Application to the Analysis of Biological Evidence, in Forensic DNA Technology 63, 77 (M.A. Farley & J.J. Harrington eds., 1991).

[11]These typically contain DNA in the semen from the assailant and in the vaginal fluid of the victim. The standard procedure for analysis allows the DNA from sperm to be separated from the vaginal epithelial cell DNA. It is thus possible not only to recognize the mixture but also to assign the DNA profiles to the different individuals.

[12]Such mixtures are detected by genetic typing that reveals profiles of more than one DNA source. See § 2:34.

[13]This source of contamination is a greater concern when PCR-based typing methods are to be used due to the capacity of PCR to detect very small amounts of DNA. However, experiments designed to introduce handling contamination into samples have been unsuccessful. See Comey & Budowle, Validation Studies on the Analysis of HLA-DQα Locus Using the Polymerase Chain Reaction, 36 J. Forensic Sci. 1633 (1991). Of course, it remains important to have evidence handling procedures to safeguard against this source of contamination. Police agencies should have documented procedures for the collection, handling, and packaging of biological evidence in the field and for its delivery to the laboratory that are designed to minimize the chance of handling contamination. Ideally, these procedures will have been developed in coordination with the laboratory, and training in the use of these procedures will have been provided. Similarly, laboratories should have procedures in place to minimize the risk of this kind of contamination. See Federal Bureau of Investigation, Quality Assurance Standards for Forensic DNA Testing Laboratories, July 15, 1998; Technical Working Group on DNA Analysis Methods, Guidelines for a Quality Assurance Program for DNA Analysis, 22 Crime Laboratory Digest 21 (1995). In particular, these procedures should specify the safeguards for keeping evidence samples separated from reference samples.

[14]Carry-over contamination is not an issue in RFLP analysis since RFLP analysis involves no amplification steps.

[15]Some laboratories with space constraints separate pre-PCR and post-PCR activities in time rather than space. The other safeguards can be used as in a space-separated facility.

[16]Standard protocols include the amplification of blank control samples—those to which no DNA has be added. If carry-over contaminants have found their way into the reagents or sample tubes, these will be detected as amplification products. Outbreaks of carry-over contamination can also be recognized by monitoring test results. Detection of an unexpected and persistent genetic profile in different samples indicates a contamination problem. When contamination outbreaks are detected, appropriate corrective actions should be taken, and both the outbreak and the corrective

depends both on the general standard of practice and on the questions posed in the particular case. There is no universal checklist, but the selection of tests and the adherence to the correct test procedures can be reviewed by experts and by reference to professional standards, such as the TWGDAM and DAB guidelines.

## § 2:40    Interpretation of laboratory results

The results of DNA testing can be presented in various ways. With discrete allele systems, it is natural to speak of "matching" and "non-matching" profiles. If the genetic profile obtained from the biological sample taken from the crime scene or the victim (the "trace evidence sample") matches that of a particular individual, then that individual is included as a possible source of the sample. But other individuals also might possess a matching DNA profile. Accordingly, the expert should be asked to provide some indication of how significant the match is. If, on the other hand, the genetic profiles are different, then the individual is excluded as the source of the trace evidence. Typically, proof tending to show that the defendant is the source incriminates the defendant, while proof that someone else is the source exculpates the defendant.[1] This section elaborates on these ideas, indicating issues that can arise in connection with an expert's testimony interpreting the results of a DNA test.

## § 2:41    Interpretation of laboratory results—Exclusions, inclusions, and inconclusive results

When the DNA from the trace evidence clearly does not match the DNA sample from the suspect, the DNA analysis demonstrates that the suspect's DNA is not in the forensic sample. Indeed, if the samples have been collected, handled, and analyzed properly, then the suspect is excluded as a possible source of the DNA in the forensic sample. Even a single allele that cannot be explained as a laboratory artifact or other error can exclude a suspect.[1] As a practical matter, such exclusionary results normally would keep charges from being filed against the excluded suspect.[2]

In some cases, however, DNA testing is inconclusive, in whole or in part. The presence or absence of a discrete allele can be in doubt, or the existence or location of a VNTR band may be unclear.[3] For example, when the trace evidence sample is extremely degraded, VNTR profiling might not show all the alleles that would be present in a sample with more intact DNA. If the quantity of DNA to be amplified

---

action should be documented. See Federal Bureau of Investigation, Quality Assurance Standards for Forensic DNA Testing Laboratories, July 15, 1998; Technical Working Group on DNA Analysis Methods, Guidelines for a Quality Assurance Program for DNA Analysis, 22 Crime Laboratory Digest 21 (1995).

**[Section 2:40]**

[1]Whether being the source of the forensic sample is incriminating depends on other facts in the case. Likewise, whether someone else being the source is exculpatory depends on the circumstances. For example, a suspect who might have committed the offense without leaving the trace evidence sample still could be guilty. In a rape case with several rapists, a semen stain could fail to incriminate one assailant because insufficient semen from that individual is present in the sample.

**[Section 2:41]**

[1]Due to heteroplasmy, a single sequence difference in mtDNA samples would not be considered an exclusion. See §§ 2:24 to 2:26. With testing at many polymorphic loci, however, it would be unusual to find two unrelated individuals whose DNA matches at all but one locus.

[2]But see *State v. Hammond*, 221 Conn. 264, 604 A.2d 793 (1992).

[3]E.g., *State v. Fleming*, 1997 ME 158, 698 A.2d 503, 506 (Me. 1997) ("The fourth probe was declared uninterpretable."); *People v. Leonard*, 224 Mich. App. 569, 569 N.W.2d 663, 666–667 (1997) ("There was a definite match of defendant's DNA on three of the probes, and a match on the other two probes could not be excluded."). In some cases, experts have disagreed as to whether extra bands represented a mixture or resulted from partial digestion of the forensic sample. E.g., *State*

for sequence-specific tests is too small, the amplification might not yield enough product to give a clear signal. Thus, experts sometimes disagree as to whether a particular band is visible on an autoradiograph or whether a dot is present on a reverse dot blot.

Furthermore, even when RFLP bands are clearly visible, the entire pattern of bands can be displaced from its true location in a systematic way (a phenomenon known as *band-shifting*).[4] Recognizing this phenomenon, analysts might deem some seemingly matching patterns as inconclusive.[5]

At the other extreme, the genotypes at a large number of loci can be clearly identical, and the fact of a match not in doubt. In these cases, the DNA evidence is quite incriminating, and the challenge for the legal system lies in explaining just how probative it is. Naturally, as with exclusions, inclusions are most powerful when the samples have been collected, handled, and analyzed properly. But there is one logical difference between exclusions and inclusions. If it is accepted that the samples have different genotypes, then the conclusion that the DNA in them came from different individuals is essentially inescapable. In contrast, even if two samples have the same genotype, there is a chance that the forensic sample came—not from the defendant—but from another individual who has the same genotype. This complication has produced extensive arguments over the statistical procedures for assessing this chance or related quantities. This problem of describing the significance of an unequivocal match is taken up later in this section.

The classification of patterns into the two mutually exclusive categories of exclusions and inclusions is more complicated for VNTRs than for discrete alleles. Determining that DNA fragments from two different samples are the same size is like saying that two people are the same height. The height may well be similar, but is it identical? Even if the same person is measured repeatedly, we expect some variation about the true height due to the limitations of the measuring device. A perfectly reliable device gives the same measurements for all repeated measurements of the same item, but no instrument can measure a quantity like height with both perfect precision and perfect reproducibility. Consequently, *measurement variability* is a fact of life in ascertaining the sizes of VNTRs.[6]

The method of handling measurement variation that has been adopted by most

---

*v. Marcus*, 294 N.J. Super. 267, 683 A.2d 221 (App. Div. 1996).

[4]See Committee on DNA Forensic Science: An Update, National Research Council, The Evaluation of Forensic DNA Evidence 142 (1996) ("[D]egraded DNA sometimes migrates farther on a gel than better quality DNA . . . ."). Band-shifting produces a systematic error in measurement. Random error is also present. See infra § 2:44.

[5]See Committee on DNA Technology in Forensic Science, National Research Council, DNA Technology in Forensic Science at 142 (1992) (Table 1.1) ("[A]n experienced analyst can notice whether two bands from a heterozygote are shifted in the same or in the opposite direction from the bands in another lane containing the DNA being compared. If the bands in the two lanes shift a small distance in the same direction, that might indicate a match with band-shifting. If they shift in opposite directions, that is probably not a match, but a simple match rule or simple computer program might declare it as a match.").

At least one laboratory has reported

matches of bands that lie outside its match window but exhibit a band-shifting pattern. It uses monomorphic probes to adjust for the band-shifting. On the admissibility of this procedure, compare *Caldwell v. State*, 260 Ga. 278, 393 S.E.2d 436, 441 (1990) (admissible as having reached the "scientific stage of verifiable certainty") and *State v. Futch*, 123 Or. App. 176, 860 P.2d 264 (1993), decision aff'd, 324 Or. 297, 924 P.2d 832 (1996) and (abrogated on other grounds by, State v. Howard, 205 Or. App. 408, 134 P.3d 1042 (2006)) (admissible under a *Daubert*-like standard), *with Hayes v. State*, 660 So. 2d 257 (Fla. 1995) (too controversial to be generally accepted), *State v. Quatrevingt*, 670 So. 2d 197 (La. 1996) (not shown to be valid under *Daubert*), and *People v. Keene*, 156 Misc. 2d 108, 591 N.Y.S.2d 733 (Sup 1992) (holding that the procedure followed in the case, which did not use the nearest monomorphic probe to make the corrections, was not generally accepted).

[6]In statistics, this variability often is denominated "measurement error." The phrase does not mean that a mistake has been made in performing the measurements, but rather that

DNA profilers is statistically inelegant,[7] but it has the virtue of simplicity.[8] Analysts typically are willing to declare that two fragments match if the bands appear to match visually, and if they fall within a specified distance of one another. For example, the FBI laboratory declares matches within a ±5% *match window*—if two bands are within ±5% of their average length, then the alleles can be said to match.[9]

Whether the choice of ±5% (or any other figure) as an outer limit for matches is scientifically acceptable depends on how the criterion operates in classifying pairs of samples of DNA. The ±5% window keeps the chance of a false exclusion for a single allele quite small, but at a cost: The easier it is to declare a match between bands at different positions, the easier it is to declare a match between two samples with *different* genotypes. Therefore, deciding whether a match window is reasonable involves an examination of the probability not merely of a false exclusion but also of a false inclusion: "[t]he match window should not be set so small that true matches are missed. At the same time, the window should not be so wide that bands that are clearly different are declared to match."[10] Viewed in this light, the ±5% match window is easily defended—it keeps the probabilities of *both* types of errors very small.[11]

## § 2:42    Interpretation of laboratory results—Alternative hypotheses

If the defendant is the source of DNA of sufficient quantity and quality found at a crime scene, then a DNA sample from the defendant and the forensic sample should

---

even measurements that are taken correctly fluctuate about the true value of the quantity being measured.

[7]See 1996 NRC Report, at 139 ("[T]he most accurate statistical model for the interpretation of VNTR analysis would be based on a continuous distribution . . . . If models for measurement uncertainty become available that are appropriate for the wide range of laboratories performing DNA analyses and if those analyses are sufficiently robust with respect to departures from the models, we would recommend such methods. Indeed, . . . we expect that any problems in the construction of such models will be overcome, and we encourage research on those models."). Forcing a continuous variable like the positions of the bands on an autoradiogram into discrete categories is not statistically efficient. It results in more matching bands being deemed inconclusive or non-matching than more sophisticated statistical procedures. See, e.g., Berry et al., Statistical Inference in Crime Investigations Using Deoxyribonucleic Acid Profiling, 41 Applied Stat. 499 (1992); Evett et al., An Illustration of Efficient Statistical Methods for RFLP Analysis in Forensic Science, 52 Am J. Hum. Genetics 498 (1993). Also, it treats matches that just squeak by the match windows as just as impressive as perfect matches.

[8]Committee on DNA Forensic Science: An Update, National Research Council, The Evaluation of Forensic DNA Evidence 139 (1996).

[9]The FBI arrived at this match window by experiments involving pairs of measurements of the same DNA sequences. It found that this window was wide enough to encompass all the differences seen in the calibration experiments. Other laboratories use smaller percentages for

their match windows, but comparisons of the percentage figures can be misleading. See D.H. Kaye, Science in Evidence 192 (1997). Because different laboratories can have different standard errors of measurement, profiles from two different laboratories might not be considered inconsistent even though some corresponding bands are outside the match windows of both laboratories. The reason: there is more variability in measurements on different gels than on the same gel, and still more in different gels from different laboratories. See *Satcher v. Netherland*, 944 F. Supp. 1222, 1265 (E.D. Va. 1996), judgment aff'd in part, rev'd on other grounds in part, 126 F.3d 561 (4th Cir. 1997).

[10]Committee on DNA Forensic Science: An Update, National Research Council, The Evaluation of Forensic DNA Evidence 140 (1996). Assuming that the only source of error is the statistical uncertainty in the measurements, this error probability is simply the chance that the two people whose DNA is tested have profiles so similar that they satisfy the matching criterion. With genotypes consisting of four or five VNTR loci, that probability is much smaller than the chance of a false exclusion. Committee on DNA Forensic Science: An Update, National Research Council, The Evaluation of Forensic DNA Evidence 141 (1996).

[11]Committee on DNA Forensic Science: An Update, National Research Council, The Evaluation of Forensic DNA Evidence 140–141 (1996); Bernard Devlin & Kathryn Roeder, DNA Profiling: Statistics and Population Genetics, in 1 Modern Scientific Evidence: The Law and Science of Expert Testimony § 18–3.1.1, at 717–718 (David Faigman et al. eds., 1997).

have the same profile. The inference required in assessing the evidence, however, runs in the opposite direction. The forensic scientist reports that the sample of DNA from the crime scene and a sample from the defendant have the same genotype. To what extent does this tend to prove that the defendant is the source of the forensic sample?[1] Conceivably, other hypotheses could account for the matching profiles. One possibility is laboratory error—the genotypes are not actually the same even though the laboratory thinks that they are. This situation could arise from mistakes in labeling or handling samples or from cross-contamination of the samples.[2] As the 1992 NRC report cautioned, "[e]rrors happen, even in the best laboratories, and even when the analyst is certain that every precaution against error was taken."[3] Another possibility is that the laboratory analysis is correct—the genotypes are truly identical—but the forensic sample came from another individual. In general, the true source might be a close relative of the defendant[4] or an unrelated person who, as luck would have it, just happens to have the same profile as the defendant. The former hypothesis we shall refer to as kinship, and the latter as coincidence. To infer that the defendant is the source of the crime-scene DNA, one must reject these alternative hypotheses of laboratory error, kinship, and coincidence. Table 1 summarizes the logical possibilities.

### Table 1.
### Hypotheses that Might Explain a Match Between Defendant's DNA and DNA at a Crime Scene[5]

| IDENTITY: | same genotype, defendant's DNA at crime scene |
|---|---|
| NON-IDENTITY: | |
| lab error | different genotypes mistakenly found to be the same |
| kinship | same genotype, relative's DNA at crime scene |
| coincidence | same genotype, unrelated individual's DNA |

Some scientists have urged that probabilities associated with false positive error, kinship, or coincidence be presented to juries. While it is not clear that this goal is feasible, scientific knowledge and more conventional evidence can help in assessing the plausibility of these alternative hypotheses. If laboratory error, kinship, and co-

---

**[Section 2:42]**

[1]That the defendant is the source does not necessarily mean that the defendant is guilty of the offense charged. Aside from issues of intent or knowledge that have nothing to do with DNA, there remains, for instance, the possibility that the two samples match because someone framed the defendant by putting a sample of defendant's DNA at the crime scene or in the container of DNA thought to have come from the crime scene. See generally, e.g., *U.S. v. Chischilly*, 30 F.3d 1144, 40 Fed. R. Evid. Serv. 289 (9th Cir. 1994) (dicta on "source probability"); Koehler, DNA Matches and Statistics: Important Questions, Surprising Answers, 76 Judicature 222 (1993). For reports of state police planting fingerprint and other evidence to incriminate arrestees, see John Caher, Judge Orders New Trial in Murder Case, Times Union (Albany), Jan. 8, 1997, at B2; John O'Brien & Todd Lightly, Corrupt Troopers Showed No Fear, The Post-Standard (Syracuse), Feb. 4, 1997, at A3 (an investigation of 62,000 fingerprint cards from 1983–1992 revealed 34

cases of planted evidence among one state police troop).

[2]§§ 2:27 to 2:29.

[3]Committee on DNA Technology in Forensic Science, National Research Council, DNA Technology in Forensic Science 89 (1992) (Table 1.1).

[4]A close relative, for these purposes, would be a brother, uncle, nephew, etc. For relationships more distant than second cousins, the probability of a chance match is nearly as small as for persons of the same ethnic subgroup. Bernard Devlin & Kathryn Roeder, DNA Profiling: Statistics and Population Genetics, in 1 Modern Scientific Evidence: The Law and Science of Expert Testimony § 18-3.1.3, at 724 (David Faigman et al. eds., 1997). For an instance of the "evil twin" defense, see *Hunter v. Harrison*, 1997 WL 578917 (Ohio Ct. App. 8th Dist. Cuyahoga County 1997) (unpublished paternity case).

[5]Cf. Morton, The Forensic DNA Endgame, 37 Jurimetrics J. 477, 480 (1997) (Table 1).

incidence can be eliminated as explanations for a match, then only the hypothesis of identity remains. We turn, then, to the considerations that affect the chances of a reported match when the defendant is not the source of the trace evidence.

## § 2:43  Interpretation of laboratory results—Alternative hypotheses— Error

Although many experts would concede that even with rigorous protocols, the chance of a laboratory error exceeds that of a coincidental match,[1] quantifying the former probability is a formidable task. Some commentary proposes using the proportion of false positives that the particular laboratory has experienced in blind proficiency tests or the rate of false positives on proficiency tests averaged across all laboratories.[2] Indeed, the 1992 NRC Report remarks that "proficiency tests provide a measure of the false-positive and false-negative rates of a laboratory."[3] Yet, the same report recognizes that "errors on proficiency tests do not necessarily reflect permanent probabilities of false-positive or false-negative results,"[4] and the 1996 NRC report suggests that a probability of a false-positive error that would apply to a specific case cannot be estimated objectively.[5] If the false positive probability were, say, 0.001, it would take tens of thousands of proficiency tests to estimate that probability accurately, and the application of an historical industry-wide error rate to a particular laboratory at a later time would be debatable.[6]

Most commentators who urge the use of proficiency tests to estimate the probability that a laboratory has erred in a particular case agree that blind proficiency testing cannot be done in sufficient numbers to yield an accurate estimate of a small error rate. However, they maintain that proficiency tests, blind or otherwise, should be used to provide a conservative estimate of the false-positive error probability.[7] For example, if there were no errors in 100 tests, a 95% confidence interval would include the possibility that the error rate could be almost as high as 3%.[8]

Instead of pursuing a numerical estimate, the second NAS committee and individual scientists who question the value of proficiency tests for estimating case-specific laboratory-error probabilities suggest that each laboratory document all the steps in its analyses and reserve portions of the DNA samples for independent testing whenever feasible. Scrutinizing the chain of custody, examining the laboratory's protocol, verifying that it adhered to that protocol, and conducting confirmatory tests if there

---

**[Section 2:43]**

[1]E.g., Bernard Devlin & Kathryn Roeder, DNA Profiling: Statistics and Population Genetics, in 1 Modern Scientific Evidence: The Law and Science of Expert Testimony § 18-5.3, at 743 (David Faigman et al. eds., 1997).

[2]E.g., Koehler, Error and Exaggeration in the Presentation of DNA Evidence at Trial, 34 Jurimetrics J. 21, 37–38 (1993); Scheck, DNA and *Daubert*, 15 Cardozo L. Rev. 1959, 1984 n.93 (1994).

[3]Committee on DNA Technology in Forensic Science, National Research Council, DNA Technology in Forensic Science 94 (1992) (Table 1.1).

[4]Committee on DNA Technology in Forensic Science, National Research Council, DNA Technology in Forensic Science 89 (1992) (Table 1.1).

[5]Committee on DNA Forensic Science: An Update, National Research Council, The Evaluation of Forensic DNA Evidence 85–87 (1996).

[6]Committee on DNA Forensic Science: An Update, National Research Council, The Evaluation of Forensic DNA Evidence 85–86 (1996); Bernard Devlin & Kathryn Roeder, DNA Profiling: Statistics and Population Genetics, in 1 Modern Scientific Evidence: The Law and Science of Expert Testimony § 18-5.3, at 744–745 (David Faigman et al. eds., 1997). Such arguments have not persuaded the proponents of estimating the probability of error from industry-wide proficiency testing. E.g., Koehler, Why DNA Likelihood Ratios Should Account for Error (Even When a National Research Council Report Says They Should Not), 37 Jurimetrics J. 425 (1997).

[7]E.g., Koehler, DNA Matches and Statistics: Important Questions, Surprising Answers, 76 Judicature at 228 (1993); Lempert, After the DNA Wars: Skirmishing with NRC II, 37 Jurimetrics J. 439, 447–448, 453 (1997).

[8]See Committee on DNA Forensic Science: An Update, National Research Council, The Evaluation of Forensic DNA Evidence 86 n. 1 (1996).

are any suspicious circumstances can help to eliminate the hypothesis of laboratory error,[9] whether or not a case-specific probability can be estimated.[10] Furthermore, if the defendant has had a meaningful opportunity to retest a sample but has been unable or unwilling to obtain an inconsistent result, the relevance of a statistic based on past proficiency tests might be questionable.

## § 2:44 Interpretation of laboratory results—Alternative hypotheses—Kinship

With enough genetic markers, all individuals except for identical twins should be distinguishable, but this ideal is not always attainable with the limited number of loci typically used in forensic testing.[1] Close relatives have more genes in common than unrelated individuals, and various procedures for dealing with the possibility that the true source of the forensic DNA is not the defendant, but a close relative have been proposed.[2] Often, the investigation, including additional DNA testing, can be extended to all known relatives.[3] But this is not feasible in every case, and there is always the chance that some unknown relatives are included in the suspect population.[4] Formulae are available for computing the probability that any person with a specified degree of kinship to the defendant also possesses the incriminating genotype.[5] For example, the probability that an untested brother (or sister) would match at four loci (with alleles that each occur in 5% of the population) is about

---

[9]E.g., Koehler, On Conveying the Probative Value of DNA Evidence: Frequencies, Likelihood Ratios, and Error Rates, 67 U. Colo. L. Rev. 859, 866 (1996) ("In the *Simpson* case, [l]aboratory error was unlikely because many blood samples were tested at different laboratories using two different DNA typing methods."); Thompson, DNA Evidence in the O.J. Simpson Trial, 67 U. Colo. L. Rev. 827, 827 (1996) ("the extensive use of duplicate testing in the *Simpson* case greatly reduced concerns (that are crucial in most other cases) about the potential for false positives due to poor scientific practices of DNA laboratories").

[10]See Berger, Laboratory Error Seen Through the Lens of Science and Policy, 30 U.C. Davis L. Rev. 1081 (1997).

**[Section 2:44]**

[1]See, e.g., B.S. Weir, Discussion of "Inference in Forensic Identification," 158 J. Royal Stat. Soc'y ser. A 49 (1995) ("the chance that two unrelated individuals in a population share the same 16-allele [VNTR] profile is vanishingly small, and even for full sibs the chance is only 1 in very many thousands.").

[2]See Belin et al., Summarizing DNA Evidence When Relatives Are Possible Suspects, 92 J. Am. Stat. Ass'n 706, 707–708 (1997). Recommendation 4.4 of the 1996 NRC report reads:

If possible contributors of the evidence sample include relatives of the suspect, DNA profiles of those relatives should be obtained. If these profiles cannot be obtained, the probability of finding the evidence profile in those relatives should be calculated with [specified formulae].

Committee on DNA Forensic Science: An Update, National Research Council, The Evaluation of Forensic DNA Evidence 6 (1996).

[3]Committee on DNA Forensic Science: An Update, National Research Council, The Evaluation of Forensic DNA Evidence 113 (1996).

[4]When that population is very large, however, the presence of a few relatives will have little impact on the probability that a suspect drawn at random from that population will have the incriminating genotype. Committee on DNA Forensic Science: An Update, National Research Council, The Evaluation of Forensic DNA Evidence 113 (1996). Furthermore, it has been suggested that the effect of relatedness is of practical importance only for very close relatives, such as siblings. Brookfield, The Effect of Relatives on the Likelihood Ratio Associated with DNA Profile Evidence in Criminal Cases, 34 J. Forensic Sci. Soc'y 193 (1994).

[5]E.g., Brookfield, The Effect of Relatives on the Likelihood Ratio Associated with DNA Profile Evidence in Criminal Cases, 34 J. Forensic Sci. Soc'y 193 (1994); David J. Balding & Peter Donnelly, Inference in Forensic Identification, 158 J. Royal Stat. Soc'y Ser. A 21 (1995); Ian W. Evett & Bruce S. Weir, Interpreting DNA Evidence: Statistical Genetics for Forensic Scientists 108–118 (1998); Morton, The Forensic DNA Endgame, 37 Jurimetrics J. at 484 (1997) (Table 1); Committee on DNA Forensic Science: An Update, National Research Council, The Evaluation of Forensic DNA Evidence 113 (1996). But see Committee on DNA Technology in Forensic Science, National Research Council, DNA Technology in Forensic Science 87 (1992) (Table 1.1) (giving an incorrect formula for siblings). Empirical measures that are not directly interpretable as probabilities also have been described. Belin et al., Summarizing DNA Evidence When Relatives Are Possible Suspects, 92 J. Am. Stat. Ass'n 706, 707–708 (1997).

0.006; the probability that an aunt (or uncle) would match is about 0.0000005.[6]

## § 2:45    Interpretation of laboratory results—Alternative hypotheses— Coincidence

Another rival hypothesis is coincidence: The defendant is not the source of the crime scene DNA, but happens to have the same genotype as an unrelated individual who is the true source. Various procedures for assessing the plausibility of this hypothesis are available. In principle, one could test all conceivable suspects. If everyone except the defendant has a non-matching profile, then the conclusion that the defendant is the source is inescapable. But exhaustive, error-free testing of the population of conceivable suspects is almost never feasible. The suspect population normally defies any enumeration, and in the typical crime where DNA evidence is found, the population of possible perpetrators is so huge that even if all its members could be listed, they could not all be tested.[1]

An alternative procedure would be to take a sample of people from the suspect population, find the relative frequency of the profile in this sample, and use that statistic to estimate the frequency in the entire suspect population. The smaller the frequency, the less likely it is that the defendant's DNA would match if the defendant were not the source of trace evidence. Again, however, the suspect population is difficult to define, so some surrogate must be used. The procedure commonly followed is to estimate the relative frequency of the incriminating genotype in a large population. But even this cannot be done directly because each possible multilocus profile is so rare that it is not likely to show up in any sample of a reasonable size.[2] However, the frequencies of most alleles can be determined accurately by sampling the population[3] to construct *databases* that reveal how often each allele occurs.[4] Principles of population genetics then can be applied to combine the estimated allele

---

[6]The large discrepancy between two siblings on the one hand, and an uncle and nephew on the other, reflects the fact that the siblings have far more shared ancestry. All their genes are inherited through the same two parents. In contrast, a nephew and an uncle inherit from two unrelated mothers, and so will have few maternal alleles in common. As for paternal alleles, the nephew inherits not from his uncle, but from his uncle's brother, who shares by descent only about one-half of his alleles with the uncle.

**[Section 2:45]**

[1]In the United Kingdom and Europe, mass DNA screenings in small towns have been undertaken. See, e.g., D.H. Kaye, Science in Evidence at 222–226 (1997). The strategy has been employed in various locations in the United States as well. See Imwinkelried & Kaye, DNA Typing: Emerging or Neglected Issues, 413 Wash. L. Rev. 76 (2001).

[2]Committee on DNA Forensic Science: An Update, National Research Council, The Evaluation of Forensic DNA Evidence 89–90 (1996) ("A very small proportion of the trillions of possible profiles are found in any database, so it is necessary to use the frequencies of individual alleles to estimate the frequency of a given profile."). The 1992 NRC report proposed reporting the occurrences of a profile in a database, but recognized that "such estimates do not take advantage of the full potential of the genetic approach." Committee

on DNA Technology in Forensic Science, National Research Council, DNA Technology in Forensic Science 76 (1992) (Table 1.1). For further discussion of the statistical inferences that might be drawn from the absence of a profile in a sample of a given size, see Committee on DNA Forensic Science: An Update, National Research Council, The Evaluation of Forensic DNA Evidence 159–160 (1996) (arguing that "the abundant data make [the direct counting method] unnecessary").

[3]Ideally, a probability sample from the population of interest would be taken. Indeed, a few experts have testified that no meaningful conclusions can be drawn in the absence of random sampling. E.g., *People v. Soto*, 21 Cal. 4th 512, 88 Cal. Rptr. 2d 34, 981 P.2d 958 (1999); *State v. Anderson*, 118 N.M. 284, 881 P.2d 29, 39 (1994).

Unfortunately, a list of the people who comprise the entire population of possible suspects is almost never available; consequently, probability sampling from the directly relevant population is generally impossible. Probability sampling from a proxy population is possible, but it is not the norm in studies of the distributions of genes in populations. Typically, convenience samples are used. The 1996 NRC report suggests that for the purpose of estimating allele frequencies, convenience sampling should give results comparable to random sampling, and it discusses procedures for estimating the random sampling error. Committee on DNA Forensic Science: An Update, National Research Council, The Evaluation of Forensic

frequencies into an estimate of the probability that a person born in the population will have the multilocus genotype. This probability often is referred to as the *random match probability*. Three principal methods for computing the random match probability from allele frequencies have been developed. This section describes these methods; the next section considers other quantities that have been proposed as measures of the probative value of the DNA evidence.

## § 2:46 Interpretation of laboratory results—Alternative hypotheses— Coincidence—The basic product rule

The basic product rule estimates the frequency of genotypes in an infinite population of individuals who choose their mates and reproduce independently of the alleles used to compare the samples. Although population geneticists describe this situation as *random mating*, these words are terms of art. Geneticists know that people do not choose their mates by a lottery, and they use "random mating" to indicate that the choices are uncorrelated with the specific alleles that make up the genotypes in question.[1]

In a randomly mating population, the expected frequency of a pair of alleles at each locus depends on whether the two alleles are distinct. If a different allele is inherited from each parent, the expected single-locus genotype frequency is twice the product of the two individual frequencies.[2] But if the offspring happens to inherit the same allele from each parent, the expected single-locus genotype frequency is the square of the allele frequency.[3] These proportions are known as *Hardy-Weinberg* proportions. Even if two populations with distinct allele frequencies are thrown together, within the limits of chance variation, random mating produces Hardy-Weinberg equilibrium in a single generation. An example is given below.[4]

Once the proportion of the population that has each of the single-locus genotypes

---

DNA Evidence 126–127, 146–148, 186 (1996).

[4]In the formative years of forensic DNA testing, defendants frequently contended that the size of the forensic databases were too small to give accurate estimates. To the extent that the databases are comparable to random samples, confidence intervals are a standard method for indicating the amount of error due to sample size. E.g., Kaye, DNA Evidence: Probability, Population Genetics, and the Courts, 7 Harv. J. L. & Tech. 101 (1993).

**[Section 2:46]**

[1]E.g., Committee on DNA Forensic Science: An Update, National Research Council, The Evaluation of Forensic DNA Evidence 90 (1996):

> In the simplest population structure, mates are chosen at random. Clearly, the population of the United States does not mate at random; a person from Oregon is more likely to mate with another from Oregon than with one from Florida. Furthermore, people often choose mates according to physical and behavioral attributes, such as height and personality. But they do not choose each other according to the markers used for forensic studies, such as VNTRs and STRs. Rather, the proportion of matings between people with two marker genotypes is determined by their frequencies in the mating population. If the allele frequencies in Oregon and Florida are the same as those in the nation as a whole, then the proportion of genotypes in the two states will be the same as those for the United

States, even though the population of the whole country clearly does not mate at random.

[2]In more technical terms, when the frequencies of two alleles are $p_1$ and $p_2$, the single-locus genotype frequency for the corresponding heterozygotes is expected to be $2p_1p_2$.

[3]The expected proportion is $p_1^2$ for allele 1, and $p_2^2$ for allele 2. With VNTRs, a complication arises with apparent homozygotes. A single band on an autoradiogram might really be two bands that are close together, or a second band that is relatively small might have migrated to the edge of the gel during the electrophoresis. Forensic laboratories therefore make a "conservative" assumption. They act as if there is a second, unseen band, and they use the excessively large value of $p_2 = 100\%$ for the frequency of the presumably unseen allele. With this modification, the genotype frequency for apparent homozygotes becomes $P = 2p_1$. If the single-banded pattern is a true homozygote, this $2p$ convention overstates the frequency of the single-locus genotype because $2p$ is greater than $p^2$ for any possible proportion $p$. For instance, if $p = 0.05$, then $2p = 0.10$, which is 40 times greater than $p^2 = 0.0025$.

[4]Suppose that 10% of the sperm in the gene pool of the population carry allele 1 ($A_1$), and 50% carry allele 2 ($A_2$). Similarly, 10% of the eggs carry $A_1$, and 50% carry $A_2$. (Other sperm and eggs carry other types.) With random mating, we

for the forensic profile has been estimated in this way, the proportion of the population that is expected to share the combination of them—the *multilocus* profile frequency—is given by multiplying the single-locus proportions. This multiplication is exactly correct when the single-locus genotypes are statistically independent. In that case, the population is said to be in *linkage equilibrium*.

Extensive litigation and scientific commentary have considered whether the occurrences of alleles at each locus are independent events (Hardy-Weinberg equilibrium), and whether the loci are independent (linkage equilibrium). Beginning around 1990, several scientists suggested that the equilibrium frequencies do not follow the simple model of a homogeneous population mating without regard to the loci used in forensic DNA profiling. They suggested that the major racial populations are composed of ethnic subpopulations whose members tend to mate among themselves.[5] Within each ethnic subpopulation, mating still can be random, but if, say, Italian-Americans have allele frequencies that are markedly different than the average for all whites, and if Italian-Americans only mate among themselves, then using the average frequencies for all whites in the basic product formula could understate—or overstate—a multilocus profile frequency for the subpopulation of Italian-Americans.[6] Similarly, using the population frequencies could understate—or overstate—the profile frequencies in the white population itself.[7]

Consequently, if we want to know the frequency of an incriminating profile among Italian-Americans, the basic product rule applied to the white allele frequencies could be in error; and there is some chance that it will understate the profile frequency in the white population as a whole. One might presume that the extent of the error could be determined by looking to the variations across racial groups,[8] but, for a short time, a few scientists insisted that variations from one ethnic group to another within a race were larger than variations from one race to another.[9] In light

---

expect $10\% \times 10\% = 1\%$ of all the fertilized eggs to be $A_1A_1$, and another $50\% \times 50\% = 25\%$ to be $A_2A_2$. These constitute two distinct homozygote profiles. Likewise, we expect $10\% \times 50\% = 5\%$ of the fertilized eggs to be $A_1A_2$ and another $50\% \times 10\% = 5\%$ to be $A_2A_1$. These two configurations produce indistinguishable profiles—a band, dot, or the like for $A_1$ and another mark for $A_2$. So the expected proportion of heterozygotes $A_1A_2$ is $5\% + 5\% = 10\%$.

Oddly, some courts and commentators have written that the expected heterozygote frequency for this example is only 5%. E.g., Thompson & Ford, DNA Typing: Acceptance and Weight of the New Genetic Identification Tests, 75 Va. L. Rev. 45, 81–82 (1989). For further discussion, see Kaye, Bible Reading: DNA Evidence in Arizona, 28 Ariz. St. L. J. 1035 (1996); D.H. Kaye, Cross-Examining Science, 36 Jurimetrics J. vii (Winter 1996).

[5]The most prominent expression of this position is Lewontin & Hartl, Population Genetics in Forensic DNA Typing, 254 Science 1745 (1991).

[6]On average, the use of population-wide allele frequencies overstates the genotype frequencies within defendant's subpopulation. See Krane et al., Genetic Differences at Four DNA Typing Loci in Finnish, Italian, and Mixed Caucasian Populations, 89 Proc. Nat'l Acad. Sci. 10583 (1992); Sawyer et al., DNA Fingerprinting Loci Do Show Population Differences: Comments on

Budowle et al., 59 Am. J. Hum. Genetics 272 (1996) (letter). This mean overestimation occurs because (1) the use of population-wide frequencies rather than subpopulation frequencies underestimates homozygote frequencies and overestimates heterozygote frequencies, and (2) heterozygosity far exceeds homozygosity.

[7]The use of the population-wide allele frequencies usually overstates genotype frequencies in the population as a whole, thereby benefitting most defendants. See Kaye, DNA Evidence: Probability, Population Genetics, and the Courts, 7 Harv. J. L. & Tech. 101, 142 (1993).

[8]On the problems in defining racial populations, compare Loring Brace, Region Does Not Mean "Race"—Reality Versus Convention in Forensic Anthropology, 40 J. Forensic Sci. 171 (1994), with Kennedy, But Professor, Why Teach Race Identification if Races Don't Exist?, 40 J. Forensic Sci. 797 (1995).

[9]*Compare* Lewontin & Hartl, Population Genetics in Forensic DNA Typing, 254 Science 1745 (1991). ("there is, on average, one-third more genetic variation among Irish, Spanish, Italians, Slavs, Swedes, and other subpopulations than there is, on average, between Europeans, Asians, Africans, Amerindians, and Oceanians"), *with* Lewontin, Discussion, 9 Stat. Sci. 259, 260 (1994) ("all parties agree that differentiation among [major ethnic groups] is as large, if not larger than,

of this literature[10] courts had grounds to conclude that the basic product rule, used with broad population frequencies, was not universally accepted for estimating profile frequencies within subpopulations. Yet, few courts recognized that there was much less explicit dissension over the ability of the rule to estimate profile frequencies in a general population.[11] Particularly in *Frye* jurisdictions, a substantial number of appellate courts began to exclude DNA evidence for want of a generally accepted method of estimating profile frequencies in both situations.[12]

## § 2:47 Interpretation of laboratory results—Alternative hypotheses— Coincidence—The product rule with ceilings

In 1992, the National Academy of Sciences' Committee on DNA Technology in Forensic Science assumed arguendo that population structure was a serious threat to the basic product rule and proposed a variation to provide an upper bound on a profile frequency within any population or subpopulation.[1] The interim ceiling method uses the same general formulas as the basic product rule,[2] but with different values of the frequencies. Instead of multiplying together the allele frequencies from any single, major racial database, the procedure picks, for each allele in the DNA profile, the largest value seen in *any* race.[3] If that value is less than 10%, the procedure inflates it to 10%. Those values are then multiplied as with the basic product rule. Thus, the ceiling method employs a mix-and-match, inflate, and

---

the difference among tribes and national groups [within major ethnic groups]"). Other population geneticists dismissed as obviously untenable the early assertions of greater variability across the ethnic subpopulations of a race than across races. E.g., B. Devlin & Neil Risch, NRC Report on DNA Typing, 260 Science 1057 (1993); Morton et al., Kinship Bioassay on Hypervariable Loci in Blacks and Caucasians, 90 Proc. Nat'l Acad. Sci. 1892 (1993) (gene frequencies cited by Lewontin & Hartl are atypical, and "[l]ess than 2% of the diversity selected by Lewontin and Hartl is due to the national kinship to which they attribute it, little of which persists in regional forensic samples").

[10]The literature on genetic differences across the globe is reviewed in, for example, Bernard Devlin & Kathryn Roeder, DNA Profiling: Statistics and Population Genetics.

[11]See Kaye, DNA Evidence: Probability, Population Genetics, and the Courts, 7 Harv. J. L. & Tech. 101, 146 (1993). The general perception was that ethnic stratification within the major racial categories posed a problem regardless of whether the relevant population for estimating the random match probability was a broad racial group or a narrow, inbred ethnic subpopulation.

[12]See cases cited, Kaye, DNA Evidence: Probability, Population Genetics, and the Courts, 7 Harv. J. L. & Tech. 101, 158 (1993). Courts applying *Daubert* or similar standards were more receptive to the evidence. E.g., *U.S. v. Jakobetz*, 955 F.2d 786, 34 Fed. R. Evid. Serv. 876 (2d Cir. 1992); *U.S. v. Bonds*, 12 F.3d 540, 38 Fed. R. Evid. Serv. 688 (6th Cir. 1993); *U.S. v. Chischilly*, 30 F.3d 1144, 40 Fed. R. Evid. Serv. 289 (9th Cir. 1994); *U.S. v. Davis*, 40 F.3d 1069, 40 Fed. R. Evid. Serv. 1036 (10th Cir. 1994).

**[Section 2:47]**

[1]See Committee on DNA Technology in Forensic Science, National Research Council, DNA Technology in Forensic Science 80, 91–92 (1992) (Table 1.1); ("Although mindful of the controversy, the committee has chosen to assume for the sake of discussion that population substructure may exist and provide a method for estimating population [genotype] frequencies in a manner that adequately accounts for it."). The report was unclear as to whether its "interim ceiling principle" was a substitute for or merely a supplement to the usual basic product rule. Years later, one member of the committee opined that the committee intended the latter interpretation. Eric S. Lander & Bruce Budowle, Commentary: DNA Fingerprinting Dispute Laid to Rest, 371 Nature 735 (1994). In any event, the interim ceiling principle was proposed as a stopgap measure, to be supplanted by another ceiling principle that could be used after sampling many "[g]enetically homogeneous populations from various regions of the world." Committee on DNA Technology in Forensic Science, National Research Council, DNA Technology in Forensic Science 84 (1992) (Table 1.1).

[2]Applied to a single racial group like whites, the basic product rule estimates the frequency of the multilocus genotype as the product of the single-locus frequencies, and it estimates each single-locus frequency as $2p_1p_2$ for heterozygotes or as a quantity exceeding $p^2$ for homozygotes, where $p$ refers to frequencies estimated from the database for that race.

[3]Actually, an even larger figure is used—the upper 95% confidence limit on the allele frequency estimate for that race. This is intended to account for sampling error due to the limited size of the

multiply strategy. The result, it is widely believed, is an extremely conservative estimate of the profile frequency that more than compensates for the possibility of any population structure that might undermine the assumptions of Hardy-Weinberg and linkage equilibria in the major racial populations.[4]

### § 2:48    Interpretation of laboratory results—Alternative hypotheses—Coincidence—The product rule for a structured population

The 1996 NRC Report distinguishes between cases in which the suspect population is a broad racial population and those in which that population is a genetically distinct subgroup. In the former situation, Recommendation 4.1 endorses the basic product rule:

> In general, the calculation of a profile frequency should be made with the product rule. If the race of the person who left the evidence-sample DNA is known, the database for the person's race should be used; if the race is not known, calculations for all the racial groups to which possible suspects belong should be made.[1]

"For example," the committee wrote, "if DNA is recovered from semen in a case in which a woman hitchhiker on an interstate highway has been raped by a white man, the product rule with the 2p rule can be used with VNTR data from a sample of whites to estimate the frequency of the profile among white males. If the race of the rapist were in doubt, the product rule could still be used and the results given

---

databases. Committee on DNA Technology in Forensic Science, National Research Council, DNA Technology in Forensic Science 92 (1992) (Table 1.1).

[4]See, e.g., Committee on DNA Forensic Science: An Update, National Research Council, The Evaluation of Forensic DNA Evidence 156 (1996) ("sufficiently conservative to accommodate the presence of substructure . . . a lower limit on the size of the profile frequency"); Committee on DNA Technology in Forensic Science, National Research Council, DNA Technology in Forensic Science 91 (1992) (Table 1.1) ("conservative calculation"). This modification of the basic product rule provoked vociferous criticism from many scientists, and it distressed certain prosecutors and other law enforcement personnel who perceived the 1992 NRC report as contributing to the rejection of DNA evidence in many jurisdictions. See, e.g., Kaye, DNA, NAS, NRC, DAB, RFLP, PCR, and More: An Introduction to the Symposium on the 1996 NRC Report on Forensic DNA Evidence, 37 Jurimetrics J. 395, 396 (1997). The judicial impact of the NRC report and the debate among scientists over the ceiling method are reviewed in Kaye, The Forensic Debut of the National Research Council's DNA Report: Population Structure, Ceiling Frequencies, and the Need for Numbers, 34 Jurimetrics J. 369 (1994) (suggesting that because the disagreement about the ceiling principle is a dispute about legal policy rather than scientific knowledge, the debate among scientists does not justify excluding ceiling frequencies).

By 1995, however, many courts were concluding that because a consensus that ceiling estimates are conservative had emerged, these

estimates are admissible. At the same time, other courts that only a short while ago had held basic product estimates to be too controversial to be admissible decided that there was sufficient agreement about the basic product rule for it to be used. See *State v. Johnson*, 186 Ariz. 329, 922 P.2d 294, 300 (1996); *State v. Copeland*, 130 Wash. 2d 244, 922 P.2d 1304, 1318 (1996) ("Although at one time a significant dispute existed among qualified scientists, from the present vantage point we are able to say that the significant dispute was short-lived."); D.H. Kaye, DNA Identification in Criminal Cases: Lingering and Emerging Evidentiary Issues, in Proceedings of the Seventh International Symposium on Human Identification 12 (1997).

In 1994, a second NAS committee was installed to review the criticism and the studies that had accumulated in the aftermath of the 1992 report. In 1996, it reported that the ceiling method is an unnecessary and extravagant way to handle the likely extent of population structure. Committee on DNA Forensic Science: An Update, National Research Council, The Evaluation of Forensic DNA Evidence at 158, 162 (1996).

**[Section 2:48]**

[1]Committee on DNA Forensic Science: An Update, National Research Council, The Evaluation of Forensic DNA Evidence 5 (1996). The recommendation also calls for modifications to the Hardy-Weinberg proportion for apparent homozygotes. The modifications depend on whether the alleles are discrete (as in PCR-based tests) or continuous (as in VNTR testing). Committee on DNA Forensic Science: An Update, National Research Council, The Evaluation of Forensic DNA Evidence 5 n. 2 (1996).

for data on whites, blacks, Hispanics, and east Asians."[2] However, "[w]hen there are partially isolated subgroups in a population, the situation is more complex; then a suitably altered model leads to slightly different estimates of the quantities that are multiplied together in the formula for the frequency of the profile in the population."[3] Thus, the committee's Recommendation 4.2 urges that:

> If the particular subpopulation from which the evidence sample came is known, the allele frequencies for the specific subgroup should be used as described in Recommendation 4.1. If allele frequencies for the subgroup are not available, although data for the full population are, then the calculations should use the population-structure equations 4.10 for each locus, and the resulting values should be multiplied.[4]

The "suitably altered model" is a generalization of the basic product rule. In this *affinal model*, as it is sometimes called,[5] the "population-structure equations" are similar to those for multiplying single-locus frequencies. However, they involve not only the individual allele frequencies, but also a quantity that measures the extent of population structure.[6] The single-locus frequencies are multiplied together as in the basic product rule to find the multilocus frequency. Although few reported cases have analyzed the admissibility of random match probabilities estimated with the product rule for structured populations, the validity of the affinal model of a structured population has not been questioned in the scientific literature.[7]

The committee recommended that the population-structure equations be used in special situations,[8] but they could be applied to virtually all cases. The report suggests conservative values of the population-structure constant might be used for broad suspect populations as well as values for many partially isolated subpopulations.[9] The population-structure equations always give more conservative probabilities than the basic product rule when both formulae are applied to the

---

[2]Committee on DNA Forensic Science: An Update, National Research Council, The Evaluation of Forensic DNA Evidence 5 (1996) (note omitted). See also C. Thomas Caskey, Comments on DNA-based Forensic Analysis, 49 Am. J. Hum. Genetics 893 (1991) (letter). For a case with comparable facts, see *U.S. v. Jakobetz*, 747 F. Supp. 250, 31 Fed. R. Evid. Serv. 1007 (D. Vt. 1990), judgment aff'd, 955 F.2d 786, 34 Fed. R. Evid. Serv. 876 (2d Cir. 1992).

[3]Committee on DNA Forensic Science: An Update, National Research Council, The Evaluation of Forensic DNA Evidence 5 (1996).

[4]Committee on DNA Forensic Science: An Update, National Research Council, The Evaluation of Forensic DNA Evidence at 5–6 (1996).

[5]Bernard Devlin & Kathryn Roeder, DNA Profiling: Statistics and Population Genetics, in 1 Modern Scientific Evidence: The Law and Science of Expert Testimony § 18-3.1.3, at 723 (David Faigman et al. eds., 1997).

[6]Committee on DNA Forensic Science: An Update, National Research Council, The Evaluation of Forensic DNA Evidence 114–115 (1996) (equations 4.10a & 4.10b); see also papers cited, Bernard Devlin & Kathryn Roeder, DNA Profiling: Statistics and Population Genetics, in 1 Modern Scientific Evidence: The Law and Science of Expert Testimony § 18-3.1.3, at 723 n.37 (David Faigman et al. eds., 1997). This quantity usually is designated $\theta$ or $F_{st}$. See generally Ian W. Evett & Bruce S. Weir, Interpreting DNA Evidence:

Statistical Genetics for Forensic Scientists 94–107, 118–123, 156–162 (1998).

[7]Questions can arise, however, as to the estimation of the parameter $\theta$. See David J. Balding, Weight-of-Evidence for Forensic DNA Profiles 63 (2005).

[8]The report explains that the recommendation to use the population-structure equations "deals with the case in which the person who is the source of the evidence DNA is known to belong to a particular subgroup of a racial category." Committee on DNA Forensic Science: An Update, National Research Council, The Evaluation of Forensic DNA Evidence 6 (1996). It offers this illustration:

> For example, if the hitchhiker was not on an interstate highway but in the midst of, say, a small village in New England and we had good reason to believe that the rapist was an inhabitant of the village, the product rule could still be used (as described in Recommendation 4.1) if there is a reasonably large database on the villagers.
>
> If specific data on the villagers are lacking, a more complex model could be used to estimate the random-match probability for the incriminating profile on the basis of data on the major population group (whites) that includes the villagers.

Committee on DNA Forensic Science: An Update, National Research Council, The Evaluation of Forensic DNA Evidence at 6 (1996).

[9]Committee on DNA Forensic Science: An Update, National Research Council, The Evaluation of Forensic DNA Evidence 115 (1996) ("typi-

same database, and they are usually conservative relative to calculations based on the subpopulation of the defendant.[10]

In a few situations, however, very little data on either the larger population or the specific subpopulation will be available.[11] To handle such cases, Recommendation 4.3 provides:

> If the person who contributed the evidence sample is from a group or tribe for which no adequate database exists, data from several other groups or tribes thought to be closely related to it should be used. The profile frequency should be calculated as described in Recommendation 4.1 for each group or tribe.[12]

Similar procedures have been followed in a few cases where the issue has surfaced.[13]

### § 2:49  Interpretation of laboratory results—Measures of probative value— Likelihood ratios

Sufficiently small probabilities of a match for close relatives and unrelated members of the suspect population undermine the hypotheses of kinship and coincidence. Adequate safeguards and checks for possible laboratory error make that explanation of the finding of matching genotypes implausible. The inference that the defendant is the source of the crime-scene DNA is then secure. But this mode of reasoning by elimination due to small probabilities is not the only way to analyze DNA evidence. Two alternatives are likelihoods and posterior probabilities.[1]

To choose between two competing hypotheses, one can compare how probable the evidence is under each hypothesis. Suppose that the probability of a match in a well-run laboratory is close to one when the samples both contain only the defendant's DNA, while the probability of a coincidental match and the probability of a match with a close relative are close to zero. In these circumstances, the DNA profiling result strongly supports the claim that the defendant is the source, for the observed outcome—the match—is many times more probable when the defendant is

---

cal values for white and black populations are less than 0.01, usually about 0.002. Values for Hispanics are slightly higher . . . ."), 116 ("For urban populations, 0.01 is a conservative value. A higher value—say 0.03 could be used for isolated villages."); cf. David J. Balding, Weight-of-Evidence for Forensic DNA Profiles 97 (2005) (recommending using values between .01 and .05 depending on the circumstances); John M. Butler, Forensic DNA Typing 507 (2d ed. 2005) (giving examples of small changes due to using small values of $\theta$); John Buckleton et al., Forensic DNA Evidence Interpretation §§ 3.2 to 3.4 (2005); Bernard Devlin & Kathryn Roeder, DNA Profiling: Statistics and Population Genetics, in 1 Modern Scientific Evidence: The Law and Science of Expert Testimony § 18-3.1.3, at 723–724 (David Faigman et al. eds., 1997) ("For [VNTR] markers, theta-bar is generally agreed to lie between 0 and .02 for most populations.").

[10]Bernard Devlin & Kathryn Roeder, DNA Profiling: Statistics and Population Genetics, in 1 Modern Scientific Evidence: The Law and Science of Expert Testimony § 18-3.1.3, at 723 (David Faigman et al. eds., 1997).

[11]See, e.g., *People of Territory of Guam v. Atoigue*, 1992 WL 245628 (D. Guam 1992), aff'd, 36 F.3d 1103 (9th Cir. 1994) (unpublished).

[12]Committee on DNA Forensic Science: An Update, National Research Council, The Evaluation of Forensic DNA Evidence 6 (1996). The committee explained that:

> This recommendation deals with the case in which the person who is the source of the evidence DNA is known to belong to a particular subgroup of a racial category but there are no DNA data on either the subgroup or the population to which the subgroup belongs. It would apply, for example, if a person on an isolated Indian reservation in the Southwest, had been assaulted by a member of the tribe, and there were no data on DNA profiles of the tribe. In that case, the recommendation calls for use of the product rule (as described in Recommendation 4.1) with several other closely related tribes for which adequate databases exist.

Committee on DNA Forensic Science: An Update, National Research Council, The Evaluation of Forensic DNA Evidence 6 (1996).

[13]§ 2:1.

**[Section 2:49]**

[1]See, e.g., Richard Royall, Statistical Evidence: A Likelihood Paradigm (1997); Taroni et al., Evaluation and Presentation of Forensic DNA Evidence in European Laboratories, 42 Sci. & Just. 21, 27 (2002) (concluding that likelihood-ratio statements "should be adopted by all European laboratories, not only for DNA, but for all aspects of forensic interpretation").

the source than when someone else is. How many times more probable? Suppose that there is a 1% chance that the laboratory would miss a true match, so that the probability of its finding a match when the defendant is the source is 0.99. Suppose further that $p = 0.00001$ is the random match probability. Then the match is 0.99/0.00001, or 99,000 times more likely to be seen if the defendant is the source than if an unrelated individual is. Such a ratio is called a *likelihood ratio*, and a likelihood ratio of 99,000 means that the DNA profiling supports the claim of identity 99,000 times more strongly than it supports the hypothesis of coincidence.[2]

Likelihood ratios are particularly useful for VNTRs and for trace evidence samples that contain DNA from more than one person.[3] With VNTRs, the procedure commonly used to estimate the allele frequencies that are combined via some version of the product rule is called *binning*.[4] In the simplest and most accurate version, the laboratory first forms a "bin" that stretches across the range of fragment lengths in the match window surrounding an evidence band. For example, if a 1,000 base-pair (bp) band is seen in the evidence sample, and the laboratory's match window is ±5%, then the bin extends from 950 to 1,050 bp. The laboratory then finds the proportion of VNTR bands in its database that fall within this bin. If 7% of the bands in the database lie in the 950–1,050 bp range, then 7% is the estimated allele frequency for this band. The two-stage procedure of: (1) declaring matches between two samples when all the corresponding bands lie with the match window; and (2) estimating the frequency of a band in the population by the proportion that lie within the corresponding bin is known as *match-binning*.[5]

Match-binning is statistically inefficient. It ignores the extent to which two samples match and gives the same coincidence probability to a close match as it does to a marginal one. Other methods obviate the need for matching by simultaneously combining the probability of the observed degree of matching with the probability of observing bands that are that close together. These "similarity likelihood ratios" dispense with the somewhat arbitrary dichotomy between matches

---

[2]See Committee on DNA Forensic Science: An Update, National Research Council, The Evaluation of Forensic DNA Evidence 100 (1996); Kaye, The Relevance of "Matching" DNA: Is the Window Half Open or Half Shut?, 85 J. Crim. L. & Criminology 676 (1995).

[3]§ 2:34. Mixed samples arise in various ways—blood from two or more persons mingled at the scene of a crime, victim and assailant samples on a vaginal swab, semen from multiple sexual assailants, and so on. In many cases, one of the contributors—for example, the victim—is known, and the genetic profile of the unknown portion is readily deduced. In those situations, the analysis of a remaining single-person profile can proceed in the ordinary fashion. "However, when the contributors to a mixture are not known or cannot otherwise be distinguished, a likelihood-ratio approach offers a clear advantage and is particularly suitable." Committee on DNA Forensic Science: An Update, National Research Council, The Evaluation of Forensic DNA Evidence 129 (1996). For refinements, see Evett et al., Taking Account of Peak Areas When Interpreting Mixed DNA Profiles, 43 J. Forensic Sci. 62 (1998); Perlin & Szabady, Linear Mixture Analysis: A Mathematical Approach to Resolving Mixed DNA Samples, 46 J. Forensic Sci. 1372 (2001). Contra R.C. Lewontin, Population Genetic Issues in the

Forensic Use of DNA, in 1 Modern Scientific Evidence § 17-5.0, at 703–705 (David L. Faigman et al. eds., 1997); Thompson, DNA Evidence in the O.J. Simpson Trial, 67 U. Colo. L. Rev. at 855–856 (1996). For expositions of this likelihood ratio approach, see David W. Balding, Weight-of-Evidence for Forensic DNA Profiles § 6.5 (2005); Ian W. Evett & Bruce S. Weir, Interpreting DNA Evidence: Statistical Genetics for Forensic Scientists at 188–205 (1998).

[4]There are two types of binning in use. *Floating bins* are conceptually simpler and more appropriate than *fixed bins*, but the latter can be justified as an approximation to the former. For the details of binning and suggestions for handling some of the complications that have caused disagreements over certain aspects of fixed bins, see Committee on DNA Forensic Science: An Update, National Research Council, The Evaluation of Forensic DNA Evidence 142–145 (1996).

[5]Likelihood ratios for match-binning results are identical to those for discrete allele systems. If the bin frequencies reveal that a proportion $p$ of the population has DNA whose bands each fall within the match window of the corresponding evidence bands, then the match-binning likelihood ratio is $1/p$.

and nonmatches.[6] They have been advocated on the ground that they make better use of the DNA data,[7] but they have been attacked, primarily on the ground that they are complicated and difficult for nonstatisticians to understand.[8]

## § 2:50 Interpretation of laboratory results—Measures of probative value— Posterior probabilities

The likelihood ratio expresses the relative strength of an hypothesis, but the judge or jury ultimately must assess a different type of quantity—the probability of the hypothesis itself. An elementary rule of probability theory known as *Bayes' theorem* yields this probability. The theorem states that the odds in light of the data (here, the observed profiles) are the odds as they were known prior to receiving the data times the likelihood ratio: *posterior odds = likelihood ratio × prior odds*.[1] For example, if the relevant match probability[2] were 1/100,000, and if the chance that the laboratory would report a match between samples from the same source were 0.99, then the likelihood ratio would be 99,000, and the jury could be told how the DNA evidence raises various prior probabilities that the defendant's DNA is in the evidence sample.[3] It would be appropriate to explain that these calculations rest on many premises, including the premise that the genotypes have been correctly determined.[4]

One difficulty with this use of Bayes' theorem is that the computations consider only one alternative to the claim of identity at a time. However, several rival hypotheses might apply in a given case. If it is not defendant's DNA in the forensic sample, is it from his father, his brother, his uncle, et cetera? Is the true source a

---

[6]The methods produce likelihood ratios tailored to the observed degree of matching. Two more or less "matching" bands would receive less weight when the measured band lengths differ substantially, and more weight when the lengths differ very little. Bernard Devlin & Kathryn Roeder, DNA Profiling: Statistics and Population Genetics, in 1 Modern Scientific Evidence: The Law and Science of Expert Testimony § 18-3.1.4, at 724 (David Faigman et al. eds., 1997). And, bands that occur in a region where relatively few people have VNTRs contribute more to the likelihood ratio than if they occur in a zone where VNTRs are common.

[7]See Committee on DNA Forensic Science: An Update, National Research Council, The Evaluation of Forensic DNA Evidence 161, 200 (1996) ("VNTR data are essentially continuous, and, in principle, a continuous model should be used to analyze them."); A. Collins & N.E. Morton, Likelihood Ratios for DNA Identification, 91 Proc. Nat'l Acad. Sci. 6007 (1994); Bernard Devlin & Kathryn Roeder, DNA Profiling: Statistics and Population Genetics, in 1 Modern Scientific Evidence: The Law and Science of Expert Testimony § 18-3.1.4, at 724 (David Faigman et al. eds., 1997).

[8]E.g., Contra R.C. Lewontin, Population Genetic Issues in the Forensic Use of DNA, in 1 Modern Scientific Evidence § 17-5.0, at 705 (David L. Faigman et al. eds., 1997). For discussion, see §§ 2:1 to 2:20.

**[Section 2:50]**

[1]Odds and probabilities are two ways to express chances quantitatively. If the probability of an event is P, the odds are P/(1–P). If the odds are O, the probability is O/(O + 1). For instance, if the probability of rain is 2/3, the odds of rain are 2 to 1: (2/3) / (1–2/3) = (2/3) / (1/3) = 2. If the odds of rain are 2 to 1, then the probability is 2/(2 + 1) = 2/3.

[2]By "relevant match probability," we mean the probability of a match given a specified type of kinship or the probability of a random match in the relevant suspect population. For relatives more distantly related than second cousins, the probability of a chance match is nearly as small as for persons of the same subpopulation. Bernard Devlin & Kathryn Roeder, DNA Profiling: Statistics and Population Genetics, in 1 Modern Scientific Evidence: The Law and Science of Expert Testimony § 18-3.1.3, at 724 (David Faigman et al. eds., 1997).

[3]For further discussion of how Bayes' rule might be used in court with DNA evidence, see, for example, Kaye, DNA Evidence: Probability, Population Genetics, and the Courts, 7 Harv. J. L. & Tech. 101 (1993); Committee on DNA Forensic Science: An Update, National Research Council, The Evaluation of Forensic DNA Evidence 201–203 (1996).

[4]See Lempert, The Honest Scientist's Guide to DNA Evidence, 96 Genetica 119 (1995). If the jury accepted these premises and also decided to accept the hypothesis of identity over those of kinship and coincidence, it still would be open to the defendant to offer explanations of how the forensic samples came to include his DNA even though he is innocent.

member of the same subpopulation? A member of a different subpopulation in the same general population? In principle the likelihood ratio can be generalized to a likelihood function that takes on suitable values for every person in the world, and the prior probability for each person can be cranked into a general version of Bayes' rule to yield the posterior probability that the defendant is the source. In this vein, a few commentators suggest that Bayes' rule be used to combine the various likelihood ratios for all possible degrees of kinship and subpopulations.[5] However, it is not clear how this ambitious proposal would be implemented.[6]

## § 2:51 Novel applications of DNA technology

Most routine applications of DNA technology in the forensic setting involve the identification of human beings—suspects in criminal cases, missing persons, or victims of mass disasters. However, inasmuch as DNA technology can be applied to the analysis of any kind of biological evidence containing DNA, and because the technology is advancing rapidly, unusual applications are inevitable. In cases in which the evidentiary DNA is of human origin, new methods of analyzing DNA will come into at least occasional use, and new loci or DNA polymorphisms will be used for forensic work. In other cases, the evidentiary DNA will come from non-human organisms—household pets,[1] livestock,[2] wild animals,[3] insects,[4] plants,[5] even bacte-

---

[5]See David W. Balding, Weight-of-Evidence for Forensic DNA Profiles (2005); David J. Balding & Peter Donnelly, Inference in Forensic Identification, 158 J. Royal Stat. Soc'y Ser. A 21 (1995).

[6]A related proposal in Lempert, After the DNA Wars: Skirmishing with NRC II, 37 Jurimetrics J. 439, 447–448, 453 (1997), suffers from the same difficulty of articulating the composition of the suspect population and the prior probabilities for its members. Professor Lempert reasons that "the relevant match statistic, if it could be derived, is an average that turns on the number of people in the suspect population and a likelihood that each has DNA matching the defendant's DNA, weighted by the probability that each committed the crime if the defendant did not." Lempert, After the DNA Wars: Skirmishing with NRC II, 37 Jurimetrics J. 439, 458 (1997). He concludes that although this "weighted average statistic" does not directly state how likely it is "that the defendant and not some third party committed the crime," it is superior to "the 'random man' match statistic" in that it "tells the jury how surprising it would be to find a DNA match if the defendant is innocent." Lempert, After the DNA Wars: Skirmishing with NRC II, 37 Jurimetrics J. 439, 458 (1997).

[Section 2:51]

[1]Brauner et al., DNA Profiling of Trace Evidence—Mitigating Evidence in a Dog Biting Case, 46 J. Forensic Sci. 1232 (2001) (mastiff excluded as the dog that attacked a six-year-old girl, but the owners were charged with negligence for not having properly restrained the animal, and the dog was impressed into service in the Israeli canine corps); Muller et al., Use of Canine Microsatellite Polymorphisms in Forensic Examinations, 90 J. Heredity 55 (1999); Pádár et

al., Canine STR Analyses in Forensic Practice: Observation of a Possible Mutation in a Dog Hair, 116 Int'l J. Legal Med. 286 (2002) (in a Hungarian case of the death of a seven-year-old boy, analysis of 10 canine-specific STR loci revealed-contrary to the eyewitness testimony—a possible dog attack and suggested two specific dogs who might have been responsible); Padar et al., Canine Microsatellite Polymorphisms as the Resolution of an Illegal Animal Death Case in a Hungarian Zoological Gardens, 115 Int'l J. Legal Med. 79 (2001) (canine DNA loci used to eliminate the zoo's German Shepard guard dogs as suspects in an animal death case); Schneider et al., Forensic mtDNA Hair Analysis Excludes a Dog from Having Caused a Traffic Accident, 112 Int'l J. Legal Med. 315 (1999).

[2]Giovambattista et al., DNA Typing in a Cattle Stealing Case, 46 J. Forensic Sci. 1484 (2001) (meat pieces and bones in butcher's home matched to remains of a cow slaughtered and removed from a farm).

[3]For example, hunters sometimes claim that they have cuts of beef rather than the remnants of illegally obtained wildlife. These claims can be verified or refuted by DNA analysis. Cf. State v. Demers, 167 Vt. 349, 707 A.2d 276, 277–278 (1997) (unspecified DNA analysis of deer blood and hair helped supply probable cause for search warrant to look for evidence of illegally hunted deer in defendant's home).

[4]Sperling et al., A DNA-Based Approach to the Identification of Insect Species Used for Postmortem Interval Estimation, 39 J. Forensic Sci. 418 (1994).

[5]Linacre, Identifying the Presence of "Magic Mushrooms" by DNA Profiling, 42 Sci. & Just. 50 (2002).

ria[6] and viruses.[7] These applications are directed either at distinguishing among species or at distinguishing among individuals (or subgroups) within a species. These two tasks can raise somewhat different scientific issues, and no single, mechanically applied test can be formulated to assess the validity of the diversity of applications and methods that might be encountered.

Instead, this section outlines and describes four factors that may be helpful in deciding whether a new application is scientifically sound. These are the novelty of the application, the validity of the underlying scientific theory, the validity of any statistical interpretations, and the relevant scientific community to consult in assessing the application. We illustrate these considerations in the context of three unusual applications of DNA technology to law enforcement:

- Although federal law prohibits the export of bear products, individuals in this country have offered to supply bear gall bladder for export to Asia, where it is prized for its supposed medicinal properties. In one investigation, the National Fish and Wildlife Forensic Laboratory, using DNA testing, determined that the material offered for export actually came from a pig absolving the suspect of any export law violations.[8]

- In *State v. Bogan*,[9] a woman's body was found in the desert, near several palo verde trees. A detective noticed two seed pods in the bed of a truck that the defendant was driving before the murder. A biologist performed DNA profiling on this type of palo verde and testified that the two pods "were identical" and "matched completely with "a particular tree and "didn't match any of the [other] trees," and that he felt "quite confident in concluding that" the tree's DNA would be distinguishable from that of "any tree that might be furnished" to him. After the jury convicted the defendant of murder, jurors reported that they found this testimony very persuasive.[10]

- In *R. v. Beamish*, a woman disappeared from her home on Prince Edward Island, on Canada's eastern seaboard. Weeks later a man's brown leather jacket stained with blood was discovered in a plastic bag in the woods. In the jacket's lining were white cat hairs. After the missing woman's body was found in a shallow grave, her estranged common-law husband was arrested and charged. He lived with his parents and a white cat. Laboratory analysis showed the blood on the jacket to be the victim's, and the hairs were ascertained to match the family cat at ten STR loci. The defendant was convicted of the murder.[11]

---

[6]See Horswell et al., Forensic Comparison of Soils by Bacterial Community DNA Profiling, 47 J. Forensic Sci. 350 (2002); Jo Thomas, Outbreak of Food Poisoning Leads to Warning on Hot Dogs and Cold Cuts, N.Y. Times, Dec. 24, 1998 (DNA testing of bacteria in food can help establish the source of outbreaks of food poisoning and thereby facilitate recalls of contaminated foodstuffs).

[7]See *State v. Schmidt*, 771 So. 2d 131 (La. Ct. App. 3d Cir. 2000), writ denied, 798 So. 2d 105 (La. 2001) (where a physician was convicted of murdering his former lover by injecting her with the AIDS virus, and the state's expert witnesses used PCR-based analysis to identify HIV strains).

[8]Interview with Dr. Edgard Espinoza, Deputy Director, National Fish and Wildlife Forensic Laboratory, in Ashland, Oregon, June 1998. Also, FDA regulations do not prohibit mislabeling of pig gall bladder.

[9]*State v. Bogan*, 183 Ariz. 506, 905 P.2d 515 (Ct. App. Div. 1 1995), as corrected, (Apr. 13, 1995).

[10]Brent Whiting, Tree's DNA "Fingerprint" Splinters Killer's Defense, Ariz. Republic, May 28, 1993, at A1, available in 1993 WL 8186972; see also C.K. Yoon, Forensic Science—Botanical Witness for the Prosecution, 260 Science 894 (1993).

[11]DNA Testing on Cat Hairs Helped Link Man to Slaying, Boston Globe, Apr. 24, 1997, available in 1997 WL 6250745; Gina Kolata, Cat Hair Finds Way into Courtroom in Canadian Murder Trial, N.Y. Times, Apr. 24, 1997, at A5; Marilyn A. Menott-Haymond et al., Pet Cat Hair Implicates Murder Suspect, 386 Nature 774 (1997).

### § 2:52 Novel applications of DNA technology—Is the application novel?

The more novel and untested an application is, the more problematic is its introduction into evidence. In many cases, however, an application can be new to the legal system but be well established in the field of scientific inquiry from which it derives. This can be ascertained from a survey of the peer-reviewed scientific literature and the statements of experts in the field.[1]

Applications designed specially to address an issue before the court are more likely to be truly novel and thus may be more difficult to evaluate. The studies of the gall bladder, palo verde trees, and cat hairs exemplify such applications in that each was devised solely for the case at bar.[2] In such cases, there are no published, peer-reviewed descriptions of the particular application to fall back on, but the analysis still could give rise to "scientific knowledge" within the meaning of *Daubert v. Merrell Dow Pharmaceuticals, Inc.*[3]

The novelty of an unusual application of DNA technology involves two components—the novelty of the analytical technique, and the novelty of applying that technique to the samples in question. With respect to the analytical method, forensic DNA technology in the last two decades has been driven in part by the development of many new methods for the detection of genetic variation between species and between individuals within a species. The approaches outlined in the appendix[4] for the detection of genetic variation in humans—RFLP analysis of VNTR polymorphism, PCR, detection of VNTR and STR polymorphism by gel and capillary electrophoresis, respectively, and detection of sequence variation by probe hybridization or direct sequence analysis—have been imported from other research contexts. Thus, their use in the detection of variation in nonhuman species and of variation among species involves no new technology. DNA technology transcends organismal differences.

Some methods for the characterization of DNA variation widely used in studies of other species, however, are not used in forensic testing of human DNA. These are often called "DNA fingerprint" approaches. They offer a snapshot characterization of genomic variation in a single test, but they essentially presume that the sample DNA originates from a single individual, and this presumption cannot always be met with forensic samples.

The original form of DNA "fingerprinting" used electrophoresis, Southern blotting, and a *multilocus probe* that simultaneously recognizes many sites in the genome.[5] The result is comparable to what would be obtained with a "cocktail" of single-locus

---

[Section 2:52]

[1]Even though some applications are represented by only a few papers in the peer-reviewed literature, they may be fairly well established. The breadth of scientific inquiry, even within a rather specialized field, is such that only a few research groups may be working on any particular problem. A better gauge is the extent to which the genetic typing technology is used by researchers studying related problems and the existence of a general body of knowledge regarding the nature of the genetic variation at issue.

[2]Of course, such evidence hardly is unique to DNA technology. See, e.g., *Coppolino v. State*, 223 So. 2d 68 (Fla. Dist. Ct. App. 2d Dist. 1968) (holding admissible a test for the presence of succinylcholine chloride first devised for this case to determine whether defendant had injected a le-

thal dose of this curare-like anesthetic into his wife).

[3]*Daubert v. Merrell Dow Pharmaceuticals, Inc.*, 509 U.S. 579, 590, 113 S. Ct. 2786, 125 L. Ed. 2d 469, 27, 27 U.S.P.Q.2d 1200, Prod. Liab. Rep. (CCH) P 13494, 37 Fed. R. Evid. Serv. 1, 23 Envtl. L. Rep. 20979 (1993) ("to qualify as 'scientific knowledge,' an inference or assertion must be derived by the scientific method").

[4]See Appendix 2A, Table A-1.

[5]The probes were pioneered by Alec Jeffreys. See, e.g., Alec J. Jeffreys et al., Individual-specific "Fingerprints" of Human DNA, 316 Nature 76 (1985). In the 1980s, the "Jeffreys probes" were used for forensic purposes, especially in parentage testing. See, e.g., Kaye, DNA Paternity Probabilities, 24 Fam. L. Q. 279 (1990).

probes—one complex banding pattern sometimes analogized to a bar-code.[6] Probes for DNA fingerprinting are widely used in genetic research in nonhuman species.[7]

With the advent of PCR as the central tool in molecular biology, PCR-based "fingerprinting" methods have been developed. The two most widely used are the *random amplified polymorphic DNA* (RAPD) method[8] and the *amplified fragment length polymorphism* (AFLP) method.[9] Both give bar code-like patterns.[10] In RAPD analysis, a single, arbitrarily constructed, short primer amplifies many DNA fragments of unknown sequence.[11] AFLP analysis begins with a digestion of the sample DNA with a restriction enzyme followed by amplification of selected restriction fragments.[12]

Although the "DNA fingerprinting" procedures are not likely to be used in the analysis of samples of human origin, new approaches to the detection of genetic variation in humans as well as other organisms are under development. On the horizon are methods based on mass spectrometry and hybridization chip technology. As these or other methods come into forensic use, the best measure of scientific novelty will be the extent to which the methods have found their way into the scientific literature. Use by researchers other than those who developed them indicates some degree of scientific acceptance.

The second aspect of novelty relates to the sample analyzed. Two questions are central: Is there scientific precedent for testing samples of the sort tested in the particular case? And, what is known about the nature and extent of genetic variation in the tested organism and in related species? *Beamish*, the Canadian case involving cat hairs, illustrates both points. The nature of the sample—cat hairs—does not seem novel, for there is ample scientific precedent for doing genetic tests on animal hairs.[13] But the use of STR testing to identify a domestic cat as the source of the particular hairs was new. Of course, this novelty does not mean that the effort was scientifically unsound; indeed, as explained in the next section, the premise that cats show substantial microsatellite polymorphism is consistent with other scientific knowledge.

---

[6]As with RFLP analysis in general, this RFLP fingerprinting approach requires relatively good quality sample DNA. Degraded DNA results in a loss of some of the bars in the barcode-like pattern.

[7]E.g., DNA Fingerprinting: State of the Science (S.D.J. Pena et al. eds., 1993). The discriminating power of a probe must be determined empirically in each species. The probes used by Jeffreys for human DNA fingerprinting, for instance, are less discriminating for dogs. A.J. Jeffreys et al., DNA Fingerprints of Dogs and Cats, 18 Animal Genetics 1 (1987).

[8]J. Welsh & M. McCelland, Fingerprinting Genomes Using PCR with Arbitrary Primers, 18 Nucleic Acids Res. 7213 (1990); J.G.K. Williams et al., DNA Polymorphisms Amplified by Random Primers Are Useful as Genetic Markers, 18 Nucleic Acids Res. 6531 (1990).

[9]P. Vos et al., AFLP: A New Technique for DNA Fingerprinting, 23 Nucleic Acids Res. 4407 (1995).

[10]The identification of the seed pods in *State v. Bogan*, 183 Ariz. 506, 905 P.2d 515 (Ct. App. Div. 1 1995), as corrected, (Apr. 13, 1995), was accomplished with RAPD analysis. The general acceptance of this technique in the scientific community was not seriously contested. Indeed, the expert for the defense conceded the validity of RAPD in genetic research and testified that the state's expert had correctly applied the procedure. *State v. Bogan*, 183 Ariz. 506, 905 P.2d 515, 520 (Ct. App. Div. 1 1995), as corrected, (Apr. 13, 1995).

[11]Primers must be validated in advance to determine which give highly discriminating patterns for a particular species in question.

[12]Both the RAPD and AFLP methods provide reproducible results within a laboratory, but AFLP is more reproducible across-laboratories. See, e.g., C.J. Jones, et al., Reproducibility Testing of RAPD, AFLP and SSR Markers in Plants by a Network of European Laboratories, 3 Molecular Breeding 381 (1997). This may be an issue if results from different laboratories must be compared.

[13]E.g., R. Higuchi et al., DNA Typing from Single Hairs, 332 Nature 543, 545 (1988). Collection of hair is non-invasive and is widely used in wildlife studies where sampling in the field would otherwise be difficult or impossible. Hair also is much easier to transport and store than blood, a great convenience when working in the field.

### § 2:53 Novel applications of DNA technology—Is the underlying scientific theory valid?

Neither *Daubert* nor *Frye* banishes novel applications of science from the courtroom, but they do demand that trial judges assure themselves that the underlying science is sound, so that the scientific expert can be found to be presenting scientific knowledge rather than speculating or dressing up unscientific opinion in the garb of scientific fact.[1] The questions that might be asked to probe the scientific underpinnings extend the line of questions asked about novelty: What is the principle of the testing method used? What has been the experience with the use of the testing method? What are its limitations? Has it been used in applications similar to those in the instant case—for instance, for the characterization of other organisms or other kinds of samples? What is known of the nature of genetic variability in the organism tested or in related organisms? Is there precedent for doing any kind of DNA testing on the sort of samples tested in the instant case? Is there anything about the organism, the sample, or the context of testing that would render the testing technology inappropriate for the desired application?[2] To illustrate the usefulness of these questions, we can return to the cases involving pig gall bladders, cat hairs, and palo verde seed pods.

Deciding whether the DNA testing is valid is simplest in the export case. The question there was whether the gall bladders originated from bear or from some other species. The DNA analysis was based on the approach used by evolutionary biologists to study relationships among vertebrate species. It relies on sequence variation in the mitochondrial cytochrome b gene. DNA sequence analysis is a routine technology, and there is an extensive library of cytochrome b sequence data representing a broad range of vertebrate species.[3] As for the sample material—the gall bladder—such cells may not have been used before, but gall bladder is simply another tissue from which DNA can be extracted.[4] Thus, although the application was novel in that an approach had to be devised to address the question at hand, each segment of the application rests on a solid foundation of scientific knowledge and experience. No great inferential leap from the known to the unknown was required to reach the conclusion that the gall bladder was from a pig rather than a bear.

The DNA analysis in *Beamish* required slightly more extrapolation from the known to the unknown. As indicated in the previous section, the use of cat hairs as a source of DNA was not especially novel, and the very factors that reveal a lack of novelty also suggest that it is scientifically valid to test the DNA in cat hairs. But we also observed that the use of STR typing to distinguish among cats was novel. Is such reasoning too great a leap to constitute scientific knowledge? A great deal is

---

**[Section 2:53]**

[1]See *Daubert v. Merrell Dow Pharmaceuticals, Inc.,* 509 U.S. 579, 590, 113 S. Ct. 2786, 125 L. Ed. 2d 469, 27, 27 U.S.P.Q.2d 1200, Prod. Liab. Rep. (CCH) P 13494, 37 Fed. R. Evid. Serv. 1, 23 Envtl. L. Rep. 20979 (1993) ("The adjective 'scientific' [in Rule 702] implies a grounding in the methods and procedures of science. Similarly, the word 'knowledge' connotes more than subjective belief or unsupported speculation."). In *Frye,* the courts determines validity indirectly, using general acceptance as the dispositive consideration. In this section, we discuss the broader inquiry mandated by *Daubert,* which includes the criterion of general acceptance in the scientific community.

[2]But cf. Committee on DNA Technology in Forensic Science, National Research Council, DNA Technology in Forensic Science 72 (1992) (Table 1.1) (listing seven "requirements" for new forensic DNA tests to achieve "the highest standards of scientific rigor").

[3]If the bear cytochrome b gene sequence were not in the database, it would be obligatory for the proponents of the application to determine it and add it to the database, where it could be checked by other researchers.

[4]There is a technical concern that the DNA extracted from a gall bladder might contain inhibitors that would interfere with the subsequent sequence analysis; however, this merely affects whether the test will yield a result, and not the accuracy of any result.

known about the basis and extent of genetic variation in cats and other mammals. In particular, microsatellite polymorphism is extensive in all mammalian species that have been studied, including other members of the cat family. Furthermore, by testing small samples from two cat populations, the researchers verified the loci they examined were highly polymorphic.[5] Thus, the novelty in using STR analysis to identify cats is not scientifically unsettling; rather, it extends from and fits with everything else that is known about cats and mammals in general. However, as one moves from well studied organisms to ones about which little is known, one risks crossing the line between knowledge and speculation.

The DNA testing in *State v. Bogan*[6] pushes the envelope further. First, the genetic variability of palo verde trees had not been previously studied. Second, it was not known whether enough DNA could be extracted from seed pods to perform a genetic analysis. Both of these questions had to be answered by new testing. RAPD analysis, a well-established method for characterizing genetic variation within a species, demonstrated that palo verde trees were highly variable. Seed pods were shown to contain adequate DNA for RAPD analysis. Finally, a blind trial showed that RAPD profiles correctly identified individual palo verde trees.[7] In short, the lack of pre-existing data on DNA fingerprints of palo verde trees was bridged by scientific experimentation that established the validity of the specific application.

The DNA analyses in all three situations rest on a coherent and internally consistent body of observation, experiment, and experience. That information was mostly pre-existing in the case of the gall bladder testing. Some information on the population genetics of domestic cats on Prince Edward's Island had to be generated specifically for the analysis in *Beamish*, and still more was developed expressly for the situation in the palo verde tree testing in *Bogan*. A court, with the assistance of suitable experts, can make a judgment as to scientific validity in these cases because the crucial propositions are open to critical review by others in the scientific community and are subject to additional investigation if questions are raised. Where serious doubt remains, a court might consider ordering a blind trial to verify the analytical laboratory's ability to perform the identification in question.[8]

### § 2:54 Novel applications of DNA technology—Has the probability of a chance match been estimated correctly?

The significance of a human DNA match in a particular case typically is pre-

---

[5]One sample consisted of nineteen cats in Sunnyside, Prince Edward Island, where the crime occurred. See Commentary, Use of DNA Analysis Raises Some Questions (CBS radio broadcast, Apr. 24, 1997), transcript available in 1997 WL 5424082 ("19 cats obtained randomly from local veterinarians on Prince Edward Island"); Marjorie Shaffer, Canadian Killer Captured by a Whisker from Parents' Pet Cat, Biotechnology Newswatch, May 5, 1997, available in 1997 WL 8790779 ("the Royal Canadian Mounted Police rounded up 19 cats in the area and had a veterinarian draw blood samples"). The other sample consisted of nine cats from the United States. DNA Test on Parents' Cat Helps Put Away Murderer, Chi. Tribune, Apr. 24, 1997, available in 1997 WL 3542042.

[6]*State v. Bogan*, 183 Ariz. 506, 905 P.2d 515 (Ct. App. Div. 1 1995), as corrected, (Apr. 13, 1995).

[7]The DNA in the two seed pods could not be distinguished by RAPD testing, suggesting that they fell from the same tree. The biologist who

devised and conducted the experiments analyzed samples from the nine trees near the body and another nineteen trees from across the county. He "was not informed, until after his tests were completed and his report written, which samples came from" which trees. *State v. Bogan*, 183 Ariz. 506, 905 P.2d 515, 521 (Ct. App. Div. 1 1995), as corrected, (Apr. 13, 1995). Furthermore, unbeknownst to the experimenter, two apparently distinct samples were prepared from the tree at the crime scene that appeared to have been abraded by the defendant's truck. The biologist correctly identified the two samples from the one tree as matching, and he "distinguished the DNA from the seed pods in the truck bed from the DNA of all twenty-eight trees except" that one. *State v. Bogan*, 183 Ariz. 506, 905 P.2d 515, 521 (Ct. App. Div. 1 1995), as corrected, (Apr. 13, 1995).

[8]The blind trial could be devised and supervised by a court-appointed expert, or the parties could be ordered to agree on a suitable experiment.

sented or assessed in terms of the probability that an individual selected at random from the population would be found to match. A small random match probability renders implausible the hypothesis that the match is just coincidental.[1] In *Beamish*, the random match probability was estimated to be one in many millions,[2] and the trial court admitted evidence of this statistic.[3] In *State v. Bogan*,[4] the random match probability was estimated by the state's expert as one in a million and by the defense expert as one in 136,000, but the trial court excluded these estimates because of the then-existing controversy over analogous estimates for human RFLP genotypes.[5] In *State v. Leuluaialii*,[6] however, the prosecution offered testimony of an STR match with a dog's blood that linked the defendants to the victims' bodies. The defendants objected, seeking a *Frye* hearing, but the trial court denied this motion and admitted testimony that included the report that "the probability of finding another dog with Chief's DNA profile was 1 in 18 billion [or] 1 in 3 trillion."[7] The state court of appeals reviewed the scientific literature on canine STR identification and concluded that it was not sufficient to demonstrate general acceptance of the underlying computations. It remanded the case for a hearing on general acceptance, cautioning that "[b]ecause PE Zoogen has not yet published sufficient data to show that its DNA markers and associated probability estimates are reliable, we would suggest that other courts tread lightly in these waters and closely examine canine DNA results before accepting them at trial."[8]

Estimating the probability of a random match or related statistics requires a sample of genotypes from the relevant population of organisms. As discussed in §§ 2:53 to 2:60, the most accurate estimates combine the allele frequencies seen in the sample according to formulae that reflect the gene flow within the population. In the simplest model for large populations of sexually reproducing organisms, mating is independent of the DNA types under investigation, and each parent transmits half of his or her DNA to the progeny at random. Under these idealized conditions, the basic product rule gives the multilocus genotype frequency as a simple function of the allele frequencies.[9] The accuracy of the estimates thus depends on the accuracy of the allele frequencies in the sample database and the appropriateness of the population genetics model.

---

**[Section 2:54]**

[1] §§ 2:40 to 2:52.

[2] David N. Leff, Killer Convicted by a Hair: Unprecedented Forensic Evidence from Cat's DNA Convinced Canadian Jury, Bioworld Today, Apr. 24, 1997, available in 1997 WL 7473675 ("the frequency of the match came out to be on the order of about one in 45 million," quoting Steven O'Brien); All Things Considered: Cat DNA (NPR broadcast, Apr. 23, 1997), available in 1997 WL 12832754 ("it was less than one in two hundred million," quoting Steven O'Brien).

[3] See also Tim Klass, DNA Tests Match Dog, Stains in Murder Case, Portland Oregonian, Aug. 7, 1998, at D06 (reporting expert testimony in a Washington murder case that "the likelihood of finding a 10-for-10 match in the DNA of a randomly chosen dog of any breed or mix would be one in 3 trillion, and the odds for a nine-of-10 match would be one in 18 billion").

[4] *State v. Bogan*, 183 Ariz. 506, 905 P.2d 515

(Ct. App. Div. 1 1995), as corrected, (Apr. 13, 1995).

[5] *State v. Bogan*, 183 Ariz. 506, 905 P.2d 515, 520 (Ct. App. Div. 1 1995), as corrected, (Apr. 13, 1995). The Arizona case law on this subject is criticized in Kaye, Bible Reading: DNA Evidence in Arizona, 28 Ariz. St. L.J. 1035 (1996).

[6] *State v. Leuluaialii*, 118 Wash. App. 780, 77 P.3d 1192 (Div. 1 2003), review denied, 154 Wash. 2d 1013, 113 P.3d 1039 (2005).

[7] *State v. Leuluaialii*, 118 Wash. App. 780, 77 P.3d 1192, 1196 (Div. 1 2003), review denied, 154 Wash. 2d 1013, 113 P.3d 1039 (2005).

[8] *State v. Leuluaialii*, 118 Wash. App. 780, 77 P.3d 1192, 1201 (Div. 1 2003), review denied, 154 Wash. 2d 1013, 113 P.3d 1039 (2005).

[9] More complicated models account for the population structure that arises when inbreeding is common, but they require some knowledge of how much the population is structured. See §§ 2:40 to 2:52.

### § 2:55 Novel applications of DNA technology—Has the probability of a chance match been estimated correctly?—How was the database obtained?

Since the allele frequencies come from sample data, both the method of sampling and the size of the sample can be crucial. The statistical ideal is probability sampling, in which some objective procedure provides a known chance that each member of the population will be selected. Such random samples tend to be representative of the population from which they are drawn. In wildlife biology, however, the populations often defy enumeration, and hence strict random sampling rarely is possible. Still, if the method of selection is uncorrelated with the alleles being studied, then the sampling procedure is tantamount to random sampling with respect to those alleles.[1] Consequently, the key question about the method of sampling for a court faced with estimates based on a database of cats, dogs, or any such species, is whether that sample was obtained in some biased way—a way that would systematically tend to include (or exclude) organisms with particular alleles or genotypes from the database.

### § 2:56 Novel applications of DNA technology—Has the probability of a chance match been estimated correctly?—How large is the sampling error?

Assuming that the sampling procedure is reasonably structured to give representative samples with respect to those genotypes of forensic interest, the question of database size should be considered. Larger samples give more precise estimates of allele frequencies than smaller ones, but there is no sharp line for determining when a database is too small.[1] Instead, just as pollsters present their results within a certain margin of error, the expert should be able to explain the extent of the statistical error that arises from using samples of the size of the forensic database.[2]

### § 2:57 Novel applications of DNA technology—Has the probability of a chance match been estimated correctly?—How was the random match probability computed?

As we have indicated, the theory of population genetics provides the framework for combining the allele frequencies into the final profile frequency. The frequency

---

[Section 2:55]

[1]Few people would worry, for example, that the sample of blood cells taken from their vein for a test of whether they suffer from anemia is not, strictly speaking, a random sample. The use of convenience samples from human populations to form forensic databases is discussed in, for example, Committee on DNA Forensic Science: An Update, National Research Council, The Evaluation of Forensic DNA Evidence at 126–127, 186 (1996). Case law on the point is collected §§ 2:1 to 2:20.

[Section 2:56]

[1]The Committee on DNA Forensic Science: An Update, National Research Council, The Evaluation of Forensic DNA Evidence 114 (1996), refers to "at least several hundred persons," but it has been suggested that relatively small databases, consisting of 50 or so individuals, allow statistically acceptable frequency estimation for the common alleles. A new, specially constructed database is likely to be small, but alleles can be a

assigned a minimum value, resulting in conservative genotype frequency estimates. Ranajit Chakraborty, Sample Size Requirements for Addressing the Population Genetic Issues of Forensic Use of DNA Typing, 64 Human Biology 141, 156–157 (1992). Later, the NRC committee suggests that the uncertainty that arises "[i]f the database is small . . . can be addressed by providing confidence intervals on the estimates." Committee on DNA Forensic Science: An Update, National Research Council, The Evaluation of Forensic DNA Evidence at 125 (1996).

[2]Weir, Forensic Population Genetics and the NRC, 52 Am. J. Hum. Genetics 437 (1993) (proposing interval estimate of genotype frequency); cf. Committee on DNA Forensic Science: An Update, National Research Council, The Evaluation of Forensic DNA Evidence at 148 (1996) (remarking that "calculation of confidence intervals is desirable," but also examining the error that could be associated with the choice of a database on an empirical rather than a theoretical basis).

estimates are a mathematical function of the genetic diversity at each locus and the number of loci tested. The formulas for frequency estimates depend on the mode of reproduction and the population genetics of the species. For outbreeding sexually reproducing species,[1] under conditions that give rise to Hardy-Weinberg and linkage equilibrium, genotype frequencies can be estimated with the basic product rule.[2] If a species is sexually reproducing but given to inbreeding, or if there are other impediments to Hardy-Weinberg or linkage equilibrium, such genotype frequencies may be incorrect. Thus, the reasonableness of assuming Hardy-Weinberg equilibrium and linkage equilibrium depends on what and how much is known about the population genetics of the species.[3] Ideally, large population databases can be analyzed to verify independence of alleles.[4] Tests for deviations from the single-locus genotype frequencies expected under Hardy-Weinberg equilibrium will indicate if population structure effects should be accorded serious concern. These tests, however, are relatively insensitive to minor population structure effects, and adjustments for possible population structure might be appropriate.[5] For sexually reproducing species believed to have local population structure, a sampling strategy targeting the relevant population would be best. If this is not possible, estimates based on the larger population might be presented with appropriate caveats. If data on the larger population are unavailable, the uncertainty implicit in basic product rule estimates should not be ignored, and less ambitious alternatives to the random match probability as a means for conveying the probative value of a match might be considered.[6]

A different approach may be called for if the species is not an outbreeding, sexually reproducing species. For example, many plants, some simple animals, and bacteria reproduce asexually. With asexual reproduction, most offspring are genetically identical to the parent. All the individuals that originate from a common parent constitute, collectively, a clone. The major source of genetic variation in asexually reproducing species is mutation.[7] When a mutation occurs, a new clonal lineage is created. Individuals in the original clonal lineage continue to propagate, and two clonal lineages now exist where before there was one. Thus, in species that reproduce asexually, genetic testing distinguishes clones, not individuals, and the product rule cannot be applied to estimate genotype frequencies for individuals. Rather, the

**[Section 2:57]**

[1]Outbreeding refers to the propensity for individuals to mate with individuals who are not close relations.

[2]§§ 2:40 to 2:52.

[3]In *State v. Bogan*, 183 Ariz. 506, 905 P.2d 515 (Ct. App. Div. 1 1995), as corrected, (Apr. 13, 1995), for example, the biologist who testified for the prosecution consulted with botanists who assured him that palo verde tree were an outcrossing species. *State v. Bogan*, 183 Ariz. 506, 905 P.2d 515, 523, 524 (Ct. App. Div. 1 1995), as corrected, (Apr. 13, 1995).

[4]However, large, pre-existing databases may not be available for the populations of interest in these more novel cases. Analyses of the smaller, ad hoc databases are unlikely to be decisive. In *Beamish*, for instance, two cat populations were sampled. The sample of nineteen cats from Sunnyside, in Prince Edward Island, and the sample of nine cats from the United States revealed considerable genetic diversity; moreover, most of the genetic variability was between individual cats, not between the two populations of cats. There was no statistically significant evidence of

population substructure, and there was no statistically significant evidence of linkage disequilibrium in the Sunnyside population. The problem is that with such small samples, the statistical tests for substructure are not very sensitive; hence, the failure to detect it is not strong proof that either the Sunnyside or the North American cat population is unstructured.

[5]A standard correction for population structure is to incorporate a population structure parameter $F_{st}$ into the calculation. Such adjustments are described §§ 2:40 to 2:52. However, appropriate values for $F_{st}$ may not be known for unstudied species.

[6]The "tree lineup" in *Bogan* represents one possible approach. Adapting it to *Beamish* would have produced testimony that the researchers were able to exclude all the other (28) cats presented to them. This simple counting, however, is extremely conservative.

[7]Bacteria also can exchange DNA through several mechanisms unrelated to cell division, including conjugation, transduction, and transformation. Bacterial species differ in their susceptibility to undergo these forms of gene transfer.

frequency of a particular clone in a population of clones must be determined by direct observation. For example, if a rose thorn found on a suspect's clothing were to be identified as originating from a particular cultivar of rose, the relevant question becomes how common that variety of rose bush is and where it is located in the community.

In short, the approach for estimating a genotype frequency depends on the reproductive pattern and population genetics of the species. In cases involving unusual organisms, a court will need to rely on experts with sufficient knowledge of the species to verify that the method for estimating genotype frequencies is appropriate.

### § 2:58   Novel applications of DNA technology—What is the relevant scientific community?

Even the most scientifically sophisticated court may find it difficult to judge the scientific soundness of a novel application without questioning appropriate scientists. Given the great diversity of forensic questions to which DNA testing might be applied, it is not possible to define specific scientific expertises appropriate to each. If the technology is novel, expertise in molecular genetics or biotechnology might be necessary. If testing has been conducted on a particular organism or category of organisms, expertise in that area of biology may be called for. If a random match probability has been presented, one might seek expertise in statistics as well as the population biology or population genetics that goes with the organism tested. Given the penetration of molecular technology into all areas of biological inquiry, it is likely that individuals can be found who know both the technology and the population biology of the organism in question. Finally, where samples come from crime scenes, the expertise and experience of forensic scientists can be crucial. Just as highly focused specialists may be unaware of aspects of an application outside their field of expertise, so too scientists who have not previously dealt with forensic samples can be unaware of case-specific factors that can confound the interpretation of test results.

# APPENDIX 2A

### 1. Structure of DNA

DNA is a complex molecule made of subunits known as *nucleotides* that link together to form a long, spiraling strand. Two such strands are intertwined around each other to form a double helix as shown in Figure A-1. Each strand has a "backbone" made of sugar and phosphate groups and nitrogenous *bases* attached to the sugar groups.[1] There are four types of bases, abbreviated A, T, G, and C, and the two strands of DNA in the double helix are linked by weak chemical bonds such that the A in one strand is always paired to a T in the other strand and the G in one strand is always paired to a C in the other.[2] The A:T and G:C *complementary base pairing* means that knowledge of the sequence of one strand predicts the sequence of the complementary strand. The sequence of the nucleotide base pairs carries the genetic information in the DNA molecule—it is the genetic "text." For example, the sequence ATT on one strand (or TAA on the other strand) "means" something different than GTT (or CAA).

### Figure A-1.

**A Schematic Diagram of the DNA Molecule. The bases in the nucleotide (denoted C, G, A, and T) are arranged like the rungs in a spiral staircase**

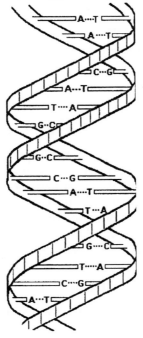

### 2. DNA Probes

A sequence specific oligonucleotide (SSO) probe is a short segment of single-

---

[1] For more details about DNA structure, see, for example, Anthony J.F. Griffiths et al., An Introduction to Genetic Analysis (8th ed. 2005); Elaine Johnson Mange & Arthur P. Mange, Basic Human Genetics 95 (2d ed. 1999).

[2] The bonds that connect the complementary bases are known as *hydrogen bonds*.

stranded DNA with bases arranged in a particular order. The order is chosen so that the probe will bind to the complementary sequence on a DNA fragment, as sketched in figure A-2.

**Figure A-2.**

**A Sequence-specific Probe Links (Hybridizes) to the Targeted Sequence on a Single Stand of DNA**

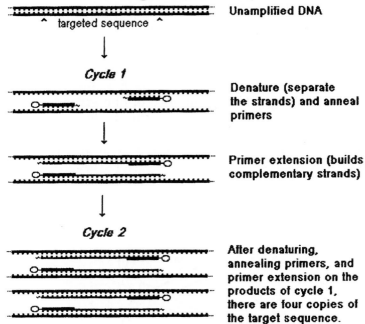

## 3. Examples of Genetic Markers in Forensic Identification

Table A-1 offers examples of the major types of genetic markers used in forensic identification.[3] As noted in the table, simple sequence polymorphisms, some VNTR polymorphisms, and nearly all STR polymorphisms are detected using PCR as a starting point. Most VNTRs containing long core repeats are too large to be amplified reliably by PCR and are instead characterized by *restriction fragment length polymorphism* (RFLP) analysis using *Southern blotting*. As a result of the greater efficiency of PCR-based methods, VNTR typing by RFLP analysis is fading from use.

**Table A-1**

**Genetic Markers Used in Forensic Identification**

| *Nature of variation at locus* | | |
| --- | --- | --- |
| Locus example | Method of detection | Number of alleles |
| *Variable number tandem repeat (VNTR) loci contain repeated core sequence elements, typically 15–35 base pairs (bp) in length. Alleles differ in the number of repeats and are distinguished on the basis of size.* | | |

---

[3]The table is adapted from Committee on DNA Forensic Science: An Update, National Research Council, The Evaluation of Forensic DNA Evidence 74 (1996).

| | | |
|---|---|---|
| D2S44 (core repeat 31 bp) | Intact DNA digested with restriction enzyme, producing fragments that are separated by gel electrophoresis; alleles detected by Southern blotting followed by probing with locus-specific radioactive or chemiluminescent probe | At least 75 (size range is 700–8500 bp); allele size distribution is essentially continuous |
| D1S80 (core repeat 16 bp) | Amplification of allelic sequences by PCR; discrete allelic products separated by electrophoresis and visualized directly | About 30 (size range is 350–1000 bp); alleles can be discretely distinguished |

*Short tandem repeat (STR) loci are VNTR loci with repeated core sequence elements 2–6 bp in length. Alleles differ in the number of repeats and are distinguished on the basis of size.*

| | | |
|---|---|---|
| HUMTHO1 (tetranucleotide repeat) | Amplification of allelic sequences by PCR; discrete allelic products separated by electrophoresis on sequencing gels and visualized directly, by capillary electrophoresis, or by other methods | 8 (size range 179– 203 bp); alleles can be discretely distinguished |

*Simple sequence variation (nucleotide substitution in a defined segment of a sequence)*

| | | |
|---|---|---|
| DQA (an expressed gene in the histocompatibility complex) | Amplification of allelic sequences by PCR; discrete alleles detected by sequence specific probes | 8 (6 used in DQA kit) |
| Polymarker (a set of five loci) | Amplification of allelic sequences by PCR; discrete alleles detected by sequence-specific probes | Loci are bi-or tri-allelic; 972 geno-typic combinations |
| Mitochondrial DNA control region (D-loop) | Amplification of control-sequence and sequence determination | Hundreds of sequence variants are known |

## 4. Steps of PCR Amplification

The second National Research Council report provides a concise description of how PCR "amplifies" DNA:

First, each double-stranded segment is separated into two strands by heating. Second, these single-stranded segments are hybridized with primers, short DNA segments (20–30 nucleotides in length) that complement and define the target sequence to be amplified. Third, in the presence of the enzyme DNA polymerase, and the four nucleotide building blocks (A, C, G, and T), each primer serves as the starting point for the replication of the target sequence. A copy of the complement of each of the separated strands is made, so that there are two double-stranded DNA segments. The three-step cycle is repeated, usually 20–35 times. The two strands produce four copies; the four, eight copies; and so on until the number of copies of the original DNA is enormous. The main difference between this procedure and the normal cellular process is that the PCR process is limited to the amplification of a small DNA region. This region is usually not more than 1,000 nucleotides in length, so PCR methods cannot, at least at present, be used [to amplify] large DNA regions, such as most VNTRs.[4]

---

[4]Committee on DNA Forensic Science: An    Update, National Research Council, The Evalua-

Figure A-3 illustrates the steps in the PCR process for two cycles.[5]

## Figure A-3.
### The PCR Process

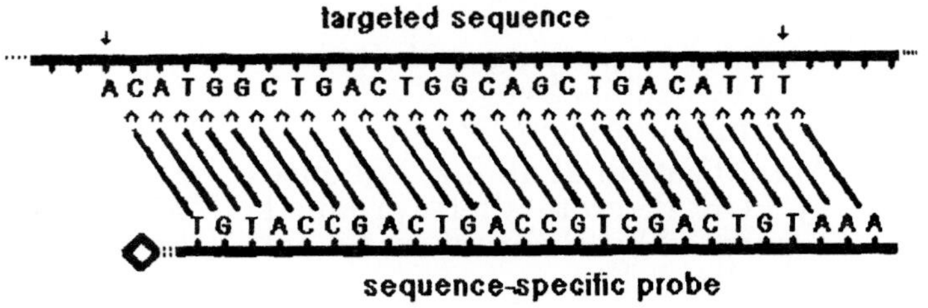

targeted sequence

sequence-specific probe

In principle, PCR amplification doubles the number of double-stranded DNA fragments each cycle. Although there is some inefficiency in practice, the yield from a 30-cycle amplification is generally about one million to ten million copies of the targeted sequence.

### 5. Quantities of DNA in Forensic Samples

Amounts of DNA present in some typical kinds of evidence samples are indicated in Table A-2. These are approximate, and the quantities of DNA extracted from evidence in particular cases may vary somewhat.[6]

### Table A-2
### DNA Content of Biological Samples[7]

| Type of Sample | | DNA Content | Success Rate |
|---|---|---|---|
| Blood | | 20,000–40,000 ng/mL | |
| | stain 1 cm × 1 cm | ca. 200 ng | >95% |
| | stain 1 mm × 1 mm | ca. 2 ng | |
| Semen | | 150,000–300,000 ng/mL | |
| | on post-coital vaginal swab | 0-3000 ng | >95% |
| Saliva | | 1000–10,000 ng/mL | |
| | on a cigarette butt | 0–25ng | 50–70% |
| Hair | | | |
| | root end of pulled hair | 1–750 ng | >90% |
| | root end of shed hair | 1–12 ng | <20% |
| | hair shaft | 0.001–0.040 ng/cm | |
| Urine | | 1–20 ng/mL | |
| Skin cells | | | |
| | from socks, gloves, or clothing repeatedly used | | 30–60% |
| | from handled objects (e.g., a doorknob) | | <20% |

ng = nanogram, or 1/1,000,000,000th of a gram; mL = milliliter; cm = centimeter; mm = millimeter

---

tion of Forensic DNA Evidence 69–70 (1996).

[5]The figure is adapted from figure 1-6 in Committee on DNA Technology in Forensic Science, National Research Council, DNA Technology in Forensic Science 41 (1992).

[6]The amounts in the table are given in nanograms (ng), ng per centimeter, or ng per milliliter (ng/mL). A nanogram is one billionth (1/1,000,000,000) of a gram.

[7]Adapted from Committee on DNA Technology in Forensic Science, National Research

---

Council, DNA Technology in Forensic Science 28 (1992) (with additions).

# APPENDIX 2B

# Glossary

***Adenine (A).*** One of the four bases, or nucleotides, that make up the DNA molecule. Adenine only binds to thymine. See Nucleotide.

***Affinal Method.*** A method for computing the single locus profile probabilities for a theoretical subpopulation by adjusting the single locus profile probability, calculated with the product rule from the mixed population database, by the amount of heterogeneity across subpopulations. The model is appropriate even if there is no database available for a particular subpopulation, and the formula always gives more conservative probabilities than the product rule applied to the same database.

***Allele.*** In classical genetics, an allele is one of several alternative forms of a gene. A biallelic gene has two variants; others have more. Alleles are inherited separately from each parent, and for a given gene, an individual may have two different alleles (heterozygosity) or the same allele (homozygosity). In DNA analysis, the term is applied to any DNA region (whether or not it constitutes a gene) used for analysis.

***Alu Sequences.*** A family of short interspersed elements (SINEs) distributed throughout the genomes of primates.

***Amplification.*** Increasing the number of copies of a DNA region, usually by PCR.

***Amplified Fragment Length Polymorphism (AMP-FLP).*** A DNA identification technique that uses PCR-amplified DNA fragments of varying lengths. The DS180 locus is a VNTR whose alleles can be detected with this technique.

***Antibody.*** A protein (immunoglobulin) molecule, produced by the immune system, that recognizes a particular foreign antigen and binds to it; if the antigen is on the surface of a cell, this binding leads to cell aggregation and subsequent destruction.

***Antigen.*** A molecule (typically found in the surface of a cell) whose shape triggers the production of antibodies that will bind to the antigen.

***Autoradiograph (Autoradiogram, Autorad).*** In RFLP analysis, the x-ray film (or print) showing the positions of radioactively marked fragments (bands) of DNA, indicating how far these fragments have migrated, and hence their molecular weights.

***Autosome.*** A chromosome other than the X and Y sex chromosomes.

***Band.*** See Autoradiograph.

***Band Shift.*** Movement of DNA fragments in one lane of a gel at a different rate than fragments of an identical length in another lane, resulting in the same pattern "shifted" up or down relative to the comparison lane. Band-shift does not necessarily occur at the same rate in all portions of the gel.

***Base Pair (bp).*** Two complementary nucleotides bonded together at the matching bases (A and T or C and G) along the double helix "backbone" of the DNA molecule. The length of a DNA fragment often is measured in numbers of base pairs (1 kilobase (kb) = 1000 bp); base pair numbers also are used to describe the location of an allele on the DNA strand.

***Bayes' Theorem.*** An elementary formula that relates certain conditional probabilities. It can be used to describe the impact of new data on the probability that a hypothesis is true.

***Bin, Fixed.*** In VNTR profiling, a bin is a range of base pairs (DNA fragment lengths). When a database is divided into fixed bins, the proportion of bands within each bin is determined and the relevant proportions are used in estimating the profile frequency.

***Bins, Floating.*** In VNTR profiling, a bin is a range of base pairs (DNA fragment lengths). In a floating bin method of estimating a profile frequency, the bin is centered on the base pair length of the allele in question, and the width of the bin can be defined by the laboratory's matching rule (e.g., ± 5% of band size).

***Binning.*** Grouping VNTR alleles into sets of similar sizes because the alleles' lengths are too similar to differentiate.

***Blind Proficiency Test.*** See Proficiency Test.

***Capillary Electrophoresis.*** A method for separating DNA fragments (including STRs) according to their length. A long, narrow tube is filled with an entangled polymer or comparable sieving medium, and an electric field is applied to pull DNA fragments placed at one end of the tube through the medium. The procedure is faster and uses smaller samples than gel electrophoresis, and it can be automated.

***Ceiling Principle.*** A procedure for setting a minimum DNA profile frequency proposed in 1992 by a committee of the National Academy of Science. One hundred persons from each of 15–20 genetically homogeneous populations spanning the range of racial groups in the United States are sampled. For each allele, the higher frequency among the groups sampled (or 5%, whichever is larger) is used in calculating the profile frequency. Cf. Interim Ceiling Principle.

***Chip.*** A miniaturized system for genetic analysis. One such chip mimics capillary electrophoresis and related manipulations. DNA fragments, pulled by small voltages, move through tiny channels etched into a small block of glass, silicon, quartz, or plastic. This system should be useful in analyzing STRs. Another technique mimics reverse dot blots by placing a large array of oligonucleotide probes on a solid surface. Such hybridization arrays should be useful in identifying SNPs and in sequencing mitochondrial DNA.

***Chromosome.*** A rod-like structure composed of DNA, RNA, and proteins. Most normal human cells contain 46 chromosomes, 22 autosomes and a sex chromosome (X) inherited from the mother, and another 22 autosomes and one sex chromosome (either X or Y) inherited from the father. The genes are located along the chromosomes. See also Homologous Chromosomes.

***Coding DNA.*** A small fraction of the human genome contains the "instructions" for assembling physiologically important proteins. The remainder of the DNA is "non-coding."

***CODIS (Combined DNA Index System).*** A collection of databases on STR and other loci of convicted felons maintained by the FBI.

***Complementary Sequence.*** The sequence of nucleotides on one strand of DNA that corresponds to the sequence on the other strand. For example, if one sequence is CTGAA, the complementary bases are GACTT.

*Cytosine (C).* One of the four bases, or nucleotides, that make up the DNA double helix. Cytosine only binds to guanine. See Nucleotide.

*Database.* A collection of DNA profiles.

*Degradation.* The breaking down of DNA by chemical or physical means.

*Denature, Denaturation.* The process of splitting, as by heating, two complementary strands of the DNA double helix into single strands in preparation for hybridization with biological probes.

*Deoxyribonucleic Acid (DNA).* The molecule that contains genetic information. DNA is composed of nucleotide building blocks, each containing a base (A, C, G, or T), a phosphate, and a sugar. These nucleotides are linked together in a double helix—two strands of DNA molecules paired up at complementary bases (A with T, C with G). See Adenine, Cytosine, Guanine, Thymine.

*Diploid Number.* See Haploid Number.

*D-loop.* A portion of the mitochrondrial genome known as the "control region" or "displacement loop" instrumental in the regulation and initiation of mtDNA gene products.

*DNA Polymerase.* The enzyme that catalyzes the synthesis of double-stranded DNA.

*DNA Probe.* See Probe.

*DNA Profile.* The alleles at each locus. For example, a VNTR profile is the pattern of band lengths on an autorad. A multilocus profile represents the combined results of multiple probes. See Genotype.

*DNA Sequence.* The ordered list of base pairs in a duplex DNA molecule or of bases in a single strand.

*DQA.* The gene that codes for a particular class of Human Leukocyte Antigen (HLA). This gene has been sequenced completely and can be used for forensic typing. See Human Leukocyte Antigen.

*DQα.* The antigen that is the product of the DQA gene. See DQA, Human Leukocyte Antigen.

*EDTA.* A preservative added to blood samples.

*Electrophoresis.* See Capillary Electrophoresis, Gel Electrophoresis.

*Endonuclease.* An enzyme that cleaves the phosphodiester bond within a nucleotide chain.

*Environmental Insult.* Exposure of DNA to external agents such as heat, moisture, and ultraviolet radiation, or chemical or bacterial agents. Such exposure can interfere with the enzymes used in the testing process, or otherwise make DNA difficult to analyze.

*Enzyme.* A protein that catalyzes (speeds up or slows down) a reaction.

*Ethidium Bromide.* A molecule that can intercalate into DNA double helices when the helix is under torsional stress. Used to identify the presence of DNA in a sample by its fluorescence under ultraviolet light.

*Fallacy of the Transposed Conditional.* See Transposition Fallacy.

*False Match.* Two samples of DNA that have different profiles could be declared to match if, instead of measuring the distinct DNA in each sample, there is an error in handling or preparing samples such that the DNA from a single sample is analyzed twice. The resulting match, which does not reflect the true profiles of the DNA from each sample, is a false match. Some people use "false match" more broadly, to include cases in which the true profiles of each sample are the same, but the samples come from different individuals. Compare True Match. See also Match, Random Match.

**Gel, Agarose.** A semisolid medium used to separate molecules by electrophoresis.

**Gel Electrophoresis.** In RFLP analysis, the process of sorting DNA fragments by size by applying an electric current to a gel. The different-sized fragments move at different rates through the gel.

**Gene.** A set of nucleotide base pairs on a chromosome that contains the "instructions" for controlling some cellular function such as making an enzyme. The gene is the fundamental unit of heredity; each simple gene "codes" for a specific biological characteristic.

**Gene Frequency.** The relative frequency (proportion) of an allele in a population.

**Genetic Drift.** Random fluctuation allele frequencies from generation to generation.

**Genetics.** The study of the patterns, processes, and mechanisms of inheritance of biological characteristics.

**Genome.** The complete genetic makeup of an organism, comprising 40,000–100,000 genes in humans.

**Genotype.** The particular forms (alleles) of a set of genes possessed by an organism (as distinguished from phenotype, which refers to how the genotype expresses itself, as in physical appearance). In DNA analysis, the term is applied to the variations within all DNA regions (whether or not they constitute genes) that are analyzed.

**Genotype, Single Locus.** The alleles that an organism possesses at a particular site in its genome.

**Genotype, Multilocus.** The alleles that an organism possesses at several sites in its genome.

**Guanine (G).** One of the four bases, or nucleotides, that make up the DNA double helix. Guanine only binds to cytosine. See Nucleotide.

**Hae III.** A particular restriction enzyme.

**Haploid Number.** Human sex cells (egg and sperm) contain 23 chromosomes each. This is the haploid number. When a sperm cell fertilizes an egg cell, the number of chromosomes doubles to 46. This is the diploid number.

**Haplotype.** A specific combination of linked alleles at several loci.

**Hardy-Weinberg Equilibrium.** A condition in which the allele frequencies within a large, random, intrabreeding population are unrelated to patterns of mating. In this condition, the occurrence of alleles from each parent will be independent and have a joint frequency estimated by the product rule. See Independence, Linkage disequilibrium.

**Heteroplasty.** The condition in which some copies of mitochondrial DNA in the same individual have different base pairs at certain points.

**Heterozygous.** Having a different allele at a given locus on each of a pair of homologous chromosomes. See Allele. Compare Homozygous.

**Homologous Chromosomes.** The 44 autosomes (non-sex chromosomes) in the normal human genome are in homologous pairs (one from each parent) that share an identical set of genes, but may have different alleles at the same loci.

***Human Leukocyte Antigen (HLA).*** Antigen (foreign body that stimulates an immune system response) located on the surface of most cells (excluding red blood cells and sperm cells). HLAs differ among individuals and are associated closely with transplant rejection. See DQA.

***Homozygous.*** Having the same allele at a given locus on each of a pair of homologous chromosomes. See Allele. Compare Heterozygous.

***Hybridization.*** Pairing up of complementary strands of DNA from different sources at the matching base pair sites. For example, a primer with the sequence AG-GTCT would bond with the complementary sequence TCCAGA on a DNA fragment.

***Independence.*** Two events are said to be independent if one is neither more nor less likely to occur when the other does.

***Interim Ceiling Principle.*** A procedure proposed in 1992 by a committee of the National Academy of Sciences for setting a minimum DNA profile frequency. For each allele, the highest frequency (adjusted upward for sampling error) found in any major racial group (or 10%, whichever is higher), is used in product-rule calculations. Cf. Ceiling Principle.

***Kilobase (kb).*** One thousand bases.

***Linkage.*** The inheritance together of two or more genes on the same chromosome.

***Linkage Equilibrium.*** A condition in which the occurrence of alleles at different loci are independent.

***Locus.*** A location in the genome, i.e., a position on a chromosome where a gene or other structure begins.

***Mass Spectroscopy.*** The separation of elements or molecules according to their molecular weight. In the version being developed for DNA analysis, small quantities of PCR-amplified fragments are irradiated with a laser to form gaseous ions that traverse a fixed distance. Heavier ions have longer times of flight, and the process is known as "matrix-assisted laser desorption-ionization time-of-flight mass spectroscopy." MALDI-TOF-MS, as it is abbreviated, may be useful in analyzing STRs.

***Match.*** The presence of the same allele or alleles in two samples. Two DNA profiles are declared to match when they are indistinguishable in genetic type. For loci with discrete alleles, two samples match when they display the same set of alleles. For RFLP testing of VNTRs, two samples match when the pattern of the bands is similar and the positions of the corresponding bands at each locus fall within a preset distance. See Match Window, False Match, True Match.

***Match Window.*** If two RFLP bands lie with a preset distance, called the match window, that reflects normal measurement error, they can be declared to match.

***Microsatellite.*** Another term for an STR.

***Minisatellite.*** Another term for a VNTR.

***Mitochondria.*** A structure (organelle) within nucleated (eukaryotic) cells that is the site of the energy producing reactions within the cell. Mitochondria contain their own DNA (often abbreviated as mtDNA), which is inherited only from mother to child.

***Molecular Weight.*** The weight in grams of one mole of a pure, molecular substance.

***Monomorphic.*** A gene or DNA characteristic that is almost always found in only one form in a population.

***Multilocus Probe.*** A probe that marks multiple sites (loci). RFLP analysis using a multilocus probe will yield an autorad showing a striped pattern of thirty or more bands. Such probes rarely are used now in forensic applications in the United States.

***Multilocus Profile.*** See Profile.

***Multiplexing.*** Typing several loci simultaneously.

***Mutation.*** The process that produces a gene or chromosome set differing from the type already in the population; the gene or chromosome set that results from such a process.

***Nanogram (ng).*** A billionth of a gram.

***Nucleic Acid.*** RNA or DNA.

***Nucleotide.*** A unit of DNA consisting of a base (A, C, G, or T) and attached to a phosphate and a sugar group; the basic building block of nucleic acids. See Deoxyribonucleic Acid.

***Nucleus.*** The membrane-covered portion of a eukaryotic cell containing most of the DNA and found within the cytoplasm.

***Oligonucleotide.*** A synthetic polymer made up of fewer than 100 nucleotides; used as a primer or a probe in PCR. See Primer.

***Paternity Index.*** A number (technically, a likelihood ratio) that indicates the support that the paternity test results lend to the hypothesis that the alleged father is the biological father as opposed to the hypothesis that another man selected at random is the biological father. Assuming that the observed phenotypes correctly represent the phenotypes of the mother, child, and alleged father tested, the number can be computed as the ratio of the probability of the phenotypes under the first hypothesis to the probability under the second hypothesis. Large values indicate substantial support for the hypothesis of paternity; values near zero indicate substantial support for the hypothesis that someone other than the alleged father is the biological father; and values near unity indicate that the results do not help in determining which hypothesis is correct.

***pH.*** A measure of the acidity of a solution.

***Phenotype.*** A trait, such as eye color or blood group, resulting from a genotype.

***Polymarker.*** A commercially marketed set of PCR-based tests for protein polymorphisms.

***Polymerase Chain Reaction (PCR).*** A process that mimics DNA's own replication processes to make up to millions of copies of short strands of genetic material in a few hours.

***Polymorphism.*** The presence of several forms of a gene or DNA characteristic in a population.

***Point Mutation.*** See SNP.

***Population Genetics.*** The study of the genetic composition of groups of individuals.

***Population Structure.*** When a population is divided into subgroups that do not mix freely, that population is said to have structure. Significant structure can lead to allele frequencies being different in the subpopulations.

*Primer.* An oligonucleotide that attaches to one end of a DNA fragment and provides a point for more complementary nucleotides to attach and replicate the DNA strand. See Oligonucleotide.

*Probe.* In forensics, a short segment of DNA used to detect certain alleles. The probe hybridizes, or matches up, to a specific complementary sequence. Probes allow visualization of the hybridized DNA, either by radioactive tag (usually used for RFLP analysis) or biochemical tag (usually used for PCR-based analyses).

*Product Rule.* When alleles occur independently at each locus (Hardy-Weinberg equilibrium) and across loci (linkage equilibrium), the proportion of the population with a given genotype is the product of the proportion of each allele at each locus, time factors of two for heterozygous loci.

*Proficiency Test.* A test administered at a laboratory to evaluate its performance. In a blind proficiency study, the laboratory personnel do not know that they are being tested.

*Prosecutor's Fallacy.* See Transposition Fallacy.

*Protein.* A class of biologically important compounds made up of smaller units (amino acids). The order of the certain base pairs in DNA determines which amino acids, and hence, which proteins are made within a cell.

*Quality Assurance.* A program conducted by a laboratory to ensure accuracy and reliability.

*Quality Audit.* A systematic and independent examination and evaluation of a laboratory's operations.

*Quality Control.* Activities used to monitor the ability of DNA typing to meet specified criteria.

*Random Match.* A match in the DNA profiles of two samples of DNA, where one is drawn at random from the population. See also Random Match Probability.

*Random Match Probability.* The chance of a random match. As it is usually used in court, the random match probability refers to the probability of a true match when the DNA being compared to the evidence DNA comes from a person drawn at random from the population. This random true match probability reveals the probability of a true match when the samples of DNA come from different, unrelated people.

*Random Mating.* The members of a population are said to mate randomly with respect to particular genes of DNA characteristics when the choice of mates is independent of the alleles.

*Recombination.* In general, any process in a diploid or partially diploid cell that generates new gene or chromosomal combinations not found in that cell or in its progenitors.

*Reference Population.* The population to which the perpetrator of a crime is thought to belong.

*Replication.* The synthesis of new DNA from existing DNA. See Polymerase Chain Reaction.

*Restriction Enzyme.* Protein that cuts double-stranded DNA at specific base pair sequences (different enzymes recognize different sequences). See Restriction Site.

*Restriction Fragment Length Polymorphism (RFLP).* Variation among people in the length of a segment of DNA cut at two restriction sites.

***Restriction Fragment Length Polymorphism (RFLP) Analysis.*** Analysis of individual variations in the lengths of DNA fragments produced by digesting sample DNA with a restriction enzyme.

***Restriction Site.*** A sequence marking the location at which a restriction enzyme cuts DNA into fragments. See Restriction Enzyme.

***Reverse Dot Blot.*** A detection method used to identify SNPs in which DNA probes are affixed to a membrane, and amplified DNA is passed over the probes to see if it contains the complementary sequence.

***Sequence-Specific Oligonucleotide (SSO) Probe.*** Also, Allele-Specific Oligonucleotide (ASO) Probe. Oligonucleotide probes used in a PCR-associated detection technique to identify the presence or absence of certain base pair sequences identifying different alleles. The probes are visualized by an array of dots rather than by the electrophoretograms associated with RFLP analysis.

***Sequencing.*** Determining the order of base pairs in a segment of DNA.

***Short Tandem Repeat (STR).*** See Variable Number Tandem Repeat.

***Single-Locus Probe.*** A probe that only marks a specific site (locus). RFLP analysis using a single-locus probe will yield an autorad showing one band if the individual is homozygous, two bands if heterozygous.

***SNP (Single Nucleotide Polymorphism).*** A substitution, insertion, or deletion of a single base pair at a given point in the genome.

***Southern Blotting.*** Named for its inventor, a technique by which processed DNA fragments, separated by gel electrophoresis, are transferred onto a nylon membrane in preparation for the application of biological probes.

***Thymine (T).*** One of the four bases, or nucleotides, that make up the DNA double helix. Thymine only binds to adenine. See Nucleotide.

***Transposition Fallacy.*** Confusing the conditional probability of A given B with that of B given A. Few people think that the probability that a person speaks Spanish (A) given that he or she is a citizen of Chile (B) equals the probability that a person is a citizen of Chile (B) given that he or she speaks Spanish (A). Yet, many court opinions, newspaper articles, and even some expert witnesses speak of the probability of a matching DNA genotype (A) given that someone other than the defendant is the source of the crime scene DNA (B) as if it were the probability of someone else being the source (B) given the matching profile (A). Transposing conditional probabilities correctly requires Bayes' Theorem.

***True Match.*** Two samples of DNA that have the same profile should match when tested. If there is no error in the labeling, handling, and analysis of the samples and in the reporting of the results, a match is a true match. A true match establishes that the two samples of DNA have the same profile. Unless the profile is unique, however, a true match does not conclusively prove that the two samples came from the same source. Some people use "true match" more narrowly, to mean only those matches among samples from the same source. Compare False Match. See also Match, Random Match.

***Variable Number Tandem Repeat (VNTR).*** A class of RFLPs due to multiple copies of virtually identical base pair sequences, arranged in succession at a specific locus on a chromosome. The number of repeats varies from individual to individual, thus providing a basis for individual recognition. VNTRs are longer than STRs.

***Window.*** See Match Window.

*X Chromosome.* See Chromosome.

*Y Chromosome.* See Chromosome.

## BIBLIOGRAPHY

### REFERENCES ON DNA

David W. Balding, Weight-of-Evidence for Forensic DNA Profiles (2005).

John Buckleton et al., Forensic DNA Evidence Interpretation (2005).

John M. Butler, Forensic DNA Typing: Biology and Technology Behind STR Markers (2d ed. 2005).

Ian W. Evett & Bruce S. Weir, Interpreting DNA Evidence: Statistical Genetics for Forensic Scientists (1998).

Elaine Johnson Mange & Arthur P. Mange, Basic Human Genetics (2d ed. 1999).

National Research Council Committee on DNA Forensic Science: An Update, The Evaluation of Forensic DNA Evidence (1996).

National Research Council Committee on DNA Technology in Forensic Science, DNA Technology in Forensic Science (1992).

# Chapter 3

# Fingerprint Identification

## I.  LEGAL ISSUES

## II.  SCIENTIFIC STATUS

## I.  LEGAL ISSUES

### § 3:1   Generally

Fingerprint identification evidence presents post-*Daubert* courts with a paradox. On the one hand, most if not all of the claims made by or on behalf of fingerprint examiners enjoy widespread and unquestioning belief among the lay public, including the bench and the bar. On the other hand, surprisingly little conventional science exists to support the claims of the fingerprint examination community. The latter point is sufficiently well appreciated within the fingerprint community that, following the decisions in *Daubert*[1] and *Kumho Tire*,[2] the National Institute of Justice was asked to support research to test the validity of some of their most important assertions, which thus far have gone largely untested. "The participants in the [National Institute of Justice Fingerprint Research Advisory Panel] included practicing latent print examiners, researchers, and senior administrators from Federal, State, and private forensic science laboratories. They reached a consensus that the field needs . . . [b]asic research to determine the scientific validity of individuality in friction ridge examination . . . ."[3] On the one hand, strong intuitions have convinced several generations of fingerprint examiners that all of their beliefs about the nature of fingerprints and about fingerprint identification are correct. On the other hand, they can point to remarkably little hard data from systematic tests of the validity of those claims. How are courts to resolve insuperable challenges to the unchallengeable?

Today, a thoughtful and scientifically literate[4] proponent of expert fingerprint identification testimony, compelled by a thoughtful and scientifically literate op-

---

**[Section 3:1]**

[1]*Daubert v. Merrell Dow Pharmaceuticals, Inc.*, 509 U.S. 579, 113 S. Ct. 2786, 125 L. Ed. 2d 469, 27 U.S.P.Q.2d 1200, Prod. Liab. Rep. (CCH) P 13494, 37 Fed. R. Evid. Serv. 1, 23 Envtl. L. Rep. 20979 (1993).

[2]*Kumho Tire Co., Ltd. v. Carmichael*, 526 U.S. 137, 119 S. Ct. 1167, 143 L. Ed. 2d 238, 50 U.S.P.Q.2d 1177, Prod. Liab. Rep. (CCH) P 15470, 50 Fed. R. Evid. Serv. 1373, 29 Envtl. L. Rep. 20638 (1999).

[3]National Institute of Justice, Forensic Friction Ridge (Fingerprint) Examination Validation Studies (March, 2000). Although this solicitation for research proposals was originally scheduled for publication in August, 1999, the FBI arranged to delay its release until after the trial of *United States v. Mitchell*. The case and the incident are discussed at §§ 3:3 to 3:18.

[4]By "scientifically literate" we mean nothing more (nor less) than having an understanding of how to ask empirical questions and how to evaluate the answers offered to those questions.

ponent to demonstrate the validity of fingerprint identification claims in front of a thoughtful and scientifically literate judge, would face a number of serious difficulties. The seminal cases admitting fingerprint evidence in American courts paid so little attention to the foundation of the asserted science that they offer no help in evaluating the admissibility of fingerprint identification evidence under *Daubert* and *Kumho Tire*. Proficiency testing does not support the claimed error rate of zero or of the unanimity of opinion asserted by fingerprint examiners.[5] Many of the most basic claims of fingerprint identification have never been tested empirically, and the field's most thoughtful research and scholarship have concluded that, in the strong form in which they usually are presented, those claims in fact are unprovable.[6] The most central beliefs of the public and the legal profession are irrelevant to the task at hand in most fingerprint identification cases.[7] The judgments whether a match exists or not and whether the latent and the known share a common origin or not have not evolved beyond subjective appraisal.[8] Finally, while the practical and realistic goal of fingerprint identification would be to make probability statements about the likelihood that a latent print which appears to match a suspect's rolled print actually came from someone *other than* the suspect (that is, the probability of a coincidental match), the fingerprinting field eschews probability statements as an "ethical" offense, and demands that its members offer only opinions of an absolute and certain nature or give no opinion.[9]

The greatest challenge, of course, is faced by the thoughtful and scientifically literate judge who has to decide whether to admit or exclude the fingerprint examiner's expert testimony. Some judges have simply taken judicial notice of the truth of the fingerprint community's beliefs, which—in the context of challenges brought under new law designed to encourage rigorous gatekeeping—would seem to be an acknowledgment of and response to the lack of more conventional scientific evidence on the issue.[10] A judge who takes *Daubert*'s commands seriously would be hard pressed to write a coherent opinion justifying a decision to admit the expert

---

[5]See David Grieve, Possession of Truth, 46 J. Forensic Identification 521 (1996) (Editor of the leading fingerprint examination journal lamenting that in the first proficiency test of fingerprint examiners, ". . . one in five [experts] would have provided damning evidence against the wrong person" and that only 44% of 156 examiners offered correct answers to all of the fingerprints in the test.). See also Collaborative Testing Services, Inc., Forensic Testing Program: Latent Prints Examination, Report No. 9808 (1998) (unpublished report). The few subsequent proficiency tests that have been conducted have the error rate averaging around 0.5%.

[6]"It is unfortunate that this approach carries the implication that a complete correspondence of two patterns might occur . . . ." " . . . it is impossible to offer decisive proof that no two fingerprints bear identical patterns." Harold Cummins & Charles Midlo, Finger Prints, Palms and Soles: An Introduction to Dermatoglyphics 154 (1943). See also Stoney, What Made Us Ever Think We Could Individualize Using Statistics?, 31 J. Forensic Sci. Soc'y 197 (1991). For a recent review of the status of the science, see Zabell, Fingerprint Evidence, 13 J. Law & Policy 143 (2005).

[7]§ 3:31. Because most comparisons are between fragments of prints, the question that needs

to be asked is whether portions of two people's fingerprints can be so alike that examiners mistake one person's print as belonging to the other person. Since such errors can occur and have occurred, the questions move on to: what are the probabilities of such errors under varying conditions.

[8]§ 3:45.

[9]§ 3:36.

[10]E.g., *United States v. Mitchell*, Crim. No. 96-407 (E.D.Pa., *Daubert* hearing held July 7–13, 1999); *State v. McGee*, No. 99-CR-277 (Superior Court of Carroll County, Ga., *Daubert* hearing held October 27, 2000). Were there adequate solid research, courts could cite it and explicate it. Moreover, it is not clear whether the courts relying on judicial notice are treating the question as one of adjudicative or legislative fact. If they are taking judicial notice of adjudicative fact (under Federal Rule of Evidence 201 or a state equivalent) they must find that the adjudicative fact at issue is "not subject to reasonable dispute" and (in a criminal case) must instruct the jury that it has the discretion to accept or reject the judicially noticed fact. Yet this kind of judicial notice seems inapplicable because the very reason for taking judicial notice on this issue is that conventional scientific evidence is lacking. If, on the other hand, these courts are taking judicial notice of legisla-

opinion.[11] Indeed, because fingerprint identification has been both oversold and under-researched it is a prime candidate for exclusion for the most conventional of reasons for requiring expert testimony to cross a high threshold in order to enter the courtroom, namely, that the jury will give it excessive weight. Some judges might feel that because their duty is to obey the law, where *Daubert* is the law the lack of data or other rigorous evidence underlying fingerprint identification claims compels them to rule that the fingerprint expert may not testify.[12] However, the very ubiquity of the public's implicit belief in the validity of fingerprint identification evidence will cause many judges to think twice before excluding the expert testimony, though perhaps not for reasons of law or science. The professional skepticism of normal scientists requires them to postpone belief until the data are sufficient to support belief. Similar postponement of belief by courts would mean that in the case at bar the expert opinion would not enter, and that has its own consequences. Still other judges might conclude that they somehow "know" the claims are correct[13] and *that* belief, however it was arrived at, it might be argued, satisfies *Daubert*.[14]

None of these is a happy resolution. Perhaps courts will begin to find more creative and practical solutions to this boggling dilemma.[15] One possibility is partial admission: the expert is allowed to testify to similarities and differences between the questioned and the known evidence, but may not offer an ultimate opinion of identification or non-identification.[16] Another possibility might be to require, as a condition of admission, that examiners give scrupulously accurate portrayals of the

---

tive fact they are on firmer legal ground because this latter type of judicial notice is applicable to facts that usually are anything but indisputable (see Federal Rule of Evidence 201, Advisory Committee's Note). Yet judicial notice of legislative fact is appropriate only for decisions that are being made as a matter of law, and which therefore would be subject to de novo review on appeal, which would be contrary to the Supreme Court's holding in *General Elec. Co. v. Joiner*, 522 U.S. 136, 118 S. Ct. 512, 139 L. Ed. 2d 508, 18 O.S.H. Cas. (BNA) 1097, Prod. Liab. Rep. (CCH) P 15120, 48 Fed. R. Evid. Serv. 1, 28 Envtl. L. Rep. 20227, 177 A.L.R. Fed. 667 (1997). Clearly, there are some legal as well as scientific conundrums to be resolved.

[11]§ 3:45 (Considering the possible application to fingerprint methods of some of the criteria courts used to evaluate DNA typing: "Woe to fingerprint practice were such criteria applied!").

[12]An example is Judge Seay's assessment of hair identification evidence in the habeas corpus review of *Williamson v. Reynolds*, 904 F. Supp. 1529 (E.D. Okla. 1995), aff'd, 110 F.3d 1508 (10th Cir. 1997) and (abrogated on other grounds by, Nguyen v. Reynolds, 131 F.3d 1340 (10th Cir. 1997)) and (rejected on other grounds by, Castro v. Ward, 138 F.3d 810 (10th Cir. 1998)). But that is a rare example. Other judges faced with forensic sciences that similarly failed to pass *Daubert* muster have striven to find ways to keep the evidence from being excluded. See, e.g., *U.S. v. Starzecpyzel*, 880 F. Supp. 1027, 42 Fed. R. Evid. Serv. 247 (S.D. N.Y. 1995) (concluding that because forensic handwriting examiners flunked

*Daubert*, they were not doing science; because they were not doing science they did not have to pass muster under *Daubert*; therefore they were permitted to testify).

[13]Scientists, and other logical people, would ask: how can one "know," when the problem is a paucity of data?

[14]Query whether this is simply judges engaging in the same ipse dixit that the Supreme Court has prohibited experts from engaging in. *General Elec. Co. v. Joiner*, 522 U.S. 136, 118 S. Ct. 512, 139 L. Ed. 2d 508, 18 O.S.H. Cas. (BNA) 1097, Prod. Liab. Rep. (CCH) P 15120, 48 Fed. R. Evid. Serv. 1, 28 Envtl. L. Rep. 20227, 177 A.L.R. Fed. 667 (1997).

[15]Some solutions simply may not be available to the judicial management of these problems, though they could be managed through proper legislation. For example, it might be expedient to grant temporary admission, that is, temporarily stay the operation of *Daubert* against a particular expertise or field of expertise, and permit continued admission of expert opinions for a limited number of years to permit belated empirical testing of the field's claims, after which period admission would be conditioned on producing the required evidence of validity. But it is hard to imagine how this can be done by courts making case-by-case decisions to admit or exclude.

[16]This has occurred in many cases where the testimony of forensic handwriting examiners has been offered. See discussion of cases at §§ 33:1 et seq. of this work.

limitations of their field and their conclusions.[17] Another solution might be judicial instruction of the jury about the limitations of a field, notwithstanding popular beliefs to the contrary.[18] If nothing else, courts should have no objection to the opponent of admission offering to the jury evidence of the weakness or lack of confirmatory science, in order to assist the jury in determining the weight that should be given to the expert's opinion.[19]

Though we hesitate to venture a guess as to the eventual outcome of this period of questioning the heretofore unquestionable, we will say this much. One likely and beneficial scenario would be that the belated empirical research sparked by the fingerprint community's fear of exclusion under *Daubert* and *Kumho Tire* will result in knowledge that will lead courts not to exclude but to require fingerprint identification expert witnesses to remain within the bounds of those data, to become aware of and be candid about the field's limitations, and to refrain from making unsupportable exaggerations—some of which virtually define the field in the popular imagination.

## § 3:2 Admissibility prior to *Daubert*

Expert testimony based upon fingerprints to prove identity is admitted in every jurisdiction of the United States.[1] That much is well known. The details of judicial acceptance of the technique during the second decade of the 20th Century are far less well known. This evidentiary development was characterized by meager judicial scrutiny combined with relatively rapid spread of acceptance among numerous jurisdictions. That swiftness is somewhat surprising considering that fingerprint identification presented the courts with a claim that was still novel (infinite and absolute individualization) in a remarkably strong form (infallibility);[2] and rapid considering the recent shortcomings and abandonment of anthropometry, the first child of scientific attempts at individualization, which had made essentially the same claims.[3]

Case law upholding the admission of fingerprint evidence begins in 1911 with

---

[17]Thus, if the data do not exist to support assertions of absolute identification, or an opinion is based on subjective probability guestimations or intuition or leaps of faith, the witness must say so as part of the opinion.

[18]Compare the court's instruction in *U.S. v. Starzecpyzel*, 880 F. Supp. 1027, 42 Fed. R. Evid. Serv. 247 (S.D. N.Y. 1995).

[19]As the Supreme Court explained in *Daubert*: "Vigorous cross-examination, presentation of contrary evidence, and careful instruction on the burden of proof are the traditional and appropriate means of attacking shaky but admissible evidence."

**[Section 3:2]**

[1]See Annotation, Admissibility of bare footprint evidence, 45 A.L.R.4th 1178.

[2]Recall that once these concepts were accepted on behalf of fingerprint identification, numerous other forensic individualization areas made the same claim by analogizing themselves to fingerprints.

[3]Anthropometry, or *bertillonage*, developed in the early 1880s by Alphonse Bertillon, a clerk in the Paris prefecture of police, relied on the measurements of 11 different physical features of prisoners to determine if they had prior arrests in spite of their giving aliases to the police. Anthropometry marked the birth of forensic individuation techniques. Although anthropometry and fingerprints share the same underlying theory, fingerprints involve many more than 11 features, the features are more likely to be independent, and therefore less likely to be in violation of the statistical principle that is at the heart of all forensic individualization. And, obviously, fingerprints can be used not only to identify and catalog suspects once they are arrested, but can be used to help find suspects who left their fingerprints at a crime scene. Bertillon's system became controversial when it was thought that some prisoners were found who, contrary to the theory, had indistinguishable anthropometric measurements. *Bertillonage* would have been replaced by fingerprinting anyway, given the latter's greater convenience and unrivaled usefulness for investigative purposes. For a history of these matters, see Jürgen Thorwald, The Century of the Detective (1965); see also John I. Thornton, Criminalistics—Past, Present, Future 11 Lex et Scientia 1 (1975).

*People v. Jennings*,[4] in Illinois. Within the decade New Jersey,[5] New York,[6] Nevada,[7] and Texas[8] joined Illinois in approving the admissibility of fingerprint evidence. These initial jurisdictions established the rationale for admissibility. Little more than the passage of time seems to have been necessary for eventual universal acceptance. In the next 10 years 12 more states joined. By the end of the 1930s all but five states were formal members of the club.[9]

These cases, germinal not only for fingerprint identification but for many other forensic individualization techniques, invested virtually no effort assessing the merits of the proffered scientific evidence, but merely cited treatises on criminal investigation, or general approval of science, or, soon, other cases admitting it.

In *Jennings*, expert opinion based on fingerprints was the sole ground of

---

[4]*People v. Jennings*, 252 Ill. 534, 96 N.E. 1077 (1911).

[5]*State v. Cerciello*, 86 N.J.L. 309, 90 A. 1112 (N.J. Ct. Err. & App. 1914).

[6]*People v. Roach*, 215 N.Y. 592, 109 N.E. 618 (1915).

[7]*State v. Kuhl*, 42 Nev. 185, 175 P. 190, 3 A.L.R. 1694 (1918).

[8]*McGarry v. State*, 82 Tex. Crim. 597, 200 S.W. 527 (1918).

[9]Following are the initial appellate cases in various jurisdictions admitting expert testimony on identification based on fingerprint examinations. In other jurisdictions, fingerprint evidence came to be admitted without specific judicial authorization.

**Second Circuit**—*U. S. v. Perillo*, 164 F.2d 645 (C.C.A. 2d Cir. 1947).

**Seventh Circuit**—*U.S. v. Dressler*, 112 F.2d 972 (C.C.A. 7th Cir. 1940).

**Eighth Circuit**—*Duree v. U.S.*, 297 F. 70 (C.C.A. 8th Cir. 1924).

**Ninth Circuit**—*Stoppelli v. U.S.*, 183 F.2d 391 (9th Cir. 1950).

**Tenth Circuit**—*U.S. v. Fujii*, 55 F. Supp. 928 (D. Wyo. 1944), judgment aff'd, 148 F.2d 298 (C.C.A. 10th Cir. 1945) and judgment aff'd, 148 F.2d 527 (C.C.A. 10th Cir. 1945); *Shigeru Fujii v. U.S.*, 148 F.2d 298 (C.C.A. 10th Cir. 1945).

**Alabama**—*Leonard v. State*, 18 Ala. App. 427, 93 So. 56 (1922).

**Arizona**—*Moon v. State*, 22 Ariz. 418, 198 P. 288, 16 A.L.R. 362 (1921).

**Arkansas**—*Hopkins v. State*, 174 Ark. 391, 295 S.W. 361 (1927).

**California**—*People v. Van Cleave*, 208 Cal. 295, 280 P. 983 (1929).

**Connecticut**—*State v. Chin Lung*, 106 Conn. 701, 139 A. 91 (1927).

**Florida**—*Martin v. State*, 100 Fla. 16, 129 So. 112 (1930).

**Georgia**—*Lewis v. State*, 196 Ga. 755, 27 S.E.2d 659 (1943).

**Idaho**—*State v. Martinez*, 43 Idaho 180, 250 P. 239 (1926).

**Illinois**—*People v. Jennings*, 252 Ill. 534, 96

N.E. 1077 (1911).

**Kentucky**—*Hornsby v. Commonwealth*, 263 Ky. 613, 92 S.W.2d 773 (1936); *Ingram v. Commonwealth*, 265 Ky. 323, 96 S.W.2d 1017 (1936).

**Maryland**—*Debinski v. State*, 194 Md. 355, 71 A.2d 460 (1950).

**Massachusetts**—*Com. v. Bartolini*, 299 Mass. 503, 13 N.E.2d 382 (1938).

**Michigan**—*People v. Chimovitz*, 237 Mich. 247, 211 N.W. 650 (1927); *People v. Les*, 267 Mich. 648, 255 N.W. 407 (1934).

**Mississippi**—*Willoughby v. State*, 154 Miss. 653, 122 So. 757, 63 A.L.R. 1319 (1929).

**Missouri**—*State v. Richetti*, 342 Mo. 1015, 119 S.W.2d 330 (1938).

**Nevada**—*State v. Kuhl*, 42 Nev. 185, 175 P. 190, 3 A.L.R. 1694 (1918); *State v. Behiter*, 55 Nev. 236, 29 P.2d 1000 (1934).

**New Jersey**—*State v. Cerciello*, 86 N.J.L. 309, 90 A. 1112 (N.J. Ct. Err. & App. 1914).

**New Mexico**—*State v. Johnson*, 37 N.M. 280, 21 P.2d 813, 89 A.L.R. 1368 (1933).

**New York**—*People v. Roach*, 215 N.Y. 592, 109 N.E. 618 (1915).

**North Carolina**—*State v. Combs*, 200 N.C. 671, 158 S.E. 252 (1931).

**Ohio**—*State v. Viola*, 51 Ohio L. Abs. 577, 82 N.E.2d 306 (Ct. App. 7th Dist. Trumbull County 1947).

**Oklahoma**—*Stacy v. State*, 49 Okla. Crim. 154, 292 P. 885 (1930).

**Oregon**—*State v. Smith*, 128 Or. 515, 273 P. 323 (1929).

**Pennsylvania**—*Com. v. Loomis*, 270 Pa. 254, 113 A. 428 (1921).

**Texas**—*McGarry v. State*, 82 Tex. Crim. 597, 200 S.W. 527 (1918).

**Vermont**—*State v. Watson*, 114 Vt. 543, 49 A.2d 174 (1946).

**Washington**—*State v. Bolen*, 142 Wash. 653, 254 P. 445 (1927).

**West Virginia**—*State v. Johnson*, 111 W. Va. 653, 164 S.E. 31 (1932).

**Wyoming**—*Waxler v. State*, 67 Wyo. 396, 224 P.2d 514 (1950).

identification. The court recognized the novelty of the expertise at issue, noting that "the courts of this country do not appear to have had occasion to pass on the question." In upholding the admissibility of fingerprint expertise, the *Jennings* court cited two general encyclopedias,[10] three treatises on crime investigation methods,[11] and one recent English case.[12] Nowhere in the opinion, however, does the court articulate the basis of the expertise it is evaluating, or discuss any scientific evidence in support of the expertise, or illuminate the technique's theoretical premises, or explain why one should believe that fingerprint examiners can do what they claim the ability to do. Nor do the cited sources fill that gap.[13] In addition, the court also referred to four experts who testified on behalf of fingerprint identification, each of whom had been studying or practicing fingerprint examination for three to four years before the trial. But the court's opinion shares nothing of what, if anything, they had to say on the question at issue.

Here is the totality of what the court had to say in its review of the science:

> These authorities state that this system of identification is of very ancient origin, having been used in Egypt when the impression of the monarch's thumb was used as his sign manual, that it has been used in the courts of India for many years and more recently in the courts of several European countries; that in recent years its use has become very general by the police departments of the large cities of this country and Europe; [of] the great success of the system in England, where it has been used since 1891 in thousands of cases without error . . . .[14]

Based on the preceding, the *Jennings* court concluded:

> We are disposed to hold from the evidence of the four witnesses who testified, and from the writings we have referred to on this subject, that there is a scientific basis for the system of finger print identification, and that the courts are justified in admitting this class of evidence; . . . .

The second American case to consider the admissibility of fingerprint evidence, *Cerciello*, neither cited nor explained anything whatsoever concerning the expertise at issue. This court's scientific assessment was nothing more than a generalized endorsement of scientific progress:

> [I]ts admission as legal evidence is based upon the theory that the evolution in practical affairs of life, whereby the progressive and scientific tendencies of the age are manifest in every other department of human endeavor, cannot be ignored in legal procedure, but that the law, in its efforts to enforce justice by demonstrating a fact in issue, will allow evidence of those scientific processes which are the work of educated and skillful men in their various departments . . . .

The court's legal reasoning amounted to this: the admission of expert opinion, "one of the prominent exceptions of the general rules of evidence," was permitted on so many other matters that the court could hardly exclude one more; moreover, the

---

[10]10 Ency. Britannica 376 (11th Ed., 1910–1911); 5 Nelson's Encyclopedia 28.

[11]Hans Gross, Criminal Investigation 277 (Adams' Transl., 1907); Leonhard F. Fuld, Police Administration 342 (1909); Albert Osborn, Questioned Documents 479 (1910).

[12]*In re Castleton's Case*, 3 Crim. App. 74.

[13]Nor would one expect them to. With the possible exception of Osborn's treatise on handwriting (which is discussed at some length at §§ 26:1 et seq.) they do not even purport to be presentations of the basic science underlying techniques of crime investigation.

[14]The allusion to "thousands of cases without error" obviously begs the question of validity. In actual disputed cases it rarely if ever is possible to tell whether the identification was correct or not; that is why the issue was before the fact-finder. This has been a major problem in validating many forensic techniques. See discussions of this problem in Congressional Office of Technology Assessment, The Scientific Validity of Polygraph Testing: A Research Review and Evaluation (1983); John Thornton, Courts of Law v. Courts of Science: A Forensic Scientist's Reaction to *Daubert*, 1 Shepard's Expert and Scientific Evidence Quarterly 480 (1994). Take *Jennings* as an example: how might one confirm whether that fingerprint identification was correct or not?

jury would give the testimony whatever weight was appropriate.

The *Roach* court did no more than to cite *Castleton* and *Jennings*, commenting of the latter that "The opinion of Chief Justice Carter in that case contains an instructive and learned discussion of this whole subject." The opinion offers no citations to any scientific materials or any discussion of the principles claimed to be the foundation of the technique. The court focused on the "qualifications" of the witness rather than the content of the science.[15] The court reasoned: "In view of the progress that has been made by scientific students and those charged with the detection of crime in police departments . . . we cannot rule as a matter of law that such evidence is incompetent."

In Texas, the *McGarry* court rested its opinion squarely on *Jennings*, literally adopting the Illinois opinion as its own. After quoting at length[16] from *Jennings*, *McGarry* held simply: "We conclude that the evidence of the witness was admissible."[17]

The quality of judicial scrutiny of fingerprint evidence rarely exceeded that of *Jennings*, and sometimes it fell far shorter. While some cases made reference to actual early scientific works on fingerprints,[18] others cited Mark Twain's novel, "Puddin' Head Wilson," as authority for the infallibility of fingerprint evidence,[19] or appealed to far higher authority:

> "God's finger print language," the voiceless speech, and the indelible writing on the fingers, hand palms, and foot soles of humanity by the All-Wise Creator for some good and useful purpose . . . . [namely,] the ultimate elimination of crime . . . [by] unquestionable evidence of identity in all cases.[20]

Before long, courts had ample precedents from sister jurisdictions to cite as authority for the infallibility of fingerprint evidence. Popular and judicial intuitions about fingerprints are so strong that not a case can be found that entertains any serious doubt about the scientific perfection that has been achieved by fingerprint examination.[21]

A modern court, compelled to apply the conventional scientific criteria outlined in *Daubert*, would find no help in these earlier cases. Indeed, it may be precisely the easy and rapid admission in those early cases that brings us to the post-*Daubert* dilemmas that today's courts are beginning to face. Because the forensic sciences have no tradition of research, little if any institutional support for doing research, and generally no cognate fields in academia or industry to do the research for them, once they are admitted to court their efforts to test themselves or prove themselves all but cease.[22] Had the early courts been more thoughtful and demanding, there would be less left untested and unproved today, and that research is likely to come

---

[15]"Before testifying to his opinion as to the identity . . . the witness explained fully his qualifications, specified the circumstances upon which he predicated his opinion, and swore that he was able to express an opinion with reasonable certainty." *People v. Roach*, 215 N.Y. 592, 109 N.E. 618 (1915).

[16]*McGarry v. State*, 82 Tex. Crim. 597, 200 S.W. 527, 528–530 (1918).

[17]*McGarry v. State*, 82 Tex. Crim. 597, 200 S.W. 527, 603 (1918).

[18]Notably, Francis Galton, Finger Prints (1900); William Herschel, The Origin of Finger Printing (1916); H. Faulds, Guide to Finger-Print Identification (1905).

[19]*State v. Kuhl*, 42 Nev. 185, 175 P. 190, 3 A.L.R. 1694 (1918); *Stacy v. State*, 49 Okla. Crim.

154, 292 P. 885 (1930).

[20]*Kuhl*, quoting approvingly from Frederic Augustus Brayley, Brayley's Arrangement of Finger Prints Identification and Their Uses, for Police Departments, Prisons, Lawyers, Banks, Homes, Trust Companies . . . and in Every Branch of Business where an Infallible System of Identification is Necessary (1909). In fairness to the *Kuhl* court it must be noted that its opinion was perhaps the most erudite, citing some of the most scholarly works on fingerprints—as well as some of the silliest.

[21]See *Stevenson v. U.S.*, 380 F.2d 590 (D.C. Cir. 1967).

[22]An Assistant U.S. Attorney has argued that it is unfair to criticize forensic sciences "for failing to develop a rigorous empirical defense of [their] theories and methods" because they "had not had

into being only if today's courts are thoughtful and demanding.[23]

## § 3:3 Post-*Daubert* challenges in federal courts

The first case in which a serious and timely in limine challenge was made to the foundational claims of fingerprint identification, and in which a *Daubert* hearing was held, was *United States v. Mitchell*.[1] At the *Daubert* hearing, both the proponent and the opponent offered briefs, witnesses, and arguments that attempted to provide the court with real information about the strengths and the weaknesses of the claims of fingerprint identification.

Because the district court wrote no opinion to accompany its ruling, details are somewhat hard to come by, and this discussion relies on the reports of participants other than the judge.[2] The proponent's major witnesses at the *Daubert* hearing were Bruce Babler,[3] Donald Ziesig,[4] David Ashbaugh,[5] Bruce Budowle,[6] and Stephen Meagher.[7] Called by the opponent were James Starrs,[8] Simon Cole,[9] and David Stoney.[10]

The proponent's witnesses explained the process of fingerprint identification and their theories of why it is believed sound by fingerprints examiners and should be by the court as well, despite limited conventional scientific testing. They presented a variety of such arguments, including the fact that identical twins do not have identical fingerprints,[11] the argument that 100 years of fingerprint casework constitutes empirical testing, efforts at developing statistical models of fingerprint identification, and they claimed that the error rate in fingerprint identification is zero.[12] Ashbaugh offered the theory that he has developed in an effort to articulate a foundation for fingerprint identification that can meet modern scientific standards.

---

any particular reason to conduct validity studies because their testimony was being admitted without them." J. Orenstein, Effect of the *Daubert* Decision on Document Examinations From the Prosecutor's Perspective, 1 Forensic Science Communications (October 1999), at http://www.fbi.gov/programs/lab/fsc/backissu/oct1999/abstrctf.htm.

[23]While the results of such research will be unlikely to lead to ultimate exclusion, it is likely to lead to a tempering of the astounding claims made by fingerprint and other forensic examiners, such as the claim of error rates of zero.

**[Section 3:3]**

[1]*United States v. Mitchell,* Crim. No. 96-407-1 (E.D.Pa., judgment entered February, 2000). A previous trial and conviction resulted in a reversal, reported at *U.S. v. Mitchell*, 145 F.3d 572, 49 Fed. R. Evid. Serv. 361, 165 A.L.R. Fed. 713 (3d Cir. 1998).

[2]Query what is signified by the judge's failure to write an opinion in so noteworthy a hearing. Our sources for what transpired at the hearing are: Press Release, Office of the U.S. Attorney for the Eastern District of Pennsylvania (Sep. 13, 1999); Simon Cole, The Myth of Fingerprints, Lingafranca, Nov. 2000, at 54; Fingering Fingerprints: Fingerprints, the Touchstone of Forensic Science, Have Never Been Subjected to Proper Scientific Scrutiny, The Economist, Dec. 16, 2000, at 69; and a summary at http://onin.com/fp/daubert_links.html#CASE1.

[3]A Professor of Physical Anthropology from Marquette University.

[4]An engineer at Lockheed-Martin Corp.

[5]A Sergeant in the Royal Canadian Mounted Police.

[6]A senior scientist at the FBI Laboratory in Quantico, who holds a doctorate in genetics.

[7]Latent Print Unit Chief at the FBI Laboratory.

[8]Professor of law and forensic science at George Washington University and co-author of Andre Moenssens et al., Scientific Evidence in Civil and Criminal Cases (4th ed. 1995).

[9]A sociologist and historian of science, and author of Simon A. Cole, Suspect Identities: A History of Fingerprinting and Criminal Identification (2001).

[10]Director of the McCrone Research Institute in Chicago, holds a doctorate in forensic science, and is the author of the Scientific Status part of this chapter.

[11]However, query which way this fact cuts. It implies that fingerprints are determined by unknown random or non-random forces in addition to whatever genetic forces may be operating.

[12]As witness Budowle explained: "I don't think error rates is the right approach. I think errors are the right approach in reviewing errors in improving upon them, discussing them and fixing them is an absolutely important thing to do. But

In addition, the government offered the findings of two studies conducted for the purposes of this hearing.

The witnesses for the opponent pointed to the subjectivity and lack of standards, lack of conventional scientific testing of the hypotheses at the root of belief in absolute identification by fingerprints, and that fingerprint casework does not constitute testing because it is not designed to falsify the examination.[13] These witnesses also pointed to errors demonstrated by proficiency testing and errors which have been found in actual cases. The debate between the experts also involved the issue of counting points of similarity between known and questioned prints (and that while point-counting is rejected by American examiners, they nevertheless engage in it in whatever idiosyncratic way each one chooses).[14]

Two studies conducted by the government in reaction to the challenge raised in this case are noteworthy on several levels. First of all, the fact that such research had not been conducted before, and had to be rushed into being for this hearing is itself astonishing. Most fields of normal science could pull from the shelf dozens or hundreds, if not thousands, of studies testing their various hypotheses and contentions, which had been conducted over the past decades or century, and hand them to the court. The need to conduct such studies at such a late date would seem to be a dilemma for the proponents (do we go to court without the studies, or do we conduct them and thereby underscore the fact that until now such research had not been done) and would seem to confirm a major point being made by the opponents.

One of the studies conducted by the government for the *Daubert* hearing in this case employed the two actual latent and the known prints that were at issue in the case. These prints were submitted to 53 state law enforcement agency crime laboratories around the country for their evaluation. Though, of the 35 that responded, most concluded that the latent and known prints matched, eight said that no match could be made to one of the prints and six said that no match could be made to the other print. This disagreement is significant, given the professional ideology of fingerprint examiners, which asserts that they are so conservative in reaching conclusions that no one of them would declare a match unless it were certain that every other examiner who looked at the same prints would also declare them a match.[15] This first test of that belief had to be shocking to the field. The FBI reacted by sending annotated blow-ups of the prints to those examiners who judged the

---

using them to calculate an error rate is meaningless and misrepresents the state of the art." Witness Meagher argued that if error is divided into "methodological error" (the errors made by the technique) and "examiner error," all of the errors would be found to be a result of the latter, and therefore the technique of fingerprint examination is flawless; it is certain examiners who err. These statements reflect the culture of fingerprinting practice which protects its doctrine by attributing errors to individual examiners, rather than by asking what might have been flawed in the field's methods. Witness Cole commented that this was like "saying automobiles have an extremely low 'scientific' crash rate. It's only when we put drivers behind the wheel that they crash." The most interesting question is why the proponents of fingerprint identification think that having a zero error rate is so essential that they will go to such lengths to insist on the proposition, while normal sciences consider error unavoidable and most of them have routine ways to measure and take account of error.

[13]Put simply, rarely is it possible to test whether an examiner in a real case is correct or incorrect. In scientific research a study is designed so that the hypothesis at issue is made falsifiable and can be tested. If the process withstands the effort at falsification, the hypothesis thereby gains strength.

[14]Prof. Starrs criticized the fingerprint field for "the claim of absolute certainty . . . the failure to carry out controlled empirical data searching experimentation, a failure to recognize the value of considerations of the error rate." He also criticized "the lack of objectivity and uniformity and systemization with respect to standards, if any, of the fingerprint analysis. It is a miasma. It just has absolutely no basis at all in solid science. There's [not] even a modicum of scientific certainty in the way in which they conduct themselves."

[15]See Simon Cole, What Counts for Identity? The Historical Origins of the Methodology of Latent Fingerprint Identification, 12 Science in Context 56 (1999). This is a sensible goal for an endeavor that relies so heavily on subjective judg-

prints unmatchable, showing the points of claimed similarity, and asking them to reconsider their original conclusion. Apparently each of these examiners then adopted the FBI's view of the prints.

A second study was an effort to obtain an estimate of the probability that one person's fingerprints would be mistaken for those of another person, at least to a computer system designed to match fingerprints. The FBI asked Lockheed-Martin, the manufacturer of its AFIS (automated fingerprint identification system), to help it run a comparison of the images of 50,000 single fingerprints against the same 50,000 images, and produce a similarity score for each comparison. The point of this exercise was to show that the similarity score for an image matched against itself was far higher than the scores obtained when it was compared to the others. As James L. Wayman,[16] later commented in a working paper discussing the case: "The comparison of images to themselves lead, of course, to extremely high scores, which researchers called the 'perfect match' score. Because in life fingerprints are always changing, no real comparison of two different images of the same finger will ever yield such a high score. By adopting, as the definition of 'in common,' the score obtained by comparison of identical images, the government very strongly biased any results in the government's favor."[17] A test more faithful to the task at hand would have used two different images of the same fingers, and no doubt would have obtained more modest result.

In a further effort to supply the data needed to answer the question about the task-at-hand-which in *Mitchell* and in most fingerprint cases, involves smeared and fragmentary latent prints—the FBI re-ran the study using cropped prints. This effort, presumably, suffered from the same flaw as the initial one, as well as sparing the computer some of the most nettling problems of trying to determine where on a finger or hand a fragment came from and its orientation.

"In short," Wayman observed, "nothing in the government study or testimony gives us any indication of the likelihood that the crime scene fingerprints were falsely identified as belonging to the defendant Mitchell or, more broadly, that any latent fingerprints might be falsely identified."[18]

Following the hearing, the district judge made no written order or opinion and gave no verbal explanation about his ruling of evidentiary reliability. He merely stated his conclusions from the bench: that the fingerprint expert testimony was admissible, that its probative value outweighed its prejudicial impact, and that the defense was prohibited from presenting witnesses to the jury who would testify about the general flaws in fingerprint identification. The only expert witnesses permitted to the defense were fingerprint examiners who would testify to their

---

ment. See § 3:45 ("The criteria for absolute identification in fingerprint work are subjective and ill-defined.") Perhaps the best indication of how troubling the findings were is that the government reportedly initially tried to withhold its findings from the defense.

[16]Director, U.S. National Biometric Test Center at the College of Engineering, San Jose State University, which tests biometric identification systems.

[17]James L. Wayman, *Daubert* Hearing on Fingerprinting: When Bad Science Leads to Good Law: The Disturbing Irony of the *Daubert* Hearing in the Case of *U.S. v. Byron C. Mitchell* (2000), available at http://www.dss.state.ct.us/digital/new s17/bhsug17.htm and http://www.engr.sjsu.edu/bi ometrics/publications__daubert.html. See also Kaye, Questioning a Courtroom Proof of the

Uniqueness of Fingerprints, 71 Int'l Stat. Rev. 521 (2003).

[18]James L. Wayman, *Daubert* Hearing on Fingerprinting: When Bad Science Leads to Good Law: The Disturbing Irony of the *Daubert* Hearing in the Case of *U.S. v. Byron C. Mitchell* (2000). Wayman, it should be noted, believes that at the end of the day fingerprints will be proven to be reliable enough to warrant admission as evidence. But, he writes, "I'm saddened, however, that the government's case had to rest on such shoddy science. I'd certainly prefer to see good law resulting from good science. We must strive to do better." James L. Wayman, *Daubert* Hearing on Fingerprinting: When Bad Science Leads to Good Law: The Disturbing Irony of the *Daubert* Hearing in the Case of *U.S. v. Byron C. Mitchell* (2000).

specific conclusions in this case.[19]

An interesting postscript to the *Mitchell* case is the discovery after trial and conviction that the FBI had prevailed upon the National Institute of Justice to delay release of its request for research proposals to test important beliefs about fingerprint identification[20] until after the conclusion of *Mitchell*'s trial.[21] Thus, at the same time the FBI was telling the *Mitchell* court that everything that needed to be known to confirm the reliability of fingerprint identification already was known, they were telling the NIJ to delay the process of funding research aimed at answering some of the unknowns, studies that it was hoped would be useful in defending against future challenges.[22]

Another federal case that considered a challenge to the admissibility of expert testimony on fingerprint identification is *United States v. Havvard*.[23] In contrast to the array of expert witnesses presented to the judge in the *Mitchell* court's *Daubert* hearing, the parties to *Havvard* offered the judge only a single expert: Stephen Meagher, the same FBI Latent Print Unit Chief who had testified in the *Mitchell* hearing. Upon ruling in favor of admission, and giving his reasons orally, Judge Hamilton reduced his reasons to "written form at the government's request because it may be useful to other courts."[24]

The defendant argued that "there is no reliable statistical foundation for fingerprint comparisons and no reliable measure of error rates in latent print identification, especially in the absence of a specific standard about the number of points of identity needed to support an opinion as to identification."[25] The government, in response, argued that "fingerprint identification is so well-established that the court should not even hold a hearing on the issue."[26]

To summarize the opinion in a nutshell, the *Havvard* court generally answered each scientific question not by pointing to research data but instead to assurances that the adversary process was operating.

Judge Hamilton began by reminding readers of the massive cultural acceptance of beliefs about fingerprint identification: "The court's decision may strike some as comparable to a breathless announcement that the sky is blue and the sun rose in the east yesterday."[27] "Nevertheless," the opinion continues," *Daubert* and *Kumho*

---

[19]Note that, with respect to attacking the weight to be given to fingerprint identification generally, the *Mitchell* court's conception of the division of responsibility for evaluation of evidence is the opposite of the *U.S. v. Malveaux*, 208 F.3d 223 (9th Cir. 2000) (unpublished), which held that such attacks went exclusively to weight and were for the jury. Neither court reflects the conventional view reiterated in *Daubert*, which is that expert evidence is subject first to gatekeeping review by the court, and second, if the court rules the evidence admissible, to the weight of the evidence. (*Daubert*: "Vigorous cross-examination, presentation of contrary evidence, and careful instruction on the burden of proof are the traditional and appropriate means of attacking shaky but admissible evidence.") It should matter to a factfinder whether the error rate of an identification technique is a fraction of a percent or 20%, even if the court regards neither level of error sufficient to exclude the expert testimony.

[20]§§ 3:1 to 3:19.

[21]See Fingerprints: No Marquis De Queensbury Rules for the F.B.I., Sci. Sleuthing Rev., Fall 2000, at 8.

[22]It is particularly ironic that a judicial truth-seeking proceeding would motivate members of one government agency to undertake to delay scheduled knowledge-building work of another government agency in order to prevent relevant information from coming to light.

[23]*U.S. v. Havvard*, 117 F. Supp. 2d 848, 55 Fed. R. Evid. Serv. 1087 (S.D. Ind. 2000).

[24]*U.S. v. Havvard*, 117 F. Supp. 2d 848, 850, 55 Fed. R. Evid. Serv. 1087 (S.D. Ind. 2000).

[25]*U.S. v. Havvard*, 117 F. Supp. 2d 848, 850, 55 Fed. R. Evid. Serv. 1087 (S.D. Ind. 2000).

[26]*U.S. v. Havvard*, 117 F. Supp. 2d 848, 851, 55 Fed. R. Evid. Serv. 1087 (S.D. Ind. 2000).

[27]*U.S. v. Havvard*, 117 F. Supp. 2d 848, 849, 55 Fed. R. Evid. Serv. 1087 (S.D. Ind. 2000). The court makes an important point here. Although the color of the sky and the rising of the sun, at least at these casual levels of precision, are apparent to anyone who looks, the accuracy of fingerprint identifications is not at all obvious, and the claims are anything but vague and gen-

*Tire* invite fresh and critical looks at old habits and beliefs."[28]

The so-called *Daubert* factors are entirely appropriate for the evaluation of empirical claims such as those made by fingerprint examiners about the nature of fingerprints and their own skills, and the court applied the factors to those claims. Unfortunately, while most of the *Daubert* factors invoke aspects of the scientific method, for each one of them the *Havvard* court substituted the crime investigation or litigation process.

On the issue of falsification, and whether the techniques are testable or have been tested, the court wrote that:

> They have been tested for roughly 100 years. They have been tested in adversarial proceedings with the highest possible stakes—liberty and sometimes life. The defense has offered no evidence in this case undermining the reliability of the methods in general. The government points out correctly that if anyone were to come across a case in which two different fingers had identical fingerprints, that news would flash around the legal world at the speed of light. It has not happened in 100 years.[29]

The court assumes that no special research effort is needed, that in the course of ordinary casework errors would become apparent. One must ask what opportunity ordinary casework affords for falsification. It is not obvious how such fortuitous testing is likely to occur. For example, where a suspect's prints are compared to crime scene prints, the circumstances do not permit such a test. In normal casework, when a match is found, the search ends, and there is no chance of finding further matches. The usual process might often or typically prevent rather than create a test of the hypothesis. A more serious problem is that this is not the relevant hypothesis given the usual task-at-hand. The more practical question is: given fragmentary or distorted latent prints and examiners of varying skills and differing judgment, how often are false positive errors made? Mistaking one person's prints for those of another person has occurred in both actual cases and in proficiency testing.[30] Normal science would pose the following sorts of questions: What is the probability of an erroneous match? Under what circumstances are errors more likely or less likely to occur?[31] It would then design research to find the answers.

On the issue of "peer review and publication" the court stated:

> Next, the methods of identification are subject to peer review. [A]nother qualified examiner can compare the objective information upon which the opinion is based and may render a different opinion if warranted. In fact, peer review is the standard operating procedure among latent print examiners.

---

eral. And yet, as the court suggests, many members of the public and the bar, as well as the bench, regard these matters as being equally obvious and certain. This is precisely why *Daubert* requires judges to undertake a skeptical, scientifically disciplined gatekeeping role. It cannot be enough to say that something is "common knowledge," that "everyone knows" something to be true. Indeed, if those statements are so, it should be easy to support them with unusually solid, rather than unusually weak, evidence. It is too easy to be lulled into accepting our uninformed or misinformed assumptions.

[28]*U.S. v. Havvard*, 117 F. Supp. 2d 848, 849, 55 Fed. R. Evid. Serv. 1087 (S.D. Ind. 2000).

[29]*U.S. v. Havvard*, 117 F. Supp. 2d 848, 854, 55 Fed. R. Evid. Serv. 1087 (S.D. Ind. 2000). But see § 3:47.

[30]For examples of false positive errors (erroneous matches), see *State v. Caldwell*, 322 N.W.2d 574 (Minn. 1982) (holding modified on other grounds by, Ferguson v. State, 645 N.W.2d 437 (Minn. 2002)); Starrs, A Miscue in Fingerprint Identification: Causes and Concerns, 12 J. of Police Sci. & Admin. 287 (1984); Grieve, Possession of Truth, 46 J. Forensic Identification 521 (1996); the recent case of Brandon Mayfield, § 32:20; and the web page of latent print examiner Ed German which, among other information, presents current examples of erroneous identifications, at http://onin.com/fp/problemidents.html. 223.

[31]Or, as Prof. Wayman puts the question: "What is a reasonable estimation of the chance of an error when comparing fingerprint images of reasonable size, position and quality? The answer, based on sound science, could have been, 'Reasonably low.' Unfortunately, the government's answer, disguised in the forms and terminology of 'statistical estimation,' was absurd."

*Daubert* refers to publication after peer review, which is important in evaluating scientific evidence because it shows that others qualified in a field have evaluated the method or theory outside the context of litigation and have found it worthy of publication. The factor does not fit well with fingerprint identification because it is a field that has developed primarily for forensic purposes. The purpose of the publication factor is easily satisfied here, however, because latent fingerprint identification has been subject to adversarial testing for roughly 100 years, again in cases with the highest stakes possible. That track record provides far greater assurance of reliability than, for example, publication of one peer-reviewed article describing a novel theory about the cause of a particular disease at issue in a civil lawsuit.[32]

The *Havvard* court confuses the process of fundamental knowledge building in a science with the quotidian practice of examiners checking each other's work.[33] The community of science subjects work to peer review and publication in part because "submission to the scrutiny of the scientific community . . . increases the likelihood that substantive flaws in methodology will be detected."[34] Regardless of whether a field was "developed primarily for forensic purposes"—or primarily for treating sick patients, or primarily for developing construction materials, or primarily for selecting people with aptitude to become pilots—one still can ask the field whether it has a research literature of some kind testing its beliefs and practices, how well designed those studies are (the principal function of peer review and publication referred to by *Daubert*), and what the studies found. Only one field in the preceding sentence is unable to produce numerous studies which a court could review to enable it to evaluate the field's various claims.

On the issue of error rates, the court wrote:

Another *Daubert* factor is whether there is a high known or potential error rate. There is not. The defense has presented no evidence of error rates, or even of any errors. The government claims the error rate for the method is zero. The claim is breathtaking, but it is qualified by the reasonable concession that an individual examiner can of course make an error in a particular case. See Moenssens, et al., Scientific Evidence in Civil and Criminal Cases, at 516 ("in a great number of criminal cases" defense experts have undermined prosecution by showing faulty procedures or human errors in use of fingerprint evidence). Most important, an individual examiner's opinion can be tested and challenged for error by having another qualified examiner compare exactly the same images the first one compared. See also *Daubert, at 596* ("Vigorous cross-examination, presentation of contrary evidence, and careful instruction on the burden of proof are the traditional and appropriate means of attacking shaky but admissible evidence.").

Even allowing for the possibility of individual error, the error rate with latent print identification is vanishingly small when it is subject to fair adversarial testing and challenge.[35]

The issue of error rate was discussed above, in relation to *Mitchell*. In *Havvard* the court concludes that the error rate is "vanishingly small" though it cites no relevant research on the issue, but has essentially accepted the notion that the error rate is zero—except when errors are made. Finally, the court again bases its belief in low or no error on the workings of the adversary process.

---

[32]*U.S. v. Havvard*, 117 F. Supp. 2d 848, 854, 55 Fed. R. Evid. Serv. 1087 (S.D. Ind. 2000).

[33]What exactly they are checking in a process that is essentially subjective is hard to know. See §§ 3:32 and 3:33. The peer "reviewer" most likely is seeing whether the two examiners' two subjective judgments reach the same result. This can be valuable if the review is conducted blind, but far less valuable if the second examiner knows what the first examiner concluded (for example, where the second examiner is given the two assertedly matching prints and is asked to confirm the match.) See Risinger et al., The *Daubert/Kumho* Implications of Observer Effects in Forensic Science: Hidden Problems of Expectation and Suggestion, 90 Cal. L. Rev. 1 (2002).

[34]*Daubert v. Merrell Dow Pharmaceuticals, Inc.*, 509 U.S. 579, 593, 113 S. Ct. 2786, 125 L. Ed. 2d 469, 27 U.S.P.Q.2d 1200, Prod. Liab. Rep. (CCH) P 13494, 37 Fed. R. Evid. Serv. 1, 23 Envtl. L. Rep. 20979 (1993).

[35]*U.S. v. Havvard*, 117 F. Supp. 2d 848, 854, 55 Fed. R. Evid. Serv. 1087 (S.D. Ind. 2000).

Despite the lack of systematic empirical answers to the empirical questions before it, and its repeated need to fill those gaps in scientific knowledge by appeal to the adversary process, the court ended up concluding that the proffered expert testimony "satisfies the standards of reliability in *Daubert* and *Kumho Tire*. In fact, after going through this analysis, the court believes that latent print identification is the very archetype of reliable expert testimony under those standards."[36]

The court's analysis overlooks the task-at-hand concerns of *Kumho Tire*, whereby the focus of inquiry would have centered on data illuminating the capability of a field to provide reliable opinions about the precise expert task at issue in the case (which in this case is never specified, but in most cases: "Latent prints are usually prints of only a relatively small portion of the friction ridges on a particular finger. Latent prints can also vary widely in terms of the quality and clarity of the image.").[37]

The difficulty judges are having with challenges to fingerprint expert testimony is not unlike that of freshman philosophy students confronted by a syllogism to evaluate, the conclusion to which they somehow "know" to be valid before they undertake any analysis. Clear-headed evaluation of the logic of the syllogism is precluded by the compulsion the students feel to preserve the one thing they are "sure" about, namely, the conclusion. They find it difficult to perform any analysis that might undermine the superhighway leading to the "obviously correct" conclusion.

With few exceptions, recent judicial opinions reacting to challenges[38] to asserted fingerprint identification expertise are united by their failure—typically, their refusal—to conduct any thoughtful analysis under *Daubert* and *Kumho Tire*.[39] Some of the opinions contain virtually no *Daubert* analysis at all;[40] others an inquiry that is no more than a parody of *Daubert* analysis; and those empty opinions then become something later cases can cite as justification for ducking their own gatekeeping responsibilities.[41] Judges, like virtually everyone else in our culture, have grown up

---

[36]*U.S. v. Havvard*, 117 F. Supp. 2d 848, 855, 55 Fed. R. Evid. Serv. 1087 (S.D. Ind. 2000).

[37]§§ 3:29 to 3:31.

[38]The challengers' case is summarized in Epstein, Fingerprints Meet *Daubert*: The Myth of Fingerprint "Science" is Revealed, 75 S. Cal. L. Rev. 605 (2002).

[39]Or other applicable test, as in *Frye* jurisdictions.

[40]For many of these cases, the entire opinion consumed only two pages.

[41]E.g., "Rather than repeating or attempting to restate what other courts have said in their evaluation of the *Daubert* factors for fingerprint identification, the court simply adopts what has been said in the following decisions. [Citing *U.S. v. Havvard*, *U.S. v. Rogers*, *U.S. v. Reaux*, *U.S. v. Joseph*, and *U.S. v. Martinez-Cintron*.]" *U.S. v. Cline*, 188 F. Supp. 2d 1287, 1294, 59 Fed. R. Evid. Serv. 99 (D. Kan. 2002), aff'd, 349 F.3d 1276 (10th Cir. 2003). Just what it is that these cases said, which the *Cline* court adopts without repeating, will be examined, infra.

The district court in *U.S. v. Cruz-Rivera* reached the conclusion that "the science or technique of fingerprint identification" met the *Daubert* criteria simply by citing a recent hearing in its own jurisdiction ("Magistrate Judge Arenas has recently denied just such a motion in this

District. *U.S. v. Martinez-Cintron*, 136 F. Supp. 2d 17, 56 Fed. R. Evid. Serv. 878 (D.P.R. 2001).") and in another jurisdiction ("[I]n two extremely detailed treatments of the law and data concerning fingerprint identification, here and abroad, Judge Pollak of the Eastern District of Pennsylvania has upheld the admissibility of such expert testimony following the principles of *Daubert* and *Kumho Tire* [citing *Llera-Plaza I and II*] [citations omitted]. It is unnecessary to revisit the topic after such a thorough treatment . . . .") The court then reasoned that, "the question of admissibility of the general technique should not vary from district to district in any event. Unless and until Judge Pollak's thorough treatment is reversed on appeal, it is law that should be followed." We are sympathetic to the district judge's reasoning. But it is directly contrary to the implications of the Supreme Court's holdings on expert evidence admissibility.

It is, of course, proper for a court to defer to the authority of courts above it in the appellate hierarchy. And there is nothing at all wrong with looking to the opinions of sister courts for persuasive evidence and arguments. But that implies thoughtfully considering the soundness of those opinions, not merely citing them for the purpose of decorating a meaningless opinion with citations to other meaningless opinions. Cf., *U.S. v. Llera Plaza*, 188 F. Supp. 2d 549, 58 Fed. R. Evid. Serv. 1 (E.D. Pa. 2002) [*Llera-Plaza I*] which gently and

believing, without evidence or critical thought,[42] that fingerprints are unique and that examiners are extremely accurate in all that they do.[43] Since the conclusion "must be" that asserted fingerprint identification expertise is everything it claims to be, an adequate basis for that conclusion "must" exist.[44] The first instinct of judges

---

respectfully dismisses much of the prattle in fingerprint opinions, explaining why they are unhelpful to a court trying to perform an intellectually honest analysis under by *Daubert*.

[42] This is what social psychologists call a "cultural truism"—an unquestioned and unquestioning belief in some proposition, widely considered true because it has so long and so widely been accepted as true. Also see, Mnookin, Fingerprint Evidence in an Age of DNA Profiling, 67 Brook. L. Rev. 13 (2001).

[43] See, Simon Cole, Suspect Identities: A History of Fingerprinting and Criminal Identification (2001), who explains the efforts the fingerprint community went to market themselves in a way calculated to insure that these would be the popular beliefs of our legal and public cultures.

[44] An instructive contrast is provided by a case in which the proffered evidence was identification by earprint, rather than fingerprint. *State v. Kunze*, 97 Wash. App. 832, 988 P.2d 977 (Div. 2 1999). The government's experts asserted that the anatomical features of an earprint left on a window at the crime scene matched the features of the defendant's ear, that there was a "very good correspondence of those features," and therefore "to a reasonable degree of scientific certainty . . . 'Mr. Kunze's left ear and cheek [were] the likely source of this [ear print] impression at the [crime] scene.' "

The trial court admitted the expert testimony on the basis of the usual assurances by the forensic science expert witnesses that they were confident that the questioned print was left by the defendant, because nature never makes two indistinguishably similar objects, so that a match means the defendant had to be the source of the questioned print, that the expert's "belief was that human ears are sufficiently unique to support a positive identification in an appropriate case," and (important in this *Frye* jurisdiction) assurances that their methods were generally accepted in the relevant community. On the question of admissibility, the trial court concluded: "[T]he principle . . . known as 'individualization' through the use of transparent overlay, applied to the comparison of the latent impression in the present case with the known standards of the defendant, is based upon principles and methods which are sufficiently established to have gained general acceptance in the relevant scientific community."

The court of appeals counted the noses of various forensic science experts who had testified on the extent of general acceptance—two from the world of earprint expertise, the rest from other realms of forensic science, constituting a somewhat "broad" *Frye* test, which usually results in a

finding of a lack of general acceptance. See, Chapter 1 of this work. The count appears to have been: two yes, three no, and eight not sure. The court's verdict: No general acceptance.

More important, for present purposes, the court probed more widely and deeply into factors bearing on the knowledge base of the claimed expertise and was not reassured by what it found. Witnesses and the court's own research disclosed: "No true scientific tests performed in making the earprint identification." "[D]id not know of any published scientific studies confirming his theory that individuals can be identified using earprints . . . ." "This identification [was] performed strictly as a comparison . . . between a known earprint and a latent earprint." "The reliability and validity of the results of comparisons of earprints are not recognized or accepted among scientists." "There appears to be no science . . . ." No "scientific research at all that would confirm [the] theory that ears are so unique that individuals can be positively identified by comparing known earprints with latent ear impressions." A book introduced by the proponent "contains no . . . scientific verification." Another expert witness knew of " 'no information' indicating whether one ear can be differentiated from another by observing the ear's gross external anatomy," and "did not 'consider [an earprint expert's] work scientific'; on the contrary, it was 'narrative,' not 'reported in a scientific manner,' and 'not subjected to any statistical analysis.' " Andre Moenssens testified that "earprint identification has [never] been tested by scientific methodology," has never been subjected to "inquiry and verification and studies to confirm or deny the existence of the underlying premise, that is, ear uniqueness," and that there has never been any "investigation in the possible rate of error that comparisons between known and unknown ear samples might produce." George Bonebrake, former chief of the FBI's latent fingerprint section, testified that he was "not aware of any study or research that would indicate . . . the uniqueness of earprints when it comes to the comparison of [known] earprint impressions . . . with the latent earprint." Another witness observed that "no study has ever been published in the world that could tell the jury how much correspondence is actually required in order to declare a match . . . ."

Parenthetically, it is interesting to note that, although the appellate court held the admission of the earprint expert opinion to be error and remanded for a new trial, the court pointed out that, "Nothing in our holding bars testimony at retrial concerning visible similarities and differences between the latent print and the exemplars." This is the solution advanced in *U.S. v.*

presented with a challenge to fingerprint identification expertise is that there cannot really be anything to analyze.[45] Judges who have had to resolve such challenges appear to have been unable to adopt the necessary posture of skepticism long enough to see whether or not the proponents of the expert testimony can lift their claims over the *Daubert* hurdle. With few exceptions, the opinions all resort to one or another sort of evasion so that they can arrive at what they already "know" to be the "correct" conclusion, namely, that asserted fingerprint identification expertise satisfies the law's admissibility requirements. What they actually do is to refrain from subjecting the proponents' claims to the rigors of *Daubert*. The following summary of recent cases is, therefore, little more than a catalog of evasions.

### § 3:4  Post-*Daubert* challenges in federal courts—Refusal to conduct a *Daubert* hearing

Some courts refused to hold a 104(a) hearing, or to provide a similar occasion on which the proponent of the expert evidence might be called upon to establish its admissibility, and through which the district court could develop an adequate record to support its decision concerning the challenged expert testimony.[1] To be sure, the standard for when a 104(a) hearing is required is unclear, and district courts are permitted considerable discretion in making the determination. But holding in limine hearings to resolve complex evidence issues is common practice, under appropriate circumstances the failure to do so has been held to be an abuse of discretion, and, because of the gatekeeping obligations of district courts, the duty to hold a 104(a) hearing has sometimes been held to be necessary even when the moving party has not requested it.[2]

In *United States v. Joseph*[3] there is no discussion of the reasons for not holding a hearing. The court simply did not hold one. Moreover, it apparently saw so little to be decided that it disposed of the whole *Daubert* challenge in an opinion running less than two pages.

In support of its motion in limine and request for a hearing, the opponent in *United States v. Reaux*[4] drew the court's attention to two publications, which are cited in the court's opinion.[5] Though the publications plainly seem to be germane, the court says nothing about them beyond citing them. The court says not a word

---

*Llera Plaza*, 179 F. Supp. 2d 492, 57 Fed. R. Evid. Serv. 983 (E.D. Pa. 2002), withdrawn from bound volume and opinion vacated and superseded on reconsideration, 188 F. Supp. 2d 549, 58 Fed. R. Evid. Serv. 1 (E.D. Pa. 2002).

   The lesson of the *Kunze* case for judicial gatekeeping of asserted fingerprint identification expertise is this: Nearly everything the *Kunze* court concluded about the basis of earprints expertise would also be concluded by a court taking a serious look into the basis of fingerprint expertise (the major exception being its "general acceptance"). Why, then, did the *Kunze* court inquire into the basis of asserted earprint expertise under a *Frye* test, while other courts are unable to carry out the obligation to inquire into the basis of asserted fingerprint expertise under *Daubert*? The answer would seem to have nothing to do with the underlying verification data, since the fingerprint courts cite no data.

   [45]"The court's decision may strike some as comparable to a breathless announcement that the sky is blue and the sun rose in the east yesterday." *U.S. v. Havvard*, 117 F. Supp. 2d 848,

849, 55 Fed. R. Evid. Serv. 1087 (S.D. Ind. 2000).

**[Section 3:4]**

   [1]*U.S. v. Joseph*, 2001 WL 515213 (E.D. La. 2001); *U.S. v. Reaux*, 2001 WL 883221 (E.D. La. 2001); *U.S. v. Nadurath*, 2002 WL 1000929 (N.D. Tex. 2002), aff'd, 66 Fed. Appx. 525 (5th Cir. 2003); *U.S. v. Ambriz-Vasquez*, 34 Fed. Appx. 356 (9th Cir. 2002).

   [2]See discussion and review of cases in Chapter 1 of this work.

   [3]*U.S. v. Joseph*, 2001 WL 515213 (E.D. La. 2001).

   [4]*U.S. v. Reaux*, 2001 WL 883221 (E.D. La. 2001).

   [5]The first was an article, Saks, Merlin and Solomon: Lessons from the Law's Formative Encounters with Forensic Identification Science, 49 Hastings L.J. 1069 (1998) (discussing the absence, in the seminal judicial opinions admitting forensic science, including fingerprints, of any evidence or analysis of the sort that would benefit a modern court required to analyze such asserted expertise under *Daubert*). The second

about why they were insufficient to trigger a 104(a) hearing to resolve the relevant problems and controversies described in those writings, as applied to the admissibility issue before the court.

On appeal, the Ninth Circuit held in *Unites States v. Ambriz-Vasquez*[6] that it was not error for the district court to refuse to hold a *Daubert* hearing. The Court of Appeals offers no evaluation of the propriety of that refusal, beyond suggesting that it would be onerous "to conduct *Daubert* hearings whenever defendants object to fingerprint evidence," and that in a previous case it similarly held that "a trial court did not commit clear error where it admitted fingerprint evidence without performing a *Daubert* analysis."[7] Whatever knowledge the court has about asserted fingerprint expertise that makes *Daubert* hearings unnecessary it keeps to itself.

If there are genuine issues raised concerning the claims of expertise made by or on behalf of fingerprint examiners (and such issues do seem to exist), some sort of occasion for adequately exploring those issues is required. The Ninth Circuit in *Ambriz-Vasquez* reasoned that to expect courts to hold *Daubert* hearings on asserted fingerprint expertise, "assumes that courts cannot take judicial notice of the general acceptance of fingerprinting analysis."[8] At some point, after courts have adequately and convincingly explored the issues under *Daubert* (which to date they have barely begun to do), it ought to be possible for subsequent courts to take judicial notice of those issues, facts, analyses, and conclusions. Even then, however, pursuant to the requirement of *Kumho Tire* that courts focus on the specific task-at-hand upon which the expert is proposing to opine (rather than a vague global approach to the whole field of claimed expertise), judicial notice similarly would have to be focused on those issues which had been adequately considered and which are *relevant to the task-at-hand* in the case at bar. The use of judicial notice therefore seems to be premature.

In *United States v. Nadurath*,[9] the court states that the opponent of admission had "not provided any information that would call into question the reliability of fingerprint expert testimony." The court provides no elaboration, not even to say that the defendant made a bare objection without support. If that is indeed what happened, that might well justify the refusal to conduct a 104(a) hearing. Some courts have held, however, that at least a preliminary assessment of any proffered expert testimony is necessary for district courts to discharge their expert evidence gatekeeping responsibilities.[10] If nothing else, courts, such as *Nadurath*, need to explain in their opinions what it is they have done to discharge their gatekeeping obligations, so courts above, and the larger society, can evaluate the adequacy of those efforts.

## § 3:5  Post-*Daubert* challenges in federal courts—Reversal of the burden of persuasion

Elementary principles of law place the burden of proof on the proponent of the

---

was a portion of a chapter by David Stoney in the present work (discussion by a fingerprint expert of areas of scientific disagreement among scientists concerning the nature and adequacy of fingerprint identification). The latter can be found in the scientific status part of the present chapter.

[6]*U.S. v. Ambriz-Vasquez*, 34 Fed. Appx. 356 (9th Cir. 2002).

[7]While the quoted statement would seem to be a complete failure to perform its gatekeeping function under *Daubert*, it would appear not to have been so in the earlier case, *U.S. v. Sherwood*, 98 F.3d 402, 408 (9th Cir. 1996), as amended,

(Oct. 28, 1996). In *Sherwood* the Court of Appeals noted that the defense conceded almost all of the issues it might have raised in the *Daubert* hearing, so there was no need to conduct a *Daubert* hearing. But in the case at bar the defense apparently did not make the *Daubert* hearing moot.

[8]*U.S. v. Ambriz-Vasquez*, 34 Fed. Appx. 356 (9th Cir. 2002).

[9]*U.S. v. Nadurath*, 2002 WL 1000929 (N.D. Tex. 2002), aff'd, 66 Fed. Appx. 525 (5th Cir. 2003).

[10]E.g., *Hoult v. Hoult*, 57 F.3d 1, 4, 41 Fed. R. Evid. Serv. 783, 32 Fed. R. Serv. 3d 281 (1st Cir. 1995).

admission of evidence. Accordingly, *Daubert* places the initial burden of production on the proponent of the proffered expert witness (not the challenger) and requires the proponent (not the challenger) to prove by a preponderance of the evidence that the criteria for admission have been met.

Some courts have shifted the burden of persuasion onto the challenger. The *Joseph*[1] court commented that "the defendant has not provided any evidence that either of these techniques are no longer generally accepted within the relevant scientific community."[2] This might have been a shortcut way of saying something like: the proponent has met his burden and the opponent has offered nothing. But the court recites no basis beyond a vague conclusory assertion that fingerprint identification techniques, whatever their details, had "proven to be a reliable science over decades of use for judicial purposes."[3] So it is not apparent that the proponent offered adequate (or any) support. Thus, the plainest reading of the opinion is that the court expected the opponent to prove that asserted fingerprint expertise does not meet the requirements of *Daubert*, rather than requiring the proponent to prove that it does. That is an erroneous application of the law.

Similarly, the Fourth Circuit on the appeal of *United States v. Rogers*[4] appears to say that the proponent's expert asserted the existence of "numerous studies" supporting the claims of fingerprint experts (though none are cited in the opinion), while complaining that the opponent failed to produce any studies disproving the claims of the proffered fingerprint expertise. It seems that the proponent's failure to provide more than a general assertion that supportive studies existed was viewed as sufficient.[5] (If the proponent did provide more, what those studies were and what they showed apparently was of little interest to the court.) Yet, on the other hand, the opponent was faulted for providing "no evidence suggesting that fingerprint evidence is unreliable."[6] While the opinion is not clear on where it placed the burden of proof, the two pages the Fourth Circuit devoted to this matter seem to indicate the court took the proponent's case as a given which was required to be knocked down by the opponent, who failed to do so. Again, this is not the correct law.

Another example of reversing the burden of proof is provided by the district court in *United States v. Cruz-Rivera*.[7] After accepting the general validity of fingerprint identification techniques, the judge framed the remaining question to be resolved in the motion to exclude as being: "[C]an the defendant establish that the Puerto Rico Police fingerprint identification practices followed in this case are so deficient . . . that the testimony must be excluded . . . ."[8]

## § 3:6 Post-*Daubert* challenges in federal courts—Ignoring *Kumho Tire's* task-at-hand requirement

Under *Kumho Tire*, district judges are required to determine with some precision what the task-at-hand is to which the expert's testimony is proposed to be relevant. The gatekeeping responsibility, then, is to evaluate whether the proposed expertise is "reliable" with respect to that task-at-hand. Thus, a court must determine what the fingerprint comparison problem is (a clear and complete latent print versus a

---

**[Section 3:5]**

[1]*U.S. v. Joseph*, 2001 WL 515213 (E.D. La. 2001).

[2]*U.S. v. Joseph*, 2001 WL 515213 (E.D. La. 2001).

[3]*U.S. v. Joseph*, 2001 WL 515213 (E.D. La. 2001).

[4]*U.S. v. Rogers*, 26 Fed. Appx. 171 (4th Cir. 2001) (Table).

[5]On the claim of uniqueness of fingerprints and, presumably, of fingerprint fragments as well, since that is usually the real issue in these cases, though the opinions rarely seem to address that.

[6]*U.S. v. Rogers*, 26 Fed. Appx. 171 (4th Cir. 2001).

[7]*U.S. v. Cruz-Rivera*, 2002 WL 662128 (D.P.R. 2002).

[8]*U.S. v. Cruz-Rivera*, 2002 WL 662128 (D.P.R. 2002).

tiny fragment versus a montage of numerous overlaid smeared latents, etc.) and whether the data show that the expert is likely to be able to perform that particular type of examination accurately. The law is not that a court is to ask about a field in a general and global way. Not one of the cases considering challenges to asserted fingerprint identification expertise gives any indication that it appreciates and applied the task-at-hand requirement.

## § 3:7 Post-*Daubert* challenges in federal courts—Avoidance of actual *Daubert* analysis

Under this heading we disregard appellate opinions which were casual about their *Daubert* analysis if they also concluded that even if the fingerprint expert testimony was admitted in error, it was harmless error given the other evidence in the case.[1] Where the expert testimony is irrelevant to the outcome of the case, there is no purpose to performing a careful *Daubert* analysis on appeal. The better course, however, is not to perform a sloppy *Daubert* analysis and then to say "but even if it was error it was harmless error." The better course would be to decline to reach unnecessary issues.[2] That is to say, if a task (here, a *Daubert* analysis) is worth doing, it is worth doing right. In any event, in this subsection we are concerned primarily with cases in which a serious *Daubert* analysis seems to have been necessary, but was performed poorly or not at all.

The court in *Joseph*[3] notes that it is required, first, to determine "whether the Government's fingerprint evidence is scientific knowledge. The court concludes that it is."[4] And, second, to determine "whether the [expert] evidence will 'assist the trier of fact to understand or determine a fact in issue'."[5] The court again concludes that the evidence will. These naked conclusions are just about all the court has to say on these subjects. Though the court began its opinion by reciting the *Daubert* "factors," those factors never are employed to analyze the admissibility of the challenged fingerprint identification expertise. Indeed, they never are even mentioned again. Apparently, the precise issue raised by the opponent of the expert testimony was whether the method used by the proffered expert was an acceptable method (in contrast to an alternative method). To this the court states: "fingerprint analysis has been tested and proven to be a reliable science over decades of use for judicial purposes; and fingerprint technicians utilizing both the Galton and ridgeology techniques follow established principles and use scientific methods that are recognized in their particular field."[6] This is a statement of faith, not legal or scientific analysis.

The *Reaux*[7] court went to some trouble to discuss the holdings of *Daubert* and *Kumho Tire* and numerous cases following in the wake of those opinions. Without explicitly saying what principles were being applied from those cases, the court's admissibility analysis had two elements. First, it discussed the qualifications of the proffered expert. Although the expert's qualifications are important for some purposes, they are irrelevant to answering the question of whether an expertise exists, which is the focus of *Daubert*.[8] Second, the court explicitly adopted the analysis

---

[Section 3:7]

[1]*U.S. v. Rogers*, 26 Fed. Appx. 171 (4th Cir. 2001) (Table); *U.S. v. Turner*, 285 F.3d 909, 58 Fed. R. Evid. Serv. 976 (10th Cir. 2002).

[2]See, e.g., *U.S. v. Martinez-Garduno*, 31 Fed. Appx. 475 (9th Cir. 2002).

[3]*U.S. v. Joseph*, 2001 WL 515213 (E.D. La. 2001).

[4]*U.S. v. Joseph*, 2001 WL 515213 (E.D. La. 2001).

[5]*U.S. v. Joseph*, 2001 WL 515213 (E.D. La. 2001).

[6]*U.S. v. Joseph*, 2001 WL 515213 (E.D. La. 2001).

[7]*U.S. v. Reaux*, 2001 WL 883221 (E.D. La. 2001).

[8]By analogy: It does not matter how well trained, how experienced, or how distinguished

of *United States v. Havvard*,[9] an exceedingly weak opinion.[10]

At trial, the *Havvard* opinion misunderstood much of what the Supreme Court has been saying in its expert evidence admissibility rulings, and offered trial process answers to most of the scientific questions posed by *Daubert*.[11] Though the district court was unable to cite a single published study, or find any kind of a systematic empirical answer to any of the questions posed about the claims of fingerprint experts, or had to invent excuses for gaps left unfilled by the fingerprint field,[12] the court concluded that fingerprint examiners passed *Daubert* and *Kumho Tire* with flying colors: "the very archetype of reliable expert testimony under those standards."[13]

## §︎ 3:8 Post-*Daubert* challenges in federal courts—Turning *Kumho Tire* on its head

On the appeal of *Havvard*,[1] the Seventh Circuit not only endorsed all of the district court's curious misunderstandings of *Daubert*, it invented its own curious misunderstanding of *Kumho Tire*. In *Kumho Tire*, a unanimous Supreme Court held that all fields, not only "scientific" fields, had to satisfy the fundamental reliability standards of *Daubert*. In responding to the appellant's argument that fingerprint evidence lacks a sufficient scientific basis, the Seventh Circuit countered by arguing:

> The standards of *Daubert* . . . are not limited in application to "scientific" testimony alone. See *Kumho Tire Co., Ltd. v. Carmichael*, 526 U.S. 137, 147, 119 S. Ct. 1167, 143 L. Ed. 2d 238, 50 U.S.P.Q.2d 1177, Prod. Liab. Rep. (CCH) P 15470, 50 Fed. R. Evid. Serv. 1373, 29 Envtl. L. Rep. 20638 (1999) (holding that 'the basic gatekeeping obligation' of *Daubert* applies to all expert testimony). Therefore, the idea that fingerprint comparison is not sufficiently 'scientific' cannot be the basis for exclusion under *Daubert*.[2]

---

an astrologer is if astrology lacks validity.

[9]*U.S. v. Havvard*, 117 F. Supp. 2d 848, 55 Fed. R. Evid. Serv. 1087 (S.D. Ind. 2000).

[10]See detailed reviews of *Havvard* above; and Comment, Evidence—Fingerprint Experts—Seventh Circuit Upholds the Reliability of Expert Testimony Regarding the Source of a Latent Fingerprint.—*U.S. v. Havvard*, 260 F.3d 597, 56 Fed. R. Evid. Serv. 900 (7th Cir. 2001), 115 Harv. L. Rev. 2349 (2002). Also see comments on *Havvard* in *U.S. v. Llera Plaza*, 179 F. Supp. 2d 492, 57 Fed. R. Evid. Serv. 983 (E.D. Pa. 2002), withdrawn from bound volume and opinion vacated and superseded on other grounds on reconsideration, 188 F. Supp. 2d 549, 58 Fed. R. Evid. Serv. 1 (E.D. Pa. 2002).

[11]For example, see *U.S. v. Llera Plaza*, 179 F. Supp. 2d 492, 57 Fed. R. Evid. Serv. 983 (E.D. Pa. 2002), withdrawn from bound volume and opinion vacated and superseded on other grounds on reconsideration, 188 F. Supp. 2d 549, 58 Fed. R. Evid. Serv. 1 (E.D. Pa. 2002), commenting on *Havvard*: " '[A]dversarial' testing in court is not . . . what the Supreme Court meant when it discussed testing as an admissibility factor."

[12]"In *Havvard*, the court stated that the publication factor 'does not fit well with fingerprint identification because it is a field that has developed primarily for forensic purposes.' While it is correct that the end purpose of fingerprint identifications is a forensic one, the reliability of

identification techniques must be assessed just as any other scientific, technical, or specialized technique under Rule 702." *U.S. v. Llera Plaza*, 179 F. Supp. 2d 492, 57 Fed. R. Evid. Serv. 983 (E.D. Pa. 2002), withdrawn from bound volume and opinion vacated and superseded on other grounds on reconsideration, 188 F. Supp. 2d 549, 58 Fed. R. Evid. Serv. 1 (E.D. Pa. 2002).

[13]*U.S. v. Havvard*, 117 F. Supp. 2d 848, 855, 55 Fed. R. Evid. Serv. 1087 (S.D. Ind. 2000).

**[Section 3:8]**

[1]*U.S. v. Havvard*, 117 F. Supp. 2d 848, 55 Fed. R. Evid. Serv. 1087 (S.D. Ind. 2000). The Seventh Circuit states that it reviewed *Havvard* de novo. Rulings on admissibility are to be reviewed deferentially. *General Elec. Co. v. Joiner*, 522 U.S. 136, 118 S. Ct. 512, 139 L. Ed. 2d 508, 18 O.S.H. Cas. (BNA) 1097, Prod. Liab. Rep. (CCH) P 15120, 48 Fed. R. Evid. Serv. 1, 28 Envtl. L. Rep. 20227, 177 A.L.R. Fed. 667 (1997). Rulings on or applications of law are to be reviewed de novo. The Seventh Circuit does not explain what it is reviewing deferentially and what it is reviewing de novo, nor can those be discerned from the rest of the opinion.

[2]See also *U.S. v. Cline*, 188 F. Supp. 2d 1287, 1295, 59 Fed. R. Evid. Serv. 99 (D. Kan. 2002), aff'd, 349 F.3d 1276 (10th Cir. 2003), asserting that *Kumho Tire* reduced, rather than reinforced, the obligation of judges to evaluate proffered expert testimony in a highly rigorous way: "The

The Seventh Circuit's statement is irresolvably incoherent. By expanding *Daubert*'s essential application to all fields, not only scientific fields, the Supreme Court closed a major hole through which some fields were trying to escape *Daubert*'s scrutiny. *Kumho Tire* did not create escape hatches, it closed them. A field amenable to evaluation by scientific criteria can readily be evaluated by the "*Daubert* factors." That is what the field of fingerprint examination is: an empirical field. That is what its practitioners claim to be: forensic scientists, people who work with observable, empirical things. Likewise that is what the *Havvard* trial court's analysis purports to find: that it is scientific, that it passes *Daubert*'s scientific criteria with flying colors. An attack on fingerprint identification claiming that its scientific basis is inadequate (e.g., insufficient testing) is directly on point. The Court of Appeals sought to remove fingerprinting from the realm of the empirical in order, apparently, to move it out of *Daubert*'s reach. Bizarrely, it relied on *Kumho Tire* to accomplish that, even though *Kumho Tire* stands for exactly the opposite proposition, namely, that there is to be no escape from appropriate scrutiny.

### § 3:9    Post-*Daubert* challenges in federal courts—Reliance on admission by other courts

Some courts made much of the fact that fingerprint expert evidence had been admitted in American courts for most of the 20th Century. Of what value is this fact in the evaluation of an asserted expertise under *Daubert*?

The Fourth Circuit in reviewing *Rogers* states that, "virtually every circuit and district court, both before and after *Daubert*, have a longstanding tradition of allowing fingerprint examiners to state their opinion and conclusions . . . ."[1] The Seventh Circuit in reviewing *Havvard* commented that, "The district court recognized that establishing the reliability of fingerprint analysis was made easier by its 100 years of successful use in criminal trials . . . ."[2] Neither appellate court says a word about how a long history of admission advances an admissibility analysis under *Daubert*. The mere existence of a long history of judicial admission does not in itself contribute anything to analysis under *Daubert*. The Supreme Court in *Daubert* did observe that, "Of course, well-established propositions are less likely to be challenged than those that are novel, and they are more handily defended." The point is not that a scientific claim gains validity by being let into courtrooms over a long period, but rather that propositions which have had time to be tested and found to have sound bases will *for that reason* be "less likely to be challenged . . . and . . . more handily defended." The Fourth and Seventh Circuits failed to say what it is, exactly, that was learned during that century of admission that lent support to the claims asserted by fingerprint experts.

Ironically, some forensic scientists and their proponents have sought to explain their fields' shortcomings by arguing that their long history of admission retarded any tendency these fields might otherwise have had to seriously test their claims in a manner that would meet the requirements of *Daubert* and *Kumho Tire*.[3]

### § 3:10    Post-*Daubert* challenges in federal courts—Reliance on general acceptance

A century of admission under older rules might have no relevance to an analysis

---

Supreme Court itself eschewed such a reading when it dismissed the argument that the trial court's gatekeeping obligation depended on whether the expert knowledge to be offered was scientific, technical or other . . . ."

**[Section 3:9]**

[1]*U.S. v. Rogers*, 26 Fed. Appx. 171 (4th Cir.

2001) (Table).

[2]*U.S. v. Havvard*, 260 F.3d 597, 601, 56 Fed. R. Evid. Serv. 900 (7th Cir. 2001).

[3]J. Orenstein, Effect of the *Daubert* Decision on Document Examinations from the Prosecutor's Perspective, 1 Forensic Science Communications (Oct., 1999), at http://www.fbi.gov/programs/lab/fsc/backissu/oct1999/abstrcte.htm.

that must be conducted pursuant stra and different rule (i.e., *Daubert*). In the present context, however, it is possible that pre-*Daubert* admissions decisions are relevant to the general acceptance "factor," which remains a consideration under *Daubert*. Several courts relied on general acceptance to admit fingerprint experts.[1] One might argue (though none of these courts did) that a century of admission impliedly informs a post-*Daubert* court that pre-*Daubert* courts were finding general acceptance, because *Frye* was the dominant test before *Daubert*. The flaw in this reasoning would be that all of the major seminal fingerprint admission cases were decided before the general acceptance test was invented. As early as 1918, courts were admitting fingerprints merely by citing opinions from sister jurisdictions which had already admitted fingerprints. And those sister jurisdictions were not employing *Frye* (or any other articulable test).[2]

What today's courts might be trying to say is that there has been *judicial* general acceptance for the better part of a century (among pre-*Daubert* courts), and so there should continue to be judicial acceptance (among post-*Daubert* courts).[3] This, of course, has never been a recognized test of admissibility, and certainly is not a criterion for admission under *Daubert* or *Kumho Tire*.

More importantly, under *Daubert*, general acceptance must be evaluated in conjunction with other factors. In fields which have been found to have a vigorous tradition of testing, that which becomes generally accepted carries more weight than in fields without such a tradition. Where inquiry into other factors (testing, methodological quality of published peer reviewed research, error rates) does not support admission, general acceptance does not become the one last hook on which an admission decision can be hung. As the Supreme Court put it in *Kumho Tire*: general acceptance does not "help show that an expert's testimony is reliable where the discipline itself lacks reliability."[4]

In short, general acceptance cannot properly secure admission of asserted fingerprint expertise when the other criteria have failed to do so.

### § 3:11 Post-*Daubert* challenges in federal courts—Emphasis on flexibility of criteria

Where application of the basic "*Daubert* factors" are not providing support for admission, some courts have turned to language in both *Daubert* and *Kumho Tire* which authorizes flexibility in the selection of criteria for evaluating proffered experts. The Fourth Circuit in *Rogers* stated: "However, the *Daubert* Court also emphasized that this inquiry should be flexible. See also *Kumho Tire* (concluding that the testing of reliability should be flexible and the five factors delineated in *Daubert* neither necessarily nor exclusively apply to every expert)."[1] The *Reaux* court said, "In *Kumho Tire*, the Supreme Court emphasized that the test of reliability is 'flexible,' and that *Daubert*'s list of specific factors does not necessarily, nor

---

**[Section 3:10]**

[1]*U.S. v. Joseph*, 2001 WL 515213 (E.D. La. 2001); *U.S. v. Salim*, 189 F. Supp. 2d 93, 58 Fed. R. Evid. Serv. 1544 (S.D. N.Y. 2002); *U.S. v. Ambriz-Vasquez*, 34 Fed. Appx. 356 (9th Cir. 2002).

[2]§ 3:2.

[3]For example, one court states: "Used successfully in criminal trials for over 100 years, fingerprint identification analysis has withstood the scrutiny and testing of the adversarial pro-

cess." *U.S. v. Cline*, 188 F. Supp. 2d 1287, 1294, 59 Fed. R. Evid. Serv. 99 (D. Kan. 2002), aff'd, 349 F.3d 1276 (10th Cir. 2003).

[4]*Kumho Tire Co., Ltd. v. Carmichael*, 526 U.S. 137, 151, 119 S. Ct. 1167, 143 L. Ed. 2d 238, 50 U.S.P.Q.2d 1177, Prod. Liab. Rep. (CCH) P 15470, 50 Fed. R. Evid. Serv. 1373, 29 Envtl. L. Rep. 20638 (1999).

**[Section 3:11]**

[1]*U.S. v. Rogers*, 26 Fed. Appx. 171 (4th Cir. 2001) (Table). (Citations omitted.)

exclusively, apply to all experts in every case."[2]

These references to "flexibility" should have been followed by an explanation of what evaluation criteria the court thought were more appropriate than the ones in *Daubert*, why they were more appropriate, and then a thoughtful application of those more appropriate factors. Instead, these two courts used the "flexibility" language as a license to select vague criteria and apply them loosely and without explanation. Three concurring Justices in *Kumho Tire* anticipated such evasions, and suggested that they were likely to constitute an abuse of discretion.[3]

The district court in *Cline*[4] as good as overruled *Daubert* and *Kumho Tire*. First, *Cline* declared that "evidentiary *Daubert* hearings were unnecessary as the reliability of the methods [of fingerprint examiners] could be properly taken for granted."[5] In criticizing decisions which had followed *Daubert* more faithfully, the court added: " . . . it seems an unreasonable stretch simply to discard this [unsystematic, unscientific] experiential testing [by fingerprint examiners] as wholly unreliable and to relegate the testifying opinions of all these fingerprint examiners to ipse dixit. Moreover, this court joins others who do not read *Daubert* and *Kumho* as elevating the scientific method to the touchstone by which all Rule 702 evidence is to be judged."[6]

Although there is no one who has "read *Daubert* and *Kumho* as elevating the scientific method to the touchstone by which all Rule 702 evidence is to be judged," the Supreme Court's opinions in *Daubert* and *Kumho Tire* were rather clear on what is, at bottom, required: a conscientious determination of the soundness of proffered expertise as a condition for its admission, and that appropriate criteria must be utilized in making that evaluation. Where scientific criteria are appropriate (the "*Daubert* factors"), they should be conscientiously employed. Where other criteria would be better and more appropriate, they should be conscientiously employed.[7]

In the field of asserted fingerprint identification expertise, there is no reason not to apply the basic *Daubert* factors. That field is dealing with empirical phenomena and making entirely empirical claims. The basic scientific criteria embodied in the *Daubert* "factors" are entirely appropriate for its evaluation.[8] Moreover, no one claims that the fingerprint field cannot perform empirical tests, only that it has not done so for the greater part of the past century. Indeed, it has begun to do so only very recently and only because of the threat of limitation or exclusion under

---

[2]*U.S. v. Reaux*, 2001 WL 883221 (E.D. La. 2001).

[3]"I join the opinion of the Court, which makes clear that the discretion it endorses—trial-court discretion in choosing the manner of testing expert reliability—is not discretion to abandon the gatekeeping function. I think it worth adding that it is not discretion to perform the function inadequately. Rather, it is discretion to choose among reasonable means of excluding expertise that is fausse and science that is junky. Though, as the Court makes clear today, the *Daubert* factors are not holy writ, in a particular case the failure to apply one or another of them may be unreasonable, and hence an abuse of discretion." *Kumho Tire Co., Ltd. v. Carmichael*, 526 U.S. 137, 159, 119 S. Ct. 1167, 143 L. Ed. 2d 238, 50 U.S.P. Q.2d 1177, Prod. Liab. Rep. (CCH) P 15470, 50 Fed. R. Evid. Serv. 1373, 29 Envtl. L. Rep. 20638 (1999) (Scalia, J., concurring).

[4]*U.S. v. Cline*, 188 F. Supp. 2d 1287, 59 Fed. R. Evid. Serv. 99 (D. Kan. 2002), aff'd, 349 F.3d 1276 (10th Cir. 2003).

[5]*U.S. v. Cline*, 188 F. Supp. 2d 1287, 1294, 59 Fed. R. Evid. Serv. 99 (D. Kan. 2002), aff'd, 349 F.3d 1276 (10th Cir. 2003).

[6]*U.S. v. Cline*, 188 F. Supp. 2d 1287, 1295, 59 Fed. R. Evid. Serv. 99 (D. Kan. 2002), aff'd, 349 F.3d 1276 (10th Cir. 2003).

[7]That is the gravamen of *Kumho Tire*.

[8]As the court notes in *Llera-Plaza I*, "In their submissions in the case at bar, both the government and the defendants have undertaken to apply the *Daubert* factors, albeit with discrepant results." The court agreed "with the parties that, with respect to fingerprint identification evidence, the *Daubert* factors constitute a proper touchstone of admissibility . . . ."

*Daubert*.[9]

## § 3:12  Post-*Daubert* challenges in federal courts—Bringing the standards down to meet the expertise

The *Cline*[1] court implicitly found that asserted fingerprint expertise is not scientific, has not been well tested, is in need of "traditional" scientific testing, lacks an adequate body of peer reviewed literature, and lacks uniform standards. Had the court reached the opposite of each of those conclusions about the fingerprint field's state of knowledge, we can safely assume that the court would have declared that fingerprint expertise passed muster under *Daubert*. But finding the deficiencies it found did not lead the court to conclude that the expertise at issue fails *Daubert*, and therefore testimony based on it must be excluded or have limitations placed upon it. Instead, the court concluded that these shortcomings meant that alternative, less rigorous, criteria needed to be employed (in order to facilitate admission). This kind of back door to admission is what *Kumho Tire* was designed to eliminate, and in many instances has eliminated.[2]

## § 3:13  Post-*Daubert* challenges in federal courts—Relegate to weight, not admissibility

Further, *Cline*[1] argued that the central dispute about fingerprint expert evidence is whether examiners are justified in testifying to extreme assertions of absolute, certain, pinpoint, identification to the exclusion of all others in the world, even when dealing with smeared fragments of latent prints. The court opined that such a debate should be left to the jury to resolve, as a matter of weight.[2]

## § 3:14  Post-*Daubert* challenges in federal courts—A short-lived exception to the usual evasions

An instructive exception to the pattern of evasion described thus far is provided

---

[9]Forensic scientists and police agencies knew that *Daubert* presented a serious challenge that they were not prepared to meet. They submitted an amicus brief in *Kumho Tire* urging that *Daubert*'s scrutiny not be extended to fields that had failed to test their propositions systematically. Brief *Amici Curiae* of Americans for Effective Law Enforcement, Inc.; Criminal Justice Legal Foundation; Grand Lodge of Fraternal Order Of Police; International Association of Arson Investigators; International Association of Chiefs of Police; Mothers Against Drunk Driving; National Association of Police Organizations, Inc.; National District Attorneys Association; National Sheriffs' Association; and Police Law Institute, in *Kumho Tire Co., Ltd. v. Carmichael*, 526 U.S. 137, 119 S. Ct. 1167, 143 L. Ed. 2d 238, 50 U.S.P.Q.2d 1177, Prod. Liab. Rep. (CCH) P 15470, 50 Fed. R. Evid. Serv. 1373, 29 Envtl. L. Rep. 20638 (1999). Though the Supreme Court unanimously rejected such arguments, these fields did not anticipate the extent to which judges would find ways to keep admitting them, notwithstanding the Supreme Court's opinions. Also, several fields of forensic science, including fingerprint identification, abruptly became interested in seeing federal funds spent on research to prove the validity of their claims. See, the solicitation, National Institute of Justice, Forensic Friction Ridge

(Fingerprint) Examination Validation Studies (March, 2000).

**[Section 3:12]**

[1]*U.S. v. Cline*, 188 F. Supp. 2d 1287, 59 Fed. R. Evid. Serv. 99 (D. Kan. 2002), aff'd, 349 F.3d 1276 (10th Cir. 2003).

[2]Compare *U.S. v. Starzecpyzel*, 880 F. Supp. 1027, 42 Fed. R. Evid. Serv. 247 (S.D. N.Y. 1995) (holding, before *Kumho Tire*, that because forensic document examination failed to meet *Daubert* it was not science; because it was not science it need not meet the requirements of *Daubert*; and therefore it was admissible under a much lower and unspecified standard) to *U.S. v. Hines*, 55 F. Supp. 2d 62, 52 Fed. R. Evid. Serv. 257 (D. Mass. 1999) (holding, after *Kumho Tire*, that because forensic document examination failed to meet *Daubert*, its opinions on identity were inadmissible).

**[Section 3:13]**

[1]*U.S. v. Cline*, 188 F. Supp. 2d 1287, 59 Fed. R. Evid. Serv. 99 (D. Kan. 2002), aff'd, 349 F.3d 1276 (10th Cir. 2003).

[2]This is the oldest device in the judicial toolbox for avoiding having to make admissibility decisions. It is surprising that is does not appear more often in today's cases.

by *United States v. Llera-Plaza*,[1] in which one court finally attempted to come to grips with the challenging dilemma posed by asserted fingerprint identification expertise. *Llera-Plaza* is actually two opinions, the first of which has been withdrawn. In *Llera-Plaza I*, the court applied *Daubert* in a relatively rigorous fashion, found numerous shortcomings of the field,[2] and ordered a limitation on the extent of the fingerprint examiner's testimony.[3] In *Llera-Plaza II*, the court reversed itself and allowed the usual form of fingerprint expert testimony.

## § 3:15 Post-*Daubert* challenges in federal courts—A short-lived exception to the usual evasions—*Llera-Plaza I*

The parties to *Llera-Plaza I*[1] asked the court to treat the record developed earlier in *United States v. Mitchell*[2] as the *Daubert* submissions in this case. The parties proposed, and the court agreed, "that, with respect to fingerprint identification evidence, the *Daubert* factors constitute a proper touchstone of admissibility . . . ."[3]

The court's opinion began by describing the theory and practice of fingerprinting identification. Next it recited the holdings of recent cases in which fingerprint identification had been challenged, all of which concluded that asserted fingerprint identification expertise was admissible under Fed. R. Evid. 702.

Next the court took judicial notice under Fed. R. Evid. 201 of the permanence and uniqueness of fingerprints. This raises three issues which deserve comment. First, it does not appear that these facts can be noticed under the "high degree of indisputability" standard of Fed. R. Evid. 201. Neither fact seems to be "capable of accurate and ready determination by resort to sources whose accuracy cannot reasonably be questioned."[4] For example, the uniqueness finding was made on the basis of a single new unpublished study conducted for the purpose of the *Daubert* hearing in *Mitchell*, the conclusion to which the court summarized thusly: "Mr. Ziesig's 50k × 50k study found the probability to be one in ten to the ninety-seventh power that two rolled fingerprints (whether taken from fingers of two different people or from two fingers of the same person) would be identical." Probabilistic data, as earlier students of fingerprints despairingly noted, are incapable of supporting a conclusion of uniqueness.[5] Moreover, a commentary by the director of the U.S. National Biometric Test Center was highly critical of the design of the study, pointing out that the defect led to exaggerated statistical values.[6] None of this looks like indisputability.

Second, it is not clear that Fed. R. Evid. 201 is properly applicable to general,

---

**[Section 3:14]**

[1]*U.S. v. Llera Plaza*, 179 F. Supp. 2d 492, 57 Fed. R. Evid. Serv. 983 (E.D. Pa. 2002), withdrawn from bound volume and opinion vacated and superseded on other grounds on reconsideration, 188 F. Supp. 2d 549, 58 Fed. R. Evid. Serv. 1 (E.D. Pa. 2002) [*Llera-Plaza I*] and *U.S. v. Llera Plaza*, 188 F. Supp. 2d 549, 58 Fed. R. Evid. Serv. 1 (E.D. Pa. 2002) [*Llera-Plaza II*].

[2]§ 32:11.

[3]"Partial admission" is one of the potential solutions suggested earlier at § 32:1.

**[Section 3:15]**

[1]*U.S. v. Llera Plaza*, 179 F. Supp. 2d 492, 57 Fed. R. Evid. Serv. 983 (E.D. Pa. 2002), withdrawn from bound volume and opinion vacated and superseded on other grounds on reconsideration, 188 F. Supp. 2d 549, 58 Fed. R. Evid. Serv. 1

(E.D. Pa. 2002).

[2]*United States v. Mitchell*, Cr. No. 96-407 (E.D.Pa. Sept. 13, 1999).

[3]*U.S. v. Llera Plaza*, 179 F. Supp. 2d 492, 57 Fed. R. Evid. Serv. 983 (E.D. Pa. 2002), withdrawn from bound volume and opinion vacated and superseded on other grounds on reconsideration, 188 F. Supp. 2d 549, 58 Fed. R. Evid. Serv. 1, 9 (E.D. Pa. 2002).

[4]Fed. R. Evid. 201(b).

[5]Harold Cummins & Charles Midlo, Finger Prints, Palms and Soles: An Introduction to Dermatoglyphics 154 (1943).

[6]See discussion of the 50k × 50k study, including summary of critique by James L. Wayman, Director, U.S. National Biometric Test Center, at § 3:3.

trans-case questions of scientific fact (as opposed to case-specific questions),[7] and therefore are more coherently treated as questions of legislative fact.[8] Conceived in that way, the standard for judicial notice is more relaxed, though the court still has a duty to do its best to reach a correct factual conclusion. On the other hand, the Supreme Court in *General Electric v. Joiner* appears to have directed that even these aspects of questions of expert evidence admissibility be treated as case-specific facts, as the court has done in this case.[9]

Third, uniqueness was not much of an issue in the hearing, because even assuming uniqueness of a full rolled print,[10] the real issue in these cases is whether fragments of prints, or smeared prints, or layers of prints one upon another, can be accurately linked to one and only one person on earth. On the one hand, that means that the issue for which judicial notice was taken was not relevant to the case. On the other hand, it means either that judicial notice was taken of the wrong issue, or that the disputed expertise was really the accuracy of matching fragmentary and unclear latents. That is a large area of uncertainty, in which examiners subjectively trade off size of fragment and clarity of image, and subjectively conclude that there is or is not enough information in the fragment print to declare that the fragment would or would not match any other fingerprint fragment in the world. Under *Kumho Tire*'s task-at-hand requirement, *fragment matching* is the expertise at issue, and that is where the focus of submissions and judicial analysis should have been directed.[11] Although the court was aware that the real issue in this case was the fragment matching claim, it did not advert to the task-at-hand requirement of *Kumho Tire* in conducting its analysis, and the opinion is directed at a more global assessment of the expertise of fingerprint examiners.

Next the court reviewed the trilogy of expert testimony admission cases decided by the Supreme Court. And then it turned to an analysis of the admissibility of asserted fingerprint expertise.

The proponent of admission claimed that, "[t]he ACE-V process has been tested empirically [in courtrooms] over a period of 100 years and in any particular case they can be tested by examination of the evidence by another expert."[12] On the latter point, the court noted that examination by another expert is simply not the kind of testing that is capable of confirming or refuting the theory or the technique.[13] On the former point, the court noted that, "'[A]dversarial' testing in court is not,

---

[7]Saks, The Aftermath of *Daubert*: an Evolving Jurisprudence of Expert Evidence, 40 Jurimetrics Journal 229 (2000); Walker & Monahan, Social Frameworks: A New Use of Social Science in Law, 73 Va. L. Rev. 559 (1987).

[8]The treatment of which is discussed in some detail in the Advisory Committee Comments to Fed. R. Evid. 201.

[9]Thus, another court could make the opposite finding in a future case, unless doing so could be held to be clear error.

[10]Something about which major founders of fingerprint identification had grave doubts. See Simon Cole, Suspect Identities: A History of Fingerprinting and Criminal Identification (2001) (explaining that Henry Faulds was highly critical of claims of being able to use fingerprints to link suspects to latents, at 174–176; and that Francis Galton never came to believe that fingerprinting was scientifically superior to anthropometry, at 92.).

[11]In other words, courts can be (and should

be, and in some areas are) fine-grained enough in their analyses that they can conclude that certain tasks are performed well enough to be admissible while other tasks do not meet *Daubert*'s dependability criteria.

[12]*U.S. v. Llera Plaza*, 179 F. Supp. 2d 492, 57 Fed. R. Evid. Serv. 983 (E.D. Pa. 2002), withdrawn from bound volume and opinion vacated and superseded on other grounds on reconsideration, 188 F. Supp. 2d 549, 58 Fed. R. Evid. Serv. 1, 9 (E.D. Pa. 2002).

[13]Said the court:

[I]t is not apparent that a result arrived at by a second examiner discrepant from a result arrived at by a prior examiner would (1) establish that the first result was erroneous, or (2) offer a secure basis for concluding that the "technique" was faulty. A scientist might be disposed to require scores, or perhaps hundreds, of observations before regarding the "technique" as having been "tested."

*U.S. v. Llera Plaza*, 179 F. Supp. 2d 492, 57 Fed. R. Evid. Serv. 983 (E.D. Pa. 2002), withdrawn from bound volume and opinion vacated and

however, what the Supreme Court meant when it discussed testing as an admissibility factor."[14] Moreover, while there were "numerous writings that discuss the fingerprint identification techniques employed by fingerprint examiners," none of them tested the technique's dependability. Reviewing all of the proponent's submissions, the court noted that, "the government had little success in identifying scientific testing that tended to establish the reliability of fingerprint identifications."

If there is no systematic empirical testing, the issue of peer review and publication to scrutinize the quality of those studies is moot.[15] Where there are no studies, there are no published peer reviewed studies. The court seems not to have understood this point, or went beyond it, suggesting that, had there been any research to publish, there is no "scientific community" within the fingerprint world to do any of the contemplated scrutinizing.[16] The court's point may be unhelpfully formalistic. The point of the peer review and publication "factor" is to help inform the gatekeeping judge, as well as the expert field, concerning the adequacy of the research. The intellectual ability to evaluate the design and analysis of research is not limited to scientists. The heart of the factor, therefore, is whether judges can find help from a field that engages in vigorous and skeptical debate in assessing the quality of research. The more adept members of the field are doing that, and the more of it they do, the more help a judge will find. In this particular community, there was little help to be found in evaluating research. But the far larger problem is that there was virtually no research to evaluate in the first place.

The third issue was error rates. The proponents of asserted fingerprint expertise divide this into two types, methodological error and practitioner error. By methodological error they mean error associated with the theory and technique of fingerprint identification, which they claim is utterly flawless, an error rate of zero.[17] Practitioner error refers to the error associated with the examiner's conclusion that

---

superseded on other grounds on reconsideration, 188 F. Supp. 2d 549, 58 Fed. R. Evid. Serv. 1, 10 (E.D. Pa. 2002).

[14]*U.S. v. Llera Plaza*, 179 F. Supp. 2d 492, 57 Fed. R. Evid. Serv. 983 (E.D. Pa. 2002), withdrawn from bound volume and opinion vacated and superseded on other grounds on reconsideration, 188 F. Supp. 2d 549, 58 Fed. R. Evid. Serv. 1, 11 (E.D. Pa. 2002).

[15]On the other hand, if the court had found there to be meaningful research testing the propositions, it might next have found that the studies were poorly designed, or that it could get no help from the critical assessment provided by a field through peer review and publication, and therefore the quality of the research was in doubt. For example, the 50k × 50k study produced by the FBI was certainly a study. But it was a study with some serious flaws, and those flaws were pointed out by at least one scientist who did similar work in another field. But where there is a paucity of research in the first place, the second *Daubert* factor is a non-issue.

[16]The government maintains that:

"[t]he fingerprint field and its theories and techniques have been published and peer reviewed during a period of over 100 years." Gov't Mot. & Resp. at 112. It is the case that there are numerous writings that discuss the fingerprint identification techniques employed by fingerprint examiners. But it is not apparent that their publication constitutes "submission to the scrutiny of the scientific com-

munity" in the *Daubert* sense. Even those who stand at the top of the fingerprint identification field— people like David Ashbaugh and Stephen Meagher—tend to be skilled professionals who have learned their craft on the job and without any concomitant advanced academic training. It would thus be a misnomer to call fingerprint examiners a "scientific community" in the *Daubert* sense. *U.S. v. Llera Plaza*, 179 F. Supp. 2d 492, 57 Fed. R. Evid. Serv. 983 (E.D. Pa. 2002), withdrawn from bound volume and opinion vacated and superseded on other grounds on reconsideration, 188 F. Supp. 2d 549, 58 Fed. R. Evid. Serv. 1, 11 (E.D. Pa. 2002).

[17]Not only is this one of the numerous claims of fingerprint examiners which has gone untested, it also is untestable because it is impossible to do fingerprint examination without humans exercising subjective judgment; the methodology and the practitioner cannot be disentangled. The attribution of zero errors to the technique and all errors to the human examiner is entirely a matter of faith or hope, but nothing that anyone can have any defensible knowledge about.

For conventional scientists, measurement and other kinds of error are a natural part of any process; they measure it and try to account for it. For reasons that are not entirely clear, the proponents of fingerprint testimony have gone to considerable lengths to try to remove asserted fingerprint identification expertise from a world in which error exists. And whenever it cannot be denied, it is moved into the past and said to have

a known fingerprint "matches" a latent fingerprint.

For the purposes of resolving the *in limine* motion before it, the court accepted arguendo the claim of zero error for the technique and focused on the question of practitioner error. Practitioner error, the government argued, is possible, but could be detected and avoided through review by another expert. The court described in some detail an informal study conducted in the earlier *Mitchell* case by the FBI in which a fingerprint was sent to several laboratories, but which produced results embarrassing to the proponent. In contrast to the claim of virtually flawless agreement among examiners, "Nine of the thirty-four responding agencies did not make an identification in the first instance."[18] When the prints were re-sent to the examiners who had not given the desired conclusions, along with an explanation regarding the importance of the identification and showing the asserted identifying points highlighted on the displays, all of the errant examiners then changed their opinions to the desired matches. The court concluded that these findings "are (modestly) suggestive of a discernible level of practitioner error."[19]

The larger problem, not emphasized by the court, is the paucity of studies, especially in light of the grandiosity of the claim of virtually error-free examinations. If there are no studies of the question, how can anyone know what the error rate really is?[20]

Next, the court turned to whether controlling standards existed for the technique's application. The court found the proffered expertise to be lacking in this regard. The process of determining that a match has been found is essentially a subjective process without "any clearly describable set of standards to which most examiners subscribe."[21] Moreover, "[t]here are no mandatory qualification standards for individuals to become fingerprint examiners, nor is there a uniform certification process."[22]

Finally, regarding general acceptance, the court found that fingerprint identification techniques were widely accepted among fingerprint examiners. But the

---

no further existence, and no implications for future testing. Much of the proponents' testimony seeking to advance these arguments borders on the absurd or incomprehensible. As the *Llera-Plaza I* court politely observed at one point in its opinion, "The full import of the quoted Budowle testimony is not easy to grasp." *U.S. v. Llera Plaza*, 179 F. Supp. 2d 492, 57 Fed. R. Evid. Serv. 983 (E.D. Pa. 2002), withdrawn from bound volume and opinion vacated and superseded on other grounds on reconsideration, 188 F. Supp. 2d 549, 58 Fed. R. Evid. Serv. 1, 14 (E.D. Pa. 2002).

[18]*U.S. v. Llera Plaza*, 179 F. Supp. 2d 492, 57 Fed. R. Evid. Serv. 983 (E.D. Pa. 2002), withdrawn from bound volume and opinion vacated and superseded on other grounds on reconsideration, 188 F. Supp. 2d 549, 58 Fed. R. Evid. Serv. 1, 16 (E.D. Pa. 2002). In *Llera-Plaza II*, the court corrected these figures to indicate that 39 agencies responded to the request to try to match two latent prints to the defendant's 10-print card. Thirty agreed with the FBI's reading of the prints. Of the remaining nine, four agreed on one of the two latents and five concluded that neither of the latents match the known prints.

[19]*U.S. v. Llera Plaza*, 179 F. Supp. 2d 492, 57 Fed. R. Evid. Serv. 983 (E.D. Pa. 2002), withdrawn from bound volume and opinion vacated and superseded on other grounds on reconsidera-

tion, 188 F. Supp. 2d 549, 58 Fed. R. Evid. Serv. 1, 16 (E.D. Pa. 2002).

[20]There are proficiency studies, some of which indicate examiner error of a troubling degree, cited by the court in a footnote. See, *U.S. v. Llera Plaza*, 179 F. Supp. 2d 492, 57 Fed. R. Evid. Serv. 983 (E.D. Pa. 2002), withdrawn from bound volume and opinion vacated and superseded on other grounds on reconsideration, 188 F. Supp. 2d 549, 58 Fed. R. Evid. Serv. 1 (E.D. Pa. 2002) at n.24. The government rejects these as not applicable to FBI personnel. The FBI also had its own proficiency studies, which it withheld from the court at the earlier hearings, but then offered for the rehearing. These will be discussed, infra.

[21]*U.S. v. Llera Plaza*, 179 F. Supp. 2d 492, 57 Fed. R. Evid. Serv. 983 (E.D. Pa. 2002), withdrawn from bound volume and opinion vacated and superseded on other grounds on reconsideration, 188 F. Supp. 2d 549, 58 Fed. R. Evid. Serv. 1, 17 (E.D. Pa. 2002).

[22]*U.S. v. Llera Plaza*, 179 F. Supp. 2d 492, 57 Fed. R. Evid. Serv. 983 (E.D. Pa. 2002), withdrawn from bound volume and opinion vacated and superseded on other grounds on reconsideration, 188 F. Supp. 2d 549, 58 Fed. R. Evid. Serv. 1, 17 (E.D. Pa. 2002).

consensus of this narrow community is not sufficient for two essential reasons, as the court explained:

> General acceptance by the fingerprint examiner community does not, however, meet the standard set by Rule 702. First, there is the difficulty that fingerprint examiners, while respected professionals, do not constitute a "scientific community" in the *Daubert* sense. Second, the Court cautioned in *Kumho Tire* that general acceptance does not "help show that an expert's testimony is reliable where the discipline itself lacks reliability." The failure of fingerprint identifications fully to satisfy the first three *Daubert* factors militates against heavy reliance on the general acceptance factor. Thus, while fingerprint examinations conducted under the general ACE-V rubric are generally accepted as reliable by fingerprint examiners, this by itself cannot sustain the government's burden in making the case for the admissibility of fingerprint testimony under Federal Rule of Evidence 702 [citations omitted].[23]

The court is correct that where a field is found wanting on the other *Daubert* factors, general acceptance does not save the field from exclusion. If that were the law, astrology would be admissible. This reasoning is reflected in the court's second point, a point made by the Supreme Court in *Kumho Tire*. So the general acceptance factor was in any event going to be of little consequence. But several comments are worth making. First, the fingerprint identification community is not irrelevant merely because it is not made up scientists, or people who otherwise know how to critically evaluate the kinds of empirical claims they are making. Fingerprint examiners probably are a necessary group for general acceptance analysis because if they of all people do not have faith in what they are doing, the courts certainly should give pause.[24] But they are far from a sufficient group. This is because, first of all, as already noted, they lack expertise at evaluating techniques or skills in a rigorous fashion.[25] As numerous courts, though not the *Llera-Plaza I* court, have noted, asking a narrow group of practitioners—whose livelihoods depend on continuing to do what they do—whether they have faith in their own skills and abilities, is not likely to produce very enlightening answers.

Based on its analysis, the court concluded that "the ACE-V fingerprint identification regime is hard to square with *Daubert*." The court was not, however, prepared to exclude fingerprint expert testimony entirely. Instead, following a solution formulated by *United States v. Hines*[26] in a case involving asserted handwriting expert testimony.[27] The court ordered the following:

> Accordingly, this court will permit the government to present testimony by fingerprint examiners who, suitably qualified as "expert" examiners by virtue of training and experience, may (1) describe how the rolled and latent fingerprints at issue in this case were obtained, (2) identify and place before the jury the fingerprints and such magnifications thereof as may be required to show minute details, and (3) point out observed similarities (and differences) between any latent print and any rolled print the government contends are attributable to the same person. What such expert witnesses will not be permitted to do is to present "evaluation" testimony as to their "opinion" (Rule 702) that

---

[23]*U.S. v. Llera Plaza*, 179 F. Supp. 2d 492, 57 Fed. R. Evid. Serv. 983 (E.D. Pa. 2002), withdrawn from bound volume and opinion vacated and superseded on other grounds on reconsideration, 188 F. Supp. 2d 549, 58 Fed. R. Evid. Serv. 1, 18 (E.D. Pa. 2002).

[24]Curiously, this is not what happened with forensic dentists, who had serious doubts about their ability to match bitemarks sufficiently accurately for legal purposes, but the courts convinced them that they could. See §§ 6:1 et seq. of this work.

[25]Much like pre-scientific physicians who used leeches and through their less rigorous observations mistakenly inferred that they had beneficial effects. Or more modern cancer surgeons who thought the same of radical mastectomy. As with most empirical phenomena, only well-designed studies can really test efficacy.

[26]*U.S. v. Hines*, 55 F. Supp. 2d 62, 52 Fed. R. Evid. Serv. 257 (D. Mass. 1999).

[27]Among the several solutions to the dilemma of admitting fingerprint identification mentioned earlier, this one is termed "partial admission." § 3:1.

a particular latent print is in fact the print of a particular person. The defendants will be permitted to present their own fingerprint experts to counter the government's fingerprint testimony, but defense experts will also be precluded from presenting "evaluation" testimony. Government counsel and defense counsel will, in closing arguments, be free to argue to the jury that, on the basis of the jury's observation of a particular latent print and a particular rolled print, the jury may find the existence, or the non-existence, of a match between the prints.

## § 3:16  Post-*Daubert* challenges in federal courts—A short-lived exception to the usual evasions—*Llera-Plaza II*

In *Llera-Plaza II*[1] Judge Pollak reversed himself and withdrew his initial opinion and order. The overarching reasoning of *Llera-Plaza II* is woven of two basic threads. One thread was to reason as though *Kumho Tire* had never been decided, that is, to refrain from subjecting all proffered expertise to the most appropriate evaluation criteria—so that where *Daubert's* empirical/scientific factors are the most appropriate criteria they may be employed. In other words, because fingerprint examination is not a science, as the court found, less need be asked of it in the way of empirical verification. This is a retreat from *Llera-Plaza I*, in which the *Daubert* criteria were viewed as the appropriate touchstone of admissibility by the parties and by the court. The second thread was a reversal of the normal burden of proof. In *Llera-Plaza I*, the proponent of the expert evidence had to meet the *Daubert* standards and, on failing to do so, the expert testimony was granted only limited admission. In *Llera-Plaza II*, the implicit analytical starting point is a set of presumptions favoring admissibility, and it is the opponent whose failures of proof allow the presumptions to decide the motion. This, of course, is contrary to the law. And yet it is not an unfamiliar implement in the toolboxes of some gatekeepers.[2] We turn now to the details.

The government petitioned the court to reconsider its earlier ruling, arguing that prosecutions "would be seriously compromised by the preclusion of opinion testimony at the 'evaluation' stage 'that a particular latent print is in fact the print of a particular person.' "[3] The court agreed to a rehearing, at which the proponent of admission offered two fingerprint experts, Stephen Meagher and Kenneth Smith. The opponent offered fingerprint expert Allan Bayle, laboratory auditor Janine Arvizu, and psychometrician Norman Haber.

One interesting development at the hearing was the government's submission of proficiency tests previously withheld. The court summarized the results of the proficiency tests by taking the total number of tests taken and the total number of errors: "In sum, the 447 proficiency tests administered in the seven years from 1995 through 2001 yielded four errors—a proficiency error rate of just under 1%."[4] The court also noted that one of these errors was a false positive (making an identification when two prints did not in fact come from the same person), which was made by one of the four FBI supervisors taking an external proficiency test. The other three were false negatives (failing to make an identification when two prints did in fact come from the same person), all made on internal tests. Gross results, such as these, may be misleading. As *Kumho Tire* directs, one needs to pay attention to the "task-at-hand" in the case at bar and to ask whether an adequate expertise exists

**[Section 3:16]**

[1]*U.S. v. Llera Plaza*, 188 F. Supp. 2d 549, 58 Fed. R. Evid. Serv. 1 (E.D. Pa. 2002).

[2]See §§ 1:1 et seq. of this work.

[3]*U.S. v. Llera Plaza*, 179 F. Supp. 2d 492, 553, 57 Fed. R. Evid. Serv. 983 (E.D. Pa. 2002), withdrawn from bound volume and opinion vacated and superseded on other grounds on reconsideration, 188 F. Supp. 2d 549, 58 Fed. R. Evid. Serv. 1, 17 (E.D. Pa. 2002).

[4]*U.S. v. Llera Plaza*, 179 F. Supp. 2d 492, 556, 57 Fed. R. Evid. Serv. 983 (E.D. Pa. 2002), withdrawn from bound volume and opinion vacated and superseded on other grounds on reconsideration, 188 F. Supp. 2d 549, 58 Fed. R. Evid. Serv. 1, 17 (E.D. Pa. 2002).

with respect to that particular task. In turn, that would mean disaggregating the tests into a subgroup that approximates the task-at-hand in this case. For example, how many of the proficiency tests involved comparisons of known non common source prints, as the defense hypothesized was an actual task in this case? The answer is, very few.[5] Further, which tests presented latents of the same type as those in the case at bar? That is, if the task in the present case is to compare a smear or a small fragment, which tests involves smears or small fragments? Finally, is the difficulty of the tests comparable to the difficulty of the task in the present case?[6] On this issue, Allan Bayle, a former senior Scotland Yard fingerprint expert testified that the FBI's tests were too easy—" . . . on the whole, markedly unrepresentative of the latent prints that would be lifted at a crime scene. In general, Mr. Bayle found the test latent prints to be far clearer than the prints an examiner would routinely deal with."[7]—and thus the apparent error rate was much more worrisome than it appeared. The court concluded: "On the record made before me, the FBI examiners got very high grades, but the tests they took did not."[8] Of course, the existence of any error rate at all tends to refute that extreme claims that often are made for the virtual infallibility of fingerprint examiners.

The court's analysis began by summarizing, in block quotations, its earlier ruling. The court emphasized that its earlier ruling had been based on the paper record introduced in the case of *United States v. Mitchell*. Now it had an additional three days of live testimony.[9] The court then summarized the scope of each of the experts, noting, for instance, that Mr. Meagher's testimony primarily concerned proficiency tests that the FBI apparently recently discovered demonstrated the reliability of fingerprint expert opinion. In the end, however, the court found the proficiency tests to be unhelpful, and did not rely on them in any way. In summarizing the other experts, the court similarly described the scope of their testimony, but mainly did not rely on any of it for its analysis.

Instead, the court, seemed to rethink the reasoning of the earlier ruling and reconceptualized the requirements for fingerprint evidence under *Daubert* and *Kumho Tire*. The court initially commented that fingerprinting "is not, in my judgment, itself a science." The court seemed to think that this judgment affected the admissibility analysis: "In adjusting the focus of inquiry from [fingerprinting's] status as a 'scientific' discipline to its status as a 'technical' discipline, one modifies the angle of doctrinal vision."[10] The court, thus, disregarded the mandate of *Kumho Tire* by finding that fingerprint identification could avoid the rigors of *Daubert* by

---

[5]A grand total of nine, it appears from Appendix A to the government's Memorandum of Law (Jan. 28, 2002). The false positive error was made in one of these nine tests.

[6]This is not unlike requiring, for eyewitness lineups, that the lineups present a real test, with foils who look similar to the description of the perpetrator. Where lineups are too easy, researchers calculate an "effective lineup size." In short, a test which on the surface may appear to involve a genuine challenge may be much less of a test, and some adjustment can be made for that fact in order to make a more reasonable assessment of the test.

[7]*U.S. v. Llera Plaza*, 179 F. Supp. 2d 492, 557, 57 Fed. R. Evid. Serv. 983 (E.D. Pa. 2002), withdrawn from bound volume and opinion vacated and superseded on other grounds on reconsideration, 188 F. Supp. 2d 549, 58 Fed. R. Evid. Serv. 1, 17 (E.D. Pa. 2002).

[8]*U.S. v. Llera Plaza*, 179 F. Supp. 2d 492, 565, 57 Fed. R. Evid. Serv. 983 (E.D. Pa. 2002), withdrawn from bound volume and opinion vacated and superseded on other grounds on reconsideration, 188 F. Supp. 2d 549, 58 Fed. R. Evid. Serv. 1, 17 (E.D. Pa. 2002).

[9]This emphasizes the view that these decisions about fingerprints are one-case-at-a-time decisions. In a future case, with different witnesses, a judge might reach the opposite conclusion about the nature of asserted fingerprint expertise. Though that is consistent with the Supreme Court's vision of the admissibility decisions, see *General Electric v. Joiner*, it is not a sensible way to make legal decisions about the admissibility of scientific evidence. See §§ 1:1 et seq. of this work.

[10]*U.S. v. Llera Plaza*, 179 F. Supp. 2d 492, 562, 57 Fed. R. Evid. Serv. 983 (E.D. Pa. 2002), withdrawn from bound volume and opinion vacated

dubbing it practitioners "specialists" rather than "scientists." This seems to be exactly the back door into court that in *Kumho Tire* the Supreme Court had closed and locked.[11]

The court's view that fingerprinting was something other than a science changed the court's analyses of the peer review and general acceptance criteria of *Daubert*. In his earlier decision, Judge Pollak was unimpressed with the fact that fingerprinting had been generally accepted by a self-interested guild. Now, this uncritical consensus impresses him:

> I conclude that the fingerprint community's "general acceptance" of ACE-V should not be discounted because fingerprint specialists—like accountants, vocational experts, accident-reconstruction experts, appraisers of land or of art, experts in tire failure analysis, or others—have "technical, or other specialized knowledge" (Rule 702), rather that "scientific . . . knowledge" (*id.*), and hence are not members of what *Daubert* termed a "scientific community."[12]

*Llera-Plaza I* undervalued the participation of the guild in the circle of fields whose beliefs are sought as a measure of the degree of general acceptance, and overvalued the inclusion of scientists. *Llera-Plaza II* overvalues the participation of the guild, and disregards the usefulness of relevant science and scientists.

The court continued to find, on the one hand, that the "testing factor [of *Daubert*] was not met."[13] Also what little testing had been done was poor. Yet the court concluded, on the other hand, that the error rate was sufficiently low to satisfy *Daubert*. How can this be? If there has been virtually no testing, then the rate of error—either in general or for the task-at-hand in the case at bar—cannot be known. How can it be found sufficient? The court found the error rate factor to be met primarily on the basis that the defendants had failed to adduce proof that the FBI had made mistakes in earlier cases:

> It has been open to defense counsel to present examples of erroneous identifications attributable to FBI examiners, and no such examples have been forthcoming. I conclude, therefore, on the basis of the limited information in the record as expanded, that there is no evidence that the error rate of certified FBI fingerprint examiners is unacceptably high.[14]

Since the proponent of evidence, not the opponent, has the burden of proof to show its proffered expert testimony has an acceptable error rate, this conclusion is reached through an incorrect application of the law. The *Llera-Plaza II* court's theory of why a reversal of the burden is desirable is essentially this: To postpone admission of fingerprint identification expertise pending research showing what it

---

and superseded on other grounds on reconsideration, 188 F. Supp. 2d 549, 58 Fed. R. Evid. Serv. 1, 17 (E.D. Pa. 2002).

[11]What *Kumho Tire* instructs is that all fields, regardless of their labels, be subjected to sound evaluation criteria. Gatekeepers are not to excuse fields for rigorous scrutiny for the very reason that they have not taken the trouble to subject themselves to rigorous testing. A field of endeavor need not "be a science" in order to be evaluated using scientific methods, which, after all, is essentially the use of rigorous logic to evaluate empirical claims.

[12]*U.S. v. Llera Plaza*, 179 F. Supp. 2d 492, 563, 57 Fed. R. Evid. Serv. 983 (E.D. Pa. 2002), withdrawn from bound volume and opinion vacated and superseded on other grounds on reconsideration, 188 F. Supp. 2d 549, 58 Fed. R. Evid. Serv.

1, 17 (E.D. Pa. 2002).

[13]*U.S. v. Llera Plaza*, 179 F. Supp. 2d 492, 564, 57 Fed. R. Evid. Serv. 983 (E.D. Pa. 2002), withdrawn from bound volume and opinion vacated and superseded on other grounds on reconsideration, 188 F. Supp. 2d 549, 58 Fed. R. Evid. Serv. 1, 17 (E.D. Pa. 2002). "I concluded in the January 7 opinion that *Daubert*'s testing factor was not met, and I have found no reason to depart from that conclusion."

[14]*U.S. v. Llera Plaza*, 179 F. Supp. 2d 492, 566, 57 Fed. R. Evid. Serv. 983 (E.D. Pa. 2002), withdrawn from bound volume and opinion vacated and superseded on other grounds on reconsideration, 188 F. Supp. 2d 549, 58 Fed. R. Evid. Serv. 1, 17 (E.D. Pa. 2002). Query how difficult it is to prove an erroneous conviction, especially before the advent of DNA typing.

can and cannot do at what level of accuracy "would be to make the best the enemy of the good."[15]

Can anything be said on behalf of the correct legal rule except that it is the law and courts have a duty to apply it? One of the virtues of the customary burden of proof is that it compels experts and proponents to work to produce data illuminating a court about the proffered evidence. If their evidence is admissible without such illumination, why would experts and proponents work to produce research? Actual data can only undermine the glowing judicial presumptions of such expertise by showing (as the few studies which have been done have shown) that the claims made on behalf of fingerprint expertise had been exaggerations. If the field of fingerprint identification had not produced studies illuminating most (or any?) of its most fundamental claims about its subject and itself in the century past—because it was being admitted without the data—why will it do so in the century to come?

At bottom, *Llera-Plaza I* and *II* reflect the dilemma highlighted earlier in this chapter, between the conventional scientific standards required by *Daubert* and the implicit standards that have prevailed for decades among fingerprint identification practitioners and consumers. Several imperfect resolutions of the dilemma are suggested, one of which, partial admission, is what Judge Pollak adopted in *Llera-Plaza I*.[16] His flipflop in *Llera-Plaza II* could be attributed to the pull of the other horn of the dilemma. Whichever direction a thoughtful and sincere judge goes on this issue at the present state of knowledge, the judge is going to regret that not having gone the other way. So, in a sense, Judge Pollak is the perfect illustration of that dilemma.

### § 3:17 Post-*Daubert* challenges in federal courts—Implications

Ironically, the failure of judges to write a coherent defense of asserted fingerprint expertise under *Daubert*, but only to seek ways to shelter it from serious scrutiny, suggests that fingerprint expert evidence actually does not meet the requirements of *Daubert*.

If the claims and assumptions of fingerprint identification expertise had been

---

[15]The court's more complete statement of its theory follows:

Having re-reviewed the applicability of the *Daubert* factors through the prism of *Kumho Tire*, I conclude that the one *Daubert* factor which is both pertinent and unsatisfied is the first factor—"testing." *Kumho Tire*, as I have noted above, instructs district courts to "consider the specific factors identified in *Daubert* where they are reasonable measures of the reliability of expert testimony." *526 U.S. at 152.* Scientific tests of ACE-V—i.e., tests in the *Daubert* sense—would clearly aid in measuring ACE-V's reliability. But, as of today, no such tests are in hand. The question, then, is whether, in the absence of such tests, a court should conclude that the ACE-V fingerprint identification system, as practiced by certified FBI fingerprint examiners, has too great a likelihood of producing erroneous results to be admissible as evidence in a courtroom setting. There are respected authorities who, it appears, would render such a verdict.

. . .

As explained in Part II of this opinion, I have found, on the record before me, that there is no evidence that certified FBI fingerprint examiners present erroneous identification testimony, and, as a corollary, that there is no evidence that the rate of error of certified FBI fingerprint examiners is unacceptably high. With those findings in mind, I am not persuaded that courts should defer admission of testimony with respect to fingerprinting—which Professors Neufeld and Scheck term "[t]he bedrock forensic identifier of the 20th century"—until academic investigators financed by the National Institute of Justice have made substantial headway on a "verification and validation" research agenda. For the National Institute of Justice, or other institutions both public and private, to sponsor such research would be all to the good. But to postpone present in-court utilization of this "bedrock forensic identifier" pending such research would be to make the best the enemy of the good.

*U.S. v. Llera Plaza*, 179 F. Supp. 2d 492, 571, 572, 57 Fed. R. Evid. Serv. 983 (E.D. Pa. 2002), withdrawn from bound volume and opinion vacated and superseded on other grounds on reconsideration, 188 F. Supp. 2d 549, 58 Fed. R. Evid. Serv. 1, 17 (E.D. Pa. 2002).

[16]§ 3:1. Judge Pollak apparently found that solution the same place we had, in *U.S. v. Hines*, 55 F. Supp. 2d 62, 52 Fed. R. Evid. Serv. 257 (D. Mass. 1999).

empirically tested, if these empirical tests were sufficiently well designed[1] so as to survive peer review leading to publication in scientifically respectable journals and had survived the more important debate in the intellectual marketplace following publication, and the data convincingly showed low error rates for the relevant task-at-hand,[2] and if these findings had come to be generally accepted among relevant scientific and professional communities beyond the circle of police technicians who practice the art—then the proponents no doubt would have eagerly offered such information to the courts and the judges would have had ample material with which to write cogent opinions. That such material appears in none of the opinions suggests that it does not exist. If the grounds for admitting fingerprint examiners' testimony were as strong and as sound as the judges assert that it is, then it should not be so difficult to write an opinion actually presenting those grounds.

Because conventional support for the admission of an asserted expertise about an empirical phenomenon do not exist for fingerprint identification, the courts have been casting about in search of persuasive justification for admission on some other basis, thus far without success.

### §3:18 Post-*Daubert* challenges in federal courts—Developments after *Llera Plaza*

From opinions that are superficial and unthinking, or which otherwise evade the obligation to conscientiously apply *Daubert* and *Kumho Tire*, we have crossed into the realm where newer opinions do little more than to cite those evasive or superficial opinions as authority for the proposition that fingerprint identification expertise is "reliable, and therefore admissible."[1] One would think that if sound science supporting the claims of fingerprint experts existed, proponents could offer courts plenty of data from well designed studies to support their claims, and courts could summarize those studies and data. Because the proponents have not been able to do so, courts look to each other rather than to any studies or data.

Recent such cases include the following.

In *United States v. Hernandez*[2] the defendant alleged error by the district court in admitting the government's fingerprint expert. At trial, the defendant had relied on Judge Pollak's original decision in *United States v. Llera Plaza*.[3] With virtually no reflection on the empirical issues, the Court of Appeals found that in permitting the fingerprint expert to testify the lower court had not abused its discretion. The Eighth Circuit pointed out that Judge Pollak reversed himself,[4] and concluded that "expert testimony regarding fingerprint evidence should, subject to sufficient trial court oversight, be regarded as satisfying [*Daubert* and *Kumho Tire*]." That is as deep as the Eighth Circuit's analysis went.

---

**[Section 3:17]**

[1]A careful reading of *Daubert*, as well as an understanding of the intellectual nature of science, suggests this to be the gravamen of the "peer review and publication" element.

[2]See *Kumho Tire Co., Ltd. v. Carmichael*, 526 U.S. 137, 119 S. Ct. 1167, 143 L. Ed. 2d 238, 50 U.S.P.Q.2d 1177, Prod. Liab. Rep. (CCH) P 15470, 50 Fed. R. Evid. Serv. 1373, 29 Envtl. L. Rep. 20638 (1999).

**[Section 3:18]**

[1]See, e.g., *U.S. v. Abreu*, 406 F.3d 1304, 67 Fed. R. Evid. Serv. 17 (11th Cir. 2005), *U.S. v. Janis*, 387 F.3d 682, 65 Fed. R. Evid. Serv. 834 (8th Cir. 2004), and the cases described in this section.

[2]*U.S. v. Hernandez*, 299 F.3d 984 (8th Cir. 2002).

[3]*U.S. v. Llera Plaza*, 179 F. Supp. 2d 492, 57 Fed. R. Evid. Serv. 983 (E.D. Pa. 2002), withdrawn from bound volume and opinion vacated and superseded on other grounds on reconsideration, 188 F. Supp. 2d 549, 58 Fed. R. Evid. Serv. 1 (E.D. Pa. 2002).

[4]Citing *U.S. v. Llera Plaza*, 188 F. Supp. 2d 549, 58 Fed. R. Evid. Serv. 1 (E.D. Pa. 2002).

In *United States v. Navarro-Fletes*,[5] the defendant argued that fingerprint evidence does not meet the *Daubert* standard. In a very brief consideration of the matter the Circuit Court found no error—asserting the buzz words that fingerprint identification had been "subject to peer review," that "there are publications in the field," and so on, without explanation of what those peer reviews or publications consist of or show. (For example, one could say as much on behalf of astrology.) In addition, the court identified the relevant scientific community for general acceptance purposes as consisting of police fingerprint examiners, in other words, a narrow definition of the community of experts as those who practice the technique for their livelihoods and excluding disinterested scientists. Narrow general acceptance of that sort would not seem to be consistent with the purposes and concerns discussed in *Daubert* and *Kumho Tire*.

The court in *United States v. Frias*,[6] responded to a challenge to fingerprint evidence by refusing to hold a *Daubert* hearing and conducting no review whatever of the basis for the proffered expertise. Instead, the court relied on the fact that "numerous circuit and district courts have permitted fingerprint examiners to state their opinions and conclusions." The court noted that the defendant had failed "to provide any particularized basis on which to hold that the NYPD's fingerprint investigation techniques fail to meet the standards enunciated by the Supreme Court in *Daubert* and *Kuhmo Tire* [sic]." In response to a letter from the defendant complaining about the court's failure to grant a *Daubert* hearing, the court reiterated that "[n]umerous cases, several of which are cited in the February 10, 2003 Memorandum Order, have permitted fingerprint examiners to state their opinions and conclusions and have overwhelmingly permitted testimony on fingerprint identification."[7]

Similarly, the district court in *United States v. Cline*[8] refused to hold a *Daubert* hearing, resting content with the observation that almost all district courts which have been presented with the issue admitted the expert testimony.

> Research shows *Llera Plaza* stands alone in rejecting fingerprint identification opinions on the standards established in *Daubert*, *Kumho*, and Fed. R. Evid. 702. The district court itself recognized that other courts addressing this issue have upheld admissibility even after the *Daubert* decision and the more recent amendment of Fed. R. Evid. 702. *Llera Plaza*, 179 F.Supp.2d at 500–501. While certainly exhaustive and informed, the analysis of the *Daubert* factors used in *Llera Plaza* does not persuade this court to depart from the well-traveled path. The decision should be applauded to the extent that it encourages empirical testing of the process within more traditional "scientific" parameters, leads to additional submissions to the relevant body of peer review literature, and possibly fosters the development of uniform standards followed and accepted by all qualified fingerprint examiners. It is the humble opinion of this court, however, that the decision in *Llera Plaza* overreaches in concluding that the current fingerprint identification analysis so utterly fails the so-called "scientific" criteria in *Daubert* as to render all fingerprint examiners' "subjective" evaluations or identifications unreliable and inadmissible under Rule 702. This court remains satisfied that general fingerprint identification analysis clears the threshold of reliability under Rule 702 after considering all relevant factors, including those from *Daubert*, and that the shortcomings argued against this analysis are more prudently treated as matters going to the weight of the evidence. [footnote omitted]

But the opinion does not explain anything of its "consider[ation] of all relevant factors." The court states: "Rather than repeating or attempting to restate what other courts have said in their evaluation of the *Daubert* factors for fingerprint

---

[5]*U.S. v. Navarro-Fletes*, 49 Fed. Appx. 732 (9th Cir. 2002).

[6]*U.S. v. Frias*, 2003 WL 296740 (S.D. N.Y. 2003), modified in part, 2003 WL 352502 (S.D. N.Y. 2003).

[7]*U.S. v. Frias*, 2003 WL 352502 (S.D. N.Y. 2003).

[8]*U.S. v. Cline*, 188 F. Supp. 2d 1287, 59 Fed. R. Evid. Serv. 99 (D. Kan. 2002), aff'd, 349 F.3d 1276 (10th Cir. 2003).

identification, the court simply adopts [the opinions of other cases]." In commending *Llera-Plaza* for "encourag[ing] empirical testing of the process within more traditional 'scientific' parameters," *Cline* seems to be saying that empirical research, science, and those sorts of things are some sort of adjunct and not essential information in determining the validity of the claims of a field—a perspective which will strike many as more than a little paradoxical.

The totality of the analysis offered by the Court of Appeals in *United States v. Rojas-Torres*,[9] to a trial court's admission of fingerprint expert testimony is the following:

> Rojas-Torres contends that the district court erred by admitting expert fingerprint evidence against him because such evidence does not meet the standards required for reliable scientific theory under Federal Rule of Evidence 702. We review for an abuse of discretion. *U.S. v. Alatorre*. The district court conducted an evidentiary hearing and considered the factors enumerated in *Daubert v. Merrell Dow Pharm., Inc.*. The court's conclusion that the evidence was relevant and reliable, and therefore admissible, was not an abuse of discretion [citations omitted].[10]

While some courts conclude that the field of fingerprint identification is built on a foundation of published, peer reviewed empirical research,[11] notwithstanding the more careful inquiry leading to the findings in both *Llera-Plaza I* and *Llera-Plaza II* that such testing is all but non-existent, other courts acknowledge the lack of testing and seek to account for its absence.[12] But the consensus of courts seems to be that fingerprint examination is valid primarily because it is generally accepted[13]—the least of what *Daubert* calls for, and perhaps insufficient under *Kumho Tire*. Still other courts have reached the conclusion that challenges can be dismissed out of hand because the validity of the assertions of fingerprint examiners can be taken for granted, and the numerous recent cases in which courts have approved admission can be cited in support of that assumption.[14]

Several cases do not fit the monotonous pattern that has been developing in the federal courts.

In *Jacobs v. Government of the Virgin Islands*,[15] the district court excluded the prosecution's fingerprint examiner, apparently because the government failed to provide any evidence or argument supporting reliability. The Third Circuit stated that this was a correct ruling, since the government has the burden of proof under *Daubert*. Failing to make any effort to meet that burden results in exclusion of the testimony. The Third Circuit affirmed the dismissal. The posture of this case, which so starkly presents the failure of the proponent of evidence to meet its burden, makes clear the contrast to other fingerprint expert cases, which have inexplicably shifted the burden of proof to the opponent of the evidence. The full text of the

---

[9]*U.S. v. Rojas-Torres*, 66 Fed. Appx. 747 (9th Cir. 2003).

[10]*U.S. v. Rojas-Torres*, 66 Fed. Appx. 747 (9th Cir. 2003).

[11]E.g., *U.S. v. Salim*, 189 F. Supp. 2d 93, 58 Fed. R. Evid. Serv. 1544 (S.D. N.Y. 2002); *U.S. v. Navarro-Fletes*, 49 Fed. Appx. 732 (9th Cir. 2002).

[12]E.g., *U.S. v. Merritt*, 2002 WL 1821821 (S.D. Ind. 2002) (explaining the lack of research and testing of fingerprint examination claims as resulting from field being not a science but instead a technical skill). Query the adequacy of such a defense of the untested, considering that the empirical claims of the "technical skill" and its foundational theory can be subjected to testing with as much ease (or difficulty) as anything else

in the non-metaphysical world. The issue, after all, is not whether something is or is not "science" (*Kumho Tire*) but whether or not it has been tested and what the results of that testing have been.

[13]E.g., *U.S. v. Merritt*, 2002 WL 1821821 (S.D. Ind. 2002); *U.S. v. Salim*, 189 F. Supp. 2d 93, 58 Fed. R. Evid. Serv. 1544 (S.D. N.Y. 2002).

[14]*U.S. v. Merritt*, 2002 WL 1821821 (S.D. Ind. 2002); *U.S. v. Frias*, 2003 WL 296740 (S.D. N.Y. 2003), modified in part, 2003 WL 352502 (S.D. N.Y. 2003); *U.S. v. Cline*, 188 F. Supp. 2d 1287, 59 Fed. R. Evid. Serv. 99 (D. Kan. 2002), aff'd, 349 F.3d 1276 (10th Cir. 2003).

[15]*Jacobs v. Government of Virgin Islands*, 53 Fed. Appx. 651 (3d Cir. 2002).

court's discussion follows:

> Under *Daubert v. Merrell Dow Pharmaceuticals, Inc.* [citation omitted], a trial judge must exercise a gatekeeping role under Rule 702 of the Federal Rules of Evidence, determining whether, as a threshold matter, the "reasoning or methodology underlying [expert] testimony is scientifically valid and . . . whether that reasoning or methodology properly can be applied to the facts in issue." *Id.* As the Government intended to present the testimony of a fingerprint identification expert in the instant case, the Government bore the burden of convincing the District Court that the methodology of its expert was reliable and could be appropriately applied to the facts at issue. *Id.* at 593 n. 10. In this case, the government did not do so. Nothing in the record or in the arguments made on appeal suggests that the fingerprint examiner involved in this case did not use acceptable methodology. But the record before the trial judge lacks sufficient evidence to permit us to disturb the trial judge's ruling that the government did not bear its burden on this element. Although the government could have satisfied its burden by providing minimal additional information, it did not do so. Therefore, we conclude that the Territorial Court did not abuse its discretion by excluding the proposed expert. After the Territorial Court ruled on the defendant's motion to exclude the fingerprint evidence, the court asked the prosecutor whether the government was able to proceed without the benefit of that evidence. In response, the prosecutor conceded that the government had no further evidence, and the court, with the prosecutor's acquiescence, dismissed the case with prejudice on the understanding that the government would appeal the exclusion of the proposed expert testimony.

*United States v. Crisp*[16] is significant because it is the first case in which a federal judge recognizes why the foundation of fingerprint expert testimony does not meet the requirements of *Daubert*.

The motion to exclude in the trial court was denied without published opinion. It is clear, however, from the opinion in the Court of Appeals that there was a hearing on the motions, but it seems that the only testimony taken was from the government's document examiner, the defense relying on cross examination and published sources. Further, it seems clear that the challenge made and responded to was of a global nature, in derogation of the requirements of *Kumho Tire*. That is not insignificant, though the point is lost in the present case. Some commentators have argued that the soundest basis for excluding fingerprint expert testimony is in cases where the evidence is of a fragmentary or poor quality latent print, because the fingerprint field has no knowledge and no standards[17] regarding how small or how poor the quality of a print can be and still provide enough dependable detail on which to draw reasonable inferences about identity. That is left entirely to the subjective judgment of the examiner, which almost certainly varies from one examiner to the next. Not that other judgments by fingerprint examiners depends on anything more scientifically sound, but the intuitions of examiners and judges alike will feel more assured to the degree that the questioned print includes more detail. How little the detail can become and an opinion of certain identification still be offered—the "boundary" problem—is altogether unclear.[18]

The majority affirmed the trial court's admission of the government's fingerprinting identification expert (in this case, actually, a palmprint), based on now familiar shallow grounds: asserted fingerprint experts have been admitted for decades and recent opinions have turned away challenges to its reliability. In response to the defendant's argument that no research supported the claims made by fingerprint examiners, the court simply stated that the defense cited "no studies demonstrating

---

[16]*U.S. v. Crisp*, 324 F.3d 261, 60 Fed. R. Evid. Serv. 1486 (4th Cir. 2003).

[17]Thus, where the majority casually speaks of "widespread agreement on standards" it is clearly mistaken with respect to this problem of

how small is too small.

[18]Denbeaux & Risinger, *Kumho Tire* and Expert Reliability: How the Question You Ask Gives the Answer You Get, 34 Seton Hall L. Rev. 15, 68 (2003).

the unreliability of fingerprinting analysis."[19] (Thus relieving the proponent of its burden of proof.) The defendant also argued that the only professional group among whom fingerprint identification is generally accepted is that group of professionals who practice the technique. The Fourth Circuit responded simply by saying that "While the principles underlying fingerprint identification have not attained the status of scientific law, they nonetheless bear the imprimatur of a strong general acceptance, not only in the expert community, but in the courts as well."[20] The court did not explain how general acceptance among courts met the requirements of *Daubert* and *Kumho Tire*. The court also pointed out that specific standards applied to fingerprint testing and that the error rate was "essentially zero."[21] As noted above, the assertion about standards is not true, certainly with respect to the boundary problem, and the claim of an error rate of "essentially zero" or "negligible," given without supporting data, is startling, and has been rejected by most courts as too fanciful a claim to be credited.

Judge Michael's lengthy and detailed dissent begins by saying:

> The majority believes that expert testimony about fingerprint and handwriting identification is reliable because the techniques in these fields have been accepted and tested in our adversary system over time. This belief leads the majority to excuse fingerprint and handwriting analysis from the more careful scrutiny that scientific expert testimony must now withstand under *Daubert* before it can be admitted. In Patrick Leroy Crisp's case, the government did not prove that its expert identification evidence satisfied the *Daubert* factors or that it was otherwise reliable. I respectfully dissent for that reason. In dissenting, I am not suggesting that fingerprint and handwriting evidence cannot be shown to satisfy *Daubert*. I am only making the point that the government did not establish in Crisp's case that this evidence is reliable. The government has had ten years to comply with *Daubert*. It should not be given a pass in this case.

This paragraph sets out the themes of the dissent, but its exact focus is not entirely clear. The rest of the opinion shows great familiarity with the literature concerning the global reliability arguments surrounding fingerprint identification, and it is very effective in eviscerating the majority's reliance on "adversary testing" as a general matter. However, it is difficult to know whether the dissent is saying that the government failed to make an appropriate showing in Crisp's case because they merely called two examiners who were not themselves familiar enough with the extant disputes and data to make an appropriate record upon which to base a finding of reliability. Or whether the dissent was arguing that the current state of the body of research on fingerprint expert evidence—that fingerprinting failed all of the *Daubert* factors, since no research had been published in peer reviewed journals, that there was no known error rate for the technique, and that the technique was generally accepted only among fingerprint examiners and not among a broader scientific community—is inadequate to establish admissibility. The dissent (like the majority) is too global in focus to comply with the mandate of *Kumho Tire* to judge reliability in regard to the particular task for which the proffer in the case is being made.

Another break from the monotonous and unthinking is *United States v. Sullivan*,[22] a relatively conscientious examination of the "*Daubert* factors" as they apply to the current state of the art of fingerprint examination. *Sullivan* rejected the notion that

---

[19]Denbeaux & Risinger, *Kumho Tire* and Expert Reliability: How the Question You Ask Gives the Answer You Get, 34 Seton Hall L. Rev. 15, 68 (2003).

[20]Denbeaux & Risinger, *Kumho Tire* and Expert Reliability: How the Question You Ask Gives the Answer You Get, 34 Seton Hall L. Rev.

15, 68 (2003).

[21]Denbeaux & Risinger, *Kumho Tire* and Expert Reliability: How the Question You Ask Gives the Answer You Get, 34 Seton Hall L. Rev. 15, 68 (2003).

[22]E.g., *U.S. v. Sullivan*, 246 F. Supp. 2d 700 (E.D. Ky. 2003).

historical acceptance of fingerprint evidence in the courtroom satisfies the general acceptance requirement, rejected the notion that review by a second examiner satisfies the peer review requirement, rejected the proponent's claim of zero error rate, rejected that notion that adversarial testing substituted for empirical testing, and rejected the idea that the fact that fingerprint examination methods were testable was sufficient (but rather that actual testing was needed). Importantly, this is another of the very few opinions to take heed of the Supreme Court's concept of task-at-hand, noting that the evidence presented by the proponent of admission did not provide evidence that no two fingerprints can share a *partial print* in common. Nevertheless, the *Sullivan* court held that these infirmities were not sufficient to render fingerprint evidence unreliable under *Daubert*. Resting heavily on general acceptance, the court held that these shortcomings did not bar admission and that they could be addressed in cross-examination.

Given the deferential standard of review mandated by the Supreme Court in *Joiner*, and the concept of harmless error, it is hardly surprising that no reversals have occurred on appeal, even when a district court refused to hold a *Daubert* hearing[23] or took the validity of the proponent's claims as a given[24] or admitted testimony on the strength of little more than untested theoretical propositions[25] or on the basis that other courts had admitted (without evaluating the strengths or weaknesses of those opinions).[26]

One curiosity in this mix is *United States v. Sutton*,[27] a case in which the defense sought to have the government's own fingerprint examination report admitted over the government's objection. The trial court excluded the report and the court of appeals affirmed the district court. Latent fingerprints taken from two places at the crime scene which witnesses had seen the robbers touch did not match the defendants' fingerprints, a fact the defense sought to have placed before the jury and which the government sought to keep out of evidence. The government argued that without an expert to explain the report (consisting of nothing more than a bare conclusion of no matching prints), the jury might misunderstand it. The court agreed, adding that if subjected to a *Daubert* analysis, the fingerprint examination report might have been found not to be the product of reliable principles and methods.

The main event among the appellate opinions is Judge Becker's review of *United States v. Mitchell*.[28] The reader will recall that *Mitchell* was the first post-*Daubert* challenge to the admissibility of fingerprint expert testimony, and was the record that formed the basis of the *Daubert* hearing in *United States v. Llera-Plaza*. The district judge in *Mitchell* had made only a conclusory ruling from the bench.[29]

Finally, it might be said that *Daubert* does not require formal science, and that

[23]E.g., *U.S. v. Turner*, 285 F.3d 909, 58 Fed. R. Evid. Serv. 976 (10th Cir. 2002); *U.S. v. Abreu*, 406 F.3d 1304, 67 Fed. R. Evid. Serv. 17 (11th Cir. 2005); *U.S. v. Williams*, 29 Fed. Appx. 486 (9th Cir. 2002).

[24]E.g., *U.S. v. Turner*, 285 F.3d 909, 58 Fed. R. Evid. Serv. 976 (10th Cir. 2002); *U.S. v. Williams*, 29 Fed. Appx. 486 (9th Cir. 2002); *U.S. v. Abreu*, 406 F.3d 1304, 67 Fed. R. Evid. Serv. 17 (11th Cir. 2005).

[25]E.g., *U.S. v. Sanchez-Birruetta*, 128 Fed. Appx. 571 (9th Cir. 2005).

[26]*U.S. v. Abreu*, 406 F.3d 1304, 67 Fed. R. Evid. Serv. 17 (11th Cir. 2005); *U.S. v. George*, 363 F.3d 666, 64 Fed. R. Evid. Serv. 10 (7th Cir. 2004); *U.S. v. Martinez-Garduno*, 31 Fed. Appx. 475 (9th Cir. 2002); *U.S. v. Gary*, 85 Fed. Appx. 908 (4th Cir. 2004).

[27]*U.S. v. Sutton*, 337 F.3d 792, 61 Fed. R. Evid. Serv. 1330 (7th Cir. 2003).

[28]*U.S. v. Mitchell*, 365 F.3d 215 (3d Cir. 2004).

[29]For a detailed commentary on the Mitchell appellate opinion, see Cole, Does 'Yes' Really Mean Yes? The Attempt to Close Debate on the Admissibility of Fingerprint Testimony, Jurimetrics J. (2005).

In an extensive opinion by Judge Becker, the District Court's ruling was upheld. The Court of Appeals reviewed in considerable detail the background, evidence and arguments presented at the *Daubert* hearing (which, as we discuss in the text, is exactly the same evidence offered in *Llera-Plaza I*). The Court of Appeals made clear the absence of formal science does not necessarily bar admission (even for an expertise that long has insisted that it is a science). But if *Daubert* means anything, it should mean that a proponent must offer, and a court must require, something more convincing than the field's bald assertions and the fact that courts of old believed those bald assertions, and that courts of today have taken note of those courts of old.

## § 3:19 Post-*Daubert* challenges in state courts

Though not officially reported, *People v. Clevenger*[1] is a still rare instance of a challenge to the admissibility of expert testimony on fingerprint identification in a state jurisdiction that shuns *Daubert* and adheres to *Frye*. Notwithstanding language to the contrary in *Daubert* and *Clevenger* themselves, in some contexts

that the standard of review it applied was abuse of discretion—the deferential standard called for by the Supreme Court in *Joiner*. The Court of Appeals went on to find that some aspects of the District Court's ruling were not erroneous, or not so erroneous as to constitute an abuse of discretion, and that others were erroneous but constituted harmless error. Of note:

> The major error found was the District Court's taking of judicial notice that human friction ridges were unique and permanent throughout the area of the friction ridge skin, including small fragmentary areas. The improper advantage gained by the Government, however, was deemed marginal because evidence could have been offered in support of the claims.

The Government's withholding, until after the completion of *Mitchell*'s trial, of a National Institute of Justice solicitation for research proposals (RFP) directed at validating the various claims long made on behalf of fingerprint identification evidence, was held not to constitute a *Brady* violation (because the "question is not whether the defendant would more likely than not have received a different verdict with the evidence, but whether in its absence he received a fair trial . . ." and because the issue does not turn on the Government's bad faith but on the import of the evidence withheld). The Court of Appeals remarked that it was "deeply discomforted" by the withholding of the RFP, if allegations about the incident were true. That release of the RFP was delayed until after the trial was not denied, but the reason for the delay was disputed. "Dr. Rau's story, if true, would be a damning indictment of the ethics of those involved."

Though many of the claims of fingerprint identification had not been tested until the occasion of this trial, and still had not been especially well tested, they were nevertheless *testable*, which permitted cross examination and satisfied the requirements of *Daubert* (because *Daubert* was viewed not as requiring testing but only testability.)

This opinion is one of the very few, perhaps the only, to recognize that the task at hand presented by the case, and the focus of the admissibility challenge, was whether sufficient evidence exists to support the proponent's claim that small fragments of limited quality could be dependably identified. Though little evidence was actually offered on that point, the Court found it to be sufficient for this case (since the one study of that question was done on the very prints at issue in this case).

The Court of Appeals was attentive to the weaknesses of the methodology of the proponent's studies. (One example: "[t]he FBI's reliance on an unspecified, subjective, sliding-scale mix of 'quantity and quality of detail' makes meaningful testing elusive, for it is difficult to design an experiment to test a hypothesis with unspecified parameters.")

The Court of Appeals misunderstood and misapplied the meaning of "peer review" as that phrase is used by *Daubert* and by the scientific literature. (For contrast, see the District Court's treatment of the "peer review" issue in *Llera-Plaza*.)

Testimony about whether latent fingerprint identification was or was not a "science" was judged immaterial to the issue of admissibility.

Relatedly, expert witnesses offered to testify at trial on "the reliability (*or lack thereof*) of fingerprint identification . . . would have been unambiguously admissible." [Emphasis added.] This became an issue in the present case, the Court of Appeals explained, because Mitchell framed the question as which witnesses—rather than which issues—would be admissible at trial to attack the weight of the fingerprint identification opinion. The District Court had barred the defense's witnesses from testifying as to the scientific status of asserted fingerprint expertise, which the Court of Appeals upheld, but the District Court would not have barred—or at least ought not to have barred—those same experts if it understood that they would have testified about the weaknesses and shortcomings of fingerprint identification. Query whether this is a distinction with a difference.

**[Section 3:19]**

[1]*People v. Clevenger*, 2003 WL 22872446 (Cal. App. 5th Dist. 2003), unpublished/noncitable, (Dec. 5, 2003).

*Frye* is a filter through which expert evidence more easily flows. That is well illustrated by this case. The appellate court in *Clevenger* noted that the California Supreme Court had explicitly rejected *Daubert*[2] and therefore *People v. Kelly*[3] remained the relevant test, that it applied to "expert testimony based upon the application of a new scientific technique," and that, as to the assessment of the underlying reliability of the proffered expert evidence, the touchstone was general acceptance.[4] Naturally, the court had little difficulty concluding that "fingerprint analysis is not a 'new scientific technique'" and that such experts had been received by California courts for decades, and were therefore not new. The appellate court might have ended the matter there. No data, no studies, no empirical analysis required. But, apparently unable to resist looking for *something* more persuasive than the free pass afforded to old but untested expertise by the "novelty" element of *Frye*, the court went on to note that one of the government's experts at trial "testified that she had testified in court as a fingerprint expert about 200 times in a span of 22 years, *and had never made a misidentification.*" (Emphasis added.) Which of the examiner's identifications had been made in error is, of course, impossible for the examiner to know.[5] What this small exercise in overreaching exposes is the fact that neither the expert nor the court has any hard evidence on how often or under what conditions fingerprint examination leads to errors—which is one of the things that *Daubert* encourages courts to find out, with the help of thoughtfully designed studies rather than by the ipse dixit of the witness.

Unsurprisingly, the state courts generally replicate the thinking of the federal courts, and that is true whether relying on *Frye* or *Daubert*. Although the latter test should present fewer barriers to admission, the fact that *Daubert* courts rely so heavily on general acceptance as the criterion of admission of fingerprint expert evidence, notwithstanding the Supreme Court's skepticism in *Kumho Tire*, reduces *Daubert* to *Frye*[6] or the obvious error of substituting judicial acceptance for general acceptance in the scientific community. Whatever route is taken, however, the destination is admission.[7]

*Barber v. State*,[8] notes that *Daubert* does not apply in Alabama (except for DNA typing) and that friction ridge examination (in this case, concerning a palm print) does not constitute scientific evidence so *Frye* does not apply either. Thus, no special filter is placed in the path of this specie of expert testimony. The court adds, however, that if *Daubert* did apply, this testimony would pass the test, and quotes

---

[2]*People v. Leahy*, 8 Cal. 4th 587, 34 Cal. Rptr. 2d 663, 882 P.2d 321 (1994).

[3]*People v. Kelly*, 17 Cal. 3d 24, 130 Cal. Rptr. 144, 549 P.2d 1240 (1976) (California's version of *Frye*).

[4]Whether "the thing from which the deduction is made" has "gained general acceptance" in the relevant field or fields.

[5]Outside of research designed to test the question.

[6]E.g., *Burnett v. State*, 815 N.E.2d 201 (Ind. Ct. App. 2004).

[7]*People v. Torres,* No. BA145133 (Superior Court of the County of Los Angeles, Oct. 10, 2000) (denied motion without a hearing); *People v. Nawi,* No. 176527 (Superior Court of the County of San Francisco, Oct. 10, 2000) (denied motion to obtain defense witnesses for a hearing on admissibility); *Georgia v. McGee,* No. 99-CR-277 (Superior Court

of Carroll County, Oct. 27, 2000) (taking "judicial notice of the fact that the fingerprints of each human being are different from those of any other human being and that said individual fingerprints are permanent and that they are not altered by the passing of time or by degenerative physical disorder or traumatic event; That the fingerprint identification of individuals has been accepted as accurate by all state and Federal courts of the United States as well as by the courts throughout the entire world for at least the past 80 years . . . ."); *People v. Ake,* No. CM14979 (Superior Court of Butte County, California, May 7, 2001) (holding that *Frye*, not *Daubert*, controls in California, that *Frye* limits only new or novel scientific evidence and that fingerprinting is not new).

[8]*Barber v. State*, 952 So. 2d 393 (Ala. Crim. App. 2005), cert. denied, (Sept. 22, 2006) and cert. denied, 127 S. Ct. 1875, 167 L. Ed. 2d 366 (U.S. 2007).

at length from the opinion in *United States v. Crisp*.[9] Other courts found that fingerprint examination is a science, is subject to *Daubert* analysis, that it clears the bar because the theory on which it is based had been tested, has been subjected to substantial peer review and publication, and has an extremely low error rate - all found without citing, much less reviewing, any studies concerning the empirical propositions.[10]

Paradoxically, what appear-from the perspective of applying *Daubert* meaningfully-to be some of the most poorly reasoned opinions are held up as models of sound reasoning by some state courts.[11] Or no analysis at all.[12]

Most often, however, counsel fails to challenge the admissibility of the government's evidence at trial, and therefore has no issue to raise on appeal, though some tried in vain to do so.[13]

The states, too, have their exceptional cases. *People v. Ballard*,[14] was an appeal claiming ineffective assistance for the failure of trial counsel to object to the testimony of the government's fingerprint expert. The expert testified that she was 99% certain that the latent fingerprint matched the defendant.[15] The expert indicated that the print had found six points of agreement between the latent and the known, which she matched at 100% each. However, she testified that she prefers to err on the side of caution and therefore requires seven points agreement before she would actually declare of match.[16] Thus, while she could not make an absolute identification, she was 99% sure it was the defendant's print because the match was so good at six points. The court found that there was no scientific foundation laid for the expert's testimony. Specifically, the challenged testimony had no demonstrated basis in an established scientific discipline. Further, the court found, the testimony rested solely on the personal opinion of the expert. Thus the defendant's conviction was reversed and remanded for a new trial.

Another exception is *State v. Hamilton*.[17] The defendant filed a motion to prohibit the introduction of fingerprint evidence. Following a hearing on the issue, the trial court determined that testimony was admissible. The appellate court noted that

---

[9]*U.S. v. Crisp*, 324 F.3d 261, 60 Fed. R. Evid. Serv. 1486 (4th Cir. 2003). See our discussion of Crisp in the preceding section, noting an important and unusual dissent which exposes very weak arguments by the majority.

[10]E.g., *State v. Cole*, 2002 WL 1397452 (Del. Super. Ct. 2002), judgment aff'd, 922 A.2d 364 (Del. 2007). In addition, this court remarked that two indistinguishably similar fingerprints have never been found. But see Cole, More Than Zero: Accounting for Error in Latent Print Identification, 95 J. Crim. L. & Criminology 985 (2005) (summarizing nearly two dozen documented instances of false positive errors in fingerprint practice).

[11]E.g., *State v. Payne*, 2003-Ohio-4891, 2003 WL 22128810 (Ohio Ct. App. 10th Dist. Franklin County 2003), appeal not allowed, 107 Ohio St. 3d 1411, 2005-Ohio-5859, 836 N.E.2d 1230 (2005) (relying on *U.S. v. Havvard*, discussed in the preceding section); *Barber v. State*, 952 So. 2d 393 (Ala. Crim. App. 2005), cert. denied, (Sept. 22, 2006) and cert. denied, 127 S. Ct. 1875, 167 L. Ed. 2d 366 (U.S. 2007) (relying on *U.S. v. Crisp*, discussed in the preceding section).

[12]*State v. Johnson*, 2003-Ohio-3241, 2003 WL 21419631 (Ohio Ct. App. 8th Dist. Cuyahoga

County 2003).

[13]E.g., *People v. Bradshaw*, 2004 WL 516545 (Cal. App. 2d Dist. 2004), unpublished/noncitable, (Mar. 17, 2004); *People v. Gomez*, 2004 WL 161441 (Cal. App. 4th Dist. 2004), unpublished/noncitable, (Jan. 27, 2004); *Peake v. State*, 133 S.W.3d 332 (Tex. App. Amarillo 2004); *Harrison v. State*, 2003 WL 21513618 (Tex. App. Fort Worth 2003); *State v. Drafton*, 2003-Ohio-4821, 2003 WL 22100469 (Ohio Ct. App. 10th Dist. Franklin County 2003).

[14]*People v. Ballard*, 2003 WL 697334 (Mich. Ct. App. 2003), judgment rev'd, 468 Mich. 920, 664 N.W.2d 211 (2003).

[15]This appears to violate the fingerprint examination field's prohibition on "qualified" (non-absolute) identifications. Since the field requires examiners to make all or nothing judgments, anything less than 100% should have been nothing. Our hunch, however, is that this examiner's principal mistake is candor.

[16]This is a matter of the personal preference of the examiner, since the field has no standards regarding any minimum number of points of agreement.

[17]*State v. Hamilton*, 2002-Ohio-1681, 2002 WL 549841 (Ohio Ct. App. 11th Dist. Lake County 2002).

during the hearing, the expert witness testified as to the potential problems with fingerprint evidence, and during trial the expert was cross-examined about error rates in fingerprint analysis. Further, the court noted that the latent print was very small.[18] The evidence was held to be admissible under the *Daubert* standards, and any shortcomings were said to go only to the weight of the evidence.

The defendant in *State v. Quintana*,[19] argued that fingerprint evidence is inherently unreliable and thus inadmissible. Although the appellate court concluded that fingerprint identification is not novel scientific evidence and has long been accepted by courts, the concurrence was more interesting. It notes that fingerprint evidence has never truly been put to any serious testing. While concurring with the decision, the judge suggested that trial courts be directed to instruct juries about the existing weaknesses of fingerprint examination.

A Montana case illustrates how the evaluation of a fairly novel scientific claim is at once both different from and yet very similar to evaluating a claim that has long been assumed true. In this situation as well, we see the difficulty courts are having as they try to follow the unfamiliar mission on which *Daubert* sends them. Montana adopted *Daubert* as its own rule in *State v. Moore*.[20] In *State v. Cline*,[21] an FBI fingerprint expert testified concerning the age of a latent thumb print. The age of the print was essential to the outcome of the case, because it would help a jury choose between competing theories of the case offered by the government and the defense. The defendant appealed, inter alia, on the ground that scientific evidence does not support the witness's claim that the age of a print can be determined. The Montana Supreme Court held that the testimony on the fingerprint's age did satisfy the *Daubert* criteria (or, more precisely, it upheld as not clearly erroneous the trial court's implicit decision that a valid basis existed for making the age determination). The following portions of the court's opinion are relevant to its *Daubert* review. The Montana Supreme Court encountered a number of problems on the way to reaching its decision.

On the issue of whether *Daubert* applies only to novel scientific evidence, the *Cline* court wrote:

> [W]e do not consider fingerprint evidence in general to be novel scientific evidence. However, in the present case the issue is whether it is possible to determine the age of a fingerprint utilizing magnetic powder. We apply the *Daubert* standard to this case because we consider fingerprint aging techniques in this context to be novel scientific evidence. Certainly all scientific expert testimony is not subject to the *Daubert* standard and the *Daubert* test should only be used to determine the admissibility of novel scientific evidence.[22]

This certainly misstates the rule announced in *Daubert*,[23] though it may now be the law of Montana. And it is questionable whether it follows the Montana Supreme Court's own adoption of *Daubert*. If *Daubert* was to be so limited in Montana, there is no Montana case that says so directly, no case that acknowledges that Montana is

---

[18]Raising the question of to what extent the claims made for full prints can be applied to small partial prints.

[19]*State v. Quintana*, 2004 UT App 418, 103 P.3d 168 (Utah Ct. App. 2004), cert. denied, 123 P.3d 815 (Utah 2005).

[20]*State v. Moore*, 268 Mont. 20, 885 P.2d 457 (1994) (abrogated on other grounds by, State v. Gollehon, 274 Mont. 116, 906 P.2d 697 (1995)) and (abrogated on other grounds by, City of Billings v. Bruce, 1998 MT 186, 290 Mont. 148, 965 P.2d 866 (1998)).

[21]*State v. Cline*, 275 Mont. 46, 909 P.2d 1171 (1996).

[22]*State v. Cline*, 275 Mont. 46, 909 P.2d 1171 (1996).

[23]"[W]e do not read the requirements of Rule 702 to apply specially or exclusively to unconventional evidence. Of course, well-established propositions are less likely to be challenged than those that are novel, and they are more handily defended." *Daubert v. Merrell Dow Pharmaceuticals, Inc.*, 509 U.S. 579, 593, 113 S. Ct. 2786, 125 L. Ed. 2d 469, 27 U.S.P.Q.2d 1200, Prod. Liab. Rep. (CCH) P 13494, 37 Fed. R. Evid. Serv. 1, 23 Envtl. L. Rep. 20979 (1993).

rejecting this aspect of the United State Supreme Court's view in *Daubert*, and no case that offers any reasons or analysis suggesting why it would make sense to limit *Daubert* gatekeeping in this way. The *Cline* court appears to think that it is bound to this position by its prior adoption of *Daubert*, though there is nothing in *Moore*, and certainly none in *Daubert* itself, supporting such an interpretation.

On the issue of whether *Daubert* is a less or a more liberal test than *Frye*, the *Cline* court stated:

> When we adopted the *Daubert* test in *Moore*, we specifically noted the continuing vitality of *Barmeyer* as that case pertained to the scientific evidence. In *Barmeyer* we held that "it is better to admit relevant scientific evidence in the same manner as other expert testimony and allow its weight to be attacked by cross-examination and refutation."[24] In *Barmeyer*, we rejected the "general acceptance" test, holding that it was not in conformity with the spirit of the new rules of evidence.[25]
>
> In *Daubert*, the United States Supreme Court also rejected the "general acceptance" standard in favor of the more liberal test embodied in Rule 702, Fed. R. Evid.[26]
>
> We noted that Rule 702, Fed. R. Evid., still requires the district court to screen such evidence to ensure that any and all scientific testimony or evidence admitted is not only relevant, but reliable.[27]
>
> In adopting the *Daubert* test, we concluded that "before a trial court admits scientific expert testimony, there must be a preliminary showing that the expert's opinion is premised on a reliable methodology."[28]

An important tension exists not only among these statements, but within *Daubert* itself. *Daubert*'s holding that Fed. R. Evid. 702 requires the testimony of a scientific expert witness to be grounded on a sound scientific basis cannot co-exist with the notion that the Federal Rules necessarily set a lower threshold than *Frye* would. Taking the scientific issue in the present case, suppose it were generally accepted among fingerprint examiners that they could reckon the age of a fingerprint but that the empirical research testing their ability to do so did not support that contention, or showed that they could not. The former fact would win admission for the testimony under *Frye*, but the latter fact would lead to its exclusion under *Daubert*.

On the merits of the issue whether fingerprint experts can reckon the age of latent fingerprints, the *Cline* court held:

> In this case, the State established the necessary foundation regarding the issue of determining the age of fingerprints. [The expert witness] referenced and quoted a number of scientific treatises on fingerprint technology. The treatises established that while the age of a latent print cannot be established with complete accuracy, experienced examiners can proffer an opinion regarding the age of a latent print based on the examiner's experience and investigation. The District Court, although not applying the *Daubert* criteria, correctly found that this was an area where experts could disagree,

---

[24]*Barmeyer v. Montana Power Co.*, 202 Mont. 185, 657 P.2d 594, 598 (1983) (overruled by, Martel v. Montana Power Co., 231 Mont. 96, 752 P.2d 140 (1988)) (quoting *U.S. v. Baller*, 519 F.2d 463, 466 (4th Cir. 1975)).

[25]*State v. Cline*, 275 Mont. 46, 909 P.2d 1171 (1996) (quoting *State v. Moore*, 268 Mont. 20, 885 P.2d 457 (1994) (abrogated on other grounds by, State v. Gollehon, 274 Mont. 116, 906 P.2d 697 (1995)) and (abrogated on other grounds by, City of Billings v. Bruce, 1998 MT 186, 290 Mont. 148, 965 P.2d 866 (1998))).

[26]*State v. Cline*, 275 Mont. 46, 909 P.2d 1171 (1996) (quoting *State v. Moore*, 268 Mont. 20, 885 P.2d 457 (1994) (abrogated on other grounds by, State v. Gollehon, 274 Mont. 116, 906 P.2d 697 (1995)) and (abrogated on other grounds by, City

of Billings v. Bruce, 1998 MT 186, 290 Mont. 148, 965 P.2d 866 (1998))).

[27]*State v. Cline*, 275 Mont. 46, 909 P.2d 1171 (1996) (quoting *State v. Moore*, 268 Mont. 20, 885 P.2d 457 (1994) (abrogated on other grounds by, State v. Gollehon, 274 Mont. 116, 906 P.2d 697 (1995)) and (abrogated on other grounds by, City of Billings v. Bruce, 1998 MT 186, 290 Mont. 148, 965 P.2d 866 (1998))).

[28]*State v. Cline*, 275 Mont. 46, 909 P.2d 1171 (1996) (quoting *State v. Moore*, 268 Mont. 20, 885 P.2d 457 (1994) (abrogated on other grounds by, State v. Gollehon, 274 Mont. 116, 906 P.2d 697 (1995)) and (abrogated on other grounds by, City of Billings v. Bruce, 1998 MT 186, 290 Mont. 148, 965 P.2d 866 (1998))).

that the testimony would be subject to cross-examination, and that the credibility of the witnesses and the weight of their testimony should be for the jury to decide, not the court.

How accurate fingerprint examiners are in their estimation of the age of a print, and whether that accuracy is within the tolerances required by a court, would seem to be a relatively easy inquiry to frame. But the answer to that question cannot be discerned from the court's opinion. The expert's testimony, to the extent it is reflected in the opinion[29] supplies no answer, and the court cites none of the studies to which it alluded. Whether or not the data alluded to—in which the witness "referenced and quoted a number of scientific treatises on fingerprint technology"— adequately supported the claims of asserted expertise is the critical inquiry under *Daubert*. There is, of course, a world of difference between someone asserting something in a treatise and that assertion being a conclusion based on sound empirical evidence. Had the Montana court's opinion summarized the relevant data, or at least cited the relevant studies, it would have been far more persuasive, as well as more helpful to other courts that may face the same issue. As it stands, the opinion has the ring of considerable equivocalness.[30]

The opinion mentions that an affidavit supporting the defense contention that the age of latent prints cannot be determined with sufficient accuracy was provided by Professor Andre Moenssens[31] in support of a defense motion for a new trial. Similarly, the present chapter suggests that divining the age of a fingerprint is "not generally possible, although some indications may be provided in extreme cases . . . ."[32] One article reviewing studies of the question concludes that the dating of a fingerprint is largely a speculative endeavor.[33] Thus, there is at least a serious difference of opinion in the expert community.[34] The need for an open-eyed examination of the actual data would seem to be essential. This case should make it apparent why it behooves a court to state the basis for its opinion with more documentation and thoughtfulness than is found in the this case.

All of the post-*Daubert* cases thus far remain foreshadowing. One day a thoughtful challenge to fingerprint identification will be met with a thoughtful defense of it in front of a thoughtful judge, and a thoughtful opinion will issue. That opinion will be extremely interesting, because *Daubert* and fingerprinting are somewhat like the mythical collision between an irresistible force (*Daubert/Kumho*) and an immovable object (belief in the infallibility of fingerprint identification).[35]

---

[29]"I think this is a fresh latent print probably about a month or two old. But, again, there is leeway either way." *State v. Cline*, 275 Mont. 46, 909 P.2d 1171 (1996).

[30]" . . . cannot be established with complete accuracy . . . [but] . . . examiners can proffer an opinion . . . an area where experts could disagree . . . ." That one "can" venture an opinion says nothing about the reliability versus speculativeness of the opinion.

[31]Prof. Moenssens is a former fingerprint examiner, now a professor of law and the director of a forensic science institute at the University of Missouri at Kansas City, and the author of Fingerprints and the Law (1969), Fingerprint Techniques (1971), and co-author of Scientific Evidence in Civil and Criminal Cases (4th ed., 1995).

[32]§ 3:42. If certain rare circumstances do permit a reliable estimate, did those conditions exist in this case at bar? *Kumho Tire* and logic would require such consideration.

[33]See materials cited § 3:42, especially Midkiff, Lifetime of a Latent Print: How Long? Can You Tell? 43 J. Forensic Identification 386 (1993).

[34]And possibly no difference of opinion. Are there data on only one side of this question and a testifying expert too eager to help "his side" win its case, or data pointing in different directions which support different conclusions?

[35]At the end of the day, the most defensible position is likely to be that there is considerable probative value in fingerprint comparisons, but that the field has cultivated an illusion of infallibility that is unsupported by available data and theory. The courts might come to require fingerprint expert witnesses to bring their claims into closer alignment with what is actually known and not known, so that juries have a chance to more accurately assess the probative value of the evi-

## § 3:20    Erroneous identifications

A discussion of erroneous identifications belongs in the "Scientific Status" part of this chapter as much as it belongs in the "Legal Issues" part. Its placement here reflects the special importance of errors found in actual cases (in addition to explicit testing of examiner accuracy in other contexts). By placing at the very end of the "Legal Issues" section, it might serve as a bridge between the legal and the scientific issues.

Numerous courts have asserted that no two fingerprints have ever been found to be indistinguishably alike or that no errors have ever been found to have been made by fingerprint examiners. Such is certainly not the actual state of affairs. Simon Cole has assembled a collection of nearly two dozen documented instances of false positive errors by fingerprint experts.[1] In addition, errors are regularly made in proficiency testing, even though most fingerprint proficiency testing presents easy problems.[2]

Although examiners argue that all errors reside not in the theory of uniqueness or the ACE-V procedures, but with the incompetence of particular examiners, where the procedure consists of the subjective judgment of an examiner it is impossible to separate one source of error from the other. Nor should its source matter to a gatekeeper or fact finder: whatever the source of the risk of error it needs to be recognized and considered.

Cole's earlier[3] review of the history and development of the field of fingerprint identification suggests that a major device for shielding the field's remarkable claims[4] from scrutiny has been to attribute all errors to the human who performed the examination leading to the erroneous conclusion—that is, to argue that the principles are flawless and that errors occur only when the principles are improperly applied. Those examiners serve as lightning rods and are sacrificed to protect the field's claims and all other practitioners. The result is that errors flare briefly and then disappear. The field is spared from having to take account of and make accommodation for any inherent limitations that might exist. Evidence of the success of the stratagem is that most people continue to believe that, in the realm of fingerprint identification, errors simply do not occur.

One recent erroneous identification seems a proper occasion for blaming bad-apple examiners. Early in 2004 in Boston, after serving six-and-a-half years of a 30-45 years sentence for the nonfatal shooting of a police officer, Stephan Cowans was exonerated by DNA. The principal evidence against him in the original trial was a latent fingerprint said by two Boston Police Department fingerprint examiners to belong to Cowans. After the DNA results became known, a re-examination of the original prints also led to the conclusion that the prints did not belong to Cowans.[5] Indeed, the difference between the latent print and Cowans's "wasn't even close."[6] "This was no simple mistake," said the Commonwealth's Attorney General after a four month investigation into the misidentification.[7] According to a news account, "[T]he investigation . . . failed to come up with a plausible explanation for

---

dence and not be overwhelmed by a fingerprint examiner's "aura of infallibility."

**[Section 3:20]**

[1]Cole, More Than Zero: Accounting for Error in Latent Print Identification, 95 J. Crim. L. & Criminology 985 (2005).

[2]*U.S. v. Llera Plaza*, 188 F. Supp. 2d 549, 58 Fed. R. Evid. Serv. 1 (E.D. Pa. 2002).

[3]Simon Cole, Suspect Identities: A History Of Fingerprinting and Criminal Identification (2001).

[4]E.g., absolute identification to the exclusion of all others in the world, and an error rate of zero.

[5]Jonathan Saltzman and Mac Daniel, Man Freed in 1997 Shooting of Officer, Boston Globe (January 24, 2004).

[6]Ralph Ranalli, Reilly Won't Charge Two Police Analysts, Boston Globe (June 25, 2004).

[7]Ralph Ranalli, Reilly Won't Charge Two Police Analysts, Boston Globe (June 25, 2004).

how the misidentification could have been an innocent error." Attorney General "Reilly declined to say whether he believed Cowans was purposely framed, but said that none of the independent fingerprint experts who reviewed the case—including experts from the FBI—could conceive of how the two prints could have been mistaken for one another."[8]

This case illustrates the difficulty of protecting against deception and fraud by forensic science examiners. Typically, everything known about the evidence is known only to the examiner, who might see an exclusion but call it inconclusive or even an identification. The court is generally stuck with whatever "opinion" the examiner chooses to offer. Fabricated fingerprint evidence is not unusual,[9] and post mortems of DNA exoneration cases suggest that forensic science expert witnesses lead all other categories of witnesses in offering deceitful testimony to courts.[10] They perjure themselves, presumably, because they think the right suspect is in hand, even though the evidence with which they are concerned does not support that conclusion, or they are pressured to "help" make the case, and because they usually can get away with it.[11] That is the first lesson offered by these cases.

Far more interesting—and arguably more troubling because it presumably is far more widespread—than outright fraud is the problem of "observer effects."[12] Forensic examiners sometimes know about other inculpatory evidence, and such extraneous knowledge operates below the level of their awareness to skew their perceptions and inferences about whether or not questioned and known prints come from the same person.

Although the problem of non-blind examinations is more widespread in the forensic sciences and not merely a problem of fingerprint examination, the best research on it has been conducted on fingerprint examiners. Dror et al.[13] presented five experienced British fingerprint examiners with pairs of latent and known prints. Each examiner was given a pair that he or she had positively identified five years earlier "as a clear and definite match." But on this viewing, Dror et al. told each examiner that these were, instead, the latent and file prints which the FBI had famously misidentified in the Madrid train bombing case. Each examiner was asked to set aside that fact, and to examine the prints and reach his own conclusion using his own expertise. The results were that only one of the five examiners reached the

---

[8]Ralph Ranalli, Reilly Won't Charge Two Police Analysts, Boston Globe (June 25, 2004). See also Franci Richardson, O'Toole Eyes Penalty vs. Print Technician, Boston Herald (June 25, 2004) ("'Clearly a grave injustice has occurred that highlights the low standards and lack of professionalism that cost a man 6 1/2 years of his life,' said Suffolk District Attorney Dan Conley.")

[9]See Giannelli, The Abuse of Scientific Evidence in Criminal Cases: The Need for Independent Crime Laboratories, 4 Va. J. Soc. Pol'y & L. 439 (1997).

[10]Saks and Koehler, The Coming Paradigm Shift in Forensic Identification Science, 309 Science 892 (2005).

[11]To say that forensic scientists are tempted to distort evidence, and that they lie more often than any other type of witness, is of course not to say that most or even many forensic scientists do so, or that those who do it do it often. How many lie and how often is obviously a question which is next to impossible to answer. But see Moenssens, Novel Scientific Evidence in Civil and Criminal Cases: Some Words of Caution, 84 J. Crim. L. &

Criminology 1 (1993). Professor Moenssens, himself a former forensic scientist, has written that forensic science experts are often tempted "to fabricate or to exaggerate" results. Moenssens, Novel Scientific Evidence in Civil and Criminal Cases: Some Words of Caution, 84 J. Crim. L. & Criminology 17 (1993). According to Professor Moenssens, all forensic science "experts are tempted, many times in their careers, to report positive results when their inquiries come up inconclusive, or indeed to report a negative result as positive . . . ."

[12]Risinger et al., The Daubert/Kumho Implications of Observer Effects in Forensic Science: Hidden Problems of Expectation and Suggestion, 90 U. Cal. L. Rev. 1 (2002); Saks et al., Context Effects in Forensic Science: A Review and Application of the Science of Science to Crime Laboratory Practice in the United States, 43 Science & Justice 77 (2003).

[13]Dror et al., Contextual Information Renders Experts Vulnerable to Making Erroneous Identifications, 156 Forensic Sci. Int'l 74 (2006).

same conclusion that he had originally.[14] In a followup study, Dror and David Charlton[15] again re-presented latent prints to the same latent fingerprint experts who had examined them earlier and at that time concluded that they were or were not identified with a suspect's file prints. In all, six examiners were presented with 48 pairs of prints. This time, half of the latent prints had previously been judged as identifications and the other half as exclusions. In half of the identifications the context information suggested exclusion and in half of the exclusions the context information suggested identification; the rest were control cases in which no contextual information was provided. Two-thirds of examiners changed at least one of their opinions; changes from identification to exclusion were more frequent than the other way around; some reversals occurred even when in the control conditions (where there was no context information given in either direction).

Where the evidence is ambiguous because the latent is a small fragment or of poor quality, or because several candidate owners of the latent print have corresponding regions on their prints that are very similar to each other, the examiner will tend to see what she hopes or expects to see. This phenomenon may have something to do with the recent case of Brandon Mayfield, an Oregon attorney erroneously identified by three FBI fingerprint examiners as the person whose partial fingerprint was on a bag found in Madrid which contained explosive detonators.[16] The bag was found pursuant to the investigation that followed the March 11, 2004, terrorist bombings of trains in Spain which killed nearly 200 people and injured 2,000.

Spanish investigators initially were unable to match the print, and sent it to the FBI for help. FBI personnel searched their 44 million person database and concluded that the fingerprint came from Mayfield. The FBI called the identification "absolutely incontrovertible," a "100 percent match." After their own tests, however, Spanish officials, told the Americans that Mayfield's print was "conclusively negative." That is lesson number two. Notwithstanding rhetoric to the contrary, disagreements can occur, and one of those interlocutors is in error.

A third lesson is that experts tend to become excessively zealous advocates for their conclusions, however honestly and sincerely that initial (erroneous) conclusion had been arrived at. "Carlos Corrales, a commissioner of the Spanish National Police's science division, said he was also struck by the FBI's intense focus on Mr. Mayfield. 'It seemed as though they had something against him,' Mr. Corrales said, 'and they wanted to involve us.'" Even after the Spanish showed the FBI discrepancies that should have been seen to exclude Mayfield, the FBI continued to insist for five more weeks that their own identification was correct. The FBI "called us constantly," said Mr. Corrales. "They kept pressing us."[17]

Relatedly—lesson four—although fingerprint examiners, like other forensic identification scientists, will say that a single unexplained difference between a questioned and a known will result in the decision that an identification is lacking, the wiggle word in that doctrine is "unexplained." The ability to explain away unwelcome differences is limited only by the imagination of the examiner.

> The Spanish officials said their American counterparts relentlessly pressed their case anyway, explaining away stark proof of a flawed link—including what the Spanish described as tell-tale forensic signs—and seemingly refusing to accept the notion that they were mistaken. "They had a justification for everything," said Pedro Luis Melida

---

[14]Three now declared the prints to be from different persons, and a fourth declared himself unable to reach a conclusion.

[15]Dror and Charlton, Why are Experts Prone to Error?, Why experts make errors, 56 J. Forensic Identification 600 (2006).

[16]Sarah Kershaw, Spain and U.S. at Odds on Mistaken Terror Arrest, New York Times (June 5, 2004).

[17]Sarah Kershaw, Spain and U.S. at Odds on Mistaken Terror Arrest, New York Times (June 5, 2004).

Lledo, head of the fingerprint unit for the Spanish National Police, whose team analyzed the prints in question and met with the Americans on April 21. "But I just couldn't see it."

[It's as if] "You're trying to match a woman's face to a picture," he said. But you see that woman has a mole, and the face in the picture doesn't. Well, maybe it's covered up with make-up, you say. O.K., but the woman has straight hair and it's curly in the picture. Maybe the woman in the picture had a permanent?"

The Americans eventually agreed with the Spanish that the print belonged to Ouhnane Daoud, an Algerian. But not until after an utterly innocent person had been taken into custody, told he was being investigated for a crime punishable by death, and jailed for two weeks.[18]

Background investigation of Mayfield had uncovered these facts: He was a Muslim convert. His wife was Egyptian. He had once visited Egypt. He had once represented in a child custody case a Portland man who was also a terrorism defendant. Records showed a "telephonic contact" on 11 September 2002 between Mayfield's home and a phone number assigned to Pete Seda, the director of a local Islamic charity, who is on a federal terrorism watch list. Mayfield's law firm was advertised in a "Muslim yellow page directory," which was produced by a man who had business dealings with Osama bin Laden's former personal secretary. He had visited a mosque that was under suspicion. In Mayfeld's home, FBI agents found a .22-caliber handgun and a .22-caliber rifle, his Koran, and what the agents described as "miscellaneous Spanish documents" (which turned out to be homework belonging to Mr. Mayfield's children).

If some of these facts had been gathered while the fingerprint examiners were comparing the latent print from Spain with the several suspects typically selected by the AFIS system for human fingerprint examiners to sort out, and if the examiners had learned of those facts, that knowledge could have contributed to the perception that Mayfield's prints were the ones that "matched" best.[19] If the examiners learned the facts after reaching their initial conclusions, that knowledge would have inflated their confidence that they had made a correct identification, much as eyewitnesses have their confidence raised by identification-irrelevant facts they learn of after making their identifications,[20] making them more resistant to recognizing their error.

A special review committee was convened by the FBI to study its error, and it concluded that:

> The power of the [computer aided selection of a candidate print], coupled with the inherent pressure of working on an extremely high profile case, was thought to have influenced the examiner's initial judgment and subsequent examination. This influence was recognized as confirmation bias (or context effect) and describes the mind-set in which the expectations with which people approach a task of observation will affect their perceptions and interpretations of what they observe.[21]

The report went on to explain that, the already heightened expectation of an

---

[18]But for the insistence of the Spanish authorities that Mayfield was not the source of the latent print, the FBI's confident but erroneous "identification" could have been strong evidence against Mayfield in a trial for participation in terrorism.

[19]FBI officials insisted that the fingerprint examiners initially knew nothing about Mayfield's background. As noted in Risinger et al., blind evidence lineups would prevent fraud as well as the inadvertent influence.

[20]Technical Working Group for Eyewitness

Evidence, United States Dep't of Justice, Eyewitness Evidence: A Guide for Law Enforcement (1999).

[21]Stacey, Report on the Erroneous Fingerprint Individualization in the Madrid Train Bombing Case, 54 J. Forensic Identification 706 (2004) (alluding to, but not explicitly citing, Risinger et al., The Daubert/Kumho Implications of Observer Effects in Forensic Science: Hidden Problems of Expectation and Suggestion, 90 U. Cal. L. Rev. 1 (2002); Saks et al., Context Effects in Forensic Science: A Review and Application of the Science of Science to Crime Laboratory Practice in the

identification was reinforced by finding a small number of matching points of comparison, which in turn caused the examiner to mistakenly interpret other points of comparison as matching. Once this "mind-set occurred with the initial examiner, the subsequent examinations were tainted. . . . especially because the initial examiner was a highly respected supervisor with many years of experience. . . ."[22] After another examiner was influenced by and agreed with the first, it became virtually impossible for anyone else to reach a contrary conclusion. This, despite the fact that the latent and the file print "were filled with dissimilarities," the effects of expectation and suggestion led all the FBI examiners involved to declare an identification.

The lack of any data on the probability of a coincidental match of fingerprints, or portions of prints, or prints of a given level of quality, makes it harder for examiners to look at a "match" and estimate the number or likelihood of others in the world population who will have similarly good matches to the latent.

And, the final lesson, is that looking for candidate suspects in ever larger databases, while relying exclusively on subjective judgment concerning how much and how good are sufficient to declare an identification, increases the risk of errors of this type.

## II. SCIENTIFIC STATUS
*by David A. Stoney**

### § 3:21 Introductory discussion of the science—The scientific questions

Fingerprints have become synonymous with the concept of absolute identification. They are applied in two ways: to establish personal identity and to prove that an individual touched a surface.

Questions of personal identity typically arise upon arrest or death. The person's fingerprints are taken and compared with previously existing fingerprint records. Historically this process depended on systematic manual classification using detailed codes based on the grosser aspects of the fingerprint patterns. Hard-copy fingerprint records were filed according to these codes building an ordered reference set. Thereafter, questions of personal identity could be addressed by coding a person's fingerprints and searching the fingerprint files under the corresponding codes. This process is now computerized and the traditional codes have been replaced by various image and comparison algorithms. Using either system, after fingerprint records are retrieved a direct manual comparison process is performed by a fingerprint expert to establish identity or exclusion.

Scientific questions related to the use of fingerprints for personal identification are:

(1) How specific are identifications made by comparing fingerprint records?
(2) Do the salient features of fingerprints (as recorded) remain constant throughout life?
(3) How can fingerprint records be stored and retrieved efficiently and reliably?

---

United States, 43 Science & Justice 77 (2003).

[22]Stacey, Report on the Erroneous Fingerprint Individualization in the Madrid Train Bombing Case, 54 J. Forensic Identification 706 (2004).

*Dr. Stoney has a Ph.D. in Forensic Science from the University of California, Berkeley, where he worked on the statistical modeling of fingerprint identifications. He worked for six years at the Institute of Forensic Sciences, Criminalistics Laboratory, in California before joining the faculty of the University of Illinois at Chicago. After serving as Director of Forensic Sciences for eight years he left to become Director of the McCrone Research Institute in Chicago, a not-for-profit corporation dedicated to teaching and research in microscopy and microscopic analysis.

The other application of fingerprints is in the proof that an individual touched a surface. These "latent" fingerprints first must be located on a surface. Often they must be rendered visible by treatment with powders or chemicals. This process is called fingerprint development. Following development of the prints, their location is documented and they are collected, often by physically lifting the print from the surface using tape and placing the tape onto a card. Subsequently the print is compared to fingerprint records of individuals to test for identity of source. Candidate "suspects" for comparison are selected either directly through case investigations, or through computer searching. Regardless of how the candidates for comparison are selected, a manual comparison by a fingerprint expert follows.

Scientific questions regarding fingerprints as proof that an individual touched a surface are:

(1)   What procedures are best to develop fingerprints on what surfaces?
(2)   How should fingerprints be collected and documented?
(3)   Were the fingerprints deposited contemporaneously with the alleged offense? How old are the prints?
(4)   Can fingerprints be forged or planted?
(5)   Does the absence of a person's fingerprints prove non-touching?
(6)   How absolute are identifications that are made by comparing developed fingerprints with fingerprint records?
(7)   What criteria are needed for a fingerprint to have utility other than for identification?
(8)   How can fingerprint records be accessed to select candidates for comparison?
(9)   Are fingerprint comparison practices reliable and/or scientific according to prevailing legal standards?

The questions posed arise in the day-to-day interaction of fingerprint practices, police investigation and the legal process. The depth of scientific study and the relevance to legal issues varies. It is useful to re-group the questions as follows.

## § 3:22   Introductory discussion of the science—The scientific questions— Specificity, constancy and reliability

This issue relates to questions 1, 2, 9, and 12. Questions 1 and 9, concerned with the specificity of fingerprint identifications, are of utmost importance. Question 2, whether fingerprints are a constant attribute throughout life, is necessary to justify the comparison of records taken at different times. These issues are central to both scientists and the law. There is considerable scientific research and experience to address the question of constancy throughout life.[1] The questions of specificity have received surprisingly little scientific attention.[2] There are various reasons for this, including

(1)   the professional practice of rendering an opinion only when it is absolute;
(2)   the history of public and legal acceptance of fingerprint practices;
(3)   the intuitively convincing variation seen in fingerprints; and
(4)   the difficulty of defining the scientific problem sufficiently for systematic study.

Question 12, regarding issues of reliability and scientific status is of direct legal

---

[Section 3:22]

[1]Harold Cummins & Charles Midlo, Finger Prints, Palms and Soles (1943); James F. Cowger, Friction Ridge Skin: Comparison and Identification of Fingerprints 146–149 (1983); Blanka Schaumann & Milton Alter, Dermatoglyphics in Medical Disorders 1–12 (1976).

[2]Stoney & Thornton, A Critical Analysis of Quantitative Fingerprint Individuality Models, 31 J. Forensic Sciences 1187 (1986); David A. Stoney, Measurement of Fingerprint Individuality, in Advances in Fingerprint Technology, 2nd Edition (Henry C. Lee & Robert E. Gaensslen eds., 2001).

concern.

## § 3:23 Introductory discussion of the science—The scientific questions— Value of fingerprints other than for identification

This issue relates to Question 10. Circumstances arise where there is legal interest in fingerprints when no identification has been made as, for example, where they could be offered to show that someone *other than the defendant* was present at a crime scene, had handled a document, etc. As such the *exclusionary value* of a fingerprint becomes important. Another circumstance is where the *placement of the fingerprint* in itself has important legal significance. Examples are where the placement of fingerprints allow reconstruction of how a weapon was handled or who was sitting where. Under these conditions, even if an identification is not possible, a fingerprint that *may* be from one or more persons, and *is not or probably is not* from one or more others, may be of probative value. There has been very little scientific consideration of these issues, largely due to the professional practice of rendering opinions only when there is an absolute identification.

## § 3:24 Introductory discussion of the science—The scientific questions— Time of deposition of the fingerprints

This issue relates to Question 6. The value of fingerprints as proof in specific case circumstances often is linked to the question of when the touching occurred or, equivalently, how long the fingerprints have been present on the receiving surface. There are two general approaches to address this: relative or absolute. Relative methods are intuitively suggested by case circumstances when timing can be related to events such as when a surface was cleaned, the breaking of a window, bleeding, or the deposition of additional prints. Absolute determinations are not generally possible, although some indications may be provided in extreme cases by consideration of the fingerprint development method and specific case circumstances.

## § 3:25 Introductory discussion of the science—The scientific questions— Fingerprint development

This issue relates to Questions 4 through 8. Recently the technical procedures of fingerprint development and collection (Questions 4, 5) have received considerable scientific study as new methods for fingerprint visualization have emerged.[1] The legal significance of this research is limited, however, because if a print is found, often it does not matter how, technically, it was recovered. Legal concerns do arise relating to the failure to search properly for fingerprints and the failure to locate (or the possible destruction of) fingerprints that could have produced exonerating evidence. Scientists have essentially restricted their attention to developing protocols for fingerprint development that maximize the possibility and efficiency of recovering prints.

The technical method of fingerprint development also influences the attempt to answer Question 6, how long fingerprints have been on a surface. Scientists have conducted experiments that address some aspects of this question and some, occasionally useful, generalizations can be made. Most of the scientific studies, however, have compared the efficacy of different development methods under controlled conditions. In a particular case the (unknown) contingencies of print deposition and other uncontrolled conditions preclude inferences based on these studies.[2]

---

**[Section 3:25]**

[1]Advances in Fingerprint Technology, 2nd Edition (Henry C. Lee & Robert E. Gaensslen eds., 2001).

[2]Midkiff, Lifetime of a Latent Print How Long? Can You Tell?, 43 J. Forensic Identification

Similarly, the law often is concerned with the possibility of inferring from the absence of fingerprints that no touching occurred (Question 7). There is no scientific basis for such an inference: depending on the condition of the hands and the nature of the contact, no detectable, usable fingerprint necessarily results from touching.

The question of forgery or planting of fingerprints (Question 8) is naturally of concern, both legally and scientifically. Setting aside the intentional falsification of evidence by investigators or laboratory personnel (fingerprint fabrication), the question of prints being planted, transferred or forged to implicate an innocent individual remains. At issue are the possibility of such prints and the detectability of their fraudulent nature during scientific examination. There is little systematic research in these areas, but there is a body of collective experience that has been reviewed recently.[3]

## § 3:26 Introductory discussion of the science—The scientific questions— Storage and retrieval of records

This issue relates to Questions 3 and 11. Although there is considerable scientific and commercial interest in mechanisms for the storage and retrieval of fingerprint records, the legal questions that arise are of very limited scope. Efficiency of the investigative process is affected by these procedures, but the conclusions drawn by the fingerprint examiners are independent of what methods were used to retrieve the stored prints. Recently, in civil actions for false imprisonment, issues have arisen regarding the failure of an electronic computer search to locate the actual offender's fingerprint records. This failure was only recognized years later when a second, supplementary search was conducted.[1]

Having given an overview of the key questions of legal and scientific concern, we will next describe the scientific methods that are used to address these questions. After this background material the specific areas of scientific agreement and disagreement will be discussed.

## § 3:27 Introductory discussion of the science—The scientific methods applied in the research

The first three parts of this section are: Fingerprint Recording and Processing; Fingerprint Filing and Record Retrieval; and Fingerprint Examination, Comparison and Interpretation. Different physical locations and different personnel are often involved in these three aspects of fingerprint work.[1] The next three parts of this section focus on the basis for absolute identification: The Generalized Case for Absolute Identification; Counting Minutiae or Points of Comparison; and Statistical Bases. The final two parts of the section discuss: Professional Rejection of Qualified Identifications; and Uses Other Than for Identification.

Fingerprints are reproductions of the ridged skin surface of the fingers (or palm) resulting from the transfer of oil or other matter to the receiving surface. A typical well-recorded fingerprint is shown in Figure 1.

---

386 (1993). See also materials cited § 3:42.

[3]Wertheim, Detection of Forged and Fabricated Latent Prints, 44 J. Forensic Identification 652 (1994); Wertheim, Integrity Assurance: Policies and Procedures to Prevent Fabrication of Latent Print Evidence, 48 J. Forensic Identification 431 (1998).

**[Section 3:26]**

[1]*Newsome v. James*, 968 F. Supp. 1318 (N.D. Ill. 1997).

**[Section 3:27]**

[1]The material in the first two sections can be found discussed in more detail in Advances in Fingerprint Technology, 2nd Edition (Henry C. Lee & Robert E. Gaensslen eds., 2001); James F. Cowger, Friction Ridge Skin: Comparison and Identification of Fingerprints 146–149 (1983).

Figure 1

Bear in mind that the absence of fingerprints does not necessarily indicate that a person did not touch the item or surface. Depending on the type and condition of the surface, the state of the finger and the manner of contact, prints may or may not be left and, if left, they may or may not be of sufficient clarity and extent to have any useful value.

### § 3:28    Introductory discussion of the science—The scientific methods applied in the research—Fingerprint recording and processing

Fingerprint records of individuals traditionally have been prepared by carefully inking a person's fingers with printing ink and rolling the fingers onto a standard "10-print" card. Direct electronic recording of fingerprints increasingly is used.

Latent fingerprints are discovered at crime scenes by various methods. Technicians may focus on specific areas where relevant fingerprints are likely to be found (such as items known to have been moved during a burglary) or there may be a more general search. The most traditional method to *discover* prints is searching with a flashlight held at a grazing angle to a surface. A modern variation is the use of laser light.

The most traditional processing method to *discover and visualize* fingerprints is dusting with fingerprint powder. Fingerprint powder adheres to the perspiration, oils and extraneous matter that are present on the fingers and that often transfer to surfaces during touching. Powders are most effective on smooth, clean, *non*-porous surfaces such as glass. After the passage of time the oily materials comprising the fingerprint may dry, leading to a poorer adherence of the powder.

Prints developed by powder may be photographed, but they are often *lifted* using tape, without prior photography. The tape is pressed onto the print and the surrounding surface. It is then pulled off, taking the powder with it. Powder adheres not only from the print, but from the background surface, often recording surface details such as scratching, printing or rain spots. The tape lift is transferred to a glossy card. Areas on the cards are provided for a technician's notes and sketch.

Another frequently encountered type of fingerprint development involves fuming. A traditional fuming method uses iodine, which absorbs into the oils present in perspiration and turns a brown color. This color fades with time, so photography is essential. Currently the widely used fuming method is cyanoacrylate or "super-glue" fuming. The fume turns fingerprints white. These prints are permanent and they can then be dusted and lifted for convenience. Super glue fuming is a particularly efficient and versatile processing method. It is applicable to surfaces that create problems for powder methods, such as plastic bags, highly polished surfaces, and textured surfaces.

A third widely used type of fingerprint development involves chemical color reactions. On porous surfaces, notably paper, the chemical *ninhydrin* is often employed, developing purple fingerprints. Ninhydrin will develop very old prints as well as recently deposited ones. Bloody fingerprints can be visualized or enhanced using other chemical methods.

Today there are many alternative chemical treatments, specialized powders and optical enhancing methods. Some may allow subsequent lifting, others can be documented only through photography. These specialized techniques have extended capabilities to recover prints on surfaces that previously had been nearly impossible, such as on adhesive surfaces and between successive layers of overlapping duct tape. Fingerprints may be detectable by one method and undetectable by another. Proper use of the methods involves consideration of the order of application and the type of documentation necessary for each.[1]

The extent of note-taking during fingerprint processing varies considerably. Frequently this is influenced by time constraints. Processing may occur at crime scenes, or alternatively portable items (including automobiles) may be recovered and processed in a laboratory setting. Depending on local policies the personnel involved may be police officers, crime scene technicians, fingerprint technicians or forensic laboratory personnel. Ideally, notes should provide documentation of what areas or items were processed, what processing methods were used, when the processing was done and how many latent lifts were recovered from each item or area. On the fingerprint lifts themselves should be a full description of the print's original location, with a sketch where appropriate.

### § 3:29 Introductory discussion of the science—The scientific methods applied in the research—Fingerprint filing and record retrieval

Traditionally the inked fingerprint cards of individuals have been physically filed according to a code that was developed during the early part of the century. This has been quite effective but has now been almost completely surpassed by computerized methods. Both are in use and small sets of hard copy files are often kept at the police department level.

Manual codes are based on the gross pattern features of fingerprints, rather than the fine detail. A set of grosser observations on each finger yield incredible variety of fingerprint classes and sub-classes when combined. Electronic "codes" vary with the particular proprietary algorithms used by the various computer systems, but much more of the finer detail within a print is used for coding. Inked fingerprint cards can be "read" optically by a computer or direct, live-scanned images can be used for input. Key features of the general pattern and local detail are extracted and serve as the basis for coding. This provides enough information so that prints of individual fingers can be processed efficiently. Optical images of the fingerprints themselves also are stored on most systems.

When *crime scene* prints (in contrast to inked prints) are to be entered into a computerized system they are first individually examined by technicians who prepare the prints for automated input. This step is necessary because latent fingerprints vary considerably in their clarity, contrast and size. A common procedure is for prints to be enlarged and traced. The tracing is then photographically reduced and this tracing, rather than the original print, is optically read by the computer. Alternatively, some systems project the crime scene print onto a screen and the technician interactively indicates the locations and nature of the fingerprint detail.

Once records have been filed (manually or electronically) they may be retrieved by the codes or simply by the name of the person the prints were taken from. In *manual systems* a record typically would be retrieved under two circumstances. The first is where a person's prints have been taken and their identity is to be checked against the previous fingerprint records. The new prints are coded and records with the same code are retrieved for manual comparison. The second circumstance is where prints have been found at a crime scene *and* a particular suspect has been developed through case investigation. The suspect's fingerprint records would then

---

**[Section 3:28]**

[1]Advances in Fingerprint Technology, 2nd Edition (Henry C. Lee & Robert E. Gaensslen eds., 2001); Ribaux et al. "Goldfinger": An Expert Computer System for the Determination of Fingerprint Detection Sequences, 43 J. Forensic Identification 468 (1993); S. A. Hardwick et al., Fingerprints (Dactyloscopy): Sequential Treatment and Enhancement, in Encyclopedia of Forensic Science 877 (J. Siegel et al. eds., 2000); S. K. Branble & J. S. Brennan, Fingerprints (Dactyloscopy): Chemistry of Print Residue, in Encyclopedia of Forensic Science 866 (J. Siegel et al. eds., 2000).

be retrieved to allow comparison with the crime scene prints. A third, more remote, possibility would be a case where an entire set of ten prints was left at a crime scene. These could be coded and this code could then be used to retrieve candidate records. *Notably absent* in the manual system was a method to go directly from single crime scene fingerprints to the selection of candidate ten-print cards from the fingerprint files. *In computerized systems* this additional capability is achieved because single crime scene prints can be entered and records can be searched. Typically the search provides a listing of candidates, ranked by a comparison algorithm. Candidate cards are retrieved (physically or on-line) and direct comparisons are made by a fingerprint examiner. In no sense is the computer doing the ultimate comparison of suspects' and crime scene prints. The process is not the same and the task is not part of the computer's design. Rather, the computer helps in the selection of candidates. The retrieval of records by the computer in no way compromises a later identification, nor does it impart any degree of proof.

Failure to recognize the latter point can be a source of confusion. One example is the view that fingerprint examiners alter or create evidence when they use tracings of crime scene prints, or designate the location and nature of fingerprint details. These practices involve expert judgment and do indeed substitute the expert's interpretation of the fingerprint for the actual evidence. As noted above, however, the search merely retrieves candidates for comparison. The actual comparison is conducted by the fingerprint examiner using the actual fingerprint evidence, not the representations used for computer searching.

## § 3:30    Introductory discussion of the science—The scientific methods applied in the research—Fingerprint examination, comparison and interpretation—Examination of fingerprints

Fingerprint examiners may or may not be involved in fingerprint processing. Often they will receive inked prints taken following arrest along with latent lifts that were processed and collected from crime scenes by others. Certification of Latent Print Examiners is conducted by examination through the International Association for Identification. This is an excellent and well-motivated program.[1]

Fingerprints are examined visually by fingerprint examiners under low power magnifiers (typically 5 to 10X). Photography may be substituted for direct examination under lenses, or may be included as part of the fingerprint development procedure (as, for example, with the use of colored filters to optically enhance a fingerprint).

Fingerprints are reproductions of the ridged skin surface of the fingers and palm. Important features are the overall patterns formed by the ridges and the discontinuities in individual ridges (see Figure 1). The patterns form the basis for the traditional fingerprint classification methods. A fingerprint card, with a person's ten fingerprints, is assigned a detailed filing code based on the ten patterns. Automated coding of fingerprint cards for computerized storage, with modified coding methods, eventually will replace the traditional methods. The legal significance of this change (in most contexts) is negligible.

## § 3:31    Introductory discussion of the science—The scientific methods applied in the research—Fingerprint examination, comparison and interpretation—Comparison of fingerprints

When comparing two fingerprints the patterns of the ridges are used for orienta-

---

[Section 3:30]
[1]International Association for Identification, Secretary of the Latent Print Certification Board, 545 Nixon St., St. Charles, IA 50240.

tion, but the comparison itself is done by noting the relative positions within the pattern where individual ridges branch or terminate. These ridge discontinuities are known as *fingerprint minutiae*. Examiners compare the type of minutiae (forks or ending ridges), their direction (loss or production of a ridge) and their relative position (how many intervening ridges there are between minutiae and how far along the ridges it is from one minutiae to the next). More subtle variations in the ridge form and ridge path are also included in the comparison.

With *latent* fingerprints found on surfaces (as opposed to standard, inked fingerprints) the initial examination addresses the suitability of the print for productive examination. The print is evaluated for clarity and for the amount of detail present. It is common for prints to be graded subjectively (for convenience) into three groups according to their "value" for identification: identifiable, no value, or possible value.

Some prints are unambiguously identifiable. Their clarity and detail are sufficient to meet prevailing standards and, if the person who made the print were found, identification would be forthcoming (barring rather extreme contingencies, such as severe scarring of the person's finger). Other prints may be poorly defined, smudged or fragmented to such a degree that a conclusion of "no value for identification" is justified. Prints of "possible value" for identification are common and the designation is capable of causing confusion when the legal community presses the scientist to decide if a given print is really identifiable or not. When examining a print, some of the detail seen may or may not be from the finger that produced the print. Smudging, dirty surfaces, dirty fingers, and contingencies of fingerprint deposition all contribute to the incomplete transfer of the finger's detail and the introduction of specious or artifactual detail. Some of the actual and artifactual detail is recognizable as such, but there is always a residual set of details that may or may not be actually on the finger that made the print. During the comparison process it may become apparent that what was believed to be an artifact or an indistinct portion of the print does, in fact, correspond to an actual feature of a suspect's fingerprint. Thus, in practice, the designation of possible value often remains until an identification is made. In the extreme, a print originally judged to be of no value for identification may later be identified.

Fingerprint comparison involves juxtaposition of two prints by a variety of possible means. Initially, the overall pattern of the ridges in the crime scene print is examined, together with any small groups of minutiae or particularly characteristic features of the print, such as scars or creases. The goal is to develop an initial search criterion that will allow efficient screening of the candidate reference fingerprints from the inked fingerprint cards, or from the electronic image database. (Formal definition of this criterion is not made, and several different criteria may be tried in difficult cases.) With the criterion in mind the reference fingerprints are considered, one by one, searching for a corresponding set of details. If each of a candidate's ten fingers is rejected then an exclusion results: the latent fingerprint was not made by the fingers represented on the card. If one or more of the candidate's fingers meet the initial search criterion then the comparison continues. Additional minutiae are sought that bear a specific, well-defined relationship to initial ones, expanding the set of corresponding detail. Minutiae must agree in their type, orientation, and relative position. Comparison of relative position includes, in effect, comparing the paths and form of all of the ridges between the two minutiae.

During the comparison process allowance must be made for differences arising from the normal contingencies of printing.[1] In general, the poorer the quality of the print, the greater the extent of these differences. As differences are encountered the question arises of whether these differences are "real," meaning they represent an actual difference in the fingers that made the prints, or "apparent," meaning that they have been introduced by the contingencies associated with the printing or developing process. The term *explainable differences* often is used for differences that may have arisen by these contingent means. The term does *not* mean that the examiner has a specific explanation for why a particular difference exists; rather it means that the difference is of the type commonly seen among prints that have originated from the same finger. An example of this sort is where, due to differences in the amount of ink or finger pressure, ending ridges may appear to be forks or vice versa.

In fingerprint comparison judgments of correspondence and the assessment of differences are wholly subjective: there are no objective criteria for determining when a difference may be explainable or not. The fingerprint examiner's judgment is based on a variety of considerations, including:

- the clarity of the fingerprint
- familiarity with the types of differences that are seen routinely in fingerprints from one individual
- familiarity with how the fingerprint development process may affect the print's appearance
- the presence and nature of other corresponding or discrepant detail in the comparison

## § 3:32    Introductory discussion of the science—The scientific methods applied in the research—Fingerprint examination, comparison and interpretation—Interpretation of fingerprint comparisons

The criteria for absolute identification of an individual through fingerprint comparison are wholly dependent on the professional judgment of a fingerprint examiner.[1] When a fingerprint examiner determines that there is *enough* corresponding detail to warrant the conclusion of absolute identification, then the criteria have been met. Many fingerprint examiners will have a second examiner review their identification, and some laboratories have made this their official policy. The formality and independence of this re-examination process varies. Usually a second examiner will know the result of the first examination, but will be asked to make an equally formal evaluation of the print.

The process of fingerprint examination and comparison has recently been articulated by Ashbaugh[2] and his terminology has gained some acceptance within the fingerprint community. There are four steps to his process, following the acronym ACE-V for Analysis, Comparison, Evaluation and Verification. In the *Analysis* step the poorer quality, latent fingerprint is examined to assess the quality and quantity of detail that is present. This includes evaluation of the clarity of the print, what part of the hand it may have come from, different kinds and levels of detail,

---

[Section 3:31]

[1]David R. Ashbaugh, Quantitative-qualitative Friction Ridge Analysis at 109–136 (1999).

[Section 3:32]

[1]Charles R. Kingston & Paul L. Kirk, Historical Development and Evaluation of the "12 Point Rule" in Fingerprint Identification, 186 Int'l Crim. Police Rev. 62 (1965); James F. Cowger, Friction Ridge Skin: Comparison and Identification of Fingerprints 146–149 (1983); Ashbaugh, The Premises of Friction Ridge Identification, Clarity, and the Identification Process, 44 J. Forensic Identification 499 (1994); Champod, Edmond Locard—Numerical Standards and "Probable" Identifications, 45 J. Forensic Identification 136 (1995).

[2]Ashbaugh, The Premises of Friction Ridge Identification, Clarity, and the Identification Process, 44 J. Forensic Identification 499 (1994).

and distortions arising from numerous causes. In the *Comparison* step the print is compared with a candidate reference print. The *Evaluation* step results in the formation of the examiner's opinion, and the *Verification* step is the re-examination of the prints by a second fingerprint examiner.

## § 3:33 Introductory discussion of the science—The scientific methods applied in the research—The generalized case for absolute identification

The argument for absolute identification begins with the observation of the extreme variability of fingerprint minutiae, even among identical twins. (In addition to overall genetic factors,[1] detail in fingerprints is determined by the highly variable dynamics of fetal hand development.) The extreme variability among fingerprints is readily appreciated if one takes prints from different individuals and an attempt is made to successively find a correspondence of a small group of three, then four, then five minutiae. To illustrate the point, correspondence of three minutiae may well be found when comparing two prints. A correspondence of four minutiae might well be found upon diligent, extended effort when comparing the full set of prints of one individual with those from another person. For a legitimate correspondence of five points between different individuals it might mean searching for weeks among many different individuals. A correspondence of six points might be a lifetime's search. Unfortunately, although there is extensive collective experience among casework examiners,[2] there has been no systematic study such as that described above.

Nonetheless, the fingerprint examiner's opinion of absolute identification is a logical extension of this process, including as its final step a "leap of faith" where, in the critical, experienced (but subjective) judgment of the examiner, it is *inconceivable* that the fingerprint could have come from another person's finger.

Important factors that enter into the professional judgment of an absolute identification are:

(1)   the extent of the print (area and number of minutiae);
(2)   the clarity of the print;
(3)   the presence or absence of dissimilarities; and
(4)   the examiner's training, experience and ethics.

## § 3:34 Introductory discussion of the science—The scientific methods applied in the research—Counting minutiae or points of comparison

The *number* of corresponding minutiae, or "points," is a convenient, somewhat objective feature to use when discussing fingerprint comparisons. For many years the use of the *number of points* has been discussed and debated among the profession, with the key focus being, "Should there be a formally established minimum number of 'points' that is needed for an absolute identification?" and, "If so, what is this number?"[1]

[Section 3:33]

[1]Danuta Z. Loesch, Quantitative Dermatoglyphics (1983).

[2]Andre A. Moenssens, Fingerprint Techniques 262 (1971).

[Section 3:34]

[1]Charles R. Kingston & Paul L. Kirk, Historical Development and Evaluation of the "12 Point Rule" in Fingerprint Identification, 186 Int'l Crim. Police Rev. 62 (1965); Champod, Edmond Locard—Numerical Standards and "Probable" Identifications, 45 J. Forensic Identification 136 (1995); Evett & Williams, A Review Of The Sixteen Points Fingerprint Standard In England And Wales, 46 J. Forensic Identification 49 (1996).

Although the number of points is a convenient summary of a comparison, it is insufficient and incomplete. Lacking are the consideration of: (1) the clarity of the minutiae; (2) the finer details that are present in minutiae, scars, or on the ridges themselves; and (3) allowance for differences in "value" that would account for unusual or special features of minutiae. In the United States these features are subjectively evaluated by fingerprint examiners. After much consideration and debate, there is (explicitly) no minimum number of points necessary for an identification.[2] Many other countries, however, *do* have a minimum point requirement for legal admissibility. In the United Kingdom, for example, there was for about 80 years a standard that required at least 16 points. This practice was discontinued in 2001.[3]

Nonetheless, there is at least historical agreement that twelve corresponding simple ridge characteristics are sufficient to prove identity.[4] In the United States it is generally regarded that six minutiae are too few for absolute identification. Seven or eight generally are regarded as enough, *if they satisfy an experienced examiner*.[5]

More recently questions have arisen regarding whether or not it is appropriate to count minutiae at all. This topic is considered more fully in §§ 3:45 to 3:52 on areas of scientific disagreement.

## § 3:35    Introductory discussion of the science—The scientific methods applied in the research—Statistical bases

From a statistical viewpoint, the scientific foundation for fingerprint individuality is incredibly weak. Beginning with Galton[1] and extending most recently to Champod[2] and to Meagher, Budowle and Zeisig[3] there have been a dozen or so statistical models proposed.[4] These vary considerably in their complexity, but in general there is much speculation and little data. Champod's recent work is the exception, bringing forth the first realistic means to *predict* frequencies of occurrence of specific combinations of ridge minutiae. Scientifically, the next step would be to assess the accuracy of the predictions. No such work currently is being done. Champod's work

---

[2]Champod, Edmond Locard—Numerical Standards and "Probable" Identifications, 45 J. Forensic Identification 136 (1995).

[3]Christophe Champod, Fingerprints (Dactyloscopy): Standard of Proof, in Encyclopedia of Forensic Science 884 (J. Siegel et al. eds., 2000).

[4]Charles R. Kingston & Paul L. Kirk, Historical Development and Evaluation of the "12 Point Rule" in Fingerprint Identification, 186 Int'l Crim. Police Rev. 62 (1965); Champod, Edmond Locard—Numerical Standards and "Probable" Identifications, 45 J. Forensic Identification 136 (1995).

[5]James F. Cowger, Friction Ridge Skin: Comparison and Identification of Fingerprints 146–149 (1983).

**[Section 3:35]**

[1]Francis Galton, Finger Prints 100–113 (1892; reprinted 1965).

[2]Christophe Champod, Reconnaissance Automatique et Analyse Statistique Des Minuties Sur Les Empreintes Digitales (1995) (unpublished Ph.D. dissertation, University of Lausanne, Switzerland); Christoph Champod & Pierre Margot, Computer Assisted Analysis Of Minutiae Occurrences On Fingerprints, in Proceedings of the International Symposium on Fingerprint Detec-

tion and Identification 305 (J. Almog & E. Springer eds., 1996).

[3]S.B. Meagher, B. Budowle & D. Ziesig, 50K vs. 50K Fingerprint Comparison Test (1999) (unpublished study submitted as evidence in *U.S. v. Byron Mitchell*, Crim. No. 96-407 (E.D. Pa., hearing of July 8, 1999)); J. L. Wayman, When Bad Science Leads To Good Law: The Disturbing Irony Of The *Daubert* Hearing In The Case Of U.S. v. Byron C. Mitchell, Biometrics Publications, http://www.engr.sjsu.edu/biometrics/publications_daubert.html; see also discussion in David A. Stoney, Measurement of Fingerprint Individuality, in Advances in Fingerprint Technology, 2nd Edition (Henry C. Lee & Robert E. Gaensslen eds., 2001).

[4]Stoney & Thornton, A Critical Analysis of Quantitative Fingerprint Individuality Models, 31 J. Forensic Sciences 1187 (1986); David A. Stoney, Measurement of Fingerprint Individuality, in Advances in Fingerprint Technology, 2nd Edition (Henry C. Lee & Robert E. Gaensslen eds., 2001). Christophe Champod, Reconnaissance Automatique et Analyse Statistique Des Minuties Sur Les Empreintes Digitales (1995) (unpublished Ph.D. dissertation, University of Lausanne, Switzerland); Harold Cummins & Charles Midlo, Finger Prints, Palms and Soles (1943).

does support *rejection* of simple minutiae counts as a realistic summary of fingerprint individuality. This is because the specific portion of the finger that the print comes from and the specific nature of each minutiae have a highly significant effect on the observed frequencies of occurrence.

## § 3:36 Introductory discussion of the science—The scientific methods applied in the research—Professional rejection of qualified identifications

Fingerprint examiners abhor qualified, "probable," identifications—to the degree that offering such opinions, except under extraordinary conditions (such as being directly ordered to do so by the court), is considered unethical by the profession.[1] In essence, *the profession* refuses *en bloc* to give testimony unless it is absolutely sure of an identification.[2] This remains despite the scientifically obvious continuity between the extremes of *no value* and *absolute identification*. In other countries practices of (legally) excluding fingerprint evidence below a conservatively large "point threshold" establishes essentially the same thing, but in the United States the accepted norm has not been determined by the courts, but rather by independent regulation within the fingerprint profession. (A more complete discussion of this topic appears in sections 3:45 to 3:52 on Areas of Scientific Disagreement.)

## § 3:37 Introductory discussion of the science—The scientific methods applied in the research—Uses other than for identification

Apart from *identification*, fingerprints can have value for two other purposes: *exclusion* and *reconstruction*. Prints have exclusionary value when it can be determined that a specific individual *did not* make them. In general, all identifiable prints also have exclusionary value, but some non-identifiable prints do as well. An example of the latter instance is where a pattern element, such as a (target-shaped) whorl, is present in the crime scene fingerprint and the individual in question lacks this pattern on all of his fingers.[1] Examinations for exclusion are dependent on complete, clear, inked prints from the individual and clear prints from the crime scene. Each possible area on the person's prints must be searched for correspondence with the crime scene print, so if the inked print set is incomplete (lacking, for example, the tips or edges of the fingers), then the examination may be inconclusive.

Exclusion results only when all areas of the person's hands have been searched and rejected. This can be very time consuming. Particular attention is given, therefore, to the overall pattern of the crime scene print, the presence of conspicuous ridge characteristics, or anything that will allow efficient screening of the different areas of the inked prints. When such indications are absent the search may be prohibitively laborious. If one proceeds systematically, however, the examinations often are *possible*. The results may be inconclusive due to the quality of the crime scene prints or reference prints, or due to incomplete reference prints.[2]

Fingerprints also have value for *reconstruction* of a crime inasmuch as they indicate where and what was touched and, from evidence of smearing or deforma-

[Section 3:36]

[1]Ashbaugh, The Premises of Friction Ridge Identification, Clarity, and the Identification Process, 44 J. Forensic Identification 499 (1994); Champod, Edmond Locard—Numerical Standards and "Probable" Identifications, 45 J. Forensic Identification 136 (1995); Champod & Evett, A Probabilistic Approach to Fingerprint Evidence, 51 J. Forensic Identification 101 (2001).

[2]"Absolutely sure," therefore, is really a statement about the examiner's subjective probability judgment.

[Section 3:37]

[1]Andre A. Moenssens, Fingerprint Techniques at 258 (1971).

[2]James F. Cowger, Friction Ridge Skin: Comparison and Identification of Fingerprints at 173–181 (1983).

tion, *how* the touching occurred. The position of a print, along with neighboring prints or smudges, is thus frequently important and requires documentation. This may be in the form of photographs, sketches or written notes. In the absence of sufficiently detailed documentation, a successful determination of the original position often can be made by comparison of the surface detail recorded on the fingerprint lift with the original surface.

Documentation of fingerprint examinations and comparisons has historically been quite limited. Often report forms are used which indicate the items examined, the examinations requested, and the results of the examination. Statements of results typically are limited to the presence or absence of a specific individual's fingerprints, usually, but not always, with reference to the individual latent lift cards. Examiners usually initial the lift cards and inked fingerprint records when identifications have been made, indicating the date and case number along with the person and finger that were identified.

More progressive documentation of fingerprint examinations is beginning to emerge, with some departments requiring a record for each latent print on each lift showing whose prints were compared and the results of each comparison (whether an identification, an exclusion, or an inconclusive or omitted examination).[3]

## § 3:38 Areas of scientific agreement

Most of the material in the sections that follow can be found discussed in more detail in the basic references in the margin.[1] More specific citations are supplied where appropriate.

## § 3:39 Areas of scientific agreement—Constancy of patterns

Fingerprint patterns remain constant throughout life with the exceptions of: (1) distortion of the pattern due to growth; (2) temporary damage to the superficial skin surface; and (3) permanent damage due to scarring of the underlying tissues of the skin.[1] Scarring, once it occurs, generally enhances, rather than detracts from, the individuality of the print. (Scars are permanent, comparatively rare, and originate in a non-systematic way. They have an abrupt appearance within the fingerprint pattern, with a specific dimension, shape and relationship to the surrounding minutiae.)

## § 3:40 Areas of scientific agreement—Sufficiency of identifying details

Comparison of a set of inked fingerprints taken from a person on one occasion with those taken on another provides a certain means of proving or disproving identity. The chance of duplication of this intricate pattern is conceived to be so small that it may be ignored. There is no known instance of failure among many, many attempts.[1] A single well-recorded fingerprint is universally considered to contain more than enough detail for this proof. (For this point of scientific agree-

---

[3]The Illinois State Police, for example, employ a "Fingerprint Matrix" form that documents these aspects of the examination. See also Daher, Documentation of Latent Print Comparisons 50 J. Forensic Identification 119 (2000).

**[Section 3:38]**

[1]James F. Cowger, Friction Ridge Skin: Comparison and Identification of Fingerprints 146–149 (1983); Advances in Fingerprint Technology, 2nd Edition (Henry C. Lee & Robert E. Gaensslen eds., 2001).

**[Section 3:39]**

[1]Harold Cummins & Charles Midlo, Finger Prints, Palms and Soles (1943); James F. Cowger, Friction Ridge Skin: Comparison and Identification of Fingerprints 146–149 (1983); Blanka Schaumann & Milton Alter, Dermatoglyphics in Medical Disorders 1–12 (1976).

**[Section 3:40]**

[1]Federal Bureau of Investigation, The Science of Fingerprints: Classification and Uses (1984), at iii–iv.

ment, we are specifically referring to clearly recorded impressions of large portions of the finger(s), in contrast to the full domain of latent fingerprints where the size and clarity of the detail vary over a considerable range.)

## § 3:41 Areas of scientific agreement—Storage and retrieval

Ten-print fingerprint records can be reliably coded and filed by manual methods so that any possible corresponding records can be retrieved efficiently and reliably checked for correspondence.[1]

Computerized methods that accomplish the same process also are reliable, have greater efficiency and can be applied not only to inked, ten-print records, but also to individual inked fingerprints and to crime scene fingerprints (when the latter are sufficiently clear and extensive).[2]

## § 3:42 Areas of scientific agreement—Crime scene prints

Physical and chemical procedures are well-established that allow for efficient, systematic discovery and recovery of fingerprints from crime scenes or items of evidence.

Fingerprint lifts and photographs almost always reveal sufficient detail regarding the surface where the print was found so that, should the issue arise, the original location of the print can be established by comparison of the lift or photograph with the surface.

Absent extraordinary circumstances, or independent events (such as cleaning), the age of a fingerprint cannot be determined.[1] In general, as prints age, they become more difficult to recover by powder methods. Fingerprints recovered chemically from paper could have been deposited at any time (they could be extremely old or extremely recent).

The absence of fingerprints does not indicate that a person did not touch the item or surface with their exposed fingers. Whether or not fingerprints are left depends on the condition of the surface, the condition of the fingers, and the dynamics of touching.

Fingerprints recovered from crime scenes or items of evidence often contain sufficient detail for absolute identification of the person making the print. Often the existence of sufficient detail, or its absence, is unambiguous. For some prints, however, it may not be possible to determine if the print is identifiable or not (before comparison) because of the ambiguity between artifactual detail in the print and genuine reproduction of the skin surface.

## § 3:43 Areas of scientific agreement—Identification and interpretation

Fingerprints from the same finger vary routinely due to the contingencies of

---

**[Section 3:41]**

[1]James F. Cowger, Friction Ridge Skin: Comparison and Identification of Fingerprints 146–149 (1983).

[2]Advances in Fingerprint Technology, 2nd Edition (Henry C. Lee & Robert E. Gaensslen eds., 2001).

**[Section 3:42]**

[1]Midkiff, Lifetime of a Latent Print How Long? Can You Tell?, 43 J. Forensic Identification 386 (1993); McRoberts & Kuhn, A Review of the Case Report, Determining the Evaporation Rate of Latent Impressions on the Exterior Surfaces of Aluminum Beverage Cans, 42 J. Forensic Identification 213 (1992); the original case report is, Schwabenland, Determining the Evaporation Rate of Latent Impressions on the Exterior Surfaces of Aluminum Beverage Cans, 42 J. Forensic Identification 85 (1992); Sampson & Moffett, Lifetime of a Latent Print on Glazed Ceramic Tile, 44 J. Forensic Identification 379 (1994); Moody, The Development of Fingerprint Impressions on Plastic Bags over Time and under Different Storage Temperatures, 44 J. Forensic Identification 266 (1994).

printing: the amount and type of residue on the fingers, the nature of the receiving surface, and the nature of contact between the finger and the surface. Allowance for this variation is made during fingerprint comparisons and is an essential part of the process. Study of these variations by direct experiment and through casework provides the expertise required to make the necessary allowances.[1]

Counting the number of minutiae is a useful, but incomplete, method of describing the individuality present in a print. Even with this qualification, 16 clear corresponding minutiae are (more than) sufficient for "absolute" identification.

Fingerprints that contain sufficient detail for identification also contain more than sufficient detail for exclusion.

### § 3:44 Areas of scientific agreement—Training, experience and ability of fingerprint examiners

Fingerprint examiners differ in their level of training, experience and ability.[1] This means that for a given fingerprint case examination, a more experienced or more highly skilled examiner may well be convinced of (and report) an absolute identification, whereas less experienced or less skilled examiners may conclude (and report) that they are unable to make an identification.

### § 3:45 Areas of scientific disagreement—The question of standards and the basis for concluding an absolute identification—Criteria range from self-evident to subjective and untested

The criteria for absolute identification in fingerprint work are subjective and ill-defined. They are the product of probabilistic intuitions widely shared among fingerprint examiners, not of scientific research.[1] Outside of the fingerprint profession this is generally unappreciated.

Given the above, it is remarkable that fingerprints are idealized as *the standard* for conclusions of absolute identity. This situation has come about through historical public and legal acceptance of fingerprint practice, combined with the intuitively convincing variation present in fingerprints.[2] Considering this tradition, the successful application of subjective methods, and the inherent difficulties in rendering the process objective, it would be difficult to fault current practices. There is, however, a mixing of scientific, legal and political judgments leading to this conclusion. This can be quite problematic when fingerprints are then held up as the standard to judge performance in other disciplines (notably DNA typing). Fingerprint identifications are a popularly held concept based on subjective criteria and empirically successful practice. They are not the product of conventional scientific experimentation and statistical evaluation.

There is no room for rational debate over the sufficiency of a reasonably complete,

---

[Section 3:43]

[1]See especially David R. Ashbaugh, Quantitative-qualitative Friction Ridge Analysis at 109–136 (1999). See also John Thornton, The One-Dissimilarity Doctrine in Fingerprint Identification, 306 Int'l Crim. Police Rev. 1 (March, 1977); Leo, Distortion versus Dissimilarity 48 J. Forensic Identification 125 (1998).

[Section 3:44]

[1]Wertheim, The Ability Equation, J. Forensic Identification (1996).

[Section 3:45]

[1]See Stoney, What Made Us Ever Think We Could Individualize Using Statistics?, 31 J. Forensic Science Soc'y 197 (1991); James F. Cowger, Friction Ridge Skin: Comparison and Identification of Fingerprints at 146–149 (1983); David A. Stoney, Measurement of Fingerprint Individuality, in Advances in Fingerprint Technology, 2nd Edition (Henry C. Lee & Robert E. Gaensslen eds., 2001).

[2]Simon A. Cole, Witnessing Identification: Latent Fingerprinting Evidence and Expert Knowledge, 28 Social Studies of Science, 687 (1998); Simon A. Cole, What Counts for Identity?: The Historical Origins of the Methodology of Latent Fingerprint Identification, 12 Science in Context 139 (1999).

well recorded, fingerprint for absolute identification. This is based on the intense variability seen in even small areas of prints, together with the observed correspondence of a much larger area, leading to the judgment that it is inconceivable that the fingerprint could have come from another person's finger. *Conceptually*, this subjective judgment is probabilistic: the chance of duplication of this intricate pattern is conceived to be so small that it may be ignored.

As the area of the finger represented or the clarity of the print diminishes, however, there necessarily comes a point where absolute identification is no longer justified on these subjective grounds. Where is this point? There is surprisingly little with which to answer, yet the issue is one that is continually faced within the profession. The criteria for absolute identification are wholly dependent on the subjective professional judgment of a fingerprint examiner. When a fingerprint examiner determines that there is *enough* corresponding detail to warrant the conclusion of absolute identification, then the criteria have been met. Period.[3]

Efforts to assess the individuality of DNA blood typing make an excellent contrast.[4] There has been intense debate over which statistical models are to be applied, and how one should quantify increasingly rare events. To many, the absence of adequate statistical modeling, or the controversy regarding calculations, brings the admissibility of the evidence into question. Woe to fingerprint practice were such criteria applied!

Much of the discussion of fingerprint practices in this and preceding sections may lead the critical reader to the question, "Is there any scientific basis for an absolute identification?" It is important to realize that an absolute identification is an opinion, rather than a conclusion based on scientific research. The functionally equivalent scientific conclusion (as seen in some DNA evidence) would be based on calculations showing that the probability of two different patterns being indistinguishably alike is so small that it asymptotes with zero, and therefore, for practical purposes, is treated as if it were zero. The scientific conclusion, however, must be based on tested probability models. These simply do not exist for fingerprint pattern comparisons.

### § 3:46   Areas of scientific disagreement—The question of standards and the basis for concluding an absolute identification—The absence of suitable measurements creates vague and flexible criteria

Counting corresponding minutiae has been an inherent part of fingerprint comparisons since they were first scientifically studied by Galton.[1] The limitations of a minutiae count have long been recognized and, over the last few decades, the traditional use of a specific threshold number of minutiae has been rejected on the grounds that there is no scientific basis for this practice.[2] Most recently some leading practitioners have denounced and denied the practice of counting minutiae entirely.[3] This view is founded in the fear that if one merely counts minutiae one

---

[3]David R. Ashbaugh, Quantitative-qualitative Friction Ridge Analysis at 103, 144–148 (1999).

[4]Stoney, What Made Us Ever Think We Could Individualize Using Statistics?, 31 J. Forensic Science Soc'y 197 (1991).

**[Section 3:46]**

[1]Francis Galton, Finger Prints 100–113 (1892; reprinted 1965).

[2]Christophe Champod, Fingerprints (Dactyloscopy): Standard of Proof, in Encyclopedia

of Forensic Science 884 (J. Siegel et al. eds., 2000); Ian W. Evett & Ray L. Williams, A Review Of The Sixteen Points Fingerprint Standard In England And Wales, 46 J. Forensic Identification 49 (1996); P. Margot & E. German, Fingerprint Identification Breakout Meeting "Ne'urim Declaration," in Proceedings of the International Symposium on Fingerprint Detection and Identification (J. Almog & E. Springer eds., 1996).

[3]See the excellent discussion by John Thornton, Setting Standards in the Comparison and Identification (May 9, 2000) (transcription of pre-

will be distracted from properly comparing all aspects of the print.[4] Stating the deficiencies of minutiae point counts, however, does not bring one closer to having a suitable replacement measure.

The next place to look for a measurement of the value of a fingerprint comparison would be to the statistical models. As noted earlier, about a dozen models for quantification of fingerprint individuality have been proposed.[5] None of these even approaches theoretical adequacy, however, and none has been subjected to empirical validation. Apart from illustration of the intense variability in fingerprint patterns, and the inability of simple minutiae counts to quantify this variability, these models *occupy no role* in the routine professional practice of fingerprint examination. Indeed, inasmuch as a statistical method would suggest qualified (non-absolute) opinions, the models are rejected on principle by the fingerprint profession.

What, then, are the standards in fingerprint identification practice? Any unbiased, intelligent assessment of fingerprint identification practices today reveals that there are, in reality, no standards. That is, the amount of correspondence in friction ridge detail that is necessary for a conclusion of identity has not been established. There is an even more basic deficiency, however. We have no methodology in place that is capable of *measuring* the amount of correspondence in a fingerprint comparison. And there is a third, corollary deficiency. We have no methodology in place that is capable of measuring the amount of detail that is available in a fingerprint for comparison to another. In summary we cannot:

(1)   measure the amount of detail in a (single) fingerprint that is available to compare;
(2)   measure the amount of detail in correspondence between two fingerprints; or
(3)   objectively interpret the meaning of a given correspondence between two fingerprints.

Controversy exists regarding the first two of the above points. Specifically, it is asserted that the Analysis phase and the Comparison phase[6] of the fingerprint examination process are objective.[7] This assertion is based on the idea that when a specific fingerprint is being considered, that print is constant and whatever characteristics it has are present and unvarying. This is oblique to the issue, confusing alternative usages of the word "objective."[8] Fingerprint examiners may be looking at the same print, but the process of determining how much detail is present and whether that detail corresponds within allowable limits is explicitly subjective. Specifically, there are no objective standards in the Analysis phase regarding the determination of what detail is reliable. Examiners rely, quite appropriately, on their expert assessment of distortions and the contingencies of printing in order to determine what

---

sentation at the 84th Annual Training Conference of the California State Division of International Association for Identification, Laughlin, Nevada), available at http://www.latent-prints. com.

[4]Ed German, http://www.onin.com/fp.

[5]Stoney & Thornton, A Critical Analysis of Quantitative Fingerprint Individuality Models, 31 J. Forensic Sciences 1187 (1986); Christophe Champod, Reconnaissance Automatique Et Analyse Statistique Des Minuties Sur Les Empreintes Digitales (1995) (unpublished Ph.D. dissertation, University of Lausanne, Switzerland); David A. Stoney, Measurement of Fingerprint Individuality, in Advances in Fingerprint Technology, 2nd Edition (Henry C. Lee & Robert E. Gaensslen eds., 2001).

[6]The Analysis, Comparison and Evaluation

steps are discussed at §§ 3:26 to 3:36.

[7]See, for example, David R. Ashbaugh, Quantitative-qualitative Friction Ridge Analysis at 148 (1999); Ed German, http://www.onin.co m/fp; Stephen B. Meagher, testimony at *Daubert* Hearing, U.S. v. Mitchell, Crim. No. 96-407 (E.D.Pa., testimony of July 8, 1999). See also, B. Darymple, Fingerprints (Dactyloscopy): Identification and Classification, in Encyclopedia of Forensic Science 975 (J. Siegel et al. eds., 2000).

[8]For example, David R. Ashbaugh, Quantitative-qualitative Friction Ridge Analysis at 148 (1999), states, "The comparison is objective, others must be capable of seeing the physical attributes one sees. If one feels his or her objectiveness has been compromised due to the consultation, one should ask a third party to carry out the verification."

portions of the print are reliable representations of the detail that is present on the finger that made the print. Similarly, there are no objective standards in the Comparison phase that determine the allowances that can be made for the minor "explainable" discrepancies that are inherent in fingerprints. Again, examiners rely, quite appropriately, on their expert assessment of these discrepancies and based on their training, experience and skill they determine the tolerances that are applied in the Comparison phase.

AFIS computer technology holds promise to provide some objectivity in these areas, but AFIS has been and remains restricted to the task of screening millions of prints and efficiently selecting candidates for fingerprint comparison.[9] Although this is an important, effective and indeed, revolutionary task, the comparison itself is reserved for the individual fingerprint examiner. The examiner applies a personal, subjective criterion that, despite all its historical precedent, legal acceptance and public confidence, is both vague and flexible.

Current practices are supported by legal and professional tradition, empirical success in millions of cases and professional self-regulation. Critical judgment is applied to the comparison examination process and to the rendering of opinions, but there is no justification based on conventional science: no theoretical model, statistics or empirical validation process.

Recognition of the above deficiencies does not mean that the fingerprint practices are discredited, that they have no foundational basis, or that the process is necessarily unreliable. The question of legal reliability is, however, a reasonable one to ask. Legal scrutiny of fingerprints is, after more than 80 years of uncritical public and judicial acceptance, entirely appropriate.

## § 3:47 Areas of scientific disagreement—Questions of standard practices, proficiency testing, self-regulation and empirical validation

One of the most controversial areas of disagreement surrounds the question of whether fingerprint procedures have been empirically validated during their long use. There are a number of related issues and topics including proficiency testing, self-regulation among the fingerprint profession, and the lack of standard practices.

One extreme (but widely held) view is that since no two fingerprints from different individuals have ever been found to be alike, with more than 100 years of experience, the empirical validity of fingerprints is established. This statement is based on the individuality of complete fingerprints and as such is nearly meaningless to the process of latent fingerprint examination. Left out is the reality that fingerprint comparisons involve prints with widely varying quality and quantity of ridge detail, ranging from near-perfect reproductions of a finger's friction ridge skin to blurred smudges that may show no ridge detail at all. The issue is not the finding of two fingerprints that are alike, but rather the finding of prints from two different fingers that can be mistakenly judged to be alike by a fingerprint examination.

Here one runs into a fundamental problem, since neither the education of fingerprint examiners, nor the process of fingerprint examination is standardized. There is a voluntary certification process,[1] which, when linked to hiring practices, serves a gatekeeping function in many jurisdictions. In no practical sense, however, can we consider the performance of fingerprint examiners to be uniform. Fingerprint examiners differ in their level of training, experience and ability, causing differences

---

[9]The one attempt to use AFIS for a fingerprint model resulted in disastrously erroneous results due to biases and deficiencies in the research design. See § 3:35.

**[Section 3:47]**

[1]§ 3:30.

in opinions regarding the same evidence.[2]

In this context, consider the assertion that the fingerprint process has been empirically validated because there have never been prints from two different fingers that have been mistakenly judged to be alike by a fingerprint examiner. This is simply not true. Mistakes have been made in casework[3] and in proficiency tests.[4] These mistakes, however, are subject to dismissal for a variety of reasons, such as:

- the specific examiner making the mistake was unqualified or incompetent
- the materials submitted for examination were incomplete
- a novice was given the proficiency test as a training exercise

In the face of demonstrable error, many in the fingerprint profession would simply explain that such errors would not be made by properly qualified fingerprint examiners. This may be true, but this means that the validation experiment itself is deficient. In effect, because the circumstances of the experiment were not sufficiently controlled, the outcome can be explained away. Similarly, when errors are made in casework (and subsequently discovered), the profession has seen the issue as exclusively one of examiner error, adopting the practice of "sacrificing the examiner" and saving the appearance of infallibility.[5]

In reality the current fingerprint examination processes are inextricably linked with the human examiner and one cannot separate the human error of the examiner (whatever the cause) from the reliability of fingerprint evidence. It has been widely and explicitly asserted that this separation is possible and that therefore fingerprint evidence has a zero error rate.[6]

Another problem with the assertion of empirical validity based on the absence of mistakes is that there is no established mechanism to uncover the mistakes. How would it be established that an error in a fingerprint identification occurred? Unless there is re-examination by a higher authority such mistakes are not uncovered. (Then when they are, as noted above, the error is attributed to a deficient examiner, not to any unreliability in the process.)

For the reasons discussed, we can set aside the experience and asserted infallibility of fingerprint examination practices as a foundation for reliability. What about more specific, objective validation studies of the (subjective) fingerprint practices? Although such tests are feasible, they have not been conducted. In the absence of such controlled, scientific testing, proficiency test results and cases of practitioner error have been cited as evidence to demonstrate the *unreliability* of the process. This evidence is disconcerting, but it in no way amounts to a fair empirical test of fingerprint identification practices. The problem is this: to test a process, the process itself must be defined or regulated in a way that the outcome of the test can be linked back to the process. We have a vague and flexible process in fingerprint identification. It varies with the individual examiner. If any examiner fails a test, this can be attributed to that particular examiner, leaving the process untested. Until we sufficiently define the process, no error rate can be measured and the process cannot be validated.

---

[2]§ 3:44.

[3]For example, *State v. Caldwell*, 322 N.W.2d 574 (Minn. 1982) (holding modified on other grounds by, Ferguson v. State, 645 N.W.2d 437 (Minn. 2002)); Starrs, A Miscue in Fingerprint Identification: Causes and Concerns, 12 J. of Police Sci. & Admin. 287 (1984); For current cases see Ed German, http://www.onin.com/fp.

[4]Grieve, Possession of Truth, 46 J. Forensic Identification 521 (1996); Christophe Champod, Fingerprints (Dactyloscopy): Standard of Proof, in Encyclopedia of Forensic Science at 889 (J. Siegel

et al. eds., 2000).

[5]Simon A. Cole, Witnessing Identification: Latent Fingerprinting Evidence and Expert Knowledge, 28 Social Studies of Science, 687 (1998); Simon A. Cole, What Counts for Identity?: The Historical Origins of the Methodology of Latent Fingerprint Identification, 12 Science in Context 139 (1999).

[6]For example, Bruce Budowle, testifying at *Daubert* hearing in *U.S. v. Mitchell*, Crim. No. 96-407 (E.D.Pa., hearing held July 7–13, 1999).

## § 3:48 Areas of scientific disagreement—The question of opinions of qualified association

As discussed in preceding sections, qualified, "probable" identifications are not accepted as valid, reportable opinions by the fingerprint profession.[1] To any scientist it is nevertheless obvious that between the two extremes of "no value" and "absolute identification" there must be some middle ground. In the absence of a well-defined scientific resolution of this problem (such as credible scientific models to support qualified associations) the fingerprint profession has adopted what amounts to an independent regulatory practice. Once ethically forbidden without exception, qualified identifications now are allowed by the fingerprint profession only under very narrow circumstances. They cannot be offered voluntarily. Suppose, for example, some poor quality fingerprints are found on a cash box at a burglary. Examination shows that the prints are "probably" from one of two defendants. The laboratory or police report would avoid conveying this finding, stating simply that "No identification was made." If called to testify, attorneys representing the other defendant might well press the fingerprint examiner to give the opinion that prints are "probably" from the first defendant. Specific allowance was made in professional ethical codes to avoid the dilemma of a choice among the alternatives of a professional ethics violation (for giving the qualified opinion), perjury (for lying about it), or contempt of court (for refusing to give it). To remain ethical the examiner must essentially offer the opinion under protest and must fully qualify the response as being outside of routine professional practice.

The abhorrence for qualified, "probable" identifications arises from a number of sources. Fundamentally, there is concern that the fact-finder would place undue weight on the evidence. It is argued that when examiners offer only absolute identifications, defendants are given the benefit of the doubt. (For the most part this latter point is true, although in some cases, such as that described above, what is a conservative lack of evidence against one may, of course, be prejudicial to others.) There is also concern that the practice of offering qualified opinions would compromise the popular acceptance of the infallible certainty of fingerprint identifications.[2] Furthermore, the practice would necessarily lead to probability questions such as, "How likely is it that a random person could have made this print?" As discussed above, there are no reasonable data and no scientific model that would allow an answer. Indeed, the practice of refusing even to consider qualified opinions is so uniform that there is no body of professional experience upon which to build.

The final leap-of-faith to absolute identification is thus an essential element of fingerprint practice. If fingerprint identification had an acceptable quantitative basis in theory or empirical validation criteria, then qualified (non-absolute) associations would be a necessary scientific byproduct. Legal admissibility, of course, would be another matter, but at least the scientists would be doing science and leaving standards of admissibility to the courts.

## § 3:49 Areas of scientific disagreement—The question of exclusionary value

There is some limited divergence of opinion over how extensive a fingerprint must

---

**[Section 3:48]**

[1]The material in this section can be found discussed in more detail in Champod, Edmond Locard—Numerical Standards and "Probable" Identifications, 45 J. Forensic Identification 136 (1995) and Champod & Evett, A Probabilistic Approach to Fingerprint Evidence, 51 J. Forensic Identification 101 (2001).

[2]Simon A. Cole, Witnessing Identification: Latent Fingerprinting Evidence and Expert Knowledge, 28 Social Studies of Science, 687 (1998); Simon A. Cole, What Counts for Identity?: The Historical Origins of the Methodology of Latent Fingerprint Identification, 12 Science in Context 139 (1999).

be to have exclusionary value.[1] Some examiners hold closely to the view that for an exclusion to be *possible* a fingerprint *must* be identifiable. This is erroneous. The issues involved are the clarity of the prints, the completeness of the reference prints and the amount of time available to study them. The crime scene prints must be clear enough to be unambiguous in their detail (we must be able to conclude that the absence of certain details means that a person did not make the print). The reference prints from the individual must also show *all* surfaces of the fingers and palms completely (otherwise the missing portions could be the source of the print).[2] An opinion of exclusion results only after all possible areas of the person's hands have been screened for possible correspondence with the print. When a print is unidentifiable (and often when it is identifiable) this can be very time consuming.

Controversy arises from several sources. One is that the time required of the fingerprint examiner is prohibitive, hence the examination is "not possible" as a practical (rather than scientific) matter. Exacerbating this is that, from a prosecution point of view, such an examination often is considered pointless. (From a defense point of view, of course, the existence of *someone else's* fingerprint in a key location may be of considerable importance.) A third source of controversy is that, when a fingerprint is unidentifiable, comparison of a print for exclusion might lead to the discovery of some corresponding detail, but not enough for a conclusive identification. This raises the specter of a *possible* identification, which as discussed above, is outside the scope of routine professional practice. This difficulty is resolved, in accordance with professional practice, by offering the opinion that "I could neither identify nor exclude this print as being made by the subject"—and offering nothing further.

## § 3:50 Areas of scientific disagreement—The possibility of forged or planted fingerprints

The question of forgery or planting of fingerprints is naturally of concern, both legally and scientifically. Setting aside the intentional falsification of evidence by investigators or laboratory personnel, the question of prints being planted, transferred or forged to implicate an innocent individual remains. Scientific debate has centered on whether fingerprint examiners could detect forged prints, if encountered. This discussion, of course, must consider the degree of scrutiny that a print receives during routine examination. The issue is resolved not so much by technical means as by practical considerations. It is extremely impractical to forge a fingerprint and to do so successfully would require an unusual amount of specific knowledge. Fabrication of prints by those having this special knowledge has, however, occasionally occurred.[1]

## § 3:51 Areas of scientific disagreement—Fingerprint documentation and reporting

As mentioned earlier, the extent of note-taking and reporting of fingerprint

---

**[Section 3:49]**

[1]Very little formal treatment of this subject has been made. See, for example, James F. Cowger, Friction Ridge Skin: Comparison and Identification of Fingerprints at 129–131, 173–174 (1983); Andre A. Moenssens, Fingerprints and the Law 115–116 (1969); and Andre A. Moenssens, Fingerprint Techniques at 258 (1971).

[2]These sets of comprehensive inked reference prints are referred to as "major case prints."

See Wertheim, Inked Major Case Prints, 49 J. Forensic Identification 468 (1999).

**[Section 3:50]**

[1]Wertheim, Detection of Forged and Fabricated Latent Prints, 44 J. Forensic Identification 652 (1994); Wertheim, Integrity Assurance: Policies and Procedures to Prevent Fabrication of Latent Print Evidence, 48 J. Forensic Identification 431 (1998); Andre A. Moenssens, Fingerprint Techniques 262 (1971).

processing and comparison varies considerably.[1] Frequently, the notes and reports that are available are insufficient to document fully what was processed, where prints were found, what comparisons were made, and what the results of these comparisons were. Indeed, to some extent, prevailing practices have the effect of hiding this information. Related controversies may arise. These are, for the most part, subject to legal, rather than scientific debate, but some discussion of the science is helpful to appreciate the significance of issues that might otherwise be overemphasized or overlooked.

Available documentation may fail to show the original position of a print with sufficient accuracy to establish the needed proof or to fully explore possible defense arguments. Under these circumstances scientists usually can conduct a comparison of the fingerprint lifts or photographs directly with the original surface in order to acquire the needed information.

Documentation of the results of comparisons is invariably complete with regard to identifications of the suspect. Reports may or may not mention identifications of co-defendants, victims and other individuals; or the presence of any prints that are definitely not the suspect's. Indirectly, there may be reference to the number of identifiable prints, or to prints of value (or possible value) for identification. The existence of these prints may help determine whether it would be worthwhile requesting a re-examination of the fingerprints for exclusions.

Given the prevailing professional practices, very seldom will reports refer to prints that might be from the suspect. (These would be prints where the examiner cannot make a definite conclusion that the print either is or is not from the suspect.) A typical approach would be to report that "no identification of the suspect's prints could be made," a statement that although true, leaves unsaid the actual results of the comparison. (Is there agreement, as far as it goes, with the suspect? Or is there absolute, apparent, or possible exclusion? Or are the prints simply too poor to compare, given time constraints?)

### § 3:52 Areas of scientific disagreement—Omission of fingerprint processing and disposal of latent lifts

Another primarily legal controversy arises regarding the destruction (or possible destruction) of evidence through the omission of fingerprint processing or the disposal of latent fingerprint lifts.[1] There is some scientific input into these issues and, as with the preceding section, it offers some help in defining the legal controversy.

As an example, consider a case where a loaded gun has been found in an automobile glove compartment. An arrest is made and the gun is booked directly into property, without a request for fingerprint processing. The defense later argues that by failing to process the gun for fingerprints and by its subsequent handling, exonerating fingerprint evidence may have been destroyed. Several findings could be construed as exonerating: finding no fingerprints of the suspect, finding someone else's fingerprints, or finding the defendant's fingerprints in some location on the gun (such as the barrel) that would support the suspect's statement regarding its use (e.g., "I was hammering in a stake with the butt when the gun went off accidentally"). Scientifically, the first of these would be specious because the absence

---

**[Section 3:51]**

[1]Andre A. Moenssens, Fingerprint Techniques at 109–112 (1971); James F. Cowger, Friction Ridge Skin: Comparison and Identification of Fingerprints at 85–88 (1983); Richard H. Fox and Carl L. Cunningham, Crime Scene Search and Physical Evidence Handbook 47–59 (1973). See also § 3:37.

**[Section 3:52]**

[1]We have frequently encountered cases where these issues have been of concern to defense counsel. However, we are unaware of any judicial opinions regarding the issue or any written discussion of the issue in the forensic science literature.

of fingerprints would not indicate that a person did not touch an item. The other two findings are a scientifically reasonable basis on which to make the legal argument.

Related arguments can occur regarding the disposal of latent lifts, or latent lifts that have become lost. Suppose a police department submits fingerprints to the laboratory and receives the finding that the prints are of "no value" (meaning no value for identification of the suspect). Subsequently the police department discards the latent lifts or they are lost. There is a scientifically valid argument that exonerating evidence may have been destroyed, as there may have been value for exclusion or reconstruction.

## § 3:53  Future directions

When this chapter was originally written (1996) the future directions were summarized briefly:

> It is unlikely that any significant current research will affect fingerprint practices over the next several years. We can anticipate that additional means of detecting fingerprints and more efficient methods of electronic processing will develop. At the academic level, there is a continuing low-level of effort into the statistical modeling of the variation in fingerprint minutiae. This has been made more feasible by the electronic storage of fingerprint patterns, and eventually models will be developed and tested. Even so, it is unlikely that these models will be readily accepted as a basis for fingerprint identification methodology.

The earlier version also noted that with respect to the scientific basis of fingerprint comparisons that there was

> . . . no prevailing scientific debate on these issues. For such a critically important discipline in forensic science there certainly ought to be. But among fingerprint professionals little point is seen in it. They would argue that the subjective standards used for identification are conservative (based on their historical record), and that there is no need for objective scientific research. The argument would continue that scientific inadequacies in the statistical models render them irrelevant to real-world practice. Since the current practices have a sufficient scientific basis to be both functionally effective and to be legally accepted, where is the impetus for scientific research? Outside the profession there is the unchallenged popular perception that fingerprints are the epitome of individual variation and that they must be individual, so what point is there in debate or study? Even the reality of the issues arising from fingerprints of diminishing size and quality has not disturbed this popular perception.

Happily we can now report that this situation has changed: we have active debate in the scientific, fingerprint practitioner and legal communities. Although the body of the fingerprint profession still sees scientific research on fingerprint individuality as unnecessary,[1] the forensic science community has explicitly recognized the need.[2] More importantly, the legal community has begun to critically examine the scientific status of fingerprint practices. We can now confidently predict significant changes in both the legal perspective on fingerprint evidence and the scientific foundations for fingerprint practices.

These changes will not reveal any startling deficiencies in the capability of fingerprints to absolutely identify individuals. They may not even change much in the way of how fingerprints are examined, compared and interpreted. The changes will nonetheless be fundamental. We will have scientifically valid systems in place to ensure reliability and we will have replaced the naive wholesale acceptance of fingerprint evidence with a critical awareness of the issues necessary for reliable

---

[Section 3:53]

[1]See, e.g., Grieve, Baiting Laws with Stars, 48 J. Forensic Identification 426 (1998).

[2]National Institute of Justice, Forensic Sciences: Review of Status and Needs 28–31 (1999).

proof.

From the scientist's perspective, there are two conceptual routes to this end. One is to approach fingerprint evidence by developing realistic models that will:

(1)  measure the amount of detail in a (single) fingerprint that is available to compare;

(2)  measure the amount of detail in correspondence between two fingerprints; and

(3)  objectively interpret the meaning of a given correspondence between two fingerprints.

These models will have flaws. They will be unable to incorporate all of the fingerprint examiner's expertise, and they will not fully incorporate the finer details that are represented in fingerprints. But they will be testable, and we will have science.

The second conceptual approach is to empirically test the reliability of fingerprint practices as they are currently conducted. A meaningful test will require:

(1)  an a priori definition of the process itself;

(2)  a set of fingerprint examiners of acknowledged, unquestionable, "consensus," expertise to conduct the process in the test; and

(3)  a realistic set of fingerprint test cases, covering a wide range of quality and extensiveness in the prints.

Neither of these approaches is particularly easy, and neither is likely to be cooperatively entered into by the fingerprint profession, but they are feasible and ultimately the issues are of paramount legal importance.

Steps will be necessary to translate the results of either of these approaches into reliable fingerprint practices. If objective measurements follow from the first approach, the methodology used for the examination, comparison and interpretation of fingerprints could be radically changed. This may seem attractive, but I suspect that such a procedural change is unnecessary. It presumes that things are bad, when in fact they are vague and flexible.

Out of the second approach there will be demonstrable reliability of fingerprint identifications when there is some minimal level of detail present in the fingerprints. Narrower, though still subjective, bounds will be placed on the identification criterion. To translate the results of this approach to reliability in the routine professional practice we need a method to ensure that any given fingerprint examiner is operating within the consensus norms that have been validated by experiment. This might follow a certification process, but I suspect that more explicit, ongoing external review is appropriate. This type of review is also appropriate to address the post-conviction issues that are sure to arise. One option is to use the acknowledged (and now tested!) panel of experts to review *any questioned casework, past or present.* If this were done a pattern of three outcomes would develop. Firstly, the work of nearly all fingerprint examiners in nearly all cases would be found to be well within the professional (and now tested) norms. Secondly, some very few cases would be uncovered where, even among the best of the best, there is controversy regarding the sufficiency of the identification. This result will produce professional debate and have the benefit of refining and narrowing the consensus norms. This result will also create interesting legal issues to be resolved. Thirdly, the work of some fingerprint examiners would be found to be either erroneous, fraudulent or outside the consensus norms.

The argument may be encountered that the above system is essentially in place, operating department-by-department, when fingerprint identifications are checked by colleagues or supervisors. This view is incorrect. Two things are missing. First there are no established, tested, normative practices. Second there is no mechanism in place to ensure local adherence to the these practices.

# APPENDIX 3A

# Glossary

***ACE-V.*** An acronym for the four articulated steps in fingerprint examination: Analysis, Comparison, Evaluation and Verification.

***AFIS.*** An acronym for automated fingerprint identification systems. These computerized databases allow retrieval fingerprint records that show electronic codes similar to a crime scene print. The system selects candidates for subsequent manual comparisons by fingerprint experts.

***Analysis.*** The preliminary assessment of the quality and quantity of friction ridge detail present in a friction ridge print. This includes examination of distortions, clarity, availability of detail for comparison, the possible part of the hand from which the print came and any internal indications of unreliability in the print. (As formally defined in the ACE-V fingerprint examination process. See Ashbaugh, Quantitative-Qualitative Friction Ridge Analysis (1999).)

***Anatomical aspects (in fingerprint analysis).*** Determination, based on the consideration of a single print, which finger or what part of the palm that the print came from.

***Bifurcation.*** A synonym for "fork," used to describe the form of a minutae that is present where there is a branching of a ridge.

***Classification of fingerprints.*** The process of assigning codes to fingerprints so that they can be efficiently organized, stored and retrieved. Historically conducted manually using prints from an individual's ten fingers. Now also performed electronically and on single fingerprints.

***Cold search.*** Beginning with a single crime scene print, the process of searching a large database of reference prints for a matching print.

***Comparison.*** The systematic comparison of all available friction ridge detail in the unknown, or latent print, to the detail present in the known, or reference print. (As formally defined in the ACE-V fingerprint examination process. See Ashbaugh supra.)

***Cyanoacrylate fuming.*** A fingerprint visualization technique, also known as super-glue fuming, which uses this chemical and is effective on a wide range of surfaces.

***Deposition distortion.*** Distortions in a print caused by the pressure of deposition, generally resulting in a flattening and broadening of each ridge.

***Development of fingerprints.*** Fingerprint development, or visualization, is the process of rendering invisible prints visible. It may employ optical, chemical or physical methods.

***Development medium distortion.*** Distortions in a print caused by the method used to render the print visible.

***Distortions.*** See Deposition Distortion, Development medium distortion, Matrix distortion, Pressure distortion, Substrate distortion.

***Elimination prints.*** Fingerprints taken for reference purposes from persons (other than the offender) who had access to a crime scene or to items of evidence. Any fingerprints taken as evidence are first compared with the elimination prints to eliminate the possibility that the prints are from these persons.

**Evaluation.** The answering of two questions by the expert: (1) Is there agreement between the latent and reference prints? and (2) Is the agreement sufficient to eliminate all possible donors in the world except this one? (As formally defined in the ACE-V fingerprint examination process. See Ashbaugh supra.)

**Exclusion of fingerprints.** A conclusion that a fingerprint did not come from a specific individual.

**Exclusionary value.** A judgement concerning a fingerprint's suitability for excluding that any particular person could have made it.

**Explainable differences in fingerprints.** Differences of a type routinely occurring among prints made by the same finger.

**Fingerprints.** Reproductions of the ridged skin surface of the fingers (or palm) resulting from the transfer of oil or other matter to a surface.

**First level detail.** General overall friction ridge pattern shape, e.g. circular, looping, arching or straight. (As formally defined in the ACE-V fingerprint examination process. See Ashbaugh supra.)

**Hypothenar.** The portion of the palm along the side between the little finger and the wrist.

**Identification of fingerprints.** The process of assigning the origin of a fingerprint to a specific individual.

**Incipient Ridges.** Fine, underdeveloped ridges that lack pores.

**Interdigital.** The upper portion of the palm at the base of the digits.

**Latent fingerprints.** Fingerprints that are invisible under normal viewing conditions. Latent fingerprints are rendered visible by fingerprint development methods.

**Lift card.** A small card used to hold pieces of tape that have lifted developed fingerprints from their original surface.

**Lifting of fingerprints.** Removal of a fingerprint from its original surface, typically using tape after the print has been dusted with fingerprint powder.

**Major Case Prints.** The result of inking and recording of every existing area of friction ridge skin present on the hands and fingers.

**Magnabrush.** A magnetic fingerprint dusting tool that employs iron filings mixed with fingerprint powder.

**Matrix.** The substance of which the fingerprint is composed, e.g. sweat, oils, blood.

**Matrix distortion.** Distortions resulting from the nature or behavior of the substance of which the fingerprint is composed.

**Minutiae.** The fine structure of fingerprint consisting of the individual branchings and terminations of ridges.

**Ninhydrin.** A chemical used to develop latent fingerprints, especially on paper. Ninhydrin reacts with amino acids in fingerprints producing a reddish purple color.

**Number of points.** The number of minutiae or other details seen in a fingerprint.

**Palmar.** Relating to the palm of the hand.

***Patterns of fingerprints.*** The overall geometry of the ridges in a fingerprint, especially useful for classification and for registration of prints prior to detailed comparison.

***Plantar.*** Relating to the sole of the foot.

***Pointsv.*** Minutiae or other details seen in a fingerprint.

***Powder development of fingerprints.*** A long-standing method of visualizing fingerprints based on the adherence of powder to perspiration, oils or other extraneous matter that has been transferred from the fingers to a surface.

***Pressure distortion.*** A smearing type of distortion caused by horizontal movement of the finger when the print is made.

***Qualified fingerprint identification.*** A less than certain opinion concerning whether a particular person made a fingerprint.

***Radial.*** Toward the thumb side of the hand.

***Second level detail.*** The specific paths of the ridges. This includes the minutiae (or points), but also includes the path of scars, incipient ridges, and flexion creases. (As formally defined in the ACE-V fingerprint examination process. See Ashbaugh supra.)

***Substrate.*** The surface on which the print is found.

***Substrate distortion.*** Distortions introduced due to the nature of the substrate. These can result from flexibility, shape, deformation or surface contamination.

***Super-glue.*** See Cyanoacrylate fuming.

***Ten-print card.*** The card used to record inked reference fingerprints of an individual.

***Thenar.*** The area of the palm nearest the thumb.

***Third level detail.*** The small shapes on the ridge, the relative location of pores, and the small details contained in accidental damage to the friction ridges. (As formally defined in the ACE-V fingerprint examination process. See Ashbaugh supra.)

***Ulnar.*** Toward the little finger part of the hand.

***Verification.*** The peer review by another expert conducted as a quality assurance step. (As formally defined in the ACE-V fingerprint examination process. See Ashbaugh supra.)

# Chapter 4

# Handwriting Identification

*by*

*D. Michael Risinger**

## I. LEGAL ISSUES

## II. SCIENTIFIC STATUS

*Professor of Law, Seton Hall University School of Law; B.A. Magna Cum Laude, Yale University, 1966, J.D. Cum Laude, Harvard Law School, 1969. Portions of this chapter appear in D. Michael Risinger (with Michael J. Saks) Science and Nonscience in the Courts: *Daubert* Meets Handwriting Identification Expertise, 82 Iowa L. Rev. 21 (1996); D. Michael Risinger, Mark P. Denbeaux & Michael J. Saks, Brave New "Post-*Daubert* World"—A Reply to Professor Moenssens, 29 Seton Hall L. Rev. 405 (1998); and D. Michael Risinger, Defining the "Task at Hand": Non-Science Forensic Science after *Kumho Tire v. Carmichael*, 57 Wash. & Lee L. Rev. 767 (2000).

## I. LEGAL ISSUES

### § 4:1 Introductory note

Document examiners do many things. They examine typewriting for signs of idiosyncratic typeface alignment and wear which might indicate a common origin for two documents. This task is a form of toolmark analysis best considered in connection with that chapter. They analyze ink to reveal its physical and chemical properties, a task best considered in connection with the subject of forensic chemistry. In addition, they scrutinize the alignment of printed lines and the overlap of handwritten lines to determine if words or phrases have been after-inserted, and they analyze the composition, method of production, and watermark of paper in order to ascertain probable origin and, in some cases, age. These functions may, in some applications, involve elements of chemistry, but in addition they almost always depend on specialized knowledge of manufacturing processes and manufacturer specifications not unlike that employed in firearms identification concerning the relative number, spacing, pitch and direction of twist, of grooves and lands in various makes of rifled barrels.

All of these functions generally share the strengths and weaknesses otherwise associated with toolmark evidence, forensic chemistry, and the like. They are not, however, what this chapter is about. This chapter concerns the asserted skill that historically formed the foundation of the document examiner's trade, and still comprises a surprisingly high percentage of the everyday work of document examiners both in and out of court.[1] This is the asserted ability to determine the authorship vel non of a piece of handwriting by examining the way in which the letters are inscribed, shaped and joined,[2] and comparing it to exemplars of a putative author's concededly authentic handwriting.

The balance of this section provides a discussion of the history of the courts' response to such asserted expertise.[3]

---

**[Section 4:1]**

[1]For instance, in his January 1993 testimony in *Matter of Extradition of Smyth*, 826 F. Supp. 316 (N.D. Cal. 1993), rev'd on other grounds, 61 F.3d 711 (9th Cir. 1995), opinion amended on other grounds, 73 F.3d 887 (9th Cir. 1995), an international extradition case involving an alleged IRA terrorist, Special Agent Richard M. Williams, an FBI agent questioned a documents examiner with 17 years of experience who testified that "the bulk of" his work dealt with handwriting. Transcript at 231, on file with author. Nearly 90%

of recent reported cases involving questioned document examiners concerned handwriting identification. See §§ 4:4 to 4:9.

[2]That is, by examining the characteristics of what is sometimes called the "static trace" left behind by the dynamic act of writing.

[3]A more extensive review of the legal history of handwriting identification expertise can be found in Risinger, Denbeaux & Saks, Exorcism of Ignorance as a Proxy for Rational Knowledge: The Lessons of Handwriting Identification "Expertise," 137 U. Pa. L. Rev. 731, 751–771 (1989).

## § 4:2  Early legal history

The notion that handwriting can be used to identify its author is very old,[1] as is the notion that a person can learn to make such an identification by study. Attempts to develop a system of such expertise appear to have started in Italy and France in the seventeenth century,[2] and by 1737 were well enough accepted in France to have been incorporated into the law. The Code du Faux (Code Concerning Forgeries) contained detailed provisions for regulating the collection of exemplars and their presentation to handwriting identification experts, which from the context of the code we may conclude formed a professional cadre of fair number.[3] However, no such claimed expertise then existed in the English speaking world. As we shall see, in Anglo-American courts a corps of asserted experts came into existence only after lawyers persuaded the courts to accept the idea that such an expertise might exist.[4]

Experts of any kind did not play a large role in litigation during the common law period, and when they occasionally did testify, they did so without a clearly defined set of legal principles governing their qualifications or their use. It was not until 1782, in the case of *Folkes v. Chadd*,[5] that a reported decision affirmed the propriety of the use of such "skilled witnesses,"[6] although the practice at trial was of course much older. The earliest trial use of skilled witnesses of which we have a record occurred in the trial of the Earl of Pembroke for the murder of Nathaniel Cony in 1678[7] (though it does not appear to have been regarded as a novelty in that case).

Until the very end of the 18th century, every example of expert testimony in the

---

**[Section 4:2]**

[1]Huntington Hartford quotes Aristotle as observing that "[J]ust as all men do not have the same speech sounds, neither do they have the same handwriting." Huntington Hartford, You Are What You Write 43 (1973) (quoting Aristotle, On Interpretation, Part I).

[2]The earliest treatise in this line, of a definite graphological cast, appears to be Camillo Baldi, Trattato Come Da Una Lettera Missiva Si Conoscano La Natura, e Qualità Dello Scrittore (Milano, Geo. Batt Bidelli, 1625) [An Essay on the Means of Examining the Character and Qualities of a Writer from His Letters].

[3]See generally Francois Serpillon, Code du Faux, ou Commentaire sur l'Ordonnance du Juillet, 1737, Avec Une Instruction pour les Experts en Matiere de Faux (Lyon, Gabriel Regnault, 1774).

[4]It appears certainly true that there was no cadre of such experts in England, and that the common law courts were strangers to such expertise. However, the same may not have been true in the ecclesiastical courts. See Philip Floyer, The Proctor's Practice in the Ecclesiastical Courts 103 (Worrall, London, 1744), under the title "Evidence": "Where either party would produce any writing and give it in evidence, it must be exhibited with an allegation, and so proved. The Hand of a party signing may be proved by letters, or other his handwriting, which are to be exhibited by an allegation, and being proved, Proctors or Approved Writers are to be assigned by the Judge to compare the same, who are to give Verdict thereon." This appears to describe more of a

special jury practice than proof by expertise. Proctors were the cadre of practitioners in the Arches courts (which included Admiralty and the Ecclesiastical Courts), but who might qualify to sit as an "Approved Writer" is both fascinating and totally unclear.

[5]*Folkes v. Chadd*, 1783 WL 29, 3 Dougl. 157, 99 Eng.Rep. 589 (K.B. 1782).

[6]In the 18th century the term "skilled witness" covered everyone we would today refer to as an expert. The term seems to have become recently used to refer to practical, as contrasted with scientific, experts. See, e.g., the original Advisory Committee Note to Fed. R. Evid. 702.

[7]The Trial of Philip, Earl of Pembroke and Montgomery, at Westminster, for the Murder of Nathaniel Cony (1678), in 6 Cobbett's Complete Collection of State Trials 1310 (1810). It appears that by the 1640s, surgeons were often, though by no means always, called upon to take part in coroners' inquests. Interestingly, the oldest surviving documentation of the practice currently known appears in the Maryland colonial records. See Helen Brock & Catherine Crawford, Forensic Medicine in Early Colonial Maryland, 1633–1683, in Legal Medicine in History (M. Clark & C. Crawford eds., 1994). In addition to the Earl of Pembroke's case, there were two other *notorious* 17th century trials in which expert testimony was given: The Trial of Robert Green, Henry Berry, and Lawrence Hill, at the Kings-Bench, for the murder of Sir Edmundbury Godfrey (1679), in 7 Cobbett's Complete Collection of State Trials 159 (1810); and The Trial of Spencer Cowper, Ellis Stephens, William Rogers, and John Marson, at Hertford Assizes, for the Murder of Mrs. Sarah

English speaking world involved witnesses whose expertise had primary application to practical affairs outside the courtroom, such as the physicians in the Earl of Pembroke's case or the engineers in *Folkes v. Chadd*. If expertise in general then played a small role in the law, claimed expertise limited to issues that were or might be involved in court cases (what one might call a dominantly forensic expertise), was non-existent. The first such forensic expertise allowed into the courtroom was handwriting identification expertise. Thus, handwriting identification expertise is the oldest "forensic science" although it did not secure a place in the common law courtroom until nearly a century after its introduction into French proceedings.

When handwriting identification expertise finally did enter the common law courtroom, it did so haltingly.[8] In 1792, Lord Kenyon, sitting as a trial judge, allowed two postal inspectors proffered by one of the parties to testify concerning authorship by comparing known exemplars of one party's handwriting to a document whose authorship was at issue in the case.[9] However, the next year Kenyon reversed himself and in two cases held such testimony inadmissible.[10] In the 1802 case of *R. v. Cator*[11] the court held that a postal inspector might give an opinion as to whether a signature was in a "feigned hand" by examination of the signature alone, but could not compare hands. This position was reaffirmed by a divided court in *Doe d. Mudd v. Suckermore*[12] in 1836, and it was not until an 1854 statute was construed to authorize it that handwriting identification expertise became admissible in English courts.[13]

## § 4:3  Admissibility in American jurisdictions

The story in the United States is even more complex. Until the passage of the English statute, most American jurisdictions followed English practice and rejected such expertise. There were some significant exceptions, however. In the 1836 case of *Moody v. Rowell*,[1] Massachusetts became the first common law jurisdiction[2] to authorize the use of such asserted expertise. The rationale of the *Moody* case is telling. Up to that time, in all Anglo-American jurisdictions, handwriting had been formally authenticated as to authorship by the recognition testimony of non-expert witnesses who were familiar with the putative author's handwriting, supplemented on occasion by direct jury comparison between challenged documents and other, authentic, writings of the putative author which might happen to be in the case for other purposes. This was taken to be such weak evidence that, without evaluating the validity of the proffered experts' claims to expertise, the *Moody* Court ruled that such asserted expert testimony should be admitted because it could not be any worse

Stout (1699), 13 A Complete Collection of State Trials 1105 (T.B. Howell ed., 1812). The expertise involved in all three trials was medical expertise. See generally T.R. Forbes, Surgeons at the Bailey: English Forensic Medicine to 1878 (1985).

[8]This story is told in more detail in Risinger, Denbeaux & Saks, Exorcism of Ignorance as a Proxy for Rational Knowledge: The Lessons of Handwriting Identification "Expertise," 137 U. Pa. L. Rev. at 751–771 (1989).

[9]*Goodtitle d. Revett v. Braham, 4 Term Rep. 497 (1792).*

[10]*Carey v. Pitt, Esq., Peake Add Cas. 130 (1793); Stranger v. Searle, 1 Esp. 14 (1793).*

[11]*R. v. Cator, 4 Esp 117 (C.P. 1802).*

[12]*Doe d. Mudd v. Suckermore, 5 A. & E. 703 (K.B. 1836).*

[13]Common Law Procedure Act, 1854, 17 & 18 Vict., ch. 125, § 27; See Risinger, Denbeaux & Saks, Exorcism of Ignorance as a Proxy for Rational Knowledge: The Lessons of Handwriting Identification "Expertise," 137 U. Pa. L. Rev. at 757–758, especially n. 116 (1989).

[Section 4:3]

[1]*Moody v. Rowell*, 17 Pick. 490, 34 Mass. 490, 1835 WL 2374 (1835).

[2]Louisiana's version of the French Civil Code provided for resort to handwriting experts, but it is not clear that at the time of its statehood there were any such experts in Louisiana. See Risinger, Denbeaux & Saks, Exorcism of Ignorance as a Proxy for Rational Knowledge: The Lessons of Handwriting Identification "Expertise," 137 U. Pa. L. Rev. at 761, n.133 (1989).

than what was traditionally relied on.[3] This seems to be the dominant rationale for the allowance of such testimony in those states which followed Massachusetts' lead over the next 50 to 75 years. While by 1900 a substantial majority of American jurisdictions accepted such testimony,[4] the prevailing attitude may be best exemplified by the opinion of the New York Court of Appeals in *Hoag v. Wright*:[5]

> The opinions of experts upon handwriting, who testify from comparison only, are regarded by the courts as of uncertain value, because in so many cases where such evidence is received witnesses of equal honesty, intelligence and experience reach conclusions not only diametrically opposite, but always in favor of the party who called them.[6]

While some courts continued to reject such expertise, and most which allowed it remained skeptical, a group of professional experts was growing up and beginning to seek greater respectability. It is ironic that when expert handwriting identification testimony was first declared admissible in America and England, there were no experts. That is to say, the lawyers seeking to utilize such testimony had to proffer various witnesses who were willing to assert a kind of ad hoc expertise acquired as a side effect of being something else, such as a postal inspector or a bank teller. No practicing forensic document examiner today would concede any expertise to such witnesses.[7] When the legal system agreed to accept such testimony, however, it created a demand which was to be met by people who turned their entire attention to filling it. Not surprisingly, that resulted in people setting out to create a standard theory and practice giving the appearance of "science." Among the first of those people was Charles Chabot,[8] who, despite his name, was English. He was originally a lithographer by trade, but developed an interest in handwriting identification about the time such expert testimony was gaining admissibility in English courts. It is unclear how much he was influenced by contemporary French theory and practice, but in 1871, at the urging of his lawyer-disciple Edward Twistleton (who wrote a lengthy theoretical introduction to the book), he published The Handwriting of Junius Professionally Investigated, which was the first book in English to assert that there was a science of handwriting identification,[9] and to illustrate its

---

[3]This was the rationale urged by the dissenters in *Doe d. Mudd v. Suckermore*. The *Moody* court concluded that "this species of evidence, though generally very slight, and often wholly immaterial, is competent evidence." 34 Mass (17 Pick.) 498.

[4]The earliest authority for the admission of such testimony in each U.S. jurisdiction is set out chronologically in Appendix 3 to Risinger, Denbeaux & Saks, Exorcism of Ignorance as a Proxy for Rational Knowledge: The Lessons of Handwriting Identification "Expertise," 137 U. Pa. L. Rev. at 788 (1989). (There is an error in that Appendix. The earliest date for Arkansas should be 1920, on the authority of *Murphy v. Murphy*, 144 Ark. 429, 222 S.W. 721 (1920). In addition, there is evidence of unchallenged use of such experts as early as 1910 in *Strickland v. Strickland*, 95 Ark. 623, 129 S.W. 801 (1910) and 1932 in *State Board of Law Examiners v. Strahan*, 44 Wyo. 156, 8 P.2d 1090 (1932), and perhaps 1835 in *Bank of Muskingum v. Carpenter's Adm'rs*, 7 Ohio 21, PT. I, 1835 WL 5 (1835) (overruled on other grounds in part by, White v. Denman, 1 Ohio St. 110, 1853 WL 2 (1853)), where such evidence is adverted to in the reporter's summary of evidence but is not mentioned in the opinion.

(Prof. Andre Moenssens called attention to these cases.))

[5]*Hoag v. Wright*, 174 N.Y. 36, 66 N.E. 579 (1903).

[6]*Hoag v. Wright*, 174 N.Y. 36, 66 N.E. 579 (1903). See also *Miles v. Loomis*, 75 N.Y. 288, 1878 WL 12743 (1878); *Mutual Benefit Life Ins. Co. v. Brown*, 30 N.J. Eq. 193, 3 Stewart 193, 1878 WL 177 (1878), aff'd, 32 N.J. Eq. 809, 5 Stewart 809, 1880 WL 236 (1880); *In re Fuller's Estate*, 222 Pa. 182, 70 A. 1005 (1908).

[7]See, e.g., Albert S. Osborn, Questioned Documents at 286–287 (2d ed., 1929).

[8]Chabot and his contemporary Frederick G. Netherclift were the first full time handwriting identification consultants in England, both beginning their practices in the mid-1850s after earlier careers in engraving and lithography. Two short reports by Netherclift on aspects of the Junius controversy appear in Chabot's book. Chabot, at any rate, was a significant enough character in mid-Victorian London to have rated an entry in the Dictionary of National Biography.

[9]Twistleton refers to Chabot's work as a "scientific demonstration." Charles Chabot, The Handwriting of Junius Professionally Examined

methodology.[10]

In the United States three books were published in the 1890s, Persifor Frazer's The Manual of the Study of Documents (1894),[11] William E. Hagan's Disputed Handwriting (1894)[12] and Daniel T. Ames' Ames on Forgery (1899),[13] but the event that was to turn handwriting identification expertise from ugly duckling to swan was the publication in 1910 of Albert S. Osborn's Questioned Documents, with an introduction by John Henry Wigmore.

Osborn's book, Osborn's personality, and Osborn's relationship with Wigmore, are the cornerstones upon which respect for asserted handwriting identification expertise in the United States was built.[14] As to Osborn's book, it set out the theory and practice of the claimed expertise so comprehensively that it is fair to say that all treatments of the subject since have simply been rearrangements or expansions of Osborn's 1910 book.[15] As to his personality, he was clearly a man of exceptional intelligence and critical abilities, but with a blind spot. He had a kind of mystical faith in the ability of the human mind to create a system of analytical expertise for the solution of virtually any class of problem. And, while he could be laudably skeptical regarding the claims of others,[16] he never seemed to notice that most of the generalities upon which he built his own system lacked empirical verification.[17] Nevertheless, he had faith in himself and his vision, and the ability to sell others on that vision, whether the audience was a jury, a group of students, or an audience of lawyers or judges. His most significant convert was Wigmore, the most influential figure in evidence theory of the last hundred years. Together, Osborn and Wigmore conducted a quarter century public relations campaign on behalf of "scientific"

---

220 (Edward Twistleton ed. 1871).

[10]Charles Chabot, The Handwriting of Junius Professionally Examined 220 (Edward Twistleton ed. 1871). The subject matter to which Chabot applied his methods was the authorship of the anonymous "Junius" letters, famed in the political controversy of late 18th century England. Interestingly, although Albert S. Osborn was a great admirer of the theoretical aspects of both Twistleton's and Chabot's writing in this book (See Albert S. Osborn, Questioned Documents 34–35 (1910); Albert S. Osborn, Questioned Documents at 1000 (2d ed., 1929)), he disagreed with Chabot's conclusion that the Junius letters were written by Sir Philip Francis, asserting that Chabot and Twistleton had been misled by "improper standards" and "planted" documents. Albert S. Osborn, Questioned Documents at 1000 (2d ed., 1929). Osborn seemed to favor John Horne Tooke as Junius. After the publication of his book, Chabot's testimony in the Tichborne Claimant case (the O.J. Simpson case of Victorian England) brought him to the attention of the general public.

Note that while Chabot's book was the first book in English on the subject, it was not the first written source in English. In 1850, in Massachusetts, under the authority of Moody v. Rowell, Nathaniel D. Gould, a teacher of penmanship for 50 years, was called on behalf of the prosecution in the famous trial of Harvard Professor Dr. John W. Webster for the murder of Dr. George Parkman. Since this trial was a sensation in its day, a verbatim transcript was made and published. In his preliminary testimony, Mr. Gould sets out the two basic principles of the field, which he claims to have derived from his own observa-

tion and reflection. See Report of the Trial of John Webster, Phonographic Report 116 (2d ed. revised, 1850).

[11]Persifor Frazer, The Manual of the Study of Documents (Lippincott, Philadelphia, 1894) (retitled Bibliotics, or the Study of Documents, in the 1901 Third Edition). Frazer's book was to have no lasting influence, as its main original theses were totally rejected by Albert Osborn and his followers. See Albert S. Osborn, Questioned Documents at 990 (2d ed., 1929).

[12]W.E. Hagan, Disputed Handwriting (1894).

[13]D.T. Ames, Ames on Forgery (1899).

[14]It also did not hurt that the book received a glowing review from Roscoe Pound, another of the legal giants of the era, in the Harvard Law Review, 24 Harv. L. Rev. 413 (1910).

[15]This includes Osborn's own 1929 second edition, which had surprisingly little new information on handwriting identification theory or practice. Most of its material on those topics is taken verbatim from the 1910 edition. Note that the text reference is only to the orthodox non-graphological literature. See § 4:13.

[16]Notably, graphologists, who claim to be able to determine personality traits from handwriting. See the quote from Osborn, 2d ed., at 442–444, set out in Risinger, Denbeaux & Saks, Exorcism of Ignorance as a Proxy for Rational Knowledge: The Lessons of Handwriting Identification "Expertise", 137 U. Pa. L. Rev. 731, 751–771 n. 13 (1989).

[17]§§ 4:14 to 4:38.

handwriting identification expertise as practiced by Osborn and described in his book.

The ultimate triumph of this vision was finally insured by the Lindbergh Baby kidnaping case, *State v. Hauptmann*, in 1936. Osborn was the chief witness called to testify that Bruno Richard Hauptmann had written all of the ransom notes found or sent after the abduction of the son of Charles A. Lindbergh. The public seemed to need to believe Hauptmann was guilty, wanted him convicted, and was grateful to those who supplied the evidence. Osborn became a celebrity. In the half century after the affirmance of *Hauptmann*,[18] no reported opinion rejected handwriting expertise, nor was much skepticism displayed towards it. Rather, it became universally accepted as scientific and dependable. This may be best summed up by the following quotation from Judge Cohalan dissenting in the 1977 case *In re Estate of Sylvestri*,[19] which contrasts sharply with the criticism found in *Hoag v. Wright*: "Since that rather cynical observation was made by our highest court in *Hoag*, examiners of questioned documents, as handwriting experts prefer to be called, have attained more respectable standing in the courtroom."[20] As a New Jersey court observed in 1957,[21] after the *Hauptmann* case, handwriting identification expertise could no longer be regarded as "the lowest order of evidence, and . . . accorded little evidential weight."[22]

## § 4:4 Recent developments

Two events stimulated a reevaluation of handwriting identification expertise. The first was the publication of an article (Risinger et al.[1]) in the University of Pennsylvania Law Review in 1989, pointing out the lack of empirical validation of the claims of the expertise. The other was the United States Supreme Court's 1993 decision in *Daubert v. Merrell Dow Pharmaceuticals, Inc.*,[2] rejecting previous approaches to acceptability of expertise under the Federal Rules of Evidence, and putting in play the validity of claims to scientific expertise[3] even for long accepted subjects. As a result there has been a significant amount of litigation concerning the

---

[18]*State v. Hauptmann*, 115 N.J.L. 412, 180 A. 809 (N.J. Ct. Err. & App. 1935).

[19]*In re Estate of Sylvestri*, 55 A.D.2d 916, 390 N.Y.S.2d 598 (2d Dep't 1977), judgment aff'd, 44 N.Y.2d 260, 405 N.Y.S.2d 424, 376 N.E.2d 897 (1978).

[20]*In re Estate of Sylvestri*, 55 A.D.2d 916, 390 N.Y.S.2d 598, 600, (2d Dep't 1977), judgment aff'd, 44 N.Y.2d 260, 405 N.Y.S.2d 424, 376 N.E.2d 897 (1978). Judge Cohalan's observation is literally accurate, but may have been intended sarcastically, since Cohalan was dissenting from a 2-1 decision (without opinion) finding that the conclusion of an asserted handwriting expert, contradicted by another such expert, was sufficient of itself to support a jury verdict of forgery in the face of contrary testimony by three disinterested witnesses to the signature. No such skepticism was entertained by the Court of Appeals in affirming the majority, however. *Matter of Estate of Sylvestri*, 44 N.Y.2d 260, 405 N.Y.S.2d 424, 376 N.E.2d 897 (1978).

[21]*Morrone v. Morrone*, 44 N.J. Super. 305, 130 A.2d 396 (App. Div. 1957).

[22]*Morrone v. Morrone*, 44 N.J. Super. 305, 130 A.2d 396, 400, (App. Div. 1957). Osborn

recognized the centrality of the *Hauptmann* case. Concerning it, he wrote in 1940, "[i]t can be correctly stated that in that little one hundred year old courtroom at Flemington, N.J., the scientific examination and proof of the facts in document cases was nationally recognized and firmly established as a New Profession." Albert S. Osborn, A New Profession, 24 J. Am. Jud. Soc. No. 1 (1940), reprinted in Albert S. Osborn, Questioned Document Problems (2d ed., Albert D. Osborn ed., 1946), at 311. For a similar evaluation, see James V.P. Conway, Evidential Documents (1959), at 210.

**[Section 4:4]**

[1]§ 4:1.

[2]*Daubert v. Merrell Dow Pharmaceuticals, Inc.*, 509 U.S. 579, 113 S. Ct. 2786, 125 L. Ed. 2d 469, 27, 27 U.S.P.Q.2d 1200, Prod. Liab. Rep. (CCH) P 13494, 37 Fed. R. Evid. Serv. 1, 23 Envtl. L. Rep. 20979 (1993).

[3]And, ultimately, "non-scientific" expertise as well. See *Kumho Tire Co., Ltd. v. Carmichael*, 526 U.S. 137, 119 S. Ct. 1167, 143 L. Ed. 2d 238, 50, 50 U.S.P.Q.2d 1177, Prod. Liab. Rep. (CCH) P 15470, 50 Fed. R. Evid. Serv. 1373, 29 Envtl. L. Rep. 20638 (1999).

reliability of handwriting identification in the last dozen years.[4] Before turning to the cases, however, we must address the potential impact of *Kumho Tire Co., Ltd. v. Carmichael*.[5]

In the case summaries that follow, quotations and specific holdings are generally given pinpoint citations, but fact summaries, though drawn from the opinions, are generally not burdened with citations. Sometimes, important facts are not specifically recited in an opinion but can be gleaned by fair inference from what is given in the opinion. Such circumstances are generally signaled by the use of the words "presumably" or "apparently."

## § 4:5    Recent developments—Implications of *Kumho Tire v. Carmichael*

*Kumho Tire* is dealt with elsewhere in some detail,[1] but for present purposes it is enough to point out two things: First, the court found a general obligation under Fed. R. Evid. 702 to determine that proffered expertise is sufficiently reliable that its admission can properly be said to aid the trier of fact in the task at hand, independent of whether that proffered expertise is appropriately classified as either "novel" or "scientific." And second, the proper focus is not on the dependability of the expertise in some global sense, but its dependability in its application to the task at hand. The question is whether the practitioners of the expertise can be shown to be able to do *what they are claiming to do in the particular case*. This latter point is important to proper understanding of *Kumho Tire*, and to proper treatment of claimed handwriting identification expertise. As evidence from research accumulates in the future, it may well show that questioned document examiners, or some subgroup of them with particular training, are good at some tasks (such as determining that a signature was not written by the person whose name the signature reflects[2]) and bad at others (such as identifying the actual author of the forged signature). Evidence with regard to dependability for one task does not establish dependability for the other, and courts have generally failed to keep this in

---

[4]Two other federal cases—*U.S. v. McVeigh*, 1997 WL 47724 (D.Colo. 1997) (Oklahoma City Bombing Case) and *U.S. v. Brown,* No. CR 99-184 (C.D. Cal.), order dated Dec. 1, 1999)—have also involved reliability challenges, but did not result in written opinions. Judge Matsch's decision in *McVeigh*, which was that unless document examiners could satisfy the requirements of *Daubert*, their testimony would be limited to pointing out similarities between the questioned document and the known exemplars, but not to give a conclusion about the authorship of the questioned document, has been influential, even though it was promulgated without formal opinion. (It was also influential in the *McVeigh* case itself, since the prosecution chose not to call its document examiner rather than to try to satisfy *Daubert*.)

*McVeigh* also illustrates the problem of defining what constitutes a "reported" "opinion" in the days of databases. The oral argument that led to Judge Matsch's decision is reported at 1997 WL 47724. The colloquy, though extensive, does not reveal sufficient facts to determine exactly what task was at issue in the case, beyond the fact that some documents were going to be attributed to Defendant McVeigh by a document examiner after comparing them with known samples of McVeigh's handwriting. There may have been an issue of printing comparison, or printing to cursive comparison, but that is not clear. Clearly,

Judge Matsch does not formulate the specific task at hand with the particularity required by *Kumho Tire*, but his result has been very influential, as evidenced by its impact on *U.S. v. Hines* and subsequent cases. See the discussion of *Hines*, at § 4:7; and *U.S. v. Santillan*, at § 4:7. *U.S. v. Brown*, which was decided by order without opinion, and is currently unreported in any sense, is also discussed at § 4:7, for the sake of completeness.

[5]*Kumho Tire Co., Ltd. v. Carmichael*, 526 U.S. 137, 119 S. Ct. 1167, 143 L. Ed. 2d 238, 50, 50 U.S.P.Q.2d 1177, Prod. Liab. Rep. (CCH) P 15470, 50 Fed. R. Evid. Serv. 1373, 29 Envtl. L. Rep. 20638 (1999).

**[Section 4:5]**

[1]See also Risinger, Defining the "Task at Hand": Non-Science Forensic Science After *Kumho Tire v. Carmichael*, 57 Wash. & Lee L. Rev. 767 (2000).

[2]This sentence was written before learning that there was to be a fourth Kam study which deals with this task, and lends some support to the claim of marginal superiority of some experts over lay persons, at least in some contexts, in performing this particular task, at least under test conditions. See the preliminary observations on that study at § 4:31.

mind, or even manifest an awareness of the problem. After *Kumho Tire* they are obliged to.

*Kumho Tire* emphasizes that the test for nonscience expertise is to be "flexible,"[3] and is to be reviewed by an "abuse of discretion" standard,[4] but reaffirms the observation made in *General Electric v. Joiner*[5] that the "ipse dixit" of the expert is insufficient.[6] Further, as pointed out by Justice Scalia in his concurrence, it is clear that failure to inquire into reliability with sufficient care and particularity may constitute an "abuse of discretion" in a given case.[7] With these points in mind, we turn to the issues of handwriting identification reliability reflected in the cases.

## §4:6 Recent developments—Admissibility of asserted handwriting expert testimony before *Kumho Tire*

*United States v. Starzecpyzel*[1] is the original handwriting expertise reliability case of the modern era. In that case Roberta and Eileen Starzecpyzel were charged with having stolen various works of art from Roberta's elderly (and now senile) aunt. They claimed that the paintings were a gift made prior to the aunt's impairment. Part of the evidence against them was the proposed testimony of a questioned document examiner who, after examining numerous authentic signatures of the aunt on checks and other documents, concluded that the aunt's signatures on deeds of gift for the artwork were forgeries. He did not claim to be able to identify either defendant as the forger.

Judge McKenna of the United States District Court for the Southern District of New York held an extensive hearing on the state of knowledge concerning the reliability of such asserted expertise. Judge McKenna's opinion examines the claims of handwriting identification expertise to scientific status at length, and rejects them.[2] Having done this, however, he concludes that since such experts are not practicing a

---

[3]*Kumho Tire Co., Ltd. v. Carmichael*, 526 U.S. 137, 141, 145–150, 119 S. Ct. 1167, 143 L. Ed. 2d 238, 50, 50 U.S.P.Q.2d 1177, Prod. Liab. Rep. (CCH) P 15470, 50 Fed. R. Evid. Serv. 1373, 29 Envtl. L. Rep. 20638 (1999). In my chapter on a legal taxonomy of expertise, at 1 Modern Scientific Evidence § 2, I have suggested that standards of reliability should depend on the kind of expertise, the kind of case and the kind of issue upon which it is being proffered. Without repeating all that was said there, I suggested that when an expertise was being offered by the prosecution in a criminal case on an issue of "brute fact guilt" such as identity, and when the expertise was of the kind where errors in normal practice were not unambiguously revealed to the practitioner by unmistakable circumstances, there should be an especially high degree of proof of dependability before the results of the application of such claimed expertise are allowed before a jury.

[4]*Kumho Tire Co., Ltd. v. Carmichael*, 526 U.S. 137, 119 S. Ct. 1167, 143 L. Ed. 2d 238, 247, 50 U.S.P.Q.2d 1177, Prod. Liab. Rep. (CCH) P 15470, 50 Fed. R. Evid. Serv. 1373, 29 Envtl. L. Rep. 20638 (1999); following *General Elec. Co. v. Joiner*, 522 U.S. 136, 118 S. Ct. 512, 139 L. Ed. 2d 508, 18 O.S.H. Cas. (BNA) 1097, Prod. Liab. Rep. (CCH) P 15120, 48 Fed. R. Evid. Serv. 1, 28 Envtl. L. Rep. 20227, 177 A.L.R. Fed. 667 (1997).

[5]*Kumho Tire Co., Ltd. v. Carmichael*, 526 U.S. 137, 119 S. Ct. 1167, 143 L. Ed. 2d 238, 247,

50 U.S.P.Q.2d 1177, Prod. Liab. Rep. (CCH) P 15470, 50 Fed. R. Evid. Serv. 1373, 29 Envtl. L. Rep. 20638 (1999); following *General Elec. Co. v. Joiner*, 522 U.S. 136, 118 S. Ct. 512, 139 L. Ed. 2d 508, 18 O.S.H. Cas. (BNA) 1097, Prod. Liab. Rep. (CCH) P 15120, 48 Fed. R. Evid. Serv. 1, 28 Envtl. L. Rep. 20227, 177 A.L.R. Fed. 667 (1997).

[6]*General Elec. Co. v. Joiner*, 522 U.S. 136, 146, 118 S. Ct. 512, 139 L. Ed. 2d 508, 18 O.S.H. Cas. (BNA) 1097, Prod. Liab. Rep. (CCH) P 15120, 48 Fed. R. Evid. Serv. 1, 28 Envtl. L. Rep. 20227, 177 A.L.R. Fed. 667 (1997).

[7]*Kumho Tire Co., Ltd. v. Carmichael*, 526 U.S. 137, 158–159, 119 S. Ct. 1167, 143 L. Ed. 2d 238, 50, 50 U.S.P.Q.2d 1177, Prod. Liab. Rep. (CCH) P 15470, 50 Fed. R. Evid. Serv. 1373, 29 Envtl. L. Rep. 20638 (1999).

**[Section 4:6]**

[1]*U.S. v. Starzecpyzel*, 880 F. Supp. 1027, 42 Fed. R. Evid. Serv. 247 (S.D. N.Y. 1995). In keeping with the severest punctilio of disclosure, it should be noted that one defense expert at the *Daubert* hearing in this case was the author's friend and co-author and one of the editors of this treatise, Dr. Michael J. Saks, and that the author was a consultant to the defense.

[2]"Were the Court to apply *Daubert* to the proffered FDE testimony, it would have to be excluded. This conclusion derives from a straightforward analysis of the suggested *Daubert* fac-

science within the meaning of *Daubert*, *Daubert*'s validation requirements therefore do not apply. He then, as already noted, analogizes such a proffered expert to a harbor pilot who learns to do something dependably by experience. As to whether the prosecution's expert would be allowed to testify to his conclusion that the signatures on the documents which were the subject of the prosecution were forgeries, based on his examination of the numerous genuine signatures of the putative victim, the court says that the defense had "presented no evidence, beyond the bald assertions [of its experts], that FDEs [forensic document examiners] cannot reliably perform this task. Defendants have simply challenged the FDE community to prove that this task can be done reliably. Such a demonstration of proof, which may be appropriate for a scientific expert witness, has never been imposed on 'skilled' experts."[3] Judge McKenna then declares himself persuaded that the inferences as to genuineness of the signature at issue in the case before him "can be performed with sufficient reliability to merit admission."[4]

It should be clear that Judge McKenna's bifurcated standard of reliability based on the classification of proffered expertise as "science or non-science" with higher standards applied to science, does not survive *Kumho Tire*.

Finally, it should be noted, however, that, in anticipation of the particularization focus of *Kumho Tire*, Judge McKenna emphasized that the only claimed skill he was dealing with in the opinion was the skill of comparing a known signature with a questioned signature to determine whether the questioned signature was really signed by the person whose name was reflected, and not any other asserted skill or global claim of expertise. This point has generally been lost on later courts and commentators, who have tended to treat *Starzecpyzel* as if it dealt with global validity.

In *Ruth I*,[5] the Court of Military Appeals faced two issues, one dealing with the reliability of forensic handwriting identification and the other with a claim that the

---

tors—testability and known error rate, peer review and publication, and general acceptance—in light of the evidence adduced at the *Daubert* hearing." *U.S. v. Starzecpyzel*, 880 F. Supp. 1027, 1036, 42 Fed. R. Evid. Serv. 247 (S.D. N.Y. 1995).

[3]*U.S. v. Starzecpyzel*, 880 F. Supp. 1027, 1046, 42 Fed. R. Evid. Serv. 247 (S.D. N.Y. 1995). The implication that the ultimate risk of non-persuasion as to reliability is ever on the opponent of a proffer of evidence is startling, in light of Fed. R. Evid. 104 and the general notion that the party seeking admission must convince the court affirmatively of admissibility once the issue is seriously put in issue. Actually, Judge McKenna seems to have been aware of the problems that would be created by formally placing the burden of persuasion on the opponent of a proffer. The actual position taken by his opinion on that issue is ambiguous and unclear, and, one must conclude, intentionally so. In the only explicit discussion of the issue, he concedes that Professor Berger takes the (standard) position that the burden is on the proponent of admissibility, citing Margaret A. Berger, Evidentiary Framework, in Reference Manual on Scientific Evidence (1995). *U.S. v. Starzecpyzel*, 880 F. Supp. 1027, 42 Fed. R. Evid. Serv. 247 (S.D. N.Y. 1995). He then cites an unexamined single line claim to the contrary from the middle of an article by a products liability practitioner whose main position is that *Daubert*'s effect should be viewed as allowing more to be admitted, not less. *U.S. v. Starzecpyzel*, 880 F. Supp. 1027, 1031, 42 Fed. R. Evid. Serv. 247 (S.D. N.Y. 1995), citing Maskin, The Impact of Daubert on the Admissibility of Scientific Evidence: The Supreme Court Catches Up with a Decade of Jurisprudence, 15 Cardozo L. Rev. 1921 (1994). However, Judge McKenna attempts not to choose between these two positions, characterizing the question before him as "legal" rather than factual, as if that made the problem go away. *U.S. v. Starzecpyzel*, 880 F. Supp. 1027, 1031, 42 Fed. R. Evid. Serv. 247 (S.D. N.Y. 1995). His later language from the passage cited in the text of this article seems to show his functional adoption of the problematical Maskin position, however, even though, as the text indicates, he goes on to say that he is affirmatively persuaded that handwriting identification testimony "can be performed" with "sufficient reliability to merit admission." *U.S. v. Starzecpyzel*, 880 F. Supp. 1027, 1046, 42 Fed. R. Evid. Serv. 247 (S.D. N.Y. 1995).

[4]*U.S. v. Starzecpyzel*, 880 F. Supp. 1027, 1046, 42 Fed. R. Evid. Serv. 247 (S.D. N.Y. 1995). Judge McKenna went on to fashion a jury instruction to be given in advance of the expert's testimony to explain that the testimony was not the result of a scientific process, so that the jurors would have no misconceptions in that regard. *U.S. v. Starzecpyzel*, 880 F. Supp. 1027, 1050–1051, 42 Fed. R. Evid. Serv. 247 (S.D. N.Y. 1995).

[5]*U.S. v. Ruth*, 42 M.J. 730 (A.C.C.A. 1995), decision aff'd, 46 M.J. 1 (C.A.A.F. 1997).

defense was denied due process of law by not being allowed to call its own expert to testify before the jury concerning the weaknesses of handwriting identification expertise. We will return to that issue in due course.[6] As to the reliability challenge, the *Ruth I* court first noted that handwriting expertise had been accepted in the military courts "for at least the past forty-four years."[7] It then declared that *Daubert* did not apply to nonscientific expertise, cited *Starzecpyzel* to establish the nonscientific nature of questioned document examination, and then declared "it has been generally understood that expert testimony on handwriting comparison can assist panel members by focusing their attention on minute similarities and dissimilarities between exemplars that panel members might otherwise miss when they perform their own visual comparison. . . . It is largely in the location of these similarities and differences that a professional documents examiner has an advantage over panel members."[8] As authority for this the court pointed to no data of any kind, but to an unpublished opinion in *United States v. Buck*,[9] and concluded on this basis that the challenged handwriting identification testimony was admissible as helpful to the trier of fact under Fed. R. Evid. 702. This unanalyzed global approach is now clearly unavailable after *Kumho Tire*. What it reflects, as much by implication as explicitly, is a combination of what may be called the "sufficient experience"[10] test, which emphasizes experience without testing to see if it has actually resulted in the claimed skill, and the "guild" test,[11] in which the existence of an organized group which supervises accreditation (and an expert's membership in it)

---

[6]§ 4:8.

[7]*U.S. v. Ruth*, 42 M.J. 730, 732 (A.C.C.A. 1995), decision aff'd, 46 M.J. 1 (C.A.A.F. 1997).

[8]*U.S. v. Ruth*, 42 M.J. 730, 732 (A.C.C.A. 1995), decision aff'd, 46 M.J. 1 (C.A.A.F. 1997).

[9]*U.S. v. Buck*, 1987 WL 19300 (S.D. N.Y. 1987).

[10]The "sufficient experience" approach is first set out in Imwinkelried, The Next Step after *Daubert*: Developing a Similarly Epistemological Approach to Ensuring the Reliability of Non-Scientific Testimony, 15 Cardozo L. Rev. 2271, 2292–2294 (1994). See also Agrimonte, The Limitations of *Daubert* and Its Application to Quasi-Scientific Experts, A Two Year Case Review of Daubert v. Merrell Dow Pharmaceuticals, Inc., 509 U.S. 579, 113 S. Ct. 2786, 125 L. Ed. 2d 469, 27 U.S.P.Q.2d (BNA) 1200, Prod. Liab. Rep. (CCH) P 13494, 37 Fed. R. Evid. Serv. 1, 23 Envtl. L. Rep. 20979 (1993), 35 Washburn L.J. 134, 152–156 (1995); and Perrin, Expert Witness Testimony: Back to the Future, 29 U. Rich. L. Rev. 1389, 1457–1462 (1995).

To be fair to Professor Imwinkelried, the test was set out as a preliminary step in an article pointing out the difficulties of formulating reliability tests for nonscientific expertise, especially "clinical" or "experience-based" expertise. Professor Imwinkelried himself well understood that *Daubert* in its general aspects required gatekeeping vigilance as to all expertise. Unfortunately, the approach he set out was easily embraced by proponents of the status quo ante *Daubert*, since all that it required was the testimony of the witness that he had had lots of experience, and that much of it was in circumstances substantially like those in the case at hand. (See, e.g., testimony of

Grant R. Sperry, Transcript of Testimony, *U.S. v. Jones*, No. Cr. 3–95–24 (E.D. Tenn. June 29, 1995), discussed infra in this section.) Practitioners of all sorts of questionable claimed skills can pass this test. It is not that the test is not sufficient for some kinds of expertise in some circumstances. It works fine for what I have called "everyday summarizational" experts, who testify to such things as industry practice from their years in an industry.

The problem is that it supplies little in the way of validation for what I have called "translational" experts, who claim that they can translate their experience into particular adjudicative inferences, such as handwriting identification experts. Here, we must worry about the reliability of not only the subjective data base, but also the subjective translational system applied to it. In short, merely showing up at the scene after auto accidents, even hundreds of times, is a weak warrant to believe a witness's inferences about what happened in the accident itself.

[11]The "guild" test goes beyond the "sufficient experience" test by focusing inquiry on the existence of a group that certifies training, experience and methodology. Acceptance by such a group establishes reliability. Note this is not the "*Frye* Test" applied to nonscientific expertise, since in the absence of such group acceptance an individual witness might be found reliable for other reasons, but, like the *Frye* test, acceptance by such a group guarantees admissibility. The problem, of course, is that astrology can pass this test. For the most extended and explicit assertion of the guild approach see Moenssens, Handwriting Identification Evidence in the Post-*Daubert* World, 66 UMKC L. Rev. 251, 291–292 (1998). See also Reavley & Petalas, A Plea for Return to

is taken as a sufficient warrant to infer reliability for admissibility purposes. As we will see, elements of these two approaches, usually conflated,[12] have commonly been invoked in an effort to justify admission of claimed handwriting identification expertise, and we will henceforth refer to this conflated rendition simply as the "guild test."

It is important to note what application of expertise was being claimed reliable in *Ruth I*. It was not the ability to determine if a signature was genuine, as was the case in *Starzecpyzel*. It was the much more questionable ability to attribute the authorship of a very small sample of writing (like a forged signature) to a particular person based on comparison to examples of the asserted forger's true writing.[13]

The facts in *Ruth* are these. Some person or persons had put together a get-rich-quick scam which worked like this:[14] Someone opened a bank account in Lichtenstein in the fictitious name "William Cooper" using a falsified copy of a passport. They then gained access to the personnel and pay records of 30–35 American soldiers stationed at a base in Bamberg, Germany. Using the information on bank accounts in those records, they sent letters to the (American) banks of the soldiers directing wire transfers of the complete balance of their accounts to the "William Cooper" account at "one a.m Eastern Time Zone on 01 May 1992." The letters were apparently typed, with handwritten signatures. The scheme was uncovered when the banks were told by their depositors that the letters were fraudulent. (It is not completely clear whether this was before or after any transfers, but appears to have been before, as a result of bank inquiries concerning these unusual balance transfer directives).

Suspicion fell upon Private Joseph M. Durocher and Specialist Jeffrey A. Ruth, who were personnel action clerks in Bamberg with access to the relevant bank information. Durocher was interrogated, and apparently cooperated with prosecutors, confessing to the scheme and implicating Ruth. Durocher's testimony was the main evidence against Ruth. The only corroboration of Durocher's story was a

---

Evidence Rule 702, 77 Texas L. Rev. 493 (1998); Capra, The *Daubert* Puzzle, 32 Ga. L. Rev. 699, 741–746 (1998); and Lathram, The "Same Intellectual Rigor" Test Provides an Effective Method for Determining the Reliability of All Expert Testimony, Without Regard to Whether the Testimony Comprises "Scientific Knowledge" or "Technical or Other Specialized Knowledge", 28 U. Memphis L. Rev. 1053 (1998). See also (or perhaps cf.) Peter B. Oh, Assessing Admissibility of Nonscientific Expert Evidence under Federal Rule of Evidence 702, 64 Def. Couns. J. 556 (1997) (explicitly advocating the *Frye* test for nonscientific evidence); Agrimonte, The Limitations of *Daubert* and Its Application to Quasi-Scientific Experts, A Two Year Case Review of *Daubert v. Merrell Dow Pharmaceuticals, Inc.*, 113 S. Ct. 2787 (1993), 35 Washburn L.J. at 155 (1995). The practical (though often inexplicit) adoption of the guild test by courts is dealt with in connection with numerous cases discussed infra at §§ 4:6 and 4:7.

[12]As will become apparent in the discussion of the cases *infra*, one often has to infer the test implicitly being used from the Court's recitation of training, experience and guild membership, followed by a conclusory declaration of reliability.

[13]Standard Osbornian theory of handwriting identification holds the latter a much easier task than the former. See Risinger with Saks, Science and Nonscience in the Courts: *Daubert* Meets Handwriting Identification Expertise, 82 Iowa L. Rev. 21, 73 (1996). In this regard, consider the following quotations from three of the most respected authorities in the standard document examination literature: "It is much easier to show that a fraudulent signature is not genuine than it is to show that such a writing is actually the work of a particular writer," Albert S. Osborn, Questioned Documents 286–287 (2d ed., 1929). [If the questioned document is not in the natural hand of the forger] " . . . the entire problem is an extremely difficult one, and if not handled carefully and cautiously, can lead to serious errors." Hilton, Can the Forger be Identified from His Handwriting?, 43 J. Crim. L., Criminology and Police Sci. 547, 547, 548, 555 (1953). And " . . . while it is often possible to express and justify a definite opinion as to whether a signature is genuine or forged, it is rarely that the identity of the forger can be established by comparing the handwriting of the forgery and specimens of the handwriting of suspects." Wilson R. Harrison, Suspect Documents: Their Scientific Examination 374 (1966).

[14]The true crime narrative here given is reconstructed from the statements of fact in both the *Ruth I* and *Ruth II* opinions. I have avoided burdening the text with specific notes to each sentence.

questioned document examiner's testimony that Ruth signed one of the thirty-odd forged signatures on letters to banks, and that Ruth wrote one (but not all) of the signatures of William Cooper on the applications used to open the bank account in Lichtenstein.

By now the reader will see the problem. Under a proper *Kumho Tire* approach, the issue would have been "what if anything establishes that questioned document examiners can reliably identify the writer of a small sample of writing comprised of only 14–16 letters, under circumstances where the writing might or might not represent an attempt to simulate the writing of the named signatory (since whoever created the scam had access to records containing their actual signatures), and where there is a high circumstantial likelihood of disguise of some sort being utilized in the writing in any event." This question was clearly neither asked nor answered by the court in *Ruth I.*

A similar problem is presented by *United States v. Velasquez.*[15] Again, the case presents both a reliability challenge and a challenge to the exclusion of a counter-expert, and again, discussion of the latter issue is deferred to a later section. As to the reliability issue, the case involved the conviction of Velasquez for a violation of 21 U.S.C.A. § 848, engaging in a continual criminal enterprise involving five people or more, which carries a very long sentence. The only evidence establishing that five people rather than three were involved in the alleged drug scheme was testimony by a government questioned documents examiner that mailing labels used to ship drugs had been written at least partly by two alleged coparticipants of defendant. Thus, under a proper *Kumho Tire* approach, the issue would be, "What establishes that questioned document examiners can reliably attribute authorship of individual parts of a document, the whole of which is extremely short, to particular individuals" or something of that nature. Again, this question was neither asked nor answered by the *Velasquez* court, which once again adopted without analysis and by default what was functionally the "guild" test. The *Velasquez* court's "reliability" analysis consists of merely reciting the document examiners training and experience, and her own assertion that she had performed the analysis properly, and declaring that this established sufficient reliability.[16] Again, *Kumho Tire's* emphasis on reliability of expertise in regard to the task to which it is applied in the particular case would seem to dispose such a "guild test" as a dispositive approach, especially when applied globally, as it was in *Velasquez.*

In many ways the 6th Circuit opinion in *United States v. Jones*[17] is the standard against which all other unsatisfactory treatments of reliability issues in any area must be judged. And it sets a very high standard of unsatisfactoriness indeed. In *Jones*, a thief obtained a credit card promotional mailing sent to Kathleen Jones's daughter's husband's aunt and uncle, on whose property the daughter and her husband lived in a house trailer. The thief then rented a postbox in the name of a third party (who happened to be a coworker of the defendant), and filled out the credit card application, requesting that the card be sent to the postbox. When the

---

[15]*U.S. v. Velasquez*, 64 F.3d 844, 42 Fed. R. Evid. Serv. 1175 (3d Cir. 1995).

[16]The *Velasquez* court initially took the position that *Daubert* did not apply to handwriting because it was not science, 64 F.3d at 45, citing *Starzecpyzel*, but then claimed that "in an exercise of caution" it would review the proffered expertise "for qualifications, reliability and fitness (sic) as those factors have been explicated in *Daubert.*" *U.S. v. Velasquez*, 64 F.3d 844, 42 Fed. R. Evid. Serv. 1175 (3d Cir. 1995). It then proceeds never to mention any reliability criteria beyond the testimony of the document examiner as to the

very standard practice which was the subject of the challenge, and her experience. *U.S. v. Velasquez*, 64 F.3d 844, 850–851, 42 Fed. R. Evid. Serv. 1175 (3d Cir. 1995).

[17]*U.S. v. Jones*, 107 F.3d 1147, 46 Fed. R. Evid. Serv. 885, 1997 FED App. 0082P (6th Cir. 1997). The facts of the true crime narrative that is to follow are taken from the Court of Appeals opinion in *Jones*, supplemented to resolve minor ambiguities by the briefs of the parties at trial and on appeal and the transcript of the trial, on file with the author. Exact footnotes have been omitted to avoid burdening the text.

card arrived, items were charged on it to the tune of $3748 over a two week period. When the credit card company came looking, somebody pointed a finger at Kathleen Jones. Part of the evidence against Jones[18] was testimony by a questioned document examiner. The exact nature of that testimony is obscured a little by the Court of Appeals right from the beginning, since the opinion states in paragraph 3 that the document examiner's testimony was that "Jones's signature was on: (1) the credit card application; (2) a post office box registration form for the post office box to which the card was sent; and (3) two Howard Johnson's motel registration forms, which contained the fraudulently procured number at issue."[19] However, Jones's signature was on none of these documents. What was on the documents was what purported to be the signature of the aunt, which the questioned document examiner attributed to Jones. So the core *Kumho Tire* reliability issue was in *Jones* virtually the same as in *Ruth* and close to the one in *Velasquez*, and as in those cases, it was neither asked nor answered. However, the way in which it was not answered is what raises *Jones* to new heights of unsatisfactory judgecraft.

The opinion first appropriately spends a page disposing of a trivial challenge to the authentication of an exemplar.[20] It then spends over five pages discussing the standard of review to be applied[21] (this was prior to the Supreme Court's opinion in *General Elec. Co. v. Joiner*[22]). It then spends two pages and a half deciding that *Starzecpyzel* was right, handwriting expertise is not science, so *Daubert* is irrelevant.[23] (This was prior to *Kumho Tire*, of course). The Court then says "Without relying on *Daubert*, we now address whether handwriting analysis constitutes "technical, or other specialized knowledge" under the Federal Rules of Evidence and whether the expert handwriting analysis offered in this case was sufficiently reliable."[24] On these core issues of the case the court spends less than two and a half pages.[25] In this sparse treatment the court initially makes two points it appears to think are persuasive on issues of general reliability: (1) Other courts and commentators have uniformly found or assumed that handwriting identification expertise is (globally) a proper subject of court testimony, and that the appellant is therefore "asking us to do what no other court we have found has done,"[26] and (2) "The Federal Rules of Evidence themselves suggest that handwriting analysis is a

---

[18]There was other evidence against Jones independent of the handwriting identification. In addition to the coincidence that the postbox was in the name of a coworker whose purse had been rifled when Jones was around, there was an identification of Jones by the motel clerk, and an identification of her (by her daughter) from a bank camera photo (at a bank where she had no account) showing her doing a transaction at the approximate time the credit card was used to obtain money from that bank. Indeed, one significant issue, had the courts bothered to go into the issues properly, would have been whether the document examiner was privy to such information, and its effect on his conclusion, consciously or unconsciously. See Risinger with Saks, Science and Nonscience in the Courts: *Daubert* Meets Handwriting Identification Expertise, 82 Iowa L. Rev. at 64 (1996).

[19]*U.S. v. Jones*, 107 F.3d 1147, 1149, 46 Fed. R. Evid. Serv. 885, 1997 FED App. 0082P (6th Cir. 1997).

[20]*U.S. v. Jones*, 107 F.3d 1147, 1149–1150,

46 Fed. R. Evid. Serv. 885, 1997 FED App. 0082P (6th Cir. 1997).

[21]*U.S. v. Jones*, 107 F.3d 1147, 1150–1156, 46 Fed. R. Evid. Serv. 885, 1997 FED App. 0082P (6th Cir. 1997).

[22]*General Elec. Co. v. Joiner*, 522 U.S. 136, 118 S. Ct. 512, 139 L. Ed. 2d 508, 18 O.S.H. Cas. (BNA) 1097, Prod. Liab. Rep. (CCH) P 15120, 48 Fed. R. Evid. Serv. 1, 28 Envtl. L. Rep. 20227, 177 A.L.R. Fed. 667 (1997).

[23]*U.S. v. Jones*, 107 F.3d 1147, 1156–1159, 46 Fed. R. Evid. Serv. 885, 1997 FED App. 0082P (6th Cir. 1997).

[24]*U.S. v. Jones*, 107 F.3d 1147, 1159, 46 Fed. R. Evid. Serv. 885, 1997 FED App. 0082P (6th Cir. 1997).

[25]*U.S. v. Jones*, 107 F.3d 1147, 1159–1161, 46 Fed. R. Evid. Serv. 885, 1997 FED App. 0082P (6th Cir. 1997).

[26]*U.S. v. Jones*, 107 F.3d 1147, 1159, 46 Fed. R. Evid. Serv. 885, 1997 FED App. 0082P (6th Cir. 1997).

field of expertise."[27] In trying to justify this latter statement, the court sets out an egregious version of what I call "the Rule 901(b)(3) fallacy,"[28] and flagrantly misquotes the rule in order to do it.

As is well known, Fed. R. Evid. 901(a) sets out the general standard for authentication of any evidence whatsoever, and Fed. R. Evid. 901(b) gives a non-exhaustive list of acceptable recurrent means of satisfying the general requirements of Fed. R. Evid. 901(a) for "evidence sufficient to support a finding that the matter in question is what its proponent claims."[29] One way of doing this is set out in 901(b)(3) "Comparison by the trier of fact or by expert witnesses with specimens which have been authenticated." This is the full text of the rule. It is neither limited to documents (much less handwriting), nor does it reference them. In common practice it has been applied whenever an area of expertise, from fingerprints to DNA analysis, is shown or conceded to be reliable to make such comparisons under the standards of 702.[30] However, 901(b)(3) most certainly does not contain any suggestion that because there is a claim that an expert is comparing specimens, the existence of Fed. R. Evid. 901(b)(3) means that he or she meets the reliability requirements of rule 702. This is flagrantly backward reasoning, whether applied to handwriting identification expertise or anything else. Pursuant to *Daubert* and *Kumho Tire*, the existence of reliable expertise must be determined under Fed. R. Evid. 702. If reliable expertise involving comparison of exemplars is found to exist under the standards of 702, then 901(b)(3) may be referenced to establish its sufficiency for authentication purposes (assuming the expertise involves a comparison of standards).

The mistaken argument from 901(b)(3) just given is the standard form of the fallacy often put forward in prosecution briefs.[31] The *Jones* court, however, takes it one step further (presumably as a result of an embarrassing failure to read the actual text of the rule) when it says that 901(b)(3) provides for authentication of a document by "[c]omparison by . . . expert witnesses with specimens which have been authenticated."[32] It then compounds its error by claiming that if handwriting identification expertise were excluded "there would be no place for expert witnesses to compare writing on one document with that on another in order to authenticate a document. In other words, appellant's approach *would render Rule 901(b)(3) meaningless*."[33] Perhaps this would be true if the rule said what the court apparently thinks it says, but plainly, it does not.

To its credit, the court does realize, in instinctive anticipation of *Kumho Tire*, that what it has written does not "guarantee the reliability or admissibility of this type of testimony in a particular case. Because this is nonscientific testimony its reliability largely depends on the facts of each case."[34] However, it then sets out an approach to "reliability" which deals with actual reliability almost not at all. Perhaps not surprisingly, it adopts a global combination of the "experience" test and the "guild test."

*Jones* was, of course, as already noted, not the first court to adopt the "guild" test.

---

[27]*U.S. v. Jones*, 107 F.3d 1147, 1159, 46 Fed. R. Evid. Serv. 885, 1997 FED App. 0082P (6th Cir. 1997).

[28]Fed. R. Evid. 901(b)(3).

[29]Presumably, by implication, it is what its proponent claims that makes the evidence relevant to a fact which is rendered material by the applicable substantive law.

[30]See Wright and Gold, Federal Practice and Procedure: Evidence § 7102 at nn. 2–15 (collecting cases applying Rule 901(b)(3)).

[31]See, e.g., the government attempt to sell this argument in *U.S. v. McVeigh*, 1997 WL 47724 (D.Colo. 1997), at 15–17. Judge Matsch catches the fallacy, at 16.

[32]*U.S. v. Jones*, 107 F.3d 1147, 1159, 46 Fed. R. Evid. Serv. 885, 1997 FED App. 0082P (6th Cir. 1997).

[33]*U.S. v. Jones*, 107 F.3d 1147, 1159, 46 Fed. R. Evid. Serv. 885, 1997 FED App. 0082P (6th Cir. 1997).

[34]*U.S. v. Jones*, 107 F.3d 1147, 1160, 46 Fed. R. Evid. Serv. 885, 1997 FED App. 0082P (6th Cir. 1997).

However, it is in the details which the *Jones* court seems to believe help justify an inference of reliability where the unintentional humor of the opinion shows forth most strongly. After describing a fairly normal training history for a government questioned document examiner, the court notes that his primary job responsibilities consist of the "examination and comparison of questioned handwriting."[35] The court then notes that the witness estimated that throughout his career, he had conducted "well over a million comparative examinations.[36] In addition he has published numerous articles in the field and testified approximately 240 times in various courts.[37] To put it bluntly, the federal government pays him to analyze documents, the precise task he was called upon to do in the district court."[38]

This may be the first case on record in which a person's government job description has been taken as evidence of the reliability of asserted expertise. Even more starkly, the passage illustrates the credulity of the court, and the collision between the court's approach and any even mildly skeptical approach to the dependability of information. This witness testified to conducting "well over a million comparative examinations."[39] If he had been doing document examination 18 hours a day every day for 50 years, he would still have to have done more than three comparative examinations per hour to reach a million.[40] Yet the court swallows the testimony without hesitation and cites it as substantiation for the reliability of his expertise. The *Jones* court then continues as follows: "See Imwinkelried, 15 Cardozo L. Rev. at 2292–2293 (stating that the reliability of non-scientific expert testimony increases with the more experience an expert has had and the similarity of those experiences to the expert's testimony)."[41] However, the cited article makes no such sweeping statement at the cited pages or anywhere else.[42]

The court then continues its unaccountable course by asserting that "handwriting examiners themselves have recognized the importance of experience"[43] (no doubt true), but it supports this with a quote from an article in the Journal of Forensic Document Examination which actually claims that the bulk of document examiner experience with handwriting forms is gotten outside the professional sphere and is common with the rest of the world. "For handwriting examiners, this experience comes mainly from the exposure we have to handwriting throughout the course of our life, the majority of which normally would occur before specializing in forensic

---

[35]*U.S. v. Jones*, 107 F.3d 1147, 1160, 46 Fed. R. Evid. Serv. 885, 1997 FED App. 0082P (6th Cir. 1997).

[36]J.A. [joint appendix] at 154.

[37]J.A. at 155.

[38]*U.S. v. Jones*, 107 F.3d 1147, 1160, 46 Fed. R. Evid. Serv. 885, 1997 FED App. 0082P (6th Cir. 1997) (Emphasis supplied.).

[39]Lest the reader believe that some transcription error has been made, the trial transcript does indeed reveal this to have been Mr. Sperry's Testimony.

[40]The real circumstances are even more extreme. Mr. Sperry began his training (a two year course) in 1979. Transcript of Testimony, *U.S. v. Jones,* No. Cr 3-95-24 (E.D. Tenn. June 29, 1995), at 121 (on file with the author). Thus, at the time of trial, June 1995, he had 16 years of experience, 14 of which were post-training. This more than triples his actual hourly output, to over nine for every waking hour. Yet, besides his "well

over a million comparative examinations" he also testified to having been assigned to "73, [or] 7400 cases" *Transcript,* at 123. This works out to at least one and a quarter cases, every day including Sundays and holidays, without a break, for all 16 years, including his training period.

[41]*U.S. v. Jones*, 107 F.3d 1147, 1160, 46 Fed. R. Evid. Serv. 885, 1997 FED App. 0082P (6th Cir. 1997).

[42]Which is not surprising, because this is the kind of unsophisticated global universal statement which Professor Imwinkelried would generally not make. The article does take the position that some kinds of inferences must be based on much experience as a precondition to any claim to reliability, but never says that such experiences alone guarantee or even necessarily increase accuracy in all cases.

[43]*U.S. v. Jones*, 107 F.3d 1147, 1160, 46 Fed. R. Evid. Serv. 885, 1997 FED App. 0082P (6th Cir. 1997).

handwriting examination."[44]

It is on these grounds, coupled with the fact that the document examiner described the process by which he arrived at his conclusions, that the court declared, "given Sperry's various training experiences, his job responsibilities, his years of practical experience, and the detailed nature of his testimony in this case, the court did not abuse its discretion by admitting his testimony."[45]

## §4:7 Recent developments—Admissibility of asserted handwriting expert testimony after *Kumho Tire*[1]

The first judicial decision on handwriting to reference *Kumho Tire v. Carmichael* was *United States v. Paul*.[2] However, this opinion came down very soon after *Kumho Tire*, and it is perhaps understandable that the opinion did not manifest a full understanding of *Kumho Tire*'s import.[3] It is cited only briefly for the proposition that Rule 702's reliability requirements apply to all proffered expert testimony, not merely to the products of science.

If *Jones's* careless handling of both sources and reasoning is unusual, *United States v. Paul* is in some ways stranger still. In *Paul*, the Court of Appeals statement of the facts and history of the case is precise and pertinent, and will be set out here in its entirety.

### I. FACTS

In May 1996, an unidentified person who stated that he was a bank investigator telephoned Ed Spearman, branch manager of Wachovia National Bank (Wachovia) at Atlanta, Georgia, and warned him that someone intended to leave a note at the bank in an attempt to extort money from the bank. The "investigator" instructed Spearman to follow the directions in the note. Spearman contacted bank security and the Federal Bureau of Investigation (FBI), who advised him to contact the agency immediately if he received an extortion demand. On the following morning, a security camera outside the entrance to Wachovia Bank videotaped a man, wearing a scarf and sunglasses, place an envelope under the front door of the bank. Inside the envelope, addressed to Spearman, was an extortion note that directed Spearman to deliver $100,000 to the men's restroom of a downtown Atlanta McDonald's restaurant. The note threatened violence if Spearman did not follow the instructions and make the payment. Spearman notified bank security and the FBI.

The investigating agents developed a plan to arrest the extortionist: an FBI agent, acting as Spearman, would drive Spearman's car to the McDonald's and place a briefcase in the men's restroom, while surveillance agents would watch the restroom and arrest the person who took the briefcase.

In executing the plan, FBI Agent Eric Bryant testified that upon his arrival at the McDonald's, he entered the men's restroom, observed appellant Sunonda Paul in a restroom stall, left a briefcase and exited the restroom. FBI surveillance agents testified that they later saw Paul sitting at a table near the restroom. As Bryant left the McDonald's, surveillance agents observed Paul enter the restroom again and then attempt to leave the establishment with the briefcase in his backpack. When confronted, Paul told the agents that he was in the area to visit a nearby gym and had stopped at

---

[44]*U.S. v. Jones*, 107 F.3d 1147, 1160, 46 Fed. R. Evid. Serv. 885, 1997 FED App. 0082P (6th Cir. 1997), quoting Bryan Found & Doug Rogers, Contemporary Issues in Forensic Handwriting Examination: A Discussion of Key Issues in the Wake of the Starzecpyzel Decision, 8 J. Forensic Document Examination 1, 26 (1995).

[45]*U.S. v. Jones*, 107 F.3d 1147, 1161, 46 Fed. R. Evid. Serv. 885, 1997 FED App. 0082P (6th Cir. 1997).

**[Section 4:7]**

[1]The opinions in *Paul*, *Battle* and *Hines* all were published after *Kumho Tire*, but sufficiently close in time that their failure to properly digest and apply it is perhaps understandable.

[2]*U.S. v. Paul*, 175 F.3d 906, 51 Fed. R. Evid. Serv. 1464, 183 A.L.R. Fed. 773 (11th Cir. 1999).

[3]*U.S. v. Paul*, 175 F.3d 906, 910, 51 Fed. R. Evid. Serv. 1464, 183 A.L.R. Fed. 773 (11th Cir. 1999)

the McDonald's for breakfast. He also told them that he decided to take the briefcase after he found it in the restroom. Paul, however, was dressed in casual street clothing and had no gym clothes or athletic equipment in his possession. The agents arrested him.

## II. PROCEDURAL HISTORY

A grand jury indicted Paul on one count of bank extortion, in violation of 18 U.S.C.A. § 2113(a), and Paul pleaded not guilty. Prior to trial, Paul moved in limine to exclude FBI document examiner Larry Ziegler's testimony regarding handwriting analysis. The district court, however, denied Paul's motion at the pretrial hearing.

The demand note left at Wachovia was the key evidence in determining whether Paul was the extortionist. Although FBI agents examined the videotape to determine the identity of the person who delivered the note, they could not identify the person conclusively. Consequently, the FBI conducted fingerprint and handwriting analysis tests on the note to establish the identity of the extortionist. A fingerprint expert concluded that the latent prints on the note and envelope did not match Paul's fingerprints.

Ziegler, the FBI document examiner, compared the handwriting on the note and the envelope to Paul's handwriting samples and concluded that Paul was the author of both. Specifically, Ziegler asked Paul to write the word restaurant. In the presence of an FBI agent, Paul misspelled the word as follows: "resturant." In the extortion note the extortionist misspelled the word restaurant the same way. Ziegler also asked Paul to write out "Spearman." Paul spelled it "Sperman," the same way the extortionist had addressed the envelope.[4]

What is odd about this is that the Court seems to have turned the case into one concerning the dependability of reasoning about the authorship of a document from misspellings in exemplars, without realizing that this is not necessarily an expertise issue, its proper role in document examiner practice is somewhat controversial even in document examiner literature, and it has little to do with the reliability of assignment of authorship based on comparison of form.

Suppose an investigator with no claimed skill in document examination notices what appears to him to be unusual misspellings in a typed robbery note. (The same misspelling, say, that was in the robbery note in Woody Allen's movie, "Take the Money and Run," which said (in part) "I am pointing a gub at you.") Acting on other information, he obtains a search warrant for the residence of a suspect and discovers numerous documents, typed or not, in which the suspect refers to "gubs" in contexts which clearly indicate he meant guns ("The NRA is right to oppose gub control legislation"). Virtually every court would receive such evidence authenticated by the investigator, though he claims no special knowledge about the uncommonness of this particular misspelling of "gun." Such a case raises interesting issues of jury notice and the accuracy of jury notice in regard to base rate occurrences of misspellings derived from common experience, but not of *Daubert/Kumho* reliability of expertise. Exactly how much a document examiner ought to rely or be influenced by misspellings is a subject of some controversy, and, as noted above, there have been warnings in document examiner literature against assuming uncommonness and making too much of misspellings.[5] All of this appears to have escaped the notice of the Court of Appeals, however, since these issues are never mentioned in the rest of the opinion.

Of course, though it is not explicitly noted by the court, the questioned document examiner in the case did perform a comparison-of-form analysis in addition to noting the misspellings, and it was that identification by comparison of form which was the subject of Paul's reliability objection. The court deals with that objection as

---

[4]*U.S. v. Paul*, 175 F.3d 906, 908–909, 51 Fed. R. Evid. Serv. 1464, 183 A.L.R. Fed. 773 (11th Cir. 1999).

[5]See Risinger, Denbeaux & Saks, Exorcism of Ignorance as a Proxy for Rational Knowledge: The Lessons of Handwriting Identification "Expertise," 137 U. Pa. L. Rev. at 770–771 (1989) and authorities there cited.

follows:

### 1. Admissibility of Handwriting Analysis

Paul argues that Ziegler's testimony is not admissible under the *Daubert* guidelines because handwriting analysis does not qualify as reliable scientific evidence. His argument is without merit. In *Daubert*, the Supreme Court held that Federal Rule of Evidence 702 controls decisions regarding the admissibility of expert testimony. The Supreme Court declared that under rule 702, when "[f]aced with a proffer of expert scientific testimony . . . the trial judge must determine at the outset pursuant to Rule 104(a), whether the expert is proposing to testify to (1) scientific knowledge that (2) will assist the trier of fact to understand or determine a fact in issue." *Daubert v. Merrell Dow Pharmaceuticals, Inc.*, 509 U.S. 579, 592, 113 S. Ct. 2786, 125 L. Ed. 2d 469, 27, 27 U.S.P.Q.2d 1200, Prod. Liab. Rep. (CCH) P 13494, 37 Fed. R. Evid. Serv. 1, 23 Envtl. L. Rep. 20979 (1993). The Supreme Court stated that "[t]he inquiry envisioned by Rule 702 is, we emphasize, a flexible one" and that "Rule 702 . . . assign[s] to the trial judge the task of ensuring that an expert's testimony both rests on a reliable foundation and is relevant to the task at hand." *Daubert v. Merrell Dow Pharmaceuticals, Inc.*, 509 U.S. 579, 594, 597, 113 S. Ct. 2786, 125 L. Ed. 2d 469, 27, 27 U.S.P.Q.2d 1200, Prod. Liab. Rep. (CCH) P 13494, 37 Fed. R. Evid. Serv. 1, 23 Envtl. L. Rep. 20979 (1993). The Court also listed several factors to assist in the determination of whether evidence is scientifically reliable. See *Daubert v. Merrell Dow Pharmaceuticals, Inc.*, 509 U.S. 579, 592–595, 113 S. Ct. 2786, 125 L. Ed. 2d 469, 27, 27 U.S.P.Q.2d 1200, Prod. Liab. Rep. (CCH) P 13494, 37 Fed. R. Evid. Serv. 1, 23 Envtl. L. Rep. 20979 (1993).

Many circuits were split at the time of trial, however, on whether *Daubert* should apply to nonscientific expert testimony. Some held that the application of *Daubert* is limited to scientific testimony, while others used *Daubert*'s guidance to ensure the reliability of all expert testimony presented at trial. Compare *McKendall v. Crown Control Corp.*, 122 F.3d 803, 62 Cal. Comp. Cas. (MB) 1100, Prod. Liab. Rep. (CCH) P 15045, 47 Fed. R. Evid. Serv. 1 (9th Cir. 1997) (limiting the application of *Daubert* to the evaluation of scientific testimony); with *Watkins v. Telsmith, Inc.*, 121 F.3d 984, Prod. Liab. Rep. (CCH) P 15074, 47 Fed. R. Evid. Serv. 950 (5th Cir. 1997) (holding that the application of *Daubert* is not limited to scientific knowledge).

Recently, however, in *Kumho Tire Company, Ltd. v. Carmichael*, the Supreme Court held that *Daubert*'s "gatekeeping" obligation, requiring the trial judge's inquiry into both the expert's relevance and reliability, applies not only to testimony based on "scientific" testimony, but to all expert testimony. *Kumho Tire Co., Ltd. v. Carmichael*, 526 U.S. 137, 119 S. Ct. 1167, 1174, 143 L. Ed. 2d 238, 50, 50 U.S.P.Q.2d 1177, Prod. Liab. Rep. (CCH) P 15470, 50 Fed. R. Evid. Serv. 1373, 29 Envtl. L. Rep. 20638 (1999). The Court further noted that rules 702 and 703 give all expert witnesses testimonial leeway unavailable to other witnesses on the presumption that the expert's opinion "will have a reliable basis in the knowledge and experience of his discipline." *Kumho Tire Co., Ltd. v. Carmichael*, 526 U.S. 137, 119 S. Ct. 1167, 1174, 143 L. Ed. 2d 238, 50, 50 U.S.P.Q.2d 1177, Prod. Liab. Rep. (CCH) P 15470, 50 Fed. R. Evid. Serv. 1373, 29 Envtl. L. Rep. 20638 (1999) (citing *Daubert v. Merrell Dow Pharmaceuticals, Inc.*, 509 U.S. 579, 592, 113 S. Ct. 2786, 125 L. Ed. 2d 469, 27, 27 U.S.P.Q.2d 1200, Prod. Liab. Rep. (CCH) P 13494, 37 Fed. R. Evid. Serv. 1, 23 Envtl. L. Rep. 20979 (1993)). Moreover, the Court held that a trial judge may consider one or more of the specific *Daubert* factors when doing so will help determine that expert's reliability. *Kumho Tire Co., Ltd. v. Carmichael*, 526 U.S. 137, 119 S. Ct. 1167, 1175, 143 L. Ed. 2d 238, 50, 50 U.S.P.Q.2d 1177, Prod. Liab. Rep. (CCH) P 15470, 50 Fed. R. Evid. Serv. 1373, 29 Envtl. L. Rep. 20638 (1999). But, as the Court stated in *Daubert*, the test of reliability is a "flexible" one, and *Daubert*'s list of specific factors neither necessarily nor solely applies to all experts or in every case. *Kumho Tire Co., Ltd. v. Carmichael*, 526 U.S. 137, 119 S. Ct. 1167, 1175, 143 L. Ed. 2d 238, 50, 50 U.S.P.Q.2d 1177, Prod. Liab. Rep. (CCH) P 15470, 50 Fed. R. Evid. Serv. 1373, 29 Envtl. L. Rep. 20638 (1999) (citing *Daubert v. Merrell Dow Pharmaceuticals, Inc.*, 509 U.S. 579, 594, 113 S. Ct. 2786, 125 L. Ed. 2d 469, 27, 27 U.S.P.Q.2d 1200, Prod. Liab. Rep. (CCH) P 13494, 37 Fed. R. Evid. Serv. 1, 23 Envtl. L. Rep. 20979 (1993)). Alternatively, *Kumho* declares that "the law grants a district court the same broad latitude when it decides how to determine reliability as it enjoys in respect to its ultimate reliability determination." *Kumho Tire Co., Ltd. v. Carmichael*, 526 U.S. 137, 119 S. Ct. 1167, 1171, 143 L. Ed. 2d 238, 50, 50 U.S.P.Q.2d 1177, Prod. Liab. Rep.

(CCH) P 15470, 50 Fed. R. Evid. Serv. 1373, 29 Envtl. L. Rep. 20638 (1999) (citing *General Elec. Co. v. Joiner*, 522 U.S. 136, 118 S. Ct. 512, 139 L. Ed. 2d 508, 18 O.S.H. Cas. (BNA) 1097, Prod. Liab. Rep. (CCH) P 15120, 48 Fed. R. Evid. Serv. 1, 28 Envtl. L. Rep. 20227, 177 A.L.R. Fed. 667 (1997)) (stating that courts of appeals are to apply "abuse of discretion" standard when reviewing district court's reliability determination).[6]

And that is the totality of the court's review of district court's decision on the reliability issue. The careful (or even careless) reader will have noted that, beyond declaring in the second line of the passage that Paul's "argument is without merit," the court never addresses the reliability issue, or addresses what if anything was before the district court which would have rendered its determination of reliability not an abuse of discretion. There is no formulation of the "task at hand," no description of a reliability test, no reference to information before the district court or the district court's reasoning concerning reliability, nothing.

Having assumed the conclusion of sufficient reliability with no analysis of the issue whatsoever, the rest of the opinion on admissibility follows as a matter of course, finding after a recitation of the experts credentials, that the testimony of a qualified expert could assist the trier of fact, and that its prejudicial effect did not substantially outweigh its probative value.[7] All of this is based on the assumed conclusion to the reliability issue never explicitly addressed, but, given the recitative as to credentials, what emerges in the end is functionally the guild test.

Next we turn to the 10th Circuit's (unpublished) opinion in *United States v. Battle*.[8] Battle was accused of coming from New York to Kansas to set up a drug distribution operation. The evidence against him was voluminous, and involved many witnesses and many episodes. The handwriting identification testimony figured in a single episode not particularly central to the case, but relevant nevertheless because, if believed, it would establish that Battle received money surreptitiously from an out-of-state source under suspicious circumstances. Western Union had a record of a money transfer showing a "Tyler Evans" as the sender and "Anthony Jenkins" as the receiver. The questioned document examiner was called to testify that he had examined exemplars of Battle's signature given when Battle was booked and, in his opinion, Battle signed the name "Anthony Jenkins" to the money transfer.

As usual, the court fails to realize that the document examiner is testifying to one of the subtasks in handwriting comparison most likely to be unreliable. There are 11 letters in "Shawn Battle" and 14 in "Anthony Jenkins" (which was signed only once). They share no capital letters and only 4 small letters (e, h, n, and t) and no letter combinations. One sample is in a presumably normal signature hand and the other is not unless someone named "Anthony Jenkins" in reality signed his own name. If the 10th Circuit had done what the Supreme Court did in *Kumho Tire*, it would have examined the reasons to believe or to doubt the accuracy of such a claimed identification. But though it cites *Kumho Tire* in a pro forma way, it does no such thing. It merely recites the document examiner's credentials (the guild test again) and declares that "[o]ur study of the record on appeal convinces us that McPhail's proffered testimony met the reliability and relevancy test of *Daubert*."[9] The opinion manifests some discomfort about its own conclusion, however, as it goes on to say, "Be that as it may, in any event any error in this regard is, in our view, harmless error when the evidence is considered as a whole."[10]

If the district court opinion in *Starzecpyzel* started the judicial struggle with

---

[6]*U.S. v. Paul*, 175 F.3d 906, 909–910, 51 Fed. R. Evid. Serv. 1464, 183 A.L.R. Fed. 773 (11th Cir. 1999).

[7]*U.S. v. Paul*, 175 F.3d 906, 911, 51 Fed. R. Evid. Serv. 1464, 183 A.L.R. Fed. 773 (11th Cir. 1999).

[8]*U.S. v. Battle*, 1999 WL 596966 (unpublished opinion, 10th Cir., 1999).

[9]*U.S. v. Battle*, 1999 WL 596966, *4.

[10]*U.S. v. Battle*, 1999 WL 596966, *4.

handwriting identification reliability, the opinion in *United States v. Hines*[11] contrasts sharply with the run of Court of Appeals opinions in taking the reliability issue seriously.

On January 27, 1997, someone robbed the Broadway National Bank in Chelsea, Massachusetts, using a demand or "stick up" note, and escaped. The teller who was robbed, Ms. Jeanne Dunne, described the perpetrator as a dark skinned black man with a wide nose and medium build. Ms. Dunne is white, and the court characterized the description as "as close to a generic identification of an African American male as one can imagine." Later, Dunne failed to pick Hines out of a mugbook where his picture appeared, and failed to positively identify him from an eight picture photo spread, though she said Hines "resembled" the robber. Months later, however, she picked Hines out of a lineup, and positively identified him at trial.

The main corroboration of this eyewitness identification came from an FBI questioned document examiner who compared the robbery note with exemplars of Hines' handwriting and concluded that Hines had written the note. A trial on this evidence ended in a hung jury. Before the retrial, Hines moved to disallow the document examiner testimony based on lack of sufficient reason to find it reliable under *Daubert*. The court (Judge Gertner), granted the motion in part, and wrote the published opinion during and after the second trial, which also resulted in a hung jury, in order to explain its ruling and give guidance to the parties in the event of a third trial.

As previously noted in regard to *Daubert*, Judge Gertner identifies what she takes to be a "mixed message" in both *Daubert* and in *Kumho Tire*, with the emphasis on reliability pointing in the direction of more rigor in the evaluation of expertise under Fed. R. Evid. 702 and the emphasis on "the uniqueness of the trial setting, the 'assist the trier' standard and flexibility" doing the opposite.[12] Nevertheless, the court concludes that the main emphasis is on insuring sufficient reliability, and that the Supreme Court "is plainly inviting a reexamination even of 'generally accepted' venerable, technical fields" such as handwriting identification.[13]

Which the court then proceeds to do, with a number of caveats. On what she has seen at the hearing which she held, and in writing, she seems inclined to bar the questioned document examiner testimony in its entirety. However, "[t]his handwriting challenge was raised at the eleventh hour. The hearing was necessarily constrained by the demands of the imminent trial and the schedules of the experts. The Court was unwilling on this record to throw out decades of 'generally accepted' testimony."[14]

In addition, the "compromise solution" Judge Gertner accepts was derived "largely from case law that pre-dated *Kumho*."[15] In other words, the court was not entirely comfortable that she had fully digested and applied the broader implications of *Kumho Tire* which might have been inconsistent with this compromise.

In any event, Judge Gertner proceeds to distinguish between a questioned document examiner's testimony comparing the robbery note with the exemplars and identifying similarities and differences, and testimony concerning the document examiner's inferences of authorship based on those similarities. In sum, she allows the former and bars the latter, essentially adopting the similar approach of Judge Matsch in the Oklahoma City bombing case, *United States v. McVeigh*, which she

---

[11]*U.S. v. Hines*, 55 F. Supp. 2d 62, 52 Fed. R. Evid. Serv. 257 (D. Mass. 1999).

[12]*U.S. v. Hines*, 55 F. Supp. 2d 62, 65, 52 Fed. R. Evid. Serv. 257 (D. Mass. 1999).

[13]*U.S. v. Hines*, 55 F. Supp. 2d 62, 67, 52 Fed. R. Evid. Serv. 257 (D. Mass. 1999).

[14]*U.S. v. Hines*, 55 F. Supp. 2d 62, 67, 52 Fed. R. Evid. Serv. 257 (D. Mass. 1999).

[15]*U.S. v. Hines*, 55 F. Supp. 2d 62, 67, 52 Fed. R. Evid. Serv. 257 (D. Mass. 1999).

quotes.[16]

There is a certain commonsense appeal to this approach. The document examiner's extensive experience looking at handwriting may have sensitized the expert to the perception and identification of similarities or differences which an ordinary person might not notice, and at any rate the document examiner will be free to spend more time isolating such similarities and differences than we could expect jurors to do pursuant to their own examination during deliberations. Viewed this way, a document examiner appears to become a sort of summarizational witness, and the notion of "expertise" becomes much less central to their function.

However, there is a serious problem with this, especially if the document examiner is allowed to recite his or her credentials, titles and job descriptions. By identifying a similarity or difference, the examiner is inevitably perceived as asserting the *significance* of those similarities or differences in regard to assigning authorship, so that the conclusions which are barred are easily inferred. In practice, this is profoundly true, since document examiners who believe they have identified the author of a writing by comparison will normally point out *only* similarities, and if differences are called to their attention they will dismiss them as not being significant or "real" differences, but merely manifestations of "individual variation."[17] Nevertheless, the Solomonic compromise of Judges Matsch and Gertner is clearly an improvement over surrendering the gatekeeping function entirely to the guild, as most other courts have done.[18] And there is evidence that it is becoming common practice, as reflected in *United States v. Santillan*,[19] *United States v. Rutherford*,[20] and *United States v. Brown*.[21]

In *Santillan*, the defendant, Rogelio Santillan, was charged with conspiracy to distribute false immigration documents. According to the opinion of the court, the prosecution's document examiner proposed to testify "that she has identified, using control samples of defendant's handwriting, Santillan's handwriting on numerous 'questioned' documents."[22] Note that, more than seven months after *Kumho Tire*, in an opinion referring to *Kumho Tire*,[23] this is as much information as we are given on the "task at hand" in the case before the court. Clearly, the requirements of *Kumho Tire* are not yet dependably appearing on the radar screens of the lower courts.

In any event, Judge Jensen then goes on to deal with the reliability issue globally. After briefly reviewing (and criticizing)[24] the extant research data, the court adopts the *Hines/McVeigh* approach.[25]

In *United States v. Rutherford* defendant Kent Rutherford was charged with bank

---

[16]*U.S. v. Hines*, 55 F. Supp. 2d 62, 70, 52 Fed. R. Evid. Serv. 257 (D. Mass. 1999), quoting decision of Judge Matsch, in *U.S. v. McVeigh*, 1997 WL 47724 (D.Colo. 1997), at 15–17. *McVeigh* is discussed in § 4:4.

[17]This was one of the main problems that led Judge McKenna to conclude that handwriting identification was not science. See the extended discussion in *U.S. v. Starzecpyzel*, 880 F. Supp. 1027, 1031–1033, 42 Fed. R. Evid. Serv. 247 (S.D. N.Y. 1995).

[18]Or perhaps not. If the law of unintended consequences holds, some court operating under the *Hines/McVeigh* approach is likely to disallow cross examination of a document examiner on known error rates, such as the 8% document examiner error rate shown on one task in Kam IV, on the ground that they are not giving an opinion, even though their implied opinion is clear to the whole courtroom. For a full discussion of Kam IV, see § 4:31.

[19]*U.S. v. Santillan*, 1999 WL 1201765 (N.D. Cal. 1999).

[20]*U.S. v. Rutherford*, 104 F. Supp. 2d 1190, 55 Fed. R. Evid. Serv. 201 (D. Neb. 2000).

[21]*U.S. v. Brown*, No. CR-184ABC (C.D.Cal. Dec. 1, 1999).

[22]*U.S. v. Santillan*, 1999 WL 1201765 (N.D. Cal. 1999).

[23]*U.S. v. Santillan*, 1999 WL 1201765 (N.D. Cal. 1999).

[24]*U.S. v. Santillan*, 1999 WL 1201765 (N.D. Cal. 1999). Judge Jensen seems especially troubled that Dr. Moshe Kam, the government's chief researcher on handwriting expertise issues, refused to share his raw data.

[25]*U.S. v. Santillan*, 1999 WL 1201765 (N.D. Cal. 1999).

fraud involving a scheme dealing with a "sale barn" and check. By reference to the opinion, this is all that one could tell. However, an inquiry to the defense attorney in the case reveals that someone registered at a cattle sale as one "George Hipke," a real person of repute. The imposter then purchased an expensive lot of cattle and paid for them with a check bearing the signature "George Hipke." He then removed the cattle. As would be expected, the crime came to light when the real George Hipke learned of the check from his bank.

Rutherford was a retired banker. Exactly why he was charged is a bit unclear, since the people at the sale barn said he was not the person who tendered the check. However, the theory was that he was the mastermind, who sent somebody else to pay for the cattle with a pre-signed check. The proposed expert testimony was that Rutherford in fact signed a "buyer registration form" in Hipke's name, that as to the check bearing George Hipke's purported signature, Hipke did not sign it (a fact that was actually not disputed), and that there was a strong probability that Rutherford did sign it, and that as to a "load out" sheet from Columbus Sale Barn, the inscriptions on the bottom of the sheet were probably written by Rutherford. Once again, although *Kumho Tire* is cited, there is no further attempt to formulate the separate tasks involved in this scenario, or to examine them individually. This is perhaps a bit surprising, given the extensive nature of the *Daubert/Kumho* hearing that was undertaken.[26] And once again, the main task at issue is the attribution of authorship of a forged signature based on the limited amount of writing involved in the signature, though in this case there were two signatures to work with.

In any event, after criticizing the highly suggestive way in which the problem was presented to the expert by the government in obtaining his original opinion,[27] the court ultimately adopts the *Hines/McVeigh* approach, allowing the proffered expert to testify only by pointing out similarities and differences, and not allowing any explicit opinions concerning authorship or probability of authorship.

Additionally, in the unreported case of *United States v. Brown*,[28] another check forgery case involving an attempted attribution of authorship of the forged signature, the court also adopted the *Hines/McVeigh* approach by order without opinion after holding a *Daubert/Kumho* hearing.

Finally, in *United States v. Fuji*,[29] Judge Gottschall of the Northern District of Illinois has rendered the first decision in a handwriting identification case in modern times which excludes document examiner testimony completely. She has also written the first opinion on asserted handwriting identification expertise to manifest a proper *Kumho Tire* "task at hand" approach.

In this case, there was an allegation that defendant Masao Fujii had been involved in a scheme to obtain the fraudulent entry into the United States of two Chinese nationals. Certain immigration forms filled out in hand printing had been tendered in connection with their attempted entry at John F. Kennedy airport in New York City in December of 1999. As evidence of Fujii's participation, the prosecution sought to call an Immigration and Naturalization Service document examiner, who would testify that she had compared the printing on the forms with exemplars of printing by Fujii, and that in her opinion Fujii printed the fraudulent forms. The defense objected on *Daubert/Kumho* grounds, and a hearing was held on the issue.

In her opinion Judge Gottschall notes that in general "[h]andwriting analysis

---

[26]In keeping with the highest demands of complete disclosure it is here noted that the defense expert in this case was the author's friend, co-author, and one of the editors of this treatise, Dr. Michael J. Saks.

[27]*U.S. v. Rutherford*, 104 F. Supp. 2d 1190,

1193, 55 Fed. R. Evid. Serv. 201 (D. Neb. 2000).

[28]*U.S. v. Brown*, No. CR 99-184 (C.D. Cal., order dated Dec. 1, 1999), on file with author.

[29]*U.S. v. Fujii*, 152 F. Supp. 2d 939, 56 Fed. R. Evid. Serv. 1029 (N.D. Ill. 2000).

does not stand up well under the *Daubert* standards."[30] However, as to general issues of reliability, she concludes that "this court need not weigh in on this question, for whether handwriting analysis per se meets the *Daubert* standards, its application to this case poses more significant problems."[31] This is for two reasons. First, virtually all data on document examiner dependability in identifying the author of handwriting has dealt with cursive and not printed writing. The single recorded proficiency test involving hand printing[32] revealed a 45% error rate on that test. Perhaps more importantly, however, Fujii is a native Japanese who learned to print in English as a second language in Japan. The defense called as a witness Mark Litwicki, Director of Loyola University's English as a Second Language program, who had substantial experience with teaching English to Japanese students in both the United States and Japan. The essence of his testimony was that Japanese learn to print in English only after years of training in the exact copying of Japanese characters where "uniformity of characters 'is an important and valued principle of Japanese handwriting'," that they "spend many years attempting to maximize the uniformity of their writing," that this carried over into their learning to write in English, and that "it would be very difficult for an individual not familiar with the English handwriting of Japanese writers to identify the subtle dissimilarities in the handwriting of individual writers."[33]

Considering all this, the court concludes:

Does Ms. Cox [the document examiner] have any expertise which would allow her to distinguish between unique characteristics of an individual Japanese handprinter and characteristics that might be common to many or all native Japanese handprinters? In an analysis that depends entirely on what is similar between writing specimens and what is different, it would seem to this court essential that an expert have some ability to screen out characteristics which might appear eccentric to the writer, compared with native English printers, but which might in fact be characteristic of most or all native Japanese writers, schooled in English printing in Japan, in printing English. There is no evidence on the record that Ms. Cox has such expertise or has even considered the problem Mr. Litwicki has pointed out.

Considering the questions about handwriting analysis generally under *Daubert*, the lack of any evidence that the identification of handprinting is an expertise that meets the *Daubert* standards and the questions that have been raised—which the government has not attempted to answer—about the expert's ability to opine reliably on handprinting identification in dealing with native Japanese writers taught English printing in Japan, the court grants the defendant's motion [to exclude].[34]

Judge Gottschall's opinion is a masterful example of particularized "task at hand" analysis under the standards of *Kumho Tire*. It provides a model for other courts in how to approach the reliability of specific applications of claimed handwriting identification expertise, and all forms of nonscience forensic science.

It is interesting to note that in this set of 12 federal cases (including *McVeigh* and *Brown*), only eight of the 12 trial judges involved held full-scale reliability hearings,[35] and of those who did, seven out of eight manifested substantial reservations

---

[30]*U.S. v. Fujii*, 152 F. Supp. 2d 939, 56 Fed. R. Evid. Serv. 1029 (N.D. Ill. 2000).

[31]*U.S. v. Fujii*, 152 F. Supp. 2d 939, 56 Fed. R. Evid. Serv. 1029 (N.D. Ill. 2000).

[32]The 1986 Forensic Sciences Foundation test, the results of which are reported in Risinger, Denbeaux & Saks, Exorcism of Ignorance as a Proxy for Rational Knowledge: The Lessons of Handwriting Identification "Expertise," 137 U. Pa. L. Rev. at 746–747 (1989), and also *U.S. v. Fujii*, 152 F. Supp. 2d 939, 941, 56 Fed. R. Evid.

Serv. 1029 (N.D. Ill. 2000) at §§ 4:15 to 4:20, and testified to in *Fujii* by Dr. Michael J. Saks as one of the expert witnesses for the defense.

[33]*U.S. v. Fujii*, 152 F. Supp. 2d 939, 941, 56 Fed. R. Evid. Serv. 1029 (N.D. Ill. 2000), quoting Litwicki.

[34]*U.S. v. Fujii*, 152 F. Supp. 2d 939, 941, 56 Fed. R. Evid. Serv. 1029 (N.D. Ill. 2000).

[35]*Ruth, Velasquez, Jones* and *Battle* were disposed of at trial either without hearing or on voir dire of the government's proposed expert.

about handwriting identification expertise even on a global level.[36] Contrast this with the Court of Appeals judges who heard these cases, all of whom were institutionally insulated from *having* to come to grips with the actual state of knowledge concerning handwriting identification by cold records and appendices, and *all* of whom felt comfortable brushing off reliability challenges with some version of the "guild" test. The inertia of a venerable tradition of admissibility appears to be a powerful incentive to turn a blind eye to the evidence on the asserted expertise. In light of *Kumho Tire*, perhaps even appellate judges will have to pay attention to the issues raised by these cases.

*United States v. Jolivet*,[37] was a mail fraud case. This case has recently been cited in cases such as *Gricco*,[38] as determining the acceptable reliability of handwriting identification expertise. *Jolivet*, however, does no such thing. It is true that the government proffered a document examiner to testify that Jolivet had written certain important documents. Jolivet's attorney, however, *neglected to object*. When the case reached the circuit court, this issue was thus governed by the plain error standard, and it is hardly surprising that the appellate court found that the district court had not committed plain error in admitting document examiner testimony to which there had been no objection.[39] Its further observation that the document examiner's qualifications would have rendered the admission no abuse of discretion even in the face of an objection must be viewed as fairly weak dictum under the circumstances, since, not surprisingly, no one bothered to define what exactly the document examiner was claiming to be able to do in the case.

The next case decided, *United States v. Saelee*,[40] is the second case to completely exclude proffered handwriting identification expertise, and does so on broader grounds than *Fujii* had. In *Saelee* the defendant was charged with mailing packages containing cocaine concealed in Butterfinger candy bars. The three packages each bore an address label with "to:" and "from:" information which had been hand printed. The government sought the introduction of a document examiner from the U.S. Postal Service who would testify that he had compared the printing on the labels to known exemplars of Saelee's genuine hand printing, and had concluded that the labels had been printed by Saelee. After an extensive hearing, the trial court ruled that the proposed testimony could not be admitted under Fed. R. Evid. 701 as non-expert opinion, that the government bore the burden of establishing that the proffered testimony was sufficiently reliable to meet the requirements of Fed. R. Evid. 702, and that both globally, and as to the particular issue of the identification of hand printing, that the government had failed to prove that the identification was "the product of reliable methods" as required by Fed. R. Evid. 702(2).[41]

The next case, *United States v. Richmond*,[42] is the polar opposite of *Saelee* in its approach. The case involved an alleged mail fraud scheme. The court does not explain what the document examiner is being called to do, in apparent derogation the requirement of *Kumho Tire v. Carmichael* that threshold reliability be judged in

---

[36]Judges McKenna, Matsch, Gertner, Jensen, Collins, Bataillon and Gottschall. Only Judge Tidwell, the trial judge in *Paul*, seemed unconcerned. Apropos all this, consider the following quotation from Judge McKenna's opinion in *Starzecpyzel*: "If forensic document examination does rely on an underlying principle, logic dictates that the principle must embody the notion that inter-writer differences, even when intentionally suppressed, can be distinguished from natural variation. How FDEs might accomplish this was unclear to the Court before the hearing, and largely remains so after the hearing." *U.S. v. Starzecpyzel*, 880 F. Supp. 1027, 42 Fed. R. Evid. Serv. 247 (S.D. N.Y. 1995).

[37]*U.S. v. Jolivet*, 224 F.3d 902, 55 Fed. R. Evid. Serv. 670 (8th Cir. 2000).

[38]*U.S. v. Gricco*, 2002 WL 746037 (E.D. Pa. 2002).

[39]*U.S. v. Jolivet*, 224 F.3d 902, 906, 55 Fed. R. Evid. Serv. 670 (8th Cir. 2000).

[40]*U.S. v. Saelee*, 162 F. Supp. 2d 1097, 57 Fed. R. Evid. Serv. 916 (D. Alaska 2001).

[41]*U.S. v. Saelee*, 162 F. Supp. 2d 1097, 57 Fed. R. Evid. Serv. 916, 1105 (D. Alaska 2001).

[42]*U.S. v. Richmond*, 2001 WL 1117235 (E.D. La. 2001).

regard to the particular function the expert is actually seeking to perform in the case. The three paragraph opinion does not discuss any evidence of reliability. Instead, it discusses recent cases calling handwriting identification expertise into question, and declines to follow them. The court ends by saying, "As a gatekeeper, the court will look to see if the expert's methods are reliable in nature and application to the facts."[43] The court says it "will" do this, but it never does it. After another sentence observing that, "cross-examination will help reveal whether the principles and methods used by the experts, as applied to the facts, are reliable,"[44] the court makes no explicit ruling on this issue even though such a determination would seem required by Fed. R. Evid. 702, but merely denies the motion in limine.

The next case was *United States v. Elmore*,[45] a decision of the United States Navy-Marine Corps Court of Criminal Appeals. Elmore was charged with abusing his position in the base post office at the Guantanimo Bay naval facility by stealing already purchased money orders out of the envelopes used to mail them to their intended recipients, and forging the intended recipient's signature in order to cash them. At issue in this case was the most troubling subtask issue in the area of handwriting identification—the assignment of authorship based on the limited writing involved in a concededly inauthentic signature,[46] though there was more writing here than usual because of the multiple forgeries involved. However, as in the previous military justice system case of *United States v. Ruth*,[47] the court was oblivious to the actual issue. In denying the defense motion to exclude the identifications under Fed. R. Evid. 702, the court appears to treat this case as an exercise in stare decisis rather than a determination of threshold reliability. Beyond making the motion, however, it is not clear that the defense attorneys gave the court much more to work with, since the only witness at the Fed. R. Evid. 702 hearing appears to have been the government's document examiner.

Even more troubling is the decision of a panel of the Ninth Circuit in *United States v. Johnson*.[48] Johnson was accused of a conspiracy to smuggle three aliens into the United States. Part of the evidence against him involved the testimony of a government document examiner that writing on certain forms was Johnson's. In two paragraphs, the court rules that the district court's rejection of the defense motion to exclude such testimony was not an abuse of discretion because, "it is undisputed that handwriting analysis is a science in which expert testimony assists a jury," citing a 1982 Ninth Circuit case to that effect, and revealing itself ignorant of (or perhaps willfully blind to) a decade of controversy over this issue since the decisions of *Daubert* and *Starzecpyzel*. In the court's defense, this appears to be another of those cases in which a defense attorney makes a pro forma motion and then provides the court with little other material on the issues. Such performances by the criminal defense bar do their clients little good and end up setting the stage for uninformed rulings by courts which impede the general progress of the development of the law in this area.

An interesting contrast to the use of case authority in *Johnson* is found in *Church v. Maryland*,[49] an employment discrimination case where, as to one aspect of the case, the district court ruled one particular document irrelevant, thus avoiding the issue of the admissibility of a proffered document examiner on the issue of the

---

[43]*U.S. v. Richmond*, 2001 WL 1117235 (E.D. La. 2001).

[44]*U.S. v. Richmond*, 2001 WL 1117235 (E.D. La. 2001).

[45]*U.S. v. Elmore*, 56 M.J. 533 (N.M.C.C.A. 2001).

[46]The reader will recall that this is a task the document examiner community regards as bordering on impossible, and on which at least one proficiency test showed massive errors by examiners. See § 4:17.

[47]See extensive discussion above regarding *U.S. v. Ruth*, 46 M.J. 1 (C.A.A.F. 1997).

[48]*U.S. v. Johnson*, 30 Fed. Appx. 685 (9th Cir. 2002).

[49]*Church v. Maryland*, 53 Fed. Appx. 673 (4th Cir. 2002).

identity of handwriting in the document. The court observes, however, that even if the documents were relevant, it would exclude the document examiner, citing *Saelee*.[50] While this invocation of case authority would be as questionable under *Kumho Tire* as those in *Johnson* or *Elmore*, it does show that in the federal courts the reliability of handwriting identification expertise has generated such divergent cases that both admission and exclusion can be undergirded by the inappropriate invocation of case authority.[51]

Another case that raises this issue is *United States v. Brewer*.[52] The defendant was charged with ripping off an elderly client of the bank for which he worked by using an ATM card to make unauthorized withdrawals. The defendant Brewer claimed he was helping out the client, who was very ill, and had been authorized to make the withdrawals. The elderly client, Steve Kruzic, told the FBI that he had no ATM card and had not authorized Brewer to make any withdrawals, but then he died. Brewer produced an authorization which bore what were purportedly signatures of Brewer, Kruzic, and Brewer's supervisor at the Bank, Donna Johnson. Johnson said she did not remember signing such a form, but the signature looked like her signature. The prosecution proposed to call a document examiner who would testify that the D. Johnson signature was a traced forgery, the source of which she claimed to have identified among various exemplars of Donna Johnson's true signature provided by Johnson. The reliability of a document examiner's methods in determining that a signature is not that of its putative author, but is, rather, traced from a determined source, has never been dealt with in any case under *Daubert* or *Kumho Tire*. Nevertheless, the district court ruled that the document examiner's testimony was inadmissible, based on its reading of *Hines*,[53] *Fujii*[54] and *Saelee*, concluding that "unless some new studies have been conducted in the past six months, the government would be hard-pressed to establish that Seiger's testimony would sufficient under *Daubert*."[55] What this overlooks is that there are proficiency tests dealing with traced forgery identification, the results of which were not dealt with in *Hines, Fujii* or *Saelee* because they were irrelevant to those cases, and one extant formal study,[56] actually bears on the general authenticity of signature issue in ways also not in play in those other cases. Whether the result would have been different after an appropriate hearing is difficult to say, but the reliance on precedent was totally misplaced.

A different criticism might be made of *United States v. Gricco*.[57] Gricco was charged with conspiracy to manufacture and distribute methamphetamine. In a search of his mother-in-law's residence, agents found two handwritten lists for ingredients and supplies used in making methamphetamine. The government proposed to call a document examiner who would testify that the handwritten lists were written by Gricco. Gricco's lawyer moved to exclude the document examiner pursuant to Fed. R. Evid. 702, but seems to have proffered little supporting information beyond a copy of a 14-year-old law review article.[58] This left the stage almost entirely to the government, which managed to have its way in mischaracterizing the

---

[50]*Church v. Maryland*, 180 F. Supp. 2d 708, 721, 87 Fair Empl. Prac. Cas. (BNA) 1513 (D. Md. 2002), aff'd, 53 Fed. Appx. 673 (4th Cir. 2002).

[51]Though it is significant to note that in only one case involving any real attempt at analysis of the problem, following competing presentations of the disputed underlying basis of the asserted expert evidence, has a district court admitted forensic handwriting experts without some substantial kind of limitation.

[52]*U.S. v. Brewer*, 2002 WL 596365 (N.D. Ill. 2002).

[53]*U.S. v. Hines*, 55 F. Supp. 2d 62, 70, 52 Fed. R. Evid. Serv. 257 (D. Mass. 1999).

[54]*U.S. v. Fujii*, 152 F. Supp. 2d 939, 941, 56 Fed. R. Evid. Serv. 1029 (N.D. Ill. 2000).

[55]*U.S. v. Brewer*, 2002 WL 596365 (N.D. Ill. 2002).

[56]See the discussion of "Kam IV," at §4:31.

[57]*U.S. v. Gricco*, 2002 WL 746037 (E.D. Pa. 2002).

[58]Risinger, Denbeaux and Saks, Exorcism of Ignorance as a Proxy for Rational Knowledge: The

Kam studies[59] and the Srihari study,[60] and which mischaracterizations were incorporated into the court's opinion. Based on these plus an invocation of the Third Circuit *Velasquez* case, the court admitted the evidence. No attempt was made to formulate the actual issue at stake in the case as required by *Kumho Tire*. This case seems to be another example of what can happen when defense attorneys make pro forma motions and then fail to do the research to back them up.

Next is *United States v. Nadurath*.[61] In the most extreme example to date of inappropriate global disposition by unexplained invocation of selective precedent, Judge McBryde disposed of a challenge in one paragraph by citing three cases. There is no way to know what was at stake in the case factually, since the opinion does not bother to define the task at hand at all.

It is becoming increasingly clear that many judges would like a global precedent-based solution to hard problems of expert reliability which would spare them from the task of actually thinking about such problems. Unfortunately, both *Kumho Tire* and the text of revised Fed. R. Evid. 702 are against them, though so far many judges have proceeded without paying much attention to those requirements of the law.

The next federal case is *United States v. Hernandez*,[62] a tax fraud case involving a tax preparer. The government proposed to call a questioned document examiner to testify that the handwriting on many tax forms was the defendant's. Defendant moved to exclude as unreliable under Fed. R. Evid. 702. The trial court, after hearing, adopted the *Hines* approach, allowing the witness to testify to similarities but not to give an opinion regarding authorship. The defendant was convicted, and appealed the failure to exclude completely. The circuit court found the lower court's approach somewhat puzzling, but not an abuse of discretion.[63]

Two district court opinions within 10 days of each other in September 2002 illustrate well how even judges attempting to be careful can arrive at opposite results. The first of these was *United States v. Lewis*.[64] In *Lewis*, the defendant was charged with mailing threatening communications to the President and others, by mailing them envelopes containing white powder after the well-known anthrax powder mailings had killed several people and disrupted many federal agencies including Congress. Although there was apparently overwhelming evidence from multiple sources that defendant Lewis had sent the envelopes in question, the prosecution desired to gild this lily with the testimony of John W. Cawley, a "questioned documents analyst" so certified by the U.S. Postal Inspection Service after training by the United States Postal Service Crime Laboratory between 1977 and 1980. Mr. Cawley would have testified that he had compared the known writings of Defendant with the writing on the envelopes, and that the Defendant wrote the addresses on the envelopes.

The District Court excluded Mr. Cawley's proposed testimony. In so doing, however, it did not base its decision on any affirmative conclusion of the limits of handwriting identification expertise (though it seemed at times fairly skeptical),[65] nor did it concentrate on the weaknesses of such expertise in regard to the task at

---

Case of Handwriting Identification "Expertise," 137 U. Pa. L. Rev. 731 (1989). A fine article it was, but a lot has happened since.

[59]See, the discussion of the studies by Kam and his colleagues, at §§ 4:27 to 4:31.

[60]§ 4:36.

[61]*U.S. v. Nadurath*, 2002 WL 1000929 (N.D. Tex. 2002), aff'd, 66 Fed. Appx. 525 (5th Cir. 2003).

[62]*U.S. v. Hernandez*, 42 Fed. Appx. 173, 89 A.F.T.R.2d 2002-3049 (10th Cir. 2002).

[63]*U.S. v. Hernandez*, 42 Fed. Appx. 173, 89 A.F.T.R.2d 2002-3049 (10th Cir. 2002).

[64]*U.S. v. Lewis*, 220 F. Supp. 2d 548 (S.D. W. Va. 2002).

[65]For instance, the court observed, "There were aspects of Mr. Cawley's testimony that undermined his credibility *U.S. v. Lewis*, 220 F. Supp. 2d 548, 554 (S.D. W. Va. 2002). Mr. Cawley testified that he achieved a 100% passage rate on the proficiency tests that he took and that all his peers *always* passed their proficiency tests. Mr.

hand (there was never any discussion of the amount of writing on the envelopes, whether it was cursive or printing, presence of disguise, etc.). Instead, having ruled that defendant's challenge to the reliability of handwriting identification in general was sufficient to trigger a *Daubert* hearing and place the burden of production and persuasion during that hearing on the prosecution, the court concluded that the prosecution failed to produce the required proof of reliability.[66] The prosecution relied entirely on the testimony of Mr. Cawley, whose lack of knowledge demonstrated during cross examination concerning the research record on reliability and error rates doomed the proffer.[67] The court is to be lauded for coming to the conclusion demanded by the logic of the *Daubert/Kumho* procedural structure, and (unlike some other courts) placing the burden of persuasion on the proponent of the expert evidence even when that is the government. The case also shows that it is not only the defense which sometimes fails to properly prepare for and marshal information in *Daubert/Kumho* challenges to handwriting identification.

A much more puzzling opinion was issued by Judge Lasnik in *United States v. Prime*,[68] and it is puzzling for unusual reasons. This was not the usual offhand opinion which characterizes many of the decisions admitting handwriting identification testimony. The charges against Michael Prime involved counterfeit U.S. postal money orders. The prosecution intended to call Kathleen Storer, a forensic document examiner for the United States Secret Service, to testify that Prime's handwriting "appeared on counterfeit money orders and other documents."[69] Later in the opinion, the court indicates that what Ms. Storer was asked to evaluate for authorship was made up of writing on 78 different documents (76 covered by her first report and two by her second report), including envelopes, money orders, "post-it notes," express mail labels and applications for postal boxes.[70] Some of the writing was cursive and some handprinting. Ms. Storer was given extensive known writings of three persons (Prime and codefendants Hiestand and Hardy), and asked if any of them wrote any of the writing on the 78 documents. She found that Hiestand wrote "portions of eight documents" and Hardy wrote "portions" of one document, and Prime wrote "portions" of 45 documents, and "probably" wrote "portions" of 14 more.[71] The documents contained 38 signatures, the authorship of which Storer indicated "could not be determined." Given these facts, it is obvious that, even in

Cawley said that his peers *always* agreed with each others' results and *always* got it right. Peer review in such a 'Lake Woebegone' environment is not meaningful." And the court further said, "Finally, while there may be general acceptance of the theories and techniques employed in handwriting analysis among the 'forensic document community,' this acceptance does not demonstrate reliability. *U.S. v. Lewis*, 220 F. Supp. 2d 548 (S.D. W. Va. 2002). If courts allow the admission of long-relied-on but ultimately unproven analysis, they unwittingly perpetuate and legitimate junk science." *U.S. v. Lewis*, 220 F. Supp. 2d 548 (S.D. W. Va. 2002).

[66]*U.S. v. Lewis*, 220 F. Supp. 2d 548 (S.D. W. Va. 2002).

[67]It should be noted that the court did not appear to believe it likely that a better prepared witness would necessarily have been able to provide the needed evidence.

[68]*U.S. v. Prime*, 220 F. Supp. 2d 1203 (W.D. Wash. 2002), aff'd, 363 F.3d 1028, 64 Fed. R. Evid. Serv. 219 (9th Cir. 2004), cert. granted, judgment vacated on other grounds, 543 U.S. 1101, 125 S.

Ct. 1005, 160 L. Ed. 2d 1007 (2005) and opinion amended and superseded on other grounds, 431 F.3d 1147, 68 Fed. R. Evid. Serv. 1288 (9th Cir. 2005) and aff'd, 431 F.3d 1147, 68 Fed. R. Evid. Serv. 1288 (9th Cir. 2005).

[69]*U.S. v. Prime*, 220 F. Supp. 2d 1203, 1204 (W.D. Wash. 2002), aff'd, 363 F.3d 1028, 64 Fed. R. Evid. Serv. 219 (9th Cir. 2004), cert. granted, judgment vacated on other grounds, 543 U.S. 1101, 125 S. Ct. 1005, 160 L. Ed. 2d 1007 (2005) and opinion amended and superseded on other grounds, 431 F.3d 1147, 68 Fed. R. Evid. Serv. 1288 (9th Cir. 2005) and aff'd, 431 F.3d 1147, 68 Fed. R. Evid. Serv. 1288 (9th Cir. 2005).

[70]*U.S. v. Prime*, 220 F. Supp. 2d 1203 (W.D. Wash. 2002), aff'd, 363 F.3d 1028, 64 Fed. R. Evid. Serv. 219 (9th Cir. 2004), cert. granted, judgment vacated on other grounds, 543 U.S. 1101, 125 S. Ct. 1005, 160 L. Ed. 2d 1007 (2005) and opinion amended and superseded on other grounds, 431 F.3d 1147, 68 Fed. R. Evid. Serv. 1288 (9th Cir. 2005) and aff'd, 431 F.3d 1147, 68 Fed. R. Evid. Serv. 1288 (9th Cir. 2005).

[71]*U.S. v. Prime*, 220 F. Supp. 2d 1203, 1206

the opinion of Storer, the questioned writings presented multiple tasks, and the record is unclear concerning the extent of the writing involved in each separable task. This is important, because, though the court is one of the few to manifest an awareness, at least formally, of its obligation under *Kumho Tire* to evaluate reliability in regard to the specifics of the particular case,[72] it later functionally lumps all of the tasks performed by Storer into a single task for purposes of its analysis.

The first three sections of the court's opinion are (except perhaps for a few details) unexceptionable, even admirable. Section I analyzes *Daubert* and *Kumho Tire*, recognizing that, while they speak of "flexibility" and "discretion," the focus of that flexibility and discretion (its "overarching subject") is "evidentiary relevance and reliability," and that a flexible standard "does not imply a lax one."[73] Section II recounts the history of handwriting identification expertise in the federal courts, pre- and post-*Daubert*, including a very thoughtful examination of Judge McKenna's opinion in *Starzecpyzel*. It quite fairly notes that the Court of Appeals decisions are generally simply affirmations of whatever the district courts have done pursuant to the abuse of discretion standard of *General Electric v. Joiner*, and therefore are of limited use as pronouncements on actual reliability. It further notes that the results in the District Courts have been "uneven," with some admitting the proffers without restriction, some excluding them, and some admitting them with restriction. It then turns to the application of the *Daubert/Kumho* requirements to the facts of *Prime*.

The court's first decision was to properly reject the defense's argument that the 1998 Department of Justice formal solicitation of research proposals "to determine the scientific validity of handwriting identification" was a binding admission by the government that "in its present state, handwriting analysis cannot pass muster under *Daubert/Kumho Tire*." Directly after this ruling, the court proceeds to make "a few general observations" before it gets down to the business of applying "the *Daubert* factors to assess the admissibility of Storer's testimony."[74] It is at this point that the opinion rolls off the edge of the table. The court says, essentially, that *Daubert* and *Kumho Tire* were directed at "novel theories in civil cases," and not at "time-tested techniques used almost universally by law enforcement," and further, where "a novel theory is presented to a court, it makes sense to demand proof of statistically significant results and strict compliance with scientific methods.

---

(W.D. Wash. 2002), aff'd, 363 F.3d 1028, 64 Fed. R. Evid. Serv. 219 (9th Cir. 2004), cert. granted, judgment vacated on other grounds, 543 U.S. 1101, 125 S. Ct. 1005, 160 L. Ed. 2d 1007 (2005) and opinion amended and superseded on other grounds, 431 F.3d 1147, 68 Fed. R. Evid. Serv. 1288 (9th Cir. 2005) and aff'd, 431 F.3d 1147, 68 Fed. R. Evid. Serv. 1288 (9th Cir. 2005).

[72]*U.S. v. Prime*, 220 F. Supp. 2d 1203, 1210–1211 (W.D. Wash. 2002), aff'd, 363 F.3d 1028, 64 Fed. R. Evid. Serv. 219 (9th Cir. 2004), cert. granted, judgment vacated on other grounds, 543 U.S. 1101, 125 S. Ct. 1005, 160 L. Ed. 2d 1007 (2005) and opinion amended and superseded on other grounds, 431 F.3d 1147, 68 Fed. R. Evid. Serv. 1288 (9th Cir. 2005) and aff'd, 431 F.3d 1147, 68 Fed. R. Evid. Serv. 1288 (9th Cir. 2005).

[73]*U.S. v. Prime*, 220 F. Supp. 2d 1203, 1204, (W.D. Wash. 2002), aff'd, 363 F.3d 1028, 64 Fed. R. Evid. Serv. 219 (9th Cir. 2004), cert. granted, judgment vacated on other grounds, 543 U.S. 1101, 125 S. Ct. 1005, 160 L. Ed. 2d 1007 (2005) and opinion amended and superseded on other grounds, 431 F.3d 1147, 68 Fed. R. Evid. Serv. 1288 (9th Cir. 2005) and aff'd, 431 F.3d 1147, 68

Fed. R. Evid. Serv. 1288 (9th Cir. 2005). One objection to the first part of the opinion is that, having said that the standard ought not to be lax, the court then implies that laxness is cured by the "equal intellectual rigor" test. *U.S. v. Prime*, 220 F. Supp. 2d 1203, 1205 (W.D. Wash. 2002), aff'd, 363 F.3d 1028, 64 Fed. R. Evid. Serv. 219 (9th Cir. 2004), cert. granted, judgment vacated on other grounds, 543 U.S. 1101, 125 S. Ct. 1005, 160 L. Ed. 2d 1007 (2005) and opinion amended and superseded on other grounds, 431 F.3d 1147, 68 Fed. R. Evid. Serv. 1288 (9th Cir. 2005) and aff'd, 431 F.3d 1147, 68 Fed. R. Evid. Serv. 1288 (9th Cir. 2005). Of course, that test tests nothing when it is the accuracy of the group practice itself that is being evaluated.

[74]*U.S. v. Prime*, 220 F. Supp. 2d 1203, 1209 (W.D. Wash. 2002), aff'd, 363 F.3d 1028, 64 Fed. R. Evid. Serv. 219 (9th Cir. 2004), cert. granted, judgment vacated on other grounds, 543 U.S. 1101, 125 S. Ct. 1005, 160 L. Ed. 2d 1007 (2005) and opinion amended and superseded on other grounds, 431 F.3d 1147, 68 Fed. R. Evid. Serv. 1288 (9th Cir. 2005) and aff'd, 431 F.3d 1147, 68 Fed. R. Evid. Serv. 1288 (9th Cir. 2005).

However, where a technique has been repeatedly applied and tested by law enforcement and the courts for over a century, the Court does not believe that the absence of scientific data, without more, should be the death knell for such testimony," citing Judge Pollak's *second Llera-Plaza* opinion.[75] In making these observations, the court comes as close to formally embracing the "civil plaintiff proffer vs. prosecution proffer" double standard as one can imagine a court explicitly doing, and does it without noting the difference between the use of a technique to generate investigatory leads and its use as evidence in a criminal trial. After these "preliminary observations" the result of the case seems a forgone conclusion.

Perhaps even more startling is the way that the court then deals with the requirements of *Kumho Tire*, which in the first part of the opinion it rightly noted requires some appropriate standards of reliability applied to the actual task the expert is performing in the case before the court, and which requirement it repeats at length at 1210–1211. How does Judge Lasnik define that task (or more properly, those tasks, since we have already noted that even Ms. Storer treated her comparison in this case as involving many discrete tasks applied to different parts of different writings with different amounts and types of writing)? Well, at first he makes no attempt. He begins his analysis with a description of the government's claims about data on handwriting uniqueness generally, but he says that he need not decide the general question of uniqueness,[76] given the extensive nature of the "known documents" available to the document examiner, whose credentials are impeccable. (If the reader cannot follow this logic, he is no worse off than the writer). He then says that the Kam data establish (globally) that Questioned Document Examiners are generally more accurate than lay persons (ignoring the problems of the application of those data to handwriting identification practice on the ground), that QDEs have a method, and that they have "broad acceptance" among law enforcement. Hence it is sufficiently reliable and properly admitted.

The closest the judge comes to defining the "task(s) at hand" occurs in two footnotes. In footnote 7 he rejects the idea that he should analyze handprinting separately as a separate task, relying in part on the testimony of Professor Kam described below, and further in footnote 5 he says his opinion is limited to situations where there are extensive "questioned and known" documents for the document examiner to work with.[77] In essence, *Prime* defines the *Kumho Tire* task-specific issue as "identifying handwriting as to authorship when there is extensive known writing," which is almost inevitably true in every criminal case, given the power to compel the creation of exemplars. In the end, *Prime* becomes a standard-issue global opinion in *Kumho Tire* clothing.

*Prime* is also the first case in which the government called Dr. Moshe Kam to testify explicitly on the issue of handprinting. The limitations of Kam's first two

---

[75]The strange story which led to the two conflicting opinions of Judge Pollak (both of them unsatisfactory) in *Llera-Plaza* is well known, even if the reasons for it remain unclear. See Denbeaux & Risinger, *Kumho Tire* and Expert Reliability: How the Question You Ask Gives the Answer You Get, 34 Seton Hall L. Rev. 15, 66–74 (2003).

[76]The court concedes in footnote 5 that the data cannot establish uniqueness.

[77]It is easy to see how the extent of the "known" documents in this case might be taken to enhance accuracy, but in reality the "questioned" documents were not "extensive" in the sense that the 3-page ransom note in the JonBenet Ramsey case was extensive, that is, displaying lots of writing in a single document clearly by the same

person. Instead, it is as if the document examiner had been given 78, or 150 or 300 different tests to do (depending on the separable sub-parts, which were clearly present given her actual results). How the extensive nature of her multiple tasks enhanced generally her accuracy is a mystery. The only document that actually appears to have been extensive was a three page document which was hand-printed, raising again the propriety of lumping printing and cursive together in making reliability judgments under the approach mandated by *Kumho Tire*. (Information on the nature of the individual documents is derived from the report of the prosecution's expert, supplied by Michael J. Saks, who testified for the defense in the case).

studies are analyzed at length at §§ 4:27 to 4:31. Dr. Kam refuses to share the data from those studies in contravention of the usual norms of science. In spite of this, courts have neither ordered that he produce those data for reanalysis as part of criminal discovery, nor have they barred him from testifying as a result of the failure to produce the data for defense inspection. It seems unthinkable that a court would follow a similar course in regard to a proffered plaintiff's expert who relied on such research in any competently litigated civil case. Be that as it may, however, in *Prime* things reached a new low. As indicated above, the court in *Saelee* excluded document examiner testimony on handprinting, concluding that handprinting identification was a task which the document examiner literature indicated was more difficult than cursive identification, and which, whatever the status of the research record in regard to cursive, there were no data indicating that document examiners could assign authorship to handprinting reliably. In *Prime* the prosecution called Kam to fill that gap. He testified, apparently,[78] that he had gone back to the original raw materials of those studies and discovered a subset of exemplars in the original materials that were (in his judgment) not in cursive script but handprinted, that he broke out that subset and analyzed it, and that document examiner performance in regard to the handprinting subset was not significantly different from performance in regard to cursive.[79] The court allowed this testimony despite the fact that the data and raw materials still were not produced for inspection and the newly discovered handprinting subset was never mentioned in the original publication of the study. In the end, however, despite formally recognizing the particularizing requirements of *Kumho Tire*, the court explicitly treated handwriting identification including handprinting as a global skill to be globally evaluated

The next case is *United States v. Kehoe*,[80] a truly horrific case involving the prosecution of Chevie O'Brien Kehoe, a white supremacist for, inter alia three capital counts of murder in aid of racketeering. The evidence against Kehoe was as overwhelming as the case was horrific. The handwriting identification testimony at trial appears to have been cumulative, and a good candidate for a harmless error characterization if error had been found. Instead, the court found no abuse of discretion in its admission, citing only *Kumho Tire's* "wide latitude" language regarding trial court discretion, and the expert's credentials. Once again, there is no way of knowing what specific claim of expertise was involved in the case, since the court does not even describe what kind of documents were the subject of the testimony.

In *United States v. Hidalgo*,[81] the district court faced a challenge to a prosecution proffered document examiner's testimony in regard to both handwriting and

---

[78]The court references his testimony at *U.S. v. Prime*, 220 F. Supp. 2d 1203, 1313 n 7 (W.D. Wash. 2002), aff'd, 363 F.3d 1028, 64 Fed. R. Evid. Serv. 219 (9th Cir. 2004), cert. granted, judgment vacated on other grounds, 543 U.S. 1101, 125 S. Ct. 1005, 160 L. Ed. 2d 1007 (2005) and opinion amended and superseded on other grounds, 431 F.3d 1147, 68 Fed. R. Evid. Serv. 1288 (9th Cir. 2005) and aff'd, 431 F.3d 1147, 68 Fed. R. Evid. Serv. 1288 (9th Cir. 2005), but does not describe it. The presumed tenor is taken from the fuller summary of the testimony in *U.S. v. Hidalgo*, 229 F. Supp. 2d 961 (D. Ariz. 2002).

[79]As if to confirm the elementary point of both science and law—that truth and accuracy are enhanced by making data public and accessible to scrutiny—it emerged at the *Daubert* hearing in *Hidalgo* that Kam's new analysis made the wrong comparison. It compared examiners' performance on handprinting to their performance on writing that was both script and *a mixture of script and handprinting*. Once that fact becomes known, it should be obvious even to nonscientists that what was tested was not the question that was at issue. Such a comparison between apples versus oranges with some apples mixed in will reduce and tend to obscure any true performance gap that might actually exist between examiner performance on handprinting compared to cursive writing. Why the simplest, most obvious and most appropriate comparison was not made, we cannot know. The procedural point here is that it was handled by the *Prime* court in a way that prevented anyone from learning of the problem and by the *Hidalgo* court in a way that made it possible for the error to become known.

[80]*U.S. v. Kehoe*, 310 F.3d 579, 59 Fed. R. Evid. Serv. 812 (8th Cir. 2002).

[81]*U.S. v. Hidalgo*, 229 F. Supp. 2d 961 (D. Ariz. 2002).

handprinting. This was the second case in which Dr. Kam has been called to testify as to the results of his newly discovered subset of handprinting tests from his earlier research. Early in the opinion the court seemed to understand that handprinting and cursive writing presented two separate tasks for evaluation, but in the end (without reference to the specificity requirements of *Kumho Tire*), like the court in *Prime*, it specifically rejects this distinction, citing the Kam testimony in a footnote. The court then evaluates the research record globally (and as if it applied to handprinting), finding that the record established that document examiners possessed an advantage over ordinary persons in accurately determining relevant similarities and differences between known writings and questioned writings generally. As a result, the prosecution proffered witness would be allowed to testify to such similarities and differences. However, the court also concludes that the theoretical basis upon which an actual declaration of authorship was made (the theory of uniqueness: "no two person write exactly alike") was not established and therefore testimony of specific authorship would not be allowed. In short, with a slightly different rationale, the court adopted the *Hines* approach globally.

*United States v. Mooney*[82] is another case in which it is not possible to frame the expert task at hand with much specificity from the opinion. Dennis Mooney was prosecuted in federal court on charges arising out of the armed robbery of a motel in Waterville, Maine. Mooney and the other participants in the robbery were intercepted some distance away, after the motel clerk worked free from restraints and called police. They still had the items taken from the robbery, and the clothes and weapons used in the robbery, with them in the car when they were arrested. The other four participants plead out and testified against Mooney at trial. In addition, Mooney fit a detailed fresh complaint description given by the clerk and was identified by the clerk both before and at trial. At some point, letters purportedly from Mooney were received by Mooney's (former?) girlfriend admitting participation, but the court does not tell us if the letters were signed (though it seems likely that they were). It also does not tell us how long the letters were, or whether they were cursive or handprinted. The prosecution wished to establish Mooney's authorship partly by circumstances, partly by testimony from the (at least by then former) girlfriend recognizing Mooney's handwriting, and partly by testimony from a document examiner based on his comparison of the letters to known writings of Mooney. The defense moved to bar the expert testimony pursuant to *Daubert/Kumho*, or at least to limit it to the identification of similarities as was done in *Hines* and the cases that have followed it. The district court denied both requests, and the First Circuit found no abuse of discretion in these denials.

In coming to this conclusion, the Circuit found that the district court properly relied globally on the credentials of the document examiner and on his testimony that "he and other forensic document examiners employ the same methodology," that "this methodology has been subject to general peer review through published journals in the field" and that "its accuracy has been tested, with one study concluding that certified document examiners had a potential error rate of 6.5%."[83] However, it would seem that the first two of these statements are of little value when, in the words of *Kumho Tire*, the question is whether "the discipline itself lacks reliability."[84] As to the statement that the accuracy of the method employed by document examiners "has been tested," that certainly is not true in regard to the great majority of its subtasks. As to the proposition that "one study concluded that certified document

[82]*U.S. v. Mooney*, 315 F.3d 54, 60 Fed. R. Evid. Serv. 60 (1st Cir. 2002).

[83]*U.S. v. Mooney*, 315 F.3d 54, 62, 60 Fed. R. Evid. Serv. 60 (1st Cir. 2002).

[84]*Kumho Tire Co., Ltd. v. Carmichael*, 526 U.S. 137, 151, 119 S. Ct. 1167, 143 L. Ed. 2d 238, 50, 50 U.S.P.Q.2d 1177, Prod. Liab. Rep. (CCH) P 15470, 50 Fed. R. Evid. Serv. 1373, 29 Envtl. L. Rep. 20638 (1999).

examiners had a potential error rate of 6.5%," this chapter contains an exhaustive review of the studies evaluating document examiner skills and, as the reader can see, no such study exists. The only studies that have ever tested document examiner skills at all in regard to actual tasks of authorship attribution have all concentrated on signature authentication alone, and have not differentiated between "certified" and "uncertified" examiners (whatever that term may mean). No studies have found "potential" error rates of any kind (since individual studies can deal only in actual error rates revealed by the data in the study), and no study has found a global document examiner error rate of 6.5%. What the witness was probably referring to was Kam II, which found that document examiners doing a sorting task (not attributing authorship as in normal practice) had a 13% false negative error rate and a 6.5% false positive error rate under conditions much more favorable than found in actual practice.[85]

But perhaps we are overanalyzing. Perhaps this is another case where the defense failed to make an appropriately detailed record. Perhaps the circuit panel can be forgiven for just going through the motions, given the overwhelming evidence against Mooney. They even seem to adopt the problematical argument that the long history of handwriting identification admissibility establishes its reliability, and the fallacious reading of Fed. R. Evid 901(b)(3)[86] which was discussed above.[87] What is a bit more troubling is their global suggestion that the *Hines* approach is never required when conclusions are based on the same methodology as observations (which is always), and that it may be the *Hines* approach which is the abuse of discretion (a conclusion which would be contrary to the 10th Circuit opinion in *Hernandez*, supra). Despite a wide following in various courts around the country, apparently there is less than universal respect for the *Hines* approach in the land of its birth.

*United States v. Crisp*[88] is the last of the federal criminal cases considered. It illustrates how bad facts and the best of a bad set of defense choices can help make bad law. On June 13, 1981, around 12:25 in the afternoon, a lone male wearing a mask and surgical gloves and carrying a handgun, entered the Central Carolina Bank in Durham, N.C. He approached a teller, threw a bag on the counter, and ordered her to fill the bag. The teller gave the gunman $7854. A car horn from the parking lot beeped twice, and the robber left the bank and was seen driving away in a purple Ford Probe. Police found a stolen purple Ford Probe abandoned on a local street later that day, which apparently contained no useful clues or evidence.

The next day authorities received a call on the Crimestoppers tip line from a man claiming to have information about the robbery. The caller agreed to meet the police at a local restaurant later in the afternoon. The caller turned out to be one Michael Mitchell, who said that the bank robbers were Patrick Crisp and Lamont Torain. The reason Mitchell knew who robbed the bank, he said, was that Crisp and Torain had tried to recruit him for the robbery, and Crisp had detailed the entire plan to him at that time. Mitchell said he declined to participate. (The opinion does not give any account concerning Mitchell's reason for coming forward and volunteering this information.) As a result of Mitchell's information, the police obtained an arrest warrant for Crisp.

The following day (June 15), in what the opinion makes out to be a totally unexpected coincidence, Mitchell and Crisp were driving together in a rented Pontiac Grand Am with Crisp at the wheel when they happened upon a police license checkpoint. Crisp had no driver's license, and gave his name as Jermaine Jackson. A search of the vehicle turned up a small amount of marijuana. While an officer or

---

[85]For a full analysis, see §§ 4:27 to 4:31.

[86]*U.S. v. Mooney*, 315 F.3d 54, 60 Fed. R. Evid. Serv. 60, 62 (1st Cir. 2002).

[87]§ 4:6.

[88]*U.S. v. Crisp*, 324 F.3d 261, 60 Fed. R. Evid. Serv. 1486 (4th Cir. 2003).

officers were interviewing Crisp, Mitchell informed another officer or officers of Crisp's real identity which led them to discover the outstanding arrest warrant. Crisp was arrested.

Another warrant was obtained for Torain, and he was also arrested. After police interrogation, Torain confessed. He admitted that Mitchell had begged off of participating in the robbery at the last minute, but he claimed that the original plan had been conceived by Crisp and Mitchell together. Initially, he had only agreed to drive the getaway car, but when Mitchell backed out, he agreed to be the one to go into the bank.

Torain was jailed in the same facility as Crisp. According to him, he passed Crisp's cell one day and a note was slid out under the door (which he then turned over to the authorities). The note read:

> Lamont
>
> You know if you don't help me I am going to get life in prison, and you ain't going to get nothing. Really it's over for me if you don't change what you told them.
>
> Tell them I picked you up down the street in Kathy's car. Tell them tht I didn't drive the Probe. Tell them Mike drove the Probe. His is the one that told on us. Tell them the gun and all that shit was Mike's That is what I am going to tell them tommorow.
>
> ~~Tell the Feds Mike drove you away from the bank.~~[89]

Patrick Crisp claimed that he had been with his cousin Cecilia Porter at the time of the robbery (and she so testified at trial). He also claimed that he was being framed by Mitchell and Torain. The viability of that claim (to the extent there was any[90] was heavily dependent on inducing belief that the note Torain gave to police had not been slid out of Crisp's cell, but was an invention of Torain's with or without police connivance. If the note were found to be written by Crisp, all of his defenses would collapse. There were two pieces of evidence proffered by the prosecution to bolster Torain's testimony that the note originated with Crisp. First, it appears undisputed that there was a palmprint on the note. The prosecution obtained an authentic palmprint from Crisp, and it was compared with the palmprint on the note by Mary Katherine Brennan, a fingerprint examiner with the North Carolina State Bureau of Investigation, who concluded that the palmprint on the note was Crisp's.

In addition, the prosecution obtained handwriting exemplars from Crisp. These were compared to the handwriting on the note by Thomas Currin, a document examiner with the same State Bureau of Investigation, who concluded that Crisp wrote the note.

Obviously, unless these witnesses were to be excluded (especially the fingerprint examiner), Crisp was unlikely to have a chance of acquittal. To that end, Crisp moved to exclude the proffered fingerprint and handwriting identifications on the ground that they did not meet the reliability standards of Rule 702. The motion was denied without (available) opinion as to both proffers. It is clear from the opinion in the Court of Appeals that there was a hearing on the motions, but it seems that the only testimony taken was from the government's document examiner, the defense relying on cross examination and published sources.

In addition, it seems clear that the attack that was made on both areas of expertise was global, in derogation of the requirements of *Kumho Tire*. In this case

---

[89]*U.S. v. Crisp*, 324 F.3d 261, 264, 60 Fed. R. Evid. Serv. 1486 (4th Cir. 2003). "Tomorrow" is spelled "tommorow" in original and strike-through in original.

[90]In addition to the testimony of Mitchell and Torain, police had found surgical gloves in the back of Crisp's girlfriend Katherine Bell's car (she was apparently the "Kathy" referred to in the note), and a bulletproof vest and sawed-off shotgun in the bedroom of her residence, which Mitchell, at any rate, said had been shown to him as intended for use in the robbery).

that is not surprising, certainly as to the fingerprint aspects of the case. Unless we are misled by the implications of the word "palmprint," it is likely that the latent print was extensive, rendering unavailable the attack on the "boundary problem," that is, the reliability of comparisons to latent prints which contain little detail. As I (and a co-author) have argued elsewhere, while a global attack on fingerprint comparison reliability for lack of formal data is interesting, it is only the boundary problem that is likely to create a viable issue under *Daubert/Kumho*.[91] We further observe there that quixotic global attacks on fingerprint identification are likely to have bad consequences downstream by making it easier for courts to dismiss skeptics as irresponsible bomb-throwers.[92] Something of that dynamic may have infected the majority's consideration of the handwriting identification issue in this case. Of course, the defense attorney really had no choice; assuming the palmprint was sufficiently extensive and clear, it was either a global attack on fingerprint identification or none at all, and he probably was obliged to take the one-in-a-million shot for his client even though it might foul up the way in which later decisions would be approached by this court, and others influenced by its opinion. As was said above, what happened was the bad result of making the best of a bad set of available choices for his client.

The majority had little trouble dismissing the global attack on fingerprinting, in a rather slipshod opinion tacking together pieces of rationale without much analysis, including the "longstanding acceptance, not only in the expert community, but by courts," and "widespread agreement on standards"[93] within the expert community (which happens not to be true in regard to the boundary problem, by the way), and most startlingly, acceptance of the testimony by examiners that the error rate "was essentially zero" or "negligible," without supporting data, as establishing a low error rate generally and apparently across all conditions.[94] The court, like many others, seems unaware that none of this is very compelling when, in the words of *Kumho Tire*, the issue is whether "the discipline itself lacks reliability."[95] Finally, the court concludes that, in the face of these factors, the defense had failed to bring forward sufficient information even to raise an issue concerning reliability.

If the opinion of the majority on the fingerprinting issue was slipshod, there was a better opinion that could have been written reaching the same result in the case before the court.[96] A long history of, among other things, successful identification of cadavers later confirmed by other evidence (combined with other fairly indisputable general propositions about the nature of ridged skin) perhaps provides an acceptable belief warrant for the reliability of the process when there is extensive questioned print material to work with (as appears to have been the case here), even though there is a lack of formal science concerning the randomization mechanism involved, and a lack of statistical work that could generate information on random match probabilities.[97] The only caveat here is that the palm print may have been smudged in such a way that it did not provide sufficient detail to justify such

---

[91]Denbeaux & Risinger, *Kumho Tire* and Expert Reliability: How the Question You Ask Gives the Answer You Get, 34 Seton Hall L. Rev. 15, 68 (2003).

[92]Denbeaux & Risinger, *Kumho Tire* and Expert Reliability: How the Question You Ask Gives the Answer You Get, 34 Seton Hall L. Rev. 15, 68 at n. 183 (2003).

[93]*U.S. v. Crisp*, 324 F.3d 261, 60 Fed. R. Evid. Serv. 1486 (4th Cir. 2003) *U.S. v. Crisp*, 324 F.3d 261, 60 Fed. R. Evid. Serv. 1486 (4th Cir. 2003).

[94]*U.S. v. Crisp*, 324 F.3d 261, 269, 60 Fed. R. Evid. Serv. 1486 (4th Cir. 2003).

[95]*Kumho Tire Co., Ltd. v. Carmichael*, 526 U.S. 137, 151, 119 S. Ct. 1167, 143 L. Ed. 2d 238, 50, 50 U.S.P.Q.2d 1177, Prod. Liab. Rep. (CCH) P 15470, 50 Fed. R. Evid. Serv. 1373, 29 Envtl. L. Rep. 20638 (1999).

[96]Denbeaux & Risinger, *Kumho Tire* and Expert Reliability: How the Question You Ask Gives the Answer You Get, 34 Seton Hall L. Rev. 15, at 60–63 (2003).

[97]Denbeaux & Risinger, *Kumho Tire* and Expert Reliability: How the Question You Ask Gives the Answer You Get, 34 Seton Hall L. Rev. 15, at 60–63 (2003).

an approach, especially considering the fact that the examiner's conclusions may have been contaminated by knowledge of other, fingerprint-domain irrelevant, evidence in the case (a point apparently never raised by the defense.)[98]

If an acceptable opinion on the fingerprint aspects of the case could perhaps have been written, the same is not so clearly true concerning handwriting identification, which lacks the characteristics of the fingerprint phenomenon which might provide the requisite belief warrant. Nevertheless, on the handwriting issue, the majority went on to reach a similar result that it reached in regard to palmprint identification (and on explicitly similar grounds).[99] First, the court observes that no circuit has ever found the admission of handwriting identification testimony to be an abuse of discretion.[100] Next, the court recites the qualifications of Agent Curran, the government's proposed witness.[101] It then notes in a footnote that the witness testified to the results of what is apparently one of the Kam studies (but the actual study does not seem to have been produced by the parties or obtained by the court).[102] Finally it says, "The fact that handwriting comparison analysis has achieved widespread and lasting acceptance in the expert community gives us the assurance of reliability that *Daubert* requires,"[103] a most breathtakingly disregard of *Daubert* and *Kumho Tire* and an explicit adoption of the "guild test."[104]

The dissent opens thus:

> The majority believes that expert testimony about fingerprint and handwriting identification is reliable because the techniques in these fields have been accepted and tested in our adversary system over time. This belief leads the majority to excuse fingerprint and handwriting analysis from the more careful scrutiny that scientific expert testimony must now withstand under *Daubert* before it can be admitted. In Patrick Leroy Crisp's case, the government did not prove that its expert identification evidence satisfied the *Daubert* factors or that it was otherwise reliable. I respectfully dissent for that reason. In dissenting, I am not suggesting that fingerprint and handwriting evidence cannot be shown to satisfy *Daubert*. I am only making the point that the government did not establish in Crisp's case that this evidence is reliable. The government has had 10 years to comply with *Daubert*. It should not be given a pass in this case.

This paragraph sets out the themes of the dissent, but it is harder than one might think to determine its exact focus. The rest of the opinion shows great familiarity with the literature concerning the global reliability arguments surrounding both fingerprint and handwriting identification, and it is very effective in eviscerating the majority's reliance on "adversary testing" as a general matter. However, it is difficult to know whether the dissent is saying that the government failed to make an appropriate showing in Crisp's case because they merely called two examiners who were not themselves familiar enough with the extant disputes and data to make an appropriate record upon which to base a finding of reliability (which would mean that the dissent was arguing for a result like *United States v. Lewis*), or whether the dissent was arguing that the current state of the research record is inadequate to establish admissibility of either fingerprinting or handwriting identification

---

[98]For a general discussion of such issues, see Risinger, Saks, Thompson and Robert Rosenthal, The *Daubert/Kumho* Implications of Observer Effects in Forensic Science: Hidden Problems of Expectation and Suggestion, 90 Cal. L. Rev. 1 (2002).

[99]*U.S. v. Crisp*, 324 F.3d 261, 271, 60 Fed. R. Evid. Serv. 1486 (4th Cir. 2003) ("Our analysis of *Daubert* in the context of fingerprint identification applies with equal force here.").

[100]*U.S. v. Crisp*, 324 F.3d 261, 270, 60 Fed. R. Evid. Serv. 1486 (4th Cir. 2003).

[101]*U.S. v. Crisp*, 324 F.3d 261, 270, 60 Fed. R. Evid. Serv. 1486 (4th Cir. 2003).

[102]*U.S. v. Crisp*, 324 F.3d 261, 270 n 6, 60 Fed. R. Evid. Serv. 1486 (4th Cir. 2003).

[103]*U.S. v. Crisp*, 324 F.3d 261, 271, 60 Fed. R. Evid. Serv. 1486 (4th Cir. 2003).

[104]For a discussion of the untenability of the guild test, see, § 4:6.

globally.[105] In addition, the dissent (like the majority) is too global in focus to comply with the mandate of *Kumho Tire* to judge reliability in regard to the particular proffer in the case. Finally, the dissent (like the majority) does not distinguish between fingerprint identification and handwriting identification when it comes to evaluating the reasons one might in many applications accept the reliability of one and not the other.

Although reliability challenges to handwriting identification testimony are mostly litigated in criminal cases, there have been a few that have arisen in civil cases. The first of these is *Wolf v. Ramsey*,[106] decided the same day as *Crisp*. This defamation case grew out of the unsolved 1996 murder of JonBenet Ramsey in Boulder Colorado. The opinion is worth reading just for its scrupulous and clear summary of the facts of that case and the subsequent investigation. To this date, as most of America knows, the case has not been solved, but various speculations about the perpetrator's identity have circulated. Those speculations directly concerned in this case involve the notion that there is reason to believe that JonBenet's mother Patricia (Patsy) Ramsey might have been the killer, and the notion that there is reason to believe that Robert Christian Wolf might have been the killer. The circumstances pointing toward Patsy Ramsey center around claims that it is unlikely that an intruder into the Ramsey home at night could have found JonBenet's room and abducted her into the basement, killed her, then had the time to draft a three page "ransom" note using materials found in the home and then make his escape without awakening somebody else in the house. The identification of Patsy Ramsey (as opposed to other members of the household such as her husband or son) is based on claimed identification of the handwriting on the ransom note as belonging to Patsy Ramsey.

On the other hand, if one accepts that the evidence establishes that JonBenet was killed by an intruder,[107] then the speculation about the identity of the intruder has tended to focus on a handful of named individuals, although almost everyone agrees that the perpetrator is at least as likely to be someone whose name has not yet surfaced to prominence. One of those named individuals was plaintiff Wolf. Suspicion in regard to Wolf resulted from the statement made by his girlfriend Jacqueline Dilson that she suspected him, based on the following facts she claimed were true: The murder occurred either near midnight on Christmas day or in the early morning of December 26, 1996. Wolf had spent Christmas day with Dilson, but then begged off from staying to have supper with her and her family. Dilson had gone to bed around 10:00 p.m. thinking Wolf had gone off on some sort of spree. Dilson was awakened around 5:30 a.m. by sounds coming from the bathroom. She realized that Wolf was just finishing a shower. Leaving dirty clothes all over the floor, Wolf climbed into bed and went to sleep. The next day Dilson and Wolf saw television news reports about the JonBenet Ramsey murder, and, to Dilson's surprise, Wolf became quite agitated. Wolf cursed and said that he believed JonBenet had been sexually abused by her father, and he brooded over the case for the rest of the night. Dilson also asserted that Wolf was fascinated with world political disputes and political violence, and hated big business. Finally, Dilson said that Wolf owned a sweatshirt with the initials SBTC (for Santa Barbara Tennis Club)

---

[105]At least as to fingerprints, it may be that the majority opinion also was based, like *Florence v. Com.*, 120 S.W.3d 699 (Ky. 2003), on the failure of the defendant to make a sufficient record regarding reliability issues, for it says at one point, "Put simply, Crisp has provided us with no reason today to believe that this general acceptance of the principles underlying fingerprint identification has, for decades, been misplaced." *U.S. v. Crisp*, 324 F.3d 261, 269, 60 Fed. R. Evid. Serv. 1486 (4th Cir. 2003). Or this may simply reflect an erroneous misplacement of the general burden of persuasion by the majority.

[106]*Wolf v. Ramsey*, 253 F. Supp. 2d 1323, 61 Fed. R. Evid. Serv. 1715 (N.D. Ga. 2003).

[107]The court makes it clear that the overwhelming weight of evidence points in this direction. *Wolf v. Ramsey*, 253 F. Supp. 2d 1323, 1353–1357, 61 Fed. R. Evid. Serv. 1715 (N.D. Ga. 2003).

which were the same initials as those used to sign the ransom note.

This information was communicated by Dilson initially to Pam Paugh, Patsy Ramsey's sister. Later it was given to the police, and they interviewed and investigated Mr. Wolf, who was never charged. In a book written by them, and on TV shows, Patsy Ramsey and her husband John Ramsey recounted the above in arguing that there were various people who were more likely to have been the murderer than Patsy Ramsey. As a result, Mr. Wolf sued.

To make a long story as short as possible, the court determined that the Ramseys' statements about Wolf suggested that he was a viable candidate to be JonBenet's murderer, and were thus presumptively defamatory, subject to two defenses: truth (which covered many of the statements) and good faith statements of opinion. To get around the "opinion" defense, the plaintiff asserted that the implications were knowingly false and malicious because the Ramseys knew for a fact that Wolf was not the killer, because they knew for a fact that Patsy Ramsey was the killer. This is where the handwriting identification experts come in.

The ransom note had been examined by six questioned document examiners during the police investigation. Four of those were commissioned by the police and two by the Ramseys. They were Chet Ubowski of the Colorado Bureau of Investigation, Richard Dusick of the United States Secret Service, and Leonard Speckin, Edwin Alford, Lloyd Cunningham and Howard Rile, all in private practice. All six agreed that John Ramsey could be eliminated as author of the note.[108] While none of the examiners eliminated Patsy Ramsey completely, all six agreed that the likelihood of her being the author of the note was very low. As the court said, "on a scale of one to five, with five being elimination, the experts placed Mrs. Ramsey at a 4.5 or a 4." However, Wolf claimed to have evidence that would satisfy the requirement of clear and convincing evidence (which was the applicable standard of proof) that Patsy Ramsey had written the note. This evidence was the testimony of two witnesses plaintiff claimed were handwriting identification experts, who had concluded that Patsy Ramsey had undoubtedly written the ransom note: Cina Wong and Gideon Epstein. In addition, apparently as part of the "peer review" of his work, Mr. Epstein had obtained affidavits from former FBI document examiners Larry Ziegler and Richard Williams, and private practitioners David Lieberman and Donald L. Lacey, approving his analysis and concurring in his results.

The Ramseys moved to strike the testimony of these two witnesses pursuant to *Daubert*, and for summary judgment. Judge Carnes first ruled globally (using what is functionally a variant of the guild test) that handwriting identification techniques used by trained forensic document examiners are sufficiently reliable in general to allow them to testify to similarities and differences to "aid the jury."[109] She then ruled that Cina Wong was unqualified.[110] Cina Wong was largely self taught, claimed 10 years experience, and had been vice president of the National Association of Document Examiners. The court noted, however, that this organization has no membership requirements beyond payment of a fee. The court perhaps goes too far in anointing the American Board of Forensic Document Examiners (ABFDE) as the "sole recognized organization for accreditation of qualified forensic document

---

[108]One interesting aspect of the case is the care that the court gives to explaining why, because of the nature of the felt-tipped pen with which the note was written, the document examiner community itself regarded the determination of authorship to be a difficult task.

[109]*Wolf v. Ramsey*, 253 F. Supp. 2d 1323, 1344, 61 Fed. R. Evid. Serv. 1715 (N.D. Ga. 2003). Given the later specific findings, the only function of the

global ruling seems to have been to allow the court to continue referring to and using the conclusions of the prosecution- and defense-hired document examiners. It should be noted that, given those conclusions, the Ramseys had no real need to press the issue of global unreliability.

[110]*Wolf v. Ramsey*, 253 F. Supp. 2d 1323, 1345, 61 Fed. R. Evid. Serv. 1715 (N.D. Ga. 2003).

examiners.["111] However, the conclusion concerning Ms. Wong, especially given her initial approach to defendant's attorneys offering to "analyze the Ransom Note and point out the weaknesses in analysis by 'Government handwriting experts' "[112] seems unexceptionable.

Judge Carnes contrasts favorably the qualifications of Mr. Epstein with those of Ms. Wong.[113] They are indeed, from the perspective of the guild, impeccable. He is a past president of the American Society of Questioned Document Examiners and a member of its accrediting branch, the aforementioned ABFDE. He was trained at the United States Army Crime Laboratory and the Post Office Identification Laboratory, and has 30 years of experience. She ruled that he was qualified to testify in order to point out similarities and differences between the ransom note and the handwriting of Patsy Ramsey.

However, she then turns (without citation) to the *Kumho Tire* part of the opinion, saying that she must "still determine the parameters of his expertise with regard to the opinions he seeks to offer."[114] It is here that Mr. Epstein strikes out. Judge Carnes notes that Epstein worked under what document examiner lore and his own previous writings hold are undesirable conditions, using photocopies instead of originals of both Patsy Ramsey's known writing and the ransom note. Still, he came to the conclusion "with absolute certainty" and "to a 100 percent certainty" that Patsy Ramsey wrote the note. Judge Carnes finds, in spite of the fact that his conclusion was joined by four other document examiners (who were not going to testify), that Epstein's methodological explanation for how he could be so sure failed to meet the required level of reliability, and on this basis she adopts a *"Hines"* result and bars him from testifying to his conclusions.[115] Without the benefit of the handwriting expert's conclusion, plaintiffs cannot prevail, and therefore she grants summary judgment.[116]

There are many interesting aspects of this opinion, among them: the two stage "global then particularized" approach, the willingness to examine the actual conditions of practice in judging reliability, and the willingness to be properly skeptical in the face of obvious overreaching. Judge Carnes' careful treatment of why it is sometimes required to treat reliability of conclusions separately from reliability of observations is in stark contrast to the First Circuit's summary declaration to the contrary in *Mooney*.[117] Would that more judges would follow her lead in criminal cases.

The next federal civil case of interest is *Deputy v. Lehman Bros., Inc.*,[118] a securities fraud action arising from the conduct of a Lehman Brothers investment advisor named Frank Gruttadauria, who had already pleaded guilty to fraud charges in regard to a scheme which the court characterized as "one of the largest scams of

---

[111]*Wolf v. Ramsey*, 253 F. Supp. 2d 1323, 1345, 61 Fed. R. Evid. Serv. 1715 (N.D. Ga. 2003).

[112]*Wolf v. Ramsey*, 253 F. Supp. 2d 1323, 1339, 61 Fed. R. Evid. Serv. 1715 (N.D. Ga. 2003).

[113]*Wolf v. Ramsey*, 253 F. Supp. 2d 1323, 1345, 61 Fed. R. Evid. Serv. 1715 (N.D. Ga. 2003).

[114]*Wolf v. Ramsey*, 253 F. Supp. 2d 1323, 1345, 61 Fed. R. Evid. Serv. 1715 (N.D. Ga. 2003).

[115]*Wolf v. Ramsey*, 253 F. Supp. 2d 1323, 1345–1348, 61 Fed. R. Evid. Serv. 1715 (N.D. Ga. 2003).

[116]*Wolf v. Ramsey*, 253 F. Supp. 2d 1323, 1363, 61 Fed. R. Evid. Serv. 1715 (N.D. Ga. 2003). Though Judge Carnes does not deal with it

directly, it seems right to say that, although jurors are authorized to compare handwriting directly without expert testimony (see *U.S. v. Alvarez-Farfan*, 338 F.3d 1043, 61 Fed. R. Evid. Serv. 1413 (9th Cir. 2003), for additional opinion, see, 71 Fed. Appx. 755 (9th Cir. 2003)), it would be too much to say that in a case like this, they could base a finding satisfying the clear and convincing evidence standard on such direct examination.

[117]*U.S. v. Mooney*, 315 F.3d 54, 60 Fed. R. Evid. Serv. 60 (1st Cir. 2002).

[118]*Deputy v. Lehman Bros., Inc.*, 345 F.3d 494, 62 Fed. R. Evid. Serv. 965 (7th Cir. 2003) (ellipses omitted).

retail investors ever committed by an individual broker."[119] Lehman Brothers moved to stay proceedings pending arbitration pursuant to an arbitration agreement purportedly signed by Ms. Deputy. Ms. Deputy denied signing any arbitration agreement. Lehman Brothers produced an option approval form dated February 20, 1993, and three client agreements from 2001, all bearing what purported to be Ms. Deputy's signature, all of which apparently contained arbitration clauses applying to transactions Ms. Deputy complained of. Ms. Deputy denied signing these (the implication being that Gruttadauria forged them). Lehman then produced a document examiner, Dianne Marsh, who testified that she had compared the four signatures on the documents to genuine signatures of Ms. Deputy and, in her opinion, Deputy signed two of the four documents containing arbitration clauses. She was unable to reach a conclusion as to the other two.

The plaintiff attacked the tenability of this opinion in a variety of ways. First, she denied that one of the signatures that was used as a "known" by Marsh was genuine (it was on a letter purporting to be from Deputy to Lehman Brothers). Second, plaintiff pointed out that Marsh originally had been given only the single disputed "known" signature, and had on that basis declared that she was unable to form an opinion at all, but that when Marsh was supplied with a photocopy of a second "known" signature (from an affidavit filed in the case) she had then concluded that two of the questioned signatures were made by Deputy. Plaintiff contended that the number of "known" signatures was insufficient for the task and that working from a photocopy was not proper. Marsh herself in her original report indicated that, "Before a conclusion can be reached, additional samples (plural) of the genuine signature of Doris A. Deputy need to be submitted for examination." (parenthetical supplied). Since the questioned documents span a time period from of February 20, 1993, through July 26, 2001, it would be advisable to have known standards covering this time frame."[120]

The plaintiff also asserted that Marsh should not be believed because her findings had once been rejected by a court. When the judge in this case asked her generally whether "any court refused to accept you as an expert witness on this subject matter," she had said "no," but later when probed about a particular case, had said that she did not remember.[121] Here is where the trial court got into trouble. The judge rejected Marsh's testimony based partially on its unreliability as a matter of technique under Rule 702, and partially on his evaluation of Marsh's lack of frankness. He apparently overlooked the fact that the defendant had a right to an actual trial on the issue of the existence of the arbitration agreement under section

---

[119]*Deputy v. Lehman Bros., Inc.*, 345 F.3d 494, 62 Fed. R. Evid. Serv. 965 (7th Cir. 2003).

[120]*Deputy v. Lehman Bros., Inc.*, 345 F.3d 494, 499, 62 Fed. R. Evid. Serv. 965 (7th Cir. 2003). In her testimony, Marsh asserted that originals were preferable, but that in the absence of an original a "good" photocopy could be used. She also doggedly insisted that handwriting identification was a "science," though not an "exact science." *Deputy v. Lehman Bros., Inc.*, 345 F.3d 494, 62 Fed. R. Evid. Serv. 965 (7th Cir. 2003). It is interesting to note that the plaintiff does not appear to have attacked Ms. Marsh on the ground of her qualifications, though her qualifications appear to be no better than those of Ms. Wong, whom judge Carnes rejected in *Wolf v. Ramsey*. Ms. Marsh was a member of the World Association of Document Examiners instead of the National Associa-

tion of Document Examiners, but neither are recognized by the Osbornian establishment. Note that Ms. Marsh was a "diplomate of the American Board of Forensic Examiners," not the American Board of Forensic Document Examiners annointed by Judge Carnes. The standards of the "American Board of Forensic Examiners" appear to be decidedly lax.

[121]It appears that the case was 20 years earlier and that Ms. Marsh had not in fact testified, but that her expert report had been proffered and rejected. When that was pointed out, Marsh replied, "I'm not familiar with that." *Deputy v. Lehman Bros., Inc.*, 345 F.3d 494, 498, 62 Fed. R. Evid. Serv. 965 (7th Cir. 2003) It is unclear whether she would have known of this rejection even 20 years earlier.

4 of the Federal Arbitration Act,[122] and that his sole role at the hearing was to determine admissibility at such a trial.[123] By basing his rejection of the handwriting expert on a mixture of reliability and credibility, he erred.[124] The circuit reversed, indicating that it was not concluding that Marsh's testimony was in fact sufficiently reliable to meet the requirements of Rule 702, but that the court had to evaluate it by proper Rule 702 standards.[125]

The next federal case is *United States v. Alvarez-Farfan*,[126] a case that deals, not with when handwriting experts can testify, but with when they are not required at all. Alvarez-Farfan was charged with selling to Rivera, a government informant, three-quarters of a pound of methamphetamine for $3750 inside a room at an Economy Inn in Winnemucca, Nevada, in what is known as a "controlled buy." After Rivera claimed to have arranged the purchase and delivery at the Economy Inn with one Blanco, agents watched Rivera go into the room without the drugs and exit with the drugs. The occupant of the room (if any) was not then arrested because the main target of the investigation was his boss, Blanco, who supplied the drugs. (Blanco was later arrested and convicted.) Alvarez-Farfan's theory of defense was that he was never in the room, that the room had been rented by Rivera, was empty at the time of the transaction, and that the drugs were placed there by Rivera as part of an attempt to satisfy his government handlers. In an attempt to get the jury to infer this, he wanted to show the jury a "confidential informant debriefing statement" written by Rivera, and also the motel receipt for the room (presumably the desk book). He would then argue that they should conclude that Rivera, not he, rented the room, based on their concluding from comparing the documents that the handwriting was the same. The trial court ruled that it would not allow this without a document examiner's testimony. The circuit reversed, ruling that such direct juror comparison was always competent, based in part on the mandate of a statute, 28 U.S.C.A. § 1731, which provides "the admitted or proved handwriting of any person shall be admissible for purposes of comparison to determine genuineness of other handwriting attributed to such person."[127] In addition, the court found that the admission was not harmless error, since the only witness against Alvarez-Farfan was Rivera, and, as an undocumented alien, Alvarez-Farfan would have had some difficulty actually renting the room himself.[128] Any other problems with the proffer might be dealt with under Fed. R. Evid. 403, but the government had made no such motion.[129]

*United States v. Jabali*,[130] is an unreported decision by Senior Judge Johnson of the Eastern District of New York which deals in part with a motion in limine by the

---

[122]*Deputy v. Lehman Bros., Inc.*, 345 F.3d 494, 62 Fed. R. Evid. Serv. 965 (7th Cir. 2003).

[123]The district court also erred in refusing to look at the signatures himself, in deciding that there was no triable issue based on juror comparison (see *U.S. v. Alvarez-Farfan*, 338 F.3d 1043, 61 Fed. R. Evid. Serv. 1413 (9th Cir. 2003), for additional opinion, see, 71 Fed. Appx. 755 (9th Cir. 2003), infra and compare with *Wolf v. Ramsey*, 253 F. Supp. 2d 1323, 61 Fed. R. Evid. Serv. 1715 (N.D. Ga. 2003), supra.), and in cutting off discovery in advance of that trial. *Deputy v. Lehman Bros., Inc.*, 345 F.3d 494, 62 Fed. R. Evid. Serv. 965 (7th Cir. 2003).

[124]*Deputy v. Lehman Bros., Inc.*, 345 F.3d 494, 62 Fed. R. Evid. Serv. 965 (7th Cir. 2003).

[125]*Deputy v. Lehman Bros., Inc.*, 345 F.3d 494, 62 Fed. R. Evid. Serv. 965 (7th Cir. 2003).

[126]*U.S. v. Alvarez-Farfan*, 338 F.3d 1043, 61

Fed. R. Evid. Serv. 1413 (9th Cir. 2003), for additional opinion, see, 71 Fed. Appx. 755 (9th Cir. 2003).

[127]*U.S. v. Alvarez-Farfan*, 338 F.3d 1043, 61 Fed. R. Evid. Serv. 1413 (9th Cir. 2003), for additional opinion, see, 71 Fed. Appx. 755 (9th Cir. 2003).

[128]*U.S. v. Alvarez-Farfan*, 338 F.3d 1043, 1044, 61 Fed. R. Evid. Serv. 1413 (9th Cir. 2003), for additional opinion, see, 71 Fed. Appx. 755 (9th Cir. 2003). By implication, the court seems to be saying that such direct comparison is presumptively sufficient to raise a reasonable doubt.

[129]*U.S. v. Alvarez-Farfan*, 338 F.3d 1043, 61 Fed. R. Evid. Serv. 1413 (9th Cir. 2003), for additional opinion, see, 71 Fed. Appx. 755 (9th Cir. 2003). Presumably, the court is referring to questions of sufficiency and speculation.

[130]*U.S. v. Jabali*, 2003 WL 22170595 (E.D.

defendant to "limit the government's handwriting expert to simply pointing out patterns of similarity between proffered examples of documents alleged to have been signed by Defendant and documents that were in fact written and submitted by Defendant to the Government" based on "several cases where other district courts have limited handwriting testimony, citing the unavailability of testing of this type of expertise, as well as the lack of general standards in this field"[131]

In giving short shrift to defendant's claim (and the *Hines/McVeigh* approach), the court fails to define the specific task facing the document examiner. Indeed, the court sets out very few facts from which the "task at hand" can be inferred with any confidence. The defendant was charged with "participating in a credit card fraud bust-out scheme which, it is proposed, is responsible for losses of 8.5 million dollars."[132] Generally in such a scheme multiple credit cards are obtained with false identities, purchases of merchandise may be made and paid for to expand the available credit line for each card, at which point large purchases of merchandise are made, the cards are charged to the limit and beyond (busted out), and the merchandise is sold to receivers (who may or may not know that the merchandise was obtained fraudulently). The cards, their balances, and the identities which they reflect, are then simply abandoned.

In this context, it is impossible without more to know what task the prosecution document examiner is being asked to perform. It might be attributing authorship for non-natural signatures written in false names. In that case, it is the same task that various courts beginning with *Ruth* have avoided analyzing, and have yet to come to grips with under the standards of *Kumho Tire*. Or the government might have seized more extensive writings pursuant to their investigation, in which case the task would be different. At any rate, Judge Johnson never undertakes the analysis required by *Kumho Tire*. In fact, he never even mentions the case (one can infer here that the defense attorney is at least partly responsible for failing to present the motion in terms of *Kumho Tire*'s requirements). At any rate, the court merely says conclusorily (and without citation) that the Second Circuit has interpreted *Daubert* to reflect a pro-admissibility approach reflecting the "liberal thrust" of the Federal Rules of Evidence. He then states that "[b]lanket exclusion is not favored, as any questions concerning reliability should be directed to weight given to testimony, not its admissibility."[133] This is a typical opinion, high on slogans, some of which are off the mark of the Supreme Court's requirements, and low on analysis.

*United States v. Oskowitz*,[134] is a case involving the "prosecution of a tax return preparer for knowingly and willfully aiding and assisting in procuring, counseling, and advising preparation and presentation of false tax returns."[135] The charged crime was in essence a scheme to obtain "Earned Income Credit" refund checks fraudulently. The "Earned Income Credit" is a program of the federal government intended to aid the working poor by in effect giving them a kind of negative income tax subsidy (a "refund" check larger than the amount of tax paid through withholding or otherwise) based on their low income and family obligations. The allegations against the defendant were that she advertised through fliers for people with children who had never before filed federal income tax returns, then worked with them to create a phony income profile that would qualify them to receive an "Earned

---

N.Y. 2003).

[131]*U.S. v. Jabali*, 2003 WL 22170595 (E.D. N.Y. 2003) (citing as examples *U. S. v. Hines*, "noting that there is no peer review by a 'competitive, unbiased community of practitioners and academics'" and U. S. v. Rutherford, *semble*).

[132]*U.S. v. Jabali*, 2003 WL 22170595 (E.D. N.Y. 2003).

[133]*U.S. v. Jabali*, 2003 WL 22170595 (E.D. N.Y. 2003) (note that it does not seem that "blanket exclusion" was being requested, merely a limitation on the form of the testimony, but the court seems oblivious to this distinction).

[134]*U. S. v. Oskowitz*, 294 F. Supp.2d 379 (E. D. N.Y., 2003).

[135]*U. S. v. Oskowitz*, 294 F. Supp.2d 379 (E. D. N.Y., 2003).

Income Credit" check, which she would then split with them.[136] The opinion by Judge Garaufis deals in part with a motion in limine to "exclude, or in the alternative to limit, the testimony of the government's handwriting expert, John Paul Osborn."[137]

This "reported" opinion, filed less than three months after the *Jabali* "unreported" opinion from the same Federal District, shows the remarkable variability reflected in trial court decisional practice under *Daubert, Kumho Tire,* and *Joiner.* Once again, there is no effort to identify the task that the expert will be asked to perform at trial, in derogation of *Kumho Tire v. Carmichael.* (And there is even less basis for speculating what the document examiner was being asked to do than in the *Jabali* case). In this case the failure to identify the "task at hand" is clearly because the defense attorney framed the attack globally, though in theory this should not alter the court's obligations. At any rate the judge is persuaded to adopt the *Hines/ McVeigh* approach, ruling that "proper scope of Mr. Osborn's testimony (as well as the testimony of any opposing handwriting expert the defense may choose to produce) extends to explaining to the jury the similarities and differences between a known example of Oskowitz's handwriting and a disputed tax return,"[138] on the authority of Hines, Rutherford, McVeigh, Santillan, Van Wyk, and *Hidalgo,* as well *Fujii* and *Saelee* (excluding all testimony). The Court concludes: "Jurors may then make a decision on the ultimate question of authorship with the benefit of that expert testimony, as well as the benefit of their cumulative experience distinguishing the penmanship of different writers."[139] While the decision is less committed to the status quo than *Jabali,* it is too much driven by reference to precedent and not enough by reference to reason and analysis.

The District Court's decision regarding handwriting in *United States v. Prime,*[140] analyzed above, was affirmed on appeal.[141] As the district court itself had noted, generally such confirmation is virtually a given no matter what decision the district court makes, given the abuse of discretion standard mandated by the Supreme Court in *General Electric v. Joiner* for review of Rule 702 decisions.[142] That being said, it should be obvious to the reader that, just as some district court opinions are more thoughtful than others, and more in tune with the language and requirements of *Daubert* and *Kumho Tire,* so the same is true of Court of Appeals opinions. The district court opinion in *Prime* is one of those opinions (like *Starzecpyzel,* or like the two *Llera Plaza* opinions, taken together, dealing with fingerprints) where the Court is clearly trying to understand the requirements of the Supreme Court's directives, and troubled by the surprising weakness (given its traditional unquestioned admissibility) of the prosecution-proffered forensic identification expertise, but in the end just can't bring itself to reject or limit this time-honored

---

[136]*U. S. v. Oskowitz,* 294 F. Supp.2d 379, 381 (E. D. N.Y., 2003).

[137]*U. S. v. Oskowitz,* 294 F. Supp.2d 379, 383 (E. D. N.Y., 2003).

[138]*U. S. v. Oskowitz,* 294 F. Supp.2d 379, 384 (E. D. N.Y., 2003).

[139]*U. S. v. Oskowitz,* 294 F. Supp.2d 379, 384 (E. D. N.Y., 2003).

[140]*U.S. v. Prime,* 220 F. Supp. 2d 1203 (W.D. Wash. 2002), aff'd, 363 F.3d 1028, 64 Fed. R. Evid. Serv. 219 (9th Cir. 2004), cert. granted, judgment vacated on other grounds, 543 U.S. 1101, 125 S. Ct. 1005, 160 L. Ed. 2d 1007 (2005) and opinion amended and superseded on other grounds, 431 F.3d 1147, 68 Fed. R. Evid. Serv. 1288 (9th Cir. 2005) and aff'd, 431 F.3d 1147, 68 Fed. R. Evid.

Serv. 1288 (9th Cir. 2005).

[141]*U.S. v. Prime,* 363 F.3d 1028, 1032–1035, 64 Fed. R. Evid. Serv. 219 (9th Cir. 2004), cert. granted, judgment vacated on other grounds, 543 U.S. 1101, 125 S. Ct. 1005, 160 L. Ed. 2d 1007 (2005) and opinion amended and superseded on other grounds, 431 F.3d 1147, 68 Fed. R. Evid. Serv. 1288 (9th Cir. 2005).

[142]*U.S. v. Prime,* 220 F. Supp. 2d 1203 (W.D. Wash. 2002), aff'd, 363 F.3d 1028, 64 Fed. R. Evid. Serv. 219 (9th Cir. 2004), cert. granted, judgment vacated on other grounds, 543 U.S. 1101, 125 S. Ct. 1005, 160 L. Ed. 2d 1007 (2005) and opinion amended and superseded on other grounds, 431 F.3d 1147, 68 Fed. R. Evid. Serv. 1288 (9th Cir. 2005) and aff'd, 431 F.3d 1147, 68 Fed. R. Evid. Serv. 1288 (9th Cir. 2005).

form of prosecution evidence. Many of the same characteristics are carried over into the opinion of the Court of Appeals in *Prime*.

The Court of Appeals opinion on the handwriting issues begins with an extended paragraph of stock phrases summarizing the *Daubert/Kumho/Joiner* line of cases, with an emphasis, perhaps rather too global,[143] on the discretion of the trial court.[144] The opinion then goes on to formally recognize the task-at-hand requirements of *Kumho Tire v. Carmichael*.[145] In a footnote, the Court notes that defendant Prime "has not raised as an issue, and we have no reason to believe, that the questioned writing samples were of insufficient length to support a valid analysis."[146] With this footnote, any real possibility of a true task-at-hand analysis goes out the window. Thereafter, the court essentially adopts (in some detail) the District Court's approach, although it is clearly troubled at the outset that there may be a different and more serious issue raised in a later case involving the attribution of authorship based on a small amount of unknown writing (initials or a signature for instance), and it is at pains to say, echoing the Supreme Court, that it can "neither rule in, for all cases and for all time the applicability of the factors in Daubert, nor can we do so for subsets of cases categorized by category of expert or by kind of evidence. Too much depends upon the particular circumstances of the particular case."[147] Finally, the Court takes what, given the near inevitability of the outcome on appeal under *General Electric v. Joiner*, is a kind of misplaced comfort in the fact it has arrived at a conclusion consistent with the other six circuits that have considered proffers of handwriting expertise (even though many of those cases were decided before *Kumho Tire*, or did not even recognize the task-at-hand requirements of *Kumho Tire*, and were weakly reasoned at best).[148]

A final note on *Prime*. One of the overlooked issues (as usual) was the extent to which the writings were submitted to the expert in a non-blind fashion. The responsibility for this omission, as well as for failure to develop a proper description of the subtasks involved, must fall at least in part upon the defense attorney. Finally, it appears likely that the district court, and perhaps the court of appeals as well, was influenced both by the large volume of known and questioned writing

---

[143]As noted above, the District Court was admirably aware that the "discretion" invoked in *Kumho Tire* was discretion to intelligently define and apply criteria of reliability properly referable to the application of the expertise in question to the task at hand in the case before the court. The Court of Appeals is less clear on this. Compare 220 F. Supp.2d 1203, 1205 (*U.S. v. Prime*, 363 F.3d 1028, 1033, 64 Fed. R. Evid. Serv. 219 (9th Cir. 2004), cert. granted, judgment vacated on other grounds, 543 U.S. 1101, 125 S. Ct. 1005, 160 L. Ed. 2d 1007 (2005) and opinion amended and superseded on other grounds, 431 F.3d 1147, 68 Fed. R. Evid. Serv. 1288 (9th Cir. 2005) (Court of Appeals).

[144]The fact that an opinion is made up in whole or in part of stock phrases is not per se a criticism of its judgecraft. Properly used, such stock phrases set out the analytic framework established by precedent, and lay the justifying foundation for the opinion. While they may provide legal justification, however, they should not become, as they often do, substitutes for legal reasoning.

[145]*U.S. v. Prime*, 363 F.3d 1028, 1033, 64 Fed. R. Evid. Serv. 219 (9th Cir. 2004), cert. granted,

judgment vacated on other grounds, 543 U.S. 1101, 125 S. Ct. 1005, 160 L. Ed. 2d 1007 (2005) and opinion amended and superseded on other grounds, 431 F.3d 1147, 68 Fed. R. Evid. Serv. 1288 (9th Cir. 2005).

[146]*U.S. v. Prime*, 363 F.3d 1028, 1033, 64 Fed. R. Evid. Serv. 219 (9th Cir. 2004), cert. granted, judgment vacated on other grounds, 543 U.S. 1101, 125 S. Ct. 1005, 160 L. Ed. 2d 1007 (2005) and opinion amended and superseded on other grounds, 431 F.3d 1147, 68 Fed. R. Evid. Serv. 1288 (9th Cir. 2005).

[147]*U.S. v. Prime*, 363 F.3d 1028, 1033, 64 Fed. R. Evid. Serv. 219 (9th Cir. 2004), cert. granted, judgment vacated on other grounds, 543 U.S. 1101, 125 S. Ct. 1005, 160 L. Ed. 2d 1007 (2005) and opinion amended and superseded on other grounds, 431 F.3d 1147, 68 Fed. R. Evid. Serv. 1288 (9th Cir. 2005).

[148]*U.S. v. Prime*, 363 F.3d 1028, 1034, 64 Fed. R. Evid. Serv. 219 (9th Cir. 2004), cert. granted, judgment vacated on other grounds, 543 U.S. 1101, 125 S. Ct. 1005, 160 L. Ed. 2d 1007 (2005) and opinion amended and superseded on other grounds, 431 F.3d 1147, 68 Fed. R. Evid. Serv. 1288 (9th Cir. 2005).

available, and by the relatively modest claims regarding levels of certainty manifested by the expert, Kathleen Storer, in rendering her various opinions as to authorship.[149] *Prime* was a case in which the problem of overclaiming the certainty of one's expertise, while perhaps still present, was much less dramatically present than in many other cases. The amount of overclaiming by an expert is properly one factor to be taken into account in determining the reliability of that expert's testimony.

The next federal case chronologically is *United States v. Rutland*,[150] a case involving an interesting and almost amusing variation on the kind of claims heretofore made in regard to handwriting identification expertise. The statement of facts in Judge Fisher's opinion makes it clear that the case against defendant Rutland was pretty overwhelming. Rutland had been a financial advisor employed by Citicorp Financial Services. In that capacity, he became the financial advisor to Helen Constans, an elderly widow, in 1990. In that capacity, Rutland had access to all of Constans's financial information, including various account numbers and her social security number. Constans declined physically, and apparently mentally, being placed in a long-term care facility in 1995. Her niece, Dorothy McCosh, attempted to sort through her documents and put some order in her finances. During this process Ms. McCosh found a mysterious annuity statement that listed one Barbara Grams as the annuitant. McCosh also knew that Rutland had been her aunt's financial advisor, and contacted him twice. At that time Rutland said he did not know a Barbara Grams, and that the annuity statement must have been generated in that name as the result of a clerical error by the company. At this point, McCosh apparently contacted the U.S. Attorney, and an investigation was instituted. The investigation revealed that Barbara Grams was Rutland's girlfriend. There turned out to be multiple financial forms and checks made out to the benefit of either Rutland or Grams, bearing the apparent signature "Helen Constans."[151]

As part of the government's case the prosecution intended to offer proof (beyond the obvious strong circumstantial inference that Constans had no apparent reason to make over $600,000 in gifts to Rutland and Grams) that the signatures were not genuine signatures of Helen Constans. To that end the government called Gus Lesnevich, who, it must be said, has sterling credentials as an Osbornian document examiner (putting aside for the moment the question of whether such credentials are strong indicators of the existence of claimed expertise).[152] The objection raised by Rutland's lawyer at the trial was neither a challenge to the reliability of handwriting expertise in general, nor to its reliability in regard to the task at issue in Rutland's case. (This would have been a very hard sell, considering the fact that declaring signatures authentic or inauthentic is the only task commonly encountered in court where there is any actual research supporting a claim of expertise by document examiners).[153] Nor was the objection a general claim like the ones in *Jabali* and *Oskowitz*, based on *Hines* and similar cases, that handwriting experts should be limited to pointing out similarities and differences, and should not be allowed to

---

[149]See *U.S. v. Prime*, 220 F. Supp. 2d 1203 (W.D. Wash. 2002), aff'd, 363 F.3d 1028, 64 Fed. R. Evid. Serv. 219 (9th Cir. 2004), cert. granted, judgment vacated on other grounds, 543 U.S. 1101, 125 S. Ct. 1005, 160 L. Ed. 2d 1007 (2005) and opinion amended and superseded on other grounds, 431 F.3d 1147, 68 Fed. R. Evid. Serv. 1288 (9th Cir. 2005); see also *U.S. v. Prime*, 363 F.3d 1028, 1033, 64 Fed. R. Evid. Serv. 219 (9th Cir. 2004), cert. granted, judgment vacated on other grounds, 543 U.S. 1101, 125 S. Ct. 1005, 160 L. Ed. 2d 1007 (2005)

and opinion amended and superseded on other grounds, 431 F.3d 1147, 68 Fed. R. Evid. Serv. 1288 (9th Cir. 2005).

[150]*U.S. v. Rutland*, 372 F.3d 543, 64 Fed. R. Evid. Serv. 833 (3d Cir. 2004).

[151]All details in this paragraph are taken from 543–544 of *U.S. v. Rutland*, 372 F.3d 543, 64 Fed. R. Evid. Serv. 833 (3d Cir. 2004).

[152]*U.S. v. Rutland*, 372 F.3d 543, 544–545, 64 Fed. R. Evid. Serv. 833 (3d Cir. 2004).

[153]See the discussion of the "Kam IV" study, § 4:31, infra.

opine on the final conclusion (in this case, genuineness of the signature). Rather, the objection was that, while a lesser qualified expert might be allowed to so opine because his or her credentials would not necessarily induce the jury to rely on those conclusions, a really well credentialed expert should be restricted to pointing out similarities and differences because of the danger that the jury would overvalue his conclusion based on his credentials.[154]

It is true that there is some reason to believe that a document examiner's years of experience are not good predictors of enhanced accuracy.[155] Whether that is necessarily the case with other indices of training and experience is an open question, but it is such a counterintuitive claim that courts are likely to find it just too much to swallow without affirmative data. And so it transpired in this case, with the court not unexpectedly declaring, in affirming the trial court's decision, "Rutland's suggestion of limiting an expert from testifying to the ultimate issue if the expert has stellar qualifications leads to an absurd result. Parties would be forced to determine if their proposed experts were overly qualified, and find less qualified experts. Expert opinions, valuable to the trier of fact because they are opinions of highly skilled and qualified experts, would be provided by less qualified experts."[156]

In *United States v. Ferguson*,[157] Judge Rice of the Southern District of Ohio writes at length, but the result must be counted as severely disappointing on a number of fronts.

The defendant, Scott Ferguson, was charged with interstate transport of a stolen motor vehicle and the sale of same, in violation of 18 U.S.C.A. § 2312 and § 2313. The vehicle in question was an armored car. When the vehicle was sold, the seller presented the buyer with a bill of sale signed "Elen Poloroman."[158] The main subject of defendant's motion in limine was the prosecution-proffered testimony of Allen Southmayd, a document examiner at the U.S Army Criminal Investigation Laboratory (USACIL).[159] Southmayd was to testify that he had compared exemplars of defendant's known writing with the signature "Elen Poloroman" on the bill of sale, and that the signature "was actually authored by the defendant."[160] Here again we see the most questionable "task at hand" to which handwriting identification

---

[154]*U.S. v. Rutland*, 372 F.3d 543, 545, 64 Fed. R. Evid. Serv. 833 (3d Cir. 2004).

[155]See Risinger, Denbeaux & Saks, Exorcism of Ignorance as a Proxy For Rational Knowledge: The Lessons of Handwriting Identification Expertise, 137 U. Pa., L. Rev. 731, 749 (1989) (quoting the 1987 Comments of the Proficiency Advisory Committee of the Forensic Sciences Foundation in regard to the results of that year's (and earlier years) handwriting identification proficiency tests "[a]s usual, there were no correlations between right/wrong answers and certification, experience, amount of time devoted to document examination, and length of time spent on this test.").

[156]*U.S. v. Rutland*, 372 F.3d 543, 548, 64 Fed. R. Evid. Serv. 833 (3d Cir. 2004).

[157]*U.S. v. Ferguson*, 2004 WL 5345480 (S.D. Ohio 2004).

[158]*U.S. v. Ferguson*, 2004 WL 5345480 (S.D. Ohio 2004).

[159]The prosecution also proposed to call Derek Hammond, another questioned document examiner at USACIL who checked Southmayd's work (presumably according to some form of the so-called ACE-V "methodology"). The defendant objected to Hammond's testimony as "irrelevant." It is hard to see how the testimony could be irrelevant if the "verification" step of ACE-V (often passed off as "peer review" in an attempt to fulfill the *Daubert* criteria) is an important step in ensuring the reliability of the product. However, Judge Rice ruled it irrelevant and excluded Hammond's testimony from the government's case in chief. *U.S. v. Ferguson*, 2004 WL 5345480 (S.D. Ohio 2004). Unnecessary cumulation, and a non-independent result likely to be overvalued in bolstering the testimony of Southmayd, which would justify exclusion pursuant to Rule 403, would probably have been a more satisfactory basis for the result.

[160]Southmayd graded his attribution of authorship as a Nine on the ASTM 9-point scale used by some document examiners. Nine is the highest level of certainty, which seems a bit much, to put it mildly, given the amount of questioned material there was to work with (two words, 13 total letter forms, seven individual letters). Even the graded ASTM scale is no guarantee against overclaiming. These cases always raise the question of how much other evidence relating to the defendant's guilt was communicated to the document examiner that might have raised his confidence inordinately. See, as always, Risinger, Saks,

expertise can be applied—attributing authorship of an exceptionally limited amount of handwriting to a particular individual by comparison of hands.[161] It is an issue for which there are absolutely no data that indicate that it can be done reliably, and that has been unaddressed or unsatisfactorily treated in varying degrees of poor analysis or lack of analysis in Ruth, Velasquez, Jones, Battle, and Elmore, and only dealt with in any way approaching the requirements of Kumho Tire in Rutherford. Judge Rice's opinion adds to the list of cases that totally fail to deal with the issue in the manner required by Kumho Tire.

The court begins by noting that "every appellate court, including the Sixth Circuit, which has addressed the question in the "post-Daubert world," has concluded that such testimony is sufficiently reliable to be admissible,"[162] citing Prime, Crisp, Hernandez, Paul, Jones, and Velasquez, and mis-citing Jolivet as usual, and failing to take into account the actual tasks at issue in any of those cases,[163] and also failing to note that Hernandez affirmed the propriety of a Hines/McVeigh limitation imposed on document examiner testimony. The opinion then goes on to concentrate on Jones, which is perhaps not surprising for an Ohio district judge, since Jones is a Sixth Circuit case, but unfortunately, both because Jones was decided before Kumho Tire and because by any analysis, as we have already seen in connection with the discussion of Jones above, the Jones opinion reached "new heights of unsatisfactory judgecraft." In its reliance on Jones, the Ferguson court swallows uncritically the Rule 901(b)(3) fallacy fully examined in connection with Jones. In addition, it makes more out of the citation to Jones in the 2000 advisory committee note than that citation can bear. The most that the citation can be used to illustrate is that, as it says, "in some fields experience is the predominant, if not the sole basis, for a great deal of reliable expert testimony."[164] It cannot be read as blessing the global and completely guild-based approach of a pre-Kumho Tire case as a proper approach to the reliability determination required by Kumho Tire's "task at hand" reliability evaluation. Yet this is exactly how the Ferguson opinion deals with the case, concluding explicitly, as Jones did implicitly, that (without any task-specific analysis of any kind, in derogation of Kumho Tire's requirements) the only criterion by which to judge the reliability of proffered experience-based expertise is "experience": ". . . the reliability of a document examiner's testimony is best ascertained by examining his or her training and experience."[165] The Court then examines Southmayd's training and experience, and (despite some deficiencies) predictably (given what has gone before) finds that his Southmayd's years as a document examiner, most of it with USACIL, are enough by themselves to allow him to testify to whatever conclusions

---

Thompson & Rosenthal, The Daubert/Kumho Implications of Observer Effects in Forensic Science: Hidden Problems of Expectation and Suggestion, 90 Cal. L. Rev. 1 (2002).

[161]The attribution seems to have been especially difficult, and questionable, in this case since the questioned signature was a combination of cursive and printed letters, and it required multiple sessions of demand exemplars to obtain samples of both cursive and printed forms that satisfied Southmayd as sufficient. U.S. v. Ferguson, 2004 WL 5345480 (S.D. Ohio 2004).

[162]U.S. v. Ferguson, 2004 WL 5345480 (S.D. Ohio 2004).

[163]This is especially egregious in regard to the Ferguson opinion's treatment of the Circuit opinion in Prime. Judge Rice spends a paragraph on the Prime opinion, declaring that "it finds the reasoning of the Ninth Circuit to be persuasive

and adopts the same," U.S. v. Ferguson, 2004 WL 5345480 (S.D. Ohio 2004), without noting (or noticing) that the Prime opinion is very careful to limit itself only to the very different task which was in front of it. U.S. v. Prime, 363 F.3d 1028, 1033, 64 Fed. R. Evid. Serv. 219 (9th Cir. 2004), cert. granted, judgment vacated on other grounds, 543 U.S. 1101, 125 S. Ct. 1005, 160 L. Ed. 2d 1007 (2005) and opinion amended and superseded on other grounds, 431 F.3d 1147, 68 Fed. R. Evid. Serv. 1288 (9th Cir. 2005) (embracing "a case-by-case review rather than a general pronouncement that in this Circuit handwriting analysis is reliable.").

[164]U.S. v. Ferguson, 2004 WL 5345480 (S.D. Ohio 2004) (quoting 2000 Advisory Committee note to Amended Rule 702).

[165]U.S. v. Ferguson, 2004 WL 5345480 (S.D. Ohio 2004).

he reaches, apparently whatever the task at hand, or however difficult it might be.[166]

Judge Koeltl's opinion in *United States v. Ojeikere*,[167] is more sparse than Judge Rice's in *Ferguson*, but employs, at least by implication, the same methodology, and reaches much the same result. Daniel Ojeikere and his wife Idongesit Ojeikere were charged with a variety of crimes arising primarily out of their alleged running of a version of what appears to be generically known as a "Nigerian advance fee fraud." Virtually every reader of this will be familiar with the typical e-mails often associated with such a scheme, though in the version with which the Ojeikeres were charged, the communications were by phone and fax. In the charged scheme, the communications alleged that the sender was a Nigerian citizen who was entitled to an inheritance worth approximately $17 million. These communications induced individuals to wire money from Boston, Massachusetts to bank accounts at banks in New York, by promising that they would receive in return 20% of the purported $17 million inheritance.[168]

In proof of the Ojeikeres' role in the scheme, the government intended to introduce, inter alia, testimony by questioned document examiner Gus Lesnevich that Mr. Ojeikere probably authored the text of certain (presumably handwritten) documents; that Mrs. Ojeikere probably signed the name "Barbara Smith" on one document; and that Mr. Ojeikere failed to use his true handwriting when he provided the Government with exemplars after his indictment.[169] The defendants moved to exclude Mr. Lesnevich's testimony as unreliable. In addition, Mr. Ojeikere moved, failing exclusion, to limit Mr. Lesnevich to describing purported similarities and differences between the questioned documents and the exemplars.[170]

The court seems totally oblivious to the fact that Mr. Lesnevich's three proposed conclusions involve three very different tasks and three very different claims of expertise—attribution of authorship for documents containing significant amounts of writing,[171] attribution of authorship for a single signature, and the inference that someone has not written in their "normal" hand when giving demand exemplars.[172]

---

[166]There seems to be some reason to doubt the care with which Mr. Southmayd makes factual evaluations of at least some kinds, though perhaps not quite to same degree of exaggeration of Mr. Sperry, the proffered expert in *Jones* itself, discussed in § 4:6. Southmayd testified to having done document examinations in 6000 cases in 28 years, or 214 cases per year (a little more than four cases a week, year in and year out). That certainly seems remarkably productive, though not so much so as Sperry's claim of 7300 cases in 14 years, which was more than a case a day without a break. However, Southmayd also testified to having "reviewed approximately 600,000 documents" in those 28 years (presumably for purposes of making handwriting comparisons). If he "reviewed" such a document every 10 minutes nine hours a day every day without a break for 28 years, he still wouldn't reach 600,000. Courts so inclined will swallow anything, but such indications of exaggeration and over-claiming should count against a witness's reliability rather than for it.

[167]*U.S. v. Ojeikere*, 2005 WL 425492 (S.D. N.Y. 2005).

[168]All specific case details in this paragraph derived from *U.S. v. Ojeikere*, 2005 WL 425492

(S.D. N.Y. 2005).

[169]*U.S. v. Ojeikere*, 2005 WL 425492 (S.D. N.Y. 2005).

[170]*U.S. v. Ojeikere*, 2005 WL 425492 (S.D. N.Y. 2005).

[171]It is actually unclear how much writing was contained in the "text of certain questioned documents" referred to by the court at *3 in connection with Mr. Lesnevich's first conclusion. I have assumed that it was reasonably extensive. Otherwise the first and second Conclusions present variations on the same task—attribution of authorship from extremely limited amounts of "unknown" writing.

[172]The fundamental testimonial nature of the provision of demand exemplars is well illustrated by the fact that writing one way rather than another will be taken as evidence of consciousness of guilt. See *U.S. v. Ojeikere*, 2005 WL 425492 (S.D. N.Y. 2005). How compulsion to "write honestly" does not violate the privilege against self incrimination is very hard to understand. The courts have analogized the provision of demand exemplars to the seizure of pre-existing specimens of writing under the Fourth Amendment, and their compelled production pursuant to Fed. R. Crim. P. 17(c), see *Ojeikere*, at *4, footnote

As discussed at length in connection with Ruth I, supra, and further in connection with Velasquez, Jones, Battle, Elmore, Rutherford and *Rutland*, the second is the most questionable task undertaken by document examiners. Further, there is absolutely no empirical evidence to support the skill claim in regard distinguishing between disguised exemplars and normal hand exemplars independent of comparison to some authenticated specimen of "course of business" or everyday writing pre-existing the obtaining of the demand exemplars.[173] The court appears unaware of any of this, and the responsibility for that lack of awareness probably should rest in great part with the defense attorneys whose job it is to make these issues clear, in the way that defense attorneys in civil cases (with ample resources) inevitably do in analogous situations in toxic tort cases.

In any event, with such an approach, it is not surprising that the court invokes the uniformity of Courts of Appeals opinions (without noting the problems of inferring much from their affirmances pursuant to an abuse of discretion standard, or the fact that appeals almost inevitably deal only with cases where the handwriting evidence was admitted below, not cases where it was excluded), and invokes the citation to *Jones* in the Advisory Committee note to the 2000 amendment of Rule 702.[174] But then, in a rather startling turn, the court does not simply declare the proposed testimony admissible, but rather says as follows:

> The Government conceded at oral argument that there are good reasons to hold a pre-trial hearing in this case pursuant to Federal Rules of Evidence 104(a) and 702, at least with respect to Mr. Lesnevich's final opinions. (*See* Tr. of Oral Argument dated Dec. 10, 2004 at 37–40.) A pre-trial evidentiary hearing will allow the parties to present expert evidence and conduct cross-examination of the proposed expert. *See Borawick v. Shay*, 68 F.3d 597, 608, 42 Fed. R. Evid. Serv. 1201 (2d Cir. 1995). Accordingly, the Court will conduct a pre-trial hearing to allow Mr. Lesnevich to explain his methodology and the bases for his specific opinions, particularly the basis for his conclusions that the defendants were probably the authors of certain questioned documents and his opinion that Mr. Ojeikere purposely concealed his handwriting when furnishing handwriting exemplars to the Government.[175]

So, instead of simply declaring the proposed testimony admissible, the court held a *Daubert* hearing at the prosecution's cautious insistence. The result of that hearing is not reported anywhere, though it seems obvious what it was overwhelmingly likely to be. Daniel Ojeikere, at least, was convicted, and the sentencing phase was not completed until July 9, 2007.[176] Hence the issues have not yet been considered on appeal as of this writing.

*United States v. Mornan*,[177] like the often mis-cited United States. v. Jolivet,[178] deals in pertinent part with the admission of handwriting identification testimony that was not objected to at trial. Defendant Mornan was accused of being a co-conspirator in a fraud scheme operating between Canada and the United States, whereby uncreditworthy persons were solicited, and promised loans if they would obtain "loan insurance." Checks and money orders made out to fictitious insurance

---

2 and authorities there cited, but the analogy is profoundly unpersuasive. For a thorough opinion on the issue in the context of a defendant who persists in refusing to co-operate in providing such exemplars, arriving at the conclusion that there is no Fifth Amendment violation, see *U.S. v. Lentz*, 419 F. Supp. 2d 837 (E.D. Va. 2006).

[173]The claim that the expert can accurately evaluate signs of disguise is an old one in the field, but it is a claim which has never been subject to empirical test of any kind.

[174]*U.S. v. Ojeikere*, 2005 WL 425492 (S.D. N.Y. 2005) The wording of this invocation is similar to that in Ferguson, and makes it appear likely that it was drawn from a standard government brief.

[175]*U.S. v. Ojeikere*, 2005 WL 425492 (S.D. N.Y. 2005).

[176]See *U.S. v. Ojeikere*, 2007 WL 2076695 (S.D. N.Y. 2007).

[177]*U.S. v. Mornan*, 413 F.3d 372, 67 Fed. R. Evid. Serv. 754 (3d Cir. 2005).

[178]*U.S. v. Jolivet*, 224 F.3d 902, 55 Fed. R. Evid. Serv. 670 (8th Cir. 2000).

companies were cashed, and neither loans nor insurance were forthcoming.[179] Because the handwriting identification testimony was not objected to at trial, the Court expends little effort in explaining exactly what the proffered handwriting expert testified to, and what claim of expertise was entailed, before it concludes that allowing her testimony in the absence of objection was not plain error.[180] The sole issue discussed beyond that, is the propriety of the lower court having allowed the document examiner to testify in terms less than absolute certainty, which the court finds to be perfectly acceptable.[181] This of course is the absolutely correct ruling. It would be a tragic irony if the legal system punished experts for being conservative in their estimation of their own certainty and rewarded only those prepared to overclaim.

In *United States v. Brown*,[182] the panel of the Second Circuit that issued the non-precedential Summary Order affirming defendant's conviction kept its consideration of the handwriting issue short and ambiguous in affirming the admission of the prosecution's expert handwriting testimony at trial. The facts appear to be as follows:[183] Judson Brown flew in from Columbia to a New York area airport, and was subject to a customs search which revealed a counterfeit $100 bill and a postal mailing receipt for a package sent from Colombia to an address in Connecticut. The package was later intercepted and contained in excess of 500 grams of cocaine. The exact nature of the handwriting testimony at issue in the case is not made clear by the opinion, except to say that it dealt with attributing to Brown "authorship of certain documents."[184] We are not told what documents, or how many, or how much writing was involved in each. The defense moved for exclusion, or in the alternative, for a *Hines/McVeigh* restriction.[185] One suspects these motions were fairly cursory. The trial court denied both.[186] The Court of Appeals notes the controversy surrounding handwriting expertise, and that the Second Circuit has yet to rule definitively (as if there could be a globally definitive ruling under the requirements of *Kumho Tire*'s "task at hand" approach), but further notes that "similar attacks on handwriting analysis have been rejected by our sister circuits," citing Prime, Crisp, Mooney, and *Jones*, (discussed above) and as usual failing to note the difficulties in characterizing such precedents given the "abuse of discretion" standard applied on appeal and the "task at hand" requirements of *Kumho Tire*.[187] Having said this, the court states that it will reverse only for "manifest error"[188] and that "[h]aving reviewed the record of proceedings relevant to the district court's decision to allow the challenged expert testimony in this case, we find no such manifest error."[189] However, the court then goes on to state that even if there had been error it was harmless beyond a reasonable doubt both because the authorship of the documents was peripheral to guilt in the charged offenses, and because the other evidence was so overwhelming that there is not reasonable probability of the result having been dif-

---

[179]*U.S. v. Mornan*, 413 F.3d 372, 374–375, 67 Fed. R. Evid. Serv. 754 (3d Cir. 2005).

[180]*U.S. v. Mornan*, 413 F.3d 372, 381, 67 Fed. R. Evid. Serv. 754 (3d Cir. 2005).

[181]*U.S. v. Mornan*, 413 F.3d 372, 3381–382, 67 Fed. R. Evid. Serv. 754 (3d Cir. 2005) (finding such admission to be no error of any kind, much less plain error; citing *U.S. v. Rosario*, 118 F. 3d 160, 163 (3rd Cir., 1997)).

[182]*U.S. v. Brown*, 152 Fed. Appx. 59 (2d Cir. 2005).

[183]*U.S. v. Brown*, 152 Fed. Appx. 59, 61 (2d Cir. 2005).

[184]*U.S. v. Brown*, 152 Fed. Appx. 59, 61 (2d Cir. 2005).

[185]*U.S. v. Brown*, 152 Fed. Appx. 59, 62 (2d Cir. 2005).

[186]*U.S. v. Brown*, 152 Fed. Appx. 59, 61 (2d Cir. 2005).

[187]*U.S. v. Brown*, 152 Fed. Appx. 59, 62 (2d Cir. 2005).

[188]Presumably this is the same as Joiner's "abuse of discretion" standard. According to A Dictionary of Modern Legal Usage (Bryan A. Garner, ed., 2d ed. 1999), "manifest . . . is one of those vague terms by which lawyers 'create an appearance of continuity, uniformity and definiteness [that does] not in fact exist,'" quoting Jerome Frank, Law and the Modern Mind (1930; 1963).

[189]*U.S. v. Brown*, 152 Fed. Appx. 59, 62–63 (2d Cir. 2005).

ferent if the handwriting testimony were excluded.[190] In short, this opinion is a standard issue routine affirmance by a federal Court of Appeals which does not address the actual issues of handwriting identification reliability as applied to the task in the case before it at all.

*United States v. Smith*,[191] is another "unpublished" per curiam Court of Appeals opinion (this time from the Fourth Circuit) giving short shrift to defense objections to handwriting expertise on appeal. The facts appear to be these: Al Smith was a convicted felon prohibited under federal law from possessing firearms that had traveled in interstate commerce. He was charged with, inter alia, purchasing such firearms from the Cumberland Pawn Shop in North Carolina, taking them to New York, and then selling them in New York. The purchase of the firearms (which constituted the actus reus of the felon-in-possession count and an important evidentiary fact in regard to the unlicensed trafficking counts upon which he was indicted) was the subject of overwhelming evidence. Smith purchased the guns using phony driver's licenses with another name but his picture on them. When his home was searched, the driver's licenses were found and seized. Various pawnshop employees testified to recognizing him as a person to whom they had sold and delivered guns under the names on the licenses. A co-conspirator in the selling operation, Reginald Currie, testified against him. (It is not specifically stated, but seems reasonably clear, that Smith was targeted after Currie was arrested for something and cut a deal to give Smith up.) The names on the firearms register book at the pawnshop matched the names on the phony licenses with Smith's picture on them.[192]

To gild the lily, the prosecution called a forensic document examiner, Agent Carl McClary of the Bureau of Alcohol, Tobacco and Firearms, to testify that the signatures on the register were in Smith's handwriting.[193] Once again, the formal task for which expertise was being claimed was the attribution of authorship from a very limited amount of "questioned" writing, which was not Smith's own signature. The court's opinion never notices this, perhaps understandably, given the inevitable conclusion of harmless error if error were found, but from such analytic sloppiness is bad jurisprudence forged. Instead of analyzing the case pursuant to the requirements of Kumho Tire, the court treats the previous Fourth Circuit opinion in *U.S. v. Crisp* as an applicable precedent for the global acceptability of handwriting identification expertise, even thought the task at issue in *Crisp* was vastly different than the one formally at issue in Smith, and even though the *Crisp* decision was 2-1 with a significant dissent.[194]

*United States v. Adeyi*,[195] is another Second Circuit Summary Order dealing with a challenge to the admissibility of prosecution proffered handwriting identification expertise. Defendant Adeyi was arrested at Kennedy Airport upon his arrival from Nigeria when a screening of his luggage revealed 30 kilograms of heroin.[196] In another exercise in lily gilding (perhaps to head off the argument that Adeyi really didn't know there were 65 pounds of heroin in his luggage) the government "called a

---

[190]*U.S. v. Brown*, 152 Fed. Appx. 59, 63 (2d Cir. 2005).

[191]*U.S. v. Smith*, 153 Fed. Appx. 187 (4th Cir. 2005), cert. denied, 546 U.S. 1221, 126 S. Ct. 1446, 164 L. Ed. 2d 144 (2006).

[192]The facts are pieced together from information given at *U.S. v. Smith*, 153 Fed. Appx. 187, 189 (4th Cir. 2005), cert. denied, 546 U.S. 1221, 126 S. Ct. 1446, 164 L. Ed. 2d 144 (2006).

[193]*U.S. v. Smith*, 153 Fed. Appx. 187, 189 (4th Cir. 2005), cert. denied, 546 U.S. 1221, 126 S. Ct. 1446, 164 L. Ed. 2d 144 (2006).

[194]*U.S. v. Smith*, 153 Fed. Appx. 187, 190 (4th Cir. 2005), cert. denied, 546 U.S. 1221, 126 S. Ct. 1446, 164 L. Ed. 2d 144 (2006). To be fair to the *Smith* panel, the *Crisp* majority did characterize their adoption of the "guild" test as global. See *U.S. v. Crisp*, 324 F.3d 261, 271, 60 Fed. R. Evid. Serv. 1486 (4th Cir. 2003). See the discussion of *Crisp* earlier in this section.

[195]*U.S. v. Adeyi*, 165 Fed. Appx. 944 (2d Cir. 2006), cert. denied, 127 S. Ct. 194, 166 L. Ed. 2d 158 (U.S. 2006)

[196]*U.S. v. Adeyi*, 165 Fed. Appx. 944, 945 (2d Cir. 2006), cert. denied, 127 S. Ct. 194, 166 L. Ed. 2d 158 (U.S. 2006)

handwriting expert to opine as to the authorship of certain slips of paper found among the packages of heroin contained in Adeyi's bags."[197] The expert "testified to his belief that, based on the handwriting in Adeyi's address book, two of the handwritten slips of paper found in the heroin packages appeared to be authored by Adeyi." We are not told how much writing was on the two slips of paper attributed to Adeyi. It may be that this case presents another example of the most questionable task avoided and unfaced. But this time the blame for it not being faced is entirely on the defense attorney, since the testimony of the expert was not objected to at trial. Hence, the Circuit reviewed it only for plain error, and by that standard, quite properly affirmed, leaving issues of ineffective assistance and harmlessness to post conviction proceedings.[198] Hence this case is in fact like the oft mis-cited *Jolivet* case, and *United States v. Mornan*,[199] which also involved unpreserved claims. For this reason neither *Jolivet* nor the Circuit decision in *Adeyi* establish anything except that it is not plain error to admit proffered handwriting identification testimony which is not objected to, hardly a surprising proposition. In a subsequent opinion by the district court in the same case, in response to Adeyi's motion for post-conviction relief for ineffective assistance of counsel based on counsel's failure to object to the prosecution's handwriting identification expert testimony, Judge Ross ruled that the failure to object did not constitute ineffective assistance of counsel because "such an objection would have been meritless." Although he recognizes that the admissibility issue was technically unsettled in the Second Circuit, Judge Ross says that "this court concludes that the great weight of authority favors admitting such testimony and thus, the objection Adeyi contends Marino should have made would have been overruled."[200] Note that the court never addresses the "task at hand," and makes a conclusion of global admissibility based entirely on precedent interpreted globally, in derogation of the requirements of *Kumho Tire*. Whether this is in part the result of post-conviction counsel's failure to frame the task-at-hand issue is not ascertainable on the face of the opinion, but this seems likely.

Judge Story's opinion in *U.S v. Campbell*[201] is another global opinion, but it must be said that it appears to have been generated, at least from what can be told from the opinion itself, in response to a fairly global objection by the defense, relying mostly on piling up citations to Lewis, Saelee, Fujii, Hidalgo, Rutherford and *Hines* with little case-specific analysis.[202] At least the court chose to treat the case as if that were the defense claim. The court responded with a stringcite of its own to Paul, Crisp, Mooney, Jones, Velasquez, and the usual mis-citation to *Jolivet*, with the added mis-citation to *Mornan*, and decided that the Eleventh Circuit opinion in *Paul* disposed of the issue globally for the court's circuit, obviating the necessity of any *Daubert* hearing.[203] The requirements of *Kumho Tire* are ignored (beyond citing it for the proposition that the court's gatekeeping function extends to non-science expertise), and it is impossible to determine what expert task the document examiner was being asked to perform. Unfortunately, there is reason to fear that the Campbell-type opinion is becoming the standard in the majority of district courts.

---

[197]*U.S. v. Adeyi*, 165 Fed. Appx. 944, 945 (2d Cir. 2006), cert. denied, 127 S. Ct. 194, 166 L. Ed. 2d 158 (U.S. 2006)

[198]*U.S. v. Adeyi*, 165 Fed. Appx. 944, 945 (2d Cir. 2006), cert. denied, 127 S. Ct. 194, 166 L. Ed. 2d 158 (U.S. 2006)

[199]See the discussions of *Jolivet* and *Mornan* earlier in this section.

[200]*Adeyi v. U.S.*, 2007 WL 203962 (E.D. N.Y. 2007).

[201]*U.S. v. Campbell*, 2006 WL 346446 (N.D. Ga. 2006)

[202]*U.S. v. Campbell*, 2006 WL 346446 (N.D. Ga. 2006).

[203]*U.S. v. Campbell*, 2006 WL 346446 (N.D. Ga. 2006).

In a reversal of the usual roles, the Fifth Circuit case *United States v. Garza*[204] deals with a defense-proffered handwriting expert. Unlike the usual case of prosecution-proffered handwriting expertise, the defense's asserted expert in Garza was excluded from testifying by the trial judge. Francisco Garza was charged in one count of a multi-count indictment alleging a conspiracy to distribute the drug known as Ecstasy and other drugs.[205] Garza was tried, convicted and sentenced to 36 years in prison, and on appeal raised only two substantive challenges to the central evidence against him, which was a confession obtained by Dallas Police Officer Barry Ragsdale.[206] The main attack was that Ragsdale had been investigated by Michael Grimes of the U.S. Department of Justice Inspector General's office when an Assistant United States Attorney prosecuting a case in which Ragsdale was a witness expressed concerns that Ragsdale had not told the truth in regard to the actual voluntariness of the cooperation of one of the defendants in that case. Grimes had investigated and interviewed Ragsdale, and concluded that Ragsdale was being deceptive during the investigation (based a lot on body language, according to the Court) but no prosecution was undertaken. Garza wanted to call Grimes as an opinion witness, pursuant to Fed. R. Evid. 608(a), regarding Ragsdale's lack of veracity. The trial court ruled that the investigation had not provided sufficient knowledge to form a reliable opinion for the purposes of Rule 608, conceding that to be "a close question." The circuit court ruled that the trial court "did not abuse its discretion" and rejected this ground of appeal.[207]

The handwriting dimension of the case also deals with the circumstances of the alleged confession. Kim Sanders (presumably another Dallas police officer or employee) signed two documents attesting to having witnessed Garza's confession (one of which presumably being signed close in time to the alleged confession itself).[208] Sanders testified in the prosecution's case-in-chief to having witnessed the confession and to signing the attestations. Garza alleged that this did not happen, and wished to call a handwriting expert, Linda James, to say that the signature on the attestation did not match known signatures of Kim Sanders. There were two objection made to Ms. James's testimony: first, that she had not been identified as a witness and had provided no report until the day she was called to testify by the defense, in violation of the judge's pretrial reciprocal discovery order; second, that the methodology she employed, relying solely on four photocopied "known" signatures and two photocopied signatures from the challenged documents, was not sufficiently reliable to satisfy Rule 702. At a *Daubert* hearing, "James testified that she did not know how many times the documents had been photocopied, but that she believed that the quality of the copies were (sic) clear enough for her to use them as the basis of her opinion," although she admitted that "to look at the origi-

[204]*U.S. v. Garza*, 448 F.3d 294, 70 Fed. R. Evid. Serv. 54 (5th Cir. 2006).

[205]*U.S. v. Garza*, 448 F.3d 294, 295, 70 Fed. R. Evid. Serv. 54 (5th Cir. 2006).

[206]*U.S. v. Garza*, 448 F.3d 294, 296, 70 Fed. R. Evid. Serv. 54 (5th Cir. 2006). Garza also claimed that his sentence had been impermissibly enhanced by the District Court in contravention of *U.S. v. Booker*, 543 U.S. 220, 125 S. Ct. 738, 160 L. Ed. 2d 621 (2005). On this claim he prevailed and the case was on that basis remanded for resentencing.

[207]*U.S. v. Garza*, 448 F.3d 294, 297–298, 70 Fed. R. Evid. Serv. 54 (5th Cir. 2006). The court also affirmed the District Court's rejection of the defense's attempt to get the same opinion in through a hearsay backdoor by characterizing

Grimes's course-of-business report of his investigation and conclusions concerning Ragsdale as an admission of a party under Rule 801(d)(2)(b) or (d) because Grimes was an agent of the Justice Department and the Justice Department was conducting the prosecution. *Id.* at 298–299. Consideration of the merits of that issue is beyond the scope of this chapter.

[208]All facts on this issue are taken from *U.S. v. Garza*, 448 F.3d 294, 299–300, 70 Fed. R. Evid. Serv. 54 (5th Cir. 2006).The court does not make clear whether the confession was written or oral. If it was written it is surprising that there appears to be no controversy concerning Garza's signature or writing, but this question does not change the admissibility issues in regard to the defense handwriting expert.

nal signatures is the best practice."[209] She also said that "she had requested original exemplars of Sanders' signature from defense counsel, but that originals were not provided." Based on this testimony, the district court ruled as follows: "I find that her testimony, based on the examination of copies, comparing them, copies, Xerox copies, without any knowledge about how often they had been copied, whether that's a second, third, fourth, fifth or tenth copy that had been made, in other words, a copy of a copy, I find her testimony would not be reliable under Rule 702."[210] The court also ruled that James's testimony should be excluded for violation of the pretrial order.

The Circuit Court declined to determine whether exclusion was a justified sanction for the violation of the pre-trial order, deeming that issue moot since they affirmed the exclusion based on rule 702 because "it cannot be said that the district court's ruling was an abuse of discretion."[211] In reaching that conclusion, the Court conceded that there were numerous cases that have held that the use of photocopies instead of originals by a document examiner goes to weight and not admissibility.[212] In addition, the Circuit did not address the District Court's apparent confusion of the issue concerning whether one can determine the how many generations of photocoping a copy represents with the issue of whether the photocopy is clear enough for use.[213]

Finally, the Circuit Court held that any error was harmless because the District Court allowed the jury to see the photocopies James would have relied upon, and to argue that the attestation signatures were forgeries based on this. This was supposedly sufficient to satisfy the defense's desire to impeach Sanders,[214] though it is difficult to see, if one believes in the existence of such expertise, how the direct juror evaluation would render the improper exclusion of the expertise "harmless."

One cannot help concluding that this is another case that reflects the systemic differences in judicial treatment of prosecution and defense proffers when it comes to

---

[209]*U.S. v. Garza*, 448 F.3d 294, 300, 70 Fed. R. Evid. Serv. 54 (5th Cir. 2006).

[210]*U.S. v. Garza*, 448 F.3d 294, 300, 70 Fed. R. Evid. Serv. 54 (5th Cir. 2006).

[211]*U.S. v. Garza*, 448 F.3d 294, 300, 70 Fed. R. Evid. Serv. 54 (5th Cir. 2006).

[212]A typical such opinion accepting the use of photocopies (by a prosecution expert) is *People v. Nawi*, 2004 WL 2944016 (Cal. App. 1st Dist. 2004), unpublished/noncitable, (Dec. 21, 2004) and review granted, (Apr. 20, 2005) and review dismissed, cause remanded, (Aug. 16, 2006), which is discussed infra. More importantly, so far as I know, there has never been another case where the sole basis for the exclusion of the testimony of a handwriting expert was the use of photocopies for comparison purposes. The closest case I have ever seen is *Todd v. Mississippi*, 806 So. 2d 1086 (S.Ct., Miss., 2001) affirming a trial court's decision not to give any weight to the testimony of a criminal defendant's handwriting expert in the context of a hearing on the authentication of a purported witness recantation letter, based both on the expert's very thin credentials and the use of photocopies. Id. at 1095. While it is perhaps suggestive that in Todd, as in Garza, it was a defense proffer that was rejected, the basis in Todd was at least more than merely the use of photocopies. Finally, there is *Bourne v. Town of*

*Madison*, 2007 DNH 65, 2007 WL 1447672 (D.N.H. 2007), a federal civil rights case in which the plaintiff's expert (whom the Court almost found unqualified as a handwriting expert of any kind) not only used photocopies but used a non-standard process of multiple photocopy blowups to obtain comparison specimens, which the defendant's document examiner claimed would lead to distortion. While there are some weaknesses in the testimony of the defendant's expert on these grounds, the court's rejection of the plaintiff's expert is certainly not a bare rejection based on using photocopies per se.

[213]A fourth generation photocopy made on high quality machines may be clearer than a third generation copy on machines of less high quality. The real issue is the clarity and quality of the photocopy in front of the examiner, not whether there are intervening generations. Of course, lurking in the background is the issue of how the authenticity of the "known" signatures was established at all.

[214]"This court has repeatedly held that juries are capable of comparing signatures to determine authenticity. Therefore Garza was able to impeach Sanders even without the expert testimony of Ms. James." *U.S. v. Garza*, 448 F.3d 294, 300, 70 Fed. R. Evid. Serv. 54 (5th Cir. 2006) (internal footnote to citations omitted).

proffered expertise which other studies have discovered.[215] In addition, it may again illustrate the difference in resources between prosecution and defense. Finally, it is not exactly clear how the defense could obtain the original known samples from Mr. Sanders the Court seems to require, and certainly it could not have been done without considerable foresight and extended discovery litigation. All in all, this opinion does not represent a shining example of judicial analysis.

This section on the Federal cases dealing with reliability challenges to handwriting identification expertise ends with a civil case, *A.V. by Versace, Inc. v. Gianni Versace S.p.A.*[216] This case involved a complicated struggle over the authority to use the Versace trademark among a number of corporate entities and two prominent Versaces, Gianni and Alfredo. The opinion deals with contempt proceedings against Alfredo for, inter alia, authorizing use of the mark by his son, failing to take steps ordered by the court to eliminate unauthorized internet trade, production of financial records, and a variety of other things, including signing a distribution agreement with John Pappettas.[217]

Alfredo claimed his signature on the agreement was a forgery. In support of this claim, Alfredo called Julia Bevaqua, an asserted handwriting expert who testified that she had compared the signature on the agreement with sixteen known exemplars of Alfredo's signature, and that the signature on the Pappettas agreement was not an authentic signature of Alfredo.[218] Gianni objected to this testimony. He did not attack the qualifications of Bevaqua, but rather globally attacked the reliability of handwriting expertise in general. The court disposed of this rule 702 attack in a footnote[219] in which Judge Leisure recognizes some controversy in the district courts about the reliability of handwriting identification, and about allowing them to testify to attributions of authorship conclusorily, but concludes: "every circuit that has considered this question has concluded that a properly admitted handwriting expert may offer an opinion regarding the authorship of a handwriting sample if the factors enumerated in *Daubert* are satisfied." citing *Prime, Crisp, Mooney, Paul, Jones* and *Velasquez*, and mis-citing *Jolivet* as usual.[220] This passage is curious by virtue of the peremptory and dismissive lack of analysis that precedes the stringcite. Of course "a properly admitted handwriting expert" can properly testify. The issue is, when is such an expert properly admitted? "If the factors enumerated in *Daubert* are satisfied," says Judge Leisure. But he never says what those factors are, or why they are satisfied in this case, and has apparently never heard of *Kumho Tire*, and its task-at-hand requirements. Under the circumstances, it is somewhat ironic that the task involved in the case was signature authentication, the only specific task for which there are some data suggesting support for the claims of handwriting expertise. It appears that the misplaced global stringcite has become the general "methodology" of courts faced with challenges to the reliability of handwriting expertise. The federal courts have by and large arrived at the place where they are most comfortable, where they can substitute slogans and stringcites for evidence and analysis, while turning a blind eye to the inconvenient requirements of *Kumho Tire v. Carmichael* and the implications of *General Electric v. Joiner* (rendering appellate opinions on these matters essentially meaningless).

The controversy over the reliability of handwriting identification expertise which

---

[215]See Risinger, Navigating Expert Reliability: Are Criminal Standards of Certainty Being Left on the Dock, 64 Albany L. Rev. 99, 110 (2000).

[216]*A.V. By Versace, Inc. v. Gianni Versace S.p.A.*, 446 F. Supp. 2d 252 (S.D. N.Y. 2006).

[217]The facts are drawn from *A.V. By Versace, Inc. v. Gianni Versace S.p.A.*, 446 F. Supp. 2d 252 (S.D. N.Y. 2006). There are lots of details in the opinion concerning contumacious behavior and al-

leged behavior by Alfredo, which are not necessary to understand the handwriting issues.

[218]*A.V. By Versace, Inc. v. Gianni Versace S.p.A.*, 446 F. Supp. 2d 252 (S.D. N.Y. 2006).

[219]*A.V. By Versace, Inc. v. Gianni Versace S.p.A.*, 446 F. Supp. 2d 252 (S.D. N.Y. 2006).

[220]*A.V. By Versace, Inc. v. Gianni Versace S.p.A.*, 446 F. Supp. 2d 252 (S.D. N.Y. 2006).

played itself out in the federal courts between *Starzekpyzel* in 1996 and *Oskowitz* in 2003 did not even arrive in state courts until it was almost played out in the federal courts. Since 2003 it is fair to say that the federal court response to the potential reliability problems of handwriting identification expertise has settled into a pattern which would be a source of melancholy for anyone who was excited by the prospects of rational task-specific reliability analysis pursuant to the teachings of *Kumho Tire v. Carmichael*. The story revealed in the state cases that have arisen from 2002 onward might be expected to be somewhat different by virtue of the fact that one would not necessarily expect *Kumho Tire* to be regarded as authoritative in the same way that one would have (wrongly) expected federal courts to regard it. But with that qualification, the two stories appear to have the same ending.

In the state courts, business has generally gone on as usual, with literally hundreds of opinions noting the presence of handwriting identification testimony in passing, but with the issue of reliability being neither raised nor dealt with. There is a growing number of exceptions, however, comprising a baker's dozen of opinions from nine states that either deal with, or might at first glance be taken to deal with, reliability challenges,[221] and it is to an examination of these state opinions we now turn.

The first explicit challenge to the reliability of handwriting identification expertise reflected in a reported opinion in a state court was in a civil case from North Carolina, *Taylor v. Abernethy*.[222] This case involved the estate of Romer Gray Taylor. Romer had for much of his life been a ne'er-do-well, failing repeatedly at farming and other ventures and generally always being taken in and bailed out by his brother Harvey. In 1978, in connection with Harvey bankrolling (to the tune of $38,000) yet another start for Romer, Harvey claimed Romer signed a contract to make a will with Harvey the sole beneficiary. Romer died in 1998. Apparently he had been looked after by a nephew, child of another sibling of Romer and Harvey. Apparently also Romer had made a will naming not Harvey, but the nephew, as sole beneficiary. Harvey sued. The controlling issue was the authenticity of Romer's signature on the contract dated in 1978. Harvey said it was genuine. Harvey called a document examiner who proposed also to say that Romer's 1978 signature was genuine. The nephew's lawyer moved to exclude the document examiner. Apparently influenced by the federal cases, especially *United States v. Hines*, the trial court said the document examiner could point out similarities but could not offer a conclusion of authenticity. The jury found the signature not to be Romer's. The North Carolina Court of Appeals reversed and declared handwriting identification expertise to be globally admissible, adopting what is essentially the guild test.[223] By so doing, the Court of Appeals has apparently insulated even the most questionable exercises of handwriting identification expertise from any threshold reliability examination in North Carolina courts.

A similar result was reached in a criminal context by the Supreme Court of Wyoming in *Williams v. Wyoming*.[224] In or around early March of 2000, Victim (his name is never given) was a cab driver who met defendant Betty Jean Williams while she was riding in his cab. In conversation, he said he was needing to have some work performed at his house, including some painting, and she said she would be interested in working for him. Some sort of arrangement was arrived at, because a

---

[221]Challenges which were dominantly challenges to the qualifications of a particular expert, or were so treated by the court, are not discussed here unless there was also a challenge to the existence of any expertise applying either globally or to the task at hand, which was resolved by sustaining a challenge to the qualifications of a particular expert, as in Judge Carnes opinion in

*Ramsey.*

[222]*Taylor v. Abernethy*, 149 N.C. App. 263, 560 S.E.2d 233 (2002).

[223]*Taylor v. Abernethy*, 149 N.C. App. 263, 560 S.E.2d 233, 240 (2002).

[224]*Williams v. State*, 2002 WY 184, 60 P.3d 151 (Wyo. 2002).

day or so later the defendant came to Victim's house and provided painting services. It is not clear from the opinion if Victim paid Williams, how he paid her, or how much he paid her.

Toward the end of March, Victim went to New Mexico for a week. When he returned he got his bank statement, and sat down to reconcile it. According to Victim, he discovered that five checks which he was sure he had not written had been cashed, totaling $900. The checks were apparently made out to cash, were signed with Victim's name, but had been endorsed with the name of the defendant. Victim called the police, who discovered that on March 23, 2000 Williams had taken the first check (which was for $150) to a local bank and initially tried to cash it, but the bank refused to handle the check unless she opened a savings account, which she did. She deposited the check into the savings account, and was allowed to take out $100 in cash. The next day she withdrew another $10. Then on March 27 and 28 she deposited four checks, one for $225, two for $275 and one for $200, and in a series of withdrawals interspersed with these deposits managed to leave the savings account with a balance of only one dollar at the close of business on March 28. When she was picked up she admitted to the officer who interviewed her that she had signed the endorsements on the back of the checks, but claimed Victim had given them to her. The checks were dated between March 24 and 28, when Victim was out of town.

It is important to note that Victim's testimony, coupled with that of the bank employees and the bank records and defendant's admission to the police concerning the endorsements, was sufficient evidence to support a conviction. Ever risk averse, however, the prosecution proceeded to supplement this evidence with the testimony of a Mr. Crivello, a document examiner with the Wyoming State Crime Laboratory. Mr. Crivello's examination and conclusions were unusual in their restraint. He did not claim to attribute either the signature on the front of the check or the rest of the entries on the front to defendant Williams. He said he had "no opinion" concerning that. He merely proposed to testify that the signature with the Victim's name on the front of the check "was not consistent with Victim's known signature, and that Victim "probably or very probably" did not write those signatures. He further testified that defendant Williams did write the endorsements in her name on the back of the checks. Thus, he proposed only to testify to the authenticity of the two apparent signatures on the checks, a subtask of handwriting identification about which some data exist. If that had been the focus of the defendant's attack, and therefore the decisions of both the trial and appellate courts, that would have been one thing. What happened was quite something else.

Wyoming has explicitly adopted the Supreme Court's approach in *Daubert, Joiner* and *Kumho Tire*.[225] The Rule 702 motion in Williams was made by the defense the day before trial was to begin. Initially, the trial court was of the opinion that Montana's version of *Daubert* doctrine did not require a hearing in regard to handwriting identification, citing *Starzecpyzel* (no one at the trial level seemed familiar with *Kumho Tire*). Finally, however, something of a hearing was held. The focus was completely global, addressing handwriting identification generally. The only witness was the state's document examiner, though the prosecution also apparently produced the Kam studies (the opinion refers to the prosecutor arguing at the hearing that "the peer-reviewed articles that we produced to the court from the Journal of Forensic Sciences also demonstrates (sic) that they come up with the right answer").[226] We are not told what, if anything, the defense produced. The document examiner testified to his credentials, and to never having failed a proficiency

---

[225]*Williams v. State*, 2002 WY 184, 60 P.3d 151, 153–154 (Wyo. 2002), citing *Bunting v. Jamieson*, 984 P.2d 467 (Wyo. 1999).

[226]*Williams v. State*, 2002 WY 184, 60 P.3d 151, 157 (Wyo. 2002).

test in 16 years, though what regime of individual proficiency testing he is referring to is not clear, since we are not familiar with such a regime of tests which issues passing and failing grades. At any rate, on this record, the trial court found handwriting identification testimony globally admissible, and the Supreme Court of Montana affirmed, saying that the record before the trial court was sufficient to find that "forensic document techniques have been and are tested and forensic document examination has been the subject of considerable peer review and publication. In addition the court found that there was adequate proof that "there existed appropriate testing procedures to assure and maintain the standards of the profession and that such profession had been accepted within the relevant scientific community for many years."[227] The court did indicate that its *Daubert*-like jurisprudence adopted the *Kumho Tire* requirement that all proffered expertise is subject to review for reliability. In addition, technically, the Supreme Court opinion was only a finding that admitting the testimony in this case was not an abuse of discretion. However, it seems clear that it will be the rare judge in Montana who does not take this opinion to be a global mandate to admit such evidence across the board, independent of the claims of expertise which were actually involved in the *Williams* case itself.[228]

At least the next case, *Spann v. State*,[229] has the virtue of reaching a similar result in a more straightforward, if no less questionable, way. The case involved a capital murder charge against Spann and others arising out of the murder of Kazue Perron, who was carjacked in order to get her car for use in a robbery, and then murdered execution-style so she could not identify the carjackers. The evidence against Spann was overwhelming, and will not be rehearsed here. Handwriting comes in, again, only peripherally. While in jail, Spann wrote to a co-defendant in an attempt to coach him on how to testify. Authorities were given the note. Initially, Spann denied writing it, but when told that a handwriting expert was going to examine it, Spann admitted writing the note. However, the prosecution still wanted the questioned document examiner to testify. Specifically, the prosecution wanted the document examiner to testify that the writing on the note showed an attempt to disguise Spann's ordinary hand. The relevance of this was assertedly "consciousness of guilt" (the relevance of "consciousness of guilt" in regard to the note is not made clear; perhaps it was to cut off any claim that the text of the note could be given an innocent construction). At any rate, the defense challenged the reliability of the document examiner to conclude that a writing was "intentionally disguised" and the trial court decided that this issue was both "novel" and "scientific" enough to raise an issue under Florida's version of the *Frye* test. After a hearing, the trial court concluded that the proffered testimony "is indeed based on scientific principle, which has gained acceptance in the field of Forensic Document Examination" and admitted the testimony.

Here is where the case becomes procedurally unusual. The Supreme Court of Florida ruled that the defense had only preserved error on the issue of the ability of questioned document examiners to determine disguise, but that on appeal it had only raised the issue of the general reliability of handwriting analysis testimony.[230] Because the only issue argued was not preserved at trial, and because the only is-

---

[227]*Williams v. State*, 2002 WY 184, 60 P.3d 151, 157 (Wyo. 2002). The court has an odd notion of a "scientific" community. These statements appear to be based on the guild test supplemented by the existence of the Kam studies, for all their weaknesses, and the assumed existence of yearly graded proficiency tests.

[228]This appears to be another example of a slap-dash defense challenge leading to a poorly

considered opinion that might place a whole jurisdiction's jurisprudence on the subject in a bad posture for the foreseeable future.

[229]*Spann v. State*, 857 So. 2d 845 (Fla. 2003).

[230]*Spann v. State*, 857 So. 2d 845 (Fla. 2003). The Supreme Court of Florida issued a revised opinion in the case, 2003 WL 22349391 (Fla. 2003), which does not differ from the original in regard to the handwriting issues.

sue preserved was not raised on appeal, the defendant was without legal standing to challenge anything.[231] If the court had stopped there, the case would be of limited interest. However, the court goes on to say (in what must technically count as dictum, a distinction unlikely to have much practical effect on practice in Florida in the near future) that "even if the alleged error had been properly preserved, this claim would fail."[232] It then goes on to declare that the trial court was right on both issues, that the general reliability of handwriting identification testimony is not novel and therefore not subject to Florida's version of *Frye*,[233] and that the lower court's handling of the disguise issue was proper.[234]

A radical optimist might see the potential seeds of a *Kumho Tire* approach in the way this case was handled, with general issues being subject to no challenge for lack of novelty, but each specific issue being regard as "novel" because it had never been the subject of a particularized *Frye* hearing before. A realist, however, would have to admit that the Florida Supreme Court's approval of using the document examiner guild as the reference group for general acceptance under its *Frye* test makes a successful challenge to even the most unreliable of this and other questionable techniques of forensic identification "science" very unlikely in Florida for the foreseeable future. The irony here is that this is the same court that showed itself so capable of rational evaluation of the weaknesses of specific proffered expertise in *Ramirez v. State*.[235]

The opinion in the next state case, *Florence v. Com.*,[236] is in many ways the most sophisticated of the current group. It deals with the general issue of what may be called the "price of admission" burden (as opposed to the ultimate burden of persuasion on the issue of reliability once it is reached, which doctrinally is always on the proponent of the evidence) which was alluded to by the Supreme Court of the United States in *Kumho Tire Co., Ltd.*.[237] It arises when a particular process or technique is one which has a long history of admission. In such a case, the obligations of Rule 702 to determine sufficient reliability of the proffer still obtain, but it is reasonable to require that the challenger bring forth more than just a paper motion. Instead, the challenger must support the motion with some basis establishing a good reason to believe that reliability is a real and not merely a formal issue in the context of the case before the court.

The facts in *Florence* were these: On March 3, 1999, someone (apparently using a State of Kentucky identification card) opened an account in the name "William C.

---

[231]*Spann v. State*, 857 So. 2d 845 (Fla. 2003).

[232]*Spann v. State*, 857 So. 2d 845 (Fla. 2003).

[233]"Forensic handwriting identification is not a new or novel science." *Spann v. State*, 857 So. 2d 845 (Fla. 2003). "Because expert forensic handwriting identification is not new or novel, *Frye* has no application." *Spann v. State*, 857 So. 2d 845 (Fla. 2003).

[234]The *Frye* hearing in the case was limited to the issue of whether the expert could testify that Spann distorted or disguised his handwriting. "[T]he trial court's consideration of the admissibility of expert testimony on the limited issue of distorted or disguised handwriting was properly considered and resolved." *Spann v. State*, 857 So. 2d 845 (Fla. 2003). The court cites no specific evidence or testimony dealing with the reliability of document examiners in performing this particular task.

[235]*Ramirez v. State*, 810 So. 2d 836 (Fla. 2001). There is in particular a stark and startling contrast between *Spann* and *Ramirez* in regard to what counts as an appropriate reference community under *Frye*, the need for actual information on error rates, and the caution with which partisan experts should be approached. See *Ramirez v. State*, 810 So. 2d 836, 847–852 (Fla. 2001).

[236]*Florence v. Com.*, 120 S.W.3d 699 (Ky. 2003).

[237]The issue concerns when the reliability of a proffer has been "called sufficiently into question" *Kumho Tire Co., Ltd. v. Carmichael*, 526 U.S. 137, 149, 119 S. Ct. 1167, 143 L. Ed. 2d 238, 50, 50 U.S.P.Q.2d 1177, Prod. Liab. Rep. (CCH) P 15470, 50 Fed. R. Evid. Serv. 1373, 29 Envtl. L. Rep. 20638 (1999), and therefore does not fall within that set of cases "where the reliability of an expert's methods is properly taken for granted." *Kumho Tire Co., Ltd. v. Carmichael*, 526 U.S. 137, 152, 119 S. Ct. 1167, 143 L. Ed. 2d 238, 50, 50 U.S.P.Q.2d 1177, Prod. Liab. Rep. (CCH) P 15470, 50 Fed. R. Evid. Serv. 1373, 29 Envtl. L. Rep. 20638 (1999).

Vance" at the Whitaker Bank in Lexington by depositing $50 in cash. On March 4, he returned to the same bank branch and cashed a counter check on the account for $35. On March 5, he deposited a check for $3740 made payable to William C. Vance drawn on the account of a business called Rooftek at the Fifth Third Bank. For whatever reason, the check was deposited to cash instead of being accepted subject to collection. The next day the perpetrator showed up at a different branch of the Whittaker Bank and cashed another counter check for $3540. On March 7, the perpetrator wrote a $903 check on the "Vance" account for the purchase of an airline ticket. Shortly thereafter, Whittaker Bank was notified by the Fifth Third Bank that the Rooftek account had been closed some time before, and the $3740 check was dishonored. The police were notified. A check of records determined that there was no "William C. Vance" with a real State of Kentucky identification card.

Defendant was apprehended by a combination of good police work and luck. When police in Hamilton County, Ohio, searched the home of defendant's half brother pursuant to an unrelated investigation, they found a State of Kentucky identification card in the name of William C. Vance. The picture on the card was defendant. When they saw a bulletin regarding the Kentucky case, they notified the Kentucky authorities. Defendant was arrested and later identified by various bank employees as the person who had opened the account, negotiated the checks, and made the withdrawals.

This state desired to call Detective Chris White, a Secret Service trained questioned document examiner, to testify that he had compared authentic exemplars of defendant's handwriting to the handwriting on the checks, and that defendant had written the checks. White's testimony was remarkable on three counts. First, he did not obtain any new exemplars of defendant Florence's handwriting. For "known" exemplars he relied on two documents: The Kentucky ID card and the application made to open the bank account. The first of these bore little if any writing besides a signature. The second may have had a few more blanks to fill in besides the signature, but it was not a "known" writing in the usual sense of the word, since its authentication depended on the testimony of witnesses that the defense, a fortiori, challenged as being mistaken in their eyewitness identification of Florence.[238] The ID card is a little better as a "known," since it appears to bear Florence's picture, but even this is an irregular way to establish the authenticity of a known exemplar, and it contained only a single signature.

Second, the "questioned" documents were four checks bearing four signatures, three of which were in the same name "William C. Vance." So, as to those, the examiner claimed to be comparing two signatures to each of three other signatures in the same name and determining that whoever wrote the first two wrote each of the others, based on very little material. In essence, what he was saying (and all he was saying) was that, based on comparing these five signatures alone, the same person wrote all five. The really important testimony, however, (if any of it was) was the testimony about the Rooftek check, which bore a signature in a name other than "William C. Vance" The claim that one can attribute authorship of a signature based on "known" exemplars comprising little more than two other signatures in a different name, and whose status as "known" documents is problematical, is one which even the document examiner literature would call into question. However, this was the testimony which undermined the argument at trial (weak as it was)

---

[238]There was, perhaps, another line of defense: that Florence had in fact opened the "Vance" account, but that someone else who looked like him had by coincidence written all the checks and stolen the money, which he failed to complain about when he found the money gone, but this is so pitiful as to not be worth arguing to a jury. As indicated in the text, Florence's real argument in front of the jury seems to have been, not that he didn't sign all the "Vance" checks, but that the jury should not conclude beyond a reasonable doubt that he knew that the Rooftek check was bad.

that defendant really believed that the Rooftek check was good. One suspects that the departure from standard procedures in this case resulted from the fact that the examiner knew of the strong evidence in the case independent of handwriting comparison, and simply operated as much on that basis as on the exercise of any expertise (the familiar problem of observer effects contaminating forensic science practice which has been documented elsewhere[239]

Finally, at trial, Detective White testified that "handwriting is even more precise than DNA for identification purposes."

All of the above circumstances were known to the defense prior to trial (except perhaps the claim of superiority to DNA identification). However, instead of doing any homework and making a proffer which would have, in a practical way, shown the judge that this testimony had serious reliability problems when evaluated either by exterior standards of empirical justification or by the field's own claims about good practice, the defense relied on a formal motion apparently proffering little in the way of specific information. While it is fair to say that the Supreme Court of Kentucky seemed suspicious of the reliability of the proffered testimony, it ruled that plaintiff's mere formal motion without more was insufficient to trigger a full scale Rule 702 hearing in regard to testimony in an area with long judicial acceptance. The court was careful to say that a more serious effort might properly trigger an obligation to hold such a hearing. The court was clearly trying to strike a balance between requiring the proper consideration of serious reliability issues, and not allowing litigants to require the expenditure of substantial resources in every case involving experts merely for the price of a few pieces of paper.

Finally, as to the "better than DNA testimony," the court was clearly troubled, but the defense had failed to object to the testimony at trial, and on that basis (perhaps also influenced by the large amount of other evidence against defendant) the court declined to rule on the issue.

*Delaware v. Jones*[240] is a case showing remarkable prosecutorial restraint. It involves yet another jailhouse note, this time an anonymous threatening note someone posted over a coffee station on "F" Tier in the Delaware Correctional Center. The note read:

> To: All Prisoners of War on Friday, April 19, 02 we as prisoners will start the elimination of all pigs, co's, cops or whatever you want to call them. On top of our list is co Hall, co Allen and co Jones. United we stand divided we fall.

Suspicion fell upon prisoner Bradford Jones. His fingerprints apparently were found on the note.[241] In addition, the note was sent for comparison to exemplars of Jones's known writing by Georgia Anna Carter, a 30 year veteran of the Delaware State Police who had been a document examiner for 17 years. Originally the state wanted Officer Carter to testify to and point out to the jury the similarities between Jones's writing and the writing on the note, and also to her conclusion that Jones had written the note. When the defense moved for exclusion and demanded a Rule 702 hearing, the prosecution voluntarily limited the document examiner's testimony to pointing out similarities, thus voluntarily limiting her to the functions of a *Hines* witness. After a hearing, the trial judge, Judge Gebelein, ruled globally that the document examiner could testify in the limited manner proposed. In so doing, his analysis was limited to the invocation of the results of other cases in which judges had accepted such testimony. There was no attempt at an independent evaluation of

---

[239]See Risinger, Saks, Thompson and Rosenthal, The *Daubert/Kumho* Implications of Observer Effects in Forensic Science: Hidden Problems of Expectation and Suggestion, 90 Cal. L. Rev. 1 (2002).

[240]*State v. Jones*, 2003 WL 21519842 (Del.

Super. Ct. 2003).

[241]The court indicates that, besides their document examiner, the prosecution intended to call a fingerprint examiner, whose proposed testimony was apparently not challenged. *State v. Jones*, 2003 WL 21519842 (Del. Super. Ct. 2003).

the reliability issue, and no attempt to frame the task before the court, even though Delaware claims to be a *Daubert* jurisdiction. (This should not be too surprising, since the defense attack appears to have been global and appears to have been supported mainly by citation to federal cases excluding handwriting identification expertise in other contexts.) *Kumho Tire* is cited only for its flexibility and discretion language, and for the "same intellectual rigor" test.[242] The judge seems to have been most persuaded by an unreported bench opinion of another Delaware judge which, having apparently skirted *Kumho Tire* by invoking its flexibility language, issued a ruling that was in essence a carbon copy of *Starzecpyzel* down to the limiting instruction.[243] So while the result is a *Hines* result, the judge clearly seems disappointed that, because of the limited nature of the prosecution's proffer, he could not admit the document examiner's conclusion as to authorship also.

The next case is the Massachusetts case of *Commonwealth v. Murphy*,[244] The case involves an appeal from a conviction for various charges springing from a series of incidents involving stolen identities of real people, which were used to open bank accounts, obtain credit cards then used to purchase goods, etc.[245] All six people whose identifying characteristics (driver's license number, social security numbers, etc.) were used in the scheme were named either "John Murphy" or "Michael Sullivan." Whoever committed the scams had left behind numerous documents (charge slips, etc.) bearing the signatures "John Murphy" or "Michael Sullivan," apparently after presenting identification in those names bearing a picture that matched the presenter,[246] and a signature that the presenter's signature at the store appeared to match. When the defendant John Murphy was arrested, various documents (credit card charge receipts, etc.) connected with the various charged crimes were recovered pursuant to a search warrant from the rented car he was driving.

During the pendency of his case, defendant had submitted seven documents to the court in connection with his case signed "John Murphy."[247] In addition, eight of the documents seized from his car documents bore the signature "Michael Sullivan" (two of which were picture IDs with defendant's picture on them.)[248] In a not uncommon act of overkill, the prosecution called a questioned document examiner, Nancy McCann, to testify that she had compared the "John Murphy" signatures and the "Michael Sullivan" signatures on the various charge slips and concluded that it was highly probable that all of the Murphy and Sullivan signatures on the charge slips were signed by the same person, and further, that she had compared the charge slips with the "John Murphy" signatures on the court documents and the "Michael Sullivan" signatures from the car, and concluded that it was more probable than not that they were all written by the same person.[249]

The whole point of the scam structure seems to have been to generate identification documents with signatures actually written by the defendant, so that the defendant could sign charge slips with matching signatures done fluidly in front of salespersons. The task before the document examiner was not really an attribution

---

[242]*State v. Jones*, 2003 WL 21519842 (Del. Super. Ct. 2003).

[243]*State v. Jones*, 2003 WL 21519842 (Del. Super. Ct. 2003).

[244]*Com. v. Murphy*, 59 Mass. App. Ct. 571, 797 N.E.2d 394 (2003).

[245]Factual details are drawn from *Com. v. Murphy*, 59 Mass. App. Ct. 571, 797 N.E.2d 394, 396 (2003) unless otherwise noted. The total retail value of the merchandise charged pursuant to the scheme (televisions, video recorders, computers, furniture, etc.) was in excess of $17,000. *Com. v. Murphy*, 59 Mass. App. Ct. 571, 797 N.E.2d 394,

396 (2003).

[246]The defendant, John Murphy, apparently stole the identities (that is, used the social security and driver's license numbers, etc.) of other John Murphys, setting up documents with their identifying information but his picture.

[247]*Com. v. Murphy*, 59 Mass. App. Ct. 571, 797 N.E.2d 394, 397 (2003).

[248]*Com. v. Murphy*, 59 Mass. App. Ct. 571, 797 N.E.2d 394, 397 (2003).

[249]*Com. v. Murphy*, 59 Mass. App. Ct. 571, 797 N.E.2d 394, 397 (2003).

of authorship task in the normal sense, but rather something closer to the easier task of "authentication" of signatures. In addition, unless extreme care was taken to mask the expertise-irrelevant circumstances surrounding the case from the document examiner (which masking rarely occurs), her conclusion was virtually foregone, because any rational person would come to that conclusion given the rest of the evidence, without the handwriting expert's testimony. So the expert's testimony was in many ways a dramaturgic exercise adding little information of any enhanced reliability to what was already before the jury. In addition, it was not objected to until the objection had already been waived, so, like *Jolivet* and *Mornan*, the handwriting issue was reviewed for plain error only (the Massachusetts formula is: error "that created a substantial risk of miscarriage of justice.")[250] So it is hardly surprising that the defendant's claim that he was entitled to a Hines/McVeigh limitation on the document examiner's testimony, limiting her to pointing out similarities and differences, was rejected.[251] However, as in *Jolivet* and Mornan, the court does in fact go beyond this (in what must presumably count as dictum) to opine that such a limitation is globally never required, given the long acceptance of handwriting identification expertise in Massachusetts.[252]

Two months later, in *Commonwealth v. Glyman*,[253] a Massachusetts trial court reached an even more global conclusion. The case involved a criminal prosecution charging falsification of a will. As usual, it is impossible to tell from the opinion (so it must not have mattered to the judge) exactly what claim of expertise was at stake in the case. It appears that it is either the genuineness of the signatures on the will (a task taken by the document examiner community to be an easy task, and a task for which there is at least some empirical evidence of skill) or it is attribution of authorship from a signature that is an attempt at forgery made by simulating an actual signature of the deceased, which is counted as either the hardest possible task or virtually impossible by standard document examiner lore, depending on who you ask.[254]

The defense made a motion in limine to exclude the handwriting identification testimony as unreliable under *Commonwealth v. Lanigan*,[255] the Massachusetts case that generally adopted the *Daubert* approach to reliability for purposes of admissibility,[256] and requested a hearing to establish the facts underlying the claim that handwriting identification expertise lacked the required reliability. To establish the required "price-of-admission" plausibility of its claim concerning the lack of reliability of this historically admissible claim of expertise, the defense submitted an affidavit from Dr. Michael J. Saks, and the prosecution responded with, inter alia, an affidavit of Dr. Moshe Kam. The court decided to deny the motion in limine without a hearing.[257]

It is clear that the attack of the defense was unfortunately global. It is also clear

---

[250]*Com. v. Murphy*, 59 Mass. App. Ct. 571, 797 N.E.2d 394, 397–398 (2003).

[251]*Com. v. Murphy*, 59 Mass. App. Ct. 571, 797 N.E.2d 394, 398 (2003).

[252]*Com. v. Murphy*, 59 Mass. App. Ct. 571, 797 N.E.2d 394, 399 (2003).

[253]*Commonwealth v. Glyman*, 17 Mass. L. Rptr 146 (Superior Ct., Worcester Co., 2003).

[254]See, e.g, James V. P. Conway, Evidential Documents 24 (1959). "The drawing process of copying from a visible model by its very nature disallows writing individuality, and excludes personal writing inclinations of the forger. A hundred simulations from visible model signatures of John Smith by a hundred different forgers would rarely be distinguishable, let alone identifiable with their authors." One of the complaints document examiners raised about the 1984 FSF proficiency test, wherein all who took it failed to properly attribute the author of the note involved to the true author, was that it presented an analogue to this task extended over a short note (not merely a signature). See § 4:16, infra.

[255]*Com. v. Lanigan*, 419 Mass. 15, 641 N.E.2d 1342 (1994).

[256]Lanigan was a DNA admissibility case that ultimately found the DNA identification at issue in the case reliable enough for admission by the prosecution.

[257]To be fair to Judge Fabricant, she did consider the extraneous preliminary proofs pro-

that Judge Fabricant misunderstood Dr. Saks's credentials, since she doesn't seem to be aware that he actually has a Ph.D. (she says merely that "Professor Saks" has "doctoral training in experimental social psychology").[258] She also says "it does not appear that he has published any empirical research of his own on any subject, or that he has published anything in the area of research design or methodology."[259] Both of these assertions are grossly inaccurate.[260]

Judge Fabricant begins her consideration by noting that handwriting expertise has long been admitted in Massachusetts and elsewhere.[261] She then notes that the opinion of the Massachusetts intermediate appellate court, in *Commonwealth. v. Murphy*,[262] decided only two months earlier, also indicated (in dictum, but nevertheless of understandably heavy influence to Judge Fabricant) that "as the courts in Massachusetts have long accepted as reliable expert testimony about the authorship of handwriting, a *Lanigan* hearing was not necessary even had one been properly requested."[263] She then notes that every federal appellate court that has considered a trial court admission of such testimony in the face of a reliability challenge has upheld the admission, citing *Crisp, Mooney, Paul, Jones* and *Velasquez*, with the usual questionable citation to *Jolivet*.[264] She then compares the affidavits from Professor Saks and Professor Kam, and concludes that the points raised by Professor Saks are insufficient even to give rise to the necessity of a hearing.[265]

Judge Fabricant's ultimate decision—that the disputes concerning the reliability of handwriting identification expertise are not even of sufficient weight and tenability to justify a full scale hearing when first raised within a jurisdiction, but are best dealt with by giving global stare decisis effect to dicta from her own jurisdiction and often poorly reasoned decisions from other jurisdictions—is increasingly typical

---

vided by the parties, but some of the misconceptions she derived from those proofs that are indicated in the text would have been dispelled had she had a hearing. However, given the tenor of the rest of the opinion, it probably would have made no difference.

[258]*Commonwealth v. Glyman*, 17 Mass. L. Rptr 146, *3, n. 3 (Superior Ct., Worcester Co., 2003).

[259]*Commonwealth v. Glyman*, 17 Mass. L. Rptr 146, *3, n. 3 (Superior Ct., Worcester Co., 2003).

[260]In the record before Judge Fabricant were Dr. Saks's curriculum vitae as well as the affidavit, which described some of his relevant research and scholarship. From those, had she read them, Judge Fabricant would have learned, contrary to what she claimed in her opinion, that Dr. Saks had conducted dozens of empirical studies and written a number of noteworthy methodological papers—including the methodology chapter in this treatise: *Scientific Method: The Logic of Drawing Inferences from Empirical Evidence*. It is troubling that Judge Fabricant or any judge could be so wrong about facts properly before her that are utterly obvious and beyond dispute. Her erroneous statements would lead an informed reader of her opinion to wonder what else in the opinion might not be as Judge Fabricant says it is.

[261]*Commonwealth v. Glyman*, 17 Mass. L. Rptr 146, *1 (Superior Ct., Worcester Co., 2003).

[262]*Com. v. Murphy*, 59 Mass. App. Ct. 571, 797 N.E.2d 394 (2003).

[263]*Commonwealth v. Glyman*, 17 Mass. L. Rptr 146, *1 (Superior Ct., Worcester Co., 2003), quoting *Commonwealth v. Murphy*.

[264]*Commonwealth v. Glyman*, 17 Mass. L. Rptr 146, *1 (Superior Ct., Worcester Co., 2003). At this point Judge Fabricant involves herself in one of those odd flights of questionable rhetoric that sometimes mark these cases. She asserts that, "These decisions rely on two principal points. First, the import of *Daubert* was not to compel 'wholesale exclusion of a long-accepted form of expert evidence' . . . Rather Daubert provides a framework for courts 'to entertain new and less conventional forms of expertise' admitting what is reliable, even if not yet generally accepted, among such new fields, but screening out the unreliable. And second, handwriting comparison, unlike some other areas of expert evidence, is accessible to jurors . . . . For that reason there is little risk of 'undue prejudice from the mystique attached to jurors.' Id at *2. The quotations for the first point are from the majority in *Crisp*, and for the second point from *Paul*, but it is more than a little exaggeration to claim that all the cited opinions rely on those two points as principal points, as a glance at the opinions or their treatment, *supra,* shows. In addition, the propositions quoted from *Crisp* are simply untenable interpretations of *Kumho Tire*, but apparently nobody cares.

[265]*Commonwealth v. Glyman*, 17 Mass. L. Rptr 146, *3–*4 (Superior Ct., Worcester Co., 2003).

of the judicial response, even if it does not comport with an appropriate evaluation of the empirical record.[266]

If the analysis in *Glyman* is not completely satisfactory, it does not compare with the treatment given the issues of handwriting identification expertise in the Louisiana case of *State v. Matthews*.[267] Matthews was charged with presenting a forged check to a supermarket employee, and then endorsing that check in the employee's presence with a fictitious name.[268] This act was recorded on a "Regiscope" camera system which showed the check presenter's face along with an image of the check and the fake driver's license that had also been presented at the time of the transaction.[269] After investigation pointed toward Matthews, a police photograph of Matthews was obtained which appeared pretty clearly to be the check presenter. The clerk at the supermarket apparently did not remember that particular transaction among all the others that she had handled. Although the Regiscope photograph might seem sufficient, the prosecution apparently felt more would be better. A demand exemplar was obtained from the defendant, and turned over to Officer Chana Pichon, who was the New Orleans Police Department's document examiner. She opined that Matthews authored the endorsement.[270]

Matthews was convicted on two counts of the indictment, one alleging "forging" and one alleging "issuing" the check. Since these are not separate crimes, the court entered judgment of conviction on only one, picking "forging" by asking the defense attorney which one he preferred.[271] Unfortunately for the trial judge, there was not sufficient evidence of "forging" under Louisiana law, since signing a false endorsement in person in a fictitious name could not qualify as "forging."[272] This circumstance precipitated a trip up and down the Louisiana appellate ladder. First, the Court of Appeal of Louisiana, 4th Circuit (the intermediate appellate court) held that the dismissal of the "forging" count created double jeopardy as to that count, and the "issuing" count could not stand because of insufficient evidence, and hence, Matthews had to be discharged.[273] Then the Louisiana Supreme Court granted certiorari and held that in such a situation, the charge was to be treated as a single charge, so that the erroneous selection of the wrong alternate theory for entry of judgment by the trial court was in essence to be treated as a clerical error.[274] The case was then remanded to deal with the remaining appellate issues. On remand, one of those issues, "pro se supplemental assignment of error No. 8" (raised under a

[266]A final Massachusetts case should be noted here. In *Commonwealth v. Meyamba*, 68 Mass. App. Ct. 1111, 862 N.E.2d 470 (Mass. App. Ct., March 8, 2007) the Defendant was charged with a conspiracy involving the use of thirty-two checks on the Defendant's closed bank account to create false balances in other accounts which were then drawn down before the closing of the first account was discovered. Defendant made a motion in limine challenging the testimony of the prosecution's handwriting expert, and demanding a hearing. This was denied on the authority of *Murphy*. However, when the case was tried, the objection was not renewed during trial, which under Massachusetts law fails to preserve a claim of error in regard to the denial of the motion in limine. Thus, the appellate court reviewed only for plain error, and predictably found none.

[267]*State v. Matthews*, 859 So. 2d 863 (La. Ct. App. 4th Cir. 2003), vacated, per Supreme Court Grant of Stay(Dec. 10, 2003).

[268]All facts are taken from the initial opinion of the Louisiana Court of Appeal, Fourth Circuit,

*State v. Matthews*, 814 So. 2d 619, 620–621 (La. Ct. App. 4th Cir. 2002), opinion reinstated, 868 So. 2d 21 (La. 2004).

[269]*State v. Matthews*, 814 So. 2d 619, 620 (La. Ct. App. 4th Cir. 2002), opinion reinstated, 868 So. 2d 21 (La. 2004).

[270]*State v. Matthews*, 814 So. 2d 619, 621 (La. Ct. App. 4th Cir. 2002), opinion reinstated, 868 So. 2d 21 (La. 2004).

[271]*State v. Matthews*, 814 So. 2d 619, 622–623 (La. Ct. App. 4th Cir. 2002), opinion reinstated, 868 So. 2d 21 (La. 2004) (Bagneris, J, dissenting).

[272]*State v. Matthews*, 814 So. 2d 619, 620 (La. Ct. App. 4th Cir. 2002), opinion reinstated, 868 So. 2d 21 (La. 2004).

[273]*State v. Matthews*, 814 So. 2d 619, 621 (La. Ct. App. 4th Cir. 2002), opinion reinstated, 868 So. 2d 21 (La. 2004).

[274]*State v. Matthews*, 855 So. 2d 740 (La. 2003), opinion recalled on reh'g, 868 So. 2d 21 (La. 2004).

procedure that apparently allows the convicted defendant to supplement counsel's assignments of error "pro se"), was that "the trial court erred in qualifying Officer Chana Pichon as an expert in handwriting analysis . . . (because) handwriting analysis failed to meet the criteria set forth in *Daubert v. Merrell Dow Pharmaceuticals, Inc.*"[275]

In disposing of this issue, the Louisiana Court of Appeals, 4th District, first indicates that the Louisiana Code of Evidence art. 702 is "based on" the Federal Rule.[276] The court further observes that the Louisiana Supreme Court had previously adopted *Daubert*, and then rather casually declares that it is now adopting *Kumho Tire*.[277] However, it then goes on to emphasize the "discretion" component of *Kumho Tire* without much discussion, and finally ends by concluding that the trial court did not abuse its discretion in determining proper criteria of reliability under 702, quoting, apparently with approval, the following performance by the trial judge in discharging that obligation:

> I do recognize, based on my experience as a lawyer—practicing lawyer—and as a judge, that there are people who receive training, knowledge, and certain experience in the filed of an analysis of handwriting. I also understand through readings that each person has a different handwriting, a different style whereby he or she makes letters and/or numbers. And that style is peculiar or typical to the individual involved who is the author of a particular document . . . .
>
> It's not general knowledge. In fact, it requires someone with some special training to get up and explain to a jury how the formation of the letters and/or numbers is peculiar to individuals and their style of writing.[278]

Based on this "evaluation," the court declared there was no abuse of discretion, citing *Velasquez*.[279] The low quality of the performance that the appellate tribunal was willing to accept as discharging the trial court's gatekeeping responsibility is sufficiently obvious that it requires no further comment.[280]

The next case is *Commonwealth v. Griggs*.[281] If the Supreme Court of Kentucky issued a fairly cautious and sophisticated treatment of both reliability jurisprudence and handwriting-related issues in *Florence v. Commonwealth*,[282] the same cannot be said of the Kentucky Court of Appeals in *Griggs*.

Derric Griggs was employed to work with the inmates of the Jefferson County Youth Center (a juvenile detention facility in Louisville, Kentucky) as a "youth program worker."[283] In a scandal that apparently hit the newspapers, Griggs was fired in September of 1999 based on allegations of sexual improprieties with one T.J., a 17-year-old who had some months earlier been an inmate at the detention center, but had been transferred to another facility (the Morehead Center) in July of 1999.[284] Griggs denied all wrongdoing, and hired an attorney to represent him in regard to the matter. At that point, he had not been charged with any criminal

---

[275]*State v. Matthews*, 859 So. 2d 863, 871 (La. Ct. App. 4th Cir. 2003), vacated, per Supreme Court Grant of Stay(Dec. 10, 2003).

[276]*State v. Matthews*, 859 So. 2d 863, 872 (La. Ct. App. 4th Cir. 2003), vacated, per Supreme Court Grant of Stay(Dec. 10, 2003).

[277]*State v. Matthews*, 859 So. 2d 863, 872 (La. Ct. App. 4th Cir. 2003), vacated, per Supreme Court Grant of Stay(Dec. 10, 2003).

[278]*State v. Matthews*, 859 So. 2d 863, 873 (La. Ct. App. 4th Cir. 2003), vacated, per Supreme Court Grant of Stay(Dec. 10, 2003) (quoting trial court).

[279]*State v. Matthews*, 859 So. 2d 863, 873 (La. Ct. App. 4th Cir. 2003), vacated, per Supreme Court Grant of Stay (Dec. 10, 2003).

[280]Once again, this criticism might be overly harsh, since there is no way of knowing what the defense attorney had put in front of the trial judge to provide the raw material upon which to base a better performance.

[281]*Griggs v. Com.*, 2003 WL 22745707 (Ky. Ct. App. 2003).

[282]*Florence v. Commonwealth*, 120 S.W.3d 699 (S. Ct Ky., 2003). See discussion *supra* in this section.

[283]*Griggs v. Com.*, 2003 WL 22745707 (Ky. Ct. App. 2003).

[284]*Griggs v. Com.*, 2003 WL 22745707 (Ky. Ct. App. 2003). The general age of consent in Ken-

offense. In October of 1999, Griggs's attorney held a press conference at which she produced what she said was a letter from T.J. exonerating Griggs of any wrongdoing.[285]

At about the same time, Cheryl Caudill, a supervisor at the Morehead Center, discovered that T.J. had been visited on September 22 by someone identifying himself as Randy Barnett, an investigator with the Jefferson County Crimes Against Children Unit.[286] Investigation revealed that there was no Randy Barnett with the Crimes Against Children Unit.[287] In addition, another inmate claimed that T.J. had been visited recently by Griggs.[288] Caudill confronted T.J with these facts. T.J. at first claimed that her visitor was Randy Barnett, but then admitted that it was Griggs, and that Griggs had given her a letter with suggestions on how to write her "exoneration" letter.[289] She admitted that she had not mailed the letter to Griggs's lawyer, as the envelope displayed at the press conference seemed to suggest, but instead had handed it to Griggs directly.[290]

Griggs was indicted for impersonating a peace officer.[291] As it turned out, an investigator for the Crimes Against Children Unit did not qualify as a "peace officer" under Kentucky law because such an investigator has no power of arrest.[292] After a hung jury resulted in a mistrial in a first trial, Griggs was convicted of the lesser included offense of impersonating a public servant (a misdemeanor).

As might be expected, the handwriting aspects of the trial revolved around the issue of who wrote the signature "Randy Barnett" in the visitor's log at the Morehead Center on September 22, 1999, but in an unexpected way. The guard on duty identified Griggs as the person who identified himself as "Randy Barnett" and signed the log.[293] In preparation for the first trial, Teddy Gordon, a lawyer who shared space with Griggs's then defense attorney (but who testified that he had never represented Griggs[294]) had elicited handwriting exemplars from Griggs and submitted them to a handwriting expert, Paul Kramer, apparently in hopes of obtaining an opinion excluding Griggs as the author. Kramer was called at the second trial by the prosecution to testify that he had concluded that the exemplars were attempts at disguise because they were "very deliberately written" and were written with such pressure that he "could feel the indentations very strongly at the bottom of the paper," and

---

tucky was 16 at the time. T.J. was awaiting disposition of underlying charges of armed robbery.

[285]*Griggs v. Com.*, 2003 WL 22745707 (Ky. Ct. App. 2003).

[286]*Griggs v. Com.*, 2003 WL 22745707 (Ky. Ct. App. 2003).

[287]*Griggs v. Com.*, 2003 WL 22745707 (Ky. Ct. App. 2003).

[288]*Griggs v. Com.*, 2003 WL 22745707 (Ky. Ct. App. 2003).

[289]*Griggs v. Com.*, 2003 WL 22745707 (Ky. Ct. App. 2003).

[290]*Griggs v. Com.*, 2003 WL 22745707 (Ky. Ct. App. 2003). The envelope was of the wrong type to have come from the facility, and no outgoing letter from T.J. had been logged under the routine practice of the facility,

[291]*Griggs v. Com.*, 2003 WL 22745707 (Ky. Ct. App. 2003).

[292]*Griggs v. Com.*, 2003 WL 22745707 (Ky. Ct. App. 2003). This was an issue on appeal because

the trial court submitted that charge to the jury instead of dismissing it. This error was found to be harmless in the face of the overwhelming evidence on the lesser included offence of impersonating a public servant, of which Griggs was convicted.

[293]*Griggs v. Com.*, 2003 WL 22745707 (Ky. Ct. App. 2003). The guard, Lewis Rose, was referred to as a "treatment coordinator" who was the "administrative officer" on duty on the night of the visit.

[294]*Griggs v. Com.*, 2003 WL 22745707 (Ky. Ct. App. 2003). This same lawyer, Gerry Ellis, apparently testified at the first trial as a witness for the defense, and was apparently central to Griggs's alibi claim at the first trial, which involved tickets to a charity event on the evening of the "Barnett" visit to the youth facility. These tickets were shown fairly conclusively in the second trial to have been forgeries. Ellis's testimony at the second trial seems to have been calculated to dispel any suspicion that he might have knowingly aided in the "alibi ticket" fraud.

that normally that indicates "an attempt at disguise."[295] The defendant objected to this as "scientifically unreliable." As noted in relation to *Spann v. State*,[296] above, the ability to determine disguise is a task concerning which there is a complete absence of research to evaluate the claims of the guild.[297] However, the court does not bother to give any thought to the task being performed, saying only:

> Griggs next argues that the testimony provided by the Commonwealth's handwriting expert, Kramer, was "scientifically unreliable" and therefore inadmissible. We reject this argument. "[H]andwriting analysis [has] long been recognized by the courts as [a] sound method[ ] for making reliable identifications."[298] Kramer testified that he was employed as an "examiner of questioned documents," and that he had approximately 35 years of experience in this field. Kramer further testified that he has performed over 400 examinations.[299] Consequently, we cannot conclude that the trial court abused its discretion by permitting Kramer to testify on direct examination that, in his opinion, the handwriting samples provided to him were "very deliberately written," and that writing hard is normally "an attempt to disguise" on the part of writer.

Again, nothing but the guild test, and a very unsophisticated version of the guild test at that.[300]

*People v. Nawi*,[301] was a California case involving murder and the heroin trade— but it is not exactly the kind of story this might at first blush conjure up. In the Fall of 1987, Virginia Lowery was a woman of wealth. She lived in a house on Brussels Street in San Francisco. She owned curios and collectibles and jewelry worth hundreds of thousands of dollars. She kept the bulk of the jewelry in a safe in her home. She was employed and two years from retirement. She intended to retire to Mexico with her husband.[302]

Now for the first twist. Her husband, William Lowery, was a convicted robber and major wholesale heroin dealer who had moved to Mexico in 1984 to, in the words of the court, "avoid drug enforcement authorities,"[303] although he was not under indictment for his activities in either 1984 or 1987, and could apparently travel between Mexico and the United States if he wished.[304]

On Thursday, October 29, 1987, the police got an anonymous telephone call from

---

[295]*Griggs v. Com.*, 2003 WL 22745707 (Ky. Ct. App. 2003). In response to a question on cross-examination by Griggs's own attorney, Kramer further said that "it was very obvious that . . . Mr. Griggs continued to disguise his normal writing habits" and that he had concluded that Griggs "was either guilty or . . . nervous about giving his specimen writing." *Griggs v. Com.*, 2003 WL 22745707 (Ky. Ct. App. 2003). The latter inferences seem clearly beyond his expertise, but given the way they were elicited, were not part of the court's analysis.

[296]*Spann v. State*, 857 So. 2d 845 (Fla. 2003).

[297]Or at least none I am aware of, or that the *Spann* opinion cited.

[298]For the quoted passage the *Griggs* court cites the majority opinion in *Crisp*.

[299]The opinion does not even tell us the nature of Kramer's training, employment or experience. That is pretty thin detail for an opinion that adopts a guild test. There does not even seem to have been much demonstration of guild membership.

[300]*Griggs* might properly have been disposed of on the authority of *Florence*, in that it did not appear that the challenge of the defense was

based on anything weightier than the general conclusory objection of counsel, and thus the "price of admission" burden for triggering a full-scale reliability determination in regard to traditionally admissible expertise was not carried. That would have been a more defensible option, but not a tack taken by the court, who didn't even cite *Florence*.

[301]*People v. Nawi*, 2004 WL 2944016 (Cal. App. 1st Dist. 2004), unpublished/noncitable, (Dec. 21, 2004) and review granted, (Apr. 20, 2005) and review dismissed, cause remanded, (Aug. 16, 2006).

[302]*People v. Nawi*, 2004 WL 2944016 (Cal. App. 1st Dist. 2004), unpublished/noncitable, (Dec. 21, 2004) and review granted, (Apr. 20, 2005) and review dismissed, cause remanded, (Aug. 16, 2006).

[303]*People v. Nawi*, 2004 WL 2944016 (Cal. App. 1st Dist. 2004), unpublished/noncitable, (Dec. 21, 2004) and review granted, (Apr. 20, 2005) and review dismissed, cause remanded, (Aug. 16, 2006).

[304]William Lowery had apparently been in California shortly before the murder for a wedding, see *People v. Nawi*, 2004 WL 2944016 (Cal. App. 1st Dist. 2004), unpublished/noncitable,

"an older male with an undistinguished voice" reporting a robbery and possible homicide at 966 Brussels Street. At that location, they found body of Virginia Lowery on the floor of the garage. She had been stabbed 34 times with an ice pick in the head, neck, and upper body, and had been dead for anywhere from one to four days. There were no signs of a struggle anywhere in the house. There was an ironing board set up in the garage near the body, along with some clothes. An iron was on the floor. The cord had been cut from the iron and wrapped around her throat. The medical examiner also found blunt force trauma to the head. She had apparently been ironing clothes in the garage when she was knocked on the head and then strangled and stabbed to death. There was no indication of forced entry. The front door was locked, but the sliding glass door was partly ajar. Lowery habitually left it ajar to let in fresh air. There was some evidence that someone had come over the back fence. There was no indication of robbery.[305] Nothing was turned over or obviously gone through. The collectibles were still in place. The jewelry was still in the safe. Her purse was on a sofa with wallet and money still inside.[306]

Virginia Lowery was an immaculate housekeeper. Her Cadillac and the other items in her garage were all apparently washed recently. However, on the rear bumper of the Cadillac, near the body, the police found latent fingerprints, which they collected. No suspects were developed at that time that the prints matched, and they were stored in a computer database of unsolved crimes for possible future use.[307]

Ten years later they matched the fingerprints to defendant Robert Nawi, who had been arrested that month after an altercation in a bar and fingerprinted as a result of that arrest.[308] Investigation turned up some very interesting things about Mr. Nawi. He had been arrested in 1988 under the name Robert Wells, aka Sam Zanca, and charged with federal drug trafficking violations. He was convicted and sent to federal prison, where he stayed until being released in 1997, shortly before the bar altercation.[309] When the police then looked further into the details of his drug arrest, they discovered that it stemmed from a traffic stop of Wendy Dietzel, aka

---

(Dec. 21, 2004) and review granted, (Apr. 20, 2005) and review dismissed, cause remanded, (Aug. 16, 2006), though he plainly appears to have been in Mexico when his wife was murdered. He returned to California shortly after the murder to be interviewed by police, *People v. Nawi*, 2004 WL 2944016 at *1 (Cal. App. 1st Dist. 2004), unpublished/noncitable, (Dec. 21, 2004) and review granted, (Apr. 20, 2005) and review dismissed, cause remanded, (Aug. 16, 2006), and was in California when first interviewed by police in 1998. *People v. Nawi*, 2004 WL 2944016 at *3 (Cal. App. 1st Dist. 2004), unpublished/noncitable, (Dec. 21, 2004) and review granted, (Apr. 20, 2005) and review dismissed, cause remanded, (Aug. 16, 2006). Thereafter he apparently refused to return to California for Zawi's trial, and his testimony was taken by means of a "conditional examination," which appears to be a deposition in Mexico obtained by means of letters rogatory or otherwise. *People v. Nawi*, 2004 WL 2944016 at *4 (Cal. App. 1st Dist. 2004), unpublished/noncitable, (Dec. 21, 2004) and review granted, (Apr. 20, 2005) and review dismissed, cause remanded, (Aug. 16, 2006).

[305]In his 1987 interview with police, William Lowery told police that he believed the motive for his wife's murder was robbery, and asserted that his wife had another jewelry case that was missing. Apparently no other relative recalled such a jewelry case. *People v. Nawi*, 2004 WL 2944016 (Cal. App. 1st Dist. 2004), unpublished/noncitable, (Dec. 21, 2004) and review granted, (Apr. 20, 2005) and review dismissed, cause remanded, (Aug. 16, 2006).

[306]All facts in this paragraph derived from *People v. Nawi*, 2004 WL 2944016 (Cal. App. 1st Dist. 2004), unpublished/noncitable, (Dec. 21, 2004) and review granted, (Apr. 20, 2005) and review dismissed, cause remanded, (Aug. 16, 2006).

[307]All facts in this paragraph derived from *People v. Nawi*, 2004 WL 2944016 (Cal. App. 1st Dist. 2004), unpublished/noncitable, (Dec. 21, 2004) and review granted, (Apr. 20, 2005) and review dismissed, cause remanded, (Aug. 16, 2006).

[308]*People v. Nawi*, 2004 WL 2944016 (Cal. App. 1st Dist. 2004), unpublished/noncitable, (Dec. 21, 2004) and review granted, (Apr. 20, 2005) and review dismissed, cause remanded, (Aug. 16, 2006).

[309]*People v. Nawi*, 2004 WL 2944016 (Cal. App. 1st Dist. 2004), unpublished/noncitable, (Dec. 21, 2004) and review granted, (Apr. 20,

Rosanna Gironda, who was Nawi/Wells/Zanca's wife. She was driving a Cadillac shown in motor vehicle records as registered to the deceased Virginia Lowery, but she was able to produce a California "pink slip" showing that it had been transferred, apparently from the estate of Virginia Lowery[310] to Rosanna Gironda and Sam Zanca. The car was impounded and inventoried. It had a variety of passports and other identification papers for what appeared to be one man photographically, but in a variety of names including Sam Zanca, Timothy Vahanian, John Ronck and others.[311] There were also keys to three safe deposit boxes. For undisclosed reasons, the federal Drug Enforcement Administration was notified. Two days later, "with Dietzel's consent"[312] a DEA agent opened one of the safe deposit boxes and found 650 grams of pure heroin. In September of 1988, Nawi was stopped by a customs official in the Vancouver airport because he was in possession of two airline tickets in two different names, David Johnson and S. Zanca. After further investigation, he was turned over to the DEA, which prosecuted him on the trafficking charges that resulted in his imprisonment.[313] When San Francisco police examined the evidence collected in the 1988 prosecution, they found an address book that had been seized from Nawi which contained a telephone number for David Lowery, William Lowery's son by a previous marriage, and also a telephone number for "Bill" in Mexico.[314]

The police then submitted the fingernail scrapings from Virginia Lowery's hands for DNA analysis. In addition, they discovered that Nawi had been arrested in Florida, and arranged to obtain a sample from him for testing. DNA was recovered from the fingernail scrapings, which turn out to be a mixed sample from which Nawi could not be excluded; further, the profile of the major contributor, as determined by the analysts, matched Nawi.[315]

Investigators also obtained from Florida authorities another address book of Nawi's, apparently dating from after his release from prison. In that book were addresses for Jack Colevris, at 966 Brussels Street, Virginia's old address.[316] Colevris was a caretaker apparently hired by William Lowery, who maintained the Brussels street house.[317] They also obtained phone records from Nawi's mother's house in Massachusetts which showed recent calls to David Lowery, and to William Lowery

---

2005) and review dismissed, cause remanded, (Aug. 16, 2006).

[310]*People v. Nawi*, 2004 WL 2944016 (Cal. App. 1st Dist. 2004), unpublished/noncitable, (Dec. 21, 2004) and review granted, (Apr. 20, 2005) and review dismissed, cause remanded, (Aug. 16, 2006). In a large irony, this appears to have been the same Cadillac that Zawi's fingerprints were taken from originally.

[311]*People v. Nawi*, 2004 WL 2944016 (Cal. App. 1st Dist. 2004), unpublished/noncitable, (Dec. 21, 2004) and review granted, (Apr. 20, 2005) and review dismissed, cause remanded, (Aug. 16, 2006).

[312]*People v. Nawi*, 2004 WL 2944016 (Cal. App. 1st Dist. 2004), unpublished/noncitable, (Dec. 21, 2004) and review granted, (Apr. 20, 2005) and review dismissed, cause remanded, (Aug. 16, 2006). "And then a miracle occurs"— ours not to reason why.

[313]*People v. Nawi*, 2004 WL 2944016 (Cal. App. 1st Dist. 2004), unpublished/noncitable, (Dec. 21, 2004) and review granted, (Apr. 20, 2005) and review dismissed, cause remanded,

(Aug. 16, 2006).

[314]*People v. Nawi*, 2004 WL 2944016 (Cal. App. 1st Dist. 2004), unpublished/noncitable, (Dec. 21, 2004) and review granted, (Apr. 20, 2005) and review dismissed, cause remanded, (Aug. 16, 2006).

[315]*People v. Nawi*, 2004 WL 2944016 (Cal. App. 1st Dist. 2004), unpublished/noncitable, (Dec. 21, 2004) and review granted, (Apr. 20, 2005) and review dismissed, cause remanded, (Aug. 16, 2006). There were many issues concerning the propriety of the DNA mixed sample interpretation, which the court spent a great deal of time on, and which need not concern us here.

[316]*People v. Nawi*, 2004 WL 2944016 (Cal. App. 1st Dist. 2004), unpublished/noncitable, (Dec. 21, 2004) and review granted, (Apr. 20, 2005) and review dismissed, cause remanded, (Aug. 16, 2006).

[317]*People v. Nawi*, 2004 WL 2944016 (Cal. App. 1st Dist. 2004), unpublished/noncitable, (Dec. 21, 2004) and review granted, (Apr. 20, 2005) and review dismissed, cause remanded, (Aug. 16, 2006).

in Mexico.[318] William Lowery gave a deposition in Mexico (called a conditional examination in California) at which he provided an alibi for Nawi, but other Mexican witnesses undermined that alibi.[319] William Lowery had maintained a private office in Virginia's house that he used from time to time to meet with associates in 1987, before her murder.[320] There was conflicting testimony concerning whether, when, and how often, Nawi had been in the house before the murder.[321]

Defendant was tried and convicted for the murder of Virginia Lowery. As one might suppose, the main issue on appeal dealt with the propriety of the DNA evidence in various dimensions.[322] However, handwriting came in for examination also, albeit somewhat peripherally. The prosecution wanted to show that Nawi had been present in San Francisco around the time of the murder (which occurred sometime after the evening of Sunday October 25, 1987).[323] Somebody had signed into the safe deposit area of the San Francisco Branch of the Bank of America on Monday, October 26, 1987 as "Sam Zanca."[324] The circumstantial inference that Nawi was the one who signed the entry ticket is pretty overwhelming, given the other evidence concerning Nawi's use of the alias, and various documents in that name found in his possession (and with his picture on them) in the 1988 drug arrest. But this wasn't good enough for the prosecution. Instead, they called a document examiner who compared the signature "Sam Zanca" on the entry ticket to the signature "Sam Zanca" on those documents found in the defendant's possession or otherwise associated with him (such as passport applications with his photograph accompanying them), and concluded that they were with "a high degree of probability" signed by the same person.[325] The defense attacked this testimony, saying that "the prosecution's handwriting expert should not have been allowed to testify without preliminary proof of the scientific reliability of handwriting comparisons."[326] The court rejected this challenge in the following terms:

> We recognize that some federal trial courts have questioned the reliability of handwriting comparisons and the admissibility of such evidence under the federal rules of evidence. (E.g., *U.S. v. Hines*, 55 F. Supp. 2d 62, 68–71, 52 Fed. R. Evid. Serv. 257 (D. Mass. 1999); *U.S. v. Saelee*, 162 F. Supp. 2d 1097, 57 Fed. R. Evid. Serv. 916 (D. Alaska 2001).) However, all federal appellate courts to consider the issue after *Daubert* have

---

[318]*People v. Nawi*, 2004 WL 2944016 (Cal. App. 1st Dist. 2004), unpublished/noncitable, (Dec. 21, 2004) and review granted, (Apr. 20, 2005) and review dismissed, cause remanded, (Aug. 16, 2006).

[319]*People v. Nawi*, 2004 WL 2944016 (Cal. App. 1st Dist. 2004), unpublished/noncitable, (Dec. 21, 2004) and review granted, (Apr. 20, 2005) and review dismissed, cause remanded, (Aug. 16, 2006).

[320]*People v. Nawi*, 2004 WL 2944016 (Cal. App. 1st Dist. 2004), unpublished/noncitable, (Dec. 21, 2004) and review granted, (Apr. 20, 2005) and review dismissed, cause remanded, (Aug. 16, 2006).

[321]*People v. Nawi*, 2004 WL 2944016 (Cal. App. 1st Dist. 2004), unpublished/noncitable, (Dec. 21, 2004) and review granted, (Apr. 20, 2005) and review dismissed, cause remanded, (Aug. 16, 2006).

[322]*People v. Nawi*, 2004 WL 2944016 (Cal. App. 1st Dist. 2004), unpublished/noncitable, (Dec. 21, 2004) and review granted, (Apr. 20, 2005) and review dismissed, cause remanded, (Aug. 16, 2006).

[323]The early evening of Sunday, October 25 was the last time anyone was known to have spoken with Virginia Lowery. *People v. Nawi*, 2004 WL 2944016 (Cal. App. 1st Dist. 2004), unpublished/noncitable, (Dec. 21, 2004) and review granted, (Apr. 20, 2005) and review dismissed, cause remanded, (Aug. 16, 2006). In addition, she failed to show up at her grandniece's school on Monday, October 26 to do volunteer work. *Id.*

[324]*People v. Nawi*, 2004 WL 2944016 (Cal. App. 1st Dist. 2004), unpublished/noncitable, (Dec. 21, 2004) and review granted, (Apr. 20, 2005) and review dismissed, cause remanded, (Aug. 16, 2006).

[325]*People v. Nawi*, 2004 WL 2944016 (Cal. App. 1st Dist. 2004), unpublished/noncitable, (Dec. 21, 2004) and review granted, (Apr. 20, 2005) and review dismissed, cause remanded, (Aug. 16, 2006).

[326]The defense also attacked the use of photocopies, an attack which was rejected, for reasons more specifically considered in connection with *U.S. v. Garza*, supra.

found handwriting evidence admissible. (*U.S. v. Crisp*, 324 F.3d 261, 270, 60 Fed. R. Evid. Serv. 1486 (4th Cir. 2003) and cases cited therein.)

Handwriting comparisons have been routinely used in California courts for decades (e.g., *People v. Storke*, 128 Cal. 486, 488, 60 P. 1090 (1900), and the Legislature has given its imprimatur to the use of handwriting comparisons to authenticate a writing. (Evid.Code, §§ 1415, 1418.) The Evidence Code expressly allows expert testimony and further allows the jurors to make their own determination of handwriting comparison without expert testimony. (Evid.Code, §§ 1417, 1418.)[327] Our Supreme Court has held that the rule of *Kelly*[328] does not apply to a procedure that isolates physical evidence whose appearance, nature, and meaning are obvious to the senses of a layperson. (*People v. Webb*, 6 Cal. 4th 494, 524, 24 Cal. Rptr. 2d 779, 862 P.2d 779 (1993) [laser reading of fingerprint]; *People v. Ayala*, 24 Cal. 4th 243, 281, 99 Cal. Rptr. 2d 532, 6 P.3d 193 (2000), as modified on denial of reh'g, (Nov. 15, 2000) [X-ray of bullet size].) [At this point the court observes in a footnote that: "The *Kelly* rule is also limited to *new* scientific methods of proof. The reliability of a long-established procedure need not be proven. (*People v. Clark*, 5 Cal. 4th 950, 1018, 22 Cal. Rptr. 2d 689, 857 P.2d 1099 (1993) (blood splatter evidence); *People v. Municipal Court (Sansone)*, 184 Cal. App. 3d 199, 201, 228 Cal. Rptr. 798 (4th Dist. 1986) (urine test for blood alcohol).]

In any event, any error in admitting the testimony of the handwriting expert without a prong one *Kelly* hearing was harmless. First, the jurors were capable of discerning handwriting similarities even without an expert. Furthermore, even aside from the comparison of signatures, there was strong evidence to suggest that defendant was the person who signed the entry ticket for the safe deposit box. Defendant had used the alias Sam Zanca on other occasions, and in fact documents in the name of Sam Zanca were found in the brown Cadillac driven by defendant's wife. Defendant had another safe deposit box at the Bank of America (though at a different branch) in which the heroin had been found in 1988—the heroin that formed the basis of the drug charges to which defendant pled guilty in 1988.[329]

A proper examination of the expert task in *Nawi* might arguably characterize it as signature authentication, and might arguably have found it sufficiently supported by the empirical record for admission on that basis, but there is not much hope for such a rational approach in the future, given what the court actually said.[330]

The next case that should be noted here is the Montana case of *State v. Clifford*,[331] not because it contains a ruling on a reliability challenge, but because it is easy to mistake it for such a case. Cheryl Clifford was convicted of one count of fabricating

---

[327]It is true that § 1418 of the California Evidence Code appears to authorize handwriting identification expert testimony, and to authorize it globally regardless of the empirical evidence for any given claim of the expert. What this illustrates more than anything is the problems that can be created by legislatively mandated rules of expert reliability. How should a court respond if it encounters a legislatively mandated rule of admission for phrenology?

[328]"Kelly" is *People v. Kelly*, 17 Cal. 3d 24, 130 Cal. Rptr. 144, 549 P.2d 1240 (1976), California's wellspring case on expert admissibility. Originally a fairly straightforward adoption of the *Frye* approach, it has become an idiosyncratic doctrine best characterized as a combination of *Frye* and *Daubert-like* subdoctrines.

[329]*People v. Nawi*, 2004 WL 2944016 (Cal. App. 1st Dist. 2004), unpublished/noncitable, (Dec. 21, 2004) and review granted, (Apr. 20, 2005) and review dismissed, cause remanded, (Aug. 16, 2006).

[330]It is probably advisable to note here the recent California case of *People v. Scott*, 2007 WL 404782 (Cal. App. 4th Dist. 2007), unpublished/noncitable, (Feb. 7, 2007) and review denied, (May 9, 2007), a case in which the defense objected to the expert testimony explicitly because it was not overclaimed. The document examiner utilized the ASTM nine-point scale and testified to conclusions of level 3 (probably authored) and level 4 (indications of authorship). The defense moved to exclude such non-positive conclusions as "irrelevant" or "without foundation." These grounds were properly rejected. Assuming the existence of the claimed expertise, the most serious problem for its forensic use is the temptation to overclaim its certainty or meaning, and the legal system could never hope to get control of that problem if a claim of perfect certainty were required as a condition precedent to any admissibility.

[331]*State v. Clifford*, 2005 MT 219, 328 Mont. 300, 121 P.3d 489 (2005).

evidence and one count of making threats in official matters.[332] The underlying facts concern an episode of bizarre mischief through anonymous letters, dozens and dozens of them, referred to by the court as "vicious and lascivious, gory and disturbed, and twisted and disgusting,"[333]sent to a variety of people in East Helena, and related to an episode that occurred in 1994 when one Michael Scott, the son of a person with whom a woman named Cynthia Hurst had occasionally left her children, was convicted of molesting them.[334] Some in the community, notably defendant Cheryl Clifford's husband, Officer Larry Clifford of the East Helena Police Department, thought Hurst herself should have been charged with reckless endangerment for leaving the children as she did where she did. He filed a citizen complaint, but Hurst, aided by a lawyer obtained for her by the LDS (Mormon) Church (of which both she and the Cliffords were members), had the charge dismissed. A few months later, in October of 1996, the letters began.

The first was sent to Bradley Peterson, a local church elder.[335] The letters continued regularly over the next four years to arrive at the homes of various church members, the Police Department, the Highway Patrol, the newspapers, and the Cliffords.[336] The police initially suspected the oldest Hurst boy, Daniel, but a search of the Hurst residence pursuant to a warrant turned up nothing.[337] They then focused on the Cliffords.[338] In 2000 they hired James Blanco, a document examiner certified by the American Board of Forensic Document Examiners, to examine the anonymous notes and various handwriting of the Cliffords.[339] In the first of his reports, he could neither identify nor rule out Larry Clifford, Cheryl Clifford or Daniel Hurst as the author of the anonymous letters. At that point, however, the police had obtained a warrant for the Clifford house, and they executed it. In the house they discovered a rubber stamp kit with all the letter in the kit still intact except the exact upper and lower case letters contained in a rubber stamped inscription on one of the anonymous letter envelopes. Thereafter, (supplied with more material and almost certainly the foregoing information) Blanco attributed the letters to Cheryl Clifford.[340]

This could have been a great "task at hand" reliability challenge, except for one thing. Neither a task-specific reliability challenge, nor one involving the non-blind aspect of the examination, was raised by the defense. Instead, the defense (at least in the eyes of Justice Leapheart, who wrote the opinion) conceded that the field was reliable, but attacked only the inability of the expert to explain specifically the exact basis of his conclusion. This the court characterizes as a complaint about the application of the methods of a reliable field by a qualified expert, which, according to the opinion, is "immaterial in determining the reliability of that expert field" under

[332]*State v. Clifford*, 2005 MT 219, 328 Mont. 300, 121 P.3d 489, 491 (2005).

[333]121 P.3d 489, 492 (Montana Supreme Court, 2005). The facts in this paragraph are all derived from the same page.

[334]In these details it is remarkably similar to the famous English case of George Edalji, which resulted in a similar result later determined through the intercession of Arthur Conan Doyle, among others, to have been a miscarriage of justice. See generally, D. Michael Risinger, *Boxes in Boxes: Julian Barnes, Conan Doyle, Sherlock Holmes and the Edalji Case*, 4 International Commentary on Evidence, http://www.bepress.com/ice/vol4/iss2/art3.

[335]121 P.3d 489, 492 (Montana Supreme Court, 2005).

[336]121 P.3d 489, 492 (Montana Supreme Court, 2005).

[337]121 P.3d 489, 492 (Montana Supreme Court, 2005).

[338]121 P.3d 489, 492 (Montana Supreme Court, 2005).

[339]121 P.3d 489, 493 (Montana Supreme Court, 2005).

[340]Compare this to the story told by Ludovic Kennedy, which he attributes to FBI Agent Thomas and others, concerning the substantial effect on the opinion of Albert S. Osborn caused by the discovery of the Lindbergh ransom money in Bruno Hauptmann's garage. See Ludovic Kennedy, The Airman and the Carpenter 178–183 (1985). For an earlier case illustrating the problems of suggestion, see *R. v. Silverlock*, 1894 WL 9904 (QBD), 1894 2 Q.B. 766, 767 (1894).

*Daubert* (as understood in Montana, at any rate).[341] "Cheryl misapprehends the force behind Rule 702, M.R. Evid. To restate this rule, *if* a reliable field helps the trier of fact, *and* the court deems the witness qualified as an expert, *then* he may testify."[342] All other considerations apparently go to weight. The court clearly conceives the process as global. It cites Kumho Tire, but gives no evidence of actually having read it.[343] Whether this unfortunate opinion is to be attributed more to the court or the defense attorney is an open question. However, the reader should note that this is a case in which virtually the only evidence against the defendant specifically (as opposed to her and her husband indistinguishably) was the handwriting identification evidence.

There is a concurrence by Justice Nelson, joined by Justice Cotter (two members of the five person court) that laments the fact that a proper reliability challenge was neither raised nor reached, due mostly to the way in which Montana decisions have "jurisprudentially, and improperly limited *Daubert*."[344] The concurrence goes on to point out that *Kumho Tire* (and perhaps *Daubert* also) reaches the validity of methods employed in a broad field much more specifically than the Montana construction of *Daubert* allows,[345] describes in eloquent detail some of the weaknesses in regard to handwriting identification that might be raised in a challenge properly brought, and calls on the Court to specifically adopt *Kumho Tire*, and also the revised version of Federal Rule 702, in order to "undo the mess we have collectively created."[346]

*State v. Cooke*,[347] is the opinion of a Delaware trial judge, Judge Herlihy, on a complex motion in limine directed to numerous issues raised in regard to a variety of areas of forensic science. The case arose out of multiple charges leveled against Defendant James Cooke in regard to a series of crimes: the rape-murder of Lindsey Bonistall, the burglary of the apartment of Amelia Caudra, and the burglary of the apartment of Cheryl Harmon.[348] In an interesting twist, many of the analyses (inter alia, fingerprint comparison, fiber comparison, toolmark comparison, and visual hair comparison) had been negative, but the prosecution wanted to admit them anyway to show their diligence to anticipatorily overcome what they feared might be jury expectations resulting from the "CSI effect," and the defendant wanted to keep them out.[349] The only challenged technique that had yielded a clearly incriminatory result was handwriting identification.

The handwriting identification testimony grew out of the fact that in the Bonistall

---

[341]121 P.3d 489, 495 (Montana Supreme Court, 2005). The concurrence claims, without citation, that Montana has adopted *Daubert* but "rejected *Kumho Tire*." Neither the majority nor the concurrence cites any authority for such a proposition, and perhaps the concurrence was referring to what it took to be the implications of this case itself.

[342]121 P.3d 489, 495 (Montana Supreme Court, 2005). The Court conceded that the trial judge never explicitly ruled that Blanco was an expert, but noted that the defendant's attorney never objected to this. 121 P.3d 489, 495 (Montana Supreme Court, 2005). The court also rejects the notion that the Hines/McVeigh approach ought to be required, which was the only actual Rule 702 challenge the court recognized as having been properly raised. *Id.*

[343]121 P.3d 489, 495 (Montana Supreme Court, 2005).

[344]121 P.3d 489, 504 (Montana Supreme Court, 2005).

[345]121 P.3d 489, 504–505 (Montana Supreme Court, 2005). The concurrence earlier asserts that previous Montana decisions limit a *Daubert* reliability challenge to "novel" "scientific" evidence, giving multiple citations, 121 P.3d 489, 501 (Montana Supreme Court, 2005), although there is no reference to any such limitation in the majority opinion.

[346]121 P.3d 489, 502, n. 2 (Montana Supreme Court, 2005) (James C. Nelson, J., joined by Patricia O. Cotter, J., concurring).

[347]*State v. Cooke*, 914 A.2d 1078 (Del. Super. Ct. 2007)

[348]*State v. Cooke*, 914 A.2d 1078, 1080 (Del. Super. Ct. 2007).

[349]*State v. Cooke*, 914 A.2d 1078, 1082 (Del. Super. Ct. 2007). The court spends considerable time on this issue, concluding that the prosecution should be allowed to show its diligence, except that he rejected any reference to less reliable tests or less "expected" tests, like voice identification and "fiber impression" evidence, and

murder and in the Harmon burglary the perpetrator left hand-printing on the walls.[350] In the Bonistall murder the printing was "KKK" which also had "White power" printed near it, with "More bodies are going to be turnin up dead" and "We want are (sic) weed back. Give us are (sic) weed back" further away. In the Harmon burglary the printing was "We'll be back" "Don't mess with my men" and "I want my drug money" (the court notes that there may be other misspellings or grammatical errors not noted in the court's account).[351] After Cooke was arrested based on other evidence, samples of his handwriting were obtained from various sources, such as employment applications and other documents.[352] It is not clear if any of these exemplars were hand-printed, but in any event they were apparently insufficient in the opinion of the expert, Georgia Carter of the Delaware State Police Crime Lab, and she obtained demand exemplars from Cooke on June 13, 2005, at the Gander Hill Prison where he was incarcerated.[353] The handprinting sample was "practically illegible" and Carter opined in regard to it that "Mr. Cooke attempted to disguise and distort his natural hand printing style."[354] Nevertheless, Carter felt she had enough to conclude that "there are strong indications that Mr. Cooke probably prepared" the writings found at the Bonistall site, based on "several individual handprinting characteristics" and "the presence of the same significant grammar error" in both the known and the questioned writing.[355] However, in regard to the printing at the Harmon site, all Carter concluded was that it "is not possible to determine with any degree of certainty if Mr. Cooke did or did not prepare" the Harmon site printing. However, she went on, "because there are some general features in agreement, Mr. Cooke cannot totally be ruled out."[356]

The task undertaken by the prosecution-proffered handwriting witness in this case is the attribution of authorship of hand printing done on an unusual surface at an unusual scale under unusual conditions, made by reference to exemplars that were characterized by the asserted expert herself to be disguised and near illegible, under conditions that were almost certainly not blind in regard to the other case evidence. The existence of a proper belief warrant for the claimed accuracy of such an exercise would have been an interesting issue to see fully litigated. And the court, earlier in its opinion, indicated its understanding that Delaware follows *Daubert* and *Kumho Tire*[357] (though the judge's understanding of *Kumho Tire* was superficial at best). However, when the court takes up the defendant's objections, the court summarizes them as follows "One, he challenged her qualifications, and two, he questioned her methods and whether those methods could reliably form the basis of her conclusions."[358] The court then addresses the question of expert qualifications before looking at the reliability of the expertise itself. Having decided (albeit with some reservations[359]) that Carter was an acceptable expert, the court had somewhat put the rabbit in the hat regarding the (global) existence of the expertise.

---

those would not be admitted merely on the "diligence" rationale. *State v. Cooke*, 914 A.2d 1078, 1082–1088, 1096, 1099 (Del. Super. Ct. 2007).

[350]*State v. Cooke*, 914 A.2d 1078, 1099 (Del. Super. Ct. 2007).

[351]*State v. Cooke*, 914 A.2d 1078, 1099 (Del. Super. Ct. 2007).

[352]*State v. Cooke*, 914 A.2d 1078, 1099 (Del. Super. Ct. 2007).

[353]*State v. Cooke*, 914 A.2d 1078, 1099–1100, (Del. Super. Ct. 2007).

[354]*State v. Cooke*, 914 A.2d 1078, 1100 (Del. Super. Ct. 2007).

[355]*State v. Cooke*, 914 A.2d 1078, 1100 (Del. Super. Ct. 2007). The problematical meaning to

be assigned to grammar and spelling, and whether any such meaning is within a document examiner's expertise, is dealt with in the discussion earlier in this chapter of *U.S. v. Paul*.

[356]*State v. Cooke*, 914 A.2d 1078, 1100 (Del. Super. Ct. 2007).

[357]*State v. Cooke*, 914 A.2d 1078, 1089 (Del. Super. Ct. 2007).

[358]*State v. Cooke*, 914 A.2d 1078, 1100 (Del. Super. Ct. 2007).

[359]The court observed that, "Carter testified and explained her background. It includes being a forensic document examiner for 20 years, attending a Secret Service school on document examination, taking several forensic document courses, being qualified in the United States District Court

As to that, this is what the court says:

> Handwriting comparison is beyond a lay person's general knowledge. As the Court in *Jones* said, echoing the earlier bench ruling in the other case, handwriting analysis is a special skill not a science. It, therefore, does not fit neatly into all the *Daubert/Kumho* holes of:
>
> 1. Whether a theory or technique has been tested;
> 2. Whether it has been subjected to peer review and publication.
> 3. Whether a technique had a high known or potential rate of error and whether there are standards controlling its operation; and
> 4. Whether the theory or technique enjoys general acceptance within relevant scientific community.

And that is the complete extent of what the court has to say on issues of handwriting identification expertise reliability, global or specific (independent of issues of the particular expert's qualifications), under Delaware's interpretation of *Daubert* and *Kumho Tire*.[360] Enough said.

The penultimate case as of this writing is *People v. Graham*.[361] This California case is another one that superficially appears to have something to do with a reliability decision, but which actually does not, at least not in any direct sense. Like the others (such as, most notoriously, *Jolivet*), however, *Graham* appears almost certain to be cited by other courts as if it does decide something about reliability.

One of the reasons the handwriting aspects of the case may have been more skirted than faced is that the facts of the case establish the defendant's guilt so overwhelmingly that virtually any issue raised was likely to be dealt with as a mere formality. The court's statement of these facts was succinct and to the point:

> Defendant's convictions arise from robberies at two banks in the city of Birmingham. The first robbery occurred on a rainy morning on December 7, 2004, at a Charter One Bank where Bradley Grekonich worked as a teller. According to Grekonich, a man wearing a black puffy coat and a baseball hat walked up to the counter and handed him a deposit slip that stated, "I have a gun. Give me the money or I'll kill you." Grekonich gave the man $1,700. The man walked out of the bank, leaving the deposit slip behind at the counter. Grekonich identified a man depicted in still photographs produced from the bank's video surveillance system as the robber, but failed to identify defendant in a pretrial lineup conducted by the police.

---

in 1989 and, in the last 18 years, having testified 27 times in her expert capacity in various courts, including this one. *State v. Cooke*, 914 A.2d 1078, 1100 (Del. Super. Ct. 2007).

"On *voir dire* from Cooke, she testified that she is the State Police's only document examiner, has no supervision from another examiner, neither she nor the State Police lab are accredited, that she has no manual or other documentation for her methodology. The *voir dire* also revealed there is a large element of subjectivity in her field." *State v. Cooke*, 914 A.2d 1078, 1100 (Del. Super. Ct. 2007). The court also later reported, "Carter testified that she is unaware if theories of handwriting comparison have been tested or subjected to peer review, that she has no knowledge of the potential error rate of examiners and that there are no standards for making comparisons." *State v. Cooke*, 914 A.2d 1078, 1101 (Del. Super. Ct. 2007).

[360]The court then goes on to a lengthy consideration of defendant's claim that giving the demand exemplars violated his privilege against self-incrimination. The court must receive an A+ for effort on this vexing question, which has precious little in the way of thoughtful authority on it from anywhere after the Supreme Court's simplistic analogy equating the compulsion of handwriting exemplars to the drawing of blood, which seemed to settle all issues (poorly) forty years ago in *Gilbert v. California*, 388 U.S. 263, 266, 87 S. Ct. 1951, 18 L. Ed. 2d 1178 (1967). Judge Herlihy collects the extant cases and gives his own analysis. The result he comes to—that dictation of things to write which leaves the defendant to choose how to spell and punctuate violates the self-incrimination privilege, while other parts of the process of producing demand exemplars do not—is difficult to understand, and seems unlikely to garner much agreement elsewhere. Speaking of difficult-to-understand, it is perhaps not inappropriate to observe that the entire opinion suffers from a certain lack of expository clarity.

[361]*People v. Graham*, 2007 WL 861173 (Mich. Ct. App. 2007), appeal denied, 479 Mich. 865, 735 N.W.2d 266 (2007).

The second robbery occurred on the morning of December 8, 2004, at a Fidelity Bank where Shareen Coles worked as a teller. Coles identified defendant as the robber at trial and in a pretrial lineup. Coles testified that defendant wore a black puffy coat and a baseball cap when he entered the bank. He wrote something on a withdrawal slip and then approached the teller station next to Coles. Because that teller was busy, Coles offered to help defendant. Defendant gave Coles the withdrawal slip, which stated, "I have a gun. Give me all the money now." Coles handed cash from her drawer to defendant. She reported the robbery to bank managers after defendant departed toward a back exit. The withdrawal slip used to commit the robbery was left at the bank.

The person whom Coles identified as the robber drove off in a red Chrysler Sebring. A bank customer followed the vehicle to Webster Street and then showed Birmingham Police Officer Matthew Baldwin the driveway where the vehicle pulled in. After Officer Baldwin determined that the vehicle was inside a detached garage at 1462 Webster Street, he and other police officers secured the area around the house. The police received information that defendant was a renter at the house. Officer Baldwin made phone contact with a female occupant to request that defendant come out. After approximately five hours, defendant exited the house. Police officers subsequently executed a search warrant of the house and garage. Parked inside the garage were a red Chrysler Sebring and a dusty black Mercury Topaz. Among the items in the Mercury Topaz were a wet, black puffy coat and a baseball cap. A wet handwritten note in the coat pocket stated, "I have a gun. Give me the money or I will kill you."[362]

On this record, it would appear that unless something was suppressed as illegally seized (which it wasn't[363]), virtually any other evidentiary error was likely to be deemed harmless. About the only worry even the most neurotic prosecutor might have is that somehow a juror might think that the video from the first robbery was not clear enough to recognize defendant, and be led to overvalue the inability of the clerk to identify the defendant (thus undervaluing all of the rest of the strong circumstantial evidence in the case, including the black puffy coat and the fact that the cap, with "MSU" (for Michigan State University) on the front, which was recovered from the car in the garage, was indistinguishable from the cap shown in the video of the first robbery[364]). However, just to dispel any possibility of such a juror brainfreeze, the prosecution hired a putative handwriting identification expert, Ruth Holmes,[365] obviously hoping to have the writing on the demand notes attributed to the defendant. This they predictably got (assuming that the expert was, as usual, informed of the other evidence in the case, a circumstance apparently neither explored nor raised by the defense attorney at trial, again as usual).

However, the defense did object to the admission of Holmes's testimony "because of the nature of the 'science,'" which, it claimed "was not helpful to the trier of

---

[362]*People v. Graham*, 2007 WL 861173 (Mich. Ct. App. 2007), appeal denied, 479 Mich. 865, 735 N.W.2d 266 (2007).

[363]This is the first issue disposed of by the Appellate Court. *People v. Graham*, 2007 WL 861173, at *1–*3 (Mich. Ct. App. 2007), appeal denied, 479 Mich. 865, 735 N.W.2d 266 (2007).

[364]I grant that MSU baseball caps may be relatively common in Michigan, but the cap, in combination with the black puffy coat, the general resemblance (at least) of the perpetrator in the video of the first robbery with the defendant, the practice demand note in the car of the same general wording as the demand notes in both robberies, the general similarities in robbery method, the fact that the robberies were on succeeding days, and the fact that the defendant was followed to his girlfriend's house from the second robbery, should have been enough to convince virtually any juror of defendant's guilt in regard to the first robbery.

[365]Ruth Holmes is a well known handwriting expert in Michigan who gives opinions both in regard to authorship, and also in regard to "graphology," or personality attribution from the examination of handwriting. Whether Ms. Holmes would be regarded as a qualified expert by members of orthodox Osbornian groups like the American Society of Questioned Document Examiners or the American Board of Forensic Document Examiners is an open question. The extent to which a court should care is also an open question, but it cannot properly be answered by a court that is not informed and does not inform itself on these issues. Neither the defense attorneys nor the trial court (and certainly not the appellate court) seem to have addressed even this global issue, much less any more specific issues in regard to the particular attribution exercise undertaken in this case.

fact."[366] This, apparently, was just about all the defense said in challenging the admissibility of the handwriting testimony, and the trial court summarily overruled the objection without exposition.[367] On appeal, the appellate court recognized that Michigan law generally required a careful reliability examination by the trial judge under its version of amended Federal Rule 702:

> The admissibility of expert testimony is governed by MRE 702, which provides:
>
>> If the court determines that scientific, technical, or other specialized knowledge will assist the trier of fact to understand the evidence or to determine a fact in issue, a witness qualified as an expert by knowledge, skill, experience, training, or education may testify thereto in the form of an opinion or otherwise if (1) the testimony is based on sufficient facts or data, (2) the testimony is the product of reliable principles and methods, and (3) the witness has applied the principles and methods reliably to the facts of the case.
>
> An essential condition for admitting expert testimony is that the testimony be reliable. *Gilbert v. DaimlerChrysler Corp.*, 470 Mich. 749, 780, 685 N.W.2d 391, 94 Fair Empl. Prac. Cas. (BNA) 315, 85 Empl. Prac. Dec. (CCH) P 41695, 14 A.L.R.6th 801 (2004), cert. denied, 546 U.S. 821, 126 S. Ct. 354, 163 L. Ed. 2d 63 (2005). "While a party may waive any claim of error by failing to call this gatekeeping function to the court's attention, the court *must* evaluate expert testimony under MRE 702 once that issue is raised." *Craig ex rel. Craig v. Oakwood Hosp.*, 471 Mich. 67, 82, 684 N.W.2d 296 (2004) (emphasis in original).[368]

However, the court points out that in order to trigger this requirement the objecting party has some "price of admission" burden of alerting the court to the nature of the grounds for objection:

> Review of the record reveals that defense counsel objected to the testimony because of the nature of the "science" and asserted that it was not helpful to the trier of fact. Because MRE 702 is not limited to "exact science" testimony, we conclude that the trial court did not abuse its discretion in denying defense counsel's objection to Holmes's testimony on the ground asserted, without further inquiry.[369]

One can perhaps understand the temptation to seize on the first idea that occurs in order to dispose of this ground given the inevitable irritation with *any* ground in light of the facts of the case. However, it would seem that the court here went both too far and not far enough. It seems that the court has concluded that objecting to the "science" of a "forensic science" that is not really based on science automatically puts one out of court. This seems to elevate form over substance. It would have been better to have said that the objecting party is obliged to formulate specifically the task presented (attributing authorship of a relatively short note,[370] especially after being exposed to domain-irrelevant information[371]) and to present some explanation for why there is reason to be skeptical of the expert's own claims of expertise, or that of the expert's guild. Failure by the defense to frame a meaningful reason to be skeptical of the proffered expertise may have been what lay behind the court's reference to the longstanding unquestioned admission of claimed handwriting identification expertise globally, citing *Crisp*.[372] At any rate, the Court held that the objection was unpreserved, and that it was not plain error to admit the testimony. It also

---

[366]*People v. Graham*, 2007 WL 861173 (Mich. Ct. App. 2007), appeal denied, 479 Mich. 865, 735 N.W.2d 266 (2007).

[367]*People v. Graham*, 2007 WL 861173 (Mich. Ct. App. 2007), appeal denied, 479 Mich. 865, 735 N.W.2d 266 (2007).

[368]*People v. Graham*, 2007 WL 861173 (Mich. Ct. App. 2007), appeal denied, 479 Mich. 865, 735 N.W.2d 266 (2007) (footnote omitted).

[369]*People v. Graham*, 2007 WL 861173 (Mich.

Ct. App. 2007), appeal denied, 479 Mich. 865, 735 N.W.2d 266 (2007).

[370]It is not clear whether the note was printed or cursive. It is also unclear what sources were used as exemplars of the defendant's normal writing.

[371]Assuming this to be the case, as it normally is in practice. The issue is rarely addressed explicitly by defense attorney or court.

[372]*People v. Graham*, 2007 WL 861173 (Mich.

held that any error was harmless. However, it must be noted that, unlike the Court in *Jolivet*, the Michigan Court of Appeals did not issue any dicta on what it predicted the proper result would have been had the objection been made properly and had a hearing been held. So the reliability issue in regard to various aspects of claimed handwriting identification expertise appears to remain an open issue in Michigan, unless lower Michigan courts do what many other courts have done in similar circumstances in this area, and take this appellate decision to mean something it does not.

This state of affairs is not changed by the last case in our examination, another Michigan case, *People v. Leiterman*.[373] This case is disturbing on a number of levels. First, it is disturbing because it deals with the brutal rape-murder of a young University of Michigan law student, Jane Mixer, in 1969.[374] Second, it is disturbing because it is a DNA cold hit case involving a the Michigan State Police Crime Lab, which, at the time it typed the DNA from stains on Mixer's pantyhose in 2001, was clearly suffering from failure to control cross-contamination between samples in the lab. In addition to Leiterman's profile, they also generated a profile from a drop of blood taken from Mixer's hand in 1969. That profile matched John Ruelas, who was four years old in 1969, but who had biological samples in the lab in an unrelated case at the time the testing on the Mixer materials was done in 2001.[375] A plausible explanation of the cold hits on both Leiterman and Ruelas is that both of their DNAs were being prepared for entry into the CODIS database at the same lab at the same time that the Mixer crime scene evidence was being tested. The Michigan Court of Appeals treated this issue rather cavalierly, saying that *"Daubert"* is a more relaxed standard than its previous *Davis-Frye*[376] test, and that *"Daubert"* left issues of "application" to the evaluation of the jury. The court never mentions the blurring of that supposed line in *General Electric v. Joiner* and *Kumho Tire*, nor did it bother to deal with the operative language of its own evidence rule (beyond a sterile quotation of the rule itself), section 3 of which makes reliable application of the principles and methods of the expertise to the facts of the case an issue of admissibility, not weight.[377]

Besides the DNA cold hit, there was very little evidence against Leiterman beyond the fact that he had actually lived in the community where the crime occurred (Ann Arbor) at the time of the crime, and had also owned a .22 caliber handgun at the time (Mixer had been shot with a .22).[378] In order to attempt to supplement the cold hit from the shaky lab, the prosecution submitted a photograph of the cover of

---

Ct. App. 2007), appeal denied, 479 Mich. 865, 735 N.W.2d 266 (2007).

[373]*People v. Leiterman*, 2007 WL 2120514 (Mich. Ct. App. 2007).

[374]*People v. Leiterman*, 2007 WL 2120514 (Mich. Ct. App. 2007).

[375]*People v. Leiterman*, 2007 WL 2120514 (Mich. Ct. App. 2007).

[376]The "Davis" in Michigan's previous "Davis-Frye" test is *People v. Davis*, 343 Mich. 348, 72 N.W.2d 269 (1955); the Frye is of course Frye v. U.S., 293 F. 1013, 34 A.L.R. 145 (App. D.C. 1923) (rejected by, State v. Walstad, 119 Wis. 2d 483, 351 N.W.2d 469 (1984)) and (rejected by, State v. Brown, 297 Or. 404, 687 P.2d 751 (1984)) and (rejected by, Nelson v. State, 628 A.2d 69 (Del. 1993)) and (rejected by, State v. Alberico, 116 N.M. 156, 861 P.2d 192 (1993)) and (rejected by, State v. Moore, 268 Mont. 20, 885 P.2d 457 (1994)) and (rejected by, State v. Faught, 127 Idaho 873,

908 P.2d 566 (1995)) and (rejected by, People v. Shreck, 22 P.3d 68, 90 A.L.R.5th 765 (Colo. 2001)).

[377]The Michigan rule is set out immediately above in the discussion of *Graham*.

[378]Leiterman owned a registered .22 caliber Ruger six-shot revolver from 1967 until he reported it stolen in 1987. The state police firearms expert testified that "bullet fragments removed from Mixer's brain during her 1969 autopsy were similar to several found in defendant's Van Buren County home in 2004 and could have been fired from a .22 caliber six-shot Ruger revolver." *Id.* at *2. The way the court quotes this testimony the reader would think it was fraught with significance. But unless the state police expert was testifying to the results of now-discredited bullet lead analysis test (which seems unlikely, considering that Leiter was unlikely to have 35-year-old rounds in his home), then the statement could be made about every .22 caliber bullet in Michigan or, indeed, the world, and a very great range of

a phone book found in the basement of the Michigan Law School in 1969.[379] Someone had written the victim's last name (Mixer) and her hometown (Muskegon) on the cover. (Ms. Mixer was supposed to be meeting someone she had contacted through a campus bulletin board in order to get a ride home when she disappeared).[380] Riley was asked to compare these two words (13 letters, 11 letter forms) to exemplars of Leiterman's handwriting. This is of course the "hard task" concerning which there is absolutely no evidence supporting any expert's claim to be able to perform it accurately. But in this case it was worse, even under standard guild theory, since the writing on the phone book (which, of course, might not have had anything to do with the disappearance) was 33 years old. Standard handwriting identification theory emphasizes that writing changes with time, and mandates the use of exemplars written near in time to the generation of the "questioned" handwriting.[381] It is unclear where and how exemplars were obtained, and of what date they were, but if they were recent the testimony is in violation of the field's own principles, not merely their application. Second, Riley claimed to be able to discern diagnostic patterns of pen pressure from the writing on the phone book, when pen pressure is thought generally to be undeterminable from photographs. Third, it is not clear, but is to be expected, that Riley generated his conclusions in the shadow of knowledge of the DNA match, a variable which undermines reliability quite dramatically.[382] Finally, Riley conceded that there were at least two significant differences between the phone book writing and the way Leiterman normally made the letters under examination, but attributed this to the postural difficulties of writing in a phone booth.

Admission of this handwriting identification testimony bears out the observation of Jane Campbell Moriarty and Michael Saks that, in the context of prosecution-proffered forensic identification expertise, "[t]here is almost no expert testimony so threadbare that it will not be admitted . . . ."[383] Nevertheless, the defense attorney *chose not to challenge the admissibility* of the prosecution handwriting testimony, and instead merely sought to counter it with the testimony of his own putative expert witness.[384] So, as in *Graham*, the issue was whether admission of the handwriting identification testimony was plain error, which the Court quite predictably found that it was not.[385] In addition, it found that the election to proceed in this manner was not an example of ineffective assistance of counsel.[386] Although one can still say that no Michigan court has ruled on a properly made challenge to handwriting expertise in regard to hard tasks such as this one, the Court's willingness to tolerate such questionable performances by prosecution witnesses does not bode well for such a challenge when and if one is ever made in Michigan.

Finally, while it does not deal with handwriting identification reliability issues

---

guns (the expert conceded three dozen makes and models).

[379]*People v. Leiterman*, 2007 WL 2120514 (Mich. Ct. App. 2007).

[380]*People v. Leiterman*, 2007 WL 2120514 (Mich. Ct. App. 2007).

[381]See, e.g., Albert S. Osborn, Questioned Documents 26 (2nd edition, 1929) (expressing chagrin at cases using exemplars "*thirty years* or more before or after the date of the disputed writing" [emphasis in original] and prescribing exemplars "as nearly as possible of the same date"); James V.P. Conway, Evidential Documents 90 (1959) (prescribing exemplars "prior to or of the same date" as the questioned documents).

[382]See, as always, Risinger, Saks, Thompson & Rosenthal, The *Daubert/Kumho* Implications

of Observer Effects in Forensic Science: Hidden Problems of Expectation and Suggestion, 90 Cal. L. Rev. 1 (2002).

[383]Saks, Forensic Science: Grand Goals, Tragic Flaws and Judicial Gatekeeping, 4 Judges' J. 16, 29 (2005).

[384]*People v. Leiterman*, 2007 WL 2120514 (Mich. Ct. App. 2007).

[385]*People v. Leiterman*, 2007 WL 2120514 (Mich. Ct. App. 2007).

[386]*People v. Leiterman*, 2007 WL 2120514 (Mich. Ct. App. 2007). Michigan is apparently one of those jurisdictions that allow certain issues which are normally raised by various post-conviction relief mechanisms, such as ineffective assistance of counsel, to be consolidated with the issues raised on direct appeal.

directly, we must note the Pennsylvania case of *In Re Estate of Presutti*,[387] a will contest in which those relying on a will did not attack the reliability of handwriting identification expertise but instead claimed that the will challengers' expert (who was called to testify that the decedent's signature was not genuine) was unqualified. In regard to qualifications, the court announced the following test: "The test to be applied when qualifying an expert witness is whether the witness has any reasonable pretension to special knowledge on the subject under investigation. If he does, he may testify."[388] It seems that the "any reasonable pretension test" may better capture the general attitude of most courts toward prosecution-proffered expertise in criminal cases more than those same courts are usually willing to admit quite so bluntly.

## § 4:8    Recent developments—Counter-testimony on FDEs' claimed skills

Another issue which was dealt with in three of these cases, *United States v. Ruth*,[1] *United States v. Velasquez*,[2] and *United States v. Paul*,[3] is the standard for admissibility of evidence tending to show the weaknesses of handwriting identification expertise after a questioned document examiner has been allowed to give testimony concerning the identification of the author of disputed handwriting in support of the prosecution in a criminal case. Stated this way, it would seem that a criminal defendant should have wide latitude in presenting counter-evidence, not merely through cross examination of the government's questioned document examiner, but through his own witnesses. *Daubert* itself emphasized the role of such counter-testimony as an important check on the unwarranted impact of expert testimony that managed to make it over the Rule 702 hurdle in spite of some doubts about its reliability.[4] Nevertheless, the handwriting cases are split 1-1 with one tie on the admissibility of such evidence. And there is nothing to account for this result except the courts' varying attitudes, since the proposed counter-expert was the same in each case and proposed to give largely the same testimony in each. One might even go so far as to say that these cases were decisions on the acceptability of Professor Mark P. Denbeaux.[5]

It is important before examining these cases to know what Professor Denbeaux claims to have information about which the average juror would not have, and what he does not claim. Professor Denbeaux has examined every empirical study on the reliability of handwriting expertise, and can review this literature, what it means and what it does not mean, for the jury. Further, he has studied the standard literature produced by questioned document examiners to explain what they claim to be doing, and he can summarize this literature, and further identify what he, upon reflection and evaluation, has concluded are the main weaknesses of the methodology there set out: high subjectivity, and no criteria to determine if any given similarity or difference between the questioned writing and the known exemplars is significant (an individualizing characteristic) or insignificant (merely intra-writer variation). Finally, he generally asserts that he can point out

---

[387]*In re Estate of Presutti*, 783 A.2d 803 (Pa. Super. Ct. 2001).

[388]*In re Estate of Presutti*, 783 A.2d 803, 807 (Pa. Super. Ct. 2001).

**[Section 4:8]**

[1]*U.S. v. Ruth*, 46 M.J. 1 (C.A.A.F. 1997).

[2]*U.S. v. Velasquez*, 64 F.3d 844, 42 Fed. R. Evid. Serv. 1175 (3d Cir. 1995).

[3]*U.S. v. Paul*, 175 F.3d 906, 51 Fed. R. Evid. Serv. 1464, 183 A.L.R. Fed. 773 (11th Cir. 1999).

[4]"Vigorous cross-examination, *presentation of contrary evidence*, and careful instruction on the burden of proof are the traditional and appropriate means of attacking shaky but admissible evidence." *Daubert v. Merrell Dow Pharmaceuticals, Inc.*, 509 U.S. 579, 596, 113 S. Ct. 2786, 125 L. Ed. 2d 469, 27, 27 U.S.P.Q.2d 1200, Prod. Liab. Rep. (CCH) P 13494, 37 Fed. R. Evid. Serv. 1, 23 Envtl. L. Rep. 20979 (1993) (emphasis supplied).

[5]In the spirit of full disclosure, it should be noted that Mark P. Denbeaux is a colleague, co-author, and longtime close friend of the author.

unaccounted-for dissimilarities between the questioned writing and the exemplars which are as apparently meaningful as the similarities upon which the document examiner witness has relied for identification. However, Professor Denbeaux claims no special skill at determining authorship or lack of authorship of any document as a result of similarities and dissimilarities. Indeed, his whole point is that it is doubtful whether those who claim such expertise possess it. Further, he makes it clear that he has never undergone whatever training document examiners undergo, and he is not a document examiner. He never asserts that any person did or did not in fact write any questioned document, and eschews any claim of special skill in that regard.

In *Ruth II*, the presiding judge at the court martial refused to authorize the defense to call Denbeaux. Instead, he directed the defense to attempt to cross-examine the government's document examiner first, using material from Risinger et al.[6] The trial attorney made no attempt to cross-examine the document examiner using the published information, and the Court of Military Appeals ruled that by this lapse counsel had failed to demonstrate that Denbeaux's testimony would have been "relevant and necessary," and so the judge did not abuse his discretion in denying the defense request for the production of Professor Denbeaux.

The Court of Appeals for the Armed Forces granted discretionary review limited to this issue. It was clearly uncomfortable with the handling of the issue by the Court of Military Appeals, given the intervening decision in *Velasquez* from which it quoted extensively on the general point that Denbeaux was an appropriate witness. Nevertheless, it affirmed the conviction, shifting grounds somewhat. The trial judge had invited the defense attorney to renew his motion to call Denbeaux at the close of the testimony of the prosecution's document examiner, and this the defense attorney had failed to do. It was *this* failure, not the cross examination failure, which the Court of Appeals found rendered the actions of the trial judge not to be "an abuse of discretion." So *Ruth II* is in fact a non-decision, with the court of appeals apparently adopting the analysis of *Velasquez*.

In *Velasquez*, the Third Circuit declared that the trial court's refusal to allow Denbeaux to testify after the prosecution was allowed to present identification testimony by a document examiner was an abuse of discretion.[7] The court observed that "[t]he mere fact that the Professor is not an expert in conducting handwriting analysis to identify particular scriveners of specified documents does not mean that he is not qualified to offer expert testimony criticizing the standards of the field."[8] In doing this, the Court rejected the most extreme version of the "guild test," which would hold that not only may guild members testify, but only guild members may criticize. The court then found that "sufficient evidence exists to show that the Professor had 'good grounds' for his rejection of handwriting analysis," and further found that Denbeaux's "criticisms of the field of handwriting analysis generally, as well as Ms. Bonjour's analysis in this case, would have assisted the jury in determin-

---

[6]Risinger, Denbeaux & Saks, Exorcism of Ignorance as a Proxy for Rational Knowledge: The Lessons of Handwriting Identification "Expertise," 137 U. Pa. L. Rev. 731, 751–771 (1989).

[7]Though the decision predated *Joiner*, the court stated the standard as follows: "We review the trial court's ruling on the admissibility of Professor Denbeaux's testimony for abuse of discretion," *U.S. v. Velasquez*, 64 F.3d 844, 847–848, 42 Fed. R. Evid. Serv. 1175 (3d Cir. 1995), though it went on to observe: "[B]ut to the extent the district court's ruling turns on an interpretation of a Federal Rule of Evidence our review is plenary," *U.S. v. Velasquez*, 64 F.3d 844,

848, 42 Fed. R. Evid. Serv. 1175 (3d Cir. 1995). However, the court never quarreled with the District Court's specific construction of a rule. Rather, it addressed what a court should be mindful of "in exercising its discretion," and concluded that Denbeaux's testimony "should have been admitted," *U.S. v. Velasquez*, 64 F.3d 844, 848, 42 Fed. R. Evid. Serv. 1175 (3d Cir. 1995), and should have been admitted "as a matter of law," *U.S. v. Velasquez*, 64 F.3d 844, 852, 42 Fed. R. Evid. Serv. 1175 (3d Cir. 1995), which is another rubric for describing an abuse of discretion.

[8]*U.S. v. Velasquez*, 64 F.3d 844, 851, 42 Fed. R. Evid. Serv. 1175 (3d Cir. 1995).

ing the proper weight to accord Ms. Bonjour's testimony,"[9] and that its exclusion was not harmless because, Denbeaux's testimony "very well might have affected the jury's verdict on Count VIII."[10]

However, in *Paul* the 11th Circuit reached a different result, on even more compelling facts. You will recall that the case involved an extortion directed at a bank officer, and Mr. Paul was the gentleman arrested after he picked up the briefcase with the money in a McDonald's restaurant men's room and put it in his backpack. His story was that he just picked up what appeared to be an abandoned or lost briefcase. The main evidence contradicting this was the document examiner's identification of Paul as the writer of the extortion note. Paul was tried and both the document examiner and Denbeaux were allowed to testify. That trial ended in a hung jury. At the retrial the judge concluded upon government objection that Denbeaux's testimony would not be helpful to the trier of fact and barred him from testifying. This time the jury convicted Paul. On appeal, the circuit court disposed of Denbeaux in four paragraphs. They dismissed his academic research in the literature, saying that "his skill, experience, training and education as a lawyer did not make him any more qualified to testify as an expert on handwriting analysis than a lay person who read the same articles." The rest of the opinion concentrated mainly on Denbeaux's lack of qualifications as a document examiner, thereby adopting the extreme "guild test," essentially holding that only those who are members of the guild may present testimony skeptical of its claims. (This would imply that only card carrying astrologers may criticize astrology.) The opinion then concluded, "because Denbeaux was not an expert on the limitations of handwriting analysis, the district court's exclusion of his testimony did not prejudice Paul." Unaccountably, the opinion does not mention the contrary conclusions, reasoning and result of the Third Circuit in *Velasquez*, or the apparent adoption of the *Velasquez* reasoning by the Court of Appeals in *Ruth II*.

What are we to say of the *Paul* opinion? True it is that Denbeaux is an "educational expert," one called to give the jury information derived from study which they might not be aware of, and which they therefore might not properly take into account. In this way he is like an experimental psychologist testifying about the problems of eyewitness identification. It is also true that some courts, and even commentators, have had problems with the acceptance of purely educational experts, though the irony is that, at least when it comes to courts, there is a certain asymmetry in their perception of the problem, with the government generally gaining admission of its educational experts and the defendant often not.[11] However, most attempts to account for the rejection of the experimental psychologist in the eyewitness cases center around some notion that the jury is somehow competent from experience to evaluate lay testimony without needing any supplementation from a person claiming to have special knowledge. While these objections are increasingly regarded as extremely weak, they would seem to disappear altogether when the witness the jurors are supposed to evaluate is being presented as an expert. There is nothing about their presumed general experience which would even notionally prepare them to evaluate the weaknesses of claims being made by the expert. An intuition about the untenability of a blanket rule excluding educational counter-expertise in such a situation probably lay behind the Court of Appeals reliance on Denbeaux's lack of guild qualifications. Presumably, someone with those guild qualifications could testify to alert the jury to the weaknesses of the claims of the field, except there are no guild members who believe that there are such weaknesses.

---

[9] *U.S. v. Velasquez*, 64 F.3d 844, 852, 42 Fed. R. Evid. Serv. 1175 (3d Cir. 1995).

[10] *U.S. v. Velasquez*, 64 F.3d 844, 852, 42 Fed. R. Evid. Serv. 1175 (3d Cir. 1995).

[11] See discussion in Risinger, Navigating Expert Reliability: Are Criminal Standards of Certainty Being Left on the Dock?, 64 Albany L. Rev. 99, 131–134 (2000).

The result of *Paul*, if followed, is not only that handwriting experts may testify, but that they are virtually unchallengeable, even though there is plenty of rational reason to be skeptical of many of their claims.

## § 4:9  Recent developments—Law review literature

Before undertaking a review of the empirical research which has been published concerning the accuracy of handwriting identification by questioned document examiners, a word should be said about the scholarly literature. There are two long articles which must be read by anyone interested in the issues raised by this chapter. They are Andre Moenssens, Handwriting Identification in a Post-*Daubert* World,[1] and Risinger, Denbeaux and Saks, Brave New Post-*Daubert* World—Reply to Professor Moenssens.[2] In general, I will not try to summarize these articles, in part because they should be read and evaluated on their own merits together, and in part because Professor Moenssens' article is in large part an attack on the work of Professors Risinger, Denbeaux and Saks, and Professor Moenssens would never agree with any summary that I might attempt. Among much, much else, the Moenssens article contains the most explicit embracement of what is essentially the guild test to be found in the literature (though he would probably object to the label), and the *Reply* examines at length the weaknesses of that approach.

The reader may also be interested in two commentaries that appear in Forensic Science Communications, the online journal of the Federal Bureau of Investigation. One of them, by Michael J. Saks, outlines three types of research which—if conducted and depending upon the findings—could provide an informed, empirical, basis for the claims of forensic document examiners.[3] The second is by Jamie Orenstein,[4] who was the Assistant U.S. Attorney who handled the document examination issue in the case of *United States v. McVeigh*, where the court refused to allow the expert opinion testimony of FDEs unless and until they could establish their dependability at a *Daubert* hearing, which the government declined to try to do. In what is ostensibly an essay on behalf of the admissibility of FDE opinion testimony, Orenstein concedes the lack of sufficient current evidence on that issue, and discusses what prosecutors can do to prove handwriting authorship without the testimony of FDEs.

## II.  SCIENTIFIC STATUS

## § 4:10  Introduction

Handwriting identification experts believe they can examine a specimen of adult handwriting and determine whether the author of that specimen is the same person as or a different person than the author of any other example of handwriting, as long as both specimens are of sufficient quantity and not separated by years or the intervention of degenerative disease. They further believe that they can accomplish this result with great accuracy, and that they can do it much better than an average literate person attempting the same task. They believe they can obtain these accurate findings as the result of applying an analytical methodology to the examination of handwriting, according to certain principles which are reflected in the

**[Section 4:9]**

[1]Moenssens, Handwriting Identification Evidence in the Post-*Daubert* World, 66 UMKC L. Rev. 251 (1998).

[2]Risinger et al., Brave New "Post-*Daubert* World"—A Reply to Professor Moenssens, 29 Seton Hall L. Rev. 405 (1998).

[3]M. J. Saks, Planning the Trip from Folk Art to Science: Why and How, 1 Forensic Science Communications (Oct., 1999), at http://www.fbi.gov/programs/lab/fsc/backissu/oct1999/abstrctf.htm.

[4]J. Orenstein, Effect of the *Daubert* Decision on Document Examinations From the Prosecutor's Perspective, 1 Forensic Science Communications (Oct., 1999), at http://www.fbi.gov/programs/lab/fsc/backissu/oct1999/abstrcte.htm.

questioned document literature.[1] They believe that this literature explains how to examine handwriting for identifying characteristics, and that by applying the lessons taught by this literature in connection with their experiences in various training exercises and in real world problems, they learn to identify handwriting dependably.

This portion of the chapter will examine the justifications for these beliefs, to determine if there exists any evidence that they are true.

Indeed, this frankly insupportable trend appears to have continued, and even been extended into the state courts. Professor Denbeaux was rejected summarily as a proposed witness on the weaknesses of eyewitness identification expertise by the Federal District Court in *Versace*, a ruling which was noted by the Court of Appeals in a footnote[2] but which was apparently not appealed. And in *State v. Clifford*[3] the Montana Supreme Court upheld a similar exclusion, but in a more circumspect opinion which nevertheless comes to the same unfortunate result as follows:

> First, arguably, Denbeaux is not an expert in the field of handwriting analysis; rather, he is an evidence professor who has, historically, criticized handwriting analysis evidence. It was within the District Court's discretion to conclude that Denbeaux did not qualify as an expert in handwriting analysis. *State v. Southern*, 1999 MT 94, ¶ 48, 294 Mont. 225, ¶ 48, 980 P.3d 3, ¶ 48. Moreover, Cheryl presented the testimony of her own handwriting expert, and performed a thorough cross-examination of Blanco. Thus, even if Denbeaux's testimony might have cast doubt on Blanco's testimony, Cheryl was able to accomplish that task through the testimony of her expert and cross-examination. Under these circumstances, the District Court did not abuse its discretion in precluding Denbeaux's testimony.[4]

How such rulings do not contravene the right to present a defense under the Fifth and Fourteenth Amendments to the U.S. Constitution remains something of a mystery.

## § 4:11   Areas of agreement: The possibility of a science of handwriting identification

The main goal of all forensic identification, including handwriting identification, is individualization. Individualization is the establishment that a person or object now held is the same person or object associated with a past event in a particular way, to the exclusion of all other candidates. The major source of individualization

---

[Section 4:10]

[1]What Osborn referred to as "true methods," Albert S. Osborn, Questioned Documents 6 (2d ed. 1929); and David Ellen refers to as "standard methods" and "proper method," David Ellen, The Scientific Examination of Documents: Methods and Techniques 9 (1989).

[2]*A.V. by Versace, Inc v. Gianni Versace S.p.A*, 446 F. Supp.2d 252 (U.S. Dist. Ct, S.D.N.Y., 2006), n. 15.

[3]*State v. Clifford*, 121 P.3d 489 (Montana Supreme Court, 2005).

[4]*State v. Clifford*, 121 P.3d 489, 497 (Montana Supreme Court, 2005). The concurrence is really more of a dissent in this regard: "Because of the limitations we have jurisprudentially placed on Daubert—limiting its application to "novel" scientific evidence—Clifford's concern that Blanco's methodology did not produce valid results could not be the subject of a rigorous Daubert hearing. Rather, under Montana law her concerns would have to be addressed via Barmeyer—i.e., through cross-examination and refutation; something she attempted to do with Mark Denbeaux's testimony. And there's the anomaly. Since the field validity of handwriting comparison, as a discipline, was presumed—i.e., since it was deemed reliable—the court effectively determined that expert scientific evidence attacking the validity of Blanco's methods was "novel" and, therefore subject to Daubert. Thus, under Montana law, it would have been improper for the trial court to admit Denbeaux's testimony in front of the jury without a pre-trial Daubert hearing. We've turned Daubert on its head. Id. at 323 (James C. Nelson, J, joined by Patricia C. Cotter, J., concurring).

evidence is what we may call a tagged residue.[1] A tagged residue exists when a person or thing leaves behind some residue of its presence at a relevant time and place, which residue contains information that can be used to conclude (with varying certitude) that a particular person or thing produced the residue. In addition, even when individualization is not confidently possible, exclusion may occur when a decision can be made that a particular source did not produce the tagged residue.

The notion of tagged residues is broader and covers more phenomena than one might at first glance conclude. For instance, eyewitness identification is a special example of the use of tagged residue information. In that case, the residue is not specifically physical, but exists as a memory in the mind of the identifier. Nevertheless, whether we are dealing with mental images or photographs or physical impressions or traces of bodily fluid, all tagged residue situations present some common characteristics and problems. The hope is that the information in the residue may be processed in such a way that one can properly conclude that one and only one object or person could have caused the residue. This hope is in one sense doomed, since all information about such factual relations is probabilistic. Thus, as Hume knew, for any identification whatsoever there is some residual probability of error. On the other hand, under some conditions, the probability of particular identification may be so great that it would be nearly deranged to worry about the probability of error.

The question becomes, what are the main circumstances that affect, or ought to affect, our confidence in particularized identification from a tagged residue, or in exclusion of an item or person as the source?

The main factors appear to be the following: First, what about the residue counts as a relevant characteristic bearing on specific identification (individualization). This question inevitably entails, consciously or unconsciously, some notion of separability and independence[2] of characteristics and some notion of base rate incidences of those characteristics in the population of candidates for the source of the residue.

Second, referring to the particular person or object that in fact caused the residue as the source, we have the problem of potential intra-source variation. Residues from the same source may differ each time a residue is caused. For instance, the passage of a bullet through the barrel of a gun not only leaves marks from the barrel on the bullet, it changes the barrel slightly by friction, so that marks left on the next bullet may be slightly different.

Third, referring to the people or objects that might have caused the residue as candidates, we have the problem of inter-candidate similarity, that is, more than one object may have been capable of causing a residue indistinguishable from the one at hand in one or all dimensions. Thus, given two nearly new screwdrivers of the same size and make, the blades may be so much alike, and the wood on a jimmied windowsill may retain detail so imperfectly, that is impossible to tell which blade left marks on the sill.

Failure to accurately separate important from unimportant characteristics, ac-

**[Section 4:11]**

[1]The term "tagged residue" to describe this class of phenomena is a neologism. No functionally similar term exists in the forensic science literature.

[2]In regard to handwriting, Albert S. Osborn was much more willing to assume total independence of characteristics than some of his successors have been. Compare Albert S. Osborn, Questioned Documents at 229 et seq. (2d ed. 1929) with W.R. Harrison, Suspect Documents: Their Scientific Examination (1958) at 306–307; and Ordway Hilton, Scientific Examination of Questioned Documents, at 9, n. 11 (revised ed., 1982; reprinted 1993). However, all seem confident that in practice there is sufficient individuality to distinguish any two adults' handwriting dependably if the samples presented are large enough. With questioned writings, of course, in contrast to known exemplars, the writing sample often consists of very little.

curately assess dependence and reflect accurate notions of base rate within the candidate population, whether conscious, analytic and quantified, or unconscious, impressionistic and unquantified, can obviously lead to error, though the fact that the conclusion is error may not be obvious. Failure to properly deal with the effects of intra-source variation or inter-candidate similarity is a further important potential source of error.

These problems are present in all tagged residue situations, though they may be at their most troublesome in the area of handwriting identification. It is obvious that each time a person writes, the individual letters are not formed with mechanical similarity to previously made letters. That creates a protean problem of intra-source (i.e., intra-writer) variation. Less obvious is that it may be that some writers write so much alike that their writing cannot be distinguished confidently, at least with limited samples.[3] This renders inter-candidate (inter-writer) similarity a significant problem. It seems fair to say that when intra-source variation, or inter-candidate similarity, or both, rise to a substantial level, dependable individualization becomes impossible.

In principle, there is nothing in the nature of a tagged residue problem that prevents a science of tagged residue individualization from being developed. For a source of asserted factual knowledge to qualify as scientific in the central modern sense, it must be the product of an enterprise displaying certain characteristics. Chief among these are:[4]

1. a systematic encouragement for gathering and publishing reproducible sense observations;

2. a taxonomy for organizing such observations which lends itself to dependable reproducibility of observation, and to quantification;

3. a process of hypothesis generation which results in statements about the world and its interrelationships which are consistent with all known observations and which are potentially amenable to falsification through empirical observation; and

4. an established regime which attempts to falsify new hypotheses empirically (and which is rewarded for doing so).

Moreover, although it is not a logical sine qua non of science, there is virtually universal recognition that academic institutions will play a significant role in the practice of science and the training of scientists in nearly every area.[5]

Some tagged residue individualization processes, such as DNA typing, are sci-

---

[3]Harris, How Much Do People Write Alike? A Study of Signatures, 48 J. Crim. L. & Criminology 647 (1958).

[4]For an expanded discussion, see Risinger, Denbeaux & Saks, Brave New "Post-*Daubert* World"—A Reply to Professor Moenssens, 29 Seton Hall L. Rev. 405, 435–439 (1998).

[5]By contrast, handwriting identification has no academic base. Training is by apprenticeship, and there is no standardization of training enforced either by any licensing agency or by professional tradition. Nor is there a single accepted professional certifying body. The Encyclopedia of Associations lists five different organizations: the National Association of Document Examiners; the National Bureau of Document Examiners; the World Association of Document Examiners; the Independent Association of Questioned Document Examiners and the American Society of Questioned Document Examiners. At least three of these organizations claim to grant certifications of competence. A glance at the credentials listed by document examiners advertising in various directories aimed at lawyers will quickly reveal at least four or five more such organizations. In an appendix to Moenssens, Handwriting Identification Evidence in the Post-*Daubert* World, 66 UMKC L. Rev. 2 (1998), Prof. Moenssens lists no fewer than *55* membership organizations involving persons who may claim competence in handwriting identification, many of which grant certifications of competence. (Moenssens describes these organizations in detail. See Risinger, Denbeaux & Saks, Brave New "Post-*Daubert* World"—A Reply to Professor Moenssens, 29 Seton Hall L. Rev. at 332–343 (1998)).

The American Society of Questioned Document Examiners, which one might characterize as the organization of the Osbornian establishment, is generally most vocal and aggressive in claiming its membership's superiority and, in fact, one

ences, because they are the application of knowledge gained through the process of science. Indeed, there might some day be a science of handwriting identification, and some small first steps have been made in that direction.[6] However, what forensic document examiners do is not science. There is nothing in the enterprise which results in or encourages organized reporting and publication of observations in a reproducible form. There is no agreed taxonomy of sufficient refinement to yield dependably quantified data, or dependably comparable observations of any refinement. There has been no theoretical revision of any significance in nearly a century, and there is no professional encouragement or reward for attempts to falsify those theories that exist.

## § 4:12 Areas of agreement: The possibility of a science of handwriting identification—Proposed principles of handwriting identification

The foundational principles of the expertise, as they were characterized by the expert relied upon by the prosecution in *Starzecpyzel*, are that no two people write exactly alike, and that no one person writes the same word exactly the same way twice.[1] It is most important to note that these two general principles are in their strong form nonscience metaphysical statements (though statements with an oddly commonsensical appeal). On some level, no two things can be *exactly* alike, and it is this intuition that underlies both statements. However, what science is concerned with is not metaphysical sameness, but *perceivable* similarities and differences that can be used to accurately assess common origin. When so recast, the statement that no two people write so alike that the differences are imperceptible is not intuitively obvious, nor is the claim that no one ever writes the same word so similarly that the differences are imperceptible. These forms are subject to potential testing by scientific methods, but they have been subjected to virtually no testing, and the small amount of data available do not provide much support for them. These were among the main reasons why Judge McKenna declared handwriting identification expertise to be nonscience in *Starzecpyzel*.[2]

What really occurs in practice is an example of the same kind of clinical empiric

---

object of the Moenssens article is to lend support to that claim. However, the certification testing program of its child, the American Board of Forensic Document Examiners (co-sponsored by the American Academy of Forensic Sciences) described by Mary Wenderoth Kelly (a member of that certifying board) in her testimony in *U.S. v. Starzecpyzel*, 880 F. Supp. 1027, 42 Fed. R. Evid. Serv. 247 (S.D. N.Y. 1995), leaves much to be desired. It was based on the administration of five from a pool of only seven or eight different test problems, only two or three of which involve handwriting identification. The same problems were used year after year on an honor system where they were sent to the candidates for certification through their teaching mentor, and left with them for a month unsupervised before the answers were returned. *Starzecpyzel Daubert* hearing transcript of testimony, 2/28/1995 at 48–59 (Kelly direct), at 175–192 (Kelly cross), 3/1/95 at 249–260 (Kelly cross), on file with the author. (Note: there may have been some changes in that certification procedure since Kelly's testimony as a result of criticisms like this one, but what, if any, the changes are is unclear, since the organization does not easily share information).

[6]See, e.g., references collected in Risinger et

al., Exorcism of Ignorance as a Proxy for Rational Knowledge: The Lessons of Handwriting Identification "Expertise", 137 U. Pa. L. Rev. 731 739, n. 31 (1989); and those referred to in *U.S. v. Starzecpyzel*, 880 F. Supp. 1027, 42 Fed. R. Evid. Serv. 247 (S.D. N.Y. 1995), and see particularly the National Institute of Justice funded project described § 4:40.

[Section 4:12]

[1]Mary Wenderoth Kelly, quoted by Judge McKenna in *U.S. v. Starzecpyzel*, 880 F. Supp. 1027, 1032, 42 Fed. R. Evid. Serv. 247 (S.D. N.Y. 1995). At the time of her testimony Ms. Kelly was a document examiner with the Cleveland Police Department with 13 years of experience. She was a director of the American Society of Questioned Document Examiners and a Fellow in the Questioned Document Section of the American Academy of Forensic Sciences. She is certified by the American Board of Forensic Document Examiners and at the time of her testimony served on that board as Vice President and Chair of the Committee on Testing. Starzecpyzel Daubert hearing transcript of testimony, 2/28/95 at 17–19 (Kelly Direct).

[2]*U.S. v. Starzecpyzel*, 880 F. Supp. 1027, 1033–1034, 1038, 42 Fed. R. Evid. Serv. 247 (S.D.

that also underlies eyewitness identification, and many other everyday processes. Such a process is at root probabilistically derived, just as is formal science, but with two important differences. First, it is not based on standardized measurements of any precision, and second, the database of examples that defines which characteristics are common and which are unusual is not public, recorded for all who will take the time to see and evaluate. Rather, it is private, based on the experiences of the individual practitioner over a long period of time, and stored internally in such a way that many or most of the individual data may be beyond conscious recall. The problem with such a process is that it is only as good as the unexaminable personal database of the practitioner, and the practitioner's not-fully-explainable method of deriving answers to such problems as, in the case of handwriting identification, what constitutes significant intra-writer variation and inter-writer similarity. The practitioner's opinion may be given the appearance of an explanation by pointing out similarities (or differences) between the questioned document and the exemplars, and by assertions that such characteristics are, in the practitioner's experience, common or uncommon. Arguably, however, any opinion of common authorship will have some similarities to support it, and any differences can be assigned to intra-writer variation (usually called "natural" variation[3]).

## § 4:13    Areas of agreement: The possibility of a science of handwriting identification—A summary of handwriting identification practice

Handwriting identification theory does have some process principles and some general rules which are at least not counterintuitive, and which, if followed, cut the ring down somewhat on saying just anything. The following is an attempt to give a fair summary of the main outlines of those asserted principles and that process in regard to its two most common general applications, signatures and anonymous writings:[1]

(1)    there is signal in a handwriting trace which will allow an observer to establish who wrote it dependably under conditions which are usually (but not always) present;[2]

(2)    this is because of the development of many personal characteristics in handwriting over time which combine to make a virtually unique individual

---

N.Y. 1995).

[3]See the discussion in *U.S. v. Starzecpyzel*, 880 F. Supp. 1027, 1031–1033, 42 Fed. R. Evid. Serv. 247 (S.D. N.Y. 1995).

**[Section 4:13]**

[1]No effort has been made to deal comprehensively with every area of handwriting examination doctrine. For instance, there is no specific treatment of disguise, juvenile handwriting, etc. The purpose of the text is to give the reader unfamiliar with orthodox handwriting examination doctrine a fair sample of its main positions and methodologies.

[2]Albert S. Osborn, Questioned Documents (1910) at 200–208. The first edition of Osborn's Questioned Documents has been chosen as the primary source of footnotes to emphasize its foundational status. Only on the rare occasions where some later book offered a clear qualification or variation is that other referenced. However, anyone wondering whether the main outlines of the summary given here still reflect current theory need only compare it to Ordway

Hilton's article on the subject in 13 Encyclopedia Americana (1992), at 765. Other works thoroughly examined in preparing this summary include: Charles Chabot, The Handwriting of Junius Professionally Examined (Edward Twistleton ed., John Murray and Sons, London, 1871), William E. Hagan, Disputed Handwriting, (Banks & Bros., Albany, 1894); D.T. Ames, Ames on Forgery (Bancroft-Whitney, San Francisco, 1899) Albert S. Osborn, Questioned Documents 6 (2d ed. 1929); Albert S. Osborn, Questioned Document Problems (2d ed., Albert D. Osborn ed., 1946); F. Breasted, Contested Documents and Forgeries (1932); Ordway Hilton, The Scientific Examination of Questioned Documents (1956); Ordway Hilton, Scientific Examination of Questioned Documents, at 9, n. 11 (revised ed., 1982; reprinted 1993); J.V.P. Conway, Evidential Documents, (1959); W.R. Harrison, Suspect Documents: Their Scientific Examination (1958) at 306–307; L. Caput, Questioned Document Case Studies (1982); David Ellen, The Scientific Examination of Documents: Methods and Techniques 9 (1989).

pattern;[3] which can be determined by observation of sufficient examples of the handwriting to derive the pattern[4] even in the face of inevitable variation around the pattern in any given piece of writing;[5]

(3)    this individual pattern is almost impossible to duplicate undiscoverably even by someone of skill trying to do so, because the variables are too numerous and inconspicuous, and also because the unconscious conflicting personal habits of the writer will manifest themselves either from the beginning or in a very short time;[6]

(4)    even when it cannot be established positively who left the trace, information in the trace may exclude a candidate writer;[7]

(5)    the best way to dependably extract information from the trace is not by gestalt exam, which is not totally useless but often misleading;[8] but by a system of atomized analysis of elements;[9]

(6)    atomized analysis breaks the trace down into components, some of which are measurable, some not.[10] The usual system is a frankly incomplete taxonomy[11] with many categories not suited to objective measurement, or to only imprecise estimate;[12]

(7)    handwriting questioned documents are either signatures alone, or other more or less extended writing, with or without signatures;

(8)    signatures generally are the most personal and uniform of writings;[13] though some people may have more than one signature for different uses or contexts;[14]

(9)    when dealing with a signature, two questions are commonly asked: Did the person whose name is reflected sign it (is it genuine)? Second, did some other particular person sign it if it is not genuine? Under most circumstances determining whether or not a signature is genuine is the easier task to perform;[15]

(10)   on the issue of genuineness, start with the questioned signature,[16] and observe:

    (a)    the signature as a whole, determining the dominant general underlying handwriting system it represents[17] (if possible; everybody learned some system to start, though some people have been exposed to more than one system even when learning by virtue of moving between schools or cultures);[18]

    (b)    the size of the writing compared to usual signatures of people in general on comparable documents;[19]

    (c)    location of words in regard to the (real or imaginary) signature line:

---

[3]Osborn, 1st ed., at 197.

[4]Osborn, 1st ed., at 196, 231.

[5]Osborn, 1st ed., at 196–197, 231.

[6]Osborn, 1st ed., at 237–238.

[7]Osborn, 1st ed., at 19.

[8]Osborn, 1st ed., at 206, 244–245, 262–263.

[9]Osborn, 1st ed., at 30, 209, 242–243, 253.

[10]Osborn, 1st ed., at 110.

[11]Osborn, 1st ed., at 209.

[12]Osborn, 1st ed., at 209.

[13]Osborn, 1st ed., at 210; see also Ordway Hilton, Scientific Examination of Questioned Documents, at 168, n. 4 (revised ed., 1982; reprinted 1993).

[14]Albert S. Osborn, Questioned Documents (1910) at 210.

[15]Albert S. Osborn, Questioned Documents (1910) at 13.

[16]Actually, Osborn takes the position that it is best to start with an analysis of the known standards before examining the questioned signature, but concedes this is often not possible in practice. Albert S. Osborn, Questioned Documents (1910) at 243–244.

[17]Albert S. Osborn, Questioned Documents (1910) at 190, 263.

[18]Albert S. Osborn, Questioned Documents (1910) at 190, 263. See generally §§ 9:1 et seq.

[19]Albert S. Osborn, Questioned Documents (1910) at 144–145.

above, below, trending up or down;[20]

(d)   any oddities of letter alignment relative to the words, above or below the general alignment;[21]

(e)   proportion of parts: the ratio of the height to the width of the various lowercase "minimum" letters (like a, o, i, c, etc.) and the base parts of the other lower case letters;[22] the proportion of tall lower case letters above the base line to the height of minimum letters;[23] the proportion of lower case letter extensions below the baseline to minimum letters,[24] and any divergences and oddities from the general pattern for individual letters;[25] proportion of capitals to minimums, and the height-width ratio of capitals;[26]

(f)   slant of writing measured with glass protractor or goniometer,[27] with any

---

[20]Albert S. Osborn, Questioned Documents (1910) at 142.

[21]Albert S. Osborn, Questioned Documents (1910) at 123–124, 142.

[22]Albert S. Osborn, Questioned Documents (1910) at 146.

[23]Albert S. Osborn, Questioned Documents (1910) at 145–148, 215, 309–310.

[24]Albert S. Osborn, Questioned Documents (1910) at 246.

[25]Albert S. Osborn, Questioned Documents (1910) at 246.

[26]Albert S. Osborn, Questioned Documents (1910) at 145–148, 215, 309–310.

[27]Albert S. Osborn, Questioned Documents (1910) at 150–154, 246. Harrison supplies the word "goniometer." W.R. Harrison, Suspect Documents: Their Scientific Examination (1958) at 330. Harrison asserts that by his date of publication (1959) most writing submitted to his laboratory in England had such variable slant (called "slope" by him) that it was not worth trying to measure. W.R. Harrison, Suspect Documents: Their Scientific Examination (1958) at 330.

Here we must consider the role in document examination of that cornerstone of modern science, actual measurement in reproducible quantified standard units of measurement. Osborn had a chapter on measuring instruments in both editions of his book, and the characteristics we are dealing with, such as proportion of parts of various letters, are potentially subject to standard quantified measurement, with mathematical expression of central tendency and variation, etc. In this regard Osborn was on some level aware of the potential value of measurement, and wrote: "The various parts of an ordinary signature when carefully measured bear a certain proportion to each other that with most writers is found to be surprisingly uniform . . . when a considerable amount of writing is in question and an adequate amount of standard writing is supplied for comparison, a system of measurements covering a sufficient number of features and examples may be very forceful evidence . . . any system of averages, to be reliable, must be based on an adequate

number of examples." Osborn 1st Ed. at 146. However, Osborn then goes on to say, "Evidence based on the very great number of measurements necessary to show a very slight divergence is not usually of much weight in this or any similar inquiry, because it is practically impossible for court and jury to review and verify the basis of such an opinion. If the difference is apparent by inspection, then the measurements are of value in making definite what is apparently a fact without such proof." Osborn 1st Ed. at 146–147. In the rest of the book, Osborn recommended the actual quantified measurement of very few handwriting characteristics (as opposed to typewriting, for instance), slant being primary among them. Though Osborn occasionally refers to the "size," "position" and "distance" of characteristics (for instance, Osborn 1st Ed. at 246–247, 309–310), in practice all characteristics but slant seem to have been subject to rough subjective estimation with no precise standard measurement at all. Instead, visual charts are relied upon to illustrate assertions of "size," "position," and "distance." Certainly there is no indication in the *Hauptmann* trial testimony of Osborn, his son, or any of the other experts, of actual quantified measurement of characteristics. Albert S. Osborn testimony, 1/11/35, Hauptmann transcript at 881–1008; Albert S. Osborn testimony, 1/14/35, at 1009–1051; Elbridge W. Stein testimony, 1/14/35, at 1074–1153; John F. Tyrell testimony, 1/15/35, at 1154–1247; Herbert J. Walter testimony, 1/15/35, at 1248–1271; Harry M. Cassidy testimony, 1/16/35, at 1279–1301; Wilmer T. Souder testimony, 1/16/35, at 1301–1336; Albert D. Osborn testimony, 1/16/45, at 1337–1386; Clark Sellers testimony, 1/16/35, at 1386–1432. Actual measurement appears to play no greater role in standard practice today than in 1935. As Ordway Hilton said in his 1974 Preface to a facsimile edition of Bibliotics, "While certain workers continued to urge the use of measurements, the method has virtually been discarded as too time consuming for the little value which might be derived from it." Persifor Frazer, Bibliotics ii (3d ed. 1901, reprinted 1974). Frazer was one of the few who championed actual measurements. It is regrettable that his view was rejected.

Interestingly, one of the earliest exercises

divergences from general slant for individual letters noted. Some slants may be nearly chaotic;[28]

(g)  presence or absence of lines connecting words or initials, and their form;[29]

(h)  presence and placement of punctuation relative to initials;[30]

(i)  character and construction of connections between letters: smalls to smalls and capitals to smalls;[31]

(j)  initial strokes, presence or absence, and how formed;[32]

(k)  presence and placement of any pen lifts within words,[33] and whether they result in discontinuities (spaces) between letters in the middle of words;[34]

(l)  forms of each individual letter: general pictorial style, existence of loops, retraces, decorations and flourishes, open tops, etc., with observation of variation in form as letters are repeated;[35] whether variation correlates with position in the word, beginning or middle;[36] forms of endings of terminal letters,[37] method of crossing t's,[38] presence and form of i-dots,[39] etc. Generally, some judgement should be made concerning the rarity of those characteristics (like undotted i's) which diverge from the underlying system.[40] Look also for abbreviated letters (letters only partially made or suggested) which are likely to be relatively personal characteristics;[41]

(m)  consider the dynamics that created the static trace.[42] Try to infer pen position and arm and finger movements from line quality[43] (much harder

---

in analytic handwriting identification in the United States involved an attempt to be quite precise both in measurement and mathematics. In the famous Howland Will Case of 1865, which involved a claim to the substantial Howland fortune by the infamous Hetty Green (then Hetty Howland Robinson), Hetty was accused of forging by tracing the signature on the will upon which she relied. Renowned Harvard mathematician Benjamin Peirce and his (later) even more renowned son Charles Sanders Peirce were hired to examine the signature on the will. They devised a method which relied on defining the beginning point of downstrokes, of which there were 30 in the signature. Comparing 42 genuine Sylvia Ann Howland signatures, each to all others (which gave 25,830 comparisons), they determined that any given downstroke start position would coincide using their measurement system only about one time in five. They then compared the challenged will signature with the signature claimed to be the tracing model and found perfect coincidence of the start position of all 30 downstrokes. Using their previous examination to provide the base rate data, they gave the random match probability of one divided by 5 to the 30th power, or one over 2666 followed by 10 zeros. Benjamin Peirce then asserted that "so vast an improbability is practically an impossibility. Such evanescent shadows of probability cannot belong to real life . . . . It is utterly repugnant to sound reason to attribute this coincidence to any cause but design." See Louis Menand, She Had To Have It: The Heiress, The Fortune and the Forgery, The New Yorker, April 23 & 30, 2001, at 62–70.

[28]W.R. Harrison, Suspect Documents: Their Scientific Examination (1958) at 330.

[29]Albert S. Osborn, Questioned Documents at 143 (2d ed. 1929).

[30]Albert S. Osborn, Questioned Documents at 143 (2d ed. 1929).

[31]Albert S. Osborn, Questioned Documents (1910) at 225–226.

[32]Albert S. Osborn, Questioned Documents (1910) at 220.

[33]Albert S. Osborn, Questioned Documents (1910) at 121–123.

[34]Albert S. Osborn, Questioned Documents (1910) at 121–123.

[35]Albert S. Osborn, Questioned Documents (1910) at 246–247.

[36]W.R. Harrison, Suspect Documents: Their Scientific Examination (1958) at 301.

[37]Albert S. Osborn, Questioned Documents (1910) at 220, 248.

[38]Albert S. Osborn, Questioned Documents (1910) at 218–219, 248.

[39]Albert S. Osborn, Questioned Documents (1910) at 248.

[40]Albert S. Osborn, Questioned Documents (1910) at 228; expanded upon in Albert S. Osborn, Questioned Documents at 264–266 (2d ed. 1929).

[41]Albert S. Osborn, Questioned Documents (1910) at 247; elaborated upon in Albert S. Osborn, Questioned Documents at 253–257 (2d ed. 1929).

[42]Albert S. Osborn, Questioned Documents (1910) at 106.

[43]Albert S. Osborn, Questioned Documents (1910) at 106.

now that nib pen writing is uncommon);[44]

    (i)      direction of stroke—this detail was revealed by shading in the days of nib pens, and was not analyzed separately by Osborn, since stroke direction was then both obvious and apparently more standard. Non-standard stroke direction is not mentioned in Osborn's first edition and is mentioned only twice in the second edition.[45] With the coming of ball point pens and the degeneration of standard writing discipline, stroke direction appears to have taken on a more important role in attempted identification, especially of block printing, and principals for its inference from various characteristics of the static trace have been proposed;[46]

    (ii)      speed—by looking at smoothness and length of curves, classifying writing from slow to rapid (sometimes has evidence of both in different parts);[47]

    (iii)      blunt or pointed beginning or ending strokes showing drawn starts and stops, or flying starts and stops;[48]

    (iv)      muscle movement[49] (very hard to infer accurately absent nib pen);

    (v)      pen alignment[50] (very hard to infer accurately absent nib pen);[51]

    (vi)      pen pressure—shown by depth of pen indentation into paper, heaviness of ink, width of line, etc.;[52]

    (vii)      impulse—sudden changes of direction, may require magnification

---

[44]Ordway Hilton, Scientific Examination of Questioned Documents, at 156, n. 11 (revised ed., 1982; reprinted 1993); W.R. Harrison, Suspect Documents: Their Scientific Examination (1958) at 330.

[45]Osborn 1st ed. at 360, 408. Both these mentions are in regard to photographic illustrations without further discussion in the text.

[46]David Ellen, The Scientific Examination of Documents: Methods and Techniques at 15–18 (1989). See also Ordway Hilton, Scientific Examination of Questioned Documents, at 211, n. 11 (revised ed., 1982; reprinted 1993).

[47]Albert S. Osborn, Questioned Documents (1910) at 110, 113, 117.

[48]Albert S. Osborn, Questioned Documents (1910) at 248.

[49]Albert S. Osborn, Questioned Documents (1910) at 105–109.

[50]Albert S. Osborn, Questioned Documents (1910) at 128, 242.

[51]Ordway Hilton, Scientific Examination of Questioned Documents, at 156, n. 11 (revised ed., 1982; reprinted 1993).

[52]Albert S. Osborn, Questioned Documents (1910) at 132–134. This is as good a place as any to talk about the great cleavage in the handwriting identification community, the gulf between the orthodox Osbornians and the graphology-influenced practitioners. The orthodox Osbornians reject any role for theories developed by those seeking to read personality characteristics from handwriting in the identification of authorship, citing, ironically, the absence of validation for those theories. The graphology-oriented practitioners tend to believe in graphology, but they assert that one doesn't have to believe specific character traits are revealed by handwriting in order to gain useful insights into identification from graphological studies. While both Osbornians and graphological practitioners assert that inferences concerning dynamic aspects of writing from the trace can be important in identification of authorship, graphological practitioners tend to make them primary, with many paying particular attention to pen pressure. A number of further ironies must be reported in this regard. First, while it is true that the Orthodox Osbornians have occupied most prominent positions in the document examiner community in the last 90 years, and have controlled the membership of the American Society of Questioned Document Examiners and certification by the American Board of Questioned Document Examiners, there may be a greater number of graphologically-oriented practitioners doing everyday work in court, being heavily represented in the numerically larger membership of organizations such as the National Association of Document Examiners, the World Association of Document Examiners and the Independent Association of Questioned Document Examiners. Second, it was only the more scientifically oriented of the graphologists, and none of the Osbornians, who performed any empirical studies on the handwriting phenomenon worthy of the name empirical from the 1920s to the 1980s, even going so far as to develop a specially instrumented pen called a graphodyne to record the dynamic aspects of writing as it was taking place, the forerunner of today's digitized pressure tablets used in academic motor control studies which utilize hand-

to be counted accurately, can be counted for individual up strokes and downstrokes;[53]

    (viii)  impulse grades into tremor—rapid shaking (important to note on what strokes present, since tremor of old age or nervousness may be less on up strokes or final stroke than tremor of fraud resulting from trying to draw a facsimile under pressure); and[54]

    (ix)  general line impression: flowing, free, rhythmic, halting, slow or drawn.[55]

  (n)  keep alert for retouching, and pen stops or lifts at angles, or on first or last stroke, or other unnatural places.[56]

(11)  at this point, even without exemplars, a signature may be classified as suspicious if it appears slow and drawn with blunt beginning and ending strokes, much retouching, odd pen lifts, many angular direction changes on what would usually be curves, coupled with tremor on other strokes, especially if all of this occurs in a signature which does not appear erratic and out of control on a gross level;[57]

(12)  to reach a firmer conclusion, one needs exemplars of genuine signatures, preferably from documents of like kind and like formality from the same time period during which the questioned signature was alleged to have been signed.[58] In addition, the examiner should know any claimed circumstances surrounding the making of the questioned signature that might affect the value of an exemplar, such as age or disease.[59] There should be as many exemplars as possible up to about 50–75,[60] though in some circumstances even one, sufficiently close in time will be enough to expose a crude forgery;[61]

(13)  the known exemplars should be analyzed just like the questioned signature, and a range of variation for each dimension should be determined, though it usually cannot be quantified, but can be observed by juxtaposition of letter examples.[62] If the characteristics of the known exemplars are consistent in every respect with the questioned signature, then it is genuine unless it can

---

writing as a convenient motor control phenomenon. See generally, H. Hartford, You Are What You Write (1973), especially his account of C. A. Trip's invention of the graphodyne, at 107–108. Third, recent academic studies tend to indicate that the dynamic aspects of handwriting may indeed be more dependably indicative of individual authorship than other characteristics, though those studies have the advantage of analyzing the dynamic characteristics directly as they are performed, not by way of problematical inference back from the static trace. See 3/1/95 *Starzecpyzel Daubert* hearing testimony of Dr. George Stelmach, transcript pages 386–387, on file with the author. Finally, since government laboratories tend to be officially Osbornian, if there are few data on the dependability of identification of authorship by Osbornian practitioners, there are none on the dependability of graphologically oriented practitioners. For a description of this universe from a thoroughly Osbornian perspective (which excoriates even the mild credit where credit is due given graphologists in this footnote), see generally Moenssens, Handwriting Identification Evidence in the Post-*Daubert* World, 66 UMKC L. Rev. 2 (1998). For a response, see

Risinger, Denbeaux & Saks, Brave New "Post-*Daubert* World"—A Reply to Professor Moenssens, 29 Seton Hall L. Rev. at 483–486 (1998).

[53]Albert S. Osborn, Questioned Documents (1910) at 111–114.

[54]Albert S. Osborn, Questioned Documents (1910) at 116–121.

[55]Albert S. Osborn, Questioned Documents (1910) at 109–110.

[56]Albert S. Osborn, Questioned Documents (1910) at 248–249.

[57]Albert S. Osborn, Questioned Documents (1910) at 18, 245.

[58]Albert S. Osborn, Questioned Documents (1910) at 18, 22.

[59]Albert S. Osborn, Questioned Documents (1910) at 23–24, 216.

[60]Albert S. Osborn, Questioned Documents (1910) at 19.

[61]Albert S. Osborn, Questioned Documents (1910) at 19.

[62]Albert S. Osborn, Questioned Documents (1910) at 203, 243.

be shown to be a tracing,[63] though even a tracing should usually show evidence of being drawn rather than written.[64] If there are significant divergences it is not genuine, though what makes a divergence significant, how many divergences are necessary and how to weigh them is not quantified.[65] It is a fact-sensitive judgment, and even one inexplicable difference might show that the signature is not genuine;[66]

(14) it is much harder to determine accurately who wrote a spurious signature than to determine that it is spurious.[67] This is because a forger is either simulating, tracing from a model, or writing with no model of the true signature. In a tracing, no personal writing of the forger is present, and an attempt at simulation will usually suppress individuality enough in the short space of a signature that no conclusions can be drawn.[68] Only when someone signs another's name in the signer's own usual hand is identification a significant possibility, and even then the small amount of writing and the usual presence of some disguise makes a positive identification difficult.[69] However, there may be enough in a signature to exclude a person as a candidate. For instance, if the signature requires more skill and muscle control than the candidate can muster as determined by a sufficient set of exemplars, exclusion would be justified, because one cannot write with more skill than one has;[70]

(15) moving beyond signatures, affirmative identification of the writer of a questioned document depends on both the quantity of the questioned writing, and the quantity and quality of authentic exemplars of a candidate's writing that can be obtained.[71] Natural exemplars showing unselfconscious writing from about the time of the making of the questioned writing are best,[72] but demand exemplars may do if the questioned document is sufficiently recent and if care is taken to guard against disguise in the demand exemplars by the amount required, variations in speed of production required, etc.;[73]

(16) the analysis of both the questioned and the known writing will be done as

---

[63]Albert S. Osborn, Questioned Documents (1910) at 257–260, 266–301, 308.

[64]Albert S. Osborn, Questioned Documents (1910) at 267.

[65]Albert S. Osborn, Questioned Documents (1910) at 212, 214–215.

[66]Albert S. Osborn, Questioned Documents (1910) at 281.

[67]Albert S. Osborn, Questioned Documents (1910) at 13–14.

[68]Albert S. Osborn, Questioned Documents (1910) at 13–14.

[69]W.R. Harrison, Suspect Documents: Their Scientific Examination (1958) at 387. How uncommon it is to be able to make such a positive identification from the one or two words in such a signature is apparently the subject of some controversy among practitioners, since many of them apparently undertake to do it rather frequently. See the discussion of *U.S. v. Ruth, U.S. v. Jones,* and *U.S. v. Battle,* at § 4:6; and *U.S. v. Rutherford,* at § 4:7. However, the authorities in the field are uniformly skeptical. See the quotations set out at § 4:32.

[70]Albert S. Osborn, Questioned Documents (1910) at 110–112.

[71]Albert S. Osborn, Questioned Documents (1910) at 321.

[72]Albert S. Osborn, Questioned Documents (1910) at 18–19.

[73]Albert S. Osborn, Questioned Documents (1910) at 24–25. Different authors have elaborate notions of the best ways to take demand exemplars. Compare Albert S. Osborn, Questioned Documents at 33–34 (2d ed. 1929), with W.R. Harrison, Suspect Documents: Their Scientific Examination (1958) at 442–451, and Ordway Hilton, Scientific Examination of Questioned Documents, at 310–322, n. 11 (revised ed., 1982; reprinted 1993). Note that both Osborn and Harrison refer to these writings as "request writings" and Hilton refers to them as "request standards," but I have used the term "demand" because in practice that is what is involved in the usual case. They are usually given under court order and failure to cooperate can result in being jailed for contempt.

above in regard to signatures.[74] In addition, such habits as the layout and margins of the writing on the page will be added.[75] If sufficient peculiarities correspond between the two writings and there are no significant differences, the writer of the exemplars will be established as the writer of the questioned writing.[76] Which peculiarities are rare enough to be significant, which ones are independent of each other in their occurrence, how many are necessary, and how to weight them is not defined, but the following general principles are instructive:

(a) system characteristics of writing systems, foreign and domestic, cannot establish identity, even in combination.[77] Thus an examiner must be conversant with a wide range of such systems and their characteristics;[78]

(b) the most diagnostic idiosyncrasies are those which diverge furthest from the underlying system, which are inconspicuous,[79] and which are not common products of carelessness or the desire for speed (such as open o's and omitted i-dots); and[80]

(c) each case is different and must be judged on its own particular circumstances.[81]

## § 4:14 Areas of disagreement: Testing document examiner expertise

Nothing in the above is mystical or visibly implausible, but, as previously noted, that does not a science make. As sensible as much of it seems, none of the assertions are self-validating, and all are amenable to formal empirical testing which has never been undertaken. Even the assertion that an atomistic analysis leads to better results is not inevitable, as any baseball player whose swing was harmed by a bad batting coach could tell you. Likewise,the notion that a learned technique of such analysis, with so many elements of subjective judgement, in an area where clear evidence of accurate conclusions is often not available, will enable all or most people completing such training to give accurate conclusions on both hard and difficult problems, is dubious.

This is not to say that all identification by comparison of hands is necessarily inaccurate. Common experience, once again, confirms that under some circumstances we can recognize a writer by handwriting. There is a tagged signal present, at least sometimes, but how specific or dependably perceived it is in various circumstances is subject to debate. It may be that document examiners, or some of them, pick up a not-fully-analyzable knack of accurate identification of handwriting just by being exposed to a lot of it. It may be that the atomized analysis called for by their method of practice improves the accuracy of some or all of them a little or a lot.

Indeed, there is evidence that not all of the propositions that underlie the claimed ability to identifying handwriting with a high degree of accuracy are shared within the field of forensic handwriting examiners. And there is even less agreement when the question is put to more scientific handwriting experts who are not forensic

---

[74]Albert S. Osborn, Questioned Documents at 322 (2d ed. 1929).

[75]Albert S. Osborn, Questioned Documents at 142–143 (1st ed. 1929).

[76]See Albert S. Osborn, Questioned Documents at 211 (2d ed. 1929).

[77]Albert S. Osborn, Questioned Documents at 169, 206, 210, 214 (2d ed. 1929).

[78]Albert S. Osborn, Questioned Documents at 214 (2d ed. 1929).

[79]Albert S. Osborn, Questioned Documents at 210, 308 (2d ed. 1929).

[80]Albert S. Osborn, Questioned Documents at 261 (2d ed. 1929).

[81]Albert S. Osborn, Questioned Documents at 308 (2d ed. 1929); see generally What Osborn referred to as "true methods," Albert S. Osborn, Questioned Documents at 249–269 (2d ed. 1929).

examiners.[1] This has implications, of course, for even the weakest prong of admissibility "general acceptance."

Since such a practical expertise does not have the internal validation of a developed science, it requires the external validation given to an instrument, a black box process, that may or may not lead to dependable results. Here is where science can again come into play, because science can examine the dependability of the results of such a process even when the process is not science. Beyond their own assertions,[2] however, what evidence, if any, exists to show that document examiners can accurately identify or exclude authorship by comparison of hands, or do so better than the average person?

The answer is, relatively little. In an article published in 1989 in the University

---

**[Section 4:14]**

[1]See Saks & VanderHaar, On the "General Acceptance" of Handwriting Identification Principles, 50 J. Forensic Sciences 119 (2005).

[2]In *General Electric Co. v. Joiner* and again in *Kumho Tire*, the Supreme Court of the United States warned the courts against the admission of proffered expert testimony based solely on the "ipse dixit of the expert," *Kumho Tire Co., Ltd. v. Carmichael*, 526 U.S. 137, 157, 119 S. Ct. 1167, 143 L. Ed. 2d 238, 50, 50 U.S.P.Q.2d 1177, Prod. Liab. Rep. (CCH) P 15470, 50 Fed. R. Evid. Serv. 1373, 29 Envtl. L. Rep. 20638 (1999), quoting *General Elec. Co. v. Joiner*, 522 U.S. 136, 146, 118 S. Ct. 512, 139 L. Ed. 2d 508, 18 O.S.H. Cas. (BNA) 1097, Prod. Liab. Rep. (CCH) P 15120, 48 Fed. R. Evid. Serv. 1, 28 Envtl. L. Rep. 20227, 177 A.L.R. Fed. 667 (1997). We must distinguish among three types of evidence derived by reference to the experts "own assertions," to use the phrase in the text. The first type is simply self faith: "We know we're good because we believe we are," or, "we know we're accurate because we follow the revealed true method in reaching our results." The second type is anecdotal: "In such and such a case, I identified the right person, or was right concerning the forged nature of the document." These anecdotes can further be divided into a number of varieties: The first variety is: "I know I was right because other evidence in the case established the facts independently." In these cases, the examiner almost always, in today's practice, may have known these facts before the examination, so that the handwriting conclusions may be more the result of revelation to the examiner of other facts than the examiner's independent analysis. For example, the opinions in the Lindbergh case are all subject to this suspicion. The second variety is: "the trier of fact agreed with me." Obviously, there may be ego gratification in this, but this factor alone does not establish accuracy. The third variety is "after my opinion, the defendant confessed, or pleaded guilty, or otherwise admitted I was right." The problem with these anecdotes is that guilty pleas do not very clearly prove factual accuracy, and that the confession or admission cases are usually built on other evidence, which tends to make them

overlap with the first kind of anecdote. All of these various versions of "taking the expert's word" as evidence of validity, are weak proxies for a third type of more defensible self-belief, based on a gold standard of empirically unmistakable knowledge of authorship against which the examiners may compare their conclusions, such as harbor pilots have in their actual practice, but which document examiners usually do not. The real risk is that the examiners themselves will make more out of the proxy feedback and self-affirmation than it is rationally worth. That is not to say that there is no anecdotal evidence of value. There are well known cases of miscarriage by document examiners, the existence of which contradicts at least the more extravagant claims concerning the dependability of the expertise, such as those attributed to FBI document section chief Ronald Furgerson by David Fisher in his book *Hard Evidence* that all "180" "certified" document examiners in the United States would reach the same conclusions in any given case as he would. See David Fisher, Hard Evidence (1995) at 196. *Vide* Albert S. Osborn's grandson Russell Osborn's mistaken authentication of Clifford Irving's Howard Hughes forgery (see Stephen Fay et al., Hoax 129–133 (1973)), the Hitler Diaries hoax, etc. See generally, K.W. Rendell, Forging History (1994). The data summarized, §§ 4:15 to 4:20, from the Forensic Sciences Foundation's proficiency studies, showing high rates of disagreement among document examiners, raise grave doubts about the validity such claims. On the other side, there are equally remarkable successes which suggest that under the right conditions and in the best hands, handwriting comparison can do remarkable things. *Vide* the proof of Michele Sindona's 1981 return to the U.S. through the writing on one customs card among thousands in an assumed name (confirmed by a fingerprint on the card), and the 1956 capture of Joseph LaMarca, the Peter Weinberger kidnapper, by identification of his handwriting from among millions of public records documents. In both these cases there was a very striking and easily recognized peculiarity in the handwriting. See Fisher, Hard Evidence, supra, at 196–198.

of Pennsylvania Law Review, Risinger, et al. reported a full literature search[3] and turned up only one published study bearing on the question, plus five unpublished studies carried out by the Forensic Sciences Foundation (FSF).[4] The only published study, Inbau's Lay Witness Identification of Testimony,[5] had such a small number of participants and was so methodologically flawed, that it yielded no informative data on any issue. Though Risinger et al. sparked controversy, in the years since there have been only a handful of new studies: one readministration of one of the FSF studies utilizing a control group of non-document examiner subjects,[6] two more relevant FSF studies,[7] and four studies by Dr. Moshe Kam and his colleagues, most commissioned by the FBI.[8] All of these will be examined in turn.[9]

## § 4:15  Areas of disagreement: Testing document examiner expertise—Forensic Sciences Foundation proficiency tests: 1975–1987

The results of the original Forensic Sciences Foundation (FSF) studies may or may not have yielded significant data, depending on one's perspective. The studies were designed as proficiency tests for government crime laboratories. They were taken only by a voluntarily self-selected group of such laboratories who, for each test, decided to request the test materials and to return their results. The necessity of having comparable test materials administered to each participating laboratory

---

[3]In their article, The "Principle of the Drunkard's Search" as a Proxy for Scientific Analysis: The Misuse of Handwriting Test Data in a Law Journal Article, 1 Int'l J. of Forensic Document Examiners 7 (1995), Oliver Galbraith, Craig S. Galbraith and Nanette G. Galbraith criticize the thoroughness of that search, and their title is even taken from the punch line to an old joke meant to ridicule the search as having looked where it was convenient to look rather than where the answer lay. Ironically, Risinger et al., Exorcism of Ignorance as a Proxy for Rational Knowledge: The Lessons of Handwriting Identification "Expertise," 137 U. Pa. L. Rev. 731 739, n. 31 (1989), took the unusual step of describing in some detail their literature search strategy, and it was a thoroughgoing one. The easiest way to prove that Risinger et al. overlooked important research, of course, would be simply to come forward with it. Despite years of grousing, it took nearly 13 years before anyone could cite a single empirical study or other test data bearing on the issue of handwriting examiner accuracy which existed at the time Risinger et al. was published which was not addressed in that article. § 4:33.

[4]In 1975, under a grant from the Law Enforcement Assistance Administration, the Forensic Sciences Foundation (FSF) set out to create proficiency tests for forensic expert specialties, among them handwriting identification. The results of the 1975 pilot test were later reported in Joseph L. Peterson, Ellen L. Fabricant & Kenneth S. Field, Crime Laboratory Proficiency Testing Research Program, Final Report (1978). A permanent yearly testing program was begun in 1978 and a handwriting component was added in 1984. See Risinger et al., Exorcism of Ignorance as a Proxy for Rational Knowledge: The Lessons of Handwriting Identification "Expertise," 137 U. Pa. L. Rev. at 740, n. 31 (1989). These tests were

"operated and maintained by Collaborative Testing Services, Inc." (a contract consultant in test design) "with assistance provided by the Forensic Sciences Foundation," and technical supervision "by the Proficiency Advisory Committee, a committee of the American Society of Crime Laboratory Directors." See the Introduction to Crime Laboratory Proficiency Testing Program, Questioned Documents Analysis, Report No. 89-5 (1989). These tests are referred to collectively as the "FSF studies."

[5]34 Ill. L. Rev. 433 (1939).

[6]Reported in The "Principle of the Drunkard's Search" as a Proxy for Scientific Analysis: The Misuse of Handwriting Test Data in a Law Journal Article, 1 Int'l J. of Forensic Document Examiners 7 (1995), Oliver Galbraith, Craig S. Galbraith and Nanette G. Galbraith.

[7]FSF tests, 1988 and 1989.

[8]Kam, Wetstein & Conn, Proficiency of Professional Document Examiners in Writer Identification, 39 J. Forensic Sci. 5 (1994) (hereinafter Kam I); Kam, Fielding & Conn, Writer Identification by Professional Document Examiners, 42 J. Forensic Sci. 778 (1997) (hereinafter Kam II); Kam, Fielding & Conn, The Effects of Monetary Incentives on Document Examination Professionals, 43 J. Forensic Sci. 1000 (1998) (hereinafter, Kam III); Kam, Gummadidala, Fielding & Conn, Signature Authentication by Forensic Document Examiners, 46 J. Forensic Sci. 884 (2001) (hereinafter, Kam IV).

[9]Because the forensic document examination field's body of systematic empirical literature is so meager, averaging a little more than one study every two years since the publication of Exorcism, and virtually none in the century of practice before that, the close examination of each new study is warranted.

meant that the test materials had to be photocopies rather than original documents, and the test-takers all knew that they were taking a test rather than working on a real case. The FSF itself officially took the position that the results were not necessarily representative of the actual level of performance in the field. However, the FSF could not have regarded the tests as so problematical as to be meaningless, or they would not have continued to administer them, and they have been continued under the supervision of the American Society of Crime Laboratory Directors.

Beyond these considerations, there is the ever-present problem of test design itself. Designing meaningful studies to test the validity and reliability of a diagnostic process like handwriting identification is not as easy as it might at first appear.[1] As we have seen, a process such as handwriting identification presents a number of potential subtasks dealing with variables such as writing instruments, forgery of various sorts, age, health, and so forth. No single test can map the abilities of any one practitioner, or any group of practitioners. A great many tests (certainly more than have yet been designed and administered) would be necessary to know what, if anything, they can do accurately, and under what conditions. A complete testing regime would have tests which covered the entire spectrum of conditions and difficulties. In addition, the law not only cares about the likely accuracy of results by putative experts, but also about whether the results obtained and testified to by the experts leads to more accurate conclusions than would result if the jurors did the comparisons directly without such testimony. "Expertise" exists only if there is a significant accuracy advantage of the putative expert over the average juror. Thus, the tests ideally should be administered to control groups of ordinary people to see if such an accuracy advantage exists.

With these caveats in mind, following is a summary of the tests and results available to Risinger et. al. through 1987 as the FSF reported them.[2]

## § 4:16    Areas of disagreement: Testing document examiner expertise— Forensic Sciences Foundation proficiency tests: 1975–1987—The 1975 test

In 1975, the participating laboratories were given a letter made up of both handwriting and typewriting. In addition, they received four examples of handwriting written by four different people. The problem was to determine whether the handwriting on the questioned document was written by any of the four "suspects." In reality, the questioned letter had been written by one of the suspects. Of the 74 laboratories that responded:

66 (89%) correctly identified the writer of the questioned letter;

1 (1%) gave a partially correct and partially incorrect answer (attributing part of the writing in the questioned letter to the right "suspect" but another part to another "wrong" suspect);

4 (5%) asserted that they could not reach any conclusion from the materials supplied them;

3 (4%) identified the wrong person.

---

**[Section 4:15]**

[1]*Vide* the problems Kam et al. have had in design, resulting in a steady refinement from Kam I through Kam IV. See discussion of the Kam studies at §§ 4:27 to 4:31.

[2]In Risinger et al. there are extensive footnotes to specific pages of the FSF reports for virtually each line of text. These have been omitted and, further, no such notes have been inserted in regard to the more recent FSF studies. The FSF reports are short and not easily obtainable. If the reader does not obtain them, page references obviously are useless; if the reader manages to obtain them, page references are unnecessary.

## §4:17 Areas of disagreement: Testing document examiner expertise— Forensic Sciences Foundation proficiency tests: 1975–1987—The 1984 test

In 1984 participating labs were supplied with three handwritten letters containing bomb threats, supposedly received by the news media and then followed by terrorist bombings. The labs were also given two pages of known handwriting samples for each of six suspects (a total of 12 pages). They were to determine if the three questioned letters had all been written by the same person, and whether any or all of the questioned letters had been written by any of the suspects. Two of the threat letters were in fact written by one person, who was not among the suspects and whose actual known writing was not given to the labs. The other threat letter was written by one of the suspects whose exemplars were in his normal hand, but who had tried to simulate the writing of the other two threat letters when producing *his* threat letter.

Forty-one labs requested the test materials but only 23 submitted answers. Of those:

17 (74%) perceived the difference in authorship of letter 3;

6 (26)% said erroneously that the same person wrote all three threat letters;

23 (100%) failed to recognize that letter 3 was written by one of the suspects for whom they had known writings.[1]

---

**[Section 4:17]**

[1]Judging from comments at a meeting of the Document Examination Section of the American Academy of Forensic Sciences (February, 1996, Nashville, TN), this question and the finding of 100% error is the single greatest object of complaint by questioned document examiners concerning the FSF tests, a complaint that has some validity, but not as much as they assert. The usual form of their objection appears to be something like, "we don't claim to be able to determine the authorship of a writing made while trying to imitate some other person's writing." (Such an attempt is called "simulation" or "simulated forgery" in normal document examiner parlance.) First, as the authorities cited at § 4:13, point number 14, supra, demonstrate, the orthodox Osbornian position is not that such attribution of authorship is categorically impossible, but merely that it is extremely difficult, because attempting to imitate someone else's writing is an effective way to disguise one's own writing, and may be so effective at suppressing individuality that identification is impossible. Second, many examiners are willing to do such attributions in practice. See discussions of *Ruth, Jones,* and *Battle* at § 4:6, and *Rutherford* at § 4:7. The real underlying complaint concerning Question 2 in the 1984 FSF test seems to be that the skill of the simulator was unusual, and even though the writing was in a fairly generous amount, the simulator managed to suppress all identifying characteristics. (It should be noted that there is no specific evidence the simulator in fact was unusually skilled. The argument is circular: since we couldn't identify the writer, he or she must have been exceptionally skilled.) Although this confirms empirically the possibility of false negatives already admitted by Osbornian theory in such cases, this level of skill (if it was exceptional) may be rare enough that the meaning of the universal failure of examiners on this question might be overstated, especially in aggregating it with the results of other tests or questions. However, standard Osbornian theory holds that the act of simulation suppresses individuality even for unskilled simulators. See quotes from Albert Osborn, Ordway Hilton, and Wilson R. Harrison set out at § 4:38. Certainly the results of Kam IV seem to indicated that document examiners are good at identifying simulations by naive and unskilled simulators as not genuine. See the discussion of Kam IV, § 4:31. However, there was no test was given to see if document examiners could attribute authorship of those simulations to the actual writer under the same conditions.

As to aggregation, it is true that all aggregation strategies applied to the FSF data are inherently flawed, since no one knows exactly how to measure either the ease or difficulty of a test task, or its statistical incidence in normal practice. However, it appears that more problems in the FSF studies as a whole come from what was assumed to be the easy end of the spectrum, so that the inclusion of the occasional hard task in an aggregation seems not as artificial as excluding it completely. Beyond aggregation objections, there can be no objection to asking the question and observing the results. In addition, it is at least a start to defining the outer limits of whatever expertise, if any, actually exists.

### § 4:18    Areas of disagreement: Testing document examiner expertise— Forensic Sciences Foundation proficiency tests: 1975–1987—The 1985 test

Participating laboratories were given 12 checks all having signatures in the same name. They were asked to decide which, if any, of the signatures were made by the same person. In fact, two of the 12 had been signed by the real person whose name appeared on them. Of the remaining ten, one was an attempted freehand forgery by a person without known experience as a forger; another was a tracing. The remaining eight were signed by eight different people in their own normal handwriting. Forty-two labs requested test materials and only 32 returned them. Of those:

13 (41%) gave correct results;

2 (6%) wrongly attributed one of the forgeries to the real signatory;

10 (31%) reported that they were unable to reach conclusions;

7 (22%) were substantially wrong, making errors beyond a single misattribution of authorship.

### § 4:19    Areas of disagreement: Testing document examiner expertise— Forensic Sciences Foundation proficiency tests: 1975–1987—The 1986 test

The 1986 test involved handwriting. Participating labs were told to assume that police had stopped a car with three known occupants. In the car they found a hand-printed holdup note and other evidence linking the note to a holdup apparently committed by only one person. The labs were given a copy of the holdup note. They were also given a copy of handwriting exemplars from the three occupants of the car. Suspect 1 had actually printed the holdup note. Suspect 2 had not, Suspect 3 had not printed the holdup note either, but he was a document examiner whose hand printed exemplar was an attempt to simulate the printing on the holdup note. Forty-eight labs requested materials and 31 returned reports. Of those:

4 (13%) gave correct answers;

3 (9%) said that none of the authors of the exemplars had written the hold-up note;

10 (32%) were unable to reach any conclusions;

14 (45%) assigned authorship to the forger.

### § 4:20    Areas of disagreement: Testing document examiner expertise— Forensic Sciences Foundation proficiency tests: 1975–1987—The 1987 test

Because of document examiner complaints concerning the difficulty of prior tests, the FSF decided to make the 1987 test easy. As its report of results said, "This test was designed to be a relatively easy and straightforward test, because of complaints about previous test design. All the writings in this test were natural and free of disguise." In this test, participating laboratories were given a copy of a handwritten extortion note. Exemplars of the handwriting of four persons were also supplied, one of whom actually had written the extortion note. The problem was to determine which, if any, of the "suspects" had written the extortion note. Fifty-five laboratories requested materials and 33 responded with reports. Of those:

17 (52%) correctly identified the writer of the extortion note;

1 (3%) incorrectly eliminated the correct suspect, asserting that none of the suspects wrote the extortion note;

0 (0%) incorrectly identified an innocent person as the author;

15 (45%) responded that their results were inconclusive.

## § 4:21 Areas of disagreement: Testing document examiner expertise—The Risinger et al. evaluation of the 1975–1987 FSF studies

Here is what Risinger et al. said in evaluating the above results:

What do all five FSF studies taken together suggest? A rather generous reading of the data would be that in 45% of the reports forensic document examiners reached the correct finding, in 36% they erred partially or completely, and in 19% they were unable to draw a conclusion. If we assume that inconclusive examinations do not wind up as testimony in court, and omit the inconclusive reports, and remain as generous as possible within the bounds of reason, then the most we can conclude is this: Document examiners were correct 57% of the time and incorrect 43% of the time.

But let us turn to more meaningful readings of the aggregate data. The pilot test in 1975 may have been unrealistically easy, like a line-up with four beefy white policemen and a skinny black person. Did this task present any real difficulty at all? There is no way of knowing whether a group of lay persons would have done any less well, since none was tested. Omitting the 1975 data, the examiners were correct 36% of the time, incorrect 42%, and unable to reach a conclusions 22% of the time. Even these results are biased in favor of accuracy because of the intentional ease of the 1987 test. Disguised handwriting fooled them all and forged printing fooled two-thirds of those who hazarded an opinion about it.

Now consider the effect on the aggregate results of the laboratories that requested test materials but did not return them. More likely than not, these nonrespondents bias the results further in favor of correct conclusions. Some of the nonresponding labs, no doubt, did not even perform the tests due to the press of daily business. But some others very likely performed the tests and then did not return their reports. Assuming that an examiner who has worked on an answer and then decides not to return it has serious doubts about its accuracy, then the sample of respondents is composed of an unrepresentatively large proportion of those who obtained—or at least think they obtained—correct answers.

If a correct answer consists of a report containing correct conclusions returned pursuant to requested and submitted test materials, then of the total submissions to laboratories in the 1984 through 1987 tests, only 18% gave wholly accurate responses (without the 1987 test the figure drops to 13%).

Finally, consider the possible effect on any aggregate conclusions of the fact that, of the more than 250 . . . laboratories that perform handwriting examination (not to mention a large number of private practitioner document examiners), only a fraction even ordered test materials in the first place. It is at least arguable that, by self-selection, the sample is inherently biased in favor of the more conscientious and capable practitioners to begin with. If this is true, the reported results would overstate the accuracy of the handwriting examination field generally.

The 1984, 1985, and 1986 tests presented examiners with a variety of challenges. The results should provide anyone with cause for concern. The examiners who returned reports on the analysis disagreed among themselves a good deal of the time, suggesting limited reliability, and many of the opinions offered were incorrect, suggesting limited validity.

In addition, the studies failed to reveal that certification or experience enhanced accuracy. The 1987 Proficiency Advisory Committee Comments state that "[a]s usual, there were no correlations between right/wrong answers and certification, experience, amount of time devoted to document examination and length of time spent on this test." Consider what this independence means for a court's likely assumptions about whether to admit a proffered expert and for the weight a fact finder is expected to give such testimony. A court is likely to assume that an examiner who is certified, who has been on the job for many years, whose caseload is nothing but document examination, and who has spent a lot of time examining the evidence, is especially likely to have something useful to say to a jury. Yet these data provide no support for these assumptions. Examiners who are uncertified, have little experience, work on document examination only part time, and spend little time on the particular document, are just as likely to be right as someone with more impressive qualifications. Does any of this suggest the existence of expertise?

These are the sorts of findings about the nature and limits of asserted handwriting identification expertise about which both document examiners and the courts need to know but which could not have been known before such studies were undertaken. Though they are not without flaws, these studies represent a step toward systematic and scientific evaluation of the claimed capabilities of this asserted expertise. Perhaps some of the considerably larger number of needed tests yet to be designed and administered would show document examiners faring better, but on the present record we must say that the underpinnings of the "expertise" have degenerated from no data to negative data.

Finally, we cannot emphasize too strongly that from the viewpoint of the law each of these studies suffers from a major omission: the absence of a control or comparison group of lay test-takers. If a jury can compare handwriting no worse than proffered "experts," then the expertise does not exist. For any given task, the level of performance of professional document examiners may be no better than that of layperson. Indeed, lay persons might perform some tasks consistently better than "experts." While such superiority may seem intuitively improbable, it remains a logical possibility and one not without analogues in other areas. For now, the kindest statement we can make is that no available evidence demonstrates the existence of handwriting identification expertise.[1]

### § 4:22    Areas of disagreement: Testing document examiner expertise—The Galbraiths' critique of *Exorcism* and their proposed reanalysis of the FSF studies

The Galbraiths' main explicit criticisms of Risinger et al. can be summarized as follows:

(1)    all the FSF studies are methodologically so flawed that they cannot be used as a proper basis for drawing substantive conclusions;[1] Risinger et al. failed to recognize this and as a result of that failure they drew inappropriate conclusions;[2]

(2)    even if the data were any good, the way Risinger et al. analyzed the data was wrong;[3] and

(3)    a proper examination of the data (which the Galbraiths claim to do in reexamination) would result in reclassification of many document examiner responses to the tests from incorrect to correct and reveal their performance to be better than Risinger et al. reported.[4]

We will examine each of these criticisms in turn.

The Galbraiths begin their criticisms by invoking "the four types of validity issues identified by Cook and Campbell" in their well respected book, Quasi-Experimentation: Design & Analysis Issues for Field Settings.[5] Unfortunately, while there are important criticisms to be made of the methodology of the FSF studies, the Cook & Campbell framework adopted by the Galbraiths is largely inapposite. The Galbraiths confused cause-effect studies (experiments and quasi-experiments)

---

**[Section 4:21]**

[1]Galbraith, Galbraith and Galbraith, The "Principle of the Drunkard's Search" as a Proxy for Scientific Analysis: The Misuse of Handwriting Test Data in a Law Journal Article, 1 Int'l J. of Forensic Document Examiners at 11 (1995). (footnotes omitted).

**[Section 4:22]**

[1]Oliver Galbraith, Craig S. Galbraith and Nanette G. Galbraith, The "Principle of the Drunkard's Search" as a Proxy for Scientific Analysis: The Misuse of Handwriting Test Data in a Law Journal Article, 1 Int'l J. of Forensic Document Examiners at 11 (1995).

[2]Galbraith, Galbraith and Galbraith, The "Principle of the Drunkard's Search" as a Proxy

for Scientific Analysis: The Misuse of Handwriting Test Data in a Law Journal Article, 1 Int'l J. of Forensic Document Examiners at 11 (1995).

[3]Galbraith, Galbraith and Galbraith, The "Principle of the Drunkard's Search" as a Proxy for Scientific Analysis: The Misuse of Handwriting Test Data in a Law Journal Article, 1 Int'l J. of Forensic Document Examiners at 11 (1995).

[4]Galbraith, Galbraith and Galbraith, The "Principle of the Drunkard's Search" as a Proxy for Scientific Analysis: The Misuse of Handwriting Test Data in a Law Journal Article, 1 Int'l J. of Forensic Document Examiners at 11 (1995).

[5]Thomas D. Cook & Donald T. Campbell, Quasi-Experimentation (1979).

with research aimed more simply at measuring some skill or ability. Cook & Campbell make clear that their validity constructs address problems of inferring that a treatment (independent variable) caused the observed effects in a dependent variable.[6] The FSF tests were simply trying to measure accuracy of performance (much like testing how well marksmen can hit targets). They were not testing which of two or more treatment conditions produced better performance (such as testing which of two training methods produced more accurate marksmen). Cook and Campbell's book is concerned with the methodological problems of the latter. The FSF studies are of the former kind. The Galbraiths struggled to apply cause-effect methodological issues to research that aimed instead to measure a single variable, test performance, making no attempt to draw causal inferences because there were no independent variables. A far more apt research tradition to inform a critique of the FSF studies would have been the literature of psychometrics (i.e., testing). Moreover, virtually all of the methodological objections raised by the Galbraiths were, in fact, dealt with by Risinger et al., either in the text or in footnotes. In the few instances where this is not true, it is generally because the Galbraiths' objections are inapposite. Their fundamental misreading of Cook and Campbell leads the Galbraiths repeatedly into confusion.

For instance, the Galbraiths assert that one ought to discount or disregard the results of Question 2 on the 1984 test (which all examiners got wrong) because of "insufficient co-variation."[7] The Galbraiths assert that "in designing or evaluating *any* test or experiment (such as the FSF tests) one must make sure that there is, or will be, sufficient covariation in the data, that is, variation in the test results must be observed in order to relate the results to the issue under investigation."[8] This is simply untrue in the universal form in which it is expressed; it depends upon what the issue under investigation is. While true for cause-effect studies (which Cook & Campbell were discussing), it is not for more basic skill measurement studies (which we, the FSF, and the Galbraiths are discussing). If all we want to know is "can most human beings hold their breath for 10 seconds" the fact that a test administered to 100 humans results in *all* participants holding their breath for 10 seconds in no way undermines the validity of the result, statistically or any other way. It is true, as Risinger et al. discussed at length, that tests that are too easy or too hard can lead to results which may be misinterpreted. It is also true that a single test designed to discriminate levels of skill has been unsuccessful if everyone does equally well or equally poorly. However, as Risinger et al. point out, handwriting identification is not a unitary operation, but rather presents "a broad variety of circumstances and tasks. Tests must be designed carefully to present discriminations of meaningful difficulty and variety. Only results from such tests could begin to paint a picture of what both lay people and experts can and cannot do . . . ."[9] Within the context of such a testing regime, it is not a criticism that some particular question or subtest

---

[6]Thomas D. Cook & Donald T. Campbell, Quasi-Experimentation (1979). This is evident throughout the book. But consider the following specifics: The second sentence of the preface: "The designs serve to probe causal hypotheses about a variety of substantive issues in both basic and applied research." Quasi-Experimentation at ix. The title of the first chapter: "Causal Inference and the Language of Experimentation." The word causation appears in 6 out of 10 section headings within the first chapter. Quasi-Experimentation at v. The first sentence of the first chapter: "The major purpose of this book is to outline the experimental approach to causal research in field settings." Quasi-Experimentation at 1.

[7]Galbraith, Galbraith and Galbraith, The "Principle of the Drunkard's Search" as a Proxy for Scientific Analysis: The Misuse of Handwriting Test Data in a Law Journal Article, 1 Int'l J. of Forensic Document Examiners at 11 (1995).

[8]Galbraith, Galbraith and Galbraith, The "Principle of the Drunkard's Search" as a Proxy for Scientific Analysis: The Misuse of Handwriting Test Data in a Law Journal Article, 1 Int'l J. of Forensic Document Examiners at 11 (1995) (emphasis supplied).

[9]Galbraith, Galbraith and Galbraith, The "Principle of the Drunkard's Search" as a Proxy for Scientific Analysis: The Misuse of Handwriting Test Data in a Law Journal Article, 1 Int'l J.

was so hard that none of the experts could do it. By themselves such data are not meaningless, as the Galbraiths seem to claim concerning Question 2 on the 1984 test. In combination with other data such results can help determine the limits of the expertise which were not known before the data were developed.[10]

Methodological misdirections aside, the Galbraiths' main critical thrust, in both parts one and two, is that Risinger et al. erred by accepting the response classifications that had been given to answers in the FSF studies initially *by the responding document examiners themselves* and then *by the FSF in its own summary of results*. Specifically, they claim that many responses that the document examiners labeled "inconclusive" when examining what turned out to be a true author's writings, ought to be treated as correct answers because the explanatory remarks accompanying the answers can be taken to indicate some level of belief that the writer of the exemplar may have written the questioned writing. They assert that these responses should be treated as examples of "qualified opinion" rather than bet-hedging "inconclusives."[11]

Even assuming the validity of their classifications of the data, however, the results do not mean what the Galbraiths go on to claim. They claim to have discovered 18 additional truly correct answers out of 192 total responses.[12] However, all but one of these answers newly classified as correct occurred in response to the two clearly easiest tests, 1975 and 1987.[13] Indeed, 13 of the new corrects were on the 1987 test alone, changing the performance on that test from 52% correct by the reckoning of Risinger et al. (based on the FSF classification) to 91% correct (based on the Galbraith reclassification). Secondly, the Galbraiths discard respondents who actually returned the test but criticized the test materials and checked off "inconclusive." These, they argue, ought to be treated as non-responses,[14] and, they argue even more vigorously, no conclusion can ever be fairly made from a non-response.[15] They then throw out the bad results of Question 2 from 1984 (which they do not like for the "lack of co-variation" reasons discussed above, that is, all responses were wrong).[16] Finally, they aggregate all the results even though the dead easy 1975 test accounted for nearly 2½ times the number of responses of the next most

---

of Forensic Document Examiners at 11 (1995) (emphasis supplied). Ironically, the Galbraiths' own footnote 14 makes the same point in very similar terms.

[10]The Galbraiths also dispute the propriety of any cogitation on how non-responses may have resulted in sample biasing which overstated the skills of document examiners as a whole. They rightly point out that the biasing results of self selection might plausibly have run the other way. The main disagreement between Risinger et al. on the one hand and the Galbraiths on the other seems really to be about who should bear the burden of persuasion and the risk of non-persuasion. The stance of Risinger et al. is clearly that validity is to be treated as unproven until there are sufficient unambiguous data supporting it. The position of the Galbraiths is that one should not doubt validity and "indict the whole field" without affirmative proof of invalidity. The Galbraiths' position appears close to that adopted by Judge McKenna in *Starzecpyzel*, and the opposite of the law's usual view that the burden is on the proponent of the evidence, as well as that of science that the burden of persuasion is on the one making the claim that some phenomenon exists.

[11]The Galbraiths show no examples of moving "inconclusives" to the "totally wrong" column.

[12]Galbraith, Galbraith and Galbraith, The "Principle of the Drunkard's Search" as a Proxy for Scientific Analysis: The Misuse of Handwriting Test Data in a Law Journal Article, 1 Int'l J. of Forensic Document Examiners at 11 (1995).

[13]Galbraith, Galbraith and Galbraith, The "Principle of the Drunkard's Search" as a Proxy for Scientific Analysis: The Misuse of Handwriting Test Data in a Law Journal Article, 1 Int'l J. of Forensic Document Examiners at 11 (1995).

[14]Galbraith, Galbraith and Galbraith, The "Principle of the Drunkard's Search" as a Proxy for Scientific Analysis: The Misuse of Handwriting Test Data in a Law Journal Article, 1 Int'l J. of Forensic Document Examiners at 11 (1995).

[15]Galbraith, Galbraith and Galbraith, The "Principle of the Drunkard's Search" as a Proxy for Scientific Analysis: The Misuse of Handwriting Test Data in a Law Journal Article, 1 Int'l J. of Forensic Document Examiners at 11 (1995).

[16]Galbraith, Galbraith and Galbraith, The "Principle of the Drunkard's Search" as a Proxy for Scientific Analysis: The Misuse of Handwriting Test Data in a Law Journal Article, 1 Int'l J.

responded-to test, and more than three times the responses of the hard 1984 test. Based on these adjustments, they claim that document examiners were correct 75% of the time.[17]

The fact remains, however, that the examiners did well at some tasks and poorly on others. The Galbraiths' own analysis (pertinent data reproduced as Table 1 below) shows that, out of six tasks with data sufficient to conduct significance tests, the document examiners could not even exceed *chance* accuracy in two of the six tasks. Think about that finding. Even where the experts do exceed chance performance, is *chance* the criterion of expertise? If a driver manages to stay on the right side of the median stripe more often than chance, if a piano student hits the correct notes more often than chance, if a student scores above sheer guessing on an exam—are they to be regarded as "experts"? And the Galbraiths found that document examiners did not even perform at that level on one third of the tests they took.

**Table 1**
Comparison of Expertise Against Chance
(Correct Versus Incorrect)

| Exam Year (Question) | Observed Proportion Correct | | Chance Proportion Correct | Exact Probability | | Conclusion |
|---|---|---|---|---|---|---|
| | (M1) | (M2) | | (M1) | (M2) | |
| 1975 | 0.9429 (66/70) | 0.9469 (70/74) | 0.2000 | 0.0001 | 0.0001 | Experts outperform chance |
| 1984 Q1 | 0.5652 (13/23) | 0.5652 (13/23) | 0.2500 | 0.0174 | 0.0174 | Experts outperform chance |
| 1984 Q2 | 0.0000 (0/23) | 0.0000 (0/23) | 0.1429 | 0.0575 | 0.0575 | Experts no different than chance |
| 1985 | 0.5900 (13/22) | 0.5517 (16/29) | 0.0002 | 0.0001 | 0.0001 | Experts outperform chance |
| 1986 | 0.1905 (4/21) | 0.2500 (7/28) | 0.2500 | 0.2652 | 0.5000 | Experts no different than chance |
| 1987 | 0.9444 (17/18) | 0.9375 (30/32) | 0.2000 | 0.0001 | 0.0001 | Experts outperform chance |

Source: Galbraith et al., Table 3.

Put simply, beating chance hardly establishes expertise. Even by the law's generous definition, in order to have expertise one must be able to outperform non-expert average jurors.[18] On that issue, even the Galbraiths concede that no statistically meaningful data existed when Risinger et al. was published.[19] In an attempt to rem-

---

of Forensic Document Examiners at 11 (1995).

[17]Galbraith, Galbraith and Galbraith, The "Principle of the Drunkard's Search" as a Proxy for Scientific Analysis: The Misuse of Handwriting Test Data in a Law Journal Article, 1 Int'l J. of Forensic Document Examiners at 11 (1995).

[18]Also, even if it could be shown that a proffered expert outperforms jurors, if both do terribly, with lay persons being right one time in a thousand and experts one time in a hundred, such

expertise still may not be dependable enough for admission.

[19]"[T]here certainly has been a shortage of studies comparing handwriting identification expertise to non-expertise . . . ." Galbraith, Galbraith, & Galbraith, The "Principle of the Drunkard's Search" as a Proxy for Scientific Analysis: The Misuse of Handwriting Test Data in a Law Journal Article, 1 Int'l J. of Forensic Document Examiners n. 7 at 7 (1995); "admit-

edy this absence of data, the Galbraiths administered the 1987 FSF test to two groups of non-experts to see how their performance compared to the document examiners who had been tested earlier. We will analyze those results below, but first we will complete the review of FSF proficiency test data by reporting the results of the 1988 and 1989 tests.

### § 4:23    Areas of disagreement: Testing document examiner expertise— Forensic Sciences Foundation proficiency tests: 1988–1989

Since the publication of Risinger et al., only two more relevant FSF studies appear to have been undertaken that we have been able to obtain. In 1988 and in 1989 the FSF again administered handwriting identification proficiency tests to document examiners at crime laboratories.[1] The results of the 1988 and 1989 FSF studies have never been published by the FSF,[2] but summary reports containing the results were issued to participating laboratories by the Forensic Sciences Foundation, and those findings are published below.

### § 4:24    Areas of disagreement: Testing document examiner expertise— Forensic Sciences Foundation proficiency tests: 1988–1989—The 1988 test

The test design for the 1988 FSF proficiency test in handwriting identification was as follows: The written instructions told the labs to assume the following case scenario: Four complaints were received from (four separate) physicians' offices about shipments of narcotics that were not received. The delivery service produced four receipts (Q1–Q4) each containing a signature in the name of a secretary for one each of the four physicians. Each secretary denied writing her own signature or any of the others. (The same driver had apparently made all the deliveries.) Handwriting samples from the four secretaries (labeled K1–K4) and the driver for the delivery

---

tedly sparse history of carefully controlled empirical studies . . . ." Galbraith, Galbraith, & Galbraith, The "Principle of the Drunkard's Search" as a Proxy for Scientific Analysis: The Misuse of Handwriting Test Data in a Law Journal Article, 1 Int'l J. of Forensic Document Examiners n. 7 at 7 (1995).

**[Section 4:23]**

[1]In 1990, after the existence of Galbraith, Galbraith and Galbraith, The "Principle of the Drunkard's Search" as a Proxy for Scientific Analysis: The Misuse of Handwriting Test Data in a Law Journal Article, 1 Int'l J. of Forensic Document Examiners at 11 (1995), became widely known, FSF quit testing on handwriting identification and began testing on such topics as rubber stamp identification (1990) and photocopying machine identification (1991). There was arguably a "handwriting" element in the 1992 test. However, comparison of form had little to do with obtaining the correct results. One could determine that the signature on the top (white) purchase order copy (copy 1) was photocopier generated and not hand signed, by direct examination without reference to exemplars (if appropriately skilled). The "carbonless carbon" on the yellow copy signature could then be determined to be a tracing of the photocopy signature by observing the ankles stylus indentation on the photocopied

signature of the white copy, and the exact correspondence between the stylus indentation and the carbonless carbon signature. The determination that a particular one of the exemplars provided had been the signature from which the photocopy on the white purchase order had been generated might be called a "comparison of form" problem, but since perfect superimposition was the key to this determination, it is not a comparison of the kind under consideration in this article. (About three quarters of the 90 respondents identified the right exemplar as the source of the photocopy, but the other quarter simply said nothing, and since they were not explicitly asked, these non-responses cannot be counted as errors, given the fact that most of them correctly identified the signature on copy 1 as a photocopy and that on copy 2 as a tracing over of the photocopy, which resolved the issue of genuineness about which they *were* asked). There have been rumors that proficiency tests with handwriting components have been renewed in recent years, but we have not been able to verify this or obtain the results of any which have been administered.

[2]Their first general publication was in the first edition of this treatise. They were, however, printed and distributed to the heads of participating laboratories and others, and were thus "semi-published."

service (K5) were requested. The delivery service also sent along two other receipts bearing signatures of "unknown persons."

The labs were supplied with six receipts acknowledging the receipt of goods. Receipt Q1 bore the signature "Sharon D. Clayborne" but in fact was written by Richard D. Osbourn, the driver. Receipt Q2 bore the signature "Lisa D. Bridgeforth" and in fact was signed by Lisa D. Bridgeforth. Receipt Q3 bore the signature "Cynthia Y. Boone" but in fact was written by Richard D. Osbourn, the driver. Receipt Q4 bore the signature "Joanna Neuman" and in fact was signed by Joanna Neuman. Receipt Q5 bore the signature "Linda N. Ninestine" and was not written by any of the five people who provided exemplars. Finally, receipt Q6 was signed "Linda D. Wentworth," but in fact was written by Richard D. Osbourn, the driver.

Sharon D. Clayborne, Lisa Bridgeforth, Cynthia Y. Boone, and Joanna Neuman each provided exemplars in which they signed their own names a number of times, and also signed all the other names appearing on the receipts a number of times. Richard D. Osbourn gave exemplars in which he signed all the names appearing on the receipts a number of times. These exemplars were provided to the labs through photographs.

These materials were submitted to 73 labs and returned by 49.[1]

For reasons set out more fully in the footnote, the 1988 FSF test must be ap-

---

**[Section 4:24]**

[1]Before examining the results of these tests, it is necessary to say something about the test design as reflected in the FSF report. The report fails to set out crucial information concerning the test design necessary to evaluate the difficulty of the task presented to the takers of the test. Fair inference from the report, however, indicates that there were in fact people named Lisa D. Bridgeforth and Joanna Neuman who signed the receipts bearing those names, and signed them in their normal signature hands. In addition, it appears that these two gave their exemplars of their own names in their normal signature hands. (If these things are not as stated in the text, the test is one of the worst that could be designed in terms of the standard internal precepts of the asserted expertise. It is a virtual postulate that signatures are special as to design, speed of execution, uniformity, etc. If supposedly authentic questioned signatures, and especially if assuredly known exemplars, are signatures by people for whom the writing is not a habitual hand, but represent someone else's name, the whole exercise would be, in the internal terms of the discipline, grossly and unfairly misleading to the test-takers.) If anything appears to correspond to reality in this field, it is that signatures are usually special manifestations of handwriting. It seems reasonable to believe that as a result of repetition, and psychological factors creating a personal stylistic identification with one's own signature, normal signatures are the most individual and uniform parts of a person's writing. This is not to say that signatures cannot be disguised. Nor is it to say that normal signatures of two people with the same name cannot evolve into confusingly similar forms. See Harris, How Much Do People Write Alike? A Study of Signatures, 48 J. Crim. L. & Criminology 647 (1958). It is merely to say

that it would presumably be rare for the normal signature of one person to look at all like another dissimilarly named person signing that name either in the second person's usual handwriting or in a disguised hand where no real signatures of person number one were available to imitate. Thus it would appear that perfect scores on Q2 and Q4 were, or ought to have been, giveaways.

In addition, the examiners being tested knew which of the sets of exemplars were from each secretary, and which set of exemplars was from the delivery man Osbourn. If they assumed that the original Clayborne and Boone signatures were natural signatures if genuine (as they had a right to do) and if they further assumed or concluded that the real Clayborne and Boone exemplars bore natural Clayborne and Boone signatures (as they had a right to do), then it would become a simple thing to eliminate all the secretarial exemplars as candidates for signing the Clayborne and Boone signatures, since none of the exemplar signatures would be likely to resemble the signatures on the receipts in any arguably significant way. This would reduce the question in regard to Q1 and Q3 to "did Osbourn sign these or not?" The difficulty of that question is presumably somewhat dependent on the nature of the writing presented (which was not reproduced in the report), but the results might also very well be influenced by the fact that Osbourn was the only candidate for those signatures left in the pool, and exterior circumstances already cast suspicion on him. Thus, his identification as the author may have resulted from the design of the test, not from the information derived from his handwriting.

Finally, the test-takers might assume (as one respondent explicitly did) that the secretaries were unlikely to be in a position to sign receipts for deliveries to other doctors, which tends to convert the question in Q5 and Q6 to a question

proached with a substantial grain of salt. Each identification is not an independent event, but rather, the test presented two connected sets of issues, one set relatively easy and one set somewhat more difficult. The easy set of issues asked: which if any of these secretaries signed a receipt bearing her name in her normal signature hand? The harder set asked: Of the four signatures left over after disposing of question one, which if any was signed by Richard Boone.

Not surprisingly, out of 48 responding labs,[2] all got each response to Q1 substantially right,[3] all but three got each response to Q2 substantially right,[4] and all but one got the answers to Q3 right. (The exception, Lab 531, eliminated Osbourn as the author of Q3.) A 49th lab was unable to reach any conclusions on any of the queries, and marked everything "inconclusive."

Apparently, Joanna Neuman has some significant intra-writer or "natural" variation in her signature, because the responses to Q4 were surprising. Out of 48 responses, 22 were right, but five were wrong in affirmatively excluding the real Joanna Neuman. Twenty-one gave various versions of "inconclusive," ranging from seven leaning toward Neuman to three leaning toward another writer. Our inclination in dealing with these responses is to throw out the inconclusives and to say that in this particular case, nearly a fifth of examiners with definite opinions were wrong. Clearly, even signatures are no guarantee of absolutely easy problems.

Up to this point the errors have been false negatives, assertions that the true writer did not write the questioned signature. Q5 presents the more troubling problem (for the legal system, especially in a criminal context) of false positives. (However, it should be noted that in a forgery case, an error asserting that a signature is not genuine when it is in fact genuine is wrongly inculpatory and in the legal context could be thought of as a false positive.) This time, only 17 labs were right,[5] but even among this group, the use of "probably did not" instead of "did not" rose in comparison to the answers to the previous questions. Only three labs manifested confidence that Osbourn did not write Q5. On the other hand, three labs affirmatively indicated Osbourn *did* write Q5,[6] and one lab (528) said Sharon D. Clayborne wrote Q5. Twenty-seven labs responded "inconclusive" to the Q5 questions, and in general these were unqualified inconclusives (not leaders in the

---

of whether or not the "Linda Ninestine" and "Linda D. Wentworth" signatures were signed by Osbourn or not. The elimination of Osbourn as the signer of the "Linda Ninestine" signature was likely to be made easier by the fact that presumably the signature was signed by a real Linda Ninestine in her real signature hand, and the Richard Osbourn exemplars would not only fail to resemble it, the examiners would already have concluded what Richard Osbourn's attempts at fake signatures looked like from Q1 and Q3. This would also assist them in identifying Osbourn as the author of the "Linda D. Wentworth" signature.

On the other hand, they might decide that since Osbourn signed all the other receipts not signed by known secretaries, he was likely to have signed Q5 also. All this raises the question of bias resulting from the presentation of unnecessary context information. Why not just present the exemplars marked questioned and known, and ask who wrote what, if anything?

[2]One lab, #517, counted as responding by FSF, responded "inconclusive" to every part of every question, and in its narrative report protested the structure of the test. While we do not believe that inconclusives are categorically mean-

ingless, under these conditions they are, and we have eliminated this lab from consideration.

[3]That is, with one exception, all answered either "did not write" or "probably did not write" to each of the secretaries and "did write" or "probably wrote" to the driver Osbourn. The one exception was lab 539, which said Osbourn probably wrote Q1, but responded "inconclusive" to all the secretaries.

[4]Labs 522, 539 and 542 failed to identify the true author of the signature, answering "inconclusive" to her.

[5]One lab was counted as right even though it had one inconclusive instead of five exclusions.

[6]Labs 516, 522, and 545. Lab 507 responded by saying that Osbourn wrote the signature also, but the accompanying narrative comments were inconsistent with an affirmative ID of Osbourn. Although this response was counted as a misidentification by the FSF, it seems to have been a typographical error, and we have not counted it. Lab 545 was counted as indicating Osbourn, even though it amended the answer from "probably" to "possibly."

Galbraith sense). Thus false positives made up 19% of the affirmative responses, and 25% of the responses with a confident finding.

Finally, as to Q6, there were 42 correct, two inconclusives that leaned toward Osbourn, three inconclusives, and one wrong exclusion of Osbourn (lab 514).

Thus, one can say that on the easy problems (Q1–Q3), document examiners gave 144 responses, of which 140 (97.2%) were correct or substantially correct, and 1 (0.5%) was an affirmative false exclusions, and 3 (2.5%) were inconclusive. Including Q6 as an easy problem, there were 192 responses, of which 181 (94.3%) were correct, 2 (1%) were affirmative false exclusions, and 9 (4.7%) were inconclusive. On the harder problems (Q4 and Q5), however, document examiners gave 96 responses, of which 39 (40.6%) were correct or substantially correct, nine (9.4%) were incorrect and 48 (50%) were inconclusive. Of the 48 answers reflecting firm conclusions on the harder problems, 19% were wrong, and of the 96 responses, only 41% were affirmatively right. The examiners did very well (but not perfectly) on the easy questions and substantially less well on the more difficult questions. And, as usual, there was no administration to a control group of non-experts to attempt to find out the relative performance advantage, if any, of experts over non-experts.

### §4:25 Areas of disagreement: Testing document examiner expertise—Forensic Sciences Foundation proficiency tests: 1988–1989—The 1989 test

If document examiners might find some comfort in the 1988 results, at least as to the easier tasks, the 1989 results were less comforting. The test was designed to see how well examiners deal with adolescent handwriting. The participating labs were asked to assume that during the final week of the school year, a high school teacher found the tires on her car slashed in the school parking lot. A handwritten note was found on the windshield. The teacher reported the matter to her principal, who in turn notified the police. On advice of the police, the teacher searched exam papers of her students and identified five students whose writing she thought similar to the threatening note. The principal refused, however, to release these exam papers to the police. The police therefore advised the teacher to ask those students to write the contents of the note to dictation five times on separate sheets of paper. Unfortunately, the instructions were misunderstood, and the writings of each student were made on only one sheet of paper. The students have since dispersed for the summer and are not available to provide additional writings. Along with these facts, the labs were provided with photographs of the note (Q) and the exemplars from the five students (K1–K5), and asked to determine if Q was written by any of the writers of K1–K5.

The questioned document and the five exemplars had been generated in the following way: The questioned document had been written by a 15–year-old female tenth grader. Sixteen other tenth grade students ages 14–16 were asked to write exemplar sheets, and the five appearing closest to the questioned document in the opinion of the testers were used as the exemplars. Three points must be made. Sixteen people is a small set from which to hope to get five confusingly similar handwritings. We are not told if the person who selected the five exemplars claimed any expertise. And none of the people who wrote the exemplars wrote the threatening note.

The test materials were submitted to 72 labs of which 53 returned the answer sheets. Of those, 13 labs answered "inconclusive" to every exemplar, and one answered "other" with no specific explanation. Of the 39 remaining labs which offered an opinion actually including or excluding anybody, 16 misidentified one of the writers of the exemplars as the culprit. (Three more leaned that way). That's 41%

false positives.[1]

## § 4:26   Areas of disagreement: Testing document examiner expertise—The Galbraith administration of the 1987 FSF test to non-experts

The Galbraiths obtained copies of the 1987 FSF handwriting test materials, and administered them twice, first to a group of 32 varied non-experts who received the materials in photocopy form, and then (much later) to a group of 33 who were given photographs of the materials. There are some methodological questions about the administration of these tests. We are told neither about the exam conditions, the time allotted, nor the instructions given to the non-experts tested. We do not know if they were administered in a way designed to prevent potential cuing. Further, it is likely that the non-expert test-takers suffered from problems of varying motivation, which are discussed in more detail in regard to the Kam et al. study, below. In addition, it seems possible that the non-experts were less likely to feel free to hedge their bets with some sort of inconclusive answer, perhaps not regarding such an answer as acceptable in the same way professional document examiners might regard it as acceptable.[1]

However, taking the data at face value, some interesting details emerge. First, even the lay people did significantly better than chance.[2] Second, if the FSF classification is utilized, the performance of the non-experts and the experts is virtually identical for true positives (17 out of 33 for the "experts," 16 out of 32 and 17 out of 33 for the two groups of non-experts). However, the non-experts were significantly worse when it came to false positives (34%, versus none for the document examiners). Finally, if we accept the Galbraith reclassification (and exclusion), document examiners significantly outperformed lay persons as a group (91% correct, no false positives, 3% false negatives; against 58% correct, 34% false positives, 8% false negatives). While these two limited and non-comparable administrations of these test materials cannot establish anything with any certainty, they seem to suggest that, at least as to the easiest tasks of handwriting comparison, the experts may have an approach which guarded against affirmative errors. The experts were no more affirmatively accurate than about half the "non-expert" population, but they were significantly less inaccurate than the other half. Any more confident conclusion as to whether this advantage truly exists, and whether it exists in relation to other more difficult tasks, must await further research.

## § 4:27   Areas of disagreement: Testing document examiner expertise—The studies by Kam and associates

In this section we begin examination of the studies undertaken by Dr. Moshe

---

**[Section 4:25]**

[1]Or 49% using the Galbraith methodology of including leaders. A strong defender of handwriting experts might say that this is the wrong way to look at the data. Each decision as to each exemplar should be treated as a separate judgment. Thus, the 39 responding labs made 195 judgements of inclusion or exclusion, of which only 16 were wrong. However, a strong critic could counter by saying two things: first, the judgements are clearly not independent. The more you are sure one wrote the note, the more you are sure the other four did not. Second, the important thing in an expertise is not absence of errors, for then a refusal to answer would be counted as establishing the existence of the expertise. The important thing is how often one makes a judgment which is wholly correct when given the op-

portunity. In this case, 72 labs were given the opportunity, and only 23 unambiguously did the job right. Of these various ways to view the data, we will stick to the position that ours is most meaningful, since it emphasizes the percentage of experts whose responses could lead to court testimony and who would then give mistaken inculpatory testimony: 41%.

**[Section 4:26]**

[1]This may reflect the instructions, or absence of instructions, on this issue.

[2]Galbraith, Galbraith and Galbraith, The "Principle of the Drunkard's Search" as a Proxy for Scientific Analysis: The Misuse of Handwriting Test Data in a Law Journal Article, 1 Int'l J. of Forensic Document Examiners at 11 (1995).

Kam and his colleagues under various FBI grants. But a word of caution as we start. Circumstances overtake us all, and if my interpretation of *Kumho Tire* is accurate, all but one of these studies have been rendered only tangentially relevant. That is because Kam I and Kam II were purposely designed to test aggregate global skills, and not to allow isolation of, much less identification of, subtasks such as identifying the handwriting of the foreign-born, adolescent handwriting, the handwriting of the aged and infirm, and so on, and Kam III was based on a readministration of Kam II. Only Kam IV is designed to test something that might be a "task at hand" in an actual case, (determination of signature authenticity). In addition, it must be emphasized that none of these studies address that most recurrent and controversial asserted skill, the ability to assign authorship based on extremely limited amounts of writing, in various contexts. With this in mind, we turn to Kam I.

### § 4:28    Areas of disagreement: Testing document examiner expertise—The studies by Kam and associates—Kam, Wetstein & Conn (1994) ("Kam I")

Under a research contract with the FBI, Kam, Wetstein and Conn designed a test intended to determine whether some professional document examiners had handwriting identification skills significantly better than those of non-experts.[1] Forty-five Drexel University undergraduates copied five test samples on to five sheets of paper. Thirteen of them copied one or another of the samples an extra time. All used their normal handwriting. Fourteen of the students wrote with whatever they had brought with them. Eighteen of the students wrote with medium point Bic pens supplied by the researchers. Thirteen students "randomly swapped pens with each other" between writings, but we are not told what the original source and type of their pens were.[2] This procedure resulted in 238 documents, from which 86 documents were randomly selected as the test materials. These randomly selected 86 documents represented the work of exactly 20 writers. These 86 were then tagged with a "non-trivial" code which would allow the holder of the code to connect each document to a particular writer.

The test consisted of handing each person taking the test the 86 documents and telling them to go into a room with a table and sort them into piles representing the work of a single writer per pile. Test subjects were not told how many writers were represented in the 86 documents, and no time limits were imposed on them. There were two groups of test subjects: seven FBI document examiners (presumably chosen by the FBI to take the test) who were administered the test in Washington, D.C. by being handed the materials and given the instructions by one of their own supervisors; and 10 graduate students in the Drexel graduate engineering and MBA programs who were selected in an unspecified manner to participate, and who had the test materials administered to them by their "supervisors" (whatever this may mean in the context of graduate students).[3]

A perfect performance on the test would yield 20 piles, each containing from one

---

impact and no apparent relevance to the issue of identification from form. For example, it may have created a distraction which the non-experts were more susceptible to, leading to inflated differences in scores between experts and non-experts.

[3]The form of test administration was selected to impress upon the participants "the importance that their respective institutions attach to these experiments." We suspect that the FBI document examiners were more impressed with this message than the graduate students.

to six documents. Each pile would contain all the documents written by a single writer and only the documents written by that writer. There were two possible types of error: a participant could put a document in a new pile when there was already a pile for that author's work. This type of error the authors called over-refinement—making distinctions that were not there.[4] Or a participant could put a document in a pile containing the work of another author. This type of error the authors called under-refinement—failing to make a distinction that should have been made.[5] Of the two, the authors observed that under-refinement errors were perhaps "more significant, since they represent a confusion between two writers," that is, they create the risk of false positives, as opposed to the risk of false negatives resulting from over-refinement.[6]

Since the test materials were not reproduced, we have no first hand way of judging whether this sorting test was inherently easy or difficult. However, since the samples were generated with no attempt to apply any standards of pictorial similarity, it would seem to be like matching photos of 20 randomly selected humans of all races and sexes: that is, many of the subtask matches would seem likely to have presented trivial challenges. In addition, as previously noted, the harder tasks are subject to confusion by virtue of the effect of the uncontrolled variable of writing instrument variation. Differences in result between two test-takers may actually reflect different assumptions concerning the test structure and the meaning assigned to writing instrument variation. In addition, we also do not know what relationship there is between the skills necessary for this test and the skills brought to bear in real-life document examination tasks, since document examiners are not called upon to do this kind of sorting task in their ordinary work. However, the ability to accurately perceive diagnostic patterns of similarity and difference in the writing represented by the test materials would seem likely to be common to both the test and to many kinds of real-life problems. At any rate, both test groups took the same test and the object was to see if there were differences in performance between the two, at least as to this test, for whatever reason.

The results obtained by the FBI document examiners are so good that one is tempted to conclude that the task was globally an easy one, especially given the differences in performance between easy and hard tasks which seem to be shown in the FSF studies. It may also be that the seven examiners selected to take the tests by the FBI were otherwise reputed to be the best in their employ. Nevertheless, taken at face value, their performance was impressive: five of the seven were perfect and the other two had only two errors each, one making one extra pile and having one incorrect inclusion, and the other making two extra piles.[7]

It is also true that the performance of the non-expert test-takers was, in the aggregate, clearly inferior to that of the FBI document examiners. However, there is another uncontrolled variable which may account for much of the difference: test-taker motivation. Clearly, knowing the growing controversy over the bare existence of any such expertise, the FBI document examiners realized that the foundation of their careers may have been at stake when they took the test. The graduate students had nothing at stake beyond some varying individual notions of personal pride at doing the best job they could, if that.[8] In line with this, the striking thing about the performance of the graduate student group was its extreme bimodality. Four of the

[4]Kam, Wetstein & Conn, Proficiency of Professional Document Examiners in Writer Identification, 39 J. Forensic Sci. at 8 (1994).

[5]Kam, Wetstein & Conn, Proficiency of Professional Document Examiners in Writer Identification, 39 J. Forensic Sci. at 8 (1994).

[6]Kam, Wetstein & Conn, Proficiency of

Professional Document Examiners in Writer Identification, 39 J. Forensic Sci. at 9 (1994).

[7]Kam, Wetstein & Conn, Proficiency of Professional Document Examiners in Writer Identification, 39 J. Forensic Sci. at 10 (1994).

[8]It would be interesting to know how much time was actually spent doing the tests by the

10 made only between nine and 14 total errors, averaging 11, which were mainly errors of over-refinement (too many piles, one person's writing counted as two persons' writing).[9] Additionally, half of the graduate students made only two or three errors of under-refinement, assigning the authorship of a document to the wrong person, and one of the FBI examiners made one such error.[10] If the top 40% of non-experts represented the properly motivated performance of non-experts, the differences in performance between the experts and non-experts, while perhaps statistically significant, is less significant in practical terms.

At the other end of the performance scale, the bottom 40% of the graduate student group made between 31 and 45 errors, averaging 38.5.[11] One person made 21 extra piles (41 total piles) and then assigned 24 of the remaining 45 documents to the wrong piles. Another made a total of 58 piles (38 extra) and assigned 6 of the remaining 28 to wrong piles. (One suspects that there was a subset of 21 or 22 documents in the set of test materials which could have been given to almost anyone as a virtually unfailable test.)

A note on the method of administering the test to the FBI agents: First, we know that the tests were administered "in Washington, D.C." and that they were "administered through the agents' supervisors." But we do not know from the published record exactly what this means. Certain obvious questions concerning the method of administering the test to the FBI agents present themselves. Were the test materials sent to Washington and kept there during the period necessary for the seven test runs, without the presence of a representative of Kam et al.? If so, this might severely undermine the validity of the results, raising as it does the distinct possibility of collaboration by substantially interested parties uncommitted to the standards of academic science. Further, while we are told that the test subjects were told nothing about the characteristics of the test materials and how they were generated, we are not told if their supervisors or others in the FBI were given such information. After all, the test was developed pursuant to an FBI contract with Professor Kam to study the methods of handwriting experts with an eye to developing a computerized scanner which could perform this work as a screening tool. If people in the FBI had information about the characteristics of the test materials, the possibility of intentional or unintentional disclosures cannot be ignored. Finally, there is the matter of the "non-trivial code" with which the test materials were inscribed, which allowed them to be matched later for statistical analysis. If it consisted merely of a randomly generated number which matched an

---

members of each group, since there were no imposed time limits, but those data are not provided and, indeed, were not kept. In his phone conversation with one of the editors, Professor Kam indicated that he was present for each of the graduate student runs, and that all expended some hours on the task. However, according to Professor Kam, the test was designed after enquiry to document examiners concerning their notions of how long tasks take, to be a full working day's project for a document examiner, so there is some mild reason to believe that the document examiners spent significantly more time than the graduate students on the task, but there are no actual data to that effect.

One can argue that it is exactly the difference in motivation to expend time examining and comparing details of questioned writings and known exemplars that justifies the admission of document examiner testimony, since the lay jury is not likely to spend the time analyzing the material assuredly necessary for peak performance

even if they could perform as well as document examiners if they spent the time. This is an interesting notion, analogous to the rationale for allowing testimony regarding summaries of voluminous material. Cf. Fed. R. Evid. 1006. How this fits in with our usual notions of expertise is not clear. At this juncture there is insufficient information on the contours of both lay and document examiner accuracy to justify rethinking the role of or justification for allowing such expertise.

[9]Kam, Wetstein & Conn, Proficiency of Professional Document Examiners in Writer Identification, 39 J. Forensic Sci. (1994).

[10]Kam, Wetstein & Conn, Proficiency of Professional Document Examiners in Writer Identification, 39 J. Forensic Sci. (1994).

[11]Kam, Wetstein & Conn, Proficiency of Professional Document Examiners in Writer Identification, 39 J. Forensic Sci. (1994).

identification key kept at all times by the researchers in Philadelphia, fine. However, if to make their computer work easier they embedded the identification information in the code itself, the entire test was compromised if the materials were sent to the FBI without researcher proctoring.

One of the editors contacted Professor Kam, who graciously filled in many of the missing details.[12] Professor Kam told us that no one in the FBI was given any information on the characteristics of the database from which the test materials were drawn, or on how they were selected. It was true that the tests were administered in Washington by sending the materials to an FBI contact after giving him instructions on how to administer the test. He was to administer the test to one agent, then return the results of the sorting to Professor Kam for scoring. Further, as to the code, it did consist of a randomly generated number, and to guard against those who had already taken the test sharing any useful tips with those who had not, the coding to the 86 papers was changed each time they were sent to Washington for administration. However, since there was nothing in the actual design of the test which would insure that the test materials were not photocopied the first time they were sent to the FBI by someone who gained access to them during the substantial time they were available for the first administration of the test, collaboration on the test by the FBI document examiners cannot be procedurally ruled out. On the other hand, the performance of the FBI document examiners was remarkable even if there was collaboration, though the results under those circumstances would be attributable only to the group, or to the best performer in the group.[13]

Where does this leave us? If the level of graduate student performance and its variation are the product of motivational differences and the artifactual impact of the writing instruments, the data could no longer be taken to support a marginal performance advantage in the experts. These artifacts cannot be ruled out as insignificant. Kam III was an effort to examine this issue, but does not lay it to rest (see § 4:30) If the variations mirror reality, then we potentially have an even stranger situation (but it is also consistent with the results of the Galbraith study). It may be that average people have a wide range of knacks, ranging from good to poor. It may be that, at least as to easy tasks, the expert is a lot better than half the

---

[12]Telephone interview by Michael J. Saks (Autumn, 1994).

[13]Before speaking to Professor Kam, we thought that there was some reason to believe that the test administration was over-supervised, not under-supervised. In 1993, Agent Richard Williams testified in a proceeding in San Francisco that he was one of the test subjects, and that during the administration of the tests he was surrounded by people in white coats with clipboards asking him questions about what was going through his mind as he did the test. See *Matter of Extradition of Smyth*, 826 F. Supp. 316 (N.D. Cal. 1993), rev'd on other grounds, 61 F.3d 711 (9th Cir. 1995), opinion amended on other grounds, 73 F.3d 887 (9th Cir. 1995). He referred to the test as a "quick and dirty" sorting. *Matter of Extradition of Smyth*, 826 F. Supp. 316 (N.D. Cal. 1993), rev'd on other grounds, 61 F.3d 711 (9th Cir. 1995), opinion amended on other grounds, 73 F.3d 887 (9th Cir. 1995). If the tests were conducted in this way, they would appear not to have been double blind, and the phenomenon of "Clever Hans" cuing (named after the famous German horse that was thought capable of solving arithmetic problems until he was tested under careful

procedures which prevented subtle cues from reaching him) cannot be ruled out. However, at the time of his testimony Williams was trying to diminish the significance of the fact that *any* mistakes had been made by the professionals. In addition, he may not actually have been one of the 7 test subjects (though he insistently testified that he was, *Matter of Extradition of Smyth*, 826 F. Supp. 316 (N.D. Cal. 1993), rev'd on other grounds, 61 F.3d 711 (9th Cir. 1995), opinion amended, 73 F.3d 887 (9th Cir. 1995)) but merely one of those document examiners "interviewed at length after the testing" to try to determine the mental processes behind document examiner performance. See Kam, Wetstein & Conn, Proficiency of Professional Document Examiners in Writer Identification, 39 J. Forensic Sci. at 13 (1994). It seems very likely that these interviews were conducted around an examination of the test materials, and that this is what Williams was involved in, not an actual run of the test itself. Williams' testimony does give rise to questions concerning the way these materials are presented to courts by document examiner witnesses, and the lengths to which they may go to bend the meaning of the tests in a desired direction.

non-experts but not much better than the other half. (This might simply result from people in the half of the non-expert population with the knack comprising most of those drawn to the work of document examination in the first place.) In the face of harder tasks, there is reason to believe tentatively that the marginal advantage may break down. What should be the law's response to a situation like that? The law is not well equipped to put such a situation into its usual paradigm, which assumes a substantial skill break between all members of the expert group and the overwhelming majority of the randomly selected population.

## § 4:29 Areas of disagreement: Testing document examiner expertise—The studies by Kam and associates—Kam, Fielding & Conn (1997) ("Kam II")

Between the beginning of May and the end of September 1996, Kam, Fielding and Conn administered a test of their own design to three groups of about 35 questioned document examiners each, a group of eight document examiner trainees, and a group of 41 untrained non-experts.[1]

Before we look at the published results of these tests, let us examine the test

---

**[Section 4:29]**

[1]All details of the Kam II test procedures are drawn from pages 779–781 of that eight-page article, §§ 4:14 to 4:38. Because the material is so short, specific footnote references to page are omitted as unnecessary and burdensome to the reader.

The test materials were generated as follows: 150 persons, ages 20 to 27, were selected by an unknown protocol to provide writing samples and they agreed to do so. Each writer worked on a wide and well lit table in a classroom setting. Each writer generated 12 documents on $8\frac{1}{2} \times 11$ in. 20 lb. white paper, copying three short assigned texts four times each. Each used pens supplied by the test designers. All writers were given both blue medium Bic pens and black medium Bic pens, and told to use both colors, switching "every 2–3 documents," so each writer created both blue and black documents in no exact fixed ratio or order. This resulted in 1800 documents, four each of three texts by 150 writers. Thirty of those writers were then selected (presumably at random) and all the documents generated by those 30 (360 documents) were placed in a set. These documents were then random number coded for writer identity. Random documents were then drawn from the set of 360 until six documents by six different writers was obtained—that is, after drawing the first document, if the second document was by the same writer, it was returned to the pool and another was drawn, and so forth, until a set of six documents by 6 different writers was obtained, which documents could represent randomly any text and either color ink. This set of 6 was then labeled "Unknown A1". The same process was repeated until 12 such sets were obtained (Unknowns A1 . . . A12) which together contained 72 documents in 12 sets of 6 each, each of the six by a different writer in each set. The remaining 288 documents were then randomly distributed into 12 sets referred to as "database packages" (database A1 . . . A12), each contain-

ing 24 random documents. The use of the label "unknown" was somewhat problematical. Among document examiners, "unknown" is the label given to a document of unknown authorship to be compared with standards of known authorship. In the Kam II test, none of the documents in either the "unknown" sets or the "database" sets were unknowns in this sense. They were in fact functionally the same from that perspective: both sets were known to the testers and unknown to the test-takers. The test was thus the same kind of sorting test involved in Kam I. A similar process was undertaken with the remaining documents not in set A, generating a set B. with the same subset characteristics, and so on for set C, until there were five such universes, A–E, containing twelve 6-document "Unknown" sets each and 12 24-document "database" sets each. Each test participant was tested by randomly selecting a Universe A–E, then within that Universe randomly selecting an "unknown" set from the 12, and randomly selecting a "database" set from the 12, explaining to the test subject that the "unknown" sets contained 6 writings by 6 different writers without disguise, and asking the test participant to determine whether any document or documents in the "database" set of 24 were written by any writer represented in the "unknown" set. Here we have a problem in figuring out the limiting conditions of the sets so generated. This is because the report of the study is a bit hazy on this point. It is inexplicit whether, once "Unknown A1" was generated, the writers there represented were removed, so that set A2 would have six writers who were different from each other and also all different from the ones in set A1, or whether the process was simply repeated on all the *documents* remaining after the generation of set A1, in which case set A2 could, in theory, contain the exact same writers as A1. It appears that the latter must be the case, because with 12 sets of four, one would need 48 writers to have no overlaps, and there were only 30 writers in the pool. But in

design, and the limits of what we might expect that it can and cannot tell us. First, like Kam I, this is a multi-document sorting test of a type encountered rarely if at all in actual practice.[2] This is not to say the results are meaningless. As noted elsewhere in regard to the similar characteristics of Kam I, "the ability to accurately perceive diagnostic patterns of similarity and difference in the writing represented by the test materials would likely be common to both the test and to many kinds of real-life problems."[3] It is merely to caution against simple extrapolation to actual practice without further thought.

Second, there are problems of motivation. Professional document examiners would be expected to put in more focused effort, given that their careers (and the fate of their profession) are in some sense on the line, than would students. This was a serious problem with Kam I.[4] However, in Kam II, the designers have made a commendable attempt to correct for this by offering the non-experts a schedule of monetary rewards and penalties. Unhappily, the schedule of rewards and penalties utilized was particularly unfortunate and problematical. The non-experts were told that they would receive a $25 participation fee, and that their payment would not go below this regardless of actual performance. They were then told they would receive an additional $25 for each true positive match, that they would lose $25 for each false positive match, that they would lose $10 for failing to see a true match, and that they would gain nothing for accurately rejecting a non-match. This payoff schedule can be schematically represented by Table 2.

### Table 2
### The Payoff Matrix Used in Kam II for Non-experts

|          |            | Reality | |
|----------|------------|---------|-----------|
|          |            | Match   | Non-Match |
| Decision | Match      | True Positive<br>+25<br>(Very Good) | False Positive<br>-25<br>(Very Bad) |
|          | Non-Match  | False Negative<br>-10<br>(Bad) | True Negative<br>0<br>(Indifferent) |

that case, it is possible (though unlikely) that each set A1 thru A12 represented exactly the same six writers, since each writer had generated 12 documents. Similarly, in regard to the "database" sets, in the event of the distribution just described, a fortiori, no "database" set would, or could, contain a document truly matching one in an "unknown" set. This theoretical (and very remote) possibility is only important to understand the real meaning of the first three tables in the Kam II report. These tables are obviously descriptive of the distribution of matches in the actual tests as given to the participants, not of the probability of such matches resulting from the distribution process described above. Thus, while there is a statistical probability that some test might be administered which had no true matches, in the 154 tests actually run there was always at least one true positive match. Similarly, at the other extreme, though there is a remote possibility of as high as 18 true matches, in the actual 154 tests administered there were never more than 10.

[2]Kam states that the "format was selected to resemble a multi-suspect case in which extensive examination of documents was required," Kam II at 780, but in fact, because there were multiple documents in each comparison set, none of which were known as to origin by the examiner, it resembles no real case. Perhaps it would be better if real cases were presented to examiners in this blind a fashion, but they are not. See Risinger & Saks, Science and Nonscience in the Courts: *Daubert* Meets Handwriting Identification Expertise, 82 Iowa L. Rev. 21, 64 (1996).

[3]Risinger & Saks, Science and Nonscience in the Courts: *Daubert* Meets Handwriting Identification Expertise, 82 Iowa L. Rev. at 60 (1996).

[4]Risinger & Saks, Science and Nonscience in the Courts: *Daubert* Meets Handwriting Identification Expertise, 82 Iowa L. Rev. at 61 (1996).

Under this regime, if their objective was to maximize their payoff, the non-experts would guess a match whenever it appeared to them to be as likely as a non-match. This is because, over the long run, it would appear that such a strategy would at least break even, whereas guessing "no match" on such an evaluation would lose an average $5 per guess over the long run. Plus, there was no real incentive to avoid false positives for fear of actually losing something they already had at the beginning of the test, because they were guaranteed their starting $25 no matter how bad their performance. This reward schedule seems guaranteed to make the non-experts risk-preferring regarding finding matches, even in the face of instructions that they should declare a match only if they were really, really sure. This effect is on top of the well-known tendency for a most people to become risk preferring in circumstances of potential high rewards and low costs, regardless of rational odds (sometimes referred to as the "lottery effect").[5]

In contrast to this, the document examiners entered the test under quite a different effective payoff schedule. For one thing, they knew that the worst thing they can do on any proficiency test is to commit a false positive error.[6] (This risk averseness to false positives on known tests is not necessarily present in normal practice.[7]) Secondly, for the document examiners, a correct discovery of a non-match is also a highly desirable indicator of affirmative expertise. The incentive matrix for document examiners taking the Kam II test might be represented as in Table 3:

---

[5]Kahneman & Tversky, Prospect Theory: Analysis of Decision Under Risk, 47 Econometrica 263 (1979); Lopes, Remodeling Risk Aversion, in Acting under Uncertainty: Multidisciplinary Conceptions 267 (George M. von Furstenberg ed., 1990); Lopes, When Time is of the Essence: Averaging, Aspiration and the Short Run, 65 Org. Berhavior & Human Decision Processes 179 (1996); Tversky & Kahneman, Advances in Prospect Theory: Cumulative Representation of Uncertainty, 5 J. Risk & Uncertainty 297 (1992).

[6]See Moenssens, Handwriting Identification Evidence in the Post-*Daubert* World, 66 UMKC L. Rev. at 315 (1998). This is because such a false positive in the real world can result in the conviction of an innocent criminal defendant, a result the official ideology of our criminal justice system disvalues much more than an inaccurate acquittal, as reflected in the requirement of proof beyond a reasonable doubt. Thus, to commit such an error on a proficiency test undermines the status of the expertise in the eyes of the law, and must be avoided at all costs *in tests*.

[7]Whether false positives must be as stringently avoided in actual practice is a different issue. It cannot be stated too often that any superiority on the part of document examiners under test conditions will not necessarily carry over to practice, where the pressures on document exam-iners, as on other forensic practitioners, are to make matches that confirm positions already arrived at by other investigators, a fact recognized by Moenssens. Consider the following: "[E]ven where crime laboratories do employ qualified scientists, these individuals may be so imbued with pro-police bias that they are willing to circumvent true scientific investigation methods for the sake of 'making their points' . . . . Unfortunately, this attitude is even more prevalent among some 'technicians' (nonscientists) in the crime laboratories, for whom the presumption of innocence disappears as soon as police investigative methods focus on a likely suspect." Moenssens, Novel Scientific Evidence in Civil and Criminal Cases: Some Words of Caution, 84 J. Crim. L. & Criminology 1, 5 (1993). And further: "The temptation to fabricate or to exaggerate certainly exists. All experts are tempted, many times during their careers, to report positive results when their inquiries come up inconclusive, or indeed to report a negative result as a positive when all other investigative leads seem to point to the same individual. Experts can feel secure in the belief that their indiscretions will probably never come to light." Moenssens, Novel Scientific Evidence in Civil and Criminal Cases: Some Words of Caution, 84 J. Crim. L. & Criminology 1, 17 (1993).

### Table 3
### The Implicit Payoff Matrix in Kam II for Experts

|          |           | Reality | |
|----------|-----------|---------|---------|
|          |           | Match | Non-Match |
| Decision | Match | True Positive (Very Good) | False Positive (Extremely Bad) |
|          | Non-Match | False Negative (Bad) | True Negative (Good) |

Thus, in a situation of equipoise, the reward structure would impel experts toward declaring a non-match, and the non-experts toward declaring a match. Hence, the non-experts and the experts took the tests under incentive structures which would be predictably expected to yield more false positives for the non-experts[8] even under equally accurate probability judgements about authorship.[9]

Third, and somewhat unaccountably, is the "ink color" variable. This problem was also present in Kam I. Why the writers of the exemplars were asked to use two different color inks is not at all clear, and the effects on the results, or on the aggregate results between groups, cannot be assumed a priori to be trivial. As noted elsewhere, this "introduced a variable into the study's design having unknown impact and no apparent relevance to the issue of identification from form."[10] Nevertheless, this is probably best regarded as simply another subtask variable of the variety inevitably present in the tests as designed, for reasons explained below.[11]

Fourth, passing beyond ink color to a much more serious problem, once again Kam et al. have apparently created the possibility that the document examiners, or some of them, had helpful information about the test in advance of its administration,[12] because apparently the earlier document examiner test subjects got to go over the results of their tests at some point before the next document examiner groups were tested.[13] Kam says he protected against this having any effect by making sure

---

[8]To correct for this, future tests should impose high disincentives on the non-experts for false positive responses, substantially higher than the reward for true positives, and equalize the value of true negatives and false negatives (missed matches).

Scientists who study decision-making of the sort done by forensic scientists, an area of research called "Signal Detection Theory," have developed ways of measuring the raw acuity of examiners separate from the subjective threshold that an observation must cross in order for examiners to decide that what they have observed is a submarine or a tumor or a handwriting "match." Such research has found that incentives for preferring to err in one way (a false negative: failing to detect a tumor) rather than another (a false positive: seeing a tumor where none is) typically have considerable impact on where the psychological threshold is placed, regardless of the raw perceptual accuracy of the examiner. See Swets, The Science of Choosing the Right Decision Threshold in High-Stakes Diagnostics, 47 Am. Psychologist 522 (1992); Phillips, Saks & Peterson, Signal

Detection Theory and Decision-making in Forensic Science, 46 J. Forensic Sciences 294 (2001).

[9]Kam III administered the Kam II test materials to four sets of laypersons under four different incentive schemes in an attempt to meet these criticisms. See discussion of Kam III, § 4:30.

[10]See Risinger & Saks, Science and Nonscience in the Courts: *Daubert* Meets Handwriting Identification Expertise, 82 Iowa L. Rev. 21, 64 n. 142 (1996).

[11]See the discussion under our fifth consideration.

[12]See the discussion, § 4:28, of this problem in regard to Kam I, which renders it impossible to know if individual performances are in fact group performances in regard to the document examiners tested.

[13]It is not fully explicit that this was the case. What Kam says is, because "unknown" and "database" pairings were never repeated "(e)ven if correct results from an early test were fully known to all test-takers in a later session, this information was practically useless. We do not believe

that no pairing of a set of "unknowns" and a set of "data base" documents was ever used twice. However, it should be obvious by now that quite a lot of useful test design information might be gleaned in such a debriefing session. For instance, if you know how the data base was generated, you can figure out pretty quickly how rich or poor in true matches the tests are likely to be, that is, what the rough probabilities are of maximum and minimum numbers of true positives, information not available to the non-experts, who might be expected to assume a universe much richer in matches, which might encourage guessing. And note that, while the document examiners were divided into three regional groups for statistical purposes, the members of at least the Northeast group were tested in at least two different subgroups at two different times, with their results being aggregated statistically. It seems especially unnecessary to have run the tests in such a way as to create this problem, since all that was necessary was to collect all the data before conducting any post-mortems.

Fifth, and finally, the actual tests presented an unknown variety of subtasks in an unknown distribution. In addition, some important varieties of subtask were clearly absent from the test, and as to those, the test can generate no direct data of any kind. Like the Kam I universe of writing exemplars, the much larger and more controlled universe generated for Kam II was generated with no attempt at isolating subtasks (comparing two exemplars with similar but unusual "class characteristics," for instance, such as the handwriting of two German immigrants of similar age and sex). Any given such subtask *might* have been present somewhere in some run of the test, but we don't know which were, which weren't, or when. This is not necessarily a criticism, but it must be kept in mind when determining what the test can tell us. Each test was a little different, presenting a different set of challenges, and the most that can be said is that the challenges are likely to be typical of a certain range of comparison situations. They are also unlikely to mirror those encountered in litigation. This is because many of the subtask problems are likely to be trivial, like distinguishing between two randomly selected humans of all races and sexes, since the exemplars were generated with no apparent attempt to make the set of materials richer in confusingly similar exemplars than random life would be.[14] Most importantly, some very critical subtasks were not under test at all, such as the effects of forgery or disguise, the particular problems of signatures or adolescent handwriting, or those of the elderly or infirm, or the like. However, with these limitations in mind, and within the range of aggregate subtasks present in the tests, the tests can generate important data, and would be expected to generate the following types of data:

- the aggregate performance of the professional document examiner group as to true positives, false positives, true negatives and false negatives
- the aggregate performance of each subgroup of professional document examiners as to the same categories of result
- the aggregate performance of the trainee group as to the same categories of result
- the aggregate performance of the non-expert group as to the same categories of result
- the distribution of performances among the professional document examiner group (best score, worst score, distribution in between, as to all categories of result)

---

that any attempt was made to record or share results from our tests between test-takers. However, if such attempts were made, they could not affect the results in a meaningful way." Kam II at 779. We take this to mean that results were provided the test-takers at some point in advance of the next group of tests. (In order to make sure this was what happened, repeated attempts have been made to obtain explicit clarification from Dr. Kam, both by e-mail and by regular mail, but Dr.

Kam has not responded. Under the circumstances we proceed on the assumption that what was written was what happened.) This is one more illustration of the hidden pitfalls of human testing that may not be immediately apparent to a researcher more accustomed to computer modeling.

[14]See the discussion, § 4:28, of the same problem in regard to Kam I.

- same for subgroups
- same for trainees
- same for non-experts

Indeed, these data are so important that, with a small domain like 154 tests, one might expect to see a frequency distribution, or even a data table giving each taker's (unidentified by name) individual scores, as was done in Kam I. In the Kam II report, however, all that is given is aggregate performance of groups, and that only in numerical averages. There is no distribution information given at all, even in the form of standard deviation values. It's not that this information does not exist or was not available to Kam et al. It just is not given. Important information is hidden (unintentionally or otherwise) behind the few aggregate statistics provided.[15]

The reader will have seen by now why Kam's conclusion that the results of Kam II "lay to rest the debate over whether or not the professional document examiners possess writer-identification skills absent in the general population" is more than a small exaggeration. A more proper conclusion would be that under test conditions not replicating actual practice in significant ways, and as to an undefined range of subtasks not including many of the most important ones of actual forensic practice, the aggregate average performance of document examiners in correctly identifying actual matches was virtually identical to layperson (layperson correctly matched authors 87.5% of the time, compared to 87.1% for experts), but document examiners were better at avoiding false positives than non-experts (layperson mistook a non-match for a match 38.3% of the time compared to 6.5% for experts), and the latter findings may be an artifact of the varying incentive and disincentive regimes applying to the two groups, perhaps compounded by other factors. More importantly, there is nothing to show that this relative advantage when performing on what is known to be a test, even if real, is robust enough to continue in the face of expectancy and suggestion effects (properly) excluded from the test, but present in normal

---

[15]Think of what this means. We do not know how well the best lay people performed, or how poorly the worst document examiners performed. Kam et al. know, but no one else does. Even the aggregate data establish that there is no significant difference in average performance in regard to true positives. (Note that the proper conclusion is "no significant difference," not "accept" the null hypothesis as Kam et al. mistakenly conclude in Kam II (tables 10, 11, 13, 15, and accompanying text). A null hypothesis is only a starting point. Based on evidence, it can be rejected. But the failure to reject it as false is not the equivalent of "accepting" it as true.) In this particular study it is in regard only to false positives, the most dangerous type of error, that document examiners have a significant aggregate advantage. However, without distribution information, we do not know if, for instance, the best half of the non-experts is as good or better at avoiding false positives as the worst half of the document examiners. Averages can conceal important variations.

This is not as farfetched as it might sound. The data from the Galbraith study and from Kam I tended to indicate that non-experts were bimodal in their accuracy distribution, including false positives. If that trend were to hold in Kam II, the best of the non-experts could still be better than the worst of the experts, but the average for non-experts would be dragged down by the truly poor performance of the worst of the non-experts.

Similarly, the high average for document examiners could conceal a cluster of very poor performers on the low end. We are well aware that the test design, which resulted in each test administered being different from every other, and each test participant therefore taking a somewhat different test, makes statements about comparative individual performance problematical, absent some way to rate the relative difficulty of particular tests. Nevertheless, other moments of performance distributions have as much claim to meaning from these data as the one Dr. Kam chose to publish, and cannot be derived without the data. These data exist but were not published. What is worse, Dr. Kam was repeatedly requested to provide it to us and others, and repeatedly refused. For details, see Risinger, Denbeaux & Saks, Brave New "Post-*Daubert* World"—A Reply to Professor Moenssens, 29 Seton Hall L. Rev. at 431–33 (1998). Finally, pursuant to an agreement, and consistent with general federal policy on data produced under federal contracts, Professor Kam and the FBI agreed to disclose the data to Dr. Michael Saks (March 28, 2000), but more than a year later, and after several reminders to send the data, the FBI explicitly reneged on its promise. Under such circumstances, one can be forgiven for suspecting that the distribution data would show bimodality for the performance of the non-experts and poor performance by a significant cluster of document examiners.

practice. Only tests specifically directed toward this issue, or a regime of blind proficiency testing, can answer this.

### §4:30 Areas of disagreement: Testing document examiner expertise—The studies by Kam and associates—Kam, Fielding & Conn (1998) ("Kam III")

Responding to criticisms concerning the confounding effect of the monetary incentives given to lay test subjects in Kam II, Kam, Fielding and Conn administered the Kam II test to four groups of 32–34 Drexel University College of Engineering sophomores, 87% of whom were receiving financial aid (and therefore might arguably respond sensitively to changes in monetary incentives). One group repeated the Kam II test with its original reward scheme intact, that is, the subject was guaranteed $25 for participation, and beyond that, correct matches gained $25, inaccurate declarations of match lost $25, failure to declare a match when one was present lost $10, and accurately declaring a non-match neither gained or lost (see extensive description and criticism at §4:29). The other three groups each took the test under different incentive schemes, which were as follows:

Group 2: correct matches gained $25, inaccurate declarations of match lost $25, failure to declare a match when one was present lost $25, accurate declaration of a non-match neither gained nor lost. $25 minimum participation fee guaranteed.

Group 3: correct matches gained $25, inaccurate declarations of match lost $50, failure to declare a match when one was present lost $5. Accurate declaration of non-match neither gained nor lost. $25 minimum participation fee guaranteed.

Group 4: Participant starts with a bank of $100. Correct matches neither gain nor lose, inaccurate declarations of match lost $25, failure to declare a match when one was present lost $25. Accurate declarations of non-match neither gain nor lose. $25 minimum participation fee guaranteed.

Kam III does not give performance data for each group, merely aggregate numbers for all four groups combined regarding "hit rate" (actual accurate declarations of match as a percent of possible accurate declarations of match) and "wrong association rate" (inaccurate declarations of match as a percent of possible inaccurate declarations of match). However, Kam III does compare those rates between individual groups statistically, and finds that, as to hit rate and wrong association rate, there were no statistically significant difference among any of the four test groups. However, there is a small impediment to any general conclusion that incentive schemes, even incentive schemes at this level of reward, and which incorporate a gain floor, do not significantly influence test-taker behavior. The aggregate performance of the four new test groups was significantly better than the original Kam II lay group. The hit rate was insignificantly lower, but the new wrong association rate was significantly better (0.227 compared with 0.338, a 41% better performance at avoiding wrong associations). Kam III attributes this to the aggregate tendency of the new groups to declare fewer affirmative matches of any kind, as if this were an explanation. But to what do we attribute this new reticence? Both reward scheme 3 and reward scheme 4 would each seem to encourage risk averseness in declaring matches of any kind, which is what was observed in the aggregate data, as compared to Kam II. So the conclusion that the different incentive schemes did not significantly affect lay performance is hardly established by Kam III.

Finally, it should be noted that none of the tested incentive schemes had the characteristics of the scheme recommended in §4:29. Number 3 came closest, by penalizing false positives more harshly than it rewarded true positives, but the penalty differential was not severe enough, and the scheme did not equalize the value of accurately perceiving a match and accurately perceiving a non-match (true positives and true negatives).

### § 4:31    Areas of disagreement: Testing document examiner expertise—The studies by Kam and associates—Kam, Gummadidala, Fielding & Conn (2001) ("Kam IV")

Between May and November of 1998, pursuant to their FBI contract, Dr. Moshe Kam and his associates initiated the first study ever designed to test the abilities of document examiners against the abilities of ordinary people in regard to a specific task that is actually a task commonly undertaken by document examiners in normal practice.[1] A number of preliminary observations must be made before dealing with the details and results of that study.

First, the task selected for examination, determining whether a signature is genuine (written by the person whose name is reflected by the signature) or nongenuine (not written by the person whose name is so reflected) is sui generis according to the standard theory of handwriting examination used by document examiners. This is because real signatures are regarded as a category of writing separate from all other writing insofar as it is common for them to manifest a high degree of personally unique characteristics, resulting from a combination of repetition and emotional or stylistic investment. If document examiners are right about this (and it is neither counterintuitive nor in conflict with existing empirical evidence), then it would be error to generalize from skill levels shown in this study to similarly high skill levels in separate and more difficult tasks, such as identifying the actual author of a concededly inauthentic signature.[2] This is in no way a criticism of design of the study. One must start somewhere, and it makes a certain sense to start with the easiest definable task and work on from there.

Determining the authenticity of a signature is an important task in many legal contexts, such as, inter alia, the probate of wills and, perhaps most commonly, asserted cases of check forgery. Broadly speaking, inauthentic signatures can be generated in three general ways. The forger can be in possession of a blank check, say, but have no model of an authentic signature to try to simulate. Signatures generated under those conditions, whether in the normal hand of the forger or in some sort of disguised hand, usually present trivial problems for determining authenticity. The new study (preliminarily titled "Signature Authentication by Forensic Document Examiners" and hereafter referred to as Kam IV) wisely did not include such circumstances.[3] Another possible way in which inauthentic signatures are generated is when the forger has a model of a genuine signature to use in attempted simulation and, in addition, is experienced in forgery, that is, has done simulations often before and has at least come to believe that they have mastered simulation skills sufficiently to do a good job. Kam IV was not designed to examine document examiner or non-document examiner skills in detecting forgeries under such conditions.

The final category of nongenuine signatures involves what we may call naive forgers, that is, people who have a model of a genuine signature for purposes of simulation, but who have no previous experience in forgery. Kam IV was designed to deal

---

**[Section 4:31]**

[1]Kam, Gummadidala, Fielding & Conn, Signature Authentication by Forensic Document Examiners, 46 J. Forensic Sci. 884 (2001).

[2]Note that this lack of generalizability is not symmetrical. To the extent significant error rates are shown on this task, it is fair to infer, at least tentatively, that error rates on harder tasks would be at least as high and probably higher, whereas good performance on this task is extremely weak evidence concerning good performance on other

tasks. And it must always be kept in mind that performance under test conditions may not measure performance under the normal conditions of practice, which are subject to substantial forces of expectation and suggestion.

[3]One weakness of Kam I and Kam II was that the tests included a substantial though not exactly known number of such trivial tests. See discussion of those studies, §§ 4:14, 4:27 to 4:30. The design of Kam IV avoids this.

only with forged signatures of this type.[4] Note that the study could have been designed only to deal with such signatures, simply by insuring that all questioned signatures presented to participants were of this type. However, again wisely, the test was designed to present both authentic and inauthentic signatures, so it is in reality two subtests, one involving the ability to declare accurately that a naive forgery is a forgery, and the other the ability to declare accurately that a genuine signature is genuine.

Within certain limits,[5] the test design was quite well conceived. Test materials were generated as follows: 64 people provided 12 signatures each in their own names on 12 identical pieces of paper, according to a procedure well designed to obtain their normal everyday signature. These 64 sets of 12 were then each randomly divided in two, yielding 64 sets of six signatures to be used as "known authentic signatures" (like six randomly selected cancelled checks from a particular person), and 64 sets of six to form the basis for the "questioned signatures." It was then randomly determined how many, if any, authentic signatures would be removed from each set, to be replaced by simulations. Two sets were to have none removed (they remained all genuine), seven sets one removed, 17 sets two removed, 21 sets three removed, 12 sets four removed, four sets five removed, and one set was to have every signature replaced by a simulation.

The simulations were then generated as follows. Seven people with no prior experience with signature simulation were hired to do all the simulations. Sets were randomly selected and assigned to a simulator, who had unlimited time to examine the six genuine signatures in the "known" set, and to generate one or at most two simulations by whatever method seemed best to the simulator. If two simulations were required, the set was then assigned to another simulator to generate one of the two simulations. If more than three simulations were required, two or three simulators were used, with no more than two signatures per simulator allowed in any given set. Care was taken to make sure the simulations were indistinguishable from the originals in every way except handwriting. A test consisted of handing a test subject a randomly selected set of "known signatures" and the associated set of "questioned signatures" and explaining that the known signatures were real normal signatures and each of the questioned signatures might be either genuine or a simulation. The subjects were provided with a microscope, a light source and a handheld magnifier. The ordinal scale of certainty represented by ASTM standard E1658 was explained to them, and the subjects were then asked to determine whether each questioned signature was genuine by the standards of the top two degrees of certainty in that standard, a simulation by reference to the bottom two degrees, or to declare themselves "unable to determine."

The test was administered to three groups of professional document examiners,

---

[4]One detail of the procedure for generating test materials might have undermined this to an unknown degree. All simulations were generated by only seven simulators, and since, on average, they had to do 25 simulations each, they would of necessity have become relatively experienced simulators by the end of the process. Whether they became better simulators is another question.

[5]Explicit detailed evaluations of the limits of the test design will await the publication of the study. However, the main ones are the ages of the providers of both the genuine signatures and the simulated signatures (19–30, with an apparent skew toward the lower end of that age range), the incentive scheme for the non-expert test subjects (which once again does not mimic the incentives

for the professional document examiner test subjects), and the allowance of the simulators to select for themselves the best method of simulation from a variety of potential methods explained to them before they undertook their simulations (including backlighting, carbon paper, overhead projection and, presumably but not explicitly, freehand simulation). Signatories of a different age group might have displayed more or less intra-writer variation in their signatures. The problems of incentives have already been discussed in connection with Kam II and Kam III, §§ 4:14, 4:27 to 4:30, and the problems presented by the unknown variation in simulation method are addressed below. Also, there was once again an unnecessary ink-color variability.

all of whom were either members of the American Society of Questioned Document Examiners or of the Southwestern Association of Forensic Document Examiners. In addition, an unknown number were certified by the ASQDE's associated certification board, the American Board of Forensic Document Examiners. The total number of document examiner test subjects was 69.

In addition, the test was administered to 50 non-experts connected in various ways to Drexel University, who were selected to resemble the educational profile of the document examiner subjects.

The resulting performance is summarized in Table 4.

### Table 4. Results from the "Kam IV" Study

| Research Participant's Decision: | | | | | | |
|---|---|---|---|---|---|---|
| | "Questioned Signature is Genuine" | | "Questioned Signature May or May not be Genuine" | | "Questioned Signature is Not Genuine" | |
| Ground Truth | FDEs | Non-FDEs | FDEs | Non-FDEs | FDEs | Non-FDEs |
| Questioned Signature: Genuine | 85.89% | 70.00% | 7.05% | 4.30% | 7.05% | 26.10% |
| Questioned Signature: Not Genuine | 0.49% | 6.47% | 3.45% | 1.40% | 96.06% | 92.00% |

Exact test format data are not given, merely statistical summaries, but a likely typical numerical distribution can be extracted from what is given, and is useful to illustrate approximately what the actual data set might have looked like. What follows is thus a typical distribution approximately consistent with the summaries given, but the real distribution is likely to have varied from these numbers by a few either way, and so what follows is for illustrative purposes only.

The universe of possible tests was comprised of 64 potential tests, which contained 384 potential judgements (6 × 64), containing 53.64% genuine signatures (206 out of 384) and 46.36% simulated signatures (158 out of 384). While individual test sets were potentially subject by random draw to as many as three repetitions between the three document examiner test groups (the lay group was tested all at once, and therefore not subject to test set repetition), we can be reasonably assume that both in the case of the 69 document examiners total 414 judgments, or the lay persons total 300 judgments, the distribution between genuine signatures and simulations should track the distribution in the total test pool fairly closely. So for illustrative purposes it is fair to say assume there were likely about 224 times that document examiners faced genuine signatures. Assuming this, of those genuine signatures, the document examiners accurately identified 192 as genuine. But they expressed no opinion as to 16 of those genuine signatures, and they affirmatively misidentified 16 of them as simulations. Similarly, using the same assumptions, the document examiners faced approximately 190 simulations, and they got 177 right, offered no opinion on 12, and made only one error.

In the case of non-document examiners, they may fairly be taken to have faced about 162 genuine signatures. Of these, they got about 113 right. They expressed no opinion at a lower rate than document examiners (4.3% of the time, or about seven cases), and they declared genuine signatures to be simulations 42 times (about 26%). Clearly, intra-writer variation creates a serious problem, making many genuine signatures appear questionable.[6] Though document examiners did better in sorting this out, they still had a fairly high rate of error.

Lay test subjects faced about 138 simulations. They correctly identified about 127

---

[6]This is consistent with the results of the   1988 FSF test discussed §§ 4:15 to 4:26.

of these as simulations. Again, they responded that they admitted inability to determine genuineness less than the document examiners (in only two cases), and they wrongly declared more simulations to be genuine than did the document examiners (nine times, as opposed to the document examiners single error in a larger universe of decisions). However, it also appears fairly clear that most simulations were not very convincing to anyone, since both document examiners and ordinary folks identified more than 90% of them as simulations (96% for document examiners, 92% for ordinary people).

Another way to express the differences in performance between document examiners and non-document examiners is to describe the error rate when you hear the conclusion "genuine" or the conclusion "simulation" (omitting any time an examiner is unable to reach a conclusion).[7]

For document examiners, the conclusion "genuine" was given 193 times, which was right 192 times and wrong once. The conclusion "simulation" was given 193 times, and which was right 177 times and wrong 16 times.

With lay persons, the conclusion "genuine" was given 122 times, which was right 113 times and wrong nine times. The conclusion "simulation" was given 169 times, which was right 127 times and wrong 42 times.

Thus, document examiners were right about 99.5% of the time when they said "genuine" and 92% of the time when they said "simulation." Lay persons were right 93% of the time when they said "genuine" and 75% of the time when they said "simulation."

What conclusions can be drawn from this study? Taken at face value, a reasonable interpretation of the results would be something like this:

- naive simulators do not on the whole appear to produce very convincing simulations. The overwhelming majority were properly identified as such by both document examiners and lay persons, though document examiners had a marginal advantage 96%–92%

- neither document examiners nor lay persons actually declare naive simulations to be genuine very often. However, simulations were found to be genuine by lay persons 6.5% of the time, and by document examiners only a half a percent of the time. The fact that one document examiner declared one of these naive simulations genuine indicates that the expert error rate even for this easy task is not vanishingly small, but it is small, both absolutely and compared to the lay group, even though the lay group did not perform poorly itself

- intra-writer, or "natural," variation among genuine signatures written by a single person poses serious dangers when trying to determine whether a signature is genuine or simulated. Thus, 8% of what document examiners declared to be simulations were in fact genuine signatures, and 25% of what lay persons similarly declared to be simulations were genuine. While the document examiners were better than the lay persons in this regard, the document examiner error rate on this supposedly easy task is substantial, and much higher that the document examiner literature would lead one to believe[8] (This conclusion is also consistent with the results of the 1988 FSF study, wherein document examiners declared a genuine signature of Joanna Neuman to be not genuine 18.5% of the time (5 of 27 responses).[9])

- Document examiners are significantly better at avoiding being fooled by genuine signature variation than lay persons, and significantly better at most

---

[7]Note that these values may differ from those in the table because these do not include inconclusives in the calculations.

[8]See, e.g., statements of Ron Furgerson, FBI Document Section Chief, quoted at §§ 4:14 to 4:38, and Todd, Do Experts Frequently Disagree?, 18 J. Forensic Science 455 (1973).

[9]§ 4:24.

authentication subtasks than are lay persons under these test conditions. However, the advantage may partly be the result of a phenomenon which has by now been repeatedly observed in testing document examiners against ordinary people. Under test conditions, ordinary people seem generally less likely to choose indecision options than document examiners.[10]

However, before generalizing these results to the real world, caveats are in order.

First, none of the Kam tests have yet resolved the incentive problem. All reward schemes for lay subjects used so far would seem to bias lay subjects toward affirmative declarations and away from inconclusives. Both Kam III and internal variations in the reward schemes used in Kam IV have led Kam to conclude that variations in reward schemes do not significantly affect lay test-taker performance. However, Kam III itself contains internal evidence of the effect from incentive scheme variation, as we have seen above.[11] Beyond that, it seems virtually certain that *some* reward schemes could change the way lay subjects responded under various levels of uncertainty. None of the schemes used by Kam so far have imposed sufficiently high penalties on affirmative error[12] to mirror document examiner motivation in tests which may affect the continued existence of their profession. However, this caveat is perhaps rendered less serious by the notion that the lay test subjects need not be as motivated to avoid error as the document examiners, merely as motivated to avoid error as jurors, and the deficiencies of the incentive schemes in the tests are much less clear in this regard.

What is more important, however, are the gross potential differences in document examiner performance between test conditions and real conditions of practice. Put simply, document examiner performance under test conditions is likely to be the best performance of which they are capable, and therefore error rates are likely to the lowest possible error rates under ideal conditions which do not apply to the real world. This is because of two linked variables: motivation and expectancy effects.

It is safe to say that, given the controversy of the last decade, there is not a document examiner in the country who does not understand that high error rates on tests, especially errors which would commonly be false positive errors in criminal cases, could lead to the widespread exclusion of document examiner testimony, and potentially, to the loss of their career. While this would be most clearly true in regard to non-blind proficiency tests, where individual performance might be discovered and compared to group norms, it is true even for tests like the Kam tests, which appear to have been designed to the extent possible to eliminate the potential for identifying and drawing conclusions about individual performance. Under conditions of normal practice, however, it is not at all clear that the sociology of the law enforcement agencies for which most of the document examiners work actually disvalues false positives to the same degree, or that inconclusive responses are as professionally acceptable in practice as on a test. The effect of different contexts with different intrinsic motivations is compounded by the highly suggestive manner in which cases are often presented to document examiners, complete with the theory of the investigators and the non-handwriting reasons for reaching one

---

[10]This was observed in the Galbraith, Galbraith and Galbraith, The "Principle of the Drunkard's Search" as a Proxy for Scientific Analysis: The Misuse of Handwriting Test Data in a Law Journal Article, 1 Int'l J. of Forensic Document Examiners 7 (1995), and in Kam II.

[11]§ 4:30.

[12]Especially error which could be identified as likely to be false positive error in criminal cases, a kind of error which all document examiners know would be the kiss of death if revealed *in*

*test data.* (As has been discussed above, it is not at all clear that they are equally motivated to avoid such error in real practice.) Interestingly, this asymmetrical motivation to avoid error of a certain type is reduced in the Kam IV test, since erroneous declarations of authenticity and inauthenticity can both lead to false convictions in criminal cases, depending on the case and its facts, though erroneous declarations of authenticity would more commonly have that result, since check forgery is such a common crime.

conclusion or another.[13] It would be startling if these circumstances did not affect performance and, consequently, error rates.

Nevertheless, these caveats are not really criticisms of the Kam IV test itself, and it is up to the legal system to fashion appropriate doctrines to take into account the difficulties in reasoning from the ideal conditions of tests to the predictably different and non-ideal conditions of practice. It may also be up to the legal system to require the conditions of practice to better mirror the ideal,[14] but failure as yet to do so cannot be laid at Dr. Kam's doorstep. Post hoc, the results of Kam IV can give some comfort to Judge McKenna, by providing evidence that, under test conditions, document examiners significantly outperform ordinary people in determining signature genuineness (which was the basic task at hand in *Starzecpyzel*).[15] And the same results can frustrate the defense attorneys in the same case, since they would have dearly loved to have had the data on the 8% document examiner error rate even under ideal conditions on the exact task that the document examiner performed in that case. And the results can give no comfort at all to the judges in all the other intervening cases where document examiner testimony was admitted on a different and more difficult "task at hand" (therefore, presumably at least, subject to much higher error rates), for which there still are no data, particularly attribution of authorship from a signature or other similarly limited sample. Kam IV shows the way. Ten or 20 further similarly designed tests devoted to different tasks will begin finally to map the contours of document examiner skill, and show other clinical forensic disciplines what is needed.

## § 4:32 Additional research

After nearly 13 years of effort by the document examiner community, a pre-1989 empirical validity study has finally been unearthed that was not reviewed in Risinger, Denbeaux and Saks's landmark article, Exorcism of Ignorance as a Proxy for Rational Knowledge: The Case of Handwriting Identification "Expertise."[1] It is a 1975 study published in German by Wolfgang Conrad,[2] the results of which do not, however, offer much support for the claims of document examiners. It will be summarized below.

In addition, three new studies and a set of studies have been obtained. One of the new studies is by two Australian practitioner-scientists, Bryan Found and Doug Rogers, who tested the accuracy of opinions of genuine, disguised, and simulated signatures among forensic document examiners in Australia and New Zealand. Another is by Jodi Sita, Found and Rogers, and once again deals with judgments of signature authenticity. The third study is by Sargur Srihari and associates, who try to test the hypothesis that all writing is unique and individualizable. The set of studies consists of the proficiency studies conducted by the Collaborative Testing

---

[13]See the court's comments in *U.S. v. Rutherford*, 104 F. Supp. 2d 1190, 1193, 55 Fed. R. Evid. Serv. 201 (D. Neb. 2000).

[14]See generally Risinger, Saks, Thompson & Rosenthal, The *Daubert/Kumho* Implications of Observer Effects in Forensic Science: Hidden Problems of Expectation and Suggestion, 90 Cal. L. Rev. 1 (2002).

[15]Or was it? Kam IV deals with the dangers of authentic signature variation with regard to a set of 19–30 year olds. What does this tell us about the dangers of similar variations with regard to infirm elderly persons in the early stages of Alzheimers, which was in fact the issue in *Starzecpyzel*. This simply and clearly illustrates

the problems of both over and under-specificity which must be dealt with carefully when formulating the "task at hand."

[Section 4:32]

[1]137 U. Pa. L. Rev. 731 (1989).

[2]Conrad, Empirische Untersuchunger über die Urteilsgüte verschiedener Gruppen von Laien und Sachverständigen bei der Unterscheidung authentischer und gefälschter Unterschriften [Empirical Studies Regarding the Quality of Assessments of Various Groups of Lay Persons and Experts in Differentiating Between Authentic and Forged Signatures], 156 Archiv. für Kriminologie 169 (1975).

Service, studies now supervised by the American Society of Crime Laboratory Directors, for the period 1990 through 2000. All will be dealt with in turn following the summary of the Conrad study.

## § 4:33  Additional research—Conrad (1975)

This study was conducted in Germany and reports comparisons among 25 professional handwriting experts, 100 laypersons who apparently were not specially motivated to perform well, 25 more motivated laypersons, and six college students who had taken courses in handwriting psychology and comparison. Each was presented with 10 known exemplar signatures and six questioned signatures (half of which were genuine and half of which were forged). With respect to the ability to identify forged signatures, judged by the respondents at any level of confidence, college students made errors of judging forged signatures to be genuine 5.6% of the time, experts made errors 17.3% of the time, highly motivated laypersons erred 12.0% of the time, and less motivated laypersons erred 21.7% of the time. Looking only at those judgments made with a confidence level "bordering on certainty," the college students erred 0.0% of the time, experts 2.7% of the time, and the motivated laypersons 5.3% of the time. With respect to the ability to identify genuine signatures, judged by the respondents at any level of confidence, college students made errors of judging genuine signatures to be forged 11.1% of the time, experts 12.0% of the time, highly motivated laypersons 28% of the time, and less motivated laypersons erred 41.6% of the time. Looking only at those judgments made with a confidence level "bordering on certainty," the college students erred 0.0% of the time, experts 5.3% of the time, and motivated laypersons 8.9% of the time.

The most important aspect of this study is that it informs the debate over the role of motivation in studies comparing experts and laypersons, suggesting that motivation is a confound in those studies. Here, the experts generally performed no better than motivated laypersons (most differences were not statistically significant). Conrad concludes that, "one cannot speak of a clear factual superiority on the part of the experts, especially since the findings did not show that experts are better defended against serious or even extreme erroneous assessments in individual cases than lay persons working under favorable circumstances, are highly motivated and with a comparable educational level." The study further suggests that there are some non-experts (in this case, college students who had studied the psychology of handwriting) who generally performed significantly better than the experts did.

## § 4:34  Additional research—Found and Rogers

The Australian study of signature identification by Bryan Found and Doug Rogers is part of a program of evaluation of forensic document examiner skills generally in which detailed feedback is provided to individual examiners to enable them to understand which specific kinds of tasks cause them difficulty.[1] The introduction to the study states:

---

**[Section 4:34]**

[1]Bryan Found & Doug Rogers, Revision and Corrective Action Package: Signature Trial 2001 (Distributed on CD-ROM by the Forensic Expertise Profiling Laboratory, School of Human Biosciences, La Trobe University, Australia). By way of introduction, the report explains:

The FEPL has evolved over the past 6 years through collaborations between the School of Human Biosciences (La Trobe University, Australia), the Special Advisory Group (which, under the direction of the Senior Managers of Australian and New

Zealand Forensic Laboratories, represents police and government document examiners in Australia and New Zealand) and the National Institute of Forensic Science.

The FEPL provides a program aimed at characterising skill and expertise associated specifically with human perceptual and cognitive processes related to forensic opinion formation. Forensic handwriting identification is a discipline that uses these processes almost exclusively when determining the authorship of questioned writings. In spite of the routine use of handwriting evidence in courts of law internationally, the nature of the skill, the expertise claimed, and the theoretical constructs articulated

Forensic handwriting examination can simply be regarded as a skill. The skill is applied to cases which vary according to the amount and complexity of both the questioned and specimen material. No one test will determine the validity of the skill. Over time, given sufficient trials, a picture of the skill for individuals should emerge. This will allow us to determine which aspects of the skill claimed by examiners are valid, which are not and what the likely error rate is for different types of examination.

The questioned signatures in the study were: 43 genuine signatures written by the specimen writer in that writer's normal signature style; 160 simulated samples (written by two forgers freehand copying the signature characteristics of the specimen writer); 47 disguised signatures written by the specimen writer. These were to be compared to known writings by the specimen writer. In all, 51 answer booklets were submitted by document examiners for analysis. These booklets included 10 peer reviewed responses, 10 experimental responses (from individuals and trainees), and 31 individual responses (including one trainee).

A total of 10,250 opinions were expressed by the group. Of these opinions 49% (5039) were correct, 7% (756) were in error, and 43% (4455) were inconclusive. If we omit the inconclusives from the computation, of the 5795 decisions offered, 87% were correct and 13% were in error.

These opinions were broken down according to whether the examiner was responding to writings that were, in actuality, genuine, disguised, or simulated. The results are presented in the following table.

### Table 5. Results from the Found & Rogers Study

| The Questioned Signatures Were | Correct | Erroneous | Inconclusive |
|---|---|---|---|
| Genuine | 92% | 2% | 6% |
|  | 98 | 2 | - |
| Disguised | 30 | 24 | 46 |
|  | 55 | 45 | - |
| Simulated | 43 | 4 | 53 |
|  | 91 | 9 | - |

The data indicate that when a signature was disguised, examiners had considerable difficulty accurately associating it to its actual author. Simulations caused 9% to offer conclusions that were erroneous. Even genuine signatures were not matched to their author 2% of the time.

Additional analyses suggested that errors tended to cluster among certain examiners, and those examiners often were from the same lab, and who often received their training under the same mentor, in the same training environment. For a field in

by the community of document examiners, until recent times, has remained almost devoid of empirical support.

Since 1994 over 30000 blind trial opinions have been collectively expressed by the participants on handwriting and signature trials. The year 2000 marked the final stage in the evolution of this program where participants were given the opportunity to express at least 500 blind trial opinions on signatures and handwriting annually. Participants are issued with a certificate that profiles the nature of their skill in terms of error, conservatism and correct rates. This certificate will provide courts of law with information regarding forensic handwriting skills that has been previously unavailable.

This package provides an overview of the first of the 2001 trials.

Forensic scientists outside of the U.S. are more likely to be trained as scientists, as in the case of these two doctoral level Australian behavioral scientists. In addition, there is more likely to be a connection between the forensic science service and university science departments. These roots in the community of science are reflected in their approach to the work and their interest in and ability to do empirical research on the topics of their professional interest. All of that is absent from American forensic document examination.

which training takes place so much by apprenticeship, this is an important finding. It suggests that students tend to acquire the same practices and understandings as their mentors—for good or for ill. That suggests that, at least for forensic handwriting examiners, courts might benefit from learning of the backgrounds of the proffered witness and the track record of that witness and that witness's teacher, or at least to demand extensive proficiency data on each examiner, and condition admission on those data.

Finally, as with the FSF studies reported above,[2] further analyses also indicated no relationship between the number of years of experience and likelihood of being correct or in error.

### § 4:35    Additional research—Sita, Found & Rogers (2002)

The participants in this study by Sita et al.[1] consisted of 17 professional handwriting examiners and 13 laypersons, all from Australia and New Zealand. Test materials consisted of 10 mock cases each containing 15 exemplar and 15 questioned signatures. The questioned signatures in different test packets contained different proportions of genuine and forged signatures. The results given in the study do not disaggregate the tasks of evaluating genuine versus forged signatures, but give combined results. Correct decisions were made by experts 54.8% of the time compared to 57.1% of the time by laypersons. This is not a statistically significant difference favoring laypersons, but it very nearly is. Similarly, experts achieved a mean number of accurate decisions of 81.9 compared to 85.6 for laypersons.

Incorrect decisions were made by experts 3.4% of the time compared to 19.3% by laypersons. Experts made a mean number of erroneous decisions of 5.0 compared to 29.0 for laypersons. Experts were unable to reach a decision 41.8% of the time compared to 23.6% of the time by laypersons. Experts averaged 63.1 inconclusive decisions compared to 35.4 by laypersons.[2]

The results of this study are similar in one way to those of the Kam IV signature authentication study, showing no superiority for experts over lay persons in calling a genuine signature genuine, but an apparent superiority among experts to refrain from calling a nongenuine signature genuine. In both studies, the superior expert performance was achieved mainly by the greater use among the experts of the "inconclusive" response. Whether the risk-averse decision threshold which generates that high percentage of inconclusives on known tests is typical of actual forensic practice is subject to doubt.

The Sita et al. study went on to evaluate the data generated for the document examiners in more detail. It found that, as the complexity of the signature goes up (and it therefore contains more information), the accuracy of document examiner performance also goes up.[3] This is the expected result correlating accuracy with the amount of information manifested in the questioned document, and it indirectly raises questions concerning tasks involving low information questioned sources (documents containing block printing, or only small amounts of writing whether or not printed).

Further, the study revealed that expert performance was by no means uniform,

---

[2]§ 4:21.

**[Section 4:35]**

[1]Sita, Found, and Rogers, Forensic Handwriting Examiners' Expertise for Signature Comparison, 47 J. Forensic Sci. 1117 (2002).

[2]Sita, Found, and Rogers, Forensic Handwriting Examiners' Expertise for Signature Comparison, 47 J. Forensic Sci. at 1119, Table 1.

[3]Sita, Found, and Rogers, Forensic Handwriting Examiners' Expertise for Signature Comparison, 47 J. Forensic Sci. at 1120 (2002), Table 1.

with five perfect performers and four with numerous errors.[4] While the same information is not given for the lay performers, it seems reasonably clear that there were some lay people who outperformed some "experts."

In addition, this study reports a higher overall error rate for document examiners than did Kam IV. In that study, when document examiners called "genuine" they were wrong about 8%[5] of the time, whereas in Sita et al. they were wrong 12.2% of the time. In Kam IV, when they said "simulation" they were wrong less than 0.5% of the time,[6] whereas in Sita et al. they were wrong 2.1% of the time. Sita et al. attribute this to likely variation in the difficulty of the tasks presented by the signatures and simulations in their test.[7]

Again, no significant correlation was found between accuracy and years of experience.[8]

## § 4:36 Additional research—Srihari, Cha, Arora, and Lee (2002)

The study published recently by Sargur Srihari and his colleagues[1] was funded by the National Institute of Justice as part of its initiative to support empirical research concerned with the bases of forensic handwriting examination. For their project they drew handwriting samples from 1568 individuals, which they desired to make representative of the United States population.[2] Computer algorithms were used to extract features from scanned images of the handwriting. Attributes of the handwriting were compared at different levels to try to distinguish writers from each other, and the automated comparison routines were able to do so at varying levels of accuracy (about 95% at the document level, about 88% at the paragraph level, about 83% at the word level, and about 91% at the character level). The authors concluded that they were able to distinguish writers with a high degree of confidence. They state:

> Based on a few macro-features that capture global attributes from a handwritten document and micro-features at the character level from a few characters, we were able to establish with a 98% confidence that the writer can be identified. Taking an approach that the results are statistically inferable over the entire population of the U.S., we were able to validate handwriting individuality with a 95% confidence. By considering finer features, we should be able to make this conclusion with a near 100% confidence.[3]

The greatest value of this study is likely to prove to be that it will lead to a system of handwriting comparison which performs much better than human examiners, does so using a finite set of objective (observable, measurable, definable) procedures, and which facilitates the computation of the probability of error in the identification or exclusion. That would be an extremely important direction in which

---

[4]Sita, Found, and Rogers, Forensic Handwriting Examiners' Expertise for Signature Comparison, 47 J. Forensic Sci. at 1121, Figure 2.

[5]§ 4:31.

[6]§ 4:31.

[7]Sita et al., at 1123.

[8]Sita et al., at 1121.

**[Section 4:36]**

[1]Srihari, Cha, Arora, and Lee, Individuality of Handwriting, 47 J. Forensic Sci. 856 (2002) ("The work was motivated by U.S. high court rulings that require expert testimony be backed by scientific methodology. Since handwriting had not been subjected to such a study, we decided to undertake this endeavor.").

[2]The study seems to assert that its sample is representative of the U.S. population. But its sampling procedures were poorly designed to accomplish that (". . . obtained samples by contacting schools in three states (Alaska, Arizona, and New York) and communities in three states (Florida, New York, and Texas) through churches and other organizations.") and at the end of the day it did not achieve a sample which reflects U.S. population with respect to the demographic variables to which the authors compared their sample. As discussed below, since the effort at obtaining a nationally representative sample is wrongheaded given the purposes of the study, the study is better for the authors having failed in their attempt.

[3]Srihari, Cha, Arora, and Lee, Individuality of Handwriting, 47 J. Forensic Sci. at 871 (2002).

to take future stages of this research.

Oddly, those important potential benefits do not seem to be the focus of the study. Srihari et al. emphasize one unwarranted and speculative conclusion which they suggest is implied by their research.[4] In conjunction with the statement quoted above, the authors assert: "Our work has employed handwriting features similar to, but not exactly the same as, those used by document analysts in the field. However, the objective analysis that was done should provide the basis for the conclusion of individuality when the human analyst is measuring the finer features by hand."[5] In other words, they assert that the notion that handwriting is infinitely variable across writers ("uniqueness") has been all but established, based on their sample of 1568 plus the assumption that because human examiners have available to them more features than were used by the computer algorithms, the human examiners will do an even better (a perfect?) job.

Their conclusion is reached by conflating two non-findings. The study itself was not able to distinguish all 1568 writers from each other. Likewise the study did not test any human examiners; comments on the capabilities of human examiners are entirely speculative. But by combining those two non-findings, the authors claim to have "provide[ed] the basis for the conclusion of individuality."

If nothing else, their conclusion would seem to be refuted both by studies of actual handwriting examiners, which usually do not find the accuracy levels Srihari et al. seem to say should be found and by Harris's study finding writings by different individuals which were indistinguishable from each other. That in turn suggests either that Srihari et al.'s inference of uniqueness is mistaken or that the algorithms outperform human examiners, or both.

Srihari et al.'s speculation relies heavily on the assumption that the more attributes taken into account, the more accurate one will be in distinguishing writers. That likely is true for computers. For humans it often leads to information overload. Research in cognitive science finds that humans often do not use the richness of information available to them. Instead, they rely inconsistently on a small number of factors to which they apply non-optimal weights.[6]

A finding of 98% accuracy does not establish unique individuality. Indeed, even a finding of 100% accuracy in Srihari et al.'s research would not establish unique individuality. That is because accuracy in this context depends upon the number and nature of features and the size of the sample. For example, if I can distinguish the writing of every student in my seminar of 10 students, that 100% accuracy would not prove anything about handwriting uniqueness (though it would affirm the obvious: that there is some amount of variability in writing). If I could accurately distinguish every one of a million writers from each other, that would be a more impressive achievement, and more useful for forensic purposes. But even that would tell us only that there is a lot of variability; it cannot assure us that the variability

---

[4]At various points in their article Srihari et al. characterize their work in the following terms: "[A] step towards providing scientific support for admitting handwriting evidence in court." "Our study is an effort to establish the individuality of handwriting." "A study was conducted for the purpose of establishing the individuality of handwriting."

This will sound to many readers more like the approach of advocates than of scientists, that is, the authors set out to prove a hypothesis in order to gain a field admission to court, rather than conducting a more disinterested inquiry into the truth or falsity of a hypothesis. But the authors'

candor probably helps us to understand why they offer speculative conclusions which reach beyond what their study can support.

[5]Srihari, Cha, Arora, and Lee, Individuality of Handwriting, 47 J. Forensic Sci. at 871 (2002).

[6]In other areas of research, as here, it was at first assumed that formal (mathematical) models of decision-making would provide a floor of accuracy below which human decision-makers would not be allowed to fall. Subsequent research, however, often found that the floor was a ceiling above which humans typically could not rise. The classic work on this topic is Paul Meehl, Clinical Versus Statistical Prediction (1954).

is virtually infinite.

Put most simply, then, Srihari et al.'s sample of 1568 is too small for a study aimed at establishing unique individuality.[7] The smaller the sample, the less likely it is that handwriting twins will be found. The extrapolation of their sample of 1568 to the population of the United States makes little sense given the goal of trying to establishing that every person's writing is distinguishably different from every other person's writing. In work of the kind done by Srihari et al., as the sample size increases (for example, approaching that of a metropolitan population), the likelihood of finding indistinguishably similar writers would rise, perhaps considerably, and the ability to distinguish those writers accurately would fall, perhaps considerably.

The attempt at maximizing writer diversity to the extent of the United States population reduced still further the ability of the study to establish infinite uniqueness among writers. The research actually benefitted from the fact that the attempt was not achieved. Maximizing the diversity of the sample of 1568 makes the task of distinguishing writers easier (for the computer or humans). By inadvertently exploiting regional, ethnic, gender, age, and whatever other differences exist, the pool of writing was made more varied than it would be if (for example) all of the "suspects" grew up in one neighborhood and all learned to write at the same school. The results would have been more impressive and more useful (for both the research question and the forensic context) if the sampling method had been to collect a representative sample of *clusters* of writers around the country, with each cluster being composed of highly *similar* writers. That would have tested the degree to which highly similar writers can be distinguished, and replicated the finding among numerous groups of such writers.

Just as the size of the sample of writers affects inferences about the ability to distinguish writers, the amount of handwriting sampled also affects the conclusion. In the present study, the writing consisted of a special 156 word letter designed to include all letters and numbers and to sample a very wide range of significant writing, such as distinctions between capitals and small letters, at the beginning and end of words, and involving certain combinations of special interest. Again, this artificially maximizes the ability to distinguish writers. Were the writing sample to decrease in size, or contain less diverse writing—that is, to approximate something more typical of crime scene writing—accuracy would decline, perhaps only a bit, perhaps considerably.

As the type of writing changes from dozens of words of script to a single signature to printed letters or numbers (again, things which are more typical of the writing in forensic case work), the accuracy level is likely to decline. Srihari et al.'s research cannot be generalized to those other situations. The research on those other writings needs to be done. (That is, there needs to be testing of smaller *writing* samples, larger and more homogeneous *writer* samples, and kinds of writing that have fewer distinguishing features.)

Strictly speaking, to establish unique individuality it would be necessary to compare every member of the population to every other member. Srihari et al.'s shortcut is unconvincing for the various reasons discussed. But the obsessive and nearly impossible search for uniqueness is also unnecessary. A more feasible and scientifically defensible approach would be to develop a method to provide empirically based statements of the extent of variability in the population and the consequent probability of a coincidental match—much as is done with DNA typing,

---

[7]Adequacy of sample size depends on the requirements of the research question and methodology. For some experiments, samples of 20 or 30 are adequate. For others, such as prospective epidemiological studies, samples in the tens of thousands often are necessary to provide useful findings.

which is highly useful and diagnostic while at the same time does not rely on the notion of uniqueness or the requirement of empirically establishing the unique individuality of DNA. The population genetics of DNA typing avoids the paradox that has been recognized by mathematicians and thoughtful forensic scientists, namely, that there is no bridge from probability theory to a conclusion of unique individuality. One can use probability theory and data sampled from populations only to reach a conclusion about the random match probability, not to declare a unique pinpoint match.

The Srihari et al. research has something far more valuable to offer than to pursue the elusive and illusory quarry of uniqueness. Srihari et al.'s research forms the basis for an improved system of handwriting comparison. That is the future toward which it could be most usefully directed.

## § 4:37   Additional research—The CTS Proficiency Tests (1990–2002)

The CTS proficiency studies have not been published and not generally made available to anyone who is not a test-taker or a part of the forensic science establishment.[1] We have been trying unsuccessfully for years to obtain these studies. They have now come to us as the result of a subpoena issued pursuant to a *Daubert* hearing. Of 15 test reports we have received, only seven concerned handwriting. The rest were about other asserted skills of document examiners (e.g., concerning photocopiers, rubber stamps, ink, typewriting, and so on).

The 1992[2] proficiency test was provided to 125 of whom 84 returned the reports of their findings. The handwriting portion of the test was designed to see whether examiners could detect that a signature on a copy of a purchase order was created by the tracing of a genuine signature. About 92% (77 of 84) of examiners correctly concluded that the signature was a tracing. About 8% (seven) mistook the tracing for an electromechanical creation.

The 1994[3] test was provided to 148 examiners, of whom 117 returned the reports of their findings. Examiners received three questioned checks and known writing standards of three people. Q1 and Q3 were written by K1 and Q2 was written by K3. This was designed to be "a straightforward handwriting identification problem," involving the writers' "natural writing." And all 100% of the respondents reached the correct answers. One interesting error, however, was that an examiner offered the conclusion that one of the writers was left-handed. There is no method of determining handedness that is recognized among document examiners. And the writer in question was in fact right-handed.

The 1996[4] test was provided to 174 examiners, of whom 137 returned the reports of their findings. This, too, was designed to be a "common handwriting problem in which the actual writer was not included in the suspect group." Examiners received one questioned note and three known writing standards of three suspects, all written in the natural writing of the writers, and all similar in skill level and overall style, so that there were no glaring differences. The correct conclusion would be to eliminate all of the suspects. Regarding suspect K1, only 38% (52 of 137) of examiners were able to exclude, 47% (64) were able to "probably exclude," about 9% (13) were in equipoise regarding inclusion or exclusion, and fewer than 1% (1) erroneously identified K1 as the author. Regarding suspect K2, only 25% (34) of examiners were able to exclude, 43% (59) were able to "probably exclude," about 15% (20) were

---

**[Section 4:37]**

[1]CTS has recently changed this policy, and now posts results on their internet website.

[2]Collaborative Testing Services, Questioned Documents Analysis, Report No. 92-6 (1992).

[3]Collaborative Testing Services, Questioned Documents Examination, Report No. 9406 (1994).

[4]Collaborative Testing Services, Forensic Testing Program, Questioned Documents Examination, Report No. 9606 (1996).

in equipoise regarding inclusion or exclusion, and about 4% (5) erroneously identified or "probably" identified K2 as the author. Regarding suspect K3, only 28% (39) of examiners were able to exclude, 40% (55) were able to "probably exclude," about 20% (28) were in equipoise regarding inclusion or exclusion, and about 6% (8) erroneously identified K3 as the author.

The 1997[5] test was provided to 131 examiners, of whom 109 returned the reports of their findings. Examiners received two questioned checks and 15 checks known to have been produced by K1. All writing on the questioned checks had been made by K1 except the amount in both words and numbers on check Q1. Regarding check Q2, about 5% (5 of 109) of examiners failed to discern that all writing was made by K1. Regarding check Q1, about 43% (47) correctly eliminated K1 as the author of the amount in words and numbers. About 31% (34) could not determine whether or not K1 wrote the amount in words and numbers. About 9% (10) refrained from venturing any opinion on the issue. And about 10% (11) erroneously identified K1 as the writer of all the writings (both Q1 and Q2).

The 1998[6] test was provided to 141 examiners, of whom 119 returned the reports of their findings. This, again, was a "routine handwriting identification case," which the test-takers thought was quite easy, as the data seem to confirm. A single writer produced handwritten material and a signature, which was sent to examiners along with the known writing samples of three suspects. All of the examiners reported that Q1 was, or probably was, written by K3. Interestingly, there was a close correspondence of opinions about the body of the receipt and the signature on the receipt, that is examiners who were less than sure about the authorship of the body also were less than sure about the author of the signature. Several examiners made clerical errors (recording an incorrect conclusion after writing a correct narrative conclusion), which most likely would have been detected before going to trial.

The 1999[7] test was provided to 155 examiners, of whom 140 returned the reports of their findings. Examiners received six questioned documents, being partially completed state auto inspection certificates on which there was handprinting and numbers, plus specimen writing from three persons, K1–K3. Items Q1 and Q4 were written by K2. Items Q2 and Q3 were written by K3. Item Q6 was written by K1. And item Q5 was written by a person whose writing was not included among the known exemplars. All participants correctly concluded who wrote, or probably wrote, Q1, Q2, Q3, Q4, and Q6. The certificate without a suspect's exemplars, item Q5, gave examiners more difficulty. Six examiners (about 0.4%) erroneously concluded that Q5 was written by K2 or K3 or both of them together. About 13% (18 examiners) could not exclude K1 as the author of Q5; about 16% (23) could not exclude K2; and about 17% (24) could not exclude K3.

The 2000[8] test was provided to 150 examiners, of whom 135 returned the reports of their findings. Examiners were provided with a set of nurses notes for three shifts (day, evening, and night) and known writing samples from three "nurses," K1–K3. The day shift notes were written by K1. The night shift notes were written by K3. And the evening shift notes were written by someone whose writing was not included among the exemplars. Nearly all examiners correctly identified the author of the day shift notes as K1 (though 10 examiners thought the identification was only "probable" and one thought no identification could be made). Similarly, nearly all examiners correctly identified the author of the night shift notes as K3 (though nine

[5]Collaborative Testing Services, Forensic Testing Program, Handwriting Examination, Report No. 9714 (1997).

[6]Collaborative Testing Services, Forensic Testing Program, Handwriting Examination, Report No. 9814 (1998).

[7]Collaborative Testing Services, Forensic Testing Program, Handwriting Examination, Test No. 99-524 (1999).

[8]Collaborative Testing Services, Forensic Testing Program, Handwriting Examination, Test No. 00-524 (2000).

examiners thought the identification was only "probable" and one thought no identification could be made). The evening shift notes, for which no correct author was among the exemplars presented examiners with some difficulty. Only 40% (54 of 135) were able to exclude (while 36% (49) were able to somewhat exclude) K1 as the author. Only 56% (75) were able to exclude (while 40% (54) were able to somewhat exclude) K2 as the author. And only 43% (58) were able to exclude (while 39% (53) were able to somewhat exclude) K3 as the author. One examiner erroneously thought that the evening shift notes "were written" by K1, and two examiners erroneously thought that these notes "probably were written" by K2.

The 2001 handwriting identification proficiency test[9] was built around a "weekend sign-in log." Apparently the log was in the normal form, with columns for "date," "name," "time arrived," and "time departed." Three such "questioned" entries were to be examined, which read as follows:

| Q-1: | 20 Jan. | Kenny Bania | 8:30 | 11:15 |
| Q-2: | 20 Jan. | Kenny Bania | 11:24 | 15:40 |
| Q-3: | 21 Jan. | Kenny Bania | 11:30 | 12:45 |

These three questioned entries were to be compared to three sets of known writings: those of Kenny Bania (K-1), Sue Ellen Mischke (K-2), and David Puddy (K-3). The known writings were apparently fairly extensive and included material from both "course of business" writings (things written in the normal course without any controversy in mind) and "dictated" writings (also called "request" or "demand" writings) provided explicitly for the purposes of comparison. In reality, Kenny Bania, who gave the known writings K-1, actually wrote the Q-1 and Q-3 entries.

The Q-2 line was written by a person whose writing was not provided. She had written the Q-2 entry after examining Kenny Bania's real handwriting, having it taken away, and then attempting to simulate it from memory. None of this person's actual known writing was provided.

Sue Ellen Mischke (K-2) and David Puddy (K-3) wrote no part of Q-1, Q-2, or Q-3.[10]

Results of the tests were submitted by 131 people. They responded on a five category scale as follows A-was written by; B-was probably written by; C-cannot be identified or eliminated; D-was probably not written by; E-was not written by.

As to Q-1, 123 participants accurately said Kenny Bania wrote Q-1, and the other eight said he probably wrote Q-1.[11]

As to Q-3, the numbers were similar, 122 positive identifications of Kenny Bania as the author and nine who said Bania had probably written Q-3. On this test, declaring these particular authentic signatures authentic gave little problem. In

---

[9]Collaborative Testing Services, Forensic Testing Program, Handwriting Examination, Test No. 01-524 (2001).

[10]Before giving the results, one detail requires comment. Though the name "Kenny Bania" appears on the sign-in sheets, it may not have been an actual signature, though there is reason to believe that it was a signature, or at least that it was in cursive, since the Manufacturer's Information mentions that the sign-in sheets contained both "printing and writing." If so, it presented a "signature authentication" problem. Signature authentication problems, of course, are supposed to present easy tests according to standard

Osbornian handwriting identification tenets. Once again, this illustrates how difficult it is to determine just how easy a "test" has been made by test designers without seeing copies of the test materials themselves. One should always remember that it was not until the materials used in the FBI fingerprint proficiency tests were actually produced and examined by the Scotland Yard expert in *U.S. v. Llera Plaza* that their unrealistically easy design was discovered. See § 4:16.

[11]Interestingly, at least two respondents positively identified Bania as the author of Q-1, but did not positively eliminate either Mischke or Puddy as the author.

this regard, the test was apparently similar to that presented by the "Lisa Bridgeforth" questioned document in the 1988 proficiency test.[12]

That leaves Q-2, and here the results are less heartening. Out of 131 responses, 16 said that Q-2 was written by Kenny Bania and four said it was probably written by him. In addition, one person said Sue Ellen Mishcke probably wrote Q-2, and another said David Puddy probably wrote Q-2. Thus, there were 22 incorrect responses. It gets worse. While 33 respondents positively eliminated Mishke, and 34 eliminated Puddy, only 20 eliminated Bania. Granted that Bania was given probable elimination by 55 respondents, the clarity of his authorship of Q-1 and Q-3 seems to have made some respondents reluctant to eliminate him altogether. Bania does not appear to have been a very good candidate for Q-2, despite the attempt at simulation from memory, since 75 respondents eliminated or probably eliminated him, compared to 63 and 66 respectively for Mishke and Puddy. All in all, more respondents refused to eliminate Mishke (66) than gave him any degree of elimination. Finally, comparing all positive responses in regard to Bania, 20 included him and 75 excluded him, for an error rate in regard to affirmative statements of 21.5%.

Some of the respondents apparently believed (correctly) that Q-2 was an attempt at simulation, or (incorrectly) disguise, and this may account for the high number of refusals to eliminate or identify. If the profession learned one thing from the 1984 proficiency test, it was to refuse to venture an affirmative opinion (at least on tests) when there are signs of simulation or disguise involved. Whether they are so circumspect in actual practice under the press of various circumstances which might generate powerful observer effects is questionable.

The 2002 proficiency test[13] contained serious design flaws. The first is attributable to the narrative "scenario" which was given with the testing materials in an attempt to put them in a realistic context (a practice that has been criticized before). Essentially, the details of the narrative made what turned out to be the true facts of the handwriting sources extremely unlikely. The fact that so many respondents failed to fall into the trap is probably more a tribute to the care and suspicion with which they approach tests and the artificial stories accompanying them than it is anything that might reflect actual practice.

The narrative was as follows:

Scenario

Wilson Temple has been divorced from his wife, Abby Newcomb, for 10 years. He was ordered by the divorce court to pay $600.00 alimony per month. His ex-wife just took him back to court, claiming that he is not paying the court-ordered alimony.

As partial proof that he has been paying the alimony, Mr. Temple produced four signed, handwritten receipts. He maintains that Ms. Newcomb wrote and signed all four of the receipts. Ms. Newcomb claims that she did not complete any part of these receipts, and has filed criminal forgery charges against Mr. Temple. As a result of this charge, the police detective sent in the disputed receipts and known handwriting samples of Mr. Temple and Ms. Newcomb for your examination. (Note that the body of the receipts was in fact hand printed, with the signature in cursive).

The answer sheet asks whether either Temple (K-1) or Newcomb (K-2) wrote the signatures on any of the receipts Q-1 through Q-4, and then asks separately whether either Temple or Newcomb wrote the body of the receipts Q-1 through Q-4. Note that under the scenario it might easily be that Ms. Newcomb wrote the body and signature on a receipt (which was in fact the case with Q-1 through Q-3), that Temple forged the body and signature on a receipt, or that Temple wrote out the

---

[12]§§ 4:23 to 4:25.

[13]Collaborative Testing Services, Forensic

Testing Program, Handwriting Examination, Test No. 02-524 (2003).

receipt for Newcomb's signature. It is not easy to imagine how Newcomb could have genuinely signed a receipt that was written out by someone other than her or Temple, but that was exactly the case in regard to Q-4. This problem was compounded by the fact that the receipts were all in handprinting using both capital letters and lower case letters, but the exemplars of Temple's writing (both "course of business" and "request") contained only capital letters, which was apparently his normal way of printing.

Once again, the signature part of the test is an authentication problem, and performance was generally very good, with nearly all the respondents identifying Newcomb as the signature on all four documents.[14] (Q-1: 119 positive, 11 probable;[15] Q-2: 118 positive, 11 probable; Q-3: 120 positive, 10 probable; Q-4: 113 positive, 14 probable, 4 no opinion. The mild rise in the "probable" and "no opinion" responses in regard to Q-4 may well be due to the clash between the details of the narrative and the circumstances of the questioned documents set out above.)

The responses in regard to identifying Newcomb as the author of the body of the first three receipts were also very good. (Q-1: 121 positive, nine probable; Q-2: 120 positive, 10 probable: Q-3: 122 positive, eight probable). However, as to the body of Q-4, results were less good, as perhaps was to be expected. Three respondents positively identified Newcomb as the author, and one positively identified Temple. In addition, four identified Temple as the probable author and two identified Newcomb as the probable author. Further, only 13 positively excluded Temple, 19 probably excluded, and 90 couldn't identify or exclude, generally because of the "all-capitals" printing exemplars. So of the 37 actual opinions rendered concerning Temple's authorship, 13.5% were erroneous. (Things were a bit better in regard to Newcomb. There were 91 exclusion opinions as to her (36 positive and 55 probable), so of the 96 opinions rendered in regard to her, only 5.2% were in error.)

In an attempt to explain the errors in this set of responses, the test administrators did not lay the blame on the test (as they well could have, but that would show the impact of observer effects flowing from non-domain specific information). Instead, they indicated that nine of the 10 respondents who made errors were from countries where English was not a first language. How this affects a handwriting identification problem under traditional handwriting identification assumptions is unclear. What it does establish, however, is that the test administrators have a lot more data about the test and its takers, at least in regard to most respondents, than they disclose. One of their prominent disclaimers on every test is that these results cannot be used to make statements about error rates because the characteristics of the respondents are not known. However, it is clear that some such information is gathered for most of the respondents, and results could be given in such a way as to obviate that problem, to the extent that it exists. Once again, it is clear that those who are in charge of the program are withholding information in order to make it difficult to establish even a minimum for the error rates that the Supreme Court in *Daubert* and *Kumho Tire* has said are important to know.

Two comments might be made about these results, one methodological and one substantive.

The methodological observation is the answer that comes from the question: why are these results, in general, so much better than the results of earlier tests? Have

---

[14]One "participant" apparently marked "could not identify or exclude" as the answer to all questions, in protest to the use of photographs instead of original writings as materials.

[15]The "probably wrote" responses are something of a problem, since they are generally linked to a refusal to completely exclude the other presented candidate (responding only "probably didn't write" for that one). Are these opinions merely properly circumspect, or improper attempts to hedge bets in the context of a case which seems to present something of a risky binary decision?

handwriting examiners improved abruptly and markedly? Or did the tests become easier? Most likely, the latter. The test manufacturers describe them as more straightforward, they appear to be simpler, and rather than complaining about test difficulty (as examiners did before the 1990s), examiners now commented about how easy the tests were. This question could be answered most usefully by seeing how well non-experts performed on the very same tasks. At the same time, that would answer the most basic question before a gatekeeping judge, namely, whether the experts provide some help beyond what a jury could do by examining the writing for itself. More important than how easy or hard the tests are, is the question *Kumho Tire* instructs courts to ask: how closely do these tasks approximate the task-at-hand that experts are offered to perform in the case at bar.[16]

The substantive finding worth noting is that document examiners have more difficulty when trying to exclude than to include (especially where the true match is not present among the knowns under consideration). The theory of forensic identification would lead one to expect the opposite, namely, that exclusion is easier than inclusion. A questioned and a known mark cannot be declared to match if there is any "unexplained" difference between them; yet the absence of any discernible differences is no assurance that the two share a common origin. But, for whatever reason—perhaps the considerable variability that exists within the writing of a single writer—handwriting examiners experience the opposite: they are more uncertain about exclusions than inclusions. This is somewhat analogous to the situation of eyewitnesses presented with a blank lineup (one from which the true perpetrator is absent). The eyewitnesses tend to make "relative judgments," that is, they ask themselves, in effect, which of those in the lineup comes nearest to looking like their memory of the perpetrator. That is a leading cause of eyewitness error. When asked to compare a questioned writing with knowns which do not include the actual match, document examiners apparently have some tendency to focus on the similarities between the known and the exemplars, rather than to exclude what in reality are non-matching exemplars. This seems to be an area of potential false positive error, much as it is for eyewitnesses. Perhaps researchers will some day take an interest in this phenomenon as it pertains to handwriting examiners. Meanwhile, it has implications for opinions in the courtroom. Where investigators have failed to provide the examiners with exemplars of the true source of the questioned writing, many examiners will not be able to confidently exclude all non-common-source suspects. (Thus, for example, on the 1996 test, only 28% of examiners were able to exclude suspect K3 as the writer of the questioned note, while about 20% were in equipoise regarding inclusion or exclusion, and about 6% erroneously identified K3 as the author.)

### § 4:38    Areas of disagreement: Testing document examiner expertise— Conclusions

In summary, what should we make of the available empirical data concerning handwriting identification expertise? First, any affirmative use of the data to support any hypothesis must be heavily qualified because of the small number of studies that have been conducted and their methodological problems. Even with this in mind, it seems fair to say that such a skill probably exists in some people for some tasks, but probably involves a large amount of inherent talent, and that while training and practice of "the true method" of atomized analysis may lead some people to become more dependable at some tasks, such credentials and experience alone do not necessarily establish the existence of a dependable skill.

Beyond this, if anything appears to be supported by the data, it is that there are

---

[16]In several instances the test manufacturer or proficiency advisory committee characterized the tests as being common handwriting problems.

many context-defined subtasks involved in handwriting identification, some easy, some very hard. Such skill as exists seems to be undependable even in many of those who have it, when it comes to many hard subtasks. Not even the most generous reading of currently available data could support a claim that we know how to define all of those subtasks. In addition, as a practical expertise, handwriting identification differs from many areas (such as Judge McKenna's harbor piloting) in that independent confirmation of the accuracy of one's results does not dependably emerge from everyday practice.

Finally, there is reason to believe that, like eyewitness identification, handwriting identification is strongly influenced by context cuing, that is, by the presentation of extraneous information to the examiner indicating the answer desired and non-handwriting reasons for its being the correct conclusion. Such presentations appear to be the norm in the submission of actual cases to document examiners, as even the materials of the FSF studies reveal.[1] Here the founding fathers of the area were quite sensible, for Hagan, Ames, and Osborn all took strong positions that it was the professional duty of the document examiner to insist that such information not be presented and to take steps to set up modes of consultation to insure against such contamination.[2]

## § 4:39   Future directions: Interdependence of research and court decisions

In the first edition of this treatise, this section emphasized that information on the actual contours of document examiner reliability would be forthcoming only to the extent the legal system forced it to be derived and produced in court, and, in its absence, was willing to reject proffered testimony. On this front there has been progress and there is reason to hope for future progress. The response of judges who have actually examined the empirical record in that regard has been overwhelmingly one of troubled concern and skepticism. The Supreme Court's decision in *Kumho Tire Co., Ltd. v. Carmichael* has made it clear that, at least for the federal

---

**[Section 4:38]**

[1]*See* the discussion of the presentation of extraneous context information by the designers of the FSF studies, and the use of such information by test-takers, at § 4:24.

[2][T]he examiner must depend wholly upon what is seen, leaving out of consideration all suggestions or hints from interested parties; and if possible it best subserves the conditions of fair examination that the expert should not know the interest which the party employing him to make the investigation has in the result. Where the expert has no knowledge of the moral evidence or aspects of the case in which signatures are a matter of contest, there is nothing to mislead him, or to influence the forming of an opinion; and while knowing of the case as presented by one side of the contest might or might not shade the opinion formulated, yet it is better that the latter be based entirely on what the writing itself shows, and nothing else.

William E. Hagan, Disputed Handwriting at 85 (Banks & Bros., Albany, 1894).

No expert should permit himself to be *retained* in the sense in which an attorney is retained, viz., for the purpose of making the most of and winning a case, right or wrong . . . .

When the services of an expert are sought, he should, so far as is possible, avoid knowing the circumstances or the relations of the party asking his opinion as to the case.

D.T. Ames, Ames on Forgery at 89 (Bancroft-Whitney, San Francisco, 1899).

It should be understood that the chief source of error in these cases is this intense partisan spirit and the spirit of advocacy surrounding the whole proceeding. The scientific examiner deliberately endeavors to keep outside the circle of these influences. Too often the investigation of what is in fact a genuine document, or, of what is in fact a crude forgery, is not taken up as a scientific investigation but every argument and every influence is brought to bear in order to get favorable opinions and assistance from those who can assist in any way . . . .

There is of course certain legitimate information that the qualified examiner should have as to alleged conditions surrounding a document that is questioned but he does not need to know, and should not be told, why this or that should have been done or should not have been done by a testator or why, for other outside reasons, it is reasonable to assume that the alleged act was, or was not, performed. One who examines a document should have information as to the condition of an alleged writer or any alleged surrounding conditions that may have affected the result, or any facts that are a legitimate part of the technical problem which is submitted to him.

What Osborn referred to as "true methods," Albert S. Osborn, Questioned Documents at 2–3 (2d ed. 1929).

courts, the nonscientific nature of a claimed expertise is no excuse for failing to evaluate its reliability by appropriate standards, and that such evaluation must be directed to the reliability of the expertise in the specific "task at hand" at issue in the particular case. Even before the lessons of *Kumho Tire* had been fully internalized, trial judges (in federal court, at any rate) had begun to place substantial restrictions on the kind of testimony that could be given by document examiners in handwriting identification cases under the *Hines/McVeigh* approach, allowing testimony concerning only similarities and differences, and forbidding conclusions. Unfortunately, this approach is flawed, in that it represents a Solomonic compromise not tied specifically to required *Kumho Tire* "task at hand" analysis and evaluation. *United States v. Fujii*, however, provides an example of proper *Kumho Tire* analysis, and shows the way for the future.

Note that, just because *Fujii* resulted in full exclusion of document examiner's testimony in regard to the task of identifying whether a particular Japanese man trained in English as a second language in Japan was the author of a limited amount of handwriting on INS forms, this does not mean that all document examiner testimony should be excluded in regard to every "task at hand." Research can provide a warrant for believing that document examiners possess sufficient skills in regard to particular tasks to warrant admission, at least under test conditions. Kam IV shows for the first time how such specific "task at hand" research can be designed and administered. While one should be hesitant to base too much on a single unreplicated study, and while Kam IV involves only writers between the ages of 19 and 30, it would not be irrational for a judge to be influenced by the results in deciding whether to allow document examiner testimony on the question of signature authenticity, leaving the weight of the testimony to cross examination or counter-testimony concerning the document examiner error rates shown by the research on this, and perhaps other, tasks.

In June of 1998 the Justice Department's National Institute of Justice issued a formal solicitation for proposals for Forensic Document Examination Validation Studies to be funded by the Institute. To date, no results of such studies have been published.[1] However, one can hope that they will follow Kam IV's lead in testing document examiner performance against non-document examiner performance in regard to particular tasks of the kind that are commonly the subject of proffered testimony. After a couple of dozen such studies, we will finally begin to know what document examiner testimony ought to be admissible under *Kumho Tire*, and what ought to be excluded. Until the studies are produced, the proper response under the terms of Fed. R. Evid. 702 and *Kumho Tire* should be total exclusion. If this is true generally, it is even more certain in regard to those tasks clearly recognized as exceptionally problematical by the leading document examiner treatises themselves, such as attributing the authorship of forged signatures, or other very limited examples of writing.

Finally, even good research of the Kam IV variety cannot resolve one huge and protean problem undermining the reliability, not only of document examiner testimony, but potentially of all forensic science: context suggestivity in the way cases are presented to the expert for evaluation. This issue is both serious, and potentially curable, at least to a large degree, by changes in the practice of crime laboratories. Once again, however, crime labs are likely to do only what courts force them to do. And once again, there is at least some mild reason to believe that at least some courts are beginning to notice, as the criticism of the suggestive presen-

---

**[Section 4:39]**

[1]Instead, the funding was apparently directed toward the development of computerized handwriting identification. § 4:40.

tation by investigators to the document examiner in *United States v. Rutherford*[2] shows. Certainly the suggestive way a particular case is presented is an appropriate factor to be considered in any *Daubert/Kumho* reliability determination.[3] Whether courts will become more appropriately sensitive to this in the future remains to be seen. And when, if ever, any of this will percolate into the consciousness of courts in criminal cases to the same degree it already has in some civil case contexts[4] is another question that only time can answer.

### § 4:40  Future directions: Computer authentication and identification of handwriting

It is appropriate to note in closing the current activities of the United State Department of Justice regarding handwriting identification expertise validation. The Federal Bureau of Investigation formed a Technical Working Group on Forensic Document Examination (TWGDOC) in May of 1997.[1] The first task undertaken by TWGDOC was to develop an agreed upon set of standard procedures for performing handwriting comparisons.[2] The National Institute of Justice (N.I.J.) noted in 1998 that "[s]uch procedures must be based . . . on more than community-based agreement. Procedures must be tested statistically in order to demonstrate that following the stated procedures allows analysts to produce correct results with acceptable error rates. This has not yet been done."[3]

In July, 1996, N.I.J. held a "Workshop for Planning a Research Agenda for Questioned Document Examination (now called Forensic Document Examination)."[4] As a result of that workshop, and in recognition that since "the seminal ruling in *United States v. Starzecpyzel* . . . the judicial system has challenged FDEs, especially handwriting identification, to demonstrate its scientific validity and reliability as forensic evidence,"[5] and further recognizing that this had not yet been accomplished, the N.I.J. solicited proposals for research concerning "the statistical validation of the individuality of handwriting,"[6] and the "statistical validation of standard operating procedures for handwriting comparison."[7] To date, no results of such research have been published. However, in an apparent attempt to explore instrumented alternatives to human document examiners, the N.I.J. funded research by a group at the State University of New York at Buffalo. This group has made some progress towards a computerized system which may one day be able to

---

[2]*U.S. v. Rutherford*, 104 F. Supp. 2d 1190, 1193, 55 Fed. R. Evid. Serv. 201 (D. Neb. 2000) ("FDE Rauscher admitted that he was not given samples of anonymous writings and then given the questioned documents for the purposes of determining which one of the anonymous writers wrote the questioned documents (Tr. 68:18–25). Instead, prior to Rauscher's analysis, the government identified the author of the exemplars (samples) and explained its theory that the writer of the exemplars and the checks was the author of the questioned documents (e.g., check and load out sheet).").

[3]See generally Risinger, Saks, Thompson & Rosenthal, The *Daubert/Kumho* Implications of Observer Effects in Forensic Science: Hidden Problems of Expectation and Suggestion, 90 Cal. L. Rev. 1.

[4]See generally Risinger, Navigating Expert Reliability: Are Criminal Standards of Certainty Being Left on the Dock?, 64 Albany L. Rev. 99 (2000).

[Section 4:40]

[1]National Institute of Justice, U.S. Department of Justice Solicitation: Forensic Document Examination Validation Studies 2 (June, 1998).

[2]National Institute of Justice, U.S. Department of Justice Solicitation: Forensic Document Examination Validation Studies 2 (June, 1998).

[3]To date, (May, 2001) TWGDOC has yet to issue a report, at least publicly, or to publish such standards.

[4]National Institute of Justice, U.S. Department of Justice Solicitation: Forensic Document Examination Validation Studies 2 (June, 1998).

[5]National Institute of Justice, U.S. Department of Justice Solicitation: Forensic Document Examination Validation Studies 2 (June, 1998).

[6]National Institute of Justice, U.S. Department of Justice Solicitation: Forensic Document Examination Validation Studies 2 (June, 1998).

[7]National Institute of Justice, U.S. Department of Justice Solicitation: Forensic Document Examination Validation Studies at 3 (June, 1998).

determine if handwriting was authored by a particular person with a defined degree of random match probability, at least under some circumstances. However, the research is still in the developmental stage.[8] Available information concerning both the design of validation tests and their results is not sufficient to evaluate the current state of their research, beyond saying that no claim is made that the system has been developed to the point that it could be confidently used in many recurrent tasks, especially those involving potential disguise. In addition, it appears clear that in any situation where the program must consider a significant number of potential candidates for authorship of a handwriting sample, its current accuracy drops precipitously. Nevertheless, future developments may lead to a system having the proven capacity to replace human document examiners with instrumentally generated information of known high validity and low error rates under the conditions actually applying to particular identification tasks in a particular case.

---

[8]A visually impressive slide show summary of the research to date may be found at www.ceda r.buffalo.edu.NIJ/pres/sld001.htm.

# Chapter 5

# Firearms and Toolmark Identification

## I. LEGAL ISSUES

## II. SCIENTIFIC ISSUES

## I. LEGAL ISSUES

### § 5:1  Generally

Reported judicial examinations of the scientific evidence on which toolmark and firearms examination (formerly, and incorrectly, termed "ballistics") expertise rests are remarkably few, and the resulting opinions tend to be both empty and opaque. While expert evidence on toolmarks and firearms identification is universally admissible,[1] this universal admissibility has come about with virtually no judicial evaluation of the validity of the underlying science or its application. One might have expected the situation to change following *Daubert*,[2] but so far that has not happened.

---

**[Section 5:1]**

[1]Cases can be found admitting testimony on a wide assortment of tools and tool markings. For some examples: Screwdrivers and crowbars on doors, sashes, and safes: *State v. Wade*, 465 S.W.2d 498 (Mo. 1971); *State v. Brown*, 291 S.W.2d 615 (Mo. 1956); *State v. Eickmeier*, 187 Neb. 491, 191 N.W.2d 815 (1971); *People v. Perroni*, 14 Ill. 2d 581, 153 N.E.2d 578 (1958) (overruled on other grounds by, People v. Nunn, 55 Ill. 2d 344, 304 N.E.2d 81 (1973)). Knives on wood: *State v. Clark*, 156 Wash. 543, 287 P. 18 (1930). Car tools: *Adcock v. State*, 1968 OK CR 147, 444 P.2d 242 (Okla. Crim. App. 1968); *State v. Smith*, 156 Conn. 378, 242 A.2d 763 (1968). Hammers: *State v. Olsen*, 212 Or. 191, 317 P.2d 938 (1957). Bolt cutters used to gain entry or on the stolen material: *Souza v. U.S.*, 304 F.2d 274 (9th Cir. 1962). Bullets: see § 5:3. See generally, Andre A. Moenssens, et al., Scientific Evidence in Civil and Criminal Cases § 6.27 (1995).

[2]*Kumho Tire Co., Ltd. v. Carmichael*, 526 U.S. 137, 119 S. Ct. 1167, 143 L. Ed. 2d 238, 50, 50 U.S.P.Q.2d 1177, Prod. Liab. Rep. (CCH) P 15470, 50 Fed. R. Evid. Serv. 1373, 29 Envtl. L. Rep. 20638 (1999) (hereafter, *Kumho Tire*).

## § 5:2  Toolmark identification

Apparently the first appellate decision to consider the admissibility of modern toolmark identification expertise was *State v. Fasick*,[1] a 1928 Washington State case which rejected the proffered testimony. In that case, a murder had been committed and the body covered with fir branches cut from nearby trees. The government offered Luke S. May, a pioneering forensic scientist who would become one of the founders of toolmark identification.[2] May had made sample cuttings of fir branches with the suspect's knife and examined the microscopic marks left by the blade, comparing them with the marks left in the branches found covering the body. He concluded that the branches had been cut with the same knife, thus placing the defendant at the crime scene. The trial court initially excluded, but then admitted, May's testimony. The Washington Supreme Court, however, found the logic behind the expert's opinion unconvincing. Wrote the Court: "You could not tell in a thousand years whether the two pieces were cut by the same knife."[3] On rehearing one year later the Court affirmed its initial rejection of toolmark identification expertise.

Eighteen months after deciding *Fasick* and only six months after re-affirming itself, the Washington Supreme Court was presented with remarkably similar evidence from the same expert. This time, in *State v. Clark*,[4] in the context of a rape case, fir boughs and saplings had been cut and used by the rapist to construct a blind from which to attack his victim. Again a knife, again cut fir branches, again Luke May the proffered expert witness. But this time the Court held that expert opinion about whether the defendant's knife cut the branches was evidence that was admissible: "The photomicrographs . . . conclusively establish, we are convinced, as doubtless the jury were, that the cuts were made with the same blade."[5] The Washington Supreme Court made no explicit effort to explain its abrupt reversal, and barely even acknowledged the contradictory opinion in *Fasick*, decided only months earlier.[6]

In an article written the same year *Clark* was decided, May discussed the case, describing what he had offered to the court. He asserted that he had "conclusively established" that the same knife was used. His inference of that identification was derived by probabilistic reasoning that is familiar[7] in the field of forensic identification:

> Invoking the law of probabilities, using the algebraic formula for determining combinations and permutations, with only one-third of the marks here shown as factors, there would be only "one" chance of there being another blade exactly like this if every one of the hundred million people in the United States had six hundred and fifty quadrillion knives each.[8]

Several years later, after praising the *Clark* Court for making an "outstanding

---

**[Section 5:2]**

[1]*State v. Fasick*, 149 Wash. 92, 270 P. 123 (1928), aff'd, 149 Wash. 92, 274 P. 712 (1929).

[2]The dust cover to his semi-autobiographical book on forensic science characterizes May as "America's Sherlock Holmes." Luke S. May, Crime's Nemesis (1936).

[3]*State v. Fasick*, 149 Wash. 92, 96, 270 P. 123 (1928), aff'd, 149 Wash. 92, 274 P. 712 (1929).

[4]*State v. Clark*, 156 Wash. 543, 287 P. 18 (1930).

[5]*State v. Clark*, 156 Wash. 543, 287 P. 18, 20 (1930).

[6]Yet the *Clark* court was ebullient in its praise of this new specie of evidence:

Courts are no longer skeptical that by the aid of scientific appliances the identity of a person may be established by finger prints. There is no difference in principle in the utilization of the photomicrograph to determine that the same tool that made one impression is the same instrument that made another impression. The edge on one blade differs as greatly from the edge on another blade as the lines on one human hand differ from the lines on another. This is a progressive age. The scientific means afforded should be used to apprehend the criminal.

Nor do the briefs to the Court give any clues as to what changed from *Fasick* to *Clark*.

[7]Saks & Koehler, What DNA "Fingerprinting" Can Teach the Law About the Rest of Forensic Science, 13 Cardozo L. Rev. 361 (1991).

[8]May, The Identification of Knives, Tools, and Instruments a Positive Science, 1 Am. J.

progressive decision," a "significant step forward,"[9] May described the *Clark* opinion as "a precedent which has already been cited in criminal trials in many other states, thereby legally advancing science in its battle against crime." While it may be that *Clark* was called to the attention of some trial judges, the opinion did not, and surprisingly so, become the talisman for the admission of toolmark expert evidence as, say, *Jennings*[10] had become for fingerprints. *Clark* was cited in only two subsequent appellate opinions, and not for propositions that would have pleased Luke May.[11] Somehow *Clark* went from standing for the "conclusive" power of toolmark identification evidence in 1930 to standing for the admissibility of "a less than exact" process in 1985.

There is nothing in the *Clark* opinion that could help a judge in a subsequent case to understand why toolmark evidence was valid and admissible, if indeed it was. The case merely offered the conclusory and unexplained enthusiasm of a Court that only months before had rendered its equal and opposite opinion on the very same question.

After so interesting a start in the case law, the subject of the validity of toolmark identification evidence has had surprisingly little appellate exposure in the decades since. From *Fasick* in 1929 to *Ramirez v. State*[12] in 1989, no other cases excluding toolmark identification evidence are to be found. For 25 years following *Clark*, there are no appellate decisions scrutinizing any aspect of toolmark identification.

Toolmark identification opinions resurfaced in 1955 with *People v. Wilkes*.[13] In *Wilkes*, the state's expert testified that although ordinarily no more than 25% of the striations correspond when a tool other than the one used in the crime is compared, in this instance 80% of the striations corresponded. He concluded, therefore, that the defendant's drift punch was the one used to help open a safe. In upholding the admission of this testimony, the court cited nothing other than a distant analogy to another case of a burgled safe in which a heel print left on an invoice at the crime scene corresponded to a shoe owned by the defendant.

A year later, in *State v. Brown*,[14] the Missouri Supreme Court upheld the admissibility of toolmark expert testimony based on no citations to legal or scientific authority. Instead, the court rested on being impressed by the expert witness's prior employment by the FBI as an analytical chemist and his hobby of carpentry. The defendant's argument that the testimony was admitted without anything that resembled scientific support was to no avail. The court relied on the notion that trial judges have discretion to admit or exclude expert testimony on myriad subjects, and the jury bears the ultimate responsibility to weigh all the evidence.[15] With so

---

Police Sci. 246 (1930).

[9]Luke S. May, Crime's Nemesis at 47 (1936). Unfortunately, he misses the chance to teach us something about the difference between the contrast in the court's thinking from *Clark* to *Fasick* because he does not mention *Fasick* at all.

[10]*People v. Jennings*, 252 Ill. 534, 96 N.E. 1077 (1911).

[11]*Hansel v. Ford Motor Co.*, 3 Wash. App. 151, 473 P.2d 219 (Div. 1 1970) (a case not involving toolmarks at all); *State v. Bernson*, 40 Wash. App. 729, 700 P.2d 758 (Div. 3 1985), opinion modified on denial of reconsideration, (June 27, 1985) (for the proposition that "[a]n expert's use of 'could have' or 'possibly' has been allowed in other cases where a less than exact scientific process is involved.").

[12]*Ramirez v. State*, 542 So. 2d 352, 83 A.L.R. 4th 651 (Fla. 1989).

[13]*People v. Wilkes*, 280 P.2d 88 (Cal. App. 1st Dist. 1955), opinion vacated on other grounds, 44 Cal. 2d 679, 284 P.2d 481 (1955).

[14]*State v. Brown*, 291 S.W.2d 615 (Mo. 1956).

[15]The U.S. Supreme Court held in *General Elec. Co. v. Joiner*, 522 U.S. 136, 118 S. Ct. 512, 139 L. Ed. 2d 508, 18 O.S.H. Cas. (BNA) 1097, Prod. Liab. Rep. (CCH) P 15120, 48 Fed. R. Evid. Serv. 1, 28 Envtl. L. Rep. 20227, 177 A.L.R. Fed. 667 (1997) that appellate review under *Daubert* is deferential—a dubious legal principle for dealing with scientific principles, which are trans-case. But even *Joiner* does not authorize deference to opinions devoid of reasons, or devoid of reasons having any substance. Moreover, it is doubtful

deferential a standard, there really was nothing for the court above to decide.[16]

The next case reviewing the admissibility of toolmark identification appears twenty years later—an appeal from a burglary conviction in North Carolina. This court in this case reasoned: "It seems abundantly clear that . . . there can be expert testimony upon practically any facet of human knowledge and experience."[17] It appears that this court mistook the phrase "can be" for "is." Whether an adequate expertise existed yet, vel non, was the issue presented. The court simply begged the question, abdicating any judicial responsibility to assure that evidence submitted to the jury has some minimum level of validity. The court merely assumed an expertise into existence.

The first federal court to opine on the question of toolmark admissibility did so in 1978 in *Fletcher v. Lane*.[18] Here, the defendant challenged a toolmark expert's positive identification—of a screwdriver found in the defendant's home as being the one that made prymarks on the victim's door, to the exclusion of all other screwdrivers in the world—as an assertion that could not be made, that was unsupportable, or at least unsupported, on scientific grounds, and therefore should not have been admitted.[19] The district court converted this challenge from one of scientific validity to one of credibility: "Petitioner's . . . contention is essentially an attack on the credibility of the expert testimony. The credibility of a witness is a matter for jury determination . . . ."[20] Again, this seems to be the kind of open door policy that *Daubert* and its progeny have sought to close, or at least to place a gatekeeper in front of.

An example of the error into which courts may fall by so casually scrutinizing expert testimony is provided by *Commonwealth v. Graves*.[21] An expert testified that scratch marks on the neck of a victim of strangulation matched the defendant's fingernail. The defendant challenged this type of identification as lacking sufficient scientific recognition to meet the *Frye* admissibility standard.[22] The court turned away the challenge, concluding:

> [T]he methods and techniques used . . . all were consistent with standards of general scientific acceptance in the field of tool-marks, of which, according to the witnesses,

---

that the actual rule in any American jurisdiction in the past century was that trial judges had the discretion, on a case by case basis, to admit or exclude what they please, without coherent explanation and reviewable only on a test of clear error. For one pre-*Daubert* analysis of the role of law and appellate courts in such matters, see *Dunagin v. City of Oxford, Miss.*, 718 F.2d 738, 10 Media L. Rep. (BNA) 1001 (5th Cir. 1983). What these cases may really reflect is the daunting challenge of having to think rationally about those myriad subjects, develop workable legal tests, and apply them consistently. It is easier for the appellate courts to pass the problem to the trial courts and the trial courts to pass the problem to the jury. At least by their terms, *Daubert* and *Kumho Tire* would seem to have brought an end to such evasions of evaluation, at least by trial judges.

[16]The same rationale can be found in *State v. Churchill*, 231 Kan. 408, 646 P.2d 1049 (1982).

[17]*State v. Raines*, 29 N.C. App. 303, 224 S.E.2d 232, 234 (1976) (quoting Stansbury's N.C. Evidence, Subject Matter of Expert Testimony, § 134 at 438).

[18]*Fletcher v. Lane*, 446 F. Supp. 729 (S.D. Ill. 1978).

[19]Cf., May, The Identification of Knives, Tools, and Instruments a Positive Science, 1 Am. J. Police Sci. 246 (1930).

[20]*Fletcher v. Lane*, 446 F. Supp. 729, 731 (S.D. Ill. 1978). The same rationale can be found in *Potter v. State*, 416 So. 2d 773 (Ala. Crim. App. 1982).

[21]*Com. v. Graves*, 310 Pa. Super. 184, 456 A.2d 561, 40 A.L.R.4th 563 (1983). The expert at issue on this point was a forensic odontologist examining a fingernail mark.

[22]*Frye v. U.S.*, 293 F. 1013, 34 A.L.R. 145 (App. D.C. 1923) (rejected by, State v. Walstad, 119 Wis. 2d 483, 351 N.W.2d 469 (1984)) and (rejected by, State v. Brown, 297 Or. 404, 687 P.2d 751 (1984)) and (rejected by, Nelson v. State, 628 A.2d 69 (Del. 1993)) and (rejected by, State v. Alberico, 116 N.M. 156, 861 P.2d 192 (1993)) and (rejected by, State v. Moore, 268 Mont. 20, 885 P.2d 457 (1994)) and (rejected by, State v. Faught, 127 Idaho 873, 908 P.2d 566 (1995)) and (rejected by, People v. Shreck, 22 P.3d 68, 90 A.L.R.5th 765 (Colo. 2001)).

testimony as to finger nail wounds is a part.[23]

But consider this comment on the case:

> The Pennsylvania reviewing court, however, completely failed to recognize that the class characteristics of the fingernail and the scratch marks, although similar, lacked the necessary individual markings to tie the accused's fingernail to the scratch marks on the victim to the exclusion of all others.[24]

In other words, there was no consideration of the possibility by the court, and apparently not by the expert either, that the marks found were characteristic of a large class of fingernails and not of one of the defendant's nails uniquely.

In rare instances a court will reject the opinion of toolmark experts on the ground that a scientific predicate was not established. In *Ramirez v. State*[25] the government sought to prove that the defendant's knife was the murder weapon "to the exclusion of all other" knives in the world by showing that microscopic striations made by the suspect's knife matched microscopic striations on the victim's cartilage. Though in most cases the forensic science expert's mere assertion that something can be done reliably is enough for a court, in this case it was not. Neither was the fact that a Kansas court had admitted such testimony,[26] nor an article by the expert concerning the technique. The Florida Supreme Court held that this testimony was erroneously admitted because "no scientific predicate was established from independent evidence to show that a specific knife can be identified from the marks made on cartilage."[27] Cases requiring an adequate scientific basis to be established before allowing opinions based on that scientific predicate to go to the jury have been rare in the courts' review of toolmark expert evidence.[28]

## § 5:3 Firearms examination

Expert testimony identifying a particular weapon as the one source of both a questioned (crime scene) bullet and known bullets (test firings) is admissible in

---

[23]*Com. v. Graves*, 310 Pa. Super. 184, 456 A.2d 561, 566, 40 A.L.R.4th 563 (1983).

[24]Andre A. Moenssens, et al., Scientific Evidence in Civil and Criminal Cases § 6.27 at 379–380 (1995). See also Starrs, Procedure in Identifying Fingernail Imprint in Human Skin Survives Appellate Review, 6 Am. J. For. Med. & Path. 171 (1985).

[25]*Ramirez v. State*, 542 So. 2d 352, 83 A.L.R. 4th 651 (Fla. 1989). Pursuant to reversal and remand, Ramirez was again tried and convicted; again the conviction was reversed and remanded. The third trip up the appellate ladder is discussed infra.

[26]*State v. Churchill*, 231 Kan. 408, 646 P.2d 1049 (1982). "We reject the state's argument that, since the Supreme Court of Kansas in *Churchill* admitted testimony that a particular knife caused the wound, without a predicate of scientific reliability, we should do likewise." *Ramirez v. State*, 542 So. 2d 352, 355, 83 A.L.R.4th 651 (Fla. 1989).

[27]*Ramirez v. State*, 542 So. 2d 352, 354, 83 A.L.R.4th 651 (Fla. 1989).

[28]The *Kumho Tire*, task-at-hand, scientific question here is whether this medium (cartilage) is capable of receiving and holding without distortion marks of sufficient detail to permit a reliable toolmark analysis. Perhaps it can, perhaps it can-

not. And what are risks of error (false inculpatory opinions or false exculpatory opinions?) associated with the imperfections of the medium. Those are among the concerns a *Daubert/Kumho* court must decide. (Interestingly, Florida was and remains a *Frye* jurisdiction, yet it insisted on a scientific basis as a precondition to admission.) Obviously, the materials with which toolmark experts usually work, metal and wood, are less elastic than cartilage, which is probably less elastic than the materials with which forensic dentists usually work, though forensic dentists are looking at far less microscopic detail than toolmark examiners are.

Though the court does not address the issue, there also is the problem of an opinion that a knife is the murder weapon "to the exclusion of all others" in the world. Though this is a common sort of conclusion among toolmark and other forensic examiners, it does not follow from the probabilistic logic underlying this form of expertise—see discussion, supra, of Luke May and the origins of toolmark analysis, and the discussion, infra, of the science, and especially the discussion of objective criteria and the study of known nonmatching comparisons, § 5:12—but is in actuality a "leap of faith" from the improbable and unlikely to the absolute and certain. See also the related discussions of all other forensic identification sciences in their chapters in this treatise.

every American jurisdiction. At least 37 jurisdictions have approved it by appellate opinion.[1] In all others, presumably, admission is a consequence of no challenge having been raised, thereby giving the courts no occasion to consider the admissibility of such evidence. But in no case has careful judicial or legislative scrutiny of the premises and performance of firearms experts occurred.

The earliest cases[2] admitting firearms identification testimony occurred more than 30 years before the admission of fingerprint expert evidence.[3] But these early cases typically permitted non-experts to testify to such matters as the identification of a gunshot as having emanated from a particular type or caliber of firearm based on its sound, or that a certain wound was caused by a firearm of a particular caliber, or that bullets matched based on their weight.

The first case admitting what we may call modern firearms identification evidence—microscopic comparison of striations left on bullets by the characteristics of the barrel of a firearm—was *Commonwealth v. Best,*[4] an opinion written by Justice Oliver Wendell Holmes for the Massachusetts Supreme Judicial Court. The comparisons were made by manually pushing a bullet through the suspect firearm rather than firing it. The defense argued that this comparison was invalid because of changes in the firearm from the time it was allegedly used in a murder and the testing, and the method of testing.[5] Justice Holmes saw no problem:

> We see no other way in which the jury could have learned so intelligently how that gun barrel would have marked a lead bullet fired through it, a question of much importance to the case. Not only was it the best evidence attainable but the sources of error suggested were trifling. The photographs avowedly were arranged to bring out the likeness in the marking of the different bullets and were objected to on this further ground. But the jury could correct them by inspection of the originals, if there were other aspects more favorable to the defense.[6]

By the 1920s, Calvin Goddard had emerged as the "father" of modern forensic firearms identification, and was certainly the most prominent thinker, writer, and expert witness on the subject. Courts which had earlier rejected such expert evidence reversed themselves, at least in part under Goddard's influence. For example, in 1923 the Illinois Supreme Court rejected firearms identification expertise, concluding that identification of a bullet as having been fired by a particular gun was impossible and "preposterous."[7] But in 1930, in *People v. Fisher*[8] the same court reached the opposite conclusion. The principal difference between the two opinions is a lengthy and detailed account of Dr. Goddard's credentials and experience in the latter opinion, as if to say that an expertise, a science, exists in the person of an expert. But, of course, the case became precedent for the technique, not only for the testimony of Calvin Goddard.

----

**[Section 5:3]**

[1]See Expert evidence to identify gun from which bullet or cartridge was fired, 26 A.L.R.2d 892; Admissibility of testimony that bullet could or might have come from particular gun, 31 A.L.R. 4th 486.

[2]E.g., *Wynne v. State*, 56 Ga. 113, 1876 WL 2941 (1876); *Dean v. Com.*, 73 Va. 912, 32 Gratt. 912, 1879 WL 5437 (1879); *Moughon v. State*, 57 Ga. 102, 1876 WL 3098 (1876); *State v. Smith*, 49 Conn. 376, 1881 WL 2185 (1881); *People v. Mitchell*, 94 Cal. 550, 29 P. 1106 (1892); *State v. Hendel*, 4 Idaho 88, 35 P. 836 (1894).

[3]*People v. Jennings*, 252 Ill. 534, 96 N.E. 1077 (1911).

[4]*Com. v. Best*, 180 Mass. 492, 62 N.E. 748 (1902).

[5]More specifically, the defense argued, without rebuttal: (1) greatly divergent pressures between firing a bullet and pushing it; (2) a period of time passed from the date of the murder until the date of testing that allowed rust to form inside the barrel; and (3) shots had been fired through the weapon after the date it allegedly was used in the murder, thereby changing its characteristics.

[6]*Com. v. Best*, 180 Mass. 492, 495, 496, 62 N.E. 748 (1902).

[7]*People v. Berkman*, 307 Ill. 492, 139 N.E. 91 (1923).

[8]*People v. Fisher*, 340 Ill. 216, 172 N.E. 743 (1930).

The Court of Appeals for the District of Columbia Circuit decided its landmark firearms identification case, *Laney v. United States*,[9] on the same day that it decided the famous case of *Frye v. United States*,[10] in an opinion written by the same Judge Van Orsdel who wrote the *Frye* opinion. But, while *Frye* announced the standard that novel scientific techniques were admissible only when the theory on which they were based had achieved general acceptance in the relevant scientific community, on that same day firearms expertise was tested by an entirely different standard, and perhaps by no standard at all:

> . . . the testimony given by the expert witnesses, tending to establish that the bullet, extracted from the head of the deceased, was shot from the pistol found in the defendant's possession, was competent, and the examination in this particular was conducted without prejudicial error . . . .[11]

By the late 1920s and early 1930s the trend toward judicial acceptance of firearms identification was clear.[12]

More modern cases have met challenges to firearms identification expertise by referring to the earlier precedents—which themselves make no inquiry of either the *Frye* or the *Daubert* type, but generally concluded merely that relevance is the test of admissibility, and other concerns go only to the weight the jury should accord the testimony.[13]

## § 5:4 Post-*Daubert* decisions

The few federal cases to address the core claims of firearms and toolmark analysis post-*Daubert* reflect contrasting approaches. One approach struggles with the shortcomings of the scientific foundation and the challenges of applying the theory in practice. These courts are trying to meaningfully assess validity under *Daubert's*. The other approach grandfathers in such testimony on little more basis than that it had been admitted for some decades pre-*Daubert*. Cases following the former approach sometimes express the concern that the latter approach risks "grandfathering in irrationality."

Two Massachusetts cases pursue the close scrutiny approach, reach different conclusions, and issue different rulings. Somewhat paradoxically, *U.S. v. Monteiro*[1] found firearms identification to meet the requirements of *Daubert*, but excluded the

---

[9]*Laney v. U.S.*, 294 F. 412 (App. D.C. 1923).

[10]*Frye v. U.S.*, 293 F. 1013, 34 A.L.R. 145 (App. D.C. 1923) (rejected by, State v. Walstad, 119 Wis. 2d 483, 351 N.W.2d 469 (1984)) and (rejected by, State v. Brown, 297 Or. 404, 687 P.2d 751 (1984)) and (rejected by, Nelson v. State, 628 A.2d 69 (Del. 1993)) and (rejected by, State v. Alberico, 116 N.M. 156, 861 P.2d 192 (1993)) and (rejected by, State v. Moore, 268 Mont. 20, 885 P.2d 457 (1994)) and (rejected by, State v. Faught, 127 Idaho 873, 908 P.2d 566 (1995)) and (rejected by, People v. Shreck, 22 P.3d 68, 90 A.L.R.5th 765 (Colo. 2001)).

[11]*Laney v. U.S.*, 294 F. 412, 416 (App. D.C. 1923).

[12]Two noteworthy opinions come from Kentucky: *Jack v. Commonwealth*, 222 Ky. 546, 1 S.W.2d 961 (1928); *Evans v. Commonwealth*, 230 Ky. 411, 19 S.W.2d 1091, 66 A.L.R. 360 (1929). Moenssens et al. characterize *Jack* as the start of "a truly objective appraisal by the appellate courts" and *Evans* as the "first exhaustive opinion treating firearms identification as a science." Andre

A. Moenssens, et al., Scientific Evidence in Civil and Criminal Cases § 6.18 (1995).

[13]E.g., *State v. Schreuder*, 712 P.2d 264 (Utah 1985); *State v. Courtney*, 25 Ohio App. 3d 12, 495 N.E.2d 472 (12th Dist. Clermont County 1985).

**[Section 5:4]**

[1]*U.S. v. Monteiro*, 407 F. Supp. 2d 351, 69 Fed. R. Evid. Serv. 156 (D. Mass. 2006). The exclusion was based on the examiner's failure to adhere to (and in some regards even to know about) the field's standards. The proffered examiner failed to make sketches or take photographs, his notes contained no description of what led him to his conclusions, and a second examiner from his lab had not reviewed his work. All of that was considered especially important given the highly subjective nature of the judgments called for and the fact that the examiner had used replacement parts when test-firing one firearm. The ruling was without prejudice, so the government had the option of having the examination redone and re-offering the results. If an expert did end up testifying, he would be barred from asserting that his

expert's testimony. *U.S. v. Green*[2] found the field did not satisfy *Daubert*, but nonetheless admitted the testimony in part.

As to the core theory and data of firearms and toolmark analysis, both courts gave the issue extensive consideration. The *Montiero* court's *Daubert* hearing lasted six days; *Green's* lasted "several days." Both courts confronted major claims of and issues about the proffered field of expertise: The claim that all firearms are uniqueness, presumably resulting from "[r]andom imperfections produced during manufacture or caused by accidental damage . . . which are unique to that object and distinguish it from all others" (Heard). That studies of (relatively small numbers of) tools are consistent with that proposition. That the indicia of that uniqueness are accurately transferred to the ammunition, though along with class and subclass characteristics common to potentially large numbers of weapons. But that firearms examiners are able to discern and distinguish class, subclass, and individualizing features to correctly declare the identity of a weapon "to the exclusion of every other firearm in the world," or at least that "the likelihood that another tool could have made the mark is so remote as to be considered a practical impossibility" (AFTE), even though there exists no generally accepted standard for distinguishing among class, subclass, and individual characteristics. That the technique is based on a subjective "threshold currently held in the minds eye of the examiner and . . . based largely on training and experience in observing the difference between known matching and known non-matching impression toolmarks" (Grzybowski et al.). That there is an "almost complete lack of factual and statistical data pertaining to the problem of establishing identity in the field of firearm identification" (Biasotti), and that the examiner's judgments result from a process that is conceded to be entirely subjective, with no standards or guidelines, no reference materials of any specificity, no national or even local databases on which to reply. Both cases cite an extensive critique of the state of firearms identification, suggesting that it cannot support the strong conclusions asserted by examiners, but neither court rests much of its opinion on the article.[3] One court noted that the *AFTE Theory* was tautological "in that it requires each examiner to decide when there is 'sufficient agreement' of toolmarks to constitute an 'identification.'" The other court found the process by which examiners reached their conclusions to be "either tautological or wholly subjective. The tautological: [The examiner] said '[t]he standard that the identifiable features, the repeatable features, that are observed under the microscope, obviously have to be such that it's identified to one firearm only to the exclusion of all others. . ..' (citation omitted). The subjective: 'it has to present with individual characteristics that satisfy me in the end that it couldn't have come from any other firearm.' (citation omitted). Indeed, [the examiner] repeated this point over and over again."

At the end of the day, despite any misgivings, the *Monteiro* court found that the "government has met its burden with regard to demonstrating that the underlying

---

conclusion is 100% certain or to give any other statistical estimate.

[2]*U.S. v. Green*, 405 F. Supp. 2d 104 (D. Mass. 2005). The court permitted the expert to testify as to his observations on similarities and differences between the known and questioned shell casings, but was prohibited from offering an opinion on whether or not they were fired from the same weapon. The court implied that the proper result under *Daubert*, in light of the findings, would have been exclusion, but: "I reluctantly come to the above conclusion [to admit partially] because of my confidence that any other decision will be rejected by appellate courts, in light of precedents across the country, regardless of the findings I have made." *U.S. v. Green*, 405 F. Supp. 2d 104, 109 (D. Mass. 2005). The court goes on to note that "[t]he more courts admit this type of toolmark evidence without requiring documentation, proficiency testing, or evidence of reliability, the more sloppy practices will endure; we should require more." *U.S. v. Green*, 405 F. Supp. 2d 104, 109 (D. Mass. 2005).

[3]Schwartz, A Systemic Challenge to the Reliability and Admissibility of Firearms and Toolmark Identification, 6 Colum. Sci. & Tech. L.Rev. 2 (2004–2005).

scientific principle that firearms leave unique marks on ammunition,"[4] and "the Court concludes that the methodology of firearms identification is sufficiently reliable."[5] It is not easy to tell from the opinion how the *Monteiro* court reached this conclusion from the evidence described in the opinion. In particular, the central claim of uniqueness, seems to have benefited from mere question begging: uniqueness is assumed at the outset and accepted despite the fact that it stands more on the ipse dixit of the community of experts than on any sort of data or meaningful theory.[6] As noted earlier, however, the *Montiero* court excluded the testimony because the examiner and his crime laboratory had not followed the principles and practices of the field.

The *Green* court seemed to find that the leap from what the firearms examiner had to work with and how he did his work, to the conclusion that a particular firearm (without the benefit of comparison to all of the other firearms sharing its class and subclass characteristics) was identified to the exclusion of every other firearm in the world, was too great a leap to accept.[7] "That conclusion—that there is a definitive match—stretches well beyond O'Shea's data and methodology."[8] As noted earlier, this court ruled that the opinion of identity was inadmissible, though the witness would be permitted to testify as to observable similarities and differences in the unknown and the test-fired ammunition.[9]

Other federal opinions generally reflect a strategy of grandfathering in firearms and toolmark identification testimony on the basis that it has been around for some decades. The court in *U.S. v. Hicks*[10] found that "the matching of spent shell casings to the weapon that fired them has been a recognized method of ballistics testing in this circuit for decades." That went on that "[b]ased on the widespread acceptance of firearms comparison testing, the existence of standards governing such testing, and [an expert's] testimony about the negligible rate of error for comparison tests, the district court had sufficient evidence to find that [the expert's] methodology was reliable."

The court's decision seems to be the same as it might have been if *Daubert* were

---

[4]*U.S. v. Monteiro*, 407 F. Supp. 2d 351, 366, 69 Fed. R. Evid. Serv. 156 (D. Mass. 2006).

[5]*U.S. v. Monteiro*, 407 F. Supp. 2d 351, 371, 69 Fed. R. Evid. Serv. 156 (D. Mass. 2006). The government had argued that "because toolmark identification evidence has been deemed admissible by many other courts, the burden of proving such evidence to be unreliable should shift to the defendants." The court rejected this argument, noting that "Because reliability under *Daubert* is among the preliminary inquiries a court must address under Fed.R.Evid. 104(a), the burden of proof with respect to reliability remains on the proponent."

[6]Ironically, perhaps, the court made a point of quoting the Advisory Committee's Comment to Fed. R. Evid. 702: "The trial court's gatekeeping function requires more than simply 'taking the expert's word for it.'"

[7]Alluding to Chief Justice Rehnquist's observation in an earlier case that "nothing in either *Daubert* or the Federal Rules of Evidence requires a district court to admit opinion evidence which is connected to existing data only by the ipse dixit of the expert. A court may conclude that there is simply too great an analytical gap between the data and the opinion proffered." *General Elec. Co. v. Joiner*, 522 U.S. 136, 146, 118 S. Ct. 512, 139

L. Ed. 2d 508, 18 O.S.H. Cas. (BNA) 1097, Prod. Liab. Rep. (CCH) P 15120, 48 Fed. R. Evid. Serv. 1, 28 Envtl. L. Rep. 20227, 177 A.L.R. Fed. 667 (1997).

[8]*U.S. v. Green*, 405 F. Supp. 2d 104, 109 (D. Mass. 2005).

[9]The judge explains the reason and the larger problem: "I reluctantly come to the above conclusion because of my confidence that any other decision will be rejected by appellate courts, in light of precedents across the country, regardless of the findings I have made. While I recognize that the *Daubert-Kumho* standard does not require the illusory perfection of a television show (CSI, this wasn't), when liberty hangs in the balance—and, in the case of the defendants facing the death penalty, life itself—the standards should be higher than were met in this case, and than have been imposed across the country. The more courts admit this type of toolmark evidence without requiring documentation, proficiency testing, or evidence of reliability, the more sloppy practices will endure; we should require more." Id.

[10]*U.S. v. Hicks*, 389 F.3d 514, 526, 65 Fed. R. Evid. Serv. 880 (5th Cir. 2004), cert. denied, 546 U.S. 1089, 126 S. Ct. 1022, 163 L. Ed. 2d 853 (2006).

not the law. Quoting *United States v. Crisp*,[11] the *Foster* court stated that the " 'imprimatur of a strong general acceptance, not only in the expert community, but in the courts as well,' carries great weight in establishing the requisite reliability." As the Supreme Court said in *Kumho Tire*, general acceptance is a dubious prong of *Daubert* when the other prongs of validity are absent. And, unless courts are part of the scientific field at issue, general acceptance by courts is irrelevant to an analysis under *Daubert* (or under *Frye*). The court also cited several other opinions[12] which themselves had engaged in no *Daubert* analysis, but which had in turn cited earlier– pre–*Daubert*–cases, finding that none of them found any unreliability in firearms identification methods. That is hardly surprising, of course, since few if any courts prior to *Daubert* would have had any occasion to ask that question. The court offered no discussion of the underlying science, cited no studies and no data. In essence, the court assumed the answer to the question posed by the challenge. The opinion does not indicate what sort of challenge the opponent of admission presented, except to say that the opponents offered no expert witness of their own, which suggests that not much of a challenge was presented.

Several other, usually more tangential, issues have been posed in firearms and toolmark cases in the post-*Daubert* era.

In *United States v. Corey*,[13] the defendant had been convicted of being a felon in possession of a firearm. The government's expert testified to his opinion that the gun found in the defendant's possession was manufactured by Smith and Wesson in Massachusetts and thus necessarily traveled in interstate commerce. The defendant was arrested in Maine. However, Smith and Wesson also had a manufacturing plant in Maine. The examination of the expert made relatively clear that he had relied heavily on a conversation he had with the manufacturer's historian.[14] In essence the defendant was arguing that the government was trying to avoid the requirements of the business records exception and was introducing hearsay through the expert testimony rules instead.[15] The court rejected this argument, finding that the expert had relied on his general experience and other factors beyond the discussion with the historian.[16] But neither the appellate court nor the trial court seemed able to explain precisely what those bases were: "Agent (sic) Cooney testified that he based the opinion, at least in part, on his own knowledge and expertise as a firearms specialist, both with the ATF and in the private sector . . . . Further, Cooney confirmed that he had handled '[h]undreds of thousands of firearms,' and had 'examined that type of shotgun . . . before.' Thus, as the district court aptly noted, Firearms Enforcement Officer Cooney himself had 'acquired this information over the years.' "[17] The failure of the court to provide a straightforward reason how the expert knew the weapon was manufactured in the Massachusetts plant rather than in the Maine plant suggests that the expert had no reason either, but was of the "it is so because I say it is so" school of expertise. A dissenting judge pointed out that the weapon's serial number could have been checked against the manufacturer's database to determine where it was produced, and that the witness should have been required to base his opinion on that kind of information, of distinctive markings on the weapon. The majority rejected this suggestion, arguing that "such a regimen would reinvent the 'best evidence' requirement which Evidence Rule 703

[11]*U.S. v. Crisp*, 324 F.3d 261, 60 Fed. R. Evid. Serv. 1486 (4th Cir. 2003).

[12]Most notably, *U.S. v. Santiago*, discussed infra.

[13]*U.S. v. Corey*, 207 F.3d 84, 53 Fed. R. Evid. Serv. 1038 (1st Cir. 2000).

[14]*U.S. v. Corey*, 207 F.3d 84, 86, 53 Fed. R.

Evid. Serv. 1038 (1st Cir. 2000).

[15]*U.S. v. Corey*, 207 F.3d 84, 86, 87, 53 Fed. R. Evid. Serv. 1038 (1st Cir. 2000).

[16]*U.S. v. Corey*, 207 F.3d 84, 89, 53 Fed. R. Evid. Serv. 1038 (1st Cir. 2000).

[17]*U.S. v. Corey*, 207 F.3d 84, 90, 53 Fed. R. Evid. Serv. 1038 (1st Cir. 2000).

was designed to relax."[18]

*Ramirez v. Artuz*,[19] stands as something of a counterpoint to *Corey*. Ramirez was a habeas corpus petitioner who had been convicted of armed robbery. Part of the case against him was the testimony of a witness who recognized the kind of nine-millimeter weapon used by one of the robbers. Such a weapon was later found in the petitioner's apartment. At trial the defendant had proffered expert testimony that the gun in question "looked similar to tens of thousands of guns in the New York metropolitan area and that there was nothing particularly distinctive about a square nose on a nine-millimeter firearm." This gets closer to the main problem of firearms identification, which is the extent to which a weapon can be pinpointed to being a particular one. The smaller the number of such weapons, as identified by the witness, the more likely it was the one owned by *Ramirez*. The larger the class of weapons that would look like what the witness saw, the less probable that it was the one owned by *Ramirez*. The district court excluded the defense expert, and with it the habeas petition. The court relied on the deferential standard of *Joiner* and applied New York's standard for expert evidence admissibility: expert testimony must "help to clarify an issue calling for professional or technical knowledge, possessed by the expert and beyond the ken of the typical juror."[20] Why that standard did not lead to admission in the original case is not clear.

The court in *United States v. Santiago*[21] explained that it had held a trial from January to March and made a number of evidentiary rulings that it now wanted to amend in part. The opinion does not contain a statement of the facts of the case, but the trial was for a criminal matter involving a group of defendants who were reputed to be part of, or associated with, the Assesino Crime Family.[22] The one expert testimony issue raised concerned the defendants' objection to the government's expert in firearms identification. The court denied the objection.

The court stated at the outset that it had "not found a single case in this Circuit that would suggest that the entire field of ballistics identification is unreliable."[23] The court's reasoning is further developed in the following passage:

> The Court has not conducted a survey, but it can only imagine the number of convictions that have been based, in part, on expert testimony regarding the match of a particular bullet to a gun seized from a defendant or his apartment. It is the Court's view that the Supreme Court's decisions in *Daubert* and *Kumho Tire*, did not call this entire field of expert analysis into question. It is extremely unlikely that a juror would have the same experience and ability to match two or more microscopic images of bullets.[24]

The court concluded, therefore, that any weaknesses attending firearms identification testimony should be the subject of cross-examination.[25] Put most simply, this court behaved as though an irrebuttable presumption of validity exists regarding firearms identification expert evidence: it must be valid and therefore it need never be scrutinized.

Considering that *Daubert* replaces one test of admissibility of expert evidence with another one, and the two pose only slightly overlapping questions, why would the court's failure to find older cases questioning the reliability of firearms identification under a previous old test be dispositive of a challenge brought under the current test? A field might pass the general acceptance test quite handily, while failing

---

[18]*U.S. v. Corey*, 207 F.3d 84, 91, 53 Fed. R. Evid. Serv. 1038 (1st Cir. 2000).

[19]*Ramirez v. Artuz*, 1999 WL 754354 (E.D. N.Y. 1999).

[20]*Ramirez v. Artuz*, 1999 WL 754354 (E.D. N.Y. 1999).

[21]*U.S. v. Santiago*, 199 F. Supp. 2d 101, 59 Fed. R. Evid. Serv. 223 (S.D. N.Y. 2002).

[22]See, *U.S. v. Santiago*, 199 F. Supp. 2d 101, 59 Fed. R. Evid. Serv. 223 (S.D. N.Y. 2002).

[23]*U.S. v. Santiago*, 199 F. Supp. 2d 101, 59 Fed. R. Evid. Serv. 223 (S.D. N.Y. 2002).

[24]*U.S. v. Santiago*, 199 F. Supp. 2d 101, 59 Fed. R. Evid. Serv. 223 (S.D. N.Y. 2002).

[25]*U.S. v. Santiago*, 199 F. Supp. 2d 101, 59 Fed. R. Evid. Serv. 223 (S.D. N.Y. 2002).

utterly the scientific dependability test. As noted earlier, there are no reported post-*Daubert* cases addressing the fundamental assumptions of firearms identification. If no court is prepared to undertake the inquiry unless it can find other courts that have done so, then it obviously will never happen.

Moreover, the court's view that "the Supreme Court's decisions in *Daubert* and *Kumho Tire*, did not call this entire field of expert analysis into question" is mistaken in at least two respects. First, the district court's view reads a grandfathering provision into the Supreme Court's decisions—such that whatever had been widely accepted under the old test must also be accepted under the new test—a view which the Supreme Court rejected.[26] Second, it utterly ignores *Kumho Tire*'s teaching that what is at issue is the admissibility of the task-at-hand in the case at bar; the issue is never the acceptability of "an entire field" considered globally.[27]

It also is possible that, under *Daubert* review, the court would find that the practices of many firearms examiners do not pass muster,[28] or that all practitioners do some things that pass muster and other things that do not. For example, the comparison of bullets may be well grounded but the drawing of inferences leading to assertions of identity may not rest on sufficiently sound ground to justify the admission of those opinions, leading to partial admission of the testimony.[29]

In any event, the court's duty under *Daubert* and Fed. R. Evid. 702 is to conduct the inquiry and see whether the proponent of the evidence can satisfy the requirements of *Daubert*.[30] This court assumed that such an inquiry could lead only to admission and, on the strength of that assumption, shirked its gatekeeping duties.

A post-*Daubert* state case that raises the core issue at the heart of a *Daubert* challenge to traditional firearms identification, *People v. Hawkins*,[31] was brought, ironically, in a *Frye* jurisdiction, where attacks based on the weaknesses of the underlying science do not carry the opponent of admission as far as they might. In response to the challenge to the scientific basis of firearms identification evidence, the firearms experts did not try to prove the validity of their field by reference to its purported scientific basis so much as they suggested they had gained a special talent for associating bullets with the guns that fired them through repeated observation of guns and bullets. Prosecution experts "conceded that ballistics identification is not an exact science. Rather, ballistics experts develop proficiency by microscopically observing a large number of bullets known to have been fired from the same gun, and from different guns, so that they acquire knowledge of when the similarities of the bullets' striations are sufficient to establish that the bullets were

---

[26]If bullet comparison techniques are as sound and reliable as the court assumes they are, it should be easy for them to demonstrate that if put to the test. As the Supreme Court stated in *Daubert*, at note 11: "Although the *Frye* decision itself focused exclusively on 'novel' scientific techniques, we do not read the requirements of Rule 702 to apply specially or exclusively to unconventional evidence. Of course, well-established propositions are less likely to be challenged than those that are novel, and they are more handily defended."

[27]Assuming the knowledge and techniques of firearms identification pass muster generally for most purposes, the specific task in the present case may not. See, e.g., *Florida v. Ramirez*, discussed infra. The only way the court can find out is to engage in the inquiry.

[28]Two schools of thought dominate firearms identification practice: an intuitive, know-it-when-they-see-it school and a slowly growing scientific school.

[29]See, e.g., *U.S. v. Hines*, 55 F. Supp. 2d 62, 52 Fed. R. Evid. Serv. 257 (D. Mass. 1999) (concerning handwriting expert testimony, discussed at § 28:7) and *U.S. v. Llera Plaza*, 179 F. Supp. 2d 492, 57 Fed. R. Evid. Serv. 983 (E.D. Pa. 2002), withdrawn from bound volume and opinion vacated and superseded on reconsideration, 188 F. Supp. 2d 549, 58 Fed. R. Evid. Serv. 1 (E.D. Pa. 2002) (concerning fingerprint expert testimoiny, discussed at § 6:15).

[30]Unless, of course, the opponent of admission did not raise sufficient concerns to warrant a *Daubert* hearing, in which case that is what the court ought to be saying.

[31]*People v. Hawkins*, 10 Cal. 4th 920, 42 Cal. Rptr. 2d 636, 897 P.2d 574 (1995), as modified on denial of reh'g, (Oct. 18, 1995) and (abrogated by, People v. Lasko, 23 Cal. 4th 101, 96 Cal. Rptr. 2d 441, 999 P.2d 666 (2000)).

discharged from the same firearm."[32] Obviously there are several empirical claims in those statements which are testable and can be found to be true or not true, but for now their mere assertion sufficed. In rebuttal the defense introduced two articles by Alfred Biasotti that call for the reform of firearm identifications by developing a statistical database. One expert "conceded that ballistics identification was to some extent more of a skill than a science, an intuition informed by extensive experience."[33] The *Hawkins* court upheld the admissibility of the firearms expert evidence under *Frye*. One would think that in a *Daubert* jurisdiction, in the wake of *Kumho Tire*, claiming that they are engaged in more of an art than science, and that there is internal consensus about their artfulness, would not be enough.

*Daubert*-type challenges to firearms testimony have also been rejected by state courts, in favor of grandfathering. *State v. Brewer*,[34] found that "[t]he testimony of the state's expert with regard to firearms and ballistics is so well established that it does not require analysis." On the other hand, the court in *Sexton v. State*,[35] rejected matching of cartridge cases based on magazine marks alone without recovery of the underlying magazine.

In ironic contrast to the *Santiago* court acting under *Daubert*, a state court which follows *Frye* perceived an obligation to scrutinize the particular application and particular variant of what was regarded to be an otherwise generally accepted field of expertise, and concluded that certain toolmark identification expert testimony was inadmissible. *Ramirez v. Florida*[36] had reached the Florida Supreme Court on two previous occasions; those earlier decisions were discussed above.[37] In *Ramirez III*, the Court held that expert testimony purporting to identify a particular knife as the one used to stab a murder victim failed to meet the *Frye* test of admissibility.

As a predicate to analyzing the admissibility of the proffered expert evidence in the case, which the court noted was subject to de novo review under its jurisprudence, the Court discussed the *Frye* test in Florida, which is somewhat more than simply asking whether a substantial number of, or most, experts in a field agree with some proposition or technique:

> When applying the *Frye* test, a court is not required to accept a 'nose count' of experts in the field. Rather, the court may peruse disparate sources—e.g., expert testimony, scientific and legal publications, and judicial opinions 10—and decide for itself whether the theory in issue has been 'sufficiently tested and accepted by the relevant scientific community.' In gauging acceptance, the court must look to properties that traditionally inhere in scientific acceptance for the type of methodology or procedure under review—i.e., 'indicia' or 'hallmarks' of acceptability. A bald assertion by the expert that his deduction is premised upon well-recognized scientific principles is inadequate to establish its admissibility if the witness's application of these principles is untested and lacks indicia of acceptability.[38]

Elements of the Court's actual analysis will have a familiar ring to students of *Daubert*: "First, the record does not show that Hart's methodology—and particularly his claim of infallibility—has ever been formally tested or otherwise verified."[39] "Second, the record does not show that Hart's test has ever been subjected to

---

[32]*People v. Hawkins*, 10 Cal. 4th 920, 42 Cal. Rptr. 2d 636, 897 P.2d 574, 588 (1995), as modified on denial of reh'g, (Oct. 18, 1995) and (abrogated by, People v. Lasko, 23 Cal. 4th 101, 96 Cal. Rptr. 2d 441, 999 P.2d 666 (2000)).

[33]*People v. Hawkins*, 10 Cal. 4th 920, 42 Cal. Rptr. 2d 636, 897 P.2d 574, 588 (1995), as modified on denial of reh'g, (Oct. 18, 1995) and (abrogated by, People v. Lasko, 23 Cal. 4th 101, 96 Cal. Rptr. 2d 441, 999 P.2d 666 (2000)).

[34]*State v. Brewer*, 2005 WL 1023238 (Conn. Super. Ct. 2005).

[35]*State v. Brewer*, 2005 WL 1023238 (Conn. Super. Ct. 2005).

[36]*Ramirez v. State*, 810 So. 2d 836 (Fla. 2001).

[37]§ 5:2.

[38]*Ramirez v. State*, 810 So. 2d 836, 844 (Fla. 2001).

[39]*Ramirez v. State*, 810 So. 2d 836, 849 (Fla. 2001).

meaningful peer review or publication as a prerequisite to scientific acceptance."[40] "Fourth, the record does not show that the error rate for Hart's method has ever been quantified. On the contrary, the State's experts testified that the method is infallible, that it is impossible to make a false positive identification."[41]

In analyzing the expert evidence in the case at bar, the Court contrasted the expert techniques and testimony here to traditional knifemark evidence. As far as technique goes, it is hard to see the differences, other than the failure of the expert in this case to document his evidence and his work with photomicrographs.[42] The differences that seem to have troubled the court most deeply about the expert evidence in the case is the following:

In general, the court was troubled by the lack of testing or data (including a lack of error rate information) supporting the dependability of the expert's methods or conclusions.

More specifically, the expert asserted that "the knife found in Ramirez's car was the murder weapon to the exclusion of every other knife in the world."[43] The Court pointed out that such extreme statements were avoided in most toolmark cases and no adequate basis was provided for believing that toolmark experts could draw such pinpoint and absolute conclusions.[44] Rather than appropriate caution, there was an ipse dixit assertion of infallibility.[45]

The receiving material, cartilege, is softer than the wood, plastic, or metal, in which toolmarks usually are found. The expert failed to offer any tests or studies to support a belief that cartilege could retain striations with sufficient integrity to permit reliable comparisons.[46]

As noted earlier, the failure of the expert to document his evidence and his work with photomicrographs was a concern, as was the lack of objective standards or criteria for reaching conclusions. The expert's "determination is entirely subjective and is based on the technician's training and experience; there is no minimum number of matching striations or percentage of agreement or other objective criteria that are used in this method."[47] "Once a match is declared under his theory, no other knives are examined because an identification under this method purportedly eliminates all other knives in the world as possible sources of the wound. Under Hart's method of identification, a team of expert technicians trained by him would be virtually impossible to challenge notwithstanding the fact that his procedure is untested and yet to be accepted by the relevant scientific community. There is [sic] no objective criteria that must be met, there are no photographs, no comparisons of methodology to review, and the final deduction is in the eyes of the beholder, i.e., the identification is a match because the witness says it is a match."[48]

In consequence of these shortcomings, the court held the expert testimony to be inadmissible, failing in numerous ways to meet the requirements of Florida's

---

[40]Ramirez v. State, 810 So. 2d 836, 849 (Fla. 2001).

[41]Ramirez v. State, 810 So. 2d 836, 849 (Fla. 2001).

[42]Ramirez v. State, 810 So. 2d 836, 850 (Fla. 2001).

[43]Ramirez v. State, 810 So. 2d 836, 842 (Fla. 2001).

[44]Ramirez v. State, 810 So. 2d 836, 846 (Fla. 2001).

[45]The assertion of an exaggerated high degree of certainty, and sometimes even infallibility is a more than occasional problem, especially worrisome in a field in which many practitioners rely on subjective criteria to make judgments about the likelihood of common source in a fundamentally probabilistic endeavor. See, e.g., Sexton v. State, 1999 WL 675442 (Tex. App. San Antonio 1999), opinion withdrawn and superseded on denial of reh'g, 12 S.W.3d 517 (Tex. App. San Antonio 1999), petition for discretionary review granted, (May 10, 2000) and judgment rev'd, 93 S.W.3d 96 (Tex. Crim. App. 2002).

[46]Ramirez v. State, 810 So. 2d 836, 848 (Fla. 2001).

[47]Ramirez v. State, 810 So. 2d 836, 847 (Fla. 2001).

[48]Ramirez v. State, 810 So. 2d 836, 847 (Fla. 2001).

*Daubert*-tinged *Frye* test.

## § 5:5  Conclusion

The case law on the admissibility of toolmark identification and firearms identification expert evidence is typified by decisions admitting such testimony with little, and usually no, reference to legal authority beyond broad "discretion" and an adroit sidestepping of any judicial duty to assure that experts' claims are valid. Appellate courts defer to trial courts, and trial courts defer to juries. Later appellate courts simply defer to earlier appellate courts.

One might have expected the scientific basis of the claims of toolmark and firearms experts, measured by whatever test the courts of a given jurisdiction had devised, to be the central issue in reviewing a challenge to their admissibility. To date, the opinions lack such scrutiny. In the long run, the provisions of *Daubert* are capable of altering that century-long pattern, and create a new and long overdue body of case law on the subject.

At a practical level, if *Daubert* can do nothing else in the criminal context, it might eventually encourage (or compel) experts to learn the data surrounding the capabilities and limitations of their fields, to share those data candidly with courts, and confine their opinions within those bounds.

## II.  SCIENTIFIC ISSUES
*by Alfred Biasotti\*, John Murdock\*\* & Bruce R. Moran\*\*\**

### § 5:6  Introductory discussion of the science

Forensic firearms examiners are concerned with such varied tasks as:

(1)  serial number restoration;

---

\*Alfred A. Biasotti (1926–1997), M.S. in Criminalistics, U.C. Berkeley, was a criminalist, supervising criminalist, and administrator from 1951 to 1990, retiring as Assistant Chief of the Bureau of Forensic Sciences, California Department of Justice. He helped establish the California Criminalistics Institute; authored numerous articles on firearms and toolmark identification; was a Fellow of the American Academy of Forensic Sciences; and a distinguished member of the Association of Firearm and Toolmark Examiners. He passed away on June 24, 1997, from complications associated with Parkinson's Disease.

\*\*John E. Murdock, M.C. in Criminalistics, U.C. Berkeley, is a Firearms and Toolmark Examiner with the Bureau of Alcohol, Tobacco, Firearms, and Explosives, San Francisco Laboratory Center. Author of a number of articles on firearms and toolmark examination, he is past president of the California Association of Criminalists, an emeritus member of the American Society of Crime Laboratory Directors, and a distinguished member of the Association of Firearm and Toolmark Examiners. Murdock served as co-chairman for the AFTE Certification Committee, whose efforts resulted in the creation of a certification program for firearm and toolmark examiners. Teaches "Criteria for the Identification of Toolmark" courses for the California Criminalis-

tics Institute (CCI).

The views expressed in this chapter are those of the authors alone; no endorsement has been sought from the Bureau of Alcohol, Tobacco, Firearms, and Explosives, or any other agency or organization.

\*\*\*Bruce R. Moran, B.S. in Forensic Science with a minor in chemistry, California State University, Sacramento, is a Criminalist / Firearm and Toolmark Examiner with the Sacramento County District Attorney's Laboratory of Forensic Services, Sacramento, CA. Author of numerous articles related to the topic of firearm and toolmark examination/identification; teaches forensic firearms and toolmark identification courses as an instructor for the California Department of Justice—California Criminalistics Institute (CCI). Past board member of the California Association of Criminalists, a life member of the International Association for Identification, and a distinguished member of the Association of Firearm and Toolmark Examiners (AFTE). Participated in the creation of the AFTE Firearm and Toolmark Certification Examination for firearm and toolmark examiners that has been implemented within the United States and is available to examiners in other countries. Served as a member of the Scientific Working Group for Firearm and Toolmark Examination (SWGGUN), 1999–2004.

(2)   examination of suspected gunshot residues;

(3)   function testing of firearms;

(4)   determination of muzzle to target distance;

(5)   determining what kind of firearm was responsible for firing recovered bullets or cartridge cases;

(6)   aiding in the reconstruction of crime scenes through the examination and evaluation of firearms evidence;

(7)   intercomparison of both unknown evidence and test fired bullets, cartridge cases, and shotshell components with one another; and

(8)   comparing toolmarks[1] on unfired cartridges and shotshells which can occur when unfired ammunition has been worked through the action of a firearm, as well as on fired bullets, cartridge cases, and shotshell components with test toolmarks produced deliberately on similar items in an attempt to identify whether a particular firearm made toolmarks on evidence items, to the exclusion of all other firearms.

Task number eight overlaps into the area of forensic toolmark examination. Members of this related profession are concerned mainly with attempting to determine whether submitted tools[2] such as screwdrivers, hammers, pliers, drill bits, punches, etc., were used to make toolmarks on portions of a crime scene or on materials found at or related to a crime scene, to the practical exclusion of all other tools. Typical toolmarks submitted in a non-firearms case would be those found on certain components of homemade bombs, on locks and window or door parts in forced entry cases, and just about anywhere that a tool has been used. The word "tool" must be considered in the broadest possible sense. Thus the steel bumper of a truck backing through an aluminum framed supermarket door may leave toolmarks on the relatively soft aluminum doorframe. The truck and bumper would be the tool and the specific portion of the bumper contacting the aluminum doorframe causing the toolmarks would be the working surface of the tool.

This chapter is concerned with the individualization of firearms and toolmarks and not with the myriad of other tasks, such as those described above, because it is the individualization process that leads to the strong associative evidence which links a defendant to a crime. The defendant is connected to the crime scene by virtue of having possessed a firearm or tool that has been identified as having made toolmarks found on submitted evidence.

### § 5:7   Introductory discussion of the science—The scientific questions

The individualization of firearms and toolmarks involves the physical comparison of one solid object with another solid object to determine through pattern recognition whether or not they were: (1) once part of the same object; (2) in contact with each other; or (3) share similar class or individual characteristics.[1]

Physical comparisons of this nature have evolved as distinct forensic disciplines,

---

**[Section 5:6]**

[1]When two objects come into contact, the harder object may mark the surface of the softer object. The tool is the harder object. The relative hardness of the two objects, the pressures and movements, and the nature of the microscopic irregularities on the tool are all factors that influence the character of the toolmarks produced.

[2]A tool is defined as an object used to gain mechanical advantage. It also is the harder of two objects, which produces toolmarks when brought into contact with the softer one.

**[Section 5:7]**

[1]*Class characteristics* are measurable features of a specimen that indicate a restricted group source. They result from design factors, and are therefore determined prior to manufacture. *Individual characteristics*, on the other hand, are marks produced by the random imperfections or irregularities of tool surfaces. These random imperfections or irregularities are produced either incidental to manufacture or are caused by use, corrosion, or damage. They are considered unique to that tool and therefore are believed to

namely, firearm and toolmark identification, tire and footwear impressions, and latent fingerprint identification.[2] This evolution as separate disciplines has occurred apparently due to differing bodies of background knowledge required, although these comparisons are based on the same physical phenomena, i.e., the imparting or transfer of a presumably unique combination of patterns or contours from one solid surface to another.

---

distinguish it from all other tools. The individualization process relies on pattern recognition, which results from complex interactions between the eyes and the brain. Taroni et al., Statistics: A Future in Toolmarks Comparison?, 28 Ass'n Firearm & Toolmark Examiners J. 227 (1996).

[2]Biasotti, Firearms and Toolmark Identification—A Forensic Science Discipline, 12 Ass'n Firearm & Toolmark Examiners J. 12 (1980); Meyers, Firearms and Toolmark Identification—An Introduction, 25 Ass'n Firearm & Toolmark Examiners J. 281 (1993).

Figure 1

## PHYSICAL COMPARISONS

### PATTERN FIT
("Physical Match")

The examination of 2 or more objects either through physical, optical, or photographic means which permits one to conclude whether the objects were either one entity or were held or bonded together in a unique arrangement. Also called Fracture Match.

### PATTERN TRANSFER
("Toolmarks and Other Impression Marks")

TWO DIMENSIONAL
(SURFACE/IMPRINT MARKS)

(1) IMPRESSION TYPE* examples:
   (a) finger, palm and foot imprints
   (b) tire and footwear imprints

(2) STRIATED TYPE** examples:
   (a) rubber wiper blade marks on glass
   (b) toolmarks in general which lack depth.

(3) COMBINATION OF (1)&(2)***

THREE DIMENSIONAL
(CONTOUR/IMPRESSION MARKS)

(1) IMPRESSION TYPE* examples:
   (a) tools, shoes, tires or other compression marks
   (b) breechblock, firing pin marks

(2) STRIATED TYPE** examples:
   (a) fired bullets

   (b) chisel, plane and other cut marks

(3) COMBINATION OF (1)&(2)***

\*    IMPRESSION denotes perpendicular movement of the "tool" relative to the surface marked.
\*\*   STRIATED denotes lateral movement of a "tool" relative to the surface marked or lateral movement of the surface marked relative to the tool.
\*\*\*  Denotes imprints or marks formed by a combination of lateral and perpendicular movements.

**FIGURE 1:** A generic classification of contemporary physical comparisons that utilize various forms of pattern recognition to identify two separated objects which were: 1) once part of the same object, 2) in contact with each other, or 3) which share some other class or individual characteristics.

The methodology applied to the various physical comparisons outlined in Figure 1 is directed to recognizing and determining whether or not a particular combination or pattern of surface characteristics is randomly distributed and, if so, whether the agreement between evidence and test grouping is greater than what has been observed in known non-matches.[3]

The methodology necessary to recognize, measure and demonstrate a unique combination of class and individual characteristics among diverse objects varies, depending on the type of objects compared, e.g., fired bullets, cartridge cases, footwear, tire impressions or fingerprints. The fundamental rationale for individualizing a mark or impression, however, is that the pattern or combination of individual characteristics is presumed to be unique to the practical exclusion of all other possible patterns or combinations of characteristics.

The physical comparisons traditionally and routinely covered under the heading of "firearms and toolmark identification" will be discussed under the two basic physical phenomena of "Pattern-Fit" and "Pattern Transfer" (Figure 1).

The "pattern-fit" category is a simple concept. This category is defined as a "physical match" by the forensic scientist, or the "jigsaw puzzle fit" by the lay person. Most people readily recognize that each piece is unique in completing a puzzle, or that the broken pieces of a once solid object uniquely fit together to make the whole. The unique character of a physical match depends on the complexity of the random contours of the separated surfaces. The greater the complexity of the contours formed by the separated surfaces, the more probable that the match is unique.

The "pattern transfer" category, in contrast, is more difficult to understand and demonstrate. Consequently, identification involving pattern transfer is subject to more challenges and controversies. Toolmarks made by firearm components, other tools, and other solid objects in the "Pattern Transfer" category in Figure 1 are, therefore, the main focus of this chapter. We will discuss both "three-dimensional" (contour/impression) and "two-dimensional" (surface/imprint) toolmarks, recognizing that the fundamental criterion for determining the probability that a toolmark is unique remains the same.

The "three-dimensional" pattern transfer-type marks are further classified into "impression" and "striated" marks.[4] Toolmarks produced by firearm components and other tools typically are a combination of both impression and striated marks. Toolmarks produced on bullets fired through a gun barrel are primarily striated.

With either two or three-dimensional toolmarks, the primary factor to consider, for individualization purposes, is the nature of the surface suspected of having made the toolmark. The portion of a tool that can come into contact with, and cause markings on other objects, is called the working surface. Toolmarks can be identified as having been made by a specific tool to the exclusion of all other tools only

---

[3]*Known non-match*: Toolmarks known to have been made by different tools, or made by the same tool but deliberately placed in a non-matching position.

[4]*Impressed toolmarks* are produced when a tool is placed against another object and enough force is applied to the tool so that it leaves an impression. The class characteristics (shape) can indicate the type of tool used to produce the mark. These marks can contain *class* or *individual characteristics* of the tool producing the marks. These also are called *compression marks*. *Impressed toolmarks* consist of contour variations on the surface of an object caused by a combination of force and motion where the motion is approximately perpendicular to the plane being marked.

*Striated toolmarks* are produced when a tool is placed against another object and with pressure applied, the tool is moved across the object producing a striated mark. *Friction marks, abrasion marks,* and *scratch marks* are terms commonly used when referring to striated marks. These marks can contain *class* and/or *individual characteristics*. *Striations* are further defined as contour variations, generally microscopic, on the surface of an object caused by a combination of force and motion where the motion is approximately parallel to the plane being marked. Additional discussion of striated toolmark striae, with regard to practical interpretation by Examiners appears in § 5:12.

when the responsible working surface has been determined to be unique and therefore capable of making unique or, in other words, individual marks. The examiner uses knowledge of: (1) machining processes; (2) the microscopic appearance of the working surface; and (3) the results of research performed on consecutively manufactured tools in making this determination.

In this context, various parts of firearms are considered simply as tools. For example, the inside of a rifled gun barrel acts as a tool when it marks a bullet fired through it; an extractor acts as a tool when it extracts fired cartridge cases or unfired cartridges from the chamber of a firearm; and a firing pin acts as a tool when it strikes the primer portion of a cartridge, and so on.

Some working surfaces are unique the moment they are produced by the manufacturer. This is because some machining processes such as grinding generally produce a uniquely finished surface. Numerous toolmark studies of ground working surfaces have demonstrated that in most instances a different random distribution of individual characteristics is formed each time a working surface is ground.[5] Other machining processes, such as those where hardened cutters are used, often produce very similar toolmarks on items consecutively manufactured. A good example of this is the persistence of matching toolmarks in .25 auto caliber cartridge case extractor grooves described by Johnson.[6] These similar (sometimes matching) toolmarks are composed of sub-class characteristics.[7] The manufacturer's goal is to produce many items of the same shape that are, within certain tolerances, the same size. They also want each of these items to have an acceptable surface finish or appearance. Items that look the same to the unaided eye are said to have the same class characteristics. The manufacturers are not, however, concerned that many or all of these items may bear toolmarks composed of subclass characteristics depending on the way in which they were manufactured. The firearms and toolmark examiner must be alert to the possibility that evidence toolmarks may have been produced by a tool working surface having subclass characteristics.

A classic example of the evaluation of the working surface of a tool and the determination of the presence of subclass characteristics was reported by Murdock in 1974.[8] In this example, the working surfaces of desk stapler rams from two different brands of desk staplers were evaluated. The ram is the tool in a desk stapler that consists of a hardened piece of metal that comes into contact with a staple when the staple is driven out of the stapler. It was determined that in the finished product, the rams in one brand of desk stapler had unique working surfaces whereas the rams in the other brand of desk stapler had matching subclass characteristics.

---

[5]Biasotti & Murdock, "Criteria For Identification" or "State of the Art of Firearms and Toolmark Identification," 16 Ass'n Firearm & Toolmark Examiners J. 16 (1984); Butcher & Pugh, A Study of Marks Made by Bolt Cutters, 15 J. Forensic Sci. Soc'y 115 (1975); Watson, The Identification of Toolmarks Produced from Consecutively Manufactured Knife Blades in Soft Plastic, 10 Ass'n Firearm & Toolmark Examiners J. 43 (1978); Cassidy, Examination of Toolmarks from Sequentially Manufactured Tongue-and-Groove Pliers, 25 J. Forensic Sci. 798 (1980); Burd & Gilmore, Individual and Class Characteristics of Tools, 13 J. Forensic Sci. 390 (1968); Diamond, The Scientific Method and The Law, 19 Hastings L.J. 179 (1967).

[6]T. Johnson, The Persistence of Toolmarks in R-P.25 Auto Cartridge Case Extractor Grooves, Presented at the Annual A.F.T.E. Training Seminar, Orlando, Florida (May 10–14, 1982). See

Biasotti & Murdock, "Criteria For Identification" or "State of the Art of Firearms and Toolmark Identification," 16 Ass'n Firearm & Toolmark Examiners J. 16 (1984), for illustrations of these toolmarks.

[7]*Subclass characteristics* are discernible surface features of an object which are more restrictive than *class characteristics* in that they are: (1) produced incidental to manufacture; (2) are significant in that they relate to a smaller group source (a subset of the class to which they belong); and (3) can arise from a source which changes over time. Examples would include: bunter *marks* (headstamps produced on cartridge cases) produced by bunters made from a common master, *extrusion marks* on pipe, etc.

[8]Murdock, The Individuality of Toolmarks Produced by Desk Staplers, 6 Ass'n Firearm & Toolmark Examiners J. 23 (1974).

When new, the desk staplers with the matching subclass characteristics probably would not be capable of leaving unique toolmarks on the top of staples driven from them. After these working surfaces become worn and the subclass characteristics become obliterated, the toolmarks produced by them would be unique.[9]

A tool may have subclass toolmarks near the working surfaces and yet because of the relative position of the subclass toolmarks they have no effect on the ability of that tool to leave unique toolmarks. For example, the teeth on slip joint pliers often are formed by a cutting process that leaves subclass toolmarks. When these teeth grip objects and the tool is used in the normal way, sliding toolmarks (from slippage) often are made 90 degrees from the orientation of the subclass toolmarks. Thus the subclass characteristics have no effect on the unique signature left behind by the pliers teeth. The examiner, must, therefore, for any specific tool, be able to: (1) recognize the presence of subclass characteristics; and (2) properly evaluate the significance of subclass toolmarks when they are present by determining whether or not they are influencing the nature of any evidence toolmarks that are under consideration.

Having considered the nature of the tool working surface suspected of being responsible for making an evidence toolmark, a critical question arises. How much agreement is needed between an evidence and test toolmark before a conclusion of identification to the practical exclusion of all other tools is justified? This is the basic question asked first by science and then by the law. We will discuss how much agreement is needed following a description of the steps taken by an examiner during a typical toolmark comparison case.

### § 5:8 Introductory discussion of the science—The scientific methods applied in firearms and toolmark examination

A typical toolmark comparison case usually starts with questioned toolmarks of some sort that are evaluated for evidentiary purposes. The submitted evidence, consisting either of actual objects or pieces of objects or replicas (casts) of suspected toolmarks found on immovable objects, is microscopically examined for toolmarks and any toolmarks found are evaluated in order to determine: (1) what type and configuration of tool was used; and (2) whether the toolmarks have potential value for comparison and identification purposes. Toolmarks have potential value for comparison and identification purposes if a sufficient number of microscopic features are present and if they possess sufficient clarity and definition. The toolmarks also are examined for the presence of trace evidence, such as paint.

If tools are submitted for comparison, they are examined for trace evidence and a determination is made as to whether the class characteristics of any specific tool agrees with the class characteristics found in the toolmarks. If the class characteristics agree, test toolmarks are made for comparison with the submitted evidence toolmarks. When test toolmarks are made, every attempt is made to duplicate the general appearance of the evidence toolmarks by varying the tool angles and degree of pressure. This is fairly easy with firearms toolmark evidence since ammunition feeds into and out of firearms in a predictable way that is usually easy to duplicate simply by operating the firearm mechanism in the normal way.

With non-firearm toolmarks, numerous test toolmarks sometimes have to be made because the first test toolmarks produced are sometimes of no value for comparison, since the angles and pressures used did not create test toolmarks having the general appearance of the evidence toolmark(s). Early test marks of no value can be, but certainly do not have to be, discarded when they have been made in a

---

[9]For a highly favorable evaluation of this forensic research, see Crime Laboratory Management Forum 177–178 (R.H. Fox & F.H. Wynbrandt eds., 1976).

relatively soft material such as lead, which will not generally cause alteration of the tool's working surface. If a relatively soft test material proves to be inappropriate because the right kind of test toolmarks are not being produced, the examiner may have to use some of the same type of material, usually harder than lead, that bears the evidence toolmark(s). If this is a relatively hard material, all test marks made in it should be retained since there is a possibility that making test marks in this harder material may alter the working surface of the tool thereby making future comparisons very difficult. As a general rule, any time the test media show any sign of causing alteration to a tool working surface, all test marks should be retained.

Regardless of the media used for test marks, the goal of test mark production is to vary the angle and pressure of the working surface of the tool so that a test mark is produced by every part of every working surface that could reasonably have been used to produce the evidence toolmark. The examiner stands the best chance of identifying the tool when a comprehensive series of test marks has been prepared, assuming that the four conditions described in the next paragraph are true. It is possible, however, that if a comprehensive series of test marks is not produced, an examiner may falsely exclude the tool.[1] A false inclusion is highly improbable because no matter how many different test marks are produced, the likelihood is remote that any of them will exhibit sufficient agreement for a positive identification if the tool was not the tool used to produce the evidence toolmark. For practical purposes, examiners regard this probability as so small that the probability of a false inclusion is considered to be zero.

Appropriately prepared test toolmarks, having the general appearance of the evidence toolmarks, are next compared to one another to see if the tool is capable of leaving reproducible toolmarks. If it is, one would expect to be able to identify the tool as having made the evidence toolmark provided that:

(1)  it was used to make the evidence toolmark;
(2)  the responsible working surface has not been damaged since having been used;
(3)  the evidence toolmark bears sufficient, unique impression or striated markings for identification purposes; and
(4)  the responsible working surface of the tool consists of an individual surface finish and not merely class or subclass features.

Subclass characteristics are toolmarks that, because of their well defined, continuous over virtually all of the tool working surface, often prominent, and sometimes equally spaced appearance without changing significantly over some distance, can be suspected of being found on other similarly manufactured tool working surfaces. The presence of toolmarks of this nature on working surfaces must prompt the examiner to conduct research, such as the desk stapler example cited above, into the effect on individuality caused by their presence.[2]

The retention of only those test toolmarks used for the identification, assuming

---

**[Section 5:8]**

[1]A false exclusion occurs when the tool actually used to produce the evidence toolmark is excluded.

[2]The consideration of subclass influence exhibited within toolmarks requires a systematic approach for differentiating between such markings and those that may be individualizing. The examiner's greatest chance for success is when the responsible tool is available for examination. The examiner must consider the following three questions: Is there potential for subclass influence present on the responsible tool working surface?

If such influence is present, is it successfully transferred to the toolmark? If present in the toolmark, will such influence preclude a conclusive identification or can a positive identification still be made despite its presence? The ability to most reliably answer these questions is dependent on a number of factors and considerations, as follows.

(1) General Knowledge in Recognition of Tool Surfaces Resulting From Machining Operations and Their Relative Potential for Contributing to Subclass Influence.

During the inspection of the working surface(s), the recognition of potential of subclass characteristics is based, in part, on the examiner's training and experience in being able to recognize various machining operations by the characteristic surfaces produced by such operations. Generally, by recognizing the machining operation responsible for producing the finish on the tool working surface, the examiner can make an assessment of its general potential for contributing to subclass influence. For example, the potential for subclass influence in a general hierarchy of decreasing order is as follows: stamping > shearing > CNC milling > lathe operations > non-controlled milling > broaching > drilling > static machine grinding > free hand grinding > free hand filing. (The preceding ordered list reflects Moran's thinking about the general decreasing order and is not based on empirical testing.) Such general knowledge would affect an examiner's caution in the interpretation of the agreement that is observed and the approach to resolving any potential for subclass influence that could be present.

(2) Direct Inspection of Tool Working Surface With Ability to Differentiate Between Subclass Features and Individualistic Characteristics.

The most reliable way to assess the potential for subclass influence in a toolmark is by direct examination of the responsible tool working surface that produced the mark. Evaluation of the responsible tool working surface upon which sufficient agreement has been found to support identification, if warranted, is conducted to differentiate between subclass features and individualistic characteristics. This is normally accomplished using some form of magnification typically with the aid of the stereomicroscope to inspect the accessible tool surfaces. Less accessible tool surfaces—such as the interior of a gun barrel or the chamber surfaces of a firearm—can be visually inspected with specialized equipment such as borescopes. Additionally, when tool working surfaces are inaccessible for direct viewing, indirect methods such as casting with Mikrosil (or similar products) and examining the surface characteristics on the cast(s) can be employed. For example, casting the face of extractors or the interior surface of a gun barrel bore. During the inspection of the working surface(s), recognition of potential of subclass characteristics is based on the examiner's training and experience in recognition of "indicators" that contribute to the possibility of subclass influence. Examples of such subclass feature indicators include but are not limited to: (a) evenly appearing (non-random) contours either impressed or striated), (b) prominent striated markings on the interior of a gun barrel bore that remain unchanged throughout the entire length of the barrel (typically the heavier the marking the greater the chance of this occurring), (c) impressed striations transferred onto the tool working surface that remain relatively unchanged across the entire working surface (typical on some ejector or breech faces, for example). These features suggest that the manu-

facturing tool responsible for placing the final finish on the tool working surface remains relatively unchanged such that it is reasonable to expect that the same features will be repeated on other tool working surfaces. The presence of such indicators should make the examiner doubt the uniqueness of these features, leaving the possibility that another tool could produce such markings.

In contrast, the examiner must be able to recognize the presence of randomly produced defects that cannot be repeated from tool working surface to tool working surface that provide a basis for the tool's individuality (or individual signature). Such individualistic features that likely are unique to the tool working surface might include: (a) nicks and gouges produced by random pieces of metal which mark the tool surface being produced because of pressures/movement coincidental to the manufacturing process, (b) machine chatter in milling operations, (c) fracture patterns caused by the mechanical separation of metal in certain machining operations such as shearing, (d) striated markings that change rapidly within the boundaries of the tool working surface, during its manufacture.

If by inspection of the tool working surface the examiner observes an absence of subclass features, he/she can be more confident that there is no subclass influence and that markings produced by this surface can be used as a basis for trying to individualize the tool.

(3) Potential for Transfer of Subclass Features Within Questioned Toolmark.

If subclass features are present on the tool working surface, the examiner must consider whether such subclass influence is actually transferred to the toolmark. This is accomplished by comparing the subclass features exhibited on the tool working surface to toolmarks produced by that surface. For example, comparing the markings on bullets test fired from a gun to Mikrosil casts of the barrel bore to see if any pre-identified subclass markings on the cast also appear on the bullets. There is generally a higher potential for the transfer of such characteristics to soft lead bullets than for copper jacketed bullets that have a relatively harder surface. It is possible that such subclass features will not transfer to the toolmark surface.

In certain cases, there may be several working surfaces on a tool, each bearing its own potential for subclass influence. For example, a standard screwdriver blade also exhibits four sides, four edges, and a tip, as well as the shank. Each of these surfaces is likely to exhibit finishes from different machining processes with differing potential for the presence of subclass influence. The orientation of the screwdriver during its application will dictate what tool working surfaces will be responsible for producing a toolmark, each with differing potential for the existence of subclass features. Likewise, the face of a pistol ejector may exhibit high potential for subclass influence while the sides or edges of the ejector may bear no subclass influence at all. Depending on the orientation of the ejector relative to the cartridge case, any of these surfaces of the ejector may contact the head of the cartridge case during the normal cycling of the firearm, imparting toolmarks from whatever surface made contact. In this case the area of the toolmark exhibiting the high potential for subclass features will be treated with more caution in its potential for uniqueness than the area of the toolmark bearing highly individualistic characteristics.

The specific orientation of the tool working surface should also be considered as an element in the potential for transfer of subclass influence to the toolmark surface. For example, if a tool with a subclass striated surface travels across a toolmark surface in a parallel fashion, there is a great chance for subclass carry over to be transferred to that surface. However, if the tool moves over the toolmark surface perpendicular to the direction of subclass striated markings, the potential for subclass markings is very low. For example, if a bullet passes parallel to potential subclass striations created by the manufacturing process in the broached groove surface of a barrel bore, while the bullet at the same time passes over the reamer markings on the tops of the lands in a perpendicular fashion, the resulting striated markings produced within the groove impressions will likely have a much higher potential for the transfer of subclass influence than on the land impressions.

Given the above considerations, if there is no transfer of subclass features from the tool working surface(s) to the toolmark, there is no subclass influence present. Therefore the tool can be considered to have been identified as the source of the mark to the practical exclusion of all other similarly marking tools. If subclass features are transferred from the tool working surface(s) to the toolmark(s) produced, the examiner must consider if such influence is sufficient to preclude an individualization of a tool. For example, if the majority of the tool working surface is comprised of subclass features, and there are insufficient individualistic characteristics present, then the tool can only be identified as a possible source of a questioned toolmark within a limited group of tools that share the subclass characteristics. Even if the potential for subclass influence cannot be ruled out, its agreement can be very significant in inferring a potential association of the questioned toolmark to the tool especially in cases where it can be determined that the number of tools in this "family" of tools with shared subclass features, is small. However, if only limited areas of the tool working surface exhibiting subclass features are present, and there are sufficient individualistic characteristics also present that

are sufficient for identification, the tool can be identified as the source of the mark despite the presence of subclass characteristics among individualizing characteristics.

Subclass Evaluation Without the Benefit of Having The Responsible Tool. It is not uncommon to compare a series of toolmarks on different items to determine if they have been produced by the same tool without having the responsible tool available. Even in the absence of the responsible firearm/tool, examiners rely on their experience in evaluating the toolmark for potential for subclass influence. This is a more difficult to do, but does not preclude being able to identify a common toolmark source without having the responsible tool. To do this the examiner must rely on: (1) general knowledge of the appearance of subclass features that stem from different machining operations as previously discussed, and (2) experience and training in recognizing the "indicators" of subclass influence from manufacturing operations that have been transferred to the toolmark surface.

In this situation, the same considerations with respect to the potential for subclass influence are applied to the toolmarks being examined as has been previously outlined. If there is no indication of subclass influence present in the markings being compared, and there is sufficient agreement of individualistic characteristics, it can be concluded that a common tool source produced them. If the potential for the presence of subclass influence cannot be eliminated, some lesser conclusion must be considered until the responsible tool can be obtained for examination of the working surface(s). The following is an example of such a conclusion:

> During the comparison of the questioned toolmarks, I observed agreement of discernable class characteristics and sufficient agreement of potentially individualistic characteristics to indicate that it is very likely that these markings have been produced by the same tool. However, without the benefit of examining the surface of the tool that caused these marks, I am unable to eliminate the possibility of subclass influence, leaving a small possibility that another tool could have produced them. If, however, an examination of the working surface of the tool reveals that it is indeed capable of leaving an individualistic toolmark, these marks can be identified as having been produced by the same tool.

An excellent discussion of this general consideration in toolmark identification can be found in Miller, An Introduction to the Forensic Examination of Toolmarks, 33 Ass'n Firearm and Toolmark Examiners J. 233, 241–244 (2001). Additionally, Nichols specifically discusses the evaluation of barrel bore working surfaces in regard to potential for subclass influence in Nichols, Firearm and Tool Mark Identification: The Scientific Reliability and Validity of the AFTE Theory of Identification Discussed Within the Framework of a Study of Ten Consecutively Manufactured

that the discarded toolmarks were made in test material softer than the tool working surface and caused no changes in the working surface, does not create a bias against an accused. Most tool working surfaces will have a number of surfaces capable of producing toolmarks. For example, one of the authors identified a hack saw blade as being used to produce a series of seven teeth marks on the end of a length of copper pipe that had been fashioned into a pipe bomb. The toolmark identified was a striated mark caused by a sidewise motion of the blade; it was not a cutmark. Many of the hack saw teeth were broken; of the approximately 173 teeth on the blade, only a seven tooth section could have been used! Approximately 300 test marks were made using sheet lead before an identification was made. It was necessary to make this many testmarks because of the saw blade length, the numerous possible blade angles when it traveled sideways during the production of approximately 24 different sets of seven teeth wide marks, and because many teeth were broken. Most of these test toolmarks have no bearing on the identification and could be remade if necessary.

When sufficient agreement is found between the evidence toolmark and a test toolmark, a positive identification of the tool is made to the practical exclusion of all other tools. All test toolmarks relied upon for the final comparison results must be retained.

The comparison process just described assumes that the examiner has the tool working surface available for comparison so that an evaluation can be made, as described above, to see whether or not it is capable of producing a unique toolmark. Situations occur where an examiner does not have a tool and is simply comparing toolmarks from a series of crimes to see if the crimes are connected. In these situations, if the toolmarks from a series of crimes *are identified* as having been produced by the same tool, the examiner is relying on general knowledge of how the working edges of such tools are produced. For example, the cutting edges of twist drills are finished by grinding. This machining process has been demonstrated to produce a microscopically unique working surface on twist drill cutting edges.[3] A series of twist drill impressions (where the hole is *not* drilled all the way through) from a series of crimes can, therefore, be determined to have been drilled with the same twist drill if sufficient microscopic agreement is present.

When there is, however, a chance that microscopic subclass characteristics, having their origin in the manufacturing process, can be present in the type of toolmarks recovered in a series of crimes, a more cautious approach should be taken. It is not uncommon in these cases for the examiner to write a report that states that sufficient microscopic agreement is present to *suggest* that the same tool made the series of toolmarks, but that a conclusive opinion can be rendered only after an examination of the responsible tool.[4] Once the examiner has the tool, the working surface can be evaluated to determine if the tool produces a unique toolmark, or is one that contains subclass characteristics that are capable of being transferred to toolmarked surfaces.

---

Extractors, 36 Ass'n Firearm and Toolmark Examiners J. 67 (2004). Moran also discusses practical considerations with reference to magazine marks and rifling impressions in the following reference. Moran, The Application of Numerical Criteria for the Identification in Casework Involving Magazine Marks and Land Impressions, 33 Ass'n Firearm and Toolmark Examiners J. 41 (2001). Moran additionally describes his approach to the consideration of subclass influence present in the grooves of the barrel bore of a questioned firearm and provides photomicrographs of these features in the following reference. Hess and

Moran, The Removal of Superficial Rust/Corrosion From the Working Surfaces of Firearms For the Purpose of Preserving Their Potentially Identifiable Signature and an Application of this Technique in a Firearms Identification, 38 Ass'n Firearm and Toolmark Examiners J. 112 (2006) (forthcoming).

[3]Reitz, An Unusual Toolmark Identification Case, 7 Ass'n Firearm & Toolmark Examiners J. 40 (1975).

[4]See footnote 2, § 5:8, for an example of such a report.

With respect to toolmarks associated with firearms evidence, Bonfanti and De Kinder have provided a comprehensive summary of the influences of manufacturing processes on the identification of bullets and cartridge cases. Their summary clearly illustrates that not every manufactured tool surface is unique and that firearm and toolmark examiners must consider the possibility of sub class (family) carry over on consecutively manufactured tool working surfaces before positively identifying a toolmark as having been made by one particular tool, to the exclusion of all other tools.[5]

We return now to the issue of how much agreement between crime scene evidence toolmarks and test toolmarks made with a suspect tool is required to determine that the working surface(s) of only one particular tool made the mark.

## § 5:9  Areas of scientific agreement

The theory of identification, as it relates to toolmarks, adopted by the Association of Firearm and Toolmark Examiners (A.F.T.E.),[1] gives a nonquantitative answer to the question of how much agreement is needed. This theory is reproduced below in its entirety.

*Theory of Identification as it Relates to Toolmarks*
   a) The theory of identification as it pertains to the comparison of toolmarks enables opinions of common origin to be made when the unique surface contours of two toolmarks are in "sufficient agreement."
   b) This "sufficient agreement" is related to the significant duplication of random toolmarks as evidenced by the correspondence of a pattern or combination of patterns of surface contours. Significance is determined by the comparative examination of two or more sets of surface contour patterns comprised of individual peaks, ridges and furrows. Specifically, the relative height or depth, width, curvature and spatial relationship of the individual peaks, ridges and furrows within one set of surface contours are defined and compared to the corresponding features in the second set of surface contours. Agreement is significant when it exceeds the best agreement demonstrated between toolmarks known to have been produced by different tools and is consistent with the agreement demonstrated by toolmarks known to have been produced by the same tool.[2] The statement that "sufficient agreement" exists between two toolmarks means that the agreement is of a quantity and quality that the likelihood another tool could have made the mark is so remote as to be considered a practical impossibility.[3]

However, A.F.T.E. did not define "sufficient agreement" in quantitative terms. Instead, it has adopted the following position statement:
   c) Currently the interpretation of individualization/identification is subjective in nature, founded on scientific principles and based on the examiner's training and experience.

Section (c) states in part that the interpretation of individualization/identification

---

[5]Bonfanti & De Kinder, The Influences of Manufacturing Processes on the Identification of Bullets and Cartridge Cases—A Review of the Literature, 39 Sci. & Justice 3 (1999).

**[Section 5:9]**

[1]Theory of Identification, Range of Striae Comparison Reports, and Modified Glossary Definitions—An AFTE Criteria For Identification Committee Report, 24 Ass'n Firearm & Toolmark Examiners J. 336 (1992).

[2]This provision makes it necessary that the examiner *know the quantitative difference between*

*an ID and a non-ID.* So it implies that examiners *must know what "best agreement" is.*

[3]The term "sufficient agreement" in this statement clearly includes both quality and quantity of agreement that must be observed so that *the likelihood that another tool could have made the mark is so remote as to be considered a practical impossibility.* This statement, therefore, does not support an absolute identification, but is a probabilistic inference of practical certainty.

is founded on scientific principles. The research directed toward criteria for identification in firearm and toolmark identification was reviewed and discussed by the authors in 1984.[4] All examinations utilizing mathematical models, mechanical models, and actual toolmarks, made with new or used tools, up to 1984 indicated that sufficient agreement of striated or impression toolmarks could be expressed by agreement of a relatively small number of individual characteristics. This research is described in some detail in §5:12. This research was carried out by adherence to the process known as the scientific method. In this process, variables were limited and observations were made that have allowed examiners to *predict* the ability to individualize "pattern-transfer" toolmarks. This *prediction* has been continually tested empirically and has stood the test of time, resulting in the general principle (Theory) adopted by A.F.T.E. in 1992.[5] The AFTE theory of identification is a working hypothesis of toolmark identification that has been empirically tested. See §5:12, note 29. By formulating this theory, AFTE anticipated one of the principal questions that would be asked of the discipline in 1993 in *Daubert*. The studies leading up to this theory have been peer reviewed, published, and thus have been available for replication by the relevant scientific community of forensic scientists. Nichols reviewed thirty-four articles that pertained to identification criteria for firearm and toolmark identification. These articles included empirical studies of consecutively manufactured barrels, firing pins, breechfaces, assorted tools as well as mathematical and computer models. Although not all of these articles generated quantifiable numbers, Nichols felt that " . . . all of these appear to be based at least in part on the scientific method . . ."[6]

Research conducted by adherence to the scientific method allows *predictions* to be made and thus serves as a guide to future situations, which in this specific instance is the identification of toolmarks. In contrast, most of the day-to-day measuring and careful observation that occurs in firearm and toolmark sections of crime laboratories is essential to the completion of casework, but is not carried out by using scientific methodology. Firearm and toolmark examiners apply science and scientific methods, procedures and instruments in a practical way, but most are more skilled in the art of applying those methods and procedures than they are in the basic sciences involved.[7] Diamond put it succinctly during a discussion of the scientific method, when he said: (1) that the value and truth of science lies in its methods, not its numbers and diagrams; and (2) determinations of specific measurements only define unique observations, but do not allow predictions to be made about future situations.[8]

As stated in section (c) of the A.F.T.E. *Theory of Identification*,[9] "currently the interpretation of individualization/identification is subjective in nature . . ." Because

---

[4]Biasotti & Murdock, "Criteria For Identification" or "State of the Art of Firearms and Toolmark Identification," 16 Ass'n Firearm & Toolmark Examiners J. 16 (1984).

[5]Theory of Identification, Range of Striae Comparison Reports, and Modified Glossary Definitions—An AFTE Criteria For Identification Committee Report, 24 Ass'n Firearm & Toolmark Examiners J. 336 (1992).

[6]Nichols, Firearm and Toolmark Identification Criteria: A Review of the Literature, 42 J. Forensic Sci. 466 (1997). Nichols brought his literature review up to date with Firearm and Toolmark Identification Criteria: A Review of the Literature, Part II, 48 J. Forensic Sci. 318 (2003).

[7]Letter from John E. Davis to John Murdock (Dec. 27, 1977) (on file with the author).

[8]Diamond, The Scientific Method and The Law, 19 Hastings L.J. 179 (1967). Moran and Murdock, in Appendix No. 2, The Application of the Scientific Method to Firearm and Toolmark Examination, [Zen and the Art of Motorcycle Maintenance—Contribution to Forensic Science (an Explanation of the Scientific Method)] in Grzybowski, Miller, Moran, Murdock, Nichols, and Thompson, Firearm/Toolmark Identification: Passing the Reliability Test under Federal and State Evidentiary Standards, 35 Ass'n Firearm and Toolmark Examiners J. 2 (2003). Moran and Murdock provide a detailed explanation of the uses of the scientific method in (1) lavys repair; (2) routine casework; and (3) research in validating the identification of toolmarks.

[9]Theory of Identification, Range of Striae Comparison Reports, and Modified Glossary

decisions are based on subjective estimates of probability, the Association of Firearm and Toolmark Examiners has adopted the following range of conclusions to be used when comparing toolmarks:[10]

*Range of Conclusions Possible When Comparing Toolmarks*

The examiner is encouraged to report the objective observations that support the findings of toolmark examinations. The examiner should be conservative when reporting the significance of these observations. The following represents a spectrum of statements:

1) *Identification*:  Agreement of a combination of individual characteristics and all discernible class characteristics where the extent of agreement exceeds that which can occur in the comparison of toolmarks made by different tools and is consistent with the agreement demonstrated by toolmarks known to have been produced by the same tool.[11]

2) *Inconclusive*:

   A. Some agreement of individual characteristics and all discernible class characteristics, but insufficient for an identification.

   B. Agreement of all discernible class characteristics without agreement or disagreement of individual characteristics due to an absence, insufficiency, or lack of reproducibility.

   C. Agreement of all discernible class characteristics and disagreement of individual characteristics, but insufficient for an elimination.

3) *Elimination*:  Significant disagreement of discernible class characteristics and/or individual characteristics.

4) *Unsuitable*:  Unsuitable for comparison.

The introductory paragraph to the A.F.T.E. *Range of Conclusions Possible when Comparing Toolmarks,* encourages examiners to report the objective observations that support their findings. This means that the examiner is free to express how he feels about the comparative evidentiary value of the toolmark comparisons. For example, a comparison conclusion of inconclusive may be further described as consisting of considerable agreement, such as that described in § 5:7, which may allow the examiner to conclude that it is very likely that the submitted tool was the tool used to make the submitted toolmark.

Since the interpretation that forms the basis for these conclusions is subjective, Murdock has suggested a series of questions designed to test the witness's qualifications for making a conclusion of identity when striated toolmarks have been identified.[12] The thrust of these questions is to evaluate the witness's knowledge of the extent of agreement that can be found when comparing striated toolmarks known to have been made by different tools. Some of these questions, together with suggested appropriate responses may be found in Appendix II. A similar line of questioning could also be developed for impression type evidence, including toolmarks. Although these fourteen questions focus on the witness's knowledge of the extent of microscopic agreement that can be found when comparing striated toolmarks known to have been made by different tools, qualified examiners need to demonstrate that they also have spent considerable time studying the extent of agreement in known matches as well as various forms of inconclusive examples.

---

Definitions—An AFTE Criteria For Identification Committee Report, 24 Ass'n Firearm & Toolmark Examiners J. 336 (1992).

[10]Theory of Identification, Range of Striae Comparison Reports, and Modified Glossary Definitions—An AFTE Criteria For Identification Committee Report, 24 Ass'n Firearm & Toolmark Examiners J. 336 (1992).

[11]This statement emphasized that the extent of agreement must exceed that which can occur in the comparison of toolmarks made of different tools. This is a quantitative inference and, therefore, all Examiners are responsible for knowing how much this is.

[12]Murdock, Some Suggested Court Questions to Test Criteria for Identification Qualifications, 24 Ass'n Firearm & Toolmark Examiners J. 69 (1992).

## § 5:10 Areas of scientific disagreement—Disagreement about the scientific foundations

The disagreement that exists in the field centers around whether objective quantifiable standards can be developed as criteria for the identification of toolmarks. While most would probably agree that the development of such criteria is desirable, some consider it impossible. John Davis[1] expressed it this way:

> Since all toolmarks are "unique" in a sense, I doubt that "universal criteria" can be found that would apply to all such marks to permit conclusions purely "objective" in nature. Since even the "application" of predetermined criteria calls for degrees of expertise itself, it is generally my position that the "minimum criteria" required for an identification must themselves vary with the degree of expertise and experience of the examiner and therefore minimum criteria cannot be fixed except in "unstable form."[2]

As early as 1977, however, Davis stated:

> If some day a computer or the like is built which will "look" at bullet striae and plot and evaluate the highs and lows, highlights or shadows, spatial relationships, etc., and "conclude" there is an identity, or a non-identity or a "don't know," perhaps we can call it another "objective" method. But it would be the "art" of the experienced examiners that would be the basis for input into the instrument—not the "science."[3]

Although the day referred to above by Davis in 1977 has not and likely never will arrive, we do have automated comparison systems that select high confidence candidates for comparison by firearms and toolmark examiners.

There is no question, however, that conclusions of identity in firearms and toolmarks are possible. The examiner qualified to render such conclusions should be familiar with:

(1) empirical studies of consecutively manufactured tools;

(2) the significance or impact upon individuality of the various means used to manufacture tool edges or working surfaces;

(3) theoretical studies where both mechanical and mathematical models have been used to study toolmark consecutiveness; and

(4) the quantity and quality of matching agreement found in comparisons of toolmarks known to have been produced by different tools. (Known non-matches.)

The authors sincerely hope that the objective quantitative criteria[4] will be applied universally to the evaluation of striated toolmarks. Progress in this area is described infra § 5:12. Until this is done, however, the correctness of subjective evaluations must continue to be based upon individual expertise gained mostly by training and experience. In addition, a working knowledge of the research that has been done in the four categories listed above will help ensure that conclusions of identity, when

---

**[Section 5:10]**

[1]Author of John E. Davis, An Introduction to Tool Marks, Firearms and the Striagraph at 35 (1958).

[2]Personal notes of John E. Davis (April 1984) (on file with the author); personal communications between Davis and the author (June, 1984).

[3]Letter from John E. Davis to John Murdock (Dec. 27, 1977).

[4]Grzybowski, Miller, Moran, Murdock, Nichols, Thompson, Firearm/Toolmark Identification: Passing the Reliability Test Under Federal and State Evidentiary Standards, 35 Ass'n Firearm and Toolmark Examiners J. 2 (2003). In addition to a comprehensive discussion of error rate in general, the authors calculated the CTS error rates for both firearm and toolmark proficiency tests from 1992 to 2002 in the same manner used by Joseph L. Peterson and Penelope N. Markham, Crime Laboratory Proficiency Testing Results, 1978–1991, II: Resolving Questions of Common Origin, 40 J. Forensic Sciences No. 6 (Nov. 1995). That is, the number of false identifications was compared to all of the comparisons reported by the responding laboratories, and these data were combined with Peterson and Markham's. For the years 1978 to 2002 the false identification rate for the firearm produced toolmark proficiency tests is 1.0% and for the years 1981 to 2002 the false identification rate for the non-firearm toolmark proficiency tests is 1.3% (non-firearm produced toolmark proficiency tests started in 1981).

made, are fully justified.

## § 5:11   Areas of scientific disagreement—Disagreement among practitioners in particular applications

In spite of the research efforts described supra §§ 34:9 and 34:12, occasionally forensic experts differ in their opinion about the identification of toolmarks. It has been the authors' experience, limited almost exclusively to striated toolmarks in firearms cases, that many of these disagreements stem from one examiner ascribing too much significance to a small amount of matching striae and not appreciating that such agreement is achievable in known non-match comparisons.

Hodge[1] discusses other sources of error, such as: (1) rushing through laboratory examinations due to excessive pressure from investigators; (2) not being thorough; and (3) trying to be helpful. Hodge goes on to discuss some ways to minimize these sources of error.

Will errors continue? We suppose so, but hope that the concept of known non-match comparisons, the thorough understanding of the influence of sub-class characteristics, and in-laboratory peer review by skilled co-workers will hold them to an absolute minimum.

Based on present data, the field is in a poor position to calculate error rates. Thornton[2] recently addressed known or potential rate of error by saying that test results hinging on judgment calls do not lend themselves to analysis by conventional statistics. No doubt Thornton was not saying that the products of human judgment cannot be measured statistically, since most if not all of cognitive science does precisely that, but rather that forensic science researchers have not managed to calculate them for the forensic specialties like firearm and toolmark comparison that depend in part on subjective judgment. With modern statistical technology, forensic science decision-making could be subjected to quantitative analysis.[3] But to date it has not been.

Some have used the results of the proficiency testing program administered by the Forensic Sciences Foundation as the major information about error rates.[4] Admittedly, this is tempting since they represent virtually the only information collected on a large scale, but it is at the same time a flawed approach. These declared (not blind) proficiency tests were designed to be used by individual crime laboratories as a quality assurance tool and were never intended to be used as the basis for a nationwide study of forensic error rates. Some crime laboratories treat them formally, requiring that they be completed by the due dates so that their results will be among the tabulated data sent out following each test. Other laboratories treat them much less formally, asking only that they be worked on as time permits, and it usually does not. Still other laboratories work harder on the proficiency tests than on their regular caseload, because they are "a test." In addition, some examiners may be more conservative when reporting the results of a declared proficiency test, feeling that they have little to gain but much to lose if they make an error. It has generally been the case that although proficiency test results have been reviewed by a supervisor before being reported, they were not peer reviewed. Peer review is an important process that is widely used in crime laboratories. This process helps prevent errors in casework from seeing the light of day. In cases where the supervisor was not a subject matter expert in the proficiency test subject there would be,

---

**[Section 5:11]**

[1]Hodge, Guarding Against Error, 20 Ass'n Firearm & Toolmark Examiners J. 290 (1988).

[2]Thornton, Courts of Law v. Courts of Science: A Forensic Scientist's Reaction to *Daubert*, 1 Shepard's Expert & Sci. Evidence Q. 480 (1994).

[3]Phillips et al., Signal Detection Theory and Decision-making in Forensic Science, 46 J. Forensic Sci. 294 (2001).

[4]Jonakait, Real Science and Forensic Science, 1 Shepard's Expert & Sci. Evidence Q. 446 (1994).

essentially, no peer review. In these circumstances, the reported error rates would, therefore, closely approximate an individual examiner's error rate. The American Society of Crime Laboratory Directors' Laboratory Accreditation Board (ASCLD/LAB) approved a program in December 1997 that suddenly moved proficiency test results into a hi-stakes game. In December 1997 ASCLD/LAB approved the Proficiency Review Program (PRP). Under this program, in ASCLD accredited crime laboratories, the results of an individual's proficiency tests must be released to a Proficiency Review Committee (PRC) established by ASCLD/LAB. The PRC will review the proficiency test results and if a discrepancy is found the laboratory will be notified and appropriate action must be taken. The type of action will depend on the level of discrepancy (class 1, 2 or 3). Failure to properly address the discrepancy may result in sanctions, which could include revocation of ASCLD/LAB Accreditation. It is clear that in such a high stakes game, laboratory administration will do everything possible including technical peer review, to ensure that the proficiency test results are correct before reporting them. Prior to the PRC it was a more low-stakes game, with the individual examiners rising or falling on their own merit. The reputation of the laboratory is now at stake. Consequently, we cannot know if pre-1998 proficiency studies overstate or understate the accuracy of examinations. But, it seems fairly certain that post-1998 proficiency studies may overstate the accuracy of the error rate of the individual examiner, but should more closely approximate the error rate of technical peer reviewed casework.

It would be more instructive if the crime laboratories completing the proficiency tests by the due dates were required to indicate if normal laboratory procedures were followed, whether this included technical peer review and supervisorial scrutiny, whether the test was used as a test for a trainee, and so on. With this additional information, more meaningful comments could be made about these proficiency test results. Or, better, that they be submitted to examiners as if they were part of the regular caseload—that is, blind proficiency testing.

Moreover, there are inherent difficulties associated with the production of toolmark proficiency tests. Due to the nature of this evidence, each sample is unique. Since there are dynamic forces involved in producing the toolmark samples, there are opportunities for variations between samples. Since all proficiency test subscribers examine unique samples, can widespread test results be used for more than a general indication of error rates? Probably not.[5]

---

[5]For further details on proficiency tests and their findings, see Peterson & Markham, Crime Laboratory Proficiency Testing Results, 1978–1991, I: Identification and Classification of Physical Evidence, 40 J. Forensic Sci. 994 (1995); Peterson & Markham, Crime Laboratory Proficiency Testing Results, 1978–1991, II: Resolving Questions of Common Origin, 40 J. Forensic Sci. 1009 (1995). Grzybowski & Murdock, Firearms and Toolmark Identification-Meeting the *Daubert* Challenge, 30 Ass'n Firearm & Toolmark Examiners J. 3 (1998), summarized Peterson & Markham's data for firearms and toolmark proficiency tests as follows: Calculating an error rate based on the total number of decisions reached (that is, including inconclusive responses, which in fact are neither correct nor incorrect), the error rate is 12% for firearms and 26% for toolmarks. But if one calculates an error rate based only on incorrect responses, as Grzybowski & Murdock believe it should be, the results are far better:

1.4% for firearms and 4% for toolmarks.

Grzybowski, Miller, Moran, Murdock, Nichols, Thompson, Firearm/Toolmark Identification: Passing the Reliability Test Under Federal and State Evidentiary Standards, 35 Ass'n Firearm and Toolmark Examiners J. 2 (2003). In addition to a comprehensive discussion of error rate in general, the authors calculated the CTS error rates for both firearm and toolmark proficiency tests from 1992 to 2002 in the same manner used by Joseph L. Peterson and Penelope N. Markham, Crime Laboratory Proficiency Testing Results, 1978–1991, II: Resolving Questions of Common Origin, 40 J. Forensic Sciences No. 6 (Nov. 1995). That is, the number of false identifications was compared to all of the comparisons reported by the responding laboratories, and these data were combined with Peterson and Markham's. For the years 1978 to 2002 the false identification rate for the firearm produced toolmark proficiency tests is 1.0% and for the years 1981 to 2002 the false

## § 5:12　Development of objective criteria for identification

In 1984, we concluded that existing research was insufficient to validate the quantitative objective criteria necessary to conclude that a working surface is unique.[1] To develop these criteria we recommended that examiners be familiar with the extent of agreement, both in quantity and quality, observed in comparisons of toolmarks known to have been produced by different tools. This recommendation, subsequently referred to as known non-match (KNM) comparisons, is an essential part of the non-quantitative theory of identification and the hypothesis adopted by the Association of Firearms and Toolmark Examiners (A.F.T.E.) in 1992.[2]

The authors added a quantitative dimension to this fundamental hypothesis. The probability that a toolmark or working surface is unique can be determined by the number and complexity (i.e., size, shape, depth) of randomly occurring matching individual characteristics in excess of the number of characteristics observed and documented in KNM comparisons.

No probability estimates were calculated for KNM comparisons because determining the maximum number of well defined matching individual characteristics in large statistical samples (i.e., more than 100) of KNMs for a variety of different types of tools is the most direct and conclusive way of determining that the probability of a false positive identification is beyond a practical possibility.

Probability estimates for the number of matching individual characteristics for known matches[3] and KNMs historically have been based on theoretical assumptions using mathematical calculations unsupported by published empirical studies of actual toolmarks. Consequently, no objective, quantitative, criteria for determining the individuality of toolmarks were presented in any of the leading texts or dissertations on this subject until 2005.[4]

The first published empirical study intended to test theoretical probability

---

identification rate for the non-firearm toolmark proficiency tests is 1.3% (non-firearm produced toolmark proficiency tests started in 1981).

**[Section 5:12]**

[1]Alfred A. Biasotti & John E. Murdock, "Criteria For Identification" or "State of the Art of Firearms and Toolmark Identification," 16 Ass'n Firearm & Toolmark Examiners J. 16 (1984).

[2]Theory of Identification, Range of Striae Comparison Reports, and Modified Glossary Definitions—An AFTE Criteria For Identification Committee Report, 24 Ass'n Firearm & Toolmark Examiners J. 336 (1992).

[3]*Match* is a term traditionally and commonly used to denote an identification between two physical objects based on the correspondence of an unspecified quantity and quality of randomly distributed individual characteristics. In a general sense, *match* simply means that two things are equal or similar to one another. In forensic identification the term *match* has come to mean that two things share a common origin. For example, two fingerprints being made by the same person, or two toolmarks, one a test and one questioned, being made by the same tool. When two toolmarks match forensically, they have been individualized to a common source; one tool to the exclusion of all others. See Biasotti & Murdock, "Criteria For Identification" or "State of the Art of Firearms and Toolmark Identification," 16 Ass'n Firearm &

Toolmark Examiners J. 16 (1984); Biasotti, A Statistical Study of the Individual Characteristics of Fired Bullets, 4 J. Forensic Sci. 34 (1959) (a summary of Biasotti's thesis, Bullet Comparison: A Study of Fired Bullets Statistically Analyzed (1955) (on file with the University of California at Berkeley)); Biasotti, The Principles of Evidence Evaluation as Applied to Firearms and Toolmark Identification, 9 J. Forensic Sci. 428 (1964).

[4]See G. Burrard, The Identification of Firearms and Forensic Ballistics (1934); Jack D. Gunther & C.O. Gunther, The Identification of Firearms (1935); A. Lucas, Forensic Chemistry and Scientific Criminal Investigation (3rd ed. 1935); J.S. Hatcher, Textbook of Firearms Investigation, Identification and Evidence (1935); J.S. Hatcher, F.J. Jury & J. Weller, Firearms Investigation, Identification, and Evidence (1957); John E. Davis, An Introduction to Tool Marks, Firearms and the Striagraph (1958); J. Mathews, 1 Firearms Identification (1962); T.A. Warlow, Firearms, the Law and Forensic Ballistics (1996); Brian J. Heard, Handbook of Firearms and Ballistics (1997). In T.A. Warlow, Firearms, the Law and Forensic Ballistics (2d ed. 2005) at 330–331, presents the quantitative CMS criteria for striated toolmark identification first introduced by Biasotti and Murdock in the 1997 first edition of the present work, along with supporting research published by Jerry Miller (citations collected in margin of § 5:12).

estimates using actual toolmarks was conducted by Biasotti and published in 1959.[5] Two groups of .38 Special Smith and Wesson revolvers were examined in this study. The first group consisted of sixteen used guns from which six to twelve 158 grain lead bullets were fired. The second group consisted of eight new guns from which six 158 grain lead bullets and six 158 grain metal-jacketed bullets were fired. The data for comparisons made between bullets fired from the same gun were obtained by considering the first bullet as the primary reference, and then comparing the succeeding five test firings with it. This made a total of 400 land and 400 groove impressions compared for the group of sixteen used guns, plus a total of 200 land and 200 groove impressions compared for each group of lead and metal-jacketed bullets from the eight new guns. The data for bullets fired from different guns were obtained by comparing the first bullet from each gun with the first bullet from a different gun, for a total of 36 different combinations, giving a total of 180 land and 180 groove impressions compared for each of the following groups of guns and tests: (1) used, lead bullets; (2) new, lead bullets; and (3) new, metal-jacketed bullets.

Two basic types of data were recorded: (1) the total line count and total matching lines[6] per land or groove impression from which the percent matching lines[7] was calculated; and (2) the frequency of occurrence of each series of consecutive matching lines[8] for which probability estimates were calculated.

For same gun comparisons, the author strictly held to the criteria for consecutive

---

[5]Biasotti, A Statistical Study of the Individual Characteristics of Fired Bullets, 4 J. Forensic Sci. 34 (1959).

[6]*Matching lines* is a term used for brevity to denote matching striae either consecutive or non-consecutive which have a unique character, i.e., width, height, length, and contour. See Biasotti & Murdock, "Criteria For Identification" or "State of the Art of Firearms and Toolmark Identification," 16 Ass'n Firearm & Toolmark Examiners J. 16 (1984); Biasotti, The Principles of Evidence Evaluation as Applied to Firearms and Toolmark Identification, 9 J. Forensic Sci. 428 (1964); and Biasotti, A Statistical Study of the Individual Characteristics of Fired Bullets, 4 J. Forensic Sci. 34 (1959).

*Lines* is a term that has largely been replaced with the term striae (or striations). Lines are two-dimensional and have length and width. They do not have height. Striations on the other hand have length, width and height.

A *striation*, viewed through the comparison microscope, consists of a segment of contour that has length, width, and height. In order for striae to have significance the striated mark must be reproducible. These are striae that are made by the tool, not by non-reproducing artifacts (i.e., lead fouling, dirt, extraneous debris). Therefore, they should also have continuity (sustained length).

[7]*Percent matching lines* denotes the percent of matching striae without regard to consecutiveness. See Biasotti & Murdock, "Criteria For Identification" or "State of the Art of Firearms and Toolmark Identification," 16 Ass'n Firearm & Toolmark Examiners J. 16 (1984); Biasotti, A Statistical Study of the Individual Characteristics of Fired Bullets, 4 J. Forensic Sci. 34 (1959).

[8]*Consecutively matching lines* are striae that correspond or match with respect to each striae's width, depth and contour and are of sufficient length to assure that striae are parallel to one another. The term *striae* is today more commonly used than "lines" although the latter term is still used by some to describe striae that are very shallow and thus appear virtually two dimensional. See Biasotti & Murdock, "Criteria For Identification" or "State of the Art of Firearms and Toolmark Identification," 16 Ass'n Firearm & Toolmark Examiners J. 16 (1984); Biasotti, The Principles of Evidence Evaluation as Applied to Firearms and Toolmark Identification, 9 J. Forensic Sci. 428 (1964); Biasotti, A Statistical Study of the Individual Characteristics of Fired Bullets, 4 J. Forensic Sci. 34 (1959).

*Consecutively matching striae (CMS)* are striae within an array of striated markings that agree in their spatial relationship, their width and their morphology. Such agreement is inherent in defining a pattern. For purposes of striated toolmark identification, it is the extent of runs of consecutively matching striae (CMS) that defines the measure of striated pattern agreement when assessing the potential for associating questioned toolmark(s) with test toolmarks produced by a submitted tool(s).

From a theoretical standpoint, all striated toolmarks are three-dimensional (3D) and have height. With sophisticated measuring equipment it is becoming increasingly possible to measure the height of any striae. While this may be possible to do, especially with today's sophisticated instrumentation, this is of little practical value for toolmark identification work using the comparison microscope. This is because such measuring equipment is not commonly used or available in forensic laboratories and, until it is, examiners

matching lines, while for different gun comparisons the criteria were liberally interpreted. To add a further subjective bias toward higher consecutive line counts, each land and groove impression of reference bullets from different guns was compared with other land or groove impressions appearing most similar in overall contour and degree of marking.

Probability estimates for the *same* gun comparisons showed a high frequency of two or more consecutive lines; however, more significantly, no more than three consecutively matching lines were found for all lead bullets, or more than four for metal-jacketed bullets from all *different* gun comparisons.

The concept of "consecutiveness" is a simplified way of expressing the matching of a segment of contour, or a pattern of matching individual characteristics in a striated toolmark. These results, therefore, support the validity of the hypothesis adopted by A.F.T.E. and further developed by the authors.

This fired bullet study also demonstrated the unsuitability of using "percent matching lines" as a criterion of identification, particularly for fired bullets where the percent matching striae in known matches can be approximately the same as the percent matching striae found in known non-matches. In this study, bullets fired from different barrels (i.e., "known non-matches") ranged from 15 to 20% matching striae, whereas bullets fired from the same barrel (i.e., "known matches") ranged from 21 to 38% matching striae. These ranges for known matches versus

---

must estimate whether they are viewing two-dimensional (2D) or 3D striae on the basis of the perceived gradations in shadow caused by contour revealed by side (oblique) lighting. If variation in contour is perceived in this way, the toolmark is 3D for CMS quantitation purposes. For the purpose of practical interpretation under the comparison microscope, the following 2D and 3D definitions are offered to assist the examiner in the interpretation of CMS runs.

*2D striated toolmarks* are any impressed or striated toolmark that lacks discernable depth or: (1) occupies only the very surface of a recording medium in which the toolmark appears; (2) has been made in a recording medium that is very thin or; (3) results from the application of the tool to the medium in such a way that only superficial markings are produced. Examples of 2D striated surface toolmarks would include rubber wiper blade marks on a glass windshield; scratches in sheet film produced by dragging a glass microscope slide across it; markings resulting from dragging a fractured edge of a wooden tongue depressor over a sheet of carbon paper; and similar processes.

*3D striated toolmarks* are any impressed or striated toolmark that displays discernable contour because the medium the toolmark is in has been displaced. Examples of potential 3D striated toolmarks would include striae appearing on fired bullets, and striae produced from chisels and screwdrivers in wood or metal softer than the tool.

Any of these examples can also be 2D if the markings are very superficial. For example, there are cases when extremely polished firearm bores produce very little information in the way of striated markings simply because there are few irregularities on the bore surface that produce striated toolmarks of any discernable depth. These

striae will be sparse and will appear as very thin "lines" with no apparent depth.

Historically, when applying these two considerations to CMS tabulations, it was found that striated toolmarks that lacked discernable depth resulted in slightly higher CMS counts among known non-matches (the best KNM being six consecutive (6X) matching striae in two dimensional toolmarks, reported by Miller and McLean, Criteria for Identification of Toolmarks, 30 Ass'n Firearm and Toolmark Examiners J. 15 (1998)) compared to striated markings with discernable depth (best KNM being 4X observed on land impressions on fired copper jacketed bullets and reported in Biasotti, A Statistical Study of the Individual Characteristics of Fired Bullets, 4 J. Forensic Sci. 34 (1959)). This difference in CMS KNMs is due to the fact that in cases where striated markings have so little depth, they appear as lines (even though they are technically striations). The lack of perceived depth of these 2D appearing striae diminishes the examiner's ability to discern differences in contour and is the likely reason for the slightly higher CMS tabulations in these cases compared to 3D striated toolmark KNM comparisons (where the element of height can be used as an additional means of critically evaluating consecutiveness).

*Tabulation of CMS*: CMS is defined as striated markings that "line up" *exactly* (close doesn't count) with one another without a break or dissimilarity in between them. These are striae that agree in their spatial relationship, width and morphology. For practical purposes CMS are counted as follows: For 2D, only striae that match exactly in relative position and width are counted. For 3D, only the ridges (which can be white/gray) are counted and not the valleys between the ridges (that are dark gray/black).

known non-matches were obtained from all the striae on all the bullets compared and appear to offer a criterion for identification. However, because of the difficulty in judging the qualitative agreement of individual striae spread over several land or groove impressions, a percent matching number often can be misleading and may result in a false identification.

Analogous studies have reported up to 28% matching striae in known non-matches produced by the ground working surfaces of tools; i.e., knives, bolt cutter blades, and tongue-and-groove pliers.[9] Striae produced by a ground working surface are typically similar in height, width, spacing (often due to grit size), and lack much three dimensional contour. Therefore they are viewed as two-dimensional parallel "lines." These type of shallow striae, combined with less than a two millimeter wide striated toolmark available for comparison, and the absence of clear class characteristic limits, can result in a false identification if percent match is the only criterion used.[10]

Other published research designed to validate quantitative probability estimates for matching striae have been conducted using mechanical or mathematical models. In one such study[11] a comparison of 1003 positions of known non-match of a 25 striae wide two-dimensional toolmark found that a five consecutive striae match occurred only at one position. No greater consecutive matching occurred and no 4X matching, but a greater number of 3X and 2X matching was found.[12] The features of toolmark depth and contour were not present in those two-dimensional toolmarks and so were not considered in this experiment.

In 1970, Brackett[13] explored the application of mathematical models to the study of striated toolmarks. This work reports an attempt to idealize striated marks in order to develop a theoretical basis (i.e., mathematical model) for their analysis. It is possible to take Brackett's ideal models and convert them into mechanical models which may be compared with actual toolmarks, the goal being to obtain sufficient information to enable establishment of objective criteria of identity of two sets of marks.

Brackett made a finding of great practical importance. Using *actual* consecutive line counts from a randomly selected example from Biasotti's bullet study,[14] he was able to demonstrate that a plot of the distribution of these actual run counts closely approximated those predicted by the general equation (i.e., mathematical model) that he derived. Brackett thus succeeded in deriving an equation which simulates the run distribution[15] properties of actual cases of randomly distributed striae. The importance of this finding is that this equation can be used to generate computer assisted programs capable of studying the effects of such crucial variables as striae density, uniformity or non-uniformity, and randomness, with a speed and efficiency not possible by conventional direct visual comparisons and evaluation. No one,

---

[9]Butcher & Pugh, A Study of Marks Made by Bolt Cutters, 15 J. Forensic Sci. Soc'y 115 (1975); Watson, The Identification of Toolmarks Produced from Consecutively Manufactured Knife Blades in Soft Plastic, 10 Ass'n Firearm & Toolmark Examiners J. 43 (1978); Cassidy, Examination of Toolmarks from Sequentially Manufactured Tongue-and-Groove Pliers, 25 J. Forensic Sci. 798 (1980).

[10]Butcher & Pugh, A Study of Marks Made by Bolt Cutters, 15 J. Forensic Sci. Soc'y 115 (1975).

[11]Conducted in 1968 by Murdock, Barnett and McJunkins, reported in Biasotti & Murdock, "Criteria For Identification" or "State of the Art of Firearms and Toolmark Identification," 16 Ass'n

Firearm & Toolmark Examiners J. 16 (1984).

[12]"5X" would be shorthand for "five consecutive striae," "4X" for "four consecutive striae," and so on.

[13]Brackett, A Study of Idealized Striated Marks and Their Comparison Using Models, 10 J. Forensic Sci. Soc'y 27 (1970).

[14]Biasotti, A Statistical Study of the Individual Characteristics of Fired Bullets, 4 J. Forensic Sci. 34 (1959).

[15]"Run count" is a term used by Brackett to describe the number of consecutive matching striae. "Run distribution" is a term used by Brackett to describe the number of striae in any given toolmark or portion thereof.

however, has pursued this line of research.

In a review of published efforts from 1990–1994 to make toolmark examinations more objective, Springer[16] concluded that, "the early 1990's shows much promise for the advancement of toolmark comparisons." He suggests that the advancements will be made by automated technology.

Research[17] performed under the direction of the authors following their 1984 *"Criteria for Identification" or "State of the Art"* paper[18] was specifically directed at examining actual two and three-dimensional striated and impression toolmarks to determine in KNM comparisons: (1) for striated marks, the maximum percent match and the maximum number of consecutive matching striae; and (2) for impression marks, the maximum number of matching randomly distributed individual characteristics.

The striated toolmark samples studied during the CCI classes consisted of:

(1) six 9 mm. Luger metal jacketed test bullets, followed by six lead test bullets fired from ten previously unfired, consecutively rifled, gun barrels. Plastic casts were made of each barrel before tests were fired. Microscopic examination of these casts revealed no subclass characteristics in either the lands or grooves in any of the ten barrels; and

(2) twelve duplicate sets of striated test marks made with the top and bottom working edges of a previously unused, three-fourths inch wide chisel having a stone-ground working edge.

For the bullet comparisons, the examiners were directed to select and compare "out-of-phase"[19] land and groove marks (fired from the same barrel), or any of the five land and groove marks (fired from different barrels) where the striae appeared most similar in density, width, and contour. Similarly, for the chisel test marks, the examiners were directed to select any test from the same out-of-phase side, or any combination of opposite side tests. These examination procedures were intended to maximize the finding of the highest percent match and highest number of consecutively matching striae for KNM comparisons.

The most significant conclusions that can be drawn from more than a thousand specifically directed, striated KNM bullet and chisel mark comparisons are:

(1) not more than three consecutive corresponding three-dimensional striae (i.e., among the bullets) were found, and the few (less than 20) apparent "fours"

---

[16]Springer, Toolmark Examinations—A Review of Its Development in the Literature, 40 J. Forensic Sci. 964 (1995).

[17]The authors were principal instructors in six forty-hour courses that dealt exclusively with "Firearms and Toolmark Identification Criteria." These were offered by the California Department of Justice Criminalistic Institute (CCI) commencing 12/10/90, 4/29/91, 5/11/92, 2/1/93, 12/11/95 and 10/96. Each course averaged twelve students, ranging in experience from one to fifteen or more years, doing comparison microscope examinations of toolmarks generated both by firearms and a hand tool. The goal of these courses was to conduct practical exercises with actual toolmarks to allow students to develop their personal criteria for identification and to further develop and refine objective, quantitative criteria. John Murdock and Frederic Tulleners (Program Manager for CCI) conducted these classes annually from 1997 to 2004. Currently John Murdock and Bruce Moran

teach these classes.

[18]Biasotti & Murdock, "Criteria For Identification" or "State of the Art of Firearms and Toolmark Identification," 16 Ass'n Firearm & Toolmark Examiners J. 16 (1984).

[19]*Out-of-Phase* refers to two possible situations: (1) two bullets which were fired from the same gun barrel are aligned on the comparison microscope so that the land and groove impressions on these bullets, which were produced by the same lands and grooves in the barrel, are *not* opposite each other. When the correct corresponding land and groove impressions are opposite one another, the bullets are said to be "in phase." This also is sometimes called *orienting* or *indexing*. See Glossary of the Association of Firearm and Toolmark Examiners (1994), at 76; or (2) when two toolmarks are lined up in such a way that they cannot possibly match, such as when clearly defined edges of two toolmarks are offset from each other.

found lacked exact qualitative agreement[20] in striae width, relative position, or contour;

(2) for striae lacking depth and therefore appearing two-dimensional (i.e., among the chisel marks), not more than five consecutive corresponding striae were found;[21]

(3) percent matching striae ranged from 15 to 30%, which is similar to values reported in previous studies,[22] thus confirming the limited value of percent match as a criterion for identification; and

(4) the nearly identical range of quantitative values found in all known non-match comparisons for all types of rifled barrels, in addition to striated marks made by the ground working surface of a chisel, demonstrates that the probability for the matching microscopic agreement of randomly distributed striae is fundamentally the same, regardless of the tool used.

Analogous studies of impression type toolmarks, such as firearm breech block markings, or models of randomly distributed individual characteristics of the same or different shape revealed no more than four matching individual characteristics. Even this small degree of chance correspondence observed was possible only if one ignored the exact shape, size, and orientation that was present in each of these randomly distributed individual characteristics. In practice, the examiner would critically evaluate impression characteristics occupying the same relative position for the extent of agreement, and conclude that evidence and test impressions were made by the same surface only where the matching[23] features are sharply defined either wholly or in part.

All research to date supports the hypothesis that it is possible to individualize toolmarks because there are practical probability limits to: (1) the number of randomly distributed consecutive matching striae; and (2) the number of randomly distributed matching individual characteristics in impression toolmarks in known non-match positions. This research also demonstrates that quantitative objective criteria can be applied with a high degree of statistical confidence in determining that a toolmark is unique if the values from KNM comparisons are conservatively applied. The authors, in advocating the following conservative quantitative criteria for identification guidelines, have considered that: (1) there is a probability that a higher number of both single and multiple groups of consecutive matching striae than empirically observed to date could occur in KNM's; (2) the occurrence of multiple groups of consecutive matching striae appearing in the same relative position in any given known non-matching toolmark becomes less probable as the number of groups increases; and (3) there may be some variance between examiners in their subjective interpretation of the qualitative and quantitative agreement observed. With these considerations in mind, the authors' conservative quantitative criteria for identification are:

(1) in three-dimensional toolmarks when at least two different groups of at least three consecutive matching striae appear in the same relative position, or

---

[20]*Qualitative Agreement* refers to the degree or extent of the agreement of striae width, relative position and contour. In practice, striae in one toolmark often will come close to matching striae in another toolmark with respect to these comparison parameters. Significant correspondence or agreement is achieved when there is *exact* agreement of these comparison parameters. Close does not count, and *very* closely agreeing striae may be ascribed greater significance than is justified, leading to incorrect identifications.

[21]Biasotti & Murdock, "Criteria For Identification" or "State of the Art of Firearms and Toolmark

Identification," 16 Ass'n Firearm & Toolmark Examiners J. 16 (1984).

[22]Biasotti & Murdock, "Criteria For Identification" or "State of the Art of Firearms and Toolmark Identification," 16 Ass'n Firearm & Toolmark Examiners J. 16 (1984); Biasotti, A Statistical Study of the Individual Characteristics of Fired Bullets, 4 J. Forensic Sci. 34 (1959).

[23]See Biasotti & Murdock, "Criteria For Identification" or "State of the Art of Firearms and Toolmark Identification," 16 Ass'n Firearm & Toolmark Examiners J. 16 (1984).

one group of six consecutive matching striae are in agreement in an evidence toolmark compared to a test toolmark; and

(2) in two-dimensional toolmarks when at least two groups of at least five consecutive matching striae appear in the same relative position, or one group of eight consecutive matching striae are in agreement in an evidence toolmark compared to a test toolmark.

For these criteria to apply, however, the possibility of subclass characteristics must be ruled out.

Research conducted thus far by the authors indicates that the practical probability limits in known non-matches for impression toolmarks are similar to those found for striated toolmarks. Some progress has been made in developing quantitative criteria for the identification of compression toolmarks. Following Stone's publication of a theoretical model for the mathematical evaluation of well defined types of impressed toolmarks,[24] Collins used and evaluated Stone's model while performing an empirical study of twenty worn hammer faces. His preliminary results show that combinations of even low numbers of simple impressed defects are, on a practical level, quite discriminating.[25] However, more research is needed involving very fine, high density, randomly distributed individual impression characteristics, viewed two dimensionally, before definitive practical probability limits can be stated confidently.

Since this chapter was first published in 1997, there have been a number of studies which have included an evaluation, using consecutive matching striae, of the numerical criteria for the identification of striated toolmarks proposed above by the authors.[26] No known non-matching (two- or three-dimensional) toolmarks were found in these studies which exhibited agreement in excess of the proposed Biasotti-

---

[24]Stone, How Unique are Impressed Toolmarks?, 35 Ass'n Firearm & Toolmark Examiners J. 4 (2003). The comparison model developed by Stone offers a springboard upon which those interested in studying the occurrence of impressed contours and establishing the basis for a quantifiable identification criterion of impressed toolmarks may now do so. His work has inspired other researchers.

[25]Collins, How Unique are Impressed Toolmarks: An Empirical Study of 20 Worn Hammer Faces 37 Ass'n Firearm and Toolmark Examiners J. 252 (2005). Collins tested the validity of Stone's theories on the statistical uniqueness of impressed toolmarks through the empirical examination of the defects observed on the faces of twenty hammers that had been subjected to various degrees of wear and abuse through normal use. These examinations were carried out under controlled conditions that would simulate those used in practical casework. The results of this study led to a re-evaluation of Stone's work and a modification of related formulae. The revised formulae were used to calculate practical but conservative probabilities associated with impressed toolmarks using the data collected from the hammers in this study.

[26]Tulleners, Giusto & Hamiel, Striae Reproducibility on Sectional Cuts of One Thompson Contender Barrel, 30 Ass'n Firearm & Toolmark Examiners J. 62 (1998); Miller & McLean, Criteria for Identification of Toolmarks, Ass'n Firearm & Toolmark Examiners J. 15 (1998) (offering a sound description of the history of criteria for identification, the use of IBIS and the scientific method; the authors used IBIS to sort single land impressions of. 38 special caliber bullets for comparison; the test firings used in their study were from firearms associated with forensic casework and thus were used firearms); Miller, Criteria for Identification of Toolmarks Part II—Single Land Impression Comparisons, 32 Ass'n Firearm & Toolmark Examiners J. 116 (2000) (extending his IBIS sorted study by examining single land impressions of.25 auto, .380 auto and 9mm calibers; because he limited his studies (Part I and II) to single land impressions, he found that he excluded some known identifications because there was not enough agreement to meet the Biasotti-Murdock criteria; no false identifications were made, however; the test firings used in this study were from firearms associated with forensic casework and thus were used firearms); Miller, An Examination of Two Consecutively Rifled Barrels and a Review of the Literature, 32 Ass'n Firearm & Toolmark Examiners J. 259 (2000) (after reviewing literature dealing with the examination of bullets fired from consecutively rifled barrels, Miller then compared test bullets pushed through two new consecutively rifled gun barrels; after determining that there was no subclass influence, he evaluated the test bullets by using the Biasotti-Murdock numerical criteria for identification described in this chapter; he found that no false identifications would be made using these criteria); Fred Tulleners, David Stoney & James Hamiel, An Analysis of Consecutive Striae

Murdock criteria.

There are indications that the concept of objective quantitative criteria for identification is gaining wider acceptance. In 1999 at the annual training seminar, approximately 300 members of the Association of Firearm and Toolmark Examiners (AFTE) voluntarily participated in a four-hour workshop on the subject.[27] In addition, workshops of varying lengths up to 12 hours duration entitled "Scientifically Defensible Criteria for the Identification of Toolmarks" have been presented by John Murdock and Bruce Moran at the 2003, 2004, and 2005 AFTE annual seminars. Approximately 87 AFTE members have attended. This same 12 hour workshop was presented at the International Association of Forensic Science in August 2005 in Hong Kong and to the Los Angeles Police Department Firearms Unit in October 2005.

On a more practical level, Bruce Moran has authored two papers which describe how he uses objective quantitative criteria in firearms and toolmark casework and how a typical question and answer session might go in court on the same subject.[28]

---

on Random and Consecutive Chisels, Paper presented at the annual meeting of the American Academy of Forensics Sciences (Feb.1999).

Miller, An Examination of the Application of the Conservative Criteria for Identification of Striated Toolmarks Using Bullets from Ten Consecutively Rifled Barrels, 33 Ass'n Firearm and Toolmark Examiners J. 2 (2001). Miller intercompared bullets test fired from ten consecutively broached gun barrels. He found that considering the results of the data for the two and three dimensional comparisons between known matches and non-matches, no erroneous identifications would be expected although some actual identifications would be excluded. He said that his study further validates the use of the conservative-numerical criteria (proposed by Biasotti and Murdock) insofar as critical evaluation of striated toolmark agreement will not result in a false identification.

Miller and Neel, Criteria for Identification of Toolmarks, Part III: Supporting the Conclusion, 36 Ass'n Firearm and Toolmark Examiners J. 1 (2004). In this study, students at the ATF National Firearm Examiners Academy evaluated two dimensional toolmarks produced with 60 grit sandpaper and recorded on 35 mm photographic film. Each kit contained known matching and non-matching toolmarks. In the three studies (12 students in each class) reported on in this research, the concept of using the Biasotti-Murdock conservative CMS criteria as a method for describing the difference between a known match and known non-match, as well as its use to support a conclusion in a striated toolmark examination, was tested. In all of the samples examined, no false identifications occurred. Missed identifications occurred only when the defined pattern area was limited, and these were rare. Although variations in counting striae and consecutive groups of striae were noted this had *no effect on* the conclusions reached by the student examiners.

[27]Objective Criteria Workshop, presented by Torrey D. Johnson (of the Las Vegas Metro Police

Department Forensic Laboratory) in Williamsburg, Virginia (July 18–23, 1999). Each participant performed a number of toolmark "photo comparisons" and were to conclude if the comparisons represented an identification, an elimination or were inconclusive of the AFTE glossary A, B or C type; see § 5:9. The hypothesis for this study was that, when toolmarks are compared, based on corresponding groups of striae, called consecutive matching striae, a level of correspondence exists which provides a satisfactory determination of identity between the marks. If it is possible to establish this level, it is possible to define quantitatively the degree of correspondence that divides inconclusive from identification. Unfortunately, the scope of this study proved too great for the time available, and no meaningful data were obtained.

[28]Moran, The Application of Numerical Criteria For Identification in Casework Involving (Ammunition) Magazine Marks and Rifling Impressions (on Bullets), 33 Ass'n Firearm & Toolmark Examiners J. 41 (2001) (including a well-illustrated discussion of subclass toolmarks on ammunition magazine lips); Moran, Firearms Examiner Expert Witness Testimony: The Forensic Firearms Identification Process Including Criteria for Identification and Distance Determination, 32 Ass'n Firearm & Toolmark Examiners J. 231 (2000) (providing helpful discussion concerning skillful and thorough presentation of this subject in court).

See also Hess and Moran, The Removal of Superficial Rust/Corrosion From the Working Surfaces of Firearms For the Purpose of Preserving Their Potentially Identifiable Signature and an Application of this Technique in a Firearms Identification, 38 Ass'n Firearm and Toolmark Examiners J. 112 (2006). This two-part paper describes: (1) a method for removing superficial rust and corrosion from the working surfaces of firearms with the intent to restore any surviving identifiable signature of the firearm and (2) casework resulting in the successful identification of several bullets to a rusted firearm treated us-

Ronald Nichols has authored two papers which have helped clarify the use of consecutive matching striae, summarized CMS validation studies, and described the validity of the AFTE Theory of Identification.[29] In addition to a well illustrated discussion of the presence of subclass characteristics which do not prevent the individuality of the working tool surfaces of ten consecutively manufactured extractors, this article collates the relevant studies, showing substantial support for the AFTE Theory of Identification, and suggesting that its scientific validity and reliability can be more than adequately defended.

Additionally, a recent paper sheds light on the astronomical probabilities, from a Bayesian point of view, of approaching KNM agreement equal to or greater than the minimum numerical criteria.[30]

## § 5:13   Future directions

It is anticipated that objective quantitative criteria for identification will eventually become widely accepted and used because of the research already conducted and published,[1] plus a commercially available system called the Integrated Ballistic Identification System (IBIS)[2] developed by Forensic Technology Industries of Montreal, Canada, for the comparison of fired bullets and cartridge cases. Barrett reported on the basic concept of the IBIS system in 1991, while Tontarski and Thompson have provided a description of the IBIS system as it was being used in 1998.[3] It has undergone several upgrades since.

The primary purpose of these automated comparison systems, as far as fired bullets are concerned, is to rapidly screen large populations of electronically stored images of fired bullets. From a comparison of the unique features of the stored images,

---

ing the procedure. The latter discussion includes a series of photomicrographs illustrating tabulations of CMS supporting conclusions of an identification involving a limited amount of striae. It also describes the approach to the consideration of subclass influence present in the grooves of the barrel bore of the questioned firearm and provides photomicrographs of these features.

[29]Nichols, Consecutive-Matching Striations (CMS): Its Definition, Study and Application in the Discipline of Firearms and Toolmark Identification, 35 Ass'n Firearm and Toolmark Examiners J. 3 (2003). A definition of CMS is presented that helps demonstrate that it is not in conflict with what has been referred to as the traditional pattern matching approach, but is simply a means of describing the observed pattern. This article also critically evaluates those articles that have questioned the conservative minimum criteria for identification approach. See also Nichols, Firearm and Toolmark Identification: The Scientific Reliability and Validity of the AFTE Theory of Identification Discussed Within the Framework of a Study of Ten Consecutively Manufactured Extractors, 36 Ass'n Firearm & Toolmark Examiners J. 1 (2004). This paper provides a summary of approximately 6,000 known non-matching striated toolmark comparisons that were conducted since publication of the conservative CMS criteria was first published in 1997. The conservative CMS criteria was not exceeded in any of these 2D and 3D comparisons.

[30]Buckleton et al., An Exploratory Bayesian Model for Firearm and Tool Mark Interpretation, 37 Ass'n Firearm and Toolmark Examiners J. 352 (2005).

[Section 5:13]

[1]Following the presentation of two CC1 "firearms and toolmark identification criteria" classes to a total of twenty eight examiners from Australia and New Zealand in November 2001 by John Murdock and Fred Tulleners, national agreed guidelines were developed regarding comparative microscopic examinations and the relevance of the conservative criteria for the identification of striated toolmarks. It was agreed that applying the criteria for Consecutively Matching Striae (CMS) was a valid tool when carrying out the comparative process and that CMS provides for a more objective approach. Firearm and Toolmark Scientific Working Group Report and Report on CMS Workshop (Australia and New Zealand), The Forensic Bulletin - National Institute of Forensic Science Australia (June 2002), at 2–3.

[2]Technical and other information available from Forensic Technology, Inc., 5757 Cavendish Blvd., Suite 200, Cote St-Luc, Quebec, Canada, H4W 2W8, 888–984–4247. Web address www.forensictechnologyinc.com.

[3]Barrett, The Microchip and the Bullet: A Vision of the Future, 23 Ass'n Firearms & Toolmark Examiners J. 876 (1991); Tontarski & Thompson, Automated Ballistic Comparison: A Forensic Tool for Firearms Identification-An Update, 43 J. Forensic Sci. 641 (1998).

these systems produce a list of bullet images ranked in order of striae agreement. An imaging comparison system called "Drugfire" was developed for cartridge cases by the Federal Bureau of Investigation.[4] Drugfire machines have been, however, phased out. They have been replaced across the United States by IBIS machines.

Automated systems do *not* make identifications, or replace the need for an expert examiner. The identification or exclusion of the images generated by these systems must be based on the informed judgement of an examiner comparing real or replica bullets or cartridge cases selected by these systems.

However, these systems will continue to make major contributions toward establishing objective quantitative criteria for identification. Objective criteria such as the number of consecutively corresponding striae, or the percent of corresponding striae, and the effect of variable qualitative dimensions of individual characteristics can be evaluated rapidly for large populations of known non-matches from a variety of different calibers, bullet and cartridge types and manufacturing methods. These automated measurements, which are inherently objective, can therefore be used to increase substantially the statistical confidence in the range of correspondence observed in direct manual known non-match comparisons.

Beyond this, it is up to individual examiners to become aware of the literature about criteria for identification and use it in their day-to-day casework. Perhaps then it will be possible to come close to the standard espoused by Paul Kirk in his syllabus to his University of California, Berkeley, Course number 151: "In criminalistic practice [forensic science], mistakes are not allowed."[5] In reality, mistakes do occur in forensic science, as in all other professions. All we can do is to try very, very hard to prevent them. It is our belief that the continued development and widespread acceptance of objective quantifiable criteria for identification will hold mistakes to a minimum, especially where limited striae are available for comparison.

The intercomparison of striated toolmarks by pattern recognition alone is a process of form perception where the goal of the examiner is to use his/her training and experience to locate sufficient matching agreement between questioned and known toolmarks to effect an identification between these toolmarks. This is a process that does *not* include a conscious tabulation of consecutive matching striae (CMS). Examiners using pattern recognition alone can describe the extent of matching striae in any given striated toolmark match position by saying that it exceeds any known non-match with which they are familiar.

Some examiners, who locate *potential* matching striated toolmark areas through pattern matching, have chosen to numerically tabulate the quantity of consecutively matching striae (CMS) in these areas and use these tabulations as a way to describe the extent of matching CMS in any given striated toolmark comparison. These numerical counts are then compared to the results of empirical research involving tabulations of CMS in both known matching and known non-matching toolmarks. Toolmark identifications are made when the tabulated CMS runs exceed the thresholds established by empirical research. The thresholds may be those proposed by Biasotti and Murdock in 1997, or lower or higher thresholds depending on examiner preference, based on their training and experience.

It should, therefore, be clear that the application of quantitative CMS criteria is not a different method than pattern matching, but is merely a quantitative way to describe the extent of striated pattern matching agreement. The use of quantitative

---

[4]Robert W. Sibert, Drugfire: Revolutionizing Forensic Firearms Identification and Providing the Foundation for a National Firearms Identification Network, 21 Crime Laboratory Dig. 63 (October 1994).

[5]Paul L. Kirk, Outline of Laboratory Work in Criminology 151 (University of California, Berkeley, 1957, reprinted 1963), at 2.

CMS criteria is simply a refinement of traditional pattern matching.

With the assumption that firearm/toolmark examiners embrace the concept of quantitative criteria for identification of striated toolmarks using consecutive matching striae, Grzybowski and Murdock have summarized the view of many examiners by concluding that:

> The firearm/toolmark identification field has all the indicia of a science: (1) It is well grounded in scientific method; (2) it is well accepted in the relevant scientific community; (3) it has been subjected to many forms of peer review and publication; (4) it has participated in proficiency testing and published error rates; and (5) it provides objective quantitative criteria that guide the identification process.[6]

Grzybowski et al.[7] comprehensively cite and summarize work that they suggest provides an approach to explaining the firearm and toolmark identification process as a reliable science under the challenges of both *Daubert* and *Frye*.

For a much less sanguine view, see Adina Schwartz, Toolmark and Firearm Identification, in Jane Campbell Moriarty, Psychological and Scientific Evidence in Criminal Trials, § 12:39, at 12–49 (2005).

---

[6]Grzybowski & Murdock, Firearms and Toolmark Identification—Meeting the *Daubert* Challenge, 30 Ass'n Firearm & Toolmark Examiners J. 3 (1998) (including a basic discussion of the scientific method as well as inductive and deductive reasoning).

[7]Grzybowski, Miller, Moran, Murdock, Nichols, Thompson, Firearm/Toolmark Identification: Passing the Reliability Test under Federal and State Evidentiary Standards, 35 Ass'n Firearm and Toolmark Examiners J. 2 (2003).

# APPENDIX 5A

## Glossary of Terms

*Drawn from a list promulgated by the Association of Firearm and Toolmark Examiners*

**Accidental characteristic.** Term formerly used to mean individual characteristic. See individual characteristics.

**Class characteristics.** Measurable features of a specimen which indicate a restricted group source. They result from design factors, and are therefore determined prior to manufacture.

**Impression.** Contour variations on the surface of an object caused by a combination of force and motion where the motion is approximately perpendicular to the plane being marked. These marks can contain *class* and/or *individual characteristics*.

**Individual characteristics.** Marks produced by the random imperfections or irregularities of tool surfaces. These random imperfections or irregularities are either produced incidental to manufacture or are caused by use, corrosion, or damage. They are unique to that tool and distinguish it from all other tools.

**Striations.** Contour variations, generally microscopic, on the surface of an object caused by a combination of force and motion where the motion is approximately parallel to the plane being marked. These marks can contain *class* and/or *individual characteristics*.

**Subclass characteristics.** Discernible surface features of an object that are more restrictive than *class characteristics* in that they: (1) are produced incidental to manufacture; (2) relate to a smaller group source (a subset of the class to which they belong); and (3) can arise from a source which changes over time. Examples include: bunter marks (headstamps produced on cartridge cases) produced by bunters made from a common master, extrusion marks on pipe, etc.

**Tool.** An object used to gain mechanical advantage. Also thought of as the harder of two objects which produces toolmarks when brought into contact with each other resulting in the softer one being marked.

**Toolmark, impressed.** Marks produced when a tool is placed against another object and enough force is applied to the tool so that it leaves an impression. The class characteristics (shape) can indicate the type of tool used to produce the mark. These marks can contain *class* and/or *individual characteristics* of the tool producing the marks. Also called *compression marks*.

**Toolmark, striated.** Marks produced when a tool is placed against another object and with pressure applied, the tool is moved across the object, producing a striated mark. *Friction marks, abrasion marks,* and *scratch marks* are terms commonly used when referring to striated marks. These marks can consist of either *class* or *individual characteristics*, or both.

# APPENDIX 5B

# Questions Designed to Test a Witness's Ability to Identify Striated Toolmarks

1. Have you had training in toolmark comparisons?

2. Please describe this training for us. I am especially interested in the specific training you have had that enables you to individualize striated toolmarks.

> (Several types of training are possible: (1) regular classroom, (2) organized on-the-job training, and (3) structured self-directed type. All of these can focus on many areas worthy of study such as note taking, photography, tool manufacturing in general, but be unrelated to the individualization process.)

3. When you are comparing striated toolmarks made by tools capable of making unique toolmarks, how much agreement do you require before you can identify a specific tool as having made a specific evidence toolmark?

> (An amount that exceeds the best known non-match agreement that I have ever seen, either in my experience or in the literature.)

4. How much agreement do other examiners require?

> (This is generally unknown but the answer to #3 above is generally accepted.)

5. What is the standard amount of agreement that is required by the profession of toolmark examiners for an identification?

> (There are no objective, quantifiable standards recognized by the profession; but there are individual subjective "standard criteria" built up in the examiners' mind's-eye.)

6. If there are no universally recognized objective, quantifiable standards for the amount of agreement that is required to individualize striated toolmarks, how do you expect this court to evaluate the propriety of your conclusion(s)?

> (There are subjective guidelines. There has been a *Theory of Identification* and *Range of Conclusions Possible when Comparing Toolmarks* (supra note 15) adopted by the Association of Firearm and Toolmark Examiners.)

7. Would you expect to find some agreement [matching striae] when comparing striated toolmarks known to have been made by different tools?

> (The answer is yes.)

8. Isn't it true that there can be, on occasion, a considerable amount of agreement in comparisons of this sort, especially if the width of a shallow (for practical purposes, two-dimensional) mark being compared is quite small [say 2 millimeters or less]?

> (The agreement referred to here should be enough agreement to pique an examiner's interest. The answer should be yes, but if no, you could refer the witness to a 1975 article on boltcutters (supra note 7) wherein quite a bit of apparent matching striae in known non-match positions are shown; or Murdock & Biasotti's "State of the Art . . ." article (supra note 7) which also contains illustrations of known non-match agreement.)

9. The match or agreement in this case has been characterized as "_____".

> (The person asking the question can either quote from pretrial oral statements or written report(s) describing the nature of the toolmark agreement. The agreement may be described, depending on the examiner, as "significant," "best seen," "textbook," etc.)

10. Since you can get striae agreement in "known non-match" comparisons, how can you be sure that the agreement in this case is any better than remarkable "non-match" agreement. If the agreement in this case is no better than that, it doesn't mean anything does it?

> (A witness who has never compared known "non-matches" is in a poor position with respect to this question. A witness who has studied known non-matches probably would

say that the agreement exceeds known "non-match" agreement, if it does.)

11. Have you ever *deliberately* compared striated toolmarks that you knew were made by different tools?

(The answer should be yes. "Deliberately" is the key word here. When you do this, you are focusing on known non-match (KNM) agreement. When you find KNM agreement incidental to casework, you are probably not so focused and probably wouldn't take the time to record agreement in KNM positions; most examiners, however, gain some experience in KNM agreement while doing striae comparison casework.)

12. If so, how many of these comparisons have you made and what was the purpose of making comparisons of this sort?

(Approximately _____, for purposes of finding maximum striae agreement in any given KNM position.)

13. Wouldn't you agree that it is important in order to properly evaluate and determine the significance of limited or less than textbook striae agreement to know what the best agreement looks like in known non-match comparisons?

(The answer is yes. This knowledge is best gained by *deliberate* KNM comparisons, and not simply by what the examiner remembers having seen while comparing striae in casework, although some knowledge as mentioned above in #11, is gained in this way.)

14. In order to make a positive identification of striated marks, it seems to me that you have to have an amount of agreement that exceeds the best known non-match agreement. Do you agree?

(Yes. A witness who acknowledges having limited or no experience critically comparing known non-matching striated toolmarks, may not be in a very good position to properly evaluate the significance of the amount of agreement in cases where limited striae are present.)

15. How much agreement is this?

(Since it has been almost 10 years since the Biasotti-Murdock conservative CMS criteria were proposed, most examiners should be familiar with it and should be able to comment on how they personally satisfy the need to have a sufficient quantity of matching striae in toolmark identifications.)

# Chapter 6

# Identification from Bitemarks

## I.  LEGAL ISSUES

## II.  SCIENTIFIC ISSUES

## I. LEGAL ISSUES

### § 6:1  Generally

The analysis of bitemarks for the purpose of identifying a criminal perpetrator is a specialized task within the broader discipline of forensic odontology. Accordingly, it presents more challenging questions to odontologists and, in turn, to courts. Forensic dentists long have been called upon to identify the remains of victims of disasters by comparing the victims' dentition with dental records.[1] In trying to identify perpetrators of crime, the forensic dentist seeks to compare a suspect's dentition with a latent mark left in the victim's flesh or in some material, usually an edible substance, found at the scene of a crime.[2]

### § 6:2  Bitemark identification and the *Daubert* factors

Like all forensic identification sciences, the claims of the field of forensic odontology clearly are empirical in nature and therefore amenable to review under *Daubert*'s[1] criteria for evaluating scientific claims. Against those criteria, bitemark identification encounters several interesting problems. Clearly the nature of dentition and the asserted skills of forensic dentists are testable. Although some of the scientific issues and claims in forensic odontology have been tested more extensively than the scientific issues and claims of most forensic individualization sciences, that is largely because most of the other forensic individualization sciences have conducted or been subjected to remarkably little systematic empirical testing.[2] Important issues about the nature of identification by bitemark comparisons remain unresolved.[3]

Some of the research that has been conducted has been published and, if not peer reviewed before publication, certainly has been afterwards. Troublingly, some of the research has not been published or otherwise made public.[4] Recall that, properly understood, "peer review and publication" is concerned with evaluating the methodology of the "testing" referred to above. The published research in forensic odontology is not without flaws, and those flaws will inevitably and properly affect the seriousness with which the findings of those studies are taken.[5]

The error rate in bitemark identification, particularly the rate of false positive errors, appears to be quite high.[6]

Finally, general acceptance is an issue in forensic dentistry with regard to the task of linking crime scene marks to the dentition of a suspect. Not long ago, many, perhaps a majority, of forensic odontologists doubted that they could make pinpoint

---

[Section 6:1]

[1]In mass disasters dentists are able to identify 20–25% of the victims. See § 6:9.

[2]The two tasks differ in important ways. In the disaster situation, there is a finite number of candidates to identify, and full dentition often is available from the victims as well as from the dental charts. In forensic bitemark cases, the number of potential suspects is huge, the bitemarks include only a limited portion of the dentition, and flesh is a far less clear medium than having the teeth (of the disaster victim) themselves.

[Section 6:2]

[1]*Daubert v. Merrell Dow Pharmaceuticals, Inc.*, 509 U.S. 579, 113 S. Ct. 2786, 125 L. Ed. 2d 469, 27, 27 U.S.P.Q.2d 1200, Prod. Liab. Rep. (CCH) P 13494, 37 Fed. R. Evid. Serv. 1, 23 Envtl.

L. Rep. 20979 (1993).

[2]See, e.g., Chapters 3 and 4.

[3]Discussed at various places in the Scientific Status section of this chapter.

[4]The results of the fourth round of proficiency testing are reported, § 6:12, but the first three have never been published. Although the results of proficiency testing in other areas of forensic science once were equally secretive (not published and circulated privately within the field), at present anonymous test results from proficiency tests sponsored by the American Society of Crime Laboratory Directors ASCLD are posted on the website of the Collaborative Testing Service.

[5]See discussion at various places in the Scientific Status portion of this chapter.

[6]§ 6:12.

identifications in more than the rare case. Due to the eager acceptance by judges of bitemark expert testimony,[7] that number has dwindled, but a significant minority of forensic dentists retain their doubts about some of the field's vital claims. Thus, general acceptance in forensic odontology is not nearly so strong as it is in other forensic science fields.

## §6:3 Divergence of opinions by bitemark experts

One pattern that has emerged from the testimony presented in bitemark cases is the persistence of forensic odontologists testifying to contrary opinions. This occurs not only for opinions about the identity of the maker of a bitemark, but also on the question of whether or not a wound was caused by a bite.

In numerous cases, forensic odontologists have disagreed about whether a particular mark on a victim was a bitemark or not.[1] An increasingly well-known article reports on a case in which an injury was initially interpreted as a "possible" bitemark.[2] A suspect was then developed and dental models were taken of his teeth. After comparing the model to the injury, two forensic odontologists "stated that not only was the injury definitely caused by a human bite, but that the individual characteristics of the injury identically matched the suspect's dentition."[3] Thereafter, it was determined through an elaborate series of tests that the injury was not a bitemark after all, even though certain areas "suggested outlines of individual tooth margins."[4] In their article, the authors, both prominent forensic dentists, state the following conclusion:

> [When an injury is initially evaluated, and consideration is given toward the possibility of a human bite origin, *the first question to be asked is*, "Is this truly a bite injury?"]. . . . *If the answer is affirmative, the next two questions are* "What portion or portions of the dental arcade does it represent and what class and individual tooth characteristics does it contain?" These [latter] two questions must be always addressed in sequence, as the application of the second query is wholly dependent upon the answer to the first. *If this process is altered, and the basic presence or absence of an actual bite pattern injury is not adequately addressed, the eventual outcome may be disastrous.*[5]

The other issue, whether a defendant was the source of a bitemark, has generated at least as much disagreement between experts.[6]

In addition to the above-cited decisions, there have been numerous reports of fo-

---

[7]See discussion infra of *People v. Marx* and its aftermath.

**[Section 6:3]**

[1]See, e.g., *Kinney v. State*, 315 Ark. 481, 868 S.W.2d 463 (1994) (state and defense experts disagree about whether mark was human bitemark); *People v. Holmes*, 234 Ill. App. 3d 931, 176 Ill. Dec. 287, 601 N.E.2d 985 (1st Dist. 1992) (same); *Davis v. State*, 611 So. 2d 906 (Miss. 1992) (same); *People v. Noguera*, 4 Cal. 4th 599, 15 Cal. Rptr. 2d 400, 842 P.2d 1160, 1165 (1992) (same); *State v. Kendrick*, 47 Wash. App. 620, 736 P.2d 1079 (Div. 1 1987) (same); *People v. Smith*, 63 N.Y.2d 41, 479 N.Y.S.2d 706, 468 N.E.2d 879 (1984) (same); *State v. Keko*, Case No. 92-3292 (Parish Plaquemines, Louisiana, 1992) (same).

[2]Sperry & Campbell, Jr., An Elliptical Incised Wound of the Breast Misinterpreted as a Bite Injury, 35 J. Forensic Science 1126 (1990).

[3]Sperry & Campbell, Jr., An Elliptical Incised Wound of the Breast Misinterpreted as a Bite Injury, 35 J. Forensic Science at 1228 (1990).

[4]Sperry & Campbell, Jr., An Elliptical Incised Wound of the Breast Misinterpreted as a Bite Injury, 35 J. Forensic Science at 1235 (1990).

[5]Sperry & Campbell, Jr., An Elliptical Incised Wound of the Breast Misinterpreted as a Bite Injury, 35 J. Forensic Science at 1235 (1990) (emphasis added).

[6]See, e.g., *Milone v. Camp*, 22 F.3d 693 (7th Cir.1994) ("at trial much evidence was adduced by both sides concerning whether Milone's dentition matched the bitemark"; defendant "presented several experts of his own to testify that he could not have made the mark found"); *Wilhoit v. State*, 1991 OK CR 50, 816 P.2d 545 (Okla. Crim. App. 1991) (eleven "well-recognized forensic odontologists" disagree with state's experts that defendant caused the bitemark on victim); *Spence v. State*, 795 S.W.2d 743 (Tex. Crim. App. 1990) ("there was truly a battle between two of today's leading experts in the field of forensic odontology at appellant's trial"); *State v. Sager*, 600 S.W.2d 541 (Mo. Ct. App. W.D. 1980) (defendant's two experts disagreed with State's experts); *Kennedy v. State*,

rensic odontologists reaching opinions that disagreed with the results of DNA and other forensic analysis.[7]

The rather frequent disagreement among forensic dentists, more common than among other forensic identification scientists,[8] could be explained in a number of different ways. Bitemark comparisons may be inherently more ambiguous than other identification types. Forensic dentists may simply be more available to defendants compared to most other forensic scientists, who are more or less exclusively in the employ of the government. Or, relatedly, board-certified forensic odontologists may inadvertently reach conclusions favorable to the party that has retained them[9]—by no means a phenomenon new to the courts. So, whether the fact of frequent disagreement reveals bitemark identification to be a peculiarly unreliable area, or whether areas of expertise that create an illusion of consistency[10] are the more worrisome, is by no means clear.

## § 6:4 The judicial response to expert testimony on bitemark identification

Though expert opinion on bitemark identification is one of the newer areas of forensic identification, having arrived in the courts only in the past generation, it was rapidly admitted in many jurisdictions throughout the United States. The great majority of those cases occurred after 1980.[1]

Several ironies accompany this legal history. One is that forensic odontologists,

---

1982 OK CR 11, 640 P.2d 971 (Okla. Crim. App. 1982) (defendant's expert disagreed with State's expert); *Harrison v. State*, 635 So. 2d 894 (Miss. 1994) (defense expert files affidavit on appeal disagreeing with state's expert); *Brown v. State*, 690 So. 2d 276 (Miss. 1996) (state and defense experts disagree); *Case v. Mississippi,* No. 91-KA-0872 (Adams Cty., Miss.) (state's expert testifies that marks on victim were bitemarks caused by defendant's dentition; defense expert testifies that he does not know whether marks were bitemarks, let alone what caused them); *Banks v. State*, 725 So. 2d 711, 101 A.L.R.5th 767 (Miss. 1997) (prosecution and defense experts disagree); *State v. Richardson,* No. A-4255-95T4 (Sup. Ct. N.J. App. Div. 1997) (State's expert testifies that defendant's teeth matched a bitemark on the victim's back while defense expert testifies that defendant could not have made the bitemark); Other Lehigh Trials Have Had A Steep Price, 1998 WL 12854106, Allentown Morning Call (7/12/98) (reporting on *Commonwealth v. Gonzalez*, a case in which state's expert concluded that woman could have bitten infant and defense expert concluded that marks were too small to have been caused by defendant).

[7]See infra § 6:7.

[8]Whose principal empirical support for their claim of expertise seems to be that they are rarely if ever contradicted by their peers. See, e.g., David Fisher, Hard Evidence 245 (1996). See § 6:3.

[9]See Nordby, Can We Believe What We See, If We See What We Believe?—Expert Disagreement, 37 J. Forensic Sci. 1115 (1992) (disagreement among honest experts often caused by "expectation-laden observations").

[10]Behind which hides an equal amount of ambiguity and disagreement.

**[Section 6:4]**

[1]By state:

**Arizona**—*State v. Garrison*, 120 Ariz. 255, 585 P.2d 563 (1978).

**California**—*People v. Marx*, 54 Cal. App. 3d 100, 126 Cal. Rptr. 350, 77 A.L.R.3d 1108 (2d Dist. 1975).

**Connecticut**—*State v. Ortiz*, 198 Conn. 220, 502 A.2d 400 (1985).

**Florida**—*Bundy v. State*, 455 So. 2d 330 (Fla. 1984) (abrogated on other grounds by, Fenelon v. State, 594 So. 2d 292 (Fla. 1992)). *Bundy v. State*, 490 So. 2d 1258 (Fla. 1986). *Bundy v. State*, 497 So. 2d 1209 (Fla. 1986). *Bundy v. State*, 538 So. 2d 445 (Fla. 1989).

**Illinois**—*People v. Milone*, 43 Ill. App. 3d 385, 2 Ill. Dec. 63, 356 N.E.2d 1350 (2d Dist. 1976). *People v. Williams*, 128 Ill. App. 3d 384, 83 Ill. Dec. 720, 470 N.E.2d 1140 (4th Dist. 1984).

**Indiana**—*Niehaus v. State*, 265 Ind. 655, 359 N.E.2d 513 (1977).

**Louisiana**—*State v. Wommack*, 770 So. 2d 365 (La. Ct. App. 3d Cir. 2000), writ denied, 797 So. 2d 62 (La. 2001).

**Michigan**—*People v. Marsh*, 177 Mich. App. 161, 441 N.W.2d 33 (1989).

**Minnesota**—*State v. Hodgson*, 512 N.W.2d 95 (Minn. 1994).

**Mississippi**—*Howard v. State*, 697 So. 2d 415 (Miss. 1997), republished as corrected at 701 So.2d 274 (holding bitemark expert testimony inadmissible). *Brooks v. State*, 748 So. 2d 736 (Miss. 1999) (holding bitemark expert evidence admissible).

**Missouri**—*State v. Sager*, 600 S.W.2d 541 (Mo. Ct. App. W.D. 1980). *State v. Kleypas*, 602 S.W.2d 863 (Mo. Ct. App. S.D. 1980). *State v.*

perhaps reflecting a grounding in scientific skepticism that is absent from the more traditional forensic identification sciences,[2] were more doubtful about whether the state of their knowledge permitted them to successfully identify a perpetrator "to the exclusion of all others." The history of other areas of forensic identification reveals no similar self doubts. Second, the courts began admitting expert testimony on bitemarks while many prominent forensic odontologists still doubted whether the necessary knowledge existed to permit them to make such identifications accurately. Third, and most remarkable, rather than the field convincing the courts of the sufficiency of its knowledge and skills, admission by the courts seems to have convinced the forensic odontology community that, despite their doubts, they were able to perform bitemark identifications after all.[3]

## § 6:5 The judicial response to expert testimony on bitemark identification—Cases before *Daubert*

The first case in the United States to confront the admissibility of expert testimony on a bitemark identification was *Doyle v. State*.[1] Doyle was charged with burglary. At the site of the burglary was found a piece of partially eaten cheese. After arresting Doyle, the sheriff asked him to bite a piece of cheese, which the suspect voluntarily did. A firearms examiner compared the two pieces of cheese to try to determine if the questioned and the known tooth marks had been made by the same person. The firearms examiner concluded that they had. At trial a dentist testified that from his own examination of plaster casts of the cheese bitemarks, he also reached the opinion that one and the same dentition had made both sets of bites.[2] The Texas Court of Criminal Appeals upheld the admission of this bitemark opinion testimony.

Although the empirical research necessary to form the scientific ground for such a conclusion had not yet been undertaken,[3] the defense in *Doyle* did not contest admissibility by raising any issue of scientific validity, but instead raised only

---

*Turner*, 633 S.W.2d 421 (Mo. Ct. App. W.D. 1982).

**New York**—*People v. Middleton*, 54 N.Y.2d 42, 444 N.Y.S.2d 581, 429 N.E.2d 100 (1981). *People v. Smith*, 63 N.Y.2d 41, 479 N.Y.S.2d 706, 468 N.E.2d 879 (1984). *People v. Smith*, 110 Misc. 2d 118, 443 N.Y.S.2d 551 (County Ct. 1981).

**North Carolina**—*State v. Temple*, 302 N.C. 1, 273 S.E.2d 273 (1981). *State v. Green*, 305 N.C. 463, 290 S.E.2d 625 (1982).

**Oklahoma**—*Kennedy v. State*, 1982 OK CR 11, 640 P.2d 971 (Okla. Crim. App. 1982).

**Rhode Island**—*State v. Adams*, 481 A.2d 718 (R.I. 1984).

**South Carolina**—*State v. Jones*, 273 S.C. 723, 259 S.E.2d 120 (1979).

**Texas**—*Doyle v. State*, 159 Tex. Crim. 310, 263 S.W.2d 779 (1954). *Patterson v. State*, 509 S.W.2d 857 (Tex. Crim. App. 1974).

**Wisconsin**—*State v. Stinson*, 134 Wis. 2d 224, 397 N.W.2d 136 (Ct. App. 1986).

[2]Compared to examiners of fingerprints, footprints, toolmarks, document examiners, firearms, and so on.

[3]In their book on scientific evidence, Andre Moenssens et al. Scientific Evidence in Civil and Criminal Cases (4th ed. 1995), they conclude

concerning the relationship between the courts and expert opinion on bitemark identification:

> The wholesale acceptance, by the courts, of testimony on bitemark identification has transformed the profession. Whereas prior to 1974 the main thrust of forensic dentistry was to prove identity of persons by means of a comparison of postmortem and antemortem dental records in mass disasters, the profession has changed direction and is now heavily involved in assisting prosecutors in homicide and sex offense cases. Having received judicial approval of bitemark comparisons, there seems to be no more limit on the extent of forensic odontological conclusions.

Andre Moenssens et al. Scientific Evidence in Civil and Criminal Cases § 16.07, at 985 (4th ed. 1995).

**[Section 6:5]**

[1]*Doyle v. State*, 159 Tex. Crim. 310, 263 S.W.2d 779 (1954). Although this was the first appellate consideration of bitemark evidence, the technique had been used for related identification purposes for decades. See §§ 6:8 to 6:33.

[2]§§ 6:8 to 6:33.

[3]As leading forensic odontologists today readily note. See studies discussed in the Scientific Status portion of this chapter.

procedural challenges.[4] Thus, the *Doyle* court did not address the scientific status of bitemark identification. Nevertheless, another Texas court relied on *Doyle* twenty years later as the basis for rejecting an appellant's contention that bitemark test results were of unproven reliability.[5] Both Texas cases seemed to take admissibility as a given, and neither addressed the scientific issues.

The cornerstone case on the admissibility of bitemark identification was decided the following year, in 1975, in California. This case undertook to grapple with the scientific issues on which admissibility of bitemark identification should turn, but in the end succeeded only in eluding them. *People v. Marx*[6] involved a brutal murder of an elderly woman who had an elliptical laceration on her nose. This mark was judged to be a human bite, and impressions were made of the wound for comparison with a cast of the defendant's teeth.

At trial, three odontologists testified that in their opinion the defendant's dentition matched the bite wound.[7] One of those experts took pains to note that in many other cases he had refused to offer a firm opinion or even to testify about an identification. This case, however, was an exception in that the dentition at issue was extremely unusual and the bitemark was exceptionally well defined. The witness characterized these bite impressions as the clearest he had ever seen, either personally or in the literature. Despite the expert's caution, and unusual case facts emphasizing the rarity of both the dentition and the bitemarks, *Marx* pried open the courtroom door for bitemark identification. Having done so, it became the admission ticket for a far wider and more dubious array of dentition in many subsequent cases.

On appeal, the defense challenged the admission of expert opinions on bite wound identification on the ground that the purported skills were not sufficiently established or generally accepted in the field of forensic dentistry. Thus, under California law following *Frye v. United States*,[8] the admission of such testimony would have been error. The field was, after all, sharply divided over the question of whether they could identify biters by the bitemarks left in crime victims. The California Court of Appeals acknowledged that there was "no established science of identifying persons from bite marks . . . ."[9] Moreover, the theory of bitemark identification is in essence based on an assessment of the probability that two or more people could leave the same bitemark,[10] yet no data existed on those probabilities. How did the Court of Appeals reach its decision to admit the testimony, despite the California Supreme Court's repeated announcement of general acceptance as the governing rule in that state, and its prohibition on evidence based on speculative probability estimates?[11] In several ways.

The Court of Appeals deflected the implications of *Frye*, by interpreting that test in these terms:

---

[4]The defense raised only the issue of whether obtaining the bitten cheese from the defendant constituted a confession and thereby violated a Texas statute prohibiting obtaining confessions without warning defendants of their likely use.

[5]*Patterson v. State*, 509 S.W.2d 857 (Tex. Crim. App. 1974).

[6]*People v. Marx*, 54 Cal. App. 3d 100, 126 Cal. Rptr. 350, 77 A.L.R.3d 1108 (2d Dist. 1975).

[7]Gerry L. Vale et al., Unusual Three-Dimensional Bite Mark Evidence in a Homicide Case, 21 J. Forensic Sci. 642 (1976).

[8]*Frye v. U.S.*, 293 F. 1013, 34 A.L.R. 145 (App. D.C. 1923) (rejected by, State v. Walstad, 119 Wis. 2d 483, 351 N.W.2d 469 (1984)) and

(rejected by, State v. Brown, 297 Or. 404, 687 P.2d 751 (1984)) and (rejected by, Nelson v. State, 628 A.2d 69 (Del. 1993)) and (rejected by, State v. Alberico, 116 N.M. 156, 861 P.2d 192 (1993)) and (rejected by, State v. Moore, 268 Mont. 20, 885 P.2d 457 (1994)) and (rejected by, State v. Faught, 127 Idaho 873, 908 P.2d 566 (1995)) and (rejected by, People v. Shreck, 22 P.3d 68, 90 A.L.R.5th 765 (Colo. 2001)).

[9]*People v. Marx*, 54 Cal. App. 3d 100, 126 Cal. Rptr. 350, 353, 77 A.L.R.3d 1108 (2d Dist. 1975).

[10]§ 6:19.

[11]*People v. Collins*, 68 Cal. 2d 319, 66 Cal. Rptr. 497, 438 P.2d 33, 36 A.L.R.3d 1176 (1968).

The *Frye* test finds its rational basis in the degree to which the trier of fact must accept, on faith, scientific hypotheses not capable of proof or disproof in court and not even generally accepted outside the courtroom. *Frye*, for example, involved the lie detector test in which the trier of fact is required to rely on the testimony of the polygrapher, verified at most by marks on a graph, to which the expert's hypothesis gives some relevant meaning . . . . [Other cases reflect] [t]he same concern that the trier of fact will be overwhelmed by "ill conceived techniques with which the trier of fact is not technically equipped to cope," sacrificing its independence in favor of deference to the expert.[12]

The paradox, of course, is that expert opinion testimony is permitted precisely because it is believed that the expert's understanding exceeds the jury's, and the expert can tell the jury truths that the jury could not otherwise grasp. Be that as it may, the court thus distinguished *Marx* from *Frye* by reasoning that *Frye* applied to evidence that was indecipherable without an expert's interpretation, whereas *Marx* involved models, X-rays, and slides of the victim's wounds and the accused's dentition, all of which were clearly visible for the jurors to view, assess, and verify on their own during court proceedings, without having to rely on the expert odontologist as a necessary intermediary. Forensic odontologists, no doubt, would be astonished to learn that once the pictures are taken and the molds cast, no special expertise or judgment is required to assess whether the wound was made by the defendant's dentition.

The *Marx* court concluded, alternatively, that the requirements of *Frye had* been met because the methods used to facilitate the bitemark identification were not really novel:

[T]he experts did not rely on untested methods, unproven hypotheses, intuition or revelation. Rather, they applied scientifically and professionally established techniques—X-rays, models, microscopy, photography—to the solution of a particular problem which, though novel, was well within the capability of those techniques.[13]

On this view, *Frye* is about the tools, not the meaning of the information collected with the help of the tools. While the reliability of the tools is by no means unimportant, the most fundamental issues in bitemark identification, as with all forensic identification, are: (a) whether the population variation in the relevant characteristics is immense; (b) whether in practice that underlying variation is adequately captured by the available tools and evidence, particularly; (c) whether the latent mark has enough distinct variation in it to allow the probability that someone else's dentition may have left the mark to fall comfortably low.[14] None of this essential knowledge was, or usually is, available to the jury. The question the court might well be focusing on, however, is whether that information is even available to the expert.[15]

Ironically, the *Marx* court appears to have believed that an inquiry about or offer of evidence on the probabilities underlying bitemark identifications would be inadmissible in California under the rule of *People v. Collins*.[16] It held that, since the experts never had actual data and did no calculations of probability, but instead remained impressionistic and intuitive, "[n]one of the witnesses engaged in a 'trial by mathematics' [citing *Collins*] on or off the stand. There was no error."

First of all, the *Marx* court overstates the *Collins* prohibition. In *Collins*, a major ground of the inadmissibility of a statistically based identification was that it was based on (a) speculative probabilities (rather than known relative frequencies of the attributes at issue), and (b) a lack of proof that the attributes of interest consisted of

---

[12]*People v. Marx*, 54 Cal. App. 3d 100, 110–111, 126 Cal. Rptr. 350, 77 A.L.R.3d 1108 (2d Dist. 1975).

[13]*People v. Marx*, 54 Cal. App. 3d 100, 126 Cal. Rptr. 350, 77 A.L.R.3d 1108 (2d Dist. 1975).

[14]§ 6:19.

[15]If it is not, in some form or fashion, then the expert is speculating.

[16]*People v. Collins*, 68 Cal. 2d 319, 66 Cal. Rptr. 497, 438 P.2d 33, 36 A.L.R.3d 1176 (1968).

independent events,[17] thereby resulting in faulty computations. In short, the evidence lacked essential foundation. Absent these flaws, such evidence might well be admissible. Second, whether a *jury* will be allowed to hear the numbers is one thing. Whether they may be heard *by a court* in deciding a preliminary question such as the admissibility of purported scientific evidence is quite another. Any court following FRE 104 or an equivalent rule plainly is authorized to do so,[18] and any court following *Daubert* apparently has a *duty* to do so.[19] Surely the experts ought to have such data, because those are what their conclusions rely upon.[20]

Most interesting, perhaps, *Marx* is one of the rare cases to realize that much forensic identification evidence invokes much the same reasoning that the California Supreme Court found so troubling in *Collins*. To believe that the experts or the court, in deciding a question of admissibility of expert evidence, should eschew consideration of the underlying data and the statistical inferences to be drawn from those data, is a deeply confused extension of *Collins*. It solves few if any of the problems that *Collins* was concerned with; it merely pretends the problems are not there. The existence and nature of probability data are at the heart of the theory of forensic identification, and a court ought to be scrutinizing them, not insisting that all is well because no one looked at or thought about them.[21]

The following year, in 1976, Illinois had its first occasion to consider the admissibility of bitemark evidence. In *People v. Milone*, the Court of Appeals held it admissible as "a logical extension of the accepted principle that each person's dentition is unique."[22] The court based this on its earlier recognition of the identification of accident victims from their dental records. In this case, expert witnesses disagreed sharply on the question of the validity and utility of bitemark identifications. The testimony of three forensic dentists was offered by the prosecution and four by the defense. The defense experts testified and cited odontological literature showing, at the least, considerable disagreement among forensic odontologists as to whether offenders could be uniquely identified from bites left in the flesh of victims. Notwithstanding the controversy in the record and in the literature, the court found that the general acceptance standard had been met.[23] In contrast to the approach a court would be expected to take today under *Daubert*, the *Milone* court held that questions about the truth of the proposition quoted above—of immense variation and unique identifiability—went to the weight of the expert testimony, not to its admissibility.

By 1978, a California Court of Appeals flatly held that the testimony of three forensic odontologists established that bitemark identification had gained the required

---

[17]In order to apply the multiplication rule to calculate the probability, each component must be uncorrelated with each other component.

[18]Moreover, in deciding such preliminary questions, the court "is not bound by the rules of evidence except those with respect to privileges." Fed. R. Evid. 104(a).

[19]Among other data to be considered is a technique's "known or potential error rate." *Daubert v. Merrell Dow Pharmaceuticals, Inc.*, 509 U.S. 579, 594, 113 S. Ct. 2786, 125 L. Ed. 2d 469, 27, 27 U.S.P.Q.2d 1200, Prod. Liab. Rep. (CCH) P 13494, 37 Fed. R. Evid. Serv. 1, 23 Envtl. L. Rep. 20979 (1993).

[20]Compare the work of experts in DNA identification. See §§ 2:1 et seq..

[21]DNA evidence is the best example of a field providing the necessary data and probability calculations, and the chief exception to the rule that the evidence offered by the forensic identification sciences resembles the evidence offered in *People v. Collins*. Forensic odontologists appreciate that these data are needed, and have been developing them. See scientific status portion of this chapter, §§ 6:8 to 6:33.

[22]*People v. Milone*, 43 Ill. App. 3d 385, 2 Ill. Dec. 63, 356 N.E.2d 1350 (2d Dist. 1976).

[23]Incidentally, as a testament to the power of weak or inapt precedents, the court cited the Texas cases of *Doyle* (which had no data) and *Patterson* (which relied on *Doyle*), as well as California's *Marx* (which dealt with highly unusual dentition, in contrast to the apparently more common dentition of the present case).

general acceptance in the relevant scientific community.[24]

Perhaps the most unusual legal development after *Marx* and before *Daubert* was a suit by the defendant who had been convicted in *People v. Milone*. Paroled after serving nearly twenty years in prison for murder, Milone continues to insist upon his innocence and continues to try to clear his name. In federal court, under both the *Frye* and *Daubert* standards, he has challenged the original decision to admit the expert bitemark testimony. Another murder victim was later found in the same area where the victim in the *Milone* case had been found. A potential bitemark from the second murder victim was linked to a suspect, Macek. The crime scene bitemarks in the two cases were judged by at least one forensic odontologist to be indistinguishable from each other.[25] Macek signed but later withdrew a confession to having killed the victim for whose murder Milone had been convicted.[26] For present purposes, more important than the question of whether or not Macek killed both victims, is the suggestion that the relevant portions of dentition of two different suspects were indistinguishably alike.[27]

The Court of Appeals for the Seventh Circuit expressed sympathy with Milone's request, in light of the new evidence presented, but declined to rule on the case for want of a constitutional basis for granting relief, and because principles of federalism precluded a federal court from reexamining an issue of fact that is reserved to the states.[28]

## § 6:6    The judicial response to expert testimony on bitemark identification—Cases after *Daubert*

In the post-Daubert era, two federal cases come within hailing distance of applying *Daubert* to bitemark identification. The first is *Burke v. Commonwealth*.[1] The plaintiff brought claims against the Commonwealth of Massachusetts alleging civil rights violations for his wrongful arrest and imprisonment, based importantly on a bitemark examination which identified him as the person whose bitemark was found on the body of a murder victim–apparently falsely, because he later was exonerated by DNA analysis. In the course of drafting recommended findings concerning the Commonwealth's motion to dismiss, the magistrate judge touched on the asserted weaknesses of bitemark identification. The magistrate judge never seemed to doubt the validity of this specie of expertise,[2] though the best the court can do to support it is to cite cases that cite cases that express the same credulousness.

---

[24]*People v. Slone*, 76 Cal. App. 3d 611, 143 Cal. Rptr. 61 (2d Dist. 1978).

[25]The forensic odontologist, later President of the American Academy of Forensic Sciences, had been a defense expert in the *Milone* case and wrote about these cases in, Lowell Levine, Forensic Dentistry: Our Most Controversial Case, in 1978 Legal Medicine Annual (Cyril Wecht, ed.).

[26]Discussed in *State v. Sager*, 600 S.W.2d 541 (Mo. Ct. App. W.D. 1980).

[27]Such findings are not unique in the identification sciences. In the present case, however, it might be noted that the comparison was not made using standard methods or procedures because of the full mouth extractions by Macek. The comparisons of the injury to x-rays of pre-extracted teeth hold little similarity to standard comparison procedures of overlaying biting edges onto the

injury patterns on the skin.

[28]*Milone v. Camp*, 22 F.3d 693 (7th Cir.1994).

[Section 6:6]

[1]*Burke v. Commonwealth*, 2004 WL 502617 (D. Mass. 2004).

[2]Even after the DNA exoneration, the court seems to place inordinate confidence not only in the soundness of bitemark identification generally but even in the false positive identification in the underlying case: "As of the present time, Dr. Levine remains of the opinion to a reasonable degree of scientific certainty that the bite mark on the breast of Ms. Kennedy matched the dentition of the plaintiff. And plaintiff has proffered no meaningful evidence to the contrary, putting to one side the mere ipse dixit of counsel for plaintiff [footnotes omitted].

In *Ege v. Yukins*,[3] in the context of a petition for habeas corpus relief, the district court found the admission of bitemark expert opinion at the original trial to be so "unreliable and grossly misleading"[4] as to constitute a fundamental denial of due process.[5] The defendant was charged with and convicted of murder nine years after the underlying crime and had served more than ten years of a life sentence by the time the federal court granted her habeas petition.

At the original trial the defendant had been convicted on the strength of evidence that she harbored considerable animus toward the victim combined with the testimony of a forensic dentist who opined that a mark on the cheek of the victim, visible in a photograph of the corpse, was a human bitemark and that the mark matched the dentition of the defendant and not that of other likely suspects. The odontologist went on the state that out of the 3.5 million people residing in the Detroit metropolitan area, the defendant was the only one whose dentition could match the asserted bitemark on the victim's cheek.

The petitioner argued that the bitemark testimony was improperly admitted because it lacked scientific foundation as well as that the statistical probability given had had an exaggerated impact on the jury. The court ruled that "there is no question that the evidence in the case was unreliable and not worthy of consideration by a jury."[6] The court's conclusion could hardly be more clear. But its reasoning, or at least its persuasiveness, is less so.

The judge's conclusions about the weakness of the bitemark testimony do not go to fundamental weaknesses of bitemark comparison, apparently argued by the petitioner and discussed later in this chapter.[7] Rather, the court's misgivings come from three other matters. One is that the comparison was made with a photograph of the wound.[8] The court says almost nothing about this. What about the photograph or its use differs from the most accepted or best comparison methods? The court does not say.

A second factor concerning the court was its perception that this particular expert witness was singularly incompetent: "Dr. Warnick thoroughly has been cast into disrepute as an expert witness and several convictions based on his testimony have been undermined and overturned."[9] Since cases occurring only recently were the basis for that conclusion it is, of course, not something that could have been obvious at trial a decade earlier. The court does not appear to know whether Dr. Warnick was doing his examinations differently or with less skill than other forensic dentists, or whether his work was no different from theirs but he merely had the bad luck of having a cluster of his cases overturned instead of just an occasional one. Thus, this case, too, assumes the general soundness of the methods of bitemark comparison, but finds fault in the particular individual performing the comparisons.

The final flaw found by the court was that Dr. Warnick expressed his opinion in

---

[3]*Ege v. Yukins*, 380 F. Supp. 2d 852 (E.D. Mich. 2005), aff'd in part, rev'd in part on other grounds, 485 F.3d 364 (6th Cir. 2007).

[4]*Ege v. Yukins*, 380 F. Supp. 2d 852, 880 (E.D. Mich. 2005), aff'd in part, rev'd in part on other grounds, 485 F.3d 364 (6th Cir. 2007).

[5]"The evidence was 'so extremely unfair that its admission violates fundamental concepts of justice.'" *Ege v. Yukins*, 380 F. Supp. 2d 852, 880 (E.D. Mich. 2005), aff'd in part, rev'd in part on other grounds, 485 F.3d 364 (6th Cir. 2007). Moreover, the trial attorney's failure to challenge the admission constituted ineffective assistance of counsel: "The flaw in Dr. Warnick's statistical opinion should have been obvious and its admissibility readily assailable." *Ege v. Yukins*, 380 F.

Supp. 2d 852, 876 (E.D. Mich. 2005), aff'd in part, rev'd in part on other grounds, 485 F.3d 364 (6th Cir. 2007).

[6]*Ege v. Yukins*, 380 F. Supp. 2d 852, 871 (E.D. Mich. 2005), aff'd in part, rev'd in part on other grounds, 485 F.3d 364 (6th Cir. 2007).

[7]See Part II.

[8]"The use of a photograph of the wound to make the comparison appears to be novel." *Ege v. Yukins*, 380 F. Supp. 2d 852, 876 (E.D. Mich. 2005), aff'd in part, rev'd in part on other grounds, 485 F.3d 364 (6th Cir. 2007).

[9]*Ege v. Yukins*, 380 F. Supp. 2d 852, 857 (E.D. Mich. 2005), aff'd in part, rev'd in part on other grounds, 485 F.3d 364 (6th Cir. 2007).

terms of a probability value. The court goes on at some length, discussing and citing numerous cases that raise doubts about inferences based on probability estimates. What the court fails to realize is that all of forensic odonotolgy (and all of forensic identification) rely on these very same notions to reach all of their conclusions of identity. The only difference seems to be that Dr. Warnick expressed his conclusion by uttering a number while his brethren typically do so by asserting in words that dentition is unique among all humans, that the defendant's dentition matches the bitemark, and therefore (explicitly stated or implied) the defendant is the only person on earth whose dentition matches the bitemark on the victim. Why is that less objectionable than Dr. Warnick's testimony? If anything, Dr. Warnick was more reserved than the typical witness. The only explanation can be that Dr. Warnick uttered a number. Do we know that extreme probabilities given in words are less misleading to factfinders than are less extreme probabilities expressed in numbers?

By attacking this particular witness and his particular testimony with such vigor, the court prevented *the field's* more general shortcomings from coming under scrutiny.

A number of state courts have evaluated proffers of bitemark expert testimony in the wake of *Daubert*, producing some interesting opinions.

*Garrison v. State*[10] notes that the trial court below did not permit the testifying forensic dentist to opine on whether the victim was the source of an apparent bitemark on the defendant because Oklahoma case law had excluded such opinions by bitemark experts as failing to meet the requirements of Oklahoma's *Daubert* decision. That precedent excluding individualizing bitemark expert testimony, oddly enough, is an unpublished opinion.[11] The lower court had only allowed the expert to opine that the wound was a "probable bite-mark," the admission of which was upheld. The court does not explain the basis for that expertise under *Daubert*, and does not seem aware of studies suggesting that even this skill is an elusive one.

The bitemark evidence in *State v. Hodgson*[12] consisted of apparent teeth marks in a suspect's arm, which a forensic dentist compared to known molds of the dentition of a murder victim. The dentist testified to "several similarities" between the bitemark on the defendant and the victim's teeth. Defense counsel objected to a question calling for the odontologist's opinion as to whether the bitemark and the victim's teeth matched, and the witness did not state her opinion.

On appeal, the defendant challenged the admission of the bitemark expert evidence on the grounds that it was not generally accepted, and therefore should not have been admitted under Minnesota's version of the *Frye* test, *State v. Schwartz*.[13] On the question of the admissibility of bitemark expert testimony, the Minnesota Supreme Court concluded as follows:

> We note that recently the United States Supreme Court, in *Daubert v. Merrell Dow Pharmaceuticals, Inc.*, held that the Rules of Evidence supersede the *Frye* or general acceptance test for the admission of novel scientific evidence. We need not address the issue of what impact *Daubert* should or will have in Minnesota. Suffice it to say, we are satisfied that basic bitemark analysis by a recognized expert is not a novel or emerging type of scientific evidence.[14]

Thus, the court disposed of the issue simply by holding that bitemark expert evi-

---

[10]*Garrison v. State*, 2004 OK CR 35, 103 P.3d 590 (Okla. Crim. App. 2004).

[11]*Crider v. State*, F-1999-1422 (Oct. 11, 2001).

[12]*State v. Hodgson*, 512 N.W.2d 95 (Minn. 1994).

[13]*State v. Schwartz*, 447 N.W.2d 422 (Minn. 1989).

[14]*State v. Hodgson*, 512 N.W.2d 95, 98 (Minn.

1994), citing C. Herasimchuk, A Practical Guide to the Admissibility of Novel Expert Evidence in Criminal Trials Under Federal Rule 702, 22 St. Mary's L.J. 181, 210–11 and n. 122 (1990) and Annot., Admissibility of evidence tending to identify accused by his own bite marks, 77 A.L.R.3d 1122 (superseded by Admissibility and Sufficiency of Bite Mark Evidence as Basis for Identification of Accused, 1 A.L.R.6th 657). for the proposition

dence was not novel.

Similarly, on appeal of the trial court's refusal to conduct a *Davis-Frye* hearing on the admissibility of bite mark expert testimony, the appellate court in *People v. Quaderer*[15] held that such an inquiry is required only when a party seeks to introduce a new scientific principle or technique. The appellate court went on, however, to find that bite mark analysis has gained general acceptance in the relevant scientific community, a conclusion based on the conclusions of another Michigan case.[16]

Whether non-novel evidence ever was insulated from fresh scrutiny under *Frye*-type tests once the issue of the evidence's unreliability, or its unproven reliability, was raised, has always been doubtful, but it certainly is not supported by any apparent logic. Why should non-novelty, by itself, shelter from reexamination erroneous scientific claims that have lost the support of the field or fields from whence they came? Under any test, the more coherent view is that novelty should serve not as a prerequisite for judicial scrutiny, but as a hair trigger for it. *Daubert* itself had this to say on the role of non-novelty:

> [W]e do not read the requirements of Rule 702 to apply specially or exclusively to unconventional evidence. Of course, well-established propositions are less likely to be challenged than those that are novel, and they are more handily defended.[17]

Though Wyoming is a *Daubert* state, a challenge to bitemark expert evidence received no more consideration there than it had in Minnesota. The defendant in *Seivewright v. State*[18] had been convicted of a burglary during which the burglar had taken a bite out of a block of cheese. At trial an orthodontist who had made an impression of the cheese and of the defendant's teeth testified that the defendant had bitten the cheese. The trial court did not hold a hearing to consider the challenge to bitemark expertise. On appeal, the Wyoming Supreme Court cited *Daubert*, *Joiner*[19] and *Kumho Tire*,[20] but did not conclude that an evidentiary hearing is required to hear a challenge to forensic bitemark evidence. Apparently it was enough to cite a number of cases in which such testimony had been admitted. On the other hand, the Court reversed the conviction because the prosecution had not provided a copy of the expert's curriculum vita or his report.

This case reflects two ironies. One, *Daubert* seems to have been adopted in Wyoming in name but not in spirit or practice. Rather than supporting inquiry into the empirical and theoretical underpinnings of bitemark opinions, both the trial and Supreme Court were content to deny a hearing and look to cases of admission in other courts as the basis for gatekeeping. Second, while the failure of the government to provide information on the expert's background and the report of his findings were sufficient for reversal, it is hard to imagine that anything in either the vita or the report could have led to the exclusion of the expert's opinion. That is to say, if the heart and soul of the expertise are of no interest or consequence, why would the details of the dentist who reached the opinion, or how he reached the

---

that bitemark expert testimony is no longer novel.

[15]*People v. Quaderer*, 2003 WL 22801204 (Mich. Ct. App. 2003).

[16]*People v. Marsh*, 177 Mich. App. 161, 441 N.W.2d 33 (1989).

[17]*Daubert v. Merrell Dow Pharmaceuticals, Inc.*, 509 U.S. 579, 593 n.11, 113 S. Ct. 2786, 125 L. Ed. 2d 469, 27, 27 U.S.P.Q.2d 1200, Prod. Liab. Rep. (CCH) P 13494, 37 Fed. R. Evid. Serv. 1, 23 Envtl. L. Rep. 20979 (1993).

[18]*Seivewright v. State*, 7 P.3d 24 (Wyo. 2000).

[19]*General Elec. Co. v. Joiner*, 522 U.S. 136, 118 S. Ct. 512, 139 L. Ed. 2d 508, 18 O.S.H. Cas. (BNA) 1097, Prod. Liab. Rep. (CCH) P 15120, 48 Fed. R. Evid. Serv. 1, 28 Envtl. L. Rep. 20227, 177 A.L.R. Fed. 667 (1997).

[20]*Kumho Tire Co., Ltd. v. Carmichael*, 526 U.S. 137, 119 S. Ct. 1167, 143 L. Ed. 2d 238, 50, 50 U.S.P.Q.2d 1177, Prod. Liab. Rep. (CCH) P 15470, 50 Fed. R. Evid. Serv. 1373, 29 Envtl. L. Rep. 20638 (1999).

opinion, make any difference?[21]

Mississippi has decided a pair of bitemark cases that are difficult to reconcile with each other or with Mississippi case law on admissibility. Mississippi is not, as of this writing, a *Daubert* state, and asserts that it follows *Frye*,[22] though it is not evident from its bitemark cases that general acceptance was a criterion the Court attended to. Despite its avowed lack of allegiance to *Daubert*, in *Howard v. State*[23] the Mississippi Supreme Court seemed inclined to critically evaluate, rather than blindly accept, the assertions of forensic odontologists concerning the scientific validity and evidentiary reliability of their field's conclusions. The Court wrote:

> This Court has never ruled directly on the admissibility or reliability of bite-mark identification evidence, though it has addressed cases in which bite-mark evidence was an issue. [Citation omitted.] While few courts have refused to allow some form of bite-mark comparison evidence, numerous scholarly authorities have criticized the reliability of this method of identifying a suspect. [Citation omitted.] It is much easier to exclude a suspect through such comparison than to positively identify a suspect. [Citations omitted.]
>
> There is little consensus in the scientific community on the number of points which must match before any positive identification can be announced. [Citation omitted.] Because the opinions concerning the methods of comparison employed in a particular case may differ, it is certainly open to defense counsel to attack the qualifications of the expert, the methods and data used to compare the bitemarks to persons other than the defendant, and the factual and logical bases of the expert's opinions. Also, where such expert testimony is allowed by the trial court, it should be open to the defendant to present evidence challenging the reliability of the field of bite-mark comparisons. [Citation omitted.] Only then will the jury be able to give the proper weight, if any, to this evidence.

Howard's initial capital murder conviction was reversed. Following retrial, he was again convicted and again sentenced to death. On the appeal of *Howard II*, the Mississippi Supreme Court again considered a challenge to the admissibility of bitemark identification expert evidence.[24] On this most recent occasion to opine on the admissibility of bitemark evidence, the Court held without explanation that such testimony "was admissible, and the trial court did not abuse its discretion in so holding" though of course "subject to challenges to weight and credibility." Without explanation, the Court had moved from its apparent awareness in *Howard I* of weaknesses and controversy in the bitemark field, to unhesitating admission in *Howard II*. At no point has any published judicial opinion in Mississippi canvassed the actual scientific data bearing on the issues raised, and explained how the proper resolution was admission. It should be said, though, that, judging from the opinion in *Howard II*, the challenge was rather lame, limited to offering legal arguments

---

[21]Indeed, one member of the Supreme Court dissented that the errors on which the reversal was based were harmless errors.

[22]See *Kansas City Southern Ry. Co., Inc. v. Johnson*, 798 So. 2d 374 (Miss. 2001), and cases cited therein.

[23]*Howard v. State*, 701 So. 2d 274 (Miss. 1997).

[24]*Howard v. State*, 853 So. 2d 781 (Miss. 2003). A dissent in the case pointed to a paucity of testing of the claims, lack of independent confirmation of the technique, the highly subjective nature of the technique, contested general acceptance in the scientific community, and it

expressed doubts about the statistical probability data claims. These considerations led the dissent to conclude that bite mark comparison is "junk science." The dissent also noted that in this particular case the defendant was wearing a partial denture which likely was mass-produced (implying that the forensic dentist might have mistook class characteristics as individual features), and that the victim's body had deteriorated for five days before the bite mark was examined (implying changes on the questioned bitemark). Finally, the dissent questioned the particular expert in the case, Michael West. See comments concerning Dr. West, infra this section. (*Howard v. State*, 853 So. 2d 781 (Miss. 2003) (McRae, J., dissenting.).

and not raising the empirical issues.[25]

In *Brooks v. State*,[26] a trial court admitted bitemark identification expert testimony and the Mississippi Supreme Court affirmed, holding that such evidence was now admissible. The majority opinion contained not the slightest review of the science (so it was not taking the *Daubert* approach), but it also did not look to the status of bitemark individualization among forensic odontologists. The opinion does little more than to announce that bitemark expert testimony is admissible because the Court says so.[27] The only reasoning behind the decision appears to be that the defense is free to cross-examine and offer rebuttal witnesses. This would appear to be no gatekeeping of any kind: everything is admissible so long as the defense is afforded the opportunity to attack the weight of the opinion during trial. Ironically and paradoxically, a concurrence implies that the opinion is consistent with *Daubert* and its progeny:

> The majority view is correct and long overdue. The U.S. Supreme Court recent decisions [citing *Kumho Tire, General Elec. Co. v. Joiner*, and *Daubert*] stress that the federal district courts must be gatekeepers on the admission of expert testimony. I am confident that our learned trial judges will properly determine, on a case-by-case basis, whether an expert may testify to certain matters if the proper procedures are followed by the parties seeking the admission of such expert's testimony.[28]

Like the main opinion, the concurrence is silent on the criteria for all of that confidence and correct gatekeeping, and does not venture to demonstrate any of it.

A dissenting opinion by one justice noted that many questions still surround bitemark identification opinions[29] and, in this instance, the expert who testified for the state.[30]

Louisiana is a *Daubert* state. In *State v. Wommack*[31] a defendant was convicted of attempted murder and burglary, and the Court of Appeals affirmed. Some of the ev-

---

[25]Which are explored in this chapter.

[26]*Brooks v. State*, 748 So. 2d 736 (Miss. 1999).

[27]"We now take the opportunity to state affirmatively that bite-mark identification evidence is admissible in Mississippi." *Brooks v. State*, 748 So. 2d 736, 739 (Miss. 1999).

[28]*Brooks v. State*, 748 So. 2d 736, 747 (Miss. 1999).

[29]"1. The timing of the bite mark injury; 2. Enhancement procedures and techniques (note that in this case, West testified that he used ultraviolet light to enhance the wound enabling him to find "several unique marks" that corresponded to the flaws on the back side of Brooks's teeth; this technique is what allowed West to be positive that only Brooks could have made the two indentations); 3. The type of material for test bites or the accuracy of test bites under various mockup conditions; 4. The pressure necessary to produce the various levels of tissue injury under normal and unusual circumstances has not been reliably measured; 5. Manipulation of various types of distortion to produce correction; 6. The problem faced by forensic dentists today is not necessarily one of matching the bite mark to a set of teeth. It is demonstrating whether another set of teeth could have produced the same or similar mark; 7. There is not universal agreement on which injuries are bite mark related; 8. Research on the minimum number of points of concordance or the minimum number of teeth marks needed in

a bite mark for certainty is not as well established as the uniqueness of the dentition." *Brooks v. State*, 748 So. 2d 736, 748 (Miss. 1999).

[30]Michael West is infamous in forensic dentistry and the courts for asserting conclusions that go well beyond what the data allow, with a confidence unsupported by the data (West is notorious for emphasizing to juries that his conclusions are "indeed and without doubt"), inventing his own unverified technique (which he termed the "West Effect"), and misrepresenting evidence and data to bolster his testimony. For his accumulated misdeeds he has been professionally punished by the American Academy of Forensic Sciences, the American Board of Forensic Odontology, and the International Association for Identification. See *Brooks v. State*, 748 So. 2d 736, 748–750 (Miss. 1999). Some may find the most remarkable things about this to be that with such a record there still are prosecutors who will hire him (owing either to ethical or tactical concerns), defense attorneys who cannot have him declared unqualified, or juries that believe him.

In a civil suit against West for damages in another case in which his fallacious testimony led to an erroneous conviction, a federal court denied West's motion to dismiss. *Keko v. Hingle*, 1999 WL 155945 (E.D. La. 1999), aff'd, 207 F.3d 658 (5th Cir. 2000).

[31]*State v. Wommack*, 770 So. 2d 365 (La. Ct. App. 3d Cir. 2000), writ denied, 797 So. 2d 62 (La. 2001).

idence against the defendant consisted of a bitemark: the victim had bitten her assailant. At trial two experts testified concerning the bitemark on the defendant, an oral-maxillofacial surgeon and a forensic pathologist. They both testified that marks on the defendant's arm came from a human bite, but they did not link the marks specifically to the victim, and they acknowledged the possibility of error and uncertainty in their opinions. On appeal the defendant challenged the experts who testified about the bitemark. The Court of Appeals held that "the *Daubert* standards do not appear to be readily applicable to the present case. Neither expert used complex testing in identifying the wound found on [the defendant's] arm . . . . Expert opinion testimony based upon personal observation and experience is admissible." Here, then, is a court—a year after the Supreme Court held in *Kumho Tire* that all expert evidence, regardless of how it is labeled or characterized, must pass a test suitably calculated to evaluate its validity—which believes that only "complex testing" but not "personal observation and experience" are subject to scrutiny, and that the latter are ipso facto admissible.

The Indiana Supreme Court, in *Carter v. State*,[32] states that, although in interpreting Indiana evidence rules it is not required to follow the United State Supreme Court's interpretation of the same or similar rules (in *Daubert* and *Kumho Tire*), Indiana had "coincidentally announced an analytical framework for Indiana procedure akin to the federal analysis declared shortly thereafter in *Daubert*."[33] Nevertheless, *Carter* held bite mark expert testimony admissible without examining the empirical data on which such a conclusion presumably must be based. Instead, the Court noted that in 1977 it had found "no reason why [bite mark] evidence should be rejected as unreliable . . . ."[34] "when bite mark evidence was a relatively new procedure," and in the present case nothing had been presented to it suggesting "that it has become less reliable." All of this language seems to suggest, incorrectly, that the burden of proof is on the opponent of the evidence. More important, perhaps, as detailed in the chapter sections below, between the mid 1970s and today, a paucity of research has been replaced by a limited body of research—earlier assumptions of accuracy have been replaced by data suggesting that moderate to high error rates are typical. These are troubling developments that require the thoughtful attention of courts.

Even at this somewhat late date and with a field that does not stand on very solid ground, some lawyers still grasp at peripheral and legalistic straws rather than inquiring into the core of the expertise. Yet these peripheral attacks sometimes are not without some effect.

In *Calhoun v. State*,[35] the defendant's objection to the bite mark evidence was that the molds and photographs used for comparison were not properly marked. The court, however, held that this objection went to the weight the evidence should be given, not its admissibility.

The defendant in *State v. Swinton*,[36] made two claims about improper admission of evidence. First, the defendant contended that the trial court improperly admitted into evidence computer enhanced photographs of the bite marks without an adequate foundation. Second, the defense argued that exhibits produced using Adobe Photoshop, which showed superimposed images of the defendant's dentition over the photographs of the bite marks, were improperly admitted. In this instance, the expert could not testify as to whether the process used was accepted in the field,

---

[32]*Carter v. State*, 766 N.E.2d 377 (Ind. 2002).

[33]Citing *McGrew v. State*, 682 N.E.2d 1289 (Ind. 1997) and *Steward v. State*, 652 N.E.2d 490 (Ind. 1995).

[34]*Niehaus v. State*, 265 Ind. 655, 359 N.E.2d 513, 516 (1977).

[35]*Calhoun v. State*, 932 So. 2d 923 (Ala. Crim. App. 2005), cert. denied, (Dec. 16, 2005) and cert. denied, 126 S. Ct. 2984, 165 L. Ed. 2d 990 (U.S. 2006).

[36]*State v. Swinton*, 268 Conn. 781, 847 A.2d 921 (2004).

whether proper procedures were followed and whether the program used was reliable. As the expert himself did not create the overlays, the court was also concerned that the effectiveness of cross-examination was seriously undermined. The court therefore found that this evidence was improperly admitted, but the error was deemed harmless.

## § 6:7   Erroneous identification and conviction

DNA typing has exposed numerous errors in the conclusions of bitemark experts. Recognition of these errors might serve, along with the error data cited in Part II of this chapter, as cautionary lessons to forensic dentists regarding the state of their art and to courts regarding the value of bitemark identification expert evidence.

In *Mississippi v. Bourne*,[1] a forensic odontologist stated that the defendant's teeth matched the bitemarks on the crime victim, but the defendant was excluded by DNA testing, hair analysis and fingerprint analysis.

After the forensic odontologist in *Mississippi v. Gates*[2] concluded that the defendant's teeth matched bitemarks on the victim, the defendant was eliminated as a suspect from investigation by DNA typing.

In *Florida v. Morris*,[3] prosecutors had first degree murder charges dismissed after the defense odontologists disagreed with the conclusion of the state's experts that a bitemark on the victim matched the defendant's dentition and subsequent DNA results also excluded the defendant.

A forensic odontologist testified at a "preliminary examination" that Otero[4] was "the only person in the world" who could have inflicted the bitemarks at issue. After spending five months in jail awaiting trial, the State dismissed the charges after a newly available DNA test excluded Otero as the source of DNA found on the victim.

Otero, a suspect in Michigan arrested based on a bitemark identification sued for false arrest after DNA tests excluded him.[5]

Twelve years after being convicted based on testimony from a forensic odontologist linking Young to a bitemark on the victim, prosecutors agreed to a new trial and dropped all charges after DNA testing excluded Young. A codefendant, Hill, was also released in a separate proceeding.[6]

More than a decade after Brewer's conviction and death sentence, DNA obtained from the decomposed victim indicated two male sexual assault perpetrators. Brewer was not the contributor of either DNA profile. The only remaining forensic evidence against Brewer was bitemark testimony that the District Attorney thought sufficient to try Brewer a second time.[7]

Raymond Milton Krone has become known as the 100th innocent person to be sentenced to death and later exonerated.[8] Krone was convicted of murder in 1992 and sentenced to death by lethal injection. After 32 months on death row, the

---

**[Section 6:7]**

[1]*Mississippi v. Bourne*, No. 93-10,214(3) (Cir. Ct., Jackson County, Mississippi).

[2]*Mississippi v. Gates*, No. 5060 (Humphrey Cty. Cir. Ct. 1998).

[3]*Florida v. Dale Morris (Pasco County, 97-3251 CFAES, 1997)*. See also, Dentist Defends His Advice in Slaying, Tampa Tribune (3/3/98), 1998 WLNR 692526 (dentist matched defendant's teeth to alleged bite on 9-year-old neighbor; "Although renowned Miami forensic odontologist Richard Souviron supported Martin's finding [of a match], they were disputed by two defense-hired experts: Phil Levine of Pensacola and Lowell Levine of Albany, N.Y."); Two Forensic Dentists Added to Wrongful Arrest Lawsuit, (St. Petersburg Times, Dec. 24, 1999).

[4]*Otero v. Warnick*, 241 Mich. App. 143, 614 N.W.2d 177 (2000).

[5]*Otero v. Warnick*, 241 Mich. App. 143, 614 N.W.2d 177 (2000).

[6]Twelve Years Behind Bars, Now Justice at Last (Chicago Tribune, Feb. 1, 2005).

[7]*Brewer v. State*, 725 So. 2d 106 (Miss. 1998) and *Brewer v. State*, 819 So. 2d 1169 (Miss. 2002).

[8]Not all of the exonerations of death row inmates have been the result of DNA typing. Krone is one of 12 who were, as of 2006.

Arizona Supreme Court overturned his conviction due to the government's failure to disclose to the defense a crucial bitemark videotape of the asserted dental match that was to be used at trial.[9] At his retrial, Krone was convicted again of murder, and this time sentenced to life in prison. After 10 years in prison in Arizona, in the spring of 2002 Krone was determined through DNA testing to be innocent of the crime and released (with the prosecution's blessings and apologies). Post-conviction DNA testing revealed that blood and saliva which almost certainly were left at the crime scene by the real killer belonged not to Krone but to another man, Kenneth Phillips, who already was in prison in Arizona for committing another sex crime, and who lived about 600 yards from the scene of the murder for which Krone had been convicted.

The strongest evidence against Krone at both trials had been bitemark identification testimony which asserted that bitemarks on the victim had been put there by Krone.[10] Judging from interviews with jurors, the forensic odontology expert testimony had a powerful impact.

> Those bitemarks on [the victim's] body had been the key to the prosecution's case against Krone. Janet Olmstead, a juror in the second trial in 1996, said forensic dentistry was what primarily convinced the jury of Krone's guilt. Although she is "delighted" that Krone is now free and that advances in DNA testing have made that possible, she believes the jury made the right decision with the information available at the time.
>
> "We had several molds of his teeth. It was pretty awful. You could roll these teeth around and they were a perfect match. The whole pattern of his teeth were significant with the match to the injury," she said.[11]

At the time of the original trial, a decade ago, little if any empirical evidence on the error rates of bitemark identification existed. That being the case, and given that the proponent of evidence has the burden of establishing its validity, one can question why the evidence was offered or admitted in the first place. Today, the government in offering such evidence, or a court in passing on its admissibility, can advert to the only body of data testing the accuracy of bitemark identifications, which shows remarkably high false positive error rates by even the most highly qualified forensic dentists.[12] Thus, it should be harder today for a proponent of bitemark identification testimony to ethically offer it or, if offering it, to succeed in having it admitted. Were the courts to enforce *Daubert*'s admissibility standards, in light of the known high error rates, one would expect to see bitemark expert testimony admitted less often or not be admitted at all.

Arizona, however, is a *Frye* state, and bitemark evidence might be admitted as readily today as it was a decade ago, notwithstanding the error rate data, provided that a sufficient number of forensic dentists disregard their field's error rate data and satisfy a court's notions of what constitutes general acceptance among the field

---

The facts recited are taken from the extensive news accounts of the case. See, e.g., Henry Weinstein, Death Penalty Foes Mark a Milestone: Crime: Arizona Convict Freed on DNA Tests is Said to be the 100th Known Condemned U.S. Prisoner to be Exonerated since Executions Resumed, Los Angeles Times, April 10, 2002, at A16; Teresa Ann Boeckel, A Measure of Justice: He Knew it Was Wrong: The Man Who Sat in Judgment on Ray Krone Disagreed with Jurors, But Felt Obliged to Let Their Ruling Stand, York Daily Record, April 13, 2002, A01; Teresa Ann Boeckel & Laura Laughlin, DNA Frees Former Death-Row Inmate: Two Juries Found Him Guilty, But New DNA Evidence Persuaded Prosecutors to Seek His Release, York Daily Record, April 9, 2002, at A01; Amanda J. Halligan, Lethal Injustice: Freeing the 100th Innocent Death Row Prisoner, Amnesty Now, Summer, 2002, at 4.

[9]*State v. Krone*, 182 Ariz. 319, 897 P.2d 621 (1995).

[10]The State's bitemark experts in both trials were Drs. Raymond Rawson and John Piakis.

[11]Amanda J. Halligan, Lethal Injustice: Freeing the 100th Innocent Death Row Prisoner, Amnesty Now, Summer, 2002, at 4. Dentist Piakis, who testified in the second trial that Krone's teeth matched the bitemark on the victim's breast, now says that "Phillips' dentition is more consistent with those bite marks on the victim's body than is Krone's."

[12]See, infra Table 2.

of forensic dentists.[13]

## II.  SCIENTIFIC ISSUES
*by C. Michael Bowers*[*]

### § 6:8   Introductory discussion of the scientific status of bitemark comparisons

The definition and breadth of forensic odontology has evolved over the centuries and now includes identification by means of dental DNA and salivary DNA.[1] "Odontology" is well established in the European dental language where it means the "study of teeth." The United States counterpart, "Forensic dentistry," is synonymous.

The initial United States historical case that utilized dental information occurred during the Revolutionary War period. Paul Revere recognized a prosthetic gold device he had previously constructed for a deceased patriot, General Joseph Warren, an American military casualty from the Bunker Hill engagement.[2] The primary duties of dentists in the medico-legal arena are to help identify the dead, apply dental facts and reliable methods to legal problems regarding identification from bitemarks, and, finally, interpretation of quality issues concerning the practice of dentistry. Dental identification of unknown persons relies on the similarities of anatomical and artificial structures (tooth restorations) and is achieved during a comparison process that focuses on shape and measured physical characteristics. Bitemark identification is a relatively recent arrival on the dental-legal scene.[3] Its inception was promoted by judicial interest in physical evidence left at crime scenes and bitemarks present on the skin of assault and homicide victims.

The materials used by forensic dentists to capture impressions of bitemarks and teeth are products accepted by the American Dental Association for the general practice of dentistry. Manufacturers stringently maintain the stability and physical duplication accuracy of these products. Dental science has progressed tremendously in the latter 20th century in its ability to create exemplars and replicas of dental structures that are used for later comparison analysis. This replication process uses materials commonly seen in dental offices.

Dental evidence collected in a bitemark case falls into two categories: (1) physical evidence that is a concert of photography and dental impression materials; and (2) biological evidence that is derived from serological swabbing of bitemarks on skin and objects that could have trace saliva DNA deposited by the biter.[4] Subsequent analysis of the latter is the realm of the biomolecular expert, while the former is the

---

[13]James McDougall, one of the judges who presided over one of Krone's trials is reported as expressing deep regret at the error, saying that he had doubts about the quality of the evidence presented at the trial, but that "It's not easy to tell a jury you think they're wrong." Another question to be asked is whether the judge's decision to admit the dental testimony rested on a sound basis.

[*]Dr. Bowers practices dentistry and law in Ventura, CA. He has been a Deputy Medical Examiner for the Ventura County Coroner's Office since 1988. He is a diplomate of the American Board of Forensic Odontology. The author would like to thank the following for their contributions to this chapter: Iain A. Pretty (University of Liverpool, School of Dentistry), John Holdridge (Justice Center, New Orleans, LA), David Sweet (Director, Bureau of Legal Dentistry, Vancouver, British Columbia), Dr. Duane Spencer (Diplomate of the ABFO), David Averill (Diplomate of the ABFO), Gary Bell (Diplomate of the ABFO), George Gould (Diplomate of the ABFO).

**[Section 6:8]**

[1]Sweet et al., PCR-based DNA Typing of Saliva Stains Recovered from Human Skin, 42 J. Forensic Sci. 320 (1997).

[2]Lester Luntz & Phyllys Luntz, Handbook for Dental Identification (1973).

[3]*Doyle v. State*, 159 Tex. Crim. 310, 263 S.W.2d 779 (1954).

[4]The effect of salivary DNA on bitemark investigations will be discussed, §§ 6:26, 6:27.

traditional bitemark venue of forensic dentists. Forensic dentists traditionally make the following postulates: the dental characteristics of teeth involved in biting are unique among individuals and this asserted uniqueness is faithfully transferred and recorded in the injury. Because these postulates and their dental science foundations constitute the field's most controversial scientific predicates, discussion of them will form a large part of this chapter.

## § 6:9 Introductory discussion of the scientific status of bitemark comparisons—Areas of dental testimony

Forensic dentists testify in court regarding medical evidence involving teeth. This involves areas of both criminal and civil law, when dental testimony might help answer a question that is at issue in the proceedings.

The predominant subject matter in criminal cases includes bitemark analysis, the identification of human remains and the dental aging of known individuals. The latter two are well founded in traditional dental and anthropological science. These use methods derived from studies of developmental dental biology and individuating characteristics of the cranial skeleton, dental structures, and dental restorations.

Human identification testimony has been utilized in the United States since the 1800s.[1] This identification of unidentified persons from their dental characteristics is the primary duty of forensic dentists. In mass disaster incidents, dentists can be expected to identify 20–25% of the victims. This is performed with a considerable degree of accuracy, due, in part, to a finite pool of candidates for identification (passenger lists) and the availability of dental records for comparison. This process emphasizes the comparison of postmortem victims to dental restorations placed during a person's life and certain anatomical structures that had been recorded in the course of radiographic examinations by medical and dental practitioners. Occasionally, old photographs showing unusually positioned front teeth may be superimposed onto postmortem images of a decedent's teeth. The forensic dentist conducts a postmortem dental examination to establish physical findings of a decedent in much the same way as with a living patient, and then compares dental records derived from investigative efforts and missing person reports.

Bitemark analysis is a product of the latter half of the 20th century. The small number of dentists in early court bitemark proceedings has increased substantially over the last twenty-five years. This is due, in part, to (1) the acceptance by the forensic odontological community of the notion that questions of reliability of methods and opinions are satisfied by their years of experience, their credentials, anecdotal reporting, and, in a display of circular logic, (2) the fact that the judiciary has allowed them to offer their opinions in trials.[2]

The physical evidence available in a bitemark case is considerably less than in dental identification. The vast array of potential biters can be large due to the fragmentary and diffuse features seen in skin injuries. The likelihood of a coincidental match of a defendant's teeth to a bitemark injury has not been quantified.

The recognition and admissibility of the discipline of forensic odontology rests on a fragile foundation of minimally relevant empirical research and a mountain of casework articles and commentaries. The caselaw evinces little doubt on the part of judges that dentists can play a role in determining questions of fact relevant to

---

**[Section 6:9]**

[1]Lester Luntz & Phyllys Luntz, Handbook for Dental Identification at 5–15 (1973) (narration of the 1850 Massachusetts homicide trial against John White Webster; a charred skull and denture fragments taken from the cellar of the defendant were identified by the first dean of the Harvard Dental School as those of the victim, Dr. George Parkman.)

[2]Rawson & Brooks, Classification of Human Breast Morphology Important to Bitemark Investigation, 5 J. Forensic Sci. 19 (1984).

identification in particular cases.

Of particular interest to readers may be § 6:13, which is intended to summarize the areas of bitemark inquiry and accumulated knowledge into various categories. This should aid the reader in determining how this material compares to the explicit reliability standards of the law announced in *Daubert* and *Kumho Tire*. Sections 6:22 to 6:25 describe recent technical efforts to improve the accuracy of bitemark opinions and the application of DNA analysis as it relates to this area of forensic investigation. § 6:12 will introduce data and interpretation regarding scientific reliability from a recent proficiency examination of dentists who have been certified by the American Board of Forensic Odontology.[3]

## § 6:10  Introductory discussion of the scientific status of bitemark comparisons—Training and professional forensic organizations

Unlike forensic pathologists, forensic dentistry is not a recognized specialty of dental practice. It may be best characterized as a subspecialty of the general field of forensic human identification. This is reflected by the lack of full time residency programs in the United States and the part-time nature of forensic dental consultants. By contrast, colleges and universities in Canada, Europe and Australia have one-year fellowships and graduate training (Masters level) devoted entirely to forensic dentistry.

The typical forensic dental expert is either: (1) a practicing dentist; (2) retired from dental practice; or (3) a dental educator. The large majority of dental forensic specialists come from the first category.

Dentists have created their own forensic organizations and have joined others. The American Board of Forensic Odontology is recognized by the American Academy of Forensic Sciences (AAFS) which has an Odontology Section with a membership of over 250 dentists. The American Society of Forensic Odontology has a membership of over 900 and meets concurrently with the AAFS once a year.

The ABFO has created Guidelines and Standards for Human Identification and Bitemark Analysis. This compilation has produced some uniformity in the methods and terminology used by dentists. But it is silent regarding reliability of comparison methods and opinions,[1] as well as the scientific validity issues often raised in court concerning bitemark methods.[2]

The regulatory nature of the AAFS and the ABFO occasionally come into play when transgressing members are expelled or are otherwise sanctioned for departures from accepted practices or ethical violations.[3]

Training for dentists interested in pursuing forensic training has remained largely

---

[3]Founded in 1976, this U.S. organization now has 113 dentists. Thirteen were grandfathered in as Diplomates. The ABFO provides a certification examination to applicants who have met qualifications of actual casework experience, participation in training seminars and presentations at the American Academy of Forensic Sciences (AAFS) meetings, and affiliations with medico-legal agencies.

**[Section 6:10]**

[1]Sweet & Bowers, Accuracy of Bitemark Overlays: A Comparison of Five Common Methods to Produce Exemplars from a Suspect's Dentition, 43 J. Forensic Sci. 362 (1998). This computer evaluation of four techniques produced recommendations to: (1) eliminate hand drawing of a suspect's teeth; and (2) use digital images of

dental characteristics. These images are placed (after flipping horizontally) onto a picture of a bitemark in order to evaluate concordance or dissimilarities between the two samples.

[2]C. Michael Bowers & Gary Bell (eds.), Manual of Forensic Odontology (3rd ed. 2001) (privately published by the American Society of Forensic Odontology).

[3]Mark Hansen, Out of the Blue, 82 ABAJ 50 (Feb.1996) (Reporting on a trial court rejection of a technique where the prosecution's dental expert positively linked metal rivets on a butcher knife's handle to marks he purportedly observed on the defendant's hand. These observations on the hand occurred during illumination by 450 nanometers visual (and blue) light. The dentist was unable to photograph the marks on the hand, but testified in court with a Xerographic copy of the defendant's

unchanged in recent years. The one U.S.-based program, at the University of Texas, San Antonio (UTSA) dental school, offers a fellowship course which is composed of on-site weekend training, take-home projects and a final exam testing the attendee's abilities. The fellowship has been met with enthusiasm but generally has only 4–6 students every two years.

The University of Montreal Institute of Legal Medicine has an online program that provides a certificate in forensic odontology. The program includes on-site class meetings necessary for a completion certificate.

The University of British Columbia has a M.Sc. program in forensic odontology. The program accepts one to two students per academic year. At this time, there are three graduates who have accomplished the program.

The Armed Forces Institute of Pathology (AFIP) has the longest running entry level short program. It is held each March and contains 5 days of presentations with short training modules. It is considered a course for introduction to forensic methods. The only equivalent program in the U.S. is the UTSA semi-annual symposium on odontology. The course contents are similar at both locales.

Professional organizations in the U.S. relevant to odontology continue to be the American Academy of Forensic Sciences (AAFS), The American Board of Forensic Odontology (ABFO) (which offers board certification and at this writing has about 100 members) and the American Society of Forensic Odontology. The American Board of Forensic Dentistry (ABFD), an affiliate of the American College of Forensic Examiners, is not recognized by the AAFS due to the ABFD's lax qualifications to achieve "diplomate" status.

The American Dental Association continues to have no interest in establishing odontology as a "dental specialty." On the other hand, the organization has used forensic dentistry as an example of the profession's "outreach" to the unidentified victims of mass disaster and terrorist caused catastrophes.[4]

## § 6:11 Introductory discussion of the scientific status of bitemark comparisons—Recognition and analysis of human bitemarks

A contemporary review of bitemark analysis techniques has summarized certain causes of unreliability in bitemark opinions used in court.[1] These include: changes in suspects' teeth from subsequent dental disease and treatment, examiner subjectivity that overvalues common tooth characteristics,[2] poor bias control,[3] lack of forensically relevant population studies to establish the frequencies of occurrence of common dental features, the dimensional accuracy of skin as a substrate for bitemark impressions made by these teeth,[4] and the multitude of unvalidated comparison methods and analytical procedures "recognized" and "generally accepted."

The issue of inter-examiner agreement and accuracy was studied briefly in the

---

hand as evidence of his findings.)

[4]Forensic teams face grim task in Katrina's wake. Dental experts called to action, ADA News, Sep. 9, 2005.

**[Section 6:11]**

[1]Rothwell, Bitemarks in Forensic Dentistry: A Review of Legal, Scientific Issues, 126 J. Am. Dental Ass'n (1995).

[2]The common debate between sparring forensic odontologists is (1) the identification value of a bitemark and (2) the degree of concordance of the injury to certain teeth of the defendant. The

proof of a positive opinion is not based on any formal population studies that state the frequency of chance random match with other members of a relevant population.

[3]The addition of a "dental lineup" of similar sets of teeth to the sample studied by the dentist has never been mandated. Some of the larger DNA labs separate extraction and comparison activities.

[4]DeVore, Bitemarks for Identification? A Preliminary Report, 11 Med. Sci. & L. 144 (1971). This study is described in detail infra at §§ 6:17, 6:21.

mid-1970s and its findings have not been altered by later research.[5] Using ideal laboratory conditions and evidence, experienced examiners who studied bitemark patterns in pig skin correctly identified the biter 76% of the time. Another author noted the subjectivity of this comparison process and has suggested that the strongest opinion linking bitemarks to suspects be limited to "possible" until the time comes that bitemark analysis is more satisfactorily tested in relation to reliability, error rate of dentists, and perhaps comes to be conducted pursuant to court appointed, rather than adversarial, expert testimony.[6]

The experimental evaluation of bitemark examiners has been attempted in the United States by the ABFO. It initiated a series of four studies, starting in 1983, and ending in 1999, where diplomates were sent sets of teeth and a series of actual bitemark photographs. They were asked to evaluate the evidence as they would in a conventional bitemark case. The cases were provided by members who attested to the identification of the true biter through means other than the bitemark evidence. The 1983 test resulted in an attempt to develop a scoring sheet that created values for specific dental features seen as concordant between the suspect and a bitemark. This led to the publication of a scoring system in 1986.[7] The quantitative values were soon discarded as being unreliable.[8] The descriptors of dental features, however, carried over into the later published ABFO Standards and Guidelines for Bitemark Analysis.

In seeking explanations for the unsatisfactorily high error rates, the previous edition of this chapter suggested that "[t]he lack of a proper match [by the examiners] was partly a reflection of the difficulty in recognizing the features found in a bitemark, partly an issue of experience and training in interpreting bitemark characteristics and matching procedures, and partly a function of the difficulty in setting up realistic situations."[9] The situations for the tests were certainly not unusual. An interesting interpretation is that, at the very least, the ABFO's membership may not generally have attained the skill necessary to achieve reliable results. The notion that experience is the key to reliability is a common theme that is seen throughout the literature.

Two subsequent studies performed after 1983 failed to generate publishable results. The difficulties have been described as a combination of poor experimental design and limited analytical prowess by the profession.[10]

The fourth test—the 4th ABFO Bitemark Workshop—was performed in 1999.[11] The results relate to a number of issues raised throughout the history of bitemark analysis in the United States. Following is a summary of the study and its findings.[12]

## § 6:12    Introductory discussion of the scientific status of bitemark comparisons—Recognition and analysis of human bitemarks—Proficiency testing of board certified odontologists

The intent of the study was to determine the ability of board certified forensic

---

[5]MacFarlane et al., Statistical Problems in Dental Identification, 14 J. Forensic Sci. Soc'y 247 (1974).

[6]C. Michael Bowers, A Statement Why Court Opinions on Bitemark Analysis Should be Limited, 4 Newsletter of the ABFO 4 (Dec. 1996).

[7]ABFO, Guidelines for Bitemark Analysis, 112 J. Am. Dental Assoc. 383 (1986).

[8]ABFO, Letter, 33 J. Forensic Sci. 20 (1988).

[9]David L. Faigman, David H. Kaye, Michael J. Saks & Joseph Sanders, Modern Scientific Evidence: The Law and Science of Expert

Testimony, Identification from Bitemarks: The Scientific Questions: Recognition and Analysis of Human Bite Marks § 24-2.1.1[2] 171 (1997).

[10]None of these studies have been published. The author gleaned this information from personal communications.

[11]The ABFO analysis is currently under review for publication by the Journal of Forensic Sciences.

[12]This description and analysis is an independent review of the raw data by this author and Dr. David Averill.

odontologists to correctly analyze bitemark evidence in a small population. All 95 board certified diplomates of the American Board of Forensic Odontology were eligible to participate in the study. Of the 60 diplomates who requested and were sent the study material, 26 returned the necessary data by the deadline and were included in the data results.

Complete case material typical of an actual bitemark case was sent to those diplomates requesting to participate. Each diplomate had six months to analyze and anonymously return findings. The study was based on four bitemark cases with known biters whose identity was substantiated by other means. Three of the cases were actual criminal cases where the bitemark was in skin. The fourth case was a fabricated bite into cheese, in which case each examiner was sent a model of the actual cheese in addition to the typical multiple color and black-and-white photographs. In addition to the four sets of models from the known biters each diplomate was sent an additional three dentitions that were selected at random from the laboratory of a unidentified dentist. These seven models made up the population from which the bitemarks were to be identified. Thus, examiners were asked to look at each unknown (3 sets of wound photos and one cheese model) and to compare each of those to the seven known dentitions, in an effort to determine which, if any, of the knowns matched an unknown.

In each case the expert was required to render an opinion in the below three areas. The expert was given the following choices in each of the three areas as defined by the ABFO Standards for Bitemark Terminology.

(1) Wound Analysis—Does the Injury Represent a Bitemark?
    (a) Definite bitemark—no doubt that teeth created the pattern
    (b) Probable bitemark—pattern strongly suggests origin from teeth but could be caused by something else
    (c) Possible bitemark—pattern may or may not have been caused by teeth; could have been caused by other factors

(2) Evidentiary Value
    (a) High forensic value—could support reasonable certainty in identification
    (b) Medium forensic value—could support possible opinion in identification
    (c) Low forensic value—would not support a linking
    (d) No forensic value—should not be used in investigation

(3) Degree of Certainty Describing the Link between the Bitemark and the Suspect
    (a) Reasonable medical certainty—virtual certainty; no reasonable or practical possibility that someone else did it
    (b) Probably—more likely than not
    (c) Possible—could be; may or may not be; can't be ruled out
    (d) Improbable—unlikely to be the biter
    (e) Incompatible—not the biter
    (f) Inconclusive—insufficient quality/quantity/specificity of evidence to make any statement of relationship to the biter

For purposes of this study, a positive linkage of the suspect's dentition to the bitemark consisted of those opinions recorded as: reasonable medical certainty, probably, and possible. Negative linkage consisted of: improbable, incompatible, and inconclusive. Conclusions could be correct in two different ways: by correctly linking an unknown bitemark to the suspect who made it (true positives) or by excluding a suspect who did not make the unknown bitemark (true negatives). Conclusions could be incorrect in two different ways: by incorrectly linking an unknown bite to a suspect who had not made it (false positives) or by excluding a suspect as having made an unknown bite when that suspect had in fact made that bite (false negatives). Table 1 graphically depicts these four possible decision outcomes.

## Table 1
## Four Possible Decision Outcomes.

|  | Reality | |
|---|---|---|
| Decision | Suspect bit victim | Suspect did not bite victim |
| Positive: Suspect bit victim | True Positive | False Positive |
| Negative: Suspect did not bite victim | False Negative | True Negative |

Table 2 summarizes the results of the study. It is important to say something, first, about the meaning of the data and the way they are presented. Suppose one were told that the overall accuracy rate for a test case was 85%. One might conclude from that number that the examiners were doing reasonably well—not as well as one might hope from a forensic science that claims the ability to connect crime scene bitemarks to suspects "to the exclusion of all others in the world," but not terrible either. In truth, however, the performance is far more troubling than is apparent. What is not made evident by that number is the fact that the poorest level of performance that examiners could achieve in this study—if they got every single answer as wrong as they could get it—would still make them appear to be accurate 71% of the time. That is because if an examiner failed to match a bitemark with the correct dentition (one error) and linked it instead with the dentition of an innocent suspect (second error) he still gets the remaining five dentitions "right" by not erroneously inculpating them.[1]

## Table 2
## Error Rates of Forensic Odontology Diplomates on the Four Test Cases

|  | Overall Error Rate (maximum possible error rate = 27%) | False Positive Errors as Percentage of Examiners Offering Opinions | False Negative Errors as Percentage of Examiners Offering Opinions |
|---|---|---|---|
| Case 1 | 14% | 62% | 38% |
| Case 2 | 7 | 42 | 4 |
| Case 3 | 12 | 65 | 15 |
| Case 4 | 13 | 65 | 27 |
| Medians | 12.5% | 63.5% | 22% |

Accordingly, Table 2 seeks to convey a more meaningful idea of how well examiners did by relating their performance to how well they could have done—or more to

---

**[Section 6:12]**

[1]Once one set of dentition is linked (correctly or incorrectly) to a bitemark, the others are not linked, and therefore are scored as "correct." In other words, given the test design, an examiner could never make more than two mistakes, and all remaining dentitions are scored as "correct." If instead of providing a set of seven dentitions from which to choose, there had been 100, then the overall accuracy rate, using this seemingly straightforward method of counting, could never be lower than 98% correct—one false positive inculpation of an innocent suspect, one overlooked guilty suspect, and 98 remaining dentitions that get scored as "correct." And, thus, the poorest possible performance would be "2% error."

the point, how poorly they did in relation to how poorly they could have done. The median overall error rate[2] is 12.5%—out of a maximum possible error rate of 27%. Thus, examiners came nearly half the way to being as wrong as they could be. More specifically, it is their false positive error rate—the tendency to conclude that an innocent person's dentition matches the bitemark—that accounts for the bulk of that overall error rate. Table 2 indicates how many examiners committed a false positive error in each test case. In their least bad performance, 42% of them gave a conclusion that inculpated an innocent person's dentition. On average, 63.5% of the examiners committed false positive errors across the test cases. If this reflects their performance in actual cases, then inculpatory opinions by forensic dentists are more likely to be wrong than right. They were, however, much less likely to overlook a true biter—reflected in a median false negative error rate of 22%.

These are not novices; these are diplomates, the most accomplished members of the field. But experience provided no assurance of accuracy. The demography of the test takers failed to disclose any correlation between years in forensic practice case work and correct results.

The results confirm Whittaker's earlier findings discussing the difficulties inherent to bitemark identification.[3] The findings of this most recent ABFO study cast serious doubt on earlier conclusions that the field has "produced a significant number of well trained and capable forensic dentists who have accepted guidelines to follow for evidence collection and analysis. The work of these organizations has contributed to the development of a systematic approach capable of producing reliable opinions."[4]

The ABFO membership opted to submit their report of the Fourth Bitemark Workshop results to the respected Journal of Forensic Sciences. Their submission was twice rejected.[5] The group then published their results in a secondary publication.[6] The ABFO subsequently reversed itself and adopted the position that the raw data were unusable and any inferences from the data were misleading.[7]

The original attempt to study accuracy and intra-examiner agreement of dentists was undertaken by Whittaker in 1975.[8] That study is cited by some writers as a validity test which proves biter identification is reliable. A more accurate description of this test's result is to say that within the four corners of the study certain types of bitemark evidence produced relatively more reliable results than other types. In Whittaker's study, two forensic dentists were tested for accuracy (choosing the correct biter) and reliability (agreement with each other) to examine bites recorded on wax, pigskin and in photographs. Dental study models were used as exemplars of possible biters. The number of possible biters was not recorded. Transparent overlays were not available, although the examiners were able to use metric analysis. The two examiners were able to correctly identify 98.8% of the impressions in wax to the appropriate study model, and achieved similar accuracy when compar-

---

[2]That is, the median of the false positives plus false negatives across the four test cases.

[3]Whittaker, Some Laboratory Studies on the Accuracy of Bitemark Comparisons, 25 Int'l Dental J. 166 (1975).

[4]David L. Faigman, David H. Kaye, Michael J. Saks & Joseph Sanders, Modern Scientific Evidence: The Law and Science of Expert Testimony, Identification from Bitemarks: The Scientific Questions: Recognition and Analysis of Human Bitemarks, § 24-2.1.1[2] 171–172 (1997).

[5]The last revision was rejected with no recommendation by JFS for resubmission.

[6]Arheart & Pretty, Results of the 4th ABFO Bitemark Workshop — 1999, 124 Forensic Sci.

Int'l 104 (2001).

[7]See ABFO Position Paper on Bitemark Workshop #4, at www.ABFO.ORG. "It has come to the attention of the American Board of Forensic Odontology, Inc. (ABFO) that some persons have misinterpreted the purpose of and statistical analysis of the ABFO Bitemark Workshop #4 conducted on February 14 and 15, 1999, in Orlando, FL. The Board has an obligation to correct these erroneous statements." The remainder of the narrative argues against the notion that the examination can be considered a proficiency review of Board Certified forensic dentists.

[8]Whittaker, Some Laboratory Studies on the Accuracy of Bitemark Comparisons, 25 Int'l Dent. J. 166 (1975).

ing to stone models produced from the wax bites. When photographs of the bites were employed, the accuracy decreased slightly to 96% when measurements were taken and fell further to 67.5% without taking measurements. When the pigskin was tested, accurate assessments hit 63.7%, but when photographs of the pigskin taken 24 hours after biting were used, accuracy fell to 16%.

The study clearly identified operational and examiner difficulties with different methods and bitten objects studied in the analyses. These difficulties still exist more than thirty years later. The use of wax test bites posed no problem. This has little if any relevance to bitemarks in human flesh. The pigskin results, clearly a better analogue to human skin, showed the diminishing accuracy of the dentists' efforts to find the correct biter.

Recently, odontology's most prolific peer-reviewed authors, Iain Pretty and David Sweet, undertook a study of the proficiency of volunteer bitemark examiners.[9] The study employed digital tooth overlays (two-dimensional outlines of suspect teeth) and simulated human bites in pigskin. The purpose of the paper was to study decision outcomes of three groups of odontologists. The methods used were restricted to the application of digital overlays of suspects' teeth to the bitemarks. The testing materials and the bitemarks created for this study were at the high end of forensic identification value. This value exceeded any actual casework most or any forensic dentists encounter because of the three dimensional depth the authors achieved in the bitten pigskin. A series of ten postmortem bites were created in pigskin using dental casts mounted in a vice-grip. Each of the bites was photographed according to ABFO guidelines. Two suspects were associated with each case, although in two of the cases, neither of the suspects supplied to the examiners was responsible for the bite. The examiners were divided into three groups based on their levels of experience and training. They were provided with photographs of the bites, the suspect's study models and transparent overlays of each suspect. The examiners were asked to reach a conclusion regarding each suspect and report their conclusions using the ABFO conclusions for bitemark analyses. The examiners conducted their examinations twice, using the same evidence samples, following a hiatus period of three months. This allowed the examiners to voluntarily change their opinion (since all sample materials were to be returned after the first test) during the subsequent testing. Thirty dentists participated, with the most experienced (all ABFO members) placed into one cohort. The other two dentist groups were those with low forensic bitemark experience and no forensic bitemark experience. The ABFO group was tested for inter-examiner reliability during the first testing. The second test studied intra-examiner reliability. Seven of the original 10 ABFO respondents were used to test intra-examiner reliability. This tests whether these same examiners, using the same evidence, changed their opinions after three months. The results for intra-examiner consistency are presented in Table 3. The performance results were considered "fair" by the reporting authors. Three of the original ten were eliminated for not returning the material to the authors after completing the first test. The study's authors, using more elaborate statistical analysis for other conclusions, considered the mean accuracy of these examiners to be 85.7% in the first test and 83.5% for the second. The percentage agreement ranged from 65% to 100%. These results underscore the variability of bitemark examiners' opinions even when given exceptionally high quality bitemark evidence with which to work.

_____

[9]Pretty & Sweet, Digital Bitemark     Forensic Sci. 1385 (2001).
Overlays—An Analysis of Effectiveness, 46 J.

## Table 3. Intra-Examiner Agreement

| Examiner | Percent Agreement |
|----------|-------------------|
| 1 | 65 |
| 2 | 70 |
| 3 | 100 |
| 4 | 100 |
| 5 | 80 |
| 6 | 95 |
| 7 | 100 |
| Mean | 87.2% |

The inter-examiner reliability results (test one) had ten diplomates returning completed answer sheets (100%). The level of agreement was considered "moderate." Two of the group were extremely conservative, with their "inconclusive opinions" heavily contributing to the group's total of this response type (12%). The remaining eight examiners used "I don't know" only two percent of the time. These two examiners scored 100% accuracy in the cases on which they did render conclusive opinions. Overall, accuracy ranged from 65% to 100% with a mean value of 83.2%. When the two most conservative examiners were removed from the testing group, mean accuracy dropped to 78.5%. False positive responses were 15.9% (ranging from 0 to 45.5%) and false negatives were 25.0% (ranging from 0 to 71.4%).

The final finding from this study was that none of the three groups (the ABFO and two non-ABFO groups) differed statistically from each other in any of the measured values of this study. These groups were given the best possible experimentally derived bitemark evidence (three dimensional bites and excellent photography protocol). The variation in individual outcomes and less than high general agreement (reliability) raises concerns about the ability of examiners presented with more forensically typical materials to identify a biter to the exclusion of all others (ABFO terminology would be that the suspect is the biter with reasonable medical/dental certainty).

Proficiency testing is a topic of discussion with a small number of concerned dentists. The intent of this testing is to insure quality control of previously qualified forensic dentists after their initial certification. This notion is prevalent in the established scientific laboratory disciplines but is not seen in the health care field per se. The onset of DNA proficiency testing of biologists and lab technicians has produced a "filter down" effect to the less rigorously scientific fields seen in forensic practice (fingerprints, ballistics, and bitemark analysis). Previous attempts by the ABFO to achieve some measure of bitemark examiner outcome calibration have repeatedly been repudiated by the organization. The ABFO is silent regarding establishing a mandatory testing of its membership. The ABFO's association with the AAFS (as in "recognition of certification. . . is for information purposes only")[10] as a forensic certification board will change this status quo due to the AAFS establishment of a Forensic Specialties Accreditation Board (FSAB).[11] The FSAB has developed criteria for the AAFS recognized boards (criminalistics, forensic pathology and psychiatry, forensic anthropology, forensic toxicology, questioned

---

[10]2005 AAFS Membership Directory, at xxiii.

[11]http://www.thefsab.org. "The goal of this program is to establish a mechanism whereby the forensic community can assess, recognize and monitor organizations or professional boards that certify individual forensic scientists or other fo-rensic specialists. This program has been established with the support and grant assistance of the American Academy of Forensic, (AAFS), the National Forensic Science Technology Center (NFSTC) and the National Institute of Justice (NIJ)."

documents, and odontology) which will demand, in the near future, ongoing proficiency review of their members' reliability in performing their analyses.[12]

The sections that follow may illuminate the reasons why accuracy has been so disappointing and what steps may improve accuracy and judicial expectations in the future.

## § 6:13 Introductory discussion of the scientific status of bitemark comparisons—Scientific methods applied to comparison techniques

A major aspect of the bitemark comparison process targets the three-dimensional characteristics of the suspect's teeth. Two studies[1] report data suggesting a high degree of variability in these features, and the authors argue that it shows bitemarks to be unique (infinitely variable) among the human population. Unfortunately, there are no studies relating this hypothesis to actual bitemarks on skin or other substrates. In addition, neither study attempted to prove the independent occurrence of each dental feature. The latter study misapplied probability theory to reach a conclusion of uniqueness of any human being.

In practice, the odontologist compares the Questioned bitemark to duplicates (exemplars) of Known teeth. The assortment of exemplar materials and methods in use are well documented in the literature. Computer imaging, hand-traced outlines, Xerographic copying, and wax impressions, among others, are used to duplicate two and three dimensional features of a suspect's teeth. These methods produce an image of the teeth, called an "overlay" since it is transferred to transparent acetate and superimposed (after being flipped horizontally), onto an image of the bitemark. The examiner studies the relationships between the two images, and reaches an opinion about their similarity.

A recent study was completed in an effort to validate the most popular of these methods.[2] This was the first attempt to compare methods in relation to a reference standard. The study obtained sample data (n=30) from plaster dental study casts of a Caucasian population pool, pertaining to tooth position and area of each tooth biting surface (also called a hollow-volume overlay) using a computer-based optical imaging method. The relative rotation of teeth in each sample was obtained using a geometric analysis. Five commonly used bitemark overlay production techniques were analyzed by computer and statistically to determine how accurately each reproduced the shape, size and rotation of the upper and lower front teeth of the research sample. (See Figure 1.) The computer-based method produced digital images of the dental plaster casts that were found to be very accurate. This method was treated as the "gold standard" and the other methods were compared to it.

[12]FSAB Guidelines, Sec. 6.2. Continuing Competency.

6.2.2. Measurement of continuing competency may include, but not be limited to, proficiency testing, case audits, relevant work experience, relevant publication, conducting training, audit of court testimony, case presentation and relevant work experience (sic)."

[Section 6:13]
[1]Reidar F. Sognnaes & Rawson, Computer Comparison of Bitemark Patterns in Identical Twins, 105 J. Am. Dental Assoc. 449 (1982); Rawson & Ommen, Statistical Evidence for the Individuality of the Human Dentition, 29 J. Forensic Sci. 245 (1984).
[2]§ 6:9.

**Figure 1**

**Overlays Produces from the Same Dental Cast Using a Variety of Different Techniques. (Note: not to scale.)**

1 = computer-generated      4 = xerographic method
2 = hand-traced from study cast      5 = radiographic method
3 = hand-traced from wax bite

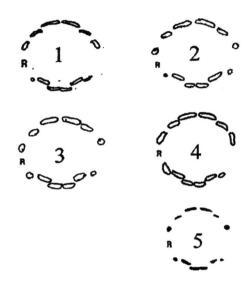

The findings established that there are significant differences among these five methods. The resulting ranking of the various methods is seen in Table 4. The authors suggested that the computer generated bitemark overlays provided the most reproducible and accurate exemplars and recommended that hand tracing of a suspect's teeth be discontinued due to its consistently low ranking for precision in both surface area and rotational accuracy. Findings such as these have played a part in the development and revision of various aspects of bitemark identification practice.[3]

**Table 4**

**Various Overlay Fabrication Techniques Ranked According to Accuracy**

| Rank | Area | Rotation |
|---|---|---|
| 1 | Computer-based | Computer-based |
| 2 | Radiopaque wax | Xerographic |
| 3 | Hand-traced from wax | Hand-traced from wax |
| 4 | Hand-traced from study casts | Hand-traced from study casts |
| 5 | Xerographic | Radiopaque wax |

After Sweet and Bowers (1998)

---

[3]Raymond Johansen & C. Michael Bowers, Digital Analysis of Bitemark Evidence (2000).

### § 6:14 Introductory discussion of the scientific status of bitemark comparisons—Scientific methods applied to comparison techniques—Analysis of suspect teeth: the conundrum of multiple methods

The issue of the multiple methods of bitemark analysis continues to thwart any attempts to standardize procedures to any sort of "gold standard." The use of digital methods in the superimposition of bitemark evidence appears to be increasing, although the older, more experienced forensic dentists still seem to resist the use of two dimensional computer methods.

> Since being introduced to the profession these new tools have had little use in certain Prosecution bitemark cases seen by this author while acting as a Defense Counsel expert. This disregard of almost 10 year old scientific literature possibly indicates the established dental experts (trained in the previous Millenium) do not consider common digital procedures will change their opinions or improve their accuracy.[1]

A recent survey study[2] of volunteering odontologists produced results indicating that 90% of the respondents used a dental exemplar (overlay) of suspect teeth. The use of digitally generated overlays was acknowledged by 70% of the respondents. The remainder of the study sample either hand drew their tooth exemplars or used some other alternative method. This flies in the face of a published findings indicating that digital methods were superior in detail and accuracy.[3]

There are three major choices of how to generate a digital dental exemplar:
1. The Naru technique.[4]
2. The Sweet method.[5]
3. The Bowers modification of Sweet.[6]

A 2005 paper[7] stated these methods are all reliable for tooth position data, but the area of the each tooth varies among the three methods. The likely reason for area variations of the dental overlays is due to operator choice of the amount to tooth structure to include in the dental exemplar. A contributing factor is that each of the three methods uses different digital "tools" available in the Adobe Photoshop computer program.

The scientific literature shows some recent advance into 3D laser scanning methods that are still experimental.[8] This bodes well for a more scientifically reproducible method of suspect dental analysis, but the knowledge and technique availability to non-university-based odontologists will be nil.

### § 6:15 Introductory discussion of the scientific status of bitemark comparisons—Scientific methods applied to comparison techniques—Analysis of a bitemark pattern

The "dental profile" physically present in a suspected bitemark injury is currently

---

[Section 6:14]

[1]Id. Raymond Johansen & C. Michael Bowers, Digital Analysis of Bitemark Evidence (2000) at S104.

[2]Pretty, A Web-based Survey of Odontologists's Opinions Concerning Bitemark Analysis, 48 J. Forensic Sci. 117 (2003).

[3]Sweet and Bowers, Accuracy of Bite Mark Overlays: A Comparison of Five Common Methods to Produce Exemplars from a Suspect's Dentition, 43 J. Forensic Sci. 1050 (1998).

[4]Naru and Dykes, The Use of a Digital Imaging Technique to Aid Bite Mark Analysis, 36 Sci. & Justice 47 (1996).

[5]Sweet, Parhar and Wood, Computer-based Production of Bite Mark Comparison Overlays, 43 J. Forensic Sci. 1050 (1998).

[6]Raymond J. Johansen and C. Michael Bowers, Digital Analysis of Bitemark Evidence, 2nd ed. (2003).

[7]McNamee, Sweet, Pretty, A Comparative Reliability Analysis of Computer-generated Bitemark Overlays, J. Forensic Sci. 50 400–405 (2005).

[8]Blackwell et al., 3-D Imaging and Quantitative Comparison of Human Dentition and Simulated Bite Marks, 4 Int'l J. Legal Med. 1 (2006).

undergoing some experimental testing. Pigskin has been used in similar testing over the last four decades as a substitute for human skin. This use of pigskin as a substrate for artificial bitemarks was revisited in 2001 by the small cadre of academic-based forensic dentists who are the source of the bulk of the contemporary peer-reviewed articles on bitemark analysis.[1] The findings indicated average agreement amongst examiners to be 80%. Reliability of the examiners (i.e., intra and inter examiner) was indicated as "not strong." This underscores the historically subjective nature of the interpretation of forensic identification value seen in bitemark injuries. The authors in the 2001 paper revisited the 1999 ABFO 4th Annual Bitemark Workshop results and found a marked agreement with their own experimental results in the area of intra-examiner reliability ranging from 86% to 59%.[2]

The threshold opinion of a bitemark investigation is what dental information or data are present in the pattern, be it on human skin or some inanimate object. The ABFO Guidelines are of no help in terms of "weighing" what is significant. Rather, these Guidelines give only descriptive terms of dental features that should be used in a written report. The actual practice of bitemark investigations commonly shows no descriptors at all and little compliance regarding data specific to the conclusions. This renders any independent examiner no help in determining the reasoning for an opposing dentist's opinion. The more experienced bitemark experts consider their opinions inviolate and therefore object to giving the specifics during the discovery phase of an actual case. This attitude, coupled with the indiosyncratic basis for bitemark evaluation nourishes the opinion of some outside the field that bitemark analysis is flawed. The lack of an appropriate "scale" of standardization for bitemark patterns makes their continued use in court a point of concern. The outcomes of a criminal trial are not a benchmark for scientific proof.

## § 6:16 Introductory discussion of the scientific status of bitemark comparisons—The scientific limitations of bitemark testimony

The phrase "evidence based" has recently been introduced into the forensic odontology literature.[1] The health care profession uses this concept to title scientifically derived proofs for established protocols and studies that provide the knowledge base for accepted treatment modalities. If we consider bitemark diagnoses as a health care method, the proof of diagnostic effectiveness should be revealed in the case history and peer-reviewed articles studying and validating the treatments normally performed by court approved bitemark experts. The bitemark literature is predominantly case reports whereas substantive proofs of both validity and reliability do not yet exist. Any argument that the primary bitemark literature is sufficient for continued court admission should be considered in the context that the actual casework observed in court has little to no relevance to the experimental studies some consider adequate. This disconnect is showing itself in the published judicial record where bitemark diagnoses have been refuted or at least severely weakened by later DNA evidence.[2]

The following section describes several scientific issues involving bitemark analysis. This is presented to illuminate the interface between the rules of scientific admissibility and reliability issues involving forensic dentistry.

---

[Section 6:15]

[1]Pretty and Sweet, Digital Bitemark Overlays—An Analysis of Effectiveness, 46 J. Forensic Sci. 1385 (2001).

[2]Arheart and Pretty, Results of the 4th ABFO Bitemark Workshop 1999, 124 Forensic Sci. Int. 104 (2001).

[Section 6:16]

[1]Pretty, The Barriers to Achieving an Evidence Base for Bitemark Analysis, 159 Forensic Sci. Int. 110 (2006).

[2]Bowers, Problem-based Analysis of Bitemark Misidentifications: The Role of DNA, 159 Forensic Sci. Int. 104 (2006).

The limitations of bitemark testimony find their origins more in legal than scientific requirements, leading very few of the early scientific papers to mention[3] pitfalls of the methods adopted by the profession. The use of bitemarks, carrying the same weight as DNA analysis, continues without any judicial scrutiny in criminal trial and appellate courts. The determination of dental profiles present in injured skin that are solely bruising is confounded by the multiple variables that exist in typical injury patterns. The checklist for these limitations continues to be the following:

1. Individual differences in victims' response to trauma.
2. The differences in the anatomical locations of the bitemarks.
3. Physical stretching and distortion of skin during the act of biting.

The effects of these variables on the appearance of a human bitemark have never been controllable and most likely are beyond domestication by any scientific application. The examiner's interpretation of the forensic value of such injuries continues to be intuitive and not the product of any scientific knowledge.

## § 6:17 Introductory discussion of the scientific status of bitemark comparisons—The scientific limitations of bitemark testimony— The accuracy of skin as a substrate for bitemarks

Central to bitemark analysis are the characteristics of the skin receiving the mark, because, in cases of physical assault having skin injuries, the anatomy and physiology of the skin, and the position of the victim, affect the detail and shape of the bitemark. DeVore[1] showed how the positioning of the test bite (actually, it was an inked circle) on a bicep varied depending upon whether the arm was flexed or pronated. (See Figure 2.) What is significant in casework and report writing is the need to experimentally control or establish the amount of positional variation in an actual bitemark case. Use of a live victim in a reenactment is difficult and a deceased individual will not be available. No important papers have been published on this subject since DeVore's in 1971.

---

[3]MacFarlane, MacDonald and Sutherland, Statistical Problems in Dental Identification, 14 J. Forensic Sci. Soc. 247 (1974).

[Section 6:17]

[1]§§ 6:11 to 6:12.

**Figure 2**

**Two Identical Marks on Human Skin. The Lower Has Been Distorted by Applying Pressure to the Area (Duplicating Devore's Test).**

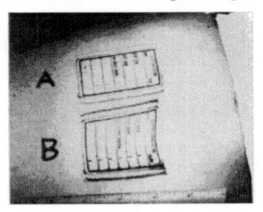

Another issue is the amount of detail present in the bitemark. Skin is a poor impression material. The injury may be a series of reddened bruises at the time of the original photograph. It is rare to see the presence of three-dimensions (i.e., tooth indentations) which could be used for increased detail.

### § 6:18  Introductory discussion of the scientific status of bitemark comparisons—The scientific limitations of bitemark testimony—Bruising and other considerations

Recognition of the fact that bruising is actually subcutaneous bleeding[1] requires that the investigator not assume that the reddened areas that appear to be teeth are an accurate representation of individual teeth.

Dailey and Bowers[2] describe the shortcomings of attempts by odontologists and other forensic experts to "age" skin injuries according to the degree of discoloration present in the mark. During the process of healing, or skin response to a sufficient force, the bruise will go through color changes before fading from visual recognition. A bruise is an "area of hemorrhage into soft tissue due to the rupture of blood vessels caused by blunt trauma."[3] Using appearance of bruises for the purpose of aging a wound has been judged to be invalid by numerous investigators. A review of research reporting controlled studies of these discolorations over time concluded that, "it would seem unlikely that a bruise could be reliably aged from appearance alone."[4]

The bitemark should be thoroughly analyzed *first*. That means measurements, angles, and other features should be exhaustively studied before the teeth of any suspect(s) are viewed.[5] This provides a modicum of control where the determinations of the forensic value of the bitemark are established prior to the dentist comparing the suspect's dental evidence. The realities of two-dimensional (i.e., bruises) bitemarks suggest that finding individualizing (i.e., unique) features in bitemarks is extremely rare. The details of intertooth spaces, rotations, and blank spaces between teeth are the principal features of this type of injury.

### § 6:19  Introductory discussion of the scientific status of bitemark comparisons—The scientific limitations of bitemark testimony—The issue of individuality of human dentition

Another foundation of bitemark analysis is the belief that the total arrangement of a person's dentition creates a dental "profile" of sorts. Attempts to determine, or demonstrate, the uniqueness of human dentition has a history in bitemark analysis that stretches over four decades. The demonstration of uniqueness is a blend of art and opinion. The probability of more than one person producing a similar or identical bitemark in a specific case is the challenge in every bitemark case.[1]

Most bitemark experts consider the human dentition to be unique to each living being.[2] A large majority of ABFO diplomates consider the dental uniqueness issue settled and the capacity of these features to be accurately reflected in human skin to be confirmed (91% support dental uniqueness and 78% believe that uniqueness

[Section 6:18]

[1]Dailey & Bowers, Aging of Bitemarks, A Literature Review, 42 J. Forensic Sci. 791 (1997).

[2]Dailey & Bowers, Aging of Bitemarks, A Literature Review, 42 J. Forensic Sci. 791 (1997).

[3]Dominick J. DiMaio & Vincent J.M. DiMaio, Forensic Pathology (1993).

[4]Langlois & Gresham, The Aging of Bruises: A Review and Study of the Colour Changes with

Time, 50 Forensic Sci. Int'l 227 (1991).

[5]Reidar F. Sognnaes, Forensic Bitemark Measurements, 55 Dental Survey 34 (1979).

[Section 6:19]

[1]Beckstead et al., Review of Bitemark Evidence, 99 J. Am. Dental Assoc. 69 (1979).

[2]Pretty and Sweet, The Scientific Basis for Human Bitemark Analysis—A Critical Review, 41 Sci. & Justice 85 (2001).

transfers faithfully to human skin).[3] Over the last 30 years, only a few papers asserting dental uniqueness (and reviewed elsewhere in this chapter) have been published.[4] They do not establish dental uniqueness or its replication onto human skin. In fact, until quite recently, no studies of this aspect of the subject of bitemarks were published in any peer reviewed journals. The assumptions of uniqueness and accurate transfer existed simply because they were convenient for court admission of bitemark analysis.

Two recent articles have added a more realistic understanding of the limits of transferability and dental uniqueness. The first article determined from other evidence that only two suspects had the opportunity to bite an assault victim.[5] The comparison of the two dentitions to the injury produced no findings that allowed either one to be excluded as the biter. The second article was a university-based project that introduced 3D laser scanning of a population of 42 study models and experimentally produced bitemarks in wax. The study's results indicated the following:

> The results of this study indicated that 15% of combinations of dentitions and bite models in this sample were categorised as a match when they were in fact a non-match, i.e. 15% of non-matching combinations were indistinguishable from the true match. This translates to six out of the 42 people in this sample at risk of being false positives, or wrongly convicted. This figure is only indicative of this particular sample and may be lower in actual casework, but this is not certain.[6]

If, however, it can be said that no two humans have the same dentition, the task is made easier, because (putting aside technical problems of the registration and reading of the bitemark[7]) the theoretical probability of a coincidental match becomes zero, and then no probability need be worried about, much less calculated. Legal commentaries from the 1970s and 80s attacked bitemark analysis as a "new and unfounded science of identification"[8] and pointed out that the "uniqueness of the human dentition hasn't been established."[9] The odontology response then and now has been to base its assertion of uniqueness on a small number of journal articles which are less than persuasive in their efforts to prove uniqueness scientifically.[10]

One approach to trying to prove uniqueness has been the comparison of identical twins.[11] The notion is that if "even" identical twins show differences, then every individual on earth "must therefore" be different from every other individual on earth. The logic that goes from the evidence to the conclusion is not especially clear, but we can understand why, as a means of proving uniqueness, it is fundamentally

---

[3]Pretty, A Web-based Survey of Odontologist's Opinions Concerning Bitemark Analysis, 48 J. Forensic Sci. 117 (2003).

[4]MacFarlane, MacDonald and Sutherland, Statistical Problems in Dental Identifications, 14 J. Forensic Sci. Soc. 247 (1974). Sognnaes et al., Computer Comparison of Bitemark Patterns in Identical Twins, 105 J. Am. Dent. Ass'n 449 (1982). Rawson et al., Statistical Evidence for the Individuality of the Human Dentition, 29 J. Forensic Sci. 245 (1982).

[5]Pretty and Turnbull, Lack of Dental uniqueness Between Two Bitemark Suspects, 46 J. Forensic Sci. 1487 (2001).

[6]Blackwell et al., 3-D Imaging and Quantitative Comparison of Human Dentition and Simulated Bite Marks, 4 Int. J. Legal Med. 1, 8 (2006).

[7]For example, Rawson & Ommen, Statistical Evidence for the Individuality of the Human Dentition, 29 J. Forensic Sci. 245 (1984), utilized teeth impressions in wax which were then hand traced and computer analyzed. Because bitemarks in skin were not the target of the 397 sets of wax teeth marks he choose to investigate out of a larger cohort of 1200, the generalizability of the findings to actual bitemarks is questionable.

[8]Wilkinson & Gerughty, Bitemark Evidence: Its Admissibility is Hard to Swallow, 12 W. St. U. L. Rev. 519 (1985).

[9]Hales, Admissibility of Bitemark Evidence, 51 S. Cal. L. Rev. 309 (1978).

[10]Sognnaes & Rawson, Computer Comparison of Bitemark Patterns in Identical Twins, 105 J. Am. Dental Assoc. 449 (1982); Rawson & Ommen, Statistical Evidence for the Individuality of the Human Dentition, 29 J. Forensic Sci. 245 (1984).

[11]See discussion, § 6:22.

unsound. When it is shown that identical twins do not have identical dentition (or fingerprints, or hair, or anything else), what that establishes is that the genotype for these traits is not isomorphic with the phenotype. Thus, genetics cannot be relied upon as a basis for concluding that these forensically relevant traits vary in accord with all that we know about genetics. Rather, it means that non-genetic, presumably random, factors introduce some disconnection between the genes and their physical expression. Rather than proving that, because identical twins show differences, everyone else must also, it proves that even the attributes of identical twins reflect these random factors and those random factors must be taken into account in determining the probability of a coincidental match. Rather than obviating the need for objective calculations, it brings us right back to the need to calculate probabilities of coincidental matches.

The heavy use of probability theory is seen in the seminal bitemark articles of the last four decades.[12] Their implication is that so much variation exists in the morphology and position of teeth that, when the product rule is applied, the probability of two being alike approaches the vanishing point. For example, some authors point to hypothetical frequencies of occurrence of more rare or "uncharacteristic" features, multiply them according to the product rule per Keiser-Neilsen, based on the assumption that these features of higher value are independent of one another, and arrive at vanishingly small probabilities.[13] Keiser-Neilsen was not, however, talking about bitemarks (far more limited representations of dentition) when he introduced the use of the "product-rule"[14] in 1960. He was offering a purely theoretical application of basic notions of probability, assuming that each dental feature was independent of the next and that the product of each frequency of occurrence could be used to establish the frequency of all the features occurring at once. He was actually talking about missing and filled teeth, not bitemarks. Thus, because bitemarks involve many fewer attributes than full sets of teeth, the probabilities can never get as small as Keiser-Nielsen's and the identifications can never be as individuating.

Another problem is that the use of the product rule requires that the separate attributes going into the calculation be independent of each other, otherwise the probability arrived at understates the improbability of the joint occurrence of the attributes. None of the studies taking the probability approach to uniqueness of dentition have achieved, or even attempted, to determine whether the attributes of dentition are uncorrelated with each other. To the contrary, some research indicates that the distribution of some tooth positions are less random than others.[15] For example, Figure 3 shows the tooth position data sets for six upper and lower teeth. The frequency of occurrence varies within each upper and lower sample. If each tooth position were occurring independently, the numbers would be similar. For instance, the lower set values of 116.0 and 153.5 are for the two lower front teeth, a considerable difference.[16] The lack of randomness of dental values (shape and posi-

---

[12]Kieser-Nielsen, Person Identification by Means of the Teeth (1980); Vale, Sognnaes & Noguchi, Unusual Three-Dimensional Bitemark Evidence in a Homicide Case, 21 J. Forensic Sci. 642 (1976); Rawson & Ommen, Statistical Evidence for the Individuality of the Human Dentition, 29 J. Forensic Sci. 245 (1984).

[13]Rawson & Ommen, Statistical Evidence for the Individuality of the Human Dentition, 29 J. Forensic Sci. 245 (1984).

[14]The product rule applied to dentition states that the probability of the joint occurrence of sev-

eral attributes is the product of each separate attribute's frequency in the relevant population. This assumes each component occurs independently, something which is not yet known to be true.

[15]Rawson & Ommen, Statistical Evidence for the Individuality of the Human Dentition, 29 J. Forensic Sci. 245 (1984).

[16]Rawson & Ommen, Statistical Evidence for the Individuality of the Human Dentition, 29 J. Forensic Sci. 245 (1984).

tion) was reported in a much earlier British paper.[17]

## Figure 3

### Number of Different Tooth Positions Found for Sets of Six Upper and Lower Teeth.

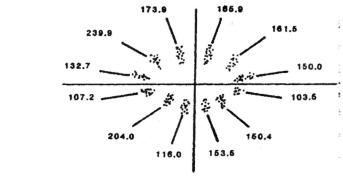

After Rawson et al. (1984).

The largest problem with using probability theory to prove unique individuality is that it is simply incapable of doing so, something that other forensic identification sciences realized some time ago.[18] Probability leads only to probabilities, never to unique, one-of-a-kind certainties. Though it may be the best route to uniqueness, it is incapable of arriving at the desired destination.[19]

What the mathematics of probability can be used for is to calculate the probability of a coincidental match, and that probability can be reported to the trial factfinder. A forensic dentist can never say that the apparent similarity between a bitemark and a suspect's dentition links the suspect with certainty to the crime scene, but the jury could be informed of the probability that a person selected at random would have so similar a match. This is exactly what DNA typing leads to: not assertions of unique matches but a probability of coincidental matches. And that is precisely what other forensic identification sciences such as odontology could do.[20] Unfortunately, forensic dentists have not yet gathered the data to perform these calculations and so their opinions and testimony cannot give such information to factfinders. Thus, while it is true that we could calculate the necessary probabilities based on "missing teeth, pattern of rotation, angulation or position of each tooth . . . if the frequency of certain positions is known for the general population,"[21] the unfortunate state of affairs is that obtaining those frequencies has not yet been accomplished by the field of forensic odontology.

In practice, then, forensic dentists have no choice but to fall back on intuition about frequencies and leaps of inference to reach their conclusions. The forensic

---

[17]§§ 6:10 to 6:12.

[18]Harold Cummins & Charles Midlo, Finger Prints, Palms and Soles: An Introduction to Dermatoglyphics (1943); Stoney, What Made Us Ever Think We Could Individualize Using Statistics, 31 J. Forensic Sci. Soc'y 197 (1991).

[19]"It is unfortunate that this approach carries the implication that a complete correspondence of two patterns might occur . . ." "it is impossible to offer decisive proof that no two fingerprints bear identical patterns." Harold Cummins & Charles Midlo, Finger Prints, Palms

and Soles: An Introduction to Dermatoglyphics (1943).

[20]Saks & Koehler, What DNA "Fingerprinting" Can Teach the Law About the Rest of Forensic Science, 13 Cardozo L. Rev. 361 (1991).

[21]David L. Faigman, David H. Kaye, Michael J. Saks & Joseph Sanders, Modern Scientific Evidence: The Law and Science of Expert Testimony, Identification from Bitemarks: The Scientific Questions: Uniqueness of the Human Dentition, § 24-2.1.1[1], 168 (1997).

dentist intuits the forensic weight (value) that various characteristics possess. The ABFO Workshop #4 data indicating a high false positive error rate may reflect an over-estimation of the individualizing value of various features. Not all bitemarks have the level of forensic value necessary to identify just one individual. Toolmark terminology was adopted early on by odontologists for discussing the types of dental features seen in bitemarks and the human dentition. A characteristic within a bitemark or in a person's dentition is a distinguishing feature, trait, or pattern. A class characteristic reflects a feature of generic value to a large population. Each human tooth has shape and position features common to the human species. Determining whether an injury is a human bitemark depends on these class characteristics being present in the injury.

Individual dental characteristics are said to be features that are unique to an individual variation within a defined group. The presence of worn, fractured or restored teeth is valued as unique features. If a bitemark possesses the reflection of such a feature, the degree of confidence in a match increases.[22] The odontological literature is silent regarding the frequency of these traits. It is actually rather counter-intuitive to assume enamel chips, fractures, and dental restorations are inherently unique. The shape of human teeth is quite constant in nature and their changes over time is based on common events. The chance occurrence of more than one person having a crooked front tooth is quite large. That is why orthodontists have such large practices.

A frequent refuge for the experienced bitemark expert is the belief that "[t]he controversy seems to hinge on how closely we look at the teeth and teeth marks."[23] This describes the odontologist's rule of thumb protection against false positive bitemark identifications. The weight given to a conclusion is based on the number of characteristics seen in the injury. Probability of a positive match is how many tooth marks are seen, not in the uniqueness value of each individual characteristic of either the defendant or the bitemark injury. Proof of uniqueness is unavailable in the scientific literature.

At the end of the day, the reliability of dental opinion historically is based on intuition derived from the expert's "experience," not scientific data. Likewise the forensic dentist's credibility with the judge or jury generally is based on factors present in the dentist's testimony other than underlying science. These factors include years of experience, demeanor on the witness stand, proper use of terminology, meticulous adherence to procedures (e.g., not forgetting to bring his/her notes), and the like.

## § 6:20  Introductory discussion of the scientific status of bitemark comparisons—Scientific literature on bitemark identification

A literature review on the subject of bitemark analysis was presented at the 2000 meeting of the American Academy of Forensic Science in Reno, Nevada.[1] This section gives an overview of the characteristics of and comments on certain seminal articles.

The material was derived from English language publications from 1960 to 1999.

---

[22]David L. Faigman, David H. Kaye, Michael J. Saks & Joseph Sanders, Modern Scientific Evidence: The Law and Science of Expert Testimony, Identification from Bitemarks: The Scientific Questions: Uniqueness of the Human Dentition, § 24-2.1.1[1], at 167 (1997).

[23]David L. Faigman, David H. Kaye, Michael J. Saks & Joseph Sanders, Modern Scientific Evidence: The Law and Science of Expert Testimony, Identification from Bitemarks: The

Scientific Questions: Uniqueness of the Human Dentition, § 24-2.1.1[1], at 167 (1997).

**[Section 6:20]**

[1]C. Michael Bowers & Iain A. Pretty, Critique of the Knowledge Base for Bitemark Analysis During the '60's, '70's and Early 80's, Invited address presented at Annual Meeting of the American Academy of Forensic Sciences, Odontology Section (2000).

The total number of articles was 120, which contained studies of empirical testing (15%), case reports (40%), technique studies (23%), commentaries (20%), and legal and literature reviews (32%). The 1970s brought out initial articles about bitemarks that were later used in the judicial system to justify the conclusion that bitemark analysis was scientific. The 1980s were the decade of greatest activity. The 90s should be considered the period where biochemical analysis of salivary DNA evidence arrived as the first independent means of confirming or invalidating bitemark opinions. Figure 4 shows the distribution of these papers by general type.

**Figure 4**

**The Bitemark Literature: Number of Publications in Various Categories (1960–1999).**

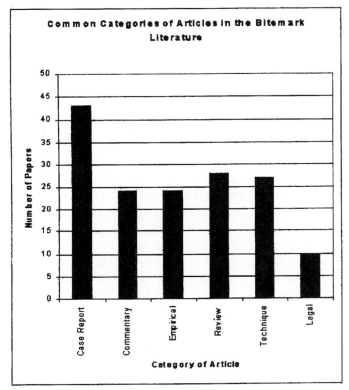

The first thing to note is the limited number of studies,[2] and the second is that only a small subset of these studies report scientific research.

The three scientific limitations and areas of controversy of bitemark analysis have been described earlier in §§ 6:14 to 6:17. The following subsections revisit these issues in relation to the literature obtained by this review.

Recent followup database searches were conducted using MedLine, ISI Web of Science, and Forensic Abstracts. The search, performed in 2003, produced a total of 1703 papers with 151 of these specifically related to bitemarks.

The earlier findings, that the vast majority of the articles were case reports, have not changed.

Very little new empirical evidence has been developed in the past several years.[3] This reflects the solo practice nature of the profession, limited training for scientific

---

[2]As a contrast, there were 1457 papers on forensic DNA during the same period of time.

[3]Pretty & Sweet, The Scientific Basis for Human Bitemark Analyses—A Critical Review,

inquiry, and limited access to scientific equipment. The use of authentic forensic materials for research is also limited, as the average bitemark caseload for individual practitioners has been found to be minimal. A recent study of 37 respondents with forensic training found that only one conducted more than 11 bitemark cases per year.[4]

The recent publications of note in peer reviewed journals have been discussed supra. The most recent published textbooks on forensic odontology and some of its methods are:

1. Digital Analysis of Bitemark Evidence Using Adobe Photoshop.[5]

   This CD-based technique book is the continuation of the 1st edition published in 2000. Simple digital methods are explained and the CD contains practice images for the reader to develop computer imaging skills.

2. C.M. Bowers, Forensic Dental Evidence: An Investigator's Handbook.[6]

   This 200 page book was written for non-dental readers. The contents outline the principles of recognition, collection and preservation of dental evidence seen in criminal and mass disaster investigations.

3. Robert Dorion, Bitemark Analysis.[7]

   This 600 page book is a compilation of contributors who discuss the history and forensic science basis of odontology, human identification from teeth, bitemark analysis, and legal issues in odontology.

### § 6:21    Introductory discussion of the scientific status of bitemark comparisons—Scientific literature on bitemark identification—The accuracy of skin as a record of bitemarks

The bulk of bitemark cases involve injuries on skin. This is not considered a good material on which to record the impression of the biter.[1] The literature shows, however, that the bulk of studies involve bitemarks in inanimate materials. Skin has considerable anatomical variation (e.g. breast tissue versus other locations) and also is affected by posture and movement at the time of biting. The 1971 study by DeVore[2] is the first of only two studies that describe and measured these factors. Figure 2 shows a replication of his simple test where inked stamps were applied at various body locations. In the figure, the lower stamp has been distorted by pressure applied at the bottom of the picture.

DeVore found both shrinkage and expansion of the skin at various positions on the body. The maximum distortion found was 60% expansion at one location. Such variability was seen that the author cautioned about the need to know the exact position of the body at the time of biting before attempting an analysis. This has been generally bypassed in actual practice due to the obvious difficulties in duplicating the dynamics of bitemarks occurring during homicides.

The second extant article on the mechanics of skin distortion appeared in 1974.[3] It reiterated the variable influence body position had on bitemarks in skin. An ad-

---

41 Sci. & Justice 85 (2001).

[4]McNamee & Sweet, Adherence of Forensic Odontologists to the ABFO Guidelines for Victim Evidence Collection, 48 J. Forensic Sci. 382 (2003).

[5]Raymond J. Johansen and C. Michael Bowers, Digital Analysis of Bitemark Evidence Using Adobe Photoshop, 2nd edition (2003) [Available from cmbowers@aol.com.]

[6]C. Michael Bowers, Forensic Dental Evidence (2004).

[7]Robert Dorion (ed.), Bitemark Evidence (2004).

**[Section 6:21]**

[1]Atsu, Gokdemir, Kedici & Ikyaz, Bite Marks in Forensic Odontology, 16 J. Forensic Odontostomatololgy 30 (1998); Stoddart, Bitemarks in Perishable Substances, 135 Brit. Dental J. 85 (1973).

[2]§§ 6:11 to 6:12.

[3]Barbanel & Evans, Bitemarks in Skin—Mechanical Factors, 14 J. Forensic Sci. Soc'y 235 (1974).

ditional revelation was the effect of healing over time on the shape of bitemarks. The researchers concluded that the changes in bitemark appearance are likely to become greater as the injury grows older. The article ended with the observation that because odontologists were "still ignorant . . . of the conditions during normal biting . . . considerable research is required" to fill that gap in knowledge.

A 1984 article by Rawson and Brooks[4] delineated a classification of breast shapes but provided no additional investigation of the actual distortion values associated with skin. They opined that "the nature of skin and its underlying structures are still of some concern and will probably be a major source of research interest during the next decade."[5]

The questions raised by these three articles remain unanswered. The lack of further research may be attributable to the difficulties of experimental design, issues regarding human research participants, funding, and training. The prevalence of judicial acceptance of bitemark evidence is ironic in light of the cautions expressed in the 1970s that have not been considered since.

## § 6:22 Introductory discussion of the scientific status of bitemark comparisons—Scientific literature on bitemark identification—Uniqueness of the human dentition

The introduction to this chapter indicated the context of dental identification of human remains, which uses the shape, type, and placement of dental restorations, root canals, and skeletal landmarks as features with individual characteristics. This identification technique has been validated and consistently produces accurate results as evidenced in mass disasters where even highly fragmented human remains may be identified dentally and later confirmed by other methods.[1]

Identification from bitemarks, however, is more problematic. It is founded on two postulates: (a) the dental features of the biting teeth (six upper and six lower teeth) are unique, and (b) these dental details can be transferred and recorded in the actual bitemark. These two postulates form the basis for bitemark admissibility as a forensic identification discipline. The overall "uniqueness" of dental characteristics is a common statement in court and in the anecdotal forensic literature. This conclusion is generally accepted though it has not been well tested by research, and it has been subject to considerable criticism.

As discussed earlier, it is impossible to prove uniqueness. It is also unnecessary. Most forensic dentists, however, rely on the unproved and unprovable assumption of uniqueness. The advantage of assuming uniqueness is that it excuses the field from quantitatively analyzing objective dental features seen in bitemarks and human teeth. Such analysis would permit the derivation of probabilities of coincidental matches in actual cases. The "probability of a match" choices now used by dentists in court are offered with no consideration of this vitally important determination, but instead are subjective estimates. Some day, forensic dentistry will follow the lead of DNA typing, forget about "uniqueness," and instead gather the necessary data and calculate the probabilities necessary to inform the factfinder. Indeed, the topic of uniqueness has to advance into the more useful question of coincidental matches, false positive identifications, and scientific proof of conclusions.

---

[4]§ 6:9.

[5]Barbanel & Evans, Bitemarks in Skin—Mechanical Factors, 14 J. Forensic Sci. Soc'y at 19 (1974).

**[Section 6:22]**

[1]The January 31, 2000, Alaska Air crash in Ventura, California, produced multiple positive identifications of victims via dental status, medical status, personal effects, tattoos, fingerprints, and DNA methods.

Still, the debate over the uniqueness of human teeth is an enduring forensic topic, fueled by a very few articles in the literature. The research that attempted to prove it (the three articles discussed below) explores this path to nowhere. The second and third of the articles are the most often cited as support for the uniqueness claim that forms the foundation of most bitemark opinions.

The first article to consider the statistical treatment of dental features appeared in 1974.[2] MacFarlane et al. studied plaster casts of 200 clinic patients. They developed two categories of features: (a) positive traits were physical shapes and rotations of teeth and (b) negative traits were an absence of teeth. The researchers subjectively inspected the plaster casts and attempted to establish base rates of occurrence of four positive dental features. These features are commonly seen in humans and consisted of (1) the number of teeth and their shapes, (2) any restorations in a front tooth, (3) shape of the jaw, and (4) rotated teeth.

The authors failed to indicate if any of these four features occurred independently of one another, and did not publish their table of results. They used the product rule to establish the likelihood of all four features occurring together and arrived at the value of eight in 100,000 people having teeth who could match a particular dental profile—an over-estimation of improbability due to the apparent violation of the product rule's assumption of independence. This figure was introduced in a later trial to much debate and eventual judicial rejection of this statistical method.[3]

The authors evidently reviewed their data and commented that some dental traits appeared to occur randomly in their study while tooth rotation and other traits were dependent. They edited their final conclusions because of this and reduced the frequency values by a factor of four for the dependent dental traits.[4] They did not claim to have confirmed the individuality of human teeth and did not relate bitemarks to their findings.

A study of five sets of identical twins was published in 1982.[5] Although the article stated that efforts were taken to standardize the production of the test bite exemplars, no details are provided. The paper concluded that the dentitions of each pair of twins could be distinguished. The authors went on to extrapolate these findings to the general human population. The fundamental flaw in the essential logic of this approach has been discussed earlier.[6] From a more practical bitemark casework viewpoint, the study is irrelevant to bitemark analysis on skin.

Rawson and Ommen's 1984 study[7] accepted 384 bitemarks in wax from 1200 submitted by contributing dentists. Selection criteria for this subset of the larger sample were not reported. Radiographic prints of the bites were created and then hand traced to produce the outline of the original teeth. This method is not the most accurate, according to a later comparison study.[8]

Several elements of tooth position were then established. It was determined that the minimum number of positions that a tooth can occupy is 150 and the greatest is 239.9. Each tooth's (x, y) coordinate on a graph was multiplied to obtain these values.[9] The authors commented that only five teeth would be necessary for a positive identification (match) of one person from the entire world's population.

---

[2]§§ 6:11 to 6:12.

[3]*State v. Garrison*, 120 Ariz. 255, 585 P.2d 563 (1978).

[4]This important limitation was overlooked by Rawson & Ommen, Statistical Evidence for the Individuality of the Human Dentition, 29 J. Forensic Sci. 245 (1984).

[5]Sognnaes & Rawson, Computer Comparison of Bitemark Patterns in Identical Twins, 105 J. Am. Dental Assoc. 449 (1982).

[6]§ 6:19.

[7]§ 6:13.

[8]Sweet & Bowers, Accuracy of Bitemark Overlays: A Comparison of Five Common Methods to Produce Exemplars from a Suspect's Dentition, 43 J. Forensic Sci. at 366 (1998). Resolution of the radiographic and hand traced methods are not optimal methods for reproducing images of teeth.

[9]Although the article as published actually gives this value as $1.4 \times 10^{14}$, and in fact gives

Present in this study was the notable use of the product rule. Again, the independence of the dental features examined was not established. But, even if the calculations were correctly based on independent attributes, the notion that if the world population is smaller than the denominator of the fraction produced by the product rule it is thereby proved that no two people on earth can have the same dental profile, is mistaken. This misconstrues the nature of probability. To believe such a conclusion requires us to assume that God (or Mother Nature)—for some unfathomable reason—gives out only one combination of traits to a customer. The error of this assumption is most easily explained with an illustration.[10] Suppose we have a lottery ticket machine that can produce 1000 differently numbered tickets. On any given push of the button it will print a ticket numbered at random somewhere between 000 and 999. And suppose we print out 10 tickets. There are, therefore, one hundred times as many numbers that can be printed as there are tickets actually printed. What law of nature or mathematics requires that each of those 10 tickets has to be different? The fact is that there is no reason the machine could not print duplicates when drawing at random from its pool of numerical possibilities. The probability of duplication is certainly low (and we can calculate how low), but it is by no means impossible. Consider a different example: There is one chance in 600 billion of any given bridge hand being dealt. Is there any reason to believe that a given hand cannot be dealt again in the next game? Or that it must wait to happen until the other 599,999,999,999 other hands have been dealt? Of course not. Decks of cards, lottery machines and gene pools have no memory for what they did a moment ago.[11]

In present light, this study does confirm that significant variability exists in the human dentition, but not that every person's dentition is distinguishable from every other person's. Although the article argued only that the human population is unique, the paper often is cited as standing for the more dubious proposition of uniqueness of *bitemarks*. But as Rawson & Ommen commented in their article: "[The question is] whether there is a representation of that uniqueness in the mark found on the skin or other inanimate object."[12]

The survey of dentists[13] asked respondents a number of questions relating to the question of dental uniqueness. Ninety-one percent of the forensic dentists questioned believed that the human dentition was unique, with only 1% stating that it was not, and 8% were unsure. No evidence from well-designed studies can be found to support such a belief. Seventy-eight percent believed that this uniqueness was replicated on human skin during the biting process. Eleven percent believed not, and 11% were unsure. Ninety-six percent of ABFO Diplomates in this survey stated that the human dentition was both unique and accurately registered on human skin during the biting process. When questioned about the product rule[14] and its application in the determination of dental uniqueness, 60% of the respondents did not

---

similar values for all of its reported probabilities, because probability can take on values only between 0 and 1, we are surmising that the quoted number is actually intended to be raised to a negative power.

[10]See Saks, Merlin and Solomon: Lesson's from the Law's Formative Encounters with Forensic Identification Science, 49 Hastings L.J. 1069 (1998).

[11]So long as the deck is kept complete throughout the process (sampling with replacement).

[12]Rawson & Ommen, Statistical Evidence for the Individuality of the Human Dentition, 29 J.

Forensic Sci. at 252 (1984).

[13]McNamee & Sweet, Adherence of Forensic Odontologists to the ABFO Guidelines for Victim Evidence Collection, 48 J. Forensic Sci. 382 (2003). This online survey received responses from forensic odontologists (experienced in actual casework). Fifty-four additional respondents had no bitemark experience. Thirty-eight percent of the respondents were ABFO Diplomates; 3% Fellows (senior level) of the American Academy of Forensic Sciences (AAFS); 33% were AAFS Members (middle level); 24% were American Society of Forensic Odontology members.

[14]See § 6:19 for a dscussion of the erroneous use of probability theory in the bitemark litera-

know what the product rule was, 22% thought that its use was justified, 9% believed that it should not be used, and 9% were unsure.

Responses regarding the validity of biter identification revealed that the mainstream opinions varied. Seventy percent believed one person alone (to the exclusion of all others) could be identified via a bitemark comparison with teeth. Five percent said it was not possible to identify a biter. Twenty-five percent said it could be done in certain circumstances.

### § 6:23 Introductory discussion of the scientific status of bitemark comparisons—Scientific literature on bitemark identification— Analytical techniques

Empirical testing of methods is an essential basis for confidence in forensic procedures. Bitemark analysis is no exception. The wide variety of comparison techniques allowed by the ABFO is not based on thorough testing to find which are the most accurate. The array of photographic methods, bitemark and suspect exemplar production, and comparison methods are largely unsupported by individual testing and validity testing. The common ground for most dentists, however, is the placement of transparent overlays of the suspect's teeth onto the image of the bitemark. The typical odontologist uses methods that are readily accessible in a dental office. This is mirrored by the technique descriptions and case reports seen in the literature. Occasionally, complex imaging systems are used (e.g., a CT scan to reproduce cross sections of dental casts that give the dentist a look at tooth shape along the length of teeth, or a scanning electron microscope to magnify a single tooth mark), but these are used relatively rarely.

The article by Sweet and Bowers,[1] discussed previously, is the sole example of testing the relative accuracy of different transparent overlay methods. See Table 3. Xerographic and radiographic methods are the ones most commonly used in the literature. This study concluded that the fabrication methods that utilized the subjective process of hand tracing should be discontinued as being the least accurate. It did not correlate any method's advantage or disadvantage in actual bitemark comparisons.

As a number of legal commentators have observed, bitemark analysis has never passed through the rigorous scientific examination that is common to most normal sciences.[2] The literature does not go far in disputing that claim. Definitive research in these areas remains for the future.

What method of comparison is most accurate remains an unanswered question. Although the American Board of Forensic Odontology (ABFO) has reported advice and guidance on many aspects of collecting bitemark evidence and terminology, the underlying question of what is the best comparison technique to use has not been addressed. This reluctance to establish a stricter protocol persists. The sole validity study of the most commonly used procedures recommended digital analysis.[3] Despite those findings, a review of the proceedings of the American Academy of Forensic Sciences since 1998 suggests that different techniques remain in use.

A recent review by the ABFO produced slight modification of the ABFO Bitemark Methodology Guidelines (see Appendices A, B, and C). The removal of the ability to identify just one person as the source of a bitemark was not supported by the Bitemark Committee tasked with summarizing suggested changes to the Guidelines.

---

ture.

[Section 6:23]

[1]§ 6:10.

[2]Zarkowski, Bite Mark Evidence: Its Worth in the Eyes of the Expert, 1 J. L. & Ethics in

Dentistry 17 (1988).

[3]Sweet & Bowers, Accuracy of Bitemark Overlays: A Comparison of Five Common Methods to Produce Exemplars from a Suspect's Dentition, 43 J. Forensic Sci. 43 (1998).

Apparently, only a minority of the review committee members agreed to this admonition. The determination of the "weight" of a bitemark comparison or how to support an analytical result using the ABFO approved methods is not discussed. The suggested methods section to the Guidelines was changed from the previous version in the following ways:[4]

*DNA Swabs from Skin.* DNA collection from a victim's skin was amplified with more scientific explanations.

*Dental Cast Exemplars.* No change was made to the section involving methods of creating dental exemplars of suspects. The current recommendations disregard primary research that shows computer generated overlays to be the most accurate method.[5] Dental exemplars may be made by the following means:[6]

   a.  Computer generated overlays.

   b.  Tracings from dental casts.

   c.  Radiographs created from radio-opaque material applied to the wax bite.

   d.  Images of casts printed on transparency film.

*Comparison of Dental Exemplars to Bitemark Injuries.* These methods continue to stress the use of dental exemplars (overlays) which are superimposed onto life-size images of the skin injury. Bitemark and dental comparison methods considered reliable by the ABFO notably show the absence of the "direct" comparison of dental study models onto the skin of a victim. This method was in vogue for decades and was utilized in a number of cases where DNA later exonerated the defendants after conviction. The methods recommended are as follows:

   1.  Exemplars of the dentition are compared to corresponding-sized photos of the bite pattern.

   2.  Dental casts to life-sized photographs, casts of the bite patterns, reproductions of the pattern when in inanimate objects, or resected tissue.

The methods to achieve a final determination using the ABFO accepted five levels of certainty (i.e. medical certainty, probable certainty, possible certainty, exclude, or insufficient data) regarding a bitemark/suspect "match" or "mismatch" are not discussed in the document.

### § 6:24 Introductory discussion of the scientific status of bitemark comparisons—Technical advancements

As explained earlier, the basis of many dental opinions (both in the identification of bodies and in bitemark analysis) is the direct superimposition of Questioned (Q) and Known (K) samples that have sufficient identification value to demonstrate features of common origin or establish an exclusionary result. These direct analysis methods demand rigorous attention to scale dimensions and the detection of photographic distortion, be they radiographs, photographic slides, negatives, or prints, or digital images. These dental techniques are generally analogous to the physical comparison of Q and K evidence in fingerprint, firearms, and toolmark studies.

The process of comparing the Questioned (Q) evidence to the Known (K) evidence is controlled by the ABFO Bitemark Standards and Guidelines. What is evident in the literature and in court is that dentists tend to adopt a method that their professional acquaintances use. Previous articles had talked about the use of digital methods. Sweet and Bowers used a desktop computer and an imaging program

---

[4]ABFO Bitemark Guidelines and Standards, 2006. [Available from www.abfo.org].

[5]Sweet and Bowers, Accuracy of Bite Mark Overlays: A Comparison of Five Common Methods

To Produce Exemplars From a Suspect's Dentition, 43 J. Forensic Sci. 1050 (1998).

[6]ABFO Bitemark Guidelines and Standards, 2006.

called Adobe® Photoshop® to create a transparent *overlay* of the biting perimeters of the teeth (obtained by scanning the dental casts). To review, the older methods included handtracing the tooth perimeters on clear acetate, Xeroxing the dental casts and then tracing the perimeters onto acetate, pushing the dental cast teeth into wax, and the use of X-ray film to capture the teeth impression which had been filled with metallic powder. The following section explains a computer method for bitemark comparison that contains tools which allow for greater control of the bitemark evidence and comparison analysis.

### § 6:25  Introductory discussion of the scientific status of bitemark comparisons—Technical advancements—Digital analysis

Identification disciplines often have the criminalist using a comparison microscope to place the Q and K evidence samples side by side. The loops, whorls, striations, indentations, accidental, and class characteristics present in the evidence samples may then be visually compared. What are difficult to assess, however, in both the crime laboratory and the dental laboratory, are the dimensional parameters of the evidence samples. In dentistry, the traditional ruler and protractor measurements and shape comparison processes are manually derived from evidence photographs and plaster casts of a suspect's teeth. These methods can vary among examiners and are therefore somewhat subjective in nature. Alternatively, some crime lab analysts ignore size comparisons and focus on similarities in class and individual features. In both situations, the possibility of error arises from examiner-subjective methods and partial selection of the total physical information available. Additional tools and protocols clearly are needed. The advent of digital technology has provided an opportunity to greatly improve the quality of comparative analyses. Working in digital format has become commonplace due to its many advantages:

- speed with which digital information can be sent (almost instantaneously)
- large amounts of digital information can be stored in a very small space
- digital images can be enhanced quickly and easily
- chain of custody issues are easily handled with digitization
- digital information can easily be duplicated and shared worldwide
- handling of digital information has proven to be very reliable
- standardization of procedures is simplified

There is no reason why forensic evaluation of dental evidence cannot avail itself of these same advantages.

The recent development of readily available digital imaging software (e.g., Adobe® Photoshop®) and image capture devices such as scanners and digital cameras have created an opportunity to allow the dentist to turn the computer monitor into a comparison microscope with the added benefit of the following functions:

- accurate means of measuring physical parameters of crime scene evidence
- correction of common photographic distortion and size discrepancies
- help eliminate examiner subjectivity—better control of image visualization—standardization of comparison procedures
- reproducibility of results between separate examiners
- electronic transmission and archiving of image data
- fabricate exemplars of the evidence and comparison techniques
- accurately demonstrate these exemplars to the trier of fact

Figure 5 shows the background image of a bitemark on pig skin. The "compound overlay" is a digitally captured exemplar of the biter's lower front teeth. The detail present in this experimentally produced comparison shows a high degree of concordance between the exemplars and the injury.

## Figure 5
### Digital Image Showing Relationship Between Underlying Bite Mark and Computer Generated Exemplar of the Biter's Lower Six Teeth.

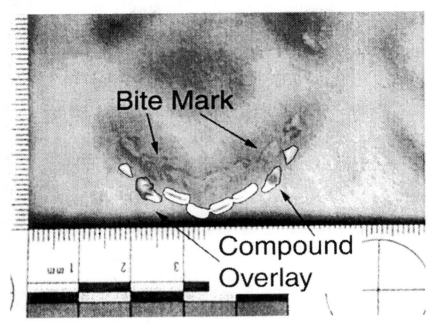

### § 6:26 Introductory discussion of the scientific status of bitemark comparisons—Technical advancements—DNA and bitemark analysis

Bitemarks have been considered possible sources of serological information since the 1970s. Swabbing of the bitemark area is considered a primary step in evidence collection, and the availability of DNA profiling of the biter's saliva has created a connection between these two areas of forensic identification.

The use of salivary DNA to analyze bitemarks is a highly objective system and offers a solution to some of the difficulties surrounding physical comparisons. However, the techniques are expensive and are subject to a number of variables: (1) failure to collect DNA; (2) ability to recover sufficient DNA; and (3) degradation of DNA from environmental factors.

An audit[1] of bitemark cases of practicing dentists found that: (1) only 18% of cases involved more than one bitemark suspect; (2) in 73% of cases the only physical evidence available was the bitemark; (3) 84% of the crimes were rated as serious assaults or higher; and (4) DNA was not involved in any of these actual cases.

But when DNA results are pending in a bitemark case, the optimum protocol is to maintain a separation between the two efforts (physical matching and DNA analysis). The literature suggests that the investigation of evidence be independent of extraneous information to prevent either intentional or expectational bias.[2] Knowing that the suspect was caught crawling through the window should not add weight to an otherwise inconclusive bitemark (or an ambiguous autorad). Knowing that the suspect's DNA matched should not add weight to an otherwise inconclusive bitemark (or vice versa). The judicial consumer of expert testimony and opinion has a right to expect odontological testing to be independent and blind to other expert conclusions.

Recent odontological studies indicate that the methods currently in use are most reliable either to exclude (exonerate) or to include (e.g., one of a group of persons who all would match the questioned bite about equally well) suspects.[3]

However, the odontological community sets no limits that restrict bitemark evidence to these two opinions. Seventy-two U.S. odontologists, 38% of whom were ABFO Diplomates, were asked if bitemarks should be used only to exclude suspects. Twenty-two percent of all respondents stated "yes," though only 6% of diplomates expressed this view.[4]

### § 6:27 Introductory discussion of the scientific status of bitemark comparisons—Technical advancements—Casework involving both DNA and bitemark evidence

Casework involving both forensic dentistry and molecular biology is increasing. Biological and toothmark evidence, when recovered from the same crime scene, will result in parallel analyses. This section reviews three recently reported instances where both forensic dentistry and molecular biology became intertwined due to the nature of evidence found at the crime scenes. This evidence may be derived from a common origin such as a bitemark on skin which possesses trace amounts of saliva,

---

[Section 6:26]

[1]Pretty, A Web-based Survey of Odontologists' Opinions Concerning Bitemark Analyses, 48 J. Forensic Sci. 1117 (2003).

[2]Nordby, Can We Believe What We See, If We See What We Believe?—Expert Disagreement, 37 J. Forensic Sci. 1115 (1992).

[3]Pretty & Sweet, Digital bitemark Overlays—An Analysis of Effectiveness, 46 J. Forensic Sci. 1385 (2001). This statistical analysis of four different dentist groups indicated "weak inter-examiner reliability" as an explanation to the contradictory opinions of bitemark experts. See also, Arheart & Pretty, Results of the 4th ABFO Workshop—1999, 124 Forensic Sci. Int'l 104 (2001).

[4]§ 6:6.

blood, or semen from the perpetrator. Similarly, an inanimate object connected to the scene might possess toothmarks and biological material that will be compared to physical and genetic data developed from a suspect.

In *State v. White*,[1] a murder victim had been bound and gagged with commercially available duct tape. Marks of five upper teeth were clearly evident on the surface of the duct tape along with the impressions of the lower front teeth showing on the inner cardboard spool. They were presumably made by the assailant using his teeth to tear the tape. A forensic odontologist was retained by the prosecution to compare the pattern in the tape to a suspect's teeth. The suspect had two fractured upper front teeth that compared favorably in size and position to the marks on the tape. Direct physical comparison and a video superimposition of the suspect's dental models were made with a duplicated model of the marks on the tape. The odontology report concluded, with a high degree of confidence, that the suspect's teeth made the indentations in the tape. Prior to the odontologist's analysis, the questioned tape had been swabbed and genomic DNA was obtained and profiled. A DNA report was submitted after the odontological result had been established. The DNA analysis confirmed the odontological findings by concluding that the suspect's salivary DNA was on the duct tape. The odontologist did not become aware of the availability of DNA evidence until after the trial.

In *State v. Brenner*,[2] a total of 22 cigarette butts were recovered from a crime scene as part of a homicide investigation. Small folds were noticed at the end of two filter tips that strongly suggested they were created by the edges of two teeth. The prosecution forensic odontologist opined that a suspect could have made the bitemarks on the filters. The defense odontologist analyzed the same evidence and excluded the suspect. PCR analysis was then performed on saliva recovered from the filter material, and DNA typing eliminated the suspect as the source of DNA on the filtertip.

In *Regina v. Driver*,[3] a murder victim had been sexually assaulted and bitten on her right breast. The body was recovered after being submerged for approximately eight hours in fresh water. A forensic odontologist recorded the bitemark injury and collected salivary DNA from the injury. Additional swabs were taken according to the normal sexual assault protocol established by the pathologist. Once a suspect had been apprehended, the odontologist performed a detailed physical comparison of the bitemark and the suspect's dentition. His conclusion indicated a probable connection between the suspect and the victim's bitemark injury. Later, PCR analysis of genomic DNA obtained from the saliva swabs was performed at a separate laboratory. The results indicated the suspect was the source of the questioned DNA.

The impact of DNA analysis in all three cases underscores the persuasiveness of results when both techniques agree. The possibility of a conflict of results also exists.

## §6:28 Areas of scientific agreement

Although the field of forensic dentistry is continually at odds over the reliability of bitemark identification conclusions, it has reached consensus on important questions of evidence collection procedure. The areas of agreement regarding these

---

**[Section 6:27]**

[1]*State v. Wesley White*, No. 5941815-3 (Contra Costa County, Cal., Sup. Ct., 1998) (suspect convicted of second degree murder).

[2]*State v. Brenner*, No. FMB01563 (San Bernardino County, Cal., Muni. Ct., East Desert District, Jan.1998), No. 099502556 (San Bernardino Coroner's Case, Jan.1998) (regarding the homicide, case dismissed before trial).

[3]*Regina v. Terry Grant Michael Driver* (Provincial Court, Abbotsford, BC. Canada, Oct. 14, 1995) (defendant convicted of second degree murder).

methods are broadly outlined in the ABFO Guidelines and Standards.[1] Refer to Appendices for details regarding these topics.

## § 6:29   Areas of scientific agreement—Evidence collection

The American Board of Forensic Odontology has well accepted protocols on the collection of evidence from both bite suspects and victims. Prior to their inception in 1988, the literature and other forensic organizations had not produced comprehensive measures on these subjects. The American Society of Forensic Odontology has a 20-year history of publishing manuals that were collaborative collections of articles on the breadth of odontology. It should be noted that the 33 contributors to the most recent version[1] all are diplomates of the ABFO. The creative process has been by agreement of the parties and, with the exception of photographic methods and techniques involving dental materials, has not been supported by extensive experimental testing. The process of judicial acceptance of this evidence, however, has developed an appellate history that supports these published ABFO protocols and even unaffiliated forensic dentists follow the concepts.

The collection of bitemark evidence is not solely the realm of dentists. This is particularly the case regarding photographic documentation. Police technicians and forensic pathologists may initially collect the evidence for later evaluation by an odontologist. Errors or omissions of certain procedures, such as specialized casting of a three dimensional bitemark, the proper excision and preservation of tissue, and collection of DNA evidence, generally result in the permanent loss of information. The weight of these transgressions are commonly debated in court.

## § 6:30   Areas of scientific agreement—Evidence collection—From the victim

The collection of bitemark evidence starts with photographic documentation.[1] This may just be a preliminary recording of the general anatomical location of the bitemark. The collection of possible DNA evidence from deposited saliva or blood must take place before any attempts are made to make the bitemark "cleaner" or otherwise more photographically acceptable. The swabbing done for salivary DNA is simple and should always be performed. The opportunity may never occur again.

Photography continues afterwards. Bitemark analysis demands that a scale or linear measuring device be placed adjacent to the bitemark[2] and parallel to the skin surface and the camera. Color film and black and white film are considered usual modes of photography. Adjunctive modes of digital, videotape, ultraviolet and alternative photography also are permitted.

The impression or casting of the bitemark completes the process. This is omitted if there are no discernible three-dimensional features seen in the bitemark. Dental materials are used throughout this process, which is both time consuming and demands particular attention to distortion control. The impressions are then used to

---

**[Section 6:28]**

[1]C. Michael Bowers & Gary Bell (eds.), Manual of Forensic Odontology at 337 (3rd ed. 2001).

**[Section 6:29]**

[1]C. Michael Bowers & Gary Bell (eds.), Manual of Forensic Odontology at 337 (3rd ed. 2001).

**[Section 6:30]**

[1]On the general subject of obtaining evi-

dence from victims, see Appendix 36A to this chapter, ABFO Guidelines on Methods to Preserve Bitemark Evidence.

[2]The ABFO No. 2 (Lightning Powder Co., Salem, Oregon) ruler is preferred due to its L-shape and circular reference targets that indicate the proper alignment of the camera to the evidence. These targets allow the image to be rectified and then properly resized to 1:1 (life-size) if there is off-angle distortion present in the original photograph.

create dental stone casts of the tissue surface. The availability of these models al-lows the odontologist to discern indentations created by specific teeth. Tissue re-moval may then occur in special circumstances and through specific methods that create a rigid framework to minimize later shrinkage of the skin. The sub-surface tissue may contain bruising that reveals additional information. The decision to dis-sect is made by the pathologist or medico-legal authorities.

## § 6:31 Areas of scientific agreement—Evidence collection—From the suspect

Properly written and signed consent of the individual suspect or an explicit war-rant must be obtained prior to collection.[1] This aspect of evidence collection focuses on the visual dental examination, intraoral photography and dental impressions. The use of a scale in appropriate photographs is also expected. It is prudent, but not an ABFO requirement, to examine the suspect for loose teeth, limited jaw opening, or abnormal chewing function. This last commonly is omitted in many odontology reports. The determination of jaw function is mandatory since the physical relation-ship of the upper and lower teeth in a bitemark must be determined to be anatomi-cally possible.

The suspect's DNA may be obtained during this exam. Swabbing of the oral tis-sues (inside of the cheek) derives a significant amount of cellular material.

## § 6:32 Areas of scientific agreement—Analysis and comparison of bitemarks

The general expectations are that odontologists see all the available evidence that is relevant to the bitemark case. Quite often this involves pre-trial discovery chal-lenges to ascertain: (1) just how much evidence (usually photographic) is available; and (2) full disclosure of the methods and overlay materials from the opposing expert.

The comparison methods that occur follow a standard pattern.[1] The bitemark is the background image that has a properly sized exemplar of the suspect's teeth placed over it. Attempts to standardize terminology are meant to control the varia-tions seen in expert expressions regarding the identification value of bitemarks. This being said, there are many versions of "acceptable" analyses and comparison methods. The attendant accuracy of each is up to the examiner to decide. The overlays showing the defendant's teeth can range from wax wafers to MRI images.

Agreement exists regarding the "exclusionary value" of bitemark evidence. If the dental characteristics in a bitemark do not have a spatial and/or shape similarity to a suspect, the expected result is an exclusion of the suspect. The other end of the spectrum is also seen, when odontolgists state that only one individual could have made a particular bitemark.

## § 6:33 Areas of scientific disagreement

The center point of disagreement amongst odontologists is the issue, "what is nec-essary to support a positive identification from a bitemark?" The odontological literature is silent on the sufficiency of evidence necessary to accomplish this task, yet this positive opinion is permitted to any dentist. Those odontologists who doubt

---

**[Section 6:31]**

[1]On the general subject of obtaining evi-dence from suspects, see Appendix 36B. ABFO Guidelines on Methods for the Collection of

Suspect Dentition.

**[Section 6:32]**

[1]See Appendix 36C, ABFO Guidelines on Methods of Comparing Bitemark Evidence.

the statement that "bitemarks are as powerful as fingerprints"[1] consider the positive identification of just one person to be quite rare and possible only when remarkable physical detail is present in a bitemark (usually *not* in skin).

The availability of probability theory as a bolster to bitemark identifications is a decades long practice. This flies in the face of aforementioned limitations to "uniqueness" determinations. This continues to be a highly controversial issue among forensic dentists.

The final, and most telling, major disagreement concerns the reliability of bitemark opinions. The proficiency results from the ABFO 4th Bitemark Workshop[2] seriously conflict with decades of assurances by odontologists that scientific reliability is possible and is in effect with bitemark analysis.

## § 6:34  Unresolved issues

What is the threshold quantum of information necessary to diagnose a skin injury as a human bitemark? The bitemark literature considers dental features seen in skin injuries or foodstuffs as "points," or uses synonyms to describe a physical finding pertaining to a tooth. This effort is rather vague since this "point" may be a complete tooth shape, a deeper bite injury showing more three-dimensional information, or only a portion of a tooth that is seen in the injury. The forensic identification value of each "point" is up to the individual dentist. It must be emphasized that many bitemark cases involve nothing more than bruising. The dental examiner must acknowledge that bruising generally creates an area of discoloration that exceeds the dimensions of the compared suspect teeth. The number of "points" necessary to conclude a human bitemark exists is not mandated in the ABFO Guidelines, and in fact is unknown. It is left to the subjective judgment of each examiner. This makes each bitemark case a potential argument between opposing dentists from the very beginning. In unfortunate cases, the question of "whether it is a human bitemark" can take place with the bitemark having been made by just one tooth—if it is a bitemark.

What is the probability that a random match has occurred between a suspect's teeth and a bitemark? The prosecution usually would like to argue that the risk of a coincidental match is so small that it can safely be ignored. The defense usually would like to argue that the risk of a coincidental match is too great not to be taken into account. But at present no one can answer this question in a scientific manner. Any assertion of a small chance is the realm of dentist judgment, even speculation.

How much detail is necessary in a bitemark analysis report?[1] Many experienced odonotologists prepare reports that contain limited and vague information, and which might later be modified at will by the odontologist, just before or even during trial.[2] The typical report contains a list of evidence (usually a single set of dental models of a suspect and bitemark photographs), possibly a copy of the overlay (if one has been used; it is not mandatory) of the suspect's teeth, and a statement regarding conclusions. Other odontologists are of the view that reports must contain specific details of the analyses, indicating exactly what the observations are and how they lead to the examiner's conclusions.

---

**[Section 6:33]**

[1]Ira A. Gladfelter, Dental Evidence: A Handbook for Police 23 (1975).

[2]§§ 6:11 to 6:12.

**[Section 6:34]**

[1]See Appendix 36D, ABFO Guidelines for Report Writing.

[2]Modifying conclusions or reports before or after they have been written in order to make the findings and conclusions more consistent with other evidence in the case is a practice specifically condemned by the Inspector General in the investigation of misconduct at the FBI Crime Laboratory. Office of the Inspector General, United States Department of Justice, The FBI Laboratory: An Investigation into Laboratory Practices and Alleged Misconduct in Explosives—Related and Other Cases (1997).

Proper documentation of image enhancements and color changes performed to evidence photographs. The permitted use of video and digital imaging creates the necessity for the examiner to quantify changes or "improvements" done to an image's color balance, brightness, contrast, and levels of hue and saturation. The lack of "before" and "after" values makes the duplication of another examiner's efforts problematic at best.

The amount of photographic distortion that precludes a bitemark analysis. It is common for dentists to receive evidence photographs from a bitemark case. This presents problems if the pictures have been taken improperly. A threshold requirement is that the bitemark be photographically reproduced in a manner that is free of controllable distortion. The literature well documents examples of less than accurate bitemark photographs. Among the common errors are: (1) the improper placement of a scale within the same plane of a bitemark, (2) the camera is not parallel to the plane of the bitemark and (3) the bitemark and the scale are not close enough to each other. The uncorrected acceptance of any of these factors means that the bitemark will not be properly sized and its shape will be distorted. This should preclude any final analysis with a suspect's teeth.

Estimates of the force necessary to create a particular injury. This is a common question from lawyers and an answer is unattainable. Another variation is "would this injury have caused pain?" Any answers are subjective as the literature is silent to both subjects.

Can a bitemark constitute "Deadly Force?" This is largely a legal question since the dental literature does not contain articles which describe someone dying from a bitemark. Communicable disease may be transmitted by a bite that breaks the skin.

The American Board of Forensic Odontology [ABFO] Guidelines and Standards for bitemark evidence were initiated in 1986[3] and have not been updated since 1995.[4] The Guidelines contain suggestions for the odontologist practicing bitemark analysis, but they lack science-based validation of suggested comparison protocols. Such validation, if achieved, would assure the accuracy of the permitted levels of confidence.[5] The intent of the document's originators was to promote uniformity of the investigative approach to bitemarks by odontologists. This has failed to materialize, since these guidelines are not sufficiently narrow in methodology to provide guidance in the analysis of bitemarks and suspect teeth. Recent discussion of the forensic dental community's adherence to certain Bitemark Guidelines and Standards has been favorable. This is limited, however, in that it related only to proper evidence collection methods.[6] The ABFO is silent about the best comparison method(s) that would improve accuracy in bitemark identification cases.

This lack of a standard protocol is an underlying reason that calibration of forensic dentists' methods and results is subject to continued debate and public

---

[3]American Board of Forensic Odontology, Inc., Guidelines for Bitemark Analysis, 112 J. Am. Dent. Ass'n 383 (1986).

[4]C. Michael Bowers & G. L. Bell, eds. Manual of Forensic Odontology (1995), at 334–357. The addition was report writing guidelines which were published in this technique manual for aspiring odontologists. They are purely voluntary in nature and are frequently ignored by practitioners.

[5]§ 6:11. Degrees of bitemark identification allowed are: virtual certainty, probable, possible, improbable, incompatible (exclusionary) and inconclusive.

[6]Pretty & Sweet, Adherence of Forensic Odontologits to the ABFO Bitemark Guidelines for Suspect Evidence Collection, 46 J. Forensic Sci. 1152 (2001). Two groups of forensic dentists (41 ABFO Diplomates and 28 non-ABFO dentists) were surveyed regarding types of dental impression materials they used and what forensic dental exam protocols they performed. There was little variation between the groups. It is notable that the original evidence collection was done by non-dentists in most active cases reported by these groups. This reflects law enforcement's role in recognizing, documenting and preserving this type of forensic evidence.

contradiction.[7] The caveat given to dentists in recent bitemark testimonials is for the evidence to be "good" before initiating a comparison to a suspect. But this remains no more than an "in the eye of the beholder" opinion for the odontologist rather than a substantive threshold having biological meaning and forensic identification value. Recent authors have confirmed the discipline's rationale that bitemark analysis is a qualitative process. They argue that it cannot be reinforced or restrained by statistical assurances of accuracy.[8]

Argument, pro and con, regarding the scientific underpinnings of bitemark identifications occasionally are superficially addressed in some trial courts. The commonly contested issue by opposing dentists, which then is typically given to the jury to resolve, is what denotes "good bitemark evidence"? The basis of this expert disagreement is, considering this author's casework, that some odontologists discuss tooth class characteristics seen in bitemarks as if they were individualizing (read: unique; one of a kind) characteristics.

Notwithstanding the occurrence of cases where DNA has shown flawed bitemark opinions leading to false convictions, the majority of the profession feels a positive identification of a given individual as a biter can be made with "reasonable doubt" not being an issue.

Research findings supporting pinpoint bitemark identification do not yet exist. This field of human identification can be considered to be in a state of flux. The recent bitemark literature contains two studies[9] that support limiting bitemark identification opinions to the more conservative categories. According to the survey mentioned above, the practitioners of the discipline (ABFO members) who adhere to the view of bitemark identification reliability outnumber the skeptics by about 3 to 1. Notable is that the non-ABFO dentists were of the view that bitemarks' usefulness is limited to including or excluding outnumber their ABFO brethren by 22% to 6%.[10]

## § 6:35  Future directions

A significant improvement of forensic education is mandatory. The bulk of U.S. forensic odontologists are self-trained products of seminars and week-long meetings. The interface between odontologists and academic programs involving pathology, criminalistics and forensic biology needs to deepen. The availability of forensic "cross-training" in these disciplines and the law would develop clearer understanding of law enforcement and the judiciary's slowly growing requirement of stringently validated protocols for methods and conclusions.

The future work of forensic odontology must focus on reliability testing of procedures, methods, and examiners. Testing the validity of such propositions as "everyone's teeth are unique" and "this bitemark shares the dental characteristics of one person in all the world" also are at the top of the list of future work the field

---

[7]*People v. Harold Hill*, Superior Court of Cook County (Illinois), PC 92CR8344 (post-conviction). This 1994 case resulted in conviction of two defendants for the sexual assault and homicide of a teenage girl. There were two possible bitemarks on the girl's body. The prosecution was heavily reinforced by an ABFO past president who stated he could positively (with medical/dental certainty) identify one defendant as a biter. He considered the other defendant as a possible biter. Appellate Counsel obtained DNA evidence in 2002 that exonerated both men. Also see *State v. Krone*, at § 6:7. Misidentification errors such as these have not yet been taken heed of by the forensic dentistry field.

[8]Kittleson, et al., Weighing Evidence: Quantitative Measures of the Importance of Bitemark Evidence, 20 J. Forensic Odontostomatol. 31 to 37 (December 2002).

[9]See, Arheart & Pretty, Results of the 4th ABFO Bitemark Workshop—1999, 124 Forensic Sci. Int'l 104 (2001). Pretty & Sweet, The Scientific Basis for Human Bitemark Analysis—A Critical Review, 41 Sci. & Justice 85 (2001).

[10]

Pretty, A Web-based Survey of Odontologists' Opinions Concerning Bitemark Analyses, 48 J. Forensic Sci. 1117 (2003).

must do. Population studies on the lines of what was accomplished in DNA typing would start to distinguish what is commonly seen in a dental profile and what features are seen less often. The assessment of independence among these features must also be undertaken.

The question of coincidental matches between a bitemark and an innocent person must be satisfied. The determinations of "likelihood ratios" to calculate the probability that one set of teeth in a bitemark could randomly match more than one person is an oft quoted wish. The confounding variables found in most bitemark patterns make experimental control that is necessary for these findings very difficult to achieve. The reality is that individualizing (only one person) dental characteristics seldom are seen in bitemarks.

A current belief exists that "the forensic dentist of today often is able to see matching characteristics that are difficult to demonstrate to other less experienced observers or jury member."[1] This axiom has apparently been gored by the ABFO Bitemark Workshop No. 4 where the findings suggest that experience has no relationship to the accuracy of bitemark opinions.

The following are several additional issues in bitemark analysis that are of some importance.

What is the threshold quantum of information necessary to diagnose a skin injury as a human bitemark? The bitemark literature considers dental features seen in skin injuries or foodstuffs as "points," or uses synonyms to describe a physical finding pertaining to a tooth mark. This effort is rather vague since this "point" may be a complete tooth shape, a deeper bite injury, or only a portion of a tooth. The forensic value of each "point" is up to the individual dentist. The number of "points" necessary to identify a human's bitemark is not mandated in the ABFO Guidelines and, in fact, is unknown. It is left to the subjective judgment of each examiner.

Considering the enormity of all these limitations, the future may contain a forensic revamping of bitemark analysis testimony where a positive identification is not allowed, but, rather, only a lesser opinion is admissible. On the other hand, if the testing methods of the forensic DNA community (the ability to calculate coincidental matches) can be imported into the odontological context, the future will be brighter.

---

**[Section 6:35]**

[1]David L. Faigman, David H. Kaye, Michael J. Saks & Joseph Sanders, Modern Scientific Evidence: The Law and Science of Expert Testimony, Identification from Bitemarks: Bite Mark Guidelines and Studies § 24-2.4.1, 181 (1997).

# APPENDIX 6A

# ABFO Bitemark Methodology Guidelines

July 2006 Updated ABFO Bitemark Standards and Guidelines

## History

This project is an update of the efforts begun at the first Bitemark workshop in 1984. This set of guidelines is not intended to invalidate the document generated as a result of previous workshops.

*Please read Bitemark Methodology with the following perspective:*

There is a need for forensic dentists to agree on basic methodology used in bitemark cases so as to maximize the quality, completeness, and validity of the collection and analysis of bitemark evidence. It is not expected that this document is ideal to all forensic dentists. However, it represents majority opinions and has the highest level of acceptance to the largest number of odontologists. All Diplomates (and other forensic odontologists) will have to make some compromises if the science of forensic odontology is to achieve the higher objective of universally agreeable methodology. There is no intention for the ABFO to mandate methods but instead to provide a list of generally accepted valid methods for this point in the development of our science. This document is not meant to stifle the development of new valid techniques that meet the criteria of the scientific method. There is every intention for the ABFO, as a credible body of experts, to present a clear and unified message as to what its members use and accept as valid methods for the collection and analysis of bitemark evidence. This document will present methods that have been agreed upon and approved as valid preservation and analysis procedures. In keeping with the commitment not to stifle the development of new methods, individuals should continue to develop new and possibly better techniques. These new techniques should be backed up by the use of accepted techniques and should satisfy the basic concepts of the scientific method.

*Please read Bitemark Terminology with the following perspective:*

Forensic dentists need to agree on language and terminology used in bitemark cases so as to avoid miscommunicating facts and opinions to attorneys, judges, juries and other dentists. This document represents majority opinion of ABFO Diplomates, and has the highest level of acceptance to the largest number of odontologists. **ALL** Diplomates (and other forensic odontologists) will have to make some compromises if the science of forensic odontology is to achieve the higher objective of universally agreeable communication.

There is no intention for the ABFO to mandate language as it is used within the body of a report or in testimony when responding to specific or hypothetical questions.

There is every intention for the ABFO, as a credible body of experts, to present a clear and unified message as to what its members mean when they state a conclusion. This document will present language that has been agreed upon and approved for communicating bitemark opinions.

## Bite mark vs. Bitemark

It is the feeling of the ABFO that the meaning of the word in any of its forms is clear and there is no need for the ABFO to endorse a particular form.

## Methods to Preserve Bitemark Evidence

General Considerations—It should be recognized that often the Forensic Odontologist is often involved in the initial examination and collection of the Bitemark evidence. This does not necessarily preclude the ability of the Forensic Odontologist to render a valid opinion. The below listed methods are not meant to be an all-encompassing list of preservation methods; however, it does list those methods that are used by the Diplomates of the ABFO. The use of other methods of documenting the Bitemark evidence should be in addition to these techniques.

Evidence collection will be done with appropriate authorization.

It should first be determined whether washing, contamination, lividity, embalming, decomposition, change of position, etc, have affected the bitemark.

A. Saliva Swabs of Bite Site
  - Aim — Acceptance of DNA evidence by the courts and the power of discrimination of current DNA testing has resulted in previous methods of salivary analysis, such as blood group antigens, being replaced by DNA methods. The aim of swabbing the bite site is now solely the collection of cells for DNA.
  - Jurisdiction — It is often unclear who is responsible to collect saliva evidence from the bite site. Since the odontologist is not usually the first to see the bite, others such as the medical examiner, coroner or police technologist might have already swabbed the area. It is the odontologist's responsibility to determine if swabs for DNA have been taken before he/she examines the site, and to take them if they were not previously recovered.
  - When — DNA degrades over time and in the presence of such things as UV light, seawater, extreme heat, acidic soil, skin decomposition, etc. Swabs should be taken as soon as possible after the bite is inflicted and before the area is cleaned or washed. If it can be determined that the bite was inflicted through clothing, attempts should be made to seize the clothing for DNA analysis.
  - Method — The double swab method will maximize the amount of DNA recovered. One swab that is moistened with sterile distilled water is used with medium pressure to wash the dried saliva from the surface over a period of 7–10 seconds. Within a few seconds of finishing with the first swab, a second swab that is dry is used as a sponge with light pressure to collect the moisture left on the surface by the first swab. The two swabs must be air-dried at room temperature prior to submission to the laboratory, or inserted into a sterile container that will allow air to circulate during storage.
  - Storage — The swabs should be submitted for analysis as soon as possible. They are kept at room temperature if submitted within 4–6 hours, or refrigerated (not frozen) if stored longer than 6 hours.
  - DNA Control Sample — A sample of the bite victim's DNA is usually collected by others for investigative purposes. This sample, usually whole blood or tissue, is also used for interpretation of DNA mixtures from the bite swabs. No other form of control sample from the victim is required to be taken by the odontologist.

B. Photographic Documentation of the Bite Site
  - The bite site should be photographed using digital and/or conventional photography. (Guidelines of the ABFO Digital Enhancement Committee will be followed)
  - The photographic procedures should be performed by the forensic odontolo-

gist or under the odontologist's direction to insure accurate and complete documentation of the bite site.

- Orientation and close-up photographs should be taken.
- Photographic resolution should be of high quality.
- Color print, and/or slide film, and black and white film may be used. If color film is used, accuracy of color balance should be assured.
- Photographs of the mark should be taken with and without a scale in place.
- When the scale is used, it should be on the same plane and adjacent to the bitemark. It presently appears desirable to include a circular reference in addition to a linear scale. (An ABFO No. 2 or an equivalent right-angle scale should be utilized).
- The most critical photographs should be taken in a manner that will eliminate distortion
- In the case of a living victim, it may be beneficial to obtain serial photographs of the bitemark
- Photographic filters, specialty film, alternate methods of illumination may be used to record the bite site *in addition to* unfiltered photographs.
- Video imaging may be used *in addition* to conventional and digital photography.

C. Impressions

- Impressions should be taken of the surface of the bitemark whenever it appears that this may provide useful information.
- The impression materials used should meet American Dental Association specifications and should be identified by name in the report.
- Suitable support should be provided for the impression material to accurately reproduce body contour.
- The material used to produce the case should accurately represent the area of impression and should be prepared according to the manufacturer's instructions.
- When a self-inflicted bite is possible, impressions of the individual's teeth should be made.
- Impressions of the bite site should be made when indicated.

D. Tissue Samples

- In the deceased, tissue specimens of the bitemark should be retained whenever it appears this may provide useful information. The bite site may be excised and preserved following proper stabilization prior to removal with appropriate approval.

# APPENDIX 6B

# Evidence Collection of Suspected Dentition

Before collecting evidence from the suspect, the odontologist should ascertain that the necessary search warrant, court order, or legal consent has been obtained, and should make a copy of this document part of his records. The court document or consent should be adequate to permit collection of the evidence listed below:

A. Dental Records

   Whenever possible the dental records of the individual should be obtained.

B. History

   Obtain history of any dental treatment subsequent to, or in proximity to, the date of bitemark.

C. Photography

   Whenever possible, good quality extraoral photographs should be taken, both full face and profile. Intraoral photographs preferably would include frontal view, two lateral views, occlusal view of each arch, and any additional photographs that may provide useful information. It is also useful to photograph the maximum interincisal opening with scale in place. If inanimate materials, such as foodstuffs, are used for test bites, the results should be preserved photographically.

   - Photographs of the dentition should be made by the forensic dentist or under the odontologist's direction.
   - A scale may be utilized during photography.
   - Video imaging may be used to document the dentition *in addition* to conventional and/or digital photography.

D. Extraoral Examination

   The extraoral examination should include observation and recording of significant soft and hard tissue factors that may influence biting dynamics, such as temporomandibular joint status, facial asymmetry, muscle tone and balance. Measurement of maximal opening of the mouth should be taken, noting any deviations in opening or closing, as well as any significant occlusal disharmonies. The presence of facial scars or evidence of surgery should be noted, as well as the presence of facial hair.

E. Intraoral Examination

   - In cases in which saliva evidence has been taken from the victim, saliva evidence should also be taken from the suspect in accordance with the specifications of the testing laboratory.
   - The tongue should be examined in reference to size and function. Any abnormality such as ankyloglossia should be noted.
   - The periodontal condition should be observed with particular reference to mobility and areas of inflammation or hypertrophy. In addition, if anterior teeth are missing or badly broken down it should be determined how long these conditions have existed.
   - It is recommended that, when feasible, a dental chart of the suspect's teeth be prepared, in order to encourage thorough study of the dentition.

F. Impressions

   Whenever feasible, at least two impressions should be taken of each arch, using materials that meet appropriate American Dental Association specifications and are prepared according to the manufacturer's recommendations, using accepted dental impression techniques. The interocclusal relationship should be recorded.

- Dental impressions should be made by the forensic dentist or under their supervision.

G. Sample Bites

Whenever feasible, sample bites should be made into an appropriate material, simulating the type of bite under study.

H. Study Casts

- Master casts should be prepared using American Dental Association approved Type II stone prepared according to manufacturer's specifications, using accepted dental techniques.
- Additional casts may be fabricated in appropriate materials for special studies. When additional models are required, they should be duplicated from master casts using accepted duplication procedures. Labeling should make it clear which master cast was utilized to produce a duplicate.
- The teeth and adjacent soft tissue areas of the master casts should not be altered by carving, trimming, marking, or other alterations.

I. Saliva Samples

- A DNA sample from the suspect is needed to enable comparison to any biological evidence at the crime scene that is thought to originate from the suspect. The best source of DNA evidence is whole blood, so usually others recover this suspect DNA sample under the provision of a warrant. There is currently no need for the odontologist to collect a saliva sample at the time of examination of the suspect.

## Standards for "Bitemark Analytical Methods"

1. All Diplomates of the American Board of Forensic Odontology are responsible for being familiar with the most common analytical methods and should utilize appropriate analytical methods.

2. A list of all the evidence analyzed and the specific analytical procedures should be included in the body of the final report. All available evidence associated with the bitemark must be reviewed prior to rendering an expert opinion.

3. Any new analytical methods not listed in the previously described list of analytical methods should be explained in the body of the report. New analytical methods should be scientifically sound and verifiable by other forensic experts. New analytical methods should, if possible, be substantiated with the use of one or more of the accepted techniques listed in these guidelines.

## Bitemark Analysis Guidelines

### Description of Bitemark

The odontologist should record and describe:

1. Identification Data (case number, agency, name of examiner(s), etc.)
2. Location of Bitemark
   - anatomical location or object bitten
   - surface contour: (e.g., flat, curved or irregular)
   - tissue characteristics
3. Shape, color, and size
4. Type of Injury (e.g., abrasion, contusion, avulsion)
5. Other Information as indicated (e.g., three-dimensional characteristics, unusual conditions, derived from excised tissue, transillumination).

# APPENDIX 6C

# Methods of Comparing Exemplars to Bitemarks

1. **Types of Overlays:**
   - Computer generated
   - Tracing from dental casts
   - Radiographs created from radiopaque material applied to the wax bite.
   - Images of casts printed on transparency film.
2. **Test Bites (wax, Styrofoam, clay, skin, etc.)**
3. **Comparison Techniques**
   - Exemplars of the dentition are compared to corresponding-sized photos of the bite pattern.
   - Dental casts to life-sized photographs, casts of the bite patterns, reproductions of the pattern when in inanimate objects, or resected tissue.
4. **Other Methods Employed For Analysis**
   - Transillumination of tissue
   - Computer enhancement and/or digitization of mark and/or teeth
   - Stereomicroscopy and/or macroscopy
   - Scanning Electron Microscopy
   - Video superimposition
   - histology
   - Metric studies

## ABFO Bitemark Terminology Guidelines

### Component Injuries Seen in Bitemarks

Abrasions (scrapes), contusions (bruises), lacerations (tears), ecchymosis, petechiae, avulsion, indentations (depressions), erythema (redness) and punctures might be seen in bitemarks. Their meaning and strict definitions are found in medical dictionaries and forensic medical texts and should not be altered. An incision is a cut made by a sharp instrument and, although mentioned in the bitemark literature, it is not an appropriate term to describe the lacerations made by incisors.

### A Characteristic

A *characteristic,* as applied to a bitemark, is a distinguishing feature, trait, or pattern within the mark. Characteristics are two types, *class characteristics* and *individual characteristics.*

*Class characteristic*: a feature, trait, or pattern that distinguishes a bitemark from other patterned injuries. For example, the finding of four approximating linear or rectangular contusions is a class characteristic of human incisors. Their dimensions vary in size depending upon what inflicted the injury: maxillary or mandibular teeth; and, whether primary or permanent teeth. Moreover, the overall size of the injury will vary depending on the contributor's arch dimension. Thus, a bitemark *class characteristic* identifies the group from which it originates: human, animal, fish, or other species.

*Individual characteristic*: a feature, trait, or pattern that represents an individual variation rather than an expected finding within a defined group. There are two types:

*Arch characteristic*: a pattern that represents tooth arrangement within a bitemark. For example, a combination of rotated teeth, buccal or lingual version, mesio-distal drifting, and horizontal alignment contribute to differentiation between individuals. The number, specificity, and accurate reproduction of these arch characteristics contribute to the overall assessment in determining the degree of confidence that a particular suspect made the bitemark (e.g., rotation, buccal or lingual version, mesial or distal drifting, horizontal alignment).

*Dental characteristic* is a feature or trait within a bitemark that represents an individual tooth variation. The number, specificity, and accurate reproduction of these dental characteristics in combination with the *arch characteristics* contribute to the overall assessment in determining the degree of confidence that a particular suspect made the bitemark (e.g., unusual wear pattern, notching, angulations, fracture).

## Distinctive — This term is variably defined as either rare or unusual.

- variation from normal, unusual, infrequent.
- not one of a kind but serves to differentiate from most others.
- highly specific, individualized.
- lesser degree of specificity than unique.

## Bitemark Definitions

*Bitemark*:

- A physical alteration in a medium caused by the contact of teeth.
- A representative pattern left in an object or tissue by the dental structures of an animal or human.

## Describing the Bitemark

A circular or oval (doughnut) (ring-shaped) patterned injury consisting of two opposing (facing) symmetrical, U-shaped arches separated at their bases by open spaces. Following the periphery of the arches are a series of individual abrasions, contusions, and/or lacerations reflecting the size, shape, arrangement, and distribution of the class characteristics of the contacting surfaces of the human dentition.

## Variations:

1. Additional features:
   - Central Ecchymosis (central contusion).
   - Linear Abrasions, Contusions or Striations
   - Double Bite—(bite within a bite)
   - Weave Patterns of interposed clothing.
   - Peripheral Ecchymosis
2. Partial Bitemarks
3. Indistinct/Faded Patterned Injury (e.g., fused or closed arches, solid ring pattern)
4. Multiple Bites.
5. Avulsive Bites.

## Terms Indicating Degree of Confidence That an Injury is a Bitemark:

*Bitemark* — Teeth created the pattern; other possibilities were considered and excluded.

- *criteria*: pattern conclusively illustrates a) classic features. b) all the characteristics, or c) typical class characteristics of dental arches and human teeth in proper arrangement so that it is recognizable as an impression of the human dentition.

*Suggestive* — The pattern is suggestive of a bitemark, but there is insufficient evidence to reach a definitive conclusion at this time.

- *criteria:* general shape and size are present but distinctive features such as tooth marks are missing, incomplete or distorted <u>or</u> a few marks resembling tooth marks are present but the arch configuration is missing.

*Not a bitemark* — Teeth did not create the pattern.

## Descriptions and Terms Used to Relate Bitemark to the Suspected Biter:

### Descriptors to indicate similarities between a bitemark and a person's dentition:

*Reasonable Dental / Medical Certainty* — beyond a reasonable doubt.

*Probable* — more likely than not.

*Exclusion* — ruled out.

*Inconclusive* — insufficient evidence to relate the bitemark to the suspected biter.

### ABFO Standards for "Bitemark Terminology"

The following list of Bitemark Terminology Standards has been accepted by the American Board of Forensic Odontology.

1. Terms assuring unconditional identification of a perpetrator, or without doubt, are not sanctioned as a final conclusion.

2. Terms used in a different manner from the recommended guidelines should be explained in the body of a report or in testimony.

3. All boarded forensic odontologists are responsible for being familiar with the standards set forth in this document.

# APPENDIX 6D

# ABFO Guidelines for Report Writing, Including Terminology

Both in the case of a living victim or deceased individual, the odontologist should determine and record certain vital information.

1. Demographics
   - Name of victim
   - Case Number
   - Date of examination
   - Referring agency
   - Person to contact
   - Age of victim
   - Race of victim
   - Sex of victim
   - Name of examiner(s)
2. Location of Bitemark
   - Describe anatomical location
   - Describe surface contour: flat, curved or irregular
   - Describe tissue characteristics
     - A. Underlying structure: bone, cartilage, muscle, fat
     - B. Skin: relatively fixed or mobile
3. Shape
   - The shape of the bitemark should be described; e.g. essentially round, ovoid, crescent, irregular, etc.
4. Color
   - The color should be noted; e.g. red, purple, etc.
5. Size
   - Vertical and horizontal dimensions of the bitemark should be noted, preferably in the metric system
6. Type of Injury
   - Petechial hemorrhage
   - Contusion (ecchymosis)
   - Abrasion
   - Laceration
   - Incision
   - Avulsion
   - Artifact
7. Other Information
   - It should be also be noted whether the skin surface is indented or smooth. At some point, the odontologist will evaluate the evidence to determine such things as position of maxillary and mandibular arches, location and position of individual teeth, intradental characteristics, etc. This may or many not be possible at the time of initial examination and will be covered below.

### Component Injuries Seen in Bitemarks

Abrasions (scrapes), contusions (bruises), lacerations (tears), ecchymosis, petechiae, avulsion, indentations (depressions), erythema (redness) and punctures might be seen in bitemarks. Their meaning and strict definitions are found in medical dictionaries and forensic medical texts and should not be altered. An incision is a cut made by a sharp instrument and, although mentioned in the Bitemark literature, it is not an appropriate term to describe the lacerations made by incisors.

The term *latent* injury or wound was preferred over occult or trace wound when referring to an injury which is not visible but can be brought out by special techniques.

### A Characteristic (as it pertains to Bitemarks)

A *characteristic,* as applied to a bitemark, is a distinguishing feature, trait or pattern within the mark. Characteristics are two types, *class characteristics* and *individual characteristics.*

*Class characteristic*: a feature, trait or pattern preferentially seen in, or reflective of, a given group. For example, the finding of linear or rectangular contusions at the midline of a Bitemark arch is a class characteristic of human incisor teeth. "Incisors" represent the class in this case. The value of identifying class characteristics is that, when seen, they enable us to identify the group from which they originate. For instance, the class characteristics of incisors (rectangles) differentiates them from canines (circles or triangles). If we define the class characteristics of human bites, we can differentiate them from animal bites. Via class characteristics, we differentiate the adult from the child bite or mandibular from maxillary arch. The original term "class characteristic" was applied to toolmarks and its definition has been modified to make it more applicable to bitemarks.

*Individual characteristic*: a feature, trait or pattern that represents an individual variation rather than an expected finding within a defined group. An example of this is a rotated tooth. The value of individual characteristics is that they differentiate between individuals and help identify the perpetrator. The number, specificity and accurate reproduction of these individual characteristics determine the confidence level that a particular suspect made the bitemark.

### Bitemark Definitions

*Bitemark*:

- A physical alteration in a medium caused by the contact of teeth.
- A representative pattern left in an object or tissue by the dental structures of an animal or human.

*Cutaneous Human Bitemark*:

- An injury in skin caused by contacting teeth (with or without the lips or tongue) which shows the representational pattern of the oral structures.

  ◆ **COMMENT:** These represent succinct, workable definitions. They lack 100% precision because they exclude the rare cases of denture markings and tooth contact marks without biting action. However, a definition that encompasses all possible tooth/mouth-to-medium contacts would be too cumbersome for practical application.

### Description of the Prototypical Human Bitemark

A circular or oval (doughnut) (ring-shaped) patterned injury consisting of two opposing (facing) symmetrical, U-shaped arches separated at their bases by open spaces. Following the periphery of the arches are a series of individual abrasions, contusions and/or lacerations reflecting the size, shape, arrangement and distribution of the class characteristics of the contacting surfaces of the human dentition.

### Variations of the Prototypical Bitemark

Variations include additions, subtractions and distortions.

1. Additional features:
   - Central Ecchymosis (central contusion)—when found, these are caused by two possible phenomena:
     - A) positive pressure from the closing of teeth with disruption of small vessels.
     - B) negative pressure caused by suction and tongue thrusting.
   - Linear Abrasions, Contusions or Striations—these represent marks made by either slipping of teeth against skin or by imprinting of the lingual surfaces of teeth. The term *drag marks* is in common usage to describe the movement between the teeth and the skin while *lingual markings* is an appropriate term when the anatomy of the lingual surfaces are identified. Other acceptable descriptive terms include radial or sunburst pattern.
   - Double Bite—a "bite within a bite" occurring when skin slips after an initial contact of the teeth and then the teeth contact again a second time.
   - Weave Patterns of interposed clothing.
   - Peripheral Ecchymosis—due to excessive, confluent bruising.
2. Partial Bitemarks:
   - one-arched (half bites).
   - one or few teeth.
   - unilateral (one-sided) marks—due to incomplete dentition, uneven pressure or skewed bite.
3. Indistinct/Faded Bitemarks:
   - Fused Arches—collective pressure of teeth leaves arched rings without showing individual tooth marks.
   - Solid—ring pattern is not apparent because erythema or contusion fills the entire center leaving a filled, discolored, circular mark.
   - Closed Arches—the maxillary and mandibular arch are not separate but joined at their edges.
   - Latent—seen only with special imaging techniques.
4. Superimposed or Multiple Bites.
5. Avulsive Bites.

◆ **COMMENT:** This list excludes variations caused by individual characteristics of the biter's teeth.

## Unique and Distinctive

*Unique:*

This term is variably defined as either one of a kind or rare and unusual. In its most conservative interpretation the following connotations apply:
- such distinctiveness that no other person could have made an identical pattern.
- to the point of persuasion of individuality.
- attributable to only one individual.
- unequaled.

To those who use a more liberal interpretation the following would apply:
- unusual.
- rare.

◆ **COMMENT:** Forensic odontologists should specify their meaning when they use the word unique.

*Distinctive:*

- variation from normal, unusual, infrequent.
- not one of a kind but serves to differentiate from most others.
- highly specific, individualized.
- lesser degree of specificity than unique.

◆ **COMMENT:** A consensus of odontologists indicated that in the hierarchy of the terminology, "unique" implies greater rarity than "distinctive".

## Terms Indicating Degree of Confidence That an Injury is a Bitemark

*Possible Bitemark*:

An injury showing a pattern that may or may not be caused by teeth; could be caused by other factors but biting cannot be ruled out.

- *criteria:* general shape and size are present but distinctive features such as tooth marks are missing, incomplete or distorted *or* a few marks resembling tooth marks are present but the arch configuration is missing.

*Probable Bitemark*:

The pattern strongly suggests or supports origin from teeth but could conceivably be caused by something else.

- *criteria:* pattern shows (some) (basic) (general) characteristics of teeth arranged around arches.

*Definite Bitemark*:

There is no reasonable doubt that teeth created the pattern; other possibilities were considered and excluded.

- *criteria:* pattern conclusively illustrates (classic features) (all the characteristics) (typical class characteristics) of dental arches and human teeth in proper arrangement so that it is recognizable as an impression of the human dentition.

◆ **COMMENT:** These terms are opinions, representing 3 zones of confidence and do not convey a statistical or mathematical measurement of precision. A lesser quality bitemark can be elevated to definite if multiple bitemarks are present or if amylase is positive (note: this is outdated since it ignores DNA evidence from saliva).

## Terms to Indicate That an Injury Represents a Bitemark

| *Ordinate Ranking of Terms* | *Connotation* |
|---|---|
| • definite | |
| • positively | no doubt in my mind it is a bitemark |
| • reasonable medical certainty | virtual certainty; |
| • highly probable | allows for the possibility of another cause, however remote |
| • probable | more likely than not |
| • possible | |

| *Ordinate Ranking of Terms* | *Connotation* |
|---|---|
| ● similar to | such a mark could have been produced |
| ● consistent with | by teeth but not necessarily and could |
| ● conceivable | have been created by something else, |
| ● may or may not be | no commitment to likelihood. |
| ● cannot be ruled out | |
| ● cannot be excluded | |
| ● unlikely | |
| ● inconsistent | less likely than not |
| ● improbable | |
| ● incompatible | no doubt in my mind it is not a bite-mark; |
| ● excluded | represents something else |
| ● impossible | |
| ● indeterminable | pattern shows insufficient |
| ● shouldn't be used | characterization to comment on teeth |
| ● insufficient | as a cause |

◆ **COMMENT:** The above ranked terms are to define the injury itself as opposed to the terms used to describe the degree of certainty that a particular set of teeth caused the wound. Please refer to the "Terms to indicate the Link Between Bitemark and the Suspect(s)" for acceptable terms used to describe the comparison opinion.

## Descriptions and Terms Used to Link a Bitemark to a Suspect

A Point, Concordant Point, Area of Comparison, Match, Consistent
*Point*:

- a singular unit or feature available for comparison or evaluation.
- an area attributable to a tooth.
- a way of counting features.

◆ **COMMENT:** This term is used as a convenience in reports to address specific components of the bitemark which are being compared to teeth. A point doesn't imply any degree of specificity and (is) not a characteristic.

*Concordant Point*:

- point seen in both the bitemark and the suspect(s)' exemplars.
- corresponding feature.
- comparable element.
- unit of similarity.
- matching point.

*Area of Comparison*:

- a dynamic or specific region to be compared.
- a complex or pattern made up of a conglomerate of several points or a group of features.

*Match*:

- nonspecific term indicating some degree of concordance between a single feature, combination of features or a whole case.

510

● an expression of similarity without stating degree of probability or specificity.

◆ **COMMENT:** This term "match" or "positive match" should not be used as a definitive expression of an opinion in a Bitemark case. The statement "It is a positive match" or "It is my opinion that the bitemark matches the suspect's teeth" will likely be interpreted by juries as tantamount to specific perpetrator identification when all the odontologist might mean is that a poorly-defined or nonspecific bitemark was generally similar to the suspect's teeth, as it might to a large percentage of the population.

*Consistent (compatible) With:*

● synonymous to "match," a similarity is present but specificity is unstated.

◆ **COMMENT:** If used to represent the odontologist's conclusion, the term "consistent with" should be explained in the report or testimony as indicating similarity but implying no degree of specificity to the match. This is necessitated by the fact that our survey showed that this term varied in meaning among odontologists to indicate everything from "possible" to "absolute certainty;" its message is unreliable. However, when used as proposed, it is an acceptable term for those odontologists who are reluctant to suggest culpability of a suspect.

*Possible Biter:*

● could have done it; may or may not have.
● teeth like the suspect's could be expected to create a mark like the one examined but so could other dentitions.
*criteria:* there is a nonspecific similarity or a similarity of class characteristics; match points are general and/or few, and there are no incompatible inconsistencies that would serve to exclude.

◆ **COMMENT:** This term is approximately synonymous with "consistent with" but has a more universally understandable meaning.

*Probable Biter:*

● suspect most likely made the bite; most people in the population could not leave such a mark.
*criteria:* bitemark shows some degree of specificity to the individual suspect's teeth by virtue of a sufficient number of concordant points including some corresponding individual characteristics. There is an absence of any unexplainable discrepancies.

*Reasonable Medical Certainty:*

● highest order of certainty that suspect made the bite.
● the investigator is confident that the suspect made the mark.
● perpetrator is identified for all practical and reasonable purposes by the bitemark.
● any expert with similar training and experience, evaluating the same evidence should come to the same conclusion of certainty.
● any other opinion would be unreasonable.
*criteria:* there is a concordance of sufficient distinctive, individual characteristics to confer (virtual) uniqueness within the population under consideration. There is absence of any unexplainable discrepancies.

◆ **COMMENT:** The term reasonable medical certainty conveys the connotation of virtual certainty or beyond reasonable doubt. The term deliberately avoids the message of unconditional certainty only in deference to the scientific maxim that one can never be absolutely positive unless everyone in the world was examined or the expert was an eye witness. The Board considers that a statement of absolute certainty such as "indeed, without a doubt", is unprovable and reckless. Reasonable medical certainty represents the highest order of confidence in a comparison. It is, however, acceptable to state that there is "no doubt in my mind" or "in my opinion, the suspect is the biter" when such statements are prompted in testimony.

## Degrees of Certainty Describing The *Link* Between the Bitemark and Suspect

| *Terms* | *Connotation* |
|---|---|
| • reasonable medical certainty<br>• extremely probable<br>• high degree of certainty | "virtual certainty; no reasonable or practical possibility that someone else did it" |
| • very probably<br>• probably<br>• most likely | "more likely than not" |
| • possible<br>• consistent (with) | "could be; may or may not be; can't be ruled out" |
| • can't exclude | |
| • improbable | "unlikely to be the biter" |
| • ruled out<br>• excluded<br>• exculpatory<br>• could not have; did not<br>• eliminated<br>• dissimilar<br>• no match; mismatch<br>• incompatible<br>• not of common origin | "not the biter" |
| • inadequate<br>• inconclusive<br>• insufficient | "insufficient quality/quantity/specificity of evidence to make any statement of relationship to the biter" |
| • evidence has no probative (forensic) value<br>• unsuitable (should not be used)<br>• non-contributory<br>• non-diagnostic | "of no evidentiary value" |

◆ **COMMENT:** Using numbers and percentages to represent opinions is inappropriate unless a specific statistical analysis on a case has been done.

## ABFO Standards for "Bitemark Terminology"

The following list of Bitemark Terminology Standards have been accepted by the American Board of Forensic Odontology.

1. Terms assuring unconditional identification of a perpetrator, without doubt, on the basis of an epidermal bitemark and an open population is not sanctioned as a final conclusion.

2. Terms used in a different manner from the recommended guidelines should be explained in the body of a report or in testimony.

3. Certain terms have been used in a nonuniform manner by odontologists. To prevent miscommunication, the following terms, if used as a conclusion in a report or in testimony, should be explained:

- match; positive match.
- consistent with.
- compatible with.
- unique.

4. The following terms *should not* be used to describe bitemarks:

- suck mark (20% of diplomates still use this antiquated term).
- incised wound.

5. All boarded forensic odontologists are responsible for being familiar with the standards set forth in this document.

# APPENDIX 6E

# ABFO Scoring Sheet for Bite Mark Analysis

(Important: Use only with scoring guide, score only reliable information.)

Case Name:

| | Features Analyzed<br>Discrepancy (if any) | Nbr. of Points | Max. | Mand. |
|---|---|---|---|---|
| **Gross** | | | | |
| | All teeth in mark present in suspect's mouth | *One per arch | | |
| | Size of arches consistent (i.e. mark not larger than dental arch) | *One per arch | | |
| | Shape of arches consistent | *One per arch | | |
| **Tooth Position** | | | | |
| | Tooth and tooth mark in same labiolingual position | *One per tooth | | |
| | Tooth and mark in same rotational position (whether rotated or normal) | *One per tooth | | |
| | Vertical position of tooth regarding occlusal plane matches depth of mark (use only in unusual case) | *One per matching tooth | | |
| | Spacing between adjacent marking edges | *One per space | | |
| **Intradental Features** | | | | |
| | Mesiodistal width of tooth matches mark (use only if individual tooth is clearly marked) | *One per tooth | | |
| | Labiolingual width of tooth matches mark OR attrition of edge matches mark | **Three per tooth | | |

514

Case Name:

| Features Analyzed<br>Discrepancy (if any) | Nbr. of Points | Max. | Mand. |
|---|---|---|---|
| Distinctive curvature of tooth incisal edge matches mark (use only in unusual case) | **Three per tooth | | |
| Other distinctive features (fractured teeth, unusual anatomy) | Three per tooth | | |

Miscellaneous

| | | | |
|---|---|---|---|
| Suspect has one edentulous arch and this is reflected in bite mark | Three | | |
| | Total, each arch: | | |
| | Grand Total: | | |

* Three points if feature is significantly distinctive.
** Only in case permitting accurate measurement.

Signature _____ Date _____
2/20/84 Committee on Bite Mark Guidelines

Note: Compilation of "points" was abandoned in January 1988.

# Chapter 7

# Talker Identification

## I. LEGAL ISSUES

## II. SCIENTIFIC STATUS

## I. LEGAL ISSUES

### § 7:1 Pre-*Daubert* decisions

Judicial opinions on the admissibility of talker identification were widely divided before *Daubert*,[1] and following *Daubert* there has been only one additional case that directly considered the admissibility of "voiceprints" or "voice spectrography," though there have been several cases on the periphery of the large central issue. Thus, no consistent or coherent judicial view can be discerned, and whether *Daubert*

---

**[Section 7:1]**

[1]*Daubert v. Merrell Dow Pharmaceuticals, Inc.*, 509 U.S. 579, 113 S. Ct. 2786, 125 L. Ed. 2d 469, 27, 27 U.S.P.Q.2d 1200, Prod. Liab. Rep. (CCH) P 13494, 37 Fed. R. Evid. Serv. 1, 23 Envtl. L. Rep. 20979 (1993).

will guide courts to increased convergence must wait for the future. The patterns and non-patterns of the courts' responses to scientific talker identification is instructive. The accompanying Table 1, Scientific Talker Identification Cases, lists the major talker identification opinions in chronological order, along with certain other information about the cases.

### Table I
### Scientific Voice Identification Cases:
### Holdings, Legal Tests, and Citations to NAS Report

| Jurisdiction | Court | Case | Cite | Date | Legal Test* | Held | NAS Report |
|---|---|---|---|---|---|---|---|
| Military | APP | Wright | 17 CMA 183 | 1967 | Reliability | IN | |
| CA | APP | King | 72 Cal.Rptr. 478 | 1968 | Frye-broad | OUT | |
| NJ | TR | Cary | 239 A.2d 680 | 1970 | Frye-broad | OUT | |
| MN | SC | Trimble | 192 N.W.2d 432 | 1971 | none | IN | |
| FL | APP | Worley | 263 So.2d 613 | 1972 | Reliability | IN | |
| FL | APP | Alea | 265 So.2d 96 | 1972 | none + [Reliability] | IN | |
| CA | APP | Hodo | 106 Cal.Rptr. 547 | 1973 | Frye-narrow | IN | |
| US-DC Cir. | APP | Addison | 498 F.2d 741 | 1974 | Frye-broad | OUT | |
| CA | APP | Law | 114 Cal.Rptr. 708 | 1974 | Frye-broad | OUT | |
| US-EDPA | TR | Sample | 378 F.Supp. 44 | 1974 | McC | IN | |
| MA | SC | Lykus | 327 N.E.2d 671 | 1975 | Frye-narrow | IN | |
| US-4th Cir. | APP | Baller | 519 F.2d 463 | 1975 | McC | IN | |
| OH | APP | Olderman | 44 OhioApp.2d 130 | 1975 | Reliability | IN | |
| US-6th Cir. | APP | Jenkins | 525 F.2d 819 | 1975 | McC + [Reliability] | IN | |
| US-6th Cir. | APP | Franks | 511 F.2d 25 | 1975 | McC + [Reliability] | IN | |
| CA | SC | Kelly | 130 Cal.Rptr. 144 | 1976 | Frye-broad | OUT | |
| US-DC Cir. | APP | McDaniel | 538 F.2d 408 | 1976 | Frye-broad | OUT | |
| NY | TR | Rogers | 385 N.Y.S.2d 228 | 1976 | McC + Rel + [Frye] | IN | |
| PA | SC | Topa | 369 A.2d 1277 | 1977 | Frye-broad | OUT | |
| MI | SC | Tobey | 257 N.W.2d 537 | 1977 | Frye-broad | OUT | |
| US-SDNY | TR | Williams | 443 F.Supp.269 | 1977 | Reliab + [Frye-broad] | IN | |
| MD | SC | Reed | 391 A.2d 364 | 1978 | Frye-broad | OUT | |
| US-2nd Cir. | APP | Williams | 583 F.2d 1194 | 1978 | McC | IN | |
| NJ | TR | D'Arc | 385 A.2d 278 | 1978 | Reliab or Frye-broad | OUT | |
| DC | APP | Brown | 384 A.2d 647 | 1978 | [Reliability + Frye] | neither | |
| NY | TR | Collins | 405 N.Y.S.2d 365 | 1978 | Reliab + Frye-broad | OUT | |
| ME | SC | Williams | 388 A.2d 500 | 1978 | Reliability-Relevancy | IN | |
| NY | TR | Bein | 453 N.Y.S.2d 343 | 1982 | Reliab + Frye-narrow | IN | no |
| IN | SC | Cornett | 450 N.E.2d 498 | 1983 | Frye-broad | OUT | no |
| OH | SC | Williams | 446 N.E.2d 444 | 1983 | Reliability | IN | no |
| AZ | SC | Gortarez | 686 P.2d 1224 | 1984 | Frye-broad | OUT | yes |
| RI | SC | Wheeler | 496 A2.d 1382 | 1985 | McC | IN | no |
| LA | APP | Free | 493 So.2d 781 | 1986 | Relevancy balance | OUT | slightly |
| NJ | SC | Windmere | 522 A.2d 405 | 1987 | Frye-broad | OUT | no |

| Jurisdiction | Court | Case | Cite | Date | Legal Test* | Held | NAS Report |
|---|---|---|---|---|---|---|---|
| CO | SC | Drake | 748 P.2d 1237 | 1988 | Frye-broad | OUT | no |
| US-7th Cir. | APP | Smith | 869 F.2d 348 | 1989 | Reliability + [Frye] | IN | slightly |
| US-DHI | TR | Maivia | 728 F.Supp.1471 | 1990 | Reliab + Frye-narrow | IN | slightly |
| US-6th Cir. | APP | Leon | 966 F.2d 1455 (table) | 1992 | McC | IN | no |
| AK | SC | Coon | 974 P.2d 386 | 1999 | Daubert | IN | no |

Note: The legal tests are abbreviated as follows: Frye with the relevant fields defined broadly (Frye-broad), or narrowly (Frye-narrow), reliability (reliab) or relevancy (relev), or McCormick weighting (McC). The Court levels are: court of last resort (SC), intermediate court of appeals (CA), trial (TR). Brackets indicate a test a court stated it was applying but where there is no indication in the opinion that the court actually applied that test.

First, we can see from the Table that the extent of agreement in recent years is no greater than in the earliest days of scientific talker identification. Of the first ten courts to consider the technique, six admitted it and four excluded it. The most recent ten to consider it were similarly divided, six for admission and four for exclusion.

Second, we can see that the legal test of admissibility applied by the courts is highly correlated with the holding.[2] Of those courts that applied the classical broad *Frye*[3] test—that is, an understanding of the relevant scientific community as consisting of a range of applicable fields[4] and not merely the one or two narrowly concerned with performing the particular application that constituted the technique at issue— not one admitted expert testimony of talker identification.[5] Of courts that employed a narrow *Frye* test—narrowing the relevant scientific field to those that performed the test at issue—not one excluded the testimony.[6] These two versions of the *Frye* test, and their predictably opposite conclusions, illustrate one of the important criticisms of *Frye*, namely, that defining the relevant scientific fields broadly or narrowly largely dictates the conclusion that will be reached.

Of courts that employed a "relevancy" or "reliability" test—frequently equated, at least in the past, with the test embodied in the Federal Rules of Evidence—eleven

---

[2]Notice that we merely say "correlated." We venture no guess as to whether the rule dictated the conclusion or vice-versa.

[3]*Frye v. U.S.*, 293 F. 1013, 34 A.L.R. 145 (App. D.C. 1923) (rejected by, State v. Walstad, 119 Wis. 2d 483, 351 N.W.2d 469 (1984)) and (rejected by, State v. Brown, 297 Or. 404, 687 P.2d 751 (1984)) and (rejected by, Nelson v. State, 628 A.2d 69 (Del. 1993)) and (rejected by, State v. Alberico, 116 N.M. 156, 861 P.2d 192 (1993)) and (rejected by, State v. Moore, 268 Mont. 20, 885 P.2d 457 (1994)) and (rejected by, State v. Faught, 127 Idaho 873, 908 P.2d 566 (1995)) and (rejected by, People v. Shreck, 22 P.3d 68, 90 A.L.R.5th 765 (Colo. 2001)).

[4]Concerning scientific talker identification, that could mean acoustical engineering, anatomy, electrical engineering, linguistics, phonetics, physics, physiology, psychology, physiology, and statistics—because the technique of voice spectrography made assumptions about or borrowed principles from each of these fields.

[5]*People v. King*, 266 Cal. App. 2d 437, 72 Cal. Rptr. 478 (2d Dist. 1968); *State v. Cary*, 99 N.J. Super. 323, 239 A.2d 680 (Law Div. 1968), aff'd, 56 N.J. 16, 264 A.2d 209 (1970); *U.S. v. Addison*, 498 F.2d 741 (D.C. Cir. 1974); *People v. Law*, 40 Cal. App. 3d 69, 114 Cal. Rptr. 708 (5th Dist. 1974); *People v. Kelly*, 17 Cal. 3d 24, 130 Cal. Rptr. 144, 549 P.2d 1240 (1976); *U.S. v. McDaniel*, 538 F.2d 408 (D.C. Cir. 1976); *Com. v. Topa*, 471 Pa. 223, 369 A.2d 1277 (1977); *People v. Tobey*, 401 Mich. 141, 257 N.W.2d 537 (1977); *Reed v. State*, 283 Md. 374, 391 A.2d 364, 97 A.L.R.3d 201 (1978); *People v. Collins*, 94 Misc. 2d 704, 405 N.Y.S.2d 365 (Sup 1978); *D'Arc v. D'Arc*, 157 N.J. Super. 553, 385 A.2d 278 (Ch. Div. 1978); *Cornett v. State*, 450 N.E.2d 498 (Ind. 1983); *State v. Gortarez*, 141 Ariz. 254, 686 P.2d 1224 (1984); *Windmere, Inc. v. International Ins. Co.*, 105 N.J. 373, 522 A.2d 405 (1987); *People v. Drake*, 748 P.2d 1237 (Colo. 1988).

[6]*Hodo v. Superior Court*, 30 Cal. App. 3d 778, 106 Cal. Rptr. 547 (4th Dist. 1973); *Com. v. Lykus*, 367 Mass. 191, 327 N.E.2d 671 (1975); *People v. Bein*, 114 Misc. 2d 1021, 453 N.Y.S.2d 343 (Sup 1982); *U.S. v. Maivia*, 728 F. Supp. 1471, 30 Fed. R. Evid. Serv. 103 (D. Haw. 1990).

admitted[7] talker identification expert testimony and three excluded it.[8] The one case that was decided after and under *Daubert* admitted voice identification expert testimony.[9] The courts varied considerably in what they required for the expertise to be found sufficiently "reliable." Most were satisfied that as long as there was something to be said on behalf of talker identification, that was enough to let it in. One court noted only that the witness was a credentialed expert and cited other jurisdictions that had admitted such testimony.[10] Using a similarly minimal threshold, however, another court excluded the evidence, concluding that its almost presumptive reliability was outweighed by its risk of being given excessive weight by factfinders.[11] Yet another court gave the scientific evidence on the proffered expertise a close and thoughtful examination, much like what the *Daubert* gloss on the Federal Rules would seem to require. That court concluded that talker identification expert testimony was inadmissible.[12]

Other courts employed the McCormick test, weighing the proffered evidence's scientific acceptability against the risks of opaqueness, error, or an exaggerated popular opinion of the technique. Every court employing this test found talker identification expert testimony admissible.[13]

Only one post-*Daubert* opinion exists, and that is discussed at length, § 7:2.

Finally, one opinion reached its conclusion without employing a discernible legal test.[14]

The refusal of some courts to admit talker identification expert evidence is an exception to the traditional receptiveness of the courts to forensic individuation techniques. Why has talker identification been treated differently? Several intercon-

---

[7]*U.S. v. Wright*, 37 C.M.R. 447, 1967 WL 4287 (C.M.A. 1967); *Worley v. State*, 263 So. 2d 613 (Fla. Dist. Ct. App. 4th Dist. 1972); *State v. Olderman*, 44 Ohio App. 2d 130, 73 Ohio Op. 2d 129, 336 N.E.2d 442 (8th Dist. Cuyahoga County 1975); *People v. Rogers*, 86 Misc. 2d 868, 385 N.Y.S.2d 228 (Sup 1976); *U.S. v. Franks*, 511 F.2d 25 (6th Cir. 1975); *U.S. v. Williams*, 443 F. Supp. 269 (S.D. N.Y. 1977); *State v. Williams*, 388 A.2d 500 (Me. 1978); *State v. Williams*, 4 Ohio St. 3d 53, 446 N.E.2d 444 (1983); *People v. Bein*, 114 Misc. 2d 1021, 453 N.Y.S.2d 343 (Sup 1982); *U.S. v. Smith*, 869 F.2d 348, 27 Fed. R. Evid. Serv. 938 (7th Cir. 1989); *U.S. v. Maivia*, 728 F. Supp. 1471, 30 Fed. R. Evid. Serv. 103 (D. Haw. 1990).

[8]*People v. Collins*, 94 Misc. 2d 704, 405 N.Y.S.2d 365 (Sup 1978); *State v. Free*, 493 So. 2d 781 (La. Ct. App. 2d Cir. 1986), writ denied, 499 So. 2d 83 (La. 1987); *D'Arc v. D'Arc*, 157 N.J. Super. 553, 385 A.2d 278 (Ch. Div. 1978).

[9]*State v. Coon*, 974 P.2d 386, 95 A.L.R.5th 729 (Alaska 1999), discussed in some detail, § 7:2.

[10]*U.S. v. Smith*, 869 F.2d 348, 27 Fed. R. Evid. Serv. 938 (7th Cir. 1989).

[11]*State v. Free*, 493 So. 2d 781 (La. Ct. App. 2d Cir. 1986), writ denied, 499 So. 2d 83 (La. 1987).

[12]*People v. Collins*, 94 Misc. 2d 704, 405 N.Y.S.2d 365 (Sup 1978). Some excerpts from the opinion:

It should be pointed out that although many of the Courts which admitted Spectrographic Voice Identification have done so based largely on the Tosi study, this study has not been replicated, and there seems to be no other formal experimentation in this area upon which the scientific community can make an informed judgment.

It is certainly reasonable to expect science to withhold judgment on a new theory until it has been well tested in the crucible of controlled experimentation and study.

[T]he entire technique is based substantially on the premise that intraspeaker variability is never as great as inter-speaker variability therefore, while each speaker's voice will be somewhat different each time he renders the same utterance, that difference will never be as great as the difference between the utterances of any two different speakers. It would seem reasonable to suppose that this is true, but this fact has not been proven to the Court's satisfaction.

The testimony however, reveals that there has been no experimentation to show that two different voices will always appear different spectrographically.

Without additional independent proof the Court cannot accept the assumption that inter-speaker variability is always greater than intra-speaker variability.

[13]*U.S. v. Sample*, 378 F. Supp. 44 (E.D. Pa. 1974); *U.S. v. Baller*, 519 F.2d 463 (4th Cir. 1975); *U.S. v. Jenkins*, 525 F.2d 819 (6th Cir. 1975); *U.S. v. Franks*, 511 F.2d 25 (6th Cir. 1975); *People v. Rogers*, 86 Misc. 2d 868, 385 N.Y.S.2d 228 (Sup 1976); *U.S. v. Williams*, 583 F.2d 1194, 3 Fed. R. Evid. Serv. 1063 (2d Cir. 1978); *State v. Wheeler*, 496 A.2d 1382 (R.I. 1985); *U.S. v. Leon*, 966 F.2d 1455 (6th Cir. 1992) (unpublished).

[14]*State ex rel. Trimble v. Hedman*, 291 Minn. 442, 192 N.W.2d 432, 49 A.L.R.3d 903 (1971).

nected explanations are plausible.

One may be that judges have gradually grown more thoughtful and discerning and less credulous about scientific offerings than their judicial ancestors had been. Numerous courts evaluating talker identification expertise were critical of witnesses testifying on behalf of the technique who were mere technicians rather than educated scientists;[15] or whose livelihoods depended upon continued admission of the technique;[16] or who came from a very small circle of proponents of the technique.[17]

Another factor is that the literature of scientific talker identification, both supporting and questioning the technique, was more quantified and qualified[18] than earlier courts had received about earlier forensic individuation techniques. This is because most of the people involved in talker identification came from fields that had a tradition of empirical testing of their ideas. Indeed, more research was available to the courts about talker identification expertise than for any forensic individuation field that preceded it. This immediately provided the courts with unusual resources with which to comprehend the shortcomings of the technique.[19] When a field provides rigorous self-critiques of its own concepts and techniques, it greatly aids the courts in making a more informed and sober assessment of the field and its likely contribution to the factfinding process.[20] Moreover, controversy tends to precipitate still more research, and a greater volume of research tends to produce a more complex and skeptical impression of the technique in the mind of the court.[21]

In the face of actual data, the courts had a real choice to make. Although the technique could reduce uncertainty in identification, it also was less than perfect. Errors were going to be made, and, unlike some other fields of forensic individuation, talker identification proponents said so.[22] The courts had concrete error rates to evaluate. How good is good enough? How much error is too much? The law provides no standards for making that assessment. Ten percent error may have been viewed by some courts as quite adequate and by other courts as not nearly good enough.

Finally, the courts may have been overwhelmed by the studies. Although more research means a greater potential to understand the scientific questions at issue, it also may have confused some courts, which had limited capacity to interpret and

---

[15]"[The expert witness's] qualifications are those of a technician and law enforcement officer, not a scientist." *People v. Kelly*, 17 Cal. 3d 24, 130 Cal. Rptr. 144, 549 P.2d 1240 (1976).

[16]"[The expert witness's] qualifications are those of a technician and law enforcement officer, not a scientist." *People v. Kelly*, 17 Cal. 3d 24, 130 Cal. Rptr. 144, 549 P.2d 1240 (1976). Compare this to the narrow version of the *Frye* test, which essentially asks the practitioners of a technique if they have sufficient confidence in their work that they should be allowed to continue to make a living at it.

[17]Of course, these shortcomings do not distinguish talker identification from most other forensic individuation techniques when they were gaining admission to the courts. Indeed, all but the third criticism continues to be true for them.

[18]In the sense of limited, restricted, circumspect.

[19]The same was true for DNA typing, and was not true for most other forensic individuation techniques.

[20]When other fields lack such critiques, is

that because there is nothing to question? Or because an uninformed and unquestioning consensus developed among members of the field? And how can courts distinguish between the two possibilities?

[21]This presents a paradox: All else equal, it appears that the better a field studies and critiques itself, the more skeptical the courts seem likely to be of it. The less a field tests its ideas and the more confidently it asserts them, the more positive an impression the courts develop of the field. For a number of the more conventional forensic individuation techniques, there still is no tradition of self-scrutiny or a literature reporting the results of rigorous testing which can inform the courts. At least in terms of their continued acceptance by the courts, those fields have nothing to gain and much to lose by adopting a tradition of inquiry, testing, and skepticism.

[22]"Possibly, no combination of methods may ever produce absolutely positive identification or eliminations in 100% of the cases submitted." Oscar Tosi, The Problem of Speaker Identification and Elimination, in Measurement Procedures in Speech, Hearing, and Language 399, 428 (Sadanand Singh ed., 1975).

evaluate the empirical studies. If this was the problem, help was on the way.

Unique assistance in evaluating the available data came into being only a decade after talker identification made its first appearance in the courts.[23] Help came in the form of a careful review of scientific talker identification by the National Academy of Sciences.[24] A panel of highly knowledgeable scientists and other experts from diverse relevant fields carefully reviewed the relevant scientific literature and concluded:

> [The assumption] that intraspeaker variability is less than . . . interspeaker variability . . . is not adequately supported by scientific data.
>
> Estimates of error rates now available pertain to only a few of the many combinations of situations encountered in real-life situations. These estimates do not constitute a generally adequate basis for a judicial or legislative body to use in making judgments concerning the reliability and acceptability of aural-visual voice identification in forensic applications.[25]

Upon publication of the Report, the FBI ceased performing talker identification for the purpose of offering testimony in court,[26] and it was expected[27] that the courts would stop admitting talker identification expert testimony, at least until the scientific support for it improved.[28] However, of the 12 judicial opinions written since release of the NAS Report,[29] seven admitted the expert testimony while five excluded it. Still more curious, only four cite the Report at all and only one seems to have actually read and learned what the Report had to say. Thus, for the most part, the courts decided the post-NAS cases as if the NAS Report did not exist.[30]

## § 7:2    State decisions post-*Daubert*

Only one case by a court following *Daubert* has considered the admissibility of expert evidence using voice spectrography. That case, *State v. Coon (1999)*,[1] is also the case through which Alaska adopted *Daubert* as its state law.

The defendant in this case was accused of making terroristic telephone calls to the husband of his ex-daughter-in-law. Part of the evidence introduced against him was expert testimony based on voice spectrograph comparisons. The trial court had held this evidence admissible under *Frye* as "generally accepted by courts," and the jury had found the defendant guilty. On appeal Alaska's intermediate appellate court held that the support for admission under *Frye* was inadequate, and remanded for further proceedings on the admissibility issue. The State appealed to the Alaska Supreme Court, which retained jurisdiction but remanded for findings under both *Frye* and *Daubert*. In its decision, the Alaska Supreme Court explicitly adopted *Daubert*, adopted a deferential standard of review, and held the voice spectrograph evidence admissible under the *Daubert* test.

Query whether, when making rulings on the admissibility of scientific evidence as

---

[23]Up until that time. There have been two NAS panels formed to review the data on the technique of DNA typing. See §§ 2:1 et seq.

[24]The NAS was created during the administration of Abraham Lincoln to provide any agency of the federal government with first rate scientific advice on issues of concern to those agencies. In this instance, the FBI made the request for a review.

[25]Bolt et al., On the Theory and Practice of Voice Identification (1979).

[26]But, as with the polygraph, they continued doing voice spectrographic tests for investigative purposes.

[27]See Andre A. Moenssens et al., Scientific Evidence in Civil and Criminal Cases 645 (4th ed. 1995).

[28]Few if any of the scientific shortcomings raised by the Report have been solved by subsequent research. See discussion § 7:26.

[29]See Table 1.

[30]Whether this reflects the shortcomings of counsel (for not drawing the courts' attention to the NAS study) or the courts (for not finding it themselves, or not appreciating its value to their decisions), we are unable to say.

**[Section 7:2]**

[1]*State v. Coon*, 974 P.2d 386, 95 A.L.R.5th 729 (Alaska 1999).

a general matter (that is, whether the science is sufficiently dependable to be admitted, not whether it has sufficient fit to the facts of the particular case at bar), the trial court is in a better position to make the decision than an appellate court. Is verbal testimony by a few witnesses (the typical mode of information gathering by a trial court) a more or a less illuminating method of learning about the underlying basis of the expertise than reading the relevant research literature, with the guidance of counsel in the form of briefs and arguments (the mode of information gathering more often used by an appellate court). The Court suggested that the main advantage of a deferential standard of review lies in the notion that a trial court would have at its disposal more up-to-date information than an appellate court could.[2]

If the Alaska Supreme Court believed that the trial court was in a better position to gather the evidence, why didn't it make the *Daubert* versus *Frye* decision, remand for the trial court to complete the case consistent with that holding, and let that specific admissibility decision be appealed if and when the parties chose to do so? Since the Supreme Court reviewed the trial court ruling on admissibility for abuse of discretion following the United States Supreme Court's opinion in *Joiner*,[3] (and ruled that the trial court's conclusions were "not an abuse of discretion"), does that mean that the admissibility of voice spectrographic evidence is not settled as a matter of precedent in Alaska, and that the State's trial courts are free to make contrary decisions when the same question of admissibility presents itself in future cases, so long as they make their rulings under the *Daubert* test? Apparently so. From the opinion it appears that the Alaska Supreme Court expects trial courts to make these decisions case-by-case, to contradict each other from time to time, and to be reviewed for abuse of discretion—yet the court hints that somehow (notwithstanding the announced rule) appellate courts will resolve the contradictions before they became an embarrassment, and that in any event the court did not expect this problem to occur very often. The court justifies its approach in part by treating all applications of science as so highly case specific, that the contradictions will be attributable to differences in the case facts.

Oddly, the opinion relied on Rule 703, rather than 702, as the foundation for its *Daubert* analysis, noting that the "commentary to the Alaska Rules of Evidence provides support for the State's view that . . . Rule 703 is also a source for an approach broader than the Frye standard."[4] The basic points the Court makes about the dependability of scientific knowledge are entirely reasonable, but finding them in Rule 703 makes little sense. Rule 703 pertains to the facts or data relied on in the *particular* case (that is, the adjudicative facts), not the general scientific

---

[2]In the present case, this clearly is not what happened. As the opinion states, " . . . no scientific literature was submitted to the trial court for review, but [the voice identification expert] testified about several articles and studies addressing voice spectrographic analysis, and conceded that the reliability of the technique was disputed among members of the relevant scientific community." *State v. Coon*, 974 P.2d 386, 402, 95 A.L.R.5th 729 (Alaska 1999). A visit to a library by a judicial clerk could unearth a far more complete review of the relevant scientific research than the selective, self-serving, and, in this instance, out-of-date sampling of research literature referred to verbally from the witness stand.

[3]*General Elec. Co. v. Joiner*, 522 U.S. 136, 118 S. Ct. 512, 139 L. Ed. 2d 508, 18 O.S.H. Cas. (BNA) 1097, Prod. Liab. Rep. (CCH) P 15120, 48

Fed. R. Evid. Serv. 1, 28 Envtl. L. Rep. 20227, 177 A.L.R. Fed. 667 (1997). The Alaska Supreme Court adopted that same position, with one of the four justices dissenting. The dissent emphasized the trans-case nature of scientific evidence, in contrast to the usual adjudicative evidence whose admissibility is being ruled upon. For further discussion of this problem, see §§ 1:1 et seq.

[4]*State v. Coon*, 974 P.2d 386, 95 A.L.R.5th 729 (Alaska 1999). Alaska Rule of Evidence 703 provides: "The facts or data in the particular case upon which an expert bases an opinion or inference may be those perceived by or made known to the expert at or before the hearing. Facts or data need not be admissible in evidence, but must be of a type reasonably relied upon by experts in the particular field in forming opinions or inferences upon the subject."

background being relied upon (more akin to legislative facts, or empirical authority) and the methods by which the expert may come into possession of those case-specific facts. In addition, query whether *Daubert* really is "broader" than *Frye*. At the same time, the opinion clearly recognizes that its adoption of *Daubert* would lead both to admitting previously inadmissible evidence and excluding previously admissible evidence (and therefore in some situations *Daubert* is "narrower" than *Frye*). The court rejected a number of arguments against the adoption of *Daubert*. It rejected the argument that *Daubert* would place too heavy a burden on trial courts, noting that courts can obtain help by appointing their own experts under Rule 706. It also rejected concerns about adversely affecting the admissibility of traditional forensic evidence like fingerprinting, handwriting, and hair comparison analyses,[5] and about opening the doors to "junk science."[6]

In examining the evidence underlying the claims of voice spectrographic identification, the Alaska Supreme Court conducted a limited and superficial review of the research on which such a decision must depend, doing little more than quoting the trial court's conclusory assertions.[7] Given that no research literature was "submitted" to the trial court, and that court did not ask for any or do any research on its own, unless the court recognized any duty to look beyond the four corners of the record from the trial's hearing on the issue, then by definition the supreme court's review will be limited to the limited review of the science conducted below. As noted above and in the original chapter, few courts have cited the National Academy of Sciences' authoritative review of voice spectrography research, the findings of which led the FBI to withdraw from offering such evidence in courts. *State v. Coon* joins that list of cases that overlooked the major scientific review of the question before them. Thus, despite the *Coon* court's own discussion of the heightened analysis of the science that is called for under a *Daubert* review, its own first outing offers a review of the scientific claims, and a review of the adequacy of the trial court's gatekeeping, that is remarkably meager.

## § 7:3    Federal decisions post-*Daubert*

A challenge by the government to the admissibility of assertedly scientific voice identification arose in *United States v. Angleton*.[1] Robert Angleton was on trial for the murder of his wealthy wife, Doris Angleton.[2] The government moved to exclude the testimony of Angleton's voice expert, who was offered to testify that the unidentified voice on a tape recording was not Robert's, and the court granted the motion.

The defense expert, Stephen Cain, had extensive training and experience in voice identification, gained while working for the United States Secret Service and the Internal Revenue Service, among other law enforcement agencies. The opposing expert offered by the government, Hirotaka Nakasone, not only had worked at similar agencies, and currently was employed by the FBI, but he was a doctoral student and protege of one of the originators of forensic voice identification, Oscar Tosi, and once an enthusiastic proponent of the admissibility of voice identification expert testimony. But now, "Nakasone testified that his initial belief that the voice

---

[5]Consult the appropriate chapters in this treatise to see how those asserted expertises have fared, or are expected to fare, under a *Daubert* analysis.

[6]Notice that these two arguments—that *Daubert*'s standard is so low that it will lead to the admission of junk science and so high that it will exclude forensic science—are at war with each other. They cannot both be true.

[7]The opinion gives a more detailed recitation of the expert's background and experience than it does the data on the underpinnings of the technique at issue (for which any facts about the particular expert are irrelevant).

[Section 7:3]

[1]*U.S. v. Angleton*, 269 F. Supp. 2d 892 (S.D. Tex. 2003).

[2]The author who interviewed Robert's brother (who later died by suicide) and others was jailed for refusing to provide the government with interview tapes and notes.

spectrographic technique is sufficiently reliable for courtroom purposes has eroded over time, as research efforts have failed to support the underlying premises of the voice identification techniques or to produce reliable testing for error rates."

The *Angleton* court took a fairly careful look at actual studies of voice identification and data their results, which data are, of course, the best and only real evidence on the dependability of the technique(s). This contrasts with the opinion of the only appellate court to admit voice spectrographic evidence after and under *Daubert*, the Alaska Supreme Court,[3] which is noteworthy for its failure to examine any studies or data, or even to be disturbed that the courts below had developed no record of those most important sources of knowledge about the expertise at issue. The *Angleton* court summarized its findings:

> General problems with the reliability of aural spectrographic voice identification raise considerable doubt as to whether these techniques meet the *Daubert* standard. The potential rate of error of the aural spectrographic method is unknown and may vary considerably, depending on the conditions of the particular application. The method has not been generally accepted by the scientific community. Peer review is increasingly difficult in a field in which there are a dwindling number of practitioners and "sparsely attended" professional meetings. (citation omitted) The Rule 702 indicia of reliability— whether the theory or technique has been tested; whether the theory or technique has been subjected to peer review and publication; the known or potential rate of error of the method used and the existence and maintenance of standards controlling the technique's operation; and whether the theory or method has been generally accepted by the scientific community—are not satisfied.

Several points of comment might be made. First, it is not clear that there is a lack of research and testing. Or, at least, we can say that far more empirical research exists on the claims of voice identification expertise than on any other forensic identification technique other than DNA testing.[4] Second, in noting that the rate of error "may vary considerably, depending on the conditions of the particular application," the court is adverting to the "task-at-hand" requirement of *Daubert* and *Kumho Tire*, though the court makes no specific reference to that concern. This court is one of the few to heed the Supreme Court's concern that however well a technique may do under other conditions and circumstances, the question at issue is how well it performs in regard to the factual issue in the case at bar. Third, the court is alert to the need for proof of the assumption in voice identification (and all other forms of forensic identification) that inter-person variation exceed intra-person variation, that the examination method must be able to dependably detect those differences, and that evidence must exist to support that both of those are true. Finally, whether *Daubert* has provoked a more open eyed scrutiny of voice identification remains to be seen. As noted in the main chapter, there are plenty of courts that ignore the data and admit the expert testimony on nothing more than the assurances of the experts that what they are offering is sound, and the realization that it has been admitted many times before in many other courts. Moreover, experts from forensic identification fields far less grounded in data are regularly admitted without nearly the scrutiny provided by this court.

In *United States v. Ramos*,[5] the Fifth Circuit summarily rejected the defendant's claim that the district court erred in excluding his expert testimony on voice identification, emphasizing clear error.

No other cases involving disputes over "classical" voice spectrography have been

---

[3]*State v. Coon*, 974 P.2d 386, 95 A.L.R.5th 729 (Alaska 1999).

[4]This is readily evident from a comparison of the present chapter to the reviews of the knowledge base in any of the other chapters in this treatise on forensic identification science (other than DNA typing).

[5]*U.S. v. Ramos*, 71 Fed. Appx. 334 (5th Cir. 2003).

reported from the federal courts subsequent to *Daubert*. But other types of voice identification expertise and some more peripheral issues were discussed and debated.

The defendant in *United States v. Salimonu*[6] was found guilty of importing heroin. Among the issues he raised on appeal was the trial court's decision to exclude expert testimony that the voice on the inculpatory tape recordings was not his. The First Circuit affirmed. The trial judge had admitted defense testimony about voice spectrographs, but excluded a linguist's testimony that was based on simply listening to the tapes in question. This expert "admitted that he had no training or special certification in voice identification or comparison, and that he had only engaged in voice recognition procedures two or three times before." Moreover, he "knew of no studies to determine the rate of error for this kind of identification," and conceded that a lay person would be able to discern the same differences between the tapes that he heard.

In *United States v. Gilbert*[7] the defendant was convicted of telephoning bomb threats to the Veteran's Hospital where she worked as a nurse. One of her arguments on appeal concerned the trial court's decision to admit expert testimony about a recording of the caller's voice, as well as an altered recording at a different speed. Since the recorded call did not sound like the defendant's voice, the government theory was that she had used toy called a "Talkboy" to change her voice. By adjusting the speed of the recording, the voice could be made to sound like that of the defendant, and her ex-husband was able to identify the voice on the modified tape as hers. On appeal she argued that such evidence should have been excluded under *Daubert*, but the First Circuit ruled that a proper objection had not been lodged at trial.

The defendant in *Virgin Islands v. Sanes*[8] was convicted of robbery and rape. Part of the evidence introduced against him at trial was the victim's identification of his voice. She selected his voice from recordings of several voices. The defendant sought to introduce the testimony of an expert who would have testified about why voice identification is not as accurate as eyewitness identification. The expert was not allowed to give this testimony, but was allowed to testify regarding the distinguishing characteristics of the defendant's voice. With little analysis, the Third Circuit held the trial court had not abused its discretion. Concerning research relevant to the scientific issues in this case, see the discussion of Earwitness Research.[9]

The defendant in *United States v. Jones*[10] had been convicted for distributing cocaine. On appeal, he argued that the trial court had improperly excluded expert testimony on voice identification. The trial court had applied the *Frye* Test, but the Ninth Circuit found that even under *Daubert* the evidence should have been excluded. The expert had developed his voice comparison technique himself, and could not cite any scientific basis for it. He conceded that no scientific studies or published research supported his theory.

The defendant in *United States v. Drones*,[11] sought, and had obtained from the district court, relief for his claim of ineffective assistance of counsel on the grounds that his attorney had failed even to investigate the availability of voice identification expert testimony to evaluate a tape that the government asserted contained the defendant's voice. The court of appeals reinstated the state court verdict. At the habeas hearing, the petitioner's expert stated that he found from his examination that there was "probably elimination" of the defendant as a source of the voice on the

---

[6]*U.S. v. Salimonu*, 182 F.3d 63, 52 Fed. R. Evid. Serv. 711 (1st Cir. 1999).

[7]*U.S. v. Gilbert*, 181 F.3d 152, 51 Fed. R. Evid. Serv. 1281 (1st Cir. 1999).

[8]*Government of Virgin Islands v. Sanes*, 57

F.3d 338, 42 Fed. R. Evid. Serv. 578 (3d Cir. 1995).

[9]§ 37:23.

[10]*U.S. v. Jones*, 24 F.3d 1177, 39 Fed. R. Evid. Serv. 1171 (9th Cir. 1994).

[11]*U.S. v. Drones*, 218 F.3d 496 (5th Cir. 2000).

recording. According to the expert, this meant that "80% of the comparable words in the samples were dissimilar aurally and spectrographically." The petitioner's expert conceded, however, that there were sundry weaknesses with this technology and that no objective criteria existed by which to check the accuracy of any conclusions an examiner might reach. Also testifying at the hearing, the government's expert echoed these cautionary words, noting that very little research had been done to validate the courtroom use of this technology. The court of appeals concluded that voice identification expertise is not competent evidence. "Given the current state of the law regarding the admissibility of expert voice identification testimony and the expert testimony presented at the evidentiary hearing, we cannot say that counsel's choice of strategy was unreasonable and therefore deficient."

One of the defendants in *United States v. Bahena*,[12] complained that the district court erred in excluding his expert on voice spectrography. The appellate court rejected this argument, and affirmed the convictions of all of the defendants. The court of appeals found that the lower court had not abused its discretion in excluding this particular witness, noting that the expert here had no college degree, was not a member of any professional association and was not familiar with the standard practices in the field of voice identification.

A Post-Script. As an investigative tool, since 9/11 and the growth of national security concerns, the net around talker identification has tightened. From news reports, it appears that federal security agencies continue to use talker identification methods, but the private practitioner market (for the defense in domestic criminal matters) seems to have dried up. At least some of the private practitioners are now old enough to be out of practice, or otherwise not inclined to contest the FBI's position that talker identification methods are not sound enough to be offered in the courts. Within the FBI and other security agencies, talker identification methods are used for investigative purposes, but discredited through obscured testimony on those occasions when the subject is discussed in court, that is, the taking of positions that preclude disclosure of methods for reasons of "national security." In short, one might say that the status of talker identification methods has less to do with what is legally accepted and more to do with what is governmentally accepted.

## II.  SCIENTIFIC STATUS

*by Raymond D. Kent\* & Michael R. Chial\*\**

### § 7:4  Introductory discussion of the science—The scientific questions— Terminology and basic concepts

Most people can easily recognize family members, friends, coworkers, and popular

---

[12]*U.S. v. Bahena*, 223 F.3d 797, 55 Fed. R. Evid. Serv. 662 (8th Cir. 2000).

\*Raymond D. Kent is Professor of Speech Science in the Department of Communicative Disorders, University of Wisconsin-Madison. His doctorate is from the University of Iowa and he did postdoctoral work in speech analysis and synthesis at the Massachusetts Institute of Technology. He has edited or written eleven books, including The Acoustical Analysis of Speech (with Charles Read, 1992), and is past editor of the Journal of Speech and Hearing Research. He holds an honorary doctorate from the University of Montreal Faculty of Medicine, is a Fellow of the Acoustical Society of America, the International Society of Phonetic Sciences, and the American Speech-Language-Hearing Association, and has earned Honors of the American Speech-Language-Hearing Association.

\*\*Michael R. Chial is Professor of Audiology in the Department of Communicative Disorders at the University of Wisconsin-Madison. His doctorate is from the University of Wisconsin-Madison. For 20 years he has worked with the American National Standards Institute and is currently working with the Audio Engineering Society to develop technical standards for forensic applications of audio recordings. He is past associate editor of the Journal of Speech and Hearing Research, and Fellow of the American Speech-Language-Hearing Association and the American Academy of Audiology.

The authors thank Lonnie L. Smrkovski for his comments on an earlier draft of this chapter.

figures from the sounds of their voices. This familiar form of personal identification finds forensic application in situations where a voice has been heard by a witness or, even better, a recording has been made of the voice in question. Talker identification may be broadly defined as a decision-making process that relies on properties of the talker's speech signal. The decision-maker's objective is to identify an individual by the characteristics of that individual's speech. The term *talker identification* is used in this chapter because it denotes the task of trying to identify a human talker. Other terms used for this application are *speaker identification* and *voice identification.*

Traunmuller[1] listed four kinds of information contained in the speech signal:

1. *Phonetic quality* refers to the linguistic content of the spoken message, i.e., the essential material from which we derive the information intended by the talker.

2. *Affective quality* is paralinguistic information, meaning that it accompanies the linguistic message of speech and may contribute to the interpretation of that message. Emotional attributes fall into this category.

3. *Personal quality* is extralinguistic, meaning that it is outside the ordinary linguistic aspects of speech. Personal quality is informative about the talker, but not the message. The information can include the talker's gender, age, state of health, and individual characteristics.

4. *Transmittal quality* gives perspectival information about the talker's location, including the distance from the one who hears the signal, orientation in space, presence of background noise, and influence of environmental acoustics that may introduce effects such as reverberation.

Talker identification rests on the assumption that intratalker variability (e.g., the variability associated with multiple productions of the same speech sample by a given talker) is less than intertalker variability (e.g., the variability associated with productions of the same speech sample by different talkers). The capability of recognizing a talker is based on two primary sources of intertalker differences: (1) anatomic differences in the size and shape of the speech organs, and (2) subtle individual differences in how speech sounds are made. The former are sometimes called *physiological differences* and the latter *behavioral differences.* Physiological differences generally are not subject to learning effects, whereas behavioral differences often are. A hardware-software analogy also has been used to distinguish these two types of differences among talkers,[2] with physiological factors being compared with the hardware and behavioral factors (including sociolinguistic and psychological factors) with the software. Presumably, the hardware is less easily altered than the software. The speech pattern produced by any one individual is a combination of physiological and behavioral factors. Differences among talkers are therefore a combination of the same factors.

Talker recognition may be subdivided into various approaches: talker recognition by listening (aural recognition), by machine (automatic recognition), and by visual inspection of spectrograms (also known as "voiceprints" or "voicegrams"). These are not necessarily mutually exclusive procedures. Forensic applications commonly

---

The opinions expressed herein are solely those of the authors.

**[Section 7:4]**

[1]Hartmut Traunmuller, Conventional, Biological, and Environmental Factors in Speech Communication: A Modulation Theory, 18 PERILUS (Phonetic Experimental Research, Institute of Linguistics, University of Stockholm) 1 (1994).

[2]Hisao Kuwabara & Yoshinori Sagisaka, Acoustic Characteristics of Speaker Individuality: Control and Conversion, 16 Speech Communication 165 (1995).

make use of both aural recognition and spectrograms, and it is possible to use all three methods in reaching a decision.

This chapter concentrates on the third approach, visual inspection of spectrograms, but some comments will be included on the first and second approaches as well. Visual inspection of spectrograms is the major source of evidence provided by trained examiners. The overarching scientific question is whether an individual talker can be distinguished from a larger group of talkers on the basis of visual patterns in a spectrogram. Because the properties of the spectrogram are essential to an understanding of their use in talker identification, some general comments on spectrograms are in order.

*Spectrogram* is a generic term for the conventional analysis of sound according to the three dimensions of frequency, time, and intensity. In the typical spectrogram, time is represented along the horizontal axis, frequency (the rate of vibration of a sound component, heard as pitch) along the vertical axis, and intensity (magnitude of a sound component, heard as loudness) as a gray (or darkness) scale. An example of a spectrogram is shown in Figure 1. These visual patterns were introduced as a practical laboratory technique in the 1940s and have been a major source of information in the study of speech. Terms synonymous with *spectrogram* are *voiceprint*, *voicegram*, and *Sona-gram*.[TM]

The term "voiceprint" was coined by Gray and Kopp[3] and reintroduced by Kersta,[4] an early proponent of talker recognition through comparisons of visual patterns. Some writers viewed the "voiceprint" as analogous to the "fingerprint." The term "voicegram" was substituted for voiceprint by others who believed that the term *voiceprint* could be misleading. Whereas a finger can leave a direct physical impression when it is pressed against a surface (hence leaving a genuine "print") the voice is given visual representation only by a series of transformations in which acoustic energy is eventually represented on paper.[5] The term *voicegram* is preferable to *voiceprint* though both have the technical disadvantage of emphasizing "voice" rather than "speech." Although voice certainly is important as the primary energy source of speech, speech is really more than voice. This is one reason why the term *talker identification* is used in preference to *voice identification* in this chapter. Energy from the voice is modified by the speech organs through resonance and other influences. Talker identification generally relies on patterns of speech including characteristics of voice, resonance, and articulation.[6] *Speaker identification* is a frequently used term, which may be gaining prominence.[7]

## § 7:5 Introductory discussion of the science—The scientific questions— Terminology and basic concepts—Instrumentation and display

Instruments for this type of speech analysis differ in several respects, but all

[3]C. H. Gray & G. A. Kopp, Voiceprint Identification, Bell Telephone Laboratories Report 1 (1944).

[4]Lawrence G. Kersta, Voiceprint Identification, 196 Nature 1253 (1962).

[5]"Voiceprint" also was used as a trademark by Voiceprint Laboratories, Inc. a manufacturer of speech spectrography equipment. A successor firm, Voice Identification, Inc., retains rights to that trademark and manufactures an analog device (Model 700) favored by some forensic practitioners.

[6]The term *Sona-gram* is a trademark of a manufacturer (Kay Elemetrics Corporation) that currently markets two digital spectrographs—the Model 5500 (a dedicated, stand-alone device) and the Model 4300B (designed for use with general-purpose personal computers). A number of other systems, especially computer programs designed for clinical research and treatment, geophysical and bioacoustical research, music and audio engineering purposes, produce spectrograms as one analysis alternative. See Charles Read et al., Speech Analysis Systems: A Survey, 33 J. Speech & Hearing Research 363 (1990); Charles Read, et al., Speech Analysis Systems: An Evaluation, 35 J. Speech & Hearing Research 314 (1992).

[7]A disadvantage to this term is that the word *speaker* has two prominent meanings, one being a human talker and the other being an electroacoustic device such as a loudspeaker.

include components that acquire sound (generally via microphones or audio recorders), edit stored signals, analyze sounds to produce spectrograms, and display results (analog units by means of facsimile technology; digital units by means of video monitors and laser or video printers). Because several systems can be used to make spectrograms, it is reasonable to ask if there are any differences among them that should be considered in the accuracy of talker identification. Unfortunately, very few comparisons of this type have been made, but Hazen[1] reported no differences between the Voiceprint Laboratories 4691C Sound Spectrograph and the Kay Elemetrics Corporation 6061A Sonagraph (neither of these analog devices is now manufactured). While contemporary digital instruments offer greater flexibility and precision than the earlier analog machines, the older devices produced hard-copy records of superior resolution. It has not been studied whether important differences exist among the various devices and computer systems currently used to make spectrograms, a problem complicated by the lack of appropriate recorded reference material (speech and speech-like signals) designed to compare alternative systems.

In this chapter, the term *spectrogram* will be used in the broad sense to include all varieties of visual displays of speech that rely on a conventional three-dimensional analysis of time, frequency and intensity.[2] In customary practice, two types of spectrograms have been used: wide-band and narrow-band. These two types are distinguished by the width of the analyzing filter which can result in different kinds of spectrograms. The bandwidth of the analyzing filter can be likened to a kind of acoustic "window" that is passed along the signal to determine the energy in various frequency regions. The narrower the bandwidth of the analyzing filter, the better the resolution of frequency but the poorer the resolution of time. Briefly, the wide-band spectrogram uses either a 250 or 300 Hz bandwidth filter and is especially useful for speech analysis because it reveals certain acoustic features that have been important in distinguishing among various types of sounds and among different talkers. In particular, the wide-band spectrogram usually is effective in displaying *formants* (acoustical energy constrained to frequency regions by vocal tract resonances). The wide-band spectrogram is particularly useful for the analysis of highly dynamic signals such as speech.[3] Figure 1 illustrates a wide-band speech spectrogram of the utterance "I said stop"; Figure 2 notes landmarks typical of speech sounds in the word "stop." The horizontal axis of both panels is time and the vertical axis is frequency in Hertz (Hz) or cycles per second. The third dimension of the spectrogram is intensity: darker areas represent greater intensity.

---

**[Section 7:5]**

[1] Hazen, Effects of Differing Phonetic Contexts on Spectrographic Speaker Identification, 54 J. Acoustical Soc'y Am. 650 (1973).

[2] Time is represented from left to right. Frequency is the rate of vibration of a sound stimulus and is expressed in the unit of hertz (Hz), which is the number of cycles of vibration per second. The acoustic energy in adult male speech is essentially contained in a frequency range (bandwidth) of about 50 to 8,000 Hz. However, speech can be understood even with much narrower bandwidths. For instance, telephone bandwidth is on the order of 3,000 Hz (500 to 3,500 Hz). The greatest concentration of speech energy for adult male voices is in the range of about 100 to 2500 Hz. Intensity is one measure of the magnitude or strength of sound energy. It is usually expressed in decibels (dB), a logarithmic scale.

[3] Smits, Accuracy of Quasistationary Analysis of Highly Dynamic Speech Signals, 96 J. Acoustical Soc'y Am. 3401 (1994).

# SPECTROGRAM

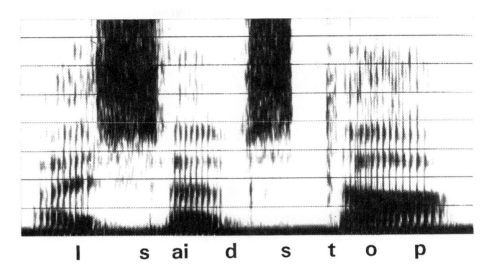

I s ai d s t o p

**Figure 1.** A spectrogram of the utterance, "I say stop." Time is represented on the horizontal axis, frequency on the vertical axis, and intensity as variations in darkness. The horizontal lines indicate frequency intervals of 1 kHz (1000 Hz).

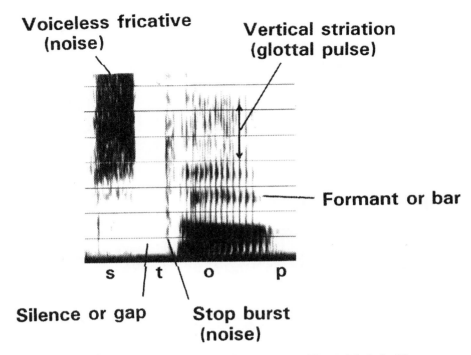

**Figure 2.** A spectrogram of the word "stop" from Fig. 1, labeled with some acoustic features that might be used in talker identification by spectrogram.

Most of the published scientific papers are based on wide-band analyses of selected words produced by adult male talkers. In this chapter, the wide-band analysis is assumed unless otherwise noted. This is also the common form of analysis used in talker identification from the visual examination of spectrograms. An advantage of many of the contemporary computer-based speech analysis systems is that they offer a range of choices of analysis filter bandwidths. The clarity of formants is influenced by interactions between bandwidth and the frequency characteristics of the speech to be analyzed. Conventional filters 250 or 300 Hz in width are generally suitable for analyzing the speech of adult males, but other bandwidths may be preferable for certain groups, including women, children, some adolescent males, and men with unusually high vocal fundamental frequency (the physical attribute most closely related to what we hear as vocal pitch). Scientific interest in the features of formants that distinguish males, females and children began in the 1940s and continues to the present.[4] Buder,[5] for example, has summarized nearly 90 years of quantitative descriptions of vocal quality. These include simple statistical summaries of fundamental frequency and voice amplitude, long and short term perturbations and covariations in both, and various spectral measures. While many of these pertain to clinical voice disorders, some have been incorporated into currently available instrumentation used in forensic practice. Differences between controlled clinical recording environments and those common to forensic practice may limit application of recent innovations in measurement, but some may prove useful. The essential point is that characteristics of the laboratory analysis should be selected to match talker characteristics in ways that recognize the limitations of recording methods to capture those characteristics.

### § 7:6  Introductory discussion of the science—The scientific questions— Terminology and basic concepts—Decision objectives

Talker recognition embraces procedures with different decision objectives and assumptions. These include *talker verification* (or authentication), *talker identification*, and *talker elimination*. Talker verification is a test of an identity claim in which a speech sample from an individual is compared to a stored reference sample previously obtained from the individual whose identity is claimed. A common application is security access. A person making the identity claim will be granted access if this person's speech sample is a satisfactory match to a stored pattern. Talker identification is a decision process in which an utterance from an unknown speaker is attributed to one speaker in a known population, such as employees in a high-security facility. Talker elimination is the inverse process of deciding that an utterance from an unknown talker cannot be attributed to a particular speaker in a known population. Most forensic applications involve speaker identification or elimination and these will be the central issues in this chapter.

Talker identification and elimination can be studied experimentally using three different comparison procedures: *closed-set*, *open-set*, and *discrimination*. Different patterns of correct and incorrect decisions are possible for each procedure. In the closed and open procedures, a sample (exemplar) of speech from an unknown talker (U) is compared to exemplars from some number (N) of talkers whose identities are known (K). Normally, each known talker ($K_n$) is represented by a single exemplar—in other words, the known talkers are independent of each other. If one of the

---

[4]Keonig et al., The Sound Spectrograph, 17 J. Acoustical Soc'y Am. 19 (1946); Peterson & Barney, Control Methods Used in the Study of the Vowels, 24 J. Acoustical Soc'y Am. 175 (1952); Hillenbrand et al., Acoustic Characteristics of American English Vowels, 97 J. Acoustical Soc'y Am. 3099 (1995).

[5]Eugene H. Buder, Acoustic Analysis of Voice Quality: A Tabulation of Algorithms 1902–1990, in Voice Quality Measurement (Raymond D. Kent & Martin J. Ball eds., 2000).

known talkers (assume it is $K_3$) is indeed the same as talker U, and if (prior to the experiment) the examiner is informed a match exits, then the procedure is closed. The procedure is open if the examiner is told that the population of known talkers may or may not actually include talker U. A common experimental strategy is to organize comparisons of unknown and known exemplars as pairs following the form: U vs. $K_1$, U vs. $K_2$, . . . U vs. $K_N$. Assuming the examiner is required to consider each pair only once, a total of N paired comparisons is possible. Each pair-wise comparison is constrained to one of two decisions: $U \neq K_n$ (a claimed identification) or $U \neq K_n$ (a claimed elimination). Examiner claims are compared to the actual configuration of pairs (known to the experimenter, but not the examiner). If a claimed identification is wrong, the decision is called a false identification or false positive. If a claimed elimination is wrong, the decision is called a false elimination or false negative.

In the closed-set procedure, the examiner is asked *which* known exemplar matches the unknown sample. Only one claimed identification ($U = K_3$ in this example) can be correct and no more than N-1 claimed eliminations can be correct. There can be only one false elimination because the pairing of U vs. $K_3$ occurs only once. Up to N-1 false identifications are possible, but because the examiner knows that only one match exists, and because at least one identity claim must be made, the closed-set procedure effectively limits the possible number of false identifications to one.

In the open-set procedure, the examiner is asked *whether* one of the known samples matches the unknown exemplar and (if so), *which* one. If the target is included among the known exemplars, there may be one correct identification, N-1 correct eliminations, one false identification, and one false elimination. In the open procedure with the target talker ($K_3$ in this example) absent, however, there can be as many as N correct eliminations and one false identification. There can be no correct identification and no false elimination because the target talker is not available for comparison. Comparison of results from open-and closed-set procedures allow study of examiner preferences for claims of elimination or identification, as well as the impact of the spectrographic cues available to the examiner upon decision-making behavior.

Systematic variations of closed and open procedures are possible in which the examiner is either allowed or required to consider each pair more than once, and in which the experimenter manipulates the size and nature of exemplars, the prior probabilities of correct identifications, the examiner's knowledge of those probabilities, or the costs assigned to false identifications and false eliminations. A common variation employs *match trials* in which coded versions of the unknown exemplar are included among the set of known samples, resulting in a comparison of the form $U_a$ vs. $U_b$. Match trials are single-blind experimental controls intended to index correct identification and false elimination. Experimental variations modify the numbers of possible correct and incorrect decisions, but not the types of error. Distinctions between closed and open procedures are pertinent to laboratory studies, but in forensic practice it may not be possible to know which condition applies.

The discrimination procedure differs from open-set and closed-set procedures in that the examiner is provided with several exemplars produced by one unknown talker and several exemplars produced by a single known talker (N = 1). The examiner's task is to determine whether the two groups of exemplars are *sufficiently similar* to have been produced by the same individual. Match trials can be used in discrimination procedures for the purposes noted above. This procedure can produce correct identifications, correct eliminations, false identifications and false eliminations. Most scientific studies can be classified according to the terms introduced to this point.

Under controlled experimental conditions, correct and incorrect decision outcomes can be described for different identification procedures based upon various data.

Rigorous quantitative comparison of decision methods is possible using techniques drawn from signal detection theory[1] and Bayesian statistics. These scientific techniques are similar to those used in research on medical diagnosis.[2]

## § 7:7 Introductory discussion of the science—The scientific questions—Terminology and basic concepts—Acoustic characteristics

A number of different acoustic characteristics are potentially useful in talker identification. An extensive and detailed listing is not possible in this brief chapter, but some commonly used characteristics can be cited as examples. Tosi et al.[1] considered the parameters of mean frequencies and bandwidths of vowel formants, gaps and type of vertical striations, slopes of formants, duration of similar phonetic elements and plosive gaps, energy distribution of fricatives, plosives, and interformant spaces.[2] Buder[3] identifies other parameters of broader scientific interest. The Voice Identification and Acoustic Analysis Subcommittee of the International Association for Identification (VIAAS-IAI) guidelines[4] specifically mentioned the following: general formant shaping and positioning, pitch striations, energy distribution, word duration, and coupling of the oral and nasal cavities. Other possibilities include inhalation noise, repetitive throat clearing, and vocalized pauses. It should be noted that these are broad categories of acoustic differences and each can include a number of variations or subtypes. The degree to which a given acoustic characteristic may contribute to an identification can vary with the talkers under examination, the quality of the recordings, and the speech sample available for inspection. The various sounds of a language differ in terms of their distinguishing acoustic characteristics, and some research studies indicate that some phonemes (the basic sound elements that distinguish among words) are better for discriminating among speakers than others.[5]

As the preceding discussion reveals, the scientific study of speech represents a number of different disciplines, including physics, physiology, anatomy, and psychology.[6]

## § 7:8 Introductory discussion of the science—The scientific questions—A model of talker identification variables

A general conceptual model, or theory, would be useful in integrating the data

---

**[Section 7:6]**

[1]See John Swets, Measuring the Accuracy of Diagnostic Systems, 240 Science 1285 (1988); John Swets & Ronald Pickett, Evaluation of Diagnostic Systems: Models from Signal Detection Theory (1982).

[2]Helena C. Kraemer, Evaluating Medical Tests: Objective and Quantitative Guidelines (1992).

**[Section 7:7]**

[1]Oscar Tosi et al., Experiment on Voice Identification, 51 J. Acoustical Soc'y Am. 2030 (1972).

[2]Individual vowel formants have two primary characteristics: the center frequency of the formant and its bandwidth (spread of energy). Vertical striations relate to the vocal pitch and to irregularities in vocal fold vibrations. Formant slopes refer to changes in the frequency of a formant during a specified time interval. Durations can be determined for a variety of acoustic segments, each of which is defined in terms of one or more acoustic features. Energy distribution typically is described in terms of the major frequency regions of sound energy, e.g., the fricative "s" in the word "stop" has the most high-frequency energy as shown in Figure 1.

[3]Eugene H. Buder, Acoustic Analysis of Voice Quality: A Tabulation of Algorithms 1902–1990, in Voice Quality Measurement (Raymond D. Kent & Martin J. Ball eds., 2000).

[4]VIAAS-IAI: Voice Identification and Acoustic Analysis Subcommittee (VIAAS) of the International Association for Identification (IAI), Voice Comparison Standards, 41 Forensic Ident. 373 (1991).

[5]Francis Nolan, The Phonetic Bases of Speaker Recognition (1983).

[6]A very readable account of this multi-disciplinary endeavor is provided by Peter B. Denes & Elliott N. Pinson, The Speech Chain (2nd ed., 1993).

from various studies and in understanding the potential interactions of the factors that influence talker identification. No unified theory of talker identification has been offered in the scientific literature, but we suggest what one might look like here.

**Figure 3**

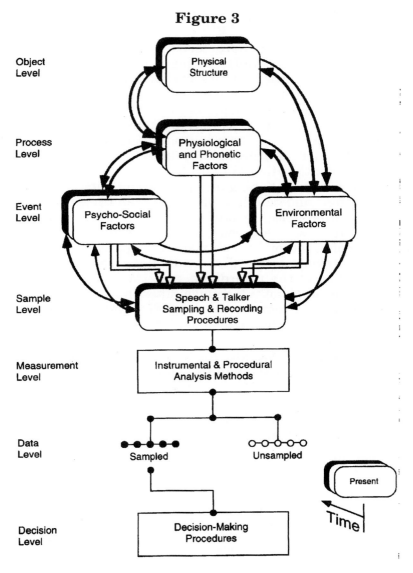

Figure 3 considers talker identification with respect to seven major levels. The first three of these (object, process, and event levels) pertain to spontaneous speech production, and the next (sample level) pertains to actions by which speech is captured or elicited for later comparison. The fifth (measurement) level relates to the methods by which recorded speech is analyzed, resulting in reports of the outcomes of such analyses (data level). The last (decision) level deals with the methods and rules by which various data are compared for the purpose of making a decision. For these purposes, decision outcomes are limited to identification and elimination, with or without qualifications of relative certainty.

The object, process, and event levels all have temporal extent, i.e., they can change with the passage of time. The curved lines with solid arrows linking the components of these levels are intended to suggest interactions or mutual influence among the components. These interactions also can change over time. Process and event levels combine to yield spoken language, depicted here with uncurved lines ending in open arrows.

Object, process, and event level components also are subject to major sources of variability, indicated in Figure 3 by curved boxes. Some of these variances change with time. For example, over relatively long periods of time, the anatomical structures involved in speech production change. An obvious change occurs at puberty when males undergo major changes in laryngeal anatomy. Less obvious are structural changes related to habits of vocal use, environmental agents, aging, and other life events (e.g., changes in dentition). These sources of variability exist both within individuals (over short and long periods of time) and between individuals at any given moment in time. Factors affecting physiological and phonetic variability include general health, state of sobriety or intoxication, and the "rules" underlying various spoken languages. Psycho-social factors include dialect, education and social status, communicative intent, speaking style, and emotional state. Another is the tendency of talkers to reflect the vocal style (changes in vocal loudness, pitch, speaking rate, and patterns of pauses) of those with whom they are communicating.

Environmental factors also can influence speech production. One such effect is the tendency of talkers to increase vocal effort (hence, vocal loudness) as the amplitude of ambient noise increases. This effect (known as the Lombard voice reflex) appears to differ between males and females.[1] Talkers also tend to change certain articulation characteristics in the presence of high levels of background noise or other interference.

The absence of temporal invariance and the presence of variability within and between talkers do not necessarily obviate talker identification if their net impact is small compared to the sources of consistency within the time frames typical of forensic identification. Two conditions seem scientifically necessary to justify talker identification by spectrographic (or any other) methods. First, the effect of interactions among physical structure, physiological and phonetic factors, and psycho-social factors must be consistent within an individual, at least over relatively short periods of time. Further, the patterns of these interactions must be sufficiently idiosyncratic to produce measurable differences among individuals under field conditions. This consistency presumably results in spoken language that differs demonstrably among individuals and is transparent to such factors as vocal disguise.

The fourth major level, sample level, is directly relevant to research design and forensic practice, and therefore is discussed infra.[2]

The decision level involves the ways in which data from different speech samples

---

**[Section 7:8]**

[1]Junqua, The Lombard Reflex and its Role on Human Listeners and Automatic Speech

Recognizers, 93 J. Acoustical Soc'y Am. 510 (1993).

[2]§ 7:12.

are compared for the purpose of identifying or eliminating individual talkers. Although standards exist to guide the procedures by which data are compared and the decision options that are allowed, standards are not always followed. Moreover, the standards themselves are somewhat arbitrary. The quality of decision-making ultimately is influenced by formal decision rules, the sufficiency of data, the accuracy and precision of measurement, and the thoroughness of procedural controls invoked while sampling speech materials and talkers.

Talker identification may resemble handwriting identification more than it does fingerprint identification. Both speech and handwriting are dynamic events, influenced by structural (anatomical) and physiological factors; both are influenced by developmental changes and by psycho-social factors. Because fingerprints are static (rather than dynamic) events, they are uninfluenced by physiology and psycho-social factors. Fingerprints are not subject to developmental change and (barring serious physical trauma) they do not change with age.

### § 7:9 Introductory discussion of the science—Scientific methods applied in talker identification research

The scientific evidence on talker identification has been obtained primarily by laboratory experimentation. The basic design of a talker identification experiment involves selection of (a) a group of talkers, (b) a type of speech material (e.g., isolated words, short sentences, or conversation), (c) one or more examiners (who may be trained or untrained), and (d) decision categories used by the examiners. However, many additional details of the experimental design need to be specified.

Because the acoustic signal of speech is shaped by a large number of factors, some of which are not under direct experimental control, the results of experiments often must be interpreted with regard to several interacting factors. The conceptual model or framework, such as that presented in Figure 3, may serve to clarify the major issues underlying talker identification by means of spectrographic comparison.[1] Figure 3 summarizes a number of variables and potential interactions that conceivably influence talker identification by spectrogram comparison.

### § 7:10 Introductory discussion of the science—Scientific methods applied in talker identification research—Variations in methods

As a result of the manifold decisions that have to be made in designing a single experiment, it is rare that any two published reports on talker identification can be directly compared with respect to size of error. As one major contributor to this field remarked, "the reader should be warned that most of the laboratory experiments on voice identification performed to date share one common characteristic—their results are very hard to compare because experimental conditions among them differ widely and data were reported differently."[1] The matter becomes further complicated in attempted extrapolations from the laboratory experiments to practical application in forensics (as discussed earlier in this chapter). These differences among laboratory experiments and between laboratory experiments and forensic examinations are major obstacles in the evaluation of the accuracy of talker identification.

### § 7:11 Introductory discussion of the science—Scientific methods applied in talker identification research—Quantity of sound studied

One reason for the difficulty of comparing various published studies is that each

---

**[Section 7:9]**

[1] With minor modifications, structurally similar models could be constructed for other systems of forensic identification such as those based on

fingerprints and handwriting.

**[Section 7:10]**

[1] Oscar Tosi, Voice Identification: Theory and Legal Applications 57 (1979).

experiment must severely limit the quantity of evidence examined in comparison to the potential amount of evidence. Speech consists of a number of speech sounds that can be combined to form words. Words, in turn, can be selected to form a potentially infinite number of sentences. On any occasion, a talker may use just a few words. The words available for examination may not be ideal for the purpose of talker identification, because some words contain better cues for identification than others. Some of the most frequently occurring words in English are short in duration and therefore limited in their acoustic cues. These words include: the, of, I, and, you, to, a, in, that, it, is, he, we. Furthermore, a word produced in different phonetic contexts (such as different sentences) will not necessarily have the same acoustic appearance from one context to the next. Finally, the production of a word even in the same context (produced in the same phrase or sentence) may vary from one time to another.

## § 7:12 Introductory discussion of the science—Scientific methods applied in talker identification research—Sampling of talkers

At the sample level of the model discussed, supra,[1] are those procedures used to select talkers to be recorded for forensic comparison, and specification of the speech to be produced by those talkers. Such selections are undertaken in circumstances in which it is normally possible to exercise some control over recording environment, language, and speaking style. If these controls are managed skillfully and thoroughly, some of the event level variances can be minimized, thus providing samples for comparison that are "fair" in the sense that the remaining variances are dominated by the presumably idiosyncratic interactions noted above. Because multiple speech and talker samples cannot be collected at exactly the same moment, temporal variables exist at the sample level. If samples are collected with proper attention to investigative technique, the identities of all but one of the talkers should be known with certainty. (This assumes, of course, that recordings are authentic and have not been edited in any way.)

Once appropriate voice samples have been collected and authenticated, a host of formal observations can be made. Some of these observations result in quantitative measurements based on visual displays of speech, others exist in the form of non-numerical observations of the visual displays themselves, and still others exist in the form of perceptual observations about the audio material under consideration. Sample duration and recording quality limit the observations that are possible. The reports of quantitative and non-quantitative observations form the data used in talker identification. Of the universe of potential data based on speech spectrograms, only a subset is used in most forensic situations. Because the subject of most forensic speech analysis is recorded material, and because the method of analysis is instrumental, temporal variances are of minimal importance.

## § 7:13 Introductory discussion of the science—Scientific methods applied in talker identification research—Differences between scientific research and forensic application

Finally, it would be helpful to compare the methods used in scientific research and those used in forensic practice. Before doing so, however, we should note that general standards or recommendations have been published for forensic examination.[1] The procedures followed by individual examiners may vary. The following discussion, however, assumes forensic procedures generally consistent with the aforementioned sources. In particular, frequent reference will be made to the

---

[Section 7:12]

[1]§ 7:8.

[Section 7:13]

[1]See Richard H. Bolt et al., On the Theory

guidelines of the Voice Identification and Acoustic Analysis Subcommittee of the International Association for Identification (VIAAS-IAI). These guidelines, published in 1991, are the most recent recommendations for forensic examination.

Published scientific research differs from forensic application in four potentially important respects:

## § 7:14  Introductory discussion of the science—Scientific methods applied in talker identification research—Differences between scientific research and forensic application—Decision categories

One difference between scientific studies and typical forensic application is that forensic examiners generally use categories of "no decision" or "uncertain" whereas most published research has required that subjects judging spectrograms choose between identification and elimination. According to VIAAS-IAI, "every examination conducted can only produce one of seven (7) decisions: Identification, Probable Identification, Possible Identification, Inconclusive, Possible Elimination, Probable Elimination, or Elimination."[1] Quantitative criteria based on decisions for the number of comparable words are associated with each of the seven decisions. Apparently, no published large-scale research project has used these decision categories. Consequently, some writers have argued that the accuracy rates in the experimental studies are conservative estimates of the accuracy to be expected in forensic examinations.

## § 7:15  Introductory discussion of the science—Scientific methods applied in talker identification research—Differences between scientific research and forensic application—Visual vs. visual-aural identification

A second difference between the scientific research on talker identification and the forensic situation is that forensic examiners routinely use aural recognition and spectrograms in reaching a decision, but published research articles have rarely, if ever, studied the joint use of aural and spectrographic procedures. Stevens et al.[1] compared spectrographic and aural presentations of stimuli. They found that the percentages of correct responses in both closed and open tests were significantly higher for aural than for visual examination. However, the examiners were not specially trained for visual examination of spectrograms, and the speech samples were brief (although exceeding the minimum number of words recommended by the VIAAS-IAI). Apparently, no published scientific report used a procedure that accords with the customary practice in forensic examination of using trained personnel to conduct combined aural and spectrographic examinations in reaching a decision of identification or elimination. Experiments have been conducted on aural and spectrographic identification separately, but it has not been established how the two methods of examination complement one another in joint application.

and Practice of Voice Identification (1979); Koenig, Speaker Identification, 49 FBI Law Enforcement Bulletin 20 (1980); Koenig, Spectrographic Voice Identification: A Forensic Survey, 79 J. Acoustical Soc'y Am. 2088 (1986) (letter); Bruce E. Koenig, Spectrographic Voice Identification, 13 Crime Lab Digest 105 (1986); Lonnie L. Smrkovski, Forensic Voice Identification (Michigan Department of State Police, 1983); Oscar Tosi, Voice Identification: Theory and Legal Applications 57 (1979); VIAAS-IAI, Voice Identification Instruction Manual (n.d.).

**[Section 7:14]**

[1]VIAAS-IAI: Voice Identification and Acoustic Analysis Subcommittee (VIAAS) of the International Association for Identification (IAI), Voice Comparison Standards, 41 Forensic Ident. at 387 (1991).

**[Section 7:15]**

[1]Stevens et al., Speaker Authentication and Identification: A Comparison of Spectrographic and Auditory Presentations of Speech Material, 44 J. Acoustical Soc'y Am. 1596 (1968).

As a partial answer to this question, Bolt et al.[2] compared the aural task performance reported by Stevens et al.[3] with the visual spectrogram performance reported by Tosi et al.[4] Bolt et al. concluded, "These results would seem to support the idea that listening and visual examination of spectrograms are comparable as single-mode methods of speaker recognition".[5] Bolt et al. also concluded that listening-only experiments on talker identification show that: (1) performance is less than perfect, with error scores for best conditions ranging from 5 to 15%; and (2) performance is fairly robust under certain types of degradation (such as filtering and addition of noise). It is not clear from this research to what degree the aural performance of experts in voice identification differs from that of laypersons. Carlson and Granstrom showed that accurate matching of unknown voices speaking different utterances can be done if the samples are sufficiently long. But they also report that listeners differ in this ability.[6] Representative studies on aural identification of talkers are given in the margin.[7] The results of selected studies are summarized in Table 2.

**Table 2**
**Summary of Selected Experiments in Talker Identification. Examples for Both Listening (Aural) and Visual (Spectrogram) Experiments Are Shown. Note: Many Important Differences Among the Studies Are Not Represented in This Table, Which Is Intended to Show the General Sizes of Error in Selected Experiments.**

| Source | Talkers | Examiners | Error rate |
|---|---|---|---|
| LISTENING EXPERIMENTS | | | |
| McGehee (1937, 1944) | 31 males, 18 females, selected to form panels of 5 talkers | 740 college students (untrained), selected to form 15 panels of listeners | 17 to 87%, depending on time elapsed between first and second sessions |
| Pollack et al. (1954) | 16, in groups of 2 to 8 | Listeners familiar with the talkers | 5% for normal voiced speech; 70% for whispered |
| Bricker & Pruzansky (1966) | 10 | 16 listeners. familiar with the talkers | 0 to 8% across judges for best condition |
| Stevens et al. (1968) | 24 highly homogeneous talkers | 6 (untrained) | Closed tests: 6 to 18% false identification; 6 to 8% false identification and 8 to 12% false elimination |

[2]Richard H. Bolt et al., On the Theory and Practice of Voice Identification (1979).

[3]Stevens et al., Speaker Authentication and Identification: A Comparison of Spectrographic and Auditory Presentations of Speech Material, 44 J. Acoustical Soc'y Am. 1596 (1968).

[4]Tosi et al., Experiment on Voice Identification, 51 J. Acoustical Soc'y Am. 2030 (1972).

[5]Richard H. Bolt et al., On the Theory and Practice of Voice Identification 118 (1979).

[6]Carlson & Granstrom, An Interactive Technique for Matching Speaker Identity, 52 Phonetica 236 (1995).

[7]Bricker & Pruzanski, Effects of Stimulus Content and Duration on Talker Identification, 40 J. Acoustical Soc'y Am. 1441 (1966); Frank R. Clarke et al., Characteristics that Determine Speaker Recognition (Electronic Systems Division, U.S. Air Force Technical Report ESD-66-636, 1966); McGehee, The Reliability of the Identification of the Human Voice, 17 J. Gen. Psych. 249 (1937); McGehee, An Experimental Study in Voice Recognition, 31 J. Gen. Psych. 53 (1944); Pollack et al., On the Identification of Speakers by Voice, 26 J. Acoustical Soc'y Am. 403 (1954); Voiers, Perceptual Basis of Speaker Identity, 36 J. Acoustical Soc'y Am. 1065 (1964).

| Source | Talkers | Examiners | Error rate |
|--------|---------|-----------|------------|
| VISUAL EXPERIMENTS | | | |
| Young & Campbell (1967) | 5 men used as known talkers in each trial | 10 examiners with 2.5 hr. of training | 63% based on two short words excerpted from context |
| Stevens et al. (1968) | 24 highly homogeneous talkers | 4–6 (untrained) | Closed tests: 21 to 28% false identification; Open tests: 31 to 47% false identification and 10 to 20% false elimination |
| Hazen (1973) | 50 males | 7 two-person panels trained over several sessions | Closed tests/same context: 20% Open tests/same context: 7% false identification, 36% false elimination |
| Smrkovski (1976) | 7 male and 7 female | 4 experts, 4 trainees, 4 novices | Match/no match decisions: 0% errors for experts and trainees; 5% false identification and 25% false elimination for novices |
| Tosi et al. (1972) | Up to 40 in individual experiments; drawn from 250 men selected from 25,000 | 29 persons trained for one month, working individually or in two- or three-person teams | For open tests, noncontemporary spectrograms and continuous speech: 6% false identification 13% false elimination |

It is likely that a combination of aural and visual identification procedures would have a lower error rate than either procedure used alone, but the amount of error reduction is unknown. The VIAAS-IAI specifies that in spectrographic/aural analysis, an "aural short-term memory comparison must be conducted . . . ."[8] and this procedure appears consistent with common forensic procedure. Indeed, it is unlikely that examiners who prepare the spectrograms for identification purposes would not listen to the tape recordings as part of the process. Forensic standards developed at the German Bundeskriminalamt use a combination of listening and spectrographic analysis.[9] The procedure includes listening and analysis by a phonetician, who identifies and characterizes dialect, pathologic features, and any other idiosyncratic properties. Acoustic analysis is performed both to provide quantitative support to the characteristics determined by listening and to supply additional information. A careful co-registration of the two kinds of analysis would enhance the validity and reliability of identification judgments.

The effects of combined auditory and visual information also have been assessed for the related purposes of speaker verification or identification. This research pertains to circumstances in which both facial and voice information are available. For speaker verification, a system using dual classifiers (acoustic features of the voice and visual features obtained from a lip tracker) outperformed single methods of classification and reduced the error rate of the acoustic classifier from 2.3% to 0.5%.[10] Fusion of audio and video information in a multi-expert decision making

---

[8]VIAAS-IAI: Voice Identification and Acoustic Analysis Subcommittee (VIAAS) of the International Association for Identification (IAI), Voice Comparison Standards, 41 Forensic Ident. at 385 (1991).

[9]Hermann J. Kunzel, Sprechererkennung: Grundzuge forensischer Sprachverarbeitung

(1987); Hermann J. Kunzel, Current Approaches to Forensic Speaker Recognition, Proceedings of ESCA Workshop on Speaker Recognition, Identification, and Verification 135 (Martigny, Switzerland, April 5–7, 1994).

[10]P. Jourlin et al., Acoustic-labial Speaker Verification, 18 Pattern Recognition Letters 853

machine was accomplished by Duc, Bigun, Bigun, Maitre, and Fischer.[11] They reported a success rate of 99.5% for speaker verification. A general review of audio-visual integration by Chen and Rao also points to the advantages of using both sources of information.[12] These results may be particularly important in the use of videotapes containing both visual and auditory signals relevant to identification of individuals.

### § 7:16 Introductory discussion of the science—Scientific methods applied in talker identification research—Differences between scientific research and forensic application—Quality of speech samples and authenticity of recordings

A third difference is, that with few exceptions, laboratory research has used high-quality speech recording systems with well-established procedures and unquestioned authenticity. Forensic applications frequently must contend with recordings obtained under less than ideal conditions and sometimes of doubtful authenticity. Recordings based on telephone conversations exhibit audio bandwidths ranging from 2000 Hz to about 3500 Hz, depending on a host of factors (telephone handset characteristics, mouth-to-microphone distance, the length of the transmission path, and intervening signal encryption, broadcasting, and switching technologies). Owen described the typical surveillance recording as having "an audio bandwidth of 300 Hz to 6000 Hz, with a maximum dynamic range of 30–50 dB."[1] These specifications are quite poor in comparison to laboratory equipment currently used in scientific studies of speech.[2] Although recent technical improvements permit surveillance recordings with much higher quality, many systems now in use remain very limited in quality. Problems with the quality of forensic recording equipment and methods may be complicated by difficulties in obtaining original recordings, for which enhancement is generally more successful.

Another problem facing the forensic specialist is the possibility that tapes submitted for analysis are nonauthentic or have been altered in some way. Owen,[3] Koenig,[4] and Hollien[5] describe procedures and criteria to ascertain the authenticity of audio tape recordings; Gruber, Poza & Pellicano[6] provide detailed treatment of legal and technical issues associated with authentication of audio recordings for evidentiary purposes. Technical authenticity analysis seeks to determine whether a particular recording was made of the events asserted by the parties who produced the recording, and in the manner claimed by those who produced it, and whether it is free from unexplained artifacts, alterations, deletions, or edits.

The issues of technical quality, enhancement and authentication go beyond the

---

(1997).

[11]Benoit Duc et al., Fusion of Audio and Video Information for Multi Modal Person Authentication, 18 Pattern Recognition Letters 835 (1997).

[12]Tsuhan Chen & Ram R. Rao, Audio-visual Integration in Multimodal Communication, 86 Proceedings of the IEEE 837 (1998).

**[Section 7:16]**

[1]Owen, An Introduction to Forensic Examination of Audio and Video Tapes, 39 J. Forensic Ident. 75 (1989).

[2]In some situations, recordings of poor quality can be enhanced by techniques such as amplitude compression or expansion, gating, simple filtering, or more complex processing (for example, adaptive predictive deconvolution, and adaptive noise cancellation) by which some background noise can be removed. See Koenig, Enhancement of Forensic Audio Recordings, 36 J. Audio Engineering Soc'y 884 (1988), for a discussion of some of these procedures.

[3]Owen, An Introduction to Forensic Examination of Audio and Video Tapes, 39 J. Forensic Ident. 75 (1989).

[4]Koenig, Authentication of Forensic Audio Recordings, 38 J. Audio Engineering Soc'y 3 (1990).

[5]Harry Hollien, The Acoustics of Crime (1990).

[6]Jordan S. Gruber et al., Audio Recordings: Evidence, Experts and Technology, 48 Am. Jur. Trials 1 (1993).

scope of this chapter but should be considered as potentially serious issues in forensic talker identification. Tape recordings should be evaluated to ascertain quality and determine authenticity before spectrograms are examined for talker identification. The VIAAS-IAI has recommended criteria for acceptable quality of speech recordings, including presence of speech energy above 2000 Hz.

## § 7:17  Introductory discussion of the science—Scientific methods applied in talker identification research—Differences between scientific research and forensic application—Selection of talkers for identification task

A fourth difference pertains to the selection of talkers for whom an identification will be attempted. Scientific experiments generally select talker subsets randomly, that is, without regard to specific similarities to a given reference talker. In contrast, forensic examination usually involves talkers who are selected because their voices have a similarity to a suspect's voice. That is, the talkers are selected to form a reasonable "lineup" of voices. Similarity among voices is not easily determined or described but this factor becomes important in evaluating error rates in talker identification. If talkers are chosen because of a similarity criterion, identification or elimination is expected to be more difficult as compared to a situation in which talkers are drawn randomly.

## § 7:18  Areas of scientific agreement

It is clear from studies of the acoustic properties of speech that marked differences may occur among various groups of talkers. For example, the acoustic patterns of speech are different among men, women and children, owing largely to differences in the size of the vocal tract, that is, the resonating system of speech that extends from the larynx up through the nose or mouth.[1] Differences within a given age-gender group are not as conspicuous as the differences across age or gender groups, but some differences exist, at least in selected comparisons. It is possible that racial differences exist,[2] but such differences have not been studied extensively. As a general conclusion, one might say that there is a high likelihood that large subgroups of talkers, particularly age-gender subgroups and some dialect subgroups, can be distinguished from one another. It is also known that certain acoustic measures of speech are correlated with physical features such as age, gender, height, and weight of talkers.[3]

The gender of a talker can be determined with high accuracy using information on vocal fundamental frequency and vocal tract length.[4] When an isolated vowel segment was analyzed according to these features, classification by gender was nearly perfect. Classification of individual talkers required information on acoustic parameters associated with vocal tract filtering (formant patterns). Essentially the same pattern of results obtained for male and female talkers, but classification rates were consistently lower for females, who were more likely to be classified as males than males were to be classified as females. This study is one of the very few to ad-

---

[Section 7:18]

[1]Childers & Wu, Gender Recognition from Speech. Part II: Fine Analysis, 90 J. Acoustical Soc'y Am. 1841 (1991); Raymond D. Kent & Charles Read, The Acoustic Analysis of Speech (1992); Wu & Childers, Gender Recognition from Speech. Part I: Coarse Analysis, 90 J. Acoustical Soc'y Am. 1828 (1991).

[2]Walton & Orlikoff, Speaker Race Identification from Acoustic Cues in the Vocal Signal, 37 J.

Speech & Hearing Research 738 (1994).

[3]Suzuki, Correlation of Speaker's Physical Factors and Speech, 41 J. Acoustical Soc'y of Japan 895 (1985).

[4]Bachorowski & Owren, Acoustic Correlates of Talker Sex and Individual Talker Identity Are Present in a Short Vowel Segment Produced in Running Speech, 106 J. Acoustical Soc'y Am. 1054 (1999).

dress gender differences in the acoustic identification of talkers.

But the essential question for talker identification by spectrograms for the usual forensic application is whether the intertalker differences are sufficient to distinguish *one* individual from a group of talkers of the same gender and roughly the same age. The relevant scientific literature pertains almost exclusively to men. Under conditions comparable to the typical forensic examination, unique identification (0% error rates for both false identification and false elimination in open tests) is unlikely. One expert in the area wrote, "no method or combination of methods will ever yield a positive result (identification or elimination) in 100% of the cases examined."[5] It is also well known that an individual talker never produces speech in *exactly* the same way in different repetitions of what is intended to be the same utterance.[6] Tokens that are recorded in the same session are more similar than tokens recorded in separate sessions.[7] For some acoustic features, intratalker variability can be as great as intertalker variability.[8]

Prospects for talker identification by spectrograms are improved if intertalker variations are large compared to intratalker variations. As will be discussed below, there are several sources of intratalker variation including emotional state, influence of intoxicants, and style of speaking. In addition, some short-term and long-term variations have been noted in the speech patterns of individual talkers.[9] The VIAAS-IAI recommends that the examiner compare "similarly spoken words within each voice sample to determine the range of intraspeaker variability"[10] and exclude the sample from comparison if considerable variability is observed. Each of the following factors can substantially affect the accuracy of spectrograms as a means of talker identification. In some cases, two or more of these factors may combine to limit the successful application of the method.

### § 7:19  Areas of scientific agreement—Signal transmission and recording

It is generally agreed that the speech signal of an individual talker can be affected to some degree by a variety of factors and circumstances in addition to robust individual characteristics of the talker such as anatomy and learned speaking habits.[1] The spectrogram is a visual record of an acoustic signal that represents a series of transformations and passages. Speech is a perishable message. The acoustic vibrations of an utterance decay rapidly in the atmosphere and are lost forever except in the memory of a listener or a storage device such as a tape recorder. Before speech can be stored in a tape recorder or computer, it must be transduced from acoustic to electrical or electromagnetic energy. This transduction process

---

[5]Oscar Tosi, Voice Identification: Theory and Legal Applications at 148 (1979).

[6]Bolt et al., Speaker Identification by Speech Spectrograms: Some Further Observations, 54 J. Acoustical Soc'y Am. 531 (1973); Richard H. Bolt et al., On the Theory and Practice of Voice Identification (1979).

[7]Aaron E. Rosenberg & Frank K. Soong, Recent Research on Automatic Speaker Identification, in Advances in Speech Signal Processing 701 (Sadaoki Furui & M. Mohan Sondhi eds., 1992).

[8]Atkinson, Inter-and Intraspeaker Variability in Fundamental Voice Frequency, 60 J. Acoustical Soc'y Am. 440 (1976).

[9]Endres et al., Voice Spectrograms As a Function of Age, Voice Disguise, and Voice Imitation, 49 J. Acoustical Soc'y Am. 1842 (1971); Rastatter & Jaques, Formant Frequency Structure of the Aging Male and Female Vocal Tract, 42 Folia

Phoniatrica 312 (1990).

[10]VIAAS-IAI: Voice Identification and Acoustic Analysis Subcommittee (VIAAS) of the International Association for Identification (IAI), Voice Comparison Standards, 41 Forensic Ident. at 384 (1991).

**[Section 7:19]**

[1]See Bolt et al., Speaker Identification of Speech Spectrograms: A Scientist's View of Its Reliability for Legal Purposes, 47 J. Acoustical Soc'y Am. 597 (1970); Bolt et al., Speaker Identification by Speech Spectrograms: Some Further Observations, 54 J. Acoustical Soc'y Am. 531 (1973); Richard H. Bolt et al., On the Theory and Practice of Voice Identification (1979); Harry Hollien, The Acoustics of Crime (1990); Oscar Tosi, Voice Identification: Theory and Legal Applications 57 (1979).

itself can degrade the quality of the signal. In addition, if the speech to be recorded is produced in a background of other sounds, these extraneous sounds usually will be recorded along with the speech signal, reducing the signal-to-noise (S/N) ratio. Some general signal quality requirements have been recommended by the VIAAS-IAI.

## § 7:20    Areas of scientific agreement—Phonetic context and duration

It is commonly accepted that speech samples chosen for use in talker identification by spectrograms should be controlled for phonetic context and should meet minimal requirements for duration. Phonetic considerations are important because speech sounds can be highly adapted to individual phonetic contexts, particularly the adjacent sounds but also more global influences such as stress pattern (stress is the degree of prominence given to syllables in an utterance) and speaking rate.[1] Words that may seem to be similar from their orthographic spelling can in fact be very different in phonetic properties. The VIAAS-IAI requires a minimum of ten comparable words between two voice samples; the Federal Bureau of Investigation requires twenty words.[2] Words can vary greatly in their total length (measured in time), number of syllables, and number of phonetic constituents. Consider, for example, the monosyllable words *a*, *the*, *it* versus the polysyllable words *telephone*, *carefully*, *explosive*. Although the number of words is a convenient index for perceptual and linguistic reasons, it should be recognized that words are not necessarily equal in their potential for talker identification.

Control for phonetic context possibly can be relaxed if talker-sensitive parameters are studied over long durations of speech. However, it should be stressed that such long durations are not always available in forensic applications. The duration of a sample is important to ensure that a sufficient number of distinguishing features can be identified in the visual pattern. Research on intertalker and intratalker variability among correlation matrices obtained from continuous speech indicates that about 30 seconds is a minimum duration of speech required for the stabilization of the correlation matrices.[3] Assuming an average speaking rate of about 170 words per minute, a 30-second sample of continuous speech should include about 85 words.[4]

## § 7:21    Areas of scientific agreement—Disguises and mimicking

Another point of consensus is that disguises or mimicking of speech can complicate the use of spectrograms in talker identification, and in some situations may preclude comparisons.[1] One of the most damaging disguises is falsetto (a high-pitched voice

---

**[Section 7:20]**

[1] Richard H. Bolt et al., On the Theory and Practice of Voice Identification (1979).

[2] Bruce E. Koenig, Spectrographic Voice Identification, 13 Crime Lab Digest 105 (1986).

[3] Li & Hughes, Talker Differences As They Appear in Correlation Matrices of Continuous Speech Spectra, 55 J. Acoustical Soc'y Am. 833 (1974).

[4] This value is given only as an example based on average speech rates; the actual number of words in a time interval can vary widely across talkers and situations.

**[Section 7:21]**

[1] See Endres et al., Voice Spectrograms As a Function of Age, Voice Disguise, and Voice Imita-tion, 49 J. Acoustical Soc'y Am. 1842 (1971); Hollien & McGlone, The Effect of Disguise on "Voiceprint" Identification, 1976 Proceedings of the Carnahan Conference on Crime Countermeasures 30, reprinted in 2 Nat'l J. Crim. Def. 117 (1976); Kathleen Houlihan, The Effects of Disguise on Speaker Identification from Sound Spectrograms, in Current Issues in the Phonetic Sciences 811 (Harry Hollien & Patricia Hollien eds., 1979); Reich, Detecting the Presence of Disguise in the Male Voice, 69 J. Acoustical Soc'y Am. 1458 (1981); Reich & Duke, Effects of Selected Vocal Disguises Upon Speaker Identification by Listening, 66 J. Acoustical Soc'y Am. 1023 (1979); Reich et al., Effects of Selected Disguises Upon Spectrographic Speaker Identification, 60 J. Acoustical Soc'y Am. 919 (1976).

quality), which can greatly obscure formants in wide-band spectrograms.[2] This result occurs because the harmonics of the falsetto voice become so widely spaced that the conventional wide-band analysis of 250 or 300 Hz resolves the harmonic pattern of the voice rather than the formant pattern. Disguises differ in the degree to which they hinder talker identification by spectrograms. Self-selected vocal disguises have been among the most effective in published research on speaker identification.[3] The VIAAS-IAI recommends that speech samples containing disguises such as falsetto or whispering be eliminated from comparison consideration.

## § 7:22 Areas of scientific agreement—Psychological or physical state of the talker

The psychological and physical state of the talker exerts a variety of influences on the speech signal. Although emotional state is not straightforwardly associated with a simple set of acoustic effects, different emotions can be distinguished by combinations of acoustic characteristics.[1] For example, Murray and Arnott[2] compared emotions such as anger, fear, sadness and disgust. Speaking rate tends to be accelerated in anger and fear but decelerated in sadness or disgust. The average pitch of the voice tends to be higher in anger and fear but lower in sadness and disgust. Vocal intensity is increased in anger but reduced in sadness and disgust. The range of vocal pitch increases in anger and fear but decreases in sadness. Tartter and Braun[3] found that listeners can accurately discriminate recorded speech produced by the same talkers while frowning, smiling or assuming a neutral facial expression. Frowning has the effect of lowering formant frequencies and increasing syllable duration. It appears that emotions have a multidimensional effect on speech. Although rate, voice pitch and intensity changes are especially notable, alterations can occur in the precision of articulation as well.[4] Very few studies of talker identification have manipulated talker emotion as a factor that might influence the accuracy of talker identification. As an additional complication, phonetic characteristics of speech may change with changes in loudness.[5]

A topic related to a talker's emotional state is the psychological stress of an individual from whom speech is recorded. Note that the word *stress* can denote two different concepts in the study of speech. One is the degree of emphasis or accent placed on a particular word or syllable in an utterance. The other meaning is a general psychological or physiological state that occurs as the result of demanding, haz-

---

[2]Endres et al., Voice Spectrograms As a Function of Age, Voice Disguise, and Voice Imitation, 49 J. Acoustical Soc'y Am. 1842 (1971).

[3]Reich et al., Effects of Selected Disguises Upon Spectrographic Speaker Identification, 60 J. Acoustical Soc'y Am. 919 (1976).

**[Section 7:22]**

[1]Hecker et al., Manifestations of Task-Induced Stress in the Acoustic Speech Signal, 44 J. Acoustical Soc'y Am. 993 (1968); Murray & Arnott, Toward the Simulation of Emotion in Synthetic Speech: A Review of the Literature on Human Vocal Emotion, 93 J. Acoustical Soc'y Am. 1097 (1993); Scherer, Vocal Affect Expression: A Review and a Model for Future Research, 99 Psych. Bulletin 143 (1986); Tartter & Braun, Hearing Smiles and Frowns in Normal

and Whisper Registers, 94 J. Acoustical Soc'y Am. 2101 (1994); Williams & Stevens, Emotions and Speech: Some Acoustical Correlates, 52 J. Acoustical Soc'y Am. 1238 (1972).

[2]Murray & Arnott, Toward the Simulation of Emotion in Synthetic Speech: A Review of the Literature on Human Vocal Emotion, 93 J. Acoustical Soc'y Am. 1097 (1993).

[3]Tartter & David Braun, Hearing Smiles and Frowns in Normal and Whisper Registers, 94 J. Acoustical Soc'y Am. 2101 (1994).

[4]Murray & Arnott, Toward the Simulation of Emotion in Synthetic Speech: A Review of the Literature on Human Vocal Emotion, 93 J. Acoustical Soc'y Am. 1097 (1993).

[5]Rostolland, Phonetic Structure of Shouted Voice, 51 Acoustica 80 (1982).

ardous, or threatening conditions. Hecker et al.[6] reported that stress could be aurally detected in the speech of some individuals and that acoustic correlates of psychological stress varied across talkers. One of the most frequently observed acoustic correlates was voicing irregularity, or an irregularity in the pattern of glottal vibration (the vertical striations in a wide-band spectrogram). The understanding of the acoustic correlates of psychological stress is incomplete owing to limitations of published research.[7] Much of the research in this area overlaps with research on the study of the emotional correlates of speech patterns.

The influence of alcohol and other substances also may induce changes in speech patterns. Alcohol inebriation is known to influence speech and it appears that some parameters are particularly sensitive to alcohol consumption.[8] Among the typical changes that have been observed in inebriated speech are misarticulations, reduced speaking rate, an increase in the ratio of voiceless to voiced sounds, a change in pitch range (either larger or smaller, depending on the talker) and an increase in pitch variability. It must be kept in mind that the group studies published in the scientific literature show that individual differences occur but the extent of these differences is not established for anything but small samples of talkers. Accordingly, care should be taken in generalizing from the limited data now in print. Moreover, very little is known about the interaction of factors such as the talker's emotional state, overall loudness, psychological stress, and the influence of intoxicants.

A talker's health, particularly the status of the upper respiratory tract, can influence speech patterns. One of the most efficient parameters proposed for talker identification relates to nasal sounds,[9] but these sounds are vulnerable to even a mild head cold.[10] Research on this topic is limited, but it seems likely that a talker's health can affect speech patterns. Normal aging processes also can influence speech production in various ways,[11] and it appears that the speech characteristics most predictive of aged speech also are frequently implicated in the speech of persons with neurologic diseases.[12] Therefore, it has been suggested that normal aging and some neurological diseases have similar effects on speech production.[13]

The implication is that the emotional and physical state of a talker ideally would be controlled in forensic applications of talker identification. However, ascertaining these characteristics and replicating them may be extremely difficult and sometimes impossible. Perhaps the best that can be done in most practical situations is to ac-

[6]Hecker et al., Manifestations of Task-Induced Stress in the Acoustic Speech Signal, 44 J. Acoustical Soc'y Am. 993 (1968).

[7]Cairns & Hansen, Nonlinear Analysis and Classification of Speech under Stressed Conditions, 96 J. Acoustical Soc'y Am. 3392 (1994).

[8]Klingholz et al., Recognition of Low-Level Intoxication from the Speech Signal, 84 J. Acoustical Soc'y Am. 929 (1988); L. Lester & R. Skousen, The Phonology of Drunkenness, Papers for the Parasession on Natural Phonology 233 (A. Bruck et al. eds., 1974); Niedzielska et al., Acoustic Evaluation of Voice in Individuals with Alcohol Addiction, 46 Folia Phoniatrica 115 (1994); Pisoni & Martin, Effects of Alcohol on the Acoustic-Phonetic Properties of Speech: Perceptual and Acoustic Analyses, 13 Alcoholism: Clin. & Experimental Res. 577 (1989); Sobell & Sobell, Effects of Alcohol on the Speech of Alcoholics, 15 J. Speech & Hearing Res. 861 (1972); Sobell et al., Alcohol-induced Dysfluency in Nonalcoholics, 34 Folia Phoniatrica 316 (1982); Chin & Pisoni, Alcohol and Speech (1997).

[9]Su et al., Identification of Speakers by Use of Nasal Coarticulation, 56 J. Acoustical Soc'y Am. 1876 (1974); Francis Nolan, The Phonetic Bases of Speaker Recognition (1983).

[10]M. R. Sambur, Selection of Acoustic Features for Speaker Identification, ASSP-23 IEEE Transactions on Acoustics and Speech Signal Processing 176 (1975).

[11]Raymond D. Kent & Robert Burkhard, Changes in the Acoustic Correlates of Speech Production, in Aging: Communication Processes and Disorders 47 (Daniel S. Beasley & G. A. Davis eds., 1981); Gary Weismer & Julie M. Liss, Aging and Speech Motor Control, in Handbook of Aging and Communication 205 (D. Ripich ed., 1991).

[12]Ryan & Burke, Perceptual and Acoustic Correlates of Aging in the Speech of Males, 7 J. Communication Disorders 181 (1974).

[13]Ryan & Burke, Perceptual and Acoustic Correlates of Aging in the Speech of Males, 7 J. Communication Disorders 181 (1974).

knowledge that these factors may limit the accuracy of the identification procedure. The number of potentially significant variables makes talker identification more complicated than fingerprint identification.

## § 7:23 Areas of scientific agreement—Earwitness testimony

There is substantial agreement on the ability of witnesses to identify individuals from the sound of their speech. This research does not speak directly to the abilities of forensic experts but rather to general earwitness testimony (i.e., testimony based on recall of auditory events, especially spoken messages uttered at the scene of a crime). Most published earwitness research focuses either on famous voices or unfamiliar voices. Recent research includes studies of memory for voices and studies of the effects of training on earwitness accuracy, both of which are relevant to gauging the role of audition in talker identification.

The recognition of famous voices improves with duration of the voice sample, with the largest gain in performance occurring within the first second and smaller gains thereafter.[1] A similar effect appears to occur for unfamiliar voices. Cook and Wilding reported that recognition memory improved with longer extracts of a stranger's voice but was not affected by increasing vowel variety (i.e., different types of vowel sounds).[2] These authors also concluded that memory for words spoken was not correlated with memory for an unknown voice. In considering these results, Cook and Wilding raise the possibility that there may be a general ability for memory-for-voices. Sheffert, however, reached a somewhat dissimilar conclusion in an experiment designed to determine whether memory for voices is distinct from episodic memory. The results of Sheffert's study were interpreted to mean that "voices are represented in long-term memory as episodic traces that contain talker-specific perceptual information."[3] Essentially the same conclusion was reached by Remez, Fellowes, and Rubin in an experiment in which natural voices were radically transformed to sinewave replicas (i.e., the formants of speech were replaced by sinusoids).[4] The results of the experiment involving six voices indicated that word recognition was affected by changes in voice for several encoding tasks. It was concluded that even with these highly altered stimuli, listeners still were able to identify ten voices. The authors viewed their results as compatible with a model in which phonetic properties of utterances carry information on both words spoken and the individuals who speak them. Although it is premature to make definitive statements, the recent research is consistent with the idea that voice identification improves with the duration of the voice sample, and that talker information is to some degree combined with information on the words spoken in a composite memory trace. These laboratory studies provide some basic information about how well listeners can identify the voices of others.

Work by Elaad, Segev, and Tobin indicates that talker identification ability is affected by training.[5] They compared identification accuracy in a mock theft study

---

**[Section 7:23]**

[1]Schweinberger et al., Recognizing Famous Voices: Influence of Stimulus Duration and Different Types of Retrieval Cues, 40 J. Speech, Language, & Hearing Res. 453 (1997).

[2]Cook & Wilding, Earwitness Testimony: Never Mind the Variety, Hear the Length, 11 Appl. Cognitive Psych. 95 (1997).

[3]Sheffert, Contribution of Surface and Conceptual Information to Recognition Memory,

60 Perception & Psychophysics 1141, 1141 (1998).

[4]Remez et al., Talker Identification Based on Phonetic Information, 23 J. Experimental Psych.: Human Perception & Performance 651 (1997). A *formant* is a resonance of the vocal tract; a particular pattern of formants characterizes individual speech sounds. A sinusoid is a pure tone, or signal containing energy at a single frequency.

[5]Elaad et al., Long-term Working Memory in Voice Identification, 4 Psychol., Crime & Law 73 (1998).

involving three listener groups: voice identification experts,[6] individuals who are totally blind, and sighted listeners without special training or experience. The highest accuracy was achieved by the voice identification experts. There also appears to be an effect of nationality on both face and voice recognition, with subjects showing better recognition for faces and voices of their own nationality.[7] The influence of interviewing technique was investigated by Memon and Yarmey in a mock abduction with 77 subjects who rated the abductor's voice for nine speech characteristics and attempted to identify his voice from an audiotaped lineup.[8] No effect of interview type was found.

In a comparison of eyewitness and earwitness identification with respect to calibration and diagnosticity analysis, Olsson, Juslin, and Winman reported that earwitness identification is poorer and is characterized by overconfidence and low diagnosticity of confidence, meaning that the witness's level or feeling of confidence had a poor relationship with accuracy.[9]

A number of issues relevant to earwitness identification have yet to be studied, including the effects of competing signals, the effects of hearing loss and the effects of linguistic accent (in particular, similarities and differences in the accents of talker and listener). Yarmey reviewed the general topic of earwitness voice identification and recommended procedures for voice lineups.[10] Although careful attention to these procedures can enhance the reliability of voice lineups, the research on earwitness identification points to general concerns about its accuracy. These shortcomings make objective identification by acoustic analysis all the more important in forensic application. This is not to detract from the combined use of perceptual and acoustic methods, as is commonly used in forensic talker identification.

## § 7:24  Areas of scientific agreement—Summary

Reviews of talker recognition published within the last five years are cited in the margin.[1] Although these reviews document several steps of progress, they also make it clear that much remains to be done to establish the scientific validity and reliability of talker identification by acoustic methods. Gruber and Poza[2] list several areas in which there are open questions or a significant lack of scientific evidence. These include knowledge about:

(1)   the uniqueness and consistency of voices;
(2)   the relative value of aural and visual methods of identification;
(3)   the relative accuracy of laypersons and experts using different methods of identification;
(4)   the specific features that pertain to visual or aural pattern matching;

---

[6]The subjects were lay individuals with no special training in talker identification.

[7]Doty, The Influence of Nationality on the Accuracy of Face and Voice Recognition, 111 Am. J. Psych. 191 (1998).

[8]Memon & Yarmey, Earwitness Recall and Identification: Comparison of the Cognitive Interview and the Structured Interview, 88 Percept. & Motor Skills 797 (1999).

[9]Olsson et al., Realism of Confidence in Earwitness Versus Eyewitness Identification, 4 J. Experimental Psychol.: Applied 101 (1998).

[10]Yarmey, Earwitness Speaker Identification, 1 Psych., Public Pol'y & Law 792 (1995).

[Section 7:24]

[1]Joseph P. Campbell, Speaker Recognition—A Tutorial, 85 Proceedings of the IEEE 1437 (1997); Sadaoki Furui, Recent Advances in Speaker Recognition, 18 Pattern Recognition Letters 859 (1997); Frederic A. Gruber & F. T. Poza, Voicegram Identification Evidence, 54 Am. Jur. Trials 1 (1995); W. Majewski, Speaker Recognition in Forensic Applications, 82 Acustica (Supp. 1) S 230 (1996); Francis Nolan, Speaker Recognition and Forensic Phonetics, in The Handbook of Phonetic Sciences 744 (William J. Hardcastle & John Laver eds., 1997).

[2]Frederic A. Gruber & F. T. Poza, Voicegram Identification Evidence, 54 Am. Jur. Trials 1 (1995).

(5)   the criteria used by forensic specialists;

(6)   error rates and accuracy in real-world forensic situations; and

(7)   effect of speaker situation on identification and elimination protocols.

This is a substantial list of unresolved issues, and although some progress has been made since publication of the Gruber and Poza volume, the list can be repeated today virtually in its entirety as an agenda for future work.

## § 7:25   Areas of scientific disagreement

Several areas of disagreement have been discussed in the literature on talker identification. Much of the literature is polarized on the relative accuracy of this method for forensic application. Among the most important publications that are generally critical or guarded concerning speaker identification by spectrograms are Bolt et al.,[1] Gruber and Poza,[2] Hollien,[3] Poza,[4] and Shipp, Doherty and Hollien.[5] Papers that take a more positive view are Black et al.,[6] Kersta,[7] Koenig et al.,[8] and Tosi et al.[9] These papers provide an overview of various disagreements concerning the use of spectrograms in voice identification or elimination.

Perhaps the most significant area of disagreement concerns the degree to which research has established the validity and reliability of talker identification by spectrograms. Much of the disagreement centers on the interpretation of published data on error rates in identification and elimination. Table 2 reports error rates for selected published studies of talker identification that have used either aural or visual (spectrogram) methods. The studies differ considerably in many features, including number of talkers, number and sophistication of judges, exemplars available for examination, and type of decision. These considerable differences preclude direct comparisons among studies, and Table 2 must be interpreted cautiously. The error rates in this table range from 0% to 85%.

The largest and most comprehensive investigation of talker identification by spectrograms was reported by Tosi et al.[10] This study includes the largest talker sample reported in the published literature: 250 men drawn from what was considered by the investigators to be a "homogeneous population" of 25,000 males speaking general American English (students at Michigan State University). The examiners were 29 individuals given a month's training in spectrographic identification. A total of 34,996 identification trials were carried out. The trials were based on subsets of 10 or 40 speakers drawn from the larger sample of 250 talkers. The experiment included several aspects: comparison of open versus closed tests, use of noncontemporaneous reference and test samples, and context variation.

The condition that probably compares most closely with forensic tests is the open

---

**[Section 7:25]**

[1]Bolt et al., Speaker Identification by Speech Spectrograms: Some Further Observations, 54 J. Acoustical Soc'y Am. 531 (1973); Bolt et al., Speaker Identification of Speech Spectrograms: A Scientist's View of Its Reliability for Legal Purposes, 47 J. Acoustical Soc'y Am. 597 (1970).

[2]Gruber & Poza, Voicegram Identification Evidence, 54 Am. Jur. Trials 1 (1995).

[3]Hollien, The Peculiar Case of "Voiceprints," 56 J. Acoustical Soc'y Am. 210 (1971).

[4]Fausto Poza, Voiceprint Identification: Its Forensic Application, 1974 Proceedings of the Carnahan Crime Countermeasures Conference (University of Kentucky, Lexington, KY).

[5]Shipp et al., Some Fundamental Considerations Regarding Voice Identification, 82 J. Acoustical Soc'y Am. 687 (1987).

[6]Black et al., "Speaker Identification by Speech Spectrograms: Some Further Considerations," 54 J. Acoustical Soc'y Am. 535 (1973).

[7]Kersta, Voiceprint Identification, 196 Nature 1253 (1962).

[8]Koenig et al., Reply to "Some Fundamental Considerations Regarding Voice Identification," 82 J. Acoustical Soc'y Am. 688 (1987).

[9]Tosi et al., Experiment on Voice Identification, 51 J. Acoustical Soc'y Am. 2030 (1972).

[10]Tosi et al., Experiment on Voice Identification, 51 J. Acoustical Soc'y Am. 2030 (1972).

test with noncontemporaneous samples extracted from continuous speech. Forensic tests frequently must use conversational speech samples (continuous speech) obtained at different times (noncontemporaneous samples) and from a suspect who may or may not be in the reference sample, or "lineup" of talkers (open test). For this condition, Tosi et al. reported error rates of 6.4% for false identification and 12.7% for false elimination. The examiners also were asked to rate the certainty of their judgments, and Tosi et al. pointed out that 60% of the incorrect judgments were associated with an "uncertain" rating. The authors suggested that if the examiners had been allowed to use a "no opinion" category of decision, the error rates would have fallen to 2.4% for false identification and 4.8% for false elimination.

Other published studies typically have used talker samples of 10–50 in open or closed tests. As noted earlier, it is difficult to make direct comparisons of reported error rates. However, as a general indication of the results, the lowest error rates (best examiner performance) across the experimental conditions used in major studies published in refereed journals were: 21.6% for comparison of single words spoken in isolation,[11] 18% for comparison of phrases and sentences,[12] 11.9% for open tests involving cue words in the same context.[13] Depending on which study one chooses, the accuracy of identifying one individual from a group of ten similar talkers under optimal conditions may be as good as 100% or as poor as 80%. By contrast, in an open test under less than optimal conditions, the accuracy may be 40% or even lower.

In their influential paper, Bolt et al.[14] remarked that, "Today's consensus suggests that talker identification by voice patterns is subject to error at a high, and as yet undetermined, rate."[15] Bolt et al. concluded, "We find, in brief, that spectrographic voice identification has inherent difficulties and uncertainties. Anecdotal evidence given in support of the method is not scientifically convincing. The controlled experiments that have been reported give conflicting results . . . . We conclude that the available results are inadequate to establish the reliability of voice identification by spectrograms." Nearly 25 years have passed since publication of the Bolt et al.[16] reports, but no research papers that resolve the question of the reliability of spectrographic talker identification have been published. The debate over the reliability of this method centers on studies published before 1980.

One disagreement pertains to the nature of decisions reached in talker identification or elimination. As noted earlier, scientific studies have relied almost exclusively on positive decisions (identification or elimination), but forensic specialists typically use categories such as "probable" or "inconclusive." Because of these differences in decision categories, it is not a simple matter to relate accuracy rates reported in scientific reports to actual practice in forensic application. It has been argued that the accuracy rates in scientific reports are conservative estimates of the accuracy expected in forensic application, especially if a "no-decision" response is used in the latter. However, this is a matter of interpretation, about which controversy is not surprising. The opposite case also can be argued, given that forensic applications

[11]Young & Campbell, Effects of Context on Talker Identification, 42 J. Acoustical Soc'y Am. 1250 (1967).

[12]Stevens et al., Speaker Authentication and Identification: A Comparison of Spectrographic and Auditory Presentations of Speech Material, 44 J. Acoustical Soc'y Am. 1596 (1968).

[13]Hazen, Effects of Differing Phonetic Contexts on Spectrographic Speaker Identification, 54 J. Acoustical Soc'y Am. 650 (1973).

[14]Bolt et al., Speaker Identification by Speech Spectrograms: Some Further Observations, 54 J.

Acoustical Soc'y Am. at 602–603 (1973).

[15]Bolt et al., Speaker Identification by Speech Spectrograms: Some Further Observations, 54 J. Acoustical Soc'y Am. at 602 (1973).

[16]Bolt et al., Speaker Identification by Speech Spectrograms: Some Further Observations, 54 J. Acoustical Soc'y Am. at 602–603 (1973); Bolt et al., Speaker Identification of Speech Spectrograms: A Scientist's View of Its Reliability for Legal Purposes, 47 J. Acoustical Soc'y Am. 597 (1970).

often contend with signals of poor quality, uncooperative subjects, and short samples of speech from which exemplars can be extracted.

Some disagreement continues over the vulnerability of the speech signal to some sources of intratalker variation. Some particular points of disagreement are over: (a) the signal quality required for identification purposes; (b) the effect of vocal disguises and the emotional or physical state of the talker; and (c) the selection of words or phonetic features for purposes of talker identification. But the importance of these disagreements is lessened by the use of forensic procedures such as those recommended by the VIAAS-IAI.

## § 7:26 Future directions

Bolt et al.[1] recommended four main categories of research in talker identification: "the origins and characteristics of variability; the relations between intraspeaker and interspeaker variability; the relations between aural and visual examination; and the potential of developments in automated methods of voice identification to make contributions to the understanding and improvement of identification performed by humans".[2] This research agenda might very well be reiterated today, only because limited progress has been made in these areas since the publication of the Bolt et al. report.

Clearly, the need remains for large-scale talker identification experiments that use procedures similar to those in forensic settings, specifically, joint use of aural and spectrographic examinations, and the use of probable or inconclusive decisions. Experiments should use spontaneous speech samples[3] as well as samples gathered using the methods of experienced forensic investigators to elicit exemplars from known talkers, which simulate the rate, vocal effort, and emotional state of the "unknown" talker to whom comparisons will be made. The intensity of debate over the validity and reliability of talker identification by spectrograms is rooted largely in the lack of experimental data collected with appropriate procedures and adequate controls.

A likely direction of future research is continued exploration of automated (or semi-automated) talker identification, possibly aided by aural recognition. Automated identification usually is a computer-based procedure. It offers the advantage of a comparatively objective process in which specified parameters are examined algorithmically and, if appropriate, assigned individual levels of statistical confidence. Automated recognition may evolve as a useful supplement to other procedures that involve more direct human observation and decision making.

One example is the linear prediction model in which different parametric representations of speech are derived.[4] An important advantage of automated procedures is the capability for analyses of long samples of speech for which variation in phonetic characteristics may be less important than for brief samples.[5] Of course, long samples of speech are not necessarily available for forensic purposes.

---

**[Section 7:26]**

[1]Richard H. Bolt et al., On the Theory and Practice of Voice Identification (1979).

[2]Richard H. Bolt et al., On the Theory and Practice of Voice Identification at 61 (1979).

[3]Hazen, Effects of Differing Phonetic Contexts on Spectrographic Speaker Identification, 54 J. Acoustical Soc'y Am. 650 (1973).

[4]One of the most promising parameters was the cepstrum, which is the inverse Fourier transform of the amplitude spectrum. Atal, Effectiveness of Linear Prediction Characteristics of the Speech Wave for Automatic Speaker Identification, 55 J. Acoustical Soc'y Am. 1304 (1974). The cepstrum and a number of other computer-implemented analyses involve highly technical issues in mathematics and signal processing. It is not possible to review these matters in this chapter, but it should be noted that they can introduce considerable complexity in discussions of automated talker identification.

[5]Li & Hughes, Talker Differences As They Appear in Correlation Matrices of Continuous Speech Spectra, 55 J. Acoustical Soc'y Am. 833 (1974).

Another advantage is the capability for relatively more straightforward statistical comparison between the recorded speech of an unknown talker and data bases drawn from large numbers of talkers and organized in ways that retain information about gender, age, dialect, speaking rate and effort level, and perhaps physiological and psychological state. This is not to say that visual examination of spectrograms should be superseded by automated methods. The pattern recognition abilities of the human visual system are not easily matched by automated systems. Yet visual recognition (like aural recognition) is a legitimate subject of study. Rosenberg and Soong[6] summarized several procedures for automated analysis, but noted that these procedures are more suited to applications in access control (i.e., security) than to speaker identification, primarily because of difficulties with uncontrolled variability in the latter. But the recent use of automated analysis with fairly large talker samples (e.g., 100 talkers in a study by Liu et al.[7]) holds promise that these techniques could have forensic relevance.

Scientific and statistical techniques used to study forensic talker identification are similar to those employed to assess decision-making in medicine. Research in clinical decision making suggests that performance depends on whether constituent information is combined in a serial or a parallel fashion.[8] In a serial decision strategy, discrete tests are conducted and evaluated one after another, typically using decision rules that dictate later steps on the basis of the outcomes of earlier steps. In a parallel strategy, discrete tests are made independently, and a decision is based on patterns of outcomes from the group of tests. It would be valuable to know how different types of information arising from talker identification can be combined most effectively to yield an ultimate decision of identification or elimination. For example, one approach is a parallel paradigm in which the outcomes of independent decisions are reached with aural identification, identification by spectrograms, and identification by automated methods. The separate decisions can be weighted, then combined into a final decision. Current approaches appear to be more serial in character: decisions are made based on if-then sequential logic suggested in part by procedural requirements. It appears that potential effects associated with the order in which comparisons are made have not been studied formally.

Similarly, additional research is needed to determine the impact on summary decision outcomes of independent replications of talker identifications by examiners with varying degrees of experience. The VIAAS-IAI standards require that an independent opinion be obtained for all decisions other than inconclusive, possible identification, and possible elimination; a third opinion is required when the first and second examiners cannot resolve differences. Post hoc reports suggest such procedures produce very small proportions of errors, and that such errors as do occur tend to be related to poor recordings, high-pitched voices, or an insufficient number of words.[9] However, these observations are based on a limited number of comparisons (2000 talkers). The examiners were sufficiently similar in training and in the analysis tools used to make comparisons that generalizing beyond them is difficult.

Future work should lead to a better specification of the parameters that are most

---

[6]Aaron E. Rosenberg & Frank K. Soong, Recent Research on Automatic Speaker Identification, in Advances in Speech Signal Processing 701 (Sadaoki Furui & M. Mohan Sondhi eds., 1992).

[7]Liu et al., A Study on Minimum Error Discriminative Training for Speaker Recognition, 97 J. Acoustical Soc'y Am. 637 (1995).

[8]Martyn L. Hyde et al., Auditory Test Strategy, in Diagnostic Audiology (John T. Jacobson & Jerry L. Northern eds., 1991); Robert Turner, Techniques to Determine Test Protocol Performance, 9 Ear & Hearing 177 (1988); Robert Turner et al., Formulating and Evaluating Audiological Test Protocols, 5 Ear & Hearing 321 (1984); Robert Turner & Donald Nielsen, Application of Clinical Decision Analysis to Audiological Tests, 5 Ear & Hearing 125 (1984).

[9]Koenig, Spectrographic Voice Identification: A Forensic Survey, 79 J. Acoustical Soc'y Am. 2088 (1986) (letter).

effective in identifying talkers. Much as fingerprint identification is based on distinguishing features such as whorls, talker identification examines particular features in the spectrogram. A number of features are potentially useful, but they probably are not equally sensitive to interspeaker differences. It would be important to know the relative value of various features for the purpose of speaker identification. One example is specification of formant tracks and other acoustic features that can be obtained from largely automatic procedures. Goldstein,[10] Sambur,[11] and Wolf[12] described certain acoustic characteristics that were useful in distinguishing among small sets of talkers but more work on larger numbers of talkers is needed. Another promising direction is to specify various phonetic characteristics that are candidates for talker identification. These might include formant patterns for vowels and vowel-like sounds, spectra of frication noise, durations of noise segments, perturbations (irregularities) in vocal fold vibrations, and covariation in selected frequency and intensity features. The large talker databases now available could be studied to construct statistical ensembles for some of these features. One recent example of such work produced long-term average speech spectra using standardized procedures and equipment for 13 languages as spoken by both male and female talkers.[13]

Kuwabara and Sagisaka[14] gave an example of a systematic approach to acoustic identification. They specified acoustic features at two levels, as follows:

*Voice source:*

1. average vocal fundamental frequency (voice pitch),
2. time-frequency pattern of vocal fundamental frequency (also known as the pitch contour),
3. fluctuations in fundamental frequency,
4. glottal wave shape.

*Vocal tract resonances:*

1. shape of spectral envelope and spectral tilt,
2. absolute value of formant frequencies,
3. time-frequency pattern of formant frequencies,
4. long-term average spectrum of speech,
5. formant bandwidths.

It should be possible to render identification or elimination decisions along different axes or dimensions, and then combine the independent decisions in a statistical decision model. Examples of different dimensions of analysis are the long-term averaged speech spectrum,[15] the cepstrum,[16] perturbation measures of vocal function,[17]

[10]Goldstein, Speaker-Identifying Features Based on Formant Tracks, 59 J. Acoustical Soc'y Am. 176 (1976).

[11]M. R. Sambur, Selection of Acoustic Features for Speaker Identification, ASSP-23 IEEE Transactions on Acoustics and Speech Signal Processing 176 (1975).

[12]Wolf, Efficient Acoustic Parameters for Speaker Recognition, 51 J. Acoustical Soc'y Am. 2044 (1972).

[13]Byrne et al., An International Comparison of Long-Term Average Speech Spectra, 96 J. Acoustical Soc'y Am. 2108 (1994).

[14]Kuwabara & Sagisaka, Acoustic Characteristics of Speaker Individuality: Control and Conversion, 16 Speech Communication 165

(1995).

[15]Atal, Effectiveness of Linear Prediction Characteristics of the Speech Wave for Automatic Speaker Identification, 55 J. Acoustical Soc'y Am. 1304 (1974); Gelfer et al., The Effects of Sample Duration and Timing on Speaker Identification Accuracy by Means of Long-Term Spectra, 17 J. Phonetics 327 (1989); Hollien & Majewski, Speaker Identification by Long-Term Spectra under Normal and Distorted Speech Conditions, 62 J. Acoustical Soc'y Am. 975 (1977); Kiukaanniemi, Individual Differences in the Long-Term Speech Spectrum, 34 Folia Phoniatrica 21 (1982); Zalewski et al., Cross Correlation of Long-Term Spectra as a Speaker Identification Technique, 34 Acoustica 20 (1975); Byrne et al., An International Comparison of Long-Term Average Speech Spectra, 96 J.

aural recognition,[18] spectrographic examination of specific phonetic features including formant pattern,[19] temporal features,[20] nasal features,[21] and turbulence noise for fricatives.[22] Some examples of multiple-factor analyses are those of Doherty and Hollien.[23] Fuzzy logic is one potential approach to combining information from several features, no one of which in itself always yields an unambiguous decision.[24]

The use of particular features in spectrograms might be enhanced if standards were available for the determination of differences related to anatomical dissimilarities as opposed to differences that reflect learned speaking patterns. Presumably, anatomy is more difficult to change than learned patterns of speech. Research along these lines may eventually establish criteria for feature selection. Nolan listed the following criteria for the selection of parameters in talker identification: high between-speaker variability, low within-speaker variability, resistance to attempted disguise or mimicry, availability, robustness in transmission, and measurability. It would be a major advance in spectrograph talker identification if a consensus were reached on the degree to which features or parameters satisfy these criteria.[25]

Published research pertains almost exclusively to male speakers, especially young to middle-aged men. Very little scientific information has been collected for female speakers, children of either gender, or elderly men. It is interesting to note that individual identity can be determined fairly well even with infant cries.[26] As it stands now, the scientific validation of talker identification pertains to less than half of the population. Moreover, the total number of speakers examined in all published research on spectrogram identification remains small.

Audio tape authentication and enhancement will experience continued refinement through technological improvements. It is important that consensus be reached concerning criteria for authentication and acceptable procedures for enhancement. Efforts by organizations such as the Audio Engineering Society to develop formal technical standards in these areas may increase the consistency with which various

---

Acoustical Soc'y Am. 2108 (1994).

[16]Atal, Effectiveness of Linear Prediction Characteristics of the Speech Wave for Automatic Speaker Identification, 55 J. Acoustical Soc'y Am. 1304 (1974); Luck, Automatic Speaker Verification Using Cepstral Measurements, 46 J. Acoustical Soc'y Am. 1026 (1969).

[17]Lieberman, Some Acoustic Measures of the Fundamental Periodicity of Normal and Pathologic Larynges, 35 J. Acoustical Soc'y Am. 344 (1963); Titze et al., Some Technical Considerations in Voice Perturbation Measurements, 30 J. Speech & Hearing Research 252 (1987); Wilcox & Horii, Age and Changes in Vocal Jitter, 35 J. Gerontology 194 (1980); Zyski et al., Perturbation Analysis of Normal and Pathological Larynges, 36 Folia Phoniatrica 190 (1984).

[18]Hargraves & Starkweather, Recognition of Speaker Identity, 6 Language & Speech 63 (1963); Reich & Duke, Effects of Selected Vocal Disguises Upon Speaker Identification by Listening, 66 J. Acoustical Soc'y Am. 1023 (1979); Stevens et al., Speaker Authentication and Identification: A Comparison of Spectrographic and Auditory Presentations of Speech Material, 44 J. Acoustical Soc'y Am. 1596 (1968); Voiers, Perceptual Basis of Speaker Identity, 36 J. Acoustical Soc'y Am. 1065 (1964).

[19]Goldstein, Speaker-Identifying Features Based on Formant Tracks, 59 J. Acoustical Soc'y Am. 176 (1976); Jassem, Formant Frequencies as Cues to Speaker Discrimination, 1 Speech Analysis and Synthesis 41 (Wiktor Jassem ed., 1968); LaRiverie, Contributions of Fundamental Frequency and Formant Frequencies to Speaker Identification, 31 Phonetica 185 (1975); Wolf, Efficient Acoustic Parameters for Speaker Recognition, 51 J. Acoustical Soc'y Am. 2044 (1972).

[20]Johnson et al., Speaker Identification Utilizing Selected Temporal Speech Features, 12 J. Phonetics 319 (1984).

[21]Su et al., Identification of Speakers by Use of Nasal Coarticulation, 56 J. Acoustical Soc'y Am. 1876 (1974).

[22]LaRiviere, Speaker Identification for Turbulent Portions of Fricatives, 29 Phonetica 98 (1974).

[23]Doherty, An Evaluation of Selected Acoustic Parameters for Use in Speaker Identification, 4 J. Phonetics 321 (1976); Doherty & Hollien, Multiple-factor Speaker Identification of Normal and Distorted Speech, 6 J. Phonetics 1 (1978).

[24]Schroeder, Speech and Speaker Recognition, 12 Bibliotheca Phonetica (1985).

[25]Francis Nolan, The Phonetic Bases of Speaker Recognition (1983).

[26]Gustafson et al., Robustness of Individual Identity in the Cries of Human Infants, 27 Developmental Psychobiology 1 (1994).

practitioners manage, describe and report results of efforts to enhance and authenticate recorded speech and other signals pertinent to forensic work.

As noted in the introduction, appropriately designed and recorded materials do not exist to promote comparison among the various instrumental systems used to produce speech spectrograms. Thus, we lack an independent physical reference by which to benchmark instruments used for talker identification by human, semi-automated or fully automated means. Such standards of comparison are common in other areas in which measurement and measurement method are important. This issue may be more technical than scientific, but it would be useful if those working in the area shared a common means by which to certify signal analyses, the results of which may be used in talker identification.

Like other areas of scientific enterprise, research in talker identification is influenced by philosophical, social and economic factors. Philosophical issues include distaste among some scientists for the adversarial and sometimes pecuniary character of the forensic enterprise and discomfort with legal standards of proof that may differ from scientific standards. One social issue involves isolation from the larger scientific community of potentially interesting analysis methods and data generated by law enforcement and intelligence agencies for reasons of national security. Another social issue has to do with reluctance among some scientists to engage in applied research and differences of opinion about the particular areas of science and engineering best qualified to address certain difficult questions. Economic factors may be the most difficult to deal with because the types of studies called for by Bolt et al.[27] and in this chapter will be costly. The fact that so few studies of appropriate scale and complexity have been performed may be due largely to lack of funds.

No compelling evidence has been produced during the early 2000s through peer-reviewed scientific literature either to enhance or detract from our understanding of the validity of talker identification methods. A possible exception is very recent work published in the *Journal of the Acoustical Society of America* which suggests more precise methods for characterizing speech via spectrographic means with possible applications in speech recognition. This may eventually have application in talker identification, but it is too soon to tell.

Finally, in the margin are major sources that are recommended to readers who seek more detailed information on various aspects of talker identification.[28] Tosi's succinct conclusion of a generation years ago seems equally applicable today:

> Possibly, no combination of methods may ever produce absolutely positive identification or eliminations in 100% of the cases submitted. Reasonably, it could be stated that the better the quality and extension of available samples, the better the qualifications of the examiner, and the more comprehensive the cluster of methods used, the better the chance of obtaining reliable decisions in a large percentage of cases.[29]

---

[27]Richard H. Bolt et al., On the Theory and Practice of Voice Identification (1979).

[28]Bolt et al., Speaker Identification by Speech Spectrograms: Some Further Observations, 54 J. Acoustical Soc'y Am. 531 (1973); Richard H. Bolt et al., On the Theory and Practice of Voice Identification (1979); Gruber & Poza, Voicegram Identification Evidence, 54 Am. Jur. Trials 1 (1995); Michael Hecker, Speaker Recognition: An Interpretive Survey of the Literature, American Speech-Language-Hearing Association Monograph No. 16 (1971); Harry Hollien, The Acoustics of Crime (1990); Manfred R. Schroeder, Speech and Speaker Recognition, 12 Bibliotheca Phonetica (1985); Oscar Tosi, The Problem of Speaker Identification and Elimination, in Measurement Procedures in Speech, Hearing, and Language 399 (Sadanand Singh ed., 1975); Special Section on Automatic Speaker Recognition, Identification and Verification, 17 Speech Communication 81 (1995).

[29]Oscar Tosi, The Problem of Speaker Identification and Elimination, in Measurement Procedures in Speech, Hearing, and Language at 428–429 (Sadanand Singh ed., 1975).

# APPENDIX 7A

## Glossary

*Acoustic.* Of or relating to the science of sound, or to the sense of hearing.

*Cepstrum.* A type of acoustic analysis defined as the Fourier transform of the power spectrum of a signal. The transform is described in terms of *quefrency* (note the transliteration from frequency), which has time-like properties. The cepstrum often is used to determine the fundamental frequency of a speech signal. Voiced speech tends to have a strong cepstral peak, at the first *rahmonic* (note transliteration from harmonic).

*Formant.* A resonance of the vocal tract, that part of the speech production system that extends from the larynx to the lips or nostrils. A formant is specified by its center frequency (commonly called formant frequency) and bandwidth. Formants are denoted by integers that increase with the relative frequency location of the formants. F1 is the lowest-frequency formant, F2 is the next highest, and so on. The first three formants are most important for speech analysis and perception.

*Fricative.* A speech sound characterized by a long interval of turbulence noise. Examples are the initial sounds in the words *thin, van, see, zoo, shoe.* Fricatives are often classified as *stridents* or *nonstridents,* depending on the degree of noise energy. Stridents have greater energy than nonstridents.

*Harmonic.* An integer multiple of the fundamental frequency in voiced sounds. Ideally, the voice source can be conceptualized as a line spectrum in which the energy appears as a series of harmonics. That is, each line represents one harmonic. The harmonics of the voice source are filtered by the vocal tract resonances.

*Interformant spaces.* The low-energy regions that fall between adjacent formants. Depending on speech characteristics, these spaces can contain noise or other energy, but usually this energy is quite weak. Consequently, the interformant spaces will appear as white or light gray on a spectrogram.

*Orthographic spelling.* The written representation of a language. Orthographic spelling may be contrasted with a phonetic transcription. The former refers to the common spelling of words with the letters of the alphabet. The latter is a specialized system in which each symbol uniquely represents a speech sound.

*Plosive gap.* The acoustic interval corresponding to articulatory closure (vocal tract obstruction) for a plosive consonant; it is identified on a spectrogram as an interval of low acoustic energy, conspicuously lacking in formant pattern or noise.

*Plosives.* Speech sounds characterized by a complete obstruction of the vocal tract that may be followed by an abrupt release of air that produces a burst noise. Examples of plosives are the initial sounds in the words *bill, pill, dill, till, gill,* and *kill.*

*Signal detection theory.* A mathematical theory dealing with the problem of detecting the presence of a signal in a background of noise. Early applications of this theory sought to statistically measure the accuracy of instrumental and sensory systems, independent of biases arising from the decision criteria of observers. Decision criteria are influenced by the observer's knowledge of the prior probabilities of target events (signals), and by the values and costs associated with correct and incorrect decisions. Accuracy is indexed graphically by means of *relative operating characteristic* (ROC) curves, and quantitatively by measures of performance such as d__ and A__. Subsequent applications of the theory have included problems in medical diagnosis, aptitude testing, weather forecasting, automated information retrieval, and forensic identification.

**Spectral envelope.** The general shape of the spectrum (the distribution of signal energy as a function of frequency). The envelope often is drawn to represent the overall form of the spectrum and may neglect minor deviations from that form.

**Spectral tilt.** The general orientation of spectral energy, or the slant of the spectral envelope.

**Spectrogram.** A graph of acoustic analysis consisting of three dimensions. Typically, time is represented on the horizontal axis, the frequency (pitch) of sound on the vertical axis, and the intensity of sound on the gray scale (shades of darkness). This is a basic form of analysis used in acoustic studies of speech, including talker identification.

**Vertical striations.** The fine-grained lines that run vertically on a wide-band spectrogram and correspond to the vocal pulses of voicing energy. The presence of these striations is an indication of voicing, and their relative pattern describes properties of the voice source, such as vocal pitch and its regularity.

**Vocal folds.** Muscles and associated tissues located in the larynx and capable of vibrating to produce voice.

**Vocal tract.** The cavities and structures above the vocal folds that are capable of modifying voice and airflow into distinctive sounds of speech; sometimes called the articulatory or articulatory-resonatory system.

**Vocal tract resonances.** The natural or resonant frequencies of the vocal tract, which can be determined mathematically from a knowledge of the length and shape of the vocal tract; also called formants.

**Voice.** The tone produced by vibration of the vocal folds and modified by adjustments of the vocal tract; sometimes used in a general sense to refer to human speech.

# Chapter 8

# Polygraph Tests

## I. LEGAL ISSUES

## II. SCIENTIFIC STATUS

### A. THE CASE FOR POLYGRAPH TESTS

## B. THE CASE AGAINST POLYGRAPH TESTS

## I. LEGAL ISSUES

### § 8:1  Introduction

In 1923, in *Frye v. United States*,[1] the United States Court of Appeals for the District of Columbia excluded the defendant's proffer of the results of an early form

---

**[Section 8:1]**

[1]Frye v. U.S., 293 F. 1013, 34 A.L.R. 145 (App. D.C. 1923) (rejected by, State v. Walstad, 119 Wis. 2d 483, 351 N.W.2d 469 (1984)) and (rejected by, State v. Brown, 297 Or. 404, 687 P.2d 751 (1984)) and (rejected by, Nelson v. State, 628 A.2d 69 (Del. 1993)) and (rejected by, State v. Alberico, 116 N.M. 156, 861 P.2d 192 (1993)) and (rejected by, State v. Moore, 268 Mont. 20, 885 P.2d 457 (1994)) and (rejected by, State v. Faught, 127 Idaho 873, 908 P.2d 566 (1995)) and (rejected by, People v. Shreck, 22 P.3d 68, 90 A.L.R.5th 765 (Colo. 2001)).

of the polygraph test because it was not "sufficiently established to have gained general acceptance in the particular field in which it belongs."[2] Seventy years later, in *Daubert v. Merrell Dow Pharmaceuticals*,[3] the United States Supreme Court ruled that *Frye's* "general acceptance" criterion is only one among many factors that federal courts should consider in deciding the determinative question of scientific validity.[4] Following *Daubert*, federal and state courts were asked in case after case to reconsider their approach to polygraphs. In particular, polygraph proponents argued that the *Daubert* standard was inconsistent with excluding this kind of testimony.[5] Some courts agreed with this argument, but most did not. In addition, the United States Supreme Court in 1998 considered the claim that a per se rule excluding polygraph testimony in criminal cases violated the Sixth Amendment.[6] The Court rejected the constitutional claim,[7] but five members of the Court noted "some tension" between *Daubert* and a per se rule of exclusion of scientific evidence.[8]

Polygraphy, as indicated by its being the subject behind the *Frye* rule, has had a long and mostly troubled history in American courts. Throughout the twentieth century, courts have been, at best, skeptical of polygraph tests and, at worst and more usual, hostile to them.[9] Courts remain wary of the technique. It must be emphasized, however, that polygraphs are used in a wide variety of contexts and under different legal circumstances. Modern courts have begun to consider the value of polygraphs in light of the complex and specific circumstances in which they are offered.[10]

---

[2]*Frye v. U.S.*, 293 F. 1013, 1014, 34 A.L.R. 145 (App. D.C. 1923) (rejected by, State v. Walstad, 119 Wis. 2d 483, 351 N.W.2d 469 (1984)) and (rejected by, State v. Brown, 297 Or. 404, 687 P.2d 751 (1984)) and (rejected by, Nelson v. State, 628 A.2d 69 (Del. 1993)) and (rejected by, State v. Alberico, 116 N.M. 156, 861 P.2d 192 (1993)) and (rejected by, State v. Moore, 268 Mont. 20, 885 P.2d 457 (1994)) and (rejected by, State v. Faught, 127 Idaho 873, 908 P.2d 566 (1995)) and (rejected by, People v. Shreck, 22 P.3d 68, 90 A.L.R.5th 765 (Colo. 2001)).

[3]*Daubert v. Merrell Dow Pharmaceuticals, Inc.*, 509 U.S. 579, 113 S. Ct. 2786, 125 L. Ed. 2d 469, 27, 27 U.S.P.Q.2d 1200, Prod. Liab. Rep. (CCH) P 13494, 37 Fed. R. Evid. Serv. 1, 23 Envtl. L. Rep. 20979 (1993).

[4]Cf. *U.S. v. Microtek Intern. Development Systems Div., Inc.*, 2000 WL 274091 (D. Or. 2000) (Court concluded that although "[p]olygraphs have come a long way," they are still not reliable enough to admit.).

[5]*Com. v. Duguay*, 430 Mass. 397, 720 N.E.2d 458, 463 (1999) (court rejected defendant's argument that Massachusetts' decision adopting *Daubert* test meant that polygraphs were admissible.).

[6]*U.S. v. Scheffer*, 523 U.S. 303, 118 S. Ct. 1261, 140 L. Ed. 2d 413, 48 Fed. R. Evid. Serv. 899 (1998).

[7]§ 8:10.

[8]*U.S. v. Scheffer*, 523 U.S. 303, 317, 118 S. Ct. 1261, 140 L. Ed. 2d 413, 48 Fed. R. Evid. Serv. 899 (1998) (Kennedy, J., concurring in part and concurring in the judgment). (Three Justices,

O'Connor, Ginsburg and Breyer, joined Kennedy's opinion that noted this tension. Justice Stevens, the fifth who joined this view, dissented. *U.S. v. Scheffer*, 523 U.S. 303, 319, 118 S. Ct. 1261, 140 L. Ed. 2d 413, 48 Fed. R. Evid. Serv. 899 (1998) (Stevens, J., dissenting)).

[9]See Charles A. Wright & Kenneth W. Graham, 22 Federal Practice & Procedure § 5169 n.67 (Supp.1995); See generally Honts & Quick, The Polygraph in 1995: Progress in Science and the Law, 71 N. Dakota L. Rev. 987 (1995); Roberta A. Morris, The Admissibility of Evidence Derived From Hypnosis and Polygraph, in Psychological Methods in Criminal Investigation and Evidence (David C. Raskin ed., 1989).

[10]See, e.g., *Ulmer v. State Farm Fire & Cas. Co.*, 897 F. Supp. 299 (W.D. La. 1995) (admitting polygraph evidence after conducting Rule 702—Rule 403 evaluation under *Daubert*); *State v. Travis*, 125 Idaho 1, 867 P.2d 234, 237 (1994) (permitting polygraph in Child Protective Act proceedings where sexual abuse is alleged and most of the evidence is secondhand).

Polygraphs are offered in a wide assortment of contexts in which the rules of evidence do not apply. There is a wide variety of possibilities, from suppression hearings to capital sentencing. Courts disagree regarding the utility of polygraphs in these contexts. Compare *State v. Domicz*, 188 N.J. 285, 907 A.2d 395, 411 (2006) (excluding the results of unstipulated polygraph examinations in suppression hearings) with *Butler v. Balal, Inc.*, 2006 WL 3375201 (Mich. Ct. App. 2006) (citing *People v. Barbara*, 400 Mich. 352, 255 N.W.2d 171 (1977)) ("[P]olygraph evidence is admissible during the preliminary stages of trial that deal with legal questions that do not directly bear on the

## § 8:2 Admissibility

In general, courts divide into three camps regarding the admissibility of polygraph evidence. First, many courts apply a per se rule of exclusion for polygraph evidence. Second, some jurisdictions view polygraph evidence more favorably, and permit it subject to the discretion of the trial court and sometimes only for limited purposes.[1] Third, a significant proportion of jurisdictions permit the parties to stipulate, prior to the test's administration, to the admissibility of the examiner's opinion concerning the results. These three approaches generally describe the division of opinion among courts whether they apply *Frye* or *Daubert* to the evidence. Because courts applying *Daubert* roughly parallel the outcomes of courts applying *Frye*, this section considers the several approaches courts use irrespective of the rule of admissibility they employ. Nonetheless, since the rule of admissibility inevitably affects the *reasons* courts give for their decisions, we explicitly examine these reasons along the way.

## § 8:3 Admissibility—Per se exclusion

Many courts, especially state courts, maintain a per se rule excluding polygraphs.[1] Courts adopting a per se rule excluding the use of polygraph evidence base this determination on a variety of reasons. These concerns can be roughly categorized into three principal objections. First, many courts find that polygraphs have not yet been shown to be sufficiently valid or reliable. Second, many courts applying the *Frye* test conclude that polygraph evidence is not generally accepted. Third, a large number of courts believe that the dangers associated with polygraphs are too great.

Although decided long before *Daubert*, the Illinois Supreme Court voiced doubt that polygraphs could meet a scientific validity test: "Almost all courts refuse to admit unstipulated polygraph evidence because there remain serious doubts about the reliability and scientific recognition of the tests."[2] More recently, a federal district court applying the scientific validity test excluded polygraph evidence on the basis of its unreliability.[3] In general, these courts find the subjective nature of the examination,[4] and the slight requirements for qualifying polygraph examiners,[5] to be factors that undermine the value of the test.

Courts also find that polygraph techniques remain highly controversial among

---

ultimate question of the defendant's guilt or innocence.").

**[Section 8:2]**

[1]For example, in *U.S. v. Piccinonna*, 885 F.2d 1529, 28 Fed. R. Evid. Serv. 1431 (11th Cir. 1989), the Eleventh Circuit held that polygraphs could be admitted for impeachment or corroboration purposes, but any other use had to be the subject of a stipulation. § 8:8.

**[Section 8:3]**

[1]*State v. Porter*, 241 Conn. 57, 698 A.2d 739 (1997); *State v. Shively*, 268 Kan. 573, 999 P.2d 952 (2000); *State v. Robertson*, 712 So. 2d 8 (La. 1998); *Tavares v. State*, 725 So. 2d 803, 810 (Miss. 1998); *State v. Hall*, 955 S.W.2d 198, 207 (Mo. 1997); *State v. Allen*, 252 Neb. 187, 560 N.W.2d 829, 833 (1997) (disapproved of on other grounds by, State v. Myers, 258 Neb. 300, 603 N.W.2d 378 (1999)); *People v. Clarence J.*, 175 Misc. 2d 273, 669 N.Y.S.2d 161 (Sup 1997); *Matthews v. State*, 1998 OK CR 3, 953 P.2d 336 (Okla. Crim. App. 1998); *State v. Sullivan*, 152 Or. App. 75, 952 P.2d 100 (1998); *Com. v. Marinelli*, 547 Pa. 294, 690

A.2d 203 (1997); *Hall v. State*, 970 S.W.2d 137 (Tex. App. Amarillo 1998), petition for discretionary review refused, (Nov. 25, 1998).

[2]*People v. Baynes*, 88 Ill. 2d 225, 58 Ill. Dec. 819, 430 N.E.2d 1070, 1077 (1981).

[3]*U.S. v. Black*, 831 F. Supp. 120, 123 (E.D. N.Y. 1993).

[4]See, e.g., *People v. Anderson*, 637 P.2d 354, 360 (Colo. 1981) (abrogated on other grounds by, People v. Shreck, 22 P.3d 68, 90 A.L.R.5th 765 (Colo. 2001)) (describing polygraph techniques as "art"); *People v. Monigan*, 72 Ill. App. 3d 87, 28 Ill. Dec. 395, 390 N.E.2d 562, 569 (5th Dist. 1979) (objecting to the subjectiveness surrounding the use of the polygraph and the "interpretation of the results"); *State v. Frazier*, 162 W. Va. 602, 252 S.E.2d 39, 48 (1979) (same).

[5]See, e.g., *People v. Anderson*, 637 P.2d 354, 360 (Colo. 1981) (abrogated on other grounds by, People v. Shreck, 22 P.3d 68, 90 A.L.R.5th 765 (Colo. 2001)) ("The absence of adequate qualification standards for the polygraph profession heighten[s] the possibility for grave abuse.").

"scientific experts" and therefore have yet to achieve "general acceptance." Courts, however, disagree concerning the scope of the "pertinent field" in which polygraphs must gain acceptance in order to be admitted. According to *Frye* itself, the fields of psychology and physiology should be surveyed for general acceptance.[6] Some courts also include polygraph examiners in this field.[7] But other courts specifically reject any reliance on polygraph examiners, because of the examiners' general lack of training and their interest in the outcome.[8]

Finally, courts express great concern about the effect polygraph evidence has on the trial process. These concerns range from the opinion that polygraphs usurp the jury's traditional role of evaluating credibility[9] to the belief that this evidence will overwhelm the jury.[10]

## § 8:4  Admissibility—Discretionary admission

Courts agree that *Daubert* applies to polygraph evidence.[1] The biggest change in form, if not in substance, since *Daubert* in regard to polygraphs is the increased number of federal courts that articulate a discretionary standard for this evidence.[2] Several states using a *Daubert*-based validity test have also moved to a standard

---

[6]Frye v. U.S., 293 F. 1013, 1014, 34 A.L.R. 145 (App. D.C. 1923) (rejected by, State v. Walstad, 119 Wis. 2d 483, 351 N.W.2d 469 (1984)) and (rejected by, State v. Brown, 297 Or. 404, 687 P.2d 751 (1984)) and (rejected by, Nelson v. State, 628 A.2d 69 (Del. 1993)) and (rejected by, State v. Alberico, 116 N.M. 156, 861 P.2d 192 (1993)) and (rejected by, State v. Moore, 268 Mont. 20, 885 P.2d 457 (1994)) and (rejected by, State v. Faught, 127 Idaho 873, 908 P.2d 566 (1995)) and (rejected by, People v. Shreck, 22 P.3d 68, 90 A.L.R.5th 765 (Colo. 2001)).

[7]See, e.g., U.S. v. DeBetham, 348 F. Supp. 1377, 1388 (S.D. Cal. 1972), judgment aff'd, 470 F.2d 1367 (9th Cir. 1972).

[8]See, e.g., U.S. v. Alexander, 526 F.2d 161, 164 (8th Cir. 1975) ("Experts in neurology, and physiology may offer needed enlightenment upon the basic premise of polygraphy. Polygraphists often lack extensive training in these specialized sciences."); but see U.S. v. Oliver, 525 F.2d 731, 736 (8th Cir. 1975) ("We believe the necessary foundation can be constructed through testimony showing a sufficient degree of acceptance of the science of polygraphy by experienced practitioners in polygraphy and other related experts.").

[9]See, e.g., U.S. v. Gianakos, 415 F.3d 912, 924 (8th Cir. 2005), cert. denied, 546 U.S. 1045, 126 S. Ct. 764, 163 L. Ed. 2d 593 (2005) ("A fundamental premise of our criminal trial system is that 'the jury is the lie detector.'") (quoting U.S. v. Barnard, 490 F.2d 907, 912 (9th Cir. 1973)); State v. Beachman, 189 Mont. 400, 616 P.2d 337, 339 (1980) ("It is distinctly the jury's province to determine whether a witness is being truthful."); State ex rel. Nebraska State Bar Ass'n v. Miller, 258 Neb. 181, 602 N.W.2d 486, 499 (1999) (noting that polygraphs duplicate purpose of trial).

[10]See, e.g., U.S. v. Alexander, 526 F.2d 161, 168 (8th Cir. 1975) ("When polygraph evidence is offered . . ., it is likely to be shrouded with an aura of near infallibility, akin to the ancient oracle of Delphi."); State v. Shively, 268 Kan. 573, 999 P.2d 952, 958 (2000) (Court noted that it had long voiced "concern about the weight a jury might place on such evidence."). When the polygraph is proffered in a bench trial, courts may be less concerned with its prejudicial effect. See, e.g., Gibbs v. Gibbs, 210 F.3d 491, 24 Employee Benefits Cas. (BNA) 1487, 53 Fed. R. Evid. Serv. 1238, 46 Fed. R. Serv. 3d 799, 172 A.L.R. Fed. 783 (5th Cir. 2000) ("Most of the safeguards provided for in Daubert are not as essential in a case such as this where a district judge sits as the trier of fact in place of a jury.").

**[Section 8:4]**

[1]See, e.g., U.S. v. Galbreth, 908 F. Supp. 877, 881, 43 Fed. R. Evid. Serv. 585 (D.N.M. 1995) (analyzing in some detail the application of Daubert to polygraph tests); See also U.S. v. Lee, 25 F.3d 997, 998, 39 Fed. R. Evid. Serv. 1004 (11th Cir. 1994) (extending Daubert to specialized technical equipment). See generally McCall, Misconceptions and Reevaluation—Polygraph Admissibility After Rock and Daubert, 1996 U. Ill. L. Rev. 363.

[2]See U.S. v. Posado, 57 F.3d 428, 434, 42 Fed. R. Evid. Serv. 1, 140 A.L.R. Fed. 777 (5th Cir. 1995); U.S. v. Beyer, 106 F.3d 175, 178 (7th Cir. 1997); U.S. v. Williams, 95 F.3d 723, 728–730, 45 Fed. R. Evid. Serv. 761 (8th Cir. 1996); U.S. v. Cordoba, 104 F.3d 225, 45 Fed. R. Evid. Serv. 1197 (9th Cir. 1997), as amended, (Feb. 11, 1997); U.S. v. Call, 129 F.3d 1402, 48 Fed. R. Evid. Serv. 339 (10th Cir. 1997); U.S. v. Gilliard, 133 F.3d 809, 48 Fed. R. Evid. Serv. 832 (11th Cir. 1998); U.S. v. Saldarriaga, 179 F.R.D. 140 (S.D. N.Y. 1998); U.S. v. Marshall, 986 F. Supp. 747 (E.D. N.Y. 1997); Meyers v. Arcudi, 947 F. Supp. 581, 71 Empl. Prac. Dec. (CCH) P 44809, 46 Fed. R. Evid. Serv. 80 (D. Conn. 1996); U.S. v. Redschlag, 971 F. Supp. 1371 (D. Colo. 1997).

that leaves polygraph admission within the discretion of trial courts,[3] but leaving discretion to trial courts rather than prescribing a per se rule does not seem to have changed practice substantially.

For example, in *United States v. Cordoba*, the Ninth Circuit held that *Daubert* requires trial courts to evaluate polygraph evidence with particularity in each case.[4] However, district courts applying *Cordoba* usually exclude polygraph evidence.[5] Indeed, courts generally are not sympathetic to proffers of polygraph evidence. They point to high error rates and the lack of standards for administering polygraphs. Moreover, Rule 403 has played a prominent part in courts' particularized analyses of polygraph evidence. Courts cite concerns about infringing on the role of the jury in making credibility assessments,[6] confusion of issues and waste of time,[7] and the problems created if the opposing party does not have a reasonable opportunity to replicate the exam or to have been present when it was given.[8] Courts seem to agree with the Ninth Circuit's conclusion that "[polygraph evidence] still has grave potential for interfering with the deliberative process."[9]

The Fifth Circuit similarly found that its "*per se* rule against admitting polygraph evidence did not survive *Daubert*."[10] The Court explained that *Daubert* changed the evidentiary standard under which the per se rule was crafted and, thus, polygraphs

---

[3]See, e.g., *State v. Brown*, 948 P.2d 337 (Utah 1997); *State v. Crosby*, 927 P.2d 638 (Utah 1996); *State v. Porter*, 241 Conn. 57, 698 A.2d 739 (1997).

[4]*U.S. v. Cordoba*, 104 F.3d 225, 229, 45 Fed. R. Evid. Serv. 1197 (9th Cir. 1997), as amended, (Feb. 11, 1997). See also *Mars v. U.S.*, 25 F.3d 1383, 1384 (7th Cir. 1994) ("[W]e have . . . decided to leave the issue of the admissibility of lie-detector evidence up to the individual trial judge, rather than formulate a circuit-wide rule.").

[5]In *Cordoba* itself, after the Ninth Circuit remanded the case to the district court for a particularized evaluation, the lower court again excluded the evidence. On appeal, the Ninth Circuit affirmed. *U.S. v. Cordoba*, 194 F.3d 1053, 53 Fed. R. Evid. Serv. 3 (9th Cir. 1999). In its opinion, the court reviewed the scientific premises of the polygraph in some detail. The appellate court noted that the district court had found that the polygraph had been subject to testing, albeit with mixed results. *U.S. v. Cordoba*, 194 F.3d 1053, 53 Fed. R. Evid. Serv. 3 (9th Cir. 1999). Also, polygraph research had been published in peer-reviewed journals. The remaining two *Daubert* factors, however, proved the polygraph's undoing. The district court determined that there was no error rate for polygraphs in various contexts, and that the field was badly divided regarding their basic validity. *U.S. v. Cordoba*, 194 F.3d 1053, 53 Fed. R. Evid. Serv. 3 (9th Cir. 1999). These conclusions, the appellate court found, were well supported. Finally, the district court also concluded that the polygraph exam administered here ran afoul of Rule 403. The Ninth Circuit agreed with this judgment. *U.S. v. Cordoba*, 194 F.3d 1053, 53 Fed. R. Evid. Serv. 3 (9th Cir. 1999). See also *U.S. v. Microtek Intern. Development Systems Div., Inc.*, 2000 WL 274091 (D. Or. 2000); *U.S. v. Orians*, 9 F.Supp. 2d 1168, 1998 WL 384731 (D.Ariz.1998); *U.S. v. Cordoba*,

991 F. Supp. 1199, 49 Fed. R. Evid. Serv. 146 (C.D. Cal. 1998), aff'd, 194 F.3d 1053, 53 Fed. R. Evid. Serv. 3 (9th Cir. 1999); *U.S. v. Pitner*, 969 F. Supp. 1246, 1252 (W.D. Wash. 1997).

[6]*U.S. v. Orians*, 9 F.Supp. 2d 1168, 1175, 1998 WL 384731 (D.Ariz.1998); *U.S. v. Cordoba*, 991 F. Supp. 1199, 1208, 49 Fed. R. Evid. Serv. 146 (C.D. Cal. 1998), aff'd, 194 F.3d 1053, 53 Fed. R. Evid. Serv. 3 (9th Cir. 1999); *U.S. v. Pitner*, 969 F. Supp. 1246, 1252 (W.D. Wash. 1997).

[7]*U.S. v. Gilliard*, 133 F.3d 809, 815–816, 48 Fed. R. Evid. Serv. 832 (11th Cir. 1998); *U.S. v. Pitner*, 969 F. Supp. 1246, 1252 (W.D. Wash. 1997).

[8]See *U.S. v. Croft*, 124 F.3d 1109, 1120, 47 Fed. R. Evid. Serv. 1048 (9th Cir. 1997).

[9]*U.S. v. Cordoba*, 104 F.3d 225, 228, 45 Fed. R. Evid. Serv. 1197 (9th Cir. 1997), as amended, (Feb. 11, 1997); see, e.g., *U.S. v. Rouse*, 410 F.3d 1005, 1011 (8th Cir. 2005); *U.S. v. Henderson*, 409 F.3d 1293, 1301–1304, 67 Fed. R. Evid. Serv. 350 (11th Cir. 2005), cert. denied, 546 U.S. 1169, 126 S. Ct. 1331, 164 L. Ed. 2d 47 (2006).

[10]*U.S. v. Posado*, 57 F.3d 428, 429, 42 Fed. R. Evid. Serv. 1, 140 A.L.R. Fed. 777 (5th Cir. 1995).

Another federal court similarly found that *Daubert* permits a more flexible approach to polygraph evidence than that permitted under the *Frye* test. In *U.S. v. Crumby*, 895 F. Supp. 1354, 42 Fed. R. Evid. Serv. 1127 (D. Ariz. 1995), the court observed that the historical concern with polygraph evidence has been twofold, reliability of the test and the prejudicial effect on the jury of admitting it. *U.S. v. Crumby*, 895 F. Supp. 1354, 1356, 42 Fed. R. Evid. Serv. 1127 (D. Ariz. 1995). The court also noted that good reasons now existed for reconsidering the admissibility of polygraph evidence. These included: (1) the fact that in this case the defendant has consistently maintained his innocence and passed a polygraph; (2) *Daubert*;

would now have to be reevaluated. The court noted "that tremendous advances have been made in polygraph instrumentation and technique in the years since *Frye*" and discussed some of these "advances."[11] Therefore, the court observed, "[w]hat remains is the issue of whether polygraph techniques can be said to have made sufficient technological advance in the seventy years since *Frye* to constitute the type of 'scientific, technical, or other specialized knowledge' envisioned by Rule 702 and *Daubert*. We cannot say without a fully developed record that it has not."[12] The court remanded to the trial court to hold a preliminary hearing to determine this matter.[13]

Several courts find that *Daubert* has not changed their approach to polygraph evidence. In *United States v. Black*,[14] for example, the court stated that "nothing in *Daubert* changes the rationale excluding evidence because of reliability concerns."[15] The court concluded that "[a]fter evaluating the standard set forth in the *Daubert* case, premised on Rule 702 of the Federal Rules of Evidence, the Court believes that nothing in *Daubert* would disturb the settled precedent that polygraph evidence is neither reliable nor admissible."[16]

## § 8:5  Admissibility—Discretionary admission—Rule 403

Although not a major part of *Daubert* itself, Rule 403 figures prominently in the federal courts' *Daubert* evaluations of polygraph evidence.[1] There is good reason for this, since research indicates that polygraphs are somewhat reliable, but courts are

---

(3) the increase in reliability in the test itself; and (4) an alternative vision of the polygraph sketched out in *U.S. v. Piccinonna*, 885 F.2d 1529, 28 Fed. R. Evid. Serv. 1431 (11th Cir. 1989). *U.S. v. Crumby*, 895 F. Supp. 1354, 1357–1358, 42 Fed. R. Evid. Serv. 1127 (D. Ariz. 1995). The court then embarked on an in-depth analysis of the polygraph and found that polygraphy now met the four factors identified in *Daubert*. *U.S. v. Crumby*, 895 F. Supp. 1354, 1361, 42 Fed. R. Evid. Serv. 1127 (D. Ariz. 1995). The court placed particular reliance on the scientific research of Dr. David Raskin in reaching its conclusions; the court, however, did not cite or even mention the substantial literature that challenges the validity of polygraph tests. Finally, the court evaluated polygraph evidence under Rule 403, finding that its probative value was not outweighed by unfair prejudice. The court stressed several factors as being important in its determination, including in particular that the defendant not the state offered it here and that it would be permitted for a limited purpose. *U.S. v. Crumby*, 895 F. Supp. 1354, 1363, 42 Fed. R. Evid. Serv. 1127 (D. Ariz. 1995). The court concluded that the defendant could introduce evidence that he took and passed the polygraph if: (1) he gave notice to the government; (2) he made himself available to a polygraph exam administered by the government; (3) he introduced the evidence only to support credibility, if attacked, under Rule 608(a); and (4) the specific questions and physiological data are not introduced into evidence, though the general science of polygraphy may be discussed under Rule 702. *U.S. v. Crumby*, 895 F. Supp. 1354, 1365, 42 Fed. R. Evid. Serv. 1127 (D. Ariz. 1995). See also *U.S. v. Galbreth*, 908 F. Supp. 877, 43 Fed. R. Evid. Serv. 585 (D.N.M. 1995) (offering a similar analysis of the issue to that of *Crumby*).

[11]*U.S. v. Posado*, 57 F.3d 428, 434, 42 Fed. R. Evid. Serv. 1, 140 A.L.R. Fed. 777 (5th Cir. 1995).

[12]*U.S. v. Posado*, 57 F.3d 428, 433, 42 Fed. R. Evid. Serv. 1, 140 A.L.R. Fed. 777 (5th Cir. 1995).

[13]*U.S. v. Posado*, 57 F.3d 428, 436, 42 Fed. R. Evid. Serv. 1, 140 A.L.R. Fed. 777 (5th Cir. 1995). Lower courts in the Fifth Circuit appear to have embraced their new responsibility to evaluate the admissibility of polygraphs under the specific facts of particular cases. See, e.g., *Ulmer v. State Farm Fire & Cas. Co.*, 897 F. Supp. 299 (W.D. La. 1995) (Applying *Posado*, the court permitted the introduction of polygraph results in a civil action in which the defendant insurance company had prompted a fire marshall to investigate the plaintiffs for arson; the plaintiffs passed the test administered by a certified, and neutral, examiner.).

[14]*U.S. v. Black*, 831 F. Supp. 120 (E.D. N.Y. 1993).

[15]*U.S. v. Black*, 831 F. Supp. 120, 123 (E.D. N.Y. 1993) (citing *U.S. v. Rea*, 958 F.2d 1206, 1224, 92-1 U.S. Tax Cas. (CCH) P 50191, 35 Fed. R. Evid. Serv. 351, 69 A.F.T.R.2d 92-918 (2d Cir. 1992)).

[16]*U.S. v. Black*, 831 F. Supp. 120, 123 (E.D. N.Y. 1993); see also *State v. Fain*, 116 Idaho 82, 774 P.2d 252, 256 (1989) (stating general rule of exclusion, because polygraphs lack validity and reliability); see also *Franklin v. Franklin*, 928 So. 2d 90, 94 (La. Ct. App. 1st Cir. 2005), writ denied, 924 So. 2d 1021 (La. 2006) (finding lower court's admission of polygraph test is an administrative hearing to be error under *Daubert* standard).

**[Section 8:5]**

[1]Rule 403 also played a prominent role in admissibility determinations prior to *Daubert*.

reluctant to find them reliable enough.[2] Since *Daubert*'s focus is primarily on relevance, reliability, and fit, polygraphs might be thought to meet the basic test. But concerns with this evidence range from friendly and thus invalid tests to invasion of the province of the jury.[3] Rule 403 has permitted courts a more discriminating tool than that permitted by Rule 702 alone. In *Posado*, for example, the court observed that "the presumption in favor of admissibility established by Rules 401 and 402, together with *Daubert*'s 'flexible' approach, may well mandate an enhanced role for Rule 403 in the context of the *Daubert* analysis, particularly when the scientific or technical knowledge proffered is novel or controversial."[4] The Sixth Circuit took a similar approach in *Conti v. Commissioner of Internal Revenue*.[5] In *Conti*, the court upheld the lower court's use of Rule 403 to exclude polygraph tests taken unilaterally. The court observed that "the prejudicial effect of [unilateral] polygraph test results outweighs their probative value under Fed. R. Evid. 403, because the party offering them did not have an adverse interest at stake while taking the test."[6]

Courts, however, have not always used the Rule 403 tool in a discriminating manner. In *United States v. Waters*,[7] the defendant appealed from his conviction for child abuse. The defendant complained on appeal, among other things, that the trial court had erred in refusing to hold a *Daubert* hearing to consider the admissibility of the defendant's polygraph results. At the government's request, the defendant had taken a polygraph, administered by a special agent of the FBI, and had "passed" when asked whether he had ever touched the alleged victim's "private areas in a sexual way."[8]

In a cursory analysis, the Eighth Circuit concluded that it did not even have to reach the *Daubert* issue, since "the district court independently excluded the evidence under Fed. R. Evid. 403, which provides for exclusion of evidence 'if its probative value is substantially outweighed by the danger of unfair prejudice, confusion of the issues, or misleading the jury, or by consideration of undue delay, waste of time . . .'"[9] It is not clear how a *Daubert* analysis can be avoided when balancing probative value against prejudicial effect, since the amount of probative value expert testimony has depends necessarily on the reliability of the evidence. The

See, e.g., *U.S. v. Piccinonna*, 885 F.2d 1529, 1536, 28 Fed. R. Evid. Serv. 1431 (11th Cir. 1989); *Wolfel v. Holbrook*, 823 F.2d 970, 972 (6th Cir. 1987); *U.S. v. Miller*, 874 F.2d 1255, 28 Fed. R. Evid. Serv. 23 (9th Cir. 1989).

[2]See, e.g., *U.S. v. Benavidez-Benavidez*, 217 F.3d 720, 54 Fed. R. Evid. Serv. 303 (9th Cir. 2000) (District court excluded polygraph evidence for failing one *Daubert* factor—general acceptance—as well as under Rule 403. Circuit Court ruled that the evidence could pass *Daubert* scrutiny, but be wholly excluded under Rule 403 alone.). *U.S. v. Ramirez-Robles*, 386 F.3d 1234, 1246, 65 Fed. R. Evid. Serv. 733 (9th Cir. 2004), cert. denied, 544 U.S. 1035, 125 S. Ct. 2251, 161 L. Ed. 2d 1063 (2005) (holding that *Daubert* analysis is unnecessary if Rule 403 excludes the evidence); *U.S. v. Ross*, 412 F.3d 771, 773, 67 Fed. R. Evid. Serv. 637 (7th Cir. 2005) ("There was no abuse of discretion here because, for one thing, the manner in which the test was administered-privately commissioned, in the eleventh hour, and without notice to the government-was highly suspect.").

[3]See, e.g., *In re Davis*, 22 F. Supp. 2 (E.D. Ill. 1938) (noting concern that polygraphs might "supplant the fact-finding function of the jury").

[4]*U.S. v. Posado*, 57 F.3d 428, 435, 42 Fed. R. Evid. Serv. 1, 140 A.L.R. Fed. 777 (5th Cir. 1995).

[5]*Conti v. C.I.R.*, 39 F.3d 658, 94-2 U.S. Tax Cas. (CCH) P 50582, 41 Fed. R. Evid. Serv. 522, 74 A.F.T.R.2d 94-6867, 1994 FED App. 0379P (6th Cir. 1994).

[6]*Conti v. C.I.R.*, 39 F.3d 658, 663, 94-2 U.S. Tax Cas. (CCH) P 50582, 41 Fed. R. Evid. Serv. 522, 74 A.F.T.R.2d 94-6867, 1994 FED App. 0379P (6th Cir. 1994); see also *U.S. v. Harris*, 9 F.3d 493, 502, 39 Fed. R. Evid. Serv. 1314 (6th Cir. 1993).

[7]*U.S. v. Waters*, 194 F.3d 926, 52 Fed. R. Evid. Serv. 1574 (8th Cir. 1999).

[8]*U.S. v. Waters*, 194 F.3d 926, 928, 52 Fed. R. Evid. Serv. 1574 (8th Cir. 1999).

[9]*U.S. v. Waters*, 194 F.3d 926, 930, 52 Fed. R. Evid. Serv. 1574 (8th Cir. 1999).

court cited *United States v. Scheffer*[10] for the proposition that there is substantial disagreement regarding the reliability of polygraphs. But *Scheffer* is not particularly good authority in this case. *Scheffer* was a constitutional challenge in which the Court ruled that it was not unreasonable for the military to adopt a per se rule excluding polygraph evidence. Rule 403, in contrast, calls upon courts to conduct a case-by-case evaluation. In *Waters*, there were several factors supporting the polygraph results, at least against government challenges. First, the government had sponsored the test and a government examiner had interpreted it. Second, in a child abuse case such as this, there is little evidence other than the child's statements, evidence not usually deemed the most dependable. The trial court refused even to hold a *Daubert* hearing, and thus never even considered the reliability (and thus the probative value) of the evidence. Without knowing the probative value of the evidence, it is impossible to say that the unfair prejudice is greater.

Rule 403 gives courts the flexibility by which they can manage scientific evidence. Rule 702, among other things, queries the scientific validity of the basis for proffered expert testimony. Yet, in reality, science does not come packaged neatly into "valid" and "invalid" containers. Sometimes, substantial testing will give courts great confidence in the validity of relevant scientific evidence; more usually, however, the testing will leave courts less sure. Rule 403 allows courts to take into account the dangers associated with a particular type of expert testimony as compared to the benefits it offers. Polygraph tests present a particularly appropriate example of the importance of Rule 403 in managing scientific evidence. As the *Posado* court noted, "the traditional objection to polygraph evidence is that the testimony will have an unusually prejudicial effect which is not justified by its probative value, precisely the inquiry required of the district court by Rule 403."[11] At the same time, the *Posado* court noted that polygraphs might possess significant probative value.[12] Hence, courts must now judge the polygraph through the lenses of Rules 702 and 403.

### § 8:6 Admissibility—Discretionary admission—Other approaches to discretionary admittance

In Massachusetts, a *Daubert* state, polygraph evidence is admissible only after the proponent introduces results of proficiency exams that indicate that the examiner can reliably discern truth-telling.[1] The Supreme Judicial Court explained the rule as follows:

> If polygraph evidence is to be admissible in a given case, it seems likely that its reliability will be established by proof in a given case that a qualified tester who conducted the test, had in similar circumstances demonstrated, in a statistically valid number of independently verified and controlled tests, the high level of accuracy of the conclusions that the tester reached in those tests.[2]

This requirement, in practice, almost certainly results in the exclusion of most polygraph evidence. Outside of the federal government, polygraph examiners do not undergo routine proficiency tests. Even inside government laboratories, it is somewhat unclear what levels of quality control exist, or whether government records would be readily forthcoming if requested.

Probably the most permissive approach to polygraph evidence occurs in New

---

[10]*U.S. v. Scheffer*, 523 U.S. 303, 118 S. Ct. 1261, 140 L. Ed. 2d 413, 48 Fed. R. Evid. Serv. 899 (1998).

[11]*U.S. v. Posado*, 57 F.3d 428, 435, 42 Fed. R. Evid. Serv. 1, 140 A.L.R. Fed. 777 (5th Cir. 1995).

[12]*U.S. v. Posado*, 57 F.3d 428, 435, 42 Fed. R. Evid. Serv. 1, 140 A.L.R. Fed. 777 (5th Cir. 1995).

**[Section 8:6]**

[1]*Com. v. Duguay*, 430 Mass. 397, 720 N.E.2d 458, 463 (1999).

[2]*Com. v. Duguay*, 430 Mass. 397, 720 N.E.2d 458, 463 (1999) (quoting *Com. v. Stewart*, 422 Mass. 385, 663 N.E.2d 255 (1996)).

Mexico. A New Mexico statute "entrusts the admissibility of polygraph evidence to the sound discretion of the trial court."[3] The court in *Tafoya v. Baca*[4] explained the operation of the rule:

> Under [Evidence] Rule 707(d), any party intending to use polygraph evidence at trial must give written notice to the opposing party of his intention. Under Rule 707(g), once such notice has been given, the court may compel . . . a witness who has previously voluntarily taken a polygraph test to submit to another polygraph test by an examiner of the other party's choice. If such witness refuses to submit, no polygraph test evidence is admissible at trial. Under [Criminal Procedure] Rule 28(a)(2), a defendant must disclose only those results of a polygraph test which the defendant intends to use at trial.[5]

In addition, New Mexico courts must determine that: (1) the polygraph examiner is qualified; (2) the procedures employed were reliable; and (3) the test administered to the subject was valid.[6]

## § 8:7   Admissibility—Admissibility by stipulation

By far the most unusual aspect of polygraph evidence is the large part the parties often play in controlling admissibility through stipulation.[1] Although, theoretically, stipulation could be a factor in a wide variety of evidentiary contexts, as a practical matter it is not. This stratagem adds an interesting wrinkle to the problem of the admissibility of scientific evidence.[2]

Although the vast majority of courts routinely exclude the results of polygraph tests, many of these courts qualify this ruling by permitting polygraph results when the parties stipulate to their admissibility prior to the administration of the test.[3] Courts typically premise the decision to permit polygraph results through prior stipulation on principles of estoppel.[4] Some courts also believe that prior stipulations increase the validity of the procedure. Many courts, however, insist that stipulations cannot cure the defects associated with polygraphy.[5] Moreover, absent stipulation, courts uniformly exclude evidence indicating the defendant's willingness[6] or unwillingness[7] to take a polygraph examination.

Most of the courts that permit polygraph results by stipulation require that

---

[3]*B & W Const. Co. v. N.C. Ribble Co.*, 105 N.M. 448, 734 P.2d 226 (1987).

[4]*Tafoya v. Baca*, 103 N.M. 56, 702 P.2d 1001 (1985).

[5]*Tafoya v. Baca*, 103 N.M. 56, 702, 702 P.2d 1001 (1985); see also *Lee v. Martinez*, 2004-NMSC-027, 136 N.M. 166, 96 P.3d 291, 306 (2004) (The Court evaluated Rule 707 under its admissibility standard—*Daubert/Alberico*—and concluded that "the control question polygraph examination is sufficiently reliable" to admit.).

[6]*Tafoya v. Baca*, 103 N.M. 56, 702, 702 P.2d 1001 (1985).

**[Section 8:7]**

[1]See generally Note, Admissibility of Polygraph Test Results Upon Stipulation of the Parties, 30 Mercer L. Rev. 357 (1978).

[2]See also Katz, Dilemmas of Polygraph Stipulations, 14 Seton Hall L. Rev. 285 (1984).

[3]See, e.g., *U.S. v. Piccinonna*, 885 F.2d 1529, 1536, 28 Fed. R. Evid. Serv. 1431 (11th Cir. 1989) ("Polygraph expert testimony will be admissible in this circuit when both parties stipulate in advance as to the circumstances of the test and as

to the scope of its admissibility."); see also *U.S. v. Gordon*, 688 F.2d 42, 44, 11 Fed. R. Evid. Serv. 1026 (8th Cir. 1982); *Ex parte Hinton*, 548 So. 2d 562, 569 (Ala. 1989); *People v. Fudge*, 7 Cal. 4th 1075, 31 Cal. Rptr. 2d 321, 875 P.2d 36 (1994).

[4]See, e.g., *Herman v. Eagle Star Ins. Co.*, 396 F.2d 427 (9th Cir.1968); *State v. Olmstead*, 261 N.W.2d 880 (N.D. 1978); *State v. Rebeterano*, 681 P.2d 1265 (Utah 1984); *McGhee v. State*, 253 Ga. 278, 319 S.E.2d 836 (1984).

[5]See *U.S. v. A & S Council Oil Co.*, 947 F.2d 1128, 1133–1134, 34 Fed. R. Evid. Serv. 380 (4th Cir. 1991); *U.S. v. Hunter*, 672 F.2d 815, 817, 10 Fed. R. Evid. Serv. 55 (10th Cir. 1982); *U.S. v. Skeens*, 494 F.2d 1050, 1053 (D.C. Cir. 1974); *Pulakis v. State*, 476 P.2d 474, 478 (Alaska 1970); *Carr v. State*, 655 So. 2d 824, 836 (Miss. 1995); *State v. Biddle*, 599 S.W.2d 182, 185 (Mo. 1980).

[6]See, e.g., *People v. Espinoza*, 3 Cal. 4th 806, 12 Cal. Rptr. 2d 682, 838 P.2d 204 (1992), as modified on denial of reh'g, (Dec. 17, 1992); *People v. Mann*, 646 P.2d 352, 361 (Colo. 1982).

[7]See, e.g., *Houser v. State*, 234 Ga. 209, 214 S.E.2d 893 (1975).

certain conditions be met. For example, in the widely followed case of *State v. Valdez*,[8] the Arizona Supreme Court established the following four conditions:

(1) That . . . counsel all sign a written stipulation providing for defendant's submission to the test and for the subsequent admission at trial of the graphs and the examiner's opinion . . .

(2) That notwithstanding the stipulation the admissibility of the test results is subject to the discretion of the trial judge . . .

(3) That if the graphs and examiner's opinion are offered in evidence the opposing party shall have the right to cross-examine the examiner respecting
   (a) the examiner's qualifications and training;
   (b) the conditions under which the test was administered;
   (c) the limitations of and possibilities for error in the technique of polygraphic interrogation; and
   (d) at the discretion of the trial judge, any other matter deemed pertinent to the inquiry;

(4) That if such evidence is admitted the trial judge should instruct the jury that the examiner's testimony does not tend to prove or disprove any element of the crime with which a defendant is charged but at most tends only to indicate that at the time of the examination defendant was not telling the truth. Further, the jury members should be instructed that it is for them to determine what corroborative weight and effect such testimony should be given.[9]

The generous reliance on stipulations to manage polygraph evidence raises substantial analytical difficulties that courts applying *Daubert* and analogous standards of admissibility should consider. Although a factual question, the validity and reliability of polygraph evidence under *Daubert* is, at heart, a legal determination under Rule 104(a).[10] Under the federal rules, judges determine the existence of preliminary facts that are necessary to the application of a particular rule under the preponderance of the evidence standard of Rule 104(a). The admissibility of polygraph evidence thus depends on a judge's preliminary determination that the technique is sufficiently valid to support expert testimony. The fact that the parties are willing to stipulate to polygraph evidence should not free the judge from making this preliminary determination of validity.[11] To be sure, parties regularly stipulate to evidence. But polygraphy is unique, in that the stipulation occurs before the real evidence—the polygraph result—exists. If polygraph results contain too large a margin of error, then a party who stipulates to their admission is playing roulette with his juristic fate. Courts might be reluctant to endorse stipulations that amount to little more than a calculated gamble.

The Illinois Supreme Court asserted that there is an "inconsistency [in] admitting polygraph evidence on the basis of a stipulation since the stipulation does little if

---

[8]*State v. Valdez*, 91 Ariz. 274, 371 P.2d 894 (1962).

[9]*State v. Valdez*, 91 Ariz. 274, 371, 371 P.2d 894 (1962). See also *State v. Souel*, 53 Ohio St. 2d 123, 7 Ohio Op. 3d 207, 372 N.E.2d 1318, 1323–1324 (1978) (adopting *Valdez* rule); *Cullin v. State*, 565 P.2d 445, 457 (Wyo. 1977) (adopting *Valdez* rule and providing, in cases of stipulation, cross-examination before admitting polygraph evidence); *State v. Rebeterano*, 681 P.2d 1265, 1268 (Utah 1984) (adopting *Valdez* rule and requiring that the defendant's participation be voluntary). See generally *Wynn v. State*, 423 So. 2d 294 (Ala.

Crim. App. 1982).

[10]*Daubert v. Merrell Dow Pharmaceuticals, Inc.*, 509 U.S. 579, 592, 113 S. Ct. 2786, 125 L. Ed. 2d 469, 27 U.S.P.Q.2d 1200, Prod. Liab. Rep. (CCH) P 13494, 37 Fed. R. Evid. Serv. 1, 23 Envtl. L. Rep. 20979 (1993).

[11]See, e.g., *Hoult v. Hoult*, 57 F.3d 1, 4, 41 Fed. R. Evid. Serv. 783, 32 Fed. R. Serv. 3d 281 (1st Cir. 1995) ("We think *Daubert* does instruct district courts to conduct a preliminary assessment of the reliability of expert testimony, even in the absence of an objection.").

anything to enhance the reliability of polygraph evidence."[12] The Illinois court refused to permit the parties to stipulate to the admissibility of results derived from a process that it considered little better than flipping a coin.[13] Other courts, however, find that the stipulation device increases the reliability of the test sufficiently to make it acceptable.[14] According to this view, the stipulation raises the subject's apprehension and leads to the selection of more impartial polygraphers, both factors leading to more accurate results.[15] Whatever the case, notwithstanding the parties' willingness to stipulate, Rules 702 and 403 probably require some preliminary determination that the polygraph test is sufficiently valid and that the agreement to admit the results does not produce excessive unfair prejudice or waste of time.

## § 8:8  Admissibility—Corroboration and impeachment purposes

Many courts do not permit polygraph results as substantive evidence (at least absent stipulation), but permit them for corroboration or impeachment purposes.[1] Several courts allow polygraphs to be used on credibility matters only when the parties stipulated to this use prior to the examination.[2] Other courts, as noted above, do not allow polygraph results for any purpose, including credibility.[3]

The suitability of employing polygraph evidence for impeachment and corroboration purposes under the federal rules and similar state codes is not obvious. In *United States v. Piccinonna*, for example, the court held that polygraph evidence may be introduced "to impeach or corroborate the testimony of a witness at trial."[4] The court established three criteria for such use: (1) notice to the opposing party; (2) reasonable opportunity for the opponent to administer a polygraph to the witness using his own expert; and (3) adherence to Federal Rule 608, which governs evidence proffered to impeach or corroborate a witness.[5]

Rule 608, however, is not well-tailored to this use of polygraph examinations. Rule 608 identifies two kinds of evidence permitted for impeachment and corrobora-

---

[12]*People v. Baynes*, 88 Ill. 2d 225, 58 Ill. Dec. 819, 430 N.E.2d 1070, 1078 (1981) (citing *State v. Dean*, 103 Wis. 2d 228, 307 N.W.2d 628 (1981)).

[13]See generally *U.S. v. Piccinonna*, 885 F.2d 1529, 1537, 28 Fed. R. Evid. Serv. 1431 (11th Cir. 1989) (Johnson, J., concurring in part and dissenting in part) ("Because the polygraph can predict whether a person is lying with accuracy that is only slightly greater than chance, it will be of little help to the trier of fact.").

[14]See, e.g., *U.S. v. Piccinonna*, 885 F.2d 1529, 1536, 28 Fed. R. Evid. Serv. 1431 (11th Cir. 1989); *Anderson v. U.S.*, 788 F.2d 517, 519 (8th Cir. 1986); *U.S. v. Oliver*, 525 F.2d 731, 737 (8th Cir. 1975); *Ex parte Clements*, 447 So. 2d 695, 698 (Ala. 1984); *State v. Montes*, 136 Ariz. 491, 667 P.2d 191, 199 (1983); *State v. Valdez*, 91 Ariz. 274, 371, 371 P.2d 894, 900 (1962).

[15]See *U.S. v. Wilson*, 361 F. Supp. 510, 514 (D. Md. 1973) (noting that without stipulation the defendant is secure in knowing that unwelcome results can be buried; "[t]his sense of security diminishes the fear of discovered deception, upon which an effective examination depends"); *McMorris v. Israel*, 643 F.2d 458, 463 (7th Cir. 1981) (rejected by, Jackson v. State, 116 Nev. 334, 997 P.2d 121 (2000)) (same).

**[Section 8:8]**

[1]See, e.g., *U.S. v. Piccinonna*, 885 F.2d 1529, 1536, 28 Fed. R. Evid. Serv. 1431 (11th Cir. 1989).

[2]See, e.g., *State v. Souel*, 53 Ohio St. 2d 123, 7 Ohio Op. 3d 207, 372 N.E.2d 1318 (1978).

[3]See, e.g., *U.S. v. Sanchez*, 118 F.3d 192, 195, 47 Fed. R. Evid. Serv. 499 (4th Cir. 1997) ("[P]olygraph evidence is never admissible to impeach the credibility of a witness."); *Robinson v. Com.*, 231 Va. 142, 341 S.E.2d 159 (1986); *State v. Muetze*, 368 N.W.2d 575 (S.D. 1985).

[4]*U.S. v. Piccinonna*, 885 F.2d 1529, 1536, 28 Fed. R. Evid. Serv. 1431 (11th Cir. 1989).

[5]*U.S. v. Piccinonna*, 885 F.2d 1529, 1536, 28 Fed. R. Evid. Serv. 1431 (11th Cir. 1989). Specifically, the court noted as follows:

> Rule 608 limits the use of opinion or reputation evidence to establish the credibility of a witness in the following way: "[E]vidence of truthful character of the witness is admissible only after the character of the witness for truthfulness has been attacked by opinion or reputation evidence or otherwise." Thus, evidence that a witness passed a polygraph examination, used to corroborate that witness's in-court testimony, would not be admissible under Rule 608 unless or until the credibility of that witness were first attacked.

*U.S. v. Piccinonna*, 885 F.2d 1529, 1536, 28 Fed. R. Evid. Serv. 1431 (11th Cir. 1989).

tion purposes, as provided under subsections (a) and (b) of the rule.[6] Rule 608(a) allows "opinion and reputation evidence of character." This appears to provide authority, since the proponent of the evidence seeks to introduce "expert *opinion*" on the witness' veracity. Rule 608(a) is ambiguous, however, because it limits opinion evidence to the witness' "*character* for truthfulness or untruthfulness."[7] It is not clear whether polygraph experts testify to subjects' characters or, rather, as the much-cited *Valdez* court remarked, only to whether the witness was or was not telling the truth "at the time of the examination."[8] Rule 608 thus does not obviously apply to the situation in which the witness states "X" on the witness stand and the polygrapher testifies as to whether the witness was truthful in saying "X" during the polygraph test. Alternatively, passing or failing a polygraph might be considered a "specific instance of conduct" that indicates the subject's character for truthfulness or untruthfulness. Rule 608(b) regulates the admission of such evidence. But subsection (b) specifically provides that "specific instances of conduct" *cannot* be introduced to support or attack credibility. Specific instances of conduct only can be inquired into on cross-examination. Under Rule 608(b), therefore, a polygraph expert would not be permitted to testify, though the opponent may be permitted to question the witness about the results of the polygraph examination on cross-examination.

## § 8:9   Confessions before, during, and after polygraph examinations

Courts generally do not exclude confessions made in anticipation of taking, or as a consequence of failing, a polygraph test.[1] Courts do not find the circumstances sur-

---

[6]Rule 608 provides, in pertinent part, as follows:

(a) **Opinion and reputation evidence of character.** The credibility of a witness may be attacked or supported by evidence in the form of opinion or reputation, but subject to these limitations: (1) the evidence may refer only to character for truthfulness or untruthfulness, and (2) evidence of truthful character is admissible only after the character of the witness for truthfulness has been attacked by opinion or reputation evidence or otherwise.

(b) **Specific instances of conduct.** Specific instances of the conduct of a witness, for the purpose of attacking or supporting the witness' credibility, other than conviction of crime as provided in rule 609, may not be proved by extrinsic evidence. They may, however, in the discretion of the court, if probative of truthfulness or untruthfulness, be inquired into on cross-examination of the witness (1) concerning the witness' character for truthfulness or untruthfulness, or (2) concerning the character for truthfulness or untruthfulness of another witness as to which character the witness being cross-examined has testified.

Fed. R. Evid. 608.

[7]Fed. R. Evid. 608(a), emphasis added. The Rule 608(a) language closely tracks the "reputation and opinion provision of Rule 405(a)." In fact, the Advisory Committee's Note to Rule 608 refers back to the Note accompanying Rule 405. The Rule 405 Note explains the expansion of the rule from the common law practice of limiting character evidence to reputation to the modern approach that allows opinion. The Advisory Committee Note indicates that the word "opinion" was intended to include expert opinion:

If character is defined as the kind of person one is, then account must be taken of varying ways of arriving at the estimate. These may range from the opinion of the employer who has found the man honest to the opinion of the psychiatrist based upon examination and testing. No effective dividing line exists between character and mental capacity, and the latter traditionally has been provable by opinion.

Advisory Committee Note to Fed. R. Evid. 405. The kind of expert opinion contemplated by this Note, however, probably does not extend to polygraph testimony, since polygraph experts do not give opinions on "the kind of person" the subject is. Instead, they offer an opinion on whether the subject was or was not lying in response to specific questions.

[8]*State v. Valdez*, 91 Ariz. 274, 371, 371 P.2d 894, 901 (1962).

**[Section 8:9]**

[1]See, e.g., *Johnson v. State*, 660 So. 2d 637 (Fla. 1995); *Smith v. State*, 265 Ga. 570, 459 S.E.2d 420 (1995); *State v. Blosser*, 221 Kan. 59, 558 P.2d 105 (1976).

In contrast, Wisconsin courts exclude "[a]nything that a defendant said during what is considered to be part of the polygraph examination." *State v. Harris*, 2007 WL 1848047 *1 (Wis. Ct. App. 2007). This rule applies even if the statement is voluntary or otherwise admissible. Id. Wisconsin courts use a multi-factored test to assess whether statements were made during, or were "closely related" to, the polygraph examination. Relevant factors include "(1) whether the post-polygraph interview was in the examination room or in some other place; (2) whether the defendant was told that the polygraph examination

rounding polygraph examinations themselves to be unreasonably coercive.[2] However, the circumstances of the polygraph examination might implicate constitutional guarantees[3] and require specific waivers of the right to counsel.[4] In addition, mental incapacity of the subject or extreme and unusual conditions imposed by the examiners, can lead to exclusion of the confession.[5] Even jurisdictions that apply a per se rule of inadmissibility allow the use of statements elicited during a polygraph examination, as long as no mention of the polygraph examination is made.[6]

## § 8:10 Polygraph evidence and constitutional guarantees

Two issues in particular arise concerning the use of polygraph tests under the United States Constitution.[1] Some defendants claim that exclusion of exculpatory polygraph results violates a defendant's Sixth Amendment right to present evidence; other defendants claim that admission of inculpatory polygraph results

---

is over; and (3) whether the polygraph examiner interrogates the defendant making frequent use of and reference to the charts and tracing just obtained in the examination." *State v. Harris*, 2007 WL 1848047 *1 (Wis. Ct. App. 2007) (citing *State v. Greer*, 265 Wis. 2d 463, 2003 WI App 112, 666 N.W.2d 518 (Ct. App. 2003) (rejected by, State v. Damron, 151 S.W.3d 510 (Tenn. 2004))).

[2]See, e.g., *U.S. v. Dupris*, 2006 DSD 4, 422 F. Supp. 2d 1061, 1071–1072 (D.S.D. 2006); *People v. Madison*, 135 A.D.2d 655, 522 N.Y.S.2d 230 (2d Dep't 1987), order aff'd, 73 N.Y.2d 810, 537 N.Y.S.2d 111, 534 N.E.2d 28 (1988).

[3]In *People v. Storm*, 94 Cal. Rptr. 2d 805 (App. 4th Dist. 2000), review granted and opinion superseded, 99 Cal. Rptr. 2d 485, 6 P.3d 150 (Cal. 2000) and judgment aff'd, 28 Cal. 4th 1007, 124 Cal. Rptr. 2d 110, 52 P.3d 52 (2002), the court found that a reasonable person would have believed himself to be in custody "when the polygraph operator told him he had badly flunked the examination." *People v. Storm*, 94 Cal. Rptr. 2d 805, 813 (App. 4th Dist. 2000), review granted and opinion superseded, 99 Cal. Rptr. 2d 485, 6 P.3d 150 (Cal. 2000) and judgment aff'd, 28 Cal. 4th 1007, 124 Cal. Rptr. 2d 110, 52 P.3d 52 (2002). The court of appeals explained that "when appellant was told he had abysmally failed the polygraph test and therefore was lying when he denied he killed his wife, the only reasonable conclusion appellant could reach was that he was then no longer free to leave." *People v. Storm*, 94 Cal. Rptr. 2d 805, 814 (App. 4th Dist. 2000), review granted and opinion superseded, 99 Cal. Rptr. 2d 485, 6 P.3d 150 (Cal. 2000) and judgment aff'd, 28 Cal. 4th 1007, 124 Cal. Rptr. 2d 110, 52 P.3d 52 (2002).

[4]*U.S. v. Leon-Delfis*, 203 F.3d 103, 109–112, 53 Fed. R. Evid. Serv. 1613 (1st Cir. 2000).

[5]See *People v. Zimmer*, 68 Misc. 2d 1067, 329 N.Y.S.2d 17 (County Ct. 1972), order aff'd, 40 A.D.2d 955, 339 N.Y.S.2d 671 (4th Dep't 1972) (subject was emotionally upset, coerced, never read his *Miranda* rights, and was told the poly-

graph results could be used against him in court); *People v. Brown*, 96 Misc. 2d 244, 408 N.Y.S.2d 1007 (County Ct. 1978) (subject was deprived of sleep and questioned for an excessive length of time); but see *Keiper v. Cupp*, 509 F.2d 238 (9th Cir.1975) (Although the test was conducted in the early morning and the subject was upset and crying, the court held that the test was not "involuntary.").

[6]See *Edwards v. Com.*, 573 S.W.2d 640, 642 (Ky. 1978); See also *People v. Ray*, 431 Mich. 260, 430 N.W.2d 626 (1988) (allowing admissions made before, during, or after a polygraph test if the admissions are voluntary); *State v. Marini*, 638 A.2d 507, 512 (R.I. 1994) (same).

**[Section 8:10]**

[1]This section does not address constitutional issues raised by the use of polygraphs in nonevidentiary contexts, such as procedural due process concerns surrounding the use of these tests in the employment context. Under federal law, the Employee Polygraph Protection Act (EPPA), private employers are prohibited from using polygraphs (or any kind of lie-detector test), except under certain highly circumscribed circumstances. 29 U.S.C.A. §§ 2001 et seq. The EPPA, however, does not apply to governmental employers or certain private companies that contract with particular agencies of the government. 29 U.S.C.A. § 2006. See generally *Veazey v. Communications & Cable of Chicago, Inc.*, 194 F.3d 850, 859, 15 I.E.R. Cas. (BNA) 1057, 139 Lab. Cas. (CCH) P 10556 (7th Cir. 1999) ("Congress intended the prohibition on the use of lie detectors to be interpreted broadly."). In addition, many states have anti-polygraph statutes. See, e.g., West's Ann. Cal. Labor Code § 432.2. To the extent state regulations conflict with federal law, the former are preempted by the latter. *Stehney v. Perry*, 101 F.3d 925, 938, 12 I.E.R. Cas. (BNA) 495 (3d Cir. 1996) (finding New Jersey anti-polygraph law preempted by EPPA to the extent the state law prohibited the National Security Agency from administering a polygraph).

violates a defendant's Fifth and Fourteenth Amendment rights to due process.[2] In general, courts uniformly hold that the Constitution does not erect per se barriers or mandate per se admission of polygraph evidence. Instead, courts find that reservations regarding polygraphs are evidentiary concerns that generally do not rise to constitutional dimensions.[3]

In *United States v. Scheffer*, the Supreme Court held that a per se rule excluding polygraph evidence does not violate the Sixth Amendment right of the accused to present a defense. The Court found that "state and federal lawmakers have 'broad latitude under the Constitution to establish rules excluding evidence from criminal trials.'" Exclusionary rules "do not infringe the rights of the accused to present a defense as long as they are not 'arbitrary' or 'disproportionate to the purposes they are designed to serve.'"[4] The Court held that the rule was not arbitrary in that it was designed to ensure "that only reliable evidence is introduced at trial, [to] preserve[ ] the jury's role in determining credibility, and [to] avoid[ ] litigation that is collateral to the primary purpose of the trial."[5] The rule, the Court concluded, was not "disproportionate in promoting these ends."[6]

According to the Court, the per se rule of exclusion had the aim of keeping unreliable evidence from the jury. This "is a principal objective of many evidentiary rules."[7] The government's conclusion that polygraphs were not sufficiently reliable was supported by the fact that "[t]o this day, the scientific community remains extremely polarized about reliability of polygraph techniques."[8]

Justice Kennedy, joined by Justices O'Connor, Ginsburg, and Breyer, wrote in

---

[2]See generally Note, Compulsory Process and Polygraph Evidence: Does Exclusion Violate a Criminal Defendant's Due Process Rights?, 12 Conn. L. Rev. 324 (1980); Note, Admission of Polygraph Results: A Due Process Perspective, 55 Ind. L.J. 157 (1979).

[3]See, e.g., *Middleton v. Cupp*, 768 F.2d 1083, 1086 (9th Cir. 1985) ("We have never held that the Constitution prevents the admission of testimony concerning polygraph verification, although we have expressed an 'inhospitable' leaning against the admission of such evidence as a matter of the federal rules of evidence.").

*Watkins v. Miller*, 92 F. Supp. 2d 824 (S.D. Ind.2000), the court held that "the prosecutor's suppression of the fact that another suspect failed a polygraph test is . . . a Brady violation that is also sufficient by itself to warrant habeas relief." *Watkins v. Miller*, 92 F. Supp. 2d 852. The court explained that "even where exculpatory information is not directly admissible, such as a polygraph result, it may still qualify as Brady material." *Watkins v. Miller*, 92 F. Supp. 2d 851.

[4]*U.S. v. Scheffer*, 523 U.S. 303, 307, 118 S. Ct. 1261, 140 L. Ed. 2d 413, 48 Fed. R. Evid. Serv. 899 (1998), (quoting *Rock v. Arkansas*, 483 U.S. 44, 55, 107 S. Ct. 2704, 97 L. Ed. 2d 37, 22 Fed. R. Evid. Serv. 1128 (1987)). But see *Paxton v. Ward*, 199 F.3d 1197, 1215–1216 (10th Cir. 1999) (Court found that the state's per se rule excluding polygraphs, applied mechanistically, violated a capital defendant's right to present mitigating evidence at the sentencing phase of the trial.).

[5]*U.S. v. Scheffer*, 523 U.S. 303, 307–309, 118 S. Ct. 1261, 140 L. Ed. 2d 413, 48 Fed. R. Evid. Serv. 899 (1998); see also *People v. Wilkinson*, 33

Cal. 4th 821, 16 Cal. Rptr. 3d 420, 94 P.3d 551 (2004), cert. denied, 543 U.S. 1064, 125 S. Ct. 892, 160 L. Ed. 2d 796 (2005) (Court cited the ongoing debate about the reliability of polygraph evidence to support its finding that a per se exclusion of such evidence was not arbitrary or disproportionate.).

[6]*U.S. v. Scheffer*, 523 U.S. 303, 309, 118 S. Ct. 1261, 140 L. Ed. 2d 413, 48 Fed. R. Evid. Serv. 899 (1998).

[7]*U.S. v. Scheffer*, 523 U.S. 303, 309, 118 S. Ct. 1261, 140 L. Ed. 2d 413, 48 Fed. R. Evid. Serv. 899 (1998).

[8]*U.S. v. Scheffer*, 523 U.S. 303, 309, 118 S. Ct. 1261, 140 L. Ed. 2d 413, 48 Fed. R. Evid. Serv. 899 (1998) (citing Modern Scientific Evidence 565, § 19-2.0, and § 19-3.0 (1997)).

In contrast, Wisconsin courts exclude "[a]nything that a defendant said during what is considered to be part of the polygraph examination." *State v. Harris*, 2007 WL 1848047 *1 (Wis. Ct. App. 2007). This rule applies even if the statement is voluntary or otherwise admissible. *State v. Harris*, 2007 WL 1848047 *1 (Wis. Ct. App. 2007). Wisconsin courts use a multi-factored test to assess whether statements were made during, or were "closely related" to, the polygraph examination. Relevant factors include "(1) whether the post-polygraph interview was in the examination room or in some other place; (2) whether the defendant was told that the polygraph examination is over; and (3) whether the polygraph examiner interrogates the defendant making frequent use of and reference to the charts and tracing just obtained in the examination." *State v. Harris*, 2007 WL 1848047 *1 (Wis. Ct. App. 2007) (citing

concurrence, stating that he would have rested the holding exclusively on "[t]he continuing, good faith disagreement among experts and courts on the subject of polygraph reliability."[9] Justice Kennedy, however, did not agree that the argument that polygraphs usurp the jury's function was especially credible.[10] This argument "demeans and mistakes the role and competence of jurors in deciding the factual question of guilt or innocence."[11] It also, according to Justice Kennedy, relies on the "tired argument," that a jury should not "hear 'a conclusion about the ultimate issue in the trial.' "[12]

Justice Stevens dissented. He began by arguing that the majority's conclusion was inconsistent with *Daubert* which, as lower courts had also read it, gave district judges "broad discretion when evaluating the admissibility of scientific evidence."[13] The core of Stevens' dissent concerned his view that the Court had "all but ignor[ed] the strength of the defendant's interest in having polygraph evidence admitted in certain cases."[14] This interest lay in the defendant's desire to introduce expert opinion that would "bolster his own credibility."[15]

Finally, Justice Stevens argued that polygraph unreliability was greatly exaggerated and that "even the studies cited by the critics place polygraph accuracy at 70%."[16] Moreover, polygraphs compare favorably to many other kinds of evidence that courts routinely admit, including handwriting, fingerprinting, and eyewitness identification. Justice Stevens concluded, "[v]igorous cross-examination, presentation of contrary evidence, and careful instruction on the burden of proof are the traditional and appropriate means of attacking shaky but admissible evidence."[17]

Although per se exclusion of polygraph evidence does not violate constitutional guarantees, the Seventh Circuit has held that in jurisdictions in which polygraphs are admissible following stipulation of the parties, prosecutors must provide valid reasons for refusing to stipulate.[18] According to this view, a prosecutor's purely tactical decision to refuse a stipulation concerning polygraph evidence violates due process.[19] In addition, courts hold that due process might also permit defense use of exculpatory polygraph results at the sentencing phase of capital cases. For example,

---

*State v. Greer*, 265 Wis. 2d 463, 2003 WI App 112, 666 N.W.2d 518 (Ct. App. 2003) (rejected by, State v. Damron, 151 S.W.3d 510 (Tenn. 2004))).

[9]*U.S. v. Scheffer*, 523 U.S. 303, 317, 118 S. Ct. 1261, 140 L. Ed. 2d 413, 48 Fed. R. Evid. Serv. 899 (1998) (Kennedy, J., concurring in part and concurring in the judgment).

[10]*U.S. v. Scheffer*, 523 U.S. 303, 317, 118 S. Ct. 1261, 140 L. Ed. 2d 413, 48 Fed. R. Evid. Serv. 899 (1998) (Kennedy, J., concurring in part and concurring in the judgment).

[11]*U.S. v. Scheffer*, 523 U.S. 303, 317, 118 S. Ct. 1261, 140 L. Ed. 2d 413, 48 Fed. R. Evid. Serv. 899 (1998) (Kennedy, J., concurring in part and concurring in the judgment).

[12]*U.S. v. Scheffer*, 523 U.S. 303, 317, 118 S. Ct. 1261, 140 L. Ed. 2d 413, 48 Fed. R. Evid. Serv. 899 (1998) (Kennedy, J., concurring in part and concurring in the judgment) (quoting *U.S. v. Scheffer*, 523 U.S. 303, 313, 118 S. Ct. 1261, 1267, 140 L. Ed. 2d 413, 48 Fed. R. Evid. Serv. 899 (1998).

[13]*U.S. v. Scheffer*, 523 U.S. 303, 321, 118 S. Ct. 1261, 140 L. Ed. 2d 413, 48 Fed. R. Evid. Serv. 899 (1998) (Kennedy, J., concurring in part and concurring in the judgment) (citing *U.S. v. Cordoba*, 104 F.3d 225, 227, 45 Fed. R. Evid. Serv. 1197 (9th Cir. 1997), as amended, (Feb. 11, 1997)).

Justice Kennedy also agreed that the majority's decision was "in tension" with *Daubert*. *U.S. v. Scheffer*, 523 U.S. 303, 118 S. Ct. 1261, 1269, 140 L. Ed. 2d 413, 48 Fed. R. Evid. Serv. 899 (1998) (Kennedy, J., concurring in part and concurring in the judgment).

[14]*U.S. v. Scheffer*, 523 U.S. 303, 330, 118 S. Ct. 1261, 140 L. Ed. 2d 413, 48 Fed. R. Evid. Serv. 899 (1998) (Stevens, J., dissenting).

[15]*U.S. v. Scheffer*, 523 U.S. 303, 330, 118 S. Ct. 1261, 140 L. Ed. 2d 413, 48 Fed. R. Evid. Serv. 899 (1998) (Stevens, J., dissenting).

[16]*U.S. v. Scheffer*, 523 U.S. 303, 331, 118 S. Ct. 1261, 140 L. Ed. 2d 413, 48 Fed. R. Evid. Serv. 899 (1998) (Stevens, J., dissenting) (citing Iacono & Lykken, The Case Against Polygraph Tests, Modern Scientific Evidence, at 608).

[17]*U.S. v. Scheffer*, 523 U.S. 303, 334, 118 S. Ct. 1261, 140 L. Ed. 2d 413, 48 Fed. R. Evid. Serv. 899 (1998) (Stevens, J., dissenting).

[18]*McMorris v. Israel*, 643 F.2d 458, 466 (7th Cir. 1981) (rejected by, Jackson v. State, 116 Nev. 334, 997 P.2d 121 (2000)).

[19]*McMorris v. Israel*, 643 F.2d 458, 466 (7th Cir. 1981) (rejected by, Jackson v. State, 116 Nev. 334, 997 P.2d 121 (2000)). But see *Israel v. McMorris*, 455 U.S. 967, 970, 102 S. Ct. 1479, 71 L. Ed.

in *State v. Bartholomew*,[20] the Washington Supreme Court held "that polygraph examination results are admissible by the defense at the sentencing phase of capital cases, subject to certain restrictions."[21] These restrictions include, first, that the test be "conducted under proper conditions," and, second, that the examiner be subject to thorough cross-examination by the state.[22]

Constitutional questions also arise when defendants claim that admission of inculpatory polygraph results violate principles of due process. Once again, in general, courts find that the evidentiary standards for polygraph examinations meet constitutional requirements. They hold, however, that the Fifth Amendment privilege against self-incrimination applies to the taking of a polygraph.[23] Thus, courts carefully evaluate a defendant's waiver of right to counsel or right to remain silent in regard to stipulation agreements concerning polygraph examinations.[24] Moreover, under the Fifth Amendment, a defendant's refusal to take a polygraph examination cannot be used against him.[25]

---

2d 684 (1982) (Rehnquist, J., dissenting from denial of certiorari) (finding the lower court's decision to be a "dubious constitutional holding"); *Jones v. Weldon*, 690 F.2d 835, 838 (11th Cir. 1982) (rejecting *McMorris* holding). Given the Court's holding in *Scheffer*, *McMorris* is unlikely to have much practical effect. Any prosecutor paying the least bit of attention could simply cite the Supreme Court's statement that there is a substantial split in authority over the validity of polygraphs to support a decision not to stipulate to a polygraph examination. See *Jackson v. State*, 116 Nev. 334, 997 P.2d 121, 122 (2000) ("[A]ny party to any criminal or civil action may refuse to agree to the stipulation of a polygraph test for any reason, or no reason at all.").

[20]*State v. Bartholomew*, 101 Wash. 2d 631, 683 P.2d 1079 (1984) (rejected by, U.S. v. Sampson, 275 F. Supp. 2d 49 (D. Mass. 2003)).

[21]*State v. Bartholomew*, 101 Wash. 2d 631, 683 P.2d 1079, 1089 (1984) (rejected by, U.S. v. Sampson, 275 F. Supp. 2d 49 (D. Mass. 2003)).

[22]*State v. Bartholomew*, 101 Wash. 2d 631, 683 P.2d 1079, 1089 (1984) (rejected by, U.S. v. Sampson, 275 F. Supp. 2d 49 (D. Mass. 2003)). These two factors come from the *Valdez* test, § 39:33, as adopted in Washington in *State v. Renfro*, 96 Wash. 2d 902, 639 P.2d 737 (1982).

[23]In a parallel context, the defendant in *State v. Castagna*, 187 N.J. 293, 901 A.2d 363 (2006) argued that the trial court violated his right to a full and effective cross-examination, as guaranteed by the Confrontation Clause, when it restricted him from inquiring about a witness' failed polygraph. The defendant sought to inquire about the examination in order to discredit the witness' testimony at trial. The witness, who had been implicated in the crime, changed her story after being told that she had failed the polygraph. The New Jersey Supreme Court agreed that the defendant must be permitted the opportunity to question the witness about her polygraph experi-

ence. The court stated, however, that "the reliability of the polygraph test results was not important." *State v. Castagna*, 187 N.J. 293, 901 A.2d 363, 373 (2006). It explained that "[i]t was [the witness'] *belief* that the polygraph results revealed she had not told the truth in her second statement that was crucial. It was apparent that [the witness] believed she needed to change her story for the State to accept her statement and to agree to offer her a plea agreement." *State v. Castagna*, 187 N.J. 293, 901 A.2d 363 (2006) (emphasis added); see also *State v. McDavitt*, 62 N.J. 36, 297 A.2d 849 (1972) (holding that unstipulated polygraph examinations are inadmissible).

See *Schmerber v. California*, 384 U.S. 757, 764, 86 S. Ct. 1826, 16 L. Ed. 2d 908 (1966); see also *Com. v. Juvenile (No. 1)*, 365 Mass. 421, 313 N.E.2d 120, 127 (1974) (abrogated on other grounds by, Com. v. Mendes, 406 Mass. 201, 547 N.E.2d 35 (1989)) ("The polygraph results are essentially testimonial in nature and therefore a defendant could not be compelled initially to take such an examination on the Commonwealth's motion.").

[24]See, e.g., *People v. Leonard*, 421 Mich. 207, 364 N.W.2d 625, 633–635 (1984) (finding that defendant did not make a knowing waiver of right to counsel at the polygraph examination to which he stipulated); see also *Patterson v. State*, 212 Ga. App. 257, 441 S.E.2d 414, 416 (1994) ("It is not required that the accused have counsel present or act only upon the advice of counsel in order to render a stipulation to the admissibility of the results of a polygraph examination valid and binding upon the accused."); *Bowen v. Eyman*, 324 F. Supp. 339, 341 (D. Ariz. 1970).

[25]See *Melvin v. State*, 606 A.2d 69, 71 (Del. 1992) ("The trial judge's reliance on [the defendant's] refusal to submit to a polygraph examination violates [his] constitutional right against self-incrimination as guaranteed by the Fifth Amendment to the United States Constitution.").

## § 8:11   The Report of the National Academies of Science on the Scientific Evidence for the Polygraph—Introduction

In January 2001, the National Academies of Science (NAS) composed a committee to consider the scientific evidence on the polygraph.[1] The principal objective of the Committee was to consider the use of the polygraph in the area of national security. The Department of Energy sponsored the Committee's work. Because the focus was on national security, the main issue to be considered by the Committee concerned the use of polygraphs for screening purposes. Screening presents special problems because the base rates are likely to be extremely low, since large numbers of employees or prospective employees are screened but few are likely to present serious security risks. However, as the report makes clear, the Committee could not simply limit the scope of its review to screening uses of polygraphs. This is so for two reasons. First, virtually all of the research conducted on the polygraph has been conducted on so-called specific incident tests. Hence, in order to generalize from the existing research to the screening situation, the weight associated with specific incident tests had to be assessed. Second, national security uses of the polygraph do not always arise in the screening context. Government agencies regularly use polygraph tests to investigate specific incidents while in the process of protecting national security. Therefore, although the NAS report does not specifically address the use of polygraphs by courts, many of the Committee's findings are highly relevant to this use. Therefore, we decided to reprint the Executive Summary of the Report in this Supplement. We strongly urge interested readers to obtain a copy of the complete Report for the detailed and exhaustive consideration of the subject provided by the Committee.

## § 8:12   The Report of the National Academies of Science on the Scientific Evidence for the Polygraph—The executive summary

For as long as human beings have deceived one another, people have tried to develop techniques for detecting deception and finding truth. Lie detection took on aspects of modern science with the development in the 20th century of techniques intended for the psychophysiological detection of deception, most prominently, polygraph testing. The polygraph instrument measures several physiological processes (e.g., heart rate) and changes in those processes. From the charts of those measures in response to questions on a polygraph test, sometimes aided by observations during the polygraph examination, examiners infer a psychological state, namely, whether a person is telling the truth or lying.

Polygraph testing is used for three main purposes: event-specific investigations (e.g., after a crime); employee screening; and preemployment screening. The different uses involve the search for different kinds of information and have different implications. A question asked about a specific incident (e.g., "Did you see the victim on Monday" or "Did you take the file home yesterday?") often has little ambiguity, so it is clear what facts provide the criterion for a truthful answer.

For employee screening, there is no specific event being investigated, and the questions must be generic (e.g., "Did you ever reveal classified information to an unauthorized person?"). Both examinee and examiner may have difficulty knowing whether an answer to such a question is truthful unless there are clear and consistent criteria that specify what activities justify a "yes" answer. Examinees may believe they are lying when providing factually truthful responses, or vice versa. Polygraph tests might elicit admissions to acts not central to the intent of the question and these answers might be judged either as successes or failures of the test. In

---

[Section 8:11]

[1]It should be noted that one of the authors

of this treatise, David Faigman, was a member of the Committee.

this regard, we have seen no indication of a clear and stable agreement on criteria for judging answers to security screening polygraph questions in any agency using them.

The use of polygraph testing for preemployment screening is even more complicated because it involves inferences about future behavior on the basis of information about past behaviors that may be quite different (e.g., does past use of illegal drugs, or lying about such use on a polygraph test, predict future spying?).

The Committee's charge was specifically "to conduct a scientific review of the research on polygraph examinations that pertains to their validity and reliability, in particular for personnel security screening," that is, for the second and third purposes. We have focused mainly on validity because a test that is reliable (i.e., produces consistent outcomes) has little use unless it is also valid (i.e., measures what it is supposed to measure). Virtually all the available scientific evidence on polygraph test validity comes from studies of specific-event investigations, so the committee had to rely heavily on that evidence, in addition to the few available studies that are relevant for screening. The general quality of the evidence for judging polygraph validity is relatively low: the substantial majority of the studies most relevant for this purpose were below the quality level typically needed for funding by the National Science Foundation or the National Institutes of Health.

### § 8:13   The Report of the National Academies of Science on the Scientific Evidence for the Polygraph—The executive summary—Scientific evidence—Basic science

Almost a century of research in scientific psychology and physiology provides little basis for the expectation that a polygraph test could have extremely high accuracy. Although psychological states often associated with deception (e.g., fear of being judged deceptive) do tend to affect the physiological responses that the polygraph measures, these same states can arise in the absence of deception. Moreover, many other psychological and physiological factors (e.g., anxiety about being tested) also affect those responses. Such phenomena make polygraph testing intrinsically susceptible to producing erroneous results. This inherent ambiguity of the physiological measures used in the polygraph suggest that further investments in improving polygraph technique and interpretation will bring only modest improvements in accuracy.

Polygraph research has not developed and tested theories of the underlying factors that produce the observed responses. Factors other than truthfulness that affect the physiological responses being measured can vary substantially across settings in which polygraph tests are used. There is little knowledge about how much these factors influence the outcomes of polygraph tests in field settings. For example, there is evidence suggesting that truthful members of socially stigmatized groups and truthful examinees who are believed to be guilty or believed to have a high likelihood of being guilty may show emotional and physiological responses in polygraph test situations that mimic the responses that are expected of deceptive individuals. The lack of understanding of the processes that underlie polygraph responses makes it very difficult to generalize from the results obtained in specific research settings or with particular subject populations to other settings or populations, or from laboratory research studies to real-world applications.

### § 8:14   The Report of the National Academies of Science on the Scientific Evidence for the Polygraph—The executive summary—Scientific evidence—Evidence on polygraph accuracy

Scientific evidence relevant to the accuracy of polygraph tests for employee or preemployment screening is extremely limited. Only one field study, which is flawed, provides evidence directly relevant to accuracy for preemployment screening. A few additional laboratory studies are relevant to preemployment or employee screening, but they are more analogous to specific-incident investigations than to screening because the deceptive examinee is given a precise recent incident about which to lie.

Of the 57 studies the Committee used to quantify the accuracy of polygraph testing, all involved specific incidents, typically mock crimes (four studies simulated screening in the sense that the incidents were followed by generic screening-type questions). The quality of the studies varies considerably, but falls far short of what is desirable. Laboratory studies suffer from lack of realism, and in the randomized controlled studies focused on specific incidents using mock crimes, the consequences associated with lying or being judged deceptive almost never mirror the seriousness of these actions in real-world settings in which the polygraph is used. Field studies have major problems with identifying the truth against which test results should be judged. In addition, they suffer from problems associated with heterogeneity and lack of control of extraneous factors and more generally, they have lower quality than could be achieved with careful study design. Moreover, most of the research, in both the laboratory and in the field, does not fully address key potential threats to validity. For these reasons, study results cannot be expected to generalize to practical contexts.

Estimates of accuracy from these 57 studies are almost certainly higher than actual polygraph accuracy of specific-incident testing in the field. Laboratory studies tend to overestimate accuracy because laboratory conditions involve much less variation in test implementation, in the characteristics of examinees, and in the nature and context of investigations than arise in typical field applications. Observational studies of polygraph testing in the field are plagued by selection and measurement biases, such as the inclusion of tests carried out by examiners with knowledge of the evidence and of cases whose outcomes are affected by the examination. In addition, they frequently lack a clear and independent determination of truth. Due to these inherent biases, observational field studies are also highly likely to overestimate real-world polygraph accuracy.

> CONCLUSION: Notwithstanding the limitations of the quality of the empirical research and the limited ability to generalize to real-world settings, we conclude that in populations of examinees such as those represented in the polygraph research literature, untrained in countermeasures, specific-incident polygraph tests can discriminate lying from truth telling at rates well above chance, though well below perfection. Because the studies of acceptable quality all focus on specific incidents, generalization from them to uses for screening is not justified. Because actual screening applications involve considerably more ambiguity for the examinee and in determining truth than arises in specific-incident studies, polygraph accuracy for screening purposes is almost certainly lower than what can be achieved by specific incident polygraph tests in the field.

The accuracy levels in the four screening simulations in our sample, which include a validation study of the Test for Espionage and Sabotage (TES) used in the employee security screening program of the U.S. Department of Energy (DOE), are in the range reported for other specific-incident laboratory studies. The one field study of actual screening presents results consistent with the expectation that polygraph accuracy in true screening situations is lower.

## § 8:15 The Report of the National Academies of Science on the Scientific Evidence for the Polygraph—The executive summary—Scientific evidence—Countermeasures

Countermeasures pose a potentially serious threat to the performance of polygraph testing because all the physiological indicators measured by the polygraph can be altered by conscious efforts through cognitive or physical means. Certain countermeasures apparently can, under some laboratory conditions, enable a deceptive individual to appear nondeceptive and avoid detection by an examiner. It is unknown whether a deceptive individual can produce responses that mimic the physiological responses of a nondeceptive individual well enough to fool an examiner trained to look for behavioral and physiological signatures of countermeasures. The available research provides no information on whether innocent examinees can increase their chances of achieving nondeceptive outcomes by using countermeasures. (It is possible that classified information exists on these topics; however, this committee was not provided access to such information and cannot verify its existence or relevance.)

> CONCLUSION: Basic science and polygraph research give reason for concern that polygraph test accuracy may be degraded by countermeasures, particularly when used by major security threats who have a strong incentive and sufficient resources to use them effectively. If these measures are effective, they could seriously undermine any value of polygraph security screening.

## § 8:16   The Report of the National Academies of Science on the Scientific Evidence for the Polygraph—The executive summary—Polygraph use for security screening

The proportion of spies, terrorists, and other major national security threats among the employees subject to polygraph testing in the DOE laboratories and similar federal sites presumably is extremely low. Screening in populations with very low rates of the target transgressions (e.g., less than one in 1,000) requires diagnostics of extremely high accuracy, well beyond what can be expected from polygraph testing. Table 1 illustrates the unpleasant tradeoffs facing policy makers who use a screening technique in a hypothetical population of 10,000 government employees that includes 10 spies, even when an accuracy is assumed that is greater than can be expected of polygraph testing on the basis of available research. If the test were set sensitively enough to detect about 80% or more of deceivers, about 1,606 employees or more would be expected to "fail" the test; further investigation would be needed to separate the eight spies from the 1,598 loyal employees caught in the screen. If the test were set to reduce the numbers of false alarms (loyal employees who "fail" the test) to about 40 of 9,990, it would correctly classify over 99.5% of the examinees, but among the errors would be eight of the 10 hypothetical spies, who could be expected to "pass" the test and so would be free to cause damage.

## Table 1. Expected Results of a Polygraph Test Procedure with an Accuracy Index of 0.90 in a Hypothetical Population of 10,000 Examinees that Includes 10 Spies

a: If detection threshold is set to detect the great majority (80%) of Spies

| Test result | Examinee's true condition | | |
| --- | --- | --- | --- |
| | Spy | Nonspy | Total |
| "Fail" test | 8 | 1,598 | 1,606 |
| "Pass" test | 2 | 8,392 | 8,394 |
| TOTAL | 10 | 9,990 | 10,000 |

b: If detection threshold is set to greatly reduce false positive results

| Test result | Examinee's true condition | | |
| --- | --- | --- | --- |
| | Spy | Nonspy | Total |
| "Fail" test | 2 | 39 | 41 |
| "Pass" test | 8 | 9,951 | 9,959 |
| TOTAL | 10 | 9,990 | 10,000 |

Available evidence indicates that polygraph testing as currently used has extremely serious limitations in such screening applications, if the intent is both to identify security risks and protect valued employees. Given its level of accuracy, achieving a high probability of identifying individuals who pose major security risks in a population with a very low proportion of such individuals would require setting the test to be so sensitive that hundreds, or even thousands, of innocent individuals would be implicated for every major security violator correctly identified. The only way to be certain to limit the frequency of "false positives" is to administer the test in a manner that would almost certainly severely limit the proportion of serious transgressors identified.

CONCLUSION: Polygraph testing yields an unacceptable choice for DOE employee security screening between too many loyal employees falsely judged deceptive and too many major security threats left undetected. Its accuracy in distinguishing actual or potential security violators from innocent test takers is insufficient to justify reliance on its use in employee security screening in federal agencies.

Polygraph screening may be useful for achieving such objectives as deterring security violations, increasing the frequency of admissions of such violations, deterring employment applications from potentially poor security risks, and increasing public confidence in national security organizations. On the basis of field reports and indirect scientific evidence, we believe that polygraph testing is likely to have some utility for such purposes. Such utility derives from beliefs about the procedure's validity, which are distinct from actual validity or accuracy. Polygraph screening programs that yield only a small %age of positive test results, such as those in use at DOE and some other federal agencies, might be useful for deterrence, eliciting admissions, and related purposes. However, in populations with very low base rates of the target transgressions they should not be counted on for detection: they will not detect more than a small proportion of major security violators who do not admit their actions.

We have thought hard about how to advise government agencies on whether or how to use information from a diagnostic screening test that has these serious limitations. We note that in medicine, such imperfect diagnostics are often used for screening, though only occasionally in populations with very low base rates of the target condition. When this is done, either the test is far more accurate than polygraph testing appears to be, or there is a more accurate (though generally more invasive or expensive) follow-up test that can be used when the screening test gives a positive result. Such a follow-up test does not exist for the polygraph. The medical analogy and this difference between medical and security screening underline the wisdom in contexts like that of employee security screening in the DOE laboratories of using positive polygraph screening results—if polygraph screening is to be used at all—only as triggers for detailed follow-up investigation, not as a basis for personnel action. It also underlines the need to pay close attention to the implications of false negative test results, especially if tests are used that yield a low proportion of positive results.

A belief that polygraph testing is highly accurate probably enhances its utility for such objectives as deterrence. However, overconfidence in the polygraph—a belief in its accuracy that goes beyond what is justified by the evidence—also presents a danger to national security objectives. Overconfidence in polygraph screening can create a false sense of security among policy makers, employees in sensitive positions, and the general public that may in turn lead to inappropriate relaxation of other methods of ensuring security, such as periodic security reinvestigation and vigilance about potential security violations in facilities that use the polygraph for employee security screening. It can waste public resources by devoting to the polygraph funds and energy that would be better spent on alternative procedures. It can lead to unnecessary loss of competent or highly skilled individuals in security organizations because of suspicions cast on them by false positive polygraph exams or because of their fear of such prospects. In addition, it can lead to credible claims that agencies that use polygraphs are infringing civil liberties for insufficient benefits to the national security. Thus, policy makers should consider each application of polygraph testing in the larger context of its various costs and benefits.

### § 8:17 The Report of the National Academies of Science on the Scientific Evidence for the Polygraph—The executive summary—Alternatives and enhancements to the polygraph

The polygraph is only one of many possible techniques for identifying national security risks among federal employees. Other techniques attempt to detect deception from facial expressions, voice quality, and other aspects of demeanor; from measurements of brain activity and other physiological indicators; and from background investigations or questionnaires. Computerized analysis of polygraph records has the potential to improve the accuracy of test results by using more information from polygraph records than is used in traditional scoring methods. This potential has yet to be realized, however, either in research or in practice.

We considered the potential to increase the capability to identify security risks by combining polygraph information with information from other screening techniques, for example, in serial screening protocols such as are used in medical diagnosis. There are good theoretical reasons to think appropriate procedures of this sort would improve detection of deception, but we found no serious investigations of such multicomponent screening approaches.

CONCLUSION: Some potential alternatives to the polygraph show promise, but none has yet been shown to outperform the polygraph. None shows any promise of supplanting the polygraph for screening purposes in the near term.

### § 8:18 The Report of the National Academies of Science on the Scientific Evidence for the Polygraph—The executive summary—Research recommendations

There has been no serious effort in the U.S. government to develop the scientific basis for the psychophysiological detection of deception by any technique, even though criticisms of the scientific grounding of polygraph testing have been raised prominently for decades. Given the heavy reliance of government on the polygraph, especially for screening for espionage and sabotage, the lack of a serious investment in such research is striking.

The limitations of the polygraph, especially for security screening, justify efforts to look more broadly for effective tools for deterring and detecting security violations. These might include modifications in the overall security strategies used in federal agencies, such as have been recommended by the Hamre Commission for DOE, as well as improved techniques for deterring and detecting security violations focused on individuals. Research offers one promising strategy for developing the needed tools.

We recommend an expanded research effort directed at methods for detecting and deterring major security threats, including efforts to improve techniques for security screening.

This effort should pursue two major objectives: (1) to provide federal agencies with methods of the highest possible scientific validity for protecting national security by deterring and detecting major security threats; and (2) to make these agencies fully aware of the strengths and limitations of the techniques they use. If the government continues to rely heavily on the polygraph in the national security arena, some of this research effort should be devoted to developing scientific knowledge that could put the polygraph on a firmer scientific foundation, develop alternative methods, or develop effective ways to combine techniques and methods. National security is best served by a broad research program on detecting and deterring security threats, not a narrow focus on polygraph research.

The research program should be open to supporting alternative ways of looking at the problems of deterrence and detection because there is no single research approach that clearly holds the most promise for meeting national security objectives. Thus, it might support research ranging from very basic work on fundamental psychological, physiological, social, and political processes related to deterring and detecting security threats to applied studies on implementing scientifically rooted methods in practical situations.

A substantial portion of our recommended expanded research program should be administered by an organization or organizations with no operational responsibility for detecting deception and no institutional commitment to using or training practitioners of a particular technique. The research program should follow accepted standards for scientific research, use rules and procedures designed to eliminate biases that might influence the findings, and operate under normal rules of scientific freedom and openness to the extent possible while protecting national security.

The mandate should be broad and should include both basic and applied research. The program should use standard scientific advisory and decision-making procedures, including external peer-review of proposals, and should support research that is conducted and reviewed openly in the manner of other scientific research. Classified and restricted research should be limited only to matters of identifiable national security. Mission agencies might well continue to conduct implementation-focused research on detecting deception, but their work should be integrated with the broader research program proposed here.

## § 8:19  Conclusion

More than most areas of scientific evidence, polygraphs present courts with substantial challenges under the rules of evidence, and implicate most of the panoply of considerations raised by testimony on ostensibly scientifically derived opinion. From the start, given its role in the formulation of the *Frye* test itself, polygraphs have been viewed with suspicion and concern by courts. A principal concern for courts has been defining the "particular field" in which polygraphs belong, especially since they have not been a subject of intense interest among scientists generally. Clearly, polygraphers cannot be the defined field, since they have a peculiar interest in accepting the validity of the trade they ply. Yet, few scientists have studied polygraphs carefully, and some fields in which we would expect interest, such as neuroscience, have ignored the matter entirely.

Under *Daubert*, polygraphs present special challenges. Unlike much expert opinion struggling under *Daubert's* expectations for data, many peer-reviewed studies have been conducted testing the validity of polygraphs. As the next two sections make clear, the research completed so far has possibly raised more dust than it has settled. In addition, under Rule 403, courts are particularly concerned with possible prejudice that might accompany expert opinion, ranging from invading the province of the jury to overwhelming it.

## II.  SCIENTIFIC STATUS*

*by Charles R. Honts,** David C. Raskin,*** & John C. Kircher****

### A.  THE CASE FOR POLYGRAPH TESTS

### § 8:20  Introductory discussion of the science—Background

Polygraph techniques for the detection of deception and verification of truthfulness have a long history of scientific research, and many prominent psychologists and other scientists have contributed to the existing literature. Following World War II, polygraph testing grew rapidly in its applications within the law enforcement, government, and commercial sectors of our society. This was soon followed by increased scientific research and intense debate within the scientific, legal, and political communities.

Critics as well as supporters of polygraph techniques have pointed out many limitations and misapplications of polygraph techniques.[1] However, we believe that the most vocal critics[2] have grossly overstated the case against the polygraph, in part because of their lack of direct research or experience with the techniques and their

---

*Scientific opinion about the validity of polygraph techniques is extremely polarized. Therefore, the editors invited scientists from the "two camps" on this issue to present their views. Consistent with classical principles of debate, we have placed the affirmative argument in favor of polygraph tests first. The argument against polygraph techniques, written by Professors Iacono and Lykken, begins at §§ 8:45 to 8:126.

**Professor Honts is the Department Head and a Professor of Psychology at Boise State University and Editor of The Journal of Credibility Assessment and Witness Psychology. He is the recipient of grants from the U.S. Office of Naval Research and from the Royal Canadian Mounted Police to conduct research on the psychophysiological detection of deception. He is a Forensic Psychological Consultant to numerous public agencies in the United States in Canada. He has been a licensed polygraph examiner for 25 years.

***Professor Raskin is Professor Emeritus, University of Utah and Editor of Psychological Methods in Criminal Investigation and Evidence and Co-Editor of Electrodermal Activity in Psychological Research. He has been the recipient of numerous grants and contracts from the National Institute of Justice, U.S. Department of Defense, U.S. Secret Service, and U.S. Army Research and Development Command to conduct research and development on psychophysiological detection of deception. He was the Co-Developer of the first computerized polygraph system. He was Past President of the Rocky Mountain Psychological Association and is an Elected Fellow in the American Psychological Association, American Psychological Society, and American Association for Applied and Preventive Psychology. He has served as a Forensic Psychological Consultant to numerous federal and local agencies and legislative bodies in the United States, Canada, Israel, United Kingdom, and Norway. He has been a licensed polygraph examiner for 27 years.

****Professor Kircher is an Associate Professor of Educational Psychology, University of Utah. He specializes in the use of computer, psychometric, and decision theoretic methods for assessing truth and deception from physiological recordings. He pioneered the development of the first computerized polygraph system and has collaborated with David C. Raskin and Charles R. Honts since 1977 on research and development of methods for the physiological detection of deception.

[Section 8:20]

[1]See, e.g., Honts, The Psychophysiological Detection of Deception, 3 Current Directions in Psychol. Sci. 77 (1994); William G. Iacono & Christopher J. Patrick, Assessing Deception: Polygraph Techniques, in Clinical Assessment of Malingering and Deception 205 (Richard Rogers ed., 1988); Raskin, The Polygraph in 1986: Scientific, Professional, and Legal Issues Surrounding Applications and Acceptance of Polygraph Evidence, 1986 Utah L. Rev. 29 (1986); David C. Raskin, Does Science Support Polygraph Testing, in The Polygraph Test: Lies, Truth and Science 96 (Anthony Gale ed., 1988).

[2]See, e.g., Gershon Ben-Shakar & John J. Furedy, Theories and Applications in the Detection of Deception (1990); David T. Lykken, A Tremor in the Blood (1981); Saxe, Detection of Deception: Polygraph and Integrity Tests, 3 Current Directions in Psychological Science 69 (1994).

applications.[3] Since the fundamental scientific question is the extent to which a psychophysiological test can differentiate truthful from deceptive individuals, much of this section is devoted to that issue and other factors that may affect the various types of polygraph tests in use today.

Scientific research clearly demonstrates that properly conducted polygraph tests have sufficient reliability and validity to be of considerable value to individuals, the criminal justice process, and society. In this chapter, we briefly review the historical development of the polygraph test along with current scientific knowledge concerning the reliability and validity of various polygraph techniques. We discuss the strengths and weaknesses of various approaches and techniques and when their application may or may not be justified on the basis of scientific research. In so doing, we comment on various problems that arise in the field, describe what has been accomplished toward correcting the problems that have plagued attempts to use psychophysiological methods to assess credibility, and suggest ways to improve their accuracy and applications.

Polygraphy is one of the oldest areas of research in applied psychology, and its history is distinguished by the stature of those who have worked in the area.[4] Modern physiological methods for assessing truth and deception began in Italy near the end of the 19th century.[5] In the United States, polygraph techniques were developed as an investigative tool for the law enforcement community, and the early work by Marston[6] and subsequent improvements by Larson[7] and Keeler[8] resulted in a portable polygraph instrument and a general method known as the relevant-irrelevant technique.

## § 8:21 Introductory discussion of the science—Psychophysiological detection of deception techniques—The relevant-irrelevant test (RIT)

In the relevant-irrelevant test (RIT), two types of questions are presented to the subject. Relevant questions directly address the matter under investigation (e.g., "Did you take that $10,000 from the safe?"), whereas irrelevant questions concern neutral topics, such as the subject's name, place of birth or residence, or simple statements of fact (e.g., "Are you sitting down?"). As in all polygraph deception tests, questions must be answered "Yes" or "No." Respiration, electrodermal, and blood pressure responses to the relevant questions are compared to those produced by the irrelevant questions. If the reactions to the relevant questions are generally stronger, the subject is judged to be responding deceptively to the relevant ques-

---

[3]See, e.g., Honts, Heat Without Light: A Review of Theories and Applications in the Detection of Deception, 30 Psychophysiology 317 (1993); Raskin & Kircher, The Validity of Lykken's Criticisms: Fact or Fancy? 27 Jurimetrics 271 (1988); David C. Raskin & John C. Kircher, Comments on Furedy and Heslegrave: Misconceptions, Misdescriptions, and Misdirections, in Advances in Psychophysiology 215 (Patrick K. Ackles et. al. eds., vol. 4, 1991).

[4]See, e.g., Roland C. Davis, Physiological Responses as a Means of Evaluating Information, in The Manipulation of Human Behavior 142 (Albert D. Biderman & Herbert Zimmer eds., 1961); David B. Lindsley, The Psychology of Lie Detection, in Psychology for Law Enforcement Officers 89 (George J. Dudycha ed., 1955); Aleksandr R. Luria, The Nature of Human Conflicts (1932); Hugo Munsterberg, On the Witness Stand (1908); Max Wertheimer & Julius

Klein, Psychologische Tatbestandsdiagnostick, 15 Archiv Fur Kriminal-Anthropolgie Und Kriminalistik 72 (1904). See also Trovillo, A History of Lie Detection, 29 J. Crim. L. Criminology & Police Sci. 848 (1939); Trovillo, A History of Lie Detection, 30 J. Crim. L. Criminology & Police Sci. 104 (1939) (a two-part detailed review of the early history of lie detection).

[5]See, e.g., Cesare Lombroso, L'homme Criminel (2d ed., 1895).

[6]See Marston, Systolic Blood Pressure Symptoms of Deception, 2 J. Experimental Psychol. 117 (1917).

[7]John A. Larson, Lying and Its Detection (1932).

[8]Leonarde Keeler, Scientific Methods of Criminal Detection With the Polygraph, 2 Kan. B. Ass'n 22 (1933).

tions. Conversely, if reactions to the relevant and irrelevant questions are similar in magnitude, the subject is considered to be responding truthfully to the relevant questions.

The RIT gained widespread use in law enforcement, government, and the private sector in the absence of any credible evidence that it can be used to distinguish truthful and deceptive answers with a reasonable degree of accuracy.[1] Fundamental flaws in the RIT argue strongly against its use in criminal investigations.[2] Most serious is the naive and implausible rationale underlying the test. Although deceptive individuals are likely to produce relatively strong physiological reactions to the relevant questions and be diagnosed as deceptive, many truthful individuals are likely to perceive the relevant questions as more threatening, causing them to react more strongly to them. As a result, the RIT can be expected to produce highly accurate decisions on deceptive subjects (true positives) and a large percentage of incorrect decisions on truthful subjects (false positives). Recent research has demonstrated that these predictions are correct. Horowitz, Raskin, Honts, & Kircher reported that only 22% of the innocent subjects in their experiment were able to produce truthful outcomes with the RIT.[3] Another study reported that none of the innocent subjects was able to pass the RIT.[4]

Use of the RIT has declined substantially in recent years, and in most jurisdictions it has fallen into disuse for forensic applications.[5] The Polygraph Protection Act of 1988 essentially eliminated its widespread use by commercial polygraph examiners. Although it offers little protection against false positive errors and the available scientific research argues against its use, the RIT is still employed by polygraph examiners in some federal programs (e.g., Federal Bureau of Investigation and National Security Agency). However, some jurisdictions have recognized the limitations of the RIT and either prohibit its use as evidence[6] or its use for any purpose.[7]

## § 8:22    Introductory discussion of the science—Psychophysiological detection of deception techniques—The control question test (CQT)

To overcome the weaknesses of the RIT, Reid devised the control question test (CQT).[1] The CQT differs from the RIT in that physiological reactions to relevant questions are compared to those produced by control (probable-lie) questions. Since control questions are designed to arouse the concern of innocent subjects, it is expected that innocent subjects will react more strongly to them than to the relevant questions. For example, if the subject were suspected of a theft, a control question might be, "During the first 22 years of your life, did you ever take something that did not belong to you?" Control questions are intentionally vague, cover a long period of the subject's life, and include acts that most individuals have committed

---

[Section 8:21]

[1]See, e.g., David C. Raskin et al., Recent Laboratory and Field Research on Polygraph Techniques, in Credibility Assessment 1 (John C. Yuille ed., 1989).

[2]See, e.g., Raskin, The Polygraph in 1986: Scientific, Professional, and Legal Issues Surrounding Applications and Acceptance of Polygraph Evidence, 1986 Utah L. Rev. 29 (1986); David C. Raskin, Polygraph Techniques for the Detection of Deception, in Psychological Methods in Criminal Investigation and Evidence 247 (David C. Raskin ed., 1989).

[3]Horowitz et al., The Role of Comparison Questions in the Physiological Detection of Decep-

tion, 34 Psychophysiology 118 (1997).

[4]Horvath, The Utility of Control Questions and the Effects of Two Control Question Types in Field Polygraph Techniques, 16 J. Police Sci. & Admin. 198 (1988).

[5]Office of Technology Assessment, Scientific Validity of Polygraph Testing: A Research Review and Evaluation (1983).

[6]N.M. R. Evid. 707.

[7]Utah Code Ann. § 34-37-1.

[Section 8:22]

[1]Reid, A Revised Questioning Technique in Lie Detection Tests, 37 J. Crim. L., Criminology & Police Sci. 542 (1947).

but are embarrassed or reluctant to admit during a properly conducted polygraph examination. During the pretest review of the questions to be asked on the test, control questions are introduced by the polygraph examiner in such a way that the subject will initially or eventually answer "No" to each of them.

Innocent subjects answer the relevant questions truthfully but are likely to be deceptive or uncertain about their truthfulness when answering the control questions. Therefore, innocent subjects are expected to react more strongly to the control questions than to the relevant questions. In contrast, guilty subjects are expected to be concerned about failing the test because their answers to the relevant questions are deceptive, and they are likely to show stronger reactions to the relevant questions.[2]

Recently, the term "control question" has been the subject of controversy and confusion in the scientific literature.[3] Control questions are misnamed because they do not function as controls in the strict scientific sense of the term, i.e., they do not elicit reactions that indicate how subjects would react if their answers to the relevant questions were truthful. Rather, they provide an estimate of how innocent subjects would react if their answers to relevant questions were actually deceptive. The fundamental issue is not whether control questions function as controls in the usual scientific sense, but whether they elicit larger reactions than relevant questions from innocent subjects and thereby reduce the risk of false positive errors.

## § 8:23 Introductory discussion of the science—Psychophysiological detection of deception techniques—The Directed Lie Test (DLT)

New question structures and examination procedures have been developed to overcome some of the problems that have plagued traditional comparison question techniques. The most promising of these is the directed-lie test (DLT) developed at the University of Utah.[1] The traditional CQT relies on the effectiveness of probable-lie comparison questions that are formulated and chosen by the polygraph examiner to suit each case. Such questions vary considerably and may also be intrusive and ineffective with some subjects. In contrast, the DLT employs a straightforward approach that has clear face validity and uses a relatively small set of simple comparison questions that are much easier to standardize.

The DLT includes questions to which the subject is instructed to lie, e.g., "Before 1998, did you ever make even one mistake?" or "Before 1998, did you ever do something that you later regretted?" The directed-lie questions are introduced during the review of all questions that follows the administration of a number test in which the subject had been instructed to choose a number and lie about the number that was chosen. The subject is told that the number test enables the examiner to determine when the subject is lying and when the subject is answering truthfully.

---

[2]For a more detailed description of the CQT, see David C. Raskin, Polygraph Techniques for the Detection of Deception, in Psychological Methods in Criminal Investigation and Evidence 247 (David C. Raskin ed., 1989).

[3]See, e.g., John J. Furedy & Ronald J. Heslegrave, The Forensic Use of the Polygraph: A Psychophysiological Analysis of Current Trends and Future Prospects, in Advances in Psychophysiology (Patrick K. Ackles et. al., eds. 1991); Lykken, The Detection of Deception, 86 Psychol. Bull. 47 (1979); Raskin & Kircher, Comments on Furedy and Heslegrave: Misconceptions, Misdescriptions, and Misdirections, in Advances in Psychophysiology 215 (Patrick K. Ackles et. al. eds., vol. 4, 1991); Raskin & Podlesny, Truth and

Deception: A Reply to Lykken, 86 Psychol. Bull. 54 (1979).

[Section 8:23]

[1]Honts & Raskin, A Field Study of the Validity of the Directed Lie Control Question, 16 J. Police Sci. Admin. 56 (1988); Horowitz et al., The Role of Comparison Questions in the Physiological Detection of Deception, 34 Psychophysiology 118 (1997); David C. Raskin, Polygraph Techniques for the Detection of Deception, in Psychological Methods in Criminal Investigation and Evidence 247 (David C. Raskin ed., 1989); David C. Raskin et al., Recent Laboratory and Field Research on Polygraph Techniques, in Credibility Assessment 1 (John C. Yuille ed., 1989).

The examiner then explains that the directed-lie questions will ensure that the subject will be correctly classified as truthful or deceptive on the subsequent polygraph test. These procedures reduce the number of false positive errors[2] and increase the standardization and ease of administration of polygraph examinations.[3]

## § 8:24  Introductory discussion of the science—Psychophysiological detection of deception techniques—Guilty knowledge tests (GKT)

The concealed knowledge or guilty knowledge test (GKT) is another method for detecting deception.[1] In contrast to the RIT and CQT, the GKT does not attempt to directly assess the veracity of a person's statements concerning knowledge or involvement in a crime. Instead, this technique is used to determine if the subject is concealing knowledge of details of the crime that would be known only to a guilty person.

The GKT consists of a series of multiple-choice questions, each of which addresses a different aspect of the crime. For example, if the subject is suspected of stealing a ring, a question on the test might be, "Regarding the type of ring that was stolen, do you know if it was: (1) a ruby ring, (2) a gold wedding ring, (3) a pearl ring, (4) a diamond ring, (5) a sapphire ring, (6) a silver and turquoise ring?"[2] A guilty subject who knows the correct alternative is expected to show a relatively strong physiological reaction to that item. However, an innocent subject who has no specific knowledge is not expected to respond differentially to correct and incorrect alternatives.

Typically, only electrodermal responses to the questions are scored, and reactions to the first alternatives are not evaluated because the first item in a series typically produces a large orienting reaction that is independent of any specific knowledge that may be possessed by the subject. Thus, for one multiple-choice question, the probability that the subject's strongest electrodermal response will occur by chance to the correct alternative is one in five, or 20%. With several multiple-choice questions, the chance probability that a subject who has no concealed knowledge will consistently react most strongly to the correct alternatives is exceedingly small.[3]

## § 8:25  Areas of scientific agreement and disagreement—Survey of the accuracy of polygraph tests

Prior to 1970, virtually no scientific research on the reliability and validity of the CQT in criminal investigation had been conducted. The first scientific study was performed in our laboratory at the University of Utah.[1] By 1983, the Office of Technology Assessment (OTA) had identified 14 analog studies and 10 field studies of the CQT, some of which can reasonably be used to make inferences about the ac-

[2]Honts & Raskin, A Field Study of the Validity of the Directed Lie Control Question, 16 J. Police Sci. Admin. 56 (1988); Horowitz et al., The Role of Comparison Questions in the Physiological Detection of Deception, 34 Psychophysiology 118 (1997).

[3]Honts, The Psychophysiological Detection of Deception, 3 Current Directions in Psychol. Sci. 77 (1994); David C. Raskin, Polygraph Techniques for the Detection of Deception, in Psychological Methods in Criminal Investigation and Evidence 247 (David C. Raskin ed., 1989).

[Section 8:24]

[1]Lykken, The GSR in the Detection of Guilt, 43 J. Applied Psychol. 385 (1959); David C. Raskin, Polygraph Techniques for the Detection

of Deception, in Psychological Methods in Criminal Investigation and Evidence 247 (David C. Raskin ed., 1989).

[2]Podlesny & Raskin, Effectiveness of Techniques and Physiological Measures in the Detection of Deception, 15 Psychophysiology 344 (1978).

[3]For a detailed description of the GKT, see David C. Raskin, Polygraph Techniques for the Detection of Deception, in Psychological Methods in Criminal Investigation and Evidence 247 (David C. Raskin ed., 1989).

[Section 8:25]

[1]Barland & askin, An Evaluation of Field Techniques in Detection of Deception, 12 Psychophysiology 321 (1975).

curacy of control question tests in the field.[2] Lykken reported the first laboratory research on the accuracy of the GKT,[3] and Elaad reported the first field study of the GKT in 1990.[4]

When scientists attempt to assess the usefulness of techniques such as polygraph tests, they are concerned with reliability and validity. In its scientific sense, reliability refers to the consistency of a technique. In studies of polygraph tests, reliability focuses on the consistency of the scoring of the physiological data. Establishing this inter-rater reliability is an important first step in evaluating any test. Reliability and validity are related in that reliability is necessary, but is not sufficient for validity. That is, if a test cannot be scored consistently (reliably), then the scores cannot be valid. The scientific issues surrounding the concept of validity are complex and scientists use the term in several different ways. However, in this context, validity may be considered simply as the accuracy of the polygraph techniques.

The reliability of scoring of the CQT has been studied extensively. Research has clearly indicated that when the performance of competent evaluators is assessed, the reliability of numerical scoring is very high. It is not unusual for agreement on decisions by independent evaluators to approach 100%, and correlational assessments of the reliability of numerical scoring are usually greater than 0.90.[5] The reliability of the GKT has not been reported in the literature, but the simplicity of scoring this test would be expected to produce very high inter-rater reliability. Computer-based statistical decisionmaking with the CQT is perfectly reliable as long as the computers are functioning properly.[6]

Assessing the validity of polygraph tests is considerably more complex than assessing their reliability. Science has generally approached such problems with different research methodologies that involve conducting research in the laboratory and in the field. Each of these approaches has strengths and weaknesses. The strength of the laboratory approach is that the scientist has control over the situation. Subjects can be randomly assigned to conditions and the scientist knows with certainty who is, and who is not, telling the truth during the polygraph examination. Variables can be manipulated with precision and strong inferential statements can often be made. However, laboratory approaches can be weak in that they may lack realism when compared to the field situation they model.[7]

The main strength of field research is that the scientist can study the phenomenon of interest in real-life settings where realism is not an issue. However, scientific control in field studies can be very difficult. A central issue for field studies is the quality of the criterion of guilt and innocence. This raises questions about how the researchers determined who was truthful and who was deceptive, which is not an easy task. If there had been strong proof of guilt or innocence in the actual cases, polygraph tests would probably not have been conducted.

Neither the laboratory nor the field approach is perfect, so the best strategy is to

---

[2]Office of Technology Assessment, Scientific Validity of Polygraph Testing: A Research Review and Evaluation (1983).

[3]Lykken, The GSR in the Detection of Guilt, 43 J. Applied Psychol. 385 (1959).

[4]Elaad, Detection of Guilty Knowledge in Real-Life Criminal Investigations, 75 J. Applied Psychol. 521 (1990).

[5]See David C. Raskin, The Scientific Basis of Polygraph Techniques and Their Uses in the Judicial Process, in Reconstructing the Past: The Role of Psychologists in Criminal Trials (Arne Trankell ed., 1982).

[6]Kircher & Raskin, Human Versus Computerized Evaluations of Polygraph Data in Laboratory Setting, 73 J. Applied Psychol. 291 (1988); Charles R. Honts & Mary K. Devitt, Bootstrap Decision Making for Polygraph Examinations: Final Report of DOD/PERSEC Grant No. N00014-92-J-1794, [available from the Defense Technical Information Center, Building 5 Cameron Station, Alexandria, VA 22304-6145].

[7]Podlesny & Raskin, Physiological Measures and the Detection of Deception, 84 Psychol. Bull. 782 (1977).

use both methodologies. To the extent that laboratory studies and field studies converge on the same results, they reinforce and complement each other in determining the true state of the world. The techniques scientists use to overcome the relative weakness of these two methodologies are discussed in the following sections.

### § 8:26 Areas of scientific agreement and disagreement—Survey of the accuracy of polygraph tests—Laboratory studies—Control question test

Laboratory research has traditionally been an attractive alternative because the scientist can control the environment. By randomly assigning subjects to conditions, the scientist can know with certainty who is telling the truth and who is lying. Laboratory research on credibility assessment has typically made some subjects "guilty" by having them commit a mock crime (e.g. "steal" a watch from an office), and then instructing them to lie about it during a subsequent test. From a scientific viewpoint, random assignment to conditions is highly desirable because it controls for the influence of extraneous variables that might confound the results of the experiment.[1] The most accepted type of laboratory study realistically simulates a crime in which some subjects commit an overt transaction, such as a theft.[2] While the guilty subjects enact a realistic crime, the innocent subjects are merely told about the nature of the crime and do not enact it. All subjects are motivated to produce a truthful outcome, usually by a cash bonus for passing the test. For example, one such study used prison inmates who were offered a bonus equal to one month's wages if they could produce a truthful outcome.[3]

The advantages of careful laboratory simulations include total control over the issues that are investigated and the types of tests that are used, consistency in test administration and interpretation, specification of the subject populations that are studied, control over the skill and training of the examiners, and absolute verification of the accuracy of test results. Carefully designed and conducted studies that closely approximate the methods and conditions characteristic of high quality practice by polygraph professionals and use subjects similar to the target population, such as convicted felons or a cross-section of the general community, provide the most generalizable results.[4] Laboratory research in general, and credibility assessment in particular, is sometimes criticized for lack of realism, which may limit the ability of the scientist to apply the results of the laboratory to real-world settings. However, a recent analysis reported in the flagship journal of the American Psychological Society examined a broad range of laboratory-based psychological research.[5] The authors concluded, "correspondence between lab- and field-based effect sizes of conceptually similar independent and dependent variables was considerable. In brief, the psychological laboratory has generally produced truths, rather than trivialities."[6] Our position with regard to the high quality studies of the CQT and DLT is similar. We believe that these studies produce important information about the validity of such tests that is not trivial and ungeneralizable, as some critics have claimed. As described below, a recent scientific survey of psychological

---

[Section 8:26]

[1]Thomas D. Cook & Donald T. Campbell, Quasi-experimentation: Design & analysis issues for Field Settings (1979).

[2]David C. Raskin, The Scientific Basis of Polygraph Techniques and Their Uses in the Judicial Process, in Reconstructing the Past: The Role of Psychologists in Criminal Trials (Arne Trankell ed., 1982).

[3]Raskin & Hare, Psychopathy and Detection of Deception in a Prison Population, 15 Psycho-physiology 126.

[4]Kircher et al., Meta-analysis of Mock Crime Studies of the Control Question Polygraph Technique, 12 L. & Hum. Behav. 79 (1988).

[5]Anderson et al., Research in the Psychological Laboratory: Truth or Triviality?, 8 Curr. Dir. Psychological Sci. 3 (1999).

[6]Anderson et al., Research in the Psychological Laboratory: Truth or Triviality?, 8 Curr. Dir. Psychological Sci. 3 (1999).

scientists who work on applied problems in psychology and the law indicates that the vast majority of them share our belief in the value of laboratory studies of the validity of the polygraph.

In 1997, a Committee of Concerned Social Scientists filed a Brief for Amicus Curiae[7] with the Supreme Court of the United States in the case of *United States v. Scheffer*.[8] They identified eight high-quality laboratory studies of the CQT,[9] the results of which are illustrated in Table 1. These high-quality laboratory studies indicate that the CQT is a very accurate discriminator of truthful and deceptive subjects. Overall, these studies correctly classified 91% of the subjects and produced approximately equal numbers of false positive and false negative errors.

## Table 1
## Results of High Quality Laboratory Studies

| Study | Guilty | | | | Innocent | | | |
|---|---|---|---|---|---|---|---|---|
| | n | % correct | % wrong | % Inc. | n | % correct | % wrong | % Inc. |
| Control Question Tests | | | | | | | | |
| Glinton, et al. (1984) | 2 | 100 | 0 | 0 | 13 | 85 | 15 | 0 |
| Honts, et al. (1994)[a] | 20 | 70 | 20 | 10 | 20 | 75 | 10 | 15 |
| Horowitz, et al. (1994)[b] | 15 | 53 | 20 | 27 | 15 | 80 | 13 | 7 |
| Kircher & Raskin (1988) | 50 | 88 | 6 | 6 | 50 | 86 | 6 | 8 |
| Podlesny & Raskin (1978) | 20 | 70 | 15 | 15 | 20 | 90 | 5 | 5 |
| Podlesny & Truslow (1993) | 72 | 69 | 13 | 18 | 24 | 75 | 4 | 21 |
| Raskin & Hare (1978) | 24 | 88 | 0 | 12 | 24 | 88 | 8 | 4 |
| Rovner, et al. (1979)[c] | 24 | 88 | 0 | 12 | 24 | 88 | 8 | 4 |
| Weighted Means | 227 | 77 | 10 | 13 | 190 | 84 | 8 | 8 |
| Directed Lie Control[d] | | | | | | | | |
| Traditional Control | | | | | | | | |
| Questions | 15 | 53 | 20 | 27 | 15 | 80 | 13 | 7 |
| Personally Relevant | | | | | | | | |
| Directed Lie | 15 | 73 | 13 | 13 | 15 | 87 | 0 | 13 |
| Trivial Directed Lie | 15 | 54 | 20 | 26 | 15 | 67 | 13 | 20 |
| Relevant/Irrelevant | 15 | 100 | 0 | 0 | 15 | 20 | 73 | 7 |
| Concealed Knowledge Tests | | | | | | | | |
| Davidson (1968) | 12 | 92 | 8 | | 36 | 100 | 0 | |
| Honts, et al. (1994)[e] | 10 | 80 | 20 | | 10 | 90 | 10 | |
| Lykken (1959) | 37 | 86 | 14 | | 12 | 100 | 0 | |
| Podlesny & Raskin (1978) | 10 | 90 | 10 | | 10 | 100 | 0 | |
| Steller, et al. (1987) | 47 | 85 | 15 | | 40 | 100 | 0 | |
| Weighted Means | 116 | 86 | 14 | | 108 | 99 | 1 | |

  **a** Countermeasure Subjects Excluded.
  **b** Traditional Control Question Subjects Only.
  **c** Countermeasure Subjects Excluded.
  **d** Data from Horowitz et al. (1994).
  **e** Countermeasure Subjects Excluded.

---

[7]Charles R. Honts & Charles F. Peterson, Brief of the Committee of Concerned Social Scientists as Amicus Curiae, *U.S. v. Scheffer*, in the Supreme Court of the United States (1997). The Amicus was co-signed by 17 individuals holding advanced scientific degrees.

[8]*U.S. v. Scheffer*, 523 U.S. 303, 118 S. Ct. 1261, 140 L. Ed. 2d 413, 48 Fed. R. Evid. Serv. 899 (1998).

[9]See Ginton et al., A Method for Evaluating the Use of the Polygraph in a Real-Life Situation, 67 J. Applied Psychol. 131 (1982); Honts et al., Mental and Physical Countermeasures Reduce the Accuracy of Polygraph Tests, 79 J. Applied Psych. 252 (1994); Horowitz et al., The Role of Comparison Questions in the Physiological Detection of Deception, 34 Psychophysiology 118 (1997); Kircher & Raskin, Human Versus Computerized Evaluations of Polygraph Data in Laboratory Setting, 73 J. Applied Psychol. 291 (1988); Podlesny & Raskin, Physiological Measures and the Detection of Deception, 84 Psychol. Bull. 782 (1977); Podlesny & Truslow, Validity of an Expanded-Issue (Modified General Question) Polygraph Technique in a Simulated Distributed-Crime-Roles Context, 78 J. Applied Psychol. 788 (1993); Raskin & Hare, Psychopathy and Detection of Deception in a Prison Population, 15 Psychophysiology 126 (1978); Rovner et al., Effects of Information and Practice on Detection of Deception, 16 Psychophysiology 197 (1979).

## § 8:27 Areas of scientific agreement and disagreement—Survey of the accuracy of polygraph tests—Laboratory studies—Directed-lie test

Since the DLT is relatively new, there are fewer studies of its validity. Seven laboratory studies have been conducted, but they are not all of high quality.[1] The Horowitz et al. study is the most carefully designed and conducted.[2] It used a mock crime that closely approximated the field situation, similar to those described for the CQT in the previous section. The Horowitz study compared the effectiveness of the DLT with the CQT and RIT. Different groups received one of two types of directed lies, personally-relevant directed lies using the procedures previously described or simple directed lies to three of the neutral questions that were used in the RIT. The results indicated that the personal directed lie produced the highest accuracy, except for the RIT with guilty subjects. The outcomes for the four types of tests are presented in Table 2. Among all question structures, the personal directed-lie produced the highest number of correct decisions on innocent subjects and among the three tests that employed comparison questions, it produced the highest number of correct decisions on guilty subjects.

### Table 2

### Test outcomes of the Horowitz et al. (1997) study

| Experimental Groups | Test Outcomes (%) | | | % Correct Decisions |
|---|---|---|---|---|
| | Correct | Wrong | Inconclusive | |
| Guilty | | | | |
|   Relevant-irrelevant | 100 | 0 | 0 | 100 |
|   Trivial Directed Lie | 53 | 20 | 27 | 73 |
|   Personal Directed Lie | 73 | 14 | 13 | 84 |
|   Probable Lie Comparison | 53 | 20 | 27 | 73 |
| Innocent | | | | |
|   Relevant-irrelevant | 20 | 73 | 7 | 22 |
|   Trivial Directed Lie | 67 | 13 | 20 | 84 |
|   Personal Directed Lie | 87 | 13 | 0 | 87 |
|   Probable Lie Comparison | 80 | 13 | 7 | 86 |

$n = 15$ for each of the experimental groups.
The %age of correct decisions was calculated by excluding inconclusive outcomes.

The U. S. Department of Defense has conducted three sets of studies concerning

---

[Section 8:27]

[1]Gordon H. Barland, A Validity and Reliability Study of Counterintelligence Screening Tests, Unpublished manuscript, Security Support Battalion, 902nd Military Intelligence Group, Fort George G. Meade, Maryland (1981); Department of Defense Polygraph Institute Research Division Staff, A Comparison of Psychophysiological Detection of Deception Accuracy Rates Obtained Using the Counterintelligence Scope Polygraph (CSP) and The Test for Espionage and Sabotage (TES) question formats 26 Polygraph 79 (1997); Department of Defense Polygraph Institute Research Division Staff, Psychophysiological Detection of Deception Accuracy Rates Obtained Using the Test for Espionage and Sabotage (TES), 27 Polygraph 68 (1998); Horowitz et al., The Role of Comparison Questions in the Physiological Detection of Deception, 34 Psychophysiology 118 (1997); Reed, A New Psychophysiological Detection of Deception Examination for Security Screening, 31 Psychophysiology S80 (1994).

[2]Horowitz et al., The Role of Comparison Questions in the Physiological Detection of Deception, 34 Psychophysiology 118 (1997).

the validity of the DLT. Barland examined the validity of the Military Intelligence version of the DLT in a mock-screening setting with 26 truthful subjects and 30 subjects who attempted deception.[3] All subjects were tested with the DLT; no other techniques were examined. Excluding inconclusive outcomes, Barland's evaluators correctly classified 79% of the subjects. Although this performance appears modest compared to that obtained in Horowitz et al. and the studies reported above for the CQT, it should be pointed out that Barland's study was conducted in a screening setting. By comparison, other mock-screening studies produced near chance performance with probable-lie tests.[4] Therefore, the performance of the directed lie in the Barland study was actually quite strong.

The other two sets of studies on the DLT concern a new test, the test of espionage and sabotage (TES) developed by DODPI for use in national security screening tests. Reed reported three laboratory mock-screening studies of the DLT.[5] Following a series of studies that indicated that the national security screening tests of the time were making an unacceptably high number of false negative errors,[6] DODPI attempted to develop a more accurate screening test. It should be noted that the primary concern in conducting national security screening tests is a desire to avoid false negative errors. Following a series of studies that are not publicly available, Reed described the product of DODPI's efforts.

In the first study, the TES test format with only directed-lie comparison questions was tested against two versions of the counterintelligence scope polygraph (CSP) test. One version of the CSP used probable-lie comparison questions (the type of comparison question used in the standard CQT) while the other used directed-lie comparison questions. The TES outperformed both of the CSP formats in terms of correctly identifying guilty subjects. The CSP with directed-lie comparisons was slightly, but not significantly, better at identifying guilty subjects than was the CSP with probable-lie comparisons. The second study produced even higher accuracy for the TES, a directed-lie comparison test format. Little information is provided about the third study, but it also appears to show considerable accuracy for the directed-lie TES. Most recently, DODPI reported a mock espionage/sabotage study that involved 82 subjects.[7] All subjects were tested with the TES. Excluding one inconclusive outcome, the examiners correctly identified 98% of the innocent subjects and 83.3% of the guilty subjects. This study also indicates that the directed-lie TES is extremely successful in discriminating between innocent and guilty subjects.

Abrams reported the only other study of the DLT. Unfortunately that study was

[3]Gordon H. Barland, A Validity and Reliability Study of Counterintelligence Screening Tests, Unpublished manuscript, Security Support Battalion, 902nd Military Intelligence Group, Fort George G. Meade, Maryland (1981).

[4]Gordon H. Barland et al., Studies of the Accuracy of Security Screening Polygraph Examinations. Department of Defense Polygraph Institute, Fort McClellan, Alabama. Available at http://truth.boisestate.edu/raredocuments/bhb.html (1989); Honts, Counterintelligence Scope Polygraph (CSP) Test Found to be a Poor Discriminator, 5 Forensic Reports 215 (1992).

[5]Reed, A New Psychophysiological Detection of Deception Examination for Security Screening, 31 Psychophysiology S80 (1994); also published as Department of Defense Polygraph Institute Research Division Staff, A Comparison of Psychophysiological Detection of Deception Accuracy Rates Obtained Using the Counterintelligence

Scope Polygraph (CSP) and The Test for Espionage and Sabotage (TES) question formats 26 Polygraph 79 (1997).

[6]Gordon H. Barland et al., Studies of the Accuracy of Security Screening Polygraph Examinations. Department of Defense Polygraph Institute, Fort McClellan, Alabama; Honts, The Emperor's New Clothes: Application of Polygraph Tests in the American Workplace, 4 Forensic Reports 91 (1991); Honts, Counterintelligence Scope Polygraph (CSP) Test Found to be a Poor Discriminator, 5 Forensic Reports 215 (1992); Charles R. Honts, The Psychophysiological Detection of Deception, 3 Current Directions in Psychological Sci. 77 (1994).

[7]Department of Defense Polygraph Institute Research Division Staff, Psychophysiological Detection of Deception Accuracy Rates Obtained Using the Test for Espionage and Sabotage (TES), 27 Polygraph 68 (1998).

so poorly designed and so methodologically flawed that the data are meaningless.[8] Although Abrams and Matte have become outspoken critics of the DLT, their criticisms lack merit and their attacks on the DLT are baseless.[9] Interested readers are referred to the research and commentary by Honts and his colleagues.[10]

### § 8:28    Areas of scientific agreement and disagreement—Survey of the accuracy of polygraph tests—Laboratory studies—Guilty knowledge test

There are many published laboratory studies of the GKT, but many of these studies used artificial and unrealistic methods that render the studies useless for providing estimates of accuracy in the field. However, a review of the scientific literature reveals five laboratory studies of the GKT that appear to have methodology realistic enough to allow some generalization to the field.[1] The results of these studies are summarized in Table 3. As with the CQT, the quality laboratory studies of the GKT indicate a high level of accuracy for the technique, but the GKT consistently produces more false negative than false positive errors. This is disturbing because the conditions for the detection of concealed knowledge with the GKT are optimized in the laboratory as compared to the field. In GKT lab studies, the experimenters usually pretest potential items for their salience and memorability by guilty subjects and for their transparency to innocent subjects, i.e., can innocent subjects guess the correct response? Although it might be possible to test the transparency of GKT items in the field, it is not possible to test the memorability of key items. Moreover, there is no clear theoretical basis for judgments about what a guilty person is likely to remember about a crime scene. Those factors likely result in an underestimation of the field rate of false negative errors when generalizing from laboratory studies of the GKT.

### Table 3
### The results of studies of the GKT

| | Guilty | | | Innocent | | |
|---|---|---|---|---|---|---|
| | n | % Correct | % Wrong | n | % Correct | % Wrong |
| **Laboratory Studies** | | | | | | |
| Davidson (1968) | 12 | 92 | 8 | 36 | 100 | 0 |
| Honts et al. (1994) [a] | 10 | 80 | 20 | 10 | 90 | 10 |
| Lykken (1959) | 37 | 86 | 14 | 12 | 100 | 0 |

[8]Abrams, The Directed Lie Control Question, 20 Polygraph 26 (1991).

[9]See Abrams, A Response To Honts On The Issue Of The Discussion Of Questions Between Charts 28 Polygraph 223 (1999); Matte, An Analysis Of The Psychodynamics Of The Directed Lie Control Questions In The Control Question Technique, 27 Polygraph 56 (1998).

[10]Honts, The Discussion of Comparison Questions Between List Repetitions (Charts) is Associated With Increased Test Accuracy, 28 Polygraph 117 (1999); Honts, A Brief Note on the Misleading and the Inaccurate: A Rejoinder to Matte (2000) With Critical Comments on Matte and Reuss (1999), 29 Polygraph 321 (2000); Honts & Gordon, A Critical Analysis Of Matte's Analysis Of The Directed Lie, 27 Polygraph 241 (1998); Honts et al., The Hybrid Directed Lie Test, The

Overemphasized Comparison Question, Chimeras And Other Inventions: A Rejoinder To Abrams (1999), 29 Polygraph 156 (2000).

**[Section 8:28]**

[1]See Davidson, Validity of the Guilty-Knowledge Technique: The Effects of Motivation, 53 J. Applied Psychol. 62 (1968); Honts, et al., Mental and Physical Countermeasures Reduce the Accuracy of the Concealed Knowledge Test, 33 Psychophysiology 84 (1994); Lykken, The GSR in the Detection of Guilt, 43 J. Applied Psychol. 385 (1959); Podlesny & Raskin, Effectiveness of Techniques and Physical Measures in the Detection of Deception, 15 Psychophysiology 344 (1978); Steller et al., Extraversion and the Detection of Information, 21 J. Res. in Personality 334 (1987).

| | Guilty | | | Innocent | | |
|---|---|---|---|---|---|---|
| | n | % Correct | % Wrong | n | % Correct | % Wrong |
| Podlesny & Raskin (1978) | 10 | 90 | 10 | 10 | 100 | 0 |
| Steller et al. (1987) | 47 | 85 | 15 | 40 | 100 | 0 |
| **Weighted Means** | **116** | **86** | **14** | **108** | **99** | **1** |
| **Field Studies** | | | | | | |
| Elaad (1990) | 48 | 42 | 58 | 50 | 98 | 2 |
| Elaad, et al., (1992) | 40 | 53 | 47 | 40 | 97 | 3 |
| **Weighted Means** | **88** | **47** | **53** | **90** | 98 | **2** |

<sup>a</sup> Countermeasure subjects excluded.

## § 8:29 Areas of scientific agreement and disagreement—Survey of the accuracy of polygraph tests—Field studies

As noted earlier, the greatest problems in conducting field polygraph studies are the development of criteria for determining who was actually telling the truth and who was lying and the lack of control that the experimenter has over the testing situation. There is a consensus among researchers that field studies should have the following characteristics:

(1) subjects should be sampled from the actual population of subjects in which the scientist is interested. If the objective is to determine the accuracy of a polygraph examination on criminal suspects, then the subjects of the study should be criminal suspects;

(2) subjects should be sampled by some type of random process, and cases must be included independent of the accuracy of the original examiner's decision or the quality of the polygraph charts;

(3) the physiological data should be evaluated independently by persons trained and experienced in the evaluation of polygraph tests who employ scoring techniques that are representative of those used in the field. The evaluations should be based on only the physiological data, and the evaluators should not have access to other case information. This provides an estimate of the accuracy of the decisions based solely on the physiological information. However, decisions rendered by the original examiner probably provide a better estimate of the accuracy of polygraph techniques as they are actually employed in the field setting by criminal investigators; and

(4) the credibility of the subject should be determined by information independent of the polygraph test. Confession substantiated by physical evidence is the best criterion for use in these studies.

## § 8:30 Areas of scientific agreement and disagreement—Survey of the accuracy of polygraph tests—Field studies—Control question test

The 1983 OTA review of the scientific literature on polygraph tests identified 10 field studies in the scientific literature that met minimal standards for acceptability.[1] However, none of the 10 studies meets all four of the above criteria for an adequate field study. The overall accuracy of the polygraph decisions in the OTA

---

**[Section 8:30]**

[1]Office of Technology Assessment, Scientific Validity of Polygraph Testing: A Research Review and Evaluation (1983); the 10 studies included by the OTA were: Gordon H. Barland & David C. Raskin, Validity and Reliability of Polygraph Examinations of Criminal Suspects 1 U.S. Department of Justice Report No. 76-1, Contract No. 75-NI-99-0001 (1976); Bersh, A Validation Study of Polygraph Examiner Judgments, 53 J. Applied Psychol. 399 (1969); Davidson, Validity and Reliability of the Cardio Activity Monitor, 8 Polygraph 104 (1979); Horvath, The Effect of Selected Variables on Interpretation of Polygraph

review was 90% on criterion-guilty suspects and 80% on criterion-innocent suspects. In spite of the inclusion of studies with serious methodological problems, accuracy in field cases was higher than is claimed by some of the most vocal critics.[2]

Subsequent to the OTA study, four field studies of the CQT that meet the criteria for an adequate field study have been reported.[3] As shown in Table 4, they produced a combined estimate of 90.5% accuracy, which is higher than that developed by OTA on the basis of the 10 less rigorous early studies.

### Table 4. The Accuracy of Independent Evaluations in High Quality Field Studies of the CQT

| Study | n | Guilty % Correct | % Wrong | % Inc | n | Innocent % Correct | % Wrong | % Inc |
|---|---|---|---|---|---|---|---|---|
| Honts (1996) [a] | 7 | 100 | 0 | 0 | 6 | 83 | 0 | 17 |
| Honts & Raskin (1988) [b] | 12 | 92 | 0 | 8 | 13 | 62 | 15 | 23 |
| Patrick & Iacono (1991) [c] | 52 | 92 | 2 | 6 | 37 | 30 | 24 | 46 |
| Raskin et al. (1989) [d] | 37 | 73 | 0 | 27 | 26 | 61 | 8 | 31 |
| Means | 108 | 89 | 1 | 10 | 82 | 59 | 12 | 29 |
| % Decisions | | 98 | 2 | | | 75 | 25 | |

[a] Subgroup of subjects confirmed by confession and evidence.

[b] Decision based only on comparisons to traditional comparison questions.

[c] Results from mean blind rescoring of the cases "verified with maximum certainty" p. 235.

[d] There results are from an independent evaluation to the "pure verification" cases.

It is interesting to note that only in the Patrick and Iacono study did the original examiners perform at a much higher level than the independent evaluators.[4] Patrick and Iacono's original examiners correctly classified 100% of their guilty subjects and 90% of the innocent subjects,[5] which was similar to the performance of the original examiners in the Honts[6] study that used examiners from the same law enforcement agency. Given the general performance of independent evaluators across these high quality field studies, it appears that the performance of the blind evaluators in Patrick and Iacono could be viewed as an outlying data point. Honts provides a

Records, 62 J. Applied Psychol. 127 (1977); Horvath & Reid, The Reliability of Polygraph Examiner Diagnosis of Truth and Deception, 62 J. Crim. L., Criminology & Police Sci. 276 (1971); Hunter & Ash, The Accuracy and Consistency of Polygraph Examiners' Diagnoses, 1 J. Police Sci. & Admin. 370 (1973); Kleinmuntz & Szucko, A Field Study of the Fallibility of Polygraphic Lie Detection, 308 Nature 449 (1984); David C. Raskin, 1 Reliability of Chart Interpretation and Sources of Errors in Polygraph Examinations, U.S. Department of Justice, Report No. 76-3, Contract No. 75-NI-0001. (1976); Slowik & Buckley, Relative Accuracy of Polygraph Examiner Diagnosis of Respiration, Blood Pressure, and GSR Recordings, 3 J. Police Sci. & Admin. 305 (1975); Wicklander & Hunter, The Influence of Auxiliary Sources of Information in Polygraph Diagnoses, 3 J. Police Sci. & Admin. 405 (1975).

[2]David T. Lykken, A Tremor In The Blood: Uses And Abuses Of The Lie Detector (1998).

[3]Honts, Criterion Development and Validity of the Control Question Test in Field Application 123 J. General Psychol. 309. (1996); Honts & Raskin, A Field Study of the Validity of the Directed Lie Control Question, 16 J. Police Sci. Admin. 56 (1988); Patrick & Iacono, Validity of the Control Question Polygraph Test: The Problem of Sampling Bias, 76 J. Applied Psychol. 229 (1991); David C. Raskin et al., A Study of the Validity of Polygraph Examinations in Criminal Investigation, 1 Nat'l Inst. of Just. (1988).

[4]Christopher J. Patrick & William G. Iacono, Validity of the Control Question Polygraph Test: The Problem of Sampling Bias, 76 J. Applied Psychol. 229 (1991).

[5]Patrick & Iacono, Validity of the Control Question Polygraph Test: The Problem of Sampling Bias, 76 J. Applied Psychol. 229 (1991).

[6]Charles R. Honts, The Psychophysiological Detection of Deception, 3 Current Directions in Psychol. Sci. 77 (1994).

discussion of this and other potential problems with the Patrick & Iacono study.[7] If the Patrick & Iacono study is excluded, the remaining three field studies produce an estimate of accuracy of 96%.

Although the better quality field studies indicate a high accuracy rate for the CQT, all of the data presented in Table 4 were obtained from independent evaluations of the physiological data. That method is desirable for scientific purposes because it eliminates possible contamination (e.g., knowledge of the case facts and the overt behaviors of the subject during the examination) that might have influenced the decisions of the original examiners. Such contamination could distort research designed to determine how much discriminative information was contained in the physiological recordings. However, independent evaluators rarely testify in legal proceedings, nor do they make decisions in most applied settings.

The original examiner renders the diagnosis of truthfulness or deception in an actual case and would testify in court. Thus, accuracy of decisions by independent evaluators is not the true figure of merit for legal proceedings and most other applications. The Committee of Concerned Social Scientists[8] presented the data from the original examiners in the studies reported in Table 4 along with two additional studies that are often cited by critics of the CQT,[9] as shown in Table 5. Those data indicate that the original examiners achieved accuracy rates of 98% on verified innocent suspects and 97% on verified guilty suspects, which are higher than the results from the independent evaluators.

| Table 5. % Correct Decisions by Original Examiners in Field Cases Using the CQT | | |
| --- | --- | --- |
| **Study** | **Innocent** | **Guilty** |
| Horvath (1977) | 100 | 100 |
| Honts and Raskin (1988) | 100 | 92 |
| Kleinmuntz and Szucko (1984) | 100 | 100 |
| Raskin, Kircher, Honts, & Horowitz (1988)[a] | 96 | 95 |
| Patrick and Iacono (1991) | 90 | 100 |
| Honts (1996)[b] | 100 | 94 |
| **Means** | **98** | **97** |

[7]Charles R. Honts, The Psychophysiological Detection of Deception, 3 Current Directions in Psychol. Sci. 77 (1994).

[8]Charles R. Honts & Charles F. Peterson, Brief of the Committee of Concerned Social Scientists as Amicus Curiae, *U.S. v. Scheffer*, in the Supreme Court of the United States (1997).

[9]Those two studies are, Kleinmuntz & Szucko, A Field Study of the Fallibility of Polygraphic Lie Detection, 308 Nature 449 (1984); Horvath, The Effects of Selected Variables on Interpretation of Polygraph Records, 62, J. Applied Psychol. 127 (1977). Neither of these studies meets the generally accepted requirements for useful field studies but nevertheless they are frequently cited by critics of the CQT as evidence that the CQT is not accurate. The study reported by Benjamin Kleinmuntz and Julian J. Szucko fails to meet the criteria for a useful field study because (1) the subjects were employees who were forced to take tests as part of their employment, not criminal suspects (2) the case selection method was not specified, and (3) the data were evaluated by students at a polygraph school that does not teach blind chart evaluation. Moreover, those students were given only one ninth of the usual amount of data collected in a polygraph examination and were forced to use a rating scale with which they were not familiar. The Horvath study also fails to meet the criteria for a useful study because (1) about half of the innocent subjects were victims of violent crime, not suspects, (2) virtually all of the false positive errors in that study were with innocent victims, not innocent suspects, (3) the independent evaluators were all trained at a polygraph school that does not teach numerical chart evaluation, and (4) cases were not selected at random. Some cases were excluded from the study because of the nature of the charts. An interesting fact that critics almost never mention is that the decisions by the original examiners in the Horvath Study were 100% correct. Also see the discussion in Raskin, Methodological Issues in Estimating Polygraph Accuracy in Field Applications, 19, Canadian J. Behaviour. Sci. 389 (1987).

| Table 5. % Correct Decisions by Original Examiners in Field Cases Using the CQT | | |
|---|---|---|
| Study | Innocent | Guilty |
| a Cases where all questions were confirmed. | | |
| b Includes all cases with some confirmation. | | |

### § 8:31  Areas of scientific agreement and disagreement—Survey of the accuracy of polygraph tests—Field studies—Directed-lie test

To date, Honts and Raskin have reported the only field study of the DLT. They conducted polygraph tests of criminal suspects over a four-year period and obtained 25 confirmed tests in which one personal directed lie was included along with typical probable-lie comparison questions.[1] Each author then performed blind interpretations of the charts obtained by the other author, scoring them with and without the use of the directed-lie question. The results of the Honts and Raskin study indicated that inclusion of the directed-lie question in the numerical evaluation of the charts had a noticeable effect on the confirmed innocent suspects, reducing the false positive rate from 20% to 0%. For the confirmed guilty suspects, it had the slight effect of changing one inconclusive outcome to a false negative. The effects of the directed-lie question on the total numerical scores were more dramatic. Inclusion of the directed-lie comparisons almost doubled the size of the total numerical scores for the confirmed innocent suspects, raising the mean score from +4.7 to +9.0. It had a lesser effect on the scores of the confirmed guilty suspects, lowering them from -13.8 to -11.5. Thus, the directed-lie question raised the mean score for innocent suspects from the inconclusive range into the definite truthful area, while the mean score for guilty suspects remained clearly in the deceptive area. The main impact of the directed-lie question was a reduction in false positive errors.

### § 8:32  Areas of scientific agreement and disagreement—Survey of the accuracy of polygraph tests—Field studies—Guilty knowledge test

The only two field studies of the GKT were published in 1990 and 1992.[1] Both are high in quality and meet the four requirements for an adequate field study of polygraph tests described above. The results of those studies are presented in Table 3. Those studies show that the GKT has a very high false negative rate (53%) in field applications. In both studies, more than half of the guilty criminal suspects passed their GKT examinations, appearing to lack knowledge of the crimes that they had actually committed. In light of the data from laboratory studies and the difficulties in developing good GKT tests as described above, the results of the field studies of the GKT are not at all surprising. Given the extensive literature on the fallibility of eyewitness memory, especially when witnesses are aroused or under stress, it is not surprising that criminals have poor memory for the details of crimes they have committed.[2]

Another factor to consider when evaluating the potential of the GKT as a field polygraph technique is the applicability of the technique to actual cases. In order to conduct a GKT, the examiner must have a number of key items of information from the crime scene to develop the test. Podlesny examined the applicability of the GKT

---

[Section 8:31]

[1]Honts & Raskin, A Field Study of the Validity of the Directed Lie Control Question, 16 J. Police Sci. Admin. 56 (1988).

[Section 8:32]

[1]Elaad, Detection of Guilty Knowledge in Real-Life Criminal Investigations, 75 J. Applied Psychol. 521 (1990); Elaad et al., Detection Measures in Real-Life Criminal Guilty Knowledge Tests, 77 J. Applied Psychol. 757 (1992).

[2]Elizabeth F. Loftus & K. Ketcham, Witness for the Defense (1991).

by studying the information available in FBI case files.[3] He estimated that a meaningful GKT could be developed in only 13%–18% of the cases examined. This study suggests that the field applicability of the GKT is extremely limited, even if it had an acceptable level of validity. Given this limitation, demonstrably low accuracy, and strong theoretical reasons why the GKT cannot work properly in the field, it is clear that the GKT is useful only as a vehicle for laboratory research.

## § 8:33  Areas of scientific agreement and disagreement—Countermeasures

Countermeasures are behaviors that an individual may use to attempt to defeat or distort a polygraph test. Countermeasures might be employed either by guilty subjects who are trying to beat the test by appearing truthful or innocent subjects who do not trust the test and want to hedge their bets. Conceptually, countermeasures fall into two major categories, general-state countermeasures that are designed to affect the general mental or physical state of the subject, and specific-point countermeasures that are used to produce physiological changes at specific points during the test. General-state countermeasures include ingestion of drugs, relaxation, and a variety of mental strategies, such as dissociation, self-deception, and rationalization. Specific-point countermeasures include physical and mental maneuvers during and following specific questions in order to increase or decrease physiological reactions to those questions.

Scientists have addressed the problem of polygraph countermeasures, primarily in the laboratory setting. The research clearly indicates that all general-state countermeasures (including drugs) and specific-point countermeasures designed to reduce reactions to relevant questions fail to produce inconclusive or false positive outcomes.[1] However, studies in which subjects have been carefully trained to use specific-point countermeasures to enhance their reactions to control questions have increased false negative rates with both the CQT and the GKT.

An initial study of the spontaneous use of countermeasures by subjects in mock crime experiments found that countermeasure usage by guilty subjects was high (61% attempted one or more countermeasures), but no guilty subject defeated the test and no innocent subject reported attempting a countermeasure.[2] That study was recently replicated by Honts and his colleagues.[3] In the context of a laboratory study of the CQT, they found that 90% of the guilty and 46% of the innocent subjects reported attempting at least one countermeasure. The spontaneous countermeasures had no significant effects with the guilty subjects, but they did produce a significant effect with innocent subjects. Innocent subjects who attempted a spontaneous countermeasure significantly shifted their scores in the deceptive direction, making it more likely that they would fail the test. It is important to note that providing the subjects with detailed information about the rationale of the control question test and suggestions concerning countermeasures that might be used did not enable them to defeat the test.[4]

---

[3]Podlesny, Is the Guilty Knowledge Polygraph Technique Applicable in Criminal Investigations? A Review of FBI Case Records, 20 Crime Laboratory Dig. 59 (1993).

[Section 8:33]

[1]See, e.g., Honts, Interpreting Research on Countermeasures and the Physiological Detection of Deception, 15 J. Police Sci. & Admin. 204 (1987); David C. Raskin, Polygraph Techniques for the Detection of Deception, in Psychological Methods in Criminal Investigation and Evidence 247 (David C. Raskin ed., 1989).

[2]Honts et al., Effects of Spontaneous Countermeasures on the Physiological Detection of Deception, 16 J. Police Sci. & Admin. 91 (1988).

[3]Charles R. Honts et al., Effects Of Spontaneous Countermeasures Used Against The Comparison Question Test, Polygraph (forthcoming 2001).

[4]Rovner et al., Effects of Information and Practice on Detection of Deception, 16 Psychophysiology 197 (1979).

## § 8:34 Areas of scientific agreement and disagreement— Countermeasures—Countermeasures and the CQT

A series of studies by Honts and his colleagues examined the effects of specific-point mental and physical countermeasures with the CQT.[1] In these studies, guilty subjects in realistic mock-crime experiments were trained for approximately 30 minutes in the use of one or more of the following countermeasures: biting the tongue, pressing the toes to the floor, mentally subtracting sevens from a number larger than 200. They were fully informed about the nature of the CQT and told that to pass the test they would have to produce larger physiological reactions to the control questions than to the relevant questions. They were instructed to begin their countermeasure as soon as they recognized any control question, stop the countermeasure long enough to answer the question, and resume and continue their countermeasure until the next question began. All subjects were motivated by the promise of a cash bonus if they were successful in producing a truthful outcome.

Across this series of studies, approximately half of the decisions with trained countermeasure subjects were incorrect. There was no significant difference between mental and physical countermeasures, and experienced examiners were unable to detect the use of countermeasures either by inspecting the polygraph charts or by observing the subjects' overt behavior. However, computerized scoring of the polygraph charts outperformed the human evaluators and was more robust in the face of countermeasures. When the discriminant analysis classification model of Kircher & Raskin was applied to these data,[2] the false negative rate was reduced by half.[3] It seems likely that statistical models can be developed to discriminate countermeasure users from innocent subjects and improve this performance. Moreover, it should be noted that all of the countermeasure research data are from laboratory studies because it would be unethical and possibly illegal to train criminal suspects to apply countermeasures in order to defeat law enforcement or defense polygraph examinations in actual criminal cases.[4] Since the task of a countermeasure subject should be easier in the laboratory than in a field setting where the relevant questions are more powerful, the findings of laboratory studies of countermeasures are likely to represent a worst case scenario with regard to the effectiveness of

---

[Section 8:34]

[1]Honts et al., Effects of Physical Countermeasures on the Physiological Detection of Deception, 70 J. Applied Psychol. 177 (1985); Honts et al., Effects of Physical Countermeasures and Their Electromyographic Detection During Polygraph Tests for Deception, 1 J. Psychophysiology 241 (1987); Honts et al., Mental and Physical Countermeasures Reduce the Accuracy of Polygraph Tests, 79 J. Applied Psych. 252 (1994).

[2]Kircher & Raskin, Human Versus Computerized Evaluations of Polygraph Data in Laboratory Setting, 73 J. Applied Psychol. 291 (1988).

[3]Honts et al., Mental and Physical Countermeasures Reduce the Accuracy of Polygraph Tests, 79 J. Applied Psych. 252 (1994).

[4]Lykken attacks polygraph evidence favorable to a defendant by repeatedly reporting the alleged results of an unpublished countermeasures field study that he designed and conducted with the aid of Floyd Fay, an Ohio prison inmate who had failed two polygraphs and was convicted of murder. See Raskin, Science, Competence and Polygraph Techniques, 8 Crim. Def. 11 (1981).

Lykken provided Fay with information to train other prison inmates to defeat polygraph tests administered during criminal investigations in the prison and claimed that he and Fay were successful in assisting 23 of 27 guilty prisoners to fool the polygraph. However, they presented no data other than Fay's claims that all of the prisoners he trained according to Lykken's instructions told him that they were guilty and that they took polygraph tests administered by the prison authorities. Fay reported that 23 of his fellow inmates told him they had used the Lykken countermeasure techniques to fool the polygraph. This claim was based on nothing more than undocumented and unsubstantiated claims by a prison inmate about what he claims other admitted felons told him about polygraph tests they claimed to have taken and beaten. Aside from the ethical issues raised by such a "study," Lykken's report violates all of the requirements for a scientific study put forward by Iacono, Lykken, and everyone else. As one of us told Floyd Fay, "If you can't trust the reports made by a convicted felon, who can you trust?" Interestingly, Fay admitted to one of us that he unsuccessfully used countermeasures on one of the tests that he failed.

countermeasures.

There is no published research on the effects of countermeasures on the DLT. However, the dynamics and scoring of the DLT are very similar to the CQT, and there is no reason to expect that the DLT is more or less susceptible to countermeasures than the CQT.

### § 8:35 Areas of scientific agreement and disagreement— Countermeasures—Countermeasures and the GKT

In 1960, Lykken made an effort to train a group of psychologists, psychiatrists, and medical students to beat a GKT.[1] He informed his subjects about the nature of the GKT and instructed them about various maneuvers designed to augment their responses to the incorrect items. Despite the sophistication of the subjects and Lykken's efforts, he failed to produce any effects of countermeasure training. However, subsequent research and analysis discovered a serious methodological flaw in Lykken's research.[2] Elaad's research was somewhat more successful.[3] Significant effects were obtained by having subjects mentally count sheep during the presentation of all of the items on a GKT, but the countermeasure effects were not dramatic.

These results and others that indicate a lack of effects of drugs on the GKT have led some proponents of the GKT to conclude that the GKT is immune to the effects of countermeasures.[4] However, a study by Honts and his colleagues has shown that conclusion to be incorrect. They examined the effects of pressing the toes to the floor and mentally subtracting sevens on the accuracy of the GKT.[5] Using methods similar to those previously described in studies of countermeasures and the CQT, they informed mock-crime subjects about the nature of the GKT. They told them that in order to pass the GKT they would have to produce larger physiological responses to the noncritical items than to the key items. Subjects were offered a monetary bonus if they could pass their GKT. Ninety percent of the subjects trained in a physical countermeasure and 60% of the subjects trained in a mental countermeasure were able to beat the GKT. The results of this study clearly demonstrate that the accuracy of the GKT is substantially reduced by countermeasures and that the GKT may be even more susceptible than the CQT to the effects of physical countermeasures. However, as with the CQT, the application of the Kircher and Raskin discriminant classification model[6] to these data dramatically improved performance.[7]

### § 8:36 Areas of scientific agreement and disagreement—The polygraph in practice—Application of comparison question tests

Comparison question tests are the most widely used techniques in criminal

---

**[Section 8:35]**

[1]Lykken, The Validity of the Guilty Knowledge Technique: The Effects of Faking, 44 J. Applied Psychol. 258 (1960).

[2]Honts, et al., Mental and Physical Countermeasures Reduce the Accuracy of the Concealed Knowledge Test, 33 Psychophysiology 84 (1994); Honts & Kircher, Legends Of The Concealed Knowledge Test: Lykken's Distributional Scoring System Fails To Detect Countermeasures, 32 Psychophysiology S41 (1995).

[3]Elaad & Ben-Shakkar, Effects of Mental Countermeasures on Psychophysiological Detection in the Guilty Knowledge Test, 11 Int'l J. Psychophysiology 99 (1991).

[4]Gershon Ben-Shakar & John J. Furedy, Theories and Applications in the Detection of Deception (1990).

[5]Honts, et al., Mental and Physical Countermeasures Reduce the Accuracy of the Concealed Knowledge Test, 33 Psychophysiology 84 (1994).

[6]Kircher & Raskin, Human Versus Computerized Evaluations of Polygraph Data in Laboratory Setting, 73 J. Applied Psychol. 291 (1988).

[7]Honts, et al., Mental and Physical Countermeasures Reduce the Accuracy of the Concealed Knowledge Test, 33 Psychophysiology 84 (1994).

investigations and judicial proceedings.[1] Almost every major federal, state, and local law enforcement agency employs such tests to reduce the number of suspects so that limited resources can be focused on likely suspects, that is, those who have failed polygraph examinations. Comparison question tests are also used to examine prime suspects and persons formally charged with criminal acts.

In many jurisdictions, prosecutors and defense attorneys make informal agreements that if the suspect or defendant passes a polygraph examination from a competent and well-qualified examiner, the prosecutor will seriously consider dismissing the charges. Alternatively, prior to the conduct of a polygraph examination, prosecutors and defense attorneys may enter into formal stipulations that the results will be admissible as evidence at trial. Under these arrangements, costly trials are often avoided by guilty pleas or dismissals based in part on the results of polygraph tests. Polygraph tests are sometimes used by prosecutors to assess the veracity of individuals involved in the crime who may testify for the prosecution in exchange for immunity or reduced charges if they demonstrate their truthfulness on the polygraph test. Also, some courts use polygraph evidence in postconviction proceedings, such as sentencing and motions for new trials. A comprehensive compilation and discussion of the federal and state case law and legislation concerning the admissibility of polygraph evidence and the polygraph examiner licensing regulations in the United States was provided by Morris.[2] Honts and Perry and others have provided a summary of the arguments in support of the use of polygraph tests in legal proceedings.[3]

### § 8:37    Areas of scientific agreement and disagreement—The polygraph in practice—Application of the guilty knowledge test

Several practical problems prevent widespread use of the GKT, some of which concern the circumstances surrounding many crimes. Consistently choosing details of a crime that are likely to be recognized by the guilty suspect during the test is an insurmountably difficult task for investigators and polygraph examiners. Details of a crime that may seem quite distinctive and memorable to an investigator or polygraph examiner may be unnoticed or forgotten by the perpetrator because of emotional stress, confusion, inattention, or intoxication during the commission of the crime. Thus, the false negative rate of the GKT in criminal investigation is likely to be high.

The utility of the GKT is also limited because innocent subjects frequently are informed about the details of the crime prior to taking a polygraph test. It is common practice for police investigators to disclose details of crimes to suspects in the process of interrogation, for news media to publicize the details of many crimes, and for defense attorneys to discuss the details of police reports and allegations with their clients. Thus, the majority of innocent and guilty criminal suspects obtain knowledge of the critical crime information after the crime was committed, which renders them unsuitable for a GKT.

Many criminal investigations do not lend themselves to the GKT because certain types of crimes characteristically have no special information that is unknown to

---

**[Section 8:36]**

[1]Raskin, The Polygraph in 1986: Scientific, Professional, and Legal Issues Surrounding Applications and Acceptance of Polygraph Evidence, 1986 Utah L. Rev. 29 (1986).

[2]Roberta A. Morris, The Admissibility of Evidence Derived From Hypnosis and Polygraph, in Psychological Methods in Criminal Investigation and Evidence 333 (David C. Raskin ed., 1989).

[3]Honts & Perry, Polygraph Admissibility: Changes and Challenges, 16 L. & Hum. Behav. 357 (1992); McCall, Misconceptions and Reevaluation—Polygraph Admissibility After Rock and Daubert, 1996 U. Ill. L. Rev. 363; Imwinkelreid & McCall, Issues Once Moot: The Other Evidentiary Objections to the Admission of Exculpatory Polygraph Examinations, 32 Wake Forest L. Rev. 1045 (1997).

potential polygraph subjects. Such situations include allegations of forcible sexual assault when the accused claims that the sexual acts were consensual, claims of self-defense in physical assault and homicide cases, and crimes in which the suspect admits having been present at the scene but denies any criminal participation. Because of its high rate of false negative errors and inapplicability in most investigative situations, the GKT is not likely to become a substitute for comparison question tests.

## § 8:38 Areas of scientific agreement and disagreement—General acceptance of polygraph testing by the scientific community

Several sources of evidence demonstrate that the validity of polygraph tests is generally accepted in the relevant scientific community. Two valid surveys of the Society for Psychophysiological Research (SPR) directly addressed the general acceptance issue.[1] The SPR is a professional society of scientists who study how the mind and body interact, which makes it an appropriate scientific organization for assessing general acceptance. The Gallup Organization survey was replicated and extended in 1994 by Amato at the University of North Dakota. The results of those surveys were very consistent. Approximately two-thirds of the doctoral-level members of the SPR who were surveyed stated that polygraph tests are a valuable diagnostic tool when considered with other available information.[2] When only those respondents who described themselves as highly informed about the scientific polygraph literature are considered, the %age who indicated that polygraph tests are a useful diagnostic tool rose to 83%. Since fewer than 10% reported being involved in conducting polygraph examinations professionally, the results were not influenced by financial interests of the respondents. These findings indicate that there is a great deal of acceptance of polygraph techniques by members of the SPR.[3]

In November 2000, Honts, Thurber, and their students conducted a telephone

---

[Section 8:38]

[1]The Gallup Organization, Survey of the Members of the Society for Psychophysiological Research Concerning Their Opinions of Polygraph Test Interpretations, 13, Polygraph, 153 (1984); Susan L. Amato, A Survey of The Members of the Society for Psycholphsiological Research Regarding The Polygraphs: Opinions and Implications (1993) (Unpublished Master's Thesis, University of North Dakota, Grand Forks) (on file with authors).

[2]Respondents in both surveys gave responses to the following question: Which one of these four statements best describes your own opinion of polygraph test interpretations by those who have received systematic training in the technique, when they are called upon to interpret whether a subject is or is not telling the truth? A) It is a sufficiently reliable method to be the sole determinant, B) It is a useful diagnostic tool when considered with other available information, C) It is of questionable usefulness, entitled to little weight against other available information, D) It is of no usefulness.

[3]A third survey of the members of the SPR was reported by Iacono and Lykken in The Scientific Status of Research on Polygraph Techniques: The Case Against Polygraph Tests, Modern Scientific Evidence: The Law and Science of Expert Testimony, (David L. Faigman, David Kaye,

Michael J. Saks, & Joseph Sanders eds. 1997); also partially available at Iacono & Lykken, The Validity of the Lie Detector: Two Surveys of Scientific Opinion, 87 J. Applied Psych. 426 (1997). Iacono and Lykken are two of the most outspoken critics of polygraph testing. However, the present authors believe that the Iacono and Lykken survey is so flawed and suspect that it cannot be used for any substantive purpose. Problems with the Iacono and Lykken study include: (1) the cover letter for the Iacono and Lykken survey described it as answering questions regarding the admissibility of polygraph evidence in court, rather than the scientific validity of the technique. They inappropriately asked the respondents to make a political and legal judgment rather than a scientific one. Few, if any, SPR members have the legal background to offer an opinion about admissibility. In contrast, Amato and Honts presented the issues in the context of whether or not the SPR should have a formal scientific policy regarding the validity of polygraph testing; (2) court-ordered discovery and cross-examination in the cases of *State of Washington v. Daniel Gallegos*, 95-1-02749-7 (1996) and *Steve Griffith v. Muscle Improvement, Inc.*, Superior Court of California, sworn deposition 21 April 1998, forced Iacono to reveal that the sample of respondents to the Iacono and Lykken survey described themselves as very uninformed about the topic of polygraph examinations. Iacono and Lykken's respondents

survey of the at-large members of the American Psychology-Law Society (AP-LS). The AP-LS is a particularly relevant scientific group because the members are highly familiar with the nature and difficulty of applied psychology-law research and because they are generally familiar with the legal requirements for the admissibility of scientific evidence. The AP-LS members were asked about a variety of issues concerning polygraph research, general acceptance, and relative validity of the polygraph. The survey required about 10 minutes, and 72% of those contacted agreed to respond. Subjects were told that their responses should take into consideration the use of the comparison question test in forensic situations.

The AP-LS respondents reported having read an average of 14 articles from peer-reviewed publications concerning the polygraph, which is nearly five times the number indicated by the SPR respondents in the Iacono and Lykken survey. The AP-LS members indicated a generally favorable attitude toward the use of laboratory data for estimating the validity of the polygraph in the real world. The majority of the respondents (89%) indicated that laboratory studies should be given at least some weight by policy makers and the courts, and a large number (49%) stated that moderate to considerable weight should be given to laboratory results.[4] This finding strikingly contrasts to the position espoused by Iacono and Lykken, who dismiss

---

were asked, "About how many empirical studies, literature reviews, commentaries, or presentations at scientific meetings dealing with the validity of the CQT have you read or attended?" Unfortunately, subjects were asked to respond on an unusual nonlinear scale. Conversion of the scale units to numbers of items indicates that the average respondent had contact with only three items dealing with the validity of the polygraph. Since the responses on this nonlinear scale are positively skewed, this means that many more than 50% of the subjects responded that they had contact with fewer than three items. In light of the large volume of scientific articles and presentations on this topic (we have either authored or co-authored more than 300 such papers and presentations ourselves), these data demonstrate that the Iacono and Lykken sample was relatively ignorant about the science relating to the polygraph; therefore, the subjects were not qualified to offer an opinion about its scientific validity. This information, which Iacono and Lykken chose not to include in either of their publications, would remain hidden were it not for compulsory discovery and cross-examination; (3) another anomaly in the Iacono and Lykken data analysis makes it impossible to compare some of their results to the other surveys in any meaningful way. In defining their "highly informed" group, Iacono and Lykken included those who chose four or higher on their seven-point scale of polygraph knowledge, whereas Amato and Honts included only those who chose 5 and above. This difference in cutting scores makes it impossible to compare these results across the two surveys. Because Iacono and Lykken included relatively ignorant respondents in their highly informed group, their entire analysis is suspect; (4) in their 1997 chapter in this volume, Iacono and Lykken described their survey as a "random sample." However, in their publication Iacono and Lykken revealed that their sampling was not random.

They deliberately excluded the authors of this chapter, and possibly other scientific supporters of the polygraph; and (5) because of Iacono and Lykken's unusual and suspicious data analyses and their misrepresentation of the survey in a publication intended for the legal profession, Amato and Honts were concerned that there might be other undisclosed problems with the Iacono and Lykken survey. Under the ethical standards of the American Psychological Association, scientists are required to make their data available for reanalysis by qualified scientists. On March 10, 1997 and subsequent occasions, Amato and Honts wrote Iacono and then Lykken requesting the data from their survey for the purpose of performing an independent reanalysis. To date, they have refused to provide their data. However, Iacono subsequently requested copies of the data from the Amato and Honts survey, which were provided to Iacono within two weeks of the receipt of their request. Iacono and Lykken have said they offered to share their data with Amato and Honts, which is misleading. They offered to provide only the summary data upon which their published analyses were based and would allow Amato and Honts simply to check their calculations. Since they would not permit discovery of other possible irregularities in their analyses and reports nor permit a reanalysis that would allow the results to be compared to the findings of the Amato and Honts survey, their offer was rejected. Iacono and Lykken's claim that they offered access to their data is simply disingenuous.

[4]Respondents were asked the following question: Laboratory mock-crime studies are often used to study polygraph tests. Consider a properly designed and conducted study that employed a realistic mock-crime paradigm (for example a guilty subject goes to an unfamiliar place and takes money from a cash box) and used techniques that are as similar as possible to actual field practice. How much weight should policy makers and

such studies. The opinions of the members of the AP-LS about laboratory research are particularly persuasive since they routinely apply the results of science to real-world problems, a process relatively unfamiliar to SPR members whose research is typically theoretically oriented. The vast majority of the AP-LS respondents (91%) believe that it is possible to conduct useful field studies of the polygraph.[5] Nearly all of them (96%) stated that the publication of polygraph studies in peer-reviewed psychology journals is indicative of a general acceptance of the scientific methodology used in those studies.[6]

The AP-LS respondents were also asked about the validity of the CQT. Two approaches were taken to that issue. Respondents were first asked to compare the usefulness of a properly conducted CQT to seven other types of frequently admitted evidence. The majority of respondents indicated that polygraph results are at least as useful as, or more useful than, psychological opinions about parental fitness, psychological opinions regarding malingering, eyewitness identification, psychological assessments of dangerousness, and psychological assessment of temporary insanity, but are less useful than fingerprint and DNA evidence. They were also asked their opinion of the impact that CQT polygraph evidence would have on the accuracy of judicial verdicts about guilt and innocence. The majority (52%) reported that judicial decision accuracy would be improved by allowing polygraph evidence, while 20% stated that polygraph evidence would have no impact on judicial accuracy. Only 28% indicated that the accuracy of verdicts would decrease if polygraph experts were allowed to testify.

The results of the AP-LS survey present an overall picture that strongly supports the usefulness of polygraph evidence in court. This relevant and knowledgeable scientific community, which is highly experienced with applied research and the requirements of the legal profession, believes that polygraph tests are at least as accurate as many types of evidence currently admitted in court. Moreover, the majority stated that introduction of polygraph evidence would improve the accuracy of judicial decisionmaking. These results replicate and extend the results reported by Gallup[7] and Amato.[8] They also underscore concerns about the findings reported by Iacono and Lykken.[9]

Another important indicator of the acceptance of the psychophysiological detection of deception in the scientific community is provided by the large number of original scientific studies published in peer-reviewed scientific journals. Studies reporting positive results for the validity of polygraph examinations have appeared in the *Journal of Applied Psychology, Journal of General Psychology, Psychophysiology, Journal of Police Science and Administration, Current Directions in Psychological Science, Psychological Bulletin, Journal of Research in Personality, Law and Human Behavior,* and many others. The review and acceptance process for these

---

courts give to the results of such studies in estimating the validity the polygraph in real world tests? Please choose one of the following: a. No weight, b. Little weight, c. Some weight, d. Moderate weight, e. Considerable weight.

[5]Respondents were asked the following question: Do you believe that it is possible to conduct a scientific field validity study of polygraph testing that can yield a useful estimate of the validity of the comparison question test? Yes or No.

[6]Respondents were asked the following question: In general, do you believe that studies of the polygraph published in peer-reviewed scientific journals (e.g., Psychophysiology, Journal of Applied Psychology, The Journal of General

Psychology) are based on generally accepted scientific methodology? Yes or No.

[7]Gallup Organization, Survey of the Members of the Society for Psychophysiological Research Concerning Their Opinions of Polygraph Test Interpretations, 13, Polygraph, 153 (1984).

[8]Gallup Organization, Survey of the Members of the Society for Psychophysiological Research Concerning Their Opinions of Polygraph Test Interpretations, 13, Polygraph, 153 (1984).

[9]Iacono and Lykken in The Scientific Status of Research on Polygraph Techniques: The Case Against Polygraph Tests, Modern Scientific Evidence: The Law and Science of Expert Testimony, (David L. Faigman, David Kaye, Michael J. Saks, & Joseph Sanders eds. 1997).

journals is lengthy and difficult. The journal editor first sends a submitted article for review by two or three independent scientists who are knowledgeable about the topic and research methods but are not personally involved with the article under consideration. These peer-reviewers comment on the quality of the literature review, the research design, the statistical analyses, the reasonableness of the conclusions drawn, and the appropriateness of the article for publication in the journal. The editor also reviews the article and incorporates the comments and recommendations of the reviewers to make a decision about publication. Minor or extensive revisions are usually required before publication. Manuscripts with unacceptable scientific methods, statistics, or insupportable conclusions are not published (assuming that the methods and data have been honestly and completely reported). For example, the *Journal of Applied Psychology* has published numerous articles on the psychophysiological detection of deception,[10] even though it rejects 85% of the manuscripts submitted for publication. The publication of numerous articles in mainstream journals of scientific psychology clearly demonstrates that the psychophysiological detection of deception is generally accepted by the community of scientific psychologists. This conclusion was supported by 96% of the AP-LS respondents in the survey described above.

## § 8:39    Major developments and future prospects

Major beneficial effects have been produced by improvements in physiological measures and examination procedures and the development and implementation of computer techniques through federally funded research that began at the University of Utah in 1970. By applying the methods and principles of human psychology and psychophysiology, Raskin, Kircher, Honts, and their colleagues refined the pretest interview, improved and developed new test methods, developed better techniques for recording and analyzing the physiological reactions, improved the reliability and accuracy of the numerical scoring system, and developed the first computerized polygraph. The latest version, the Computerized Polygraph System (CPS), is based on the methods and findings of their 30 years of scientific research on the physiological detection of deception.[1] The resulting examination procedures and computer methodology have simplified and improved the standardization of the polygraph examination, enhanced the quality of the polygraph recordings, increased the reliability and accuracy of the polygraph results, and provided higher quality printouts and documentation of the entire procedure. These improvements have generally raised the quality of training and practice of polygraph examiners in agencies such

---

[10]Some of the articles on the polygraph published in the Journal of Applied Psychology are as follows: P. J. Bersh, A Validation Study of Polygraph Examiner Judgments, 53 J. Applied Psychol. 399 (1969); Davidson, Validity of the Guilty Knowledge Technique: The Effects of Motivation, 52 J. Applied Psychol. 62–65 (1968); Elaad, Detection of Guilty Knowledge in Real-Life Criminal Investigations, 75 J. Applied Psychol. 521–529 (1990); Elaad et al., Detection Measures in Real-Life Criminal Guilty Knowledge Tests, 77 J. Applied Psychol. 757–767 (1992); Ginton et al., A Method for Evaluating the Use of the Polygraph in a Real-Life Situation, 67 J. Applied Psychol. 131–137 (1982); Honts et al., Effects of Physical Countermeasures on the Physiological Detection of Deception, 70 J. Applied Psychol. 177–187 (1985); Honts et al., Mental and Physical Countermeasures Reduce the Accuracy of Polygraph Tests, 79 J. Applied Psychol. 252–259

(1994); Horvath, The Effect of Selected Variables on Interpretation of Polygraph Records, 62 J. Applied Psychol. 127–136 (1977); Kircher & Raskin, Human Versus Computerized Evaluations of Polygraph Data in a Laboratory Setting, 73 J. Applied Psychol. 291–302 (1988); Patrick & Iacono, Validity of the Control Question Polygraph Test: The Problem of Sampling Bias, 76 J. Applied Psychol. 229–238 (1991); Podlesny & Truslow, Validity of an Expanded-Issue (Modified General Question) Polygraph Technique in a Simulated Distributed-Crimes-Roles Context, 78 J. Applied Psychol. 5 (1993).

**[Section 8:39]**

[1]Information about the CPS can be obtained from the Stoelting Company, 620 Wheat Lane, Wood Dale, IL 60191, at http://www.stoeltingco.com.

as the U.S. Secret Service, Royal Canadian Mounted Police, other federal, state, provincial, and local law enforcement agencies, and private examiners in the United States, Canada, and many other countries.

As a result of efforts by scientists and policy makers, many of the most objectionable applications of polygraph tests have been eliminated or severely curtailed by recent legislation and administrative decisions.[2] Along with the reduction in undesirable applications, a large number of the least competent polygraph practitioners were forced to leave the profession. This raised the level of competence and practice in the field and also fostered an increase in research funds and growth of research programs in universities and government agencies. These programs have also served to improve the training and competence of government, law enforcement, and private polygraph examiners.

*Automated Test Administration.* In an effort to reduce problems that may be associated with examinations performed by human polygraph examiners, Honts and Amato designed a completely automated polygraph test.[3] In the context of a preemployment screening polygraph examination, they compared the accuracy of polygraph tests conducted by an experienced human polygraph examiner to a standardized examination conducted by tape recording. Automated examination outcomes were significantly more accurate than human-administered examinations. Although these results were obtained from preemployment type polygraph examinations that are not directly generalizable to forensic settings, they suggest a promising area of research. If similar results can be obtained with forensic polygraph examinations, then a major source of variability and possible bias in polygraph examinations (the examiner) can be greatly reduced. The resulting increase in standardization and decrease in variability would be highly desirable.

*The Impact of Outside Issues.* Polygraph examiners have long been concerned that outside issues may reduce the accuracy of a polygraph examination. Consider a subject taking a polygraph test for the theft of a small amount of money from a convenience market. The subject had taken the money but is also guilty of a more serious, undiscovered crime of armed robbery and shooting. Many in the polygraph profession believe that the subject's secret concern about the more serious crime might overshadow the relatively minor issue of theft of money and result in a false negative outcome (a guilty person producing a truthful outcome). These examiners attempt to counter the potential effects of outside issues by asking outside-issue questions, e.g., "Is there something else you are afraid I will ask you a question about even though I told you I would not?" Until recently, neither the effects of outside issues nor the effectiveness of outside-issue questions had been studied scientifically.

Honts and his colleagues examined the effects of outside issues in a laboratory

---

[2]The most important development was the passage of the Employee Polygraph Protection Act of 1988, 29 U.S.C.A. §§ 2001 to 2009. The regulations promulgated by the Department of Labor [29 C.F.R. § 801; 56 Fed. Reg. 9046 (1991)] resulted in the elimination of more than one million tests that were conducted each year on applicants for jobs in the private sector and the consequent reduction in the number of polygraph examiners whose primary income was derived from such undesirable and abusive practices. One of us (Raskin) served as the expert for the U.S. Senate Committee on Labor and Human Resources in drafting the legislation and testifying at the Senate hearings.

[3]Charles R. Honts & Susan L. Amato, The automated polygraph examination: Final report of U. S. Government Contract No. 110224-1998-MO. Boise State University (1999). Also reported as: Charles R. Honts & Susan L. Amato, Human V. Machine: Research Examining The Automation Of Polygraph Testing. Paper presented at the annual meeting of the Rocky Mountain Psychological Association, Fort Collins Colorado (April, 1999), and Susan L. Amato & Charles R. Honts, Automated Polygraph Examination Outperforms Human In Employment Screening Context. Paper presented at the annual meeting of the Midwestern Psychological Association, Chicago, Illinois (May, 1999).

mock-crime experiment.[4] Half of the subjects stole $1 and half did not. Half of the innocent subjects and half of the guilty subjects then committed another crime, the theft of $20. All subjects were given a standard CQT concerning only the theft of $1. Half of the polygraph tests included two outside-issue questions and half contained none. Subjects were told that if they passed their polygraph test, they could keep the money they had stolen. Subjects who stole neither the $1, nor the $20, were offered a $1 bonus if they could pass their polygraph test. Performance was very high for subjects tested with a standard CQT and who did not have the outside issue. With innocent subjects, 91.7% were correctly classified and there were 8.3% false positive errors. With guilty subjects, 91.7% were correctly classified and 8.3% of the outcomes were inconclusive. There were no false negative errors.

The presence or absence of an outside issue produced results that failed to support the traditional beliefs of the polygraph profession. In contrast to the concerns of the polygraph profession, the outside issue manipulation had a minimal and insignificant impact on subjects who stole the $1 (the actual topic of the examination). However, the presence of an outside issue had a major impact on subjects who were innocent of stealing the $1. For those subjects, correct classification rates dropped from 91.7% to 25.0%, a highly significant and powerful result. Furthermore, the outside issue questions were ineffective for detecting the presence of outside issues. These findings might explain some of the variability in false positive errors in field studies of polygraph validity. If the subject population of an agency includes many subjects who have outside issues, then the false positive rate would be expected to be higher and vice versa. The laboratory findings further support the notion that greater confidence can be placed in truthful outcomes of polygraph examinations, whereas failed polygraph examinations should be viewed more cautiously. Finally, the results of the outside issue study suggest that the exact wording of relevant questions is not critical for the detection of subjects who are attempting deception. These results suggest that even if specific details included in a relevant question were incorrect (for example, dates, amounts of money, or specific sexual acts), a subject attempting deception in the matter under investigation would still respond to those relevant questions and would very likely fail the examination. The results are consistent with, and extend the similar findings of Podlesny and Truslow.[5]

### § 8:40 Misconceptions about control (comparison) questions

Iacono and Lykken have provided numerous and lengthy arguments attacking the CQT and the DLT while they promote the GKT. Their arguments and analyses rely on a combination of (1) incorrect assumptions and misunderstandings of the conceptual bases of the CQT and DLT; (2) selective presentation of the available scientific and professional literature; (3) flawed theoretical speculation based on an incomplete understanding of actual applications of polygraph techniques and other critical aspects of law enforcement investigations and the criminal justice process; and (4) inaccurate and misleading descriptions of virtually all of the research they selected to present (including their own).

The Iacono and Lykken attack on CQT theory centers on the so-called control questions, which they claim "do not serve as strict controls in the scientific sense of this term; the subject's responses to the CQT's control questions do not predict how

---

[4]Charles R. Honts et al., Outside Issues Dramatically Reduce The Accuracy Of Polygraph Tests Given To Innocent Individuals, presented at the American Psychology-Law Society Biennial Meeting, New Orleans, Louisiana (March 2000).

[5]Podlesny & Truslow, Validity of an Expanded-Issue (Modified General Question) Polygraph Technique in a Simulated Distributed-Crime-Roles Context, 78 J. Applied Psychol. 788 (1993).

this subject should respond to the relevant questions if he is answering truthfully."[1] In fact, the control (comparison) questions are designed to predict how the subject would respond to the relevant questions if he were answering *deceptively*.[2] This is the very heart of the CQT and the DLT, and Iacono and Lykken's failure to understand this fundamental principle renders their entire analysis moot. The problem is compounded by their apparent failure to understand how control questions are actually formulated. Rather than demanding great examiner skill, as Iacono and Lykken claim, control questions require only basic knowledge to formulate and properly present to the subject. They also speculate that guilty subjects may react more strongly to the control questions because they encompass other criminal activity that they have not disclosed, thereby beating the test. However, for many laboratory subjects, their lies to the control questions encompass prior criminal acts far more serious than the mock crime, yet they routinely fail the CQT even though there is only a few dollars at stake when they lie to the relevant questions.[3]

## § 8:41 Misconceptions about control (comparison) questions— Inconsistency, selectivity, and misrepresentations

Iacono and Lykken change their requirements for valid research studies to fit the current circumstance. When it suits their purpose, they dismiss laboratory studies as useless for estimating polygraph accuracy in real life, stating that only field studies published in peer-reviewed scientific journals are useful. Their position is not supported by the science[1] nor by the opinions of the members of the American Psychology-Law Society as was described above. Furthermore, they ignore a powerful structural analysis demonstrating the fundamental correspondence between the psychophysiological processes underlying laboratory and field polygraphs,[2] as well as a meta-analysis[3] that indicated similar high levels of accuracy of well-executed field studies and laboratory studies that realistically simulate the field polygraph situation. On the other hand, when laboratory findings suit their immediate purposes, Iacono and Lykken frequently rely on carefully selected studies, presentations at scientific meetings, published abstracts, and unpublished studies to support their current argument.

When they are unable to find any basis for dismissing studies that contradict their position, Iacono and Lykken resort to more extreme solutions. Lykken testified that studies reporting higher accuracy rates than he claims are possible must have flaws in their research designs or analyses, even though he is unable to identify any flaws.[4] This unsupported backward inference defies science and simple logic. When

---

**[Section 8:40]**

[1]Iacono & Lykken, The Validity of the Lie Detector: Two Surveys of Scientific Opinion, 87 J. Applied Psych. at 597 (1997).

[2]See the discussion in Podlesny & Raskin, Physiological Measures and the Detection of Deception, 84 Psychological Bull. 782 (1977).

[3]See the review in Kircher et al., Meta-analysis of Mock Crime Studies of the Control Question Polygraph Technique, 12 Law & Hum. Behav. 79 (1988).

**[Section 8:41]**

[1]C. A. Anderson et al., Research in the Psychological Laboratory: Truth or Triviality?, 8

Curr. Dir. Psychological Sci. 3 (1999).

[2]See David C. Raskin et al., Recent Laboratory and Field Research on Polygraph Techniques, in Credibility Assessment 1 (John C. Yuille ed., 1989). See also Honts, et al., Mental and Physical Countermeasures Reduce the Accuracy of the Concealed Knowledge Test, 33 Psychophysiology 84 (1994) (reaching a similar conclusion through a different analysis).

[3]See Kircher et al., Meta-analysis of Mock Crime Studies of the Control Question Polygraph Technique, 12 Law & Hum. Behav. 79 (1988).

[4]*California v. Parrison and Parrison*, San Diego Superior Court, August 20, 1982.

confronted with the publication of the Honts field study,[5] which contradicted their major arguments against the CQT, they did not re-examine their position. Instead, they resorted to a series of baseless attacks against the editor and the editorial board of a respected peer-reviewed scientific journal that has been published for more than 70 years.[6]

In the 1997 edition of this volume, Iacono and Lykken presented misdescriptions of criminal investigative processes, how polygraphs are used, and the typical circumstances of confessions to create a basis for their argument that it is impossible to accurately assess the accuracy of field polygraph tests. Neither of them has any training or experience in these areas (collectively, we have more than 50 years of such experience), and they employed false assumptions that formed the basis for their erroneous analysis. They claimed that polygraphs are used by police when "there is no hard evidence against a suspect and no arrest has been made" and by defense attorneys when their clients have already "been arrested and there is sufficient evidence to warrant a trial. The rate of guilt thus must be higher for those who are defendants rather than suspects."[7] In reality, the opposites are true. Polygraphs are frequently used by police when they have reason to believe that the suspect is guilty and may confess, and by defense attorneys whose clients may or may have not been arrested or facing trial. Since most criminal cases are resolved by guilty pleas, a large proportion of those who demand a trial are actually innocent. Neither the failure to obtain a confession following a deceptive polygraph nor the suspect passing a polygraph is an automatic end to the investigation of that suspect or any other suspect. The police must continue to pursue investigations in spite of these factors, and many such suspects confess later in the investigation.

Iacono and Lykken used their erroneous assumptions to argue that field studies include only those cases where "a guilty suspect failed a CQT and subsequently confessed . . . [but] all polygraph errors in which an innocent person failed a test are omitted . . . [and] all cases in which a guilty subject erroneously passed a test would also be excluded. Thus, confession studies rely on a biased set of cases . . . where the original examiner was shown to be correct."[8] On the contrary, the field studies presented above in Table 4 included both types of cases where the original examiner was shown to be incorrect. Moreover, their argument inescapably leads to the conclusion that all field studies must show 100% accuracy on guilty and innocent subjects alike. Instead of examining the facts and data related to their assumptions, Iacono and Lykken then proposed a totally impractical study in which no suspect would be given any test results, none would be interrogated after failing the test, investigators would be deprived of any polygraph outcomes that would help them investigate or solve their cases, and innocent people would be forced to continue as suspects even after passing the polygraph. Such a study raises serious ethical and legal questions.

The above arguments are a variant of an illusory analysis that Iacono invented to attack the field studies based on confessions.[9] He suggested that a sampling anomaly allows a technique with only chance accuracy to produce an estimate that the

[5]Honts, The Psychophysiological Detection of Deception, 3 Current Directions in Psychol. Sci. 77 (1994).

[6]Iacono & Lykken, The Validity of the Lie Detector: Two Surveys of Scientific Opinion, 87 J. Applied Psych. at 227 (1997) (Pocket Part 2000). Lykken even went so far as to write one of Professor Honts' undergraduate students and suggest there was impropriety in the peer-review process that allowed publication of the Honts study. A copy of this letter is available from Dr. Honts on request.

[7]Iacono & Lykken, The Validity of the Lie Detector: Two Surveys of Scientific Opinion, 87 J. Applied Psych. at 599 (1997).

[8]Iacono & Lykken, The Validity of the Lie Detector: Two Surveys of Scientific Opinion, 87 J. Applied Psych. at 602 (1997).

[9]William J. Iacono, Can We Determine the Accuracy of Polygraph Tests? in 4 Advances in Psychophysiology (J. Richard Jennings et al., eds., 1991).

technique is 90% accurate. Iacono invented a set of circumstances to illustrate this possibility without any data to support his speculation. Although it cannot be tested empirically, Iacono and Lykken have treated this creation as if it were fact. Armed with this unsupported and misleading argument, they confuse triers of fact and lead them to question the value of all field studies of polygraphs. Therefore, Iacono's formulation requires a detailed analysis to expose its fundamental flaws.

Iacono made the following assumptions for his illusory analysis:

(1)  400 innocent and 400 guilty criminal suspects are tested;

(2)  the polygraph is not better than chance in identifying innocent or guilty subjects;

(3)  each crime has only two suspects;

(4)  a guilty suspect is tested first in half of the cases;

(5)  if the first suspect fails the test, the second suspect will not be tested;

(6)  neither innocent suspects nor guilty suspects who pass the test will ever confess; and

(7)  only 20% of the guilty who are interrogated will confess.

For the illusory analysis to produce the desired result, the following implicit assumptions are required:

(8)  the polygraph is the only source of information about who is guilty; and

(9)  guilty people confess only after failing a polygraph test.

Careful examination of Iacono's assumptions yields the following conclusions:

(1)  a base rate of 50% is statistically neutral, but may not be representative of field conditions. The base rate of guilt in criminal cases varies widely depending upon how and when the polygraph is used. If it is used early in an investigation, there are likely to be many more innocent than guilty subjects; if it is used late in an investigation, there may be many more guilty than innocent subjects. Changes in the base rate will dramatically alter the outcome of the thought experiment;

(2)  chance accuracy was assumed for the sake of argument and is contrary to research findings;

(3)  Iacono's assertion that this assumption can be made without a loss of generality is obviously incorrect;

(4)  this assumption is tenable only if the base rate is 50%, and then only if the order of testing subjects in forensic cases is random. Law enforcement typically tests subjects who are most likely guilty before they test those more likely to be innocent. They never select subjects by a formally random process;

(5)  this assumption is not in accord with common police practices. If the first suspect fails and does not confess, it is likely that other suspects will be tested. If other suspects pass their tests, more pressure will be brought to bear on the suspect who failed. Further investigation and interrogation often produce a confession from this suspect. Investigations continue until the cases are solved or found to be unsolvable;

(6)  this assumption is not in accord with standard police practice and forensic experience. The guilty individual may not confess after the polygraph (passed or failed), but may decide to confess later. This often occurs as the result of additional investigation revealing further evidence or as part of an agreement to resolve the case. Recent research suggests that false confessions by innocent people may be a significant problem;[10]

(7)  this assumption grossly underestimates the confession rate. The Department

---

[10]Kassin & Kiechel, The Social Psychology of    False Confessions: Compliance, Internalization,

of Defense reported a confession rate higher than 70% following failed polygraph tests;[11] the Federal Bureau of Investigation reported 56% confessions by deceptive suspects, the U.S. Secret Service reported that 70% of deceptive results were confirmed by admissions and confessions and more than 90% of polygraph examiners' decisions were later confirmed, and the Drug Enforcement Administration reported that 65% confess following a deceptive polygraph result and 85% of those found truthful are later confirmed by investigations;[12]

(8) This assumption is also incorrect. There are many other sources of information available to police. Honts and Raskin[13] and Raskin and his colleagues reported field studies in which evidence other than confessions was used to confirm polygraph results,[14] and Honts explored the use of that information in confirming polygraph test outcomes.[15] He found that approximately 80% of case files contained inculpatory information independent of confessions. The assumption that cases are solved only through polygraph tests is clearly not correct, but it is necessary for Iacono's thought experiment to work as described; and

(9) this assumption is contradicted by data. In the Honts field study,[16] *none* of the confessions that confirmed the innocent subjects was obtained from polygraph testing situations. This analysis clearly reveals that the Iacono illusory analysis is a post-hoc formulation designed specifically to support Iacono's unscientific hypothesis.[17]

In summary, the Iacono analysis lacks logic and contradicts established facts and produces a misleading conclusion. This is sophistry, not science.

## § 8:42    Misconceptions about control (comparison) questions—The friendly polygrapher

In discussing law enforcement and privileged polygraph tests, Iacono and Lykken stated, "The more usual case for an evidentiary hearing is one where the defense counsel arranges a privately administered or 'friendly' polygraph test . . . there is not a single study demonstrating that friendly tests are valid."[1] This argument was

---

and Confabulation, 7 Psycholological Sci. 125 (1996).

[11]Honts, The Emperor's New Clothes: Application of Polygraph Tests in the American Workplace, 4 Forensic Reports 91 (1991) and the sources cited therein.

[12]Scientific Validity of Polygraph Testing: A Research Review and Evaluation—Technical Memorandum, 111 (Washington, DC: U.S. Congress, Office of Technology Assessment, OTA-TM-H-15, November 1983).

[13]§ 8:30.

[14]§ 8:30.

[15]§ 8:30.

[16]§ 8:30.

[17]Iacono's hypothesis is literally "unscientific" in the sense that it cannot be falsified. There is no way to prove that any field study was not the result of processes similar to those invented by Iacono.

**[Section 8:42]**

[1]Iacono & Lykken, The Validity of the Lie

Detector: Two Surveys of Scientific Opinion, 87 J. Applied Psych. at 599 (1997). Unfortunately, Iacono and Lykken's lack of consistency is not restricted to academic arguments. Although they argue against the CQT and its use by defense attorneys, they themselves devised and performed a CQT on Wounded Knee criminal defendant Russell Means to be presented as evidence for the defense at Means' federal trial in Sioux Falls, South Dakota. This came to light after Lykken testified for the prosecution against the validity of polygraph techniques and the admission of such evidence on behalf of defendant William Wong (*R. v. Wong (No. 2)*, 1977 WL 58794 (B.C. S.C. 1976), Reversed by, 1978 WL 162930 (B.C. C.A. 1978)). During cross-examination, Lykken admitted under oath that he had never received training in the administration of polygraph tests and he did not believe in them. He admitted that he believed defendant Means was "guilty of the specific allegations against him . . . and was probably lying," but he was prepared to testify on his behalf in court because "in my opinion the application of the standard polygraphic inference rules would lead to the conclusion that he [Means] was telling

developed by Orne,[2] who speculated that a guilty suspect who takes a non-law enforcement polygraph examination on a confidential basis might beat the test because of a lack of fear that an adverse result will be disclosed to the authorities. This speculation was based solely on the results of an unrealistic laboratory study in which college students were given only card tests and not a CQT.[3] Orne argued that a suspect who expects that only favorable results will be reported has little at stake and is more confident, the examiner is more supportive, and the lack of fear of failure and subsequent disclosure will enable a guilty person to pass the test. However, Raskin demonstrated that the scientific literature provides no support for the friendly examiner hypothesis and generally contradicts it.[4]

As noted above, laboratory studies where there is little at stake routinely produce detection rates of approximately 90%, and laboratory studies using placebos and other procedures designed to make guilty subjects believe they can pass the polygraph test showed no reduction in detection rates even for the GKT, which is easier to beat than the CQT.[5] If Orne's hypothesis were correct, laboratory studies of the CQT would produce relatively more false negative than false positive errors, which is contrary to the data. Honts reviewed 20 laboratory studies of the CQT with a total of 567 guilty subjects and 490 innocent subjects.[6] The false negative rate was 12% and the false positive rate was 16%. This outcome is opposite to the prediction generated by the friendly examiner hypothesis. Notably, 6 of the 20 studies reported no errors with guilty subjects, even though they had no fear of any negative sanctions associated with failing the test.

Criminal suspects have no assurance that adverse results will remain confidential since most examiners advise them of their rights and obtain a written waiver prior to the test.[7] However, suspects have a great deal at stake. A favorable test may help to obtain a dismissal or acquittal on the charges, and an unfavorable outcome may result in increased legal costs, personal stress, and disruption of their relationship with their defense counsel. These are far greater motivations than the small amount of money guilty subjects have at stake when they routinely fail laboratory polygraph tests. Furthermore, in order to pass a CQT, the guilty suspect must show stronger physiological reactions to comparison (control) questions than to the relevant questions about the allegations. There is no known mechanism or logical argument that explains how a low level of fear or concern about the test outcome can selectively reduce the reactions to the relevant questions so as to produce the pattern of stronger reactions to the comparison questions that is indicative of truthfulness. In fact, fear is not a necessary part of any modern scientific polygraph theory.[8] The laboratory data and logical analysis contradict the "friendly examiner" hypothesis.

---

the truth." Lykken justified his actions by stating, "I felt that Mr. Means deserved and needed all the help he could get . . . the test interpreted in the usual way would come out in his favor. It seemed to me possible that it would come out that way precisely because I don't much believe in the test."

[2]Martin Orne, Implications of Laboratory Research for the Detection of Deception, in Legal Admissibility of the Polygraph 94 (N. Ansley ed. 1975).

[3]For a complete description and analysis, see Raskin, The Polygraph in 1986: Scientific, Professional, and Legal Issues Surrounding Applications and Acceptance of Polygraph Evidence, 1986 Utah L. Rev. 29 (1986).

[4]Raskin, The Polygraph in 1986: Scientific, Professional, and Legal Issues Surrounding

Applications and Acceptance of Polygraph Evidence, 1986 Utah L. Rev. 29 (1986).

[5]Timm, Effect of Altered Outcome Expectancies Stemming from Placebo and Feedback Treatments on the Validity of the Guilty Knowledge Technique, 67 J. Applied Psychol. 391 (1982).

[6]Charles R. Honts, Is It Time to Reject the Friendly Polygraph Examiner Hypothesis (FEPH)?, A paper presented at the annual meeting of the American Psychological Society, Washington, D.C (1997, May). Available at: http://truth.idbsu.edu/polygraph/fpeh.html.

[7]David C. Raskin, Polygraph Techniques for the Detection of Deception, in Psychological Methods in Criminal Investigation and Evidence 255 (D. Raskin ed. 1989).

[8]See Podlesny & Raskin, Physiological Measures and the Detection of Deception, 84

There are two published sets of data from tests of criminal suspects that strongly contradict the friendly examiner hypothesis. Raskin presented complete data from 12 years of his confidential CQT examinations for defense attorneys and nonconfidential tests for law enforcement, courts, and stipulated situations.[9] He reported that 58% of suspects who agreed in advance that the results would be provided to the prosecution passed their tests, but only 34% of those who took confidential defense tests were able to pass. In addition, the numerical scores were significantly more negative (in the deceptive direction) for confidential tests compared to the more positive scores (in the truthful direction) for nonconfidential tests. Honts recently presented a similar, complete set of data from 14 years of confidential and nonconfidential examinations.[10] He reported that 70% of the non-confidential tests were passed, while only 44% of the confidential tests were passed. These data also contradict the predictions of the friendly examiner hypothesis. The friendly examiner hypothesis fails on all counts. It is illogical, unsupported by laboratory studies, and contradicted by data from actual field cases.

## § 8:43    Misconceptions about control (comparison) questions—The polygraph and juries

One of the major issues addressed by the Court in *Scheffer*[1] concerned the potential impact of expert polygraph testimony on jury decisions. Opponents of the admission of polygraph evidence have long argued that such evidence will have an undue influence on jury decision processes, usurp the jury function, confuse the issues, and mislead the jury.[2] However, the majority of justices rejected those arguments in *Scheffer*. Their position is consistent with courtroom experiences in actual cases and the published scientific evidence. Numerous scientific studies have been performed on this topic using mock juries, post-trial interviews with jurors who were presented with expert polygraph testimony, and surveys of prosecutors and defense attorneys in cases where polygraph evidence was presented at trial.[3] The results consistently demonstrate that jurors are cautious with polygraph evidence, and they do not give it undue weight. Also consistent with the majority of the *Scheffer* court, the results show that polygraph testimony does not unduly prolong trials or jury deliberations. Prosecutors and defense attorneys who tried cases with polygraph evidence were highly satisfied with polygraph testimony and they did not believe that it had a disruptive impact on the trials or that the judge or jury disregarded significant evidence because of the polygraph testimony. Like other

---

Psychological Bull. 783 (1977); Rosenfeld, Alternative Views of Bashore and Rapp's (1993) Alternatives to Traditional Polygraphy: A Critique, 117 Psychological Bull. 159 (1995).

[9]Raskin, The Polygraph in 1986: Scientific, Professional, and Legal Issues Surrounding Applications and Acceptance of Polygraph Evidence, 1986 Utah L. Rev. at 62 (1986).

[10]See Charles R. Honts, Is It Time to Reject the Friendly Polygraph Examiner Hypothesis (FEPH)?, A paper presented at the annual meeting of the American Psychological Society, Washington, D.C (1997, May).

**[Section 8:43]**

[1]§ 8:26.

[2]See Abbell, Polygraph Evidence: the Case Against Admissibility in Federal Criminal Trials, 15 Am. Crim. L. Rev. 29, 38 (1977).

[3]Barnett, How Does a Jury View Polygraph

Examination Results?, 2 Polygraph 275 (1973); Brekke, et al., The Impact of Nonadversarial Versus Adversarial Expert Testimony, 15 Law & Hum. Behav. 451 (1991); Carlson et al., The Effect of Lie Detector Evidence on Jury Deliberations: An Empirical Study, 5 Police Sci. & Admin. 148 (1977); Cavoukian & Heslegrave, The Admissibility of Polygraph Evidence in Court: Some Empirical Findings, 4 Law & Hum. Behav. 117 (1980); Markwart & Lynch, The Effect of Polygraph Evidence on Mock Jury Decision-Making, 7 Police Sci. & Admin. 324 (1979); Meyers & Arbuthnot, Polygraph Testimony and Juror Judgments: A Comparison of the Guilty Knowledge Test and the Control Question Test, 27 J. Applied Soc. Psychol. 1421 (1997); R. Peters, A Survey of Polygraph Evidence in Criminal Trials, 68 A.B.A. J. 161 (1982); Vondergeest et al., Effects of Juror and Expert Witness Gender on Jurors' Perceptions of an Expert Witness, Modern Psychological Studies 1 (1993).

types of evidence, in some cases juries reached decisions that were contrary to the polygraph evidence. Thus, there are no scientific data to support the claims of critics that polygraph evidence is disruptive to the trial process, and the evidence and our own extensive experience in actual cases supports the usefulness of competent polygraph evidence at trial. More detailed analyses of these studies can be found in Raskin[4] and the Amicus Curiae Brief of the Committee of Concerned Social Scientists submitted in *Scheffer*.[5]

## § 8:44 Conclusions

We have spent much of our scientific careers conducting scientific research and development on polygraph techniques for the physiological detection of deception.[1] We have received numerous grants and contracts from federal agencies and universities in the United States and Canada for this research, and we have authored hundreds of scientific articles, chapters, books, and scientific presentations on these topics. Two of us have conducted polygraph examinations in more than 2,000 criminal and civil cases, including many of the most celebrated cases of the past three decades, and we have provided expert testimony hundreds of times in federal and state courts. On the basis of the extensive scientific evidence and our personal experiences in actual cases, we firmly believe that polygraph techniques and evidence are of great value to the criminal justice system and the courts. However, general acceptance by our legal system has lagged far behind the science and its applications.

Although virtually all federal, state, and local law enforcement agencies and prosecutors rely heavily on polygraph results, they have routinely opposed the admissibility of polygraph evidence at trial. This has been a major determiner of the long history of rejection by our courts. After the *Daubert* decision, it appeared that there was a new opportunity for the courts to correctly recognize the scientific basis for polygraph techniques.[2] Some influential law review articles argued for admissibility, but a flurry of attempts to admit polygraph evidence met with only limited success.[3] In spite of the strong scientific basis for admitting polygraph evidence at trial, the current status of polygraph evidence in our courts remains relatively unchanged. We believe this is the result of ingrained institutional impediments to the admission of such evidence.

Our judicial system is founded on the premise that jurors have both the ability and sole responsibility to judge the credibility of the testimony of witnesses who appear before them. However, a large and compelling body of scientific literature demonstrates the inability of people, including jurors, to make accurate judgments

---

[4]Raskin, The Polygraph in 1986: Scientific, Professional, and Legal Issues Surrounding Applications and Acceptance of Polygraph Evidence, 1986 Utah L. Rev. 29 (1986).

[5]Available through *Polygraph Law Resource Pages* at http://truth.idbsu.edu.

**[Section 8:44]**

[1]In is of interest to note that Raskin initiated the research program at the University of Utah after being asked to testify in 1970 in a capital case in which he criticized prosecution polygraph evidence based on police administration of an RIT. Raskin embarked on a scientific program that he expected would demonstrate that polygraph tests were not accurate. However, results of the first laboratory study of the accuracy of the CQT (see Barland & Raskin, An Evaluation of Field Techniques in Detection of Deception, 12 Psychophysiology 321 (1975)) contradicted the commonly held belief about polygraph inaccuracy, and he was obliged by the ethics and principles of science to revise his beliefs to be consistent with the data. Unfortunately, many of today's vocal critics of polygraph maintain their positions in spite of the large body of scientific data to the contrary.

[2]§§ 8:1 to 8:19.

[3]See McCall, Misconceptions and Reevaluation—Polygraph Admissibility After Rock and Daubert, 1996 U. Ill. L. Rev. 363; Imwinkelreid & McCall, Issues Once Moot: The Other Evidentiary Objections to the Admission of Exculpatory Polygraph Examinations, 32 Wake Forest L. Rev. 1045 (1997).

of credibility.[4] In spite of this evidence, law schools continue to train students in the outmoded, traditional belief, and many courts continue to use it as a basis for excluding polygraph evidence.

Courts often raise the old specter of the "scientific aura" of polygraph evidence overwhelming the jurors and preventing them from properly considering other evidence. The jury research evidence previously described demonstrates the error of that thinking. After considering the available scientific evidence, the majority of the *Scheffer* court rejected the argument that jurors would be unable to give proper weight to polygraph evidence.[5] This has not prevented most courts from continuing to use the old excuse for rejecting polygraph evidence. If there were merit in this argument for exclusion, then all courts should uniformly exclude DNA and fingerprint evidence. This inconsistency is highlighted by the Supreme Court decision in *Barefoot*.[6] Although the Court acknowledged that two-thirds of psychiatric predictions of future dangerous behavior are incorrect, they ignored the opposition of the American Psychiatric Association to such testimony and affirmed the admission of a psychiatrist's prediction of future dangerous behavior that resulted in defendant Barefoot being executed. When we compare the handling of polygraph evidence with the routine admission of more influential and sometimes erroneous evidence, it is clear that the courts are biased against polygraph evidence.

Another major impediment for polygraph evidence is the fact that polygraph evidence is almost always proffered by the defendant. Many prosecutors oppose it for this reason and their desire to totally control its use in the criminal justice system, especially when the results of polygraphs they have secretly conducted on prosecution witnesses would be helpful to the defendant. This generally hostile attitude of prosecutors is met with sympathy from the majority of judges who have been drawn from the ranks of former prosecutors.

When all else fails, many courts take refuge in the fact that one party (usually the prosecution) has presented expert testimony that attacks the polygraph. The mere appearance of one inflexible, well-known and well-paid critic of the polygraph provides the excuse for the court to exclude the proffered evidence. Sometimes the expert does not have any scientific credentials to testify in a *Daubert* hearing, but hostile courts will admit and rely on testimony in spite of a record that fails to rebut the scientific basis of the evidence presented by a highly qualified scientific expert.[7] They also may accept an argument that a dispute about the polygraph evidence will become a trial of collateral issues and will consume too much time, even though that argument was also rejected by the *Scheffer*[8] Court. It is time that the courts recognize the legitimate scientific evidence and reject the specious arguments put forth by polygraph critics for personal gain and furtherance of their political agendas.[9]

It is instructive to note that only the New Mexico courts have extensive experience with polygraph evidence. Since 1975, polygraph evidence has been admissible

---

[4]Aldert Vrij Detecting Lies and Deceit (2000).

[5]§ 8:26.

[6]*Barefoot v. Estelle*, 463 U.S. 880, 103 S. Ct. 3383, 77 L. Ed. 2d 1090, 13 Fed. R. Evid. Serv. 449 (1983).

[7]See *U.S. v. Cordoba*, 991 F. Supp. 1199, 49 Fed. R. Evid. Serv. 146 (C.D. Cal. 1998), aff'd, 194 F.3d 1053, 53 Fed. R. Evid. Serv. 3 (9th Cir. 1999). The court admitted the testimony of two FBI agents in a *Daubert* hearing. Neither witness had any scientific credentials or training. However, the judge relied on their testimony and openly attacked the uncontradicted scientific testimony of the defendant's expert, whom the judge himself described as "a pioneer psychophysiologist, nationally known scholar in forensic polygraphy, and generally acknowledged as the nation's foremost polygraph expert." We found the court's rulings, to say the least, disheartening.

[8]§ 8:26.

[9]§ 8:42.

at trial in New Mexico.[10] After eight years of generally positive experience with such evidence in trials, in 1983 the Supreme Court of New Mexico adopted a comprehensive rule that specifies the requirements for admitting polygraph evidence at trial.[11] Although polygraph admissibility has been vigorously challenged by prosecutors numerous times in the 18 years since its adoption, the New Mexico Supreme Court has not reversed its stance. We wonder why almost all other state and federal courts have chosen to ignore the 25 years of positive experience of the New Mexico courts while they continue to exploit all legal devices to exclude polygraph evidence. Clearly, the well-regulated approach to the admission of polygraph evidence has been of benefit to the judicial process in New Mexico courts. There is no logical or practical reason that the situation should be any different in the rest of the United States.

In conclusion, we note that during the summer of 1997 a group of scientists formed the ad hoc Committee of Concerned Social Scientists and submitted a Brief for Amicus Curiae[12] to the United States Supreme Court in *United States v. Scheffer*.[13] That Amicus was signed by 17 professionals with advanced degrees (15 doctoral level). They concluded as follows:

> For the foregoing reasons, the members of the Committee of Concerned Social Scientists respectfully submit that polygraph testing is a valid application of psychological science and that it is generally accepted by the majority of the informed scientific community of psychological scientists as such. Polygraph testing has a known but acceptable error rate that has been well defined by scientific research. Furthermore, there is no scientific evidence that suggests the admission of the results of a polygraph examination before lay jurors will overwhelm their ability to use and value other evidence. Overwhelming the trier of fact is particularly unlikely when the quality and training of the members of a court martial are considered. Many of the traditional objections to the polygraph have been shown by science to be without merit. Although there are problems with the quality of practice in the polygraph profession, such problems are not unique to polygraph tests. They are likely to occur in any situation where a human evaluator is needed to interpret data. In any event, the problems of examiner practice are easily remedied by the traditional means of cross-examination and evidentiary rule.

It is our sincere hope that eventually the courts will recognize the merits and wisdom of this position and accord polygraph evidence its rightful place in the judicial process.

## B.  THE CASE AGAINST POLYGRAPH TESTS
*by William G. Iacono[*] & David T. Lykken[**]*

### § 8:45  Introductory discussion of the science

Psychophysiological interrogation is based on the plausible assumption that various involuntary physiological reactions to salient questions might reveal truths that

---

[10]*State v. Dorsey*, 88 N.M. 184, 539 P.2d 204 (1975). Polygraph evidence was admitted by the New Mexico Supreme Court under the constitutional right for a defendant to present a defense.

[11]N.M. R. Evid. 707.

[12]§ 8:43.

[13]§ 8:26.

[*]Distinguished McKnight University Professor, Professor of Psychology, University of Minnesota, Director, Clinical Science and Psychopathology Research Training Program, recipient of the American Psychological Association's Distin-

guished Scientific Award for an Early Career Contribution to Psychology, the Society for Psychophysiological Research's Distinguished Scientific Award for an Early Career Contribution to Psychophysiology, Past-President of the Society for Psychophysiological Research (1996–1997) and former Member, Department of Defense Polygraph Institute's Curriculum and Research Guidance Committee.

[**]David T. Lykken, who died in 2006, spent his stellar career, spanning more than five decades, as a Professor of Psychology at the University of Minnesota. He authored A Tremor in the

the person being questioned is attempting to conceal. Psychophysiological Detection of Deception (PDD) is based on assumptions regarding how guilty and innocent individuals respond differentially to accusatory questions about their involvement in a crime and their character. We shall demonstrate that the assumptions of PDD are in fact implausible, unsupported by credible scientific evidence, and rejected by most members of the relevant scientific community. PDD is widely used in the U.S. both in criminal investigation and for pre- and post-employment screening, mainly by federal police and security agencies. Although claims about its accuracy are unfounded, we shall show that PDD has been embraced by law enforcement agencies because it has utility as an interrogation tool, eliciting confessions or damaging admissions from naïve but guilty suspects. On the other hand, however, we shall show that unjustifiable faith in conclusions based on PDD has permitted sophisticated guilty suspects to escape detection while unsophisticated innocents have been condemned and punished.

Another method of psychophysiological interrogation is for the purpose of detecting the presence of guilty knowledge as opposed to the detection of lying. The guilty knowledge test is used in criminal investigation in Japan and in Israel but is, so far, seldom used in the United States. We shall demonstrate that the assumptions of the Guilty Knowledge Test are quite plausible and that the limited research concerning its validity has so far been encouraging.

### § 8:46 Introductory discussion of the science—Background—Instrumentation

The polygraph instrument consists typically of four pens recording physiological responses on a moving paper chart. Two "pneumo" pens, driven by pneumatic belts fastened around the subject's chest and abdomen, record thoracic and abdominal breathing movements. A third pen is connected to a blood pressure cuff or sphygmomanometer around one upper arm. During questioning, this cuff is inflated to partially occlude the flow of blood to the lower arm. Each heart beat then causes this "cardio" pen to briefly deflect while changes in blood pressure cause the entire tracing to move up or down on the chart. The fourth, the GSR or "electrodermal" pen, is connected to two metal electrodes attached to the fingerprint area of two fingers of one hand. This pen records changes in the electrical resistance of the palmar skin, which are caused in turn by sweat gland activity. Thus, the polygraph provides continuous recordings of breathing movements, blood pressure changes, and the sweating of the palms.

The restriction of blood flow in the arm produces ischemic pain after several minutes, which limits the number of questions that can be asked during one "chart" to about ten, after which the cuff pressure must be released. Depending on the polygraph procedure used, a typical test involves several "charts," usually with the same questions repeated in the same or different order, with a rest of several minutes between charts.

At the present time, nearly all polygraphic interrogation is intended to determine whether the respondent is answering a specific question or questions deceptively. Contrary to popular belief, however, the polygraph is not a "lie detector." Although some practitioners claim that certain patterns of physiological response recorded on

Blood: Uses and Abuses of the Lie Detector (2d ed. 1998), as well as scores of other scholarly work. Among many honors, Dr. Lykken received the American Psychological Association's Award for a Distinguished Contribution to Psychology in the Public Interest (1991) and for Distinguished Scientific Contributions for Applications of Psychology (2001). He served as President of the Society for Psychophysiological Research (1980–81), and received that Society's Award for Distinguished Scientific Contributions to Psychophysiology.

the polygraph chart are specifically indicative of lying,[1] there is no serious scientific support for this view.

Most polygraph examiners, therefore, employ a technique that provides an opportunity to compare physiological responses to different kinds of questions, including questions directly relevant to the issue at hand.

### § 8:47 Introductory discussion of the science—Background—The control question technique (CQT)

For most forensic applications, a procedure known as the "control question test" is used to evaluate a subject's truthfulness. The CQT is actually a collection of procedures which, although differing from one another slightly in format, all involve the comparison of a subject's responses to relevant questions with responses to interspersed "control" or comparison questions. The CQT is a descendant of the relevant-irrelevant test (RIT), a technique that although widely discredited for criminal applications is still used for employee screening.

The criminal application of the RIT involved two types of questions. The relevant questions focused on the matter of interest and were presented as implicit accusations. In a criminal investigation, the relevant questions usually dealt with a single issue and asked about involvement in an alleged crime, e.g., "Did you rob the First National Bank?" or "Were you involved in any way in the robbery of that bank?" Interposed among these relevant questions were irrelevant questions dealing with innocuous issues unlikely to be of much concern to anyone. Sample irrelevant questions include, "Are you sitting down?" and "Is today Wednesday?" Subjects were expected to answer these questions truthfully, so the physiological responses they elicit served as a baseline against which to compare the responses to the relevant questions. If the responses to the relevant questions were larger than those to the irrelevant queries, then the subject would be deemed deceptive. A truthful verdict required the two types of questions to yield reactions of similar size. The major criticism of this technique is that the irrelevant questions provide no "control" for the psychological impact of being asked the relevant question. The relevant question differs from the irrelevant question both in that it conveys an emotionally loaded accusation and the subject may be lying in response to it. There is no way to determine that a larger response to the relevant question is not due simply to the subject's nervousness about being asked this question. Because of this serious shortcoming, innocent criminal suspects were likely to fail the RIT.

The CQT attempts to improve on the RIT format by keeping the relevant questions and replacing the irrelevant questions with so-called control questions. The control questions refer in a deliberately vague or general way to possible misdeeds from the subject's past, misdeeds that may be chosen so that they deal with a theme similar to that covered by the relevant question. Typically, qualifying phrasing is added to the control question so that it does not involve the same period of time covered by the relevant question. Examples of control questions used with relevant questions dealing with theft and sexual abuse might be: "Prior to last year, did you ever take something of value from someone who trusted you?" and "Before age 25, did you ever engage in an unusual sex act?"

### § 8:48 Introductory discussion of the science—Background—The control question technique (CQT)—Theory of the CQT

Critical to the outcome of the CQT is the manner in which the control questions

---

**[Section 8:46]**

[1]John E. Reid & Fred E. Inbau, Truth and Deception 61–71 (2d ed. 1977).

are introduced. After the relevant questions have been formulated and reviewed, the control questions are presented to the subject with the explanation that they are intended to assess the subject's basic character with regard to honesty and trustworthiness in order to make sure that the subject has never done anything in the past similar to what the subject currently stands accused of doing.[1] The subject is actually told by the examiner that the expectation is that the subject will answer the control questions with a denial. If he or she answers such a question "Yes," the examiner responds in a way that suggests disapproval. Thus, the examiner creates a dilemma for the subject by simultaneously creating the expectation that the subject will be honest and yet answer the control questions "No." As Raskin observes, this manipulation "leads the subject to believe that admissions [to the control questions] will cause the examiner to form the opinion that the subject is dishonest and is therefore guilty. This discourages [further] admissions and maximizes the likelihood that the negative answer [to the control question] is untruthful."[2] Raskin goes on to explain that it is important to get the subject to believe that deceptive answers to the control questions "will result in strong physiological reactions during the test and will lead the examiner to conclude that the subject was deceptive with respect to the relevant issues" concerning the alleged crime. However, he acknowledges, "in fact, the converse is true."[3]

CQT theory, therefore, is based on the premise that stronger responses to the control than to the relevant questions indicates that the latter have been answered truthfully. The theory assumes that the guilty person, who must answer the relevant questions deceptively, will be more disturbed by those questions than by the control questions and that his physiological responses will be stronger to the relevant than to the control questions. The theory also assumes that an innocent person, answering the relevant questions truthfully, will be relatively more disturbed by the control questions, because only the answers to these questions involve deception or significant concern.

### § 8:49    Introductory discussion of the science—Background—The control question technique (CQT)—Scoring the CQT

Some polygraphers use a "global" procedure to help decide the outcome of the examination. With this approach, the examiner takes into account the relative size of the responses to the relevant and control questions as well as all other available information, including the case facts, the subject's explanation of the facts, and his or her demeanor during the examination. Most contemporary practitioners eschew the global approach, preferring instead a semi-objective quantitative method, referred to as "numerical scoring," to decide truthfulness. Each relevant response is compared with the response to an adjacent control question; each such comparison yields a score of -3 if the relevant response is much larger than the control response, a score of +3 if the control response is the much larger of the two, a score of zero if the two responses are about equal, with scores of 1 or 2 for intermediate values. For a typical CQT, the total score might range from +30 to -30 with positive scores interpreted as indicating truthfulness and negative scores indicating deception. Scores in some narrow range about zero, typically between +5 and -5, are interpreted as inconclusive. An increasingly common practice is to feed the polygraph data into a

---

[Section 8:48]

[1]David C. Raskin, Polygraph Techniques for the Detection of Deception, in Psychological Methods in Criminal Investigation and Evidence 247, 254 (David C. Raskin ed., 1989).

[2]David C. Raskin, Polygraph Techniques for the Detection of Deception, in Psychological Methods in Criminal Investigation and Evidence at 255 (David C. Raskin ed., 1989).

[3]David C. Raskin, Polygraph Techniques for the Detection of Deception, in Psychological Methods in Criminal Investigation and Evidence at 255 (David C. Raskin ed., 1989).

computer that is programmed to score the responses according to some standard algorithm.[1]

## § 8:50 Introductory discussion of the science—Background—The control question technique (CQT)—The "Stimulation" test

As part of the CQT, examiners commonly employ a stimulation ("stim") test, the purpose of which is to convince subjects that their physiological responses do in fact give them away when they lie. This procedure is typically administered either prior to asking the first set of CQT questions or after the list of CQT questions has been presented once (i.e., after the first "chart"). Some examiners have the subject select a card from a covertly marked deck and then instruct him or her to answer "No" to questions of the form: "Is it the 10 of spades?" Because the examiner knows in advance which card was selected, he can ensure that he identifies the correct card irrespective of the subject's polygraphic reaction. Other examiners have the subject choose a number between, say, one and seven, and then openly tell the examiner which number was chosen. The subject then is told: "Now when you answer 'No' to the number you selected, I will be able to determine what your polygraphic response looks like when you lie." Some examiners will show subjects the physiological tracings that gave them away in order to prove that they can be detected, perhaps mechanically manipulating the deflection of the pens when the critical item is presented so the subject can easily identify the response. In fact, because people do not show distinctive or characteristic physiological responses when they lie, this form of stim test is also deceptive, falsely suggesting that the examiner has somehow calibrated the test to work optimally on this particular subject.

## § 8:51 Introductory discussion of the science—Background—The control question technique (CQT)—The directed lie test (DLT): A variant of the CQT

The DLT is a form of the CQT in which the subject is instructed to answer each control question deceptively.[1] "You've told a lie sometime in the past, haven't you? Well, I'm going to ask you about that on the test and I want you to answer 'No.' Then you and I will both know that that answer was a lie and the tracings on the polygraph will show me how you react when you're lying." The DLT is scored in the same way as a standard CQT. Advocates believe that the DLT is an improvement because there is greater certainty that the subject's answers to control questions are false. The DLT involves a slightly different assumption, namely, that innocent persons will be more disturbed while giving—on instruction—a false answer to a question about their past than they will while truthfully denying a false accusation about a crime of which they are currently suspected.

## § 8:52 Introductory discussion of the science—The scientific questions and methods—What branch of science is relevant to the evaluation of CQT theory and application?

Polygraphy is unusual in that it has evolved without formal ties to any scientific discipline. Practitioners are graduates of polygraph trade schools. The faculty at

---

[Section 8:49]

[1]David C. Raskin, Polygraph Techniques for the Detection of Deception, in Psychological Methods in Criminal Investigation and Evidence at 260–261 (David C. Raskin ed., 1989); see also Kircher & Raskin, Human versus Computerized Evaluations of Polygraph Data in a Laboratory Setting, 44 J. Applied Psychol. 291, 291–302 (1988).

[Section 8:51]

[1]David C. Raskin, Polygraph Techniques for the Detection of Deception, in Psychological Methods in Criminal Investigation and Evidence at 271 (David C. Raskin ed., 1989).

these schools are usually polygraphers or law enforcement professionals. Few are trained as scientists and few have the background necessary to be able to provide competent evaluations of their discipline. As we shall see, even examiners with long experience have no way of knowing how often their decisions are correct. What feedback they do receive is limited to confessions obtained from suspects whom they have diagnosed as deceptive and then interrogated. These events necessarily confirm the examiner's conclusion and, thus, provide the examiner with a grossly misleading impression of consistent accuracy. Because polygraph testing is used for making psychological inferences or diagnoses, we conclude that psychology is the branch of science that is relevant to its evaluation.

### § 8:53 Introductory discussion of the science—The scientific questions and methods—Is the CQT a test?

*Standardization* and *objectivity* are essential to the definition of a psychological test. A test is considered standardized when its administration and scoring is uniform across examiners and situations. If the outcome of polygraph tests is to be trusted for different subjects and examiners, it is essential that the procedure is always the same. As Anastasi points out, this requirement is "only a special application of the need for controlled conditions in all scientific applications."[1] A technique that is not standardized cannot easily be evaluated; each of its variants would have to be evaluated separately to determine if, as it is generally applied, it is accurate. A test is objective insofar as its administration, scoring, and interpretation are independent of the subjective judgment of a particular examiner.[2] The validity of a test that was not objective would be undermined by individual differences in judgment that varied from one examiner to the next. We conclude that the CQT is neither standardized nor objective and therefore fails to meet the scientific definition of a psychological test.[3]

### § 8:54 Introductory discussion of the science—The scientific questions and methods—Does the CQT produce consistent (reliable) results?

In psychological science, reliability refers to the likelihood that the test yields results that are consistent and reproducible. Would another examiner score the charts in the same way? Would another test administered to the same subject yield the same results? A test can be reliable and yet inaccurate but a test that is not reliable cannot be accurate.

There are two ways to evaluate the reliability of a polygraph test. *Test-retest* reliability refers to whether the test produces the same result when it is repeated on a second occasion. The other form of reliability, *inter-scorer* reliability, asks whether two examiners can obtain the same result when they independently score the same set of charts. We conclude that inter-scorer reliability can be high (but is not always high in practice) and that test-retest reliability has not been (and probably cannot be) validly assessed.

### § 8:55 Introductory discussion of the science—The scientific questions and methods—Is CQT theory scientifically sound?

It is generally agreed that the accusatory relevant questions used in the CQT will tend to produce emotional responses (and associated physiological reactions) in both

---

**[Section 8:53]**

[1] Anne Anastasi, Psychological Testing 25 (6th ed. 1988).

[2] Anne Anastasi, Psychological Testing at 27

(6th ed. 1988).

[3] Polygraph examiners, in recognition of this fact, often refer to the CQT as the control question "technique" rather than "test."

truthful and innocent suspects. The theory of the CQT is that a truthful suspect will react still more strongly to the comparison questions that refer with deliberate vagueness to possible past misdeeds. We conclude that these "control" questions are not controls in the scientific sense and that the theory of the CQT is not scientifically plausible.[1]

## § 8:56 Introductory discussion of the science—The scientific questions and methods—Can CQT theory be tested?

The scientific method requires that hypotheses be testable empirically. In the case of the CQT, these hypotheses are that guilty suspects will consistently display stronger physiological reactions to the relevant (than to the control) questions, and that innocent suspects will consistently be more disturbed by the control questions. We conclude that existing data permit a reasonably fair test of the second hypothesis but that the first hypothesis, concerning the validity of the CQT in detecting deception in guilty suspects, cannot be adequately tested with the available data.

## § 8:57 Introductory discussion of the science—The scientific questions and methods—What scientific standards must a study satisfy to provide a meaningful appraisal of CQT accuracy?

There are hundreds of studies on polygraphy, many of which are controversial because of the way they were conducted and the results they obtained. Some of these reports are unpublished, many have been published in polygraph and police trade publications, and many have appeared in scientific journals. Conclusions about polygraphy will depend in part on which of these reports are accepted as scientifically credible. Among this array of papers, how do we decide which to use to evaluate polygraph testing? We conclude that the only studies worth consideration are those that have appeared in peer-reviewed scientific journals.

## § 8:58 Introductory discussion of the science—The scientific questions and methods—Is the CQT accurate (valid)?

Validity is a synonym for accuracy. Determining the degree to which the examiner's decisions about the truthfulness of subjects agree with ground truth assesses validity. We conclude that the validity of the CQT in detecting truthfulness is negligible and that no acceptable method has yet been implemented for assessing the validity of the CQT in detecting deception.

## § 8:59 Introductory discussion of the science—The scientific questions and methods—Can guilty persons be trained to use "countermeasures" to defeat a CQT?

Countermeasures are deliberately adopted strategies used to manipulate the outcome of a polygraph test. Effective countermeasures should be aimed at enhancing one's response to control questions. This might be accomplished by unobtrusive self-stimulation such as biting one's tongue or thinking stressful thoughts when confronted with this material on a polygraph test. The effectiveness of countermeasures can be determined by instructing guilty subjects on polygraph theory and encouraging them to use these strategies with the appropriate questions as they arise during the examination. By subsequently determining how many of these individuals escaped detection, it is possible to evaluate the effectiveness of different countermeasure maneuvers. We conclude that effective countermeasures against

---

**[Section 8:55]**

[1]Faced with this valid criticism, proponents

now often refer to the CQT as the "comparison question technique."

the CQT are easily learned and that no effective means of defeating such tactics have as yet been demonstrated.

### § 8:60    Introductory discussion of the science—The scientific questions and methods—Has the computerization of the CQT improved its accuracy?

An increasingly common practice in polygraphy is to use a computer to record the physiological responses of subjects. With some computer systems, software is included to score the physiological data and even interpret it. We conclude that computerization of the CQT lends an aura of objectivity and accuracy that is almost entirely specious.

### § 8:61    Introductory discussion of the science—The scientific questions and methods—Why do law enforcement agencies use the CQT?

A question that frequently arises concerns why the CQT is used so pervasively if its accuracy is questionable. The simple answer is that under the pressure of taking the CQT, many guilty people confess, thus resolving a case that often could not be resolved through any other means. We conclude that the CQT can be very useful as a tool for inducing confessions (i.e., it has utility) even though its accuracy as a test is negligible.

### § 8:62    Introductory discussion of the science—The scientific questions and methods—What is the prevailing scientific opinion about CQT theory and testing?

As will become apparent, it is difficult to provide straightforward answers to many of these questions by conducting scientific investigations. However, polygraph testing, as it is currently practiced, has been around for more than 40 years, providing ample opportunity for scientists to consider the questions posed here. The views of the relevant scientific community can be surveyed to determine whether there is a consensus of expert opinion regarding the major questions about polygraphy. We provide data showing that the prevailing opinion of the relevant scientific community is that the CQT is not based on sound scientific principles and that the results of CQT should not be relied upon.

### § 8:63    Introductory discussion of the science—The scientific questions and methods—Is polygraph screening of federal employees and job applicants scientifically justified?

PDD is often used to determine if a job applicant or employee is of good character and would represent a reasonable security risk. There are no credible scientific demonstrations of the accuracy of this PDD application. However, often employees, pressured by polygraphers to divulge everything in their background relevant to such an assessment, make damaging admissions concerning past misbehaviors. We conclude that these tests are used only because employers have found them to be an effective tool for eliciting such information.

### § 8:64    Introductory discussion of the science—The scientific questions and methods—Is there an accurate psychophysiological test for identifying criminals?

Often scientists are criticized for undermining PDD, thus hampering law enforcement efforts, without offering any workable alternative procedure for identifying criminals. The implication is that scientists find deception detection procedures inherently objectionable and hold a philosophical objection to PDD. In fact there is an alternative to traditional PDD that has a solid scientific foundation, is broadly embraced by scientists, but is ignored by the polygraph profession. We conclude that this alternative, known as the guilty knowledge test, appears to have great promise as a forensic investigative aid.

### § 8:65  Areas of scientific agreement and disagreement—The relevant scientific community—Scientists at arms length

Polygraph tests are psychological tests that use physiological reactions to psychological stimuli (questions) as a basis for inferring a psychological process or state (e.g., deception or guilty knowledge). This means that polygraphic interrogation is a form of applied psychology and, hence, that psychologists constitute the scientific community relevant to polygraph testing. Because polygraphy involves psychophysiological recordings, members of the premier organization composed of psychophysiologists, the Society for Psychophysiological Research, constitute an important part of the relevant scientific community. Members of this organization have been repeatedly surveyed to determine their opinions about polygraph testing.

There is little scientific controversy surrounding the physiological aspects of polygraphy. That is, there is no debate about the adequacy of the instrumentation or the physiological measurements. The controversy about polygraphy concerns its psychological and psychometric aspects, i.e., its properties (e.g., reliability, validity) as a diagnostic technique. Most psychologists are capable of evaluating the psychological principles on which a procedure is based and are knowledgeable about the problems of psychological measurement and should be capable of understanding the scientific questions at issue in this area. Psychologists recognized for distinguished achievement by election as Fellows to the American Psychological Association have recently been surveyed regarding their opinions of polygraph testing. We will review the results of these various surveys near the end of this chapter, after we have completed our analysis of polygraph theory and practices.

### § 8:66  Areas of scientific agreement and disagreement—The relevant scientific community—Polygraph examiners are not scientists

It must be stressed that professional polygraph examiners do *not* constitute the relevant scientific community. Few polygraph examiners have any psychological or scientific training. Polygraph schools provide a curriculum lasting from seven to 12 weeks and the only admission requirement is, in some cases, law enforcement experience. Moreover, even the most experienced polygraph examiner has been systematically misled by the peculiarities of his trade. He seldom discovers for certain whether any given test result is right or wrong. The only certain feedback he does get is when a suspect, whom he interrogates because that suspect "failed" the test, is induced to confess.[1] But these confessions necessarily confirm the test just given. Since suspects are either lying (guilty) or not (innocent), a test as invalid as a coin toss would fail guilty suspects about half the time and some of these would confess after interrogation. Since their experience is thus selectively misleading, polygraph examiners are perhaps the group whose opinions concerning the technique are, paradoxically, of the least value.

### § 8:67  Areas of scientific agreement and disagreement—Why the CQT is not a test—Question construction and administration are not standardized

As we noted in our description of the CQT, it is not a uniformly applied technique

---

[Section 8:66]

[1]William G. Iacono, Can We Determine the Accuracy of Polygraph Tests?, in 4 Advances in Psychophysiology (J. Richard Jennings et al., eds., 1991).

but rather a collection of related procedures. These procedures differ in what kinds of questions, other than relevant and control questions, appear on a test, how questions are ordered and grouped, how best to word relevant and control questions, how to conduct oneself during the interview phases of the interrogation, and how to score and interpret charts. The actual structure of a given CQT depends on what polygraph school a polygrapher attended and the examiner's own preferred practices. The only feature all CQTs have in common is the inclusion of control and relevant questions. Because there is no single CQT format, the CQT is clearly not a standardized procedure.

In order to conduct a CQT, the examiner must review the case facts, consider the subject's account of the case, and decide how best to formulate relevant questions that clearly cover the issue at hand. What is required under these circumstances is a series of subjective assessments regarding question development. Different examiners reach different conclusions about what questions to ask; this fact again demonstrates the lack of standardization of the CQT.

The examiner also must succeed in deceiving the subject regarding the purpose and function of the control questions. In the case of the CQT, the subject must be led to believe that his being disturbed by these questions might result in his failing the test when, in fact, the reverse is true. In the case of the DLT, he must be led to believe that his directed-lie responses will show the examiner what his responses to the relevant questions will be like if he answers the latter questions deceptively; this claim is of course untrue. Failure to adequately deceive the subject in these ways invalidates a basic assumption of the test. Because some examiners are better deceivers than others, and some examinees are more easily deceived than others, this problem represents a serious failure of standardization.

### § 8:68 Areas of scientific agreement and disagreement—Why the CQT is not a test—Subjectivity of chart interpretation

The interpretation of the polygraph charts is also problematic. Those employing the global scoring approach are by design using a non-objective, nonstandardized procedure. Although numerical scoring is supposed to be based solely on the physiological data, the examiner scoring the chart, just like those adopting the global approach, is aware of the case facts and the subject's behavior during the examination. Patrick and Iacono showed that this information can compromise the examiner's objectivity.[1] Working with real-life cases from a major police agency, the Royal Canadian Mounted Police (RCMP), these investigators found that the examiners often ignored their own numerical scoring when interpreting charts. For instance, when the numerical scoring indicated deception, 18% of the time examiners concluded the test outcome was either inconclusive or truthful. When the scoring fell in the inconclusive range, the examiners actually classified subjects as guilty or truthful 49% of the time.[2]

### § 8:69 Areas of scientific agreement and disagreement—Why the CQT is not a test—Absence of controlling standards

In *United States v. Scheffer*,[1] the Supreme Court noted that "there is simply no way to know in a particular case whether a polygraph examiner's conclusion is ac-

---

**[Section 8:68]**

[1]Patrick & Iacono, Validity of the Control Question Polygraph Test: The Problem of Sampling Bias, 76 J. Applied Psychol. 229, 229–238 (1991).

[2]Patrick & Iacono, Validity of the Control Question Polygraph Test: The Problem of Sampling

Bias, 76 J. Applied Psychol. at 233 (1991).

**[Section 8:69]**

[1]*U.S. v. Scheffer*, 523 U.S. 303, 312, 118 S. Ct. 1261, 140 L. Ed. 2d 413, 48 Fed. R. Evid. Serv. 899 (1998).

curate, because certain doubts and uncertainties plague even the best polygraph exams." We would add that there is no standard in the field regarding what constitutes the "best polygraph exams." The accuracy of a test that is administered with no controlling standards cannot be determined. This is in effect what the court ruled in a *Daubert* hearing in *United States v. Cordoba*.[2] The court, after reviewing manuals and practice codes from various professional polygraph organizations and agencies, and after hearing the testimony of Dr. David Raskin, noted that particular polygraph practices are followed more out of custom or habit than because examiners follow a prescribed set of standards.[3]

### § 8:70 Areas of scientific agreement and disagreement—The CQT has unknown reliability—Inter-scorer agreement

The only systematic studies of polygraph reliability have focused on the CQT. There is general agreement that examiners trained in numerical scoring can produce reasonably consistent numerical scores. The Patrick and Iacono findings cited above, however, show that the original examiner, influenced by his knowledge of the case facts, will sometimes disregard the physiological data when reaching a decision. In addition, Patrick and Iacono showed that when another examiner blindly scored the same charts, he would sometimes reach a decision that differed from that of the original examiner. For example, of the 72 charts that the original examiner both scored truthful and judged to be from a truthful person, only 51 (71%) were scored truthful by the blind examiner. Because the blind examiner who rescored the charts based his decision solely on the physiological data, the discrepancy in the number of subjects scored truthful by the two examiners roughly reflects the extent to which the original examiner's chart scoring was influenced by his knowledge of the case facts. That is, for the original examiner to score many more charts truthful than the blind examiner who relied exclusively on the physiological data, the original examiner's chart scoring was likely affected by his knowledge of the case facts

---

[2]*U.S. v. Cordoba*, 104 F.3d 225, 45 Fed. R. Evid. Serv. 1197 (9th Cir. 1997), as amended, (Feb. 11, 1997).

[3]For instance, the court noted that the Department of Defense Polygraph Institute, which is the most prestigious training facility for polygraphers, "teaches that if a subject fails one relevant question, the subject fails the entire test. Dr. Raskin, however, follows a standard where a subject who fails one relevant question may still pass the test." The court recognized Dr. Raskin as "probably the strongest and best informed advocate of polygraph admissibility" yet expressed the following opinion regarding his testimony about the adequacy of the CQT administered in this particular instance:

The evidence shows, and the court finds, Defendant's test contained many factors which would be considered defects under various versions of industry "standards." The duration and substance of the pre-test interview was not preserved. No tape or video was made of the pre-test interview or the polygraph exam. The examiner didn't calibrate the machine at the prison test site. Although the examiner asked four supposedly "relevant questions," only one was really relevant: two involved undisputed facts, one was marginally relevant, and the wording of the truly relevant question was arguably too ambiguous to be helpful. The examiner found deception in the marginally-relevant question's answer (while Dr. Raskin did not), but the examiner scored it as truthful after obtaining Defendant's explanation for the answer. The examiner's report was filled with errors and defects: the report was drafted before the test, it did not include a fingertip test, according to Dr. Raskin it lacked attention to detail, it omitted Defendant's response to whether he was under drugs or medication, it misstated the machine used, and it says the stimulation test was done after the first test when it was obviously done first. Although there was movement on a response, the examiner scored the response. The examiner did not record a significant breath. The examiner did not ask if defendant had proper sleep before the exam. The examiner acknowledged the exam was conducted in a poor setting with many distractions. Although each of these occurrences is a defect under various expressions of the industry's standards, Dr. Raskin declined to criticize the test in any meaningful way, and found the test to be entirely acceptable. Confronted with each defect, Dr. Raskin staunchly stuck to his view that the test was reliable and acceptable . . . If pro-polygraph's best expert declines to find any fault with an obviously faulty examination, that is strong evidence that there are insufficient controlling standards . . . The court finds there are no *controlling* standards to ensure proper protocol or provide a court with a yardstick by which a defendant's examination can be measured. *U.S. v. Cordoba*, 45 Fed. R. Evid. Serv. at 1207–1208 (emphasis added).

and therefore was not entirely objective.

The case of the Los Alamos Laboratory scientist accused of mishandling nuclear bomb secrets is illustrative. According to three Department of Energy polygraphers, Dr. Wen Ho Lee passed a polygraph test administered December 23, 1999, but, after suspicions grew that he had passed secrets to China, FBI polygraphers rescored those original charts and concluded that they indicated deception. Nevertheless, when Richard Keifer of the American Polygraph Association examined Lee's polygraph charts, he said "he had never been able to score anyone so high on the nondeceptive scale."[1]

### § 8:71   Areas of scientific agreement and disagreement—The CQT has unknown reliability—Test-retest agreement

No good scientific data are available that can be used to evaluate the consistency of results when separate CQTs are administered to the same subject by different examiners. A different choice of control questions, a different wording of the relevant questions, even a different manner displayed by the examiner, might influence the emotional responses to the questions and thus change the test outcome, whether computer scoring is in use or not. Moreover, the CQT relies on the subject's confidence in the accuracy of the procedure; an innocent suspect who has lost confidence in the test may react more strongly to the relevant questions in consequence while a guilty suspect, who has avoided detection on the first test, might be still less disturbed by the relevant questions on the second test. Thus, mistakes on the first test may be likely to be repeated on the second due to their effect on the suspect's confidence. Finally, the psychophysiological phenomenon of habituation could impact repeated testing. Habituation refers to the fact that physiological reactions diminish with repeated exposure to stimuli. It is reasonable to expect that a subject would be less responsive to the questions asked in a second polygraph test, and that such habituated responding might influence the outcome.

In real life, it is not uncommon for a second polygraph to be administered in order to confirm or check the results of the first test. In our experience, these retests provide no useful data about reliability because the polygrapher conducting the second test is always aware of the results of the first test. This knowledge is likely to affect how the examiner conducts and scores the second test; the results of the second test are thus not independent of the results of the first. Under the circumstances, obtaining the same outcome on two polygraph examinations should not be taken as convincing evidence of innocence or guilt.

### § 8:72   Areas of scientific agreement and disagreement—Implausibility of CQT theory

The scientific plausibility of the CQT can be determined by appraising the psychological assumptions on which it is based. These assumptions, analyzed below, concern what causes the response to relevant questions to be larger or smaller than the response to the "control" or comparison questions.

### § 8:73   Areas of scientific agreement and disagreement—Implausibility of CQT theory—Control questions do not work for the innocent

At the heart of the CQT is the assumption that truthful subjects will respond more strongly to the control than to the relevant questions. For this to occur, it

---

**[Section 8:70]**

[1]Wen Ho Lee's Problematic Polygraph, Sharyl Attkisson, http://www.cbsnews.com/now/st

ory10,1597,157220-41200.shtml (last visited March 27, 2001).

must indeed be the case, as the proponents of the CQT assert, that innocent subjects will be more disturbed by this question than by the relevant question. As we noted in our discussion of the RIT, it is important that the comparison question that is paired with the relevant question should control for the emotional impact of simply being confronted with an accusatory question. For that to happen, the answer to the comparison question should be just as important to the subject as the answer to the relevant question.

Being asked the relevant questions is likely to evoke large physiological reactions regardless of one's guilt. The theory of the CQT is implausible because the so-called control questions actually used do not serve as strict controls in the scientific sense of this term; the subject's responses to the CQT's control questions do not predict how this subject should respond to the relevant questions if he is answering truthfully.

## § 8:74 Areas of scientific agreement and disagreement—Implausibility of CQT theory—A genuine control question

How might we design a polygraph test in which the comparison question would provide a true control for the relevant question? One approach would be to lead subjects to believe that they are plausible suspects in two different crimes, both of which bear similar consequences if guilty. However, unknown to the subject, one of the crimes never occurred, so the examiner is certain the suspect did not commit it. A polygraph test containing a true control question could be derived from this scenario by using as the comparison question the "relevant" question pertaining to the nonexistent crime. From the suspect's vantage point, the test would now contain two types of equally threatening relevant questions. The only reason for a stronger response to be elicited by the real relevant question would be because it was answered with a lie. Such genuine control questions are not employed in real life, however.

## § 8:75 Areas of scientific agreement and disagreement—Implausibility of CQT theory—Polygraphers cannot protect the innocent from failing the CQT

Proponents of the CQT argue that the apparent imbalance in the emotional impact of the relevant and control questions fails to take into account the subtle manner in which examiners manipulate subjects into believing that the control questions are just as important as the relevant questions to the outcome of the test. Recall from Raskin's characterization of how control questions are introduced to the subject that the examiner attempts to convince the subject that the test will be failed if the control question is answered deceptively and that the subject is manipulated to hold back admissions about material covered by these questions so that he is likely to be answering them deceptively.[1] The assumption is that this manipulation will protect innocent subjects from failing a CQT.

There are several problems with this assumption:

(1) Regardless of how skilled the examiner is, subjects may not be concerned about their responses to the control questions. Subjects might feel comfortable with their denials to them or, perhaps, because they cannot recall an instance indicating that their response would be untruthful.

(2) Even when the manipulation works exactly as CQT theory requires, it is still the case that the relevant question deals with the material that is of greatest signifi-

---

**[Section 8:75]**

[1]David C. Raskin, Polygraph Techniques for the Detection of Deception, in Psychological Methods in Criminal Investigation and Evidence, at 254–255 (David C. Raskin ed., 1989).

cance, the only material that could directly link the subject to the crime. Given its perceived significance, it is likely to arouse stronger responses than control questions.

(3) The manipulation is obviously difficult to accomplish. It may be impossible to achieve the desired result in many instances, either because the examiner is not skilled enough to deceive subjects in this way or because sophisticated subjects see through the deception.

(4) Finally, any procedure that is predicated on the examiner's ability to deceive the subject in this fashion is vulnerable to the possibility that the suspect may have learned prior to the testing how the procedure is supposed to work and therefore be immune to the requisite deceptions. It is noteworthy that a trained polygraph examiner, who finds himself suspected of some crime, could not be expected to generate a valid CQT, whether innocent or guilty, since he could not be deceived in the required ways.

### § 8:76 Areas of scientific agreement and disagreement—Implausibility of CQT theory—How overreacting to control questions makes guilty suspects appear truthful

Another basic assumption of the CQT is that the deceptive subject will respond more strongly to the relevant question than to the control question. This assumption requires that suspects not use physical or mental strategies to augment their responses to the control questions. However, as we have already noted, given an explanation of CQT test structure plus coaching on how to willfully enhance physiological reactivity, guilty subjects *can* defeat a CQT. Another problem with this assumption arises from the examiner's attempt, when control questions are introduced, to discourage admissions concerning the topics covered in these questions. For example, if a guilty subject had a history of undetected criminal activity and kept this secret during the examination, he may indeed be lying in response to the control questions, causing larger responses to these than to the relevant questions. It is important to note that anyone familiar with CQT theory would understand that they should not make admissions to the examiner concerning the content of control questions, and that they should in fact think of the worst transgressions when asked these questions. This simple strategy can be used by anyone to help insure a truthful outcome on a CQT.

### § 8:77 Areas of scientific agreement and disagreement—Implausibility of CQT theory—Adversarial vs. "friendly" CQTs

The notion that a deceptive response to the relevant question will provide a stronger reaction than that to a control question is, according to CQT theory, dependent on the subject's fear of the consequences of detection. If the subject has little to fear, the significance of lying to the relevant question would be diminished and the strength of the physiological reaction to this lie would be reduced. When the police give a CQT, the results of which are public (at least they would be known to the police), the consequences of detection are serious, and the physiological reactivity associated with lying would be expected to be substantial. But such CQTs, administered under adversarial circumstances, seldom become the basis of an evidentiary hearing in court. The more usual case for an evidentiary hearing is one where the defense counsel arranges a privately administered or "friendly" polygraph test. If the subject fails, he has little to lose because the results, protected by attorney-client privilege, will remain secret. If the test is passed, defense counsel releases the results and attempts to get them into evidence in court. Under these "friendly" conditions, the fear of detection assumption is largely violated, responsivity to relevant questions can be expected to be diminished, and guilty suspects are more likely to be scored truthful. There are other reasons why friendly tests have reduced probative value. The fact that there is no assurance that the suspect would not "shop around," taking several tests from different examiners, before achieving a favorable result, indicates further that friendly tests cannot be safely relied upon. When a test is taken under "friendly" circumstances, the examiner knows that he can earn witness fees only if the results are favorable. Without necessarily impugning the integrity of polygraph examiners, this factor would skew the results of such tests.

Despite the fact that the results of friendly, rather than adversarial, tests are likely to be the subject of *Daubert* hearings, research on the validity of polygraph tests has focused on adversarial tests. There is not a single study demonstrating that friendly polygraph tests are valid. Proponents of the polygraph defend the admissibility of friendly tests by claiming that examiners in private practice who conduct tests for both the police and defense attorneys fail about the same proportion of subjects referred from both sources. Besides the fact that polygraph examiners seldom back up such assertions with an independent audit of their own records, thus leaving open the possibility that their claims are inaccurate, to make sense of a finding of equal proportions of failed tests from these two sources requires consideration of the likelihood that subjects from these two settings are guilty. When the police conduct a polygraph test, usually there is no hard evidence against a suspect and no arrest has been made. When a defense attorney offers his client for a polygraph, usually the suspect has been arrested and there is sufficient evidence to warrant a trial. The rate of guilt thus must be higher for those who are defendants rather than mere suspects, and these defendants should be expected to fail CQTs at a rate that is substantially higher than that for suspects tested by the police. For both groups of suspects to fail CQTs at the same rate, a substantial number of guilty suspects would have to pass friendly tests.

### § 8:78 Areas of scientific agreement and disagreement—Implausibility of CQT theory—The implausibility of the directed lie test (DLT)

The only differences between the DLT and the standard CQT are as follows: (1) for the CQT, the examiner assumes the control answer is deceptive while, for the DLT, both the examiner and the suspect know that these answers are false; and (2) the subject answers the control questions deceptively on instruction rather than by choice. The DLT assumes that, when instructed to answer falsely a question about some past and trivial misdeed, an innocent suspect will be more disturbed than while truthfully denying his guilt in a crime of which he stands accused. Just as for the CQT, the "control" questions are not controls in the scientific sense and there is no discernible reason for supposing that innocent persons will be reliably more disturbed while lying on instruction about some past event than while telling the truth about a recent and serious event that poses a genuine threat.

Proponents of the conventional CQT argue that one of its strengths derives from the fact that control questions are never identified as such to subjects.[1] Indeed, they are deliberately misled to believe that lying to the control questions will generate a deceptive verdict. To the extent that this deception is successful, an advantage of this approach is that unsophisticated guilty subjects may not figure out that it is to their advantage to try to augment their responses to these questions. However, it *is* obvious that even unsophisticated guilty suspects would be able to identify and understand the significance of the directed-lie questions. They could easily self-stimulate (e.g., bite their tongues) after each directed-lie answer in order to augment reactions to these control questions and thus defeat the test.

---

[Section 8:78]

[1]David C. Raskin, Polygraph Techniques for the Detection of Deception, in Psychological Methods in Criminal Investigation and Evidence at 254 (David C. Raskin ed., 1989).

### § 8:79   Areas of scientific agreement and disagreement—Intractable problems inherent to the evaluation of CQT theory

Determining if polygraph theory is testable requires evaluation of the methods that have been used to test it. Two types of studies have been used to determine whether polygraph tests work. In laboratory or analog studies, volunteer subjects, often college students, commit or do not commit mock crimes and are then subjected to polygraph tests. These tests are scored and the percentage of subjects assigned to the innocent and guilty conditions is determined. The great advantage of the analog method is that one has certain knowledge of "ground truth," of which subjects are lying and which are being truthful.

### § 8:80   Areas of scientific agreement and disagreement—Intractable problems inherent to the evaluation of CQT theory—Disadvantages of laboratory studies

The disadvantages of laboratory studies include the following:

(1)   the volunteer subjects are unlikely to be representative of criminal suspects in real life;

(2)   the volunteers may not feel a life-like concern about mock crimes that they have been instructed to commit and about telling lies that they are instructed to tell;

(3)   the CQT is an attempt to assess emotions by measuring the physiological reactions associated with lying; laboratory studies have no way of reproducing the emotional state of a criminal suspect facing possible prosecution for a crime; compared to criminal suspects, the volunteers are unlikely to be as apprehensive about being tested with respect to mock crimes for which they will not be punished, irrespective of the test's outcome; and

(4)   the administration of the polygraph tests tends not to resemble the procedures followed in real life; for example, unlike real-life tests, which are most often conducted well after the crime took place, laboratory subjects are typically tested immediately after they commit the mock crime; moreover, in laboratory research, to make the study scientifically acceptable, there is an attempt to standardize the procedure (e.g., all subjects are asked identical questions), a factor that distinguishes these from real-life tests.

The many problems with laboratory studies indicate that their results are not generalizable to real-life applications of polygraph testing. Consequently, these studies cannot be used to determine the accuracy of polygraph tests.

### § 8:81   Areas of scientific agreement and disagreement—Intractable problems inherent to the evaluation of CQT theory—Field studies

Another approach to evaluating the validity of polygraph tests is to rely on data collected from field or real-life settings. Since the original examiner possesses knowledge of the case facts and can observe the demeanor of the suspect during interrogation, this extraneous information might influence his scoring or interpretation of the test. Therefore, field studies have used a design in which different examiners, ignorant of the case facts, "blindly" rescore polygraph charts produced by suspects later determined to have been either truthful or deceptive.

Although free of the disadvantages of the analog design, real-life studies must confront the problem of determining ground truth. Most commonly, confessions have been used as the criterion, either establishing that the person tested was lying, because he subsequently confessed, or that some alternative suspect in the same crime, cleared by another's confession, was telling the truth during his polygraph test. Unfortunately, relying on confessions to establish ground truth has serious drawbacks that may not be apparent at first glance. The problem is not with the confession per se, but with the consequences of the method used to get the confession.

## § 8:82 Areas of scientific agreement and disagreement—Intractable problems inherent to the evaluation of CQT theory—Field studies—How confessions are obtained

In CQT studies that have used the confession method to try to estimate polygraph accuracy, confessions are obtained when the examiner interrogates a suspect whom he has just scored as deceptive on a completed CQT. As indicated above, being told that one has "failed the lie detector" often leads a guilty suspect to conclude that continued denials will be futile and that he may as well confess and make the best deal possible. Because they are obtained pursuant to interrogation after "failing" the CQT, these confessions invariably verify *that* test as accurate. In cases with more than one suspect, such a confession may also clear other suspects; if another suspect has "passed" a CQT prior to the confession, that prior test will also be verified as accurate.

## § 8:83 Areas of scientific agreement and disagreement—Intractable problems inherent to the evaluation of CQT theory—Field studies—Problems with the confession criterion

Because field studies must rely on confessions to determine ground truth, the only cases selected for study are those involving a guilty suspect who failed a CQT and subsequently confessed. All the polygraph errors in which an innocent person failed a test are omitted from the study because, absent a confession, none of these cases would qualify for inclusion. Similarly, because there would be no confession, all the cases in which a guilty subject erroneously passed a test would also be excluded. Thus, confession studies rely on a biased set of cases by systematically eliminating those containing errors and including only those where the original examiner was shown to be correct.

As we noted previously, polygraph scoring is reasonably consistent from one polygrapher to another. Consequently, when this biased set of confession-verified cases, all chosen in such a manner as to guarantee that the original examiner was correct, is rescored blindly by another examiner, it should be no surprise that the second examiner is also correct. Nothing can be concluded about the accuracy of the CQT from a study like this. The consequence of reliance on the confession criterion is that such studies must overestimate the validity of the CQT both in the case of truthful and of deceptive suspects.

## § 8:84 Areas of scientific agreement and disagreement—Intractable problems inherent to the evaluation of CQT theory—Field studies—Independent criteria of guilt

This problem with confession studies is caused by the fact that the confession obtained following a failed CQT is not independent of the outcome of the CQT. That is, the only way to get a confession is first for the subject to have failed the polygraph. To determine if they could overcome this problem, Patrick and Iacono carried out a field study with the RCMP in Vancouver, British Columbia.[1] These investigators began with 402 polygraph cases representing all of the cases from a designated metropolitan area during a five-year period. Rather than rely on confessions that were dependent on failing a polygraph test to determine ground truth, they searched

---

[Section 8:84]

[1]Patrick & Iacono, Validity of the Control Question Polygraph Test: The Problem of Sampling Bias, 76 J. Applied Psychol. 229, 229–238 (1991).

police investigative files for ground truth information uncovered after the polygraph test was given, such as non-polygraph-related confessions or statements indicating no crime was committed (e.g., something reported stolen was really lost and subsequently recovered by the owner). These authors found only one case out of more than 400 that independently established the guilt of someone who took a polygraph test.

It is interesting to consider why it was not possible to establish independent evidence of ground truth for guilty persons in this study. The reason lies in how law enforcement agencies use polygraph tests. Typically, a lie detector test is not introduced into a case until all the leads have been exhausted and the investigation is near a dead end. If one of the suspects fails the test, it is hoped that the subsequent interrogation will lead to a confession, thereby resolving the issue at hand. However, if the test is failed and there is no confession, there will be no new leads to follow, so the police, assuming that the person who failed the polygraph is guilty, do not investigate the case further. Hence, there is almost no opportunity for additional evidence establishing ground truth to emerge. This disappointing finding indicates that, as polygraphy is now employed in law enforcement, it is virtually impossible to establish ground truth in a manner that is independent of polygraph test outcome. Consequently, the accuracy of the CQT for guilty subjects cannot be reliably determined from the research thus far reported.

### § 8:85   Areas of scientific agreement and disagreement—Intractable problems inherent to the evaluation of CQT theory—Field studies— Independent criteria of innocence

Interestingly, if all the suspects in a case pass a polygraph, because the guilty person could potentially still be identified through further police work, the file is kept active and additional leads are investigated if they arise. Hence, Patrick and Iacono were able to identify 25 cases where no suspect failed a test but where, for example, subsequent police work led to confessions from suspects who never took a polygraph test but whose confession established as innocent those who had.[1] Because these confessions were not dependent on someone having failed a CQT, they could be used to establish the accuracy of the CQT for innocent people by having the physiological charts blindly rescored. The results of this rescoring are presented in the validity section below.

### § 8:86   Areas of scientific agreement and disagreement—Intractable problems inherent to the evaluation of CQT theory—Field studies— Summary

Laboratory studies, because they do a poor job of simulating the emotionally laden scenario that exists in real-life criminal investigations, cannot be relied on to estimate polygraph accuracy. Field studies that employ confessions following a failed polygraph also cannot be relied on for this purpose. Credible field studies would be possible, but difficult to implement. To date, no scientifically credible field study of the validity of the CQT in detecting guilty suspects has been accomplished. On the other hand, as Patrick and Iacono showed, because police practices differ between cases that yield at least one failed test and those that yield only passed tests, it is possible to collect data that bears on the accuracy of the CQT for innocent

---

[Section 8:85]

[1]Patrick & Iacono, Validity of the Control Question Polygraph Test: The Problem of Sampling Bias, 76 J. Applied Psychol. at 234 (1991).

subjects.[1]

### § 8:87 Areas of scientific agreement and disagreement—How to identify scientifically credible studies

Because the theory of the CQT is so implausible, a heavy burden of proof rests on those who would claim that this procedure can validly distinguish truth from falsehood in the interrogation of criminal suspects. In spite of decades of extensive use in the United States, by federal agencies and local law enforcement, as we have seen, no scientifically acceptable assessment of CQT validity has yet been published. This is due in part to the fact that the real value of the polygraph in criminal investigation is as an interrogation tool, an inducer of confessions, rather than as a decision-making tool or test. Post-test interrogations that elicit a confession necessarily confirm the CQT result that prompted the interrogation. In the absence of systematic evidence concerning the accuracy of CQT results that do *not* lead to confessions, examiners have been able to sustain the belief that all their diagnoses are extremely accurate.

### § 8:88 Areas of scientific agreement and disagreement—How to identify scientifically credible studies—Criteria for a credible validity study

It will be useful to consider the minimum requirements for an acceptable study of CQT validity. These include the following:

(a) subjects should be a representative sample of suspects tested in the course of criminal investigation;

(b) since one wishes to estimate with reasonable precision both the CQT's validity in detecting truthful responding and its validity in detecting deception, test results from at least 100 guilty (deceptive) and 100 innocent (truthful) suspects should be available for the assessment;

(c) for reasons reviewed earlier in discussing the problems of the confession criterion, the innocence or guilt of these study subjects must be determined subsequent to the CQT procedure by investigative methods that are wholly independent of the outcome of the CQT; and

(d) finally, to permit generalizability of the findings, the study would be replicated in a different context (e.g., by a different investigative agency using different examiners).

### § 8:89 Areas of scientific agreement and disagreement—How to identify scientifically credible studies—Plan for a credible validity study

A scientifically credible study of CQT validity might be accomplished by an investigative agency such as the FBI in the following manner:

(1) for a period of months or years, until the necessary number of verified cases had accumulated, *all* suspects under investigation would be given a CQT without post-test interrogation by the examiners;

(2) the test results would be filed separately and not revealed to anyone, including criminal investigators so as not to bias their investigative decisions;

(3) as cases were resolved, the CQT results would be validated against the independent investigative findings; and

(4) should the results prove favorable enough to warrant further study, the project would be replicated by a different investigative agency.

---

**[Section 8:86]**

[1]Patrick & Iacono, Validity of the Control Question Polygraph Test: The Problem of Sampling Bias, 76 J. Applied Psychol. at 234 (1991).

### § 8:90  Areas of scientific agreement and disagreement—How to identify scientifically credible studies—Example of a non-credible validity study

In contrast to this systematic and unbiased research design, we might consider the study by Raskin, Kircher, Honts, and Horowitz of CQT results selected from the files of the United States Secret Service.[1] Despite this study's having been completed in 1988, it has not been published in or even reviewed by a scientific journal. Instead, what the authors did must be pieced together from unpublished reports and book chapters in which the procedures and results are selectively presented.

A complication of this study that makes it difficult to compare to others is that it was not possible to verify subjects as truthful or deceptive to all of the questions they were asked on the CQT. Instead, they were classified as "verified deceptive" if at least one CQT question elicited a confession and the answer to no other question could be confirmed truthful. Likewise, they were "verified truthful" if an alternative suspect admitted guilt to the issue covered by a single question and the subject did not admit to guilt on the issues covered by the other questions. Hence, for many subjects, only partial verification of guilt or innocence was obtained.

From a total of 2,522 CQTs administered, 66, or about 3%, resulted in post-test confessions which verified at least one question on the test that prompted the interrogation, and 39 confessions verified the truthfulness of other suspects regarding their response to at least one test question. The 39 verified-truthful CQTs were administered to persons in multiple-suspect cases who were tested prior to some alternative suspect who later confessed. Thus, in this study, only about 4% of the CQTs administered were "verified" as indicating guilt or innocence, and this verification was incomplete, pertaining only to a single relevant question for many of the subjects. The representativeness of these partially verified cases is obviously open to question.

However, a more serious concern is that the method of verification virtually guaranteed that the original examiners' diagnosis would have been correct. That is, the 66 verified deceptive CQTs were verified because the examiner diagnosed deception, interrogated on that basis, and obtained a confession. Similarly, we know that the 39 CQTs verified as truthful by the confession of an alternative suspect would have been classified as truthful by the original examiner, else he would have had little reason to test the alternative suspect who later confessed.

We can therefore conclude that at least 4% of the suspects tested by the Secret Service produced CQT results like those predicted by the theory (deceptive suspects more disturbed by relevant than by control questions, truthful suspects more disturbed by the control questions). We can also conclude that other examiners, asked to score these same polygraph charts, were likely to get results similar to those obtained by the original examiners. But these results are entirely compatible with the assumption that there is no relationship whatever between the veracity of the suspect and his score on the CQT!

Let us suppose that 50% (1,261) of the 2,522 suspects tested were in fact guilty. Let us assume further that the CQT identified deception in these individuals with only chance accuracy. This would result, by chance alone, in 630 of the guilty suspects being classified as deceptive. All or most of these 630 would be interrogated and, as in this case, some 66 of them might confess their guilt. Since some of these 66 would be involved in cases with multiple suspects, their confessions would exculpate the alternative suspects. These alternative suspects were most likely

---

[Section 8:90]

[1]David C. Raskin et al., A Study of the Validity of Polygraph Examinations in Criminal Investigations (May 1988) (unpublished manuscript, on file with the University of Utah, Department of Psychology).

tested and diagnosed truthful prior to the testing of the guilty suspect who confessed, otherwise the suspect who confessed would most likely not have been tested because the guilty party would already have been identified. Note that under these circumstances, the testing of these subjects would be correct 100% of the time even though the test itself has only chance accuracy. If we now take the charts from these cases and have them blindly rescored, because scoring is reliable, we are likely to obtain nearly the same results that the original examiners obtained. However, these results, suggesting near infallibility, are totally misleading and tell us nothing about CQT accuracy.

Raskin et al. emphasize a unique feature of their study as though it represents a significant methodological refinement over other reports. In addition to requiring a confession to substantiate guilt, they also required the presence of "independent corroboration" of the confession in the form of some type of physical evidence. Although this requirement would appear to eliminate the occasional false confession, it does not deal with the fundamental problem inherent in using confessions to establish ground truth. The problem with this requirement is that the corroborating physical evidence is not independent of test outcome. Had the suspect not failed the CQT, there would be no confession, and had there been no confession, there would have been no opportunity to recover the physical evidence. Hence, there is nothing "independent" about the corroborating evidence. Just like the confession, it too is dependent on having failed the polygraph test.

In short, although much has been made of the Secret Service study, as if it had demonstrated a high degree of accuracy for the CQT, when properly analyzed it can be seen to be wholly without probative value. The fact that this study has not been accepted for publication in a peer-reviewed scientific journal illustrates the utility of impartial peer-review as a minimum criterion for consideration of scientific claims.

### § 8:91    Areas of scientific agreement and disagreement—CQT accuracy: Claims of CQT proponents are not supported—Laboratory studies

The studies that have achieved publication, although none of them meets the criteria set out above for an adequate validity assessment, do permit certain limited conclusions to be drawn. First, there are a number of studies in which volunteer subjects, usually college students, are required to commit a mock crime and then to lie about it during a CQT examination.[1] Control subjects do not commit the crime and are truthful on the CQT.[2] Instead of fear that failing the CQT will lead to punishment (such as criminal prosecution), subjects in these studies were motivated by a promise of a money prize if they were able to be classified as truthful on the CQT.[3] In these highly artificial circumstances, CQT scores successfully discriminated between the two groups.

When the circumstances are made somewhat more realistic, however, even this mock crime design produces results similar to those reported in the better field studies (discussed below). Patrick and Iacono, for example, using prison inmate volunteers, led their subjects to suppose that their failing the CQT might result in the loss to the entire group of a promised reward and thus incur the enmity of their

[Section 8:91]

[1]Barland & Raskin, An Evaluation of Field Techniques in Detection of Deception, 12 Psychophysiology 321, 321–330 (1975); Raskin & Hare, Psychopathy and Detection of Deception in a Prison Population, 15 Psychophysiology 126, 126–136 (1978).

[2]Barland & Raskin, An Evaluation of Field Techniques in Detection of Deception, 12 Psycho-

physiology 321, 321–330 (1975); Raskin & Hare, Psychopathy and Detection of Deception in a Prison Population, 15 Psychophysiology 126, 126–136 (1978).

[3]Barland & Raskin, An Evaluation of Field Techniques in Detection of Deception, 12 Psychophysiology 321, 321–330 (1975); Raskin & Hare, Psychopathy and Detection of Deception in a Prison Population, 15 Psychophysiology 126, 126–136 (1978).

potentially violent and dangerous comrades.[4] Under these circumstances, nearly half of the truthful subjects were classified erroneously as deceptive.[5] In another study, Foreman and McCauley permitted their volunteer subjects to choose for themselves whether to be "guilty" and deceptive or "innocent" and truthful.[6] Those who elected to be truthful knew that their reward would be smaller but presumably more certain.[7] This manipulation is analogous to crime situations where an individual is confronted with an opportunity to commit a crime with little likelihood of getting caught, e.g., an unlocked car with a valuable item in sight, or a poorly watched-over purse or briefcase, and must decide whether to take advantage of the opportunity. By thus increasing the realism of the test conditions, Foreman and McCauley probably also obtained a more realistic result, with about half of their truthful subjects being erroneously classified as deceptive.

Thus, although mock crime studies with volunteer subjects clearly do not permit any confident extrapolation to the real life conditions of criminal investigation, it does appear that the designs with the greater verisimilitude, which threaten punishment or which merely permit subjects to decide for themselves whether to be truthful or deceptive, demonstrate that the CQT identifies truthful respondents with only chance accuracy.[8]

## § 8:92 Areas of scientific agreement and disagreement—CQT accuracy: Claims of CQT proponents are not supported—Field studies

All reputable scientists acknowledge the importance of the peer-review process as a first line of defense against spurious claims. Studies published in archival scientific journals will have passed the scrutiny of independent scientists knowledgeable in the given area of investigation. No one believes that this process is infallible. Spurious results and dubious conclusions can and do find their way into the scientific literature from time to time. Most scientists consider publication in a peer-reviewed scientific journal to be a necessary but not sufficient basis for the serious consideration of a scientific finding or interpretation. This requirement applies as well to polygraph research as it does to other types of scientific inquiry.

Appearance in a peer-reviewed journal, however, is no guarantee of scientific quality. For example, Honts[1] undertook to evaluate the validity of CQTs administered by the RCMP, using extra-polygraphic criteria of ground truth. The plan was to obtain 75 criminal cases with extra-polygraphic confirmation of guilt and 75 cases in which the suspects had been confirmed to be innocent, also independently of polygraph results. Yet only 13 (rather than the proposed 150) tests were rated as having been strongly confirmed and in all of these cases polygraph-induced confessions of the perpetrator determined ground truth. All of the seven guilty suspects were scored as deceptive and the six innocent suspects were scored either truthful or inconclusive. Apart from these very small and unrepresentative samples, this study

---

[4]Patrick & Iacono, Psychopathy, Threat, and Polygraph Test Accuracy, 74 J. Applied Psychol. 347, 348–349 (1989).

[5]Patrick & Iacono, Psychopathy, Threat, and Polygraph Test Accuracy, 74 J. Applied Psychol. at 350 (1989).

[6]Forman & McCauley, Validity of the Positive Control Test Using the Field Practice Model, 71 J. Applied Psychol. 691, 691–698 (1986).

[7]Forman & McCauley, Validity of the Positive Control Test Using the Field Practice Model, 71 J. Applied Psychol. at 693 (1986).

[8]Raskin et al. do not include these more ecologically valid studies by Patrick and Iacono and Forman and McCauley in their lists of "high quality" laboratory studies (first edition). All but one of the studies they cite is the work of Raskin and his students. The one study not from their laboratory [Ginton et al., 1984] included only two guilty subjects and thus has no bearing on their calculation of CQT accuracy with guilty subjects in laboratory investigations.

**[Section 8:92]**

[1]Honts, Criterion Development and Validity of the CQT in Field Application, 123 J. Gen. Psychol. 309–324 (1997).

failed utterly to assess CQT validity with criteria of ground truth that were independent of the polygraph results, thus guaranteeing a misleading, high accuracy rate. Because this study adds nothing to the sum of our knowledge about the real accuracy of the CQT in criminal investigation, we were surprised that it would be accepted for publication in an archival scientific journal, even the journal edited by a colleague of Honts' at Boise State University. The quality of the peer-review that the Honts paper received may be suggested by the following facts: 1) errata were subsequently published to correct obvious arithmetical mistakes pointed out by a reader; 2) the number of subjects in the various groups studied by Honts is inconsistently reported between the published version of this work and the technical report from which the publication was derived;[2] and 3) the *Journal of General Psychology* was ranked 82nd in "impact" among the 97 general psychology journals analyzed by the Institute for Scientific Information.[3]

Four other studies have been published in scientific journals.[4] All four include cases where the verification of guilt and innocence was not entirely dependent on polygraph-induced confessions. In one of these studies, Bersh determined ground truth by relying on the consensus of a panel of attorneys who evaluated the available evidence on each case.[5] Since this evidence included reports of polygraph-induced confessions where they occurred, this criterion is contaminated and, moreover, the evidence did not always permit a confident verdict. In addition, this study, which relied on global chart scoring, did not employ blind chart review. Because the polygraph operators in this study adopted the global approach to chart scoring, their decisions regarding guilt and innocence were based on the same information the panel was given. Given these serious methodological flaws, it is not surprising that the panel and the polygraph operators agreed with each other.

Although not published in a peer-reviewed journal, Barland and Raskin extended the Bersh study using the same research design except that numerical scoring and blind chart review were used.[6] The importance of this study, which its authors have repudiated, is that it reveals that the principal scientific advocate of the CQT, Dr. Raskin, who independently scored all the charts, classified more than half of the innocent suspects as deceptive.[7]

The studies by Horvath and by Kleinmuntz and Szucko both used confession-

---

[2]Although this problem was been pointed out to Dr. Honts in a letter of 15 May 1998, in his reply of 24 May 1998, he refused to explain the discrepancies across these different versions of his work. Dr. Honts refused a request for the data on which this report was based. Letter from Charles Honts to William Iacono (May 24, 1998) (on file with author).

[3]Social Sciences Citation Index, 1993, *Journal Citation Reports*. Philadelphia: Institute of Scientific Information. "Impact factor" is a measure of the frequency with which articles published in a journal are actually cited by other authors. For the *Journal of General Psychology*, the average paper was cited only about 0.1 times, indicating that for every 10 articles published by this journal, only one is cited. Hence, scientists ignore most articles in this publication. Competitive peer-review occurs in journals that reject most submissions made to them. The field studies that we have identified as the best (which can be found in footnote 1 source, Table 1, p. 608) are published in the *Journal of Applied Psychology* and *Nature*, journals that reject 85% or more of the submissions made to them and whose impact

factors rank them as among the very best scientific journals.

[4]Bersh, A Validation Study of Polygraph Examiner Judgments, 53 J. Applied Psychol. 399, 399–403 (1969); Horvath, The Effect of Selected Variables on Interpretation of Polygraph Records, 62 J. Applied Psychol. 127, 127–136 (1977); Benjamin Kleinmuntz & J.J. Szucko, A Field Study of the Fallibility of Polygraphic Lie Detection, 308 Nature 449, 449–450 (1984); Patrick & Iacono, Psychopathy, Threat, and Polygraph Test Accuracy, 74 J. Applied Psychol. 347, 348–349 (1989); Honts, Criterion Development and Validity of the CQT in Field Application, 123 J. Gen. Psychol. 309–324 (1997).

[5]Bersh, A Validation Study of Polygraph Examiner Judgments, 53 J. Applied Psychol. 399, 399–403 (1969).

[6]Gordon H. Barland & David C. Raskin, U.S. Dep't of Justice, Validity and Reliability of Polygraph Examinations of Criminal Suspects (1976).

[7]Gordon H. Barland & David C. Raskin, U.S. Dep't of Justice, Validity and Reliability of

verified CQT charts obtained respectively from a police agency and the Reid polygraph firm in Chicago.[8] The original examiners in these cases did not rely only on the polygraph results in reaching their diagnoses but also employed the case facts and their clinical appraisal of the subject's behavior during testing.[9] Therefore, some suspects who failed the CQT and confessed were likely to have been judged deceptive and interrogated based primarily on the case facts and their demeanor during the polygraph examination, leaving open the possibility that their charts may or may not by themselves have indicated deception. Moreover, some other suspects were cleared by confessions of others, even though the cleared suspects, judged truthful using global criteria, could have produced charts indicative of deception. That is, the original examiners in these cases were led to doubt these suspects' guilt despite the evidence in the charts and proceeded to interrogate an alternative suspect in the same case who thereupon confessed. For these reasons, some undetermined number of the confessions in these two studies were likely to be relatively independent of the polygraph results, revealing some of the guilty suspects who "failed" it. The hit rates obtained in these studies are indicated in Table I.

## Table I
## Summary of Studies of Lie Test Validity that Were Published in Scientific Journals and that Used Confessions to Establish Ground Truth

|  | Horvath (1977) | Kleinmuntz & Szucko (1984) | Patrick & Iacono (1991) | Mean |
|---|---|---|---|---|
| Guilty Correctly Classified | 77% | 76% | 98% | 84% |
| Innocent Correctly Classified | 51% | 63% | 57% | 57% |
| Mean of Above: | 64% | 70% | 77% | 70% |

In a study by Patrick and Iacono, 65% of the innocent suspects were confirmed as such independently of polygraph results (e.g., the complainant later discovered the mislaid item originally thought to have been stolen).[10] As can be seen in Table I, 43% of these innocent suspects were wrongly classified as deceptive by the CQT. Only one guilty suspect could be confirmed as such from file data independent of CQT-induced confessions; his charts were classified as inconclusive by the CQT. The remaining guilty suspects in the Patrick and Iacono study were all classified solely on the basis of having been scored as deceptive on the polygraph and then interrogated to produce a confession.[11] Understandably, when examiners trained in the same method of scoring independently rescored these charts, they agreed with the

Polygraph Examinations of Criminal Suspects (1976).

[8]Horvath, The Effect of Selected Variables on Interpretation of Polygraph Records, 62 J. Applied Psychol. 127, 127–136 (1977); Kleinmuntz & Szucko, A Field Study of the Fallibility of Polygraphic Lie Detection, 308 Nature 449, 449–450 (1984).

[9]Horvath, The Effect of Selected Variables on Interpretation of Polygraph Records, 62 J.

Applied Psychol. at 129–130 (1977); Kleinmuntz & Szucko, A Field Study of the Fallibility of Polygraphic Lie Detection, 308 Nature 449, at 449 (1984).

[10]Patrick & Iacono, Validity of the Control Question Polygraph Test: The Problem of Sampling Bias, 76 J. Applied Psychol. at 234 (1991).

[11]Patrick & Iacono, Validity of the Control Question Polygraph Test: The Problem of Sampling Bias, 76 J. Applied Psychol. at 234 (1991).

original examiners in 98% of cases.[12] This 98% figure is inflated because only charts that the original examiner decided indicated deception were used in its calculation.[13]

### § 8:93 Areas of scientific agreement and disagreement—CQT accuracy: Claims of CQT proponents are not supported—Conclusions

While none of the available studies meet the criteria listed earlier, certain useful conclusions can be drawn. First, the accuracy estimates shown in Table I must all be overestimates of the real accuracy of the CQT since there was at least some reliance in each study on polygraph-induced confessions as the criterion for ground truth. (Where there is total reliance on the confession criterion, as in the Secret Service study reviewed above, then the apparent accuracy achieved by the examiners who independently rescore the charts is really just a measure of the inter-scorer reliability—an impressively high value but wholly uninformative regarding actual CQT validity.)

Because all the validity estimates are overestimates, a second conclusion permitted by the studies in Table I is that an innocent suspect has little more than a 50% chance of being classified as truthful by an adversarially administered CQT. Thus, had the prosecution offered to drop charges if these suspects passed the polygraph, on the stipulation that adverse results would be admitted as evidence at trial, at least half of these innocent suspects would have heard a polygraph examiner testify before a jury that they had been deceptive in denying their guilt.

Finally, it must be recalled that the polygraph tests involved in these three studies were all administered prior to about 1985, before the existence of an easily learned method of beating the CQT was widely known.[1] It is a safe assumption that few, if any, of the guilty suspects involved in these four studies employed these effective countermeasures. We know that the 84% average success in detecting deception, shown on the right of Table I, is already an overestimate due to criterion contamination. In the future, as the method to "beat the lie detector" becomes more widely known within the criminal community (instructions on how to beat the polygraph are now available in any public library and also on the internet), we can expect further deflation of the CQT's success in detecting deception.

The burden of proof remains on the advocates of the control question polygraph technique to demonstrate empirically that a method based on such implausible assumptions can have useful accuracy. That proof has not appeared and what relevant data are available, data that permit us at least to set an upper limit on CQT validity, indicate clearly that the accuracy of the CQT is too low for it to qualify as a courtroom aid.

### § 8:94 Areas of scientific agreement and disagreement—How guilty persons can learn to produce truthful CQT outcomes

Drugs that act to decrease responding in a general way will not normally affect

---

[12]Patrick & Iacono, Validity of the Control Question Polygraph Test: The Problem of Sampling Bias, 76 J. Applied Psychol. at 234 (1991).

[13]Raskin et al., in David L. Faigman, David H. Kaye, Michael J. Saks & Joseph Sanders, Modern Scientific Evidence: The Law and Science of Expert Testimony, 627 (1997), argued that it is the accuracy of the original examiner in these studies summarized in Table I that "is the true figure of merit" when evaluating CQT accuracy because it is the original examiner's decision that would be presented in court. However, when confessions are used to select cases, because a confession can only follow a test scored deceptive by the original examiner, the only cases of the original examiner selected for study will be the ones where he is correct. Citing such figures as legitimate accuracy estimates is thus grossly misleading.

[Section 8:93]

[1]Honts et al., Effects of Physical Countermeasures on the Physiological Detection of Deception, 70 J. Applied Psychol. 177, 177–187 (1985); Honts et al., Mental and Physical Countermeasures Reduce the Accuracy of Polygraph Tests, 79 J. Applied Psychol. 252, 252–259 (1994).

the accuracy of polygraph tests because the CQT is scored by comparing the subject's response to two types of questions. Therefore, successful countermeasures rely on the subject's efforts to artificially augment his response to the control questions. Certain techniques of covert self-stimulation, such as biting the tongue, flexing the toes, or performing mentally stressful arithmetic exercises, can augment the physiological response to a question. To employ such countermeasures, the subject must understand the principle on which the test is based and be able to identify which are the control questions.

Research, as well as a consensus among scientists, supports the view that persons with rather brief training or explanation can covertly self-stimulate so as to augment their responses to CQT control questions, that even experienced examiners cannot detect these countermeasures, and that they may be successful in preventing a guilty suspect from being classified as deceptive on the CQT.[1] There is no good evidence as to how well these countermeasures work under real life conditions and no evidence at all concerning how frequently such countermeasures are successfully employed in real life by sophisticated subjects.

## § 8:95    Areas of scientific agreement and disagreement—Why computerization does not boost CQT accuracy

In this increasingly common practice, the physiological responses of the suspect to the questions of a CQT are measured by a computer which then scores the result and compares that score to a table of scores from known truthful or deceptive subjects, stored in the computer's memory. The result of this comparison is a computer-generated statement indicating the probability of truthfulness or deception. For instance, Dr. Raskin testified in *United States v. Clayton*, based on a computer determination, that the probability that the defendant was truthful was 0.993.[1]

Substantial scientific controversy surrounds three assumptions underlying computer scoring:

(1)  that the probability of truth or deception in real-world situations can be determined from the score on a CQT (this is the basic assumption of lie detection);

(2)  that the scores stored in the computer accurately represent the scores to be expected from truthful or deceptive subjects obtained under circumstances similar to those obtaining in the instant test; and

(3)  that 50% of those who are tested with this instrument are deceptive.

To satisfy the second assumption of computer scoring, the database stored in the machine would have to contain the results of polygraph tests administered under real-life conditions to a representative sample of criminal suspects who had been subsequently proven to be innocent, and also a representative sample of suspects later proven to be guilty. Because of the problems of the confession criterion, outlined above, these tests would have to have been verified by some means other than by polygraph-induced confessions. The results of tests administered in the mock crime conditions of laboratory experiments, or tests administered privately to criminal suspects, would not be appropriate to use in this application because such differ-

---

[Section 8:94]

[1]Honts et al., Effects of Physical Countermeasures on the Physiological Detection of Deception, 70 J. Applied Psychol. 177, 177–187 (1985); Honts et al., Mental and Physical Countermeasures Reduce the Accuracy of Polygraph Tests, 79 J. Applied Psychol. 252,

252–259 (1994).

[Section 8:95]

[1]*U.S. v. Clayton*, U.S. District Court, Phoenix, Arizona, March 22, 1994, No. 92-374-PCT-RCB at 109 (trial transcript of the direct examination of Dr. David Raskin).

ences in the conditions of testing will yield differences in the distribution and meaning of the scores. It should be emphasized that *no such database currently exists* and that, absent this necessary basis for comparison, the attachment of probability values to results of polygraph tests, whether calculated by a computer or in any other way, is necessarily spurious and misleading. With regard to the third assumption, there is no way of knowing that 50% of those tested will be in fact guilty, nor is it likely that this number does not vary across jurisdictions, settings, and applications. To the extent that considerably fewer or more than 50% of subjects are actually guilty, computer-determined probabilities of truthfulness can be quite misleading.

This marriage of the myth of the "lie detector" to the mystique of the computer is a particularly insidious development. When an alleged expert testifies that a defendant's denials of guilt have been scientifically assessed by a computer, which has reported a high probability that these denials are not truthful, one must expect the average juror to give considerable weight to such evidence. However, there does not exist (and may never exist) the database required to yield accurate estimates for computerized chart interpretation. These requirements cannot now be met for criminal suspects tested either under adversarial conditions or privately by an examiner engaged by the defense.

### § 8:96 Areas of scientific agreement and disagreement—The limited research on the directed lie version of the CQT

Only two studies are available that examine the accuracy of the DLT. Horowitz et al.[1] conducted a laboratory investigation, which like other laboratory studies, produces results that cannot be generalized to real life because the testing circumstances are too artificial. This leaves a field study by Honts and Raskin[2] as the only investigation that can be used to support the forensic use of the DLT. This study has several important shortcomings. The most serious concerns the use of confessions to establish ground truth. As we have pointed out before, those real-life studies in which tests given to criminal suspects are confirmed by polygraph-induced confessions, and the polygraph charts are later scored blindly by different examiners, must overestimate polygraph accuracy. The other serious shortcomings of this study are that only 12 guilty subjects were included (too small a sample for thorough evaluation of the effectiveness of a new technique) and that the test administered was not a DLT. Instead it was a CQT with one directed-lie control question. We can only agree with Honts and Raskin when they concluded their paper with the following remarks: "It is not known whether an examination with only [directed lie control questions] would be valid."[3]

### § 8:97 Areas of scientific agreement and disagreement—Why law enforcement agencies use polygraph tests despite their limitations

Given all of the controversy that exists surrounding polygraph testing, why is it that law enforcement and national security agencies make extensive use of polygraph tests? The answer to this question lies with the fact that they have been found to have considerable utility because of the admissions that some subjects make under the stress of these procedures.

---

**[Section 8:96]**

[1]Horowitz et al., The Role of Comparison Questions in Physiological Detection of Deception, 34 Psychophysiology 108–115 (1997).

[2]Honts & Raskin, A Field Study of the Directed Lie Control Question, 16 J. Police Sci. & Admin. 56–61 (1988).

[3]Honts & Raskin, A Field Study of the Directed Lie Control Question, 16 J. Police Sci. & Admin. at 61 (1988).

### § 8:98　Areas of scientific agreement and disagreement—Why law enforcement agencies use polygraph tests despite their limitations—The polygraph as an inducer of confessions

There is no doubt that being told that one has "failed the polygraph" or "seems to be having difficulty with certain questions" is a powerful inducement to confessions or damaging admissions, especially among unsophisticated criminal suspects. Since even innocent suspects have been known to confess in this situation, unsubstantiated confessions pursuant to polygraph testing should be treated with great caution. Examiners often tell suspects that anything they feel guilty about may produce an adverse outcome and, in this way, damaging admissions are often elicited that do not specifically acknowledge guilt in the matter under investigation. Such damaging admissions are sometimes counted as verifications of the polygraph test that produced them; this is, of course, erroneous and may have led to overconfidence in the validity of the CQT. Even if a polygraph technique had only chance accuracy, 50% of the truly guilty would be expected to fail the test and, upon being interrogated, the more unsophisticated of these guilty persons may confess. Those who believe that the utility of polygraphy justifies its use should recognize that the CQT's utility would be even greater if *all* subjects were interrogated as if they had "failed" the test. Guilty suspects who pass the CQT would then not escape interrogation and some of them would respond by confessing.

### § 8:99　Areas of scientific agreement and disagreement—Why law enforcement agencies use polygraph tests despite their limitations—The polygraph test as an interrogation tool

The polygraph can also be a useful aid to criminal investigation. Should a suspect exhibit an unusual emotional and physiological response to questions that would not be expected to disturb him if his story is a true one, investigators can be led to look for evidence in new directions. It must be emphasized, however, that the utility of the polygraph in criminal investigation or interrogation does not imply nor depend on the accuracy of the procedure. By the same token, endorsement by scientists that the polygraph might be useful in these ways does not imply that these scientists believe the CQT to be accurate as a test for truth.

An example of a government agency that finds that polygraph testing has utility even though its validity is unproven is the FBI. Despite the FBI's extensive use of polygraph testing, according to James K. Murphy, former Chief of the FBI Laboratory's Polygraph Unit in Washington, D.C., "The United States Department of Justice and the FBI oppose any attempt to enter the results of polygraph examinations into evidence at trial because the polygraph technique has not reached a level of acceptance within the scientific community and there is no existing standard for training or conducting examinations under which all polygraph examiners must conform."[1]

### § 8:100　Areas of scientific agreement and disagreement—Scientists are skeptical of the CQT

We have already stressed that, in the absence of wholly adequate empirical studies of the validity of either the CQT or the GKT, decisions about when and whether to rely on the results of these techniques must be based largely on the scientific plausibility of the respective assumptions on which they are based. For this reason, accurate assessments of the opinions of members of the relevant scientific com-

---

**[Section 8:99]**
　　[1]Affidavit of James K. Murphy, Chief of

Polygraph, Federal Bureau of Investigation (March 3, 1995) (on file with the authors).

munity, concerning the plausibility of these two techniques, would seem to be of special importance.

In 1994, Amato and Honts reported findings from a survey of the opinions about lie detection of members of the Society for Psychophysiological Research (SPR). This report, based on a response rate of only 30%, was published as an abstract that did not undergo scientific peer-review. It followed on the heels of another survey of the members of SPR that also was not published in a scientific journal. Because of these (and other) inadequacies, we conducted new and more extensive surveys of SPR members and also of general psychologists distinguished by election as Fellows of Division 1 of the American Psychological Association (APA1). The results of these surveys, which achieved return rates of 91% (SPR) and 74% (APA1), were published as a peer-reviewed article in a first-rank journal. These findings show that the vast majority of both groups surveyed expressed grave doubts about the validity of polygraphic lie detection and therefore opposed the introduction of lie test results as evidence in courts. Another recent study found that psychology textbooks express a "strongly negative" opinion of the scientific status of the lie detector. Finally, in September 1999, a panel of senior scientists and engineers from the Department of Energy's weapons laboratories published a detailed appraisal of the scientific status of polygraphy, especially as used in the screening of federal employees. In this section, we review these several sets of data.

## § 8:101   Areas of scientific agreement and disagreement—Scientists are skeptical of the CQT—Methodologically flawed surveys of scientists

Two prior surveys of members of the Society for Psychophysiological Research (SPR) have been conducted. The first was a 1982 telephone survey of 155 members by the Gallup Organization on behalf of a litigant who wished to introduce into evidence the results of a polygraph test.[1] The unpublished results of this survey are difficult to evaluate because few details have been provided about how the survey was conducted. In particular, there was no indication how many SPR members could not be contacted or refused the telephone poll, information that is essential to evaluating the generalizability of the results.

The second survey, by Amato and Honts,[2] was sent by mail to 450 members of SPR. Only 30% responded. Both surveys asked a single question requiring an appraisal of the "usefulness" of polygraph testing in which respondents were asked to choose one of four statements that best described their "opinion of polygraph test interpretations" to determine "whether a subject is or is not telling the truth." The responses this question received in both surveys is reproduced in Table II.

Proponents of polygraph testing have drawn special attention to the fact that about 60% of respondents in both surveys endorsed alternative "B" indicating that polygraph interpretation "is a useful diagnostic tool." This finding led Amato and Honts to conclude that the membership of SPR consider polygraph tests "useful for legal proceedings,"[3] even though the question does not ask for an opinion concerning the use of polygraph results in court. In fact, the meaning of the response is

---

**[Section 8:101]**

[1]The Gallup Organization, Survey of Members of the American Society for Psychophysiological Research Concerning Their Opinion of Polygraph Test Interpretation (1982).

[2]Susan L. Amato, A Survey of the Society for Psychophysiological Research Regarding the Polygraph: Opinions and Implications (1993) (unpublished Master's thesis, University of North Dakota); Susan L. Amato & Charles R. Honts, What Do Psychophysiologists Think About Polygraph Tests? A Survey of the Membership of the Society for Psychophysiological Research (1994) (poster presented at the Society for Psychophysiological Research's Annual Meeting).

[3]Susan L. Amato, A Survey of the Society for Psychophysiological Research Regarding the Polygraph: Opinions and Implications (1993) (un-

ambiguous.[4] We have already noted that there is general agreement that polygraph testing has utility as an investigative aid, and there is no reason to suppose that respondents who chose option B considered their response to refer to anything more than investigative applications. Since these surveys made no distinction between the CQT, which most scientists consider to be based on implausible assumptions, and the guilty knowledge test (GKT), which many consider to be scientifically credible, there is also no way of knowing to what type of polygraph test the question refers. Because of the many ambiguities associated with the interpretation of responses to this question coupled with concerns about the representativeness of survey respondents, we undertook our own independent surveys to determine the views of the scientific community concerning deception detection.[5]

## Table II
## Opinions of Members of the Society for Psychophysiological Research Regarding the "Usefulness" of Polygraph Test Interpretation in Three Surveys

| | Response Options: | Gallup (1982) | Amato & Honts (1993) | Iacono Lykken (1995) |
|---|---|---|---|---|
| A. | Sufficiently reliable method to be the sole determinant | 1% | 1% | 0% |
| B. | Useful diagnostic tool when considered with other available information | 61% | 60% | 44% |
| | * Between "B" and "C" | 2% | - | 2% |
| C. | Questionable usefulness, entitled to little weight against other available information | 32% | 37% | 53% |
| D. | No usefulness | 3% | 2% | 2% |

* Note: Although not offered as an option, in two of the surveys respondents indicated a choice that fell between alternatives B and C.

### § 8:102    Areas of scientific agreement and disagreement—Scientists are skeptical of the CQT—An accurate survey of society for psychophysiological research members

We conducted a mail survey of a random sample of 50% of the nonstudent members of SPR who had United States addresses according to a SPR membership list provided to us by the Society in October 1994.[1] To insure anonymity and encour-

---

published Master's thesis, University of North Dakota); Susan L. Amato & Charles R. Honts, What Do Psychophysiologists Think About Polygraph Tests? A Survey of the Membership of the Society for Psychophysiological Research (1994) (poster presented at the Society for Psychophysiological Research's Annual Meeting).

[4]Another question on the Amato and Honts survey is less ambiguous in its intent and obtained results indicating substantial doubt about CQT accuracy. It asked: "How accurate is the control question test when administered to a guilty suspect during a criminal investigation?" Subjects answered on a 1–5 scale anchored with "no better than chance" (i.e., 50%) at the low end and "nearly perfect (100%)" at the high end. The mean re-

sponse was 3.08, at the approximate midpoint of the scale, corresponding to about 75% accuracy. This accuracy estimate is much lower than the 95% claimed by Raskin, Honts, and Kircher, and similar to the upper-bound accuracy estimate we made for criterion guilty subjects in the best field studies on CQT validity (see Table I).

[5]Iacono & Lykken, The Validity of the Lie Detector: Two Surveys of Scientific Opinion, 82 J. Applied Psychol. 426–433 (1997).

**[Section 8:102]**

[1]Because we conducted the surveys so we could include the results in the Modern Scientific Evidence (1st ed.) chapter to which Raskin, Honts, and Kircher were co-contributors, we did not consider it appropriate to include either them or

age responsiveness, respondents were asked to return, under separate cover from their questionnaire, a postage-paid postcard indicating that they had returned the survey. Those who did not return the postcard received up to three subsequent mailed prompts in an effort to obtain as complete a sample as possible.[2]

Of the 214 SPR members surveyed, 91% returned questionnaires. According to the former US Office of Statistical Standards, response rates of 90% or more can generally be treated as random samples of the overall population and response rates above 75% usually yield reliable results.[3] Significant caution is recommended when response rates drop below 50% as they did in the Amato and Honts survey.[4]

Included with each questionnaire was a letter explaining that the survey was prompted in part by *Daubert* and the likelihood that Federal courts might hold hearings to determine the admissibility of polygraph evidence, hearings that would consider in part the general acceptance of the technique by the scientific community. Because *Daubert* hearings are most likely to consider the admissibility of CQT results, respondents were told that all but a few of the survey questions dealt specifically with the CQT.[5]

An abbreviated listing of other key questionnaire items is presented in Table III.[6] The first item asked if respondents would agree that the CQT "is based on scientifi-

---

ourselves in the surveys. In addition, to avoid the possibility that our surveys would be unduly influenced by the inclusion of respondents from our own department (who agree with our views), we eliminated members of our department from both the SPR and APA surveys. The most likely effect of these exclusions was to reduce the overall negativity of the survey results. Because Raskin, Honts, and Kircher are not members of APA, this would be especially true of the APA survey results.

[2]A difference between our survey and that of Amato and Honts was that they did not prompt SPR members in an effort to obtain a representative sample. It is possible that had we not prompted our survey subjects, we would have obtained a sample that was more supportive of polygraph testing. To test this possibility, we contrasted the responses of those who responded early to our survey with those who responded late (after prompting). There were no statistically significant differences between these two groups in their opinions to survey questions.

[3]*See* Raskin et al., in David L. Faigman, David H. Kaye, Michael J. Saks & Joseph Sanders, Modern Scientific Evidence: The Law and Science of Expert Testimony, at § 5-1.0 (1st ed.) (1997).

[4]*See* Raskin et al., in David L. Faigman, David H. Kaye, Michael J. Saks & Joseph Sanders, Modern Scientific Evidence: The Law and Science of Expert Testimony, at § 5-1.0 (1st ed.) (1997).

[5]Raskin, Honts, and Kircher have incorrectly asserted that we have refused to share our survey data, implying that we have something to hide. See Brief of the Committee of Concerned Social Scientists as Amicus Curiae in Support of the Respondent, filed in the Supreme Court of the United States, October term 1996 (No. 96-1133), *U.S. v. Scheffer.* (Raskin, Honts, Kircher and their colleagues prepared this brief.) In fact, when we offered to share our data with Drs. Honts and

Amato in 1997, they rejected the terms of our offer. They then contacted the editor of the journal in which the survey was published, asking him to mediate a data sharing arrangement that satisfied the ethical guidelines of the American Psychological Association. Guided by the journal editor, who characterized our data-sharing proposal as a good-faith effort that he found acceptable, we once again offered to share our data with Honts and Amato. They once again rejected our offer. In April 1998, we requested the data from the Amato and Honts survey. Although they sent copies of the questionnaires completed by those participating in their survey, 22 of the questionnaires were reproduced with such poor quality that the responses to questions on them were illegible. This problem was brought to Dr. Amato's attention in a letter on 4 June 1998. Although she apologized for and promised to correct this problem, despite follow-up phone and mail requests for better reproductions of these questionnaires, we have not yet received them. Consequently, what we received from them is useless because it is not possible to analyze the complete data set to check it for accuracy.

[6]Our surveys provided respondents with information about the methods and assumptions of polygraph testing, quoting directly from the work of Raskin, Honts and Kircher when appropriate. We defined each type of polygraph test and gave the rationale underlying each by quoting verbatim Dr. Raskin's characterization of the CQT and the DLT from his past writings. We also provided examples of what hypothetical questions might look like using information from the O.J. Simpson and Unabomber (Ted Kaczynski) cases which were in the news at the time the surveys were done, although in neither case had the trials for these individuals begun. Unfortunately, the Gallup and Amato and Honts surveys did not similarly make unambiguous the terminology used in

cally sound psychological principles or theory." Sixty-four percent of SPR members denied that the CQT is based on sound principles. The next two questions inquired separately whether respondents would "advocate that courts admit into evidence the outcome of control question polygraph tests, that is, permit the polygraph examiner to testify that in his/her opinion, either the defendant was deceptive when denying guilt" or "truthful when denying guilt." Over 70% of SPR members would oppose the use of CQT results as evidence in court under either circumstance. Question 5 revealed that respondents were in overwhelming agreement with the "notion that the CQT can be 'beaten' by augmenting one's response to the control questions." For this question, respondents were divided into two groups based on their familiarity with the publication of Honts et al.[7] on countermeasures. Those responding to this question in both groups were almost unanimous in their opinion that the CQT could be beaten in this manner.

Proponents of polygraphy typically assert that the CQT is better than 90% accurate. For example, in *United States v. Clayton*,[8] David Raskin testified that an experienced examiner could be expected to identify correctly "about 95% of the deceptive" and "about 90% of the truthful people." As the responses to Question 6 indicate, the SPR membership disagrees with this claim: only about 25% agree that the CQT is accurate as often as 85% of the time.

For the next item, survey subjects were asked whether, all things being equal, it was more likely that a defendant awaiting trial would pass a friendly test arranged by defense counsel or a test administered by a police examiner. Three fourths of respondents thought a friendly test would be more likely to be passed. The final CQT item results showed that SPR members found it unreasonable for judicial proceedings to give substantial weight to the classification hit rates obtained in mock crime studies.

### Table III

### Opinions of Distinguished Members of the American Psychological Association about CQT Polygraphy

| | Questionnaire Item | % Agree | % Disagree |
|---|---|---|---|
| 1. | CQT is scientifically sound | 36 | 64 |
| 2. | GKT is scientifically sound | 77 | 23 |
| 3. | Would admit failed tests as evidence in court | 24 | 76 |
| 4. | Would admit passed tests as evidence in court | 27 | 73 |
| 5. | CQT can be beaten | 99 | 1 |
| 6. | CQT is at least 85% accurate | | |

their polls. Scientists knowledgeable about the methods and problems of psychological testing can evaluate the plausibility and probable accuracy of lie detection, but only if they are clear about the procedures employed and the rationale supporting the use of these tests. The 30% of SPR members who replied to the Amato and Honts survey doubtless included all of the professional polygraphers who belong to that organization (e.g., Raskin, Honts, and Kircher themselves) and it is their small and unrepresentative survey that in fact was biased by their failure to describe lie detection techniques so that SPR members who are not polygraphers could offer an informed opinion. An advantage of our survey of APA Fellows was that this distinguished group, none of whom were polygraphers, was able to provide an evaluation of polygraph techniques unmotivated by self-interest.

[7]Charles R. Honts et al., Mental and Physical Countermeasures Reduce the Accuracy of Polygraph Tests, 79 J. Applied Psychol. 252, 252–259 (1994).

[8]§ 8:95.

| Questionnaire Item | | % Agree | % Disagree |
|---|---|---|---|
| a. | for guilty | 27 | 73 |
| b. | for innocent | 22 | 78 |
| 7. | Friendly test more likely to be passed than adversarial test | 75 | 25 |
| 8. | Reasonable to use laboratory studies to estimate CQT validity | 17 | 83 |

We also asked the same question that the Gallup poll and Amato and Honts asked. The results are summarized in the third column of Table II. Compared to the earlier surveys, a substantially smaller fraction endorsed option B in our sample and a substantially larger proportion felt that polygraph test interpretations have "questionable usefulness." Possible explanations for these different endorsement frequencies lie with our having made clear that our survey dealt primarily with the CQT (although we did not alter the wording of this question from that of the previous surveys) and our having a representative sample of the SPR membership. Even the minority of SPR members who thought the CQT might be a "useful tool" was unenthusiastic about the CQT. When this selected subset's responses to other questions were examined, fewer than 40% were found to believe that the CQT's validity was as high as 85% and 51% opposed admitting CQTs as evidence in court. Seventy-three percent thought a friendly test was more likely than an adversarial test to be passed.[9]

### § 8:103 Areas of scientific agreement and disagreement—Scientists are skeptical of the CQT—A survey of distinguished psychologists

Not all SPR members are psychologists and, indeed, not all of them are scientists. A number of practicing polygraph examiners, including the editor of the trade journal *Polygraph*, for example, hold membership in SPR. To more clearly characterize the opinions of psychological scientists, we thought it appropriate to conduct a similar survey of an elite group of psychologists, persons who had been elected Fellows of the General Psychology Division of the American Psychological Association. Of the 226 Fellows surveyed with addresses in the United States who were still professionally active, 74% responded. This response rate, although quite high for mail survey research,[1] was lower than that in our SPR survey, most likely because this group, honored for their accomplishments by election to the status of Fellow, was less likely to respond because of the demands their careers place on their time.

---

[9]Raskin et al. have implied that our obtaining results to the question in Table II that differed from those of the other surveys may be due to our inclusion of illustrative CQT questions that hypothetically could have been used in the O.J. Simpson case. They assert that somehow the mention of Simpson led otherwise rational scientists to instantly develop a negative view of polygraphy as they completed their surveys. Because polygraph testing was not a part of the Simpson trial,

it is difficult to see how the mention of Simpson is connected to one's views on polygraphy, and if they were connected, why they would be any more likely to lead to negative than positive views about the polygraph.

**[Section 8:103]**

[1]*See* Raskin et al., in David L. Faigman, David H. Kaye, Michael J. Saks & Joseph Sanders, Modern Scientific Evidence: The Law and Science of Expert Testimony, at 5-4.7.3 (1st Ed.) (1997).

**Table IV**
**Opinions of Distinguished Members of the American Psychological**
**Association about CQT Polygraphy**

|     | Questionnaire Item | % Agree | % Disagree |
|-----|--------------------|---------|------------|
| 1.  | CQT is scientifically sound | 30 | 70 |
| 2.  | Would admit failed tests as evidence in court | 20 | 80 |
| 3.  | Would admit passed tests as evidence in court | 24 | 76 |
| 4.  | Confident could learn to beat the CQT | 75 | 25 |
| 5.  | CQT is standardized | 20 | 80 |
| 6.  | CQT is objective | 10 | 90 |
| 7.  | If innocent, would take an adversarial test | 35 | 65 |
| 8.  | If guilty, would take a friendly test | 73 | 27 |
| 9.  | DLT is scientifically sound * | 22 | 78 |

* Asked of half of the APA members.

Abbreviated results of this survey are presented in Table IV. The first three questions were repeated from our SPR survey and replicated the results of that survey by yielding almost identical endorsement frequencies. The fourth question from the Table asked how confident respondents were that they could personally learn to use physical or mental countermeasures to defeat a CQT. Over 70% felt they could do so with moderate to high confidence. The next two questions dealt with whether the administration of the CQT could accurately be considered standardized and was independent of differences among examiners in skill and subjective judgment. The CQT came up short on both counts.

Questions 7 and 8 dealt with the subjects' confidence in the CQT and the friendly polygrapher issue. Subjects were first asked if they personally would take a CQT administered by a police officer if they were *"wholly innocent"* and "the results would be admitted into evidence" before a jury. Only about a third of respondents would be inclined to take such a test, indicating that their confidence that the CQT can be used to fairly assess the truthfulness of innocent individuals is low. The second question required respondents to assume they were *"guilty"* and that their defense attorney arranged a private test by an examiner with expertise equal to that of the police examiner in the preceding question. Would they take this friendly test? Almost three-fourths would, indicating that they felt they were risking little under the circumstances.[2] The final question dealt with the scientific justification for the DLT. The APA fellows were overwhelmingly of the opinion that the DLT was

---

[2]To determine if those with greater expertise about polygraphy had opinions that differed from those less well informed in our two surveys, we divided our SPR and APA respondents into two groups based on their own appraisal of how informed they were about CQT validity. The results of these analyses are summarized in detail in our journal article. Iacono & Lykken, The Validity of the Lie Detector: Two Surveys of Scientific Opinion, 82 J. Applied Psychol. 426–433 (1997). Briefly, these two groups did not differ in any important respect regarding how they endorsed responses to the questions in Tables II–IV. We also examined the respondents who might be judged as most informed because they reported reading/attending at least six articles/presentations specifically about the accuracy of CQT polygraphy. Even among those in this select group (which made up 23% of the total respondents), there was little enthusiasm for the CQT. For instance, 66% believe the CQT is not based on sound scientific principles and 62% believe that passed CQTs should not be admissible in court. In this regard, it is important to note that the number of papers a scientist has read on CQT validity does not measure the value of his or her opinion about the accuracy of the technique. It would be a mistake to restrict the analysis of sci-

not scientifically sound.[3]

### § 8:104  Areas of scientific agreement and disagreement—Scientists are skeptical of the CQT—Further evidence of scientific opinion: Attitudes toward polygraphy in psychology textbooks

Honts and colleagues at Boise State University have established a website called the *Journal of Credibility Assessment and Witness Psychology*. One of the few essays to appear on this site was an analysis by Devitt et al. of the treatment of polygraphic detection of deception (PDD) in 37 different introductory psychology textbooks published between 1987 and 1994. This essay reports that "PDD received strongly negative treatment in the texts."[1] Only 16% of the texts provided any positive citations to polygraphy, with the ratio of negative to positive citations exceeding 15 to one. The authors complain that textbook writers tend to cite mainly critics of the lie detector (including us) and various factual errors are commented upon. The one error cited in the text concerns one author's discussion of the demonstration by Honts et al.[2] that college students can be easily taught to beat the lie detector. That author mistakenly reported that the method taught for producing augmented responses to the control questions involved pressing on a tack in one's shoe. In fact, Honts et al.'s subjects were instructed to press their toes on the floor after answering the control questions.

The tack-in-the-shoe method would undoubtedly work as well or better than the methods employed by Honts et al.[3] Floyd Fay used this technique while serving two years of a life sentence for aggravated murder prior to the discovery of the real killers, which led to his release.[4] Fay's false conviction resulted from testimony that he had failed two stipulated polygraph tests and this led him to make a study of polygraphy while in prison. The institution in which he was incarcerated used the

entific opinion to just those few scientists who practice polygraphy or are otherwise involved in this profession. Such individuals, who are likely to consider themselves highly informed and would thus be disproportionately represented in any group selected for familiarity with this topic, are not capable of dispassionate evaluation of polygraph techniques because their livelihood depends on the use of these procedures. Finally, polygraph techniques are based on very simple principles that the vast majority of psychologists are capable of evaluating provided they know what they are. As previously noted, a strength of our surveys is that these principles were presented to respondents by directly quoting from the work of Raskin, Honts, and Kircher so there could be no argument regarding whether they were fairly characterized. Our survey results showed that regardless of how well informed respondents were about this topic, most hold decidedly negative views about CQT polygraphy. The Gallup survey of SPR members also failed to find any difference between SPR members who were more versus those who were less informed about polygraph testing. Our findings thus confirm that highly knowledgeable as well as less informed scientists were equally skeptical about the CQT.

[3]We have been informed that Honts has been conducting a telephone survey of opinions about polygraphy of the members of the American Psychology and Law Society, a group whose membership includes non-scientists (our infor-

mant was a surveyed attorney with no scientific training).

**[Section 8:104]**

[1]Devitt, et al., Truth or Just Bias: The Treatment of the Psychophysiological Detection of Deception in Introductory Psychology Textbooks, as 1 J. Credibility Assessment, 9–32 (1997) (This journal is a publication of Charles Honts' website.).

[2]Honts, et al., Effects of Physical Countermeasures on the Physiological Detection of Deception, 70 J. Applied Psychol. 177–187 (1985).

[3]This line of research has shown that various techniques can be used to defeat the CQT. In addition to toe pressing, biting the tongue and mentally counting backwards when presented with a control question have been identified as effective covert methods that enable guilty persons to pass a CQT. Honts, et al., Effects of Physical Countermeasures on the Physiological Detection of Deception, 70 J. Applied Psychol. 177–187 (1985); Honts, Raskin, & Kircher, Mental and Physical Countermeasures Reduce the Accuracy of Polygraph Tests, 79 J. Applied Psychol. 252–259 (1994).

[4]Adrian Cimerman, "They'll Let Me Go Tomorrow," The Fay Case, 8(3) Criminal Defense 7–10 (1981).

lie detector to adjudicate charges against inmates of violating prison rules. Before his release, Fay managed to train a number of inmates to beat the lie test by pressing on a tack in their shoe after each control question. These and other examples have been reviewed by Lykken.[5]

The main impression left by this review of Devitt et al. is that the authors of psychology textbooks were nearly unanimous in concluding that the lie detector has poor scientific credentials and negligible forensic utility except, perhaps, as an inducer of confessions. As such, this review corroborates the findings from our SPR and APA1 surveys by illustrating that another group of broadly informed psychologists are overwhelmingly negative in their appraisal of polygraph testing.

### § 8:105  Areas of scientific agreement and disagreement—Scientists are skeptical of the CQT—Summary of scientific opinion

These findings make it clear that the scientific community regards the CQT to be a nonstandardized, nonobjective technique, based on implausible assumptions, a technique that can be easily defeated by sophisticated guilty suspects, and which is unlikely to achieve good accuracy in detecting either truthfulness or deception. Scientists do not believe that either inculpatory or exculpatory CQT results have sufficient probative value to be introduced as evidence in court and they are especially skeptical about the validity of friendly tests. They do not believe that laboratory studies should be used to estimate CQT accuracy. Further, they do not believe that the recent CQT variant, the Directed Lie Test, provides a credible solution to the defects of the CQT. These same scientists believe that the GKT, in contrast, is scientifically credible.

### § 8:106  Areas of scientific agreement and disagreement—Scientifically based forensic psychophysiology: The Guilty Knowledge Test (GKT)

The major problem with conventional psychophysiological detection of deception (PDD) techniques is that their validity depends on being able to measure complex human emotions to determine if a person is guilty or innocent. Because individual differences in the expression of emotion are substantial, causing the same stimulus to elicit quite different emotions in different people, and specific emotions produce similar physiological reactions, it may never be possible to develop a PDD technique with high accuracy. It is primarily because PDD is an emotion-based assessment that it is not possible to use laboratory studies to gauge accuracy because real life emotion cannot be reproduced adequately in laboratory simulations.

An alternative to PDD involves developing procedures that are not emotion-based. One such technique, the guilty knowledge test (GKT) provides a measure of the cognitive processing associated with memory, something that can be determined using psychophysiological procedures. The GKT answers the question: What does this person know about the crime? Laboratory studies can be used to show how well certain memories can be detected because the assessment of memory in the laboratory does not differ in any important way from the assessment of memory in the field. Two types of measures have been used to assess recognition memory with the GKT. The traditional GKT has involved the measurement of autonomic nervous system responses, especially the galvanic skin response (GSR). More recently, a version of the GKT has been introduced that relies on the monitoring of brain electrical activity.

---

[5]David T. Lykken, A Tremor in the Blood: Uses and Abuses of the Lie Detector (1981); David T. Lykken, A Tremor in the Blood: Uses and Abuses of the Lie Detector (2nd ed. 1998).

### § 8:107 Areas of scientific agreement and disagreement—Scientifically based forensic psychophysiology: The Guilty Knowledge Test (GKT)—Rationale behind the traditional GKT

The GKT provides an assessment of an individual's memory about crime-relevant information, i.e., knowledge about the crime that the perpetrator would be expected to have. Such "guilty knowledge" can only be assessed in situations in which the examiner knows certain facts about the crime that would also be known to a guilty—but not to an innocent—suspect. These facts or "keys" can be presented in the form of multiple-choice questions: "If you killed Mr. Jones, then you will know where in the house we found his body. Did we find him: In the kitchen? In the basement? In the living room? On the stairway? In the bedroom?" A traditional GKT might involve five to 10 such multiple choice questions, each with keys and foils covering a different memory about the crime.

The GKT assumes that the guilty person's recognition of the correct alternative will cause him to produce a stronger physiological response to that alternative. The incorrect alternatives provide an estimate of what the response to the correct alternative would look like if the subject did not know which alternative was correct; thus, unlike the comparison questions used in the CQT or DLT, the incorrect alternatives of the GKT questions provide genuine controls.

An innocent suspect would have about one chance in five of giving the largest response to the correct alternative in such a five-choice question; thus, the probability of false detection (a false-positive error) on a single GKT item would be 0.20. This probability of error decreases rapidly, however, for each additional GKT item that can be devised; an innocent person would have about four chances in 100 of "hitting" on both of two items, eight chances in 1,000 of giving the largest response to the correct alternative on three consecutive items, and so on.

### § 8:108 Areas of scientific agreement and disagreement—Scientifically based forensic psychophysiology: The Guilty Knowledge Test (GKT)—Measuring brainwaves with the GKT: "Brain fingerprinting"

In the last decade, scientists have refined the GKT by measuring brain electrical activity rather than the galvanic skin response to assess recognition memory. This GKT application, referred to as "brain fingerprinting" in the popular press, involves attaching electrodes to the scalp and measuring event-related potentials (ERP). An ERP is a brainwave generated every time a person is presented with a discrete stimulus. This complex wave has multiple components, but one aspect of the signal, called the P300 or P3 wave (because it has a latency of over 300 milliseconds and is the third positive component of the ERP), is especially useful for assessing recognition memory. A P300 wave arises every time a stimulus stands out as different from other stimuli a person is presented with. In the context of the GKT, the key alternatives will stand out to the guilty person because they are recognized as guilty knowledge. For the innocent person, none of the alternatives has distinct meaning, so none will evoke a P300 wave.

For the typical adult, the P300 wave has an amplitude of only about 15 microvolts, far smaller than the background electrical activity that is continuously present in the brain. In order to measure P300, the same stimulus must be repeatedly presented, each time recording the brain's electrical response. All the responses to this stimulus are eventually averaged together. The background electrical activity of the brain varies randomly around the time a stimulus is presented. Averaging this random activity causes it to disappear from the averaged signal. Because the ERP is "time locked" to the stimulus (i.e., its shape and latency is the same to every stimulus presentation beginning the moment the stimulus is presented), averaging enhances the ERP signal. Hence, averaging makes it possible to measure accurately this tiny response by strengthening the representation of the ERP while causing the brain's random background electrical activity to fade away. The implications of this for the GKT are several. First, the stimuli must be presented with precise timing and for very short durations. Typically, a computer is used to present them, and they appear on a computer monitor for about 50 milliseconds. Second, to facilitate averaging, the same stimuli must be presented repeatedly, perhaps 20 or more times. Because a stimulus can be presented every few seconds, this requirement poses few logistical problems because hundreds of stimuli can be presented in a 15 minute recording session.

Because the shape of ERPs vary from person to person, it is important to know what a P300 wave looks like for the given individual. It is also important to make certain that individuals being tested pay attention to the stimuli. Hence, the ERP-GKT includes some special stimuli that the person being tested admits knowledge of and must respond to. Assume, for instance, that one ERP-GKT item deals with knowledge of the weapon used to kill someone. The examiner and the person being tested agree that the item used was not a gun. The actual crime weapon was a hammer. These words, gun (the target) and hammer (the probe) are flashed every two seconds or so on a computer screen, randomly interspersed with the irrelevant words knife, rope, and poison. The subject is told to press a red response key every time gun appears on the screen and a green response key every time another word is presented. This manual response requirement forces the person to pay attention because it compels cognitive processing of each word in order to be able to press the correct key. Because the word gun stands out as memorable, when the ERPs to this word are averaged, a distinct P300 wave will be seen. Knife, rope and poison have no special meaning, so ERPs averaged to these words will not contain a distinct P300 wave. The important question concerns whether the probe word hammer produces an ERP with a P300 wave that resembles that produced by the target word gun or a wave that looks indistinguishable to that of the irrelevant foils. If it resembles gun, the subject is attaching special meaning to the presentation of the word representing the murder weapon, i.e., the subject has guilty knowledge. If the ERP resembles that of the foils, there is no evidence of guilty knowledge for the murder weapon. Statistical procedures have been developed to determine the degree to which the ERP to the probe word more closely resembles that of the target or the irrelevant foils. Just as with the regular GKT, the ERP-GKT involves the presentation of multiple items that may include as stimuli words, phrases, and visual displays such as pictures of the crime scene, victim, weapon, etc.

The ERP-GKT has several advantages over the traditional GKT. First, because of the inclusion of the target word, it is possible to determine that the test was properly administered to the subject. We can make this determination by a) showing that the proper button was pressed in response to this word; and b) showing that this word elicits an ERP that is distinctly different from that to the irrelevant foils. If either of these features is absent, the test of the particular subject would not be valid. Second, a built-in control for individual differences in how a person's brain responds to memorable information is included in the test. It would be possible to drop the target condition from the test and simply determine if the probe ERP differs from the irrelevant ERPs. However, we would not know how different it would have to be to signal the typical recognition response of this person's brain. By including the target condition, we know what a given person's recognition response should look like. Third, the ERP-GKT is not dependent on the measurement of autonomic nervous system responses like the GSR. These responses are not always reliably produced and they can be generated by extraneous factors like unintentional movements or provocative thoughts. The ERP is an involuntary response that is always present if the subject is paying attention. Fourth, the ERP-GKT is unlikely to be easily defeated by employing countermeasures. Because ERPs are derived from brain signals that occur only a few hundred milliseconds after the GKT alternatives are presented, and because as yet no one has shown that humans can selectively alter these brain potentials at will, it is unlikely that countermeasures could be used successfully to defeat a GKT derived from the recording of cerebral signals.

### § 8:109  Areas of scientific agreement and disagreement—Scientifically based forensic psychophysiology: The Guilty Knowledge Test (GKT)—Evidence supporting GKT accuracy

There are two distinct questions to ask concerning GKT accuracy. The first concerns whether this technique can be used to determine whether someone has recognition memory for an item or event. This question can be answered with laboratory research. The second concerns what items and events it is reasonable to expect a person who has committed a crime to remember. This question is best addressed from field studies that determine what criminals pay attention to and remember as aspects of a crime they commit. As we show below, studies of the GKT are clear in demonstrating that this is a highly accurate technique for determining if an individual recognizes information. However, at present there are no field studies demonstrating what people who commit a crime are likely to remember.[1] Consequently, we can confidently determine whether a subject has recognition memory, but we cannot determine scientifically whether someone who committed a crime should necessarily have certain memories.

### § 8:110  Areas of scientific agreement and disagreement—Scientifically based forensic psychophysiology: The Guilty Knowledge Test (GKT)—Evidence supporting GKT accuracy—Traditional GKT

A virtue of the GKT is that its validity with innocent suspects can be estimated *a priori*. With five equally plausible alternatives in each GKT question, an innocent person would have a 20% chance of giving his strongest response to the correct alternative on one question, a 4% chance of appearing guilty on both of two questions, and so on. With a 10-question GKT, if we require five items to be "failed" to classify a person as guilty, more than 99% of innocent suspects can be expected to be correctly classified. The GKT's validity with guilty suspects cannot be predicted with such confidence because we cannot be certain that each suspect will have noticed and remembered all 10 of the items of guilty knowledge.

The ability of the GKT to detect both innocence and guilt decreases when there are fewer items and also when there are fewer alternatives per item. The validity estimates that have been obtained in the laboratory studies of the GKT that have been published to date have been close to those predicted from the numbers of items and alternatives-per-item used in each study. For instance, a review of eight GKT

---

**[Section 8:109]**

[1]Although they were not studies designed to determine what criminals remember from a crime scene, Elaad et al. have carried out field studies using the traditional GKT. Elaad et al., Detection Measures in Real-Life Guilty Knowledge Tests, 77 J. Applied Psychol. 757, 757–767 (1992); Elaad, Detection of Guilty Knowledge in Real-Life Criminal Investigations, 75 J. Applied Psychol. 521, 521–529 (1990). These studies, carried out in Israel, showed that innocent suspects responded to GKT items as predicted by theory. Guilty suspects seemed to remember about 70% of the guilty knowledge facts used for GKT items, as compared with about 88% for subjects involved in the mock crimes of laboratory studies where the details of the crime scene were still fresh in their minds. The Israeli field studies achieved 97% detection of innocent suspects but only 76% detection of guilty suspects, which has been cited as indicating a defect of the GKT. But this is an erroneous conclusion. Elaad et al. used GKTs with only one to six items (mean = 1.8), each repeated typically three times, so that their detection efficiencies were predictably less than would be expected with GKTs constructed from six to 10 different guilty knowledge facts.

laboratory studies revealed that the GKT had an accuracy of 88% with guilty study subjects and 97% with innocent subjects.[1]

The GKT is unlikely to be suitable for the investigation of all crimes. Its results will be dependent on what the perpetrator pays attention to and remembers and how well the examiner is able to determine what that may be.[2] Premeditated crimes and those for which it can be determined what exactly the perpetrator did would make good GKT cases. These would include a planned murder, a theft involving unrecovered items, and a sex crime where the victim can give a good account of what happened.[3]

### § 8:111 Areas of scientific agreement and disagreement—Scientifically based forensic psychophysiology: The Guilty Knowledge Test (GKT)—Evidence supporting GKT accuracy—ERP-GKT

The ERP-GKT received its impetus from the work of Dr. Lawrence Farwell. In an initial report by Farwell and Donchin,[1] 20 laboratory subjects were exposed to guilty knowledge about one of two espionage cases. Hence, each subject possessed guilty knowledge regarding one case and not the other. Excluding inconclusive test outcomes, the ERP-GKT was 100% accurate. That is, it was possible to determine for every subject which espionage scenario he was familiar with and which scenario he had no knowledge of by showing that guilty knowledge probes produced ERPs that closely resembled targets when individuals were guilty and that closely resembled irrelevant foils when individuals were innocent. Allen, Danielson, and Iacono[2] carried out three studies of the ERP-GKT using a different method to determine whether a probe ERP better resembled the target or the irrelevant foil ERPs, a method that did not allow for the possibility of inconclusive outcomes. Examining a total of 60 subjects across three studies, they obtained an overall classification accuracy of 96%. Allen and Iacono[3] later reanalyzed their data using the scoring method of Farwell and Donchin. Excluding inconclusives, they obtained 100% accuracy. Allen and Iacono varied the motivation their subjects had to try to conceal their guilty knowledge and avoid being detected by giving them varying degrees of incentive to try to "beat the test." They found that as incentive was increased, fewer subjects were classified as inconclusive. These results suggest that

---

**[Section 8:110]**

[1]David T. Lykken, A Tremor in the Blood: Uses and Abuses of the Lie Detector (1981); David T. Lykken, A Tremor in the Blood: Uses and Abuses of the Lie Detector (2nd ed. 1998).

[2]Just as fingerprint evidence, when absent at a crime scene, is not exculpating, a passed GKT indicating no recognition of crime scene information also cannot establish innocence. A failed GKT, on the other hand, indicating the presence of knowledge a suspect claims not to have, is potentially as incriminating as fingerprints found at a crime scene.

[3]Podlesny et al. have concluded, after a review of FBI files, that only a small fraction of cases would be suitable for GKTs [Podlesny, Is the Guilty Knowledge Applicable in Criminal Investigations? A Review of FBI Case Records, 20 Crime Laboratory Dig. 59 (1993); John A. Podlesny et al., A Lack of Operable Case Facts Restricts Applicability of the Guilty Knowledge Deception Detection Method in FBI Criminal Investigations: A Technical Report, U.S. Dept. of Justice, FBI, Forensic Science Research and Training Center,

Quantico, Virginia (1995)]. We expect that a search of Scotland Yard files prior to 1900, when the Galton-Henry system of fingerprint classification was established, would also have failed to find many instances where this powerful forensic tool could be employed retrospectively. When police investigators are trained to search crime scenes for items on which GKT questions might be based, they will in many cases find them.

**[Section 8:111]**

[1]Farwell & Donchin, The Truth Will Out: Interrogative Polygraphy ("Lie Detection") with Event Related Potentials, 28 Psychophysiology 531, 531–547 (1991).

[2]Allen et al., The Identification of Concealed Memories Using the Event-Related Potential and Implicit Behavioral Measures: A Methodology for Prediction in the Face of Individual Differences, 29 Psychophysiology 504, 504–522 (1992).

[3]Allen & Iacono, A Comparison of Methods for the Analysis of Event-Related Potentials in Deception Detection, 34 Psychophysiology 234, 234–240 (1997).

in real life, the ERP-GKT may work even better than in the laboratory.

Other studies also suggest that the ERP-GKT is likely to work well in the real world. Several clinical studies have been carried out to determine the validity of amnesia claims made by different types of study participants. In one study, four patients with multiple personality disorder (also called dissociative identity disorder) were assessed to determine if the memories of one personality can be recognized by an alter personality that claims amnesia for them.[4] This study involved presenting to the alter personality memorized information learned by the other personality. This memorized information provided the material for the GKT's probe stimuli, while information memorized by the alter personality served as the source of target stimuli. Other meaningless stimuli served as irrelevant foils. The results showed that the alter personalities generated probe ERPs resembling the target ERPs, indicating recognition memory for the alleged amnesic information in all four cases. A similar study evaluated hypnotized individuals with profound recognition memory amnesia. Again, the ERPs to the memory probes closely resembled those of targets, not irrelevant foils.[5]

Farwell and colleagues have also shown the ERP-GKT is likely to be effective in field applications.[6] In one study, subjects admitted to arrests for minor crimes like public drunkenness. They were queried about the details of the event (e.g., who they were with, where they were) and GKT probes, targets, and irrelevant foils were developed. Each subject was tested for guilty knowledge related to his crime and also for guilty knowledge related to a crime of one of the other participants. Again, no errors of classification were evident. In another investigation, individuals reported to a laboratory with a close friend.[7] The friend was interviewed regarding the details of an important event in the life of the study subject, and this information was used to develop memory probes. When subjects were tested, their ERPs to the probe material provided by their friends matched the target ERPs, not those of irrelevant foils. Again, there were no classification errors.

In *Terry Harrington v. State of Iowa*,[8] the results of an ERP-GKT were introduced in court for the first time as part of an evidentiary hearing. Dr. Farwell administered two separate tests to Terry Harrington, a man who, although steadfastly maintaining his innocence, was convicted of murder more than 20 years ago. Farwell thoroughly investigated the nature of the crime scene, paying particular attention to unusual obstacles the perpetrator would have been confronted by during his flight from the murder scene. This information was not presented at trial, and Harrington claimed no knowledge of these details. Dr. Farwell was able to demonstrate that Harrington's ERP to probe words characterizing these crime facts resembled his ERPs to irrelevant phrases. The target word phrases produced an ERP with a distinct P300 wave, making it distinctly different form the ERPs associated with the other two types of words. Dr. Farwell also tested Harrington on the details of his alibi on the night of the crime. The probe words, representing information Harrington should have remembered about the events surrounding his alibi, evoked an ERP that matched the ERP of the target words and not the ERP of the irrelevant foils. Taken in combination, these results show that Harrington did not have memories

---

[4]Allen & Movius III, The Objective Assessment of Amnesia in Dissociative Identity Disorder Using Event-Related Potentials, 38 Int'l. J. Psychophysiology 21, 21–41 (2000).

[5]Allen et al., An Event-Related Potential Investigation of Posthypnotic Recognition Amnesia, 104 J. Abnormal Psychol. 421, 421–430 (1995).

[6]Farwell & Donchin, The Truth Will Out: Interrogative Polygraphy ("Lie Detection") with Event Related Potentials, 28 Psychophysiology 531–547 (1991).

[7]Farwell & Smith, Using Brain MERMER Testing to Detect Knowledge Despite Efforts to Conceal, 46 J. Forensic Sci. 1, 1–9 (2001).

[8]*Terry Harrington v. State of Iowa*, PCCV073247, 5 March 2001.

related to the commission of the crime but he did recognize information associated with his alibi. The fact that his brain response showed recognition of alibi-relevant information clearly demonstrated that he was able to remember details of the night in question. Judge O'Grady, who held an evidentiary hearing to review the science supporting the ERP-GKT ruled that while the P300 evidence was "arguably merely cumulative or impeaching, it may be material to the issues in the case," but that Harrington "failed to meet his burden to prove that the P300 evidence probably would have changed the result of the trial."[9]

### § 8:112   Areas of scientific agreement and disagreement—Scientifically based forensic psychophysiology: The Guilty Knowledge Test (GKT)—Scientific opinion

In the surveys conducted by Iacono and Lykken of members of SPR and APA, respondents were asked their opinions regarding the GKT. The results are summarized in Table V. The members of both organizations clearly believed the GKT to have a solid scientific foundation. They also believed that GKT results have probative value. When asked if it was reasonable to believe that a person who failed eight of 10 GKT items was guilty, the vast majority of both organizations agreed that it was. Finally, asked what was more believable, a failed GKT or a passed CQT administered through a defendant's attorney, respondents found the GKT to offer the more credible result. These results establish two important points. First, scientists find the GKT to be a theoretically sound forensic tool with great potential. Second, scientists are able to distinguish between different forensic uses of psychophysiological procedures. It is not the case that they are opposed in principle to forensic applications of psychophysiology; they are opposed only to those that have a weak scientific basis.

### Table V
### Opinions of Members of the Society for Psychophysiological Research (SPR) and Fellows of the American Psychological Association (APA) about the GKT

| Questionnaire Item | % Agree | % Disagree |
|---|---|---|
| 1.   GKT is scientifically sound. | | |
|     SPR | 77 | 23 |
|     APA* | 72 | 28 |
| 2.   Reasonable to believe a suspect is guilty if eight out of 10 GKT items were failed. | | |
|     SPR | 72 | 28 |
|     APA* | 75 | 25 |
| 3.   If a suspect failed a GKT but passed a CQT dealing with the same crime, which result would be more believable? | | |
|     GKT result more believable** | 73 | 27 |

Note: *Asked of half of APA members; **Asked of SPR members only

---

[9]*Terry Harrington v. State of Iowa,*   PCCV073247, 5 March 2001.

### § 8:113 Areas of scientific agreement and disagreement—Polygraph screening of federal employees and job applicants—National security screening

In view of the federal Employee Polygraph Protection Act of 1988,[1] which prohibits requiring employees or job applicants in the private sector to submit to polygraph testing, it is ironic that the federal government is the principal employer of polygraph examiners. Applicants for positions with the FBI, CIA, NSA, Secret Service, and similar agencies are required to undergo lie detector tests intended to supplement or substitute for background investigations. Current employees of some of these agencies, military personnel who hold high security clearances, and civil employees of defense contractors doing classified work may be required to undergo periodic tests for screening purposes. The Department of Defense conducted some 17,970 such tests in 1993.[2] Most of these tests, which are based on the relevant/irrelevant polygraph technique, are referred to as counterintelligence scope polygraph tests by the government.

As a consequence of Public Law 106-65 (S. 1059) passed as part of the National Defense Authorization Act of 2000, potentially thousands of scientists and security personnel employed at U.S. weapons labs at Lawrence Livermore, Sandia, or Los Alamos must submit to polygraph tests as part of an effort to improve nuclear security. A relatively new procedure, the Test for Espionage and Sabotage (TES), or a nearly identical variant of this procedure, the Test for Espionage, Sabotage, and Terrorism (TEST), is used.

As outlined in the recently promulgated Department of Energy (DOE) Rule 709 these counterintelligence polygraph examinations are to be limited to coverage of six topics:[3]

(1) espionage;
(2) sabotage;
(3) terrorism;
(4) intentional unauthorized disclosure of classified information;
(5) intentional unauthorized foreign contacts; and
(6) deliberate damage or malicious use of a U.S. government or defense system.

Rule 709 has a number of interesting features that are similar to those governing the use of polygraph tests by other federal agencies and that are likely to stimulate law suits.[4] These include the following:

- Prospective employees of the DOE or its contractors who refuse to take a polygraph cannot be hired and incumbent employees must be denied access to secret information.

- Using the results of a polygraph test as an "investigative lead" can result in an administrative decision that denies or revokes an employee's access to classified information and may lead DOE to "reassign the individual or realign the individual's duties within the local commuting area or take other actions con-

**[Section 8:113]**

[1]29 U.S.C.A. §§ 2001 et seq.

[2]Dept. of Defense Polygraph Institute, A Comparison of Psychophysiological Detection of Deception Accuracy Rates Obtained Using the Counterintelligence Scope Polygraph and the Test for Espionage and Sabotage Question Formats, 26 Polygraph 79–80 (1997) (hereafter DoDPI Study 1).

[3]Part 709 "Polygraph Examination Regulations'" in Chapter III of Title 10 of the Code of Federal Regulations.

[4]In anticipation of the DOE regulations, attorneys representing government employees and employee prospects have indicated a desire to sue the government based on adverse employee decisions made as a result of polygraph examinations.

sistent with the denial of access."

- These tests will be conducted at least every five years and also on an a periodic basis.
- Public comment on the proposed regulations revealed widespread opinion that "that polygraph examinations have no theoretical foundation or validity." DOE decided, however, that "as a matter of law," the agency is mandated to conduct polygraph examinations, and "is no longer free to act favorably on comments arguing against establishment of a counterintelligence scope polygraph examination program because of information and claims about deficiencies in polygraph reliability."

The TES[5] is a type of DLT that includes four irrelevant questions (e.g., "Do you sometimes drink water?" "Is today _____?") and the following four relevant questions: "Have you committed espionage?" "Have you given classified information to any unauthorized person?" "Have you failed to notify, as required, any contact with citizens of sensitive countries including China?" "Have you been involved in sabotage?" The responses to the relevant questions are compared to the responses to four "directed lie" questions that serve as "controls" or comparisons by providing an example of a response to a known lie. The directed lies are questions that both the examiner and the examinee know will be answered falsely. These four questions are chosen from a list of acceptable alternatives, but may include any of the following, which the examinee is directed to answer "No": "Did you ever violate a traffic law?" "Did you ever say something that you later regretted?" "Did you ever lie to a co-worker about anything at all?" Examinees who show greater autonomic disturbance following the questions about espionage and sabotage, than they show following these directed lies, are classified as deceptive.

The field validity of counterintelligence scope polygraph examinations, including the TES, is unknown. However, the Department of Defense Polygraph Institute (DoDPI) has reported two laboratory studies of the validity of the TES.[6] These both employed paid volunteers, 115 of whom were innocent while 60 others were each required to enact simulated acts of espionage or sabotage. Of the innocent subjects, 14, or 12.5%, responded in the deceptive direction. Of the "guilty" subjects, 10, or 17%, were misclassified as innocent.

It is obviously likely that innocent scientists or other persons with high security clearances would be more disturbed by the TES relevant questions asked during an official screening test than were these volunteers for whom the test carried no threat to their reputations or careers. The disturbance produced by the directed-lie questions, on the other hand, might be expected to be no greater in real-life than in simulated conditions of testing. Therefore, when innocent, loyal government employees with top-secret classifications are subjected to the TES, one might expect many more to be classified as deceptive than the 12.5% suggested by the DoDPI studies. The actual rate of false-positive diagnoses is probably close to the 44% level indicated by the real-life studies summarized in Table I.

When DOE scientists are subjected to the planned TES (or TEST), these data indicate that large numbers of innocent employees would be classified as deceptive if the test scores were relied upon. DOE's polygraph examiners avoid any such disastrous result because they know that the base rate of spying (the proportion likely

---

[5]Because the government has published information only on the TES, we will refer to this procedure in the remainder of this section.

[6]Dept. of Defense Polygraph Institute, A Comparison of Psychophysiological Detection of Deception Accuracy Rates Obtained Using the Counterintelligence Scope Polygraph and the Test for Espionage and Sabotage Question Formats, 26 Polygraph 79–80 (1997); Dept. of Defense Polygraph Institute, Psychophysiological Detection of Deception Accuracy Rates Obtained using the Test for Espionage and Sabotage, 27 Polygraph 68–73 (1998).

to be spies) among such a highly screened and dedicated group is likely to be tiny. Consequently, they cannot fail 44% or even 12.5% of scientists without undermining their own credibility, creating a personnel management nightmare, and wreaking havoc on employee morale.

Therefore, subjects who are more troubled by "Have you committed espionage?" than by "Did you ever say something that you later regretted?" are invited by the examiner to explain why they might have responded in this way. If the respondent's answer and demeanor satisfy the examiner, his "fail" is converted to a "pass." Thus, by permitting the polygraph operator to be the ultimate arbiter, relying on whatever clinical skills or intuitions the examiner may (or may not) possess, the frequency of false-positive diagnoses is kept to a low value. Nevertheless, if as few as 2% of the 10,000 workers potentially covered by Rule 709 receive final diagnoses of "deception indicated," 200 highly trained but probably innocent scientists would be implicated as spies in the first round of testing.[7]

Although the controversy surrounding the DOE polygraph screening program has focused on the high likelihood that innocent individuals will be judged to be spies, there is little evidence that the program will actually catch spies. The laboratory studies of the TES, which reported only 83% accuracy in identifying persons "guilty" of committing mock-espionage, overestimate accuracy for the real-life guilty in two important ways.

First, consistent with real-life screening test practices that help to keep the number failing these tests low, these studies did not conclude that deceptive polygraph tests were in fact failed if, during a posttest interview, an examinee offered information that reasonably justified why the test might be a false positive outcome. However, the design of the studies allowed only innocent test subjects this opportunity to "talk their way out of" a failed test because guilty people were instructed to confess as soon as the examiner confronted them with their deceptive test results. We do not know how many guilty individuals would have been mistakenly judged "false positives" had they been allowed to try to "explain away" the outcome of their examinations.

Second, these DoDPI studies did not account for the likelihood that real spies would use countermeasures to defeat the TES. DOE scientists are not simpletons: if one or two are in fact spies, surely both they and their foreign handlers would have sense enough to be prepared to bite their tongues after each directed-lie question. Thus it is to be expected that the *only* weapons-lab scientists, with their highly specialized skills, who fail the projected DOE polygraph screens, will be truthful, honorable people who cannot offer a plausible excuse for failing their polygraphs. The most likely result of Rule 709 will be their ruined reputations and the government's loss of skilled, dedicated employees.

Besides the facts that these tests are not justified on scientific grounds and that they are clearly biased against truthful employees, there is no evidence that person-

---

[7]The Department of Defense Polygraph Program report to Congress for Fiscal Year 2000 illustrates how polygraphers adjust the outcomes of their tests to minimize failing anyone. Department of Defense Polygraph Program Annual Report to Congress, Fiscal Year 2000, Office of the Assistant Secretary of Defense (2000); available at http://www.fas.org/sgp/othergov/polygraph/dod-2000.html. For fiscal year 2000, 7,688 individuals were given counterintelligence scope polygraph tests but demonstrated "no significant physiological response to the relevant questions and provided no substantive information." In other words, some undetermined number provided a substantial physiological response but passed because they did not make incriminating revelations. An additional 202 individuals produced significant physiological reactions and provided "substantive information." Of these, 194 received "favorable adjudication" with the remaining eight cases still pending decisions, with no one receiving "adverse action denying or withholding access" to classified information. These data confirm that the government goes to extreme lengths to ensure no one fails these tests, but they also demonstrate that the tests have no utility.

nel screening tests have any true utility.[8] No spy has ever been uncovered because of a failed polygraph test. Although the government has argued that the admissions individuals make when undergoing these tests provide valuable information, there is no evidence documenting that vital or even important information has been uncovered as a result of polygraph tests. It is possible that employee screening has a deterrent effect in that knowledge that one must pass such tests may discourage would be spies from seeking employment, and it may discourage the currently employed from entertaining thoughts about becoming a spy. However, there is no evidence to support such an assertion. Given the ease with which individuals can learn to defeat these tests coupled with the fact that almost no one is judged to have failed them, it is unlikely that they have any serious deterrent effect.

### § 8:114 Areas of scientific agreement and disagreement—Polygraph screening of federal employees and job applicants—Opinions of DOE national laboratory senior scientists regarding employee screening

Concerned by the requirement that national laboratory employees submit to periodic lie detector tests, a panel of the more senior national laboratory scientists and engineers undertook a detailed appraisal of the existing literature relating to the nature and validity of polygraph screening methods. Sandia's Senior Scientists and Engineers ("Seniors") provide a service to the Laboratories as independent, experienced, corporate evaluators of technical issues. They are available as a group to assist Sandia management with technical reviews of particularly significant issues and programs. Implementation uses subpanels of the Seniors (helped as necessary by other Sandia staff) to conduct the initial, detailed review of issues or programs. The reports of the subpanels are then made available for review by all other Seniors prior to submission to management. The report of the subpanel studying polygraphs and security at Sandia was circulated in the fall of 1999.[1]

These Seniors, whose expertise is in physics, chemistry, or mathematics, do not pretend to be psychologists, psychophysiologists, or psychometricians. But they do know how to read research reports and to evaluate statistical evidence and probabilities. In their Executive Summary, they concluded that:

(1)  there were no adequate studies to support polygraph screening;

(2)  it is impossible to predict what error rates to expect;

(3)  polygraph testing could drive away existing innocent, talented workers who have provided value to national security programs, and it would deter prospective, talented employment candidates from considering a career in the national laboratories; and

(4)  because few spies are likely to be detected, real subversives may be more likely to become insiders—particularly if overreliance on polygraph testing leads to reduced emphasis on other security and counterintelligence methods.

---

[8]In the Clinton Administration's Joint Security Commission Report ["Redefining Security," A Report to the Secretary of Defense and the Director of Central Intelligence, February 28, 1994, Joint Security Commission, Washington, D.C. 20505; available at http://www.fas.org/sgp/library/jsc/index.html], it is noted that "the most important product of the polygraph process is more likely to be an admission made during the interview than a chart interpretation . . . While senior officials at the CIA and the NSA acknowl-edge the controversial nature of the polygraph process, they also strongly endorse it as the most effective information gathering technique available in their personnel security systems."

[Section 8:114]

[1]Polygraphs and Security, A Study by a Subpanel of Sandia's Senior Scientists and Engineers, October 21, 1999, Sandia, NM; available at http://www.fas.org/sgp/othergov/polygraph/sandia.html.

## § 8:115 Summary of areas of agreement: Topics for future research

The concept of the "lie detector" is so deeply entrenched in American mythology that it has proved difficult to eradicate. This aspect of American culture has never caught on in European countries although polygraphy is used by law enforcement in Canada, Israel, and Japan. However, CQT results are not admissible in the courts of these countries and, at least in Israel and Japan, police polygraphers seem to prefer to use the GKT where possible, in place of the discredited methods of "lie detection." However, because it is effective, as a "bloodless 3$^{rd}$ degree," in inducing confessions, the polygraph is likely to continue to be valued in police work.

There is general agreement on a number of scientific issues relevant to the use of polygraph tests.

The polygraph machines used to monitor physiological responses, provided they are in good working order, provide adequate recordings.[1]

(1)  When these physiological signals are computerized, a properly programmed computer can provide an adequate representation of the signals. However, computerized polygraph testing does nothing to resolve any of the controversies surrounding polygraph accuracy because these controversies concern the lack of scientific support for PDD theory and the fact that the results depend on how questions are formulated and asked, unpredictable individual differences in how a person responds emotionally to control and relevant questions, and the likelihood that a guilty person will use undetected countermeasures.

(2)  PDD procedures are not standardized or objective. This is true about their administration and scoring.

(3)  The proper administration of a CQT requires the examiner to deceive the examinee by leading the examinee to believe that "failing" the control questions will lead to an deceptive verdict when in fact the opposite is true. Unless innocent people have great concern about failing the control questions, they will inadvertently respond more strongly to the relevant questions and be judged deceptive. Left unresolved is how the test can be valid for an innocent person who is unconvinced by this deception.

(4)  The comparison or control questions on a CQT or DLT are not controls in the scientific sense in that there is no reason to assume that relevant and control questions have equivalent psychological significance.

(5)  Basic questions about the reliability or consistency with which polygraph tests produce the same result remain unanswered. In particular, it is not known how likely it is that two different examiners testing the same person would obtain the same result (referred to as test-retest reliability).

(6)  There are no field studies of CQT accuracy with unambiguous criteria for ground truth that have overcome the confession bias problem. Consequently, there are no studies that both proponents and opponents of polygraph testing can point to as providing a valid estimate of CQT accuracy.

(7)  Countermeasures can be employed successfully by guilty individuals to pass a polygraph test, and the use of these countermeasures is not detectable.

(8)  The GKT is a scientifically sound alternative to PDD. Whether based on the measure of autonomic nervous system responses like the GSR or on brain potentials, this technique can accurately determine if someone has recognition memory for information they claim to have no knowledge of.

(9)  Polygraphers are not scientists, and their opinions regarding polygraph test-

---

[Section 8:115]

[1]Christopher J. Patrick & William G. Iacono, A Comparison of Field and Laboratory Polygraphs in the Detection of Deception, 28 Psychophysiology 632–638 (1991).

ing are not relevant to how scientists appraise polygraphy. Psychologists, especially those trained in psychophysiology, have the requisite knowledge to evaluate these psychologically based PDD techniques.

(10) Personnel screening cannot be scientifically justified. These PDD procedures are biased against the innocent, and have not even been shown to have the kind of utility that the CQT has.

## § 8:116    Summary of areas of agreement: Topics for future research—The future of the "lie detector"

Because the CQT and its progeny are based on such implausible assumptions, it is unlikely that future research will do more than confirm the present view of the scientific community that these techniques have negligible validity.[1] As we have seen, the fatal defects of the CQT are: (1) innocent suspects are likely to be more disturbed by the relevant questions than by the comparison questions, while (2) sophisticated guilty suspects can easily (and without being detected) self-stimulate so as to augment their responses to the comparison questions and thus to beat the test. Whether scientifically supportable alternative lie-detection techniques can be developed remains to be seen. It is well established that cognitive effort produces pupillary dilation and that the greater the effort, the larger the pupillary change. Building on this fact, it has recently been shown that giving a narrative (rather than a Yes or No) answer to a question produces greater pupillary dilation when the answer is deceptive rather than truthful.[2] Although such work requires replication and study in real-life applications, it illustrates that it may be possible to develop instrumental lie-detection techniques that circumvent the weaknesses of CQT polygraphy.

## § 8:117    Summary of areas of agreement: Topics for future research—The future of the guilty knowledge test

The detection of guilty knowledge, on the other hand, is entirely feasible from a scientific point of view and the limited research so far conducted with the GKT indicates that this technique works just as the theory would predict. The GKT cannot be employed in many situations where lie-detection is now used. Its utility is limited to those instances in which the investigator can identify a number of facts about the crime scene that are likely to be recognized by a guilty suspect but not by one without guilty knowledge. But it is important to realize that many celebrated criminal cases, including those involving espionage, could have been solved with dispatch and a high level of statistical confidence had the defendant been administered a GKT.

One example is the case of the missing computer hard drives at the Los Alamos nuclear facility.[1] These laptop drives, about the size of a deck of playing cards, contained nuclear secrets and were missing for as long as six months. They reappeared in a package behind a photocopying machine in one of the nuclear facility buildings. The members of the Los Alamos "X Division" that was entrusted with the security of the drives were flown to Albuquerque for a day and polygraphed, but the mystery regarding who placed the drives behind the photocopier remains unsolved.

---

**[Section 8:116]**

[1] A recent analysis of CQT polygraphy in light of *Daubert* has reached a similar conclusion. Saxe & Ben-Shakar, Admissibility of Polygraph Tests: The Application of Scientific Standards Post-Daubert, 5 Psychol., L., & Pub. Pol'y., 203 (1999).

[2] Dionisio et al., Differentiation of Deception Using Pupillary Responses as an Index of Cognitive Processing, 38 Psychophysiology 205–211 (2001).

**[Section 8:117]**

[1] FBI Ends Inquiry in Los Alamos, New York Times, January 19, 2001.

Had the FBI not publicized the recovery of the drives, the information regarding their whereabouts could have been used to develop a GKT which then could have been administered to X Division personnel. For instance, only the guilty individual would know in what building and room the drive was deposited, that it was placed behind a photocopier, and that it was in a certain type of packaging.

The GKT also has screening applications. For instance, notorious FBI spy Robert Hanssen reportedly hacked into a secure computer to access secrets.[2] Hanson and any agent could be routinely asked to take an ERP-GKT where various words and pictures would be flashed, including those associated with information the tested person should not have memory for. Probe words in such a test might include the classified computer password that was last in effect, file names, pictures of computer screens that would have to be processed to access information, and other items that would be salient to someone who gathered information from the computer. To an innocent person, all of these stimuli, mixed in with foils, would evoke no memories or P3 wave. A guilty person, by contrast, would show a P3 recognition response to the probe items.

The GKT has not been used by U.S. law enforcement for two reasons. First, there remains a strong, albeit unjustified, faith in "lie detection" which is so much easier to employ. Secondly, use of the GKT requires that the person who will identify the facts to be used in GKT items must visit the crime scene with the original investigative team. Polygraph examiners do not visit crime scenes and criminalists are not yet being trained to develop GKT items that might later be used by polygraph examiners. It is possible, however, that the apparent possibilities of this technique will come to be exploited in the future. If that time does come, the courts may have occasion to consider such questions as the admissibility of GKT results or whether requiring a suspect to undergo a GKT examination is equivalent to requiring him to permit a photograph or a blood sample to be taken.

### § 8:118 Summary of areas of agreement: Topics for future research—To accept the pro-polygraph arguments, one must believe...

Scientists have often noted that extraordinary claims demand extraordinary supporting evidence. With no solid scientific foundation and a lack of methodologically sound supporting research, the claims that polygraph tests are up to 95% accurate demand close scrutiny. As a convenience to the reader, we conclude by summarizing what would be required to accept the proponents' conclusions about lie-detector tests in preference to ours, as follows:

(1) That two surveys, one by Amato and Honts and the other by the Gallup organization, neither of which was published in a scientific journal, and neither of which asks directly about the scientific soundness of the CQT or the desirability of using it in legal proceedings, are to be preferred over our surveys of two different scientific organizations, each yielding very similar and overwhelmingly negative results, a study that was published in a scientific journal that regularly rejects over 85% of submitted papers.
That the SPR survey of Amato and Honts, which obtained a response rate of only 30%, did a fairer job capturing the opinions of the relevant scientific community than our survey, to which 91% responded.

(2) To accept the pro-polygraph arguments, one must believe that, in real life, subjects cannot be expected to learn how to employ countermeasures despite the widespread availability of information, in the library or on the internet, on how to accomplish this objective, and in Raskin, Honts, and Kircher's

---

[2]A Search for Answers: The Suspect; FBI Never Gave Lie Test to Agent Charged as Spy, New York Times, February 22, 2001.

published work showing that guilty subjects can successfully employ countermeasures with no more than a half-hour of instruction.[1]

(3) To accept the pro-polygraph arguments, one must believe that the results of the directed-lie test, a procedure that has received little systematic scientific study and that is not even generally accepted by the professional polygraph community,[2] meets the *Daubert* standards for credible scientific evidence.

(4) To accept the pro-polygraph arguments, one must believe that polygraph tests arranged by a suspect's defense counsel, the results of which are protected by attorney-client privilege, involve the same degree of fear of detection as adversarial tests administered by the police, the results of which are available to the prosecution.

To accept the pro-polygraph arguments, one must believe that friendly tests meet the *Daubert* standard despite the absence of even one empirical study attesting to the accuracy of these tests.

(5) To accept the pro-polygraph arguments, one must believe that laboratory studies in which participants are passive recipients of instructions to carry out mock crimes, and which are without the fear of detection that exists in real-life polygraph tests, can be used to accurately estimate the validity of lie-detector tests in real life.

(6) To accept the pro-polygraph arguments, one must believe that those field studies in which polygraph-induced confessions are the basis for determining ground truth can be used to estimate CQT accuracy when the only cases selected for study are likely to be the ones that were scored correctly by the original examiner.

(7) To accept the pro-polygraph arguments, one must believe that polygraph testing is standardized enough to constitute a scientific test when in fact there are no standards as to what constitutes an acceptable test and the nature of individually administered CQTs varies substantially from one examiner to another.

(8) To accept the pro-polygraph arguments, one must believe that government use of screening tests is justified despite their being strongly biased against the innocent and a complete lack of evidence that they either catch or deter spies.

---

**[Section 8:118]**

[1]Besides countermeasure information being available in university libraries, in texts such as this, it is also available in public libraries and bookstores in Lykken's books (cited in footnote 73), and on the worldwide web under http://www.polygraph.com, http://www.antipolygraph.org, and http://www.nopolygraph.com.

[2]Responding to a request for information made under the Freedom of Information Act, the Department of Defense Polygraph Institute's Dr. Gordon Barland noted in October of 1996 that "we do not teach, nor do we advocate, [the directed lie test's] use in criminal testing."

# Chapter 9

# Fires, Arsons and Explosions

## I. LEGAL ISSUES

### § 9:1 Introduction

The frequency of reliability challenges to fire investigations has steadily increased since the decision in *Daubert*,[1] and many of them have resulted in exclusion of testimony. The fire investigation community has teetered and tottered with the push of major decisions. Following *Daubert* and leading up to the 11th Circuit's decision in *Benfield*,[2] the International Association of Arson Investigators urged courts to regard fire investigation as being something other than a science and therefore not subject to evaluation under *Daubert*. Between *Benfield* and *Kumho Tire*, insurance defense attorneys frequently advised fire and arson experts to avoid the "S" word like the plague in an effort to avoid *Daubert* scrutiny. After *Kumho Tire*, it appeared there was no escape, scrutiny increased, often resulting in exclusion, and the result has been that fire examiners have grown more cautious about what it is they say when they climb onto the witness stand. Now they work harder to make sure that what they have to say is supportable with serious evidence and methods. These developments are described in greater detail in the sections that follow.

Even in the wake of *Kumho Tire*, judicial scrutiny is not consistent. Courts appear to scrutinize more thoroughly and write more detailed opinions when they exclude proffered expert evidence; exclusion on the basis of minimal scrutiny and a superficial opinion is a virtual null set. Decisions to admit evidence are accompanied by less apparent scrutiny. Which is the chicken and which the egg is a puzzle. Do courts fail to exclude because they fail to scrutinize rigorously? Or do they work harder to justify a decision to exclude? In either event, and paradoxically given the law's formal presumptions and burdens of proof, it appears that the real starting point is a presumption of admission, with exclusion occurring only with effort.

Fire and explosion investigation consists of a highly varied mixture of methods, techniques, and principles. Consequently, there is not just one actual or potential body of relevant scientific research on which experts may depend, but many, some of which are more sound and others which are less sound.[3] Fire investigators can be found who rely on such tools as electronic sniffers, accelerant detecting canines, and

---

**[Section 9:1]**

[1]*Daubert v. Merrell Dow Pharmaceuticals, Inc.*, 509 U.S. 579, 113 S. Ct. 2786, 125 L. Ed. 2d 469, 27, 27 U.S.P.Q.2d 1200, Prod. Liab. Rep. (CCH) P 13494, 37 Fed. R. Evid. Serv. 1, 23 Envtl. L. Rep. 20979 (1993).

[2]*Michigan Millers Mut. Ins. Corp. v. Benfield*, 140 F.3d 915, 49 Fed. R. Evid. Serv. 549 (11th Cir. 1998).

[3]This state of affairs contrasts with most of the kinds of expertise with which the chapters of this book are concerned. But it is not unique. For

gas chromatography; examination of electrical arc beads, metallurgical examination, burn patterns, crazed glass, concrete spalling; and consideration of reports of the color of the smoke and the fire, blood chemistry, and other indications from human remains found at the fire scene. Some of these clues are derived from sound science. Others are nothing more than a set of more or less shared beliefs that may or may not be true.[4] An opinion is then reached by these clues being processed through each investigator's personal experience, beliefs and assumptions—in addition to or instead of any well tested model for analyzing fire evidence.[5]

Such profusion presents courts with a dilemma. In considering admissibility, should members of a field of expertise be required to elucidate each of the components on which they rely, and to establish the validity of each component? Or should the courts make a general, global, judgment about the field, and trust the expert, under questioning by counsel, to spell out the details? Historically, the courts generally followed the latter strategy, and experts, once permitted to testify, were given wide latitude to offer opinions based on whatever the expert thought reasonable.[6] The task-at-hand analysis called for by *Daubert* and elaborated upon by *Kumho Tire* would appear to have brought those carefree days to an end. Task-at-hand analysis requires a court to identify the precise knowledge and skills invoked by an expert witness and to focus its gatekeeping responsibilities on those particular expert claims. The approach elaborated by *Kumho Tire* follows from the logic of *Daubert*. *Daubert* requires a finding of validity of the basis for an expert witness's opinion. That gatekeeping requirement would be defeated if multiple techniques were allowed to hide behind a global claim of expertise. In other words, *Daubert* appears to require that an expertise be unpacked, so that the court can permit those methods and principles it is persuaded are valid, and only those, to be offered to the factfinder. *Kumho Tire* makes that requirement explicit.

Expert testimony on the causes of fires went through a period of initial judicial resistance as being an inappropriate subject matter for expert opinions.[7] Gradually, the courts began to reverse themselves, allowing fire investigators and others to of-

---

example, the testimony of medical examiners or accident reconstructionists depends on the witness bringing together a potentially wide range of principles or assumptions on which an opinion is based.

[4]As the field begins to test its beliefs, some are confirmed and others are found to be false. See §§ 9:29 et seq.

[5]"As circumstantial proof of the incendiary origin of a fire, arson investigators rely most heavily upon a rather amorphous group of so-called burn or arson indicators." Andre A. Moenssens et al., Scientific Evidence in Civil and Criminal Cases 416 (4th ed. 1995).

[6]Thus, it is not possible to list the pivotal or leading case by which each jurisdiction permitted each component of the expertise. And after *Daubert v. Merrell Dow Pharmaceuticals, Inc.*, 509 U.S. 579, 113 S. Ct. 2786, 125 L. Ed. 2d 469, 27, 27 U.S.P.Q.2d 1200, Prod. Liab. Rep. (CCH) P 13494, 37 Fed. R. Evid. Serv. 1, 23 Envtl. L. Rep. 20979 (1993) (hereafter, *Daubert*), and *Kumho Tire Co., Ltd. v. Carmichael*, 526 U.S. 137, 119 S. Ct. 1167, 143 L. Ed. 2d 238, 50, 50 U.S.P.Q.2d 1177, Prod. Liab. Rep. (CCH) P 15470, 50 Fed. R. Evid. Serv. 1373, 29 Envtl. L. Rep. 20638 (1999) (hereafter, *Kumho Tire*) the case law admitting fire and

explosion experts under a notion of broad, global expertise has been rendered irrelevant to future fire admission decisions, at least in *Daubert/Kumho* jurisdictions.

[7]*State v. Watson*, 65 Me. 74, 1876 WL 4091 (1876) (testimony of a fireman on the spread of fire and aspects of fire behavior excluded as within the scope of common experience); *Neal v. Missouri Pac. Ry. Co.*, 98 Neb. 460, 153 N.W. 492 (1915) (fireman's opinion as to where a fire started excluded as invading the province of the jury); *People v. Grutz*, 212 N.Y. 72, 105 N.E. 843 (1914) (an assistant fire marshal should not have been permitted to express his opinion about the origin of a fire because the physical facts could be readily understood by the jury when properly described); *Sawyer v. State*, 100 Fla. 1603, 132 So. 188 (1931) (witness in arson case, in this instance the chief of a fire department, may not as a general rule give an opinion whether fire was of incendiary origin because this is "a question for the jury to determine, and upon which they can usually form their own opinion without any need of expert advice"); *Beneks v. State*, 208 Ind. 317, 196 N.E. 73 (1935) (expert witness cannot give his opinion as to origin of fire because jury can draw conclusions from observable facts that can be testified to by expert).

fer expert testimony on causes of fires.[8] The courts came to focus more on the training and experience of the proffered expert rather than on the validity of the proffered expertise, their assumption being that valid knowledge existed and the only issue was whether the witness possessed it in sufficient quantity. Of course, the line that divides enough training and experience[9] from not enough[10] may not be a very bright one. But deciding on an expert witness's "qualifications" is easy compared to evaluating the validity (or lack of validity) of the knowledge held by the field represented by the witness.[11]

As this chapter explains, some of the scientific predicates long relied upon by investigators and admitted by courts were later found by research on those investigative methods to be less valid than the experts or the courts thought them to be.[12] In some instances, principles of fire investigation that lacked a sound scientific basis led to convictions for arson and homicide by arson that later were vacated.[13]

Consider the courts' responses to some specific elements of fire investigation lore. Concrete spalling has been allowed as conclusive evidence that a fire was started by incendiary means, typically with little or no question raised about the validity of the asserted relationship between spalling and arson.[14] Crazed glass has been relied upon as "indicating a fast spreading fire."[15] Expert testimony about burn patterns has been admitted as providing evidence that a fire was of incendiary origin.[16] These and other beliefs of fire investigators have since been called into doubt by empirical research.[17] Similarly, some courts recently have been admitting dog "alerts" as evidence of arson without requiring hard evidence of the accuracy of the canines, and in particular without considering empirical evidence of the level of false positive errors in the method—data which have given great pause to many arson evidence

---

[8]An example of testimony by an "other": *Brown v. Eakins*, 220 Or. 122, 348 P.2d 1116 (1960) (an electrician who regularly investigated fires was qualified as an expert on the causes of fires, despite lack of any formal fire investigation training).

[9]*Billings v. State*, 503 S.W.2d 57 (Mo. Ct. App. 1973) (fireman with 4.5 years experience and investigation of two dozen fires found to be qualified); *State v. Wilbur*, 115 R.I. 7, 339 A.2d 730 (1975) (seven years experience as firefighter, several months arson investigation training, and three years as a fire inspector found qualified).

[10]*Sperow v. Carter*, 8 Pa. D. & C.2d 635, 1957 WL 6357 (C.P. 1957) (a part time fire chief who had been fighting fires for 20 years found not qualified); *State v. Barnett*, 480 A.2d 791 (Me. 1984) (a fire chief with 18 years experience fighting fires, extensive formal training in fire fighting, and fire investigation experience as a consultant to the Air Force and several large corporations found not qualified).

[11]For example, consider an astrologer with a successful practice for 25 years, extensive education and training, and numerous certifications and awards.

[12]§ 9:30.

[13]See, e.g., *State v. Knapp*, No. CR78779 (Superior Court of Arizona, Maricopa County, Feb. 11, 1987); *State v. Girdler*, No. 9809 (Superior Court of Arizona, Maricopa County, Jan. 3, 1991); see also, *Girdler v. Dale*, 859 F. Supp. 1279 (D. Ariz. 1994). Arson Review Committee, Report on

the Peer Review of the Expert Testimony in the Cases of State of Texas v. Cameron Todd Willingham and State of Texas v. Ernest Ray Willis (2006), available at www.innocenceproject.org.

[14]See, e.g., *Reed v. Allstate Ins. Co.*, 376 So. 2d 1303 (La. Ct. App. 2d Cir. 1979), writ denied, 378 So. 2d 1382 (La. 1980); *Security Ins. Co. of Hartford v. Dudds, Inc.*, 648 F.2d 273 (5th Cir. 1981); *State v. Danskin*, 122 N.H. 817, 451 A.2d 396 (1982); *LeForge v. Nationwide Mut. Fire Ins. Co.*, 82 Ohio App. 3d 692, 612 N.E.2d 1318 (12th Dist. Clinton County 1992); *American Mfrs. Mut. Ins. Co. v. General Motors Corp.*, 582 So. 2d 934 (La. Ct. App. 2d Cir. 1991) (unlike the other cases in this note, the expert drew a negative inference: because there was no spalling, the fire at issue was thought not to have been arson). But see § 9:30.

[15]*McReynolds v. Cherokee Ins. Co.*, 815 S.W.2d 208 (Tenn. Ct. App. 1991). But see § 9:29.

[16]*People v. Thomas*, 65 Cal. 2d 698, 56 Cal. Rptr. 305, 423 P.2d 233 (1967); *People v. Swain*, 200 Cal. App. 2d 344, 19 Cal. Rptr. 403 (4th Dist. 1962); *Com. v. Wisneski*, 214 Pa. Super. 397, 257 A.2d 624 (1969); *State v. Kelley*, 901 S.W.2d 193 (Mo. Ct. App. W.D. 1995); *State v. Swanson*, 1995 WL 238853 (Minn. Ct. App. 1995); *State v. Bouchillion*, 1995 WL 75444 (Tenn. Crim. App. 1995); *State v. Bernier*, 13 Conn. L. Rptr. 498, 1995 WL 70337 (Conn. Super. Ct. 1995); *State v. Haggood*, 36 Conn. App. 753, 653 A.2d 216 (1995); *Adams v. Tennessee Farmers Mut. Ins. Co.*, 898 S.W.2d 216 (Tenn. Ct. App. 1994). But see 9:14 and 9:22.

[17]§ 9:30.

professionals.[18]

These examples might make clear why courts could profitably unpack this broad area of forensic expertise into its component sub-areas and separately consider the validity of each. Judicial skepticism is expected to return to some of these areas.

## § 9:2 Before *Kumho Tire*: Are fire experts subject to *Daubert* scrutiny?

In deciding whether asserted fire and arson expertise had to be tested under *Daubert*, some courts made a distinction between whether the expert was offered as, or claimed to be, a "scientific" expert, in which case *Daubert* was applied, or whether the expert was sailing under the flag of "technical or other" expertise, in which case the expert was tested by a lesser standard.

The most interesting of these cases is *Michigan Millers Mutual Insurance Corp. v. Benfield*.[1] The Millers had sought a declaratory judgment against its insured, Benfield, precluding payment of fire insurance benefits on several grounds, notably that the fire had been intentionally set. The district judge excluded the testimony of the insurance company's expert, finding that his proffered testimony did not meet *Daubert*'s reliability criteria, adding that the testimony did not meet the requirements of *Frye*[2] either.

Michigan Millers appealed to the 11th Circuit,[3] arguing that its expert should have been admitted—not because the expertise was scientific, but because it was *not* scientific, therefore should not have been subject to *Daubert*, and should instead be admissible on a lesser standard as "experience-based" expertise.[4] Appellants cited several cases where testimony had been admitted over *Daubert*-based objections.

The International Association of Arson Investigators (IAAI) submitted an amicus brief urging the admission of the expert testimony. The brief argued that a fire and arson expert who is qualified by conventional criteria and who is not presenting any novel scientific evidence should not have to pass *Daubert* scrutiny. That argument was based on the clearly mistaken (but surprisingly common) belief that *Daubert* was narrowly focused on novel scientific techniques and methodologies. Since fire investigation is not a novel scientific technique, the amicus argued, *Daubert* should not apply.[5] The IAAI brief also argued that fire and arson investigation is neither a science nor strictly based on science, but its asserted validity rests instead on training and experience, and for that reason as well *Daubert* was inapplicable—a view

---

[18]§§ 9:7 and 9:23.

**[Section 9:2]**

[1]The opinion of the United States District Court for the Middle District of Florida, No. 93-1283-CIV-T-17A, is unreported.

[2]*Frye v. U.S.*, 293 F. 1013, 34 A.L.R. 145 (App. D.C. 1923) (rejected by, State v. Walstad, 119 Wis. 2d 483, 351 N.W.2d 469 (1984)) and (rejected by, State v. Brown, 297 Or. 404, 687 P.2d 751 (1984)) and (rejected by, Nelson v. State, 628 A.2d 69 (Del. 1993)) and (rejected by, State v. Alberico, 116 N.M. 156, 861 P.2d 192 (1993)) and (rejected by, State v. Moore, 268 Mont. 20, 885 P.2d 457 (1994)) and (rejected by, State v. Faught, 127 Idaho 873, 908 P.2d 566 (1995)) and (rejected by, People v. Shreck, 22 P.3d 68, 90 A.L.R.5th 765 (Colo. 2001)).

[3]*Michigan Millers Mut. Ins. Corp. v. Benfield*, 140 F.3d 915, 49 Fed. R. Evid. Serv. 549 (11th Cir. 1998).

[4]"Millers argues that *Carmichael v. Samyang Tire, Inc.*, 131 F.3d 1433, Prod. Liab. Rep. (CCH) P 15137, 48 Fed. R. Evid. Serv. 334 (11th Cir. 1997), judgment rev'd, 526 U.S. 137, 119 S. Ct. 1167, 143 L. Ed. 2d 238, 50, 50 U.S.P.Q.2d 1177, Prod. Liab. Rep. (CCH) P 15470, 50 Fed. R. Evid. Serv. 1373, 29 Envtl. L. Rep. 20638 (1999) made clear that the *Daubert* criteria apply only to scientific testimony, and the testimony of their expert was not based on scientific principles but rather was based on his years of experience, and on his skill and experience-based observations." *Michigan Millers Mut. Ins. Corp. v. Benfield*, 140 F.3d 915, 920, 49 Fed. R. Evid. Serv. 549 (11th Cir. 1998).

[5]Cf. *Daubert v. Merrell Dow Pharmaceuticals, Inc.*, 509 U.S. 579, 593 n.11, 113 S. Ct. 2786, 125 L. Ed. 2d 469, 27, 27 U.S.P.Q.2d 1200, Prod. Liab. Rep. (CCH) P 13494, 37 Fed. R. Evid. Serv. 1, 23 Envtl. L. Rep. 20979 (1993).

later rejected unanimously in *Kumho Tire*.[6]

In addition, a member[7] of the IAAI, upon seeing the organization's amicus brief, wrote and submitted his own amicus brief, in which he argued that although the field once was unscientific, it has been making important strides in recent years, and that judicial toleration of unscientific arson investigation certainly would not inspire the field to continue to develop itself as an empirically grounded science.[8]

The Court of Appeals applied an analysis following its decision in the case of *Carmichael v. Samyang Tire, Inc.*[9] It concluded that because the fire investigator in question had held himself out as an expert in fire science, *Daubert* criteria did indeed apply to the issue of the admissibility of his testimony, and the Circuit Court upheld the District Court's exclusion of the testimony. The expert had performed no tests, taken no samples, and could not adequately explain how he had reached his conclusion. The court cited *General Electric v. Joiner* for the proposition that courts are not required to admit opinions based on nothing more than the ipse dixit of the expert.[10] On the other hand, it held that the "experience-based" testimony of a different expert, the local fire investigator employed by Sarasota County, could be admitted for the jury's consideration. Because the fire in question was an obvious arson fire, however, the Court set aside the trial court's directed verdict and remanded the case for a new trial.

The case ultimately was settled prior to a second trial, but the repercussions of the case continued to reverberate through the fire investigation community. As a result of the 11th Circuit's reliance on the witness's self-characterization as either a scientific witness or an experience-based witness, some insurance company attorneys began counseling fire investigators to identify themselves as "experience-based" experts, in an effort to avoid scrutiny under *Daubert*.

Still trying to avoid judicial scrutiny of its asserted expertise, the IAAI again submitted an amicus brief when *Carmichael v. Samyang Tire* (of which *Benfield* had been progeny), now known as *Kumho Tire Co., Ltd. v. Carmichael*[11] was heard by the United States Supreme Court. Joining an amicus brief filed by the International Association of Chiefs of Police, Mothers Against Drunk Driving, the National District Attorneys Association, and numerous other organizations, their brief in *Kumho Tire* argued that the trial judge's gatekeeping responsibility should not serve as an obstacle to testimony based on "technical" or "specialized" knowledge or it would threaten much of the expert evidence that law enforcement organizations offer.[12]

The Supreme Court in *Kumho Tire*, of course, unanimously rejected such

---

[6]The Supreme Court's view implies that these questions could and should be put to those who claim a valid expertise on the basis of training and experience: What knowledge was imparted to you in your training? How can we know if it was valid? What knowledge did you acquire through your experience? How can we know if it was valid? (After all, if training and experience without further inquiry establish expertise, then astrology would be admissible.)

[7]John Lentini, author of the scientific status portion of this chapter.

[8]Copies of both the IAAI brief and Lentini's brief are on file with the author.

[9]*Carmichael v. Samyang Tire, Inc.*, 131 F.3d 1433, Prod. Liab. Rep. (CCH) P 15137, 48 Fed. R. Evid. Serv. 334 (11th Cir. 1997), judgment rev'd, 526 U.S. 137, 119 S. Ct. 1167, 143 L. Ed. 2d 238, 50, 50 U.S.P.Q.2d 1177, Prod. Liab. Rep. (CCH) P 15470, 50 Fed. R. Evid. Serv. 1373, 29 Envtl. L.

Rep. 20638 (1999), later to be known as *Kumho Tire v. Carmichael*.

[10]*General Elec. Co. v. Joiner*, 522 U.S. 136, 118 S. Ct. 512, 139 L. Ed. 2d 508, 18 O.S.H. Cas. (BNA) 1097, Prod. Liab. Rep. (CCH) P 15120, 48 Fed. R. Evid. Serv. 1, 28 Envtl. L. Rep. 20227, 177 A.L.R. Fed. 667 (1997).

[11]*Kumho Tire Co., Ltd. v. Carmichael*, 526 U.S. 137, 119 S. Ct. 1167, 143 L. Ed. 2d 238, 50, 50 U.S.P.Q.2d 1177, Prod. Liab. Rep. (CCH) P 15470, 50 Fed. R. Evid. Serv. 1373, 29 Envtl. L. Rep. 20638 (1999).

[12]Brief Amici Curiae of Americans for Effective Law Enforcement, Inc.; Criminal Justice Legal Foundation; Grand Lodge of Fraternal Order of Police; International Association of Arson Investigators; International Association of Chiefs of Police; Mothers Against Drunk Driving; National Association of Police Organizations, Inc.; National District Attorneys Association; and

arguments. Had the decision gone the other way, and "technical and other specialized" experts were exempted from scrutiny under *Daubert*, their experience, intuition and ipse dixit would have been transformed from shortcomings into the very basis of their expertise. As a result of *Kumho Tire*, *Daubert*-based objections to fire investigation testimony not based on good science have increased.[13] Few of the rulings on *Daubert* challenges to fire investigators have reached the appellate level, but decisions affecting admissibility are quickly and widely circulated among fire investigators through trade publications and electronic bulletin boards.

In still another repercussion of the *Benfield* decision, the National Fire Protection Association Technical Committee on Fire Investigations, the committee responsible for the preparation and maintenance of NFPA 921, *Guide for Fire and Explosion Investigations*, received several public proposals to eliminate from the *Guide* any reference to science or the scientific method. (This despite the fact that *Kumho Tire* had rendered that means of evading scrutiny unavailing.) The proponents of this change wanted to substitute the words "systematic approach" for "scientific method." The Technical Committee rejected these proposals, while attempting to deal with the misperception that a scientific fire investigation requires a complete reconstruction of the fire. The 2001 edition of NFPA 921 makes reference to "cognitive" testing as well as experimental testing as a means of testing a hypothesis within the structure of the scientific method. Cognitive testing, as used in this context, means mentally comparing all of the collected data with the proposed hypothesis, and rejecting the hypothesis if it cannot account for all of the data.

The *Benfield* court was not alone in the question it pondered, as fire investigators sought shelter from *Daubert*. Before *Kumho Tire* unanimously resolved the confusion about whether *Daubert*'s gatekeeping requirement applied only to the "scientific" prong of Rule 702, or whether it applied to all kinds of expert opinion evidence, a number of courts struggled with the question in the context of fire causation. Typically, these cases relied on an expert's "experience" to substitute for systematic empirical or theoretical knowledge on the facts in dispute, and allowed the asserted expert to testify.[14] After *Kumho Tire* and after the recent revision to Fed. R. Evid. 702 it is doubtful that the cases cited in the margin could be regarded as following the requirements of Federal evidence law.

### § 9:3 Other aspects of admissibility and exclusion of fire experts

A number of other aspects of the problem of what is required for proffered fire expert testimony to be admitted, some of them hinted at in the *Benfield* discussion, supra, are considered next.

---

National Sheriffs' Association; and Police Law Institute, submitted to the United States Supreme Court in *Kumho Tire Company, Ltd. v. Carmichael* (October 19, 1998).

[13]§§ 9:10 et seq.

[14]*Talkington v. Atria Reclamelucifers Fabrieken BV*, 152 F.3d 254, Prod. Liab. Rep. (CCH) P 15288, 49 Fed. R. Evid. Serv. 1184 (4th Cir. 1998) (holding *Daubert* inapplicable to expert testimony about the cause of fire in a house, because the defendant acknowledged the testimony was not science and was not based on scientific principles or data, but was based instead on the expert's training and experience); *Polizzi Meats, Inc. v. Aetna Life & Cas. Co.*, 931 F. Supp. 328 (D.N.J. 1996) (holding that the lack of any scientific or other systematic empirical basis for their testimony on the origin and cause of fire at insured's building did not preclude testimony of insurer's expert witnesses); *Patterson v. Conopco, Inc.*, 999 F. Supp. 1417 (D. Kan. 1997) (holding it acceptable for an expert to "rely on his experience," though he had never actually conducted any tests on whether human hair could sustain a fire and, presumably, could point to no data on the question); *Fireman's Fund Ins. Co. v. Xerox Corp.*, 30 F. Supp. 2d 823, 51 Fed. R. Evid. Serv. 98 (M.D. Pa. 1998) (holding *Daubert* inapplicable and admitting an expert's opinion on how a fire started at a copy machine, concluding that the expert was "not relying on any particular methodology or technique," and that he had "reached his . . . conclusions by drawing upon general electrical engineering principles and his twenty-five years of experience investigating electrical accidents."). For a further discussion of experience-based expertise in fire cases, see § 9:6.

### § 9:4 Other aspects of admissibility and exclusion of fire experts—The qualifications of the expert

The Supreme Court's admissibility cases make clear that the admissibility of claimed expertise is distinct from the qualifications of the expert. Qualifications of fire and arson experts vary considerably, and the courts have done little to distinguish among the various kinds of proffered experts, ranging from fire department employees with minimal science training to bachelors level engineers to chemists with doctorates. Even with a given subspecialty, unlike experts in medicine or economics or many other fields, courts cannot rely on a fire investigation expert to have completed an established curriculum. Suitable qualifications are necessary but not sufficient for the admission of the proffered expert testimony.[1] *Kumho Tire* went further, emphasizing the need to evaluate the precise "task at hand"—the factual issue which expertise is being offered to resolve. The implications of *Kumho Tire* suggests that the proffered expert must be qualified on precisely the expert issue at bar, rather than some general or global expertise in fire investigation.

Though fairly superficial scrutiny usually is involved in passing on qualifications, it may be worth noting that one can only be qualified as an expert in a subject on which an expertise exists. In other words, one cannot be an expert on something in which there is no expertise. Thus, where a technique (e.g., dog sniffing for accelerants) is being challenged, qualifications and admissibility of the expertise will be entangled.

One example of rather stringent scrutiny of qualifications, interwoven with scrutiny of doubtful foundations for the experts' proffered opinions, is *Weisgram v. Marley Co.*,[2] where the Court of Appeals for the Eighth Circuit found the district court's wholesale admission of various types of fire causation experts to constitute reversible error. The Court of Appeals judged all three experts to be "unqualified" and their opinion testimony "speculative." A city fire captain who investigated the fire in the home was held not qualified to give expert testimony as to whether or not the baseboard heater in the home malfunctioned, or how the heater might have ignited other objects, and his opinions were found to be without foundation. A fire investigator's testimony that the baseboard heater was defective and caused the fire was held to be unsupported by sufficient foundation because no studies had been conducted to test the investigator's theory; the Court found that instead it was based on pure speculation. Finally, the Court held that the expert testimony of a metallurgist that thermostat contacts on the baseboard heater were defectively designed was not supported by sufficient foundation because the metallurgist had little knowledge about this particular model heater or this type of heater. Moreover, upon excluding the testimony of these witnesses, the Court of Appeals directed that judgment be entered against the proponent of this expert evidence, which decision was appealed to the United States Supreme Court.

Specifically, the plaintiffs complained that it was "unfair" to direct a verdict against them without giving them a chance to procure admissible expert testimony. The Supreme Court rejected this argument: "Since *Daubert*, . . . parties relying on expert evidence have had notice of the exacting standards of reliability such evidence must meet. It is implausible to suggest, post-*Daubert*, that parties will initially present less than their best expert evidence in the expectation of a second chance should their first try fail. We therefore find unconvincing [the plaintiff's] fears that

---

**[Section 9:4]**

[1]Cf. *Allstate Ins. Co. v. Maytag Corp.*, 1999 WL 203349 (N.D. Ill. 1999), discussed in more detail infra, a case which illustrates reliance on credentials and no scrutiny of the basis of the proffered testimony.

[2]*Weisgram v. Marley Co.*, 169 F.3d 514, Prod. Liab. Rep. (CCH) P 15475, 51 Fed. R. Evid. Serv. 76 (8th Cir. 1999), aff'd, 528 U.S. 440, 120 S. Ct. 1011, 145 L. Ed. 2d 958, Prod. Liab. Rep. (CCH) P 15745, 53 Fed. R. Evid. Serv. 406, 45 Fed. R. Serv. 3d 735 (2000).

allowing courts of appeals to direct the entry of judgment for defendants will punish plaintiffs who could have shored up their cases by other means had they known their expert testimony would be found inadmissible."[3] On the specific procedural question presented, the Court held "that the authority of courts of appeals to direct the entry of judgment as a matter of law extends to cases in which, on excision of testimony erroneously admitted, there remains insufficient evidence to support a jury's verdict."[4]

## § 9:5 Other aspects of admissibility and exclusion of fire experts—Novelty

Occasionally a court mistakenly treats *Daubert* as applying only to "novel" types of expertise, and in effect grandfathers in a non-novel yet questionable expertise by refusing to scrutinize it. The district court in *Polizzi Meats, Inc. v. Aetna Life & Casualty Co.*[1] did so with remarkable vehemence considering that the court was misreading *Daubert*. The defendant insurer refused to pay the plaintiff's claims resulting from a fire that had destroyed its place of business. Aetna asserted that the plaintiffs had set the fire intentionally. In a partial summary judgment motion, the plaintiffs argued that Aetna's experts had not produced "scientific proof" of the cause of the fire, and therefore they should be barred from testifying. The district court held that this "astounding contention is based on a seriously flawed reading of . . . *Daubert* . . . . [which] addressed the standards to be applied by a trial judge when faced with a proffer of expert scientific testimony based upon a novel theory or methodology. Nothing in *Daubert* suggests that trial judges should exclude otherwise relevant testimony of police and fire investigators on the issues of the origins and causes of fires."[2] Apparently the district court overlooked the gloss on novelty given in *Daubert*, namely: "[W]e do not read the requirements of Rule 702 to apply specially or exclusively to unconventional evidence. Of course, well-established propositions are less likely to be challenged than those that are novel, and they are more handily defended."[3]

An even more confused opinion is *Jugle v. Volkswagen of America, Inc.*[4] This case involved a young man who was burned to death in a Volkswagen Jetta. The defendant sought in limine to exclude the plaintiff's experts' testimony, but that motion was denied. One expert offered the opinion that the catalytic converter had caused a wax used on the floor pan to ignite, which in turn had caused plastic fuel lines to melt and burn. A second expert offered the opinion that the converter had ignited the fuel lines directly, even though this theory was contradicted by the first expert's data. The *Jugle* court held *Daubert* inapplicable to the expertise or to the opinions at issue in the case. "Because the opinions of Dr. Jacobson and Mr. Cole are not based on novel scientific techniques, the Court need not test their opinions against *Daubert*'s four factors."[5] The opinion went on to say that "[t]he Court must, however, still assess the reliability and fit of the proposed experts' opinions,"[6] and for this proposition it quoted the language in *Daubert* which explained that Rule 702's

---

[3]528 U.S. 440, 456, 120 S.Ct. 1011, 145 L.Ed.2d 958 (2000).

[4]*Weisgram v. Marley Co.*, 528 U.S. 440, 457, 120 S. Ct. 1011, 145 L. Ed. 2d 958, Prod. Liab. Rep. (CCH) P 15745, 53 Fed. R. Evid. Serv. 406, 45 Fed. R. Serv. 3d 735 (2000).

**[Section 9:5]**

[1]*Polizzi Meats, Inc. v. Aetna Life & Cas. Co.*, 931 F. Supp. 328 (D.N.J. 1996).

[2]*Polizzi Meats, Inc. v. Aetna Life & Cas. Co.*, 931 F. Supp. 328, 336, (D.N.J. 1996).

[3]*Daubert v. Merrell Dow Pharmaceuticals,*

*Inc.*, 509 U.S. 579, 593 n.11, 113 S. Ct. 2786, 125 L. Ed. 2d 469, 27, 27 U.S.P.Q.2d 1200, Prod. Liab. Rep. (CCH) P 13494, 37 Fed. R. Evid. Serv. 1, 23 Envtl. L. Rep. 20979 (1993).

[4]*Jugle v. Volkswagen of America, Inc.*, 975 F. Supp. 576, Prod. Liab. Rep. (CCH) P 15191, 48 Fed. R. Evid. Serv. 115 (D. Vt. 1997).

[5]*Jugle v. Volkswagen of America, Inc.*, 975 F. Supp. 576, 580, Prod. Liab. Rep. (CCH) P 15191, 48 Fed. R. Evid. Serv. 115 (D. Vt. 1997).

[6]*Jugle v. Volkswagen of America, Inc.*, 975 F. Supp. 576, 580, Prod. Liab. Rep. (CCH) P 15191, 48 Fed. R. Evid. Serv. 115 (D. Vt. 1997).

gatekeeping requirements, explicated in *Daubert*, were not limited to novel or unconventional scientific evidence. Finally, the court found the methodology of the experts reliable, though it provided virtually no description of it in the opinion.[7]

## § 9:6 Other aspects of admissibility and exclusion of fire experts—Basis in experience versus in empirically tested knowledge

It is clear, after *Kumho Tire*, that no expert witness of any kind may pass through the *Daubert* gate unless and until the court is properly satisfied that the testimony is based on valid principles. What is not yet clear is what criteria courts may or must use in making this assessment, especially since they will vary to a greater or lesser extent with the specie of expert evidence being offered.

In the area of fire and arson, as in other areas, courts have been presented with the dilemma of deciding whether expertise must be based on adequate empirical testing or whether a looser accumulation of individual "experience" is sufficient. One such case is *Patterson v. Conopco, Inc.*[1] This was a wrongful death case involving a woman who died from burns and smoke inhalation in a bathroom fire. The decedent's plaintiff's claim was that hair spray made by the defendant had caused this fatal accident. The trial court denied challenges to the expert testimony of a chemist and a fire investigator. The chemist's report concluded that the hair spray contained flammable materials that are easily ignited and will propagate a fire. The fire investigator's testimony purported to explain how the accident could have occurred. The defendant argued that the chemist's conclusion depended on the assumption that human hair by itself could not sustain combustion, a "fact" based only on the chemist's "experience," not any systematic testing. The court held, nevertheless, that it was acceptable for an expert to "rely on his experience" and to take that more casually acquired knowledge into account in forming an opinion.[2] This decision may or may not have survived *Kumho Tire*'s emphasis on the need of a court to evaluate the specific "task at hand."

Because *Allstate Insurance Co. v. Maytag Corp.*[3] was decided after *Kumho Tire*, the magistrate judge had no doubt that *Daubert* applied to fire experts, yet he appears to have been content to rely on the credentials and experience of the experts, rather than scrutinizing with particularity the basis of their asserted knowledge, the content of the knowledge, and determining whether it was sufficiently sound that the opinions flowing from it would be dependable. The judge also did not find the objection that one expert's theory of causation was unsupported by any testing to raise any barriers to the witness offering his opinion on causation. On the other hand, the judge did draw some lines. Because the defendant's expert was a mechanical engineer with a great deal of experience with the cooktops which were the disputed source of a house fire, and not an expert in fire causation, the judge limited his testimony to the nature of the cooktop and why in his opinion it could not have been the source of the fire. In admitting the testimony of both experts, the magistrate judge ruled that they were "based on deductions from various known technical facts which appear to have at least a theoretical basis."[4] One might have expected the judge to follow the example of Justice Breyer in *Kumho Tire* and state with

---

[7]*Jugle v. Volkswagen of America, Inc.*, 975 F. Supp. 576, 581, Prod. Liab. Rep. (CCH) P 15191, 48 Fed. R. Evid. Serv. 115 (D. Vt. 1997).

**[Section 9:6]**

[1]*Patterson v. Conopco, Inc.*, 999 F. Supp. 1417 (D. Kan. 1997).

[2]"It is true, as *Conopco* asserts, that Armstrong's conclusion was based in part on his stated opinion that human hair by itself (i.e. without an outside fuel source) will not sustain combustion and that this view in turn was founded in large part on Armstrong's personal experience. That fact alone, however, does not make it an illegitimate basis for consideration." *Patterson v. Conopco, Inc.*, 999 F. Supp. 1417, 1420, (D. Kan. 1997).

[3]*Allstate Ins. Co. v. Maytag Corp.*, 1999 WL 203349 (N.D. Ill. 1999).

[4]*Allstate Ins. Co. v. Maytag Corp.*, 1999 WL 203349 (N.D. Ill. 1999).

some particularity what the underlying knowledge was, and why it was or was not sound.

This is an issue that undoubtedly will continue to be confronted. Courts would be well advised to unpack the claimed "experience" in order to discover what was learned from it and whether that something supports a valid and reliable expert opinion. As stated in the commentary to Fed. R. Evid. 702, "the witness must explain how that experience leads to the conclusion reached, why that experience is a sufficient basis for the opinion, and how that experience is reliably applied to the facts."[5]

## § 9:7  Accelerant-detecting canines

Without requiring evidence of the ability of dogs in general to detect accelerants, or data concerning the accuracy of the particular dog in question, some courts have allowed the dogs' handlers to testify concerning the presence of accelerants at fire scenes based on the "alerts" of their dogs. This has occurred despite the newness of the technique and the applicability of *Daubert* in those jurisdictions.[1] Such research as has been conducted suggests canines used in this capacity are prone to making false positive errors.[2] Accordingly, the professional association of arson investigators has cautioned against reliance on canines for the detection of accelerants.[3]

Though most courts admitting canine accelerant detection evidence have done so without awareness of the research and professional association prohibition on the evidence, the U.S. Court of Appeals for the Second Circuit has gone to considerable lengths to twist the data and the cautions into unrecognizable form so as to uphold a district court's admission of dog sniff evidence. In *United States v. Marji*,[4] the Court of Appeals evaluated the district court's admission of dog alert evidence and

---

[5]Advisory Committee Notes, Amendments to Fed. R. Evid. 702 (effective December 1, 2000).

**[Section 9:7]**

[1]Admission of evidence of dog alert evidence was upheld in: *Reisch v. State*, 628 A.2d 84 (Del. 1993); *State v. Buller*, 517 N.W.2d 711 (Iowa 1994). Evidence from canine arson investigation was admitted in other cases, but the admissibility was not challenged. See e.g., *Auto-Owners Ins. Co. v. Ogden*, 667 So. 2d 743 (Ala. 1995) (table) (aff'd; rehearing denied; all opinions withdrawn); *State v. Bernier*, 13 Conn. L. Rptr. 498, 1995 WL 70337 (Conn. Super. Ct. 1995); *State v. Interest of W.T.B.*, 771 So. 2d 807 (La. Ct. App. 2d Cir. 2000).

[2]The Illinois State Police Bureau of Forensic Sciences conducted an experiment in which they placed known quantities of known substances in containers, and tested the sensitivity (how small a sample can be detected) and selectivity (distinguishing accelerants from other pyrolyzed substances) of both dogs and gas chromatographs or mass spectrometers. They found that while one dog did quite well, other dogs "were indicating on the pyrolyzed carpeting and foam padding samples, as well as on pine wood . . . ." They conclude that because dogs are "not very selective," "a positive alert must always be corroborated by the laboratory." George Dabdoub et al., Accelerant Detection Canines and the Laboratory, 1995 Proceedings of the American Academy of Forensic Sciences 19. § 9:16.

[3]The International Association of Arson Investigators adopted an official position which stated that until there is sufficient research to confirm that canines actually can discriminate between real accelerants and the wide array of other ignitable compounds, "[a]ny alert or indication not confirmed by laboratory analysis must be considered a false positive . . . for the purposes of origin and cause determination." They concluded: "If the forensic laboratory examination of the sample is negative for the presence of identifiable ignitable liquids, any positive indication by the canine of that sample *must* be deemed as *not relevant*." IAAI Forensic Science Committee Position on the Use of Accelerant Detection Canines, (Sept. 1994). § 9:16.

[4]*U.S. v. Marji*, 158 F.3d 60, 63, 49 Fed. R. Evid. Serv. 1522 (2d Cir. 1998) ("Although the defendant cites some studies and a proposed amendment to the National Fire Protection Association's Guide for Fire and Explosion Investigations to the effect that dog-sniff evidence is not always reliable, all that these sources suggest is that special weight should not be assigned to dog-sniff evidence in the absence of any corroborating evidence. We conclude that the trial judge did not abuse his broad discretion under *Daubert* in admitting the testimony. We note further that, even if we were to assume arguendo that the district judge's decision to allow this expert testimony was erroneous, there was substantial additional evidence offered at trial demonstrating

found no error.

The Court of Appeals seems to have presumed the soundness, and therefore the admissibility, of dog sniff evidence. The Court misconstrues the nature of error rate data when it states that dog alerts are "not always reliable," and it implies that the dogs usually are reliable. The Court essentially begs the empirical question to be decided. Reliability of a technique cannot be measured on an instance-by-instance basis but only in the aggregate, and the aggregate measure inevitably will show some level of accuracy (hits and correct rejections) and some level of inaccuracy (misses and false alarms). By the standard used by this panel, few if any techniques could ever be found so unreliable that they would have to be excluded. When the Circuit Court states that "all that these sources suggest is that special weight should not be assigned to dog-sniff evidence in the absence of any corroborating evidence," it misrepresents what those sources say and what they mean. The fire and arson field regards dog sniff evidence as merely a preliminary screening test that gives leads to an investigator but which ought not be offered as evidence unless and until it has been confirmed by laboratory testing. That is a far cry from cautioning against giving "special weight" "to dog-sniff evidence in the absence of any corroborating evidence." The Court transforms the field's advice that the evidence should be given no weight into a conclusion that it should be given no more than normal weight.

Finally, the Circuit Court concluded that "even if we were to assume arguendo that the district judge's decision to allow this expert testimony was erroneous" the error was harmless. The Circuit Court would have accomplished the same result, while placing itself on ground more consistent with the empirical evidence on dog alerts, to have concluded that, although the district court erred by admitting the dog-sniff evidence without sufficient basis for believing in its dependability, the error was harmless in light of other evidence in the case on the question of the presence of accelerants.

In other cases, courts found the use of dogs to establish the presence of accelerants to be unreliable and therefore inadmissible.[5]

### § 9:8    On whom can fire experts rely for the data on which they base their conclusions?

The case-specific information on which fire and arson experts base their conclusions sometimes includes the observations or inferences of others. To what extent can a fire investigator rely on the statements and conclusions of others? In *Westfield Insurance Co. v. Harris*,[1] a fire marshal relied for most of his information upon the investigator hired by one of the parties, thereby making his own conclusions the product of someone else's investigation and less than independent. In light of this, the district court had the fire marshal's evidence stricken from the record. The Court of Appeals vacated and remanded, holding that "it is within the fabric of the State Fire Marshal's official duties to receive and rely on insurance company information about fires within his jurisdiction."

### § 9:9    Who bears the burden of proof in a *Daubert* hearing?

At one level the answer to the question in the heading should be obvious: the

---

that an accelerant was used by the defendant to start the fire.").

[5]*People v. Acri*, 277 Ill. App. 3d 1030, 214 Ill. Dec. 761, 662 N.E.2d 115 (3d Dist. 1996); *Carr v. State*, 267 Ga. 701, 482 S.E.2d 314 (1997); *Farm Bureau Mut. Ins. Co. of Arkansas, Inc. v. Foote*, 341 Ark. 105, 14 S.W.3d 512 (2000) (adopting

*Daubert* as the test for admissibility of expert evidence in Arkansas, and finding that dog sniff evidence for the detection of accelerants failed the test).

**[Section 9:8]**

[1]*Westfield Ins. Co. v. Harris*, 134 F.3d 608, 48 Fed. R. Evid. Serv. 887 (4th Cir. 1998).

proponent of evidence always bears the burden of persuading the court that the conditions for its admission are met. But the question has nevertheless led to confusion in *Daubert* hearings on a variety of expert areas, and one particularly confusing instance arose in the context of a proffer of expert evidence on fire causation.

*Maryland Casualty Co. v. Therm-O-Disc, Inc.*[1] involved a fire that began in a clothes dryer, allegedly due to a malfunctioning part. The district court initially placed the burden on the opponent of the expert witness to show that the testimony could not meet the requirements of *Daubert*. Here is the Fourth Circuit's recitation of what happened:

> Neither party disputes that, at the beginning of the *Daubert* hearing, the district court told Jim Rothschild, counsel for Therm-O-Disc, "[y]ou have the burden of proof" with regard to Rodems's testimony. However, counsel immediately corrected the district court on this point, and from then forward it appears that the district court understood both the demands of *Daubert* and its own role as "gatekeeper," and conducted the hearing accordingly. Immediately after the objection, the district court withdrew its call for Mr. Rothschild to come forward and show that Rodems's testimony was not admissible, and called Rodems himself to the stand to explain the basis for that testimony. This Rodems did under both direct and cross-examination. After several hours of testimony, the district court determined that, although it had some reservations about the proffered basis for Rodems's opinion, "the defendant has failed to establish . . . [that] Mr. Rodems relied upon a scientific principle that was not valid."[2]

Although the Court of Appeals goes to considerable (and confusing) lengths to try to establish both that there is no burden of persuasion in a Rule 104(a) hearing and that the district court did not err because it placed the burden where it was supposed to be, the final sentence in the quotation above—offered in support of the correctness of the district court's hearing process—should leave readers wondering if, at the end of the day, the district judge did understand who bore the burden of persuasion, if there is a burden of persuasion.

The confusion in *Daubert* hearings is perhaps understandable, because the first voice heard is that of the *opponent* of proffered expert testimony. This has given some lawyers and judges the impression that the opponent has the burden of convincing the court that the witness does not meet *Daubert*'s requirements. This impression may be all the more compelling when the expertise being challenged is a type that has become familiar to the courts. But the correct procedure is the opposite of that.

The opponent of expert evidence need only make a showing sufficient to convince a trial court that the objection to the evidence is not frivolous; this triggers a *Daubert* hearing under Rule 104(a). In a Rule 104(a) hearing on the question of admissibility of expert evidence, "These matters should be established by a preponderance of proof."[3] This statement of a standard of proof implies that the hearing is analogous to a civil bench trial. The proponent has the initial burden of production and the ultimate burden of persuading the court that the proffered expert evidence satisfies Rule 702, as interpreted by *Daubert* and *Kumho Tire*. The trial judge serves as the factfinder.[4] And the judge must believe the expert's opinion

---

**[Section 9:9]**

[1]*Maryland Cas. Co. v. Therm-O-Disc, Inc.*, 137 F.3d 780, 48 Fed. R. Evid. Serv. 780 (4th Cir. 1998).

[2]*Maryland Cas. Co. v. Therm-O-Disc, Inc.*, 137 F.3d 780, 784, 48 Fed. R. Evid. Serv. 780 (4th Cir. 1998).

[3]*Daubert v. Merrell Dow Pharmaceuticals,* *Inc.*, 509 U.S. 579, 593 n.20, 113 S. Ct. 2786, 125 L. Ed. 2d 469, 27, 27 U.S.P.Q.2d 1200, Prod. Liab. Rep. (CCH) P 13494, 37 Fed. R. Evid. Serv. 1, 23 Envtl. L. Rep. 20979 (1993).

[4]Note that Rule 104(a) also provides: "In making its determination [the court] is not bound by the rules of evidence except those with respect to privileges."

by a preponderance of the evidence.[5] Thus, if both parties sat mute, the court would have to rule against the party with the burden of persuasion, namely, the proponent of the evidence. If at the end of the hearing, the evidence on the evidence were in equipoise, again the court would have to rule against the proponent of the evidence.

## § 9:10   Nature of scrutiny following *Kumho Tire*

Because *Kumho Tire* closed off the major route by which fire and arson experts had been seeking to evade scrutiny under *Daubert*, one might expect courts to be subjecting experts of many kinds, including fire and arson experts, to more rigorous inspections following *Kumho*. Though limited in number, and revealing a ratio of about 50:50 (close scrutiny to relaxed scrutiny), it does seem that the courts are indeed beginning to step up the level of rigor employed in their evaluations of fire and arson expertise under *Daubert* and *Kumho Tire*. It might be misleading to point out that most of the cases of more vigorous scrutiny and exclusion occurred in the context of a civil action, because most of the cases in which the expertise was challenged were civil cases.

## § 9:11   Nature of scrutiny following *Kumho Tire*—Excluded due to lack of adequate scientific foundation

In *Weisgram v. Marley*,[1] discussed in greater detail above, the Eighth Circuit Court of Appeals found plain error in the admission of three expert witnesses who had been permitted to testify by the District Court. A fire department officer who investigated the fire in the home was held not qualified to give expert testimony as to whether or not a baseboard heater in the home malfunctioned, or how the heater might have ignited other objects. A fire investigator's testimony that the baseboard heater was defective and caused the fire was held to be unsupported by sufficient foundation because no studies had been conducted to test the investigator's theory. Finally, the Court held that the expert testimony of a metallurgist that thermostat contacts on the baseboard heater were defectively designed was not supported by sufficient foundation because the metallurgist had little knowledge about this type of heater or this particular model heater. The rulings of the Court of Appeals were affirmed by the Supreme Court.[2]

In *Pride v. BIC Corp.*[3] the plaintiff's three experts were excluded by the District Court (following the recommendation of a Magistrate Judge), and the exclusion was upheld by the Sixth Circuit Court of Appeals. The plaintiff's husband had burned to death in a fire which the plaintiff argued had been caused by the defendant's defective cigarette lighter. In a thoughtful and detailed opinion, the Court of Appeals upheld the exclusion of a mechanical engineer, an analytical chemist, and a fire inspector, all of whose methods it found inadequate to support their opinions.

---

[5]This still does not answer the question of how much error is too much error to be admissible. For example, would expert predictions that are shown by all of the available evidence on the evidence to be correct only 51% of the time be sufficiently "reliable" to be admissible? Would expert predictions that are wrong more often than they are right be admissible?

**[Section 9:11]**

[1]*Weisgram v. Marley Co.*, 169 F.3d 514, Prod. Liab. Rep. (CCH) P 15475, 51 Fed. R. Evid. Serv. 76 (8th Cir. 1999), aff'd, 528 U.S. 440, 120

S. Ct. 1011, 145 L. Ed. 2d 958, Prod. Liab. Rep. (CCH) P 15745, 53 Fed. R. Evid. Serv. 406, 45 Fed. R. Serv. 3d 735 (2000).

[2]*Weisgram v. Marley Co.*, 169 F.3d 514, Prod. Liab. Rep. (CCH) P 15475, 51 Fed. R. Evid. Serv. 76 (8th Cir. 1999), aff'd, 528 U.S. 440, 120 S. Ct. 1011, 145 L. Ed. 2d 958, Prod. Liab. Rep. (CCH) P 15745, 53 Fed. R. Evid. Serv. 406, 45 Fed. R. Serv. 3d 735 (2000).

[3]*Pride v. BIC Corp.*, 218 F.3d 566, Prod. Liab. Rep. (CCH) P 15844, 54 Fed. R. Evid. Serv. 1428, 2000 FED App. 0222P (6th Cir. 2000).

*Werner v. Pittway Corp.*[4] was a suit alleging defective smoke detectors. The District Court excluded the plaintiff's expert witness, finding that the expert offered nothing but a "bare conclusion" regarding the type of detector the plaintiffs' used, and offered no explanation whatsoever regarding the reasoning process that would have permitted him to reach this conclusion.

In *Donnelly v. Ford Motor Co.*[5] the plaintiff claimed that his Ford had a defective ignition switch, which caused the automobile fire in which he was injured. The expert's report asserted his experience and his conclusion to "a reasonable degree of engineering certainty" that "any fire in [one of the defendant's vehicles], in which arson has been eliminated as the cause, that has its origin under the driver side dash and in the area of the steering column can be directly linked to the vehicle ignition switch and system."[6] The report lacked any explanation of the expert's reasoning. A supplemental report contained an explanation insofar as the expert rebutted the defendant's experts, but the court held that "is not a substitute . . . for setting forth the reasoning or methodology by which he formed the opinions in his own reports . . . ."[7]

Finally, in *Comer v. American Electric Power*,[8] the plaintiff claimed a power surge caused a fire that seriously damaged his house. The defendant power company's expert agreed that arcing in a panel distribution box led to the fire, but the two sides's experts disagreed about the cause of the arcing condition. Awaiting guidance from the Supreme Court in *Kumho Tire*, the district court delayed ruling on the motion until after the jury returned a verdict for the plaintiff. In granting a motion for judgment as a matter of law the court held the plaintiff's expert evidence inadmissible. The court held that the plaintiff's expert's testimony was based only on personal knowledge and experience, lacked a more sound basis, and therefore his opinions were nothing more than unsupported speculation, inadmissible under *Daubert, Joiner* and *Kumho Tire*. In commenting on the "lack [of] factual, technical, or scientific support,"[9] the court expressed particular disapproval of the expert's flexibility in reaching opinions:

> Indeed, one marvels at the breath-taking ease with which [the expert] offers his 'expert' opinions, surpassed only by his apparent ability to change them based on nothing more than the mere suggestion of counsel. With such an approach, unshackled as it is to any sort of factual, scientific or technical analysis, [the expert's] testimony easily accommodates whatever theory or time interval is needed by his client.[10]

In *Travelers Property & Casualty Corp. v. General Electric Co.*, an insurance company, as subrogee of its policy holders, sued the manufacturer of a clothes dryer which is alleged to have been defective and caused 23 fires.[11] The defendant challenged the plaintiff's expert in engineering and fire investigation, arguing that his methods were unreliable. The expert had conducted no tests or experiments to test his hypothesis of fire causation, but limited himself to "analyzing the burn patterns in each dryer and then ruling out potential alternative explanations." In deciding that the expert met the requirements of *Daubert*, the court emphasized the need to ensure that the expert uses in the case the "same level of intellectual rigor that

---

[4]*Werner v. Pittway Corp.*, 90 F. Supp. 2d 1018 (W.D. Wis. 2000).

[5]*Donnelly v. Ford Motor Co.*, 80 F. Supp. 2d 45 (E.D. N.Y. 1999).

[6]*Donnelly v. Ford Motor Co.*, 80 F. Supp. 2d 45, 49 (E.D. N.Y. 1999).

[7]*Donnelly v. Ford Motor Co.*, 80 F. Supp. 2d 45, 49 (E.D. N.Y. 1999).

[8]*Comer v. American Elec. Power*, 63 F. Supp. 2d 927 (N.D. Ind. 1999).

[9]*Comer v. American Elec. Power*, 63 F. Supp. 2d 927, 937, (N.D. Ind. 1999).

[10]*Comer v. American Elec. Power*, 63 F. Supp. 2d 927, 935, (N.D. Ind. 1999).

[11]*Travelers Property & Cas. Corp. v. General Elec. Co.*, 150 F. Supp. 2d 360, Prod. Liab. Rep. (CCH) P 16181, 57 Fed. R. Evid. Serv. 695 (D. Conn. 2001).

characterizes the practice of an expert in the relevant field,"[12] and the expert's "experience, knowledge and training, taken together with the process he described during the [*Daubert*] hearing of analyzing the burn patterns in each dryer and then ruling out potential alternative explanations . . . ."[13] Qualifications are a separate issue from the *Daubert* admissibility analysis. The two issues reflect the distinction between the expertise (is there a body of knowledge that can dependably address the factual issue at hand?) and the expert (is this person qualified to employ and apply the expertise?). The "same intellectual rigor" test, though mentioned by the Supreme Court, has the shortcoming of failing to recognize that if the field has no intellectual rigor, then an expert who employs the "same" lack of rigor as that used in the field should still be excluded. Even this minimally sound criterion is unavailing in the case of fire experts because there is no relevant field outside of litigation to which to compare the work of a fire investigator.[14] To quote one of the briefs in *Benfield*:[15]

> in some fields, the consequences of error makes the errors obvious to all. Thus, auto mechanics who cannot fix cars, plumbers who cannot stop pipes from leaking and harbor pilots who run ships aground can be seen to lack expertise without the necessity of subjecting their beliefs and techniques to scientific testing. Simple, obvious tests suffice. But fire investigators who have failed to learn at least the rudiments of what is known of the science of fire chemistry and fire dynamics can continue offering opinions based on misconceptions without detection or consequence.

On the most relevant aspect of its evaluation of the expert's admissibility, the court observed: "Importantly, although [the expert] did not test his theory experimentally, his theory is capable of being tested, so that GE's experts could employ testing to undercut it and, indeed, have engaged in such efforts."[16] On another aspect of the expert's offerings, the court vehemently criticized the "woefully inadequate" three-page report provided by the expert, which required 12 days of depositions to find out what the expert concluded and why. The court stated that if the only basis for the expert's opinion had been what was contained in the report, then the expert testimony would have been excluded. However, the court decided that it would also take into consideration the expert's testimony at the *Daubert* hearing. The court did, however, find that the skimpy report amounted to bad faith and awarded sanctions.

The plaintiff in *Snodgrass v. Ford Motor Co.* sued for an allegedly faulty ignition switch which started a fire in the plaintiff's vehicle.[17] The defendant challenged the admissibility of the testimony of two of the plaintiff's expert witnesses. As part of the causation argument, one expert witness, a statistician, sought to show that the type of ignition switch used in the plaintiff's vehicle was associated with a higher frequency of fires. The court found that the database that was the foundation for the expert's analysis was of uncertain validity, having been developed by plaintiff's counsel. Because the database could not be shown to be valid, any conclusions based on it were ruled inadmissible. The second expert was a fire origins expert. This expert's testimony was admitted, largely because of the care he took in looking at

---

[12]*Travelers Property & Cas. Corp. v. General Elec. Co.*, 150 F. Supp. 2d 360, Prod. Liab. Rep. (CCH) P 16181, 57 Fed. R. Evid. Serv. 695 (D. Conn. 2001).

[13]*Travelers Property & Cas. Corp. v. General Elec. Co.*, 150 F. Supp. 2d 360, Prod. Liab. Rep. (CCH) P 16181, 57 Fed. R. Evid. Serv. 695 (D. Conn. 2001).

[14]Or almost any forensic scientist for that matter.

[15]Brief Amicus Curia submitted by John Lentini in *Michigan Millers Mut. Ins. Corp. v. Benfield*, 140 F.3d 915, 49 Fed. R. Evid. Serv. 549 (11th Cir. 1998).

[16]*Travelers Property & Cas. Corp. v. General Elec. Co.*, 150 F. Supp. 2d 360, Prod. Liab. Rep. (CCH) P 16181, 57 Fed. R. Evid. Serv. 695 (D. Conn. 2001).

[17]*Snodgrass v. Ford Motor Co.*, 2002 WL 485688 (D.N.J. 2002).

the reports and the many cases on which he had been lead investigator.[18] No doubt careful attention is welcome in an expert witness. But in this case that merely provided the input information to which an expertise is to be applied. Where is the assurance that sufficiently sound expertise is being applied? Furthermore, why does having investigated 900 vehicle fires assure that the inferences drawn about the cause of those fires had validity? Suppose an astrologer has done 900 charts. How does that make the astrologer's conclusions more valid? As the commentary to the most recent amendments to Fed. R. Evid. 702 states, "If the witness is relying solely or primarily on experience, then the witness must explain how that experience leads to the conclusion reached, why that experience is a sufficient basis for the opinion, and how that experience is reliably applied to the facts. The trial court's gatekeeping function requires more than simply 'taking the expert's word for it.' "

The plaintiff in *Knotts v. Black & Decker, Inc.*[19] sued for damages in a house fire which led to the deaths of two people. The official arson investigation report concluded that "the fire 'was accidental and all indications point[ed] to a [sic] electrical battery charger used for charging cordless tools.' " The defendants filed several motions in limine, including challenges to the plaintiffs' experts and for summary judgment. The court granted all of the defendant's motions. In excluding the plaintiff's experts the court closely follows the task-at-hand mandate of *Kumho Tire* and focuses on the specific theory of fire causation and the particular battery charger, insisting on relevant data. As to one of the plaintiff's proffered experts, an electrician and fire investigation expert, the court noted that the plaintiffs claimed that this expert, Dolence, would assist the jury in understanding "how an origin of a fire is determined and will provide a forensic analysis to establish this fire's origin."[20] The court found, however, that Dolence had conducted no independent investigation but had merely relied on reports and statements in the record. Moreover, the court observed, Dolence had failed to rule out other possible causes, such as the possibility that one of the children in the house had set the fire. The court concluded that "[h]aving carefully viewed the factors upon which Dolence premises his opinion, the Court finds that his opinion is not grounded on anything other than the fire investigation report and the witness statement contained therein. There is no independent basis or analysis grounded either in scientific methodology or reliable procedures to support his theory as to the origin of the fire."[21] Thus, the court held, the expert would be excluded. The second expert, Kramerich, an electrical engineer, sought to testify that defendant's product could "overheat and potentially cause a fire due to a lack of thermal protection in its design." As to this proffered expert, the court summarized its findings and conclusions as follows:

> Considering Dr. Kramerich's testimony as a whole, the Court concludes that this testimony shows at best the possibility of a failure mode on the part of all battery chargers but does not establish a probability as to the Black & Decker VP130 sufficient within the dictates of *Daubert*. As acknowledged in his deposition, there was no independent testing of the product in order to validate Dr. Kramerich's assertions that the Defendant's product could cause the battery to overheat and the plastic charger case to ignite. Rather, the expert's theory was based upon articles and documents which involved battery chargers of several types, made by varying manufacturers, all for the proposition that the "same technology" was applicable to the Black & Decker VP130 for

---

[18]"Mr. Hagerty reviewed the complaint accounts, deposition transcripts, and evidentiary documents, most of which described the fire incidents as occurring under conditions and with burn patterns resembling those fires attributable to ignition switch defects, according to his report. Indeed, Mr. Hagerty's vast experience as lead investigator in over 900 vehicle fires provides him with the capability and expertise to diagnose many different kinds of vehicle fires." *Snodgrass v. Ford Motor Co.*, 2002 WL 485688 (D.N.J. 2002).

[19]*Knotts v. Black & Decker, Inc.*, 204 F. Supp. 2d 1029 (N.D. Ohio 2002).

[20]*Knotts v. Black & Decker, Inc.*, 204 F. Supp. 2d 1029, 1038 (N.D. Ohio 2002).

[21]*Knotts v. Black & Decker, Inc.*, 204 F. Supp. 2d 1029 (N.D. Ohio 2002).

the purpose of asserting this possible scenario with the alleged offending product. This extrapolation theory when coupled with the lack of any independent testing qualifies Dr. Kramerich's opinion as tenuous at best because "there is simply too great an analytical gap between the data and the opinion offered." *Joiner v. General Electric Co., 522 U.S. at 146, 118 S.Ct. at 519.*[22]

Upon ruling the experts inadmissible, the court granted the defendant's motion for summary judgment.

*Lockridge v. Scripto-Tokai*[23] is a good example of a court thinking in some depth about the proffers, and writing an opinion which provides considerable detail about what the parties are offering. Ten year-old Patrick Lockridge was injured when his t-shirt caught fire at home, a fire that may or may not have been caused by the defendant's butane lighter which may or may not have been defective. The child gave conflicting accounts of what happened, including whether the fire he started resulted from misuse of the lighter (which on the plaintiff's theory released butane gas when it should not have, building up prior to ignition) or from misuse of matches.

The plaintiffs proffered as one of their two experts a prominent figure in fire science, Patrick Kennedy, one of the principal authors of the National Fire Code, NFPA 921—Guide for Fire and Explosion Investigations (much cited in the present chapter), and other works, and holder of various positions in the field. The second expert, on consumer product safety, based his conclusions on those of Kennedy. Though reciting the credentials of the plaintiffs' expert, the court clearly paid attention mostly to what the evidence was, and what the proffered experts on both sides did with it.

Kennedy did not consider contradictory elements of the child's story nor did he consider other available evidence from medical and emergency responder records which suggested alternative theories of the fire's origin. He did perform tests of whether the t-shirt would ignite without an accelerant (it did not), whether the shirt would ignite in a beaker along with butane (it did), but he did not perform tests of whether the shirt would ignite in open air under the circumstances described by the child.

The defendant's experts[24] did conduct a series of tests such as whether the butane would remain concentrated in the air in order to start the shirt on fire as described by the child (several such tests, such as inverting the beaker for one second and attempting to ignite a t-shirt on a mannequin in open air, found that the butane from the lighter could not ignite the shirt), and how much concentrated butane in how rich of a mixture would be required to ignite the shirt, and chemical tests of what materials had come into contact with the shirt and areas which the shirt had burned on (a carpet).

In short, the plaintiff's expert's hypothesis testing was inadequate to support the plaintiffs' theory against alternative theories, while the defense experts conducted tests which explored the range of possibilities, yielding evidence which drew the plaintiff's theory into serious doubt. Although the court excluded the plaintiff's experts on a *Daubert* motion, as well as ruling in the defendant's favor on a motion for summary judgment, it is hard to tell whether the court excluded the plaintiffs' experts for reaching the wrong answer or for not using proper scientific theory and methods. An alternative basis, as or more coherent, for granting summary judgment might have been insufficiency of the evidence: the plaintiffs' proffers could not have provided an adequate basis for a rational jury to have found for the plaintiff.

---

[22]*Knotts v. Black & Decker, Inc.*, 204 F. Supp. 2d 1029 (N.D. Ohio 2002).

[23]*Lockridge v. Scripto-Tokai*, Case No. 3:03-CV-1058 (M.D. Tenn 2005).

[24]One of whom is the author of the scientific status portion of this chapter.

*Truck Ins. Exch. v. MagneTek*,[25] raises an important issue, which applies across the spectrum of expert evidence admissibility contexts. When deciding on the admissibility of general principles of scientific evidence, is the court's duty to reach a scientifically correct answer, a task in which the parties merely assist,[26] or is the court's role merely to consider the evidence presented by the parties and to rule on that record. If there is genuine controversy over the validity of a scientific proposition, is the court's job to decide which view is correct (and rule on admissibility accordingly) or to admit the testimony so the parties can debate their claims to the jury?

The district court in *MagneTek* excluded the testimony of plaintiff's two expert witnesses who would have opined that a restaurant fire was caused by a fluorescent light ballast manufactured by the defendant. The district court found, following a *Daubert* hearing, that the proffered testimony was not based on a sufficiently reliable scientific theory. The appellate court affirmed the evidentiary ruling as well as the summary judgment ruling (since, without the testimony, the plaintiff had insufficient evidence to persuade a jury).

As to qualifications, the first expert had advanced degrees in physics and had been studying the cause of fires for over 20 years. The court found his theory of long-term, low temperature ignition[27] to be unproved and therefore "unreliable."[28] The court noted that the expert failed to show that experiments were conducted to prove that a fire could be started under his theory in the actual conditions present in the case. The court found three articles submitted in support of the theory cast doubt on its general acceptance, and on the methodology and the adequacy of the experimentation.

The second expert, an investigator with the Fire Protection District, also offered an opinion as to the cause and origin of the fire. The court found that the expert failed to offer evidence that the ballast in question could generate enough heat to ignite combustibles in the ceiling. Therefore the court found that the opinion was based on assumption and speculation and not reliable principles and methods.

If in another case the plaintiff's experts did a better job of explaining the evidence for pyrophoria, a court might admit it. But should the soundness of a scientific concept be accepted or rejected depending on the varying eloquence or clarity of particular witnesses? The question of whether debatable expert evidence is to be admitted or not is governed by *Daubert* and its sequella: if the proffered expert evidence is demonstrated to be more likely than not sound in relation to the specific task at hand, then it is admissible.

The court in *McCoy v. Whirlpool Corp.*[29] granted a post-trial defense motion for judgment as a matter of law. An earlier trial had ended in a mistrial. The present trial had resulted in a jury verdict for the plaintiffs. In granting the post-trial motion, the court noted that the defendant had not presented a timely or effective challenge to the defense experts, but that the court would reconsider the expert testimony nonetheless.[30]

At trial, plaintiffs alleged that a fire, which destroyed their home and killed their

[25]*Truck Ins. Exchange v. MagneTek, Inc.*, 360 F.3d 1206, Prod. Liab. Rep. (CCH) P 16918, 63 Fed. R. Evid. Serv. 948 (10th Cir. 2004).

[26]See Advisory Committee Comments to Fed. R. Evid. 201.

[27]Known as "pyrophoria," though the court calls it "pyrolysis."

[28]For discussion of the scientific debate about pyrophoria, see § 9:40.

[29]*McCoy v. Whirlpool Corp.*, 379 F. Supp. 2d 1187 (D. Kan. 2005).

[30]"Even at trial, the Court noted that if defendant had raised the issue in a more timely manner and presented competing scientific testimony as to Martin's methodology, the Court might have rejected his testimony as unreliable. [Citation omitted.] Absent competing scientific testimony, however, and without the opportunity to conduct a pre-trial Daubert hearing, the Court accepted Martin's own testimony that his methodology was reliable. [Citation omitted.] On further

daughter, originated in a Whirlpool manufactured dishwasher. Four expert witnesses testified as to the origin and cause of the fire. Three testified that the fire originated in the upper door of the dishwasher in the door latch assembly area. The fourth expert, Martin, testified that the fire resulted from a manufacturing defect in the current flow path of the assembly, which caused excessive resistance heating. All objections to the testimony at trial were overruled.

The defendant argued that it was entitled to judgment as a matter of law because the verdict was founded on mere speculation and conjecture in violation of *Daubert*. Specifically, the defendant contended that the court abused its discretion by allowing Martin to testify. Whirlpool presented evidence that the washer was equipped with a black microswitch that is designed to melt at 160 degrees so that no electrical current can flow through the dishwasher to generate excessive resistance heating. The court found that Martin ignored undisputed evidence about the thermal properties of black microswitches. Absent a theory on the issue, Martin could not test it. The court also found that the plaintiffs failed to present reasonably reliable evidence that one of the two alleged defects actually raised the temperature in the dishwasher high enough to ignite surrounding combustibles. Thus, the court belatedly excluded Martin's testimony, held that the plaintiffs now lacked a sufficient evidentiary basis to support their theory of causation, and entered a judgment as a matter of law in favor of Whirlpool. The *McCoy* court also recognized NFPA 291 as the "gold standard."

In *103 Investors I, L.P. v. Square D Co.*,[31] the defendant manufacturer moved to exclude the testimony of the plaintiff's expert witness. After testing the busway in which a fire originated, the expert testified that manufacturing contaminants caused the fire. The court held a *Daubert* hearing on the issue. The court found that the expert could testify as to the cause of the fire (that it resulted from short circuiting in the bus duct which occurred due to contaminants within the system) because he followed the established methods of inquiry in his field (NFPA 921) to deduce the cause. However, the court also found that the plaintiff was unable to establish any expertise relevant to how contaminants got into the system (does not have knowledge of the original manufacturing process or standards utilized during that process). Also, the plaintiff had not demonstrated any generally accepted scientific methodology for addressing the question. Note that this court is attentive to the specific task-at-hand issues in the case. The court also found the permeability test conducted by the expert to be flawed because it did not take into account an important factor. Based on these rulings, the court granted the manufacturer summary judgment on the manufacturing defect because there was no expert opinion on that issue.

The plaintiffs in *Fireman's Fund Ins. Co. v. Canon U.S.A., Inc.*[32] asserted that a defective copier caused a fire that destroyed several stores along a business strip. The court found that the lower court was correct in finding that the experts did not comply with NFPA standards. NFPA 921 requires that any hypothesis of fire origin must be carefully examined against empirical data obtained from the fire scene analysis and appropriate testing. Originally, the experts testified that the copier's upper fixing heater assembly was the cause of the fire. Their experiments, however, were not able to create a situation in which the proposed malfunction could create a fire. Also, they were unable to explain the malfunction in theory or replicate it in

---

reflection, the Court finds that Martin did not adequately explain under what scientific principles he concluded that a product defect created excessive resistance heating which caused the McCoy fire." *McCoy v. Whirlpool Corp.*, 379 F. Supp. 2d 1187 (D. Kan. 2005).

[31]*103 Investors I, L.P. v. Square D Co*, 2005

WL 1124315 (D. Kan. 2005), aff'd, 470 F.3d 985, Prod. Liab. Rep. (CCH) P 17641, 71 Fed. R. Evid. Serv. 1224 (10th Cir. 2006).

[32]*Fireman's Fund Ins. Co. v. Canon U.S.A., Inc.*, 394 F.3d 1054, Prod. Liab. Rep. (CCH) P 17274, 66 Fed. R. Evid. Serv. 258 (8th Cir. 2005).

any test. Further, analysis of the burned copier revealed that no electrical current was flowing to the heating element when the fuse was opened. Thus, the experts did not apply the principles of NFPA 921 reliably to the facts in the case, and therefore the lower court did not abuse its discretion.

## § 9:12 NFPA as a standard in fire investigation

Numerous courts have been confronted with *Daubert* challenges to fire experts for failing to follow the scientific methodology set forth in NFPA 921,[1] or proponents claiming that by following NFPA 921 the proffered expert met the requirements of *Daubert*. The growing body of case law suggests that courts are generally ruling that NFPA 921 does embody the standards of the field.

The court in *Travelers Property & Casualty Corp. v. General Electric Co.*[2] found the "NFPA 921, [to be] a peer reviewed and generally accepted standard in the fire investigation community."

The *Royal Insurance Company of America v. Joseph Daniel Construction, Inc.*,[3] stated that, "The NFPA 921 sets forth professional standards for fire and explosion investigations. . . ." In the case at bar, the court held: "A comparison of McGinley's methodology and the six steps of the NFPA 921 methodology reveals that his conclusions were based on these recognized standards and not merely his subjective belief." "Therefore, McGinley's testimony satisfies the standard of reliability under *Daubert* and Fed. R. Evid 702."

The treatment of NFPA 921 is illustrated in more detail in *American Family Insurance Group vs. JVC Americas Corp.*:[4]

In 1995, the National Fire Protection Association adopted Standard 921, entitled "Guide for Fire and Explosion Investigations (NFPA 921)." NFPA 921 specifically endorses the scientific method for use in fire investigations. For example, NFPA 921 states: "The systematic approach recommended [for a fire investigation] is that of the scientific method, which is used in the physical sciences. This method provides for the organizational and analytical process so desirable and necessary in a successful fire investigation." NFPA 921 § 2-2, at 921-9. Further, "use of the scientific method dictates that any hypothesis formed from an analysis of the data collected in an investigation must stand the challenge of reasonable examination." NFPA 921 § 12-6, at 921-79 (citing Daubert). Plaintiff and Choudek debate whether NFPA 921 is actually a "standard," or merely a "guide." Regardless, the NFPA, of which Choudek is a member, emphasizes that the use of the scientific method is appropriate in reaching conclusions as to fire cause and origin. The NFPA allows for some flexibility in analytical methods, however as defendant's expert Richard Dyer testified: "if you do not use certain portions of the document on certain investigations, that is acceptable but then you should be able to explain why it wasn't necessary." Similarly, Daubert and its progeny make clear that "proposed [expert] testimony must be supported by appropriate validation." *Daubert v. Merrell Dow Pharmaceuticals, Inc.*, 509 U.S. 579, 590, 113 S. Ct. 2786, 125 L. Ed. 2d 469, 27 U.S.P. Q.2d 1200, Prod. Liab. Rep. (CCH) P 13494, 37 Fed. R. Evid. Serv. 1, 23 Envtl. L. Rep. 20979 (1993).

Numerous other courts, cited in the margin, have similarly embraced the NFPA 921 as expressing the standards of the fire investigation field.[5]

Failure to follow NFPA 921 guidelines is not, however, necessarily fatal to a prof-

---

**[Section 9:12]**

[1]National Fire Protection Association 921 Guide for Fire and Explosion Investigations.

[2]*Travelers Property & Cas. Corp. v. General Elec. Co.*, 150 F. Supp. 2d 360, Prod. Liab. Rep. (CCH) P 16181, 57 Fed. R. Evid. Serv. 695 (D. Conn. 2001).

[3]*Royal Ins. Co. of America v. Joseph Daniel*

*Const., Inc.*, 208 F. Supp. 2d 423 (S.D. N.Y. 2002).

[4]*American Family Ins. Group v. JVC Americas Corp.*, 2001 WL 1618454 (D. Minn. 2001).

[5]*Allstate Insurance Co. v. Hugh Cole Builder, Inc.*, 137 F. Supp. 2d 1283 (M.D. Ala. 2001) ("the court finds that Boyer's education and experience, his discussions with other experts, and especially, the discussion of conductivity in the NFPA 921

fered expert's admission.[6]

## § 9:13 Nature of scrutiny following *Kumho Tire*—Excluded with little analysis

On the other hand, a number of other cases admitted expert witnesses with minimal scrutiny of the methodology and reasoning (if any) underlying the proffered testimony to determine if it rested on a valid, and therefore admissible, foundation. These include the following cases.

*Call v. State Industries*[1] involved a claim that the defendant's water heater caused the fire that destroyed the plaintiffs' home. The trial resulted in a jury verdict for the plaintiffs. On appeal, the defendant challenged, inter alia, the admissibility of the plaintiff's expert witnesses. The Tenth Circuit Court of Appeals offered only a cursory review of the challenged expert testimony, never explaining how it, or the lower court, reached the conclusion that the testimony was reliable, or what factors it used to reach that conclusion. This would seem to be the very abuse of discretion (a failure to explain what factors were used, why they are appropriate, and why they lead a court to its conclusion on admissibility) that Justice Scalia warned

---

establish that Boyer's testimony is a product of reliable principles."); *Zeigler v. Fisher-Price, Inc.*, 2003 WL 1889021 (N.D. Iowa 2003) (referring to "the strict standards of NFPA 921"); *Abon, Ltd. v. Transcontinental Ins. Co.*, 2005-Ohio-3052, 2005 WL 1414486 (Ohio Ct. App. 5th Dist. Richland County 2005), appeal not allowed, 107 Ohio St. 3d 1408, 2005, 2005-Ohio-5859, 836 N.E.2d 1228 (2005) (NFPA 921 "is a peer reviewed and generally accepted standard in the fire investigation community."); *Booth v. Black & Decker, Inc.*, 166 F. Supp. 2d 215, Prod. Liab. Rep. (CCH) P 16184 (E.D. Pa. 2001) ("Given NFPA 921's comprehensive and detailed treatment of fire investigations, it appears that NFPA 921 might have contained a methodology upon which Thomas could have relied, but he failed to state that he applied any specific methodology contained in NFPA 921. In discussing his methodology in his testimony and reports, he did not refer to any specific section in NFPA 921. Furthermore, Thomas pointed to nothing in that document that provided a methodology for investigating the hypothesized cause of the fire in this case; the spontaneous welding of contacts, resulting in the overheating of an electrical appliance. Thus, NFPA 921 offers no help to Thomas."); *Indiana Ins. Co. v. General Elec. Co.*, 326 F. Supp. 2d 844 (N.D. Ohio 2004) ("NFPA-921 is a recognized guide for assessing the reliability of expert testimony in fire investigations."); *McCoy v. Whirlpool Corp.*, 214 F.R.D. 646, 55 Fed. R. Serv. 3d 740 (D. Kan. 2003) (". . . the parties agree [that NFPA 921] represents the national standard with regard to appropriate methodology for investigation by fire science experts." "The 'gold standard' for fire investigations is codified in NFPA 921, and its testing methodologies are well known in the fire investigation community and familiar to the courts."); *TNT Road Co. v. Sterling Truck Corp.*, Prod. Liab. Rep. (CCH) P 17063, 2004 WL 1626248 (D. Me. 2004) ("The parties and their experts are in agreement that a proper investigation of the subject fire should have

conformed with standards set forth in the National Fire Protection Association's publication number 921. . . ." "It appears that Adams's investigation substantially complied with the NFPA standard."); *Tunnell v. Ford Motor Co.*, 330 F. Supp. 2d 707 (W.D. Va. 2004) (". . . Daubert requires that the expert's methodology be established, scientifically sound, and subject to testing and peer review. That is clearly the case with Crim's opinion as he testified that he employed the fire origin methodology spelled out in the definitive fire origin standard published by the National Fire Prevention Association, Inc.'s NFPA 921. . . ." "Crim's testimony was based on his investigation of the cause of the fire, an investigation which was conducted in accordance with the professional standards and scientific methodology used by experts in fire and explosion investigations, and set forth in NFPA 921. A comparison of Crim's methodology and the NFPA 921 methodology reveals that his conclusions were based on these recognized standards and not merely his subjective belief."); *Workman v. AB Electrolux Corp.*, 2005 WL 1896246 (D. Kan. 2005) (". . . the Court is satisfied that plaintiffs have established that Martin's methodology was reliable." ". . . Martin developed his opinions based on the methodology set forth in NFPA 921, which represents the national standard with regard to appropriate methodology for investigation by fire science experts."); *Ficic v. State Farm Fire & Cas. Co.*, 9 Misc. 3d 793, 804 N.Y.S.2d 541 (Sup 2005) (recognizing NFPA 921 as an authoritative source of procedures and substantive facts about fires and their investigation).

[6]See, e.g., *Torske v. Bunn-O-Matic Corp.*, Prod. Liab. Rep. (CCH) P 17079, 2004 WL 1717649 (D.N.D. 2004).

**[Section 9:13]**

[1]*Call v. State Industries*, 221 F.3d 1351 (10th Cir. 2000) (Table).

against in his concurrence in *Kumho Tire*.

*Allstate v. Maytag*,[2] discussed in more detail above, relied entirely on the qualifications of the experts and made no assessment of the basis of the proffered knowledge to opine whether a cooktop was the source of a house fire.

*Abu-Hashish v. Scottsdale Insurance Co.*[3] allowed the defendant's experts to testify from their observations of burn patters that the fire at issue was not accidental, with no deeper scrutiny of how they could infer causation from what they observed.[4]

*Cooper v. Toshiba Home Tech. Corp.*[5] admitted a plaintiff's expert who would opine that the fire was caused by a defective kerosene heater made by the defendant. The court admitted the expert on the basis that he was qualified, having "written or presented on issues of fire and arson over three hundred times . . . [and] he holds a patent for an anti-flareup device for kerosene heaters."[6] As to the expert's failure to test his hypothesis that a flareup had caused the fire in this case, the court held that such testing was not required, but only that "[t]he expert's conclusions simply must not be 'subjective belief or unsupported speculation.'"[7]

*Gross v. DaimlerChrysler Corp.*[8] Plaintiff sued auto manufacturer for injuries suffered when his vehicle caught on fire. The court found that the testimony regarding a specific product defect should be excluded because of the methodological and logical gaps in the expert's opinion. The court noted that the investigator had followed the accepted fire investigation protocol. But the court found a lack of proof to support the expert's testimony that the cause of the fire was electrical in nature. The court said the expert's opinion was rooted in pure speculation because there was no identification of the source of the alleged overcurrent.

Of course, not much analysis is needed when an expert concedes his or her own lack of expertise or inability to answer the question posed by the task-at-hand, not surprisingly, courts readily grant motions to exclude.[9]

### § 9:14 Nature of scrutiny following *Kumho Tire*—Admitted with little analysis

In *Reberger v. Bic Corp.* the plaintiff sued the manufacturer of a cigarette lighter that exploded, causing injury and damage.[1] The defendant challenged the admissibility of the plaintiff's expert witness in chemistry as unreliable testimony. The court rejected certain arguments in support of admission: that credentials alone justified admission and that the plaintiff's chemist was not subject to *Daubert* review. The plaintiff's expert believed that the "the lighter was a non-extinguishing lighter that suddenly failed due to polymer contamination." The defendant's theory of the case, in contrast, was that the plaintiff had placed the lighter too near a lightbulb (contrary to explicit warnings on the package) and the heat caused it to explode. In order to support his theory of the explosion, the plaintiff's expert had interviewed witnesses and examined the pieces of the lighter. The plaintiff argued that there was no more elaborate protocol available to make the determination of cause and

---

[2]*Allstate Ins. Co. v. Maytag Corp.*, 1999 WL 203349 (N.D. Ill. 1999).

[3]*Abu-Hashish v. Scottsdale Ins. Co.*, 88 F. Supp. 2d 906 (N.D. Ill. 2000).

[4]Fire and arson experts have subscribed to numerous beliefs about the relation of features of a burned structure's remains and the cause of the fire, later determined to be unreliable indicators. § 9:30.

[5]*Cooper v. Toshiba Home Tech. Corp.*, 76 F. Supp. 2d 1269 (M.D. Ala. 1999).

[6]*Cooper v. Toshiba Home Tech. Corp.*, 76 F. Supp. 2d 1269, 1278, (M.D. Ala. 1999).

[7]*Cooper v. Toshiba Home Tech. Corp.*, 76 F. Supp. 2d 1269, 1278, (M.D. Ala. 1999).

[8]*Gross v. DaimlerChrysler Corp.*, 2003 WL 23305157 (D. Md. 2003).

[9]E.g., *Cook v. Sunbeam Products, Inc.*, 365 F. Supp. 2d 1189 (N.D. Ala. 2005); *New York Central Mut. Fire Ins. Co. v. Toyota Motor Sales, U.S.A., Inc.*, 2004 WL 2643172 (W.D. N.Y. 2004).

[Section 9:14]

[1]*Reberger v. Bic Corp.*, Prod. Liab. Rep. (CCH) P 16256, 57 Fed. R. Evid. Serv. 1194 (N.D. Tex. 2001).

that, indeed, the defendant's own expert had used the same methods. The experts, the court observed, had essentially employed the same methods, but had relied on different versions of the facts. At summary judgment, the court held, it would be inappropriate to rule on the admissibility issue, "since the gatekeeping function required from the district court under *Daubert* must be 'tied to the facts' of a particular case." (Citing *Daubert*). The court summarized its view of the matter as follows:

> [I]t appears from the record that while [the plaintiff's expert] believed the "crazing" he saw in the microscope could only be caused by pre-existing polymer contamination, the Defendant's experts concluded that the explosion could have been caused only by proximity to an external heat source. The resolution of these two conflicting opinions directly rests on whether or not a jury finds credible Ms. Reberger's testimony that she did not put the lighter directly next to the lamp in her bedroom, and that the lamp had only been turned on for a few minutes before the explosion.

The court is correct that a disputed fact question exists so that summary judgment may not be proper. However, the parties, under *Daubert*, still must demonstrate that their expert's testimony is reliable. There are several jury outcomes possible here. If the jury believes the defendant's theory, then all of the experts seem to agree that heat could have caused the lighter to explode. The plaintiff would thus lose because of her contributory negligence. However, if the jury believes the plaintiff's testimony, then it must also believe the cause of the explosion was the polymer contamination that Rippstein testified to. The defendant could still win if the jury believes the plaintiff but the plaintiff's expert's testimony is unreliable (i.e., some third reason caused the explosion, not attributable to the defendant). But the court here never explained whether the expert's testimony was admissible given this possible outcome. It merely observed that both plaintiff's and defendant's experts had used the same methods. But since the plaintiff bears the burden of proof, excluding both experts' methods results in a win for the defendant. Thus, it is not at all clear that the court was correct in believing that it did not have to reach the expert witness reliability question.

The plaintiffs in *Tolliver v. Naor*[2] brought suit after a Ryder truck, operated by one of the defendants, crashed into the back of their 1990 Plymouth Acclaim, which allegedly sat in an emergency lane after suffering a flat tire. The accident resulted in several deaths and severe injuries for most involved in it. Most of the plaintiffs' claims settled. Claims against DaimlerChrysler under product liability remained. In this opinion, the court considered a litany of objections regarding an assortment of experts offered by both plaintiffs and defendants. These proffered and challenged experts included: For the plaintiffs: an expert in forensic engineering and failure analysis; an expert in automotive fuel system design; and an expert in forensic pathology and occupant kinetics. For the defendant: an expert in accident reconstruction, fuel system performance and design and fire analysis; an expert in fire cause and analysis; an expert in vehicular kinematics and injury causation; and an expert in automotive seating systems and automotive body design. As to the plaintiff's objections to the defense expert witnesses, the court concluded that they were not directed at the qualifications or the reliability of the methods used by the experts, but merely with "the controverted facts of the case," which were for the factfinder to determine. These challenges, therefore, were denied. The defendant challenged the plaintiff's forensic engineer as being unqualified and using unreliable methods. The court did not reach the merits of the objections but took the issue under advisement. The plaintiff's expert in fuel system design was challenged as being unqualified and having conducted no tests on the subject of his testimony. The

---

[2]*Tolliver v. Naor*, 2001 WL 1345735 (E.D. LA. 2001).

court's full analysis of this challenge is this:

> Although Mr. Rosenbluth is not an engineer, the Court finds that he is qualified by both education and experience to render an expert opinion in this case. The Court recognizes that Mr. Rosenbluth is a thirty-year veteran of the automotive industry with the benefit of both practical experience and graduate study in industrial design. Furthermore, the theories proposed by Mr. Rosenbluth are not so complex or specialized to require formal degrees in engineering or another highly-specialized discipline. The Court finds that the witness satisfies Rule 702 and the "*Daubert* test."[3]

The reader should note that the court's analysis is a superficial and conclusory one that does not come to grips with the methods or knowledge on which the expert's opinion must stand. Finally, as to the plaintiff's forensic pathologist, who was challenged because his proffered testimony was said to lack a factual foundation and not be based on an adequate scientific methodology, the court concluded that "Defendant's challenges to Dr. Burton's opinions are based largely on disputed issues of fact and are more appropriately resolved by the trier of fact." In all, the court's evaluations of the challenged experts were cursory.

*Royal Insurance Co. of America v. Joseph Daniel Const.*[4] The plaintiff insurer brought this action against defendant construction company to recover in subrogation for amounts it paid for fire damage to property owners' garage. The plaintiff claimed that the fire was caused by the negligence of the defendant's employees while doing construction on the garage. The defendant filed motions to exclude the plaintiff's fire investigation expert and for summary judgment. The court denied both motions, finding the fire investigator's testimony to be admissible. In reviewing its gatekeeping obligations under the *Daubert* line of cases, the court noted that *Daubert*'s "list of factors is not exhaustive, and the court, in its discretion, may consider different factors to test reliability."[5] The court did not, however, propose any additional factors that it might rely upon in the fire investigation context. The court then turned to the question of how plaintiff's expert fared under *Daubert* scrutiny. It explained that his "testimony was based on his investigation of the cause of the fire, an investigation which was conducted in accordance with the professional standards and scientific methodology used by experts in fire and explosion investigations, and set forth in the National Fire Protection Association, Inc.'s 'Guide for Fire and Explosion Investigations' (NFPA 921),"[6] as well as other professional publications. The court quoted the six steps investigators should follow, according to the NFPA 921[7] and then summarized what the expert did in accord with those six steps.[8] The court's discussion is at such a level of generality that it borders on useless. Even investigations relying on poorly tested and highly erroneous

---

[3]*Tolliver v. Naor*, 2001 WL 1345735 (E.D. La. 2001).

[4]*Royal Ins. Co. of America v. Joseph Daniel Const., Inc.*, 208 F. Supp. 2d 423 (S.D. N.Y. 2002).

[5]*Royal Ins. Co. of America v. Joseph Daniel Const., Inc.*, 208 F. Supp. 2d 423 (S.D. N.Y. 2002).

[6]*Royal Ins. Co. of America v. Joseph Daniel Const., Inc.*, 208 F. Supp. 2d 423 (S.D. N.Y. 2002).

[7]"(1) recognize that a need exists to determine what caused the fire; (2) define the problem; (3) collect data; (4) analyze the data; (5) develop a hypothesis based on the data; and (6) test the hypothesis." *Royal Ins. Co. of America v. Joseph Daniel Const., Inc.*, 208 F. Supp. 2d 423 (S.D. N.Y. 2002).

[8]In following the NFPA 921 methodology, McGinely recognized that, in order to determine whether plaintiff had a viable cause of action against defendant, it was necessary to determine the cause of the fire. He then defined the problem and collected data, which included: (i) obtaining color copies of the photographs taken by the Magee family; (ii) obtaining the reports from Earl Sheldon (investigator, Investigative Resources Global, Inc.) and Jerome Levine (consulting engineer, Jerome G. Levine, Inc.); (iii) taking the depositions of Patrick Magee, Sr., Patrick Magee, Jr., Linda Magee, Earl Sheldon, Sean Tichenor (JDC employee) and Detective Barry Sherry (Rockland County Police Department); and (iv) personally interviewing Patrick Magee, Sr., Earl Sheldon, Paul Kaczmarczik (electrical engineer) and Jerome Levine. McGinely then analyzed the data and developed his hypothesis that the fire in the Magee's garage was caused by smoldering molten slag resulting from the carelessness of

"principles" could pass this sort of scrutiny.[9] Of greater value is that after identifying the possible causes of the fire, the investigator undertook by a process of elimination to zero in on the most likely. But, again, the court's summary of this process is so vague and general as to be meaningless.[10] The defendant argued, however, that according to governing standards, if the origin of the fire cannot be determined, then the cause cannot be identified. The court responded to this argument by saying that when it is impossible to locate the origin of a fire then an origin need not be determined and an opinion on causation can still be offered.[11]

The plaintiff in *Farris v. Coleman Company, Inc.*[12] claimed that a fire was caused by a short circuit in the electric cord to a refrigerator which was connected to the cigarette lighter in his truck. The defense moved to exclude the plaintiff's expert testimony. The expert's reasoning went no further than his observation that there was fire damage where the connecting cord was located, and that there was a short in the cord. Whether the short was the cause or a consequence of the fire, he could not say. The court granted the motion to exclude, noting that this logic had been "condemned by the Fifth Circuit" in several other cases.

The court in *Torske v. Bunn-O-Matic Corp.*[13] sidestepped its own dilemma over admissibility by opening the gates and letting the parties debate research methodology to the jury. The plaintiff alleged that a coffee maker caused a fire that destroyed his home. The defendant moved to exclude the plaintiff's expert testimony. The court found that the expert was qualified in fire investigation, although whether his expertise extended to the design of coffee makers was unclear. The court concluded, after a careful review of the deposition testimony, that it could not dismiss the expert testimony as unreliable. Further, the court said that during trial the defense would have an opportunity to question the expert about his methodology. Though the Supreme Court has observed that cross-examination at trial is the proper place to confront "shaky but admissible" evidence. The question remains whether proffered testimony is sufficiently dependable to be admissible.

---

JDC's employees. Finally, in developing his hypothesis, McGinley relied on deductive reasoning, a method recognized as "scientific", and identified all of the potential ignition scenarios. Technical Committee on Fire Investigations, National Fire Protection Association, Inc. 921: Guide for Fire and Explosion Investigations, 9 (1998). *Royal Ins. Co. of America v. Joseph Daniel Const., Inc.*, 208 F. Supp. 2d 423 (S.D. N.Y. 2002).

[9]§ 9:30.

[10]He eliminated the heating system as a cause of the fire through his discussions with Levine and Sheldon. He eliminated the electrical system as the cause of the fire through his discussion with Kaczmarczik. Commonplace causes, such as careless disposal of cigarettes, and incendiary causes, such as arson and lightning, were eliminated based on a reasonable analysis of the circumstances. After examining all of the evidence, McGinely concluded that molten slag was "most probably" (although not conclusively) the cause of the fire on plaintiff's property. *Royal Insurance*, at 4.

[11]However, a careful reading of the NFPA 921 shows that it does not require that the exact point of origin be determined and McGinley does provide a reasoned explanation of his identifica-

tion of the area of origin of the fire. According to his theory, the molten slag was projected from one of many areas of the garage where JDC employees were cutting beams. The molten slag then became embedded in a floorboard and smoldered there until eventually igniting and starting the fire. Consequently, McGinely hypothesizes that it is impossible for anyone to determine the exact point of origin because the floorboard where the fire originated has been destroyed. Based on this logical analysis coupled with McGinely's extensive professional experience as a fire investigator, McGinley's conclusion passes the threshold of admissibility mandated under *Daubert* and the Fed. R. Evid. However, defendant may challenge the degree of credibility a trier of fact ought to accord McGinley's conclusion and present counter-evidence to refute the scientific veracity of McGinley's hypothesis. *Royal Ins. Co. of America v. Joseph Daniel Const., Inc.*, 208 F. Supp. 2d 423 (S.D. N.Y. 2002).

[12]*Farris v. Coleman Co., Inc.*, 121 F. Supp. 2d 1014 (N.D. Miss. 2000).

[13]*Torske v. Bunn-O-Matic Corp.*, Prod. Liab. Rep. (CCH) P 17079, 2004 WL 1717649 (D.N.D. 2004).

In *Tunnell v. Ford Motor Co.*[14] a car started on fire after a crash. The testimony of fire origin experts was admitted for the most part. The testimony was found to be grounded in NFPA 921 and supported by some facts. With respect to the first expert, the "flying lighter theory" and "smoking materials theory" were found "not so baseless as to be stricken at this stage." (The flame did reportedly start as small and blue as would be expected from a butane lighter.) Also, the window was cracked (weather outside was extremely cold) suggesting the passengers might have been smoking. In addition, the experts' crash dynamic theory, which suggested that electrical arcing would need to be present to support the plaintiff's theory, was sufficiently grounded in scientific methodology to be admitted. The second expert's testimony as to where the fire started based on burn patterns was allowed because "such an analysis is consistent with NFPA standards." However the expert's theory that the fire source was highly flammable liquor was not allowed because there was no evidence such material was present in the car.

Another example of a case admitted on apparently superficial analysis of the proffered expert evidence is *Galentine v. Estate of Stekervetz.*[15] A fire broke out on the defendants boat and spread to the plaintiffs boat. The defendant challenges the qualifications as well as the reliability of the plaintiff's expert testimony. First the court found that the expert had the experience and training to qualify as an expert. The expert had taken a 10-hour course for cause and origin in fire investigation. Also, he has his national certification in residential wiring for code enforcement officials. The expert examined the wiring on the defendants boat the morning of the fire. The court found that because the expert had experience in electrical work and examined the wiring the morning of the fire, his testimony is sufficiently reliable. Also, the court notes that the defendant did not challenge the methodology of the expert. At bottom, the court seems to have relied, improperly, on the qualifications of the expert.

In *Savage v. Scripto-Tokai Corp.*[16] the plaintiff's expert testified that it was likely that the plaintiffs' child started the fire using the defendant's lighter. The defendant sought to exclude the expert testimony proffered by the plaintiff. The plaintiff's expert found no plausible alternative cause and the fire started in the sofa where both the child and lighter were found nearby. The court was concerned that some of the testimony involved statistical analysis, but this was acceptable because the expert did not hold himself out as a student of statistics and he did not claim his theory to be true beyond all possible doubt. Ironic on two counts: If one entirely intuits one's probabilistic inferences, courts tend not to see problems. Second, probability almost never leads to a conclusion beyond all doubt; it illuminates and makes explicit the existence of uncertainty. The testimony was admissible because it was "grounded in methods and procedures of science."

The court in *Bitler v. A.O. Smith Corp.*[17] admitted a fire investigator's testimony despite finding it "not susceptible to testing or peer review," and stating that the expert's "personal experience, training, method of observation, and deductive reasoning sufficiently reliable to constitute 'scientifically valid' methodology."

Additional cases belonging in this category are cited in the margin.[18]

---

[14]*Tunnell v. Ford Motor Co.*, 330 F. Supp. 2d 731 (W.D. Va. 2004).

[15]*Galentine v. Estate of Stekervetz*, 273 F. Supp. 2d 538 (D. Del. 2003).

[16]*Savage v. Scripto-Tokai Corp.*, 266 F. Supp. 2d 344, Prod. Liab. Rep. (CCH) P 16660 (D. Conn. 2003).

[17]*Bitler v. A.O. Smith Corp.*, 391 F.3d 1114, 1122, Prod. Liab. Rep. (CCH) P 17225, 65 Fed. R. Evid. Serv. 1223 (10th Cir. 2004), as clarified on reh'g, 400 F.3d 1227 (10th Cir. 2004), cert. denied, 546 U.S. 926, 126 S. Ct. 395, 163 L. Ed. 2d 274 (2005).

[18]*Hartford Ins. Co. v. Broan-Nutone, LLC.*, Prod. Liab. Rep. (CCH) P 16977, 2004 WL 842516 (N.D. Ill. 2004) (finding that investigator's use of burn patterns to deduce an opinion was reliable

## § 9:15 Nature of scrutiny following *Kumho Tire*—Admitted with thoughtful analysis

The plaintiffs in *Hynes v. Energy West, Inc.*[1] were injured in a natural gas explosion caused by a leaking pipeline near their apartment building. They sued the gas company and others alleged to be responsible for the explosion. After a trial verdict for the plaintiffs, the gas company appealed, arguing that the trial court had erred in admitting expert testimony about the odorant used by the company to warn of gas leaks. The expert had opined that the gas "may have lost its odor through either or both of two different chemical reactions: neutralization and oxidation." The appellate court held that the trial court had not abused its discretion under *Daubert* and *Kumho Tire*. The expert "had extensive scientific credentials and he was able to articulate a scientific process by which neutralization and oxidation occurs . . . . In addition, evidence of adherence to a practice within an industry [here using an alternative odorant in areas containing alkaline soils] implies a significant degree of reliability." Credentials aside—since in *Daubert* review the focus is on the expertise, not the expert—the expert appears to have been offering a theory relevant to a contested factual issue bearing on whether or not the defendant was liable for a defect in its product. If the expert's theory had a sound basis, then it would be proper to admit.

*Allstate Insurance Co. v. Hugh Cole Builder, Inc.*[2] involved a house which was destroyed by a fire which started near the fireplace. The plaintiff's theory was that the fire was started by a metal pipe that conducted heat off the fireplace and ignited wood outside the firebox. To advance this theory the plaintiffs proffered an expert in engineering and fire investigation. The defendants initially argued that the expert's theory that metal pipe could get hot enough to ignite wood was not based on reliable general principles.[3] The court observed that the defendants are correct that the expert had not specifically relied on any general authority to support the assertion that metal pipe could ignite wood, but that this general principle is contained in reference books and, at trial, the expert can be expected to rely on this authority. Hence, this general principle is sufficiently accepted in the relevant scientific community. The defendants' next argument was that the expert's test did not support his opinion. The court found that the test was inadequate, since it demonstrated only that the metal pipe could conduct heat, not that it could ignite wood, because the expert "did not measure the surface temperature of the pipe to determine whether the temperature rose to a level that could ignite wood"[4] nor did he "see if the surface temperature of the pipe could ignite wood by placing a piece of wood in contact with the pipe."[5] Nevertheless, the court concluded that his "testimony is a product of reliable principles" based on the expert witness's general experience and education. The court next turned to an analysis of the sufficiency of the facts supporting the expert's opinion. The court found that although there were

---

because it the analysis of burn patterns is a method used by fire analysts in determining the origin of a fire; lack of testing by the experts did not render their opinions inadmissible); *TNT Road Co. v. Sterling Truck Corp.*, Prod. Liab. Rep. (CCH) P 17063, 2004 WL 1626248 (D. Me. 2004); *Becerra Hernandez v. Flor*, 2002 WL 31689440 (D. Minn. 2002); *Florists' Mut. Ins. Co. ex rel. Battlefield Farms, Inc. v. Ludvig Svensson, Inc.*, 2003 WL 1856552 (W.D. Va. 2003); *U.S. Xpress, Inc. v. Great Northern Ins. Co.*, 2002 WL 31789380 (D. Minn. 2002); *Hartley v. St. Paul Fire & Marine Ins. Co.*, 118 Fed. Appx. 914, 2004 FED App. 0184N (6th Cir. 2004) (district court admitted and court of appeals affirmed).

[Section 9:15]

[1]*Hynes v. Energy West, Inc.*, 211 F.3d 1193, 54 Fed. R. Evid. Serv. 501 (10th Cir. 2000).

[2]*Allstate Insurance Co. v. Hugh Cole Builder, Inc.*, 137 F. Supp. 2d 1283 (M.D. Ala. 2001).

[3]This is analogous to the distinction between general and specific causation in toxic tort litigation.

[4]*Allstate Insurance Co. v. Hugh Cole Builder, Inc.*, 137 F. Supp. 2d 1283 (M.D. Ala. 2001).

[5]*Allstate Insurance Co. v. Hugh Cole Builder, Inc.*, 137 F. Supp. 2d 1283 (M.D. Ala. 2001).

no direct facts supporting the expert's theory, sufficient circumstantial facts did support it. Finally, the court considered the expert's application of the principles to the facts of this case. The court was somewhat troubled by the expert's failure to rule out other possible causes for the fire, though he did consider several possibilities. In particular, the expert did not rule out a gas leak as an alternative cause. In the end, however, the court concluded that "the fact that a large gas leak remains uneliminated as a possible cause of the fire goes to the weight rather than the admissibility of [the witness's] testimony."[6] The court ruled, therefore, that the expert's testimony should be admitted. It might be noted, as regards the final issue of the court's discussion—the application of principles to the particular facts—that this issue is much like that in toxic tort cases, where experts are expected to rule out other possible causes, and their failure to do so often results in their exclusion. It is not clear why engineers should not also be required to display the same ability given the similarity of the two contexts.

## § 9:16 Nature of scrutiny following *Kumho Tire*—Admitted and excluded with careful parsing

*Thurman v. Missouri Gas Energy*[1] provides an example of a case in which the court engaged in careful parsing of the basis of various expert witnesses' proffered testimony, and fashioning of orders reflecting its conclusions about what each witness could or could not testify to. The plaintiff was injured in a gas explosion while working in a telecommunications vault. Both plaintiff and defense sought to exclude expert testimony. One defense expert was limited to testifying about general engineering principles and corrosion control. He was not permitted to testify about the cause of the accident. Said the court: "In order to be able to state an opinion of the cause of the pipeline's failure, [the expert] must be able to offer a credible explanation as to why he supports one theory of failure over another." A second defense expert was allowed to testify about a stress analysis he had conducted on the pipeline even though his methodology was contested, but he was not allowed to testify about what caused the pipe to fail. "Since the pipeline was not excavated after the accident, no expert can offer a reliable opinion on the issue of ultimate causation." A third defense expert was offered on a variety of issues. His opinions about gas odorization and manhole venting were found admissible despite inconsistencies with testimony from fact witnesses. This expert also was barred from testifying about the cause of the accident, but he was allowed to testify about the corrosion control systems that historically were in use, and about what procedures a telecommunications worker should have followed. As to the plaintiff's experts, one who had been an official in the Department of Energy was allowed to testify about Federal regulations governing pipelines. The court ruled that his background as a (non-lawyer, non-scientist) government official made "him a qualified witness who can help the jury understand the importance of the regulations." (Under what circumstances, if any, should an expert witness be testifying to the jury about the law.) This witness was not, however, allowed to testify about a theory that odorant had been "scrubbed out" when the gas passed through soil. A second plaintiff expert was permitted to enumerate the possible causes of the pipeline's failure, but could not opine on which was the actual cause because neither he not anyone else had been able to examine the pipe. His reliance on statistical analysis was found inappropriate in that he did not have sufficient data. This expert was al-

----

[6]*Allstate Insurance Co. v. Hugh Cole Builder, Inc.*, 137 F. Supp. 2d 1283 (M.D. Ala. 2001).

**[Section 9:16]**

[1]*Thurman v. Missouri Gas Energy*, 107 F. Supp. 2d 1046 (W.D. Mo. 2000).

lowed to testify

> regarding historical operations of the pipeline, the typical causes of failure in a pipeline as it ages, the historical frequency of these typical causes, why he believes some of the typical causes did not occur here, the facts which he believes support corrosion as a cause, and the importance of excavation in determining pipeline failure . . . . In short, he will be permitted to testify as to the basis for his opinion but will not be permitted to state the opinion.

He also was permitted to testify about possible odorant stripping in the soil. His dispute with a defense expert about the methodology to use in doing stress analysis was for the jury to decide. A third plaintiff expert was allowed to testify about how corrosion occurs in general, but not about the specific cause of failure in this case. He "does an adequate job of reciting articles he uses to arrive at his opinion but does nothing to show how other corrosive engineers make conclusions of pipeline failures without examining the pipeline or the soil around it." The final expert proffered by the plaintiffs, a chemist, was allowed to testify about the odorant issue and about possible sources of ignition, but was not permitted to offer an opinion that static electricity caused the explosion, or that the defendant had acted willfully. The court ruled that merely because the defendant had "failed to perform a failure analysis of the pipeline and the odorant, Plaintiff should not be penalized for presenting evidence that helps the jury understand what conditions may have occurred to cause the accident."

In *Zeigler v. Fisher-Price, Inc.*[2] the plaintiff alleged that a toy vehicle manufactured by the defendant started their house fire. The defendant sought to exclude the testimony of the plaintiff's two expert witnesses. The first expert was a fire investigator. After doing an extensive walkthrough and analysis of the fire scene, discussing the fire with the fire fighters on scene and learning of a recall on the toy, the expert concluded that the toy was the source of the fire. The court found that any challenges by the defendant based on NFPA standards were hypertechnical. The court also found that the expert followed a generally accepted methodology and that his reasoning suggests they are reliable.

The second expert based his opinions on photographs and fire scene reports. The expert testified that overheating of the H connector in the toy vehicle likely caused the fire. The court found that there was very little evidence in the record to provide a scientific basis for his deduction. He performed no tests on the toy, but rather based his opinion on the fact that in the recall a new type of connector replaced the original H connector and that after the recall there were significantly fewer fires associated with the toy. The court held that the expert's observations represented common sense deductions, not scientific opinions and therefore should not be admitted into evidence.

## § 9:17　Nature of scrutiny following *Kumho Tire*—Criminal cases

*United States v. Norris*[1] is a fire case that actually is an appeal of a perjury conviction. The defendant appealed his conviction, arguing that expert testimony and a video tape should not have been admitted into evidence. The defendant had testified in other proceedings that he had burned almost $500,000 in $100 bills, and therefore the money was not available for him to pay back to his former law

---

[2]*Zeigler v. Fisher-Price, Inc.*, 302 F. Supp. 2d 999, Prod. Liab. Rep. (CCH) P 16788 (N.D. Iowa 2004).

**[Section 9:17]**

[1]*U.S. v. Norris*, 217 F.3d 262, 54 Fed. R. Evid. Serv. 632 (5th Cir. 2000).

partners. "The government sought to prove the perjury charges . . . , in part, through a video tape of, and testimony relating to, [an ATF] re-creation of the burning of the currency as [the defendant] had described it . . . . In particular, the government intended the re-creation to demonstrate that most of the cash could not have burned under Norris's description of the incident." The witness at issue was a fire investigation expert who had re-enacted the steps the defendant said he took to burn the cash. The trial court had held *Daubert* was applicable only to the expert's qualifications. This is plainly erroneous and the Fifth Circuit so held. The Court of Appeals held, however, that it was not error to admit the videotape evidence because the trial court had determined it was reliable and relevant. So, although the trial court had not applied the *Daubert* factors, its analysis of the substantial similarity between the expert's currency burn and the defendant's alleged burn were tantamount to a *Daubert* review.

In *United States v. Gardner*,[2] a criminal case, the court engaged in no apparent scrutiny of the government's expert, but merely asserted by ipse dixit that the government's proffered expert met the standard for admission.

The defendant in *United States v. Diaz*[3] appealed his conviction for arson, challenging the admission of expert testimony, attacking the validity and reliability of the methodology used by fire investigators. The court held that the defendant did not adequately preserve his challenge to the expert witness testimony, leaving him only with plain error review on appeal. The court found that the expert's examinations yielded sufficient detail supporting preferred theories of causation and refuting alternative theories; that their methods were fully explained; that there was no need for additional testing of electrical outlets because the experts had explained how they eliminated the possibility of an electrical fire. Finally, the court notes that all of these issues were fully explored in cross-examination.[4] In short, the court found no plain error in the admission of the testimony.

## § 9:18 State cases

Several fire cases from the state courts are noteworthy.

## § 9:19 State cases—*Daubert* states

We divide the cases in this subsection into civil and criminal. First the civil cases.

In *Mensink v. American Grain*,[1] the Iowa Supreme Court confronted the same question the United States Supreme Court did two years later, in *Kumho Tire*, namely, whether (Iowa's version of) *Daubert* applies to all experts or only to "scientific" experts. The plaintiff had been seriously injured by a dust explosion in a grain elevator that was struck by lightning. The plaintiffs argued, inter alia, that the elevator could have and should have installed lightning protection devices, and offered a retired professor of electrical engineering to testify to that opinion. The jury found for the plaintiff. The defense appealed, and the case was reversed and remanded on grounds other than the expert witness issue.

As to the expert issue, the defendants argued unsuccessfully that the plaintiffs' expert should have been excluded under *Daubert* because he had no experience with grain elevators, though he had extensive experience in lightning protection. The court also rejected the argument that the basis of the expert's opinion failed

---

[2]*U.S. v. Gardner*, 211 F.3d 1049, 54 Fed. R. Evid. Serv. 788 (7th Cir. 2000).

[3]*U.S. v. Diaz*, 300 F.3d 66 (1st Cir. 2002).

[4]The relevance of cross-examination is somewhat puzzling in the context of an admissibility assessment. If cross-examination were a substi-

tute for gatekeeping, there would be no need for Rule 702 or *Daubert*.

**[Section 9:19]**

[1]*Mensink v. American Grain*, 564 N.W.2d 376 (Iowa 1997).

*Daubert*'s reliability criteria and was inadmissible for that reason. *Daubert* was held to be inapplicable because, the Court concluded, it is limited to "evidence of a complex nature," which the Court took to mean scientific evidence as opposed to "technical or other specialized knowledge." In this case, the expert had considered factors like the type of building construction and topography of the surrounding area, which the court believed were readily understood by lay jurors. This narrow reading of *Daubert* limits it to "complex" or "scientific" expert evidence, and to the explicit "*Daubert* factors:" rather than taking the case to stand for the more general proposition that all expert testimony must be found to be valid before it can be admitted. *Kumho Tire*, of course, took this latter tack, holding that all expert evidence, regardless of how it is labeled, must be found to be valid before it can be admitted. Whether Iowa or other state courts will follow the Supreme Court's broader reading in *Kumho Tire* remains to be seen.

At trial in the Texas case of *Doyle Wilson Homebuilder, Inc. v. Pickens*,[2] the plaintiffs won damages for the value of their 18-month old home which had burned to the ground while they were away. Their theory of the fire was that defective or improperly installed wiring caused the fire, and their claim was brought against the general contractor. Though it reversed on other grounds, the Court of Appeals rejected the defendant's challenge to the admissibility of the plaintiffs' electrical engineer (no challenge having been made against the plaintiffs' other expert, a fire investigator). The case is interesting for the remarkably thoughtful and detailed care the court of appeals gave to reviewing the details of the experts' testimony. Yet despite that detailed care, the court nevertheless accepted without question the soundness of whatever theory or empirical data or experience underlay the opinions offered. This case highlights the difficulty counsel have in seeing that some experts may (or may not) be offering poorly grounded opinion (where in this case counsel for the defense challenged one but not the other expert). And the difficulty judges sometimes have in looking underneath the opinions and procedures of experts to try to discern the validity of the knowledge upon which it purports to stand.

The primary plaintiff in *Darbonne v. Wal-Mart Stores, Inc.*[3] was a man who was injured when an automobile battery exploded. The plaintiff's expert testified that the explosion was caused by improper welding between the plate tab and strap in one of the battery cells. The defendant manufacturer's expert testified that the explosion was caused by overcharging due to a faulty voltage regulator. After a trial court verdict for the plaintiffs, the defendant appealed, arguing that the plaintiffs' expert should not have been allowed to testify. Though Louisiana is a *Daubert* state, it is not apparent that the trial court engaged in much explicit gatekeeping. The trial court had accepted the expert testimony without even specifically noting that the witness was an expert. The Court of Appeals affirmed admission, on the manifest error standard, holding that, although the expert had "no formal expertise in battery design or manufacture, he has been formally educated in mechanical engineering and explosions" and he had extensive experience in the investigation of explosions. The courts' focus seems to be on qualifications rather than the foundations of the expertise or the substantive foundations of the testimony.

Courts have excluded fire experts in numerous cases, sometimes with opinions that reflect careful consideration of the scientific issues, other times with far less consideration. An example of a well considered submission is *Podrasky v. T&G, Inc.*[4] The plaintiff contended that the water heater manufactured and installed by the defendant caused his house fire. The defendants moved to exclude the testimony of the

---

[2]*Doyle Wilson Homebuilder, Inc. v. Pickens*, 996 S.W.2d 387 (Tex. App. Austin 1999).

[3]*Darbonne v. Wal-Mart Stores, Inc.*, 774 So. 2d 1022 (La. Ct. App. 3d Cir. 2000).

[4]*Podrasky v. T&G, Inc.*, Prod. Liab. Rep. (CCH) P 17223, 2004 WL 2827710 (Del. Super. Ct. 2004).

plaintiff's expert based on *Daubert* principles and, finding a series of weaknesses in the expert proffer, the court agreed. A fire marshal had determined that the fire started near the heater and was caused by the proximity of the wooden platform below the heater. The plaintiff's expert devised an experiment to test his causation hypothesis. The court found several problems with the circumstances of the experiment that led its results to be of doubtful application to the case. The defendant questioned the lack of peer review, publication and general acceptance of the methodology and testing procedures used by the plaintiff's expert. The court found inconsistencies between the expert's report, depositions and affidavits, which created concern for the witness's reliability. Finally, the court found that the portions of the expert's opinions that were based on "pyrolysis" were not sufficiently grounded in science.[5]

Sometimes the proffers are so weak that courts have no real decision to make, if they are being at all true to their charge. The challenged expert in *Hart v. Resort Investigations & Patrol*,[6] simply had no basis for his opinion. The theory of the plaintiff was that the accelerant used to start a fire at a construction site which destroyed their home was from the construction company's materials, and was filched due to their and their security service's negligence. The expert opined on the soundness of this theory even though no evidence of any kind was offered to link the fuel from the on-site tank to the fire, nor was the type of accelerant used ever determined. The court excluded the expert testimony as failing the tests of reliability and relevancy.

In *Carnell v. Barker Management, Inc.*,[7] the trial court, affirmed on appeal, ruled that the proffered expert evidence did not meet the minimum threshold of explanation of methods. The plaintiffs claimed that faulty wiring in their basement caused a fire, which killed their two children. Defendants filed a motion to strike the second affidavit submitted by the plaintiffs' expert. The court found that the affidavit provided no explanation of the methodology the expert used to determine the cause of the fire or to exclude other possible causes. In addition, the affidavit did not contain information pertaining to the expert's education, training and experience in the area of fire investigation, and thus could not be found qualified to testify as to the cause of the fire. Therefore, the Supreme Court found that the lower court properly struck the second affidavit because it did not meet the threshold requirements for admissibility.

Another apparently easy case for the courts was *Safeco Ins. Co. of America v. Chrysler Corp.*[8] Plaintiffs claimed that the fire which destroyed their house started in a van manufactured by the defendant. The trial court found an expert's proffered testimony inadmissible as to the origin and cause of a fire even though he had a degree in electrical engineering. The expert identified four photographs which he believed showed that the fire was caused by electrical wiring outside of the van. Upon close inspection, however, those electrical wires turned out to be pine straw. The court found that such a glaring error raised doubts about the entire foundation of the testimony and the plaintiff's theory of causation. Upheld on appeal.

Cases admitting expert testimony seem to tend to involve less searching consideration of the scientific basis of the testimony. For example, the court in *Abon, Ltd. v. Transcontinental Ins.*,[9] went into depth on the legal standard but barely touched on the science. The plaintiffs submitted a fire loss claim to their

---

[5]See discussion of low temperature ignition in § 9:32.

[6]*Hart v. Resort Investigations & Patrol*, 2004 WL 2050511 (Del. Super. Ct. 2004).

[7]*Carnell v. Barker Management, Inc.*, 137 Idaho 322, 48 P.3d 651 (2002).

[8]*Safeco Ins. Co. of America v. Chrysler Corp.*, 834 So. 2d 1026 (La. Ct. App. 3d Cir. 2002).

[9]*Abon, Ltd. v. Transcontinental Ins. Co.*, 2005-Ohio-3052, 2005 WL 1414486 (Ohio Ct. App. 5th Dist. Richland County 2005), appeal not allowed, 107 Ohio St. 3d 1408, 2005-Ohio-5859,

insurer, which was denied. The plaintiffs challenged the expert testimony provided by the defendant regarding the cause of the fire. The court concluded: "Appellant does not contest Churchwell's expert qualifications. Rather, appellant contends that his testimony did not comply with Evid.R. 702 because it was not based upon generally accepted investigatory and scientific principles and procedures and there was no evidence that his conclusions were based on valid and reliable information resulting from an adequate investigation. We disagree."

On infrequent occasions, given the deferential standard of review applicable to expert evidence admissibility, trial courts exclude testimony and are reversed on appeal. One example is *Baker Valley Lumber, Inc. v. Ingersoll-Rand Co.*[10] The plaintiff sued the manufacturer of a compressor, claiming that it allowed oil to escape which then ignited and burned down their lumber mill. The trial court excluded the plaintiff's expert testimony. The New Hampshire Supreme Court found that the lower court abused its discretion in excluding the fire investigator's testimony, saying that the trial court was requiring too extreme a level of specificity in order to testify on a subject. The high court also found that, to the extent that *Daubert* was relied on by the court in assessing admissibility, the lower court erred by focusing on the reliability of the expert's conclusion, rather than on the reliability of the used to reach that conclusion.

*Perry Lumber Co. v. Durable Services, Inc.*[11] presents an issue of implicit waiver of a *Daubert* challenge. The defendant's expert devised and conducted an experiment to test the theory that fiberglass insulation was not combustible. The trial court excluded the expert's testimony concerning his test results. On appeal of the exclusion, on which the loss of the case turned, the Nebraska Supreme Court ruled that because the plaintiff's expert had discussed the experiment and explained why he believed it to be inaccurate, prior to the exclusion of the defense expert, the plaintiff effectively waived any objection to its admissibility. The high court held that the defense expert's testimony was, therefore, erroneously excluded and ordered a new trial.

In the criminal cases, expert fire causation testimony proffered by the prosecution rarely is excluded.

*State v. Interest of W.T.B.*[12] involved a Louisiana juvenile who was an adjudicated delinquent for setting fire to a high school building. On appeal he argued that the trial court should not have accepted expert testimony that the fire in question was started with an accelerant. An engineer employed by the school's insurer concluded the fire was caused by an electrical problem. But the Louisiana Court of Appeals affirmed. Citing *Daubert*, the court noted that the fire investigator was well qualified and had 23 years training and experience. His opinion was "based upon the pattern of damage in [the area where he determined the fire had started] and the reaction of the dogs used in the investigation that were trained to sniff the presence of accelerants."[13] Since some of the field's beliefs about burn patterns have been found to be fallacious[14] and dog sniff evidence produces what the field regards as an unacceptably high risk of false positive errors,[15] this is a good example of why a court ought not to be relying on vague assurances from the expert witness but should require hard evidence on the soundness of the proffered testimony before admitting it. As to the contradictory report by the insurer's engineer, that was properly treated

---

836 N.E.2d 1228 (2005).

[10]*Baker Valley Lumber, Inc. v. Ingersoll-Rand Co.*, 148 N.H. 609, 813 A.2d 409 (2002).

[11]*Perry Lumber Co., Inc. v. Durable Services, Inc.*, 266 Neb. 517, 667 N.W.2d 194 (2003).

[12]*State v. Interest of W.T.B.*, 771 So. 2d 807

(La. Ct. App. 2d Cir. 2000).

[13]*State v. Interest of W.T.B.*, 771 So. 2d 807, 813 (La. Ct. App. 2d Cir. 2000).

[14]§ 9:30.

[15]§§ 9:7 and 9:23.

as competing evidence which the finder of fact has the duty to weigh and judge.[16]

In *Commonwealth v. Goodman*,[17] defendants appealed their conviction for arson. The defense argued that the state's expert did not lay a proper foundation for his testimony. The expert testified as to the general approach he followed and explained his conclusions based on the evidence. The court noted that providing the actual standards followed (NFPA 921) would have been helpful, but that the methodology followed by the expert was sufficiently commonsensical to be accessible to the jurors without a foundation.

A more discerning example is provided by *State v. Campbell*,[18] The defendant's girlfriend accused him of pouring lighter fluid on her and setting it on fire. The defendant argued that expert testimony was erroneously admitted against him. The appellate court found that the expert's testimony as to the origin of the fire and elimination of other possible causes outside of an open flame was helpful and admissible. However, the expert should not have been permitted to testify that the defendant started the fire. That causation conclusion was based solely on the victim's statement, leading to an inference that the expert was no more qualified to make than a juror was. Moreover, the physical evidence failed to indicate the use of any accelerant. Thus, the case was reversed and remanded for a new trial.[19]

Sometimes the challenge mounted by the defense is so weak that the court can do little else but admit the testimony. At the trial at which the defendant in *State v. Jackson*[20] had been convicted, no challenge to the fire expert was raised. Thus, in an appeal challenging admission of the expert testimony the court, the court ruled that it would have to apply a plain error analysis. Because the defendant did not point to any reason why the testimony was unreliable and the court did not see any support for the contention in the record, it held that the testimony had been properly admitted.

## § 9:20 State cases—Non-Daubert states

In *Bailey v. Cameron Mut. Ins. Co.*,[1] the insured is suing the insurer after a claim was denied. On appeal, the plaintiffs argued that the defendant's expert had not satisfied Mo. Rev. Stat. § 690.065 and should have been excluded. The court of appeals noted that both of the experts investigated the scene of the fire and determined that the blaze was intentionally set. To be admissible, the Missouri rule requires that the "facts or data in a particular case upon which an expert bases an opinion or inference . . . be of the type reasonably relied upon by experts in the field in forming opinions or inferences upon the subject and . . . be otherwise reasonably reliable." The court ruled, with very little discussion of the investigation and inference methods used, that the facts and data upon which the experts relied were of the type reasonably relied upon by experts in the field. *Ficic v. State Farm Fire & Casualty Co.*[2] was another case of an insurer refusing to pay a claim on the grounds that the fire (causing total loss of a vehicle) resulted from arson. The N.Y. Court of

---

[16]When a trier of fact "is confronted with a decision of which expert opinion to credit, a determination of the weight of evidence is a question of fact which rests solely with the trier of fact." §§ 9:7 and 9:15.

[17]*Com. v. Goodman*, 54 Mass. App. Ct. 385, 765 N.E.2d 792 (2002).

[18]*State v. Campbell*, 2002-Ohio-1143, 2002 WL 398029 (Ohio Ct. App. 1st Dist. Hamilton County 2002).

[19]On retrial, the defendant was convicted again, and on appeal of that conviction the expert

testimony was held to have been admitted without error. *State v. Campbell*, 2003-Ohio-7149, 2003 WL 23022038 (Ohio Ct. App. 1st Dist. Hamilton County 2003).

[20]*State v. Jackson*, 2003-Ohio-6183, 2003 WL 22725287 (Ohio Ct. App. 10th Dist. Franklin County 2003).

**[Section 9:20]**

[1]*Bailey v. Cameron Mut. Ins. Co.*, 122 S.W.3d 599 (Mo. Ct. App. E.D. 2003).

[2]*Ficic v. State Farm Fire & Cas. Co.*, 9 Misc. 3d 793, 804 N.Y.S.2d 541 (Sup 2005).

Appeals struck the opinion of the insurer's expert as not reliable, saying that the expert's conclusion that the fire was "suspicious" was not a generally accepted opinion recognized by the fire investigative community, and that the expert's "opinion was based on conjecture and speculation."

The defendant in *People v. Sorah*[3] was convicted of arson. He sought post-conviction relief on the ground that his attorney was ineffective for stipulating to the government's expert witness's status as an expert. The defendant on appeal argued that the expert reached the conclusion that the fire was caused by arson based solely on his failure to find any accidental cause for the fire. The court rejected that argument in a conclusory fashion, without offering any support that the expert provided proper and adequate investigation, analysis, and findings. Moreover, the court thought that any shortcomings of the expert would go to the weight of the evidence and not its admissibility; and this the court held that defense counsel had not acted unreasonably.

## II.  SCIENTIFIC STATUS
*by John J. Lentini*[*]

### § 9:21  Introductory discussion of the science

The scientific study of fires, arsons, and explosions is unique among the forensic sciences for two reasons. First, the fire or explosion tends to destroy the very physical evidence that can be used to establish the cause, so in the case of arson, it is first necessary to prove that a crime has been committed. Second, the majority of practitioners of this "scientific" endeavor are not scientists and have little, if any, scientific training or education. While there are other forensic disciplines where technical skills learned on the job may provide adequate training (e.g., fingerprints, firearms identification, and handwriting comparison), it is difficult to argue that individuals who have a limited understanding of the chemistry and physics of fire development can draw reasonable conclusions about fires. Yet, the most practitioners do not possess a bachelors degree. With the exception of fire debris chemists, who spend most of their time in the laboratory and most of their efforts on detecting minute quantities of ignitable or explosive material, the people who investigate fires and explosions got their experience one fire at a time, as firefighters, and later as fire investigators.

The skills and mindset required to extinguish a fire are quite different from those required to investigate a fire. Firefighters are accustomed to being given a straightforward, albeit dangerous and difficult task and accomplishing it. The task of determining the origin and cause of fires is far more intellectually challenging than the task of extinguishing fires, and as a result, the success rate in determining the cause is often lower than the success rate in extinguishing the fire. All fires go out eventually. It is a difficult transition from firefighter to fire investigator, and in many cases, newly minted fire investigators are reluctant to call a fire "undetermined" even if that is the correct classification based on what they know. An "unde-

---

[3]*People v. Sorah*, 2002 WL 31941520 (Mich. Ct. App. 2002).

[*]John J. Lentini is a fire investigator and chemist who manages the fire investigation division of Applied Technical Services of Marietta, Georgia. He is a fellow of the American Academy of Forensic Sciences and the American Board of Criminalistics, holds certificates from the National Association of Fire Investigators and the International Association of Arson Investigators. He chairs the ASTM Committee E30, which is responsible for developing forensic science standards, and is a principal member of the National Fire Protection Association's Technical Committee on Fire Investigations. Mr. Lentini has investigated more than 2000 fires, analyzed more than 20,000 samples of fire debris, and testified on more than 200 occasions. He can be contacted at johnlentini @yahoo.com.

termined" call is perceived as a failure by one not accustomed to failure.

Because the knowledge, skills, and abilities of fire investigators differ from forensic scientists in general, the literature in fire investigation is divided into two parts: the scientific literature, and anecdotal reports of field investigators. In recent years, increasing numbers of fire protection engineers, scientifically trained individuals with an understanding of the behavior of fire, have demonstrated an interest in fire investigation, and the literature is beginning to reflect the influence of this group. Much of the work of fire protection engineers in this area, however, is still beyond the technical grasp of the average fire or arson investigator.

Because of the extensive destruction of physical evidence, those who investigate fires in the field, known as "cause and origin investigators," rely heavily on eyewitness testimony. In the absence of that, a frequent occurrence, or sometimes even in spite of contradictory eyewitness testimony, fire investigators rely heavily on their previous experiences in analyzing small bits of evidence. Fire investigation has been likened to putting together a jigsaw puzzle, where the pieces are all scattered but additionally the pieces are frequently missing, and those that are present are frequently unrecognizable.

A fire investigator puts this puzzle together and reaches conclusions by comparing observations with expectations. The expectations have been developed from training and experience, but that training and experience may not necessarily have a solid scientific foundation. For this reason, it is imperative that before an investigator's opinion is taken seriously, the efforts taken to "calibrate" the investigator's expectations should be scrutinized. Most importantly, the presumptions that the investigator carries into each fire scene should be determined, as these presumptions will have a significant impact on the investigator's credibility as an expert.

Observations that one investigator will use to show incontrovertible evidence of an incendiary fire might be found by another investigator to be an unimportant indicator of a secondary event that occurred long after the fire started. There are major areas of disagreement on the ability of investigators to "read" burn patterns, particularly in fires that have burned for extended periods of time. There is also disagreement about an investigator's ability to interpret the condition of wires as evidence of electrical arcing, which might have caused the fire or may be a result of the fire. There are numerous other chicken-and-egg problems that arise in fires, due to the destructive nature of the event.

A major consequence of the destruction of the physical evidence is that very few criminal arson cases are brought. District attorneys are usually not interested in bringing arson cases, unless they are also homicide cases. Most of the litigation surrounding fires occurs in the civil arena. Insurance companies are much more likely to deny a payment based on the belief that their insured committed arson than is a prosecutor to bring an arson case against that same individual with the same evidence. This is at least partly due to the lower standard of proof in civil cases. Likewise, in cases where a product or service defect is alleged to have caused a fire, the impetus to settle based on overwhelming evidence is frequently absent, because the evidence is seldom overwhelming, at least as compared to other cases. In the case of arson, the first task of the prosecutor is to prove that a crime has been committed—a task that in most other cases is much more easily accomplished, or hardly even necessary.

There is reasonably good agreement among forensic scientists regarding the proper testing of physical evidence in the laboratory. Consensus standards exist for most routine tests of fire debris. Standardization of field practices, however, is still controversial, though many courts have recognized NFPA 921 as the appropriate "standard" by which to judge the methodology of fire investigator.[1] One impetus for the standardization of the fire investigation field is the realization by fire investigators (and, indeed, most forensic scientists) that standards may be the key to admissibility. Another impetus for standardization springs from efforts at certification of both laboratory and field investigators. Because examinations are required to grant certification, a standard body of knowledge from which to develop such examinations also is required. Laboratory analyst certification did not become universally available until 1993. Field investigators may obtain certification from either the International Association of Arson Investigators (IAAI) or the National Association of Fire Investigators (NAFI). Laboratory analysts may obtain certification from the American Board of Criminalistics (ABC).

## § 9:22    Introductory discussion of the science—Field investigations

Just as the type of evidence examined and the type of people examining the evidence differ from the field to the laboratory, the approach to the scientific analysis of fire behavior is often radically different between the field and the laboratory.

## § 9:23    Introductory discussion of the science—Field investigations—Test burns

During the 1970s and 1980s, the Center for Fire Research at the National Bureau of Standards, now known as the National Institute of Standards and Technology (NIST), conducted hundreds of excellent test burns, and characterized the behavior of fire up to the point of *flashover*. Flashover is a transitional phase in compartment fires in which temperatures rise to a level sufficient to cause ignition of all exposed combustible items in the compartment. Most structure fires will eventually achieve flashover, unless there is intervention by firefighters or unless there is an unusual occurrence that allows the release of the fire gases, thus preventing the heat build-up.

In a typical flashover scenario, an item of burning fuel, typically a piece of furniture, releases heat and smoke into the room, but in its early stages, the fire is unaffected by the room itself. This is known as the "free-burning" stage, and the behavior of the fire at this stage is relatively simple and easily explained (heat rises). When the fire begins to interact with its enclosure, its behavior becomes much more complex. As the fire progresses, a layer of hot gases forms at the ceiling, and gradually banks down, becoming thicker and more charged with energy. Once the gas layer reaches a temperature of approximately 1100°F, the radiant heat coming from the gas layer is sufficient to ignite common combustibles.[1]

---

**[Section 9:21]**

[1]See cases cited in § 9:12.

**[Section 9:23]**

[1]National Fire Protection Association, Guide for Fire and Explosion Investigations (Pub. No. 921) (2004), at § 5.5.4.2.6.

# Figure A

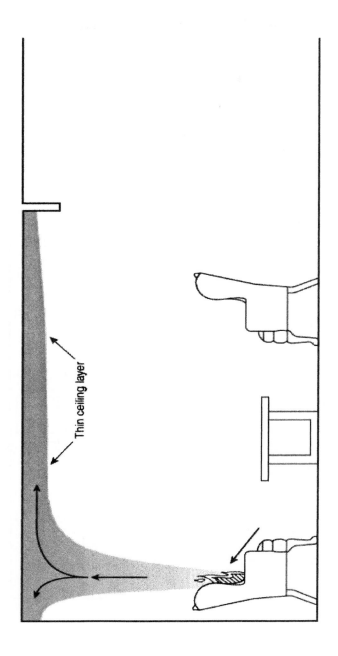

**Figure B**

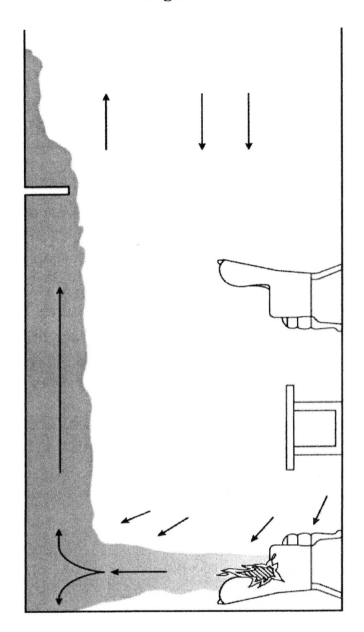

# Figure C

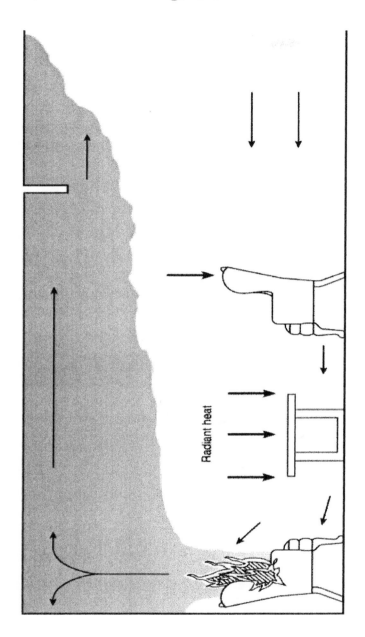

**Figure D**

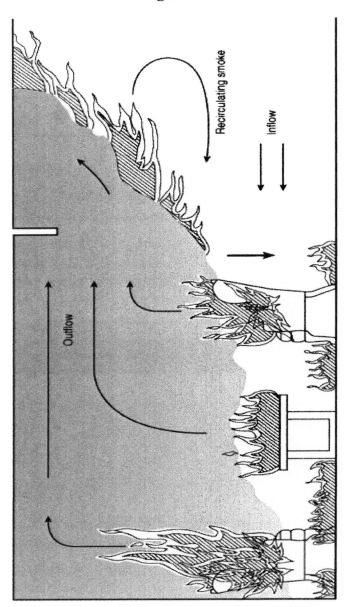

## Figure E

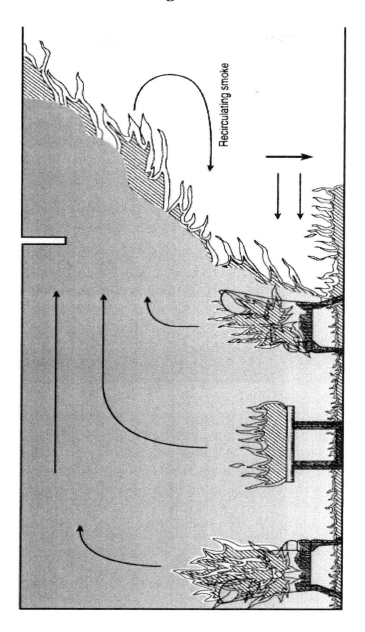

Prior to flashover, the fire can be described as "a fire in a room." After flashover, the fire is more accurately described as "a room on fire." Flashover is actually a transition point, not an end point, and the damage that results from flashover is actually the result of *full room involvement* rather than the result of the flashover itself. Prior to flashover, the fire increases in size as more fuel is involved, and is said to be a "fuel-controlled" fire. Once flashover occurs, all of the exposed fuel is already involved, so the growth of the fire is controlled by the amount of oxygen available. The fire is said to be "ventilation-controlled."

The research conducted at NBS and NIST in the 1970s and 1980s was designed to characterize the behavior of materials up to point of flashover, for purposes of improving the safety of structures and contents. Of the hundreds of fires conducted, none were examined to look at the aftermath, so from that era, there are almost no data from scientifically conducted test burns that give the field investigator any clues about what type of "burn patterns" remain behind after flashover has been achieved.

Other test burns take place on a regular basis, and are usually conducted at weekend seminars sponsored by local chapters of the International Association of Arson Investigators (IAAI). The reproducibility, and therefore, the validity of these tests varies widely from test to test, depending on the knowledge and dedication of the test organizers. Many of these "burn exercises" are conducted merely to familiarize new investigators with what an ignitable liquid pour pattern looks like (how to recognize arson), and to provide extinguishment exercises for fire crews.[2] The vast majority of burn exercises conducted over the years have been performed with these limited goals in mind. This approach has resulted in many trainees getting a one-sided view of fire investigation, which has unfortunately been passed on to each successive generation of investigators.

As a result of criticism of this practice, fire investigation groups are now beginning to try to stimulate accidental fires, and to collect more data from the fires they set. A properly instrumented test burn may have as many as two hundred thermocouples and several radiometers collecting data. A typical test burn conducted by professional fire investigators has fewer than ten thermocouples and no radiometers. The behavior of the fire is usually recorded on videotape.

Two types of test burns have been attempted. The vast majority of test burns are set up to test one or more hypotheses about the general behavior of fire. If the test burn is narrowly focused in terms of the questions it seeks to answer, it is possible for useful information to be derived. Frequently, however, because structures that are available to burn are a rare resource, multiple burns are scheduled for the same structure, so the validity of subsequent tests is questionable.

The second type of test burn aims to reconstruct a particular fire, even though it is generally accepted that no two fires are alike, and an exact reconstruction is impossible. A simple change, such as leaving an interior door open when it should be closed, can drastically affect the development of a fire. About the best that can be hoped for is to reasonably reproduce a fire in a single compartment. This requires an exact match of interior finish and furnishings, something that is difficult to ascertain after a severe fire. Because of the time and enormous expense ($10,000–$100,000) involved in full-scale test burns, they are usually conducted only when there have been multiple deaths or when the damages are in the millions of dollars.

The United States Fire Administration (USFA) released a new report on the

---

[2]National Fire Protection Association, Standard on Live Fire Training Evolutions in Structures (Pub. No. 1403) (2002).

study of fire patterns in July 1997.[3] The Fire Pattern Research Committee conducted ten full-scale fire tests, four at NIST headquarters in Gaithersburg, Maryland, two in residences in Florence, Alabama, and four in residences in Santa Ana, California. All of the test fires were instrumented and recorded, and the results of the tests are presented in a 210-page report. Many of the concepts, investigative systems, dynamics of pattern production, and pattern analysis concepts put forward in NFPA 921 were confirmed by the testing. Several of the "old fire investigators' tales" and fire investigation misconceptions that are repudiated in NFPA 921 were also shown to be unsubstantiated by the testing.

The "old investigators' tales" whose repudiation was confirmed by this testing included:

* wide V's versus narrow V's (which were erroneously thought to reflect the "speed of a fire")
* crazing of window glass (which was erroneously thought to indicate rapid heating—it actually indicates rapid cooling—a much less significant phenomenon)
* char blisters and speed of fire (large, shiny blisters were thought to indicate a rapid fire, while small flat blisters were thought to indicate a slower fire)
* window sooting/staining (formerly thought to signify the type of fuel that had burned)
* color of smoke and flame (also thought to be indicative of the type of fuel that was burning)

Throughout the ten test burns, it became apparent that a major factor in fire pattern development, namely ventilation, was the least understood. They study concluded that much more research needs to be directed at studying the effects of ventilation on the development of fire patterns. Funding for such tests, however, is difficult to obtain.

A second series of test burns, conducted by Anthony Putorti at NIST was reported by the Justice Department in 2001. Putorti's goal was to characterize the appearance of floor surfaces on which he had started fires using 250–1000 ml of gasoline or kerosene. Many of the patterns produced did not live up to the expectations of many investigators. This was particularly true with the fires set on nonporous surfaces.[4]

### § 9:24 Introductory discussion of the science—Field investigations— Accelerant detecting canines

In the early 1980s, the Bureau of Alcohol, Tobacco & Firearms and the Connecticut State Police pioneered the use of accelerant detecting canines (ADCs). This practice has spread as its efficacy has become more apparent.[1] One of the central problems in fire investigation, particularly in arson investigation, is the location of suitable samples for submission to a laboratory so that hypotheses about the presence of ignitable liquids can be tested. Because most ignitable liquids have an odor, it is surprising that it took as long as it did until the concept of accelerant detecting canines was explored. The canines have the ability to improve the efficiency of a fire

---

[3]Federal Emergency Management Agency, U.S. Fire Administration, USFA Fire Burn Pattern Tests-Program for the Study of Fire Patterns (FA 178) (Jul. 1997).

[4]Anthony Putorti, Flammable and Combustible Liquid Spill/Burn Patterns (March 2001) (NCJ Number 186-634), available online at www.ncjrs.org.

**[Section 9:24]**

[1]Melissa F. Smith, Evidentiary Issues Surrounding Accelerants Detected by Canines,

Proceedings of the Annual Meeting of the American Bar Association (Aug. 9, 1993); Kurz et al., Evaluation of Canines for Accelerant Detection at Fire Scenes, 39 J. Forensic Sci. 1528 (1994); George Dabdoub et al., Accelerant Detection Canines and the Laboratory, Proceedings of the Annual Meeting of the American Academy of Forensic Sciences 19, (1995).

investigation, by indicating the location of the ignitable liquid residue, and decreasing the frequency of the submission of negative samples to the laboratory, thus saving an enormous amount of resources. Like many scientific advances, however, the law has jumped ahead of the science, and there are now individuals testifying as to the presence of ignitable liquids at a fire scene based on "alerts" from their canines, even though the laboratory has failed to confirm the indication. Given that there have been few scientific studies and even fewer published research papers on the subject of canine proficiency, this is a disturbing trend.[2] Most scientists in the fire investigation field hold that unless there is a positive laboratory analysis to confirm a canine alert, the alert is not useful in determining the cause of the fire, and is, therefore, irrelevant, both to the fire investigator and to the trier of fact.[3]

This widely held view has subsequently been codified in NFPA 921, as discussed below. Because of concern over some misguided court decisions allowing the testimony of dog handlers regarding unconfirmed alerts, the NFPA passed a "Tentative Interim Amendment" (TIA) to its 1995 edition of the GUIDE FOR FIRE AND EXPLOSION INVESTIGATIONS, fearing that if they waited to voice their concerns in the 1998 edition of the document, the rapidly developing law on the subject would be difficult or impossible to change. Consequently, the Technical Committee on Fire Investigations declared (and the NFPA Standards Council agreed) that a "judicial emergency" existed. The TIA stated that the only legitimate uses for a canine were the selection of samples that had a higher probability of testing positive, and the establishment of probable cause for a warrant to search further. The TIA echoed the concerns expressed by the IAAI Forensic Science Committee, and was carried forward into future editions of NFPA 921.[4]

As a result of the publication of the TIA, judges began to follow the guidance of the fire investigation community, and exclude evidence of unconfirmed alerts. In a murder case in Georgia a conviction was overturned because the trail judge allowed testimony about unconfirmed alerts into evidence.[5]

The utility of canines as a tool for detecting ignitable liquids was introduced at a meeting of the American Academy of Forensic Sciences in the late 1980s when Maddie, the first operational ADC, was brought to a meeting for a demonstration. Six crime laboratory directors were selected from the audience and asked to stand on a stage. One of them had a drop of gasoline placed on his shoe, and when Maddie came into the hall, she immediately alerted on the appropriate shoe. One astute crime laboratory director asked his colleague to hand him the shoe and brought it up to his nose at which point he exclaimed "I can smell that!" The value of accelerant detection canines is not so much in the sensitivity of their noses, but in their willingness to spend their entire day sniffing the floor of a 4,000 sq. ft. fire scene, something that the average fire investigator is not willing to do.

### § 9:25   Introductory discussion of the science—Field investigations— Sniffers

Dogs were preceded into fire scenes by electronic sniffers, devices that had been developed to detect combustible gases in mines and in utility installations. These devices, while useful in eliminating negative samples, are widely believed to be prone to providing false positive alerts. A positive alert by an electronic sniffer is generally not accepted as an indication of the presence of ignitable liquids.

---

[2]*State v. Buller*, 517 N.W.2d 711 (Iowa 1994).

[3]IAAI Forensic Science Committee, Position on Accelerant Detection Canines (adopted Sep. 1994), 45 Fire & Arson Investigator 22 (1994).

[4]See National Fire Protection Association,

Guide for Fire and Explosion Investigations (Pub. No. 921) (2004), at § 16.5.

[5]*Carr v. State*, 267 Ga. 701, 482 S.E.2d 314 (1997).

Commercially available electronic sniffers generally incorporate detection devices similar to those used on gas chromatographs. The simplest sniffers use thermal conductivity detectors. Flame ionization, photo ionization and solid-state models have been used. The more complex detectors are sometimes unable to withstand the harsh conditions of the fire scene environment. Solid-state units with comparison modules, sold by Pragmatics, are probably the most popular unit in use today.

### § 9:26 Introductory discussion of the science—Laboratory analysis— Classification of petroleum products

Most of the people with science degrees who are interested in the study of fires conduct their investigations in the laboratory, where they examine samples brought to them by field investigators. The laboratory analysis of fire debris is one area of forensic science where there is a near consensus on methodology and terminology.[1] Because of this consensus, there has been a considerable amount of research published on the characterization of ignitable liquid residues recovered from fire debris. Much of the credit for this general consensus goes to the International Association of Arson Investigators Forensic Science Committee and ASTM Committee E30 on Forensic Sciences, which publishes Standard Test Methods for the separation and identification of ignitable liquid residues.[2]

The gas chromatograph (GC) has been the primary instrument used in the identification of petroleum-based hydrocarbon liquids, which are the most commonly used accelerants. An identification not based at least in part on GC is probably invalid. Gas chromatographic techniques that are significantly at variance with the ASTM standards have a lower likelihood of being valid.

As is the case with many of the forensic sciences, the identification is based on pattern recognition and pattern matching. The "pattern" arises because petroleum distillates are complex mixtures of up to five hundred different compounds. There is, for example, no such entity as a "gasoline molecule." Gasoline, and most petroleum distillates, are resolved by the chromatographic column into separate compounds, usually in ascending order by boiling point or molecular weight. (Lighter compounds pass through the chromatographic column more quickly than heavier compounds.) The laboratory analyst comes to recognize the patterns produced by particular classes of petroleum products, and the "match" is made by overlaying the chromatogram from the sample extract onto the chromatogram of a known standard. This comparison can be made on a computer screen, but the traditional method involves laying one paper chart over another on a light box.

There is some room for judgment in this pattern matching, and it is for this reason that the use of mass spectrometry, coupled with gas chromatography, has gained much wider acceptance in recent years. While gas chromatography produces a pattern of peaks, the mass spectrometer is capable of identifying the compounds that produce the peaks. With gas chromatography, it may be possible to confuse patterns produced by background materials with patterns of petroleum-based liquids. This is less likely to happen when gas chromatography-mass spectrometry (GC-MS) is used, because there is much less guesswork about the identity of the compounds causing the peaks on the chart. Caution is still required, however because a piece of carpeting (or any combustible solid) pyrolyzing in the process of combustion may produce compounds that also are found in petroleum distillates.

---

**[Section 9:26]**

[1]U.S. DOJ, Forensic Sciences: Review of Status and Needs (Feb. 1999), at 40, available at http://www.ncjrs.org/pdffiles1/173412.pdf.

[2]ASTM International, Standard Test Method for Ignitable Liquid Residues in Extracts from Samples of Fire Debris by Gas Chromatography (Pub. No. E 1387) (2001); ASTM International, Standard Test Method for Ignitable Liquid Residues in Extracts from Samples of Fire Debris by Gas Chromatography/Mass Spectrometry (Pub. No. E 1618) (2001).

Thus, ASTM E 1387 and E 1618 advise analysts that merely *detecting* benzene, toluene, and xylenes, or higher molecular weight aromatics is not sufficient for identifying gasoline. The relative concentrations of all of the compounds of interest must be such that *a recognizable pattern is produced.*

The forensic analysis of ignitable liquid residues thus differs significantly from "identifications" made by environmental scientists, for whom quantifying benzene, toluene and xylene equates to quantifying gasoline. The forensic analysis of ignitable liquids also differs significantly from the forensic analysis of drugs, where detection, not pattern recognition, is the analytical question. Fire debris analysis conducted by drug chemists or environmental chemists is worthy of increased scrutiny, because the skill sets required for fire debris analysis are different.

In recent years, proficiency tests, manufactured by Collaborative Testing Services (CTS) and sponsored by the American Society of Crime Laboratory Directors (ASCLD), have revealed that the error rate for laboratories using gas chromatography alone is significantly higher (50 to 100% higher) than laboratories using GC-MS.[3] These same CTS studies show a decreasing reliance on GC alone (at least among CTS subscribers—arguably the better laboratories in the field), and may result in future changes in ASTM standards.

### § 9:27    Introductory discussion of the science—Laboratory analysis—Identification (individualization) of petroleum products

Considerable work has been done regarding the individualization of ignitable liquids in order to tie a suspect to a source. Matching of gasolines has been demonstrated, but as a fire progresses and the gasoline becomes more evaporated, the identification becomes more difficult. In 1987, Mann was able to correctly identify the source of fresh gasoline based on the relative concentrations of light hydrocarbons.[1] Recent work by Dolan and Ritacco demonstrates that it is possible to make successful comparisons, or at least exclusions, of gasoline samples that have weathered to more than fifty percent.[2] This identification is carried out by analyzing pairs of minor components that have very similar boiling points, and thus are equally affected by evaporation. Both Mann and Dolan and Ritacco used a 60–meter column and conventional gas chromatography-mass spectrometry. A new technique, which is in use in the United Kingdom, is said to be capable of not only comparing gasolines, but determining their manufacturer based on the characterization of additive packages using highly sophisticated time-of-flight mass spectrometry. These additives are not volatile, and are said to remain even after all of the volatile materials in a sample have evaporated. Because of privatization of the forensic sciences in the U.K., however, the one laboratory that claims the capability of performing it has not yet published this technique.[3]

Individualization of petroleum distillates other than gasolines has not been extensively studied, due mainly to the difficulty of the task. Unless there is some unusual compound dissolved in the petroleum distillate, identification is generally regarded as difficult, but exclusions are possible.

---

[3]Collaborative Testing Services, Flammables Analysis Report No. 9716 (1998); Collaborative Testing Services, Flammables Analysis Report No. 9816 (1999); Collaborative Testing Services, Flammables Analysis Report No. 99-536 (2000).

[Section 9:27]

[1]Mann, Comparison of Automotive Gasolines using Capillary Gas Chromatography: I Comparison Methodology, 32 J. Forensic Sci. 606 (1987).

[2]J. Dolan and C. Ritacco, Gasoline Comparisons by Gas Chromatography/Mass Spectrometry Utilizing an Automated Approach to Data Analysis, Proceedings of the American Academy of Forensic Sciences Annual Meeting, Atlanta, Georgia (Feb. 16, 2002), at 62.

[3]Rebecca Pepler, Petrol Branding, Presentation at Gardner Associates International Fire and Arson Investigator Conference (June 29, 2005).

Recent studies by environmental chemists, attempting to measure the age or source of petroleum discharges, have identified several classes of higher molecular weight compounds, more likely to survive a fire, which can be used for individualization. Considerable additional work is required before this technology will be applicable to fire debris analysis.[4]

With the enormous financial incentives related to the identification of responsible parties in environmental cases, the field of environmental forensics has moved forward in ways that indicate that the day when it will be possible for petroleum products to be linked to a particular source is not far off. *Introduction to Environmental Forensics*[5] goes into great detail on the chemical "fingerprinting" of hydrocarbon, and the scientific theory that makes such fingerprinting possible. New techniques to accomplish this task include two-dimensional gas chromatography, high-resolution mass spectrometry and isotope ratio mass spectrometry. While generally too expensive to be used routinely in routine fire cases (and usually the question of individualization does not present itself) these techniques promise to assist in the individualization of even highly weathered residues, such as those found at fire scenes.

## § 9:28 Introductory discussion of the science—Sources—Authoritative publications

The industry standard for fire investigation is known as NFPA 921, GUIDE FOR FIRE AND EXPLOSION INVESTIGATIONS. The National Fire Protection Association is a nonprofit organization founded in 1896 that promulgates all types of codes related to fires, including building codes, equipment specifications, guidelines for certification of individuals, and a guide for fire investigation. NFPA 921 is produced and maintained using the NFPA consensus process, which has been approved by the American National Standards Institute (ANSI). The Technical Committee on Fire Investigations, which drafted NFPA 921, consists of no more than 30 individuals, with membership strictly regulated by NFPA guidelines, including specified numbers of public officials, academics, insurance industry representatives and private experts. The general public has the opportunity to propose changes to the standard, and to comment the Committee's disposition of proposed changes. (In general, however, only NFPA members are made aware of pending standards.) The committee then votes on whether to accept or reject the proposals or comments from the individual submitters, some of whom may be members of the committee. The first edition of NFPA 921 was published in 1992. The document, which took six years to produce, was passed with no dissenting votes from Committee members.[1]

When this chapter was first published in 1997, the industry standard for fire investigation was the 1995 edition of NFPA 921, GUIDE FOR FIRE AND EXPLOSION INVESTIGATIONS. As a result of the receipt of more than 150 proposals for changes, the 1998 edition, which became effective in February of 1998, contained many substantial changes and clarifications. The document was extensively revised in 2001 and 2004. The next revision will be printed in early 2008.

One of the more interesting changes between 1995 and 1998 was the removal of

---

[4]S. A. Stout & A.D. Uhler, Chemical "Fingerprinting" of Highly Weathered Petroleum Products, Proceedings of the American Academy of Forensic Sciences (Feb. 2000).

[5]Brian L. Murphy and Robert D. Morrison, Introduction To Environmental Forensics (2002).

**[Section 9:28]**

[1]Disclaimer: The author is a member of the

NFPA Technical Committee on Fire Investigations, and has attempted to accurately describe the contents and appropriate interpretation of NFPA 921, Guide for Fire and Explosion Investigations. Nothing in this text, however, should be interpreted as a formal interpretation or the official position of NFPA or the Technical Committee on Fire Investigations.

the word "misconception" from the titles of many sections. A significant portion of the fire investigation community was offended by the use of the word "misconception" in the first two editions of the GUIDE. Proponents of the change argued (with, it turns out, unjustified optimism) that while misconceptions might exist in a few investigators' minds, the first two editions had cleared up many of those misconceptions. In most cases, the text of the chapter section was left intact, but the title was changed. For example, the sections entitled "Misconceptions about Char" and "Misconceptions about Spalling" had their titles changed to "Interpretation of Char" and "Interpretation of Spalling." The cautions regarding the potential for misinterpretation of these two artifacts, however, remained in the text.

Another significant change between 1995 and 1998 was the removal of the section on certainty of opinions. A consensus within the Committee developed regarding removal of these various levels of certainty. The Committee felt that they had been mistakenly equated by the legal community with burdens of proof—an easy mistake to make since some of the terms and their definitions plainly adopted terminology that borrowed from and tracked legal burden of proof concepts. Whatever the intention of the fire and arson community may have been, they provide an example of how to invite (and get) confusion. An attempt had been made to clear up the confusion between the 1992 and 1995 editions, but it was not successful. Elimination of the terminology altogether was judged to be the best available course at that time. Many Committee members, however, felt that some expression of the "comfort level" that an investigator had with his opinion was in order. In the 2001 edition, the discussion was unchanged, but in the 2004 edition, the following text was added:

> "Two levels of confidence have significance with respect to opinions: 1. Probable. This level certainty corresponds to being more likely true than not. At this level of certainty, the likelihood of the hypothesis being true is greater than fifty percent.

> 2. Possible. At this level of certainty the hypothesis can be demonstrated to be feasible but cannot be declared probable." If two or more hypotheses are equally likely then the level of certainty must be "possible."[2]

In the 1998 edition, the chapter on electricity and fire and the interpretation of electrical artifacts was significantly expanded and improved. A chapter was added on fuel gas systems, and a large number of references were added to the explanatory material in the appendix.

Between 1998 and 2001, the NFPA received 183 proposals for changing the NFPA 921, and over 500 comments on the Technical Committee's handling of those proposals. The level of discourse in the standards development process descended to a level commonly associated with party politics. There was a serious conflict between the old guard "arson investigators," and the proponents of the scientific method. The proponents of science prevailed.

The 2001 edition of NFPA 921, released in February 2001, included a rewritten chapter on vehicle fires, and new chapters on fire deaths, human behavior in fires, analytical tools (including computer assisted fire modeling), wildfire investigations and building systems. Additionally, the GUIDE was reorganized into three sections outlining what a fire investigator should know, how a fire investigator should conduct a routine investigation, and special topics in fire investigation.

In the 2001 edition, language was added to the section on hypothesis testing under the scientific method to allow for "cognitive" testing in addition to, or in lieu of, experimental testing. This change was made because many people in the fire investigation community misunderstood the scientific method, and believed that in order to be "scientific," it was necessary to rebuild the structure and recreate the

---

[2]National Fire Protection Association, Guide    921) (2004), at § 18.6.
for Fire and Explosion Investigations (Pub. No.

fire, which was never the intent of the document. (Actually, this wrongheaded argument was usually advanced disingenuously by attorneys opposing the introduction of scientific methodology and resisting *Daubert* challenges.) Some fire investigators, however, took the new language on "cognitive" testing as a license to go back to the old ways of declaring a fire to be caused by arson or some other cause based on nothing more than their "training and experience" rather than on deductive reasoning. Consequently, for the 2004 edition, the Technical Committee on Fire Investigations has added definitions of inductive reasoning and deductive reasoning, and has added an explanatory appendix item to this paragraph in order to explain exactly what is meant by "cognitive testing."

Other significant additions to the 2001 edition included a discussion of spoliation of evidence, and a definition of those necessary activities that should not be considered spoliation, as well as a discussion of the process of elimination, an attempt to come to grips with the so-called "negative corpus" determination.[3]

By far the most significant controversy for the 2001 edition was a movement led by the International Association of Arson Investigators and certain insurance defense attorneys to remove any mention of the word "science" from the document. Despite the fact that the *Kumho* decision rendered the effect of such a change moot, the rear guard took this fight to the NFPA, and, as happened in the Supreme Court, they were roundly defeated. The Technical Committee and the NFPA as a whole continued to endorse the scientific method as the way to investigate fires. The vote was 29-0 in the Technical Committee and unanimous by a voice vote at the NFPA annual meeting. The rejection of the IAAI *amicus* brief by the *Kumho* court and the rejection of the proposals to eliminate science from NFPA 921 finally caused a change in the attitude in the IAAI leadership. The 2001 edition of NFPA 921 was the first officially endorsed by the President of the IAAI on behalf of his 8,000 members. The same attorneys who had counseled investigators to avoid using the "S" word subsequently began advising the investigators to embrace the document and using it as a means of getting their testimony accepted by trial courts.

Compared to the technical, legal, and ideological battles that surrounded the production of the 2001 edition, the proposals to make changes in the 2004 edition were relatively minor, at least from a substantive standpoint.

The 2004 edition of NFPA 921 also has a different format, because NFPA has decided to conform all of its standards to International Organization for Standards (ISO) guidelines. Additionally, the document has separated the chapter on cause into two separate chapters, one dealing with the circumstances that bring together an ignition source, an oxidizer, and a fuel, and another chapter dealing with the "cause" of fire spread, injuries, deaths, and other issues that go beyond the traditional "cause" of the fire.

The chapter on legal considerations was been completely rewritten and reorganized to provide more information on discovery procedures, and the impact of the *Daubert* decision on fire investigation. The chapter has also been reordered so that the paragraphs generally follow the temporal path of a legal case, beginning with investigative considerations, followed by the filing of a complaint or indictment, discovery, and trial.

Work is underway on the 2008 edition of NFPA 921. New chapters will be added on marine fires, and the Origin, Basic Fire Science, and Patterns chapters are slated for a major rewrite. The revision of the chapter on Origin Determination is designed to bring the recommended procedures more in line with the temporal flow of the scientific method.

The general, yet grudging, acceptance of NFPA 921 as the standard of care in fire

---

[3]§ 9:47.

investigation is reflected in the growing number of *Daubert* challenges to fire investigators who fail to follow its guidance, particularly with respect to interpretation of fire scene evidence. It is the misinterpretation of fire effects and fire patterns (as opposed to incorrect procedures) that account for most of the incorrect determinations of fire origins and causes. *Daubert* rulings on the admissibility of fire investigation opinions almost invariably cite NFPA 921.[4]

Additional support from the law enforcement community for the use of NFPA 921 as the standard of care in fire investigations began in late 1997, when the Justice Department started work on national guidelines for fire and arson scene investigation.

These guidelines were modeled after NATIONAL GUIDELINES FOR DEATH INVESTIGATION, a research report published by the National Institute of Justice (NIJ) in December of 1997.[5] The Technical Working Group assembled by NIJ at first recommended that the Justice Department simply purchase 15,000 copies of NFPA 921 and mail them to the nation's law enforcement agencies and fire departments. This suggestion was not adopted. Work on the national guidelines continued for three more years, culminating in the publication of a finished pamphlet in June 2000. These national guidelines recommend a general procedure for the handling of fire and arson scenes, and specifically direct responsible officials to find a fire investigator capable of conducting a scientific scene inspection according to the recommendations of NFPA 921. While the term "standard of care" does not appear in the Justice Department document it does say the following about NFPA 921. "It has become a benchmark for the training and expertise of everyone who purports to be an expert in the origin and cause determination of fires."[6]

A similar guide was published at the same time dealing with the responsibilities to explosion or bombing scenes.[7]

Most fire investigators will, on cross-examination, concede that NFPA 921 represents the industry standard for the conduct of fire investigations although it is "only a guide." These words "only a guide," suggest that somewhere in the investigation, the investigator has elected not to accept the proffered guidance.

The most important concept embodied in NFPA 921 is the recognition that fire investigation must be based upon the scientific method.[8] This may seem obvious, but until recently, fire investigators based their conclusions upon their "technical knowledge" gained through training, and experience. The existence of NFPA 921 makes it more difficult for the investigator to rely solely upon anecdotal experience. As stated by the Joiner court, "nothing in either *Daubert* or the Federal Rules of Evidence requires a district court to admit opinion evidence which is connected to existing data only by the *ipse dixit* of the expert." This ruling disappointed many fire investigators, but it has had a salutary effect on the practice of fire investigation.

There exist a few other authoritative sources or learned texts in the field, but other than NFPA 921, there is only one text that any group of fire investigators will be likely to agree upon as being "authoritative," and that is KIRK'S FIRE INVESTIGATION, by John D. DeHaan.[9] This excellent basic text, which is understandable to nonscientists, explains most of the aspects of fire investigation that a typical

---

[4]See cases cites in § 9:12.

[5]National Medicolegal Review Panel, National Guidelines for Death Investigation (NCJ 167568) (1997).

[6]Technical Working Group on Fire/Arson Scene Investigation, USDOJ, Fire and Arson Scene Evidence: A Guide for Public Safety Personnel (Jun. 2000), available at http://www.ojp.usdoj. gov/nij/scidocs2000.htm.

[7]Technical Working Group for Bombing Scene Investigation, USDOJ, A Guide for Explosion and Bombing Scene Investigation (Jun. 2000), available at http://www.ojp.ussdoj.gov/nij/scidocs 2000.htm.

[8]National Fire Protection Association, Guide for Fire and Explosion Investigations (Pub. No. 921) (2004), at § 4.2.

[9]John D. DeHaan, Kirk's Fire Investigation

investigator is likely to encounter. Paul Kirk, perhaps the most respected forensic scientist of the 20th century, in 1969, authored the first edition of this book[10] and it was the standard reference text for over a decade. To appreciate the changes and improvements in the understanding of fire dynamics and fire investigation that have occurred since 1969, a review and comparison of the successive editions of this book is useful. This popular reference text on fire investigation came out in its fifth edition in 2002. There were several additions to the text, as DeHaan attempted to bring it more in line with NFPA 921.

As with most "standard" texts, KIRK'S FIRE INVESTIGATION, while moving the profession gradually forward, defines where the consensus is rather than leading the way. The evolution of the thinking of mainstream fire investigators can, in fact, be followed by reviewing the changes in KIRK'S FIRE INVESTIGATION through its five editions, as it gradually embraces a more rigorous approach, and finally disposes of some of the myths and misconceptions that appeared in earlier editions.

### § 9:29 Introductory discussion of the science—Sources—Periodical literature

There are several periodicals to which fire investigators may subscribe, and the reliability of the information in these periodicals varies widely. FIRE TECHNOLOGY, a peer-reviewed journal, usually deals with highly technical aspects of fire behavior, such as computer modeling, the behavior of large liquid pool fires, or the response of fire protection systems. Fire investigation articles appear occasionally in FIRE TECHNOLOGY, as fire protection engineers publish results of test fires that may (or may not) validate computer models.

The most widely read fire investigation publication is THE FIRE & ARSON INVESTIGATOR, the official publication of the International Association of Arson Investigators. Publication in this journal may reflect a thorough peer review (for the more technical articles) or simply editorial review (for news reports or "op-ed" pieces). Peer review began only in 1996. The IAAI Board of Directors, until then, elected to publish more of a newsletter than a scientific journal, in the belief that everyone is entitled to their own opinion and that the exclusion of articles, even highly technical scientific articles, because of the objections of peer reviewers was equivalent to "censorship". The introduction of peer review to THE FIRE AND ARSON INVESTIGATOR has not been without its difficulties. Some reviewers report that, while they have made comments and suggestions for changes to technical articles, the articles were eventually published in their original form.

FIRE FINDINGS,[1] an independent publication based in St. Joseph, Michigan, publishes topical articles on fire investigation. While not strictly peer-reviewed, it is generally worth reading. Issues contain directions to resources, reports of experiments, and explanations of how things work. Each issue also contains a section on product recalls, book reviews, a report on a particular type of fire (for instance, neon sign fires), and a discussion of some part of NFPA 921.

The internet is gaining popularity as a resource for fire investigators. Particularly useful sites include CFI Trainer, http://www.cfitrainer.net, an online training center, and an independent forum for fire investigators, http://www.forumworld.com/arson-investigations, where fire investigators exchange information (and sometimes barbs).

A recent development in fire investigator training holds the potential for dramatically improving the quality of fire investigations. The IAAI, funded by the Department of Homeland Security's Assistance to Firefighters Grant Program and working with the Bureau of Alcohol, Tobacco, Firearms and Explosives, the Insurance Com-

---

(5th ed. 2002).

[10]Paul Kirk, Fire Investigation (1969).

**[Section 9:29]**

[1]Available at http://www.firefindings.com.

mittee for Arson Control and NIST, now offers at no cost training modules of interest to both fire investigators and the attorneys who employ them. This training is available at http://www.cfitrainer.net. As of August 2006, programs were available on the application of *Daubert* to fire investigations, an introduction to fire dynamics and fire modeling (in terms understandable to lay audiences) the Scientific Method in Fire Investigations and digital photography for fire investigators. Information obtained from this page should meet the requirement of "general acceptance."

## § 9:30    Areas of scientific agreement and disagreement—Field investigations

There are few fields where the ability of experts to disagree after viewing the same evidence is more of a problem than in fire investigation. Because a fire destroys so much of the physical evidence, it is a rare fire that can be examined by more than one expert yet have only one conclusion reached about it. Generally, the more severe the fire, the less likely two individuals are to agree as to its cause. Certainly, the more thorough the investigation and the more information that is actually collected, the more likely these individuals are to be able to agree as to the cause of a fire.

Some opinions are a cause for particular concern. When the fire investigator opines that the artifacts he sees are the result of the burning of an ignitable liquid, and the laboratory analysis fails to confirm the presence of ignitable liquid residue, additional scrutiny of the investigator's methodology is warranted. This is especially true if the investigator bases his interpretation on one or more of the many discredited myths about fire investigation. These myths were first collected and published by the Law Enforcement Assistance Administration in 1977[1] and include the following:

*Alligatoring effect*: Checking of charred wood, giving it the appearance of alligator skin. Large rolling blisters indicate rapid intense heat, while small flat alligatoring indicates long, low heat.

*Crazing of glass*: Formation of irregular cracks in glass due to rapid intense heat—possible fire accelerant.

*Depth of char*: Depth of burning of wood—used to determine length of burn and thereby locate the point of origin of the fire.

*Line of demarcation*: Boundary between charred and uncharred material. On floors or rugs, a puddle-shaped line of demarcation is believed to indicate a liquid fire accelerant. In the cross-section of wood, a sharp distinct line of demarcation indicates a rapid, intense fire.

*Sagged furniture springs*: Because of the heat required for furniture springs to collapse from their own weight (1150°F) and because of the insulating effect of the upholstery, sagged springs are believed to be possible only in either a fire originating inside the cushions (as from a cigarette rolling between the cushions) or an external fire intensified by a fire accelerant.

*Spalling*: Breaking off of pieces of the surface of concrete, cement or brick due to intense heat. Brown stains around the spall indicate the use of a fire accelerant.[6]

In addition to the misconceptions listed in the LEAA report, the following myths have also been widely promulgated:

*Fire load*: Knowing the energy content (as opposed to the energy release rate) of the fuels in a structure was believed to allow an investigator to calculate the damage that a "normal" fire should produce in a given time frame.

---

[Section 9:30]

[1]Aerospace Corp., Arson and Arson Investigation: Survey and Assessment (USDOJ, National Institute of Law Enforcement and Criminal Justice, 1977), at 87.

*Low burning and holes in the floor*: Because heat rises, it was widely believed that burning on the floor, particularly under furniture, indicated an origin on the floor.

*V-pattern angle*: The angle of a V-pattern was supposed to indicate the speed of the fire.

*Time and temperature*: By estimating the speed of a fire, or establishing the temperature achieved by a fire, it was believed that an investigator could determine whether it was accelerated.[2]

The authors of the LEAA publication, to their credit, acknowledged that the burn indicators listed had not been scientifically validated, and urged a series of experiments to test their reliability. They further urged the production of a handbook after the tests were run.

Unfortunately, no tests were run, but a handbook was published anyway. Using information provided by the U.S. Fire Academy, no less an authority then the U.S. National Bureau of standards published a collection of old wives' tales in 1980.[3] Given the undisputed authority of the NBS, these myths were widely cited in the fire investigation literature.

Despite the fact that nobody now employed at The National Fire Academy or at NIST (the successor to NBS) still believes the myths, neither agency has yet "officially" repudiated the misinformation that they promulgated. This is particularly disturbing in the case of the NFA, because nearly all public sector fire investigators, and especially the senior members of the profesion were trained (or mis-trained) at the NFA.

## § 9:31 Areas of scientific agreement and disagreement—Field investigations—The behavior of fire

With respect to the behavior of fire, all investigators will agree that there is a fire triangle consisting of heat, fuel, and oxygen. Some investigators will expand the triangle into three dimensions, and describe a fire tetrahedron, the fourth point of which is a sustained chemical reaction.[1] Fire investigators will all agree that heat rises, and that the primary means of fire spread are conduction, convection, and radiation.

When they actually begin to describe how a *particular* fire spread, however, many fire investigators ignore everything but convection, that is, the phenomenon that causes warm air to rise. This phenomenon also causes a fire to spread out in a "V" shaped pattern until it reaches an obstruction. Thus, seeking the bottom of the "V" shaped burn pattern should lead one to the origin.[2]

Unfortunately, this indication of a fire's origin is useful only when the fire is extinguished prior to achieving total room involvement. Once a fire has progressed beyond a certain point, items that were located near the top of the room catch fire and fall down, causing secondary ignitions, and additional "V" shaped burn patterns.[3] These may be falsely interpreted as evidence of a second point of origin. Since everyone agrees that an accidental fire can begin in only one place, multiple points of origin are generally considered to be an indicator of arson.

There is considerable disagreement in the fire investigation community, however, about the ability of fire investigators to credibly determine multiple origins when

[2]See John J. Lentini, The Mythology of Fire Investigation, in Scientific Protocols for Fire Investigation (2006).

[3]Francis Brannigern et al. (eds.), Fire Investigation Handbook (1980).

[Section 9:31]

[1]National Fire Protection Association, Guide for Fire and Explosion Investigations (Pub. No. 921) (2004), at § 5.1.2.

[2]National Fire Protection Association, Guide for Fire and Explosion Investigations (Pub. No. 921) (2004), at § 6.6.2.5.

[3]National Fire Protection Association, Guide for Fire and Explosion Investigations (Pub. No. 921) (2004), at § 22.2.1.

the fires have burned together. Some fire investigators insist that they have the ability to determine multiple points of origin even if a room has flashed over. They do this by looking at holes in the floor, and because holes in the floor represent "low burns," these are equated with multiple origins. NFPA 921 advises the investigator to be wary of numerous conditions that could result in "apparent" multiple origins.[4]

Low burns are also taken (or mistaken) as an indication of the presence of ignitable liquids. Because heat rises and fire burns up, the presence of a low burn is sometimes taken as an indication that there was "something" on the floor that held the fire down. While ignitable liquids will accomplish this task, radiation is even more effective at burning floors. If total room involvement has been achieved, there is no reason for a floor not to be burned.[5] The failure to take into account the effects of radiation may be a result of a general lack of understanding of this common and important means of heat transfer.[6]

When the floor is burned, there is a tendency on the part of some fire investigators to believe that, unless it has burned in a perfectly uniform manner, radiation can be ruled out as the cause of the low burning. This is based on the misperception of flashover as being a uniform phenomenon.[7] Actually, the uniformity of the flashover event breaks down within the first few seconds. Additionally, most synthetic floor coverings have a tendency to tear open during a fire, thus leaving parts of the floor exposed and other parts of the floor covered. The alternating exposed and covered areas can result in the production of patterns, particularly on combustible surfaces, which look remarkably like patterns that people associate with flammable liquids.[8] This is a fact that is not yet accepted by many fire investigators, but the exposure of these misperceptions has led to several well-publicized reversals of convictions.[9] The current edition of NFPA 921 contains several photographs of what one would expect a flammable liquid pour pattern to look like, but which were actually created by radiation alone.[10]

The series of test burns conducted under the auspices of the USFA, discussed above, has generated much interesting data, but there has not been unanimous agreement on the correct interpretation of the data. The NFPA Technical Committee on Fire Investigations received several comments critical of the series of tests when it proposed citing the final test report in NFPA 921.[11] Many of these criticisms cited the "incomplete" nature of the data, because funds ran out before all of the proposed tests could be completed. These arguments really did not focus on the quality or the interpretation of the data. Other, more legitimate, criticisms of the report focused on its conclusions about the cause of certain types of burn patterns, believed to have been caused by unique ventilation parameters, and on the suggestion of the report's authors that much meaningful data could be found in the depth of the "calcination" of gypsum wallboard.

Scientists at the Building and Fire Research Laboratory (BFRL) at NIST conducted a series of tests to identify the characteristics of flammable and

---

[4]National Fire Protection Association, Guide for Fire and Explosion Investigations (Pub. No. 921) (2004), at § 22.2.1.2.

[5]National Fire Protection Association, Guide for Fire and Explosion Investigations (Pub. No. 921) (2004), at § 6.19.1.

[6]John D. DeHaan, Kirk's Fire Investigation 36 (5th ed. 2003).

[7]Barker Davie, Flashover, 11 Nat'l Fire & Arson Rep. 1 (1993).

[8]National Fire Protection Association, Guide for Fire and Explosion Investigations (Pub. No.

921) (2004), at § 6.17.8.2.5.

[9]*State v. Knapp*, No. CR 78779 (Superior Ct. of Arizona, Maricopa County, Feb. 11, 1987); *State v. Girdler*, No. 9809 (Superior Ct. of Arizona, Maricopa County, Jan. 3, 1991).

[10]National Fire Protection Association, Guide for Fire and Explosion Investigations (Pub. No. 921) (2004), at § 6.17.8.2.

[11]Technical Committee Documentation, NFPA, Report on Proposals for the Fall, 2000, Meeting, at www.nfpa.org.

combustible liquid burn patterns on horizontal surfaces.[12] The findings reveal several interesting facts about the resulting patterns:

* that the spill area can be predicted from fuel quantity
* that the quantity of gasoline spilled can be determined by the burn pattern area on nonporous flooring such as carpet
* that the heat release rates of spilled liquids on carpeted surfaces are approximately equal to the steady heat release rate of the equivalent diameter pool fires, but on nonporous surfaces the heat release rates are much lower
* that on carpeted surfaces, a "donut" pattern is frequently the result when ignitable liquid burns on the carpet

The study also found that significant quantities of the fuel were present after extinguishment on carpeted fires because the carpet melted and protected the unburned liquids. On nonporous surfaces, some of the burn patterns look remarkably unlike those typically expected from a flammable liquid pour. It turns out that radiation from burning solids can create "puddle-shaped" patterns when no liquids are present. A photograph of such a puddle shaped pattern was added to NFPA 921 as a caution to fire investigators against "over interpreting" (a euphemism for misinterpreting) the burn patterns that they see on floors.

## § 9:32 Areas of scientific agreement and disagreement—Field investigations—Accidental fires

Even though 80% or more of all fires are accidents, the vast majority of fire scene investigators receive their training as "arson investigators." Accidental fires frequently result in civil litigation. The trend toward subrogation in the insurance industry picked up considerable strength in the late 1980s and shows no signs of abating. Thus, arson investigators are now called upon to determine accidental causes, with an eye toward pinning the blame on a manufacturer, or a provider of a service, or anyone other than the name insured. Competent investigators have the good sense to call in the appropriate engineering discipline once they have determined that a particular device is located at the origin. Most engineers are unable to determine the origin of a fire, but most fire investigators are unable to independently determine the cause of failure of an appliance or system.

## § 9:33 Areas of scientific agreement and disagreement—Field investigations—Electrical activity

Fire investigators generally agree that the electrical system can be used as a fire detector, in that the first point on an energized electrical circuit that is compromised by a fire is likely to be the first and only point on that circuit where arcing occurs.[1] There is some disagreement, however, about the characterization of arcing. There are many fires where one investigator will point to a piece of melted copper and identify it as evidence of arcing, while another investigator will look at the same piece and state that the copper was heating above its melting point (1981°F). The determination as to whether a bead of melted copper was caused by electrical or thermal activity can usually be resolved through an examination by a practiced

---

[12]Anthony Putorti, Flammable and Combustible Liquid Spill/Burn Patterns (NCJ Number 186-634) (March 2001), available online at www.ncjrs.org.

**[Section 9:33]**

[1]Richard Underwood & John J. Lentini, Appliance Fires: Determining Responsibility, 7

Nat'l Fire & Arson Report 1 (1989).

investigator.[2] The essential test for determining whether the copper was melted by electrical or thermal activity is the existence of a sharp line of demarcation between a localized area of melting and unmelted wire.

Some study has been conducted on the examination of arc beads, to determine whether they were created in an atmosphere full of smoke or in a smoke-free atmosphere. The thus far unproved theory is that if the arc was created toward the beginning of the fire, it might have been the cause of the fire.[3] The ability to determine the elemental content of the atmosphere at the time an arc bead was created, however, has not been repeatedly demonstrated, and the significance of the atmospheric chemistry is a subject of debate.[4] Arcing occurs in almost all fires, and almost all arcing events are the result of a fire, rather than the cause of it. The search for the "primary" arc, however, has resulted in many disagreements among fire investigators and electrical engineers. The fact is that electrical arcing is not responsible for a large number of fires, but an arc can be shown to be a competent ignition source, although the typical arc lasts less than a hundredth of a second. Thus electrical arcs are often mistakenly blamed for causing fires.[5] Electricity does cause fires, but almost all electrical fires are caused by "series arcs." These arcs occur when the electrical current is traveling in its intended path, but encounters a lose connection. The current jumping across that connection generates locally high temperatures sufficient to ignite surrounding combustibles. Series arcs typically can last for hours or days. Ground fault arcs, where the current moves out of its intended path are frequently extinguished in one cycle (1/60th of a second) or less. Thus, the utility of looking for evidence of a "primary" arc is questionable, at best. The analytical technique required for this "test," auger electron microscopy, is quite expensive, and is unlikely to be encountered in routine cases.

In addition to "arcing," other electrical sources are frequently cited, correctly or incorrectly, as the cause of a fire. Heat producing appliances (portable space heaters and kitchen ranges) are the most frequent causes of fires started with electrical energy.[6] Ballasts from fluorescent lights are probably the most frequently falsely accused electrical devices. When we consider the millions of these devices in use, it is not hard to imagine that there will be a ballast found within ten feet of the origin of almost any commercial fire. If a fluorescent light ballast truly has caused a fire, it will likely have a hole melted in the ballast case.

Electronic equipment such as computers, stereo systems, and televisions often are blamed for fires. Television sets manufactured in the early 1970s were responsible for a very large number of fires. By 1993, the Consumer Product Safety Commission (CPSC) estimated that incidence had fallen to 0.4% of all residential fires, 2100 incidents annually, causing 30 deaths.[7]

Each proposed electrical fire cause deserves careful evaluation. Some "indicators" of electrical causation, like some indicators of arson, have been studied and shown to be less valid than previously thought. Oversized fuses or breakers, unless very much larger than required, are generally incapable of supplying sufficient current to overheat a circuit. A 30-amp fuse or breaker located in a panel where there should be a 20-amp fuse or breaker is interesting, but almost certainly meaningless. The condition of insulation on a cable may yield some information about overcurrent, particularly if the insulation has melted loose from the conductor. A comparison

---

[2]Bernard Beland, Examination of Electrical Conductors Following a Fire, 16 Fire Tech. 252 (1980).

[3]Anderson, Surface Analysis of Electrical Arc Residues in Fire Investigation, 34 J. Forensic Sci. 633 (1989).

[4]Bernard Beland, Examination of Arc Beads, 44 Fire & Arson Investigator, Jun. 1994, at 20.

[5]John D. DeHaan, Kirk's Fire Investigation at 335 (5th ed. 2003).

[6]U.S. Consumer Product Safety Commission, 1986 National Fire Loss Estimates (Oct. 1988).

[7]John D. DeHaan, Kirk's Fire Investigation at 271 (4th ed. 1997) and at 340 (5th ed. 2002).

must be made with a similar unheated wire, however, to determine the original "tightness" of the insulation. The lack of loose insulation does not rule out overcurrent.[8] Overcurrent in branch circuit wiring, however, is not a frequent cause of fires. Sometimes, overcurrent causes undersized extension cords to overheat.

The most frequently encountered problem in the examination of electrical evidence is one of cause and effect. Did the wire short and start the fire, or did the fire burn the insulation and cause the wire to short?

The laboratory examination of an appliance suspected of causing a fire will usually allow for a definitive ruling in or out of the appliance as the cause. An essential component of such a laboratory examination is the acquisition of an exemplar product. A detailed description of the procedures for examining various types of appliances suspecting of causing fires may be found in SCIENTIFIC PROTOCOLS FOR FIRE INVESTIGATION.[9]

### § 9:34  Areas of scientific agreement and disagreement—Field investigations—Cause and effect

The same type of chicken-and-egg, or cause and effect, argument applies to other systems found in buildings, as well. The gas system, for instance, is frequently compromised by a fire, resulting in leaks observed during and after the fire. It is the goal of the fire investigator to determine whether the leak existed before the fire. This is often a more difficult question than the science is capable of handling, particularly if the leak occurs in a combustible line. Metallurgists can be of some assistance in determining the reason for a fracture, and can sometimes tell whether the metal broke while it was hot or cold.

The compromise of electrical and fuel systems by fire, and the confusion that it creates, is even more evident in vehicle fires. As a general rule, fire investigators will agree that, while fires can start in the engine compartment and move to the passenger compartment, the reverse is seldom true. Some of the early fire investigation literature pertaining to vehicles suggested that almost all vehicle fires were intentionally set, as all of the fires contained certain "indicators" of excessive heat.[1] These texts are now generally regarded as incorrect, as it has been shown that regardless of ignition method, the temperature achieved by a vehicle fire will approach 2000°F, resulting in buckling and warping of body panels, melting and flowing of window glass, and a loss of seat spring temper. Thus, the intensity and duration of a vehicle fire cannot be interpreted as indicating or not indicating the presence of accelerants.[2]

In a structure fire, an investigator who can narrow the origin down to a three by three foot square is considered a hero. In a vehicle fire, a three by three foot square is the starting point, and unless the exact cause can be determined, the fire investigator will be looked upon as a failure. Thus, frequently investigators will seize upon a burned fuel line, or an arced electrical wire as the cause of a fire, when the evidence argues equally that the observed "causative" phenomenon is actually an effect.

It has been recently accepted that a determination of the compartment of origin (engine compartment versus passenger compartment) can be made by observing burn patterns on the exterior surfaces of the car. These so-called *radial burn pat-*

[8]John D. DeHaan, Kirk's Fire Investigation at 271 (4th ed. 1997) and at 340 (5th ed. 2002).

[9]John J. Lentini, Evaluation of Ignition Sources, in Scientific Protocols For Fire Investigation (2006).

[Section 9:34]

[1]National Automobile Theft Bureau, Manual for Investigation of Vehicle Fires (1986).

[2]John D. DeHaan, Kirk's Fire Investigation 287 (5th ed. 2003).

*terns* indicate the direction of fire movement.[3]

A special case of vehicle fire can be usually be determined without even looking at the vehicle. This is the case where a vehicle is reported stolen and recovered burned. The possibility that it sustained an accidental fire right after it was stolen is almost not worth considering.

### § 9:35    Areas of scientific agreement and disagreement—Field investigations—Black holes

Perhaps no type of fire is more difficult than the "black hole," a structure fire in which everything is reduced to ashes. Despite the difficulties of these investigations, fire investigators have been known to claim the ability to detect multiple origins in completely consumed structures, or to state, based on "indicators," that a fire burned "hotter than normal" or "faster than normal."

The studies done by the Center for Fire Research have tended to put to rest the diagnosis of "faster than normal." If a piece of upholstered furniture is ignited, it can bring a room to total involvement in less than five minutes. Time to flashover as low as ninety seconds has been reported.[1] Once flashover occurs in a particular room, extension into nearby rooms can be exceedingly rapid, involving entire houses in as little as fifteen minutes.

The editors of Fire Findings have explored the reliability of witnesses who report on the speed of a fire. Such reports are generally unreliable.[2] Fire Findings offers a videotape entitled "What Witnesses Don't See" that describes the event preceding a fire's detection. Often, witnesses only notice a fire when it breaks out a window, a sign that flashover has just occurred. The witnesses to the event have no clue as to when the fire started.

The fire that burns "hotter than normal" has, in the past, been identified by examination of the metals and other noncombustible materials within a structure, in order to get a handle on the temperature that the fire achieved. In 1969, Kirk advised noting melted metals because:

> The investigator may use this fact to his advantage in many instances, because of the differences in effective temperatures between simple wood fires and those in which extraneous fuel, such as accelerant, is present.[3]

Contrast this advice with DeHaan, Kirk's successor:

> While such melted metals cannot and should not be used as proof that the fire was incendiary, the fire investigator should note their presence, extent and distribution. Such information can be of help in establishing differences between normally fueled and ventilated accidental fires and those produced by enhanced draft conditions or unusual fuel loads from accelerants in incendiary fires.[4]

While DeHaan recognizes the importance of ventilation, he still maintains that unusual temperatures may be caused by enhanced draft conditions *or* unusual fuel loads while the data only support the former. Nonetheless, the modern text of KIRK's at least recognizes what blacksmiths and metallurgists have known for centuries: increased ventilation causes increased temperatures. Despite this knowledge, fire investigators continue to rely on the presence of melted copper to indicate a "hotter than normal" (therefore accelerated) fire. This is particularly true of fires

---

[3]National Fire Protection Association, Guide for Fire and Explosion Investigations (Pub. No. 921) (2004), at § 25.8.

**[Section 9:35]**

[1]National Fire Protection Association, Guide for Fire and Explosion Investigations (Pub. No. 921) (2004), at § 5.5.4.2.11.

[2]Jack Sanderson, Fire Timing Test Results: Fires May Only Appear to Spread Rapidly, 3 Fire Findings 1 (1995).

[3]Paul Kirk, Fire Investigation 145 (1969).

[4]John D. DeHaan, Kirk's Fire Investigation, at 173 (4th ed. 1997) and at 218 (5th ed. 2002).

when the melting is found at floor level.

Melted steel was considered to be even more indicative of a "hotter than normal" fire. Steel has a melting temperature of 2100–2700°F, depending on its elemental content. Multiple areas in a structure that exhibit melted steel have been considered as indications of the use of ignitable liquids to accelerate a fire.

Actually, it has been demonstrated that the flame temperature above a burning pool of ignitable liquid is no greater than the flame temperature of a well-ventilated wood fire.[5] The purpose of an accelerant is to make the fire burn faster, by involving more materials sooner than they would be otherwise involved. These fires do not burn at higher temperatures. The *rate* of heat release is higher in an accelerated fire, as the BTUs or joules are released over a shorter period of time. The *temperature* of the fire, however, and its ability to melt items such as steel and copper, is actually no different from that of an unaccelerated fire.

Although the concept of an accelerated fire burning hotter than an unaccelerated fire is an appealing notion, like many of the other myths in fire investigation it is easily disproved. The purpose of an accelerant is to involve materials sooner. Consider a birthday candle. We can use a thermocouple to measure the temperature of the candle. If we light ten candles, the energy released by the burning candles will be 10 times higher, but the temperature of the individual candle flames will be exactly the same.

After the catastrophic Oakland fire of 1991, Lentini, Smith, and Henderson conducted a study to determine the validity of the "indicators of arson." They studied copper, steel, and glass in fifty of the 3,000 houses that had been burned to completion. Most of the houses exhibited multiple "indicators" of arson, even though they are known to have burned in an accidental fire.[6]

### § 9:36 Areas of scientific agreement and disagreement—Field investigations—"Melted" steel

Metallurgical laboratory analysis conducted as a follow-up to the Oakland study revealed that it is not possible to determine by visual inspection alone whether a piece of steel, particularly a low mass piece of steel such as a bedspring, has melted or merely oxidized. This distinction can only be made by microscopic examination of a polished cross-section of the metal. Thus, steel that had been characterized as "melting," at temperatures of up to 2700°F, may have actually been exposed to temperatures no higher than 1300°F for a long period of time, and gave an appearance that was wrongly interpreted as melting.[1]

### § 9:37 Areas of scientific agreement and disagreement—Field investigations—Crazed glass

Glass is another material that changes as a result of exposure to the heat of a fire. Many texts have referred to the crazing of glass as an indication of rapid heating, and one widely circulated handbook went so far as to state that crazed glass

---

[5]Richard Henderson & George Lightsey, Theoretical Combustion Temperature, 3 Nat'l Fire & Arson Report 7 (1985).

[6]John J. Lentini et al., Baseline Characteristics of Residential Structures Which Have Burned to Completion: The Oakland Experi-

ence, 28 Fire Technology 195 (1992).

**[Section 9:36]**

[1]John J. Lentini et al., Baseline Characteristics of Residential Structures Which Have Burned to Completion: The Oakland Experience, 28 Fire Technology 195 (1992).

was an indicator of nearby accelerants.[1] Crazed glass was used as an important "indicator" in the trial of Ray Girdler, whose conviction was later overturned based on new scientific evidence.[2] Experiments conducted after the Oakland fire study revealed that no amount of rapid heating would cause crazing, but that rapid cooling, caused by the application of a water spray, would cause crazing in all cases, whether the glass was heated rapidly or slowly.[3] Crazed glass is meaningless in determining the cause of a fire. Investigators who cite crazed glass as an indicator of an incendiary fire should be easily discredited.

### § 9:38    Areas of scientific agreement and disagreement—Field investigations—Concrete spalling

Spalling is the explosive breaking of concrete, caused by the application of heat. This phenomenon has been the subject of more rhetoric, and probably less research, than most of the other issues in fire investigation. It is one of the most misunderstood and improperly used evidentiary features in the field,[1] and was the basis of an unfortunate case in Alabama that resulted in a record punitive damage award against the insurance company, which presented spalling as evidence of incendiary origin. In that case, the fire had reduced a two-story house to a pile of rubble about a foot deep on top of the concrete slab basement floor. The fire investigator (the second one hired by the insurance company) cleared off a narrow area about ten feet in length and discovered that the floor was spalled. He then declared that a "trail of spalling" existed, and was incontrovertible proof of an incendiary fire. Despite the fact that the defendant's investigator found that the entire slab was spalled, this "trail" evidence was presented, resulting in the court rendering and the Supreme Court upholding the following characterization: "The presentation of his [the investigator's] testimony borders on the perpetration of a fraud upon the Court."[2]

There is an "old school," which holds that concrete spalling is an indication of the presence of ignitable liquids, as well as a cadre of scientists (none of whom have published in a peer reviewed journal) who hold that it is impossible for a flammable liquid to cause spalling.[3] In the middle are the vast majority of fire investigators, who believe that spalling is just another facet of the "burn pattern," which may or may not indicate the presence of a ignitable liquid, depending on the situation. Most fire investigators have seen containers of ignitable liquids that have spilled their contents onto a concrete floor, and in the exact place where the liquid was located, spalling has occurred. The extrapolation of this anecdotal experience to all fires is, of course, an error, as is the contention that ignitable liquids cannot cause spalling under any circumstances.

### § 9:39    Areas of scientific agreement and disagreement—Field investigations—Colors of smoke and fire

Other indicators of unusual fire behavior that have fallen by the wayside include the color of smoke and the color of the flame. When these indicators first were promulgated by the teachers of fire investigation, they were considerably more valid than they are today. Wood and cellulose products tend to have a gray to white

---

[Section 9:37]

[1]John Barracato, Burning, A Guide to Fire Investigation 4 (AETNA Casualty and Surety Company) (1986).

[2]*State v. Girdler*, No. 9809 (Superior Ct. of Arizona, Maricopa County, Jan. 3, 1991).

[3]Lentini, Behavior of Glass at Elevated Temperatures, 37 J. Forensic Sci. 1358 (1992).

[Section 9:38]

[1]National Fire Protection Association, Guide for Fire and Explosion Investigations (Pub. No. 921) (2004), at § 6.6.2.

[2]*United Services Auto. Ass'n v. Wade*, 544 So. 2d 906 (Ala. 1989).

[3]Dennis Canfield, Causes of Spalling Concrete at Elevated Temperatures, 34 Fire & Arson Investigator, Jun. 1984, at 22.

smoke, and burn with a yellow flame. Petroleum based products, such as most common ignitable liquids, burn with a sooty orange flames and produce large quantities of black smoke. In the past, it was thus possible to reach conclusions about what was burning, particularly in the early stages of a fire. In the modern structure, however, a large portion of the interior finish and furnishings consists of petroleum-based products in the form of plastic films, foams and fibers. A burning couch is just as likely to produce thick black smoke as is a burning pool of gasoline or kerosene.

Once again, it is useful to contrast Kirk in 1969 with DeHaan in 1991 and later. According to Kirk, "The presence of much black smoke, especially in the early stages of building a fire, is highly indicative of the presence and burning of a highly carbonaceous material, typical of many fire accelerants."[1] DeHaan, on the other hand, advises, "The combustion of [such] polymers contributes largely to the formation of greasy or sticky dense soot found at many fire scenes, and is responsible for the dense black smoke more frequently noted during the early stages of structure fires."[2] Not only is smoke color an unreliable discriminator between normal and abnormal fuels, it has lately been found that even ordinary wood fires can produce black smoke in the low oxygen conditions which occur following flashover.[3]

## § 9:40 Areas of scientific agreement and disagreement—Field investigations—Low temperature ignition

Under ordinary circumstances, solid materials, particularly wood, will not ignite unless they are heated to their ignition temperature. The theory of low temperature ignition proposes that prolonged exposure to a source of energy that does not raise wood to its ignition temperature, but some temperature tens or hundreds of degrees below that ignition temperature will cause the ignition temperature to decrease. At some point, the theory goes, the wood is transformed into "pyrophoric carbon," which is subject to ignition at lower temperatures. This theory has it origins in the observation of wood members ignited by high-pressure steam pipes in industrial settings. There are reported cases of ignition by steam pipes in residential settings as well. The temperature of the steam pipes is allegedly well known, and below the ignition temperature of wood. Therefore, the theory goes, prolonged exposure to the low temperature has caused a reduction in the ignition point of the wood. This was the theory advanced by a group of investigators in the case of *Truck Insurance Exch. v. MagneTek*. In that case, however, the investigators proposed that the ignition source was not a steam pipe, but a fluorescent light ballast operating at approximately 325°F. Further, the ballast was insulated from the wood target fuel by a layer of gypsum drywall.

The phenomenon of low temperature ignition is also known as "pyrophoria." This phenomenon was studied by Cuzzilo[1] and has been reported on extensively by Babrauskas[2] who takes issue with the Appeals Court in the *Truck case*.[3]

Cuzzilo claims that his research has proven the pyrophoria hypothesis to be false. Babrauskas argues that there are simply too many reported cases of low temperature ignition to ascribe to poor fire investigation. Babrauskas admits that there is

**[Section 9:39]**

[1]Paul Kirk, Fire Investigation 61 (1969).

[2]John D. DeHaan, Kirk's Fire Investigation 111(5th ed. 2003).

[3]National Fire Protection Association, Guide for Fire and Explosion Investigations (Pub. No. 921) (2004), at § 5.6.7.

**[Section 9:40]**

[1]Bernard Cuzzilo, Pyrophoria (unpublished manuscript, University of California, Berkley (1997).

[2]Vytenis Babrauskas, Ignition Handbook, SFPE (2004), at 955.

[3]Vytenis Babrauskas, Truck Insurance v. MagneTek: Lesson to be Learned Concerning Presentation of Scientific Information, 55 Fire & Arson Investigator 9 (Oct. 2004).

no scientific theory underpinning low temperature ignition, at least not one that we understand now. He compares this lack of scientific theory to the lack of a geological theory as to why Mt. Saint Helens exploded on May 18, 1980, instead of May 15. Essentially he says, "We know it happens but we don't know why." Scientists generally eschew this kind of thinking, and since *Daubert*, courts do as well.

The scientific controversy has directed much attention to the possibility of low temperature ignition, and this has resulted in more, not fewer, determinations that low temperature ignitions took place. In some situations, the results are similar to what happens when a fire investigator is unable to find an ignition source and determines the fire to be incendiary. In the industrial situation where arson is eliminated, low temperature ignition is the next obvious suspect.

### § 9:41  Areas of scientific agreement and disagreement—Field investigations—Computer modeling

As a result of years of research conducted at the Center for Fire Research, several computer programs have been developed to predict the spread of a fire, given certain assumptions.[1] If certain facts are known about the configuration of the compartments and fuel packages in a building, a model can predict how a fire can behave and the model's predictions can be compared with fire patterns and witness observations. Fire modeling is a way to test hypotheses, and to answer questions about which factors might have affected the growth and development of a fire. Because the fire models were developed at taxpayer expense, these models are free and becoming quite popular. All of the models available from NIST[2] come with a disclaimer similar to the one that accompanies fire Dynamics Simulator:

> The US Department of Commerce makes no warranty, expressed or implied, to users of the Fire Dynamics Simulator (FDS), and accepts no responsibility for its use. Users of FDS assume sole responsibility under Federal law for determining the appropriateness of its use in any particular application; for any conclusions drawn from the results of its use; and for any actions taken or not taken as a result of analyses performed using these tools.

> Users are warned that FDS is intended for use only by those competent in the fields of fluid dynamics, thermodynamics, combustion, and heat transfer, and is intended only to supplement the informed judgment of the qualified user. The software package is a computer model that may or may not have predictive capability when applied to a specific set of factual circumstances. Lack of accurate predictions by the model could lead to erroneous conclusions with regard to fire safety. All results should be evaluated by an informed user.[3]

There are currently two types of computer modeling programs for fires: zone models and field models. A zone model divides each compartment into an upper zone and a lower zone, and predicts the conditions in each zone as a function of time. Zone models are useful for situations where a rough approximation will do, and have been used to closely predict, for instance, when flashover will occur, given a specific fire on a specific fuel package. A proficient modeler can run zone models in a few hours on a personal computer. A typical zone model assumes that every part of the zone is uniform with respect to temperature and smoke concentration. Consequently, while the model may be able to predict when any sprinkler head might activate, it will be less reliable in predicting the activation of a particular sprinkler head.

Field models (also known as computational fluid dynamics or CFD models) are

---

[Section 9:41]

[1]Harold Nelson, FPETOOL Users Guide (NIST Pub. No. 4439) (1990).

[2]http://www.bfrl.nist.gov.

[3]Kevin McGrattan and Glenn Forney, Fire Dynamics Simulator (Version 4) User's Guide (NIST Special Publication 1019) (Feb. 2005).

much more complicated. They divide each compartment into thousands or tens of thousands of small volumes, and calculate the fire's progress through each volume. This makes the field models much more precise, but they are much more difficult to work with compared to zone models. In the recent past, a multi-compartment field model required days or weeks of mainframe computer time, but now can be run on reasonably fast personal computers, although the model may still take days or weeks to run.

The information required for both field and zone models is the same. A good description of the required inputs, as well as the limitations of computer models was added to NFPA 921 in 2001.

As in other areas of fire investigation, two experts provided with the same program can plug in different assumptions and reach different conclusions about the spread of fire. This is because of the large number of variables that affect the fire's behavior. Although computer modeling has been touted as a method for testing an investigator's hypothesis, the vast majority of computer models that are likely to be presented to a jury will demonstrate, but not prove, an expert's opinion.

Because of their ability to graphically present the growth of a fire, computer models are becoming commonplace in fire litigation. It is necessary to distinguish whether an expert is presenting a simulation or an animation. Animations are used to demonstrate what an expert thinks happened, while a simulation is the actual output of the model. Formerly, the output of models was numbers of graphs. The development of a program called Smokeview by engineers at NIST[4] now allows for computational fluid dynamics models as well as zone models to be presented graphically on a 3D CAD drawing of a building. These make powerful exhibits, but need to be checked carefully against the facts. As with any computer program, the rule "garbage in, garbage out" still applies.

### § 9:42 Areas of scientific agreement and disagreement—Field investigations—Fatal fires

Fires that involve fatalities are more likely to become the subject of civil or criminal litigation than fires that cause only property damage. The methodology of investigating a fatal fire is exactly the same as the methodology involved in investigating a property fire, except that there is one important piece of evidence provided in the fatal fire: the body. In those cases where the victim dies at the scene, the body can provide invaluable information as to the condition of the atmosphere at the time of death.

A careful forensic autopsy and toxicology including carboxyhemoglobin (COHb), blood alcohol and drug readings are imperative for a proper understating of what occurred. Low carbon monoxide content in a victim's blood suggests that they were rapidly overcome by heat, and died from burn injuries, rather than smoke inhalation, the most common cause of fire death. Higher carbon monoxide concentrations (around 50%), on the other hand, suggest exposure to a gradual build-up of smoke. Still higher levels of CO suggest brief exposure to very high concentrations of toxic smoke. Such exposures are typical of victims found away from the origin of a fire. Those intimate with the originating fire are unlikely to be still breathing by the time the fire produces high concentrations of CO. Fire extending from the room of origin undergoing flashover can rapidly spread deadly concentrations of CO throughout the building.[1]

---

[4]Glenn P. Forney and Kevin B. McGrattan, User's Guide for Smokeview Version 4—A Tool for Visualizing Fire Dynamics Simulation Data (NIST Special Publication 1017) (Aug. 2004).

[Section 9:42]

[1]John D. DeHaan, Kirk's Fire Investigation 492 (5th ed. 2003).

Low carbon monoxide (CO) concentrations have been interpreted by fire investigators as indicating arson, rather than an accidental fire.[2] The problem with this indication is that, like fire damage itself, carbon monoxide poisoning is a result of both the intensity of the exposure (carbon monoxide concentration) and the duration of the exposure. Exposure to a high concentration for a short period of time may result in the same carboxyhemoglobin level as exposure to a low concentration for a long time. For instance, exposure to a concentration of 0.05% CO (500 parts per million) for two to three hours will result in a COHb level of 30%. The same result is achieved by exposure to a concentration of 1% CO (10,000 parts per million) for one to five minutes.[3] Of course, a COHb concentration of zero is an indication that the victim was not breathing and indicates that death preceded the fire.

An excellent review of carbon monoxide data compilations has been published by Gordon Nelson.[4]

The effects of incineration can lead to mischaracterization of the events leading up to the victim's death. Muscle contraction caused by exposure to heat results in a "pugilistic pose," which has led investigators to see the victim as fighting off an assailant.[5] Other artifacts of incineration include neck contusions, which have been interpreted as evidence of strangulation, and skull fractures, cause by the expansion of cranial contents, which have been misinterpreted as evidence of bludgeoning.[6] The knowledge and experience of the medical examiner with burn victims should be carefully scrutinized before allowing these sorts of conclusions into evidence.

## § 9:43   Areas of scientific agreement and disagreement—Field investigations—Explosions

Procedures for investigating an explosion are similar to those used in fire investigations. A more detailed examination of the surrounding area is generally required, particularly in the case of chemical explosions.[1]

Historically, explosions have been difficult to define because there are several types of explosions, some of which are difficult to distinguish from rapid combustion. For this discussion, let us describe an explosion as an event having the following four characteristics: high pressure gas, confinement or restriction of the pressure, rapid production or release of the pressure, and change or damage to the confining or restricting structure or vessel.

Two major types of explosions may occur: mechanical explosions, such as steam boiler explosions, and chemical explosions, which encompass combustion explosions and the detonation of high explosives.

In a mechanical explosion, no chemical or combustion reaction is necessary, although mechanical explosions caused by boiling liquid and expanding vapor (BLEVE) frequently happen as a result of heating a sealed container of liquid in a fire. If the liquid is flammable, a chemical explosion may follow the mechanical explosion.

Chemical explosions may be caused by the sudden ignition of dusts, gas/air mixtures, or vapor/air mixtures. These are known as combustion explosions. An explosion in a cloud of smoke from a pre-existing fire is known as a backdraft. Most

---

[2]See, eg., *Pennsylvania v. Han Tak Lee* (Court of Common Pleas of Monroe County, 43rd Judicial District, No. 577 Criminal, 1989), testimony of Robert Jones.

[3]John D. DeHaan, Kirk's Fire Investigation 491 (5th ed. 2003).

[4]G.L. Nelson, Carbon Monoxide and Fire Toxicity: A Review and Analysis of Recent Work, 34 Fire Technology 39 (1998).

[5]John D. DeHaan, Kirk's Fire Investigation 483 (5th ed. 2003).

[6]*State v. Girdler*, No. 9809 (Superior Ct. of Arizona, Maricopa County, Jan. 3, 1991).

**[Section 9:43]**

[1]John D. DeHaan, Kirk's Fire Investigation 380 (4th ed. 1997).

of the explosions described so far are accidental in nature. Explosions fueled by chemicals whose primary function is to explode are more likely intentional.

All explosions, whether mechanical or chemical, are grouped into two categories: low order and high order. Low order explosions are characterized by a widespread "seat" or no "seat," and by the movement of large objects for short distances. High order explosions are characterized by a well-defined "seat," where the energy of the explosion creates a shattering effect, and typically a crater. High order explosions tend to project small objects for long distances.

Determination of the origin or epicenter of an explosion is carried out by searching the perimeter of the scene; locating and documenting projected debris, and developing force vector diagrams. This task may be complicated by secondary explosions, which appear to have more than one "origin." Once the origin is observed, conclusions can be drawn about the type of fuel involved and, if necessary, samples selected for laboratory analysis.

While the types of materials involved in commercial or industrial explosions are too numerous to cover in this chapter, the potential fuels for residential explosions are very limited. Unless the explosion is a backdraft, easily recognized by the smoke staining on the projected objects, the potential sources of fuel are limited to natural and LP gas, and flammable liquid vapors.

NFPA 921 contains an excellent discussion of the techniques of explosion investigation, and a recent National Institute of Justice guide dealing with the responsibilities of responders to explosion or bombing scenes contains much useful information.[2]

### § 9:44 Areas of scientific agreement and disagreement—Field investigations—Smoke detectors

According to statistics compiled by the National Fire Protection Association, residential fire deaths in the United States have dropped from a high of 6,015 in 1978 to 3,145 in 2003.[1] The National Smoke Detector Project—a joint project among the Consumer Product Safety Commission, the Congressional Fire Services Institute, the U.S. Fire Administration, and the National Fire Protection Association—issued a major report in October 1994 on the use of home smoke detectors, and characterized the home smoke detector as the fire safety success story of the decade. According to the 1994 report, smoke detectors cut the risk of dying in a home fire by roughly 40%. In the ten years ending in 1995, the death rate from fires in homes with a smoke detector present was 45% lower than the death rate from fires in homes with no smoke detector present.[2]

Of course, once technology comes into being that can save lives, certain failures of the technology become occasions for tort litigation.[3] The National Smoke Detector Project study found that nearly all of the smoke detectors that failed to operate did so because their batteries were either dead or disconnected. Some research, however, has indicated that for certain types of smoldering fires, the most common type of detector, the ionization detector, does not respond as quickly to the large particles generated by smoldering fires as a different type of detector, the photoelectric detector.[4] The general consensus of the scientific community involved in smoke

---

[2]§ 9:28.

**[Section 9:44]**

[1]Fast Facts, http://www.nfpa.org.

[2]Consumer Product Safety Commission, Smoke Detector Operability Survey: Report on Findings (1994).

[3]See Grady, Why Are People Negligent? Technology, Nondurable Precautions, and the Medical Malpractice Explosion, 82 Nw. U.L. Rev. 293 (1988).

[4]R.G. Bill, The Response of Smoke Detectors to Smoldering-started Fires in a Hotel Occupancy (Factory Mutual Research, Norwood, MA) (1988).

detector research, and the vast majority of the literature,[5] however, supports the proposition that the differences in response time are not significant with respect to smoldering fires, and the ionization detector's faster response to the more immediately dangerous flaming fire makes it the detector of choice. In recent litigation, smoke detector manufacturers have been sued for failing to incorporate a photoelectric detector into their smoke alarms, and the plaintiffs have had some success.[6]

Most smoke detectors use a small amount of radioactive material to ionize particles of air in the detection chamber. The ionized air conducts a very small current between a pair of electrodes. The presence of small particles of smoke in the ionization chamber interferes with this passage of current and triggers an alarm. In photoelectric detection chambers, there is a light emitting device and a light-detecting device. The light-emitting device is aimed away from the detection device, but the presence of smoke particles causes light to be reflected to the detection device, which sets off the alarm. Photoelectric detectors are not as sensitive to particles smaller than one micron (characteristic of flaming fires) as are ionization detectors. Ionization detectors are not as sensitive to particles larger than one micron (characteristic of smoldering fires) as are photoelectric detectors. All fires produce a wide range of particle sizes, and both types of detectors have been evaluated and found to provide adequate warning.[7] It is possible to build a smoke alarm that utilizes both types of detectors, and the argument has been advanced that alarms that incorporate only ionization detectors are therefore dangerous and defective. Unfortunately, when the smoke detector manufacturers put combination units on the store shelves, they stayed there. Consumers seem to be motivated largely by cost in the selection of smoke alarms. Litigation surrounding smoke detector design is likely to continue, but as of this writing, there have been few appellate decisions on the subject.

Recent work by Worrell et al.[8] describes ways of determining whether smoke detectors sounded during a fire. This involves looking for a ring of agglomerated soot particles on the hole in the center of the horn. The techniques described work well in fires in which soot-producing material, such as polyurethane, are involved, and not so well in fires fueled by paper and other materials that produce white or gray smoke. In the presence of black smoke, determinations could generally be made. In the past, smoke patterns known as Chlandi figures, have been cited, without the benefit of any research, as an indication that the vibrating disc of a smoke detector has sounded, and the absence of such figures, which can theoretically take the shape of concentric rings, a wagon wheel, or variations of the two, could be used as an indication that a smoke detector did not sound. This particular hypothesis has failed to gain any acceptance, and Worrell et al. seem to disprove the hypothesis. Once a smoke alarm has been significantly damaged by fire, the telltale ring of agglomerated soot particles around the horn may no loner be visible.

## § 9:45    Areas of scientific agreement and disagreement—Field investigations—Stolen autos recovered burned

This common scenario requires almost no investigation to determine that the fire

---

[5]R. Bukowski & N. Jason (eds.), Int'l Fire Detection Bibliography 1975–1990 (NIST 4661, Building and Fire Research Laboratory, Gaithersburg, MD) (1991).

[6]See, e.g., *Gordon v. BRK Brands, Inc.*, No 992-0771 (Circuit Ct. of the City of St. Louis, July, 1999) (settled after a $50 million verdict) or *Mercer v. Pittway Corp.*, 616 N.W.2d 602, Prod. Liab. Rep. (CCH) P 15925 (Iowa 2000) ($16.9 million trial verdict for compensatory and punitive damages,

reversed in part and remanded for new trial).

[7]Ionization Versus Photoelectric: Choosing the Right Smoke Detector, 30 Building Official & Code Admin., Nov./Dec. 1996, at 17.

[8]C.L. Worrell et al., Effect of Smoke Source and Horn Configuration on Enhanced Deposition, Acoustic Agglomeration, and Chlandi Figures in Smoke Detectors, 39 Fire Technology 309 (Oct. 2003).

was intentionally set. The chance that a vehicle happened to catch fire accidentally after it was stolen is almost not worth considering. The question in cases such as this is not whether the care was set on fire, but who did it. If an insurance company can prove that it was their insured that set the fire, or arranged the theft and fire, the company can avoid payment. Historically, this has been difficult to prove.

A new technique, bearing some resemblance to traditional toolmark analysis, purports to be able to determine the "last key used" to move a vehicle. This technique has no support in the relevant scientific community of firearms and toolmark examiners, but has nonetheless proven popular with insurers, and has been admitted over *Daubert* objections in several jurisdictions. Challenges are rare because the stakes are usually too low to support the involvement of adverse experts to refute the claim of the "forensic locksmith."

The proponents of this technique submitted a proposal to the NFPA to include it as a tool for vehicle fire investigations, but the Technical Committee rejected the proposal because there was no scientific evidence supporting the validity of the technique.[1]

## § 9:46 Areas of scientific agreement and disagreement—Field investigations—Presumption of accidental cause

Because the investigator making an arson case frequently lacks scientific training, the presumptions that individual carries into a fire scene should be closely scrutinized. Just as the assumptions that are plugged into a computer model can affect the outcome of the analysis, so will the assumptions that a fire investigator carries with him into a fire scene affect the outcome of his investigation.

Because of the large amount of evidence destroyed in a fire, it is possible to "prove" almost any fire scene to be the result of arson, if one is bent on doing so. This idea is conveyed by DeHaan: "If an investigator decides that a fire is arson before collecting any data, then only data supporting that premise are likely to be recognized and collected."[1] DeHaan, of course, was inspired by Holmes (Sherlock not Oliver Wendell), who stated, "It is a capital mistake to theorize before one has data. Insensibly, one begins to twist facts to suit theories, instead of theories to suit facts."[2]

Many fire investigators will state that they carry no presumptions into a fire scene with them, and rely on an objective evaluation of the evidence to reach their conclusions. NFPA 921 urges upon investigators the scientific method of hypothesis development and hypothesis testing. The question is: Should there be a hypothesis before all of the evidence has been observed? It could be argued that the proper presumption to carry into a fire scene is a presumption of accidental cause, i.e., all fires are presumed accidental until proven otherwise. Such a presumption protects the presumption of innocence accorded to individuals. Many states[3] have codified this presumption of accidental cause into the standard jury charge for arson, but whether codified in a particular jurisdiction or not, the fire investigator who fails to apply the presumption of accidental cause to all fires will eventually make an erroneous declaration of arson.

The error will result from a misinterpretation of circumstantial evidence. In nearly every fire case, it is circumstantial evidence that allows the cause of the fire

---

**[Section 9:45]**

[1]See Technical Committee Documentation, NFPA, Report on Comments for the Fall, 2000, Meeting.

**[Section 9:46]**

[1]John D. DeHaan, Kirk's Fire Investigation

4 (5th ed. 2003).

[2]Arthur Conan Doyle, A Scandal in Bohemia, in The Annotated Sherlock Holmes (William S. Baring-Gould ed., 1967).

[3]AR, GA, HI, IN, MD, MI, MO, MT, NE, NC, OR, PA, TN, TX, VT, VA, WA, WV.

to be deduced. Likewise, in nearly every arson case, the *corpus delicti* is proven by circumstantial evidence, and the jury is read the standard circumstantial evidence charge. Mr. Holmes described the perils of circumstantial evidence in *The Boscombe Valley Mystery*:

> Circumstantial evidence is a very tricky thing. It may seem to point very straight to one thing, but if you shift your own point of view a little, you may find it pointing in an equally uncompromising manner to something entirely different.[4]

In many instances, if there is one survivor of a fire, particularly a fatal fire, and the fire is determined to have been the result of arson, then only one conclusion can be reached—the survivor did it. This is because, in the investigator's "opinion," the survivor's account of events, which typically describes an accidental fire, is "impossible," and therefore, the survivor is lying. This is exactly what happened to Ray Girdler. Judge James Sult, who presided over the first trial and sentenced Girdler to life in prison, wrote in his opinion remanding the case for a new trial:

> The newly discovered evidence would probably change the verdict upon a retrial of this case. Several considerations support this finding: . . . At the trial of the case, the State claimed, based on then understood fire investigation evidence, that Mr. Girdler's account of the fire was impossible and, therefore, false. The new evidence shows that Mr. Girdler's observations of the fire are consistent with a flashover fire of innocent origin.[5]

If the state's investigator had the proper scientific approach to fire investigation, or even admitted the possibility that an explanation other than burning flammable liquids (none were detected in laboratory analysis) existed, the erroneous conviction, which cost Ray Girdler eight years in prison, might have been avoided.

Ray Girdler's experience is unfortunately not unique. A recent review of expert testimony in two Texas death penalty cases[6] found that the evidence used to obtain the convictions had no value in helping the Court understand how the fires actually started. In one case, the defendant was freed after 17 years on death row.[7] In the second case, the defendant was executed.[8]

### § 9:47    Areas of scientific agreement and disagreement—Field investigations—The "negative corpus"

Since the advent of scientifically based fire investigation, one of the thorniest issues for fire investigators has been the determination of fire cause when the evidence has either burned up or been taken from the scene by the fire setter. "Negative corpus," short for negative *corpus delicti*, is fire investigator shorthand for the determination that a fire was incendiary based on the lack of evidence of an accidental cause. Such determinations come from investigators who fail to heed Carl Sagan's warning, "Absence of evidence is not evidence of absence." The proponents of scientific fire investigation have generally held "negative corpus" determinations in low regard, but that has not prevented their introduction into evidence. The case of *Michigan Millers Mutual Insurance Corp. v. Benfield*[1] was a classic "negative corpus" determination. When fire investigators testify that a fire was intentionally

---

[4]Arthur Conan Doyle, The Boscombe Valley Mystery, in The Annotated Sherlock Holmes (William S. Baring-Gould ed., 1967).

[5]*State v. Girdler*, No. 9809 (Superior Ct. of Arizona, Maricopa County, Jan. 3, 1991).

[6]Discussed at www.innocenceproject.org.

[7]Arson Review Committee, Report on the Peer Review of the Expert Testimony in the Cases of State of Texas v. Cameron Todd Willingham and State of Texas v. Ernest Ray Willis (2006),

available at www.innocenceproject.org.

[8]Arson Review Committee, Report on the Peer Review of the Expert Testimony in the Cases of State of Texas v. Cameron Todd Willingham and State of Texas v. Ernest Ray Willis (2006), available at www.innocenceproject.org.

**[Section 9:47]**

[1]*Michigan Millers Mut. Ins. Corp. v. Benfield*, 140 F.3d 915, 49 Fed. R. Evid. Serv. 549 (11th Cir. 1998).

set, "the elimination of all potential accidental causes" is frequently added to other evidence of incendiary activity.

The NFPA Technical Committee on Fire Investigations struggled with the concept of "negative corpus" for several years. Despite the lack of a demonstrable ignition source, many fires can be stated to have been set based on the absence of any other possibilities. The Committee's challenge was to limit the abuse of the negative corpus determination, and to put legitimate determinations of incendiary activity into the context of the scientific method. The result of the Committee's work, first published in the 2001 edition of NFPA 921 is as follows:

> Process of Elimination. Any determination of fire cause should be based on evidence rather than on the absence of evidence; however, when the origin of a fire is clearly defined, it is occasionally possible to make a credible determination regarding the cause of the fire, even when there is no physical evidence of that cause available. This may be accomplished through the credible elimination of all other potential causes, provided that the remaining cause is consistent with all known facts.

> For example, an investigator may properly conclude that the ignition source came from an open flame even if the device producing the open flame is not found at the scene. This conclusion may be properly reached as long as the analysis producing the conclusion follows the Scientific Method as discussed in Chapter 2.

> "Elimination," which actually involves the testing and rejection of alternate hypotheses, becomes more difficult as the degree of destruction in the compartment of origin increases, and is not possible in many cases. Any time an investigator proposes the elimination of a particular system or appliance as the ignition source, the investigator should be able to explain how the appearance or condition of that system or appliance would be different than what is observed, if that system or appliance were the cause of the fire.

> There are times when such differences do not exist, for example, when a heat producing device ignites combustibles that are placed too close to it, the device itself may appear no different than if something else were the ignition source.

> The "elimination of all accidental causes" to reach a conclusion that a fire was incendiary is a finding that can rarely be scientifically justified using only physical data; however, the "elimination of all causes other than the application of an open flame" is a finding that may be justified in limited circumstances, where the area of origin is clearly defined and all other potential heat sources at the origin can be examined and credibly eliminated. It is recognized that in cases where a fire is ignited by the application of an open flame, there may be no evidence of the ignition source remaining. Other evidence, such as that listed in §§ 39:45 to 39:126, which may not be related to combustion, may allow for a determination that a fire was incendiary.

> In a determination of an accidental cause, the same precautions regarding "elimination" of other causes should be carefully considered.

Note that nowhere in the above quotation does the term "negative corpus" appear.

The above language represents a compromise between the presumption of accidental cause, and the knowledge that in many cases, particularly where the ignition source is an open flame, incendiary fires may leave behind little physical evidence of their cause.[2] As with many other additions of compromise language, this section of NFPA 921 has been the subject of some misconstruction. The term "clearly defined" is not itself clearly defined. What the Committee meant by "clearly defined" was an area of origin that even an untrained person could easily discern. Abuses of this language have occurred when the clear definition of the area of origin existed only in the mind of the investigator.

Computer modeling has lately started to be used in "negative corpus" cases. The investigator posits "hypotheses" even though no evidence supports them. These

---

[2]National Fire Protection Association, Guide for Fire and Explosion Investigations (Pub. No. 921) (2004), at § 18.2.

"hypotheses" are then run through the model and the scenario that provides the "best fit" with the post-file artifacts is declared the winner. Thus the model is used to manufacture "data". Because computer modelers are highly skilled and highly educated, carts may be easily hoodwinked.[3]

### § 9:48 Areas of scientific agreement and disagreement—Field investigations—Certainty of opinions

Few legal issues other than the cause of fires rely so heavily on the opinion of the investigator. Even in the case of explosions, which may be equally destructive or more destructive than fires, the fact that an explosion occurred drastically limits the number of potential causes.

Fire investigators have grappled with the question of certainty for years, raising such questions as whether an investigator's "comfort level" with his opinion should be stronger in a criminal case than in a civil case. On cross examination, many investigators will admit that they are not infallible, yet nevertheless go on to assert that there is no other possible explanation for their observations than what they have offered.

The uncertainty about certainty has generated much discussion in the fire investigation community, as illustrated by the discussion in the previous edition of this chapter. Because it seemed impossible to separate a codification of "comfort level" from legal burdens of proof, the Technical Committee on Fire Investigations voted in 1998 to remove the discussion about levels of certainty from the document. As discussed previously, the concepts of probable and possible were added back into the document in the 2004 edition.

### § 9:49 Areas of scientific agreement and disagreement—Field investigations—Conflicting opinions

There is a curious notion in the fire investigation community that every fire investigator is entitled to his own opinion about the cause of a fire. There is even a tacit recognition of the possibility of investigators reaching different conclusions after making the same observations of the same fire scene in the International Association of Arson Investigators CODE OF ETHICS, which includes the rule, "I will remember always that I am a truth seeker, not a case maker."[1]

Unfortunately, due to the lack of scientific training in the discipline, many investigators do not understand the difference between a "personal" opinion and a "professional" opinion. Certainly, very few investigators will grant their physicians the right to make a misdiagnosis based on their observation and interpretation of a set of symptoms. If two doctors disagree on a diagnosis, the doctors regard it as their duty to cooperate and attempt to reach the correct conclusion. They would be uncomfortable knowing that one of them was wrong if they did not do so. Such cooperation in the search for the truth, particularly when arson is alleged, is so far a relatively rare occurrence in fire investigations. Fire investigators with differing views most often leave it up to the trier of fact to decide who is right, even though the legal fact finder is likely to be even less knowledgeable about the substance of the expert testimony than either investigator.

With the growing acceptance of NFPA 921 as the standard of care in fire investigation, some investigators are learning to accommodate the standard without really changing the way they do business.

---

[3]See, e.g., Louisiana v. Hypes, Criminal Docket No. 265,037 (9th Judicial Cir., Rapides Parish, Jun. 27, 2006).

**[Section 9:49]**

[1]International Association of Arson Investigators, IAAI Code of Ethics (1949).

A curious circular logic seems to be gaining currency with respect to the "elimination" of particular causes of fire. The fire investigator first determines the point of origin, sometimes with arresting specificity, even in rooms that have gone well beyond flashover and have been completely involved in fire for tens of minutes. In such compartments, it is difficult, if not impossible to determine what burned first. It is possible to determine only what burned the most. This frequently has nothing to do with the origin of the fire; but, upon declaring a particular point to be the origin of the fire, the fire investigator then states that he has "eliminated" everything on the north side of the room because he has "determined" that the origin is at the south side of the room. In this way, it is possible to avoid examining just about anything, but still be in a position to state that even without the examination, a particular system or appliance has been eliminated.

Some fire investigators continue to follow the "Emperor's New Clothes" school of reporting, by showing a photograph and stating that there are "obvious pour patterns" in the photograph, when all anyone, even another fire investigator, can see is a burned surface. There is a frequent overuse of the words "clear" and "obvious." If the artifact that the investigator is pointing at is neither clear nor obvious to an untrained individual, the investigator should be challenged.

### § 9:50 Areas of scientific agreement and disagreement—Laboratory analysis

Unlike the field investigation of fires, there are considerably more areas of agreement and fewer areas of disagreement in the laboratory analysis of fire debris, and since the early 1990s, a near consensus has developed in the scientific community regarding the proper techniques to be applied to samples of fire debris in which it is suspected that ignitable liquid residues are contained. Two chemists, looking at the same data from a fire debris sample, are more likely to agree on its interpretation than are two field investigators looking at the same fire scene, but disagreements still occur, and these are usually due to one of the chemists failing to follow industry standards.

### § 9:51 Areas of scientific agreement and disagreement—Field investigations—Conflicting opinions—Standard methods of sample preparation

The industry standard for the laboratory analysis of fire debris is embodied in ASTM E 1618, Standard Test Method for Identification of Ignitable Liquid Residues in Extracts from Samples of Fire Debris by Gas Chromatography-Mass Spectrometry[1]. It is agreed almost unanimously in the forensic science community that gas chromatography is an essential requirement for the identification of common petroleum-based products. Gas chromatography-mass spectrometry and gas chromatography-infrared spectrophotometry, known as "hybrid" or "hyphenated" techniques, provide more information, but are basically more sophisticated versions of gas chromatography. Gas chromatography has been the accepted method of analyzing petroleum products since the 1960s, but there have been considerable improvements in the field. These improvements and variations on the technique of gas chromatography are reported in peer-reviewed journals such as the Journal of Forensic Sciences, Science and Justice, Analytical Chemistry, and others.

There have also been numerous improvements in sample preparation techniques over the years. These improvements are also likely to be documented in the literature, and all of the commonly used sample preparation techniques are

---

**[Section 9:51]**

[1]§§ 9:25 to 9:26.

described in ASTM standards.

Headspace analysis (ASTM E 1388) is the simplest of the sample preparation techniques. This method is rapid, but not highly reproducible, and not highly sensitive to the heavier hydrocarbons such as those found in diesel fuel. The sample is warmed and a syringe is used to withdraw a small volume of the air above the sample, known as the headspace. This headspace is then injected directly into the gas chromatograph.[2]

Steam distillation (ASTM E 1385) is a classical technique, which relies on the immiscibility of oil and water. A visible oily liquid can be separated from the sample and then diluted or injected directly into the gas chromatograph. This technique is time consuming, and is not sensitive to very low concentrations of ignitable liquids, which are often all that remains in fire debris samples. When applied to a sufficiently concentrated sample, the visible liquid that the technique produces, however, can make a very convincing exhibit.[3] When the jury can actually see the recovered liquid, and perhaps smell it and see it burn, they will not likely feel the need to understand the intricacies of gas chromatography mass spectrometry.

Solvent extraction (ASTM E 1386) is another classical technique which is highly sensitive, but which has the disadvantage of dissolving materials other than the ignitable liquid residues of interest. It is also expensive, dangerous, and destructive of evidence. This is a technique best applied to very small samples and to the problem of determining what was inside a now empty container.[4]

Headspace concentration techniques (ASTM E 1412 and E 1413) employ an adsorbent to trap volatile materials present in the headspace above a warmed sample. These adsorption/elution techniques are highly sensitive, highly reproducible, and the passive headspace concentration technique is both simple to use and essentially nondestructive of evidence. The sample can be analyzed repeatedly, by different laboratories, if necessary, and the carbon strips used in the analysis can be archived and repeatedly re-tested. Because of its simplicity and non-destructive nature, passive headspace concentration has become the "method of choice" in modern forensic science laboratories.[5]

All of the above sample preparation techniques are scientifically valid. Sample size, ignitable liquid concentration, and the analyst's experience and preference will determine which method of separation is selected. Regardless of separation technique, the analytical methods recognized as valid are limited to those involving gas chromatography.

## § 9:52 Areas of scientific agreement and disagreement—Field investigations—Conflicting opinions—Classification of ignitable liquids

Beginning in 1982, fire debris chemists used a numbered "petroleum distillate classification system" to characterize petroleum products found in fire debris samples.[1] Classes 1 through 5 described light petroleum distillates, gasoline, medium petroleum distillates, kerosene, and diesel fuel. New products coming to

---

[2]ASTM International, Standard Practice for Sampling of Headspace Vapors from Fire Debris Samples (Pub. No. E 1388) (2000).

[3]ASTM International, Standard Practice for Separation and Concentration of Ignitable Liquid Residues from Fire Debris Samples by Steam Distillation (Pub No. E 1385) (2000).

[4]ASTM International, Standard Practice for Separation and Concentration of Ignitable Liquid Residues from Fire Debris Samples by Solvent Extraction (Pub. No. E 1386) (2000).

[5]ASTM International, Standard Practice for Separation and Concentration of Ignitable Liquid Residues from Fire Debris Samples by Passive Headspace Concentration (Pub. No. E 1412) (2000).

**[Section 9:52]**

[1]AA Notes, 6 Arson Analysis Newsletter (Systems Engineering Associates, Columbus, OH) (1982).

the market in the 1980s and 1990s led to the addition of a new class, Class 0, which was initially entitled "Miscellaneous Products," and then was broken down into Classes 0.1, 0.2, etc., to describe the newer products. Eventually, the miscellaneous sub-classes outnumbered the traditional classes, and it was the decision of ASTM Committee E30 on Forensic Sciences to restructure the classification system in 2001,[2] doing away with the class numbers, and relying instead on the class name. Under the new system, for example, gasoline is simply called gasoline, rather than a "Class 2 petroleum product."

Distinctions within any one of these classes are very difficult, and often impossible.[3] Once an ignitable liquid has been exposed to a fire, its character changes to the extent that its source is very difficult to identify. Some work has indicated that source identification is possible if a sample is less than 30% evaporated (i.e., at least 70% of the original weight remains). There are times, however, when ignitable liquids are mixed, producing a unique pattern that can conceivably be identified with a source. There also exist occasions when it is possible to unequivocally eliminate a suspected source of an ignitable liquid residue.

The exposure of a petroleum distillate to a fire results in its evaporation, with the lower boiling point compounds being preferentially evaporated over the higher boiling point compounds. This results in an increase in the average molecular weight of the mixture. It is also generally recognized that it is not possible to distinguish whether a sample has been exposed to a fire or to room temperature evaporation. A sample of petroleum distillate that has burned to 50% of its original volume or weight will give a gas chromatographic pattern that is indistinguishable from a sample that has evaporated to that point.

### § 9:53 Areas of scientific agreement and disagreement—Field investigations—Conflicting opinions—Detection of explosives

Because of the relative rarity of explosion incidents (compared to fire incidents) and because bombing incidents are exclusively criminal, scientists regularly dealing with the detection and identification of explosives are almost exclusively concentrated in law enforcement laboratories, particularly federal laboratories (FBI and ATFE). Most private laboratories have only primitive explosive detection capabilities, and most state and local government laboratories are not much better equipped. Techniques for explosive detection and identification appear in the literature, but few laboratories are capable of repeating the published analyses. Techniques used by explosive chemists are as varied as the explosives themselves. The following are techniques used in the federal laboratories on a routine basis: thin layer chromatography, gas chromatography, gas chromatography-mass spectrometry with chemical ionization, infrared spectrophotometry, high performance liquid chromatography, energy dispersive x-ray analysis, x-ray diffraction, and capillary electrophoresis, one of the newer techniques.

As in the analysis of petroleum distillates in fire debris, the critical first step in the analysis of explosive residue is the separation of the residue from the debris. The salts that are the products of the explosive reaction are removed from the debris by a cold water extraction, while the unreacted or partially reacted residue of the explosive itself is removed using an organic solvent. These concentrated extracts are then analyzed by one, or usually several, of the techniques listed above.

For explosions caused by fuels other than chemicals designed to explode, gas

---

[2]ASTM International Standard Test Method for Ignitable Liquid Residues in Extracts from Fire Debris by Gas Chromatography-Mass Spectrometry (Pub. No. E 1618) (2001).

[3]ASTM International, Standard Test Method for Ignitable Liquid Residues in Extracts from Samples of Fire Debris by Gas Chromatography (Pub. No. E 1387) (2001).

chromatography is the usual method of analysis. Gasoline, the most common fuel for explosive vapor/air mixtures, is detected as described previously. Gas chromatography is required to detect ethane, and higher molecular weight gases, which are found in natural gas, but not in sewer gas. Odorization of natural and LP gases is frequently an issue in explosion cases. The National Fuel Gas Code requires that consumer fuel gases be odorized so that they are detectable at a concentration of one-fifth of the lower explosive limit. Quantitation of the odorant level may be accomplished by gas chromatography or through an "odor panel," five people with an unimpaired sense of smell. Reagent tubes can also be used to detect the ethyl mercaptan or thiophane used to odorize fuel gases.

## § 9:54  Future directions

The laboratory analysis of fire debris is about as "settled" as any forensic science is ever likely to be. The gas chromatograph-mass spectrometer can provide almost total characterization of complex mixtures to allow for unequivocal identification of the petroleum products that are likely to be used as accelerants. The techniques of sample preparation have reached the practical limit of what is desirable to detect. More sensitive levels of detection increase the risk of identifying ignitable liquid residues that are part of the normal background.[1] The simplicity of the techniques available to achieve current levels of detection provides little impetus to improve the techniques. The impetus in the field is general to improve the quality of work done by laboratories that have yet to adopt techniques that are generally recognized as valid. Laboratories that fail to follow these minimum standards can expect to see their results challenged frequently and more vigorously.

With the lack of a frontier, more laboratory scientists are stepping out into the field, and applying their scientific skills to the understanding of the behavior of fire. The National Fire Protection Association (NFPA) and the National Institute of Standards and Technology (NIST) are both looking at ways to repeat the experiments of the 1970s and 80s, but this time, the researchers will look at the aftermath, rather than just the fire itself. Numerous test burns should be recorded in the next few years, and the information that comes out of them should greatly improve the quality of field fire investigation work.

As more canines are brought into the field of accelerant detection, a body of knowledge, including peer-reviewed research, is likely to come into being. The use of accelerant detecting canines may free up large amounts of fire investigators' time, allowing overworked state and local officials to concentrate on those fire scenes most likely to result in prosecutable arson cases.

Computer modeling is likely to assume a much larger role in the future, particularly as data come in from more test burns. These data can be used to validate a model's predictions. As with any new technique. The potential for error or abuse is present. Determinations that rely heavily on modeling should be carefully challenged.

Certification of field investigators by the International Association of Arson Investigators or by the National Association of Fire Investigators is becoming more common. Neither certification program guarantees the competence of the witness or the correctness of their findings, but the programs do serve a useful purpose in encouraging the fire investigation community to identify some areas of agreement and to study areas of disagreement. Many states require fire investigators to be licensed as private investigators, but in most cases these requirements only serve to

---

[Section 9:54]

[1]Lentini et al., The Petroleum-Laced Background, 45 J. Forensic Sci. 968 (2000).

restrain trade and raise revenue. Kentucky is the first state to require that private investigators that conduct fire and arson investigations be certified by either IAAI or NAFI.

Certification of laboratory analysts through the American Board of Criminalistics began only in 1994, so it will be some time before there is a large cadre of certified fire debris chemists. As more scientists leave the laboratory to do field research in the area of fire behavior, the understanding of fire behavior is likely to improve, and the quality of fire investigations is likely to benefit from the application of a scientist's natural skepticism to the outdated or unsupported beliefs held by many field investigators. While there are still far too m any cases of incorrect fire analyses, the profession is moving incrementally toward a more accurate "calibration" of expectations. Training available over the internet from Interfire and CFItrainer has the capacity to rapidly improve the level of knowledge in the field.

The entry of fire protection engineers (FPEs) into the fire investigation business is a hopeful sign. These highly educated scientists and engineers are bringing a new level of rigor to the field, which can only improve the situation. Individuals and organizations that formerly ignored or even looked down upon the contribution of these engineers are beginning to appreciate what they have to offer.

The process of fire investigation continues to improve, though the vast majority of practitioners still possess no formal education in chemistry and physics, despite the fact that society asks them to make sophisticated decisions about exactly those subjects. Ensuring that those who hold themselves out to be fire experts, and those considered qualified to testify at trial, are competent in the relevant science is one future direction that still remains to be taken.

# APPENDIX 9A

## Glossary

**Accelerant.** An agent, often an ignitable liquid, used to initiate or speed the spread of fire.

**Adsorption/elution.** A method of concentrating ignitable liquid vapors onto an active surface, usually a small (10 × 10 mm) square of carbon impregnated polytetrafluoroethylene (PTFE) tape, or c-strip. Once the vapors are trapped on the active surface, they are removed (eluted) by placing the c-strip in a solvent. The resulting solution in the analyzed by GC-MS.

**Arc.** A luminous electric discharge across a gap. If the arc generates sufficient energy, an arc bead may be formed. An arc bead is a round globule of re-solidified metal at the point on an electrical conductor where the arc occurred.

**Area of Origin.** The room or area where a fire began. While "area" of origin is a common term of art, the fire occurs in three-dimensional space, and this term actually means "volume" of origin. *(See also Point of Origin.)*

**Capillary Electrophoresis.** An analytical separation technique, which utilizes electric charge to separate and analyze sub-milligram quantities of chemical substances. Capillary Electrophoresis is useful in many types of analytical chemistry, including the detection of explosives and gunshot residues.

**Cause.** The circumstances, conditions, or agencies that brought about or resulted in the fire or explosion incident, damage to property resulting from the fire or explosion incident, or bodily injury or loss of life resulting from the fire or explosion incident.

**Compartment Fire.** Any fire that occurs inside an enclosure. Once a fire has progressed beyond the initial free-burning stage, it interacts with the floors, walls, and ceilings of the enclosure and behaves differently from a free-burning fire.

**Flashover.** A transition phase in the development of a compartment fire in which surfaces exposed to thermal radiation reach ignition temperature more or less simultaneously and fire spreads rapidly throughout the space.

**Gas Chromatography (GC).** An analytical method for separating and identifying mixtures of compounds. A compound's solubility in a stationary phase versus its solubility in a mobile phase allows separation of similar compounds due to subtle differences in physical or chemical properties. Most gas chromatography performed on ignitable liquid residues relies on differences in boiling points to effect the separation. GC is the fundamental first step in the analysis of any ignitable liquid residue. The output of the GC is known as a chromatogram.

**Headspace.** The volume of air above a sample of debris in a container.

**Infrared Spectrophotometry (IR).** An analytical method that measures the absorbance of radiation having a wavelength slightly longer than the wavelength of visible light. This method is used to characterize the functional groups present in a sample, and is frequently applied to polymers and drugs. The utility of IR is limited in ignitable liquid residue analysis because most ignitable liquids are mixtures, and infrared spectrophotometry requires pure or nearly pure compounds in order to yield meaningful data. The output of the IR spectrophotomer is known as an absorbance spectrum.

***Mass Spectrometry (MS).*** An analytical method that begins with the breaking up of the compounds of interest by the application of chemical or electrical energy, followed by a measurement of the size and number of ions produced in the ionization step. Like other spectral techniques, mass spectrometry requires pure compounds in order to yield meaningful data. The purification for most mass spectral analysis is accomplished via gas chromatography. Typically, the MS is attached to the output side of a gas chromatograph (GC-MS) column. The output of the mass spectrometer is known as a mass spectrum.

***Odorization.*** The addition of small concentrations of substances to a fuel gas in order to make it detectable by smell. The two common fuel gases, natural gas and LP gas, have no odor. Odorants such as ethyl mercaptan or thiophane must be added to fuel gases in order to make them detectable at a concentration not over one-fifth of the lower limit of flammability.

***Point of Origin.*** The exact physical location in three-dimensional space where a heat source and a fuel come in contact with each other and a fire begins.

***Radiometer.*** A collection of thermocouples encased in a solid conductive metal jacket (e.g., copper), which is cooled by water. By measuring the voltage difference between the thermocouples exposed to the fire and the thermocouples exposed to the water, and taking into account the surface area of the case, the radiative flux in watts per square centimeter (or kilowatts per square meter) can be measured directly.

***Thermocouple.*** A device consisting of two dissimilar metal wires, which convert heat energy into electrical energy. A voltage-measuring device is attached to the wires and the temperature at the junction of the wires can be calculated. This is usually accomplished electronically, and the thermocouple readout, known as a pyrometer, reads directly in °F or °C.

***Thin Layer Chromatography (TLC).*** A chemical analytical procedure, which separates compounds by their solubility in a solvent, and the tenacity by which these compounds adsorb (adhere) to a thin sheet of silica gel spread out on a glass plate. Once separated, the spots of analyte can be further characterized by exposure to a developing agent, which causes the spots to change color. As in all chromatographic analyses, a comparison is made between a known substance and an unknown substance. TLC may be used for the separation of drugs and explosives, and also for the characterization of dyes in automotive gasoline.

# Table of Laws and Rules

―――――――

## FEDERAL ARBITRATION ACT

## UNITED STATES CODE ANNOTATED

## UNITED STATES PUBLIC LAWS

## CODE OF FEDERAL REGULATIONS

## FEDERAL RULES OF CRIMINAL PROCEDURE

## FEDERAL RULES OF EVIDENCE

# Table of Cases

118 S. Ct. 512, 139 L. Ed. 2d 508, 18 O.S.H. Cas. (BNA) 1097, Prod. Liab. Rep. (CCH) P 15120, 48 Fed. R. Evid. Serv. 1, 28 Envtl. L. Rep. 20227, 177 A.L.R. Fed. 667 (1997)—3:1, 3:8, 4:5, 4:6, 4:14, 5:2, 5:4, 6:6, 7:2, 9:2

General Elec. Co., Travelers Property & Cas. Corp. v., 150 F. Supp. 2d 360, 57 Fed. R. Evid. Serv. 695 (D. Conn. 2001)—9:11, 9:12

General Motors Corp., American Mfrs. Mut. Ins. Co. v., 582 So. 2d 934 (La. Ct. App. 2d Cir. 1991)—9:1

George, U.S. v., 363 F.3d 666, 64 Fed. R. Evid. Serv. 10 (7th Cir. 2004)—3:18

Gianakos, U.S. v., 415 F.3d 912 (8th Cir. 2005)—8:3

Gianni Versace S.p.A., A.V. By Versace, Inc. v., 446 F. Supp. 2d 252 (S.D. N.Y. 2006)—4:7, 4:10

Gibbs v. Gibbs, 210 F.3d 491, 53 Fed. R. Evid. Serv. 1238, 46 Fed. R. Serv. 3d 799, 172 A.L.R. Fed. 783 (5th Cir. 2000)—8:3

Gibson v. State, 915 So. 2d 199 (Fla. Dist. Ct. App. 4th Dist. 2005)—2:7, 2:20

Gibson, Van Woudenberg ex rel. Foor v., 211 F.3d 560 (10th Cir. 2000)—2:19

Gilbert v. California, 388 U.S. 263, 87 S. Ct. 1951, 18 L. Ed. 2d 1178 (1967)—4:7

Gilbert, U.S. v., 181 F.3d 152, 51 Fed. R. Evid. Serv. 1281 (1st Cir. 1999)—7:3

Gilliard, U.S. v., 133 F.3d 809, 48 Fed. R. Evid. Serv. 832 (11th Cir. 1998)—8:4

Girdler v. Dale, 859 F. Supp. 1279 (D. Ariz. 1994)—9:1

Girouard, Com. v., 436 Mass. 657, 766 N.E.2d 873 (2002)—2:14

Glass v. State, 255 Ga. App. 390, 565 S.E.2d 500 (2002)—2:14

Glover v. State, 787 S.W.2d 544 (Tex. App. Dallas 1990)—2:3

Glyman, Com. v., 17 Mass. L. Rptr. 146, 2003 WL 22956121 (Mass. Super. Ct. 2003)—4:7

Gomez, People v., 2004 WL 161441 (Cal. App. 4th Dist. 2004)—3:19

Goodman, Com. v., 54 Mass. App. Ct. 385, 765 N.E.2d 792 (2002)—9:19

Gordon, U.S. v., 688 F.2d 42, 11 Fed. R. Evid. Serv. 1026 (8th Cir. 1982)—8:7

Gore, State v., 143 Wash. 2d 288, 21 P.3d 262 (2001)—2:3

Gortarez, State v., 141 Ariz. 254, 686 P.2d 1224 (1984)—7:1

Graham, People v., 2007 WL 861173 (Mich. Ct. App. 2007)—4:7

Graves, Com. v., 310 Pa. Super. 184, 456

A.2d 561, 40 A.L.R.4th 563 (1983)—5:2

Great Northern Ins. Co., U.S. Xpress, Inc. v., 2002 WL 31789380 (D. Minn. 2002)—9:14

Green, State v., 305 N.C. 463, 290 S.E.2d 625 (1982)—6:4

Green, U.S. v., 405 F. Supp. 2d 104 (D. Mass. 2005)—5:4

Greer, State v., 265 Wis. 2d 463, 2003 WI App 112, 666 N.W.2d 518 (Ct. App. 2003)—8:9, 8:10

Gricco, U.S. v., 2002 WL 746037 (E.D. Pa. 2002)—4:7

Griffin v. California, 380 U.S. 609, 85 S. Ct. 1229, 14 L. Ed. 2d 106 (1965)—2:19

Griggs v. Com., 2003 WL 22745707 (Ky. Ct. App. 2003)—4:7

Gross v. DaimlerChrysler Corp., 2003 WL 23305157 (D. Md. 2003)—9:13

Grutz, People v., 212 N.Y. 72, 105 N.E. 843 (1914)—9:1

Guzman, People v., 80 Cal. App. 4th 1282, 96 Cal. Rptr. 2d 87 (4th Dist. 2000)—2:19

## H

Haggood, State v., 36 Conn. App. 753, 653 A.2d 216 (1995)—9:1

Hall v. State, 970 S.W.2d 137 (Tex. App. Amarillo 1998)—8:3

Hall, State v., 955 S.W.2d 198 (Mo. 1997)—8:3

Hamel v. State, 803 S.W.2d 878 (Tex. App. Fort Worth 1991)—2:19

Hamilton, State v., 2002-Ohio-1681, 2002 WL 549841 (Ohio Ct. App. 11th Dist. Lake County 2002)—3:19

Hammond, State v., 221 Conn. 264, 604 A.2d 793 (1992)—2:41

Harbold, People v., 124 Ill. App. 3d 363, 79 Ill. Dec. 830, 464 N.E.2d 734 (1st Dist. 1984)—2:19

Harris, State v., 2007 WL 1848047 (Wis. Ct. App. 2007)—8:9, 8:10

Harris, U.S. v., 9 F.3d 493, 39 Fed. R. Evid. Serv. 1314 (6th Cir. 1993)—8:5

Harris, Westfield Ins. Co. v., 134 F.3d 608, 48 Fed. R. Evid. Serv. 887 (4th Cir. 1998)—9:8

Harrison, Hunter v., 1997 WL 578917 (Ohio Ct. App. 8th Dist. Cuyahoga County 1997)—2:42

Harrison v. State, 2003 WL 21513618 (Tex. App. Fort Worth 2003)—3:19

Harrison v. State, 644 N.E.2d 1243 (Ind. 1995)—2:3

Harrison v. State, 635 So. 2d 894 (Miss. 1994)—6:3

Hart v. Resort Investigations & Patrol, 2004

## I

8:4

Marsh, People v., 177 Mich. App. 161, 441 N.W.2d 33 (1989)—6:4, 6:6

Marshall, U.S. v., 986 F. Supp. 747 (E.D. N.Y. 1997)—8:4

Martin v. State, 100 Fla. 16, 129 So. 112 (1930)—3:2

Martinez-Cintron, U.S. v., 136 F. Supp. 2d 17, 56 Fed. R. Evid. Serv. 878 (D.P.R. 2001)—3:3

Martinez-Garduno, U.S. v., 31 Fed. Appx. 475 (9th Cir. 2002)—3:7, 3:18

Martinez, Lee v., 2004-NMSC-027, 136 N.M. 166, 96 P.3d 291 (2004)—8:6

Martinez v. State, 549 So. 2d 694 (Fla. Dist. Ct. App. 5th Dist. 1989)—2:7

Martinez, U.S. v., 3 F.3d 1191, 37 Fed. R. Evid. Serv. 863 (8th Cir. 1993)—2:3, 2:8

Martinez, U.S. v., 937 F.2d 299, 33 Fed. R. Evid. Serv. 334 (7th Cir. 1991)—2:19

Marx, People v., 54 Cal. App. 3d 100, 126 Cal. Rptr. 350, 77 A.L.R.3d 1108 (2d Dist. 1975)—6:4, 6:5

Maryland, Church v., 180 F. Supp. 2d 708 (D. Md. 2002)—4:7

Maryland, Church v., 53 Fed. Appx. 673 (4th Cir. 2002)—4:7

Maryland Cas. Co. v. Therm-O-Disc, Inc., 137 F.3d 780, 48 Fed. R. Evid. Serv. 780 (4th Cir. 1998)—9:9

Massey, U.S. v., 594 F.2d 676 (8th Cir. 1979)—2:8

Matthews, State v., 859 So. 2d 863 (La. Ct. App. 4th Cir. 2003)—4:7

Matthews, State v., 855 So. 2d 740 (La. 2003)—4:7

Matthews, State v., 814 So. 2d 619 (La. Ct. App. 4th Cir. 2002)—4:7

Matthews v. State, 1998 OK CR 3, 953 P.2d 336 (Okla. Crim. App. 1998)—8:3

Maytag Corp., Allstate Ins. Co. v., 1999 WL 203349 (N.D. Ill. 1999)—9:4, 9:6, 9:13

McCaughtry, Bergmann v., 65 F.3d 1372 (7th Cir. 1995)—2:19

McCoy v. Whirlpool Corp., 379 F. Supp. 2d 1187 (D. Kan. 2005)—9:11

McCoy v. Whirlpool Corp., 214 F.R.D. 646, 55 Fed. R. Serv. 3d 740 (D. Kan. 2003)—9:12

McDaniel, U.S. v., 538 F.2d 408 (D.C. Cir. 1976)—7:1

McDavitt, State v., 62 N.J. 36, 297 A.2d 849 (1972)—8:10

McDonald, People v., 37 Cal. 3d 351, 208 Cal. Rptr. 236, 690 P.2d 709, 46 A.L.R.4th 1011 (1984)—2:17

McGarry v. State, 82 Tex. Crim. 597, 200 S.W. 527 (1918)—3:2

McGhee v. State, 253 Ga. 278, 319 S.E.2d 836 (1984)—8:7

McGrew v. State, 682 N.E.2d 1289 (Ind. 1997)—6:6

McMorris, Israel v., 455 U.S. 967, 102 S. Ct. 1479, 71 L. Ed. 2d 684 (1982)—8:10

McMorris v. Israel, 643 F.2d 458 (7th Cir. 1981)—8:7, 8:10

McNickles, Com. v., 434 Mass. 839, 753 N.E.2d 131 (2001)—2:8, 2:12

McReynolds v. Cherokee Ins. Co., 815 S.W.2d 208 (Tenn. Ct. App. 1991)—9:1

McVeigh, U.S. v., 1997 WL 47724 (D.Colo. 1997)—4:4, 4:6, 4:7

Melvin v. State, 606 A.2d 69 (Del. 1992)—8:10

Mensink v. American Grain, 564 N.W.2d 376 (Iowa 1997)—9:19

Mercer v. Pittway Corp., 616 N.W.2d 602 (Iowa 2000)—9:44

Merrell Dow Pharmaceuticals, Inc., Daubert v., 509 U.S. 579, 113 S. Ct. 2786, 125 L. Ed. 2d 469, 37 Fed. R. Evid. Serv. 1 (1993)—1:34, 2:2, 2:52, 2:53, 3:1, 3:3, 3:19, 4:4, 4:8, 6:2, 6:5, 6:6, 7:1, 8:1, 8:7, 9:1, 9:2, 9:5, 9:9

Merritt, U.S. v., 2002 WL 1821821 (S.D. Ind. 2002)—3:18

Meyers v. Arcudi, 947 F. Supp. 581, 46 Fed. R. Evid. Serv. 80 (D. Conn. 1996)—8:4

Michigan Millers Mut. Ins. Corp. v. Benfield, 140 F.3d 915, 49 Fed. R. Evid. Serv. 549 (11th Cir. 1998)—9:1, 9:2, 9:11, 9:47

Microtek Intern. Development Systems Div., Inc., U.S. v., 2000 WL 274091 (D. Or. 2000)—8:1, 8:4

Middleton v. Cupp, 768 F.2d 1083 (9th Cir. 1985)—8:10

Middleton, People v., 54 N.Y.2d 42, 444 N.Y.S.2d 581, 429 N.E.2d 100 (1981)—6:4

Miles v. Loomis, 75 N.Y. 288, 1878 WL 12743 (1878)—4:3

Miller v. District Court In and For City and County of Denver, 737 P.2d 834 (Colo. 1987)—2:19

Miller, State ex rel. Nebraska State Bar Ass'n v., 258 Neb. 181, 602 N.W.2d 486 (1999)—8:3

Miller, People v., 173 Ill. 2d 167, 219 Ill. Dec. 43, 670 N.E.2d 721 (1996)—2:3

Miller, State v., 666 N.W.2d 703 (Minn. 2003)—2:3

Miller, U.S. v., 874 F.2d 1255, 28 Fed. R. Evid. Serv. 23 (9th Cir. 1989)—8:5

Miller, Watkins v., 92 F. Supp. 2d 824 (S.D. Ind. 2000)—8:10

# Index